Everyone Had Cameras

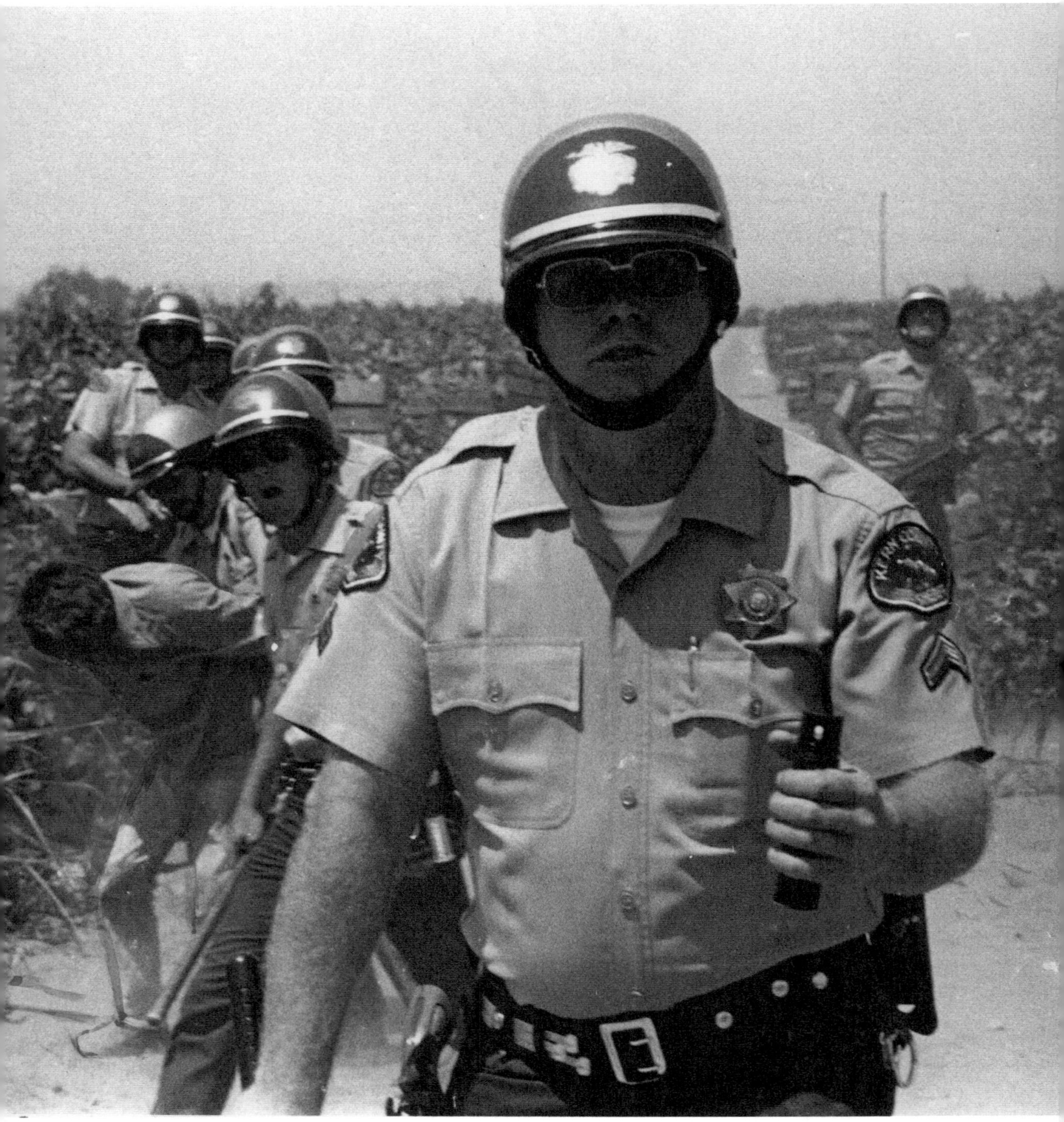

Everyone Had Cameras

Photography and Farmworkers in California

1850–2000

RICHARD STEVEN STREET

MIN
NE
SO
TA

UNIVERSITY OF MINNESOTA PRESS
MINNEAPOLIS • LONDON

Publication of this book has been aided by a grant from the Wyeth Foundation for American Art Publication Fund of the College Art Association.

FRONTISPIECE: A Kern County deputy sheriff threatens to spray Mace on a United Farm Worker union photographer, August 7, 1973. Photographer unknown. Author's collection.

Published by the University of Minnesota Press
111 Third Avenue South, Suite 290
Minneapolis, MN 55401-2520
http://www.upress.umn.edu

Library of Congress Cataloging-in-Publication Data

Street, Richard Steven.
Everyone had cameras : photography and farmworkers in California, 1850–2000 / Richard Steven Street.
p. cm.
Includes bibliographical references and index.
ISBN 978-0-8166-4966-2 (hc : alk. paper) — ISBN 978-0-8166-4967-9 (pb : alk. paper)
1. Documentary photography—California—History—19th century. 2. Documentary photography—California—History—20th century. 3. Agricultural laborers—California—History—19th century—Pictorial works. 4. Agricultural laborers—California—History—20th century—Pictorial works. I. Title.
TR820.5.S8475 2008
779′.99794053—dc22

2007051643

Printed in the United States of America on acid-free paper

The University of Minnesota is an equal-opportunity educator and employer.

15 14 13 12 11 10 09 08 10 9 8 7 6 5 4 3 2 1

In memory of Colonel Oscar Richard Street,
the crews of Big Job, B-24D,
and the Duchess, B-24D,
especially Colonels David Thompson and Walter Stewart,
and the members of the Eighth Air Force,
330th Squadron,
93rd Bombardment Group (heavy),
"Ted's Traveling Circus,"
Benghazi, North Africa, and Hardwick, England,
1943–1945

Shooting has many meanings when you think about farmworkers, including the murders over the years. . . . Striking farmworkers shot at Wheatland. Farmworkers shot during the Great Depression. Juan de la Cruz shot on the United Farm Workers union picket line at Arvin. In those early Delano years every cop—Kern or Tulare or Highway Patrol—had a camera to shoot farmworkers and their supporters. Every volunteer support group that came to Delano with food, supplies, and money had cameras to shoot. Labor leaders that came to visit and consult with César Chávez had their cameras at the ready. Freelancers, assignment photographers carried several cameras slung around their necks—all to shoot César and his farmworkers. Even some young five-dollar-a-week volunteers had cameras to shoot. Everyone had cameras.

—LEROY CHATFIELD, friend and associate of César Chávez,
National Farm Workers Association/United Farm Workers union, 1964–73

Contents

Preface

This book narrates the long and complicated relationship between photographers and farmworkers in California. It takes the story from before photography into the first daguerreotypes of farmworkers during the gold rush era through the break with commercial norms and development of humanistic photography during the Great Depression and into experimental forms of digital documentary photography at the end of the millennium. Observing a vast, still-evolving historical epoch spanning more than a century and a half, photographers take us on a surprising journey through a visual medium, a dispersed industrial machine, and an ever-changing class of people. The experience of these photographers provides a unique forensic opportunity to explore how we see ourselves and others. It is a prismatic journey, refracting the tensions and trends, triumphs and tragedies, strengths and weaknesses of three-eyed people who as frontline witnesses create what Howard Chapnick, the founder of the photo agency Black Star, calls the ultimate in anthropological and historical documents, "a visual time capsule for our generation and those to follow."[1]

As one of those three-eyed people, I occupy an odd position. Photographing the farmworker story since 1975, I approach this subject as a scholar, observer, and participant. Because this subject is so close to my heart, I have had to probe my own experiences and examine my images the same way that I have probed the work of predecessors and colleagues. Aware that my biases and prejudices might impede a view of the larger picture rather than contribute to it, I have tried to advance its unfolding by extracting insights gained in living the life I describe and by photographing side by side with many of the modern photographers of California farmworkers.

To produce a truly multidisciplinary and interdisciplinary work, I have taken the long view in order to fracture a tendency to think about photographic coverage of California farmworkers as falling into various camps and categories. Dates and labels only approximate a complicated process in which nothing proceeds in a linear manner. Photographers appear, disappear, and reappear over the course of decades. Old distinctions and trends blur and break down, with each one overlapping and intermingling so completely with others as to suggest more of a continuum than a series of dramatic breaks.

Everyone Had Cameras rejects approaches that see photographers as merely artists endowed with an "aura." Building on Allan Sekula's idea that "the photograph, as it stands alone, presents merely the *possibility* of meaning," with the book in hand I try to present all of the "encoding factors" that help viewers understand the people who have photographed farmworkers. I accomplish this by reconstructing the setting, sequence, and venues in which photographers have interacted with farmworkers and by probing the principles, perceptions, and assumptions governing their work. Along the way, I provide clues helpful in "reading" their images. Above all, I try to understand what they did and why they did it. I believe that we can learn from them, and I hope that we can use their images to think about ourselves, where we stand, where we have been, where we are going, and how we communicate.[2]

My concern for context is aligned with the work of Roland Barthes, Lili Bezner, Gail Buckland, James Curtis, Vicki Goldberg, Jim Hughes, Estelle Jussim, Michael Lesy, Ken Light, John Loengard, David M. Lubin, John G. Morris, Martha Sandweiss, Charles Shindo, David Levi Strauss, Carole Squires, Sally Stein, and Alan Trachtenberg (among others), who try to understand how photographers behave by merging biography, history, and photographic criticism. Although the theme of photographers-as-artists is well-worked, consideration of what kind of artists they are (as well as how they use their medium as a powerful instrument of insight and oppression, liberation and control, titillation and reflection) is still evolving.

My goal is to free photographers from insular and problematic dimensions and return them to their original locations. By revitalizing our appreciation of photographers, I hope to highlight the powerfully energizing and ubiquitous emotional, intellectual, and political role that they play in an overwhelmingly visual culture in which, as the critic Andy Grundberg has said, "camera-based images have become the common coin of representation and the means by which we receive most of our information about [the] workings of the world."[3]

No single theory of visual culture or labor relations explains how photographers have interacted with farmworkers, explored social conditions, and shaped social values or the way farmworkers have reciprocated and viewers have filtered images through their own biases. That interaction has involved a dialectical process that externalizes internal visions and raises issues about the boundary between aesthetics and politics, whether or not beautiful photographs undermine action by inspiring excessive admiration, and the extent to which subjects learn from and shape forms of visual representation.

Certainly there is nothing objective about the way photographers work. We all have clients. We all have a point of view. We are full of prejudices and biases, hopes and dreams, anger and sympathy. We record, document, capture, and idealize. Sometimes we do it all at the same time. There is nothing neutral about our images. Commercial and government employers want one thing; private individuals, quite another. Each requires us to advance a particular goal—to look good, capture some aesthetic quality, commemorate a moment, honor a loved one, attract tourists, justify a government program, record a newsworthy event, build sympathy, document evil, inspire action, or incite change.

Whether we are amateurs or professionals, documentarians or commercial artists, we filter the world of farm labor through a lens influenced by psychology, moral values (or lack of them), the market, the client, the employer, technology, deadlines, politics, ambition, and so on. Distorting and selecting, we make countless choices, many of them instantaneous, overlapping, and impossibly complex. Existing in a shifting cultural matrix, we are magicians engaged in an intricate, constantly evolving performance. With light as our wand and a camera bag full of tricks, we produce work that is both solid and highly opaque, work that projects the illusion of capturing what is seen and "speaks for itself" but in fact achieves full impact only when surrounded by substantial decoding information, especially captions. Our work involves a large element of chance, that accidental moment when emotion, content, and composition all come into balance and a masterpiece is created. Knowing all of this, we cannot avoid questioning the fidelity of photographs as documents, even as we marvel at their detail and continually extract new meaning from old images once thought familiar but now seen in a new light.

Following semiotic analysis, we discover in these photographers both indices and icons, reflections of larger forces and mechanisms for asserting power, and, of course, extensions of our hopes and fears, experiences, and points of view. Just plain curious, we want to know who such people are, what makes them tick, and why they focus their attention on people who are radically different from themselves. Alongside those questions are the nuts and bolts of how photographers go about their tasks, the sources of their inspiration, the evolution of their ideas, the nature of the problems they encounter, the ways in which they overcome those problems, and, above all, what they accomplish and whether or not they make a difference. Visiting with such people, we see them developing a photographic discourse following a process that historian John Mraz describes as "people making something out of what their situation is making of them."[4]

Many of these photographers are ordinary people, going about their ordinary business, making ordinary images. Many are familiar names who have produced compelling images that have embedded themselves deeply in the American psyche, disrupted the system, and become symbols for an age. Whatever their background and skill, they are at once historians and what Robin D. G. Kelley calls "high-tech griots." They freeze movements in time and peek behind the mirror. The best do not allow us to forget. Their work affirms what the Roman poet Horace said of pictures, that they are poems without words. This is also the main characteristic of the single most important, influential, and widely recognized image in all of American photography and California farmworkers: Dorothea Lange's *Migrant Mother.* Great art, it touches the human spirit much like a painting by one of the masters. But there are many other photographers, images, and photo essays of equal power and depth, many of them undeservedly obscure, some of them presented here for the first time.[5]

Such work is always substantive, never disappointing. This is another reason why the photographers of California farmworkers are so important. Probing the fissures and wounds of society, we sometimes find ourselves confused and wondering, Am I allowed to see such things? No matter what their talents or defects, fame or obscurity, photographers continue to instruct and inspire nonphotographers, humanists, and activists, even in a world saturated with images. None of this dynamic would have developed if so many of these photographers had not been such great emblematic figures and completely unique and worthy individuals—visually creative, physically active, and emotionally engaged guides through a farm labor system that *Nation* editor Carey McWilliams described as "California's most profound and vexatious social problem."[6]

Abbreviations

AFBF	American Farm Bureau Federation
AFL–CIO	American Federation of Labor and Congress of Industrial Organizations
ALRA	California Agricultural Labor Relations Act
AWA	Agricultural Workers Association
AWOC	Agricultural Workers Organizing Committee
BAE	Bureau of Agricultural Economics
Caltrans	California Department of Transportation
CAWIU	Cannery and Agricultural Workers Industrial Union
CCIH	California Commission of Immigration and Housing
CMM	California Migrant Ministry
CORE	Congress of Racial Equality
CRLA	California Rural Legal Assistance
CUCOM	Confederación de Uniones Campesinos y Obreros Mexicanos
EAS	Emergency Farm Labor Program
FAP	Federal Arts Program
FERA	Federal Emergency Relief Administration
FSA	Farm Security Administration
FTAWU	Food, Tobacco, and Allied Workers Union
FVPU	Fruit and Vegetable Packers Union
GSA	Growers and Shippers Association
GSVA	Grower Shipper Vegetable Association
IATSE	International Alliance of Theatrical Stage Employees
ILA	International Longshoremen's Association

ILWU	International Longshoremen's and Warehousemen's Union
INS	International News Service
IWW	Industrial Workers of the World
MALDEF	Mexican American Legal Defense and Education Fund
NACFL	National Advisory Committee on Farm Labor
NAM	National Association of Manufacturers
NAWU	National Agricultural Workers Union
NEA	National Enterprise Association
NFLU	National Farm Labor Union
NFWA	National Farm Workers Association
NIRA	National Industrial Recovery Act
OEM	Office for Emergency Management
OWI	Office of War Information
PBA	Public Buildings Administration
PCML	President's Commission on Migratory Labor
PWA	Public Works Administration
PWAP	Public Works Art Project
RA	Resettlement Administration
SDP	Southern Documentary Project
SDS	Students for a Democratic Society
SERA	California State Emergency Relief Administration
SNCC	Student Nonviolent Coordinating Committee
STFU	Southern Tenant Farmers Union
UAW	United Automobile Workers
UCAPAWA	United Cannery, Agricultural, Packing, and Allied Workers of America
UFFW	Union of Farm and Field Workers
UFW	United Farm Workers
UFWOC	United Farm Workers Organizing Committee
UP	United Press
UPI	United Press International
UPWA	United Packinghouse Workers of America
USIA	U.S. Information Agency
UXA	Unemployed Exchange Association
WIR	Workers' International Relief
WPA	Works Progress Administration
WRA	War Relocation Authority

I

ORIGINS AND PATTERNS

1767–1934

1

Before Photography

Images from the Era of Conquest and Colonization

Photographers have inspired more attention than any other chroniclers of California farmworkers except for John Steinbeck and Carey McWilliams. Contemporaries found models of behavior in photographers' lives and creative vision in their work, and subsequent generations have turned to them again and again for insight. Today, politicians, lawyers, and labor organizers draw on their work, as do advertising agencies, farmers, and journalists. Across the United States, biographers, labor relations specialists, and historians of California and the American West endlessly scrutinize them, and art historians draw parallels spanning the centuries—how one photographer has used a shaft of light the same way that Vermeer used it to illuminate a subject and how another has captured in faces of union members a look seen in Dutch portrait paintings from the seventeenth century. Although activist photographers have long dominated in the realm of American farmworkers, masters who are known for their landscapes and commercial work and are thought never to have gone near farmworkers have also made substantial contributions. At the same time, cherished icons have been deconstructed, assigned new meanings, and shown to be no more (or less) representative of the truth than any other documents used by historians and, in some cases, even more unreliable; figures once thought familiar are now appreciated from new and more complicated perspectives. All of this has occurred not just because photographers have produced stunning images to be hung on museum walls, published in books, commemorated on postage stamps, and later sold at auction (sometimes for astronomical prices), although that is certainly part of their allure. The more profound reason these photographers command such attention is the immense reassurance they give to creativity, that mysterious ability that always benefits from a human-centered perspective focused on substantive matters.

Photographers working among California farmworkers are devoted to accomplishing difficult goals—some complicated and shifting combination of art and documentation, income and political engagement, self-expression and a desire to witness history up close. Engaged with farmworkers over an immense span of time, they take us on a complicated journey. One part of that journey moves through vast alterations in the photographic profession. At the beginning, photographers recorded farmworkers by coating sheets of highly polished metal with vapors of iodine and bromine, inserting them into a camera for exposures of up to several minutes, then developing their precious, jewel-like images over dangerous mercury vapors. Such images were not reproducible. Seldom seen by more than one or two people, daguerreotypes were slow, expensive, and did not elicit much interest among farmworkers themselves. Today,

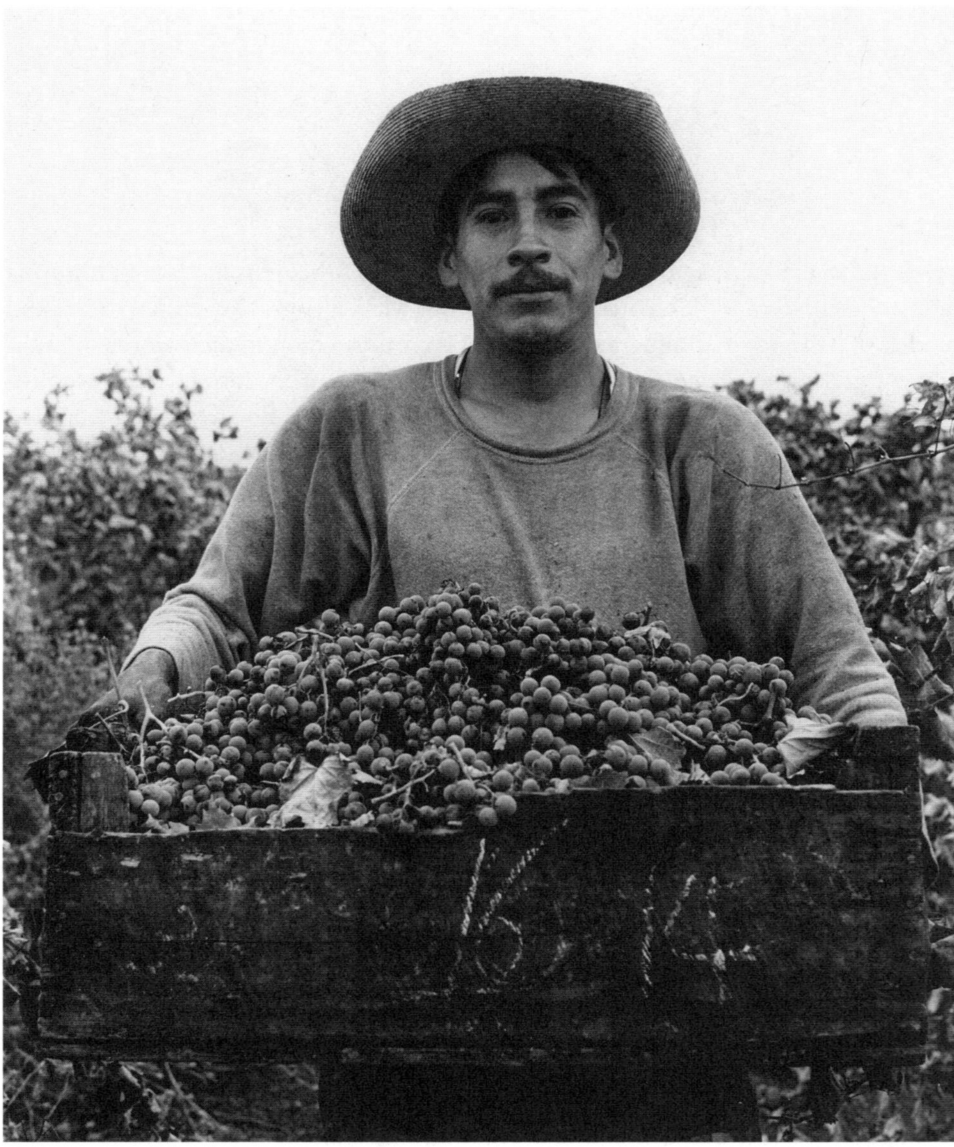

Grape picker bringing in the last harvest in the Berryessa Valley, fall 1955. From *Death of a Valley.* Photograph by Pirkle Jones. Courtesy of Pirkle Jones.

cheap, instantly recorded digital images are multiplied exponentially. Sent halfway around the world by computer and satellite, they often capture the deepest emotions, reflect the most intimate insights and experiences, and are seen by millions of people. At the beginning, no one questioned why anyone photographed farmworkers. Today, socially motivated photographers are criticized, and fundamental concepts like truth and objectivity are challenged. At the beginning, photographers recorded a fragmentary picture. Today, they have amassed an enormous record. For every shot that has been published, many more remain unseen. Amounting to perhaps the single most substantial and extended visual account of the American laboring classes, the cumulative outcome of this effort is something one commentator likened to a Ken Burns–type newsreel and another described as the California counterpart to Michael Lesy's *Wisconsin Death Trip.*[1]

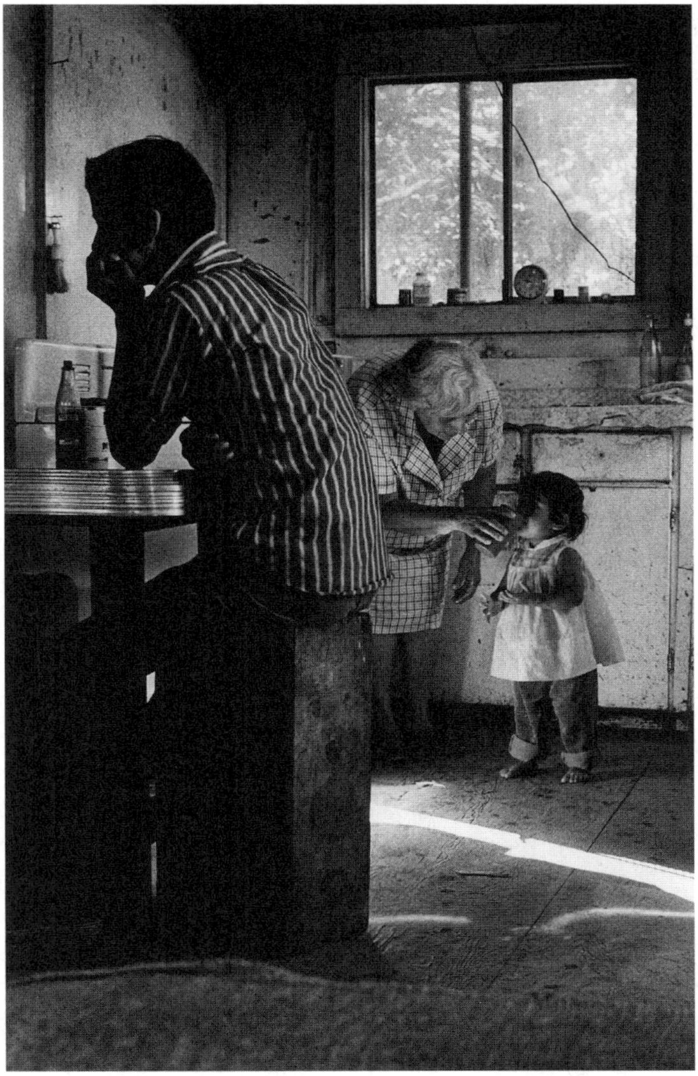

Waiting for work at the Gilroy ranch, Gilroy, September 1971. Photograph by Morrie Camhi. Courtesy of Morrie Camhi.

On their journey through the farmworker landscape, photographers have demonstrated an unusual resilience, as well as an ability to incorporate European ideas, move in new directions, and remain innovative and pragmatic while exploring the ever-changing face of farm labor. They have helped to establish new ways of seeing, especially the social documentary and "concerned" perspectives, which have a profound effect on public perceptions of the world; proved the value of new camera technology, like the 35-millimeter Leica; and applied new visual techniques, like the photo essay. Watching them move in and out of the fields, we quickly realize their diverse and eclectic nature. Every species of photographer is here, professionals and amateurs alike: great canonical figures and anonymous journeymen; geniuses whose work has remained undeservedly obscure and young children using inexpensive cameras to explore family roots. Left-wing photographers tiring of highly profitable work shooting catsup bottles and spoons are here alongside voyeurs "day-tripping into someone else's nightmare" (as British photographer Anthony Lloyd has said of certain war photographers covering Bosnia in 1993). Also here are idealists on the lam from Nazi Germany; Spanish expatriates landing in Mexico wearing cameras and rags; social scientists pioneering the camera as a means of visual note taking; freelancers establishing a reputation; union activists employed by farmworker unions; teenage dishwashers grabbing their Kodak on the spur of the moment; fashion photographers expanding their portfolios; famous photo essayists on extended assignment; town photographers going through their everyday routine; portrait photographers moving out of the studio into the fields; and digital manipulators generating insights that traditional photographic techniques will not yield. These photographers embody every type of personality, from the cool and detached to the passionate and political, from the shy and retiring to the assertive and aggressive, from wild men who dress in tatters to pretenders sporting the latest Domke gear and big dangling telephoto lenses. Women also make a disproportionate contribution, often far in advance of their male counterparts, as do husband and wife teams in collaborations of creative intimacy.[2]

Nothing about these photographers is simple, straightforward, self-evident, one-way, or objective. Masters of light and shadow, with the capacity to educate as well as inspire, to represent as well as misrepresent, these photographers have been responsible for creating degrading and stereotypical caricatures of people naturally inclined to stoop labor (as seen in the many examples of photographic propaganda and advertising that perpetuate racist and sexist stereotypes) as well as counterimages of success and ambition, laughter and play, hard work and family life, selflessness and the struggle to develop countervailing power, and the exercise of personal responsibility at political events and social functions. Some of these photographers have done all of this and more. Others have kept to one approach and never changed.

Watching photographers going about their business, we confront life's dilemmas and the difficult decisions that we all must face: the conflict between business and conscience, the struggle between selflessness and ambition, and the challenge of maintaining high aesthetic values without compromising content. Getting to know such people, we often discover ourselves admiring their physical, emotional, and intellectual bravery. Whether shooting advertising or covering a strike, they are addicted to the "golden hours" around sunrise and sunset. In pursuit of that light, they follow the same routine. Rising before dawn, they put in a long day and collapse in exhaustion, then drag themselves out of bed or the back seat of their automobile to photograph again at first light. We sometimes want to direct them this way, point out some obstacle, save them from some stupid error, remind them to eat and rest, or warn them away from a deputy about to spray them with tear gas. We hope they linger in a field, ask more questions, shift their perspective, switch lenses, and drive on a little farther to the next camp. But we must let them encounter farmworkers as they do in order to understand something about the photographic passion. As Hegel said, passion is at the core of human attributes, because without it we fail to have the energy and character required for attainment of purpose. Time and again, passion, coupled with the kind of luck known to gamblers and hunters, carries these photographers past the feelings of inertia and helplessness that conspire against accomplishment and places them at the right place at the right time. Seeing them there, we begin to appreciate them as emblematic, even universal, figures.[3]

By studying these photographers, we approach that which we all seek—understanding of ourselves. Observing photographers crippled by hunger and poverty, stalled by mud and heat, struggling against loneliness and betrayal, facing down all kinds of dangers, begging for money, and venturing off the well-worn paths of their profession simply to take a good picture or record something of interest, we glimpse those qualities of spontaneity and calculation, loyalty and empathy, which are at the core of all accomplishing personalities. Also present in abundance are such human qualities as tenacity, patience, determination, stamina, and resolve. With a deep love of history and an understanding of the value of historical images, one photographer rescued from the garbage heap at the very last minute a key archive of glass-plate negatives produced by a predecessor who covered life and labor in the fields around Modesto early in the twentieth century. Two other photographers would wait fifty years before finally publishing two highly original photographic essays that barely interested anyone when they were first created.

These are not negative and despairing artists. We are amazed by their imagination and novelty, their complete commitment to their craft, the uniform quality of their work, their skill, and their emphasis on fundamentals. Even the most commercial among them are forward looking and hopeful. Seldom willing to settle for mere snapshots, even if that is all that is required, they love their craft and always try to go beyond their predecessors by constantly pushing the limits of camera technology and asking the questions: What is important? How do I capture it? So often we find ourselves looking at their work and wanting to know, What was in their hearts as they photographed blood flowing from gunshot wounds, heads smashed by police truncheons, and mummified human remains? How did they keep control as the tear gas hit them? Did they cry or break down upon seeing those bodies in the desert? What was it like in the middle of that cloud of DDT? How long did the nightmares continue? Did they later develop leukemia, or worse, from that cloud of looper poison?

One of the ways these photographers affect us most powerfully is in dissolving anonymity and underscoring byline. *California Farmer,* the Farm Security Administration (FSA), or United Press International (UPI) did not take these images. Human beings have stood in these spots, looked this way, and engaged in an intellectual process involving intricate, concurrent decisions, many of them intuitive, all coming together when finger and intellect joined forces in a fraction of a second. Human beings have paid a price to take these pictures. They sweat bullets. They sleep somewhere other than in a bed for days. They stink and have no time to eat a proper meal. In the early years of photography, they packed thousands of pounds of glass plates, coated them inside dark tents, and composed their pictures on viewing screens that inverted their compositions. They drive thousands of miles. They cross borders. They climb trees and telephone poles. They have been sprayed with Mace. Foremen have threatened them. Supervisors have fired them. Thugs have smashed their cameras. Film laboratories have lost their film. News media have refused to look at their work. To do their best, they have had to quit and strike out on their own.

Whether they are commercial, artistic, social documentary, or news photographers, or some combination thereof, and wherever their journey takes them, such people greet

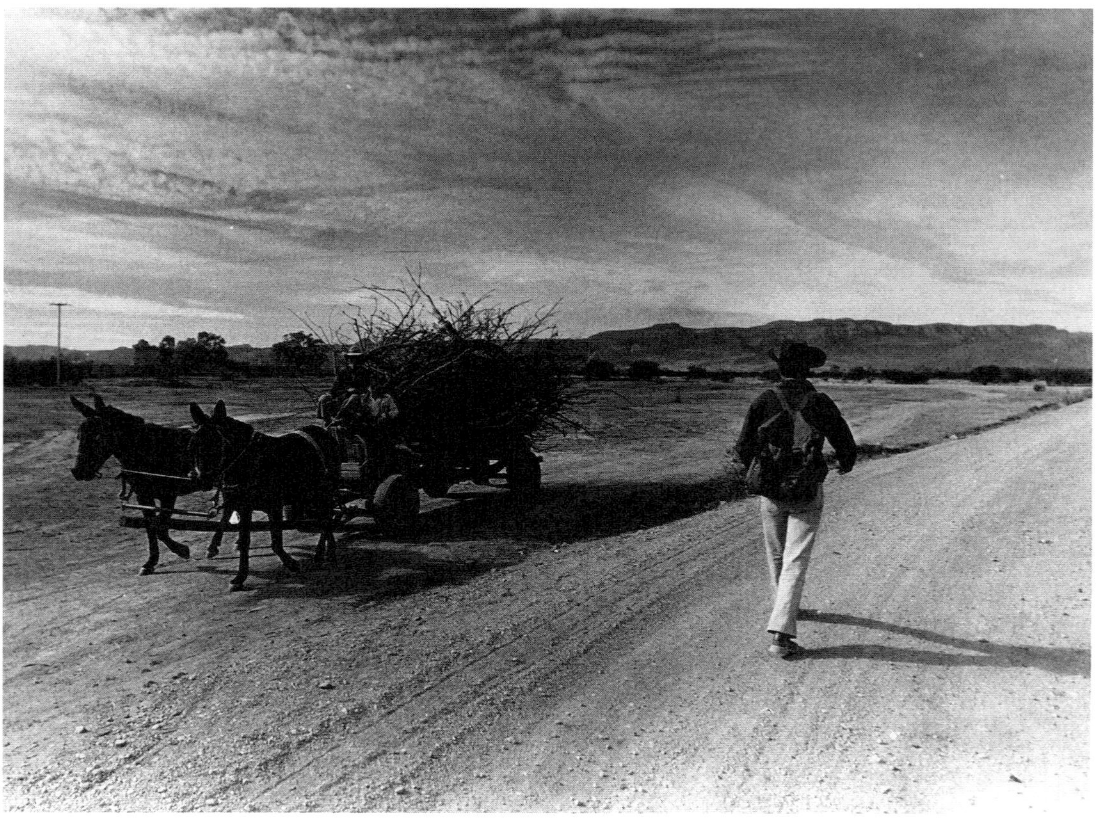

A farmworker from south of the border begins his journey north, March 1980. From *Faces beyond the Border.* Photograph by Len Lahman. Courtesy of Len Lahman.

us as worldly individuals now coming back with experiences and insight. No matter how long they have been away, we throw up our arms and embrace them. At day's end, it is like sitting around the campfire. We delight in their stories and adventures and wonder if we would have been up to the task.[4]

Another way they affect us is in conveying some of the excitement underlying their visual journeys. In viewing their work, we follow them on assignment, which can take us on a dark trek into the valley of the shadow of death, a reality tour off the beaten paths, or an enlightening journey of self-discovery. Through these photographers we appreciate many of the defining characteristics of their profession. The discovery that so many California photographers have photographed in the fields—including those not ordinarily considered in the same vein, such as Ansel Adams and Max Yavno—holds great significance and sheds new light on old masters we once thought we knew, adding to the debate over what makes this group of photographers unique. Along with the often cited inspiration provided by a dramatic landscape, environmental concerns, technical virtuosity, and the drive to achieve personal freedom in a new social setting, California photographers, to a degree that is surprising and heretofore unacknowledged, have been drawn en masse to farmworkers.[5]

But the dimension that provides the greatest meaning and depth to their journey and their accomplishments is what they show us. Photographers make farmworkers real to millions of Americans. Their images are pregnant with information and launch us on the second part of an amazing journey. Through their work, we overcome geographic separation—the schism between farm and suburb—discovering a nexus of nature and culture, myth and reality, petro farming and advanced irrigation, and the industrialization of resources and human beings on a gigantic scale. We shake hands not only with people of color and immigrants moving north from Mexico and Central America and east from China, Japan, India, and the Philippines, but also with dispossessed American-born drifters, European immigrants, Okies and Arkies, people variously labeled as wetbacks, illegals, and bindle stiffs. Quickly we become aware of the ever-changing face of rural California. We confront exploitation and cruelty, generosity and courage. We witness triumph and tragedy, the ordinary and the extraordinary, alongside joy and sorrow, birth and death, family and loneliness.

Whatever their background and orientation, whatever the era in which they have worked, and regardless of their employers, politics, and working methodology, photographers have not been able to avoid questions of class, class conflict, power, exploitation, social justice, and the exertions of hard physical labor under the sun. They show us that the 350,000 farmworkers currently employed in California agriculture are as important to fruit and vegetable farmers as the sun, water, soil, and technology. Their images reveal the human cost of cheap food: arthritic backs, children maimed by exposure to pesticides, impoverished and dysfunctional rural communities, and people long excluded from the social and legal privileges enjoyed by most Americans. Shattering an immense advertising system's facade of Mediterranean images superimposed on large-scale, commercial farming, photographers underscore the extent to which food production rests on the backs of successive waves of landless peasants.

Through photographers we become more fully conscious of the origins of agricultural abundance and the true nature of modern food culture.[6]

In assessing the impact of photographers' work, one cannot produce any quantifiable proof that they have changed anything or made a difference. A few critics routinely assert that photographers, in order to build their own careers, distort and misrepresent a picture that is actually not so bad or, conversely, they make too pretty that which is ugly in order to garner large commercial fees. Some people might argue that images of immigrant field hands living in caves and shelters made of garbage during strawberry harvest remind us of the growing gap between rich and poor and the existence of a variety of American apartheid. Others might say that after being exposed again and again to such images we suffer a kind of "compassion fatigue" in which the I've-seen-it-before syndrome can be overcome only by seeking ever more sensational images. Most people would probably agree with what we intuitively know and see from common experience: that even more than writers, journalists, and novelists, photographers have the capacity to change thinking, that they matter very much to farmworkers, that their work has a compelling and subversive effect. One could also argue that such work exerts its most profound impact not on the public but on the photographers themselves. Can you remain aloof while constantly confronting violence and oppression as a photojournalist? What does it mean to turn a blind eye and camouflage or consciously distort injustice and exploitation as a commercial photographer? Even the most consummate professionals cannot claim to be unaffected by what they see and how they record it. Few shrug it all off as just part of life.[7]

Although social documentary photographers employed by the Farm Security Administration during the Great Depression are usually hailed for contributing the most to public understanding, their successors and modern counterparts have done much more with much less over a much longer period of time. Largely through the efforts of these later photographers, the farmworker movement gained an audience. During the Delano grape strike from 1965 to 1970, a small group of audacious photographers played a key role in projecting the conflict far beyond the vineyards into the larger public arena, allowing farmworkers to launch a boycott of table grapes that disrupted the American conscience as much as any striking group of coal miners or auto workers. As important to the United Farm Workers union (UFW) as politicians, picket captains, labor leaders, reporters, and the usual array of volunteers and sympathetic bystanders, these photographers shaped the organizing struggle along with such traditional labor relations factors as the nature of the workforce, the structure of the industry, characteristics of employers, and the role of government. Just as scenes of police billy clubs and fire hoses unleashed against peaceful civil rights protesters in the American South seem incredible to many citizens, scenes of mass marches, fasts, arrests, and nonviolent protests affect and galvanize public attitudes toward the farmworker struggle in California and across the United States. Through photographers the American public first glimpsed the emergence of La Raza and sensed the pride and solidarity among a small band of union members and community activists who were forging new identities, creating new lives, and seizing political power. With the exception of the civil rights movement, few other struggles and few other classes have been so strongly impacted by photographers and photography.

Today, photographers are acutely aware of the role they play. Many regard themselves as visual historians. They try to avoid duplication by taking the story to new levels. Often at the very instant they compose a picture, they find themselves comparing what they see in their viewfinders with hundreds of similar scenes recorded by their predecessors. While some have consciously avoided replicating earlier work, others are impelled to record such images precisely because they directly confront questions of change and continuity. To accomplish these goals, photographers have become a ubiquitous presence. No organizing activity, no strike, no protest, no boycott is set in motion without ample photographic coverage, notification of all possible newspaper photographers, or contact with all variety of freelancers. So deeply imbedded in the farmworker story are photographers that it cannot be told, studied, or understood without paying attention to their still-evolving vision. So common are they as witnesses on picket lines and at strikes and demonstrations that it is normal to see not only photojournalists and social documentary photographers but also security guards, police, growers, farmworkers, and assorted bystanders, all armed with cameras, each awaiting some decisive or incriminating moment.

Visual representation of California farmworkers unfolds as an extended parable of the American West and an epic subplot in photographic history. It has roots stretching back to the earliest forms of exploratory visual representation at the beginning of the Spanish frontier in North America, as well as to older graphic art forms and broader practices of picture making as a whole, and it embraces a wide spectrum of artistic expression and personalities, ranging from the quickly sketched pencil drawings of rank amateurs to the carefully executed paintings of acknowledged masters. Even before photographers appeared on the scene, California farmworkers had attracted the attention of three groups: artists and foreign visitors to Alta California; landscape painters whose harvest scenes set the countryside aglow but could not omit the people at the center of the action; and magazine illustrators who captured scenes of wonder and curiosity in the era before halftone photographic reproduction began. Dealing with the rhythms of life, the nature of work, and the imperatives of the natural and altered environment, they established views, popularized techniques, and, most important, inaugurated a discourse vacillating between realism and fantasy, agony and ecstasy, and the beautiful and the sublime, which shaped the picture of farm labor well into the era of photography.[8]

The first artist to paint California farmworkers was perhaps the most unlikely of all, Father Ignacio Tirsch. A thirty-four-year-old, Bohemia-born Jesuit, Tirsch had arrived in San José del Cabo, Baja California, in 1762. The settlement along the Bay of San Bernabé was at the southern tip of the peninsula, straight across the Sea of Cortez from Culiacán, Mexico, a convenient layover on the trade route followed by Spanish and Filipino traders across the Pacific Ocean. Taking charge of Mission Santiago, about fifty miles north, Tirsch began painting and sketching for pleasure and relaxation and, in 1767, devoted spare moments to creating a series of idyllic drawings and watercolors of the animals, plants, people, and places that he encountered in the area. A full-time padre busy ministering to his mission, Tirsch was anything but accomplished in his avocation. His pictures had a cartoonlike quality, vividly colored but amateurish in execution.

Sometime during his painting, Tirsch turned his attention to Mission San José del Cabo. Sketching it first in ink and later coloring it by brush, he adopted an elevated perspective, looking at the community as if seen from the roof of a church or the coastal foothills. Only peripherally concerned with depicting the local Pericú Indians who tended crops in the fields, Tirsch placed the mission outbuildings, sheep pen, dogs, cemetery, and living quarters for farm hands on the right, bisected the picture with a beautiful flowing stream, and placed the fields, oxen, and granary on the left. Field hands appear as small and dark figures in submissive roles, carrying sacks of grain, working land near the beach, toting their burdens, and bending over their tools. Mounted riders, some carrying swords and wearing fancy hats and archaic costumes, direct them in their work. A Philippine sailing vessel is anchored just offshore

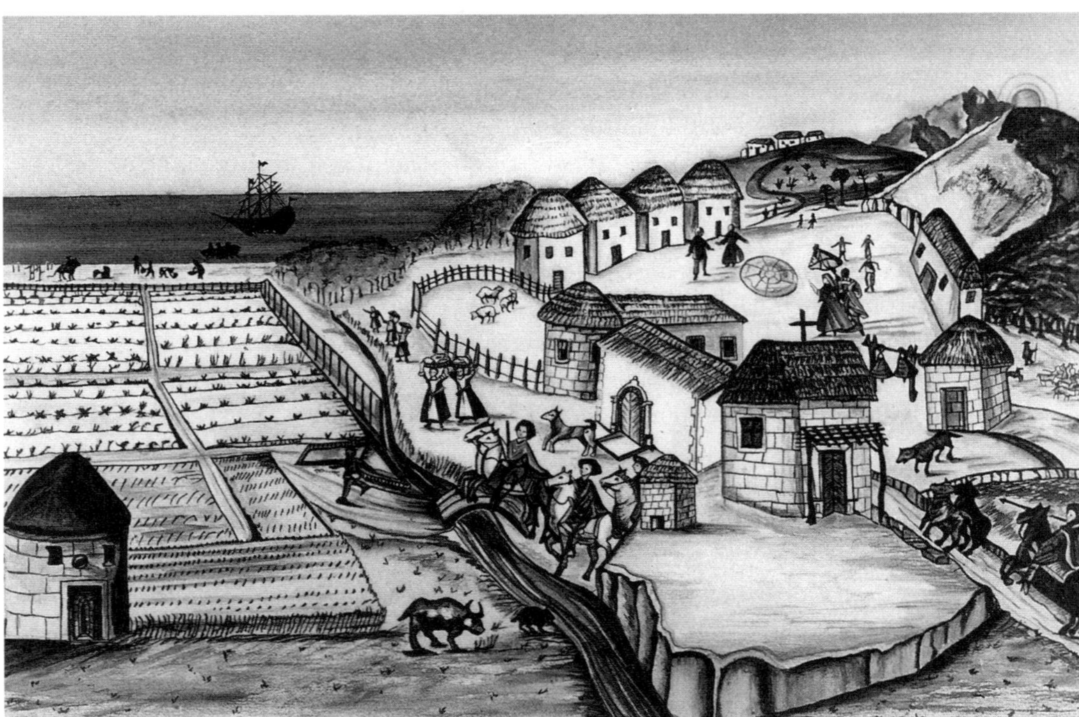

Field hands at Mission San José del Cabo, Baja California. Watercolor by Joanne Crosby after an original 1767 drawing by Padre Ignacio Tirsch, S.J., in Doyce B. Nunis, ed., *The Drawings of Ignacio Tirsch: A Jesuit Missionary in Baja California,* trans. Elizabeth Schultz-Bischof (1972). Original color illustration in the State Library of the University of Prague, Czech Republic. Watercolor facsimile courtesy Joanne Crosby, from Harry W. Crosby, *Antigua California* (Albuquerque, 1994).

awaiting resupply. Bathed in soft, golden light of the sun setting behind the coastal hills, the scene projects a sense of ordered prosperity, suggesting a lively, self-sufficient medieval town.[9]

As the earliest surviving picture of natives who were forced to abandon hunting and gathering, indoctrinated in the mysteries of the Catholic religion, and set to clearing land, constructing irrigation systems, planting and tending crops, Tirsch's watercolor captures the key role that native field hands played in creating an agricultural surplus. Without that surplus, the padres could not have established a series of self-sufficient outposts, expanded their influence northward, attracted ever-larger numbers of natives, converted them to field hands, and secured vast amounts of territory that extended Spanish influence throughout the Western Hemisphere. But in all other facets, the watercolor is a completely fictitious distortion of a colonial institution that, for native peoples, fit into an archipelago of incarceration. Nowhere in the pretty picture of a happy place well integrated into the natural landscape is there any sense of the stinking reality of open latrines, native peoples ravaged by measle epidemics, or the pervasive presence of church-imposed routine. Seen through this padre's eyes, the tiny Indian field hands dwarfed in the picture's background exemplify what art historian Brian Lukacher describes as "the spectacle of national power and its pleasurable integration within the natural order."[10]

Had Tirsch remained at his beloved post, he might have considerably expanded the picture of mission field hands. Such a picture would have been especially valuable in filling a void in Jesuit recollections stressing the inherently lazy and incompetent nature of their agricultural recruits. But what could have been, never was. The following year Tirsch was arrested and expelled from Baja California, just as all of the other Jesuit missionaries were purged from power in Mexico and South America. Packing his precious paintings into a chest, he shipped out under cover of night, sailed across the Gulf of California, and walked overland for seven weeks to Veracruz, Mexico. Catching a ship for Belgium, he returned to his home in Prague and lived out the remainder of his life in a monastery, dying in such complete obscurity that his death and place of burial went unrecorded.[11]

Never published, transferred to prints, or otherwise made available for a wide audience, Tirsch's precious picture remained an intensely personal and solitary record locked away in the Clementinum Library. It did not see the light of day for several centuries, until the Clementinum was absorbed into the Czech State Library at the University of Prague. Only then did it become apparent that Tirsch had produced something truly historic while also establishing a precedent, later adopted by photographers, for recording field hands not as people worthy of documentation on their own merits but as elements of scale and decorations in a bucolic landscape.[12]

To these distortions, the Spanish soon added a kind of visual amnesia. Documenting or even acknowledging the work of Baja California field hands was not so much as an afterthought in the mind of José de Gálvez, the megalomaniacal *visitador general* (inspector general) of New Spain and the greatest Spanish expansionist in the Western Hemisphere. After arriving at San José del Cabo on July 5, 1768, Gálvez, along with the Mexican viceroy Marqués de Croix and King Carlos III, dreamed of large territorial strategies. Hoping to block English fur trappers venturing south from Canada and west from Louisiana, as well as Russian fur trappers sailing east into Alaska inevitably to make their way down the west coast, Gálvez and King Carlos III devised a plan to secure Alta (Upper) California, which then encompassed the entire swath of land from the northern portions of the Baja California peninsula through present-day Oregon, by planting missions at Monterey and San Diego, then adding a string of additional missions thirty to sixty miles apart along the coast.

From several centuries of mission building throughout the Western Hemisphere, the Franciscans knew there would be a massive amount of work clearing and planting fields, building and maintaining irrigation works, converting Indian hunter–gatherers to European-style agriculture, and creating self-sustaining agricultural enterprises. To accomplish this, expedition leaders rounded up a force of eighty-six of the most loyal and trusted natives from the Baja California missions. Becoming the core of two large overland expeditions under the spiritual command of Padres Junípero Serra and Juan Crespí, these campesinos marched three hundred miles north through the Central Desert to found Mission San Diego in the spring of 1769 and then another three hundred miles north to found Mission Monterey later that summer. Digging fresh graves daily, they buried sixty of their own by the end of July, endured a series of Indian attacks that killed many others, and lost six more from their ranks to some combination of exhaustion, exposure, and overwork that winter. But even though they performed countless tasks, played a critical role in teaching agriculture to native Californians, and died in droves, no Spanish padre, soldier, or official thought Baja California field hands important enough to commemorate or acknowledge their efforts in even the crudest sketch or drawing.[13]

As the padres expanded their realm, thousands of Indians were gathered into a chain of missions scattered between San Diego and Sonoma. Lured, enticed, dragooned, and otherwise baptized and converted to Catholicism, they were transformed from hunters and gatherers into vaqueros, masons, and other types of workers whose labor was absolutely essential for creating what were, in effect, self-sufficient religious plantations. Field hands were by far the most important of these new mission workers. At first trained by Baja California campesinos, they learned to plant, cultivate, and harvest and soon grew into the largest single group of mission workers, about one-third of the labor force by most estimates. Without them the missions could not have survived. But as with their predecessors from the Baja California missions, their indispensability did not inspire artistic treatment, even of the rudest sort. This would have important consequences. With plenty to say about the nature and character of their new converts, especially their lazy, backward ways, and the almost total absence of any competing views, either written or visual, the padres completely controlled the dialogue.[14]

But the power of the padres was not the only thing that allowed them to impose their view. They were also aided by their extremely isolated location. At the northernmost extension of the Spanish Empire, more than two thousand miles away from the nearest colonial center in Mexico City, California was sealed off on the east by the

Sierra Nevada and the wide swampy valley of the San Joaquin and on the west by the vast Pacific Ocean. From the missions to civilization was a long, long way. Only two routes existed. One was by sea and required supply ships to tack their way north around Cabo San Lucas up the coast. Lasting four months or more, these voyages could meet with disaster at any point along the way. Some did not arrive at all, and those making it all the way with their cargo frequently disgorged entire crews sick with scurvy. The other route was little more than a mule train along the perilous north–south trail known as El Camino Real. Few who took this route actually rode mules, which were overburdened with supplies. To reach the missions, padres, soldiers, and settlers walked most of the way from Mexico, much of it through deserts.[15]

Under such conditions, no established class of artists could exist. Nor did any of the padres, soldiers, majordomos, or Spanish and Mexican officials evidence any talent for illustration. Even if they had, how could they have gone about it? They lacked the paint, ink, pencils, brushes, paper, canvas, and other supplies necessary for executing even rudimentary sketches. And even if someone possessed the will, ability, and supplies to sketch and paint, it is unlikely that they would have turned their talents to the mundane realities of life and labor in the fields. Who would want to see such pictures? Only the native Californians outside the missions, with their finger-painted rock art and pictographs, and those leaving subaltern graffiti inside the churches produced images at this time. No artist explored farmworkers the same way that the influential European painter Pieter Brueghel the Elder (1525–1569) had explored reaping and harvesting scenes two centuries earlier. No one began to produce anything that even remotely touched on the lives of mission farmworkers until successive waves of explorers sailed into California. These explorers did not encounter mission field hands in a single given time frame. Theirs was a purposeful process of discovery and rediscovery extending over three generations.[16]

Exploration was a complex hit-and-miss business, preliminary and unsystematic, a confrontation with the unknown, a path along a river, a voyage down a coast, a foray inland, usually to be followed by a more thorough, comprehensive, and systematic survey. The explorers who ventured into California had very specific goals serving larger imperial agendas. Their expeditions were intelligence-gathering operations, career-building adventures, preliminary steps toward colonization, often inoculated with a large dose of Enlightenment ideas about knowledge. Each conducted investigations. From the maps and notes, the collected specimens and the drawings, the flora and fauna, grew a series of observations and conclusions that guided and shaped not only the destiny of the newly encountered locations and their inhabitants but the explorers as well. These observations and conclusions were published in reports, usually several years after the explorers returned home, a kind of first step before taking possession or, in rare cases, avoiding further contact. Such reports yielded different images of California as a great empty place, a land of savages and worm eaters, a New Spain, Devonshire reincarnate, and many more. To accomplish their country's goals, explorers always made sure to take along plenty of scientists, astronomers, geologists, cartographers, botanists, and physicians. Their specialized information would inform the expedition's findings and contribute to a more precise understanding of a single location. Explorers also understood the usefulness of the visual arts in bringing attention to and illustrating their work, so they always employed at least one artist. These artists are of central importance to the early picture of native peoples and early California farmworkers. In the course of their more general work, they established categories, used techniques, set objectives, and produced images that diverged from or amplified the work of their compatriots, had lasting impact in their own right, and shaped perspectives well into the nineteenth century.[17]

The first of these exploring expedition artists was Gaspard Duché de Vancy, a member of a handpicked crew assembled with great fanfare by French explorer Jean-François Galaup de La Pérouse for his around-the-world exploration. Vancy had departed with La Pérouse from the French port of Brest on August 1, 1785, onboard *La Boussole* or *L'Astrolabe,* intent on spending four years at sea, visiting every continent, gathering intelligence, and exploring trade opportunities for King Louis XVI. When Vancy arrived at Monterey on the morning of September 14, 1786, he had already sailed across the Atlantic Ocean, around Cape Horn, and up the Pacific Coast as far

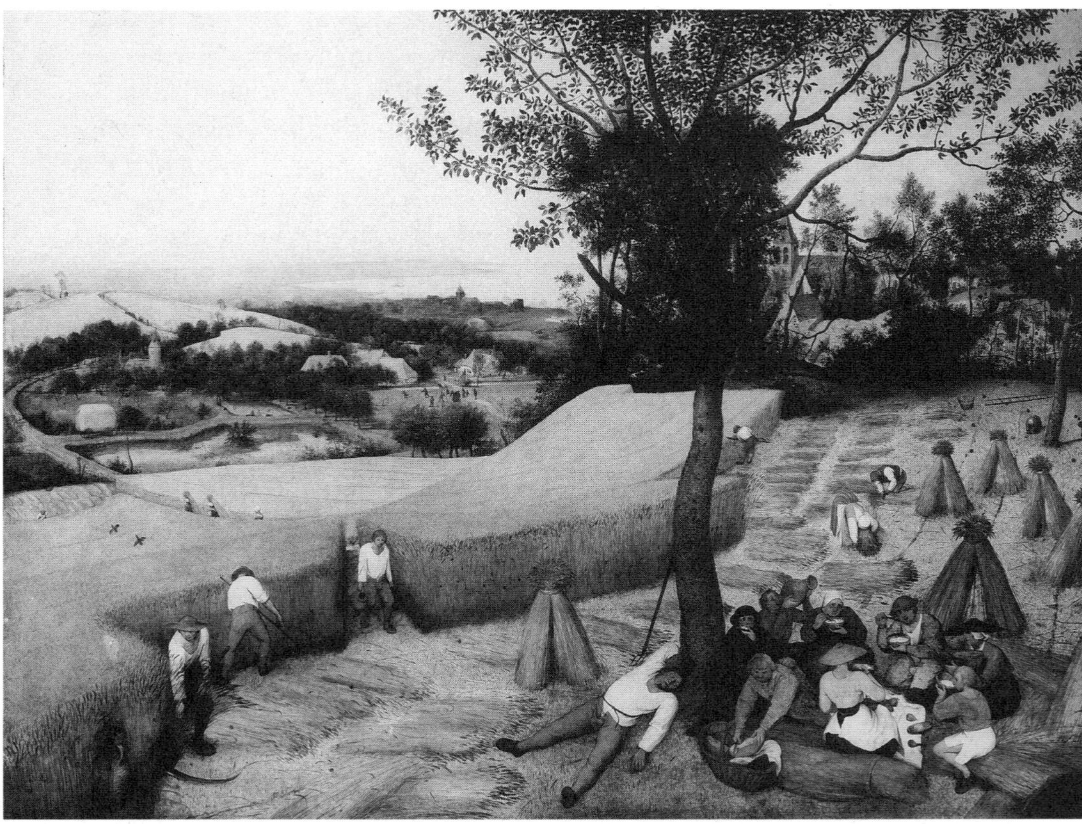

Phases of grain harvesting depicted in *The Harvesters,* 1565. Oil on wood painting by Pieter Brueghel the Elder. Courtesy of The Metropolitan Museum of Art, Rogers Fund, 1919. Image copyright The Metropolitan Museum of Art.

north as Alaska, with layovers in southern Chile, on Easter Island, and in Hawaii. Rowing ashore through the fog in longboats with the sailors, scientists, physicians, engineers, mapmakers, and other members of the expedition, he was amazed to see a landscape similar to that of southern France. Received like a visiting lord and given the run of Mission San Carlos, he unpacked his sketch pads and went to work. He would spend the next ten days with fifty-year-old Padre Fermín Lasuén, a handful of Spanish soldiers, and 711 baptized Indians, all living together in squalor.

As an expedition member, Vancy had grown accustomed to making quick preliminary sketches and then later fleshing them out onboard ship. Impressed by the plenitude of native wildlife, a healthful climate, great natural beauty, and the large crops of maize, barley, wheat, and peas, he began sketching sturdy *soldados* (soldiers) and various birds, fish, and animals. But a few days after landing, Vancy had a chance to become a kind of journalist with a sketch pad. Watching a reception in the mission courtyard, he shortly thereafter created a memorable sketch that would become a central icon in the debate over mission life and mission farmworkers. This sketch adopted a slightly elevated vantage point to depict a line of pitiful-looking Indians. Wearing nothing but loincloths, these Indians, many of whom no doubt were field hands, stand for inspection before the padres, La Pérouse, and his staff. On the right, a dark form that may be a statue of the Virgin Mary watches over the event from a drab chapel. In the background, an attendant rings bells on a makeshift scaffold. Although organized to impress the visitors, it was not a pretty sight. "In a word, everything reminded us of a habitation in Sait Domingo [*sic,* Santo Domingo], or any other West Indian colony," La Pérouse later recalled. "The men and women are assembled by the sound of the bell, one of the religious conducts them to their work, to church, and to all other exercises. We mention it with pain, the resemblance is so perfect, that we saw men and women loaded with irons, others in the stocks; and at length the noise of the strokes of a whip struck in our ears."[18]

Accusations of slavery, exploitation, and abuse dogged the missions from the beginning, with subsequent anti-Franciscan writers characterizing the missionaries as monsters presiding over something that journalist Carey McWillams described as a kind of "Auschwitz with roses," and pro-Franciscan scholars defending the missions as the morally uplifting products of self-sacrificing Catholic padres. Although Vancy captured something of the power that the Franciscans held over their field hands, he was not at the mission long enough to sketch field hands at work and further explore themes of exploitation, failure, and denial of freedom. Nor was he able to share his ideas among freedom-loving French citizens back home. Departing from Monterey on September 22, Vancy sailed across the Pacific Ocean with La Pérouse. He reached Macao, on the south coast of China, in late December, then continued to Manila, the Kamchatka Peninsula, and Samoa. On March 10, 1788, after sketching around Botany Bay, Australia, he departed for France but was never seen again. Somewhere east of the Solomon Islands, both *La Boussole* and *L'Astrolabe* hit a reef and sank. Vancy either died in the wreck or struggled ashore with a group of survivors to live out his last days among natives, some of whom perished in a futile attempt to reach Manila in a handmade boat. His journals from Mission San Carlos survive because La Pérouse gave many of them to homeward-bound sailors he encountered along the way. His sketches survive because he left three with Padre Lasuén, who protected them long enough for a subsequent visiting artist to make copies.[19]

Five years after Vancy looked askance at field hands caught in what seemed to be a kind of religious penal colony, two other expedition artists, José "Pepe" Cardero and Tomás de Suría, arrived at Monterey with a Spanish expedition commanded by Alejandro Malaspina. Cardero was a diminutive twenty-five-year-old who had joined the expedition two years earlier as a lowly *criado,* or cabin boy, and worked his way up to novice artist before being assigned to mapping duties as a last-minute replacement for an ill officer. Suría, a Mexico City–based artist–engraver on loan from the Mexican mint, had joined the expedition near Acapulco. Sometime between September 10 and September 25, 1791, these artists produced at least nineteen detailed pen-and-ink drawings in and around the presidio and mission. Seldom deviating in their routine, they not only surveyed the flora and fauna and the exotic and common but also drew amply endowed Indian women wearing traditional braided tule skirts and sea otter robes, handsome native men displaying common tools, modest and tidy Hispanic women in short frocks, strong *soldados* with broad-brimmed hats and finely tooled leather jackets, newly constructed buildings, the stockade, the plaza, and various tribal customs

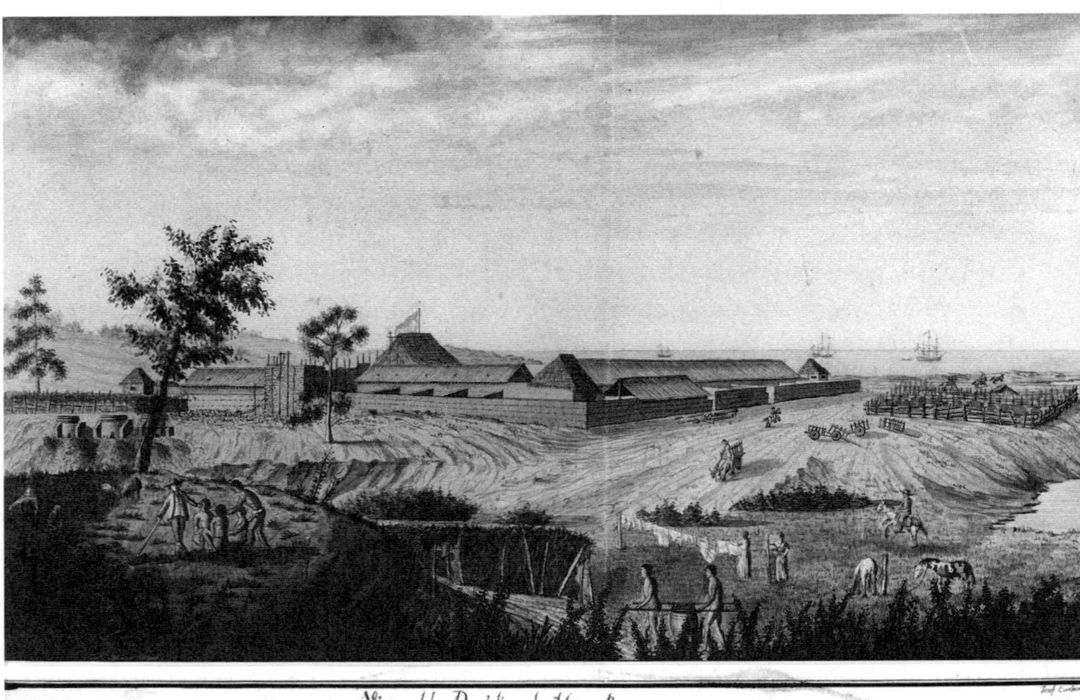

Vista del presidio de Monte Rey. Pen and ink drawing by José ("Pepe") Cardero, September 10, 1791. Original in El Museo Naval de Madrid, Spain; copy in the Robert Honeyman Collection, Bancroft Library, University of California, Berkeley. Courtesy of El Museo Naval de Madrid.

and rituals. Intended as an easily comprehended and highly flattering visual inventory revealing the suitability of the territory for agriculture, mining, and settlement, these pictures ignored the displacement of Indian communities, the disruption of tribal relations, and the lethal effects of introduced germs and diseases. And while most of this work suggests that mission Indians were a people eagerly awaiting the spark of European enlightenment, at least three images deviate from formulaic approaches to add important new dimensions to the picture of mission field hands at this time.[20]

One of these is a watercolor, probably by Cardero. Adopting a distant perspective overlooking the presidio garden, *Vista del presidio de Monte Rey* depicts an overseer astride a horse who supervises two men carrying a water barrel to a field near what appears to be vineyards. In the foreground, Indian women hang out the day's wash. Behind them a field hand drives a *carreta* (cart). Everything suggests a colony throbbing with activity. Only the intersection of the imposing presidio walls extending nearly into the fields hints at the need for protection in this otherwise Arcadian vision of Spanish mission agriculture, which is apparently the earliest picture of natives toiling in the fields. A second pen-and-ink sketch, also attributed to Cardero, depicts Indian field hands and other natives mingling with Hispanic colonists and explorers in the courtyard of Mission San Carlos de Borromeo. While ignoring such essential activities as weeding, planting, and threshing (performed by one-third of the mission population, according to most estimates), Cardero's view, with its wide perspective and attention to symmetry, nevertheless broke new ground, capturing a sense of where field hands ventured daily as they walked to and from Mass and communal meals and also identifying salient environmental details, including a *ranchería* (a native settlement) in the background of one image. The third drawing, done in pencil and attributed to Suría, is titled *Modo de pelear de los Indios* (How the Indians Fight). It shows Indian men armed with bows and arrows outside their conical, thatched reed house, defending themselves and what appears to be their wives and daughters against a mounted Spanish dragoon. Whether or not this drawing originated in something the two artists witnessed or was completed later as a composite arising from information they had received is open to debate. So, too, is the motivation. By now Indians were beginning to flee the missions in droves, and the drawing well captures a typical encounter between *huidos* (runaways) and mounted patrols sent out either to bring them back or to raid Indian villages for new converts.[21]

At the outset, neither Vancy nor Cardero and Suría were biased against the Spanish missions. Before they left on their expeditions, they were instructed that their role was to extract the best from what they saw and not to undermine their hosts. This admonition created a significant restraint on how they worked and what they saw. But on-site, despite the instruction, Vancy's powers of observation overruled his original lack of bias against the missions and led him to capture scenes that were hardly celebratory. Cardero and Suría, while hired propagandists, were also accomplished artists, with artists' sensibilities that kept them, too, from completely toeing the line. Despite their predisposition to a positive view, what they saw led them away from their intended purpose.

One talented amateur artist, however, never broke from his predisposition. While on the British around-the-world expedition commanded by sea captain George Vancouver, John Sykes, a seventeen-year-old master's mate and amateur artist, produced a more soothing picture when he visited the missions. His record also centered on field hands in and about the presidio and mission at Monterey, but its emphasis on beautiful pictures celebrating the land hardly resembled the pictorial records produced by Vancy, Cardero, and Suría.

Sykes arrived in San Francisco onboard the *Discovery* in November 1792, when Captain Vancouver stopped to repair and resupply his ship. Sykes had been selected as chief expedition artist two years earlier, along with two other "young men of the quarter-deck" whose naval instruction had included drawing and who therefore might be able to supplement the expedition's written records. Expected to produce pictures strengthening English claims to Alta California, Sykes got busy after traveling from San Francisco (Yerba Buena) to Mission Santa Clara, then sketched and painted at Monterey in December before sailing to Mexico. He returned for a second visit in the fall of 1793 and a third between September 17 and December 9, 1794, when the *Discovery* stopped in Monterey on its way back to England.

Of these visits, the last layover in Monterey yielded a number of dreamy and celebratory watercolors transforming the dry, rugged, manzanita-covered countryside around the mission and presidio into a sparsely populated, Edenic woodland, studded "with the true old English Oak," that seemed lifted intact from Cornwall or Devon, England. Dwarfed by this environment and stripped of their humanity, mission Indian field hands are pictured as small figures who herd cattle in the distance or work in small huts beside large, European-style farm buildings set in a magnificent grand emptiness. Numerous other examples of these views were gathered in two principal publications: the atlas to Vancouver's *Voyage of Discovery to the North Pacific Ocean and round the World* (1798), and the three volumes of Vancouver's narrative.[22]

Providing European and American readers with their most extensive picture of the environment in which field hands lived and worked, Sykes embedded the idea that missions were fragile institutions clinging to an uncertain existence in an untamed environment. His emphasis was on environment, not people. It was the beginning of a split in focus and approach that would grow and expand to other forms of visual representation as artists grappled with what was important, place or people, and how to best show them, critically or uncritically. For the next eight years, however, no visiting artist added anything to these approaches. During this time, no other paintings, watercolors, drawings, or sketches of field hands, the missions, or the California landscape were produced. Georg Heinrich von Langsdorff, a German physician who arrived in San Francisco on April 5, 1806, was the first artist to add to this picture. As part of an around-the-world expedition led by Russian–American Fur Company representative Count Nikolai Petrovitch Rezanov, Langsdorff visited both Mission San José and Mission San Francisco de Asís (aka Mission Dolores) sometime between April 5 and May 19, 1806. He had been on the seas for three years and arrived from Alaska onboard the *Juno* as part of an effort to obtain supplies for the desperate Russian colony at Sitka.

At Mission San José, Langsdorff discovered that Padre Pedro de La Cueva had locked up all of the ornaments and other articles that field hands used in their ritual dances. When La Cueva released them to give a command performance for the expedition, Langsdorff watched the Indians smear their bodies with charcoal dust, chalk, and red clay and then start dancing to an enchanting music created by "singing and the clapping of sticks at one end." Less interested in colonization than in fur trapping and fishing, Langsdorff became fascinated with what seemed to be a thriving culture, hardly altered by Spanish colonization. Reflecting this perspective, one of his ink drawings, *Dance of the Indians at Mission San José,* focused on six highly decorated, stocky Indians wearing elaborate headgear and native costumes. Seen as interesting natural history specimens more animal-like than human, these mission Indians hardly seemed to be the well-assimilated people and potential citizens required for a successful colony. A similar perspective emerges from Langsdorff's drawing of Costanoan Indians paddling a tule reed boat across San Francisco Bay. What historians would praise as the earliest illustration of Indians living at Mission San Francisco de Asís is in fact an extremely unflattering picture, officially incorporated into *Langsdorff's Narrative of the Rezanov Voyage to Nueva California in 1806,* which branded field hands as "small, ugly . . . pigmies."[23]

Langsdorff reversed the perspective of Sykes, placing native peoples front and center in his pictures. Ten years later, when the French artist Louis Choris arrived in San Francisco on October 2, 1816, with the Russian expedition led by Otto von Kotzebue, it was more of the same. Choris had left Alaska onboard the *Rurik* on September 14, bound for California, where Kotzebue hoped to obtain fresh provisions necessary to continue his explorations. Neither he nor Choris admired the Spanish. Both had a clear disdain for missionizing, not just in California, but everywhere they had seen it. Nor did either much admire the California natives, whom Choris condemned as lazy, miserable, rat-eating savages. "I have never heard one laugh," he would later write in his memoir. "I have never seen one look one in the face." These biases strongly shaped his art.[24]

Greeted by Governor Luis Arguello on the morning of October 4, Choris toured the mission with Kotzebue and the *Rurik* officers and scientific corps and found the Indian quarters stifling and dirty. Groups of neophytes (Indian converts) addicted to gambling and games of chance hunkered beside buildings and entertained themselves by playing a game with half-round sticks and shell money, apparently in defiance of the Franciscans. After attending Mass on October 9, Choris watched hundreds of feathered and painted Indians perform a dance for the crew of the *Rurik.* Sometime later he witnessed a group of Indians being rounded up and herded off under the guard of mounted Spanish lancers. This was followed by a bull and bear fight at the presidio. Sometime during these encounters, Choris began working these sights into scenes. By the time the *Rurik* departed for the Sandwich Islands on November 1, he had completed several watercolors.[25]

It took six years for Choris to have his paintings published. Appearing in Paris as lithographs by Firmin Didot under the title *Voyage pittoresque autour du monde*

(Pictures of the World by the Author), the book had 105 lithographs, two maps, and descriptive texts by the artist, expedition naturalist Adelbert von Chamisso. Of the ten plates and thirteen pages pertaining to the California missions, most were the usual variety: tattooed Indian field hands, groups of field hands and others gambling beside their quarters, northern Yokuts, who refused to become field hands and remained free to hunt the shores with bows and arrows, and Costanoan (Ohlone) men paddling the water of San Francisco Bay in tule canoes lashed together with vines. The most provocative watercolor in *Voyage pittoresque* shows Indian workers under guard at the presidio. It is a sorry sight, depicting a group of ten natives marching across a field under the lance point of a mounted soldier, another group of five or six Indians behind them, warming themselves around a fire, and off in the distance, a third group of three Indian men being herded at lance point, with a second mounted soldier racing to the scene. Except for the identifying caption, the viewer might easily assume the picture depicts slaves. Once again the treatment of mission field hands inspired visiting artists and scientists to invoke images reminiscent of plantations in the American South or the Caribbean.

As Choris transferred his images to lithographic plates and waited for them to be published, the mission system reached its apogee. Following a volley of musketry on the morning of July 4, 1823, José Altimira dedicated the last mission, San Francisco de Solano (Sonoma). Now there were twenty-one missions extending from San Diego north to Sonoma, each roughly a day's ride apart, with a population of about twenty-one thousand Indians. Drawn from tribes in a thirty-mile-wide swath of land extending inland from the Pacific Ocean, the mission neophytes varied widely in native customs but followed a remarkably similar existence in the missions. By some measures, their lives had improved vastly over those of earlier generations of mission neophytes. No longer living in crude mud and brush shelters, they enjoyed the benefits of substantial adobe-walled dormitories with tile roofs, and they now worshiped in beautiful churches with resplendent bell towers. Dozens of stone storehouses held stockpiles of wheat grown on thousands of acres; cellars were stocked with wine; the missions possessed 14,973 cattle, 193,234 sheep, 5,772 horses, and 2,011 mules; and dozens of orchards and gardens yielded fresh fruit, vegetables, and olive oil.[26]

Such progress did not mean that Indian field hands knelt respectfully—as later mythmakers such as writer Helen Hunt Jackson would contend—to receive the benefits of a superior culture while in the background the church bells rang the padres to Mass. Mission field hands died off in droves, falling to the effects of *mal galico* (syphilis), measles, chicken pox, small pox, influenza, the common cold, and all varieties of European microbes to which they lacked previous exposure and immunity. As their population dwindled, they began running away in increasing numbers, sometimes by the hundreds. Their many escapes into the interior prompted the padres to send ever larger expeditions out to retrieve the *huidos,* who did not always submit meekly and often fought deadly battles with soldiers to maintain their freedom. After fleeing Mission San Rafael, Alcalde Pomponio attacked missions north and south of

San Francisco for three years until he was captured and executed on January 12, 1824, at Mission San José. A few weeks later, hundreds of Chumash field hands at Mission Santa Barbara led a huge uprising that spread to Missions La Purísima and Santa Inez, and then fled to the interior, where they established a maroon colony along the Kern River, far out of the reach of Spanish soldiers. Similar colonies of marooned mission Indians accumulated around Lakes Buena Vista and Tulare.[27]

No artist witnessed any of these developments, even though hundreds of ships plied the waters of the Pacific and landed their crews at San Francisco and Monterey to take on supplies and haul away huge cargoes. All business, these crews lacked the curiosity of the exploring expeditions preceding them. They were not interested in mission affairs or in the status of the California Indians. No one made a single sketch, drawing, or painting of a mission Indian between 1818 and 1826. Even such mountain men as Harrison Rogers, who stumbled into Mission San Gabriel after exploring a route from the Rocky Mountains across the Mojave Desert with trapper Jedediah Smith in late 1826, and James Pattie, whose incredible and highly embellished *Personal Narrative* detailed his 1827 confinement at Mission San Diego in the first complete, but possibly highly fictionalized, description of an Alta California mission by an American, did not include any drawings or pictures of field hands or farming operations among the pages of their voluminous writings.[28]

This visual void would not be filled until the English explorer Captain Frederick Beechey anchored his ship the *Blossom* in San Francisco Bay on November 6, 1826. Having sailed from England a year earlier with a crew of one hundred, Beechey brought along a scientific corps of botanists, zoologists, and geographers, among them Bydges Beechey, a midshipman, third son of British portrait painter William Beechey, and brother of the expedition commander, and William Smyth, who was listed in the ship's log as a mate. Serving as the expedition's general illustrators, Smyth and Bydges Beechey accompanied their captain on exploratory treks around the bay and attended Mass with him at Mission San José late in the month. Finding the missions "tedious and insipid," Smyth confined himself to documenting specimens until the expedition hauled anchor in late December and headed for Monterey Bay, where the *Blossom* remained for five days, cutting spars and obtaining supplies from the mission there and from vessels in port. During their layover in Monterey, Bydges Beechey and Smyth turned their attention to field hands and the larger agricultural environment in which they worked. After a journey that took them from the Sandwich Islands to the Arctic Ocean, they returned to Monterey a second time between October 29 and December 17, 1827, again sketching and painting, before sailing for home on January 3, 1828.[29]

When Smyth and Beechey first arrived at Monterey, the mission farms had reached a critical juncture. Change had been flowing north through a series of edicts, one after another. These edicts originated in Mexico after it had achieved independence from Spain in August 1821, following eleven years of bloody guerrilla warfare, anarchy, and chaos. As royal control of New Spain ended, the viceroy in charge there resigned, and, following 302 years of Spanish oppression and exploitation, Mexico took charge of all North American territories, including the vague and distant province of Alta California. One of the first changes by Mexican administrators was to terminate the Spanish ban on foreign trade and to generate income by taxing anchorage fees and charging duties on imports. All but ignoring the Mexicans, more than twenty British, American, and Russian merchants worked the Alta California coast that first year, exchanging manufactured goods for cattle hides, and New England whaling ships sailed into San Francisco Bay to stock up on water, fruit, and vegetables. As these changes occurred, Mexico began to replace the Franciscan missionaries slowly with parish priests and to annex mission property to existing pueblos. Mexican administrators announced plans to emancipate all mission Indians and integrate them into the province of Alta California as equal citizens under the democratic principles of the revolutionary constitution. To accomplish this, administrators subject to the supervision of town councils and territorial governments sold church property and used the income to pay the salaries of teachers and maintain public institutions. Scholars later referred to this phase in mission history as secularization. Padres called it spoilage.

Secularization pushed field hands into an ever deepening catastrophe. Struggling with the transition to their newfound freedoms, they descended into disorganization and drunkenness. Many refused to work, declaring their freedom and departing from the southern missions so quickly and in such great numbers that Padre Francisco Gonzales de Ibarra, at Mission San Buenaventura, could only lament, "The crops cannot be sown at the regular time and even those that are sown are lost, for there is no one to harvest them." At Monterey, where farming operations seemed in chaos, field hands neglected their prayers, skipped Sunday Mass, allowed their dress and appearance to degenerate, and evidenced little desire to continue as they had in the past. Still others begged, stole, and wandered aimlessly about the mission. Writing in his journal, Captain Beechey described how many field hands had become "so obnoxious to the peaceable inhabitants, that the padres were requested to take some of them back to the missions, while others whom had been guilty of misdemeanor were loaded with shackles and put to work."[30]

An English romantic, Brydges Beechey did not incorporate these insights into his watercolors. He ignored the poor soil and rundown conditions around the mission and imbued it with vivid colors and signs of prosperity. In his paintings, half-starved cows appear fat, and dull, broken terra-cotta tiles become vivid red roofs. Days are sunny and turquoise in color. There is no trace of the constant fog. Although frequently painting the same subjects, Smyth was a very different artist. With a more realistic perspective, Smyth did not ignore the brown and dead grass of early winter or the soft and muted colors and dull, overcast skies characteristic of the coastal environment. His paintings capture a sense of a farm labor class unraveling and an agricultural industry falling apart. They also go beyond the mission farther than any others before, lingering even in Indian temescals, sweat houses where field hands (following traditional recreational techniques) socialized while driving out the pains from a hard day's labor.

Smyth found one of his strongest images while wandering around a long line of adobe apartments near Mission San Carlos. The winter rains had not yet arrived, and everything was dusty, hardly the picture of prosperity. Two vaqueros are approaching the mission, which is seen not from the front but from the side. A half dozen field hands lounge outside their quarters, and a group of natives, possibly field hands, sit on the ground. They are animated and absorbed in their diversions, apparently gambling under the watchful eye of a soldier, while a padre strolls away toward the church. Visitors described such activity, hinting at the broader social life that field hands now enjoyed, but for the first time, Smyth visually documented just how far Indians were straying from the holy embrace of the missionaries. He did not stop there, though.

Hiking into the grassy hills east of the settlement, Smyth found one vista from which he could illustrate the entire settlement, but far more critically than Sykes had similarly done thirty-four years earlier. He places himself in the lower right-hand corner of the picture, with a portion of his sketch pad visible just over his left shoulder. Two assistants are also present. One looks at Smyth's sketch; the other peers over his shoulder, comparing his work with the scene spreading below. In the distance, fences wind their way across the undulating terrain, enclosing groups of buildings, adobe dormitories, storehouses, and a church, whose bell tower rises dead center in the picture. It may well be the most sublime image ever to depict mission agriculture.

Smyth underscores a sense of loneliness that is at odds with what one expects to see. A single rider moves across the landscape, and a field hand, a mere dot on the landscape, tramps a dusty trail. Although the area should have been bustling with noontime activity, Smyth presents the verdant and plentiful territory as a deserted and pristine landscape. It is an utterly subversive image, referring not only to the shiver and thrill and the extraordinary power of the place but also to the untapped potential it held. His work asks viewers: Why does this landscape look this way? As much as what is seen in the present, the picture suggests what might be seen in the future when that empty landscape, through the efforts of British overseers, would throb with energetic Indian field hands bringing in profitable harvests by the wagon load.[31]

Highly lyrical and complex, these pictures are the only visual records of the rapidly changing nature of life and labor on the mission farms at the beginning of secularization. They assume a wider audience and a more involved role for painting than any previous art, and they act as a kind of moral guide, injecting a charged meaning into pictures of agricultural landscape. There is nothing else like them. Over the next few years, new groups of artists sketched and painted in and around the missions. They were not the members of the government surveys that had visited before secularization but rather private individuals who rowed ashore in launches from trading ships to stare in astonishment and draw in great detail naked Indians and mission architecture, with a good bit of the landscape dolloped into various scenes.

Of these artists, the most important was an obscure German physician–horticulturist and amateur artist involved in the hide and tallow business. Ferdinand Deppe had been wounded fighting against Napoleon at the battle of Waterloo. During his recuperation he had studied drawing and painting and, in 1825, left Germany for Mexico, where he began acquiring artifacts for exhibition and sale to collectors in Berlin, London, Paris, and Copenhagen. As part of his collecting work, Deppe also sketched

Indian costumes and Palenque sculptures, a practice he continued after 1830, when he began working as a supercargo (commercial agent) for Heinrich Virmond, a German trader with headquarters in Mexico City. Somewhere around San Diego, Deppe met Alfred Robinson, a clerk in the hide and tallow trade, who in 1831 alone sold over seventy-nine thousand dollars worth of goods shipped from Boston. The two began traveling a circuit among the missions. Riding north together, they soon encountered a hillside covered with choya cactus, also known as prickly pear. Their horses became hobbled by the barbed cactus spines, and when Robinson dismounted and attempted to remove the barbs, he was kicked in the groin and laid up for several days. This was just the first of many adventures the two shared, including a horrible flea-infested, sleepless night spent at Mission San José.[32]

While taking orders, settling accounts, keeping an eye on the competition, and negotiating their way through government regulations, Robinson and Deppe somehow found time to sketch, paint, and observe mission feasts, attend bull and bear fights, and collect ethnographic material, including Indian ornaments, carved bone, featherwork, and basketry. Robinson's crude and predictable drawings of missions, pueblos, and presidios were transferred to stone for reproduction in his 1846 memoir, *Life in California,* but they added nothing to the picture of the life of field hands. Although Robinson was well aware that Indians were descending into a life of crime and alcoholism and even mentioned this in his writing, he did not document their plight in his drawings. Deppe would follow this pattern, although his work is more difficult to evaluate, because his sketch pads disappeared, and his drawings never made it into print. All that survive from his years in Alta California are two magnificent paintings based on sketches he made while observing a religious procession exiting the church at Mission San Gabriel on a warm and cloudless spring day.[33]

To make his paintings, Deppe first set up his easel on a small rise, then sketched what is essentially a landscape. Emphasizing the mission plantation in all its glories, he placed the snow-capped summit of San Bernardino Mountain in the background. In the foreground he added a padre who chats with a foreign trader, perhaps Robinson. To their left, Deppe included a child who crawls alongside a dog and a Californio conversing with a nearly naked Indian. Nearby, several women in their bayetas of flannel visit with one another outside their conical reed home. Midpicture, Deppe drew three rows of neat adobe houses where field hands live beside the imposing mission church and attached quadrangle. Here and there, he added vaqueros who round up and lead horses about the gently sloping plain and Indian women who contemplate the activities. As a final touch, he included a stream meandering from left to right between the church and Indian quarters.[34]

By the time of his visit, Mission San Gabriel was no pastoral Eden. Like other missions, it had little income, and the padres for some time had been unable to maintain the required upkeep. The place was falling apart. Written records indicate that the tile roofs on the church and the field hand quarters that Deppe included in his painting were cracking and in need of repair; the vines in La Vina Madre, the Mother Vineyard, which was the largest in California, were scraggly, demanding proper pruning, and did not appear in the painting. Demoralized majordomos, nowhere seen in Deppe's composition, could not maintain the farms and orchards, now choked with weeds, because their field hands refused to work. Many field hands were destitute, homeless, and addicted to *aguardiente,* a cheap and powerful liquor made from fermented leftovers, leaves, stems, pomace, and seeds. Hundreds lived in wretched conditions on the outskirts of Los Angeles, a vast body of vagrant laborers whose only salvation lay not in the mission but in the parsimonious charity of the Mexican citizenry and the thin possibility of finding work mucking out the *zanjas* (irrigation canals) on small farms and wineries strung out alongside the Los Angeles River.[35]

None of this interested Deppe, although he surely glimpsed much of it as he traveled about Los Angeles. Deppe was following convention. Having trained in the German school of landscape painting, he was interested in aesthetics, not the labor history of a setting. He wanted pictures of breathtaking beauty, dramatic terrain, broad vistas, distinctive flora, colorful natives, brilliantly colored wildflowers, whitewashed buildings, a welcoming God, creaking carretas, and nice running streams, not too large and easily bridged, beneath a welcoming sun. Above all he wanted everything to seem unworked, to appear as if it were natural, even if it was quite the opposite. The considerable sweat and blood that sustained this colonized landscape could not have been further from his mind.

Working from his sketches, Deppe inverted reality to create two oil paintings of mission farm life, each measuring 38 × 28 inches, later praised by the *Los Angeles Star* as "the only proper painting[s] ever made of one of the missions during their flourescence [*sic*]." Triangulated by Spanish architecture, verdant hillsides, and a benevolent Mediterranean climate, these pictures of mission life were so at variance with the facts that California historian Kevin Starr would mockingly describe them as deceptions in which "grateful Indians, happy as peasants in an Italian opera, knelt dutifully before the Franciscans to receive the baptism of a superior culture, while in the background the angelus tolled from a swallow guarded campanile and a choir of friars intoned the *Te Deum.*"[36]

Only one painter at this time adopted a completely realistic perspective on mission farms and farmworkers. French naval officer François Edmond Pâris had learned how to draw and paint watercolors at the French naval school at Agoulmême. After accompanying Captain Cyrille Pierre Théodore Laplace on an around-the-world voyage from 1830 to 1832, Pâris rejoined Laplace again in 1837 and visited Monterey in August 1839, on the *Artémise.* Riding over the coastal foothills to Mission San Carlos, Pâris found the padres hardly in control and the mission in sad shape. The gardens and orchards languished in ruin. All the looms stood silent, the baking ovens were cold, the threshing floors choked with debris, and several adobe walls had collapsed and washed away. Painting several watercolors on that autumn day, Pâris captured the decaying mission, portraying it as an overgrown and depopulated outpost, now wrapped in solitude and decay, filled with bleached bones, and overrun with cattle. With the roofs of some buildings entirely missing and even the church cross askew, it was indeed a forlorn sight of a once great agricultural endeavor now in its final throes of death.[37]

By the time Pâris painted at Monterey, the locus of farm labor and agriculture had shifted from the missions to more than seven hundred private land grants known as ranchos. Ranging in size from several hundred to over fifty thousand acres, ranchos covered nearly one-quarter of the land in California. Retired soldiers, sons of soldiers, well-favored Californios, and Americans and Europeans acquired these principalities as gifts from the Mexican governors or through marriage or purchase. Most were concentrated in Southern California, as far south as San Diego. But ranchos extended as far north as the upper Sacramento Valley, along Chico Creek, where John Bidwell set up operations; Deer Creek, where Danish trapper Peter Lassen established his holding; and Cottonwood Creek, where Pierson B. Redding's holding spread out below Mount Shasta. Near the confluence of the American and Sacramento rivers, Swiss-born ranchero John Sutter pronounced death sentences, maintained a private army, and built an agricultural and trading empire on the backs of natives caught in a credit-and-debt system. While every rancho maintained orchards, vineyards, and gardens, they were not farming enterprises. Cattle were their main business; hide and tallow, were their only products. Traders from New England, Europe, and China picked up more than one million hides and countless tons of tallow every year, often in exchange for shoes, other leather products, soap, and candles, made from the raw materials the ranchos provided. Such was the lack of progress and enterprise on the Mexican ranchos that Harvard-educated *bostoño* Richard Henry Dana had little hope. "There are no people to whom the newly invented word 'loafer' is more applicable than to the Spanish Americans," he wrote in *Two Years before the Mast.* "In the hands of an enterprising people, what a country this might be!"[38]

While the ranchos should have inspired considerable attention among Spanish Mexican Californios and pioneer settlers, none of them produced even a single drawing. Well into the 1840s, most pictures still originated among outsiders who uncritically glorified the leisurely ranchos just as Deppe had glorified the missions. This was the state of affairs until 1846, when the Bear Flag Revolt and war with Mexico brought a succession of American military artists to California. Like most soldiers arriving in Monterey to occupy the territory and secure it for the United States, these soldier–artists were deeply imbued with what later came to be known as the concept of Manifest Destiny. As they rode about the country and noted its abundant natural resources, they returned with a feeling of "California mad," as one of them put it. They saw their mission as a benevolent influence, now fulfilling its God-given purpose, to extend the boundaries of the United States all the way to the Pacific coast. They would bring the rule of law, freedom, and equal opportunity to a wonderful place, heretofore under the thumb of a lazy group of inbred slave owners who needed to be pushed aside. To such people, the rancheros were immoral, backward, and un-American, and they had to be exposed, pictured for what they were.

Among the most important military artists to expose rancho life was William Rich Hutton, a Philadelphia-born soldier who arrived in California in 1847 as a twenty-one-year-old clerk for his uncle, William Rich, a paymaster with the American volunteer troops in Monterey. Traveling widely through the state, Hutton produced dozens of the usual watercolors of Mission San Luis Rey, the city of Los Angeles, and the water system at Mission Santa Barbara. Like artists before him, he bathed his pictures in a warm light at the dawning of the American era. But sometime in 1848, when the treaty ending the war with Mexico made California a territory of the United States, Hutton had an epiphany. His epiphany came at a *matanza,* in which Indian field hands rounded up cattle, drove them into corrals, and slaughtered and butchered the animals in bloody, industrial-scale operations.[39]

Hutton watched as one group of Indians quickly skinned the cattle, rolled their hides into bundles of twenty-five, soaked them in brine for days, unrolled them to dry on platforms, then later spread the hides on the ground where they stretched and staked them, skin side up. The activity was nonstop. From sunrise until noon, men knelt and scraped the hides clean, then turned them over, restaked and stretched them, and repeated the process. Continuing for many weeks, the Indians salted the hides for a brief period of storage, then hauled them to the tannery, submerged them in large brick-and-mortar vats full of lime and ground oak bark, then washed, rewashed, and bundled them for shipment as "California bank notes" and "leather dollars," worth from one to three dollars each. While all of this unfolded, Hutton observed another group of Indians stripping suet and large globs of fat from the cattle carcasses. Carrying the fat to large cauldrons, they boiled it in lime water, rendered it, poured it into white-washed bags, loaded the bags into wheel barrows, and hauled them off

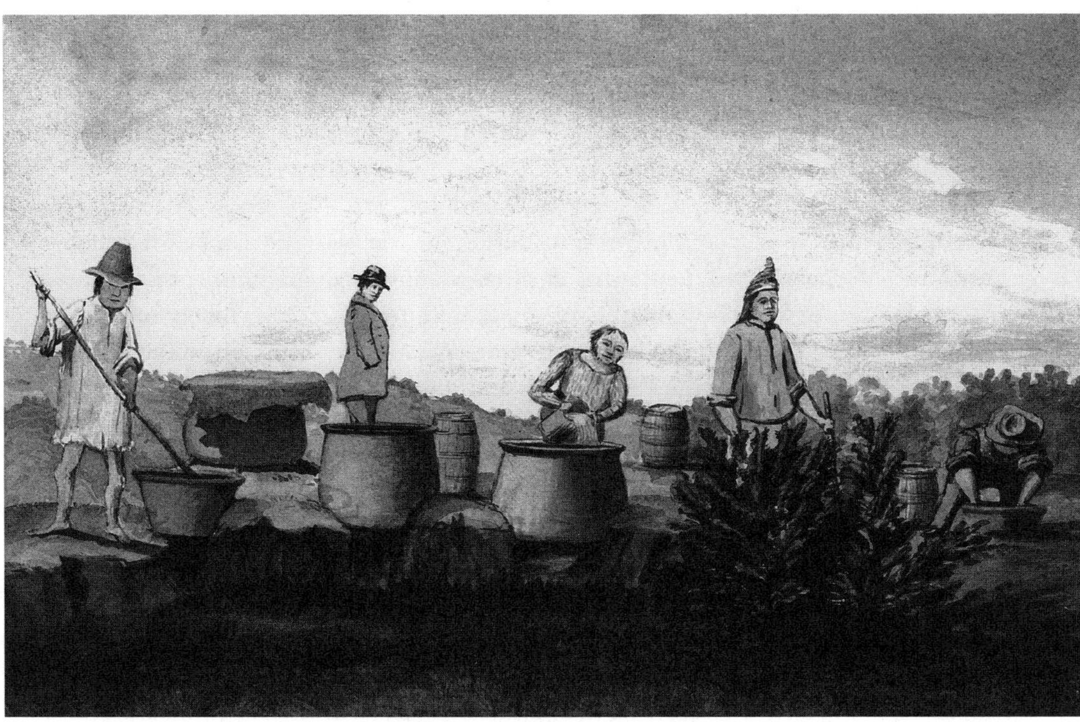

Tying Out the Tallow, Monterey, 1833, watercolor by William Rich Hutton. Courtesy of The Huntington Library, San Marino, California.

to underground warehouses. At the same time, another team of Indians mixed the tallow with potassium wood ash to make a foamy scum, then skimmed it off and poured it into molds to make soap. Throughout the activity, woodcutters came and went, and children ran about gathering up small pieces of fat amid great fields of bleached skulls and skeletons.[40]

Leaving Indians stinking and covered in blood and the countryside strewn with the thousands of rotting cattle carcasses, the *matanza* reminded Hutton of something out of Dante's *Inferno* and inspired him to produce two watercolors that constitute the single most important visual record of rancho field hands before the gold rush. One watercolor, titled *Tying Out the Tallow, Monterey,* shows Indians tending fires and busily stirring huge, boiling iron cauldrons resting on boulders, all under the watchful eye of an overseer. Another, titled *Matanza, Monterey,* pictures a cattle slaughter, including animal parts and hides hung up to dry on racks, with vultures circling overhead and apparently the same overseer surveying the work. Both watercolors capture an extremely primitive and makeshift operation. Waste and inefficiency are everywhere. The ground is strewn with debris. The site appears to be out in the bushes. Californios rest and talk as if all is normal. And the barefoot Indians, dressed in ill-fitting clothes, seem downtrodden and forlorn. It is as if in composing his picture, Hutton had just read Edwin Bryant's *What I Saw in California,* in which he describes how, at a typical *matanza,* the "bones of cattle were thickly strewn in all directions, showing a terrible slaughter of the four-footed tribe and a prodigious consumption of flesh."[41]

Hutton was not alone in capturing such scenes. At least one other military artist went beyond him, unintentionally mocking the rancheros in a colorful picture of illiterate and primitive people lording over field hands and property. That artist was a twenty-eight-year-old son of famous Philadelphia portrait artist Thomas Sully. One of nine children, Alfred Sully had attended West Point and then served as a second lieutenant commanding troops in Veracruz during the war with Mexico before being posted to California as chief quartermaster, where he turned out a number of picturesque watercolors of Monterey and the surrounding countryside. His golden moment came when he traveled to Rancho Jimeno, a cattle operation covering several thousand acres between the mouth of the Pajaro River and the coastal foothills in the vicinity of present-day Watsonville. Don Manuel Jimeno, a Mexican who had arrived in California in 1830, lived there with his vivacious wife, doña Augustias, and their beautiful fifteen-year-old daughter, Manuela. Sully fell in love with Manuela and became engaged to her. As a consequence, he visited Rancho Jimeno often. On a cool winter morning, he apparently painted the entire family of six along with five field hands and three Indian children arranged about the veranda of their home.[42]

At first glance, Sully's watercolor is charming. A señorita, perhaps Manuela, sits sidesaddle on a golden horse with a gallant caballero, possibly Sully himself. Don and doña Jimeno stand nearby with an anonymous serape-clad individual, who engages the couple in conversation. Two Indian children run across the courtyard hand in hand, and a third marvels at the beautifully outfitted horse. That much seems fairly normal, just a lovely day at the rancho. Also normal, but not so pretty, is the activity transpiring all around. Directly in front of the rancheros, an Indian kneels to gut, skin, and butcher a steer. The dead animal lies on its back, legs in the air, pigs and chickens poised by its tail, dogs looking on. In the background another Indian raises a huge axe and brings it down on another animal. All of this occurs in the midst of everyday life, just a few feet from well-dressed rancheros, in such close proximity as to suggest the routine nature of such gruesome activity. A clear division of labor separates the field hands, who perform the difficult and bloody business of the farm, from the rancheros, who do nothing but watch and talk.[43]

As Sully was painting at Rancho Jimeno, word of the discovery of gold at Sutter's Mill seeped out. Soon a rush to the diggings began. By May, San Francisco was deserted; by June, few adult males remained in Monterey; by July, gold fever had reached Los Angeles and San Diego, with similar results. By August 6, when word reached Monterey that a peace treaty signed earlier at Guadalupe Hidalgo had made California a part of the United States, about five thousand Californians were prospecting for gold in the Sierra Nevada between the Trinity and the Tuolumne rivers. By the fall, California's obscurity was ending. A rush for gold began when thousands of people poured in from Oregon, Hawaii, and Sonora. Between April 1849 and March 1850, over sixty thousand passengers arrived in San Francisco by ship. On the westward trails, thirty-two thousand overland immigrants made the trek to California by October 1849, quickly dispersing throughout the mining territory. Late starters who did not reach the Sierra until September sometimes veered north and, after an ordeal of several months, struggled through the first mountain snowstorms to make their way to the Sacramento Valley. This was the path followed by a no-nonsense man of unflagging energy who, after being abandoned in the mountains and left to starve, made his way to Lassen's rancho and, while recuperating there, produced the last and most important picture of rancho field hands before statehood.[44]

On first glance, Joseph Goldsborough Bruff seems to belong more to the story of gold mining and overland immigration than to the visual history of California farmworkers. He left Washington, D.C., for the goldfields on April 2, 1849, leader of sixty-six men who called themselves the Washington City and California Gold Mining Association. His main qualifications consisted of his West Point education, cut short when he wounded a classmate in a duel, followed by seven years on the high seas as a merchant sailor and twenty years of service as a draftsman for the United States Bureau of Topological Engineers, during which time he never left Washington, D.C. But along the way, Bruff proved himself to be an able leader who kept his men together through squabbles that shattered less well-commanded outfits. He sketched everything from hail storms to cast-iron pots heating over an open fire and once climbed high above his campsite to record a large panorama. Like many immigrant leaders, he made the mistake of following the Lassen Trail, a shortcut from the California Trail that snaked its way north through Nevada's Black Rock Desert before looping back into California near the Oregon border. On a ridge two days' march from safety, Bruff volunteered to remain behind to guard the company property and take care of an abandoned four-year-old boy while his company made its way south, all but abandoning him without food and then returning six weeks later to strip him of all supplies. Surviving the winter on a diet of candles, coffee grounds, and woodpeckers, he refused to kill and eat his dog. Then, during an early April thaw, he buried his sketches and diaries and made his way to Deer Creek, collapsing one hundred yards from Peter Lassen's twenty-six-thousand-acre Rancho Bosqueto.

Bruff spent the next year recuperating at Rancho Bosqueto. During this time he was assaulted by bears and wolves, witnessed Sacramento destroyed by fire, experienced an earthquake, staggered into the aftermath of a lynching, and filled many diaries with drawings and observations, enough to warrant several biographies. Among his most important sketches are a series of the Maidu Indian field hands who lived and worked in Lassen's vineyards and wheat fields. Having been chased by George Fremont during his march north two years earlier, the Maidu were surviving largely on wages that seldom exceeded a lump of beef, shelter, and some cheap cloth. Bruff found all of this fascinating and became the first artist to depict, however crudely, something of the daily routine on one of California's largest interior ranchos. With no particular axe to grind, he drew and sketched for himself, not as part of a government survey.

What attracted Bruff's attention more than anything else was not the beautifully dressed Californios directing lowly underlings but the life and customs of American ranchers and Maidu field hands going about their everyday business. His sketches are devoid of the trappings associated with people claiming to be *sangre de azul* (blue blood). Non-Indians on the rancho look more like trail drivers than *gente de razón* (people of reason). Overseers do not sit regally on horses decorated with silver reins. Everyone wears work pants and work clothes, at best, and often much less. No Indians are drawn as feathered and painted specimens of a survey. The Maidu appear as culturally wounded people, even worse off than their counterparts on the Mexican ranchos, yet far more independent. They do everything: chop, carry, dig, clean, build, plant,

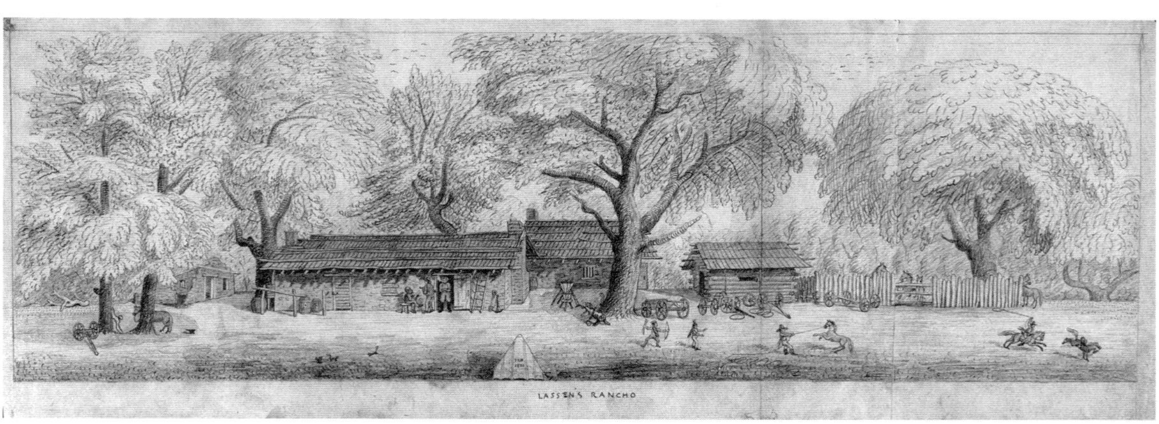

Maidu Indian field hands at Lassen's ranch, 1850. Pencil drawing by Joseph Goldsborough Bruff. Courtesy of The Huntington Library, San Marino, California.

harvest, weed, and tend. They are everywhere: in the countryside, about the buildings, in front of Lassen's house. Bruff's drawings give a sense of being in Maidu territory, not in a replica of Spain. Instead of Beechey's land of dreamy Indian maidens and enchanting mission architecture, Bruff recorded tribal chiefs, a sweat house, and dusty hitching posts. He was entirely preoccupied with adobe huts, seeming to melt before his eyes. Grinding stones, arrows, woven baskets, and pottery are all on display in his sketch book beside mounted field hands, hunters, mothers, grandfathers, and children.

Bruff injected Indians into the story of agriculture along the immigrant path into the northern Sacramento Valley, people heretofore omitted from the record. He left the impression of a land densely populated by natives, not a wilderness, but a fully settled and inhabited place, a valley that belonged to its original inhabitants. He seemed to be saying that the people living there must be appreciated along with the geography, resources, and opportunity. While his drawings are sometimes crude and reduce the Maidu to sticklike figures, they accept these people not as subjects to be incorporated into Anglo culture but as independent, fully capable predecessors with a completely developed culture. Though hardly social criticism on the order of Jean-François Millet's *The Gleaners,* Bruff's work is the first realistic portrait of California farmworkers during the entire eighty years of Spanish rule and Mexican colonization. It does not reject the concern for natural beauty and culture that characterized earlier artists but attempts to show Maidu field hands as part of the larger setting, along with crops, buildings, and farms.

Bruff's art stands midway between the sublime agricultural landscapes that Cardero and Sykes made at the missions and the disturbing watercolors of the *matanza* that Hutton painted near Mission San Carlos. His goal was to establish a more secularized appreciation of ranchos in the northern Sacramento Valley while acknowledging that the Maidu had already claimed the land and would be absolutely essential to unlocking its potential. But Bruff was a unique artist. His torturous journey and long recuperation kept him out of the mines long enough to look around and see a bigger picture. This was his unique gift. And while his perspective was enough to delight numerous biographers and have a county named in his honor, it largely went unknown. On his return to Washington, D.C., in 1852, Bruff contacted several publishers who rejected his diaries and sketches as all too familiar. Remaining unseen long after his death in 1889, his illustrations did not see the light of day until his diaries were published nearly a century later. Nearly seven generations would pass before another artist produced a similar picture, amalgamating California field hands into the larger agricultural environment.[45]

2

Competing Visions

Photography and Painting

On a warm morning in early May 1858, thirty-one-year-old Alfred Doten sat for some portraits taken by Charles E. Hamilton, an Irish immigrant and real estate speculator who was one of the most successful photographers in San Francisco. Young Doten had come to California with the Pilgrim Mining Company, on the bark *Yeoman,* around the Horn from Plymouth, Massachusetts, and set out to try his luck after a brief fling in the Mother Lode. Life in California had been hard. Doten had abandoned mining after an accident laid him up. But like many other forty-niners who refused to return home a failure, he had remained in California, eventually finding employment as a farmhand and ranch manager at Mountain View in the Santa Clara Valley. After two years of working twelve to fifteen hours a day, plowing, planting, threshing and harvesting wheat, and building fences, Doten took leave of his task of suckering peach trees and cutting barley and oats and rode a stagecoach north to San Francisco, then a thriving city of more than forty thousand. He wanted to purchase some supplies and, while in town, obtain some pictures, a routine he had followed during his career as a miner. He wanted the best photographs possible, so he visited Hamilton's gallery on Washington Street, most likely because Hamilton was a well-known, widely exhibited, and established photographer who had been doing business for six years. For his portraits, Doten dressed in a tidy but rugged outfit consisting of a clean shirt and overalls and stood still for the several seconds of exposure required for each of three pictures. The entire session likely took less than a half hour, but Hamilton or an assistant probably needed several hours to develop and process the "pictures on Patent leather" that Doten recalled in his diary. They cost Doten five dollars.[1]

Countless numbers of Euroamerican farmhands followed the same routine. Drifting out of the diggings by the tens of thousands, they looked around for some way to make a living in gold rush California. They saw a booming agricultural industry taking shape before their eyes. With apples going for five dollars each, peaches and pears commanding twice that, a spoonful of spinach cooked with bacon drippings earning fifty cents, and dried figs at one dollar a pound, miners who had been farmers were realizing that there was great opportunity in their old profession, and they were trading pistols, mining equipment, indeed anything they owned, for a yoke of oxen, plows, other farm animals, and seeds. Ex–gold miners like Doten read advertisements in the *Alta California* employment sections. "Wanted—by a farmer at San Jose," read a typical solicitation, "four or five sober and steady men, acquainted with farming." Soon large numbers of failed gold miners, Doten among them, were working on abandoned mission property, old ranchos, land along the east bank of the Sacramento River, around San Francisco Bay, in the fertile bottomlands close to mining camps, along Putah Creek, and beside Chico Creek in the northern Sacramento Valley. Alone in California, they began thinking of their friends and family back

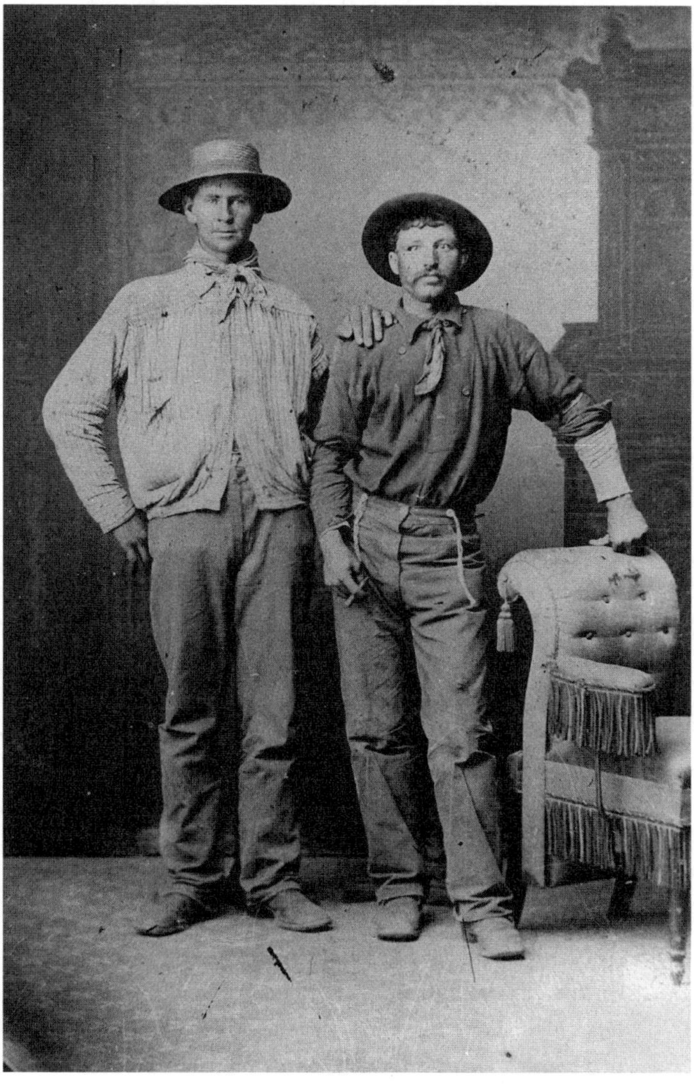

Gold rush–era field hands posing for a tintype portrait in an unknown photographer's studio, circa 1852. Courtesy of Peter Palmquist.

home. Inevitably they tired of their demanding routine harvesting and threshing grain, plowing fields, erecting buildings, hauling hay, and performing countless other tasks. Seeking rest and recreation, they headed to town, often capping such trips with a visit to a studio to sit for a portrait to be mailed back home, sometimes with a lock of hair enclosed, as proof of a prosperous new life, whether real or illusory.[2]

A mixed bag of more than fifty photographers operated studios in San Francisco and various towns throughout the diggings. These photographers came from every background, persuasion, and nationality—Swiss-born portrait painters, New England booksellers, San Francisco grocery store owners, brash young men seeking adventure, sailors on the lam. They tended to be individuals of the jacks-of-all-trades type, with several previous careers and advertisements that invariably stated how they were "prepared" to take likenesses in a "superior style" or in the "highest perfection of the art" or in the "latest and most approved style" and urged all to have a visit and "inspect" specimens. Where studios were scarce, field hands saw traveling photographers, or "sun painters." Driving into town in horse-drawn studio wagons, also known as saloons, these photographers unhitched their teams and opened shop in the back room of a saloon or in a tent erected in a vacant lot or park. These "saloons" ranged from austere canvas-covered trailers to lavishly outfitted houses on wheels that were the equal of more permanent galleries in San Francisco and Sacramento. One "circuit rider," as traveling daguerreotypists were known, was Perez M. Batchelor, who deployed a stable of wagons according to the fluctuations of the trade. Another, working out of the St. Charles Hotel in Shasta, placed an advertisement in the local newspaper that read, "an excellent opportunity for young gentlemen to procure a most acceptable present for some loved friend in the East. Perhaps a sister, or mother, or more likely some 'bonnie blue-eyed lassie.'" A competitor asserted that his images provided an even greater opportunity "to give their friends in the States an idea of the effect which a rough and tumble life, and a California sky and climate has upon their personal appearance."[3]

Most of these images were daguerreotypes. Invented in 1839 by Louis Daguerre in France, the daguerreotype process imprinted small, direct-positive images on silver-plated copper sheets, usually measuring two or three inches square, but often as large as 6 × 8 inches. Jewel-like, one-of-a-kind works of art, daguerreotypes were hard to see except when held at just the right angle. To make them, photographers went through a complicated sequence. They began by placing a sheet of polished copper over vapors of iodine crystals in a closed box. After the plate took on a golden yellow hue, they placed it in a dark slide and inserted it into a camera. To help sitters remain still during long camera exposures in low light, which could take as long as fifteen minutes, photographers sometimes resorted to various devices and supports, including heavy iron head rests with adjustable horns in a semicircle that humorists described as tools of torture. There were no shutters or light meters, and the exposure was made by simply removing the camera lens cap. After making one exposure, the photographer next placed the plate in a closed box with fumes of heated mercury, then washed the plate in hyposulphite of soda, dried it, and sealed it under glass. This yielded a mirror image with white areas of pure mercury, midtone areas of a mercury–silver amalgam, and dark areas that were nearly pure silver.[4]

By sitting for a daguerreotype, field hands reversed the visual practices of the past three-quarters of a century. No longer were they the passive subjects of visiting artists who arranged them as parts of larger pictures or recorded them as elements in surveys. Now they themselves were important. They were making the decision to have their pictures taken. Plunking down dollars, they wanted what pleased them. They wanted to project a certain image. They wanted to look good. They did not want to be shown as haggard, sweating, exhausted men dressed in dirty and worn clothes. And they seldom settled for one picture. Multiple images were the norm, all concocted. With their curling mustaches and flowing beards, field hands appear as happy, proud, stiff, and heroically confident people, indistinguishable from barkeepers, roustabouts, gold miners, murderers, bandits, and others, like them, who had once mined for gold. Many adopted the common habit of wearing sombreros and displaying big revolvers, knives, and tools such as hatchets and hoes.

Only in death were field hands accurately represented. Succumbing to "Panama fever," cholera, a work accident, a ruptured appendix, exposure, overwork, malnutrition, poisoning, or some other affliction, farmworkers, like the rest of the population, provided ample opportunities for one variant of the daguerreotype trade known as death portraiture. During the cholera epidemics that swept through California, the San Francisco mortuary firm of Johnson and Selleck erected a small building at Yerba Buena Cemetery, where daguerreotypists took views of the deceased and their last resting place, to be sent east to relatives. The practice of postmortem portraits, or "posthumous portraits," as they were called, stuck. But even when the body of a fallen farmworker could not be daguerreotyped, friends and relatives would commission a daguerreotype at grave side, often with mourners standing nearby, heads bowed, hats in hand.[5]

Studio portraits depict only Euroamerican field hands. Indians are entirely absent, for obvious reasons. The most important was their complete desperation. While some Indians employed on the new gold rush farms worked willingly and were treated well by conscientious employers, many others did not work voluntarily or happily. They were employed under an April 9, 1850, law called the Act for the Government and Protection of Indians, later referred to as the Indian Indenture Act. Assuring a continual supply of labor, this law—the first piece of business conducted by the California legislature—controlled and coerced Indians in the same way that the Black Codes compelled newly freed black slaves to work in the fields of the post–Civil War American South. Twelve of the act's twenty sections were designed to compel Indian labor. Several created conditions of legalized peonage. One section prohibited Indians from testifying against whites in court, making it impossible for native field hands to win legal redress for mistreatment. Another provided a way for employers to obtain Indian labor under the pretext of vagrancy; any farmer could have an unemployed or otherwise "vagrant" Indian arrested. Those convicted and fined for their crimes would be bailed out and set to work for a prescribed period of time, that is, until they repaid the amount of their fine. This proved especially convenient for employers around Los Angeles. Employing a local variant of the state law, they rounded up and arrested unemployed or drunk field hands found about the town or those determined to be leading a promiscuous, wasteful, or "licentious" existence. Paraded before rancheros on Monday mornings, the Indians would be sold to the highest bidder, then set to work mucking out the *zanjas* and bringing in the grape harvest.[6]

Such people had no knowledge of or contact with photographers. Barely able to survive, none could afford a daguerreotype. And what would they do with a likeness? But even those Indians who were treated better and lived more comfortable lives while working for good employers had no use for pictures. They were not going to send them to loved ones. Nor were they about to stroll into a studio and sit for a white photographer. Photographic studios—the so-called temples of photography—were structured, organized, and located in such a way as to discourage people of modest means from entering them or to make them feel uncomfortable. The only studios that would have appealed to them even slightly were those set up by traveling photographers, whose improvised tents attracted a clientele drawn from among the working classes. But even then, Indian farmworkers were photographed only by photographers who visited them in the fields, and only a few of the most talented and productive photographers working at the time had the initiative to make such images.[7]

Of these photographers, by far the most important was a twenty-six-year-old Baring, Maine, native who was labeled "the Matthew Brady of the West" by one photographic historian. As a young man, Robert H. Vance learned portrait photography while employed at several studios in Boston and New Hampshire, but after his Gallery Row business dissolved in the winter of 1846, Vance traveled to Valparaíso, Chile, in March 1847, where he established a daguerreotype business specializing in silver mining operations. Vance began thinking about California during the fall of 1849, when he saw men departing from the coastal ports of South America for the diggings. Hoping to cash in on something big, he headed north by way of Panama City and Acapulco, Mexico, arriving in San Francisco in November 1850, one of thirty-six thousand argonauts stepping ashore in California that year. He quickly established a gallery on Clay Street and then tried to capitalize on the growing interest in and thirst for images of the gold rush by making hundreds of daguerreotypes of the most interesting people, places, and scenes in the state. He intended to create a daguerrean panorama in which images were mounted end to end in long frames. Such displays in New York City galleries often attracted large audiences, who viewed the images after enjoying a lecture. Vance believed such an exhibition would attract huge audiences and earn him a tidy profit.[8]

Indian field hands assumed a prominent position in Vance's project, because his list of important people and sites to be documented included John Sutter. No survey of California could omit Sutter, a man often described as the father of California. Born in Germany and raised in Switzerland, Sutter had arrived in San Francisco in 1839 and, after ingratiating himself with the Mexican government, obtained a grant of forty-eight thousand acres at the junction of the Sacramento and American rivers, largely because the Mexican governor Juan B. Alvarado wanted to check the power of his uncle and relative, Mariano Guadalupe Vallejo, then presiding over his own empire around the town of Sonoma. At the center of Sutter's empire was Nueva Helvetia, a fort with walls three feet thick and fifteen feet tall, surrounded by wheat fields, orchards, and vineyards worked by Indians. To the north, more of Sutter's Indians worked on Hock Farm, along the banks of the Feather River near present-day Marysville. Vance seems to have arrived at Hock Farm sometime in early spring of 1851 while photographing along a broad loop running roughly between San Francisco, Sacramento, Stockton, and Marysville. He remained at the farm long enough to make at least seven views: three focusing on the farm itself, four depicting the Indian village and Indian huts where field hands resided.[9]

After finishing sometime in June, Vance packed up his daguerreotypes, booked passage on a ship, and headed east by way of the Isthmus of Panama. He reached New York in August and immediately paid seven hundred dollars to have his daguerreotypes beautifully mounted and framed in rosewood. In September, he put them on display at 349 Broadway, above Jesse Whitehurst's daguerrean gallery, introducing them not as painted representations, subject to artistic distortions, but as "the real thing itself." Few people, however, were willing to spend several hours weaving their way through a display that the editor of the *Photographic Art-Journal* described as a "circuit of scenery." Although several of Vance's images were soon published as woodcuts, including one titled *Indian Rančheria—Hock Farm,* the originals, which historian Martha Sandweiss has called "one of the great lost collections of western photography, a holy grail for historians and collectors alike," were sold to St. Louis daguerrean artist John H. Fitzgibbon in 1853. Fitzgibbon displayed the immense collection, lit up by gaslight at night, in his studio as late as 1856. They were last seen in 1857, on display at the St. Louis Museum. Among the missing images are not only precious views of San Francisco, Chile, and the diggings but also all of the images of Indian field hands at Hock Farm.[10]

It was a spectacular loss that left a large hole in the early photographic record of California farmworkers and might have been even more catastrophic had it not been for a mysterious, Philadelphia-born country lawyer and jack-of-all-trades, John Wesley Jones. Indian field hands encountered Jones as he went about the business of compiling his own ambitious picture of California. Jones's images of the field hands would not be lost, because he conceived of his project with the energy and thoroughness of a desperate man who had pulled himself and others across the country. His great ordeal had occurred in the spring of 1850 while serving as a lieutenant with an overland immigration company that counted among its members the artist William Newton Bartholomew. Arriving in Hangtown (Placerville), penniless, hungry, exhausted, and half-dead, Jones went to work as a lawyer and immediately won a lawsuit that brought enough money to feed his company. After a brief stint as a store owner at Cold Springs and Diamond Spring and a census agent for Calaveras County, he established a studio in Marysville, where he began amassing a pictorial record of every interesting building, person, or place in the western environment, including the

California Trail. To accomplish that goal, he and daguerreotypist Seth Louis Shaw formed Shaw, Jones, and Company, obtained thirty thousand dollars in financial backing from a group of silent partners, and began working on what was then known as a pantoscope. Often described as precursors to movies, pantoscopes were essentially large painted canvases that were slowly unrolled and drawn across a stage before a large audience. Already several such travelogue panoramas exploiting the popular thirst for images of the world and the growing fascination with California and the West had opened to rave reviews in the eastern United States. Part theatrical art, part entertainment, part education, and part hyperbole, these grand, unfolding stories were accompanied by spoken narrations, even music, and often required as much as three hours to view.

To produce *Pantoscope of California, Nebraska, Utah, and the Mormons,* Jones and Shaw followed much the same route as Vance had. They started by photographing in San Francisco in mid-April and arrived in Sacramento on May 6. Following a dispute over misuse of funds, Shaw left the project. Within a day Jones resumed control and hired Marysville daguerreotypists William and Jacob Shew, two brothers who had arrived in San Francisco in 1850 after learning their trade in Boston and Baltimore from the great chain-studio operator John Plumbe. After augmenting the company's finances by pausing briefly to make a series of commissioned pictures of local homes and businesses, Jones and the Shews proceeded to the gold country. Somewhere between Nevada City and American Bar, the team experienced a number of misadventures with their mobile studio, the "California Delta," which continually broke down and once had to be yanked from a mud hole by Indians driving a team of oxen.[11]

Jones and his team reached Hock Farm in July 1851. Celebrating their arrival, Sutter's field hands covered themselves in mud, tar, and paint and danced in remembrance of the dead. "It is a time of much hilarity and sport," Jones later recalled, "and for a grand display of all the trinkets and gew-gaws of the tribe." Over the next week, the team made daguerreotypes of the Indian huts, their village, and the farm itself. After attending an Indian council meeting on July 18, they bid Sutter and his Indians farewell and headed east over the Sierra Nevada. The company of fourteen dropped to seven following a scrape with Indians near Salt Lake City early in August, reached St. Louis in October, and arrived in Massachusetts in December with some fifteen hundred images. Jones spent most of the next year supervising a team of artists engaged in painting the *Pantoscope of California.* When the mammoth panorama was unreeled in Boston on December 1, 1852, Jones himself delivered a lecture on topographic features, native peoples, animals, and the scenes from Independence, Missouri, to California, emphasizing the sufferings of the immigrants and the spectacular riches and landscape they discovered at journey's end, notably the farming operations at Hock Farm. His main selling point was that through the use of daguerreotypes he had imparted the stamp of faithful representation to the *Pantoscope of California.*[12]

Large audiences viewed the *Great Pantoscope of California* during its initial six-month run. Interest remained strong while the panorama toured throughout the

Northeast in 1854 and 1855. The *Pantoscope of California* was last seen in Chicago in 1856, retitled as *Fremont's Travels*. After that, it disappears from the historical record along with all of the daguerreotypes, including those taken at Hock Farm, either discarded or sold off piecemeal. Leaving photography, Jones served as a Union officer in the Civil War, held a post as a U.S. Customs agent, and ran unsuccessfully for a congressional seat representing Brooklyn, New York, in 1890. He passed away from a stroke on December 15, 1905.

Despite the disappearance of the daguerreotypes, images of the Indian field hands at Hock Farm did not vanish completely. They survive because of the work of two artists. One was fellow overland immigrant and project artist T. C. Bartholomew, who used the daguerreotypes to make a number of 4 × 6–inch pencil drawings on clay-coated paper, which were intended to serve as illustrations for a projected series of *Harper's New Monthly Magazine* articles. These articles were never published or, apparently, completed. Among the twenty-four surviving drawings, two—*Indian Rancheria, Sutter's Farm* and *Hock Farm, Home of Captain John Sutter, California*—give some sense of the crude living and working conditions of the times. The other artist was German-born Charles Christian Nahl, another failed gold miner who had worked his way up from sign painter and newspaper illustrator to a well-regarded San Francisco artist. In 1855, Nahl used several of the Hock Farm daguerreotypes to make a number of illustrations for a *Hutchings' California Magazine* article. One image in particular suggested that the formerly wild Indians at Hock Farm had been easily transformed into docile and productive field hands. In this drawing Wahla, chief of the Yuba tribe, stands fully dressed beside a partly clothed "civilized" native, with a "wild" Indian to the left. "Like a series of time-lapse photographs," wrote art historian Claire Perry, "the images sequentially erased readers' conception of the Indian as untamed—on the right—or degenerate—in the middle. These second- and third-rate models were replaced with a first-rate subject suited up and ready for work. The figure on the left fulfills promoters' promises; his dark outfit, that of a domestic servant, indicates his role in the community, while the emptiness of his hands and his attentive posture allude to his readiness to serve."[13]

A year after Jones had visited Hock Farm, a daguerreotypist visited Rancho Chico and made what would become the only surviving daguerreotype of field hands from that era. The name of the daguerreotypist is open to speculation. He may have been one of the traveling sort just passing through, but a good guess would be Moses Hanscom, a daguerreotypist who operated a Marysville branch gallery for Robert Vance. Whoever the daguerreotypist was, he certainly was acting at the direction of John Bidwell, a successful farmer and respected leader of the first overland journey to California, who employed local Mechoopda Indians on his twenty-two-thousand-acre rancho. Close to his Indian workers, Bidwell probably asked Hanscom to record him standing with a group of his field hands and their families outside his store and post office. What makes the image so important today is that Bidwell preserved it among his family papers, making it the oldest surviving daguerreotype of California farmworkers.[14]

Bidwell's daguerreotype holds great documentary value. But like all other images of farmworkers at this time, it was not taken primarily for documentary purposes. Such images contain within them a symbolic order that both sends and receives messages. Daguerreotypes like Bidwell's do not document any important fact about farmworkers. They are not evidence, and they do not even attempt to represent social reality accurately at a particular moment in time. While they all contain documentary value, they are not part of that particular variety of social commentary that focuses on social reality and human existence. Strong ethical values and feelings do not infuse these images. None of the photographers who took them evidenced even the slightest concern for the nature of life and labor in the fields. Politics and issues never entered into their thinking. When Vance, Jones, the Shews, and Hanscom ventured beyond their studios into the fields, they did not do so out of concern for others. They were not bearing witness or giving visual testimony. Rather, they were acting as businessmen. Either they were fulfilling an assignment for a client, or they were after images that sold. What interested them were the same things that had interested previous artists: notable personalities and scenes of wonder and curiosity. Accidents, planting, plowing, class distinctions, even the drama of men swinging scythes, threshing wheat, or living in hovels held no value next to dramatic images of mining and miners at work, panoramas of San Francisco, and a miscellany of scenes ranging from

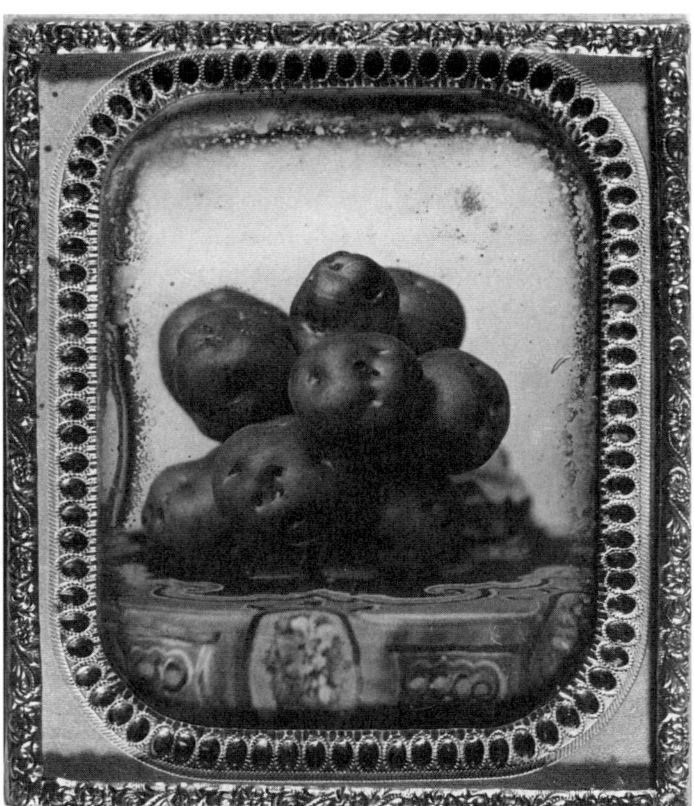

Daguerreotype of potatoes harvested at John Horner's ranch, near Mission San José, in 1851. Courtesy of Peter Palmquist.

wharves and hotels to waterfalls and dead whales. One exception was images of agricultural productivity that underscored size and productivity. Aware that views showing the best side of California were guaranteed to bring a profit, some daguerreotypists neatly reversed the farming process and recorded the result of hard field labor: a stack of jumbo potatoes from John Horner's record harvest near Mission San José; a pear weighing two and three-quarter pounds, exhibited at the California State Fair. Published as woodcut illustrations, such images offered to eastern readers indisputable visual proof of agricultural productivity that strained credulity.[15]

Several important new photographic technologies were introduced in the mid-1850s. Tintypes (also known as ferrotypes) were chocolate brown or black pieces of thin iron sheeting coated with black lacquer, with bleached collodion glass negatives sandwiched on top of them. Ambrotypes were made by placing dark paper behind collodion glass negatives bleached with mercuric chloride to produce a positive image. Collodion glass-plate negatives, also known as wet plates, were aptly named and absolutely essential to making tintypes and ambrotypes. To make collodion negatives, photographers engaged in what came to be known as the "black art," also aptly named, because the process left practitioners with stained fingers and blackened fingernails that instantly identified them as photographers. They began by cleaning a piece of glass with a compound such as decomposed limestone, then added a few drops of alcohol and rubbed and polished the glass with a flannel cloth, being careful not to touch its surface with their fingers. After removing any remaining particles with a sable or camel hair brush, they moved into a darkened room and coated the glass with a photosensitized, syrup-like, gelatinous mixture of collodion made of egg white (albumen) or gun cotton, silver bromide, and sulphuric ether.[16]

The awkward process called for dexterity and care. Holding the glass by its edges between the thumb and forefingers of one hand, a photographer poured the collodion in the far left-hand corner of the plate, then tilted the plate to work the thick fluid slowly over its surface until the fluid reached the near right-hand corner. This was difficult to do even in a studio. But so adept were some photographers that they seldom spilled a drop or had to return any collodion to the bottle. When the collodion was tacky and the ether had evaporated, the photographer then made the glass plate light sensitive by immersing it in a bath of silver nitrate, waiting five minutes, then draining the plate. This left behind a transparent, colorless, sticky film full of light-sensitive silver salts that remained most light-sensitive while still damp. Next the photographer slipped the damp plate into the holder and exposed it while wet for a fifth of a second to a few seconds. Following exposure, the photographer removed the plate from its holder and took it to a dark area, developed and rinsed it, fixed the image by immersing it in a solvent of silver iodide, then rinsed the plate again to rid it of chemicals. After drying the plate by air or by passing it carefully over a lamp flame and then protecting the image with varnish, the photographer permanently sandwiched it in front of dark iron sheeting to make a tintype or in front of a piece of black paper to make an ambrotype.[17]

These new photographic technologies had an important impact on farmworker portraiture. Farmworkers, who had previously avoided more expensive daguerreotypes, flocked to studios for tintype and ambrotype portraits. Low cost and portability were the main attractions. Tintypes sold for ten to twenty-five cents each. They usually measured 2¼ × 3¼ inches, but they came in a variety of sizes, including some no bigger than a postage stamp, and could be ordered in bulk. Ambrotypes could be purchased for as little as twenty-five cents per dozen. These characteristics made tintype and ambrotype photography far more accessible to financially strapped classes. But they also had large defects. The technology was too cumbersome for outdoor work, and the one-of-a-kind images required farmworkers to sit through portrait sessions in studios that were a kind of labyrinth of conformist tyranny.

When farmworkers arrived at a tintype or ambrotype studio, they passed through a reception area with comfortable sofas and chairs and perhaps mirrors they might use to inspect their appearance. Somewhere in the background the workroom where all of the processing was done remained off limits, vaguely discernable from its strange odors and the muffled voices of men working with chemicals. Farmworkers spent most of their time in the sitting room, which one photographic historian described as "a theatrical set erected in the middle of the props department." All variety of contraptions conjured up illusions, created deceptions, and assisted photographers in using their wizardry and sleight of hand to flatter farmworkers and other clients with the same old tricks and tried-and-true procedures. Seated or standing in front of painted backdrops, under light entering through a large window and diffused through sheets, white curtains, screens, or baffles, farmworkers recorded on tintypes and ambrotypes look no different from farmworkers sitting for dageurrean portraits.[18]

Outside the studio, it was a different matter. Glass-plate collodion photographers employed a staggering amount of cumbersome equipment that was awkward to use in the field and took hours to unpack and set up. The wet plates had to be made within minutes of being exposed, and the resulting images had to be developed while the plates were still wet, requirements that forced photographers to pack their chemistry with them into the fields. Contemporary accounts often mention several thousand pounds of equipment and at least one or more assistants. A dark tent was essential, and everything began inside, where the photographer or assistant coated glass plates with collodion. Cameras were little more than large, tripod-mounted boxes. A smaller accordion box in front of the larger box held a lens, and the photographers adjusted focus by covering the apparatus with a black cloth, ducking underneath, and sliding the accordion box in and out to compose an image that appeared upside down on a ground glass at the back of the large box. The photographer simply removed the lens cap, basing exposure on experience and intuition. With exposures of a few seconds to a minute or more in low light, capturing action was technically impossible.

During the early 1860s, an even more popular and economical process pushed aside tintypes, ambrotypes, and daguerreotypes and dramatically changed the relationship between photographers and farmworkers. That process used glass-plate negatives to make contact prints on photo-sensitized paper. Making a clean print was not easy.

Photographers preferred aluminized paper, because its smooth, glossy surface produced sharp, detailed prints with a full range of gray tones. Usually the photographer began by coating paper with albumen (egg whites), then floating it in a solution of silver nitrate, citric acid, alcohol, and water. After five minutes, the paper was lifted out and hung to dry. The next step was to load the glass-plate negative in a frame with the albumen paper, lock the frame, then place the sandwiched plate and paper in the sunlight. Unloading the frame in a darkened room under a subdued yellow light, the photographer then rinsed the print, moved it from one water bath to another, immersed it in a toning solution, removed the print again and rinsed it in hot water, fixed it either in cyanide of potassium or hyposulfite of soda, rinsed it again for several hours to remove all fixer, then hung the print to dry for the last time.

Within a few years, wet-plate photography and paper prints pushed aside all other image types and became the standard mode for recording farmworkers and everyone else in California. Now a farmworker could have an unlimited number of paper prints from a single exposure. Each print could then be sold under various arrangements and distributed through an infinite number of channels. This multiplication significantly reduced production costs, a saving that was passed on to consumers. Unlike direct positive daguerreotypes, tintypes, and ambrotypes, which reversed left and right, paper prints made by contact printing with glass-plate negatives exactly represented the scene as it was recorded. Collodion photography also contained delicate half tones not so easily seen in the falsified daguerreotype images reflected off silver or black backgrounds. Easily manipulated during sun printing, with various areas given more or less exposure, prints could also be trimmed or cropped to eliminate extraneous details and blurred areas. Most important, the collodion process required far less exposure time than daguerreotypes, tintypes, and ambrotypes.[19]

As the cost of photographs dropped, farmworkers began posing for a brand-new type of portrait, small and economical photographic prints known as cartes de visite. Measuring 2 × 4 inches, about the same size as a calling card, and costing about twenty-five cents, cartes de visite were vertically composed compositions that invariably showed the subject standing, leaning against a column, or sitting in a chair. Soon becoming the most common type of photograph, cartes de visite led to a proliferation of portraits and a certain democratization that opened photography to the masses in the 1860s. Besides cartes de visite, farmworkers could also sit for larger cabinet card portraits, measuring 4 × 6 inches and costing about fifty cents. Whichever image type they chose, farmworkers usually had friends and relatives in mind as recipients, since both cartes de visite and cabinet cards were small and could easily be mailed home. But even though they became the most popular methods for making portraits, cartes de visite and cabinet cards did not substantially alter the type of images that photographers produced. As with earlier approaches, farmworkers dressed in neat clothes, sat on a stool amid props, and projected an air of accomplishment that might prove they were still alive and doing well in California. Hardly authentic representations of everyday life and individuality, such cartes de visite and cabinet cards, noted one critic, have a certain "resistance to meaning."[20]

Wet-plate glass negatives, however, allowed photographers for the first time to make pictures that were large enough to convey a sense of the agricultural environment. Photographers quickly began accepting commercial assignments documenting record crops, verdant orchards, and the latest farm machinery. While farmworkers might be present, these photographs were really about something else. They commemorated the first grape crush or celebrated a successful harvest. Or they portrayed a proud farm owner at some important moment surrounded by his workers. These moments had gone largely unrecorded during the 1850s. But in September 1864, a dynamic young Los Angeles photographer, William M. Godfrey, would turn one such celebration into a picture the likes of which had never been seen before in the rural districts. He was hired by German-born winemaker L. J. Rose and taken by wagon to Sunny Slope Vineyards, on the edge of the old San Pasqual land grant in the San Gabriel Valley, near present-day Pasadena. He immediately saw all the possibilities. Mexican laborers and Indian field hands from a *ranchería* near La Presa had cleared the land, planted thirteen hundred acres of grapevines, and now, after four years of hard labor, were about to harvest the first crop of grapes and make the first vintage. He knew exactly how to commemorate the event.

Godfrey, owner of the Sunbeam Gallery, was thirty-four years old, still a young man. He had been a photographer for almost half of his lifetime. He was well-established in his studio at 55 North Main Street (or Calle Principal), in Los Angeles, a dusty agricultural outpost with a booming wine industry and about seventy-five small, irrigated vineyards. At five feet seven inches tall, with fair skin, brown eyes, and sandy hair, he had the energetic constitution of the typical self-made man of the time. Although he had trained as a dentist, his real love was daguerreotype photography, which he learned while practicing dentistry in Ann Arbor, Michigan. In the spring of 1850 he had driven an ox team across the plains to Placerville (then Hangtown), arriving in the fall. After briefly trying his hand at mining, he had leased equipment from a photographer in the grips of gold fever and then proceeded to work his way through Folsom, Placerville, and other mining towns, paused in Sacramento and San Francisco, then continued south to Los Angeles, where in 1860 he established a business specializing in street scenes, new buildings, and emerging businesses. Although he used all of the various photographic technologies, Godfrey quickly became famous for his work with a stereographic view camera. With two lenses mounted about two inches apart (approximating the average distance between human eyes), stereographic cameras were all the rage at the time, a kind of poor man's movie gallery, allowing people to experience the wider world from the comfort of their homes. Their great appeal was that they created the optical impression of seeing things in relief. They accomplished this by making twin pictures of the same scene. After making contact prints, a photographer such as Godfrey cut the prints apart, mounted them side by side on 3 × 7–inch cards with the prints reversed, left side prints mounted on the right side and vice versa, and printed information on the sides and bottom. Viewed simultaneously through an optical device held to the eyes like a pair of binoculars, such images gave a three-dimensional effect that the public found enticing. As the market for stereographs expanded, Godfrey tried to exploit the demand for what has been called "the first visual mass medium" by amassing a huge file of images ranging from San Pedro in the north to San Diego in the south.[21]

Godfrey might have folded his Sunny Slope assignment into his regular routine, if it had been just an ordinary expedition to amass pictures and if he had been just another photographer. But he regarded the assignment as something quite extraordinary. He gathered a group of sixteen Mexican and Indian harvesters around a two-thousand-gallon vat, posed some of them beside fifty-pound boxes of grapes, and directed others to hold baskets full of grapes overhead. In the middle of the scene he positioned Rose atop the vat, with his trusted overseer on the right. With Rose dressed in a white shirt, dark vest, and fancy hat, the picture was not primarily about the workers or their labor but rather had everything to do with recording Rose's triumphant moment. Although several of the field hands shortly dumped grapes into the vat, stripped naked, and began tramping out the vintage, Godfrey did not record that work. Like the daguerreotypist who twelve years earlier had recorded Bidwell with his field hands, Godfrey was basically commemorating an event and creating a memento, not exploring life and labor in the fields. But in the course of this commemoration, he captured for the first time a sequence of three images of farmworkers bringing in the harvest.[22]

Even as Godfrey was laying the foundation for a more engaged visual relationship with farmworkers, painters and sketch artists continued to follow tradition. Typical of these artists was English-born Frederick Whymper, one of those itinerant artists who were packing into California to capture its beauty for profit. Whymper had been in the state for two years and was apparently in such great demand as an artist that Agoston Haraszthy, the dynamic Hungarian refugee and "father of California viticulture," who had been attempting to grow fine, European varieties of wine grapes in Wisconsin and at Crystal Springs in San Mateo, invited him to paint the harvest at Buena Vista Vineyard and Winery, his sprawling 560-acre grape-growing and wine-making operation two miles east of the Sonoma town plaza. Like Yosemite Valley, Alcatraz Island, and Sutter's farm, Buena Vista Vineyard and Winery presented Whymper with the same kind of prominent landmark that photographers had been prospecting since the start of the gold rush. Whymper is not mentioned in the local press or in the records of the winery, and very little is known about him as a person or artist, even less about his sojourn to Buena Vista Vineyards and Winery. His surviving 11 × 13–inch painting, however, makes clear that he was no different from his predecessors. Prevailing artistic convention guided Whymper and prevented him from producing anything other than another uplifting, even inspiring, pastoral scene that relegated farmworkers to the margins.[23]

Whymper visited Buena Vista on October 21, 1864, at the height of the wine-grape harvest. He placed his easel on a road leading into the vineyards, thus lending a sense of perspective that leads the viewer into his painting. Buena Vista was situated in a lovely valley surrounded by the rugged Mayacamas Mountains, and Whymper made every effort to capture the dramatic setting, including Haraszthy's villa and winery buildings. He depicts the harvest as a rather bucolic affair, with four Chinese packing grapes into wooden lug boxes under the direction of a well-dressed overseer, possibly Haraszthy.

While many European artists were variously painting peasants as beasts of burden and workers given to hard drinking and sloth, Whymper all but ignores such themes. No one seems fatigued. None strains at his work. Not one farmworker displays a hardened body and the bulging muscles associated with field labor. There is no indication that these field hands sweat or that their arms and hands have become covered with sticky grape juice. In Whymper's view, Buena Vista Vineyard and Winery is a kind of very large, productive, cultivated garden. Bathed in beautiful, luminous light and rendered in subtle watercolors, pencil lines, and ink, field hands do not appear as industrialized workers. They hardly seem to work at all. They are people enjoying a truly promised land where man lives in harmony with nature.[24]

It is unclear whether Whymper ever exhibited his picture, as was common practice, or if it became the basis for woodcut prints, also a common practice. He found cultural practices at Buena Vista to be strange. On the back of his painting he writes that the vines were "staked as in Europe but further apart and more luxuriant," that pickers placed grapes in boxes, not wicker baskets, and that they were Chinese, while a "white man or two may be looking on directing the operation." Haraszthy subsequently

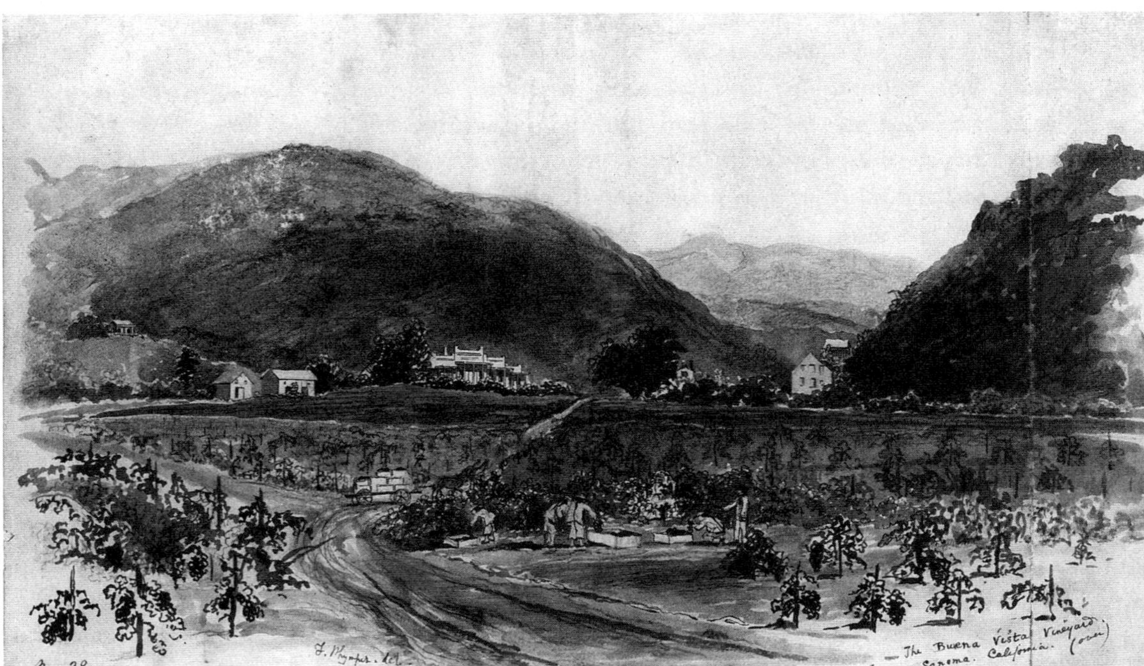

The Buena Vista Vineyard, Sonoma, California, 1857. Pen, pencil, and wash drawing by Frederick Whymper, showing Haraszthy's stone wine cellars and villa in the background and Chinese field hands harvesting grapes in the foreground. Courtesy of Brian McGinty and the Frank H. Bartholomew Foundation.

changed his vineyard layout, shifting to closer spacing to increase production. As for the Chinese, he regarded them as ideal laborers and employed them everywhere.[25]

Apparently Whymper made only one painting at Buena Vista. All that is known is that the following July he sailed north as a sketch artist with the Russian–American Telegraph Exploring Expedition and subsequently completed a series of sketches along the Central Pacific Railroad and a book, *The Fisheries of the World* (1884). Hardly the most skilled of artists, Whymper disappeared into the Bohemian Club, of which he was a charter member, and the San Francisco Art Association, which he helped to found. He is important because he continued an older approach to farmworkers that would vie with photography over the next ten years and because he personified the way late Victorian style slowed down the din and frenzy of the harvest into perfectly inaccurate preconceived notions. If those Chinese grunted and winced, if they bled and ached, Whymper was not going to show it. Nor were any other California painters going to break with tradition. Confronted with hard labor, they were incapable of registering expressive faces.[26]

This approach to portraying farmworkers was also shared by a thirty-seven-year-old Birmingham, England, native, Thomas Hill, who one year later painted an even more fantastic picture. He had been practicing his brand of landscape painting since he had moved to San Francisco five years earlier. His early training in Baltimore, Boston, and Philadelphia (where he studied at the Pennsylvania Academy of the Fine Arts) aimed at producing genre still life paintings and landscapes, the most famous depicting Muir Glacier, the Rocky Mountains, the White Mountains, Yellowstone, and Yosemite Valley. Just before traveling to Paris for a year's stay in 1865, Hill completed *Irrigating at Strawberry Farm.* Measuring 12 × 19 inches, the oil painting depicts a well-dressed gentleman presiding over a small crew of Chinese. Although it is not known who commissioned Hill, where he executed his painting, or if it is a concocted image, the low foothills in the background suggest a location along the coast, perhaps in the Santa Clara Valley. Here, if Hill's painting is to be believed, gentlemen farmers in dress coats lived in beautiful Spanish-style mansions, farmed fields watered by artesian wells, and went about their business without ever getting their hands dirty. Hill's picture of happy Chinese workers busily weeding the furrows beside a beautiful pond is a fanciful suggestion of an idyllic plantation setting. In fact, at this time, hundreds of Chinese worked not for well-dressed Anglos on sprawling estates but for fellow Chinese on small tenant farms, where shelters were little more than some shacks and piles of brush to shade workers.[27]

Created to grace the drawing rooms, dining rooms, and parlors of well-to-do art patrons, works like this continued to emphasize timeless rituals of rural life and familiar themes of agricultural success while ignoring questions of landownership and labor exploitation. The same is true of the work of Edward Deakin, a thirty-two-year-old, self-taught artist and a native of Sheffield, England. After four years in Chicago, Deakin arrived in San Francisco in 1870 and promptly set about painting outdoor scenes, among them *Farming in the Livermore Valley,* a luminous, 24 × 30–inch oil on canvas painting. Carrying forward the idea of California as the quintessence of the

American agrarian ideal, *Farming in the Livermore Valley* looks through a clearing framed by tall valley oaks, across a lovely tree-shaded pond, toward a pristine valley. An alfalfa field resembling a lawn takes up the foreground. Midscene, a farmer leads a team of oxen pulling a wagon load of alfalfa, with two children playing on top. Everything is precisely ordered and moves the viewer's eye from wilderness in the background to middle ground, where agricultural operations are under way, to the comfortable and substantial homes in the center of the composition. The whole picture is entirely concocted. At this time no farmers used oxen as beasts of burden, alfalfa farms were anathema to such valley locations, and no farmer would permit his children to ride on top of a teetering stack of alfalfa. Somewhat reminiscent of the English countryside (minus the oxen), the romantic composition, with its lush green colors and familiar, enticing rural imagery, is a kind of prospective view, a variety of landscape painting in which the viewer is given an assuring glimpse into the future. Demonstrating the bountiful, prosperous rural communities awaiting settlers north, south, and east of San Francisco, *Farming in the Livermore Valley* is essentially a reassuring visual pastiche in which field hands bask in harmony and enjoy the fruits of material progress on the California frontier.[28]

Whymper, Hill, and Deakin might have superimposed their artistic views on reality if William Godfrey had not returned to the field in 1872 and produced the first photo essay exploring the day-to-day operations on one of the most modern diversified farms in the state. Godfrey had been biding his time since his work at Sunny Slope. On April 25, 1866, he had married Lucia Huntington, a sixteen-year-old woman and the daughter of a prominent Mormon family. Providing for his family absorbed most of his energy during the intervening years, but he still continued to prospect for stereographic scenes. During 1869 he photographed extensively in San Pedro and at a camp meeting at Los Nietos, where he and his wife set up a rough burlap tent in which they lived and photographed. During 1870 he fully documented Mission San Juan Capistrano. The following year he returned to Los Angeles, reopened his Sunbeam Gallery, and accepted a large commission from the Army Corps of Engineers to photograph the Los Angeles Harbor. His work brought him into contact with Jonathan Bixby, a Yankee pioneer who, after arriving from Norridgewock, Maine, in 1850, had amassed a ranching and farming empire in Los Angeles, Monterey, and Orange counties. One of his largest ranches was Rancho los Cerritos (Ranch of the Little Hills), near present-day Long Beach. Originally part of Manuel Nieto's 1786 land grant, the property subsequently had passed first to Nieto's heirs, then to Massachusetts native John (Jonathan) Temple (1843–1866), and finally to Bixby. After finishing a massive renovation and improvement effort, Bixby hired Godfrey to survey the property.[29]

Godfrey apparently devoted a great deal of time to the project, which he seems to have regarded as both a specific assignment and part of his more general business of amassing and publishing stereographic images. In photographing with his stereographic camera, Godfrey employed a form of environmental portraiture that always placed one or more persons in the foreground to create a sense of perspective and lend scale and three-dimensional realism to pictures of outbuildings, corrals, and barns. These images have a marvelous, stage-managed quality, but they accomplish much more. Rancho los Cerritos had a full-time workforce of more than thirty vaqueros and farmhands, and Godfrey's stereographs clearly identify their position in the ranch hierarchy and the nature of their work. Some are accorded special status, none more so than Bixby's head Chinese cook, Ah Ying, who with another Chinese assistant prepared six meals a day for the Bixby family and the Los Cerritos ranch hands. Apparently influenced by Bixby's high regard for the man, Godfrey made several views of the cook standing outside a spacious two-story adobe home, surrounded by a formal garden and orchard. His most dramatic stereographs focus on large-scale, industrialized sheep-dipping and sheep-sheering operations and the vaqueros and farmhands engaged in this work. In one stereograph, Godfrey arranges the entire sheep sheering in front of a barn. It is a precious photograph, with nearly every man holding a pair of very large sheep sheers in one hand. In another, Jonathan Bixby himself stands to the right of a sheep-dipping tank. Capturing a sense of the action and hard labor, these images are without precedent. They may be the first photographs of their type. No other photographer had produced anything even vaguely resembling these scenes or paid such close attention to the Chinese presence on farms and ranchos.[30]

Although hardly motivated by a desire for social betterment, stereographic photographers like Godfrey were having an effect. Besides counteracting the distortions of painters and sketch artists and emphasizing realism, Godfrey helped set in motion a business that would dramatically expand the number of images of farmworkers. Because that business had such a high overhead—workshops employing skilled workmen ("photoprinters") who processed, trimmed, and pasted prints onto cards, then dried and labeled them—success hinged on amassing a large and growing archive of interesting regionally oriented views. Everything that seemed interesting became fodder for stereographic publishers: animals, bridges, catastrophes, clouds, daredevils, factories, food, exhibitions and expositions, fires, Indians, lakes, machinery, medicine, monuments, people of various occupations, parades, personalities, prisons, railroads, churches, rivers, schools, sports, ships, towns, weather, and countless other subjects. Agriculture and ranching were very important categories. Stereographic publishing houses, such as Lawrence and Houseworth, a San Francisco firm, amassed over one thousand views. Sold through outlets in optical shops, art studios, and mail order operations, these stereographs themselves prompted photographers to further explore the state and its people, including those who tilled the land and cultivated and harvested crops.[31]

Taking the lead in this effort was a heavy-boned, rough-looking, egocentric, go-getter, Eadweard Muybridge, who, at the height of his success, murdered his wife's lover, was acquitted at trial, and then emerged as one of the originators of the motion picture. Muybridge was one of those incredibly inventive and energetic individuals who led several lives simultaneously. He had been born Edward James Muggeridge, the second of four sons of a corn and coal merchant in Kingston-upon-Thames, just upriver from London. Immigrating to the United States in 1851, the twenty-year-old arrived in San Francisco four years later, another bushy-bearded argonaut, and promptly became a book dealer and, as a sideline, an agent dealing in photographs under the name E. J. Muygridge. Strongly influenced by Vance and the Shews, he determined to photograph California's wonders, returning to England in 1860 to study the latest photographic techniques and to secure outlets for his work. While traveling overland through Texas onboard a Butterfield Overland Mail Company stagecoach, he was tossed from the coach and sustained a severe head injury. Apparently he took up photography while recovering his sense of smell and taste and overcoming double vision back in England, years that are a complete blank in his biography. Returning to California in 1867, he changed his name for the second and last time to Eadweard Muybridge and launched his career by using his twenty-five-hundred-dollar settlement with the Butterfield company to finance a photographic survey of the Yosemite Valley, then selling his views under his trademark nom de plume, "Helios, the Flying Studio."

With American landscape photographers just beginning to supply the nation's demand for pictures of the American West, Muybridge could not have had better timing; he soon received numerous commissions and assignments for his "views," as photographs were then called. Beginning in 1868, he was engaged first by Major General Henry W. Halleck to photograph military ports and harbors in Alaska, just acquired by the United States from Russia, then engaged by the Lighthouse Board and the Treasury and War departments to photograph the west coast. At the end of this work, he returned to Yosemite Valley. Packing his usual stereographic and small-view cameras in addition to a large 18 × 22–inch view camera, other photographic equipment, and camping provisions, Muybridge traveled to key points and executed a series of spectacular photographs that established his reputation as one of the preeminent landscape photographers of the American West.[32]

While he built his portfolio of landscapes, Muybridge also amassed a similar portfolio of all the most interesting sites in Northern California, including those around San Francisco Bay, which he titled San Francisco Views. Advertising that he was prepared "to accept commissions to photograph Private Residences, Views, Animals, Ships etc., anywhere in the city, or any portion of the Pacific Coast," Muybridge traveled widely. As sales and commissions rolled in, he shut down his old gallery, divorced his wife, and opened a new studio with painters Carl (Charles) Christian Nahl and Hugo Wilhelm Arthur Nahl. In the spring of 1871, Muybridge married Mrs. Flora Stone, a photo retoucher who was half his age. The following year he returned to the Sierra Nevada and rephotographed all the best scenes in Yosemite Valley; he also added new ones in the Canyon of the Merced and the Mariposa Grove, among them forty-five gigantic prints measuring 18 × 22 inches that represented the epitome of technical and artistic perfection.[33]

During an image-vacuuming expedition sometime that fall, Muybridge made the first of two visits to Buena Vista Vineyard and Winery. Arriving toward the end of the long harvest season, he used his large-view camera and stereographic camera to photograph the harvest and crush. One large-view picture captures a crew of twenty-five men in the vineyards at about the same spot where the harvesters worked in Whymper's painted picture. Unlike Godfrey's earlier pictures of the grape harvest at Sunny Slope, Muybridge's shot appears to be unposed. Since glass-plate technology of the time did not yet allow field photographers to freeze action with a shutter speed of one twenty-fifth of a second or faster, it is likely that Muybridge asked all of the crew members to hold still at some dramatic moment while they went about their tasks picking grapes, packing them into boxes, and stacking the boxes in a horse-drawn wagon.

Sometime that fall or winter, Muybridge returned to complete a series on off-season work about the winery. While making these pictures, he operated much like Godfrey and was especially attentive to creating optimum visual effects by including items of interest in both the foreground and the background. That winter, Muybridge collected his Buena Vista views under the title of The Vintage in California and offered them for sale in *Catalogue of Photographic Views Illustrating the Yosemite, Mammoth Trees, Geyser Springs, and other Remarkable and Interesting Scenery of the Far West.* All but five of the views in The Vintage in California series include farmworkers. Most are Euro-Americans. They pick grapes; inspect boxes of grapes headed for the crusher; drive wagons; haul pomace away from the winery; label wine bottles; disgorge sediment from champagne bottles and recork them; make barrels; plow, plant, and fertilize young grapevines; and run grapes through a crusher and destemmer. Together these images amounted to the first comprehensive picture of the labor cycle at a large California winery.

One other dimension of Muybridge's work at Buena Vista also broke new ground. This was the way he paid close, even sympathetic, attention to Chinese field hands. Sympathy for the Chinese ran against rising waves of Sinophobia. Already the state's white workers were developing strong anti-Chinese sentiments. As deepening economic depression filled the cities with unemployed and disillusioned men who blamed the Chinese for their problems, images that had once been neutral and even positive became highly polarized. There seemed no middle ground. Chinese workers were either characterized in derogatory and demeaning portraits and cartoons, or they were omitted entirely from the picture. Many photographers simply ignored them. Commemorating the meeting of the Central Pacific and Union Pacific railroads at Promontory Point, Utah, photographers A. J. Russell and Charles Savage relegated Chinese railroad workers so far to the margins of their famous photographs that they effectively wiped from the historical record those laborers who built 90 percent of the line from California.[34]

At Buena Vista Vineyard and Winery, Muybridge did not banish the Chinese to the margins. He made them central to his portrait. They appear everywhere in his portfolio of stereographic images. The picture he presents is one of constructive labor by a group breaking into agriculture on a large scale. Already well known was their work building a huge winery, planting vineyards, and, most important, excavating storage caves. Muybridge paid hardly any attention to this work, preferring instead to capture their wine-making duties. One of his stereographs shows Chinese bottling the vintage. Another is titled *The "Heathen Chinee" Bottle Washer.* Notwithstanding the description, these images are unprecedented in the way they sympathetically represent Chinese as central parts of the day-to-day operations of the state's preeminent winery. And they did not go unseen. Muybridge reached a wider public early in the following spring when the firm of Bradley and Rulofson, the San Francisco art dealers who marketed his work, began displaying the Buena Vista portfolio at public exhibitions and fairs.[35]

With Muybridge's work at Buena Vista, photography finally, and for the first time, fulfilled its latent potential for capturing a realistic picture of California farmworkers. Other changes were on the horizon. One of the most important occurred a year later, two hundred miles south. An unlikely individual was responsible for it. This

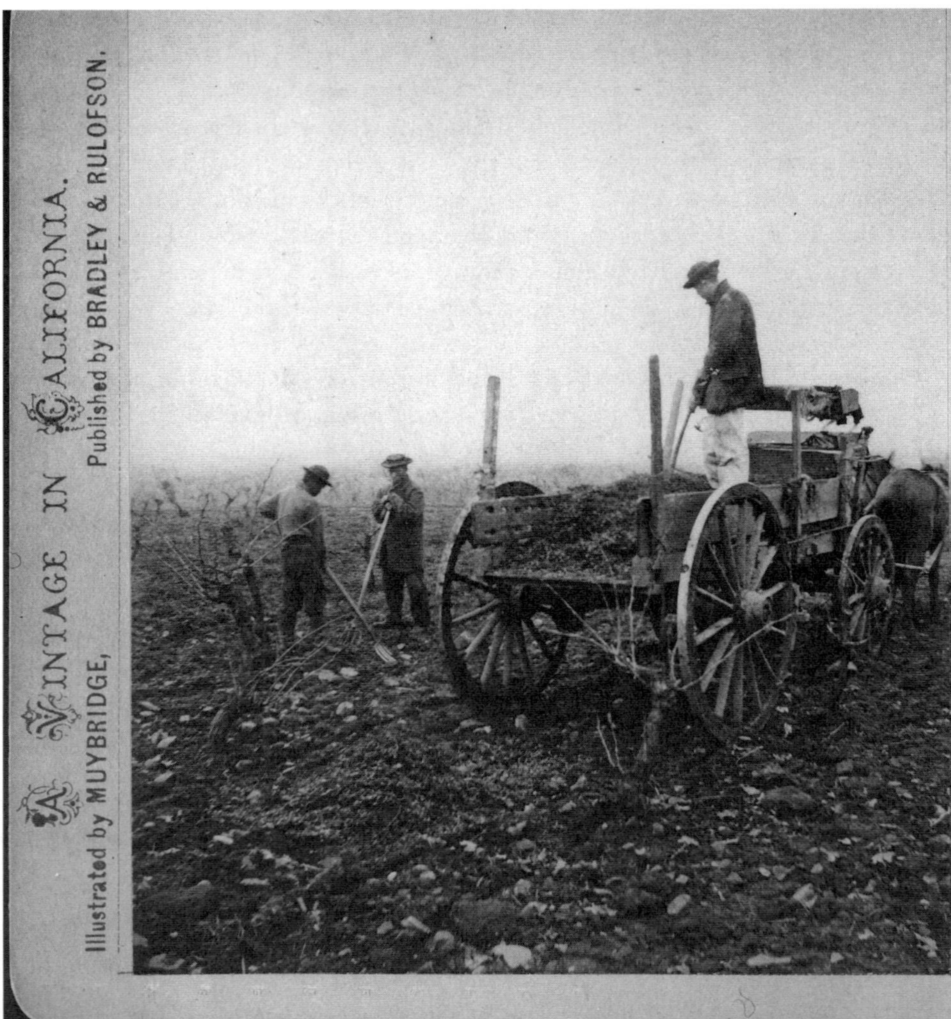

Left frame of stereographic photograph of manuring operations at Buena Vista Vineyard and Winery, 1872, by Eadweard Muybridge. From The Vintage in California. Courtesy of the Bancroft Library, University of California, Berkeley.

individual was not a photographer; he was an orphaned Indian farmworker named La-Ache, also known as Jack. His actions emerged as the logical consequence of his hard life and his indenture twelve years earlier to Fresno farmer Ira McRay. A man of decidedly parsimonious disposition, McRay paid La-Ache little more than food, clothing, bedding, medicine, and "other necessities of life." For this meager compensation, La-Ache worked faithfully "in the capacity of Domestic Servant and general laborer, until he . . . attained the full age of Twenty-five Years." At the time of his emancipation, La-Ache received a horse and fifty dollars. He apparently decided to celebrate his new freedom by going to Centerville, a small town astride the Kings River southeast of Fresno. His reasons for entering a studio and sitting for a portrait are unclear. Such behavior was uncharacteristic of Indian field hands. Certainly the money La-Ache paid for his carte de visite took a big chunk of his earnings. Perhaps he feared arrest and wanted some form of identification. Perhaps he simply wanted to celebrate the occasion and was testing the boundaries of his freedom. La-Ache was certainly not seeking sympathy. And he would get none. But in requesting a photograph, he asserted his own independence and humanity and initiated a process that widened the scope of photographic coverage.[36]

Photographers themselves were not yet prepared to make such a statement with their work. If any were bothered by the legacy of Indian indenture, they never said so. Nor did any photographer seem bothered by any aspect of farm labor in California. When someone like La-Ache walked in for a portrait, the photographer handled the encounter as another everyday transaction. Photographers were, above all, trying to make a living by satisfying a market, a client, or both. None thought about making a social statement. While visually involved, photographers remained politically neutral, if not completely aloof. Preoccupied with profit, they concentrated on developing a lucrative business. But this concern for business and profit was beginning to lead many local photographers into an industry in which farm labor was central to every image: the booming wheat industry. No photographer in rural California could ignore it. Wheat growers were the largest and most colorful group of farmers in California.

By 1873, California farmers were producing wheat on virtually every farm in a 125-mile crescent north, south, and east of San Francisco Bay. In the Santa Clara Valley, wheat farms with a new crop of sprouting stalks were described somewhat breathlessly as "beautiful green islands in a golden sea." During the American Civil War, when California wheat growers dramatically expanded exports to the eastern United States and opened a second market in England, a species of large-scale growers known as bonanza farmers, sand lappers, and sky farmers exploited the market and, blessed with the wet years of 1866 and 1867, began producing bumper crops. By 1872, the state had tripled its wheat acreage. On this basis, a triangular trade quickly developed: British manufactured goods to Australia; Australian coal to San Francisco; and California wheat to England. California quickly emerged as the largest wheat-exporting state in the country. To service the trade, new wharves, docks, and warehouses were constructed. Railroad lines extended the areas under cultivation from around San Francisco Bay into the interior and south along the coastal valleys. A series of wheat-shipping towns—Willows, Traver, Hanford, Newman, and countless others—grew up to service the big bonanza farms that were fast spreading over the Sacramento and San Joaquin valleys. With production topping twenty million bushels in 1870, the saying was that men would no longer harvest gold; now they were beginning the golden harvest of wheat.[37]

No other segment of agriculture promised photographers such a dramatic amalgamation of artistic challenge and commercial opportunities. The organization of the work, the controlled chaos, the way light fell on the wheat, and the great drifting clouds of wheat chaff always made for interesting photographs that satisfied all but the most jaded photographers. At the center of everything, photographers found the largest and most colorful group of farmworkers in the state: the roustabouts who planted, harvested, and threshed grain. They were a rogue's gallery of Chilean sailors on the lam, ex–gold miners just getting by, newly arrived German immigrants still in satin pants, failed landscape painters, criminals, drunks, and family members supplementing their income with a summer spent threshing. With their faces darkened by long days under the sun, threshermen projected the look of a criminal gang. But it was not just their coarse appearance and their colorful attire—overalls, well-worn hats, dirty bandanas sagging beneath their chins, gloves stuffed into pants pockets—that explain why photographers developed such an abiding fascination with wheat threshers. Mechanization also certainly added to the allure.

On smaller farms, self-binding reapers drawn by a pair of horses were driven by one field hand and accompanied by a crew of "shockers," who gathered and hauled bundles of wheat to the threshing site. But on most of the larger wheat farms of the 1870s, headers cut the grain a few inches below the kernel and conveyed it up an endless apron and onto a low-sided header wagon, which then took the grain to the thresher. A typical header crew consisted of sixteen to twenty-one men who tended a thresher, one or two water wagons, seven headers, fourteen header wagons, a steam engine, a portable cook shack, hay derrick, feeder table, and countless other pieces of equipment. Commercial photographers in Healdsburg, Sacramento, Marysville, Fresno, Stockton, and San Francisco found such machinery to be both fascinating and highly marketable. Not only the owners and manufacturers of these machines wanted pictures; so too did various rural and national news journals, as well as the many state publications seeking to promote California agriculture. Fulfilling that demand, photographers issued a steady stream of pictures depicting giant belching steam threshers, huge stacks of hay, and perfectly arranged threshing outfits with all the crew members at their various stations, flags flying, horses at the ready, large pyramids of sacked grain rising in the foreground.[38]

Often photographers did not even have to visit the wheat farms to take pictures. Men came to them. The season usually got under way in mid-June, when the first blast of hot weather brought desperate, unemployed common laborers out of the towns and into the wheat districts. Stealing rides on trains and traveling on the weekly steamers, these men piled out of boxcars and disembarked at river landings in Sacramento, Stockton, Fresno, and countless other towns, where they booked a room for the night and often visited a studio for a portrait commemorating the occasion. After a few weeks on the job, these men could also be counted on to contribute more to the area's revenues by leaving their remote wheat camps and returning to town for a weekend spent in wild excess, which often began more or less innocently with a shave and bath to spruce up for another portrait session and then an evening of complete drunkenness, sport, and debauchery.[39]

Toward the end of the harvest, photographers kept busy making group pictures. These images were the heart of their business, and they expended considerable energy on them. The procedure seldom varied. Early morning provided the preferred soft, warm lighting, which made the best pictures, so photographers usually arranged to meet threshermen at sunrise. Arriving on scene, they brought all activity to a halt and quickly organized a composition, often resorting to formula. If they were in a hurry, they simply arranged the men in two or three rows in front of their machinery, such as the thresher and the steam engine. Otherwise, a few men always lounge on large stacks of bagged grain. Some kneel. Some stand. Some strike highly animated poses. Some hold up stumps showing fingers lost in an accident, like so many trophies or badges of honor. A dog or two always sits in the foreground. Prominently stationed in front or to the side, sometimes on horseback, is the foreman or farm owner, identified by his clean clothes and white shirt. Shooting from a wagon, photographers sometimes achieved an elevated perspective on scenes that tended to float in great open skies.

Conditions in the wheat fields were seldom ideal, and photographers sometimes had to make do with whatever they encountered. If it was midday, so be it. If it was the end of the day and everyone was tired and dirty, that only added to the aura of the picture, projecting a roughness often associated with bandits, outcasts, and revolutionaries. Ample opportunities for creativity existed everywhere. W. R. Nutting, a Vacaville-area photographer and San Francisco publisher, documented crews waking from a night's sleep on a pile of wheat straw. He called one of these pictures *Sleeping Beauties*. Not to be outdone, a Healdsburg photographer recorded a quiet moment when crewmen paused for a meal on the steps of a cook wagon. A young girl, perhaps the daughter of the cook, plays with two pet rabbits on leashes. A sign on the side of the cook wagon identifies it as belonging to "C. J. Aydt, Thresherman." Other photographers recorded threshing crews moving through town with their cavalcade of equipment, caught them waiting beside their equipment as it was being repaired, and photographed men extracting steam engines that had fallen through wooden bridges or rolled off a ferry while crossing a river. One of the most repeated compositions focuses on field hands hauling heavily loaded wagons full of sacked wheat to river landings.[40]

Photographing wheat threshers was not easy. During the summer, out on the open plains, photographers were burned by the sun, covered in dust, and constantly itching from the wheat chaff that settled over everything. Even while performing a number of difficult technical operations, they had to fight off black gnats and swarms of biting flies, no easy task while coating a glass plate with collodion inside a hot dark tent. Just reaching a wheat crew usually involved a long wagon ride over dusty roads and frequently an overnight camping trip. The reward for such efforts was multiple sales. Crew members and bosses fat with cash usually wanted at least one image to commemorate the season's work. So too did the proud farmer, who invariably wanted prints for family and friends. One farmer, after obtaining a group portrait by San Francisco photographer George G. Coffom, framed it and mounted it on his farmhouse wall. Titled *Harvester on the Pete Garnett Ranch near Willows in 1899,* it had the names of every crew member written on the margins.[41]

Capturing a world of feeling among men joined in hard physical labor under rough and often dangerous circumstances, these group portraits display important details of everyday life, especially intimate association and the bonds of male friendship and workplace camaraderie. Men hold hands, wrap their arms around one another's shoulders, rest a palm on the shoulder of the man in the front row, recline against the knees of those behind them, and bring a beloved cook front and center in the picture. Such images are so common as to suggest that, while autonomy may well have been the main value of late nineteenth-century field hands, they also adhered to an older value: what Anthony Rotundo, the historian of premodern American masculinity, has labeled "communal manhood."[42]

A few of the more intrepid photographers recorded pictures that appear to attempt a commentary on farm labor. Sometimes this was conveyed by a particular setting. Or a piece of machinery. Or the work itself. One photographer exercised considerable dexterity and bravery; climbing up onto the steam thresher, he re-created a view the men had as they looked out over the threshing scene from their machinery. Full of long belts and large gears, the picture has a rare quasi-documentary quality.[43]

Although such efforts at visual poetry, irony, and social commentary remained largely excluded from their repertoire, these photographers were very different from their predecessors of the previous generation. One can follow in their work the evolving images of the countryside as a whole and see a kind of heightened oscillation between efforts to romanticize the wheat industry and expository efforts to describe it in all its complexity. These latter efforts always fell short. Threshing and harvesting involved a landscape of such expanse that it could not fit easily into the arbitrary, rectangular dimensions of most cameras. Too many people were always spread out too far across the flat fields. A photographer standing at ground level or even on top of a wagon could never accurately represent wheat threshers and harvesters in their relationship to the environment. Early wet-plate photographers, struggling with their chemicals and limited by their equipment and technology, failed to accommodate the wide perspective required to fully convey the nature of life and labor in the fields. This was something that only the imagination could wrap around. As a result, well into the era of wet-plate photography, landscape painters and sketch artists continued to shape the picture of California farmworkers.[44]

Perhaps the most famous painters of farmworkers at this time were German-born William Hahn, a classically trained artist inspired by Europeans working in America, and Virgil Williams, an artist born in Dorchester, Massachusetts, in 1830, and a descendant of Roger Williams. Virgil Williams had studied in Italy and then come to California in 1862, where he applied his talents and established the San Francisco School of Design in 1874, becoming a major influence on California painting in the years before his death in 1886. Hahn came to San Francisco from Boston in 1872, where he met Williams, who by then was living in a cottage near Calistoga in the Napa Valley. Over the next year, Hahn established his reputation with paintings of the Russian River, the Sierra Nevada, Yosemite Valley, and various developing communities, as well as re-created scenes from California's recent history. During that time, Williams concentrated on the Napa Valley and produced a series of undated oil-on-canvas paintings. Among his most important paintings were: *Calistoga Barnyard* (1870), 11 × 15 inches; *Wine Cart Burro, Napa Valley* (no date), 13 × 10 inches; *Landscape* (no date), 14¾ × 10¾ inches; *Girl with Hayfork in Landscape* (1870), 5 × 3 inches; and *Winnowing Grain, California* (1872), 18 × 25 inches.[45]

Concentrating on haying and threshing, these last two paintings brought the artist into contact with themes that had by now become familiar to photographers. In *Harvest Time, Sacramento Valley* (1874), Hahn, too, shifted attention from the rich green colors and lush surroundings of irrigated farming around San Francisco Bay to the golden hues of the flat, dry, interior valleys. Much like Thomas Hill's *Irrigating at Strawberry Farm* and Deakin's *Farming in the Livermore Valley,* Hahn's *Harvest Time, Sacramento Valley* pushes California's genius for invention and advancement and reinforces every nostalgic cliché that Hahn had learned while studying at the Royal Academy of Art in Dresden. Unlike New England painters of the time, who focused on a bucolic past and emphasized rural folk engaged in individual tasks and time-honored rituals, Hahn invoked a glorious future in which animals and machines would relieve the farm population of the burden of tedious, back-breaking toil. While filled with accurate details regarding the technology of horse-powered threshing operations, Hahn's painting is in fact a capricious fantasy projecting the idea that children could enjoy a picnic next to a threshing crew. This would have struck any wheat thresher as ridiculous. Children never went near threshing operations; they were far too dangerous and completely polluted with wheat chaff. But this apparently made little difference to Hahn.[46]

Hahn and Williams were accomplished painters, but they did not always adhere to reality. Neither, in fact, ever witnessed the harvest scenes they painted. This would all change, and change in a big way, in 1875. The artist responsible for this change possessed only marginal talents. Andrew P. Hill would never be compared to William Hahn. He was no great master. After arriving in California from Porter County, Indiana, in 1867, he had worked as a carriage painter and studied art at the Santa Clara College Academy of Art and in San Francisco with the Italian artist Domenico Tojetti. He had exactly one commissioned painting to his credit when Colusa County wheat farmer George W. Hoag contacted him. Hoag was one of the largest wheat farmers in the northern Sacramento Valley and had been fabricating new agricultural machinery to streamline his business. His greatest creation was the Monitor, a thirty-five-foot-long grain separator that combined three threshers and a single feeder table. Painted barn red, the gigantic machine became one of the most famous of all California agricultural inventions when Hoag's crew used it on August 8, 1874, to thresh and sack 5,779 bushels of wheat in a twelve-hour period, a new world record. Hoag, proud of his accomplishment, commissioned the twenty-two-year-old Hill to commemorate the event. Some evidence suggests that Hoag may have hired Hill by mistake, confusing him with Thomas Hill, the far more accomplished and famous painter of Yosemite Valley scenes. Whatever the reasons for his choice, it led Hill to create what many regard as the most important painting of California farmworkers.[47]

In July 1875, Hill traveled north from San Francisco to Willows, in Colusa County (later Glenn County). From Willows, Hill took a buggy ten miles east to the land that Hoag leased from wheat magnate Hugh Glenn. Witnessing a reenactment of the record-setting threshing operation, he spent an entire day photographing and sketching, then returned to San Francisco the following day. Throughout the winter he worked on his painting, finally completing it the following March. Visitors to Snow and May's Gallery on Kearney Street in San Francisco were the first to see *A California Harvest Scene* when it went on exhibit in April 1876. Mounted in a massive gilded frame, which added another foot to its 34 × 38–inch size, the painting almost immediately achieved a kind of mythic status as a vision of technological triumph. Newspaper reporters urged readers to visit the gallery and see Hill's amazing work before Hoag took permanent possession of the painting. The *Pacific Rural Press* wrote:

> It is a peculiarly California scene. The immense separator and the engine to drive its hungry jaws and rattling beaters, and shelving screens, the ever widening circle of the headers and wagons, the mules dragging away the quickly accumulating straw, the owner in his carriage, and the overseer on horseback supervising the small army of men required to do the work, the bright sunlight flooding the scene—all these characteristics of our peerless harvest scenes.[48]

As an example of landscape painting, Hill's work seems a contradiction. Like most of that genre, it projects a scene of sublime beauty, soft dramatic lighting, and beautiful tones of earth and sky. But it also projects a sense of a highly mechanized and modern, large-scale industrial regimen that is as real as any photograph. Men and machines sprawl across the landscape in a way that photographers of the time could not capture, even on large glass-plate negatives. In the foreground, wearing a high silk hat and frock coat and driving a black buggy pulled by two fancy trotting horses, is George Hoag. To the right of the painting's center, powered by a belt running from a fifteen-horsepower steam engine, stands the Monitor, also known as the big red grain eater. A long line of header wagons encircle the threshing area, waiting to disgorge their cuttings. Crews of Chinese sack the threshed wheat, sew the sacks shut, and stack them. Almost invisible in the painting are the headers, only one of which is displayed in the left foreground. Although Hoag's original record-breaking threshing crew had consisted of fifty-six men, seven headers, twenty-one header wagons, and ninety-six horses and mules, Hill's painting cuts down the numbers by about one-quarter. Apparently, the scale of the original operation was simply too large to capture on canvas.[49]

Praised as "symbolic of California agriculture" and celebrated as "a stirring embodiment of enterprise, of action, of success," Hill's painting, only the second of his young career, is especially valuable for its capture of easily overlooked details. For example, rather than stacking the cut grain, Hoag's men pitch wheat directly onto a conveyor that feeds the cylinder. This became the standard technique on wheat farms from that point forward. But for all its value as a document, the painting remains basically celebratory. While modern viewers sometimes construe hidden meanings in the painting, at the time it suggested nothing critical of either the wheat industry or labor under industrialized conditions.[50]

It is not a well-executed painting. Foreground figures are somewhat large and sticklike. Hill took the liberty of moving the sun around to the northern sky so as to sculpt the scene with a soft, golden light that hits men and machines at a perfectly impossible angle. He also moved the Sutter Buttes into a prominent position, shifting them much farther north, obscuring them in a grayish blue haze (much as they appear on the horizon fifty miles to the south). But these defects were far outweighed by the cultural debate that the painting provoked. By depicting "the grand onslaught on the sea of yellow grain," *A California Harvest Scene,* for all its amateurish aspects, marks another turning point in the visual representation California farmworkers.[51]

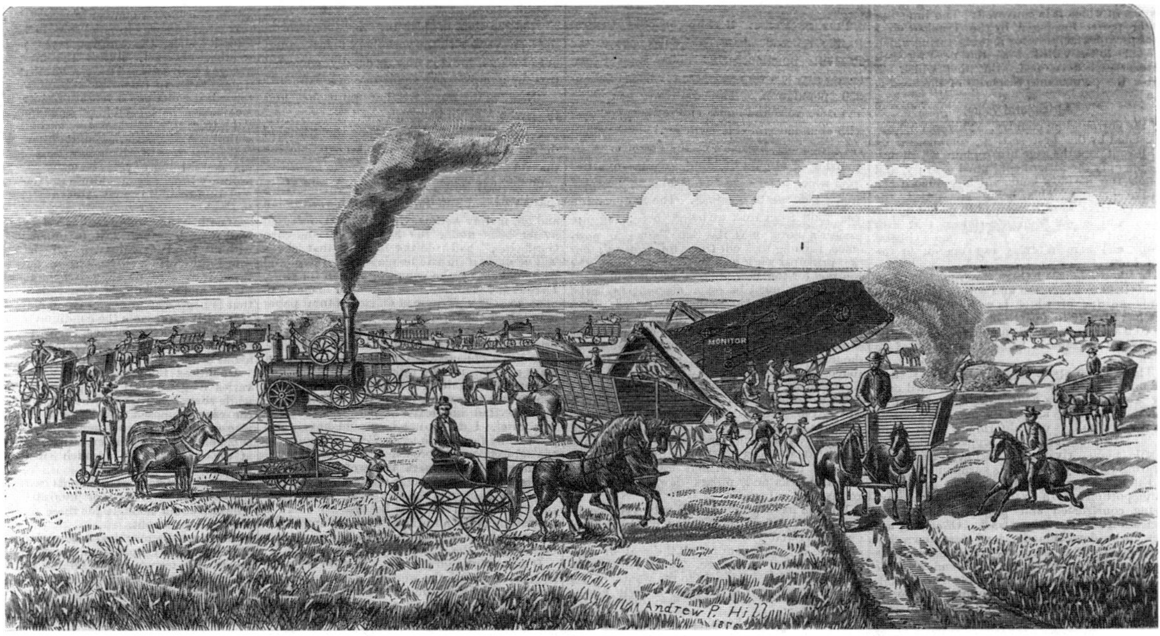

Engraving print of Andrew P. Hill's oil painting *A California Harvest Scene,* 1875. From Pacific Rural Press, April 1, 1876. Author's collection.

Like so much of the early visual record of California farmworkers, Hill's work could not be directly reproduced and initially had limited impact. That quickly changed. Although not widely used at the time, engravings and woodcuts allowed newspapers and journals to publish excellent facsimiles of paintings. An extremely slow and expensive process, engraving required an intermediate line drawing that had to be transferred to a steel plate. Very few California publications could afford the technology. Among them, only the *Pacific Rural Press,* a leading farm publication in the state, used engravings extensively. On April 1, 1876, the journal spread Hill's painting across its front page. Two years later, Marcus Hawley and Company, one of California's leading farm equipment manufacturers, transferred the painting to a colored lithograph to advertise its own work in building threshers, harvesters, plows, rakes, harrows, pumps, winches, and other agricultural machinery. For the first time, a large number of everyday folk saw and began seriously discussing the nature of industrialized wheat farming, its effect on land and society, and, most important, its consequences for farmworkers. The reaction was overwhelmingly positive.[52]

Commemoration played a central role the following year, when General Henry M. Naglee, one of the leading citizens in San Jose, sought someone to paint the grape harvest in his vineyard. Naglee had come to California as an army officer during the war with Mexico and, in 1852 purchased land in San Jose. After serving for the Union army during the Civil War, he returned to California and became interested in the production of wine and brandy. In 1868, he constructed a large winery and distillery, planted fine European varieties of wine grapes, and soon earned a reputation as the state's preeminent brandy maker, as well as a man whose sexual appetite made him the talk of San Jose. By 1877, Naglee was producing a hundred thousand gallons of wine annually. When the grapes ripened in his prize vineyard that year, he hired local artist John R. Key to paint the harvest along Coyote Creek, on the southeast corner of his property. Using the conventional method of looking out from between trees toward the vineyard, Key focused on a crew of five Mexican harvesters picking grapes into wicker baskets and loading them onto a horse-drawn wagon for shipment to the winery. Although the harvest for what was then the largest brandy operation in California must certainly have been a frantic one, it was not portrayed this way in Key's painting. With the coastal foothills looming dramatically in the background and baskets full of grapes cooling in the shade of a large oak tree, Key's pastoral scene reversed Hill's and represents farm labor as placid, easy work in which men hardly break a sweat.[53]

At about the time that Key was painting the grape harvest, publishing firms such as Thompson and West, the largest of several county history publishers, were sending out pairs of extremely talented artists. While executing sketches for various local and county histories, these so-called mug book artists drew pictures of countless farms on which farmworkers appear about the property. These artists drew their scenes from a ubiquitous bird's-eye view, like those in a Victorian children's storybook. Their sharp and detailed 9 × 12–inch, full-page drawings provide a bonanza of information about bunkhouses and other outbuildings, homes, crops, fields, orchards, modes of transportation and dress, and various routine activities. But while so meticulously attentive to detail that one can see every clapboard, shingle, and gingerbread finial on a building and every picket on a fence, their sketches also have an odd, prefabricated look. Orange groves, walnut orchards, and vineyards are invariably free of weeds; roads and lanes are arrow-straight; lawns are clipped and manicured; dogs, sheep, and cows frolic; horses prance about; and human figures, including the patron and his family, some drawn to scale, others not, project all the animation of wooden chess pieces.[54]

Mug book illustrators often depicted farmworkers in the middle of the grain harvest or while plowing, planting, or weeding. Farmworkers appear quite small and usually in black outline, with Euro-Americans clearly distinguished from Chinese, who usually appear in loose, square-cut blouses and baggy pants, with queues wound around their heads or trailing out from under a traditional hat. These are entirely cheerful images, without impact, and seldom elicited much controversy or even aroused much response at all. But in a different format and different venue and in the hands of

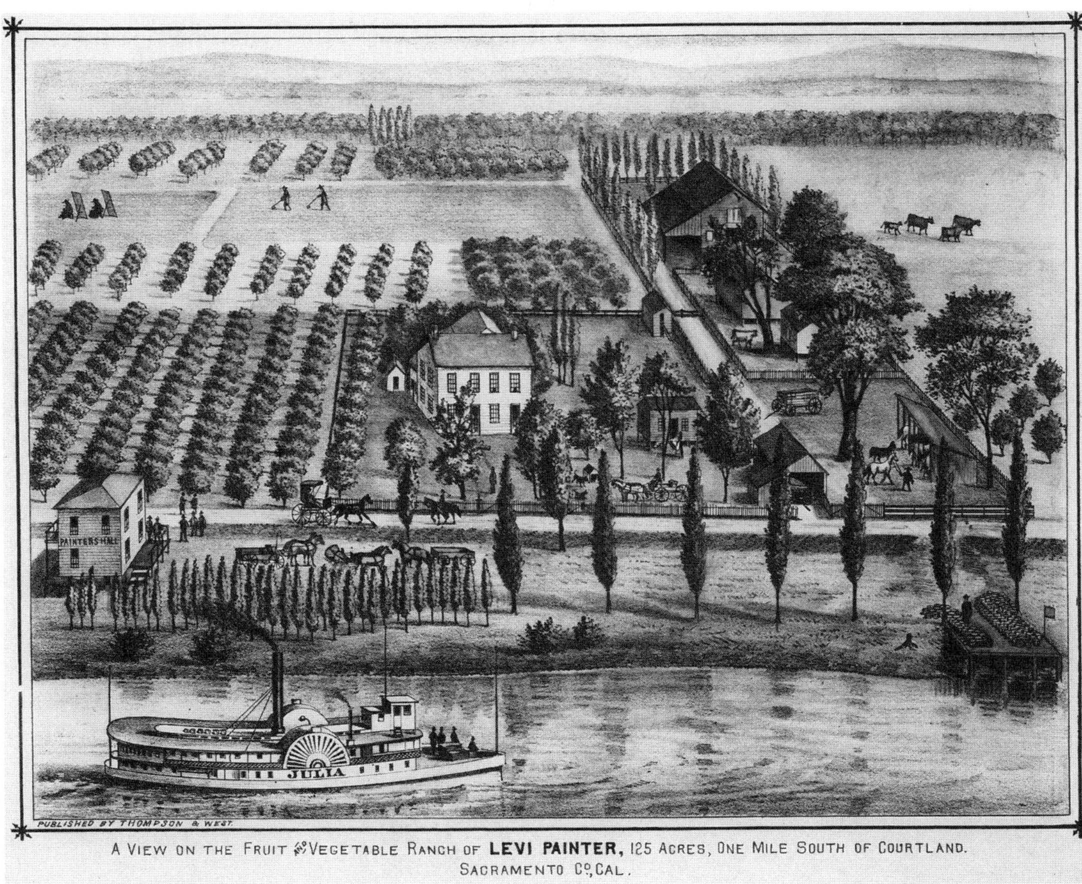

A View on the Fruit and Vegetable Ranch of Levi Painter, 125 Acres, One Mile South of Courtland, Sacramento Co., Cal., 1880. Note farmworkers in distant fields. From [Thomas A.] Thompson and [Albert Augustus] West, *History of Sacramento County, California, with Illustrations*, 1880. Author's collection.

different illustrators, drawings of farmworkers could and did have an impact equal to that of the best painting or photograph. Nothing more clearly demonstrates this than work done by illustrator Paul Frenzeny, who in 1878 was assigned to illustrate a long and detailed story on California wine making. After visiting the Sonoma Valley, he produced a wonderful image of wine-making activities to accompany an article titled "The Vintage in California." Translated into a wood engraving by Allen Meason, the drawing went a long way toward solidifying California's reputation as the premier wine-making region in America. But Frenzeny's carefully composed sketch—which contains all of the elements of wine making, from presses and juice pumps to great storage casks and mule carts bringing grapes in from the vineyards—caused a storm of controversy when it appeared on October 5, 1878.[55]

Before Frenzeny's drawing, neither *Harper's Weekly* nor any other journal or mug book had ever published an agricultural image suggestive of anything besides a pastoral ideal. Typical of these late nineteenth-century engravings, J. W. Ehninger's *Gathering Pumpkins—an October Scene in New England* rounded up every farm-related cliché to create a blissful scene in which a farm family and a few hired hands heft beautiful pumpkins into a wheelbarrow and wagon. As this transpires, horses happily pause to nuzzle, and a husband takes a refreshing drink. The scene is portrayed as so delightful that the man's wife and child, who are seated at his feet, exude contentment.

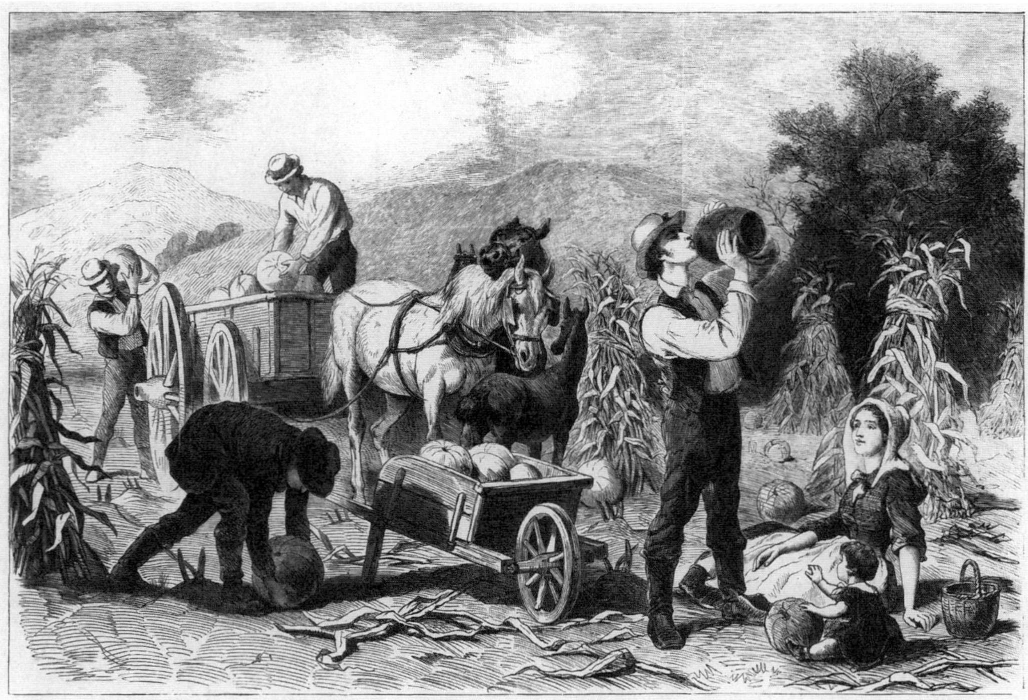

Gathering Pumpkins—an October Scene in New England, 1867. Woodblock print from a drawing by J. W. Ehninger, *Harper's Weekly,* October 26, 1867. Courtesy of the Library of Congress, Prints and Photographs Division.

Not so with Frenzeny's work. Hardly catering to the nostalgic yearnings of a city-based audience that knew no better, Frenzeny broke dramatically with the pastoral ideal and enraged Sonoma Valley residents. For one thing, Frenzeny featured Chinese field hands prominently in his scene. By now they had established themselves in vineyards and wineries throughout the Sonoma and Napa valleys and as far south as Los Angeles. Vintners even praised them for "their no drinking and general steadiness and adaptation for the work." But because California's reputation for quality wine was becoming established, many winemakers did not in any way want to jeopardize this position by mentioning the role that the Chinese were playing as wine blenders, fermentation masters, and assistant winemakers. Knowing all too well what anti-Chinese zealots were capable of, no one wanted to risk opening the industry up to issues of cleanliness, disease, and immigration policy, which might lead to violence, arson, boycotts, or other threats.[56]

What upset winemakers most was Frenzeny's quite inaccurate depiction of Chinese stomping the grapes with their bare feet. Winemakers had long since discarded that technique in favor of modern screw presses and highly sanitary wine-making procedures. In fact, so concerned with cleanliness were some wineries that they hired Chinese to stand alongside conveyor belts and pick out unripe grapes, stems, leaves, and other debris. Now it seemed to many winemakers not only that their reputation for innovation and quality was being tarnished but additionally that the drawing might link their product to the unsavory image of Chinese field hands stomping out the vintage.[57]

To a man, California winemakers denounced *Harper's Weekly* and demanded that the magazine immediately drop all further references to the Chinese. Frenzeny himself drew the strongest fire. "He has libeled the state," blasted a writer for the *San Francisco Call.* "The tendency of such a picture is not likely to weaken the prejudice which some Eastern dealers have endeavored to create against the wine produced in this state." In truth, two-thirds of California's five-million-gallon annual vintage actually sold within the state; slightly less than one million dollars in California wine sold to markets on the East Coast. Hence, California wine merchants had little or nothing to fear from the *Harper's Weekly* drawing. Nevertheless, none could stomach the picture of "dirty Oriental laborers, reeking with perspiration," depositing various unmentionable pollutants from between their toes into the latest vintage. Concerned that *Harper's Weekly,* with its circulation of well over a hundred thousand, might reprint the image, vintners made their intentions clear. Should the magazine ever again publish Frenzeny's drawing, they vowed revenge on the magazine and the artist. *Harper's Weekly* never printed a retraction, and Frenzeny, who never apologized, continued working for the magazine well into the 1880s.[58]

A year after the Frenzeny controversy, one of California's most honored artists, Scottish-born William Keith, painted *Haying in Marin County.* Although it is essentially a landscape in which farmwork is but a small element of the composition, the painting depicts a crew of field hands loading a hay wagon in the shade of a stand of redwood trees while three young children watch. The painting had little to do with agriculture or labor and everything to do with finding another way to highlight a bucolic scene in a beautiful valley in the same way that Keith had made colorful, romantic canvases of Yosemite and the High Sierra. Another mellow contemplation of farm labor in 1879 was American-born artist Peter Moran's *Threshing Wheat, San Juan,* which shows several field hands driving horses around a threshing corral near San Jose. Another promised land picture, it features the usual golden fields of wheat and human figures, hardly breaking a sweat, in peaceful harmony with the natural setting as they bring in the harvest.

After 1880, great landscape painters all but abandoned technological agriculture in general, and wheat threshing in particular, in favor of still lifes of the state's famous fruits and vegetables. Three genres emerged. One stressed compositions of luscious cherries and plump grapes as they would be seen at the dinner table of wealthy and middle-class patrons. A leading painter of such still lifes, Samuel Marsden Brooks, did a good business filling the parlors and local galleries with various arrangements. A second genre focused on local produce in the distribution process. These paintings used the California setting in conjunction with a plethora of produce to suggest that technological changes were now in the past and the state had come of age. A third genre was really a variation of a style fashionable in eighteenth-century England: the outdoor conversation piece. Gone were the great lumbering combines and threshers. Painters recoiled from their belching smokestacks, and no patrons wanted paintings of such things. As the era of bonanza wheat farming and pioneering in wine making passed, farmers in need of a commemorative picture turned to laudatory promised land paintings. Surrounded in picturesque, orderly, productive, and sunny landscapes, the state's preeminent farmers emerge as a respectable and sophisticated horticultural elite, who seem to will the crops out of the ground independent of field hands.[59]

From dead nature still lifes and promised land portraiture, it was but a small step to paintings of the cornucopia of the world. Southern Pacific Railroad took the lead in this effort. Hiring teams of artists to create promotional posters, the company appealed to cherished republican values, played up the agrarian myth, and attracted American go-getters with hundreds of brochures, broadsides, advertisements, and newspaper illustrations. On the cover of one brochure titled *California for the Settler,* artist Arthur Cahill painted a wholesome farmer holding a young blonde girl. Splashed across a famous lithographic poster, another artist painted an irrigation spigot releasing streams of water that spirals through a cornucopia and gushes forth as pineapples, oranges, grapes, bananas, and peaches tumbling toward the viewer. It did not matter that California did not even grow pineapples and that the few banana groves were of no commercial significance. This art was not about reality. It was about a dream. And a myth. Whether looking forward to a promised land or backward to a mythical Spanish Arcadia, images in *Sunset* magazine, various publications from the State Board of Trade, and local chambers of commerce appealed to the needs and interests of targeted audiences in the eastern United States. As for the laborers whose lives were contradicted by themes of lush abundance and easy pickings, they appear nowhere in the cornucopia but logically should have been listed in the brochures as one of the state's assets, along with 43,795,000 acres of government lands, a climate of health and wealth, railroad and private land for a million farmers, and an environment without cyclones or blizzards.[60]

By the late 1870s, art no longer served as a means to understand farmworkers. In truth, it rarely had done so. Painters and sketch artists had almost always suppressed scrutiny of agricultural labor relations in favor of what looked pretty. Now they became complete propagandists for clients who banished farmworkers from the field of vision. Absent competitors, photography emerged as the default medium for representing farmworkers. Far easier and cheaper to produce, it created an illusion of objective reality. But like all categories of communicators, the photographers who focused on farmworkers were hardly of one mind. If they provided new perspectives on farmworkers, they also followed old ways of seeing. If they now helped explain and interpret a class of people, they also helped to create new stereotypes. If they photographed with sympathy and insight, they also consigned farmworkers to insignificance as objects and decorations in their landscapes. Photographers would see farmworkers in new ways and in new settings, but they would also maintain, and in some cases amplify, the distortions and misrepresentations of their predecessors.

3

An Old Master in a New Place

Carleton E. Watkins in the Fields

One day in the fall of 1886, grape grower George C. Husmann trained his camera on Vina, Leland Stanford's gigantic, ultramodern wine-making operation in the northern Sacramento Valley. A native of Germany who had immigrated to the United States in 1837, Husmann was the leading viticultural authority in the United States at the time, a former professor of pomology and forestry at the Missouri State University and the author of the 1880 book *Grape Growing and Wine Making.* He had acquired several view cameras four years earlier to document his work at the Talcoa Vineyards in the Napa Valley and subsequently proceeded to photograph all aspects of wine making and grape growing. Now, as manager of Vina, he was in charge of more than one hundred French workers who tended 3,825 acres of vineyards, and one thousand Chinese who picked a crop that yielded two million gallons of wine and about 20 percent of the nation's brandy. Although perhaps the unlikeliest of early farmworker photographers, Husmann nevertheless seems to have captured everything and done it well. Surveying the complex work arrangements, he recorded bunkhouse quarters and "cellar rats" at work in the winery as well as draymen hauling grapes to the presses and harvest crews posed in the vineyards under the watchful eye of a foreman astride a white horse. The thick, gold-embossed maroon album that he presented to Leland Stanford was filled with sharp, well-composed, and perfectly exposed images suggesting the work of a master photographer. And there within lies the importance of his effort. Husmann was not a professional photographer. He was a rank amateur, albeit a very good one. And yet, with just a few years' experience and no formal training, he produced images of farmworkers as good as those from any commercial photographer.[1]

Several new technological developments made it possible for Husmann and other amateurs to duplicate, and in some cases improve on, work that had once been so complicated that only a select group of professionals could master it. At the heart of their ascendency was the introduction in the early 1880s of factory-made dry-plate, glass negatives. Precoated with a silver-bromide gelatin emulsion, dry plates were far easier to use and far more light-sensitive than wet plates. By eliminating the need for transporting huge quantities of chemicals to process exposed negatives on-site and by allowing photographers to employ much faster shutter speeds, dry plates laid the foundation for a revolution in the way photographers worked. High-speed shutters coupled with more sensitive film emulsions created even more possibilities by eliminating the "cap, uncap" method of photography, which often lasted several seconds; the new features allowed photographers to freeze action with exposures as quick as 1/250 of a second. For the first time, agriculturists, indeed, anyone, could easily and quickly record farmworkers.[2]

There was plenty to photograph. Following completion of the transcontinental railroad in 1869 and construction of a system of interconnected rail lines within the state, perishable agricultural products became available to a wider market, both within California and as far away as the larger cities of the eastern United States. As a result, California agriculture experienced a rapid and dramatic spurt of growth. Average farm size fell from 462 acres in 1880 to 397 in 1900, but the number of farms more than doubled, from thirty-six thousand to over seventy-two thousand. Wheat farming gave way to irrigated fruit and vegetable farming. By 1900 California was producing 25 percent of the nation's canned fruits and vegetables, 65 percent of its prunes and plums, 18 percent of its pears, 95 percent of its apricots, most of its oranges, lemons, figs, and olives, and a significant portion of its sugar beet crop. With native field hands dying out and Euro-American settlers increasingly avoiding farmwork, a large number

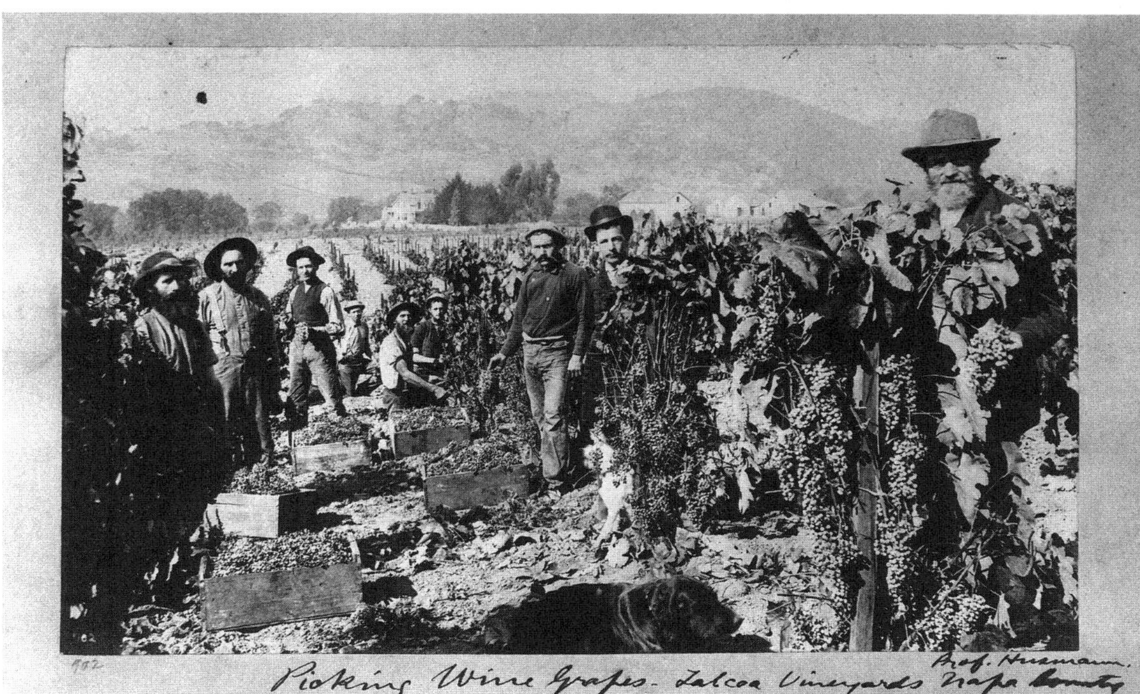

Picking Wine Grapes, Talcoa Vineyards, Napa County, 1888, by George C. Husmann. Courtesy of the California Historical Society.

of Chinese and Japanese immigrants were working in the fields, expanding the farm labor force from 16,231 in 1870 to 76,493 in 1900.[3]

Not quite gone from the scene, a small group of painters focused on these dynamic changes. Among them was Virgil Williams, the Massachusetts native who had first come to California in 1862 after completing his artistic training in Rome. Sometime in 1885, Williams photographed a woman on a ladder picking fruit near St. Helena, which was to become his silver gelatin print *Picking Fruit, Foothills of St. Helena* and the basis of his genre oil painting *Farm Yard Scene,* which was more reminiscent of a harvest in Tuscany than anything in California. Williams died the following year, and in his absence no one seems to have carried on the tradition established by William Keith, Andrew P. Hill, and William Hahn. In truth, their day had already passed. The telephone, phonograph, and telegraph were changing conceptions of time and space, and the new speed and ease of visualization were launching the modern world. Williams and other artists who belonged to a bygone era were left in the wake. In the new technological West, they could not compete with photographers, who pushed them aside and dominated the emerging picture of California farmworkers.[4]

During the 1880s and 1890s dozens of photographers kept busy executing assignments for the *Pacific Rural Press* and numerous other agricultural journals. Most were prominent local photographers. Familiar with their territory, they matter-of-factly documented important technical innovations, unusually large or record harvests, and various newsworthy events. They seldom received a byline for their work when their images appeared as translations into woodcuts, drawings, and engravings. Then, an identifying caption typically stated, "We here within submit an engraving which has been faithfully prepared from a photograph . . . which can't lie."[5]

Around 1888, farmworker images began appearing in books as colored lithographic plates. San Francisco's W. R. Nutting, owner and manager of the California View Publishing Company, pioneered this effort. Producing a series of illustrated books on different regions in the state, Nutting in 1885 hired Edward J. Wickson, editor of the *Pacific Rural Press,* to write *California Illustrated No. 1: The Vacaville Early Fruit District,* a lively and informed account detailing every aspect of fruit culture, as well as various crop varieties, the method by which farmers shipped fruit by railroad lines to markets on the East Coast, and countless agricultural operations along with the challenges, geography, and day-to-day activities of fruit farming in what was, at that time, the state's premier agricultural district. After Wickson completed the text, Nutting, who had learned to photograph for the specific purpose of illustrating this book, used it as a shooting script and made several hundred photographs documenting everyone and everything Wickson had mentioned.

Commencing with the first apricot and cherry harvests, Nutting began photographing in June 1886. He continued into the following seasons and concluded his sojourn with two shots in the late fall of 1887. When *Vacaville Early Fruit District* was published the following spring, all three thousand first-edition copies sold out at one dollar each. Pronounced "The Best Advertising Work ever produced in California or any other country," a second edition, published in May 1888, also sold out, along with individual photographs, bound volumes, and combinations of photographs and albums purchased by various farmers featured in views or mentioned in the text.[6]

What particularly attracted readers were the eighty-six colored lithographs produced by San Francisco printer H. S. Crocker and Company, which were made by artists who visited the location of every scene with the original photographs in hand in order to note the proper colors. Filling the front of the book, these images—the first sustained effort to capture farm labor in color—provoked extensive praise as the equal of anything done in the Atlantic Coast states. Many reviewers professed that they had never seen anything like them. Admiring the way text and images worked together in sequence, the *Vacaville Reporter* praised the collection as "a most delightful impression of the beauty and fertility of the country, and of the variety and attractiveness of its characteristic features." While no one used the term *photo essay* to describe the layout, Nutting's technique in essence mirrored the way photo essays would be produced by magazines such as *Life* and *National Geographic* a half century later. Contrasting *Vacaville Early Fruit District* with the profusion of cheap, quickly forgotten pamphlets being produced by various communities at the time, one writer summarized the book as something that would be "saved up, read and re-read by the seekers after knowledge of this country."[7]

Nutting's well-composed images are packed with information revealing salient details of harvest work. They are extremely important as historical documents because Vacaville was the premier fruit-growing district in California, both in importance and in its early development, and because it was one of the locations where Chinese field hands appeared in large numbers. At the time that Nutting photographed, Chinese field hands were becoming scarce throughout the state, largely as a result of a growing anti-Chinese movement and a series of restrictive immigration laws, but apparently not in the Vaca Valley. Although Nutting's photographs were marred by long exposures of one-half second or more, which blurred the faces of those Chinese who moved slightly while being photographed, they show that, despite many outbreaks of violence against the Chinese, Vaca Valley farmers continued to value and protect these workers, who appear completely integrated into farming operations. In the photos, none works alone; most are interspersed among Euro-American men, women, and children. This is true of various harvest and field operations as well as processing and packing operations. If Nutting's photographs are accurate documents—and there is no reason to doubt their veracity—then it appears that the Vaca Valley was an alcove of safety where the Chinese continued to work even while being driven from other farming districts.[8]

Besides spotlighting the Chinese, Nutting also devoted considerable attention to the fruit-drying yards, where Vacaville growers found a way to dispose of their surplus as well as undersized or flawed peaches and apricots that failed to meet grade. His photographs undermine a central myth of farmworker history, according to which, migratory farmworkers who followed the ripening crops over long distances were now handling most of this work. But Nutting captured a more complex situation in the fruit-drying yards around Vacaville. Virtually the entire Vacaville community is seen nailing up fruit boxes, driving fruit wagons, picking, packing, cutting, pitting, and drying fruit, or performing some other associated chore. Also present are families from nearby towns. Children as young as four years of age are everywhere. One photograph of drying yards on the W. J. Pleasants farm in Pleasants Valley shows thirty-five workers, many of them boys, cutting, peeling, spreading, and placing peaches on the drying grounds. Another depicts children as young as six cutting and packing peaches. Those too small to reach the cutting table can be seen standing on boxes. According to prevailing thought, their dexterity, nimble fingers, good eyes, and ability to squeeze into narrow spots proved especially valuable when carrying trays loaded with fruit to vacant spots in the drying yards, where they turned and rotated trays full of split fruit.[9]

Of all the photographers using the new dry-plate technology to document California farmworkers at this time, none was more famous, talented, or prolific than Carleton E. Watkins. Among landscape photographers of the era, Watkins stood alone. He was the acknowledged preeminent figure. Born in Oneonta, New York, in 1829, he came to California in 1851 and, after several years as a merchandise store owner and carpenter in Sacramento, made his first daguerreotypes in 1854, while employed as an apprentice to San Francisco photographer Robert Vance. Over the next decade he

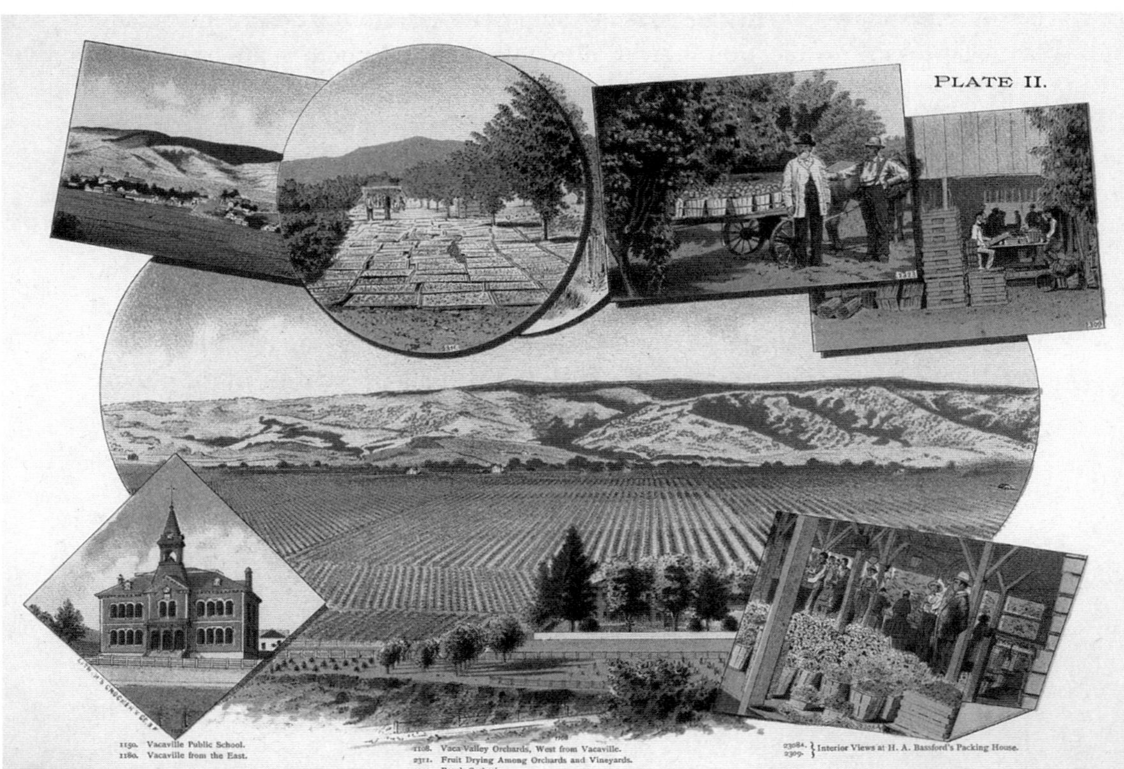

Plate II from Edward Wickson, *California Illustrated No. 1: The Vacaville Early Fruit District,* 1888. Photographs by W[illiam] R. Nutting. Originals in color. Courtesy of the Vacaville Museum.

photographed the Farallon Islands, the New Almaden Mines and the Mendocino coast, Mt. Hood, Mt. Shasta, Mt. Lassen, the North Bloomfield Gravel Mine, the Columbia River, the Central Pacific Railroad, and various sites for the Oregon Steam Navigation Company, and scenes as far north as British Columbia and as far south as Mexico. Although work and workers do not appear in most of his photographs other than as incidentals—the odd miner pushing his ore cart and the railroad engineer beside his locomotive—those photographs that do feature workers with their drooping mustaches and stoic poses have the power of a Walt Whitman poem. Watkins made his reputation in 1861 with a series of extraordinary and technically breathtaking 20 × 24–inch mammoth-plate photographs of the Yosemite Valley, which made their way east into the hands of congressmen, who, in 1864, declared Yosemite "inviolate"—the first step in preserving it as a national park. These images, which Watkins duplicated in 1865, constituted something that historian Weston J. Naef characterizes as "the first body of work to systematically present the landscape as a wilderness before the arrival of man." He accomplished much of his fieldwork by traveling the railroads in two special cars; one served as living quarters and housed his photo studio, and the other carried his photo wagon and horses. Watkins unhitched the cars, leaving them at sidings along the way, and used his dark-colored photographic wagon to range far and wide. An advertisement on the side of his wagon read: "C. E. WATKINS, Landscape Photographer. YOSEMITE GALLERY. 22 & 26 MONTGOMERY ST. Views to Order in any Part of the STATE OR COAST."[10]

Watkins was the first great visual poet of the American West. His photographs were full of radiant and mysterious qualities, the harmoniously arranged world that all hoped existed but could not find among the promotional deals, political intrigue, mining booms, Sinophobic outbreaks, riots, hangings, and catastrophes. He worked with such energy and artistry that many contemporaries acknowledged him as America's greatest landscape photographer, essentially the Ansel Adams of the late nineteenth century, whose subjects and vistas Adams would later revisit and reinterpret. Such a self-made man, with all his success and status, was never associated with the mundane and commonplace. He was a man of soaring vistas. When people thought about his work, they did not associate him with the dirty aspects of farming and the sweat-stained faces of field hands. They did not think of haystacks and steam threshers or of Chinese irrigating fields of alfalfa. Nor did they think of Watkins as someone who had even the slightest contact with farmworkers. But like most working photographers, Watkins was adept at every facet of his craft. While practicing photography as an art form, he never referred to himself as an artist. He could photograph hydraulic mining operations and lumber mills as well as the lavish homes of California's nouveaux riches and the great unspoiled West. But he did not photograph solely in the quest of beauty. Watkins was a businessman. His need for income and assignments grew acute after 1876, when a series of business failures resulted in the loss of his entire studio and its contents. To regain financial stability, Watkins created his New Series and undertook even more wide-ranging assignments, reshooting old scenes and accepting numerous commercial assignments.[11]

An assignment for Southern Pacific Railroad brought Watkins into the San Joaquin Valley for the first time in 1877, when he was hired to photograph the railroad as far south as Los Angeles. He passed through a second time in 1880 during an extended journey along the route of the Southern Pacific Railroad, a long, grueling, and difficult assignment that brought him as far south as Tucson, Arizona, and resulted in much new material for his New Series offerings, including a sequence on the missions. It was during this trip that he first photographed agriculture and farmworkers, the former around Pasadena, where he documented citrus fruits, walnut groves, banana trees, vineyards, a bee ranch, and farms in the San Gabriel Valley; the latter mostly centered on Indian field hands and winemakers at Sunny Slope. His friendship with millionaire landowner and prominent San Francisco attorney James B. Haggin resulted in his third visit to the San Joaquin Valley.

Son of a prominent Kentucky slaveholding family, Haggin had come to California in 1850 and, with his brother-in-law, Lloyd Tevis, became involved in transportation, banking, manufacturing, and construction businesses throughout the American West. Watkins had met Haggin eight years earlier at the San Francisco Art Association, and Haggin had subsequently employed Watkins to photograph various enterprises, such as the Anaconda Copper Mine in Montana and the Comstock Mine in Nevada. By hook and crook but mostly by exploiting land laws, such as the Desert Land Act, and through friendship and alliance with William B. "Billy" Carr, a leading Republican Party official often referred to as the Napoleon of the Railroad Company, Haggin had obtained over one hundred thousand acres of Kern County railroad lands north and south of Bakersfield. By purchasing surrounding water rights and many small irrigation canals, Haggin eventually gained control over a large portion of Kern River water. This soon brought Haggin and Carr into conflict with two other land barons, Henry Miller and Charles Lux, who along with James C. Crocker, had secured some eighty thousand acres surrounding Buena Vista Slough and launched an equally vast land reclamation project centered on a huge canal that diverted the Kern River's main flow onto their farmlands.

In 1879, Miller and Lux sued Haggin and Carr to establish riparian rights (their rights to have water continue flowing into Buena Vista Slough). With Haggin and Carr contending that no water course existed, a court case of vast proportions shaped up. With Haggin's attorneys claiming that Miller and Lux could not benefit from riparian rights because Buena Vista Slough was simply part of a vast, undefined swamp, and Miller and Lux attorney, Hall McAllister, arguing that Buena Vista Slough was a clearly defined waterway that had run uninterrupted from time immemorial, a vast number of witnesses were summoned to describe its size, flow, and location. To make his case clear, McAllister employed photographs, which he obtained from Watkins, whom he hired to make eighteen mammoth prints and provide expert court testimony.[12]

Watkins photographed the various diversions, weirs, and canals around Buena Vista Slough, at Tracy's Crossing, and near the Kern River Bridge on January 9, 10, and 11, 1881. Summoned to the Bakersfield district courtroom of Judge Benjamin

Brundage to describe his photographs during the seven-week trial that spring, Watkins first offered his photographs as an objective record of the river system and irrigation diversion facilities. Aggressively interrogated by opposing counsel, Watkins got into a drawn-out debate over whether his photographs accurately represented the scale of the objects they depicted. Eventually he escaped back to San Francisco, having left behind a pile of mounted images that contributed substantially to a four-foot-high stack of court documents. The last witness was heard on June 2, when Watkins was hard at work photographing the United States Geodetic Survey's Yolo Base Line near Davis. To what extent his photographs influenced the eventual outcome of the court case is unclear. On November 3, 1881, Brundage ruled in favor of Haggin and Carr. The court determined that no continuous channel flowed into Buena Vista Slough, and therefore Haggin and Carr had the right to appropriate water. Over the next two years, Watkins finished a series of images along the coastline between Los Angeles and San Francisco, documented the del Monte Hotel in Monterey, and photographed in the Washington Territory, Pacific Northwest, and British Columbia. In 1884, while Watkins was working on a huge photographic reconnaissance in Oregon, Idaho, Montana, and the Yellowstone area, the California Supreme Court overturned the 1881 decision and, in 1886, affirmed Miller and Lux's riparian rights. As a result, in 1887, Miller and Haggin concluded a private agreement guaranteeing Miller and Lux sufficient water from the Kern River and retaining the remaining flow for Haggin and Carr.[13]

With water rights finally settled, Haggin and Carr formulated plans in the summer of 1888 to promote and sell vast tracts of farmland around Bakersfield. As a first step, they needed a visual inventory of Kern County. They could have hired a local photographer from Bakersfield, because by this time several portrait galleries existed in the southern San Joaquin Valley. Particularly outstanding was C. A. Nelson, whose studio opposite the Kern Valley Bank in Bakersfield advertised cabinet-sized photographs at three dollars per dozen, plus "instantaneous" photographs even on cloudy days, as well as baby pictures. Although Nelson did landscape work for valley farmers, producing views comparable to those of Watkins, Haggin and Carr chose Watkins, probably because he was already known to them, had done good work, and had just completed a series of views of Sonoma County farms and ranches near El Verano. Haggin and Carr wanted Watkins to do more or less the same, then organize his photographs into albums. These would be presented to various company officials and made available as illustrative material for promotional pamphlets. Since the inventory would document farms, crops, equipment, agricultural assets, irrigation works, and water resources, many of the photographs inevitably depict farmworkers in different phases of their work or as elements of scale or decorations, as was the custom in landscape and inventory photographs.

By now a veteran of many far-ranging assignments, Watkins took great care in packing and loading equipment for the 315-mile journey from San Francisco to Bakersfield. He probably followed his well-established pattern of leasing two railcars and, once in Bakersfield, parked them on a siding. Since both Haggin and Carr maintained residences in Bakersfield, Watkins may have stayed with them while on assignment in the valley, probably residing on the different ranches, using each as a base of operations, then moving on to the next location.[14]

Watkins was briefly noted in the July 7, 1888, issue of the *Kern County Californian,* a weekly newspaper long hostile to every aspect of Haggin's schemes; it described Watkins as a "eminent photographer" and advised that this was "an unusual opportunity for those who want photographs of their property to have them taken. Mr. Watkins will visit any place desired. His charge is only $6 per dozen for the 8 × 10 size, and others in proportion." Watkins apparently photographed around Bakersfield from early July until mid-September. A small group of men from the Haggin–Carr–Tevis land operations, as well as foremen and managers from the Miller and Lux empire, guided Watkins, his all-around packer and cook, Charlie Staples, and his young photographic assistant, Jessie Miller.[15]

Temperatures on the plains surrounding Bakersfield hovered between 100 and 110 degrees throughout July and August. This must have drained the fifty-eight-year-old photographer, who for many years had suffered from rheumatism and leg problems. The work proceeded very slowly, in part because of Watkins's age, ill health, and the heat, but also because of the size of the photographic party and extensive equipment that needed to be transported, unpacked, set up, and repacked at various, widely scattered ranches.[16]

Watkins averaged about ten photographs each day, with between three and six scenes at each site. He produced a total of 726 views. Unlike any other photographs of California at this time, these arresting images are unique historical documents evoking the texture of rural life in an area just as it was being opened and intensely promoted for settlement and development. Exactly how Watkins made them is still a mystery. He apparently photographed at least one farmworker or group of farmworkers at each site, usually as they were preparing for work, engaged in some aspect of agricultural labor, posing beside some favored asset, or displaying an array of equipment and farm animals. It was very deliberate photography, under less than ideal conditions. But while the subject matter was conventional and prescribed, Watkins did not treat the images as routine. A true master of his craft, Watkins always approached his subjects with a careful eye for composition, lighting, and the imprint of humanity on the raw landscape. Containing a heightened sense of a particular time and place, his photographs are akin to pages in a diary. A close reading reveals heretofore hidden aspects of Watkins's working methodology and vision of farmworkers. Some of his images are surprising, and many are far in advance of their time.[17]

Most of the pictures Watkins made in Kern County suggest a routine of taking an overview, photographing the entrance to the farm, then moving on to document barns, stables, orchards, and fields. He was extraordinarily well organized. If the ranch had a special cow, an artesian well, a champion race horse, or a fine garden, Watkins carefully recorded it. "Some of the photographs . . . rows of cheeses drying in their racks, a close-up of cling peaches, show a formalism, a regard for pattern, verging on the abstract," observes historian Kevin Starr. "There is an ambition, an inclusiveness, in Watkins that contrasts dramatically with the California painters of the period, riveted as they were to landscape."[18]

Farmworkers apparently qualified as among the special assets worthy of documenting. Watkins seems to have moved among them freely, as can be seen in one photograph of horse and mule teams hitched and ready to pull mowers and headers through the alfalfa and grain fields. Besides photographing farmworkers in the fields or in the midst of activities like hitching up teams, irrigating, and plowing or cutting hay, Watkins also photographed them in barnyards, alongside canals, among equipment, and resting in the shade at ranch headquarters or on the porches of various farm buildings. Unlike previous photographers, who found it useful to photograph farmworkers only at work, Watkins was interested in depicting them in a broader range of circumstances that situated field hands within the region's larger industrial transformation.

Watkins had always done this. Whether he was photographing the New Almaden Mine or the Tehachapi Loop, he was ever attentive to the relationship among industrialization, the physical surroundings, and the people who did the work. Watkins also seems to have been fascinated by the various ethnic groups he encountered in Kern County, and he went to great pains to produce a number of unusual photographs highlighting their work. Outside El Tejon Ranch headquarters, he posed a Mexican in full regalia with a gigantic knife. The man is clearly a figure of authority, perhaps a majordomo (foreman) who supervised a large number of men. The man appears in a number of photographs taken on the ranch in several different locations, both alone and with many different groups, an amount of attention that suggests he was a key and valued employee and that perhaps he was traveling with Watkins and was responsible for logistics.

Watkins also took many photographs of Chinese. After making their way into Kern County while building the Southern Pacific Railroad route through the Tehachapi Mountains, so many had remained behind in Bakersfield that two separate Chinatowns had developed. As agriculture expanded in the region, the Chinese found work in constructing irrigation canals and as irrigators, hay stackers, milkers, and, perhaps most important, cooks. Watkins posed one Chinese cook alongside a family on the porch of a fine building in a way that suggests the man played a key role and had an elevated status in farm operations. Next in importance is a series of photographs of Chinese irrigators, ankle deep in water as they go about their task of diverting water to alfalfa fields and orchards. But Watkins also photographed Chinese operating hay rakes in the fields, driving hay rakes out of a ranch yard early in the morning, and using special California derricks to stack hay in piles two stories high. Among his most distinctive shots is a portrait of a Chinese boiler tender, stoking the furnace of a steam engine that pumps irrigation water from deep wells. No other photographer recorded images of Chinese in positions of prominence or portrayed them so artfully and with so much respect and dignity in so many different farm-related activities.[19]

Besides overseers and Chinese field hands, Watkins photographed all varieties of farmworkers: ditch diggers, sheep shearers, and wagon drivers. He also became engrossed by wheat threshers and alfalfa harvesters, especially their machinery, work methods, camps, and the huge stacks of hay and grain they produced. To illustrate their work, Watkins executed several traditional views of grain fields dotted with massive harvest machines and proud, strategically placed workers. But he also made a number of photographs that were completely unique. As Nutting had done in Vacaville, Watkins used long, medium, and close-up shots to unfold his stories of wheat harvesting in a sequence closely resembling that of modern photo essayists. In one sequence depicting wheat threshers, Watkins moved progressively closer in executing a series of five shots, concluding with a group portrait of four men. Framed by heavy, black machinery and obscuring clouds of dust, the last image is a haunting portrait of nineteenth-century men engaged in hot, dirty, noisy, dangerous, exhausting work.[20]

One of his most imposing photographs focuses on haying at Buena Vista Farm. In this photograph a crew of twenty Chinese cut and haul hay from the fields to a large derrick and erect a stack thirty feet high and more than one hundred feet long. Overseeing this monumental operation are three men, who appear in the foreground seated on their horses. The more distant of the three is an unnamed Chinese crew boss. The other two men, facing the camera, are S. W. Wible, who supervised all of the various ranch managers and canal foremen in the southern division of Miller and

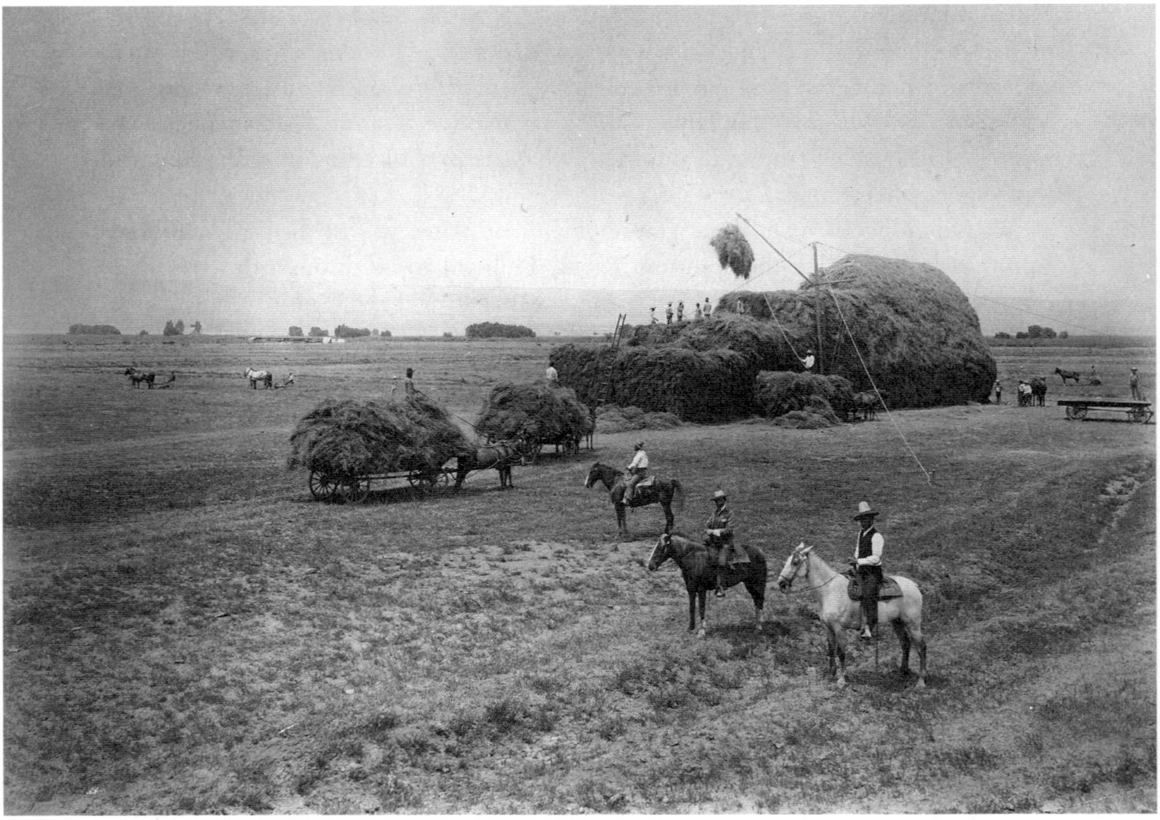

Haying at Buena Vista Farm, Kern County, Cal., 1888, photograph by Carleton E. Watkins. Courtesy of the Library of Congress, Prints and Photographs Division.

Lux's operations and who had a canal named in his honor, and Rafael Cuen, a skilled Mexican vaquero, recently with the Haggin and Carr farming operations, who sports a tall white hat and sits astride a massive white horse. Over twelve hundred migrant workers toiled on the Miller and Lux empire, and men like Wible and Cuen were absolutely essential to the company's large-scale industrialized farming operations. They appear in a half dozen photographs.[21]

Unlike present-day photo essayists, Watkins was unable to arrest action. Instead, he had to simulate work by posing his subjects appropriately, acting more or less as a director of his scenes. This limitation makes his work even more admirable. His farmworker photographs frequently document men at the apex of action or in the midst of some key activity—the instant when the hay fork swung into position or the moment near daybreak when a wheat harvest crew paused before moving out of the ranch enclosure into the fields. He probably used a "cap, uncap" procedure in making these photographs. His exposures in the open sunlight lasted about one-fifth to one-half of a second. Had they been longer, in the range of two or three seconds, most of the animals and some of the men would have moved and become blurs. His exposures were never short enough to freeze action totally, as the blurred blades of the whirling windmills, silky water in irrigation canals, and two-headed horses clearly demonstrate.[22]

A careful evaluation of Watkins's farmworker photographs reveals another little-known aspect of his photographic technique: his habit of photographing from the roof of his traveling wagon, a height of about fifteen feet. Particularly well-suited to the flat and unspectacular Kern County landscape, this method was somewhat reminiscent of the elevated perspective adopted by mug book sketch artists and helped transform undramatic views of farmworkers into interesting scenic vistas rich with information.

Like most landscape photographers, Watkins was up before sunrise to begin work early in the morning. This not only allowed him to bathe his subjects in a soft, warm, sculpting light but also was an accommodation to the realities of farm life, in which people rose early and started work just after dawn. Group pictures portraying harvesting were best done at this time, although in many scenes Watkins clearly had to wait several hours before harvesters erected the giant haystacks that figure prominently in many photographs. Watkins's use of early-morning light, however, also originated in his desire to avoid working in the searing July and August heat and the harsh, unflattering light of midday. Additionally, his early-morning work freed him to do portraiture in the open shade of farm buildings during the afternoon and in the evening when people had returned from the fields, had washed up and rested, and had time to pose.[23]

Watkins often recorded his own shadow and the shadow of his tripod and the dark camera drape in his photographs. These are prominently seen in his picture of Chinese milkers at the Mountain View Dairy. He also left behind other evidence of his presence. Some views of men irrigating alfalfa fields reveal the ears and heads of horses, because Watkins shot them from his wagon. Others show his traveling buggy parked on a bridge or in the middle of a field to provide a sense of scale for various elements in the landscape. One photograph taken by his assistant may even include Watkins himself. It shows a group of men camped in front of a large tree. A photographic wagon is on the right. In the center is a white-bearded man wearing a large smock and big hat. This view probably includes Charlie Staples, Jessie Miller, and Watkins.[24]

Watkins probably processed his glass plates when he returned to his railcar studio in Bakersfield, then shipped them back to his San Francisco studio at 427 Montgomery Street. Twelve years earlier he had lost his chief printer, Policarpo Bagnasco, who left to print for rival Isaiah Tabor after Tabor had taken control of Watkins's business as payment for debts owed. Watkins then relied on Ah Fue, an accomplished Chinese printer who remained with him for twenty years. After printing the images, Ah Fue mounted them on heavy rag board and added extensive typeset captions to the boards along with the New Series label.

Who wrote these lively, informative, and substantial captions is unclear. Each one unfolds a story that molds the viewer's interpretation of the image: the history behind the photograph, the importance of what is portrayed, the location of the picture, and the names and significance of the people depicted. Glued below each print so the viewer can easily shift from photograph to words, these captions are nothing less than short, well-written promotional essays on the history, prominent leaders, and landscape of Kern County, with vast amounts of additional information on all aspects of farm labor, agricultural technology, cultivation techniques, and harvest practices.[25]

One typical caption, accompanying a photograph of Chinese irrigating alfalfa fields on the two-thousand acre Panama Ranch, twelve miles southwest of Bakersfield, makes the unfamiliar work seem less strange by explaining:

> The alfalfa fields here are checked for irrigation by levees or ridges thrown up about one foot high with plows and buck scrapers usually, but as shown here with a hone, which is really a twelve-inch plow, having an adjustable mold-board twelve feet long. This is so adjusted as to cut a narrow furrow the first round, being widened each subsequent round, until the fifth round completes a check, with a base of four feet. Each check is laid out about five inches lower than the one above. The area between the checks to be flooded is about twenty-five acres. This varies by the slope of the land, from one to one hundred acres. The illustration shows how each check is filled, then the levee is cut, and the overflown water is let off, flooding the next lower check and so on until the whole field is flooded. Men barefooted perform this labor with shovels. The labor for this irrigation costs five to ten cents an acre, the water belonging to the proprietors. The trees as seen in the center and background . . . willows, poplars, and cottonwoods have all grown up in ten years. To the uninitiated in irrigation, this irrigating scene shows its practical utility and proves its economy when we state that four men as seen here, will irrigate according to circumstances from fifty to one hundred and fifty acres a day.[26]

Another caption, accompanying a photograph of alfalfa hay stacking on the 13,500-acre Bellevue Ranch, eight miles southwest of Bakersfield, explains that, with water from the James, Plunkett, and other canals,

> alfalfa hay is put up is such large quantities that ordinary methods of handling it will not suffice. Stacks usually range from 100 to 300 feet in length, twenty-five to thirty feet high, and twenty-five to thirty feet wide, containing from 100 to 300 tons. Sometimes 750 tons are put in one stack. Twenty to thirty stacks have been counted from one view on a ranch. The scene above shows the operation of stacking. The derrick and fork, a California invention, worked by horses, is the principal implement employed. The fork has four prongs, four feet long, and eighteen inches apart, and will lift from 200 to 500 pounds at once. It requires six teams to supply one derrick, and with these appliances, sixty tons per day can be stacked.[27]

During September 1888, the Kern County Board of Trade purchased two dozen of these extensively captioned photographs, including several showing farmworkers stacking hay and harvesting alfalfa. Mounted behind glass in attractive wooden frames, the prints were exhibited the following year in San Francisco at the Mechanic's Institute Industrial Fair. Trade journals praised the way they were displayed, flanked by jars of preserves, stacks of jumbo peaches, mounds of fine vegetables, stands of corn, and drapes of colorful bunting and paper streamers. In October, several volumes of the Kern County photographs, bound in hefty albums adorned with maroon covers and gold embossed titles, went on sale at A. C. Maude's Stationery Store in Bakersfield for thirty dollars per album. Not surprisingly, the most extensive use of Watkins's Kern County images was made by the Haggin and Carr land development operations. Beginning in late 1888, the two promoters started issuing pamphlets, brochures, and booklets illustrated with Watkins's photographs, particularly the scenes featuring productive fields and men at work in them. The photographs were proof, one claimed, that Kern County "does not partake of the wild and wooly west."[28]

Although Watkins provoked curiosity and admiration, his work among field hands in the southern San Joaquin Valley was never a probing force for change. Living conditions received especially radiant treatment. Under one image of the mess house at Mt. View Dairy, an extended caption offers a glowing description of housing that asserts:

> It is the custom of the owners of ranches to provide separate dwelling houses, kitchen and dining-room for employees. This is two-stories, fifty-eight ft. long by twenty ft. wide and twenty six ft. high, with a porch on the west side, and contains three rooms upstairs and three downstairs. The upper rooms are all sleeping rooms, one of which is also used as a sitting room and contains a stove. Downstairs are dining room, kitchen, and store-room and pantry. The superintendent's house is just visible among the trees and the ventilations of the dairy house can be made out among the distant tree tops. The neatly white washed five-board fence divides the grounds into separate fields and corrals, and trees and grass adorn and make them comfortable to man and beast.[29]

Like most other photographers, Watkins did the bidding of his employers. He had not been hired to question the status of farmworkers. He apparently saw no reason to stress exhausting work, had no interest in exposing the difficulties farmworkers faced, regarded them essentially as part of the landscape he was documenting, not much different from the fields, orchards, or farms he was photographing. His work pays little attention to living conditions other than to survey bunkhouses and chuck wagons as evidence of wholesome, up-to-date accommodations. His close-ups of wheat threshing are excitingly innovative in the way they frame work, zero in on men and machines, and lead the viewer in through a telescoping sequence, but they were ultimately produced for propaganda purposes.

Even if Watkins felt otherwise, his work indicates that he was disinclined to see farmworkers as a cause or a class distinct from other working people. Employing every trick in his bag of photographic techniques, he transformed people engaged in hot, dirty, exhausting work into noble, productive, rustic field hands, thereby feeding romantic and distorted late nineteenth-century notions of life and labor in the fields. Amassing a record that documented a region at a critical juncture in its development, Watkins was frankly promotional. On the grounds that his Kern County photography conveyed an event or revealed something significant about that region, his work there can be considered part of the earliest, broad-based phase of documentary photography, during which photographers rushed off to capture views of distant places, the natural setting, and other facets of the American West. Such places could be visited personally only by the most well-off members of society. Such views, by providing a clear representation, were regarded as both evidence and art—a literal picture or document of reality that does not lie. However, this does not make Watkins a social documentarian of Kern County. His work does not show concern with exploring the human condition, shining a light on the world's ills, attempting a deeper commentary, or holding up a mirror to society. Several generations would pass before a photographer would produce images of farmworkers that indicate those goals.[30]

Although many of Watkins's Kern County images were quickly converted to lithographs and published in books and newspapers, comparatively few people ever saw them. Only those who attended the Mechanic's Institute Industrial Fair really had a chance to see his work, which for the next century remained an isolated Kern County document known to only a few local historians. To reach the general public, Watkins would have had to convert his images and captions into stereographs or a slide show. Just then becoming popular, slide shows (also called salon lectures) combined a lecture with hand-tinted glass-plate images projected onto a wall or screen.

One of the most popular slide shows containing images of farmworkers at this time was presented by wine writer Frona Eunice Wait. Astounding readers in 1889 by producing *Wines and Vines of California,* the first book on the wine industry by a woman, Wait became so successful that William Randolph Hearst asked her to produce a special supplement on California wine that appeared in the April 12, 1890, *San Francisco Examiner.* As part of her writing process, Wait collected dozens of photographs depicting all aspects of wine making and grape growing throughout the state. But instead of using the pictures to enhance her publications, she converted the black-and-white prints to glass lantern slides, had them tinted by some unknown artist, and then used them to illustrate her wildly successful lectures on the wine industry and grape growing.

Among the black-and-white images converted into Wait's lantern slides were those of Harvey Lewelling, a Napa Valley winemaker who photographed in his vineyards extensively between 1885 and 1920, and H. H. Alexander, a Fresno-based photographer who worked at about the same time in the San Joaquin Valley. Considerably enhanced by the addition of color, Wait's lantern slides brought the harvest to the public in a new and vivid format. Effectively capturing the drama of large crews spread across both sides of a vineyard lane, one beautifully colored photograph displays horse-drawn wagons overflowing with lug boxes of lush, purple grapes. Several colored slides also focus on Chinese field hands in their unique domed hats while harvesting wine grapes in the Napa Valley. One captures Japanese raisin-grape harvesters on A. B. Butler's 480-acre vineyard east of Fresno in 1900. Another documents Mexicans harvesting

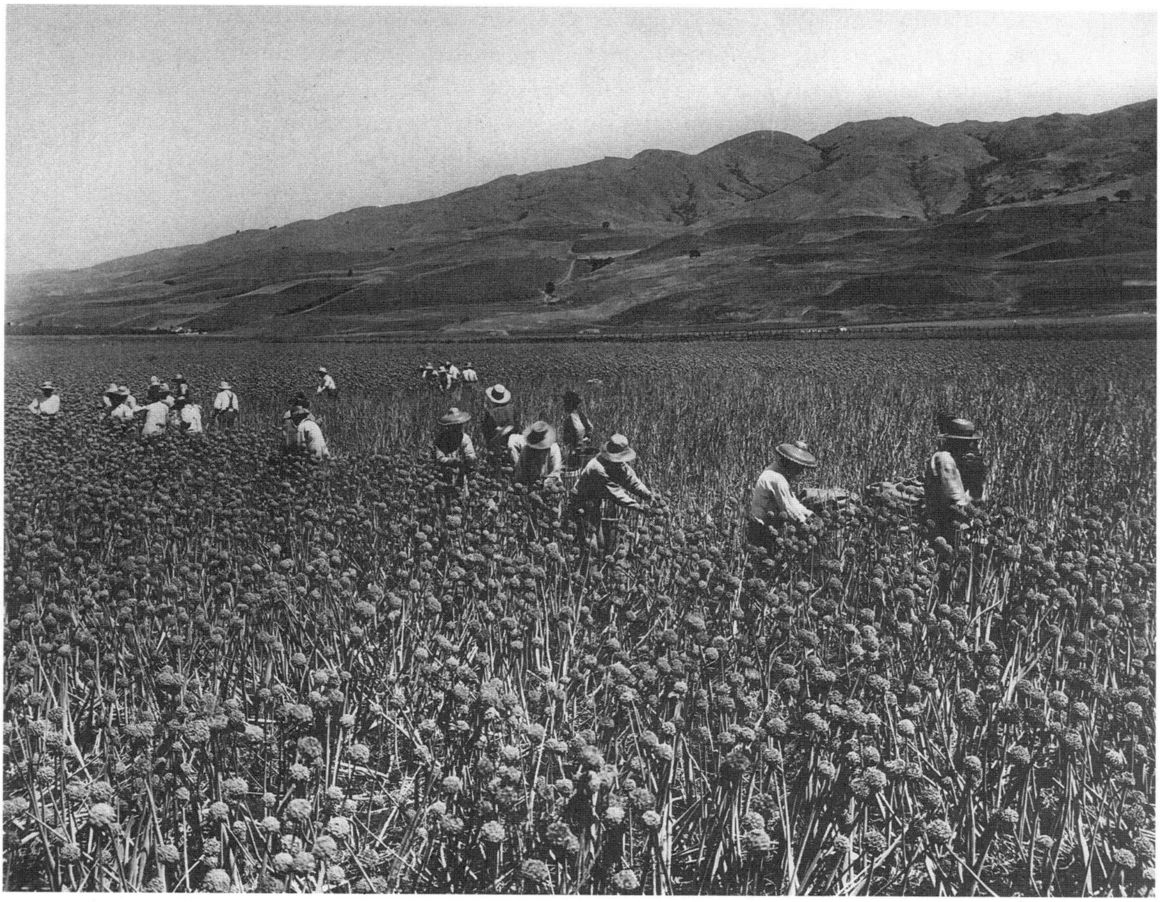

Chinese Onion Seed Harvesters, Morse Seed Farm, Santa Clara County, ca. 1902, photograph by Mrs. Alice Hare. Courtesy of the California Historical Society, North Baker Research Library, FN-22166.

wine grapes near Los Angeles, possibly near Cucamonga. Audiences, fascinated by the images, flocked to Wait's lectures. But it was not a thirst for informing the public about farm labor that inspired Wait to hold such lectures. Her entire motivation centered on wine, not work. Field hands were adjuncts of the larger story. They were never important in and of themselves.[31]

Wait's slides, and others like them, enjoyed only a brief period of popularity that ended with the introduction of motion pictures. Far more important as a mechanism for conveying pictures of farmworkers to the general public were new techniques that allowed images to appear routinely in newspapers, books, and magazines. Photomechanical reproduction technology, especially the halftone process, made this change possible. Far more accurate than any previous process, halftones (in which the gradation of tones from black to white is reproduced by a system of minute dots) preserved a wealth of detail and most of the tonal qualities of the original images while allowing publishers to publish limitless quantities of photographs quickly, faithfully, and economically. As agricultural journals such as the *Pacific Rural Press* eliminated woodcuts, engravings, and other lithographic techniques and quickly incorporated halftone reproductions onto their front pages, photographers discovered a new and expanding outlet for images of virtually every kind of agricultural activity. With the halftone process, farmworkers became common sights in the pages of the farm press.[32]

Adoption of halftones did not change how or why photographers photographed farmworkers. It did not cause publications to begin running images exposing deplorable living and working conditions. Nor did it raise questions about the place of farmworkers in the agricultural industry. To the contrary, halftones had little if any effect on the content or orientation of farmworker photography or on the issue of farmworker treatment. While farmworkers now appeared frequently in print, the ways in which they were depicted and described did not change. Knowing what sold and what did not, those employed by the agricultural press were not above concocting scenes that presented the hard, hot work of grape picking as a kind of big picnic for young boys and girls. Often these images depicted children working barefooted amid the vines, displaying gigantic grape clusters, and sitting beside raisin-drying trays while women wearing long dresses and straw hats and men in overalls supervise their work. The full meaning of such images was seldom if ever evident. The different meanings these scenes had for the workers, the growers, and the consuming public had to be assigned. Without exception, editors followed industry practices, which meant not mentioning hard labor. Caption writers always put a happy spin on images. Some of their picture captions were incredible. Some projected a meaning entirely skewed from anything that could have pertained to the workers. Rather than describing a picture of harvesters buckled under the weight of seventy-pound boxes while carrying grapes out of El Portal Vineyard near San Jose, an editor for the *Pacific Rural Press* emphasized the beautiful surroundings, the huge grape clusters, and a sense that field hands were exerting little effort while working in a modern Garden of Eden. "Men and women, youths and maidens, boys and girls, all go out to earn the liberal reward," proclaimed the caption. "It is inspiring work."[33]

Among photographers active worldwide at this time, only one far-sighted individual, the ardent British photographer and medical doctor Peter Henry Emerson, seems to have broken from the pattern of tame imagery and banal captioning. Emerson's production of realistic pictures of farm labor that possessed the directness and honesty found in the work of French painters of the time, such as Jean-François Millet, was no accident. By every account he was an extraordinary individual. Born in 1846 in Cuba of an American father and an English mother, he spent his first eight years on the family's La Palma Estate. When he was eight years of age, Emerson moved to Massachusetts, the family's original home and, after his father's death, returned briefly to Cuba, finally relocating permanently to England, where he embarked on a long period of study, eventually graduating from King's College, Cambridge University, where he amazed everyone by earning a medical degree while also winning honors in theology and football. Described by one of his biographers as "clear thinking, highly intelligent, logical and [with] an enormous capacity for hard work," Emerson became involved in photography in about 1881. Independently wealthy, arrogant, insufferably patronizing, and hauntingly condescending, Emerson soon began criticizing efforts by the photographic establishment to emulate contemporary painters through artificiality, soft focus, and sugar-sweet allegorical styles. Embarking on a radical departure from existing pictorialist approaches, holding that photographs should aspire to be high art, Emerson attempted to prove the value of photography as a medium unique in its own right. To accomplish that, he devoted the next eight years to the task of realistically photographing the tidal areas of East Anglia. Calling his work naturalism, he explored the difficult existence of the rural English poor while simultaneously documenting their rapidly changing customs and traditions.[34]

While following the grain harvest in the summer of 1888, Emerson came upon a group of barley harvesters resting and sharpening their scythes. His description of his picture *In the Barley Harvest* reveals a deep sense of documentary purpose, reading in part:

> Here one man is honing his scythe, while another, his face streaming with perspiration, has taken off his hat with which to fan himself, and now stretches forth his hand to his mate, who, leaving his rake in the field, has brought the bottle of "homebrewed" from which they will quench their thirst. Through the hot day they will work under the broiling summer sun until 4:30 p.m., when they rest and have tea, or "fourses," as is now locally called, its name formerly being "beavers." After half an hour's grace they again fall to, and work hard till seven in the evening, when it is a common sight to meet gangs of these tired labourers going home with scythes and rakes, empty bottles and baskets, probably a few rabbits killed that day in the fields.[35]

Exulting in honest labor and revealing the quiet beauty of the surrounding fields, Emerson's attention to details such as a sweat, sun, and liquor serves as a convenient demarcation point in the relationship between photographers and farmworkers. At a time when no photographers in California were expressing such concerns, a small group of English photographers, artists, and intellectuals affiliated with Emerson were attempting to zero in on the nature of life and labor in the fields. This provoked an acrimonious debate over naturalism versus pictorialism and inspired scores of English photographers to drift away from contrivance toward a more natural and realistic approach. But Emerson was almost unknown to photographers of California farmworkers. He had no effect on their work. After 1890, when he renounced photography and moved on to writing mystery novels, Emerson was forgotten. His attempt at creating honest and direct pictures of farm life became submerged in the renewed trend toward contrived and celebratory images.[36]

Certain farmworkers themselves bore some responsibility for these misrepresentations. Common field hands seldom had any way to influence how, when, where, or why photographers chose to portray them at their work. But one group, Chinese labor contractors and farm cooks, had both the money and the opportunity to sit

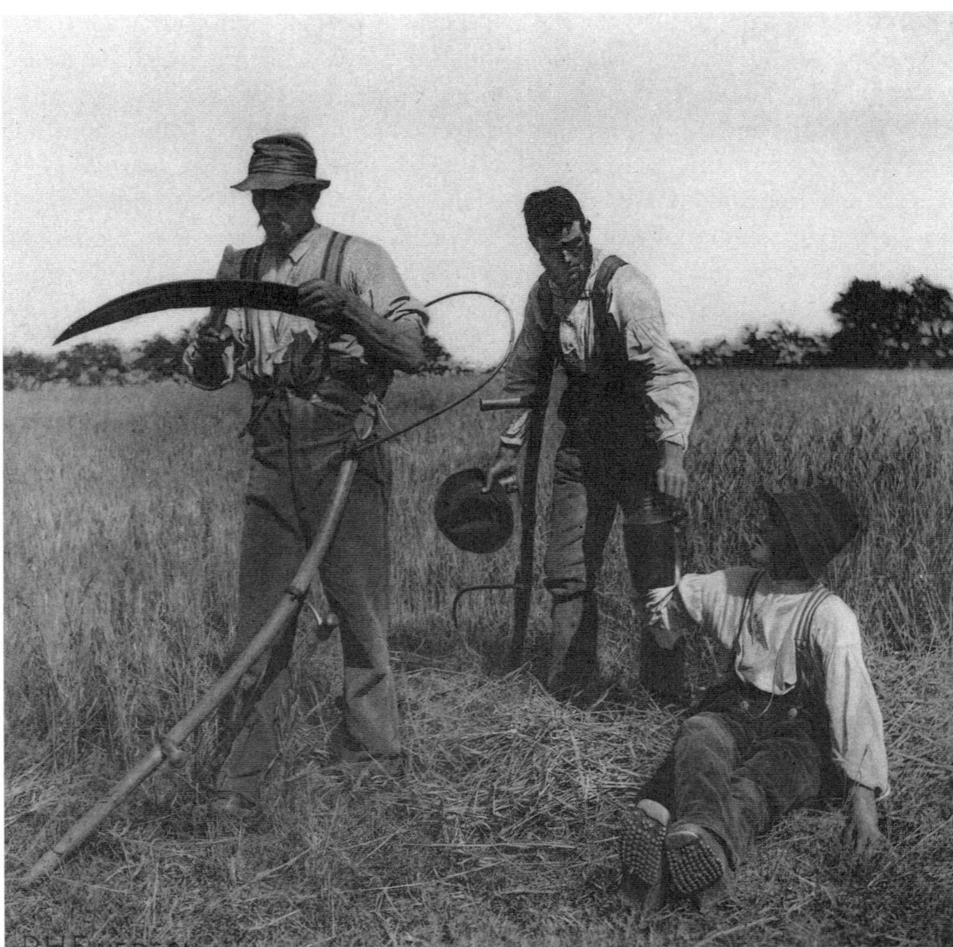

In the Barley Harvest, 1888, photograph by Peter Henry Emerson. From P. H. Emerson, *Pictures of East Anglican Life,* 1888. Courtesy of Norfolk and Norwich Millennium Library, England.

for studio portraits. Standing in front of painted, orientalized studio canvases that presented them in the most favorable and often unrealistic light, Chinese cooks and contractors stare straight into the camera in medium close-ups, lean against a fake Roman column with perhaps a fan held in one hand or folded across their laps, or pose holding bouquets and wearing their best silk pants and jackets. In photographs taken outside the studio, they have stationed themselves on front steps of their employer's ranch house, surrounded by family members and precious children, or they stand at the door to a cook wagon as if pausing from their duties preparing meals.[37]

Of all the images of Chinese farmworkers at this time, however, the most common are disembodied head shots tacked onto identification documents. These became common after 1891, when anti-Chinese zealots began calling for all Chinese present in the United States to be photographed and given certificates of residence. When it appeared that every Chinese immigrant, not just laborers, would have to comply, photographers in San Francisco opened a thriving business photographing not only those Chinese who were in need of documents but also those who had been taken into custody for violating provisions of the Chinese Exclusion Act. Ordered to surrender themselves before a U.S. marshall, detainees had to provide two certified copies of the judgment of remand, each containing a tintype, usually with the name of a lawyer etched across the lower edge and a red wax seal to prevent tampering. Chinese returning from a visit to their homeland also had to affix these images to their documents as proof that they were legally entitled to reenter the country. Thousands of these images reside in Immigration and Naturalization Service archives. Looking into the eyes of each man and reading his expression, one sees the fear, trepidation, and uncertainly that these men no doubt felt while wondering about their future.[38]

A final element in the scenario originates in the way late nineteenth-century Southern California photographers such as Adam Clark Vroman, George Wharton James, Frederic Hamer Maude, and others like them focused on the demoralized, impoverished, and declining numbers of Indians who existed on the edges of white communities and survived as seasonally employed farm laborers. As sociologists, anthropologists, and humanitarians collected their artifacts, studied their culture, and made them cause for concern, photographers saw a market for images. These photographers were not social scientists with cameras. There was no scholarly component to what they did. None had more than a passing interest in the lives, struggles, contributions, and exertions of Indian field hands. Their goal was to accumulate images of a race before it died out. And they never passed up an opportunity. Anything would do: Indians trooping in from their *rancherías* to pick hops, Indians camping out in the brush during the harvest, Indians threshing grain by flail, Indians handling various other agricultural activities. This was picturesque and salable material for a market in rare memorabilia premised on the assumption that the Indians were a people in the last throes of their extinction process.[39]

A few photographers were not beyond concocting images. Foremost among these were photographers capitalizing on the commercial appeal of Helen Hunt Jackson's 1884 novel *Ramona.* The novel culminated Jackson's long career as a reformer and regionalist and reflected her long-standing desire to "write a story that would do for the Indian a thousandth part what *Uncle Tom's Cabin* did for the Negro." Created over a three-month period at the rate of two thousand to three thousand words per morning from an idea that formed over a five-minute explosion of inspiration, *Ramona* was the story of Ramona Ortenga, the beautiful Scottish-Indian half-breed, and Alessandro, a noble, full-blooded descendant of mission Indians and captain of the Indian sheep shearers. The two lovers elope against the wishes of Ramona's parents. Driven from place to place by hostile Americans who steal Indian land and kill Alessandro, Ramona returns to her home on Moreno Rancho, an idyllic Garden of Eden setting. She lives there for a brief but happy period packed with colorful incidents centered on field hands living under a fading lifestyle, then is forced to sell out and flee to Mexico, where she dies heartbroken.[40]

One of the first photographers to recognize the entrepreneurial opportunities of the story was Ventura County photographer John Calvin Brewster, who built a thriving business by exploiting the belief that the fictional Moreno Rancho, "home of Ramona," was actually Rancho Camulos, near Piru, in Ventura County. On June 10, 1887, Brewster visited Rancho Camulos and created a series of thirteen staged images. Among the most popular was one depicting Alessandro's first glimpse of Ramona as she washed an altar cloth in the ditch outside her home. Offering all thirteen mounted prints for six dollars, Brewster sold thousands of these totally fictitious images. And he was not alone. A year later, Los Angeles photographer Charles F. Lummis, an editor

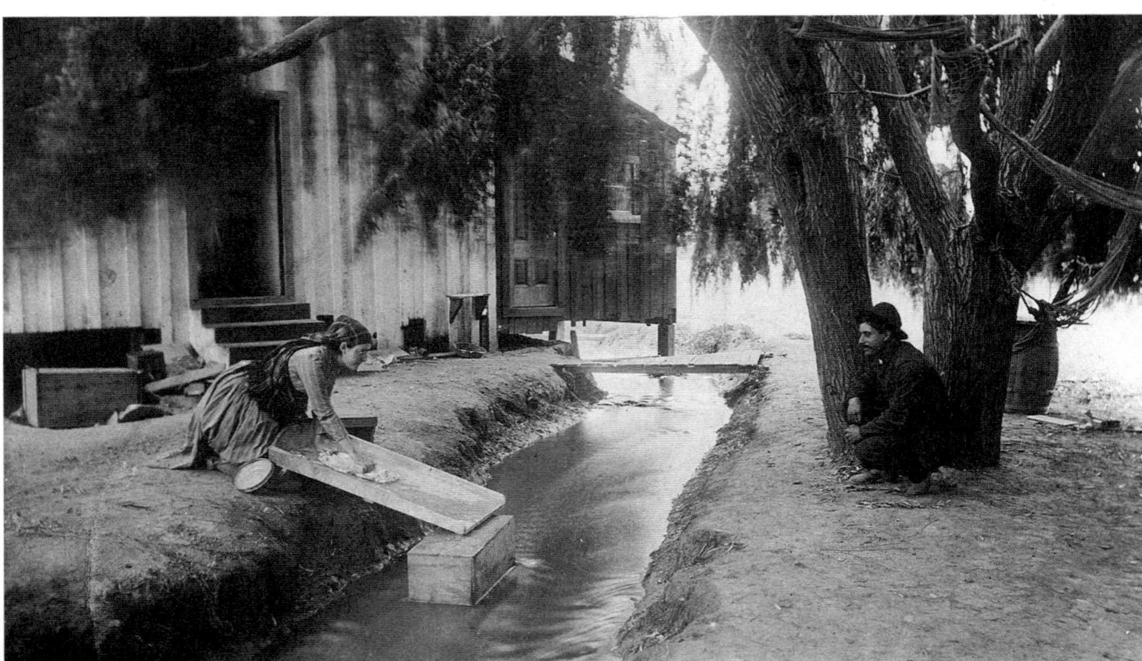

Alessandro's First Glimpse of Ramona as She Washes the Altar Cloth, 1887, photograph by J[ohn] C[alvin] Brewster. View no. 13. Courtesy of the Ventura County Museum of History and Art.

at the *Los Angeles Times* and a leading figure in the effort to preserve the art and culture of the California Indians, published a small book of photographs entitled *The Home of Ramona: Photographs of Camulos, the fine old Spanish Estate Described by Mrs. Helen Hunt Jackson as the Home of "Ramona."* The book paired quotes from *Ramona* with images in and around Rancho Camulos. At least a half dozen other photographers produced similar images featuring ranch hands from Rancho Camulos simulating scenes from *Ramona.* Expanded to include postcards and even fruit box labels (such as Home of Ramona Brand), these appropriations projected a highly romantic and totally fraudulent picture of farm labor that continued well into the twentieth century.[41]

4

Progressive Photography Takes Hold

Strikes, Murders, and Mexicans

An auburn-haired, hazel-eyed high school student named Lorraine Collett worked in the Griffin and Skelley Packing Company shed in Fresno in September 1914. Griffin and Skelley belonged to the California Associated Raisin Company, as did the neighboring Pacific Coast Company shed, and both were developing a label. Spotting Miss Collett, two plant superintendents pulled her off the packing line and asked her to go to the nearby Maxwell Studio and sit for a portrait. Dressed in the usual blue cap and apron worn by packing shed workers, Miss Collett posed for the photographer but had little idea of how the images would be used. Hearing nothing more, she was surprised the following year when the packing plant supervisors, having seen the in-house publicity stills, asked her to work in the raisin booth at the Panama–Pacific International Exposition in San Francisco. Her job consisted of passing out raisin samples and, every afternoon, dropping a rainfall of raisins from a small airplane when it flew over the exposition.

Returning to Fresno in May, Miss Collett was preparing for the annual Raisin Day parade when one of the superintendents spotted her wearing a red sunbonnet. Griffin and Skelley, Pacific Coast Packing, and hundreds of other Fresno-area raisin growers and packers had just merged into the Sun-Maid Raisin Cooperative and were embarking on an advertising campaign. Instantly recognizing Miss Collett as the image they wanted for their raisin boxes, Sun-Maid executives sent her to Fanny Scafford's art studio in San Francisco to have her portrait painted. Hustled off again to work the rest of the day in the Panama–Pacific International Exposition raisin booth, Miss Collett was paid sixteen dollars a week but received nothing for her time posing for Fanny Scafford. At a third portrait session at Scafford's Studio, Miss Collett posed holding a large tray of grapes in front of a large painted sun. Out of that session, the Sun-Maid raisin girl was born. "At one point they said they didn't want so much of my teeth showing," Miss Collett told a *Los Angeles Times* reporter many years later. "There were even discussions on whether or not the bonnet strings should be tied, and whether they should be in front or the back." When finished, the watercolor of a smiling Miss Collett, with a sunburst glowing behind her, was first hung at the exposition, then transformed into a trademarked logo that would be stamped on millions of boxes of raisins. So great was excitement over the picture that a Fresno newspaper dispatched a photographer to document the event by arranging twenty-five brokers and salesmen for the California Associated Raisin Growers outside a Fresno packing plant on June 16, 1916. Directing them to hold up giant, specially constructed raisin boxes with the new Sun-Maid logo, the photographer snapped a picture of the smiling salesmen displaying the highly calculated and totally fictitious image of what raisin growers hoped would pass for a grape picker.[1]

Continuing to see farmworkers as uncritically as ever, commercial photographers were not inspired to produce more realistic and sympathetic images, despite many technological advances that simplified and somewhat democratized their work. In fact, their approach differed little from that of the artist who painted the Sun-Maid girl. Independent photographers such as Augustus W. Ericson, who covered Humboldt County, followed this pattern, along with C. C. Pierce, who went on to amass the

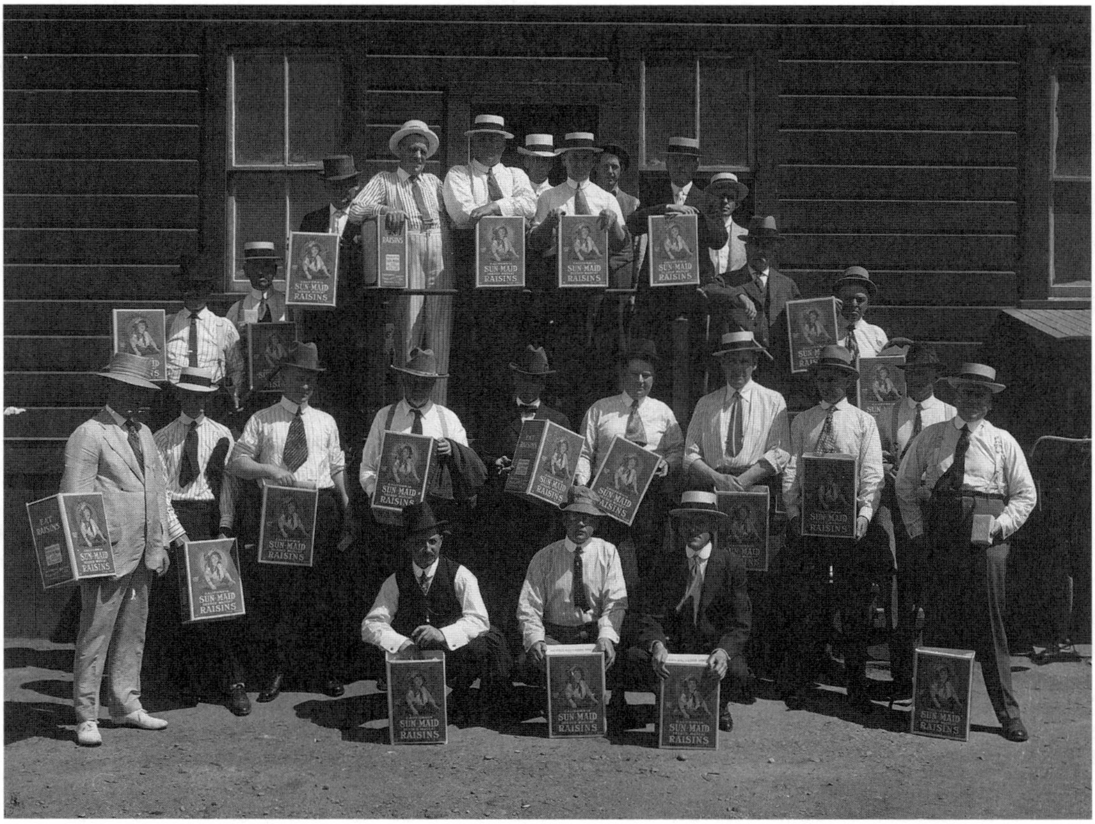

Brokers and salesmen of the California Associated Raisin Growers Company, June 16, 1916, photograph by Claude "Pop" Laval. Courtesy of Jerome D. Laval, Laval Company, Inc., and Fresno County Historical Society.

single finest photographic record of Los Angeles County after arriving there in the winter of 1886, H. C. Tibbets, who shot commercial assignments throughout Southern California, and Alice Hare, who photographed extensively in the Santa Clara Valley between 1900 and 1910 for clients such as W. J. Fosgate, owner of a five-hundred-acre seed farm along the Guadalupe River. Other photographers employed by the Garden City Photo Company, Keystone View Company, Underwood and Underwood, and countless other large photographic firms during the first quarter of the twentieth century rarely saw farmworkers as sufficiently important to warrant separate treatment.[2]

It was a different story outside California, where older Victorian concepts were beginning to link up with newer reform attitudes to produce a new way of photographing. This approach emerged in response to the poverty-stricken immigrants living in disgraceful conditions in New York City's tenement slums or on the streets themselves. One man was largely responsible for forging this new visual sensibility. A police reporter for the *New York Herald,* Jacob Riis prowled a malignant New York City slum known as Mulberry Road. Using his camera to prove the truth of his words, he focused on vagrant children, squalid housing, and disgraceful police lodgings for the homeless. His goals were to establish a relationship between poverty and social behavior and to raise public concern, which he did to great effect in his muckraking exposé, *How the Other Half Lives: Studies among the Tenements of New York,* an amalgamation of personal reportage illustrated by forty plates, including seventeen halftone reproductions, which appeared in 1890. Although Riis was an outsider looking in, his work was neither casual nor superficial. *How the Other Half Lives* presents a slice-of-life realism that persuaded viewers of the need for social reform and a renewed commitment to humanitarian ideals. After it appeared, photographic "evidence" became a fundamental element in all publications dealing with social problems, and the social documentary concept became an established way of seeing the world.[3]

A seminal publication in the history of American photography, *How the Other Half Lives* had a great impact on contemporaries and inspired several disciples. One was sociologist Lewis Hine, who enlarged on the work of Riis by photographing immigrants at Ellis Island and children in the coal breakers of Pennsylvania and the spinning mills of Georgia. With an even stronger and more forceful style and far greater technical virtuosity, Hine produced detailed, informative photographs of child laborers, bathed in somber light and living in a kind of miniature netherworld of "deadening . . . monotony." After documenting factory life and industries such as mining, textiles, and manufacturing, Hine moved outdoors. In 1910 he photographed child labor in agriculture and, in a famous essay titled "Roving Children," created a bitter picture of migrant workers, "herded together like animals," who lived in sheds and shacks owned by labor contractors and canneries. At a time when a central myth of the Gilded Age held that children were merely little capitalists who, through industry and light, easy farm chores, acquired the skills needed to rise from rags to riches, Hine's images of seven-year-old sugar beet toppers hooking themselves in the knees with beet knives, child cannery workers wading in filthy muck, and children struggling through cranberry bogs with heavy buckets shocked the public and lent ammunition to reformers seeking to regulate farm work. Another reform photographer, Episcopal minister James McCook, photographed migrants riding the rails and living in hobo jungle camps in the eastern states. The most intriguing of this new breed of photographers was also the most mysterious and least known. He went by the name of Saffo and packed a camera while following the migrant trail, developing his negatives in jungle camps.[4]

If any California photographer had even the slightest awareness of Riis, Hine, McCook, Saffo, and photographers like them, none indicated it. Even though California was in the forefront of the Progressive movement by 1910, the state's political unrest did not generate any reform-oriented photography in general or a specific focus on farmworkers or any other segment of the working class. Consequently, at a time when a penetrating form of social documentary photography was employed by reform organizations such as the National Child Labor Committee, the "human element" in photography, as Hine described it, was almost entirely missing in California. Not believing in the power of photography to alter circumstances and vanquish evil, California photographers at this time did not explore the state's farm labor camps, focus on the thousands of bindle men drifting with the harvests, dissect the nature of work in the fields, or attempt to convey social realities to middle-class viewers.[5]

Nowhere was this willingness to overlook hardship more pronounced than among those photographers whose business centered on the Southern California citrus industry. After the turn of the century, California's citrus culture prospered, thanks to expanded train routes and the development of boxcars that would keep produce fresh during transport. Promoting "Oranges for Health, California for Wealth," a class of well-educated, wealthy, and genteel midwestern and eastern entrepreneurs settled around the city of Riverside, which soon emerged as the per capita wealthiest town in the United States. Benefiting from and, to a very large extent, influencing the American dietary shift from traditional European foods such as potatoes and wheat to Mediterranean and subtropical fruits, the Southern California citrus industry in the early twentieth century entered a period of rapid and sustained growth. As citrus culture spread to Pasadena, Azusa, and Duarte, and to Covina, Ontario, Pomona, and Redlands, a new group of commercial growers perfected spraying, fumigation, and orchard heating techniques; employed modern business methods; and introduced scientific farming methods based on information developed at the University of California's Citrus Experiment Station. By 1900, the Southern California citrus industry extended throughout a crescent-shaped, frost-free belt stretching from Santa Barbara through portions of Ventura, Los Angeles, Orange, San Bernardino, and Riverside counties. With its fragrant blossoms, annual citrus fairs, and carefully cultivated mission traditions, the citrus industry—unlike the sugar beet industry, whose dominant images were factory smoke stacks and laborers slaving in shadeless fields—etched on the American mind an image of Spanish fiestas and happy workers gathering "golden globules of health."[6]

Accommodating themselves to the commercial needs of their clients, leading photographers around Los Angeles went to great lengths to concoct an endless stream of images that placed farmworkers at the center of what was essentially an industrial landscape of ordered productivity and overwhelming beauty. Following a standard formula, these photographers typically arranged dozens of pickers in an orchard to produce an image titled *World's Largest Lemon Grove* or *Sunny Orchards beneath Snow-Capped Peaks.* Although many of these photographers produced images with residual documentary value, none ever attempted to analyze work motion, focus on physical strength and prowess, record the mundane realities of rural life, zero in on sweat and exhaustion, or move beyond the work environment. Photographers knew that there was no market for such images. As always, they were after images that sold products and glorified an industry. When their work appeared in promotional pamphlets, illustrated fruit company booklets, or accompanied advertising messages, viewers had no idea that farmworkers were not anything but eternally happy.[7]

Among the photographers who made citrus workers look pretty, one achieved mythic status. Burton Fraser, a former fruit box maker turned photographer, followed the fresh fruit industry up and down the West Coast from San Diego to Washington. Before settling into a studio in Pomona in 1905, he made over sixty thousand pictures, many of which portrayed citrus workers in somewhat theatrical poses, even when he captured them fumigating orchards at night. With no thought of revealing anything significant about power relationships or scrutinizing the nature of orchard labor, Fraser concentrated on capturing a sense of wholesome, well-ordered productivity. If citrus pickers ever got dirty, seemed tired from the exertions of climbing up and down ladders all day, or suffered the dangers of falling to the ground while wrestling a heavy canvas bag full of oranges, it was not apparent in Fraser's photographs.[8]

Transforming hard-working citrus harvesters into props standing on sets, photographers of the Southern California citrus industry had such a huge impact that, when one Los Angeles photographer came out to the orchards of the Covina Citrus Association early in the morning in 1902, crews had become so well-rehearsed and accustomed to being photographed that they readily simulated a picking scene, playing their roles like actors on a stage. Long before a day's work left the men grimy and unsmiling from fatigue, this photographer had packed up and left the orchard. But it was not just citrus industry photographers who concocted harvest scenes. Whether they were locals or outsiders, photographers in other agricultural industries continued to follow a similar formula.[9]

At Segundo Guasti's Italian Vineyard Company, the promotional bias achieved epic proportions. Comprising some four square miles of vineyards in the Cucamonga Desert, east of present-day Pomona and Ontario, Guasti's company was the largest contiguous vineyard in the world. At harvest time over one thousand Japanese, Mexican, white, and African American harvesters carefully packed Guasti's wine grapes in boxes, nailed on lids, and stacked them eight to ten boxes high at the end of each vineyard row to be loaded into wagons and hauled to the winery. With one-third of his harvest labor force busy loading, transporting, and emptying boxes rather than picking the crop, Guasti purchased a narrow-gage railroad in the winter of 1907, complete with forty gondola cars and a fifteen-ton locomotive called the *Italia.* At the beginning of the 1908 harvest, when he started using the railroad to haul grapes out of the vineyards,

Guasti hired a Pasadena photographer to commemorate the harvest. Arriving late in August, the photographer first posed a long line of men carrying lugs full of grapes out of the vineyards, then photographed them pitching the grapes from the lugs into the gondolas. Once the gondolas were overflowing, the photographer followed the train into the winery and photographed the gondolas being tipped sideways to send their cargo cascading directly into great concrete troughs. After making a series of images documenting men pitchforking grapes onto chain conveyors that fed the stemmers and crushers, the photographer moved inside the fermenting room and made flash shots of men directing the grapes down long sloping chutes into huge redwood tubs. While modern viewers find huge documentary value in the sequence of images, they were in fact propaganda extolling a picture of unparalleled agricultural industrialization, innovation, and creative thinking.[10]

A similar adulatory approach informed the agricultural photography of William Henry Jackson. Ranked alongside Carleton E. Watkins as one of the greatest American landscape photographers, Jackson is another example of a great photographer who, for some reason, at some time, photographed farmworkers in the Golden State. Before his sojourns to the orchards and vineyards, Jackson had traveled throughout the West for thirty years as a photographer for many of the great exploring expeditions. To stave off bankruptcy, he had joined the Detroit Photographic Company in 1897, bringing with him over twenty thousand of his negatives and instantly catapulting the company into a position from which it could compete with such popular giants as Keystone View Company and Underwood and Underwood. After supervising the process by which many of his views were converted into postcards, Jackson began traveling widely to obtain additional views and update old ones. His goal was to acquire dramatic, picturesque, and scenic landscapes, including vineyards, orchards, and packing plants throughout California, as well as tourist sites, domesticated landscapes, and industrial activity. He photographed California farmworkers for the first time in 1899 at the end of a twenty-thousand-mile photographic trip that took him across the country in search of images. While in Southern California, he photographed in a Redlands orange-packing shed and among cottages for citrus workers in Riverside, then stopped in Fresno to photograph a raisin-drying yard on the way north. He was sixty-six years old at the time but still had plenty of energy. In the Redlands packing shed, he opened up the shadows with flash powder, and at Fresno he got up before dawn to direct farmworkers into position for his early-morning shot of the raisin-drying yard. It was not easy work. His diary recorded his exhaustion and the hectic pace of work as he fought a "hazy atmosphere . . . rain . . . [and] occasional banks of fog . . . so that no general work can be done." Constantly frustrated by washed-out, cloudless skies, Jackson confided that he found less satisfaction "in looking for special things that one feels one must get than in reaching out for anything that offers."[11]

Sold by the millions as postcards, agricultural photographs like those by William Henry Jackson soon glutted the market. Burton Fraser's work was so prolific that he became known as the Postcard King of the West. Because of their wide distribution, tinted postcards had the potential to educate the public about the role that California

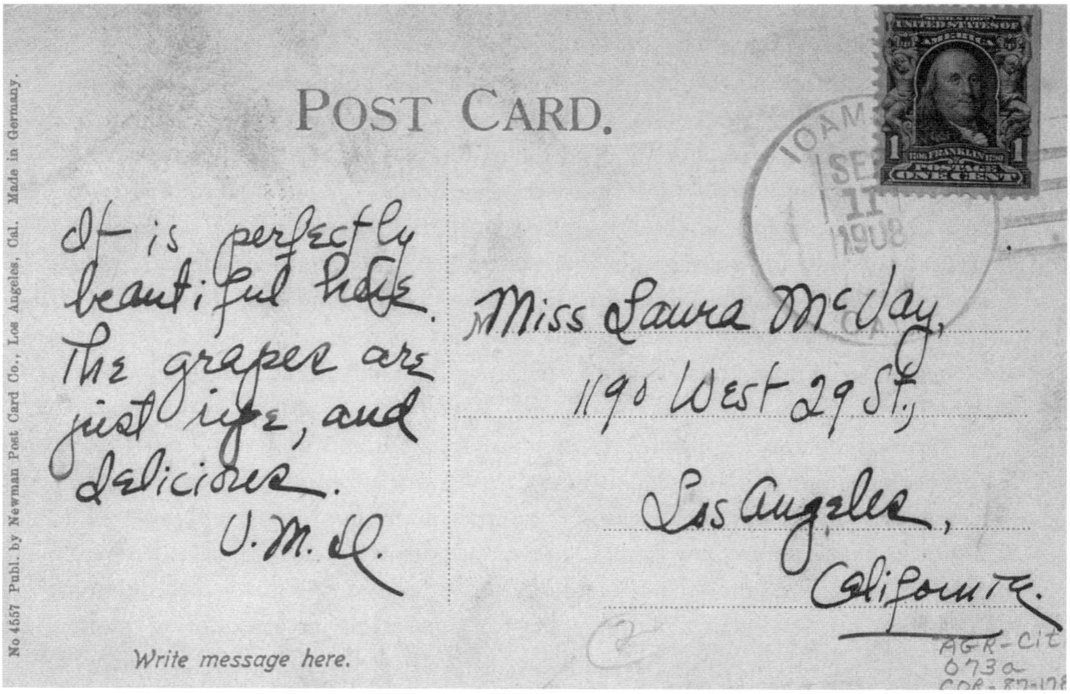

Picking Oranges in California, ca. 1908, photographer unknown. Author's collection.

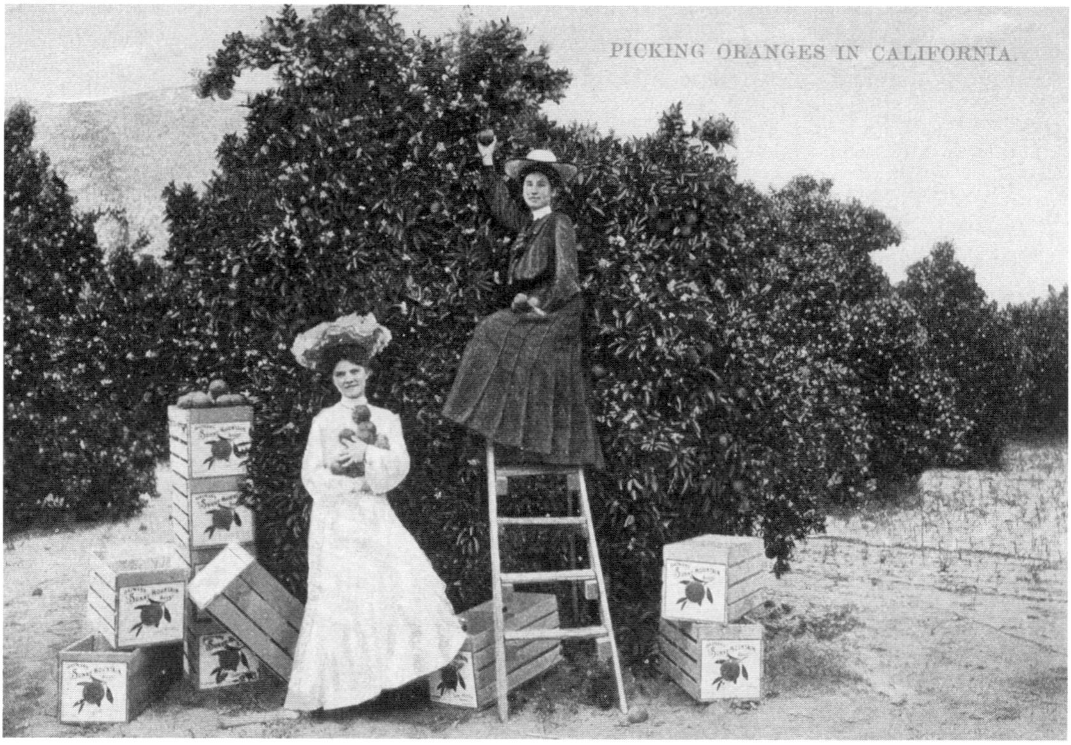

farmworkers played in the American food production system. But they were basically commercial items and depended for their success on attractive imagery and idealized realities. After tourist sites and leisure activities, agriculture forms the largest category of postcard images. Most show orange groves in bloom, palms dangling huge clusters of dates, massive fruit displays at county fairs, and occasionally a cherry or strawberry the size of a small house resting on a flatcar with a humorous caption about the size of the fruit grown in this particular locality.[12]

Postcards had little effect on the public conscience or public understanding of farm labor or agriculture. Far smaller in size than most photographs, they made farmworkers themselves largely irrelevant other than in their usual function as elements of scale to a landscape. Compounding these problems was the loss of subtle tonal qualities and overall richness inherent in standard photographic prints and the almost posterlike effect and exaggerated compositions suitable to the postcard format. Often discarded soon after being seen, postcards provoked no dialogue and served mainly to reinforce prevailing agricultural mythologies. Hardly documents of social history, they served as brief reminders of a moment during a vacation when the sender purchased a postcard, thought of a friend or relative, dashed off a few sentences on the reverse side, and dropped it in the mail. Out of thousands of surviving mailed postcards with scenes of farmworkers, I have not found one message on the reverse side that contains a reference to the people seen on the front.[13]

Postcard trivialization was not unique. Fruit box labels were an even more ubiquitous source of artificial images. This was not their original intent. When growers started using fruit labels on their shipping crates, they hoped to differentiate their products in an increasingly crowded marketplace. Well-known commercial artists and lithographers met the challenge by designing and producing beautiful and eye-catching 10 × 11–inch orange box labels and 9.5 × 12–inch lemon box labels. But citrus growers were not alone in these efforts. Everyone who sold fresh fruit and vegetables needed a label and devoted considerable attention to either designing one or selecting from among a wide variety of stock templates in all sizes and shapes. Most of these labels featured exotic animals and luscious landscapes. Gold Medal, Silver Medal, Silver Moon, Pure Gold, Golden West, California Dream, California Beauty, Land of Sunshine, Sun-Kist, Fog-Kist, Old Mission, Cornucopia, and Miracle were common, but virtually everything and everyone from the swastika and the Greek god Mercury to Pocahontas and Tom Sawyer appeared on a label. Fantasy characters also made their appearance, such as the red-haired maiden who holds a bunch of grapes while exclaiming, "Squeeze Me," a big-mouthed boy shouting, "Hey Look," and well-endowed, scantily clad women variously labeled Nudist, Phun-Enuf, Buxom, Shocking, and Eva.[14]

Farmworkers appear everywhere in fruit and vegetable box labels, large and small, in many guises. An amazing label for the Maywood Colonies Fruit Association features among the six small pictures arranged around a landscape panorama a single hand-stippled picking scene every bit the equal of a William Keith or a Thomas Moran painting, except it is the size of three dimes. Reality, of course, is not part of this advertising imagery. Farmworkers appear on labels as genies glowing with health and holding silver plates of oranges and as seductive maidens who dance through the orchards. Racial stereotypes appear on a surprisingly large number of labels. Mexican caricatures are the most common. Laziness and "mañana society" are the themes. Plump and slow but happy campesinos, usually wearing sombreros and sometimes displaying a pistol, bandolier, and guitar, are variously titled "Lazy Peon," a label used by Index Mutual of la Habra, "Cactus Pete," "Felixo," the label of the Felix Cohen Company of Oakland, and "Señor Vocado," one of the labels of the CAL-ROYAL Company, Inc., Vista. Hardly innocuous, these caricatures moved across the country and around the world, becoming a ubiquitous and deeply embedded everyday matter-of-fact source of demeaning images that shackled farmworkers with notions of inferiority.[15]

Given such promotional deception, it was inevitable that commercial photographers would manipulate views. If a new raisin destemming mechanism or a unique apricot dehydrator appeared in the region, photographers on assignment for this or that farm publication or agricultural implement company made sure to take a picture with farmworkers posed nearby as happy people whose work had now been made immeasurably easier. Even if the men were involved in some task, such as shoveling debris from an almond-shelling operation or filling bags full of refined beet sugar, compositions always stressed the equipment. Perfect examples of this approach are photographs taken in various well-equipped fruit-drying yards. With rail lines running down the middle and trays stacked ten and twenty feet high, fruit-drying yards of the first decade of the twentieth century had grown far beyond their modest beginnings a generation earlier around Vacaville. Many were gigantic operations that stretched as far as the eye could see. Seemingly always inspired by their design elements, photographers frequently used an elevated perspective to photograph them. And by taking additional images of women posed in neat rows at their fruit-cutting tables or children lined up according to height, photographers could assure themselves multiple secondary sales to the people in the scene.[16]

Fruit shed workers often preserved these photographs for generations, handing them down as miniature picture diaries. To them, there was nothing to be ashamed of here. Such images were cherished mementos. Many wrote on the backs or in the side margins of their pictures, supplying the kind of additional information that historians so cherish. Writing short captions—"Dipping & Peeling Peaches with Mother and Sisters" or "Packing House, Shipping grapes to Chicago"—they singled out childhood friends, job foremen, and coworkers who were of interest. On the back of one such photograph from Fresno, under the initials E. M. E., someone left the following inscription:

> Somewhere in the group is Laura Compadonica before her marriage to Peter Drago of Drago Fruit Company. My guess is that she is the girl 3rd. from the right, in the white blouse and dark skirt.[17]

Only two California photographers during the first decade of the twentieth century deviated from these approaches. One was Marysville commercial photographer

Clara S. Smith. From September 1900 until June 1908, Smith earned between two and twenty-two dollars per month making "mug shots" of criminals, many of whom were farmworkers. While photographic documentation of prisoners had been around for generations, Smith's efforts to classify "the dangerous classes," including chronically underemployed migrant workers and criminal paupers, represented a pervasive form of visual repression. Photography critic Allan Sekula sees this as something akin to fingerprinting. The goal of such imagery, he argues, is to define the criminal body—to "establish and delimit the terrain of the *other* . . . of deviance and social pathology."[18]

During her years defining the criminal body, Smith recorded a full range of social deviants. She photographed them year-round but seemed to have more to deal with as the hop harvest neared. Since emerging as a center for hop farming, Marysville and the nearby towns of Wheatland and Yuba City were overrun with harvesters every July. Several thousand people were required to bring in the crop on one of the largest ranches, that of E. Clements Horst. While families from Sacramento and elsewhere made up much of the harvest force, plenty of desperate and penniless bindle men and people like them always participated. Arrested for robbery, forgery, "working a flim-flam," stealing a roll of blankets, "nipping a new coat," and various other crimes, these poor souls were sentenced to prison terms of a few months to many years, although many were given "a floater," a heavy sentence suspended on condition that

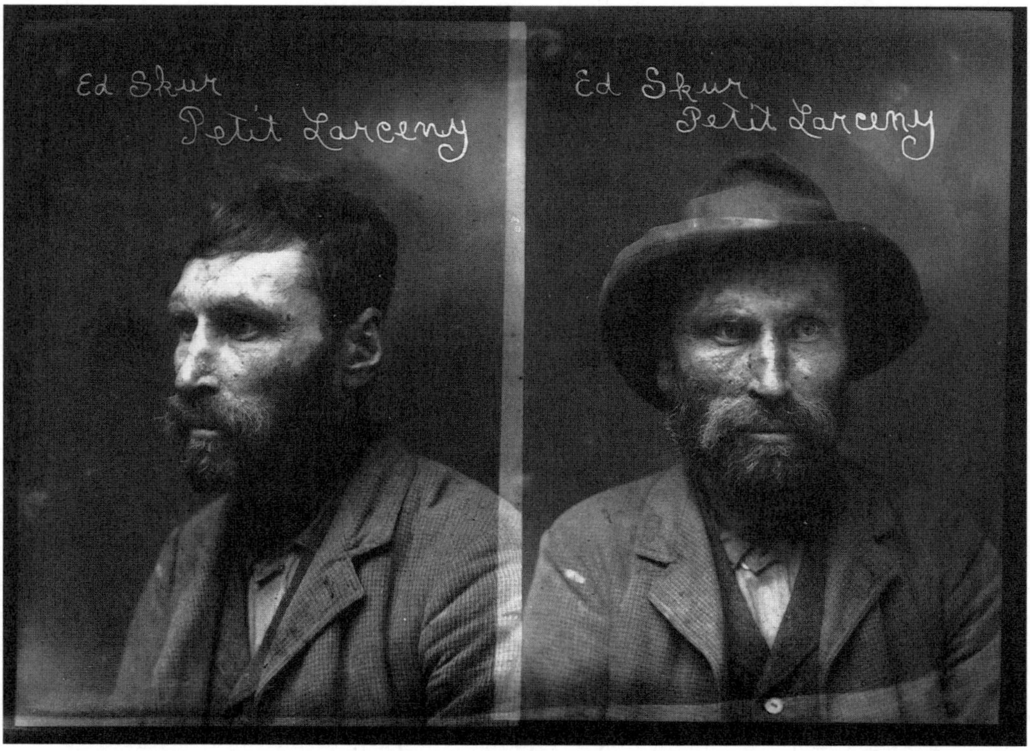

Ed Skur, Petit Larceny, 1906, photograph by Clara Smith. From Arne Svenson, *Prisoners,* 1997. Courtesy of Arne Svenson.

the undesirable person leave town permanently. Although not documentary photographs, Smith's studio images of these people—front and side shots on a single glass-plate negative—hold tremendous documentary value for later observers. Not only do they capture the disheveled look of migrant laborers; they also reflect a difficult and marginal existence in which crime often emerged as a last desperate effort at survival.

But Smith's photographs do even more than that. They also humanize people in a way that goes beyond words. Sometimes they document stories that were almost unbelievable. Nothing better accomplished this than the photograph Smith made on July 23, 1904, of fourteen-year-old Claude Hankins, "an average sized lad" with a lisp, who had been working on the George Thompson farm, six miles east of Marysville. Young Hankins sat for Smith's mug shot in both left profile and staring straight ahead, completely contradicting postcard pictures, fruit box labels, and commercial concoctions. This haunting picture of a teenaged farmworker hints at something going on below the surface and of the tensions and difficulties of child labor.

Over the next four months, the local press reported the incredible story behind Smith's photograph. Sent to Marysville for reform by his brother and sister after they had read a San Francisco newspaper advertisement praising the beneficial effects of wholesome work in the countryside, the troubled Palo Alto boy, whose mother had recently died and whose father had deserted the family, grew lonely after only ten days of working on the farm. Consequently, Hankins fell under the control of George Morse, a middle-aged foreman, braggart, and self-described "Guatemalan insurrectionist." After Morse subjected Hankins to a "crime against nature," the teenager stole Morse's revolver, crept up behind him as he walked back from milking, and blew out his brains. Hankins then took $68.30 from Morse's dresser drawer and fled to town on foot. He was discovered and arrested in the Golden Eagle Hotel, registered under the name of Johnny Larkin. Although claiming at trial in October that Morse had forced him to endure all kinds of indignities and that Morse had told him "he would just as soon cut his head off as he would to whittle a piece of wood," Hankins was convicted of murder. Apparently influenced by the testimony of numerous witnesses describing Morse's cruelty, the jury initially advised Judge E. P. McDaniel that it could not render a verdict. Only after the judge threatened to lock the jury up for the night did its members find Hankins guilty of second degree murder, with recommendations for extreme mercy. Because of his age, Hankins escaped hanging and was sentenced to sixteen years in San Quentin Prison.[19]

Two years later, another of Smith's photographs further hinted at the dark underside of farmworker life. This one captures the sad face of Thomas Gordon. The *Marysville Appeal* described the circumstances that led to Gordon's arrest:

> Thomas Gordon, twenty-two-years old, was arrested by Officers McCoy and Burroughs last evening and charged with forgery. He admits the truth of the charge and stands to serve a term in a penitentiary. Gordon came here from Wheatland, where he had been working on the Horst hop ranch. He asked for and was given three blank checks of the Rideout Bank at the store of the W. T. Ellis Company yesterday. Later he tried to pass

> one of them, which had been filled out for $27.60 at the store of M. Schwab. The name of the Rideout Bank had been cancelled and the words "Farmers' and Merchants' Bank of Wheatland" had been written. The check did not look good to Mr. Schwab and he investigated, learning enough to cause him not to accept it in payment of a pair of shoes. In the evening the young man passed the check at the saloon of Joseph Whyler at Second and C streets. Officer McCoy had been on the trail since the appearance of Gordon at Schwab's store and he finally succeeded in getting S. E. Conrad, foreman of the Horst ranch, on the telephone. He learned that the only check given Gordon had been cashed in Wheatland and that the paper passed here was undoubtedly a forgery. Upon this the arrest was made. The name of Mr. Conrad had been signed to the check, but it was written "Samuel" Conrad instead of "S. E. Conrad," the latter being the way the gentleman signs his checks. The name of the bank was wrong, too. It is the Farmer's Bank of Wheatland. The endorsement on the back of the check is in a different handwriting, but Gordon claims he wrote both sides of the check. He had $17.60 left when arrested, showing that he had spent $10.[20]

The second person attempting to inject reality into the visual record of California farmworkers at this time was University of California economics professor Ira B. Cross. A descendant of Plymouth Colony founder William Bradford, the Illinois-born Cross had received his AB and MA degrees from the University of Wisconsin. An ardent socialist whose academic work focused on the laboring classes, Cross was finishing his PhD at Stanford University in 1908 when his dissertation adviser, Harry A. Millis, hired him to gather information on migrant laborers for the United States Immigration Commission (1907–9). As he traveled through the San Joaquin and Santa Clara valleys and several other unnamed agricultural areas, Cross photographed Chinese, Indian Sikhs, Italians, and Japanese at work in the fields, including some using short-handled hoes. Paying special attention to farmworker quarters, Cross documented large, well-equipped communal bunkhouses as well as tent shelters and rundown shacks, along with such salient details as beds and cots. Moving into the ethnic enclaves around Fresno, Palo Alto, Ryde, Visalia, and Woodland, he also scrutinized employment offices, pool halls, alleyways, and bathhouses frequented by farmworkers and, around Los Angeles, photographed Mexicans during the shape-up in the city plaza.[21]

At the end of the summer, Cross returned to Stanford with over one hundred photographs, which he apparently offered to Millis and the United States Immigration Commission. Although the commission would issue an exhaustive study of the effects of immigration on American life, it used photographs only to illustrate an introductory overview. Written by H. Parker Willis, an editorial adviser to the commission, the introduction featured a selection of images by Lewis Hine, all of them taken in the eastern United States. With no use for his photographs, Cross filed them away in his personal papers. They languished unseen and unappreciated until 1950, when, following his retirement from teaching, Cross donated his papers to the Bancroft Library. Another half century would pass before scholars finally saw the photographs and realized that Cross had broken dramatically with prevailing photographic orthodoxy, compiled the first photographic collection to focus on life and labor in the fields, and inaugurated a tradition of using photography as a tool of social science.[22]

Four years after Cross left the fields, two photographers—a veteran professional and a rank amateur—recorded the first images of organizing and protest. The professional was Harold McCurry, a successful commercial and landscape photographer who founded and operated McCurry Foto Company of Sacramento. As the largest photography business in the Sacramento Valley, McCurry and his assistants regularly photographed farmers, agriculture, crops, and agricultural products. Early in August 1913, McCurry visited the huge labor camp that had assembled at the Ralph Durst hop ranch, about one mile east of Wheatland. Normally such photography was fairly routine, just part of the annual circuit. But on arriving for what he believed was a typical shoot, McCurry found himself photographing one of the most extraordinary scenes imaginable.[23]

Spread out across part of Durst's 641-acre hop ranch was a temporary tent city composed of Native American bindle men, Indian Sikhs, Japanese, Mexicans, Puerto Ricans, "quasi-gypsies," and middle-class families from nearby towns. Lured by advertisements that Durst had published in dozens of newspapers throughout the state, they swarmed into Wheatland expecting three or four weeks of work, under good conditions, with high wages. With twenty-eight hundred hop pickers living in the camp, McCurry recognized an opportunity for massive sales and, during the first few days of the harvest, made at least a half dozen group portraits of children, women, and men, as well as various views in and about the camp. Taken together, these images mark another milestone in the photographic history of California farmworkers: the first systematic photographic survey of a large farm labor camp.[24]

Sharp, detailed, well-composed, and recorded on big glass-plate negatives, McCurry's images illustrate many aspects of life in the Durst camp. One image displays a row of fifty people in front of tall hop vines. Hop baskets and dump boxes line the edge of a dusty road. Trellis wires stretch overhead. A small group of men clump together in the background. Young girls in long dresses stand in front of women wearing fancy straw hats. A father holds a baby in his arms, and children of various ages peek out from between the adults. A look of quiet dignity is etched on every face. Harvesting is under way, and children are either helping with the work or tagging along with their parents. Technically and aesthetically very fine, the image is extremely valuable for its documentation of both child and family labor.[25]

A few days later, McCurry captured an even more dramatic and important photograph. To make this one, he climbed to the roof of a barn or the top of a water tower. From there he executed a picture that surveyed the entire hop pickers' camp. No detail escapes his camera's all-encompassing gaze, which probably constitutes the earliest quasi-aerial photograph of a harvest labor camp. In composition, McCurry's photograph is essentially a landscape, with fully one-quarter of the upper half given over to the sky and horizon. The rest of his image shows a temporary worker city sprawling over several acres of a dusty, unshaded field. At the center are a commissary store and several small, canvas-topped structures housing shops selling equipment and various necessities ranging from food to picking sacks. Tents, brush shelters, timber stockades called bull pens, gunny sacks stretched over fence posts, camp wagons, and little "hooches" (many of them no more than shades against the sun) are scattered about, some in neat rows, others in haphazard fashion. Men stroll along well-worn paths. People clump together. A child and adult carry a water tub from the communal trough. A water tower rises in the background. Barely visible behind the tower on the edge of the camp is the town of Wheatland. Here, in one broad perspective, McCurry captures a nearly perfect view of a large farm labor camp. Any cinematographer seeking to re-create the Wheatland hop camp would do well to copy the image.

Another of McCurry's photographs displays a crew of several hundred men and boys dressed in their Sunday best. They pose in the midst of the Durst camp and look directly into the camera with an air of pause and attention. The image reveals details of the sort historians crave: precisely what kind of clothing, hats, shirts, suspenders, boots, and so on are worn by field hands; what kinds of facial expressions workers put on when being photographed; how children mimic adults in stance and manner; and the difference in appearance between the laborers and their supervisors, who stand nearby, dressed in white shirts and dark ties. Above all, McCurry's photograph shows the look of plain people engaged in hard labor. McCurry may not have recognized it as such, but his composition is a metaphor that encapsulates the spectrum of races and nationalities then working in the fields.[26]

Probably the most intriguing image of all shows a group of about twenty-five Mexican and Anglo children standing on the steps of a temporary shelter. The boys are dressed in overalls, but the girls wear long dresses, a most uncomfortable requirement in the August heat. All display the look of young people accustomed to adult work. This was something new. While children had been working in fruit-drying yards for a generation and had been photographed by Nutting and others, they had seldom been seen in big farm labor camps, women only slightly more frequently. That was because most of the work up to that time had been performed by single males: bindle stiffs, Chinese, and Japanese field hands. But as the agricultural industry had grown, harvest labor demands, especially in the hop industry, so overwhelmed local farm labor pools that children were released from school to help bring in the local crop, and married couples from nearby towns began drifting into the agricultural districts with their children in tow. Not full-time migratory workers, they would remain at Wheatland for the brief but intense harvest, which many regarded as something of a holiday and an opportunity to supplement their income. Although their children sometimes participated in the hop harvest, only those older than ten or eleven years of age worked in any meaningful way. Younger children simply accompanied their parents because they had no place else to go. While playing at harvest work, they seldom contributed much to the family income and usually slowed down whichever parent whose duty was to watch over them. This was the situation that McCurry caught at Wheatland. Signs at left, right, and center, as well as the presence of adults in the background and a scattering of books among the children, suggest that this is probably a combination Sunday school, church, library, day care center, and letter-writing service.[27]

Besides delineating for the first time the elements of a large, racially segmented farm labor camp, McCurry's photographs are important also because they provide some sense of the crowded, unsanitary living conditions that workers faced at the Durst hop camp. Outhouses overflowed with human waste; piles of garbage rotted in the sun; pickers slept in the open air on piles of straw; wells dried up; and drinking water became contaminated. Typhoid and dysentery soon decimated the pickers. Dissatisfied with conditions, hop pickers began protesting. On the morning of August 3, Richard "Blackie" Ford, Herman Suhr, and a delegation of other discontented hop pickers met with Ralph Durst. When Durst rejected their demands for more toilets, better pay, clean, cool drinking water, an end to the "hold back" system (wherein a portion of their pay was held until the end of the harvest), and reinstatement of "high pole men" (who went through the hop yard cutting the vines so that the harvesters could more easily pick from them), pickers returned to camp and convened a series of meetings that lasted throughout the afternoon.[28]

McCurry may actually have captured one of these meetings in a ground-level shot of the camp as viewed from the east. Close examination of a ragged print, rescued from the trash bin by Wheatland historian Juanita DeValentine after the image had

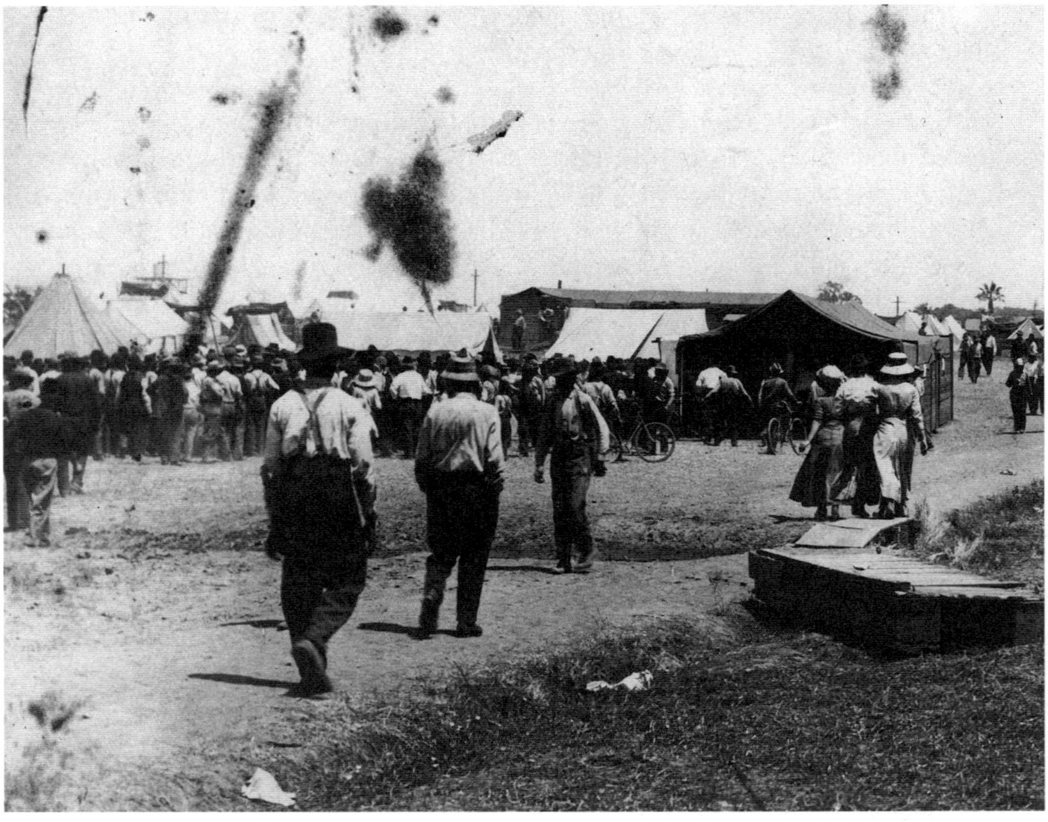

Camp of hop pickers, Durst ranch, Wheatland, August 6, 1913, photograph by Harold McCurry. Unretouched image. Courtesy of Juanita N. DeValentine.

been used as evidence in the subsequent court trial and then discarded, reveals some words written in ink and barely visible beneath a patch of mold in the upper left corner: "1913—Durst [some people read this as 'Just'] before the riot." Further scrutiny yields another unexpected discovery. To the left of a canvas-roofed commissary sporting a large sign advertising "Near Beer" and other refreshments, a cluster of several hundred people mill about. Enlargement identifies the focus of their attention as a speaker who addresses the crowd from a wooden platform. This may, in fact, capture part of the dialogue preceding the strike vote, making it the earliest known photograph of protesting agricultural workers in California, possibly even the United States.[29]

The amateur who photographed on that fateful day was seventeen-year-old Elizabeth Carney, who for about a year had been photographing with a new Kodak Ensignette Number One that she had received as a high school graduation present. One of the millions who picked up snapshot photography following the introduction of the roll-film Kodak in 1888 and the Brownie camera in 1901, young Carney had set about doing exactly what other amateurs had done: she proceeded to take pictures of birthdays, grandparents, friends, neighbors, and the town. Never giving a thought to photographing violence, illness, murder, insanity, divorce, or the people who paraded before Clara Smith, young Carney, like most amateurs, used her camera to construct an ideal view of life. But on Sunday, while she was washing dishes and doing chores in the Wheatland Hotel, a meeting was taking place at the hop picker's camp. At least one source claims that during the height of the meeting a member of the Industrial Workers of the World (IWW) reached down from his speaker's platform, took a sick infant from a mother's arms, and held the child up to the crowd, saying, "It's not so much for ourselves that we are fighting, as that this little baby may never see the conditions which now exist on this ranch!" Shortly thereafter a riot erupted; the sheriff, district attorney, and two hop pickers were shot and killed; and many pickers were injured, one of whom lost an arm. As the melee escalated, young Carney noticed the commotion, grabbed her Kodak, leaned out the window, and snapped several pictures. She then went onto the streets and photographed pickers with their bedding piled high on wagons fleeing town and congregating at the train depot. Over the next few days she also recorded the arrival of sheriff's deputies and various National Guard units setting up camp and patrolling about town.[30]

But young Carney did not stop there. After becoming the first person to use a small, handheld camera to record some aspect of a farmworker strike in California, she continued her reconnaissance and resumed her work during the August hop harvest the following year. When workers again flocked into the Durst hop ranch and the IWW attempted to organize them, she waded into the action with her Kodak, recording events with a candid and spontaneous quality heretofore unseen in photographs of farmworkers. In doing so, she provided the first photographs of a farm labor union hall and the first photographs of protest marches by agricultural workers and their sympathizers.[31]

Carney took a total of a dozen pictures: six on August 3 and 4, 1913, and six more on about the same dates the following year. Fuzzy and improperly exposed, these snapshots nevertheless demonstrate a remarkable understanding of the Wheatland episode. In fact, when arranged in sequence, they present much more than a mere record of events. A photograph of the National Guard equipped in full fighting regalia plus gas masks shows the state's fears of rebellion and violence and its determination to suppress the strikers, and an image of hop kilns silhouetted against the evening light symbolizes something of the dark terror that swept through Wheatland and poisoned the atmosphere for years following the riot.

One of Carney's photographs stands out from the others. It is a plain photograph of IWW strike headquarters at 501 Main Street. In front of the office, amid various signs and banners, is a poster that declares in Spanish: "Give us freedom. We are men. We shall not be slaves." Reiterated and put into slightly stronger wording on hundreds of separate occasions and in dozens of languages up and down the length of California, that simple declaration would grow until, during the 1980s, it became a rhetorical cornerstone for César Chávez and the United Farm Workers union.[32]

Overlooked in accounts of California's photographic heritage, Carney's snapshots of events at Wheatland nonetheless represent a giant step away from concocted imagery and toward a more realistic and spontaneous picture of California farmworkers. Over the preceding sixty years, the photographic record had been the product of professional or semiprofessional photographers using heavy, large-format, glass-plate view cameras to produce orderly and impressive studies that mostly bore testimony to the glories of agriculture. Now that older, more traditional approach was challenged. For

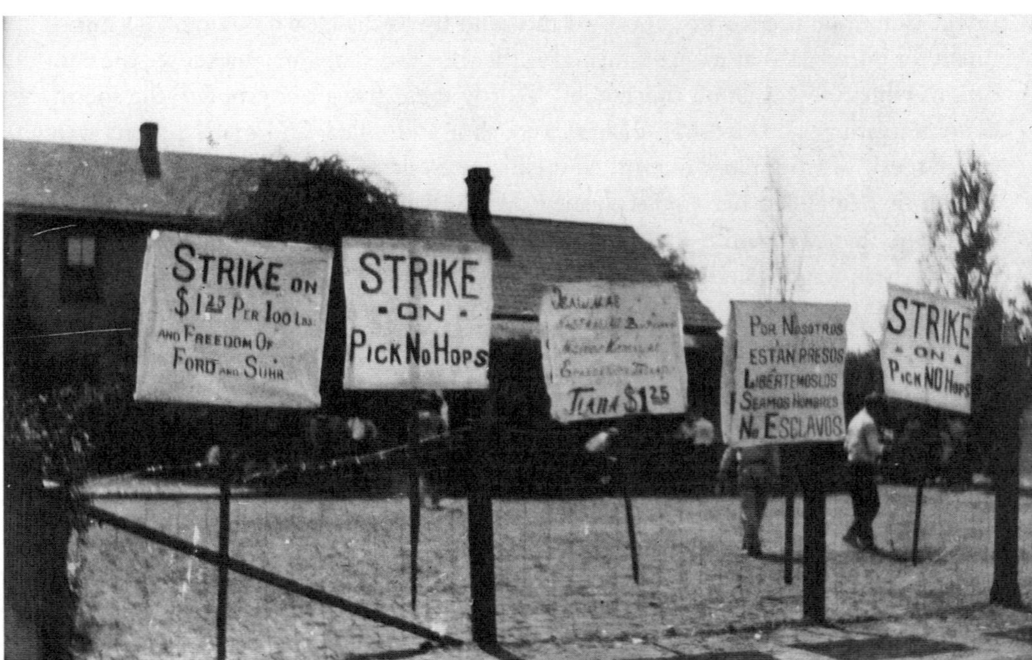

Strike and boycott signs protesting the imprisonment of Richard Ford and Herman D. Suhr, August 7, 1914, photograph by Elizabeth Carney. Courtesy of Juanita N. DeValentine.

the first time, photographers could work spontaneously. They could follow action, respond to news, and dispense with posed pictures. Small, handheld, roll-film cameras would supplement more traditional equipment and allow both amateurs and professionals alike to capture spur-of-the-moment images that begin to yield a far more complex picture of the state's farmworkers.[33]

This more complex picture became evident during the January 1914 trial of Richard "Blackie" Ford, Herman D. Suhr, and two other alleged Wheatland hop riot leaders. Unaware of Carney's work, defense attorneys and prosecutors introduced into the record dozens of Harold McCurry's photographs. Though primarily used to identify the camp layout and locate certain key landmarks, McCurry's photographs also served as objective evidence of the type of living conditions and housing arrangements that hop pickers endured, as well as the exact location where various events occurred. At the same time, magazines such as *Harper's Weekly* and newspapers such as the *Sacramento Bee* illustrated stories on the hop riot, court proceedings, and agricultural labor with photographs of Ford and Suhr, troops moving in and out of Wheatland, and conditions in farm labor camps around the state.[34]

Over the next few years, photographs also became a key element in efforts to prevent (or at least deflect) any further incidents. While probing the riot and conditions in the state's farm labor camps, members of the newly formed California Commission of Immigration and Housing (CCIH) bolstered their findings with photographic evidence. Using dozens of photographs borrowed from the McCurry Foto Company and other commercial photographers, CCIH's *Advisory Pamphlet on Camp Sanitation* displayed both abysmal and exemplary farmworker housing around the state, as well as images of standardized model camp plans. Dozens of other CCIH photographs either ran in state pamphlets and reports dealing with farmworker housing or were made available to journalists investigating the issue. While fairly banal, these images nevertheless influenced public perceptions and government attitudes in California and the nation. Juxtaposed to commercial scenes of engineered, gorgeous beauty, they emphasize a side of the California Dream that historical geographer Don Mitchell describes as having "been there all along, but . . . easy to overlook from atop the hill."[35]

Oddly, CCIH images seldom include any people. The focus is almost always on buildings and facilities, interiors of barns serving as bunkhouses, and rude hovels of gunny sacks and brush in which hop pickers shelter themselves from the sun. Without exception, every one of these images is aesthetically flat, even boring, and fails to connect on a fundamental human level. At a time when urban reformers were initiating vast photographic surveys of steelworkers and immigrant groups in the eastern United States, no member of the CCIH ever proposed the same kind of rigorous photographic reconnaissance as part of its program. None even seemed to be aware of these efforts.[36]

To counteract all of the bad publicity, Southern California citrus ranchers began using photography to aggressively record every improvement they made to farmworker housing. When C. C. Leffingwell constructed a new and extremely modern "white man's dormitory" and a separate dormitory for Japanese workers in his La Habra orange groves, he hired Los Angeles photographer Bertha Smith to make a series of views. Spending a day on the ranch in December 1914, Smith composed her pictures to emphasize the beautifully landscaped grounds, large shade trees, and fine shrubbery. "I am not particularly proud of them," she wrote to Leffingwell, "but I send them to you for what they are worth."[37]

At no time in the years between the Wheatland hop riot and the beginning of World War I did any professional photographer anywhere in the state break from this approach. Studio portraits seldom added much to the picture. Sitting for a photographer in front of a dark cloth, farmworkers spruced up in new clothes with their hair nicely clipped, struck proud poses, and projected images of success, happiness, even sexuality. Snapshots taken by family members revealed the most. Unconcerned with producing marketable images suitable for advertising purposes, amateurs snapped pictures that years later still seem vivid, evoking strong if not always fond memories. Often they captured the small details of life, such as the afternoon when a father brought home a used automobile, along with warm moments at birthday parties, family reunions, and picnics, as well as sad moments at funerals.

Farmworkers recorded in snapshots taken by other farmworkers look self-reliant and capable. They are proud of who they are. They seldom appear to be impoverished and victimized. Nor do they appear as orderly and subservient workers arranged robot-like in rows beside machines and among the vines and trees. Abandoning prevalent compositional strategies, snapshot photographers documented fellow farmworkers as one might see them around the farm. Pasted into family albums or sent to friends as tokens of a memorable summer spent cutting and drying apricots, snapshots were visual mementos of everyday life. While seldom breaking new ground or recording anything as newsworthy as the images shot by young Carney at Wheatland, amateur snapshots were beginning to yield an important and voluminous record that had meaning not only to those involved but also to subsequent generations of historians. Through snapshots, catching at least a glimpse of how workers lived became possible for the first time, and for the first time farmworkers themselves could record the telling details that would have been dismissed by a commercial photographer as not worth the effort.[38]

Professional photographers altered their approach to farmworkers with the advent of World War I, which became the driving force for this change. With large numbers of jobs opening up in the industrial sector, over one hundred thousand men on the Pacific Coast shifted out of farm labor into lumber, construction, munitions, shipbuilding, and dock work. To fill the resulting farm labor shortage, a number of organizations began bringing harvesters into the countryside and quickly captured the attention of photographers. Boy Scouts, schoolchildren, and members of the Young Men's Christian Association (YMCA) were always good for a picture or two while they camped out in the peach orchards. Even more photogenic were members of the Women's Land Army and the Boys' Working Reserve, two experimental programs of the National Council of Defense and the U.S. Department of Labor. Supervised by University of California agricultural economist Richard L. Adams, the Women's Land

Army created wholesome camps in nineteen counties north of the Tehachapi Mountains. Here, eager young boys and girls willing to help out with the harvest lived and worked under the supervision of house mothers. Camps featured tent cabins with wood floors, showers, screened dining halls, and various other amenities seldom enjoyed by many field hands.[39]

Photographers had a field day documenting young girls attired in new boots and dresses or trousers and blouses, giggling as they held up clusters of big grapes, posed with hoes, and squirted one another with hoses in camp. At day's end they were always good for at least one nice swimming shot when they retired to a nearby irrigation canal before a shower. None ever seemed to sweat or get dirty. After washing their hair and putting on nice clothes to head into town for a Saturday night dance, the women harvesters were indistinguishable from local school girls and, in fact, were often one and the same. Photographers had an equally good time with the Boys' Working Reserve, which brought thousands of teenagers into the fields in 1918. Photographers again stressed themes of wholesomeness and camaraderie. None depicted a ranch or camp that did not seem like a vacation spot, where otherwise idle youngsters engaged in healthy outdoor work.[40]

Though local photographers and those hired by various government agencies found plenty of work documenting these newcomers, they did not devote the same degree of attention to the beginning of the most significant farm labor development of World War I. This came in May 1917, when the U.S. Department of Labor waived the customary head tax and literacy test that had long impeded Mexicans from immigrating north. Within months, large numbers of Mexicans could be found harvesting every crop throughout the state. Many had been there all along, working not only in agriculture but also in railroad construction and other industries throughout the Southwest, but the labor shortage of 1917–18 opened a flood tide of immigration from Mexico that did not abate after the war. Whereas around 50,000 legal immigrants had come north between 1901 and 1910, the figure rose to 459,257 between 1921 and 1930, the so-called Mexican decade. Following the cotton harvest into the San Joaquin Valley and taking over the winter lettuce crop in the Imperial Valley, Mexicans settled in isolated rural settlements known as *colonias* and urban enclaves known as barrios, from which they ventured forth by automobile to follow a sequence of harvest jobs that provided them with employment nearly twelve months of the year.[41]

Identification cards were one exception to the general omission of Mexican immigrants from photographic coverage. Both the United States and Mexican governments issued them, but for different reasons. In the cards of both countries, an immigrant's photograph was pasted into a box on the left-hand side, which also bore an official stamp, along with the date, the name, age, birthplace, and destination of the individual. An identification number also appeared on the right side, opposite the photograph. American photographers employed by the U.S. Immigration Service closely cropped the head shots just below the chest, creating decapitated pictures of armless, bodyless men. Mexican photographers employed by the Servicio Emigratorio produced standard portraits, often showing well-dressed individuals wearing ties and coats. American

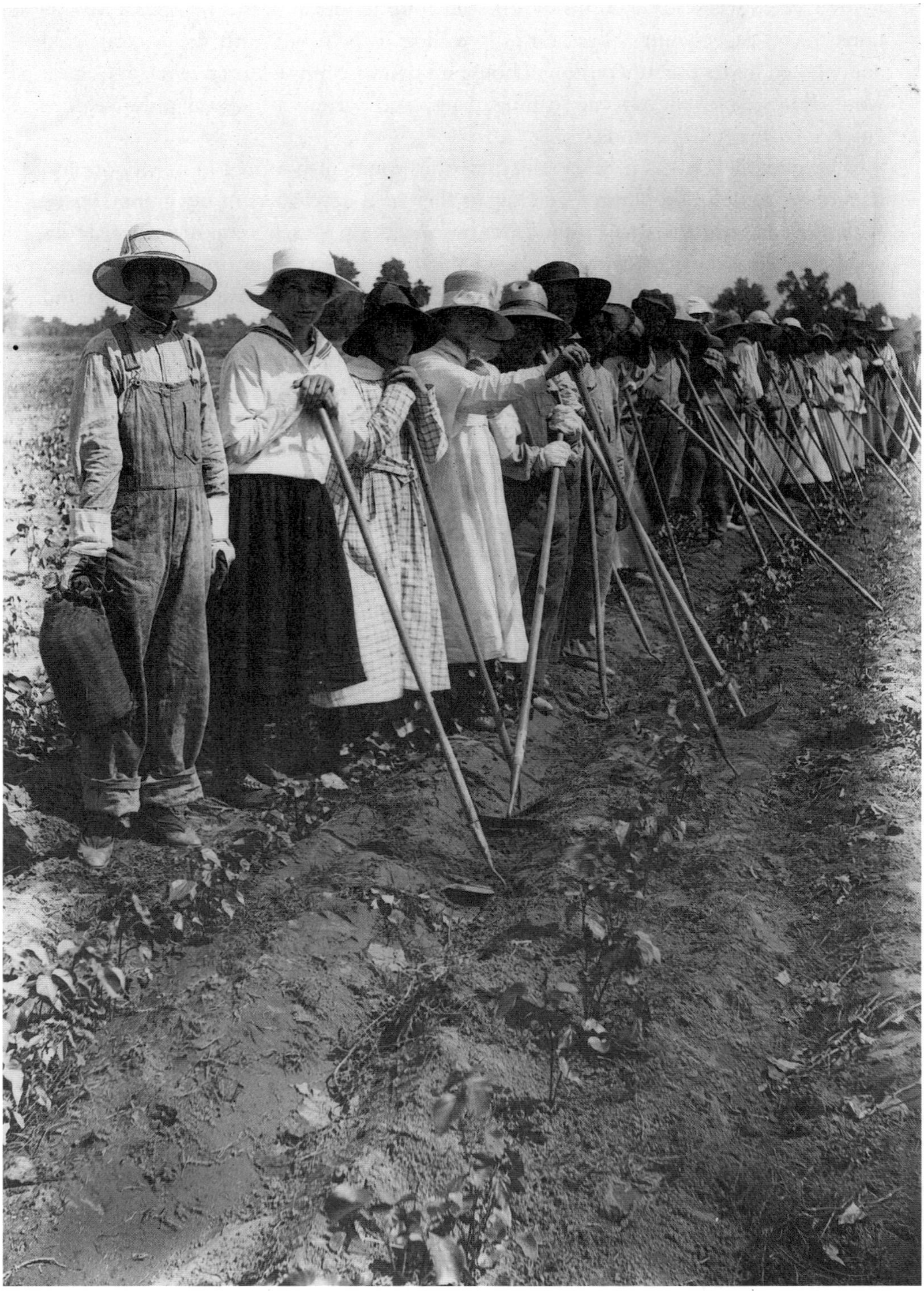

Women's Land Army hoeing a field near Bakersfield, ca. 1916, photographer unknown. Author's collection.

identification cards measured 3 × 5 inches, whereas Mexican cards were larger, usually measuring 5 × 5 inches. But much more than size and appearance differentiated them. American cards officially granted the bearer all the rights and privileges of the Department of Labor circular of June 12, 1918, essentially allowing them to enter the country legally to work. Mexico curtailed emigration by granting a limited number of identification cards, which were necessary to leave the country and work in the United States.[42]

Once past the border, Mexicans attracted the most photographic scrutiny when they moved into the citrus industry, where growers regarded them as an answer to their dreams. For years citrus farmers had been plagued by labor turnover. With the arrival of Mexicans and their families, conditions stabilized. Resolving to do everything in their power to maintain the status quo, growers embarked on a massive program to construct farmworker housing. Taking the lead in this effort, University of California, Riverside, plant pathologist Archibald D. Shamel began analyzing various programs launched by the California Fruit Growers Exchange. An intensely broad-minded man's man with supreme confidence in the industry's ability to overcome every obstacle, Shamel was a complicated individual who believed that the citrus growers of Southern California could create an agricultural paradise where basic tenets of corporate capitalism and scientific management extended into every sphere of operations. His goal, like that of citrus leader G. Harold Powell, was to combine the profits of orange and lemon culture and the lessons of modern management to create a bountiful, plantation-like society that integrated beauty and profit in a landscape that was at once industrial and suburban, pastoral and productive. To promote those goals, Shamel did more than write speeches, publish scientific papers, and conduct agricultural experiments. Beginning in February 1918, he also employed a camera to produce a remarkable series of photographic essays on housing projects at Limoneira Company and Rancho Sespe in Ventura County and the Upland Citrus Association in San Bernardino County. These essays ran sequentially over the next decade in the *California Citrograph* and were read and seen by the entire citrus industry.[43]

Often photographing early in the morning from a perspective that enhanced the architectural details or natural setting of a citrus village, Shamel recorded what amounted to luxury housing, especially when measured against that provided by other segments of the agricultural industry. Besides communal baths for Japanese citrus workers and bunkhouses designed by Pasadena architects, Shamel presents a methodology of site selection, construction standards, and various interior details, as well as porches and even gardens and flower boxes. Citrus workers allowed to live in such "quaint," comfortable, and sanitary (if isolated) villages were the envy of farmworkers throughout the state, in Shamel's view. Children growing up in these surroundings, particularly those with public schools teaching Americanization classes, formed, according to Shamel, a second generation of loyal, grateful, English-speaking workers.[44]

Creating a pleasing picture, Shamel's images of high-quality housing and auto camps that met or exceeded state standards depict an appealing version of farmworker community life. Cottages and dormitories equipped with running water, gas, and electricity and shaded by eucalyptus, sycamore, and oak trees projected a model of paternalistic concern requiring no government regulation. Happy and well-housed in the aesthetically pleasing, inexpensive, comfortable, company-owned housing constructed by liberal-minded citrus growers, citrus workers rewarded their employers with exemplary work habits and a strong sense of loyalty. So charming and attractive are Shamel's pictures of these farmworker alcoves that district and local citrus exchanges, on seeing them, were inspired to copy and even improve on the industry's model facilities.[45]

As more and more citrus villages were built, Shamel used his camera to record the change. He was alone in these efforts. Despite the drama inherent in the rapidly growing Mexican American community and the considerable artistry of Shamel and the staff members of the *California Citrograph* who laid out his images, no photographers were inspired to explore, even in a superficial way, the triumphs, challenges, and hardships faced by Mexican immigrants, the nature of the work they were doing, the reasons why they had come north, the places where they settled, and their various adaptive responses. While Mexicans were the first farmworkers to use automobiles extensively as a means to migrate between crops and were also the first to work as permanent family units in the fields, neither aspect of their lives attracted much more than passing photographic coverage. Although the twenty thousand Mexicans in the Imperial Valley constituted one-third of its entire population in 1929, they remained excluded from local photo studios in El Centro, the valley's largest town; those in the San Joaquin Valley, where Mexicans composed 56 percent of the farm labor force, attracted hardly any photographic attention. Although they created communities ranging from isolated collections of shacks in unincorporated areas to vibrant sections of town packed with pool halls, stores, movie theaters, and mutual aid societies, Mexicans never attracted much photographic attention.[46]

Only three rural photographers after World War I photographed Mexicans with any depth or regularity, and they did so largely while producing informational pictures for the agricultural industry. The most important of these photographers was Claude "Pop" Laval. A New York native who moved to Fresno in 1911, Laval established a commercial photography business that focused on agriculture. While photographing in the fields, he often captured images of farmworkers, many of them Mexicans picking grapes, driving tractors, and handling every other conceivable task. But Laval was also on hand on the evening of August 18, 1918, when Francisco Palomares, manager of the San Joaquin Valley Agricultural Labor Bureau and a representative of the CCIH, addressed a group of 160 recently arrived Mexicans seated in the Nippon Building in Fresno. Standing on the stage and speaking in Spanish, Palomares urged them to practice economy in war times, to avoid labor disputes, and to subscribe to the Red Cross. Laval, who was famous for his shots of large groups, fired several flashes and recorded the moment. He would go on to record numerous other news events, including various farm labor housing projects, Red Cross activities among Indian field hands near Clovis, and members of the Women's Land Army flailing away with hoes and trying to pick grapes, which is work that actually requires skills learned from experience.[47]

Frank D. Robinson was another San Joaquin Valley photographer who routinely photographed farmworkers. Born on a farm near Merced Falls in 1875, Robinson took up photography in 1912. Shooting mostly glass-plate negatives, he recorded everything in the Merced area, including the Yosemite Valley and the construction of various dams, as well as schools, sports, early canal building, and numerous aspects of farming and farm-related activities reproduced by the Farm Bureau as postcards and glass slides. It was in the course of his everyday agricultural photography recording planting and harvest activities that Robinson, like Laval, candidly recorded Mexican field hands. Although he occasionally posed them against a particularly spectacular or heavily laden fruit tree, Robinson more commonly made what later came to be known as environmental portraits. Photographed while building canals or planting grapevines far out in the middle of a San Joaquin Valley vineyard, field hands are often seen in his work as very small, dark, silhouetted figures, indistinguishable from other ethnic groups.[48]

Also documenting farmworkers at this time was the Imperial Valley photographer Leo Hetzel. A "bread and butter photographer" who covered the valley with his 6 × 10–inch box camera, Hetzel, known for his motto "Anything in Photography," worked for farmers and surveyors, photographed corpses for the coroner, and shot advertising for local businesses. As a two-time president of El Centro Chamber of Commerce and small-scale grower of grapefruit and alfalfa, he was not disposed to provocative images. Certainly his clients wanted nothing if not positive images, typically captioned "The Annual Cantaloupe Crop Fills from 16,000 to 21,000 Railroad Cars." About the closest Hetzel ever came to anything suggesting hard labor during the 1920s was a group portrait of Japanese women and children dressed in their best clothes and standing by while their husbands, sons, and brothers pick winter strawberries under the direction of a foreman and labor contractor.[49]

During and after World War I, commercial photographers like Laval, Robinson, and Hetzel did what they had always done. Accustomed to producing promotional images for the booming agricultural industry, they seemed to consciously avoid barrios, mutual aid societies, and other aspects of Mexican immigration, despite their growing importance. When the *Saturday Evening Post,* a strong advocate of restricting Mexican immigration, ran a series of articles by novelist Kenneth L. Roberts that reflected the magazine's view, editors illustrated the text with photographs of "a bit of a Mexican section" of one Imperial Valley town and Mexicans riding to the fields in automobiles. The images were not shot on contract for the magazine but picked up from Ewing Galloway, Underwood and Underwood, Garden City Photo Company, and other photo agencies. Such stock agencies ventured into the fields among Mexicans only as an ancillary to assignments to promote a town, industry, crop, or product or, most commonly, while collecting stock photographs to sell under their bylines to *Sunset* and other magazines. About the only aspect of Mexican farm labor that interested these photographers was the shacks set up just south of Calexico, where residents of the Imperial Valley could drink bootleg mescal.[50]

Poverty, conflict, and hard labor did not interest photo agency photographers, although they surely saw plenty of these things on their way to the mescal shacks. They continued to relegate Mexicans and other ethnic field hands to bit parts in promotional scenes. Captions attached to their images seldom mention the race or ethnic identity of the people depicted. "Harvesting Hops in American River Basin," "Digging Irish Potatoes with a Potato Digger," and "Cantaloupe Picking from an 800-Acre Field near Brawley," were typical.[51]

Sometime during the early 1920s, farmers themselves, in the course of recording their daily operations, began photographing farmworkers. One of the first to do so on a regular basis was Kenneth Keller. Manager of the Thousand Acre Rancho in Colusa County, Keller recorded various aspects of work in and around his farm and often sent his 2¼ × 3–inch images to company superiors as part of his weekly reports. Another of these farmer–photographers was John Sparhawk Appleton. A successful Simi Valley honey farmer, Appleton photographed with a 6 × 8–inch mahogany view camera made by Rochester Optical Company. With no motive beyond the enjoyment of a hobby, he recorded field hands on neighboring ranches as well as on his own operations. Merging the best technical aspects of commercial photography with the insight of someone familiar with his surroundings, Appleton's images have a unique look and feel. And while they do not expose poverty and injustice, they are nonetheless revealing in the way that they move into places and record details not normally captured by photographers of the day.[52]

None of this amounted to anything close to an investigative approach to farm labor in general or to Mexican farm labor in particular. When the first inkling of a

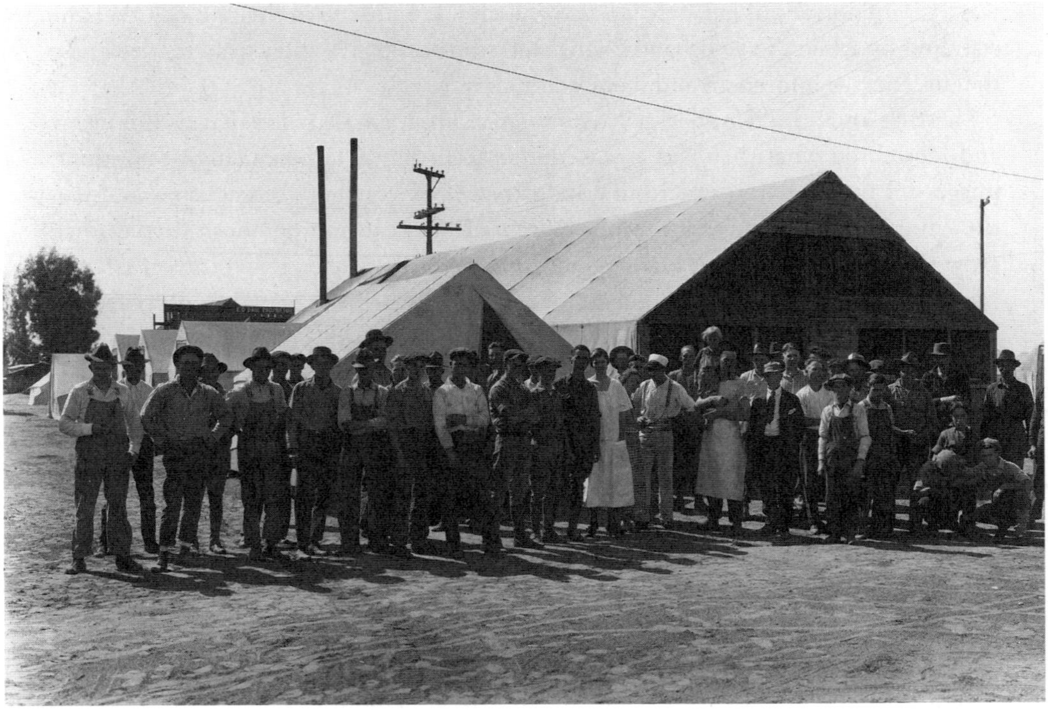

Group at Community Camp no. 1, Fowler, September 28, 1920, photograph by Claude "Pop" Laval. Courtesy of Jerome D. Laval, Laval Company, Inc., and Fresno County Historical Society.

change occurred, it emerged not in California but far to the east, in Texas, a popular crossing point for Mexican immigrants seeking work in the western United States. After venturing as far north as El Paso and San Antonio, the newcomers were inspected by the Public Health Service, and the feeble or disabled were barred. Those remaining were, if necessary, vaccinated, then deloused, fumigated, and discharged. Making their way to any one of dozens of labor agencies, they paid a job fee and were then dispatched throughout Texas and as far west as Arizona and California. Many ended up in Southern California, where the wages were highest.[53]

Large crowds of immigrants often gathered outside labor agencies while waiting for work. On March 22, 1924, San Antonio photographer Hugo Summerville, who specialized in large group portraits, encountered a particularly desperate group of Mexicans outside the Alamo City Employment Agency. Several hundred men and even some women stood on the street, in obvious distress. Nearby were a few boxes of donated food. So evocative was the scene that Summerville felt compelled to capture it with his best camera, a Kodak Cirkut that rested on a heavy tripod, used roll film that was six to twelve inches wide, made a panoramic picture of at least 180 degrees without distortion, and produced a negative ranging from forty-two inches to twenty feet in length. After making his first exposure, Summerville reloaded his camera and made a second picture. As was the custom with Cirkut camera photographers, Summerville carefully captioned the photographs, writing in white ink on the bottom of each print: "THE C. CAMPA LABOR AGENCY AND W. J. LEWIS OF THE ALAMO CITY EMPLOYMENT AGENCY, DISTRIBUTING BREAD THREE TIMES A DAY TO MEXICANS WHO ARE IN DISTRESS, WAITING TO BE SENT TO A JOB. MARCH 22, 1924."[54]

A sign featured prominently on a building in each photograph reads: "SALIDAS PARA TODAS PARTES DE ESTADOS UNIDOS" (Office to Hire Workers for All Parts of the United States). The sign also contains two other important pieces of information. One is the term *bracero,* which comes from *brazo,* the Spanish word for "arm." Loosely translated, a bracero is a farmhand, a man who works with his arms. Literally translated, a bracero is an "arm-man," someone supplying a pair of arms. Besides these definitions, there is also the implied meaning: cheap laborers who impose few obligations on growers. The other term is *enganches,* which literally means "hooks" but in fact referred to a contract from which one could not escape. Within a few years, Mexican workers coming north under contract to work in the sugar beet fields would refer to themselves as *los enganchados,* "the hooked ones," whereas farmworkers brought north to plug the farm labor shortage of World War II would be referred to as braceros, and the program that brought them north, as the bracero program.

Straightforward, extremely detailed, and richly composed, Summerville's panoramas were probably reassuring to the city's leaders, who at the time were more concerned about supplying cheap labor than any humanitarian issues related to the migrants. But to historians of photography, the images are haunting; Jennifer Watts and Claudia Bohn-Spector describe them in their book *The Great Wide Open: Panoramic Photographs of the American West* as "a provocative glimpse at a group of disenfranchised souls staring back at us through time and space."[55]

Summerville was not alone in using a Cirkut camera to document the Texas component of the California farmworker story. Probably the greatest practitioner was rival Eugene O. Goldbeck. After opening up a photographic studio in San Antonio with the catchy slogan "We cover the United States and then some," Goldbeck recorded every aspect of life in and around the city, from soldiers and Mexican revolutionaries to members of the Elks Club and various high school graduating classes. Two years after Summerville photographed the C. Campa Labor Agency, Goldbeck traveled to Laredo to photograph the Border Patrol. Established on May 28, 1924, as part of the Johnson–Reed Immigration Act, the Border Patrol had a budget of one million dollars and was just beginning to police the southwestern border with Mexico. Granted unusual and sweeping powers of search, seizure, and arrest, the initial force of 472 men, many of whom saw themselves as embodying the traditions of the Texas Rangers, was equipped with the latest technology, including motor vehicles and various weapons. Recruited from a mix of cowpunchers, ranch hands, roustabouts, military veterans, and former Texas Rangers, the Border Patrol tried to dispel an image of trigger-happy, ruthless patrolman and project an image of tough professionalism. To accomplish that, Supervising Inspector M. M. Hanson hired Goldbeck to photograph him posed with twenty-six members of his Border Patrol unit. Arranging the men next to their vehicles in front of banners proclaiming "Stop: U.S. Officers," Goldbeck had the unit display various high-powered firearms in a way that suggests the seriousness with which they went about the work of ending the illegal entry of the very class of immigrants being fed by the Alamo City Employment Agency.[56]

Goldbeck took pride in his photograph, realizing that it was a one-of-a-kind image. Even the great drama of his picture, however, inspired no other photographers to break with tradition and begin producing edgy, documentary images centered

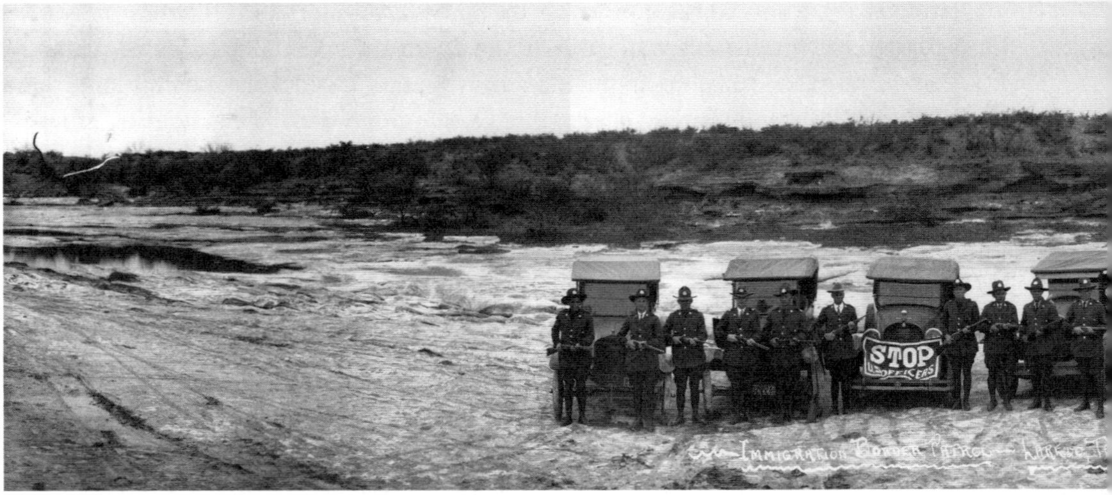

Immigration Border Patrol, Laredo, Texas, M. M. Hanson Inspector in Charge, February 1926, photograph by Eugene O. Goldbeck. Courtesy of the Photography Collection, Harry Ransom Humanities Research Center, University of Texas at Austin.

on the influx of Mexican labor. His photograph of men deployed to intercept immigrants on their way to the fields was anomalous. Of the hundreds of other photographers in Texas, very few were inspired to use the new technology to peer below the surface. Goldbeck soon understood that he would probably never again take such a picture. Within a few months he would be far from the border, high in a tower, directing thousands of massed army troops arranging themselves like dots in an expressionist painting. But as the decade progressed, Goldbeck could see changes under way.

All around him new groups of photographers were moving into the profession. Many refused to work with large-view cameras and photographed for noncommercial reasons. Less engaged in commerce and less beholding to the agricultural industry, their politics and values were independent of their employers. Although they did not participate in any explicitly ideological displays, neither did they turn their backs on the issues of the day: housing, hunger, immigration, hard work. Their portraits diverge from earlier romantic approaches by displaying considerable respect for farmworkers and immigrants on their way to becoming farmworkers and by emphasizing the attentive work and valuable contributions of these people and their devotion to their families. Smoke, light, danger, and dust—all the drama of the industrial environment—are visible. Police control, violence, poor housing, and efforts at reform appear. These photographers were beginning to inject social values into their work. It was a subtle change, but it was also very real and lasting. They were doing so because of an implicit belief in the profound educational power of photography. Soon they would begin exploring, however tentatively, heretofore overlooked aspects of life and labor in the fields, bringing fresh eyes and a social conscience to a task that Goldbeck, Summerville, and so many others like them still regarded as basically a business.

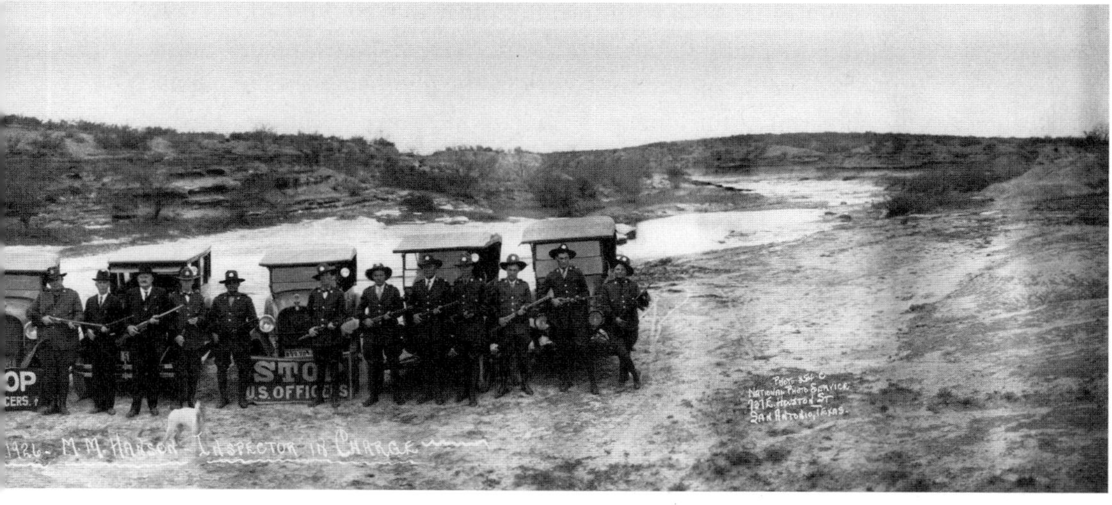

5

An Attitude of Engagement

Photography Takes the Side of the Poor

The annual May Day parade was under way in 1926 when Tina Modotti, a beautiful and mysterious young Italian activist, femme fatale, and sometime actress, climbed to the roof of the Mexico City home of artist Pablo O'Higgins. Thousands of Mexican peasants wearing big sombreros filled the streets below, and Modotti intended to photograph the scene. Having just returned to Mexico from California, the financially strapped Modotti had recently traded in her big Korona view camera for a handheld, highly portable Graflex. Shifting away from photographing flowers, delicate objects, and other subjects in the style of her lover and teacher, Edward Weston, she was beginning a period of intensive political photography that explored peasant life in the nation following the Mexican Revolution, which she had passionately supported. Prowling the countryside with her camera in order to record life in the raw, she was trying to capture this tumultuous period with unique contemporary documents. Now focusing her Graflex on the crowd below, she photographed the pulsating, jostling sea of campesinos, put humanity under a microscope, and captured a powerful sense of class solidarity. The resulting image, soon known as *Workers Parade,* was published in the August–September 1926 issue of *Mexican Folkways,* a bilingual magazine that spotlighted the "creative spirit" of indigenous Mexico. Often described as campesinos in motion toward the goal or target of asserting their human rights, *Workers Parade* is a unique contemporary document that melded Modotti's formalist concerns with her growing revolutionary politics.[1]

Continuing to photograph over the next four years, Modotti joined the Mexican Communist Party, had an affair with the Cuban exile revolutionary Julio Mella, saw him assassinated as she walked by his side along a street in Mexico City, and yet managed to develop her own artistic identity while compiling a remarkable record of the peasant society that was moving north to work in the fields of California and the Southwest. But in 1930, all of this ended. Modotti was deported. Traveling first to Berlin and from there to Moscow, Paris, and Spain, she abandoned photography for dangerous, underground, revolutionary politics. She did not return to Mexico until 1942, when she died in the backseat of a taxi cab, under an assumed name, apparently of a congenital heart condition, although rumors circulated that she was assassinated. But long before Modotti had passed from the scene, her photograph of campesinos on the march, with its slightly blurred sense of motion and sunburstlike patterns of light falling on the sombreros, was hailed as the first really symbolic work of revolutionary photographic reportage dealing with California farmworkers or, more precisely, peasants who would soon become California farmworkers.[2]

Modotti was not the only visual artist who adopted an explicitly political point of view at this time. While she was photographing people moving north into the fields of California, one of the oddest of all farmworker chroniclers was portraying immigrants arriving from the East. That man was Henry "Yoshitaka" Kiyama, a Japanese student who, after arriving in San Francisco in 1914, studied at the San Francisco Art Institute and then began earning a living as a portrait painter. At some point, however, Kiyama became fascinated with cartoons and comic strips, then enormously popular. About 1927, he began drawing cartoons depicting the trials and tribulations of four Japanese immigrants. Creating a 104-page, integrated story, Kiyama gathered these cartoons into *The Four Immigrants Manga.* Printed in Japan and sold extensively in San Francisco in both Japanese- and English-language editions, *The Four Immigrants* was essentially an autobiographical tale of Kiyama and his three friends after they arrived by boat in San Francisco in 1904.

Although many of the cartoons were set in San Francisco, one referred specifically to an incident in another California town, Turlock, from which Japanese field hands had been run out, while others focused on bunkhouse life, gambling, and work in the Colusa rice fields. Among the most gripping is one twelve-panel sequence about two buddies, Frank and Charlie, who leave the cold and foggy environs of San Francisco seeking warmth, work, clean air, and lots of money as "blanket boys" in the Sacramento Delta. Much to their consternation, they choke in the dusty fields, gag on fly-infested rice soup, and are housed in hot, mosquito-filled quarters next to the stable. Awakened one night by what they believe is an earthquake, Frank and Charlie are humiliated when the farm owner informs them that the shaking was only horses bucking in their stalls. Leaving for better work irrigating orchards, they get drunk, fall asleep, flood the orchards, and, calling themselves "crows trying to be cormorants," move on to another job. Thereafter, they become farm cooks and forget to remove the insides of a chicken before baking it, resulting in their firing after their employer cuts into the bird and an awful skunk smell overtakes everyone. After various other humiliations, including wages lost to liquor and gambling, Frank and Charlie manage to save two thousand dollars, which they are tricked into investing in a Colusa rice farm, where they slave all year only to lose their crop to torrential rains. Fed up, one of them returns to Japan in 1924, no richer for the experience but certainly wiser.[3]

While Japanese cartoonists and revolutionary photographers were graphically depicting the dilemmas of immigrants about to become farmworkers, Ventura County sheriff's photographer Carl J. Wallace was adding yet another dimension to the evolving picture. Assigned the task of recording the aftermath of various suicides, murders, and accidents, Wallace compiled a dossier of shocking images chronicling mayhem on a scale heretofore unimaginable in photographs: men lying in pools of blood in bunkhouses with pistols pressed to their stomachs; field hands dead from blows to the head, with their pruning shears still in their hands; body parts scattered about the railroad where a field hand had slipped beneath a moving train; autopsy photographs; despondent men who had hanged themselves in their jail cells; men crushed when a truckload of hay bales fell on them. Hinting at an ugly underside to life and labor in the citrus orchards of Ventura County, Wallace's photographs also signal the continuing shift away from dominant photographic approaches stressing beauty and, for the first time, introduce shock and uglification into the picture. Eighty years after photography first interacted with farmworkers, someone was confronting death.[4]

Pasted into Ventura County coroner Oliver Reardon's Book of Violent Deaths, these images were completely unpublishable. The dead have gaping mouths. Many are caught in last gasp. Some are in pieces. Or hanging. They are shriveled and caked in dirt. Often their pants are stained with urine and blood. Some of the images are postmortem pictures and include evidence of autopsy work, with extensive suturing.

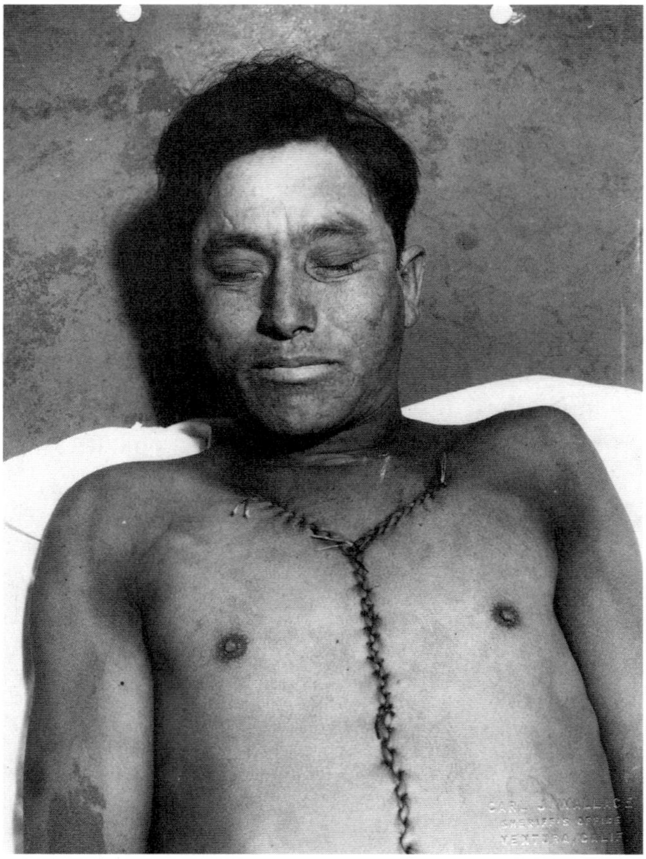

Antolin Ramos, Death from Overdose of Whiskey, 1926, photograph by Carl J. Wallace. Ventura County Coroner's Office, Book of Violent Deaths. Courtesy of John Nichols Gallery, Santa Paula, California. www.JohnNicholsGallery.com.

A few look as if they were taken in some awful torture chamber. Accompanying documentation lists the possessions of the dead: some coins, a few dollars, a small knife, a silver cross, a medallion of the Virgin of Guadalupe.

Preceding each photograph, a cryptic commentary summarizes the circumstances of death. One summary, of Antolin Ramos, discloses that he had been

> brought into Ventura County at 10:00 AM by brother Cepomar Ramos, had been attended for several days prior by Dr. G. O. Grenhoved, Santa Paula. Eight days prior to death he was suffering from a cold, friends told him to get some whiskey to cure himself. He went to the Teke Pool Hall at Santa Paula and bought three pints of Old Creek Whiskey. It is believed that he drank all three pints. When brought to the County Hospital [he] was suffering from failing vision. His throat and larynx were burned and scarred and raw, [he] was treated at the hospital by Dr. Gilman and Dr. James W. Moore. Stomach contents and specimens were sent to Pathological Laboratory of Bremm, Zeiler and Hammerk, Los Angeles for examination. Their diagnosis was chronic nephritis, suspected wood alcohol poisoning. Examination of tissue failed to show any wood alcohol. However, according to Dr. Hammack that due to the length of time that had lapsed (8 days) it was impossible to determine by analysis whether wood alcohol was present.

Another report on the death of John (Juan) Griego describes how

> Griego and his father had left the evening of the 21st from their home in Camarillo to go to Hueneme to get the separated wife Elinor Griego who had agreed to return to him. Her brothers apparently started trouble and called Constable Forter of Hueneme who took him to the Oxnard Jail about 7:45 PM, Aug. 21. Officer Harris at about 5:00 opened [the] cell to put [in] another prisoner [and] found him hanging by his belt to the grating about 9 feet from the floor. He had stood on the toilet seat and put one foot on the disinfectant can and hooked the belt and stepped off. He had been drinking when he went to Hueneme but was not drunk. Ignacio Seja and other boys at the Camarillo Ranch stated that he said that he was going to kill himself.[5]

By the mid-1920s a few photographers and artists were clearly beginning to create a visually stunning body of uncomfortable images that focused directly on farmworkers themselves, especially their struggles and tragedies. The term *documentary,* coined in 1926 by British film producer and sociologist John Grierson to describe the educational and persuasive aspects and the larger purpose that he had found in Robert Flaherty's film *Moana,* encapsulated some of the new visual sensibility that was crystalizing in California around farmworkers. At its core, this new approach delved into the commonplace, into everyday life and human problems. Created in the service of larger social matters rather than pure art or commerce, this style of imagery aimed at making a difference. This was not aloof photography. Nor was it something that later became known as photojournalism; there was at this time no such word.

This was engaged photography that grabbed a viewer's attention. A number of news-related developments contributed to this emerging sensibility. These ranged from the push toward content-oriented photography in the gravure magazine supplements of various newspapers to the beginning of news picture services such as Wide World Photos (1919), International News Pictures (1919), Acme Newspictures (1923), and the Associated Press News Photo Service (1927). Going far beyond cataloging, surveying trends, and conveying information, the new sensibility was centered on people and issues, not places or things, and amounted to more than a photographer's personal concerns. Above all, it aimed at bearing witness, giving testimony, approximating "truth," and provoking a wide audience to experience a sense of sadness, pity, and despair that moved people to new awareness and sometimes action. Those who practiced this kind of photography tended to be skeptical of the intellect. As the historian William Stott has said, they resembled artists in their belief that "a fact to be true and important must be felt."[6]

Over the next eight years, a diverse lot of photographers and artists focusing on farmworkers considerably expanded this approach. These quintessentially modern

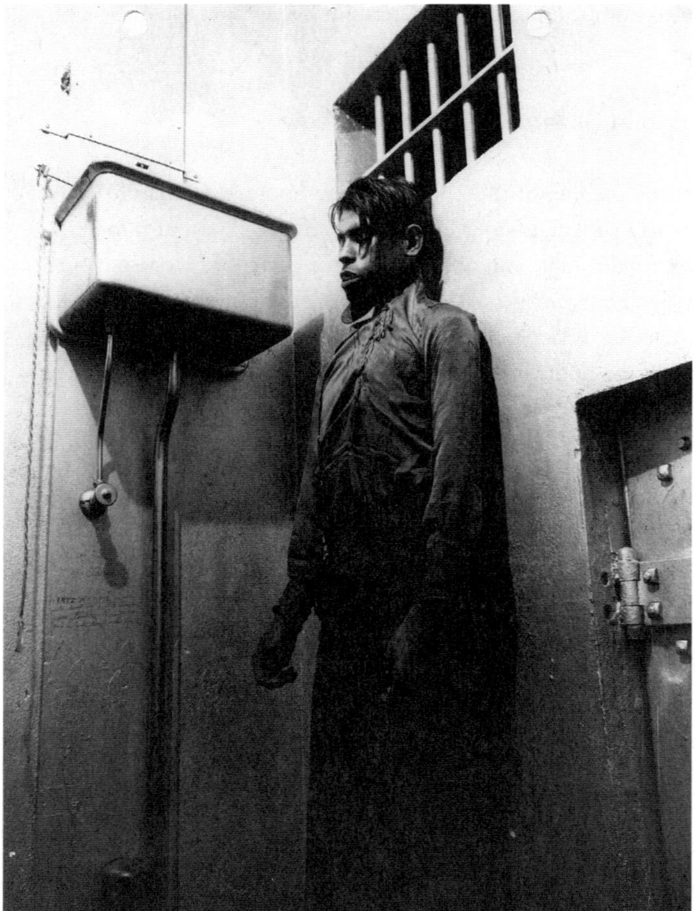

Juan [John] Griego, Death by Hanging in the Oxnard Jail, 1928, photograph by Carl J. Wallace. Ventura County Coroner's Office, Book of Violent Deaths. Courtesy of John Nichols Gallery, Santa Paula, California. JohnNicholsGallery.com.

people, who included a university economist, a renowned landscape photographer, two German refugees, a seventeen-year-old high school student, a handful of commercial photographers, several photojournalists, and a labor activist painting in a drunken stupor on the walls of his basement, created a body of work eliciting a complicated spectrum of insights, questions, and reflections. Hardly of one view, they embraced a sometimes incongruous mix of elements: scholarship and advocacy, communism and democracy, commerce and art, independence and teamwork, anger and alcoholism. Several were women who operated in a man's world, far removed from the safe and prescribed fields of fashion photography and studio portraiture. A few went well past common photographic practices, leaving behind detailed written records of their work, politics, values, motivation, and experiences. All shared an approach to imagery that critic Antonio Rodríguez calls "glorification of the insignificant." By glorification, Rodríguez means portraying the poor as actors in their own right rather than as mere subjects or victims. Disruptive as well as educational, such images are hardly a cold or even an objective record. They attack well-seasoned clichés about the worthy or noble poor. Eventually this type of photography would become a distinct form of communication and a prime method of inquiry into the lives of California farmworkers. But at the moment, no one had yet applied a label. All anyone knew was that it now seemed time to explore social reality and human activity visually in the hope of awakening public understanding of life and labor in the fields.[7]

Of all the various photographers grappling with this visual impulse, University of California economics professor Paul S. Taylor is by far the most important. A popular professor whom University of California president Clark Kerr later recalled as "a very unusual breed of what might be called economic anthropologists with an interest in labor problems," Taylor was a worldly, battle-toughened professor, a pioneer in oral history interviewing techniques, and a Mexican immigration expert who broke the artificial barriers separating history from economics and synthesized the two in his own investigations. Born in Sioux City, Iowa, in 1895, he had absorbed a strong dose of progressive thinking while growing up in a middle-class family of English–German–Swiss lineage. In 1913 he entered the University of Wisconsin at Madison, an experience that he later recalled "gave the bent to [his] whole life." Madison offered a stimulating intellectual environment, and Taylor was strongly attracted to the school's controversial and challenging economists: Richard T. Ely, E. A. Ross, and John R. Commons. Finding these men appealingly broad-minded rather than narrowly academic and drawn to their view of economics as a flexible field of study embracing history, law, sociology, and political science, Taylor was particularly impressed by their belief that knowledge could be a tool for solving contemporary social problems. Studying with these men, Taylor found economics to be a lively discipline rather than the proverbial "dismal science." Above all he was stimulated by concepts identified with Commons and his associates: that political, historical, and social circumstances determine economic reality, that the economist must reject arbitrary academic disciplines and work from real conditions rather than theorizing from books, that facts so discovered suggest courses of action, and that ethical decisions are the essence of the discipline.[8]

Visual research had not been part of Taylor's undergraduate training, although Commons had urged his students to purchase the copiously illustrated *Pittsburgh Survey,* then considered a model of social science investigation. In 1919, Taylor became interested in photography while convalescing from a mustard gas attack suffered while serving as a Marine Corps second lieutenant during the battle at Belleau Wood, France. Reflecting on the grainy, poorly focused photographs shot with his vest-pocket Eastman Kodak camera, Taylor discovered a communicative power that surpassed all of the words in all of the letters he had written home. Taylor worked on sharpening his photographic talents while studying for his doctorate at Berkeley between 1919 and 1922, and his interest in photography further deepened when, after becoming an assistant professor in the Berkeley Economics Department, he became aware of the pioneering work being done by Paul Kellogg and *Survey* magazine.[9]

Often described as a precursor to the great modern illustrated magazines, *Survey* was something like a well-illustrated version of the *Nation* or the *Outlook.* Kellogg edited the journal in spare moments stolen from his job as secretary to the New York Charity Organization Society, the largest charity organization in the country. He had created the magazine in 1909 out of *Charities and the Commons,* another innovative magazine that often published the work of Lewis Hine and other "social photographers," as they were then known. He named it *Survey* in order to suggest its new investigative methodology and soon transformed it into an unabashed champion of social science research focused on industrial workers and their environment, especially those

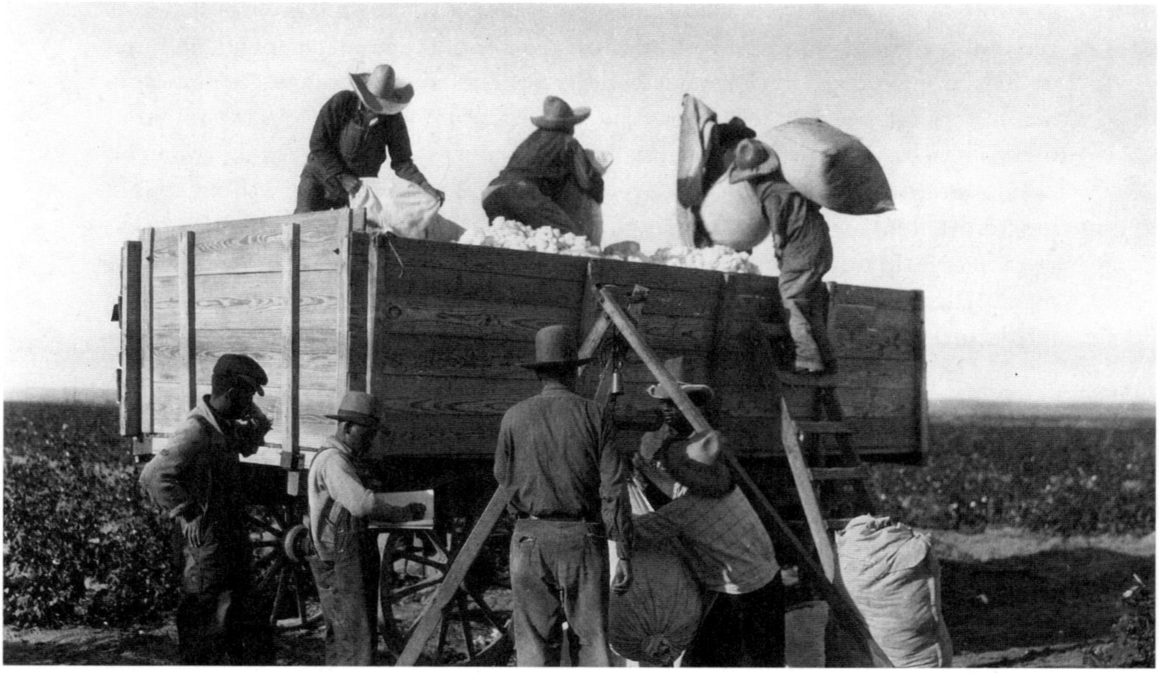

Weighing and loading cotton in the Imperial Valley, 1928, photograph by Paul S. Taylor. Courtesy of Paul S. Taylor and John Dixon.

employed in the steel industry. Using clear essays written in an engaging style that avoided recriminating words and political rhetoric, *Survey* advanced a concept of industrial sociology that became the driving force behind the Pittsburgh Survey, which used funding from the Russell Sage Foundation to produce a six-volume study of living and working conditions in the steel industry. Illustrated with 525 photographs, drawings, charts, and tables, the effort rested on the assumption that social science discoveries might inform public policy and lead to reform. In 1923, Kellogg further promoted the idea of illustrated social science by publishing alternate issues of *Survey* as the copiously illustrated *Survey Graphic.*[10]

Taylor was among those who read *Survey Graphic* and absorbed its message about using photographs to understand social problems. "I was interested professionally in immigration, in labor—those were both included in Paul Kellogg's interests," he recalled. "So it was quite natural that I should find myself establishing some kind of connection with him." Energized by Kellogg's approach, Taylor immediately began exploring more deeply the history of photography and its applicability to his field of interest, labor economics. As a result, in 1926, when the Social Science Research Council funded Taylor's proposal to produce his multivolume monograph series Mexican Labor in the United States, Taylor decided to photograph while interviewing and gathering data in the field.[11]

Having begun in earnest during World War I, Mexican immigration had reached a flood tide and was provoking extensive commentary and debate. Realizing that his subject merged contemporary history with journalism, Taylor refused to restrict himself to the usual methods of academic inquiry. He was a restless and unconventional academic. Hardly content to sit in dusty archives, he liked to get out among his subjects. During his tour of duty in the trenches, Taylor had developed the habit of taking notes and using them as the basis for detailed narratives, and he had also drawn on first-person experiences working on the docks in San Francisco while writing his doctoral dissertation on the Sailors' Union of the Pacific. Determined to discover what was really happening in the fields while other economists fiddled with theoretical models, Taylor employed these methods in February 1927, when he launched his pioneering and panoramic project on Mexican labor and Mexican immigration. Because so much of what he encountered could not be expressed merely in words and numbers, he immediately decided to elevate photography from the periphery of academic research to one of the "tools of social science," from an adjunct of his work to a central element in his repertoire of data-gathering techniques.[12]

Taylor began photographing Mexican immigrants in their peasant villages and *ejidos* (communal lands), the sugar beet fields and processing plants of Colorado and Utah, the steel mills and meat-packing plants of Illinois, Michigan, and Pennsylvania, and the lush farm lands of Arizona and the lower Rio Grande Valley of Texas. His most challenging photography occurred in Southern California, especially in the Imperial Valley. Carved out of the raw desert eighty miles east of San Diego and watered by means of a canal tapping into the Colorado River, the Imperial Valley was a place of vast potential and extreme social stratification along ethnic lines, where farming was controlled by Anglo owners, many of them absentees, and most of the fieldwork was handled by Mexican laborers, who constituted about one-third of the population. "What I saw hit me in the face," Taylor explained fifty years later. "I found myself in the midst of an agricultural society with a labor pattern the opposite of all that as a youth I had known in the Middle West."[13]

Probing that society, Taylor employed an approach that was at once casual, indirect, and sympathetic, which inspired confidence and put people at ease. By appearing to be no more than a harmless gringo (academic researcher), Taylor was received warmly. Welcomed into cabins and brush shelters, tolerated by labor contractors, and allowed to roam freely in the barrios and *colonias,* he was treated to cold beer in pool halls and bars, invited to pass time in mutual aid societies, taken to recruitment sites where Mexicans found employment, invited to relax in the company of friends, and fed in the small sitting rooms of tiny shacks. Under these conditions, Taylor's small handheld camera proved especially valuable, allowing him to compose scenes documenting the intimate details of life as well as the pride and struggles of a people living on the bare margin. In contrast to the large, heavy, view cameras still being used by many photographers, the roll-film Eastman Kodak camera, just then beginning to impact news photography, did not require an intrusive, analytical working method. With high-speed shutters and more sensitive film than that of view cameras, the Kodak made photography easier, allowing Taylor to work quickly. Unencumbered by tripods, film packs, and the usual complement of photographic equipment, Taylor could raise his camera and in a few seconds make several candid pictures in a melon field or at an early-morning shape-up, when a foreman left the area or even when supervisors were present. Any errors of composition or extraneous details could later be edited out of the image during the printing process, although Taylor seldom cropped his prints.[14]

One obstacle that Taylor faced daily was the searing summer heat, which cracked his film and rendered midday photography a sweaty ordeal. Another was the ever-present dust and sand, which gummed up Taylor's camera and dirtied his lens. Finally, there was the harsh sun, which created such sharply contrasting shadow and light that Taylor found it difficult to calculate his film exposures. Lacking a photo electronic meter (none would be available until 1931), he was forced to rely on memory, printed exposure tables, and practical experience, with predictable consequences. Some negatives were improperly exposed. Others, especially work portraits, lost important facial details in black shadows. Lacking fine equipment, Taylor was no darkroom guru and could not produce prints with great detail and tonal qualities. His photography was further marred by a flaw in the lens or shutter of his Kodak camera, which produced a hairlike mark in the upper left corner of every negative. But this was not of great concern. Late at night, in free moments, after his family was asleep, he would edit his negatives and print the best images, sometimes continuing with the task into the early-morning hours. "I used to pull the shades down in one of the rooms in our 1075 Cragmont house and turn it into a darkroom at night," he recalled many years later to Regional Oral History Project interviewer Suzanne B. Riess. "I never developed negatives, but I did enlarge prints quite a lot."[15]

Modest as these efforts were, they placed Taylor in the forefront of the changes that were inaugurating a new era of photographic representation of farmworkers in California. By emphasizing clarity and realism and by associating with *Survey Graphic,* Taylor was moving toward a commitment to the modern photo essay (a narrative sequence of photographs accompanied by text or extended captions focusing on a single subject), although he never articulated such a view, used the phrase, or saw himself as part of any particular photographic movement. As he went about his business, few in the agricultural hierarchy worried very much that Taylor and others like him might subvert the rural status quo and generate a countervision beyond that of big peaches and orchards in full bloom. After all, Taylor was a mere university professor, with a limited audience and limited resources. Uncomfortable images could easily be countered with advertising campaigns, a technique that had previously worked so well in establishing, selling, and maintaining a view of agricultural tranquility achieved without reference to the human effort. No matter how disturbing the images, farmers knew that photographers would tire and move on or be bought off, time would pass, everything would be forgotten, and the industry would continue to pursue profits as usual.[16]

That had always been the pattern, but with Taylor's work, old ways of seeing dissipated. More than any other single individual, Taylor would push farmworker photography in a more creative and socially oriented direction. But while hooked

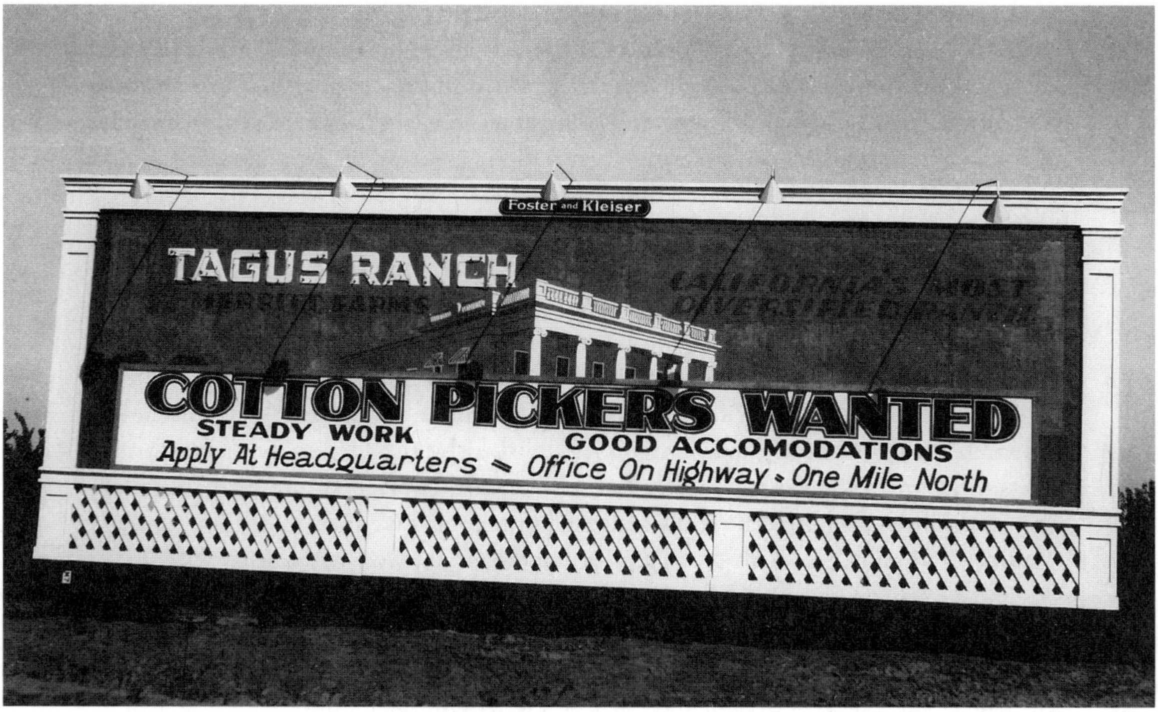

Tagus Ranch sign along Highway 99, near Fresno, 1929, photograph by Paul S. Taylor. Courtesy of Paul S. Taylor and John Dixon.

on photography as a medium for conveying his ideas, Taylor at this time never tried to label his work. Although familiar with the earlier efforts of Jacob Riis and most certainly with Lewis Hine's images in *Survey Graphic,* Taylor was nevertheless completely unaware of what Tina Modotti was doing in Mexico or the images that Hugo Summerville had made in Texas. Taylor's stated conviction, "no amount or quality of words could convey . . . the situation . . . that I was studying," influenced his approach, which developed almost entirely from his drive to present and organize facts pertinent to Mexican labor, his push to describe the struggle to overcome human-made problems, his quest to find "another language" for the social sciences, his great desire to move people to action, and his commitment to overcoming the great sin of economics that his predecessor, Berkeley economics professor Carleton E. Parker, had identified: "the divorce of its work from reality."[17]

While busy publishing his pioneering, multivolume Mexican labor series, Taylor did not abandon what he later described as his "slow climb up the ladder towards an appreciation of photographs." While completing his study of Mexicans in Chicago, Taylor met Kellogg at Hull House and received further encouragement to use photography as part of his presentation. After he moved to south Texas, Kellogg came down to Carrizo Springs following a conference of social workers, and the two spent several days together in the fields. Carrizo Springs is a small town and county seat in the Wintergarden district, and Kellogg did not at first understand what Taylor was doing there or why he had asked Kellogg to visit. "If you will wait an hour or so," Taylor explained, "I think you'll have the answer to the question." About twenty minutes later, he saw Mexican laborers in industrialized agriculture. "He had been familiar with the European immigrants in the urban slums and ghettoes in New York and the towns of the Pennsylvania steel industry," recalled Taylor. "But this was his first glimpse of rural Mexican labor."[18]

Slowly such experiences were leading Taylor into the kind of work that absorbed his attention and pointed him toward the use of photography as a fundamental tool of social science research. This did not abate when he resumed teaching duties at Berkeley in the fall of 1929. By then Taylor had approximately 450 negatives, which he planned to print and integrate into his scholarly studies. As he familiarized himself with the latest camera equipment, Taylor began to link text and images closely in his publications. He would use images in all thirteen monographs in his series Mexican Labor in the United States, ten published by the University of California Press, one by the University of North Carolina, and two remaining in manuscript form. Although Taylor did not fully realize it at the time, his efforts to document rural California visually, especially its changing demographics, were without parallel.[19]

Large urban newspapers in Los Angeles and San Francisco had been employing photographers and running news pictures of agricultural labor since the 1920s. But photographic journalism in the Central Valley and other farming districts lagged, with only the *Fresno Bee, Stockton Record,* and *Sacramento Bee* employing photographers at this time. Most photographers for rural newspapers were known as photo-correspondents or photo-reporters, not photojournalists. Their work was called photo-reportage. Their working methodology consisted of attempts to obtain one or two pictures in time for their news deadlines. Few ever dwelled at a scene beyond the time required to complete an assignment, and they had little say in what was selected for publication or how it was used, cropped, placed, or captioned. When a mob, led by the local police chief, attacked Filipinos near Exeter, in Tulare County, during the 1929 Kadota fig harvest, the *Exeter Sun* failed to dispatch a photographer to cover the violence, said to have occurred after the workers had brought white female "entertainers" to the camp; the newspaper also made no effort that day, October 26, to cover mob attempts to burn the barn where the men bunked. Three months later, when mobs chased Filipinos down the city streets of Watsonville and forced them to seek refuge in the City Council room, the *Watsonville Pajaronian* failed to visually document any aspect of the violence. It did, however, prominently quote the racist remarks that a Monterey County justice of the peace made about Filipino workers: "Little brown men attired like Solomon in all his glory, only a decade removed from the bolo and the breechcloth, were strutting like peacocks through the towns of the region to attract white and Mexican girls." Eleven days later no news photographer documented anti-Filipino riots that raged throughout Watsonville; nor did any record the aftermath of an attack on a labor camp that left Fermin Tobera dead from a shot through the heart and sixty other Filipino field hands wounded. On January 29 the following year, Stockton photographers did not document a Filipino clubhouse that had been blown up; nor were photographers on top of anti-Filipino violence that flared up in Salinas and San Jose. And when striking Mexican and Filipino lettuce harvesters were rounded up, beaten, and arrested en masse in the Imperial Valley, not one local photographer captured any aspect of the violence.[20]

Although Taylor was in no position to cover these events, he did make every effort to use photography in the cause of reason. This became apparent early in 1931, when Mexican repatriation programs were returning the first of over four hundred thousand Mexicans south of the border. As public opinion raged back and forth on the issue, Taylor accepted Paul Kellogg's invitation to shed light on the so-called Mexican Question by writing a comprehensive article on Mexican immigration. After assembling his notes, Taylor also printed dozens of his photographs, wrote an accompanying text, and, in March, shipped the package off to *Survey Graphic.* Integrating words and pictures in a dramatic and effective narrative that was at once moving and informative, the article, titled "Mexicans North of the Rio Grande," appeared in May. Six of Taylor's pictures were published, along with four by environmental photographer Ansel Adams.[21]

Ansel Adams is an odd name to associate with the beginning of socially motivated photography among California farmworkers. A child of privilege, he was born in San Francisco in February 1902 and grew up in a Craftsman bungalow in the Golden Gate headlands in an area that would soon become the exclusive Sea Cliff district. His parents were educated, progressive, belonged to the Sierra Club, and gave Ansel everything, including a Brownie camera, which he used to photograph the seashore and sand dunes of Baker Beach. By age fifteen he was an accomplished photographer, a fortunate young man, too young for service in World War I, healthy, enjoying a world of peace and beauty. He had fallen in love with Yosemite on his first trip there and maneuvered to return often and then remain there permanently from 1919 to 1927 as custodian of the LeConte Memorial. While hiking in Yosemite, he met the woman who would become his wife. He went everywhere in the valley, hauling a big 8-inch view camera and shooting everything with a yellow or red filter over the lens to darken the sky. By 1928 or 1929 he was beginning to perfect his concept of "previsualization," whereby the artist sees the picture he wants to create before he takes it. His stunning vistas and interpretations earned him large commissions, led him to abandon a career as a concert pianist, and brought him to the attention of important patrons. Among these patrons was Albert Bender, who bought a portfolio of his images and published them as *Parmelian Prints of the High Sierra,* Adams's first book.[22]

Oddly, it was the widened horizons of his success and the important art patrons that he met that conspired to bring Adams into the cotton fields near Fresno. Considerable confusion and speculation surround the exact sequence. Toward the end of his life, Adams himself simply could not remember the assignment, which was but one of many, and feared that the negatives had been destroyed in a 1937 darkroom fire. He gave Oakland Museum curator Therese Heyman a slightly different and inaccurate explanation for his sojourn to Fresno, stating that he had done the series for Paul Taylor and that the images had appeared in the *New Statesman.* But from fragmentary sources, this much is known: Sometime in 1930, Mrs. Charles Felton, scion of one of the leaders of San Francisco society and a leading art patron, telephoned Adams and commissioned him to photograph Mexican cotton pickers for the forthcoming *Survey Graphic* article. Traveling into the San Joaquin Valley during the October 1930 cotton harvest, Adams split his time between the fields and a labor camp near Fresno. To complete his assignment, he abandoned his large view camera in favor of a handheld Speed Graphic or Crown Graphic camera fitted with a film pack. Besides recording cotton picking, Adams made a number of portraits and surveyed the cotton camp where the Mexicans lived. He paid special attention to housing conditions and documented children at play, as well as everyday activities such as hanging out the wash. On returning to San Francisco, he delivered a portfolio to Mrs. Felton, who paid him for his work. After receiving the prints, Mrs. Felton forwarded them to Paul Kellogg.[23]

Although *Survey Graphic* published most of his images as contact prints, Adams enlarged, cropped, and straightened at least one image—a dramatic cover shot of cotton pickers dumping their sacks into a wagon. A second photograph of a cotton picker ran in large format inside and was followed by photographs of men bringing their sacks to the weigh master and older girls caring for younger children in a labor camp. As portraits, the photographs were beautiful, and Kellogg used them to carry the story. While Adams was no documentary photographer, he well captured the essence of his assignment and conveyed a good sense of the nature of cotton picking, camp life, and Mexican labor.

Placed together in sequence and accompanied by a sparse text to produce a picture story on a single subject, the photographs by Taylor and Adams anticipated the kind of layouts later popularized by W. Eugene Smith, Margaret Bourke-White, and Leonard McCombe in *Look* and *Life* magazines. Although by contemporary standards the images seem slightly static and posed, especially when compared with modern images emphasizing movement and freezing action, one must remember that these pictures were the first of their kind. Taken with cameras not well-suited to candid photography, they amounted to the first photo essay on California farmworkers, the logical outgrowth of the love that Ansel Adams had for his craft and Paul Taylor's reformist orientation, role as witness to history, and determination to develop a visual language capable of explaining contemporary issues to a general audience.[24]

Following this initial foray into the fields, Adams did not abandon farmworkers. Although he often expressed his discomfort with social documentary photography and explained that he was temperamentally incapable of devoting himself to contemporary social problems, Adams always had a strong sense of social purpose. He eventually linked his views with his love for the outdoors, but in pursuing that focus he included attention to farmworkers. Over the next forty years while completing many commercial assignments for wineries and large corporate farmers, Adams frequently photographed field hands, harvest hands, plowmen, and braceros. Taylor also continued his photographic work but, lacking good equipment and darkroom skills,

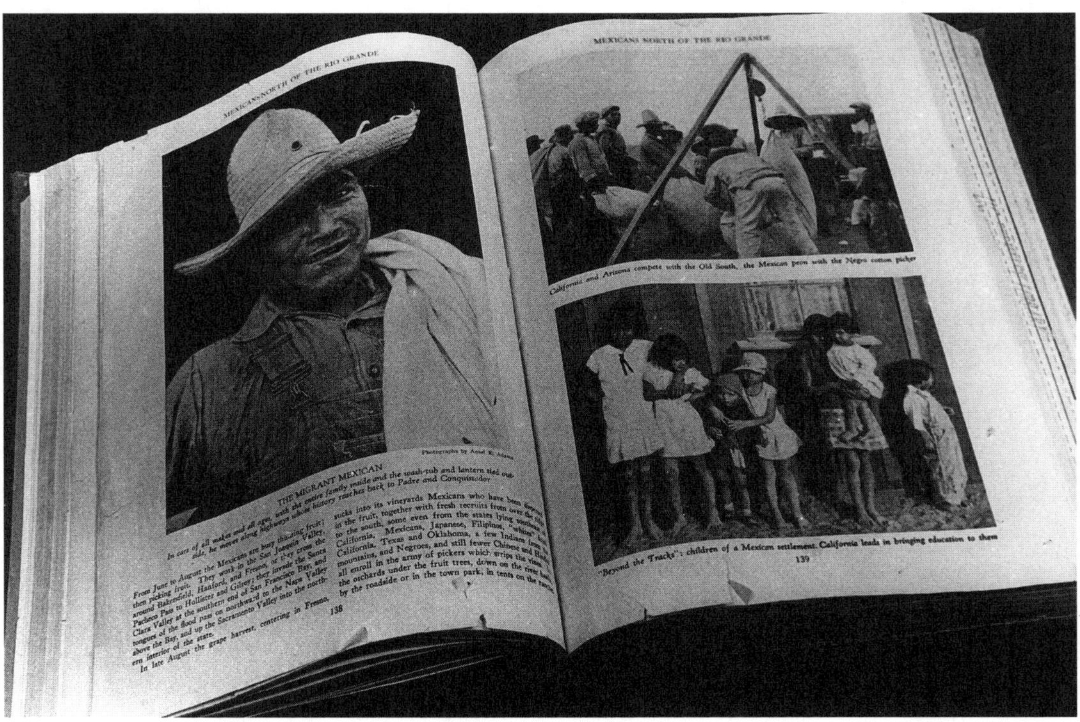

Layout of photographs by Ansel Adams illustrating Paul S. Taylor, "Mexicans North of the Rio Grande," *Survey Graphic* 19 (May 1931): 138–39. Photograph by Richard Steven Street.

never produced prints with the qualities that Adams found essential. Oddly, Taylor at this time did not know Adams. After Taylor finished working on "Mexicans North of the Rio Grande," four years passed before they met. But their collaboration had lasting effects. Verifying Taylor's thesis concerning the value of pictures in social science research, it stimulated more photographic work, which Taylor undertook during 1932 while studying in Mexico on a Guggenheim Fellowship.

When fellow historian Leslie Simpson showed Taylor a new Rolleiflex twin-lens camera, Taylor was amazed by the new equipment. In contrast to his old Kodak, which provided only a rough and approximate method for previsualizing the scene, the new Rolleiflex allowed Taylor to see exactly what he was going to photograph. Attracted to this more precise way of photographing, to the square film format (as opposed to the rectangular format of the Kodak), and to the waist-level method of operation (the Kodak was brought to eye level), Taylor immediately purchased a Rolleiflex, retiring his Kodak to backup status. With these tools, he hoped simply to "provide some kind of record of what [he] was about to see." But the decision, he later wrote, "transformed" his relationship to photography. "I took more pictures; and with the products found ways of persuading academic publishers to print some of my photographs along with my text."[25]

By the time Taylor returned from the field and resumed teaching duties at Berkeley late in 1932, he had compiled a comprehensive photographic record of immigration. But while hooked on photography as a medium for conveying his ideas, Taylor did not summarize his work in a single word or phrase. Nor did he refer to it as documentary photography or realize the pivotal role that he was playing in the medium. But a decade later, after Taylor's photography and that of his predecessors had been labeled documentary, he attempted to define the genre more fully in a statement that Ansel Adams used in his book *A Pageant of Photography.* Drawing on his early photographic experiences, Taylor described a type of photography that recorded the social scene, mirrored the present, and documented the human condition. He stressed that documentary photography

> records our customs at work, at war, at play . . . through twenty-four hours a day, the cycles of the seasons, or the span of a life. It portrays . . . institutions—family, church, government, political organizations, social clubs, labor unions. It . . . seeks to reveal the manner in which they function, absorb the life, hold the loyalty, and influence the behavior of human beings. It is concerned with the methods of work and the dependence of workmen on each other. . . . Documentary photography stands on its own merits and has validity by itself. A single photographic print may be "news," a "portrait," "art," or "documentary" and any of these, all of them, or none. . . . Among the tools of social science—graphs, statistics, maps, and text—documentation by photograph now is assuming [its] place.[26]

What Taylor later described as his "slow climb up the ladder towards an appreciation of photographs" did not end after he published his pioneering, multivolume series on

Mexican labor and returned to the university. Having familiarized himself with the latest camera equipment, Taylor broadened the focus of his work beyond Mexican labor and began photographing in the cities, among the unemployed, the down-and-outers, and the San Francisco longshoremen. He also practiced two other dimensions of what later became cornerstones of documentary photography: taking extensive notes on the situations he encountered, so that subsequently he could closely link text and images in his publications, and gathering massive amounts of on-site material ranging from fliers and newspaper clippings to posters and anything else that appeared pertinent. But Taylor did not confine his work merely to taking photographs, writing captions, and producing informed commentary. He also recognized the value of photographs as evidence and historical documents. This understanding could not have come at a more opportune moment.[27]

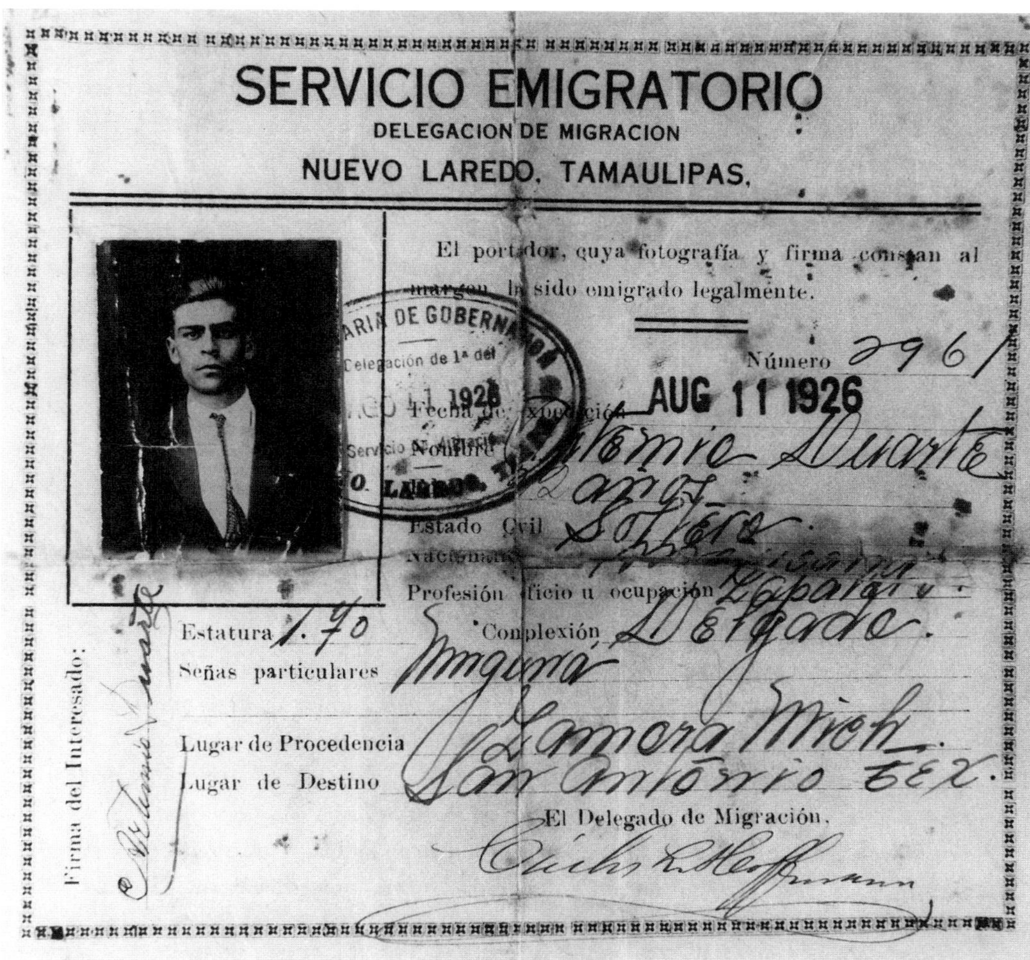
SERVICIO EMIGRATORIO

DELEGACION DE MIGRACION

NUEVO LAREDO, TAMAULIPAS.

El portador, cuya fotografía y firma constan al margen ha sido emigrado legalmente.

Número 2961

AUG 11 1926

Fecha de expedición

Nombre Artemio Duarte

Estado Civil Soltero

Nacionalidad Mexicana

Profesión oficio u ocupación Zapatero

Estatura 1.70 Complexión Delgado

Señas particulares Ninguna

Lugar de Procedencia Zamora Mich.

Lugar de Destino San Antonio TEX.

El Delegado de Migración.

Firma del Interesado:

Mexican government immigration document photograph for Artemio Cerada Duarte, August 11, 1926, photographer unknown. Courtesy of Security Pacific National Bank Photograph Collection, Los Angeles Public Library.

With Taylor devoting himself to his university duties and Adams concentrating on the natural landscape, two talented German émigré photographers, Otto Hagel and Hansel Mieth, stepped into the picture and began photographing farmworkers with remarkable power and insight. An avid reader of Jack London's novels and stories of high adventure, Otto Fritz Hagel was born in 1909 into a working-class family in Oppelsbohm, Germany, a small provincial village near Stuttgart. Nearly six feet tall, with blue–gray eyes and fair skin, he was interested in music but had to make do sweeping floors in a piano factory. After spending a year in his father's construction business, during which time he lost the end of his left thumb in an accident, Otto left school at fourteen to be apprenticed to a watchmaker in Stuttgart. A year later, he met Johanna Mieth, a stocky blonde girl from the neighboring town of Fellbach. She had already noticed Otto. "Many times," she recalled in her autobiography, "I saw Otto sitting on a rooftop putting shingles down with one hand and holding a book in the other. His father would shout up at him, 'get back to work, you lazy bastard!'" Otto later affectionately renamed her Hansel, and except for those times when they were on solo assignments, when Otto preceded her in immigrating to the United States, and during a brief separation in the early 1930s, they would remain inseparable for the rest of their lives.[28]

As the eldest of three daughters of outgoing working-class parents who ran a general store and rented out rooms to make ends meet, Mieth had recently been forced to leave school for lack of funds and helped to support her family with income earned in a dressmaking shop. Dreamers and idealists, she and Otto did not fit into small-town German life. When Mieth turned fifteen, the two left Germany one cold, wintry Sunday in 1926 "to find truth in life," as Mieth put it. Like other restless, rambling Europeans (among them Endre Friedmann, aka Robert Capa), Otto and Hansel flirted with the gypsy life as social refugees in such cities as Paris and Budapest. Over the next two years they bicycled through Austria, Bulgaria, France, Hungary, Italy, Spain, Turkey, and Yugoslavia. As they traveled, both shot photographs and wrote and sold small articles to newspapers. Often living on the road with groups of teenagers, they spent the spring of 1928 living under a bridge that crossed the Danube River in Vienna. Mieth later recalled:

> There was this bunch of us kids with musical instruments. I played a little guitar, and Otto played a violin. . . . We played our instruments on the street and in front of restaurants and apartment houses, and [*sic*] would give us money. We scraped by that way, and by taking pictures and selling them and writing articles for local newspapers when we passed through. For about six weeks we lived in a Cistercian monastery in Yugoslavia. I dressed in short leather pants so that I could pass as a boy and we could stay there.[29]

When they returned home from their adventure, Hagel and Mieth found themselves ostracized, regarded with great suspicion and hostility, and labeled as people infected with foreign ideas. Already possessing a far richer adolescence than most, the two had chosen an unconventional and exhilarating life and distanced themselves from their families. Wandering through Europe and exploring whatever crossed their paths, they had experienced many adventures, seen many things, inverted the passive behavior of other German citizens, and probed the world around them as they saw it, not as others told them about it. Their interest in photography corresponded to a heightened awareness of the medium and its potential, not only in Germany, but throughout Europe. Their cameras had become instruments of freedom and provided them with a new photographic language. Mieth's experiences in dressing as a boy had given her an opportunity that the opposite sex took for granted. She wondered how to expand the freedom she had found, refusing to give it up.[30]

Although Hagel and Mieth did not then realize what was happening, the same thoughts were occurring to an entire generation of photographers struggling to find their place in Weimar Germany. On the surface, German photographers captured a world of calm and elegant beauty. But beneath the facade, all was not well. Following the end of World War I, Germany had attempted to find its way through a succession of governments that left the population suffering through incessant spells of mass unemployment. Reacting against an aristocratic mentality that seemed both unable and unwilling to shed its commitment to regaining lost empire, politically oriented and socially engaged photographers tried to go beyond the charming surface conformity and nonjudgmental images they were seeing. Both individually and collectively, they launched a number of efforts addressing the world around them. One group of left-leaning photographers formed a collective dedicated to combatting what they labeled bourgeois picture lies. Calling themselves worker photographers, they focused on the injustices of society and the lives of common workers. By composing extensive captions, these photographers amplified the power of individual photographs and posed crucial questions that pointed to conditions demanding change. But many went further. Through photo-sequences or photo-reports, they clumped groups of images together to project a larger picture that might contribute to social revolutionary goals.[31]

Berlin was a hotbed of experimentation. Transylvania surrealists, French expressionists, Jewish cubists, Hungarian social documentarians, Polish sentimentalists, Belgian landscape photographers, Russian constructivists, Dutch cabaret dancers, communist revolutionaries, and avante-garde weirdos of every stripe all shared the same tables and cheap lodgings while using inexpensive cameras to learn their craft and photograph for themselves and for dozens of newspapers, magazines, book publishers, and independent photo services. New ideas proliferated. There was a vast expansion in visual media, including art magazines and dozens of weekly illustrated picture magazines such as *Berliner Illustrirte Zeitung, Münchner Illustrierte Presse, Schweitzer Illustrierte,* and, perhaps most important, *Arbeiter Illustrierte Zeitung* (Workers Illustrated News). At the center of the action, the *Deutsche Hochschule für Politik,* a liberal school founded in 1920 to provide practical political training to postwar Germans, offered darkrooms and inexpensive evening photography classes taught by a first-rate faculty.

All of this attracted a stampede of aspiring photographers. While less explicitly political than the worker photographers, talented photographic reporters, including the impressive Felix Mann, Harold Lechenperg, Walter Bosshard, and Kurt Hübschmann, created a charged sense of excitement with their coverage of the oddities of daily life and people of all kinds, from potato harvesters to avante-garde entertainers, from factories to the beauty of Luna Park. At the same time modernists like Germaine Krull were experimenting with sexuality and exploring the dark underworld at the center of Berlin, neo-Dadaists like Simon Guttman were bringing the very best and most versatile photographers into Dephot (German Photo Service), and photographic reporters like Dr. Erich Salomon (a German lawyer-turned-businessman-turned-photographer who would die in a Nazi concentration camp) were dressing in formal clothes to infiltrate diplomatic parties and insinuate themselves into privileged situations in order to make artless but surprising records of Europe's power elite. Similar trends were under way in Hungary, where a half dozen bright "Szociofoto" (Sociophoto) photographers affiliated with the socialist magazine *Munka* (Work) were focusing their cameras on dehumanizing aspects of industrial labor, impoverished farmers, and inadequate housing.[32]

While it was all very heady stuff and very exciting to those who were there, neither Hagel nor Mieth seemed to be more than vaguely aware of these developments. If their curiosity and questioning nature seemed to parallel that of the emerging German left, and if their attraction to photography mirrored what was happening across the country, their provincial existence impeded contact with worker photographers, and their years of wandering kept them geographically separated from Berlin, Munich, and other centers of visual excitement. Hagel and Mieth did share the same unease with life in Germany that bothered other photographers. And like their counterparts in Berlin, they increasingly thought about seeking greater employment and artistic opportunities elsewhere. Eventually an entire generation of German photographers would join photographers from France, Hungary, and Austria in leaving Europe for the United States, where they exerted a profound impact on their medium and profession. Some would leave shortly after the American stock market crashed and Europe began to slide into depression. Most would wait until Hitler began consolidating power. Many of those who remained paid the ultimate price. As street fights broke out between socialists and proto-Nazis, the young lovers saw the dangers of staying in Germany and decided to flee.[33]

Otto was the first to go. Seeing no future in his hometown or Germany in general and disgusted with the bourgeoisie, which seemed to be working his parents to death, Otto headed to the United States. Details about his journey are cloudy and confused by Mieth's foggy and sometimes deliberately skewed recollections. While Mieth always maintained that Hagel had no relatives or friends to contact in the United States, FBI documents reveal that an uncle who was a member of the police department in Brooklyn, New York, provided an early destination and safe haven. According to most accounts, Otto made his way across the Atlantic Ocean as a deckhand on a German freighter or a roustabout on a banana boat, although some evidence suggests that he may have crossed as a sailor in the German navy. He jumped ship in Baltimore either in November 1928 or January 1929. With twenty-five cents in his pocket, he headed for New York and found work at eighteen dollars a week in a packing room. Learning that he could earn double that as a window washer, he changed jobs, then nearly died when one of the safety hooks on his belt broke, leaving him dangling hundreds of feet above the ground before someone opened a window and pulled him inside. When it was discovered that his employer had been bribing building inspectors not to report safety violations, Otto received a large settlement and headed west. Traveling across country by foot and by stealing rides on freight trains, he reached San Francisco early that summer and again took a job as a window washer and maintenance man for A. Crosetti Brothers and Company. Taking a picture of himself cleaning a window in the Pacific Gas and Electric Building, he sold it to the *New York Times Magazine* for ten dollars, his first photograph published in the United States.[34]

After Otto settled in, he sent a telegram to Hansel asking her to follow on a ship, then take a Greyhound bus across the country. Details about her journey are as skimpy as those about Otto's. Hansel did not really want to go to the United States. She wanted to live in Yugoslavia. But she had been stuck in a garment factory working twelve-hour days and was glad to join Otto. She left for New York City onboard the *Albert Ballin* on December 11 and arrived on December 21, 1930. Her aunt's daughter met her at the docks. Many years later, Hansel told a story about getting into a fight with the young woman. When she left to call her mother, Hansel grabbed a taxi. She could not speak English, so she took out an address book of Esperanto-speaking people in New York. Addressing the driver in Esperanto, she gave him an address in Brooklyn. It was 2 A.M. when she arrived and rang the doorbell. A women stuck her head out and wanted to know who she was. "Oh, you want my son," she said. He came running down, soon followed by another ten people. They welcomed Hansel, paid the taxi driver, and partied all night. Hansel stayed a week and had a great time. Finally she went to Philadelphia and saw her aunt, who was in a cast. She had stood on a chair while putting up a Welcome sign and fallen and broken her hip. "She didn't like me very much," Hansel recalled.[35]

After a few days in Philadelphia, Hansel sold a boat ticket she had purchased for passage through the Panama Canal to San Francisco, perhaps intending to travel by Greyhound bus after all, but on the way back to her aunt's she bought a second-hand, yellow Maxwell automobile for fifty dollars. Without ever having driven an automobile before and speaking little English, she set off for California, reaching it after a freezing, eighteen-day, cross-country drive in the dead of winter. (It's unknown whether she returned to her aunt's before leaving.) Along the way the car top flew off and the windshield collapsed, but people took pity on her and donated food, coats, and scarves. When she finally arrived in San Francisco, the Maxwell died. "Otto couldn't understand how that sardine can had made it across the country," Hansel recalled to fellow photographer John Loengard.[36]

Of her arrival in California "looking like a mummy," Hansel later told photo historian Sally Stein that her new home was a photographer's paradise, with a wide and varied canvas and much more freedom to travel and photograph than she had known before coming to America. "It was a relief from the stultification of Europe.

We, ourselves felt: here you are free, you might die of hunger, but you are free to let yourself go—to reach out, to experiment, to mix with people, to learn." Like other European photographers, Otto and Hansel brought with them a good measure of daring and chutzpah born of fear and a desperate desire to succeed. Hansel's chutzpah on arrival in San Francisco nearly jeopardized her reunion with Otto. Wandering over to a political meeting just as it was being raided by the police, she was promptly arrested. Otto bailed her out, and the two put all of their possessions into Otto's red Ford and left to prospect for gold, but after several months returned to San Francisco seeking work. Hansel immediately went to work for six dollars a week doing piecework sewing. When she learned that the woman next to her received twelve dollars, she asked her boss for a raise. When he said no, Hansel quit. Over the next six months, she lived with Otto while he worked on the Wawona Tunnel in Yosemite National Park. Leaving their tent, they would drive into Fresno on Sunday mornings to buy supplies. "We bought a few rolls of film and as soon as Otto got a little money—we also worked in the fields then—we payed *[sic]* down on a movie camera," Hansel later recalled. "And that's how we really started out."[37]

After the Wawona job, Otto and Hansel went on the road as migrant farmworkers, photographing along the way in what amounted to an early version of the participant–observer approach to reporting. There was plenty to see. California agriculture by this time had become highly industrialized. Although irrigated, intensively cultivated fruit and vegetable farms were not the large-scale operations often described by polemicists, they were, nevertheless, extremely concentrated, with one-tenth of all farms producing over half of the crops and small farmers accounting for only about 6 percent. Regardless of farm size, however, harvest operations could not be mechanized. As long as they kept their car running and kept moving, Otto and Hansel could expect to find work for at least half of the year. Seldom receiving more than fifteen cents an hour, neither ever earned more than $450 a year, or about half of what state relief officials calculated as the minimum living wages. But by pooling their wages and wintering on the cheap in San Francisco with friends, Otto and Hansel were able to make ends meet, if just barely.[38]

While moving with the crops, Hansel again escaped the confines of her gender by disguising herself as a boy. She passed as Otto's younger brother until she became pregnant and began to show in late 1931. Sometime during their wanderings they spent some time in north Sacramento. Working at house painting and cleaning there, they daily passed by a huge refuse dump, where the city's poor picked through the garbage. One day they encountered two young boys, knee deep in the raked-over dump. The two boys had rescued an apple or onion from the pile, and Otto and Hansel photographed them displaying their unappetizing find. Over a period of several weeks, they returned to the dump and photographed its residents struggling to survive. Printed on cheap paper, many of their early prints of the Indian residents of the dump came out pink, so Otto and Hansel always referred to them as "pink Indians." What little extra money they had during this time enabled them to continue their photography, paying for gasoline, film, chemicals, and photographic paper.[39]

Hansel gave birth to a baby girl early in 1932, somewhere on a sand dune in the Imperial Valley. Named Maria, after Hansel's deceased little sister, the child grew up a migrant. While busy with their infant, Otto and Hansel did not take any photographs. Newspaper photographers, failing to rise to the challenge of recording farm labor problems, remained as distant from them as ever. Ignoring pea pickers who went on strike near Half Moon Bay in May 1932 and cherry pickers who struck near Mountain View in June, press photographers failed to cover any farm labor strike until November, when four hundred orchard pruners, under the leadership of the newly organized Cannery and Agricultural Workers Industrial Union, struck against Vacaville fruit growers. Dispatched to cover the action, one *Sacramento Bee* photographer missed the masked mob that broke into the Vacaville jail, hauled out strike leaders, drove them into the countryside, flogged them, shaved their heads, and poured red enamel paint over the strikers. But he did manage to produce several pictures of club-wielding growers gathered to celebrate the mob action.[40]

Aware of the void in photographic coverage, Otto and Hansel resumed their photography early in 1933. "Otto said we must record the situation now—all the people who have no homes, who have no roof over themselves, who have dishes and who have nothing to cook, and who are on the road," Hansel explained to photographer Ken Light fifty years later. Developing and printing proved especially difficult for them. Periodically returning to San Francisco, they stayed with friends and improvised their darkrooms in closets and bathrooms. Of their migratory existence, Hansel later recalled, "We were living the same as the people we photographed. We lived out of our car. We kept all our grub in the rumble seat and cooked on a stove made out of a five gallon tin can. When we stopped, we could set up camp and have a meal going in no time at all." What especially affected Hansel was the feeling of togetherness and comradeship born of evenings sitting around a campfire. One incident in particular stayed with Hansel for the rest of her life. She recalled, "There was the family in their tent next to ours. The father was in jail for stealing a used tire. It was between seasons, we were camped in the desert. The desert was hot, oppressively hot. Children played in the dust with a sickly puppy. Moans came from the inside of the tent. 'Mommy's going to have a baby,' one life-wise toddler explained. We helped as best we could and later there was gladness over the birth of one more man."[41]

While traveling through the countryside, Otto and Hansel struggled to define what they were doing. Hansel would later assert that she and Otto did not fit any political category, never joined anything because they were so undisciplined, but did regard themselves as "spiritual cousins of Lewis Hine." Basically, they were just idealistic liberals exploring the class distinctions and injustices around them. However, among photographers then active in California, Otto and Hansel were generally considered to be the most left leaning and technically proficient. Fluent in the latest professional trends, both were artists who aspired to take aesthetically excellent images; however, above all they were concerned with content. Engaged in a socially oriented form of self-expression, they valued the most trivial, common, and flawed photograph if it accomplished its purpose. Hoping that their photographs would advance understanding of the human condition, they intended to point out inequities and support political reforms that would shrink the gap between the classes. Their images reflect a sense of trust, human decency, and at the same time a deep hatred for the inequitable circumstances they encountered and the people who profited from those circumstances. Although such an approach sounds tame enough by modern standards, at the time it represented a dramatic, if not a radical, departure from others photographing in the fields.[42]

Like Paul Taylor, they had no terminology to summarize what they were doing. But they were thoroughly modern in their thinking and completely engaged. What mattered to them was the humanistic dimension of their work. Identifying with their subjects in an "overwhelmingly emotional way," they were also practicing social documentary photography at least five years before the term became part of the photographic lexicon. Social documentary as it would be practiced focused on the underclass, the disenfranchised, the poor, the helpless, the exploited, and the "common man" in need of sympathy and understanding. To Hansel, this was nothing more than simply doing what seemed right. But it was really much more. Hansel was after the truth. She valued honest and straightforward photographs. She claimed to photograph free from manipulation. In fact, her straight photographs were very complex, ideologically based, and designed to arouse an emotional and intellectual response. She later explained: "We wanted somehow to contribute to an understanding of the inequities of the world, we wanted somehow to help to bring about a change in the world through our photographs, through our reporting. . . . In a vaguely sentimental and never analyzed fashion we knew that we wanted to bring about a better understanding through the showing of the reality of human existence, and by reality we meant the contrast and the chasm between rich and poor. Our sympathy was always on the side of the poor, of the working class, and we never abandoned that sympathy."[43]

6

Photography and the Great Depression

A New Way of Seeing

A few months after they resumed photographing, Otto Hagel and Hansel Mieth discovered that their large cameras impeded their work. Both their Speed Graphic and Graflex cameras, then considered state-of-the-art equipment, were about the size of a breadbox and held bulky sheet-film magazines. After Hansel's 4 × 5–inch view camera was stolen, they began looking at a whole range of equipment. A big change came quite unexpectedly. Otto found a broken Rolleiflex camera while cleaning someone's attic. Introduced in 1928, the Rolleiflex was the first of the modern twin-lens, reflex cameras. Highly portable, the Rolleiflex used roll film that allowed a photographer to make twenty-four pictures, each measuring 2¼ × 2¼ inches. By looking down into a retractable hood, the photographer composed images as they appeared through the upper camera lens on a ground-glass focusing screen. Tripping the shutter recorded an image that was captured through the lower lens, making the whole process much easier, faster, and cheaper than earlier camera technologies.[1]

After his employer gave the Rolleiflex to him, Otto disassembled and repaired it. Hansel used that Rolleiflex exclusively during the first year they resumed their photography, and Otto continued to shoot with an old Ermanox compact camera brought over from Germany. About the size of a modern 35-millimeter camera, the Ermanox was perfect for making candid shots in poor lighting conditions. But it had its limits. Using only 2 × 3–inch glass plates, the Ermanox required Otto to insert an individual plate for every picture. It was also difficult to focus accurately. But its fast f/2 lens allowed Otto to work without special lighting, make candid shots of daily events, and engage in extended pictorial storytelling until the fall of 1932, when he left the camera on the running board of a car and lost it and all his glass plates along a highway in Southern California.[2]

Early in the following winter, Otto headed to San Francisco in search of a camera and purchased a used Leica from a Chinese boy for ninety dollars. Originally developed as a way to make light-exposure tests for film footage, the Leica had been invented in 1911 by Oscar Barnack, an expert technician in the E. Leitz microscope factory in Wetzlar, Germany. World War I had interrupted work on the camera, but in 1924 Barnack resumed his experiments, and in 1925 the Leitz factory began producing the camera in large quantities. By 1932 the Leica had been fully refined. Even more compact than the Rolleiflex, the Leica was a masterpiece of design and organization that could be held firmly against the eye, thus allowing the photographer to compose a scene through a built-in range finder that produced a greater registration between human vision and camera sight. Rather than using glass plates or large pieces of sheet film, it recorded pictures on 35-millimeter roll film that yielded thirty-six exposures in a rectangular format. With its rapid film-advance lever, film could be advanced almost instantaneously with the flick of a thumb, allowing a photographer to make exposures in rapid succession. Once familiar with its operation, a photographer could find, focus, and determine distance automatically. No longer bound by the single-picture technique of the standard news photographer with the larger, less portable camera, the Leica user could move quickly and make multiple exposures, thereby extending the range of work and the odds for taking a successful picture. European photographers quickly adopted it as their primary camera, and it quickly made its way to San Francisco, where Peter Stackpole began using a Leica with an f/3.5 lens to cover news events for Bay Area newspapers in 1932.[3]

Although Hansel continued to work with her Rolleiflex, Otto quickly switched over to the Leica. Besides speed of operation and the ability to capture sequential action by advancing film instantly with the flick of a thumb, Otto loved the way his Leica allowed him to cut his photographic expenses considerably. Too poor to afford preloaded, individual 35-millimeter film magazines, Otto bought one hundred feet of film, or whatever length he could find on the cheap, and rolled it into individual film cartridges inside a changing bag.

Using their Leica and Rolleiflex cameras and more light-sensitive films, Otto and Hansel became the first photographers to systematically exploit new, miniaturized cameras while documenting life and labor in the fields. This freed them from static approaches and safe situations and allowed them to take pictures almost everywhere. Slowly and without really understanding what they were doing, Otto and Hansel began to incorporate into the photographic coverage of California farmworkers a new aesthetic that emphasized flexibility, control, and spontaneity in the service of social criticism, made possible now with the smaller, more manageable cameras.[4]

Most of the time, labor contractors and foremen did not object to being photographed. "Picture taking was like seeing," recalled Hansel Mieth. "You take a picture, you are hungry, you are thirsty, you eat, and you think, it was such a part of us that we didn't think." On those occasions when they attempted to photograph surreptitiously, Otto and Hansel found that their pictures were weak. But photographing openly sometimes had painful consequences. "Quite a few times we had to leave without getting paid," Hansel later recalled. "We knew we were about to get beaten up. Very often it happened with a vehicle, usually a truck making a swerve, cutting a corner short, knocking you down, forcing you to jump out of the way. That happened many times." There were worse encounters. "Pretty soon an overseer saw you and came up and said 'get the hell out of here,'" Hansel told filmmaker Nancy Schiesari, with perhaps some exaggeration. "If you didn't go, he went for the whip. They were swinging that thing around and every so often you got something in your ear. And sometimes I would get it on my fingers. A very sharp pain where they hit you. They were beasts." But Otto and Hansel persisted. "It was understood what we were doing and that we were trying to show with our photographs how bad the times were and that they shouldn't get any worse," Hansel later stressed. "If the times ever got better, the photos would be a warning that at any time it could get bad again, and so we should stick together."[5]

Following prevalent style, Otto and Hansel often photographed early in the morning, when field hands arrived at first light. But life on the move severely restricted their audience. "I remember that we had a whole series on picking fruit in which we showed living conditions in the camps, and many times we had the negatives but we had no ways and means of printing them because we lived in a tent," Hansel told an interviewer forty years later. "We had no place where we could do the printing, because you needed running water—or at least some clean water and most of the time we camped either near a cemetery, where they had water, or in some kind of slough near the dump." But for all their dedication and innovations, Otto and Hansel never had a specific market in mind for their images. Had they known anyone in the newspaper industry or magazine business, they might have sold their photographs. "We didn't know what to do with the photographs we took," Mieth explained to Ken Light. "I said there might come a time when they would be useful. At the time we took them there was really no use for them."[6]

A new group of photographers joined Otto and Hansel in 1933, drawn into the countryside to cover some thirty-seven different farmworker strikes involving 47,575 farmworkers—still the most violent and dramatic year in the history of farm labor organizing. Slow as ever to cover the conflicts, newspaper photographers from San Francisco and Los Angeles at first focused their cameras on growers and law enforcement efforts suppressing the orchard pruners around Vacaville, who were still on strike in January. Not until a few weeks later, when six thousand Mexican berry pickers went on strike in El Monte, a small farm town on the banks of the San Gabriel River where natural springs made farming easy, did some local activists affiliated with the Film and Photo League attempt to cover the action.[7]

Photographers for the Film and Photo League beat press photographers to the scene of the conflict because they were highly motivated individuals. With deep roots in the Depression and in radical politics of the era, Film and Photo League photographers were in the forefront of the emerging documentary impulse. They belonged to a New York–based organization that had been founded in 1930 as a cultural appendage of the Workers' International Relief (WIR), headquartered in Berlin, a kind of leftist Red Cross that assisted strikers and labor organizers, especially those caught in legal cases. Creating branches called Workers' Camera Leagues throughout Europe and the United States, WIR sponsored a New York City branch that aimed at producing documentary films on the class struggle and still pictures for such publications as *New Masses* and the Communist Party newspaper *Daily Worker.* Committed to social change, Photo League members tended to come from the school of hard knocks. Many if not all had life stories as tough and demanding as the people they documented. As people who lived in walkups where the coal was not ignited until late afternoon and breakfast might be a roll dipped in a cup of coffee, they were inspired by the example of Lewis Hine and were absolutely uninterested in the technical matters that concerned Ansel Adams. Although hardly a monolithic group, Film and Photo League members agreed that Hollywood was to be scorned and vowed to "struggle against and expose reactionary film; to produce documentary films reflecting the lives and struggles of the American worker; to spread and popularize the great artistic and revolutionary Soviet productions."[8]

Soon after the berry strike began, one of the most active Film and Photo League members in East Los Angeles began filming the strike and followed events well into July. Director–producer Louis Siminow captured little of the drama. His unconvincing, if not embarrassing, docudrama features heavy-handed direction, including not very believable reenactments of workers leaving the fields. Opening with an affluent lady driving to a fruit stand and asking for some nice berries, his film cuts to lovely shots of berries in a bowl on a table followed by not so lovely scenes of workers stooped over picking in the fields. A dramatized sequence then contrasts a farmer drinking a cool glass of water and relaxing with a cigar as a field hand attempts to drink from a muddy ditch and then walks out of the fields to protest his low pay and abominable working conditions. In the next scene, a Mexican berry picker cuts a small piece of bread into four parts to feed his family, commenting, "We raise food and we starve." Meeting a woman organizer for the Cannery and Agricultural Workers Industrial Union (CAWIU), the field hand joins a strike, and the grower is seen exclaiming, "What! They can't strike. How can starving people afford to strike?" Negotiations break down, and at the end of the film, the staged scenes give way to actual documentary footage taken in a union hall and outside a Mexican bar. The film then follows pickets into the fields, where they are confronted by deputies. Titled *Berry Pickers,* the film ends with workers returning to the saloon and voting to continue the strike. For all its faults and resemblance to earlier labor–capital melodramas, such as *The Passaic Textile Strike,* of 1926, the film is notable as the first such filmmaking venture among farmworkers in California.[9]

Several months later, a larger strike erupted in the table-grape vineyards between Lodi and Fresno. From mid-September until the end of the month, strikers clashed with replacement workers and sheriff's deputies on a daily basis. Then on October 4, these clashes became deadly. Vineyard foreman Matt Beroni (in some accounts Beronio) was shot and killed by John Glouck when Beroni stepped onto the porch of his cabin. Blaming the murder on strikers, several hundred vigilantes threw up an armed cordon around the town, closed restaurants frequented by strikers, and launched a manhunt for Glouck. In a scene that librarian of California Kevin Starr describes as "straight from Eastern Europe under the Nazis," a lynch-mad mob herded all itinerants, strangers, and suspects into the town plaza, loaded them onto trucks, and sent them on their way.[10]

Photographers from the *Stockton Record, Oakland Tribune, Sacramento Bee,* and National Enterprise Association (NEA)—a Scripps Howard newspaper subsidiary—broke with old patterns and followed the action for several weeks. Now acting as eyewitnesses, they found themselves engaged in the kind of industrial-strength photography that is the essence of modern photojournalism. Taking the lead in this paradigm shift was a *Stockton Record* photographer whose byline never appeared in his newspaper. After first recording scenes of officers examining the porch where Beroni was shot, the photographer moved on to cover deputized citizens stopping and searching cars on the highway near Lodi. His last images record vigilantes rounding up strikers and searching them for weapons. One of his more remarkable images captures strike leaders Orrin Powell and Ray Gogan surrounded by a crowd. Another focuses on deputized vigilantes being placed under the command of Colonel Walter Garrison

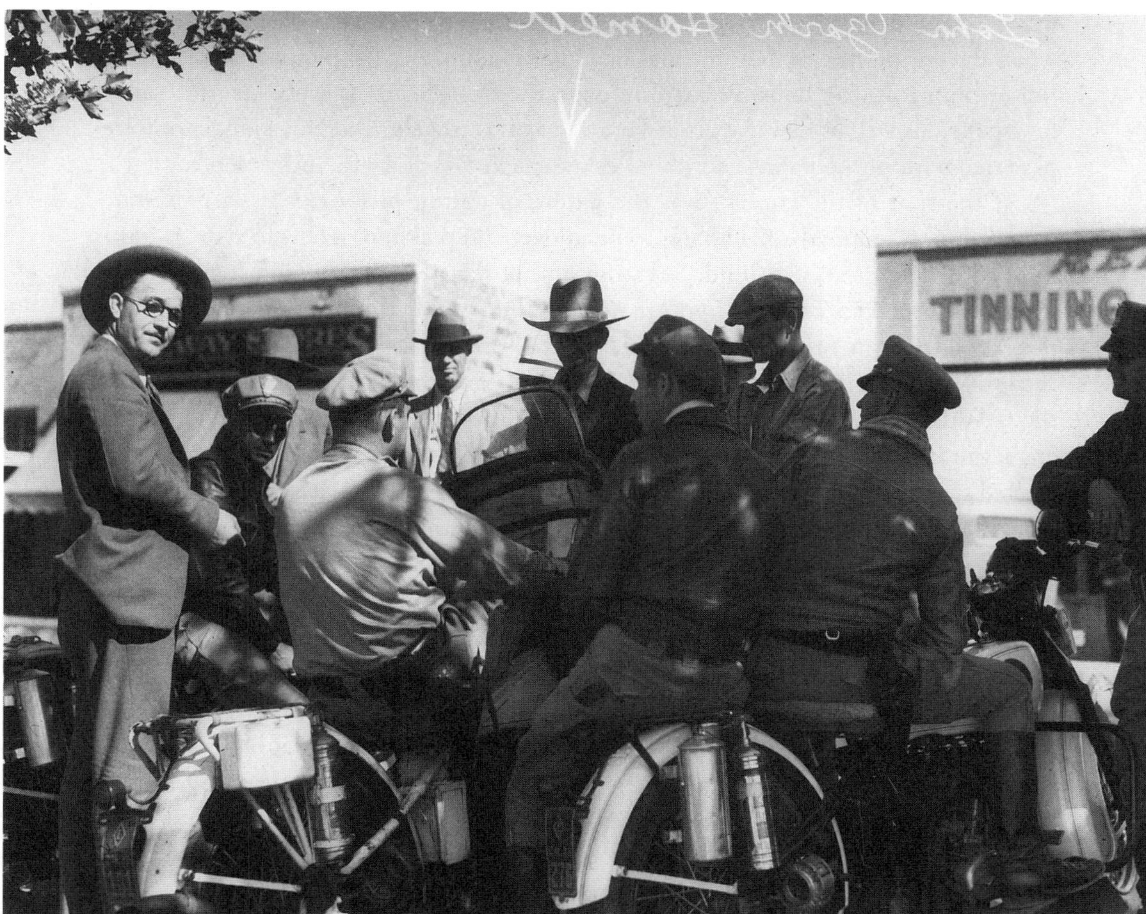

Deputy John "Ozark" Hamett and San Joaquin County deputy sheriffs at the strike of grape pickers at Lodi, October 25, 1933, photographer unknown. Courtesy of *San Francisco Examiner.*

and Garrison's two daughters, Bobbie and June, each armed with a rifle, "prepared for any emergency." His most important images present a kind of before-and-after series. Taken five minutes apart, the first one focuses on a crowd of two thousand strikers assembled in downtown Lodi, and his last picture records the same men walking down the railroad tracks about to board an outbound freight train after vigilantes had driven them off. Also focusing on the aftermath, an *Oakland Tribune* photographer produced a sequence of images. Arranged in a large block, sequencing from left to right and top to bottom, the layout unfolded key developments in the conflict.[11]

No such sequence of images had ever before appeared in the pages of a California newspaper. For the first time, reportage took on aspects of the photo essay. These essays seemed to originate spontaneously in the minds of rural news editors confronting an event the likes of which they had never seen before. Peaking toward the end of the month, this coverage then petered out into individual images. When the grape harvest ended and Mexican farmworkers throughout the Central Valley paused for a day-long fiesta in honor of Mexican independence, editors and photographers covered the celebrations with the usual single image of happy and contented farmworkers. Meanwhile, when the cotton harvest began, rural newspapers ran the usual pictures of vast fields full of plump cotton bolls. But within days, the front pages of every Central Valley newspaper, as well as newspapers as far away as Los Angeles and San Francisco, were plastered with photographs and photo essays packed with death and violence.

At the root of the conflict was the nature of cotton picking. Classic piece-rate stoop labor, it required a field hand to bend over and pick into a ten- to sixteen-foot-long bag, which trailed behind. Sweating on hot days and freezing on foggy mornings, cotton pickers earned $1.60 for stuffing four hundred pounds of Acala cotton into these bags in 1933, down from $1 per hundred pounds in 1926. Fed up with the low pay, crews began walking out of the fields on October 4 under the banner of the CAWIU. One day later, twelve thousand field hands were on strike. After growers began evicting strikers from their labor camps, pickers took over vacant lots and erected strike camps. The largest of these camps, dubbed Little Mexico City, held about three thousand strikers and sprawled across four acres of land around Tulare Lake, near Corcoran. With a community kitchen, improvised schools, sentries, and a nine-member strike committee presiding over affairs, the camp even featured a Mexican circus, Circo Azteca, which entertained camp residents for several days.[12]

Complicating matters was the multiethnic nature of the strike. Mexicans had dominated cotton picking for a decade, but now a new component was added to the work force. The one–two blow of economic and natural disaster that had struck the Great Plains during the previous three years had depressed farm prices and caused massive foreclosures at the same time that a dry weather cycle created swirling dust storms that transformed parts of Oklahoma, Arkansas, Texas, Kansas, Colorado, and New Mexico into a dust bowl. Tens of thousands of small farmers gave up and fled in overloaded jalopies. Dubbed Okies and Arkies, they headed to California, hoping to reestablish their roots as small farmers. To make ends meet, they became migrant workers and began squatting in improvised shantytowns and camps referred to as

Little Oklahomas, where a new Okie subculture stressing fundamentalist Protestant values took root. By the fall of 1933, thousands of Okies were working in the cotton fields and often experiencing discrimination, typified by a sign in a San Joaquin Valley movie theater that read "Negroes and Okies upstairs." While lacking the traditions of protest, solidarity, and mutual aid that sustained the Mexican communities, Dust Bowl migrants became a significant part of the fledgling union movement and played important roles in leading the cotton strike.[13]

At first these developments drew little photographic coverage. But when strike leaders were arrested by the hundreds on vagrancy charges and sheriff's deputies began seizing truckloads of food bound for the strike camps, tensions rose, and dozens of still and motion picture photographers from all over California and as far away as New York descended on the cotton district. Many worked under conditions resembling combat. On October 9 headlines in the *Los Angeles Times* screamed, "Strike War Flares Up; Cotton Growers Oust Agitators; California Roads Patrolled to Block Picketing in Four Counties; Workers Driven off Farms and Vigilantes Urged to Keep Them on the Run." That day, some photographers were close enough to the action to be in the line of fire. But they got the pictures.

Among the most important photographs from the strike was one of a murdered farmworker. Taken on October 10 by NEA photographer Fred Smith twenty miles east of Corcoran in the Tulare County town of Pixley, the horrible image shows a striker, Dolores Hernández, attempting to prop himself up while lying in a pool of blood on

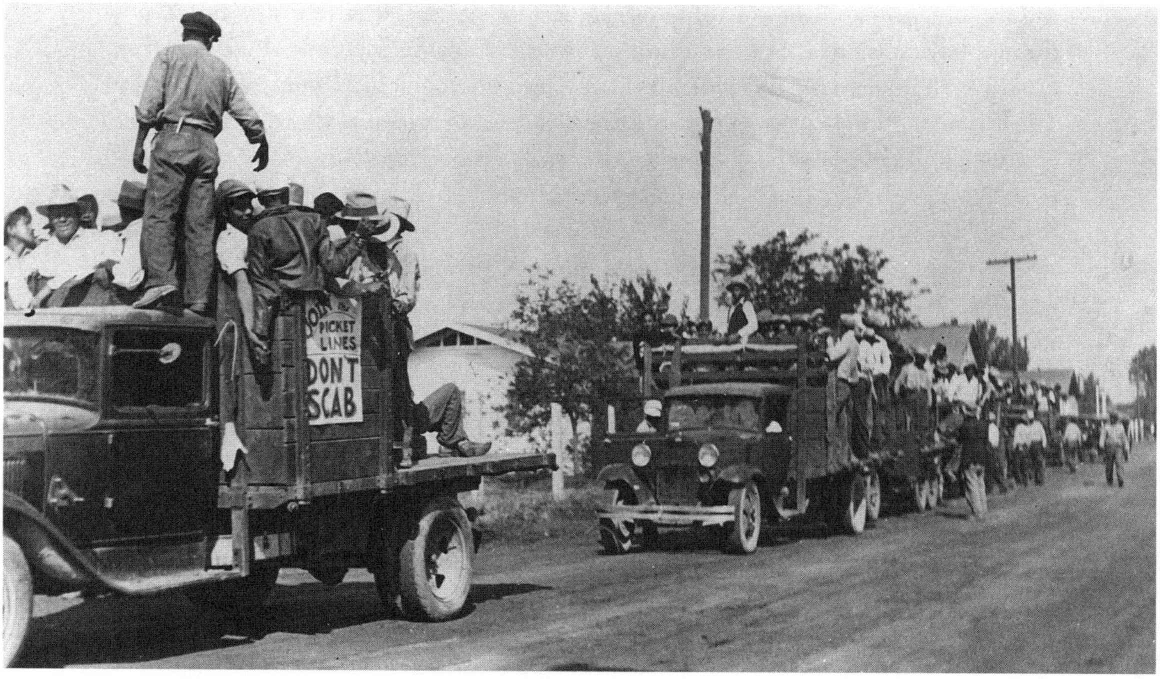

Join the Picket Lines, Don't Scab, October 10, 1933, photograph by R. H. Powell. Courtesy of R. W. Powell.

a street. When strike leader Pat Chambers climbed into a pickup truck bed to address strikers, about forty growers arrived and took up positions across the road from the red brick building where CAWIU was meeting. After a scuffle, the growers first shot Mexican consular representative Delfino d'Avila, then unleashed a fusillade that wounded twenty strikers and cut down Hernández. Mortally wounded, Hernández collapsed and died shortly after Smith snapped his picture. "A small army of ranchers fired point-blank into a crowd of striking cotton pickers," reported *San Francisco Chronicle* correspondent Clifford Fox, and the *San Francisco News* reporter described how he "saw eleven unarmed persons shot down in cold blood. One was a woman. Two were killed."[14]

As the first, but not the last, image of a farmworker killed in the course of a farm labor struggle, Smith's photograph would exert a powerful impact by "embalming" death as it was occurring. At the time that Smith photographed that dying farmworker, newspapers had just started running strike images. Editorial guidelines regarding what was to be seen and not seen, what was news and what constituted good taste, had not yet been worked out. Since the start of the American Civil War, photographs of U.S. war dead had never appeared in major publications, and bodies of the foreign dead only rarely intruded onto the pages of newspapers. Publication of Smith's photograph thus broke new ground on several levels. After his horrific photograph appeared, not only did photographers go on to capture gruesome details; they also saw their work shifted from the inside pages to the front pages. Reporting also shifted perspective. Whereas prestrike reports had stressed the role of agitators, the inclination of strikers toward violence, and the role of law-enforcement personnel in restoring order, now the emphasis was on lawlessness among growers. Sympathetic editors at the *San Francisco News* underscored these themes with large photographic layouts consisting of a half dozen photographs spliced together, and newspapers such as the *Sacramento Bee,* which initially had been hostile to the strike, did an about-face and reproduced two photographs of the "Pixley Massacre," as it was called, taken from a distance just before it erupted.

One of the most dramatic sequences captures growers beating up Pat Chambers. Taken by Fred Smith in Pixley on October 10, these images were accompanied by a sequence showing Chambers addressing cotton pickers just before his arrest, then the pitched battle that followed, and finally the fatally wounded Hernández. Many other newspapers ran the sequence, although several dropped the image of the mortally wounded striker as too gruesome. Subsequent layouts in the *Los Angeles Times* showed a group of strikers carrying a sign reading "General Strike. Stay away from the Cotton Fields and Join the CAWIU. Help win the strike." Equally dramatic, the *San Francisco Chronicle* published pictures of a volunteer teacher holding classes for children in the makeshift camp and a "martyr's funeral" in Tulare.[15]

Over the next few days, more photographs filtered back to urban newspapers. One was by *San Francisco Examiner* photographer Harold Ellwood. A small man with a dark mustache and hair parted on the right side, so that most of it fell over the left side of his forehead, Ellwood was always dressed in a smart business suit. Although a veteran newspaper photographer, he was photographing his first farmworker strike when he caught a group of strikers standing, unsmiling and unarmed, in front of their union hall. Essentially documenting the survivors of the onslaught, Ellwood's photograph elicited considerable sympathy for the strikers. It would not be the last important photograph that he would take at a farmworker strike.

Two unattributed photographs had an even greater effect on newspaper readers. One was essentially a close-up of union pickets carrying wooden staves to guard their camp. The other was a close-up of a handsome union leader, Leroy Gardiner, alias Leroy Gordon, addressing strikers. The first image captured a sense of the futility of facing off against growers armed with rifles and shotguns; the second revealed the feelings of unity between Okies and Mexicans in what was clearly a multiethnic strike.[16]

Precisely who made many of these and other photographs remains unclear and the source of much speculation. Fred Smith, Harold Ellwood, *Fresno Bee* photographer Lew Hegg, and several anonymous freelancers, along with Otto Hagel and Hansel Mieth, were all present for most of the twenty-four-day strike. But some of the best, most widely reproduced, but heretofore unattributed images were the work of an unlikely photojournalist, seventeen-year-old high school student Ralph H. Powell.[17]

Young Powell was assisting his father, long-time San Joaquin Valley photographer Lewis Powell. He was in his father's studio one morning when a California Highway Patrol captain from the Hanford office next door suggested that someone head over to the strike and take pictures. "I had a Graflex, Telegraflex, a 5 × 7–inch Eastman view camera, and a Cirkut camera that made a print thirty-six inches long and nine-inches wide," Powell later recalled. "I went over to the strike camp near Pixley, got permission to climb on top of a tower at a service station just across the railroad tracks from the camp, and took a panorama from the platform running around the outside." So clear is Powell's panorama that the eye can travel endlessly through the various rows of tents and burlap shelters where thirty-five hundred people lived in primitive squalor. Also visible are segments of a waterpipe system, with various outlets, about a dozen wooden privies, and an irrigation canal that served as a collective bathing facility for camp residents. Because of the long exposure time, many figures are blurred as they walk about the camp. But the photograph is so rich that every viewing reveals a new detail.[18]

Of his experiences at the camp, Powell recalled:

> My old Graflex roll camera wasn't right. It vibrated when the mirror went up, and the film wasn't fast enough. Someone told me that this farmer over in Corcoran had a camera for sale, and it turned out it was a 4 × 5–inch Graflex camera. You could tell he'd been selling off. His wife had left him. He was broke. He sold me a three hundred dollar camera for twenty-five dollars on installment. He had been pretty well off; now he was broke. Here I was taking his camera to photograph all of these strikers talking about rich farmers. . . . Both sides were very fair to me. I was young. They let me do pretty much what I wanted. . . . I tried to be friendly and nonpartisan. . . . Those days we used the exposure system based on experience. If you didn't know exposure you overexposed and developed under. That was because we couldn't afford an exposure

> meter, or they weren't too good at that time. . . . I got a little irked because some of the agitators who wanted photographs were living in this hotel in Tulare, going around in old clothes, pretending to be poor and unarmed while the Highway Patrol was picking guns out of cars.[19]

After finishing his work on the water tower, Powell climbed down and moved into the camp. "You had to be kind of careful in the camp because that was private property, and they didn't have to let you in," he recalled. "I promised to give the strikers prints. That won their confidence. I never had any trouble. I think they were kind of glad to see a photographer taking pictures. I was able to photograph on the picket lines and follow their roving picket activities without any interference." At least one striker, Edward Bañales, retained one of Powell's prints three-quarters of a century later.[20]

From the camp, Powell photographed a CAWIU funeral parade through downtown Corcoran. He then followed strikers out to the picket lines. In one photograph, about twenty Mexican women are crowded into the back of a truck. The driver has opened the cab door and is looking out, smoking a cigarette. The women, barely tall enough to see over the slatted wooden side rails on the pickup bed, stare unsmiling toward Powell. Prominently displayed on the truck is a sign that declares: "The Governor Sends Aid to Pixley. 24 Deputy Sheriffs. 11 Highway Patrolman. WE WANT FOOD!" Another photograph captures a truckload of strikers stopped to call workers out of the fields. Down the road, two highway patrolmen and someone who appears to be a detective or district attorney stand by another patrolman's motorcycle, monitoring the action. Featured prominently in the foreground, a beefy, denim-clad Anglo striker, possibly a displaced Okie tenant farmer, blows on a bugle, his cheeks puffed up as he tries to increase volume. Beside him, a thin Mexican field hand bends forward at the waist as he waves his hat and calls to the strikebreakers. Between them and the highway patrolmen, another striker, with his sleeve rolled up, stands and waves to the strikebreakers from the fender of a car. All three men are highly animated, and standing together, they project an image of ethnic solidarity and determination that evokes considerable sympathy.[21]

After photographing the strike, Powell moved into his father's business. Specializing in family portraits, weddings, and high school yearbooks, he never again photographed in the fields, even though Hanford, the community where he would reside for the next sixty years, was prime farm country. But while Powell seemed to regard his essay as but a passing phase, Paul Taylor instantly recognized it as an extraordinary visual document. A week into the strike, Taylor visited the San Joaquin Valley with Clark Kerr, a new research assistant who had just arrived at Berkeley from Stanford University. First meeting with jailed strike leader Pat Chambers, then with growers arrested following the Pixley Massacre, Taylor began amassing nearly two thousand pages of oral interviews, various fliers, documents, and newspaper clippings for a massive documentary history of the cotton strike. As he went about his business, Taylor also collected images, acquiring a set of Powell's prints, which he probably first saw in the *Los Angeles Times, La Opinion,* the *Sacramento Bee,* and the *Fresno Bee,* where they were featured prominently in full-page stories on the strike and the Corcoran tent city. Taylor then incorporated the set of Powell's images into his documentary history of the cotton strike. He also deposited a second set in the Library of Congress and a third in the Bancroft Library, where they would be consulted and used by countless historians without proper attribution or payment.[22]

While Powell and Taylor went about their business, Otto Hagel and Hansel Mieth, who were also present at the strike, shot footage with the 16-millimeter movie camera they had purchased several years earlier. Describing Hagel's approach, Mieth told Ken Light, "He thought maybe a film could have given them a little presence and not them individually, but the whole idea, a movement, and show it a little better than in still pictures."[23]

While filming, Hagel and Mieth worked closely with Hungarian-born Lester Balog. A naturalized citizen who had arrived in New York City with his mother in 1912, Balog was a member of the New York Film and Photo League and in 1930 had led an effort to add film production to the league's activities. Producing films documenting the struggles of workers in the eastern United States, Balog, like Hagel and Mieth, possessed a keen sense of social justice coupled with a belief that film could

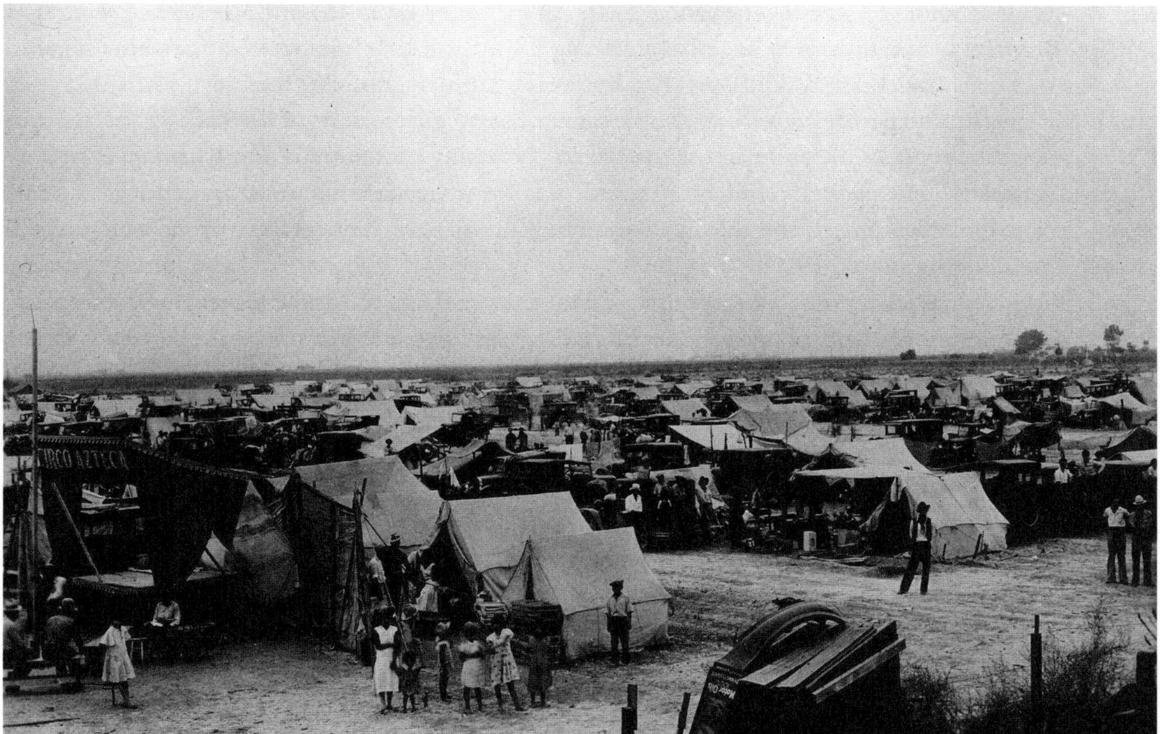

Corcoran camp, Circo Azteca, October 10, 1933, photograph by R. H. Powell. Courtesy of R. W. Powell.

be used to convey information and reach a wide audience. On September 7, he left New York with a projector, a print of Pudovkin's *Mother* (based on a Maxim Gorky novel of the same title but called *1905* in some publicity advertisements), and several Film and Photo League newsreels. In Chicago he acquired Leo Seltzer's film of the Chicago World's Fair and in Milwaukee shot his own footage of an antifascist demonstration. Along the way, Balog showed his films fifty-one times to an estimated twelve thousand people.[24]

Balog arrived in San Francisco on October 7. He was accompanied by Eddie Royce, whom Mieth recalled as "a speech maker" and "good talker." Royce would serve as the featured speaker at various film showings. The two were so impoverished that Balog had to leave behind his watch and Royce his sweater to pay the toll on the Vallejo Bridge. That night they showed their films to an audience of a thousand at the Fillmore Workers' Center. Heading south to Carmel, an artist's colony whose residents included muckraking writer Lincoln Steffens and farm labor organizer Ella Winter, Balog showed his films to an audience that seemed to enjoy the shorts but not the features. On October 9, he helped print fifteen thousand publicity leaflets.[25]

On October 10, Balog and Royce headed into the San Joaquin Valley, accompanied by Sam Darcy, regional head of the Communist Party. Stopping off briefly in Fresno, the group witnessed a guilty verdict against one of the leaders of the Lodi grape strike. After camping for the night outside Tulare, they headed south to cotton strike headquarters in the town. On October 11, Balog joined five thousand strikers marching to Visalia, the Tulare County seat, to protest the murders in Pixley the previous day. "They had no parade permit so I got the camera ready," Balog wrote in his diary. "They marched right to the court house and began a meeting on the steps. Pat Chambers, against whom a warrant had been issued, was the chairman. There were plenty of troopers and deputies, and the only reason they didn't arrest Pat was the very militant mood of the strikers."[26]

Later that day, Balog made a ten-foot banner to be displayed at the funeral for one of the murdered cotton pickers. Spending that night at the home of a strike sympathizer, Balog found himself bunked near Caroline Decker, executive secretary of the striker's union, whom Ella Winter recalled as a petite blonde woman who "looked like a dancer, but . . . talked like an economics professor," and a man named Applebough, whom Balog thought "a crazy nut." About 2 A.M., Applebough launched into a heated lecture on nonviolence, so Balog was unable to get to bed until about 3 that morning. On October 12, Balog attended strike meetings, avoided police, followed pickets, and continued making leaflets, cranking them out by hand on an old mimeograph machine. The following day, Balog was out on the picket lines filming when Sheriff R. L. Hill spotted him, walked over to his car, and explained that he was going to warn the pickets and that he wanted Balog to film the warning. "When I told him that my assignment was to take pictures of strikers picketing," Balog later recalled, "he got red in the face, and I got pale, but I was lucky for just then a cameraman came there (Frisco news guy) and he took the picture. And I decided that from now on it will be healthier for me to keep away from Sheriff Hill." Returning to town that night, Balog participated in a strike meeting at which he made four large oilcloth banners and twenty-five posters to be displayed at the funeral for the two murdered cotton pickers.[27]

At some point during the cotton strike, Hagel and Mieth suffered a tragedy that would haunt them the rest of their lives. The incident centered on their two-year-old child, Maria. Although mired in controversy, legend, and contradictory statements given by Mieth at various points in her career, certain key facts are clear. While Hagel was photographing in the nearby fields, Mieth remained behind in camp. Busy washing clothes, she barely noticed her daughter crawling about the open tent, playing with a kitten. Holding the kitten in her hands, the little girl skipped out the entrance and was run over by a truck driven by a drunken foreman. Hansel fell upon her dead child, and when Otto heard the news he threw down his camera, rushed to the scene, and collapsed to his knees. A red-faced man gave Hansel a shove with his boot and told her to stop whimpering. Camp residents inquired about the couple, whether they were Americans. Interrogated by the police, Otto was asked if he was German. The word filled Hansel with fear.[28]

Guilt-ridden, shattered by the loss of her child, and blaming her preoccupation with photography for the tragedy, Hansel could not look Otto in the eyes. Fleeing the camp, she vowed never again to pick up a camera. In a note, Hansel explained to Otto:

> I left you. Don't search for me. I no longer can look at your accusing eyes. My heart has been torn to shreds. I lost all I had. My love child has been taken from me. Killed by a drunken bum. They used him to do the deed. Our child had to pay the price. We had been warned, but you wanted to save the world. You have made the camera an instrument of fear for me. I don't think I can ever take another picture. I feel surrounded by hate and fear. I go crazy, for I do want my child—nothing else. *She is dead.* I am alone. Nobody can help me.[29]

Otto remained behind until October 23, when a fact-finding commission recommended that pickers return to work for seventy-five cents per hundred pounds. The commission refused to recognize the CAWIU. Quickly ratifying the settlement, pickers returned to the fields on October 25. Hansel disappeared into San Francisco. Tracing her activities at this time is extremely difficult. Her FBI file indicates that she married window washer Avendano Montroni on October 31, 1933, and that the two shared a flat at 280 Union Street. She never mentioned this marriage in any of her writings or interviews. She may have been desperate and resorted to marriage as a way to remain in the United States. But in other statements she explained that Otto found her in San Francisco and the two rented an apartment at 910 Carolina Street on Telegraph Hill, near North Beach, paying $8.25 a month. Apparently she continued to see Otto even while married to Montroni.[30]

Early in the following spring, Balog moved in with Hagel and Mieth, and the three spent many long nights working on a documentary that aimed at dramatically exposing class tensions and differences. They wanted to present a picture radically different from the one seen in Movietone News features shown in American theaters. The catalog for the San Francisco Workers School, later described by *San Francisco Chronicle* writer Jesse Hamlin as "a hotbed of labor activism that offered a range of classes to working people," lists Balog and a P. Otto (most likely a pseudonym for Otto Hagel) as cinematography instructors in a class on Soviet newsreels, documentary films, and working-class film. As they proceeded with editing, Hagel, Mieth, and Balog added shots of urban labor and WPA work, "Hoovervilles," police attacks on striking longshoremen, cotton strikers marching to protest the Pixley murders, union organizing, and picketing in the fields. "I remember the nights sitting together with friends, splicing, editing, going out to bring home 'filler,'" Mieth recalled in a letter to film historian Tom Brandon forty years later. After splicing in a controversial sequence that juxtaposed scenes of the Chicago World's Fair with pictures of men scavenging through a garbage dump, Hagel, Mieth, and Balog added various scenes from labor camps, farmwork, the lifestyles of the rich and famous in San Francisco, and billboard shots extolling "The Highest Standard of Living in the World." Titled *Century of Progress,* after the Chicago World's Fair title, their film ended with a caravan of cars, trucks, and old jalopies carrying hundreds of strikers to Sacramento to petition the State of California for better wages and more humane working and living conditions.[31]

Even before Hagel, Mieth, and Balog began working on *Century of Progress,* photography again came to the forefront of the farmworker story when a strike broke out among pea pickers and lettuce harvesters in the Imperial Valley. At the start of the organizing drive late in November 1933, the *Los Angeles Times* dispatched photographer Eddie Collias to the valley, where he photographed Mexican consul Joaquín Terrazas discussing strategies with Mexican field hands. Maintaining coverage, the *Times* sent Collias to the valley the following March, when organizers from San Diego and Los Angeles met with local farmworker union leaders dissatisfied with Terrazas. Published in the *Calexico Chronicle,* these tame but important photographs put a human face on the growing confrontation and illustrate the split in leadership between the conservative and grower-approved Terrazas and the more militant CAWIU.[32]

When violence erupted during the spring, a *San Francisco Chronicle* photographer arrived in the valley but missed the action. He could do little more than produce posed pictures of vigilantes manning highway checkpoints. And when vigilantes attacked and broke up mass meetings and burned a strikers' camp to the ground and thugs abducted attorney A. L. Wirin from his hotel room and dumped him twenty miles out in the desert, no photographers were around to record the crime. However, Campbell MacCulloch, a member of a National Labor Relations Board Investigating Commission charged with examining the violence, concluded that the attacks could not be understood without reference to photographs. "Conditions are unimaginable to those who have not investigated Imperial valley . . . at first hand," wrote MacCulloch to the National Labor Relations Board. To drive home his point, MacCulloch obtained photographs of the charred remains of the incinerated labor camps and of the conditions under which field hands lived and worked. Sending the images to other members of the Investigating Commission, he hoped to provide vital evidence supplementing his analysis. By amassing the kind of proof that would support his stinging report, MacCulloch believed he could avoid being accused of reacting hysterically. Photographs would support his conclusion that farmworkers were mistreated and abused and that law enforcement literally stood by as this happened.[33]

A few months later, Balog and Hagel began showing *Century of Progress,* as well as various Russian documentaries, to labor audiences throughout the San Joaquin Valley, but not without opposition. Awaiting them was the Associated Farmers, a notorious antilabor group funded by a coalition of the largest agricultural and industrial organizations in California, among them the Bank of America and the Pacific Gas and Electric Company. At exactly the same time that Balog and Hagel were using photographs to educate farmworkers, the Associated Farmers was accumulating an excess of six hundred photographs of alleged communist leaders together with their descriptions, fingerprints, and other records, all neatly filed on more than five thousand index cards. So extensive was the photographic surveillance of agitators, communist sympathizers, and farmworker organizers that Associated Farmers executive secretary Guernsey Frazer

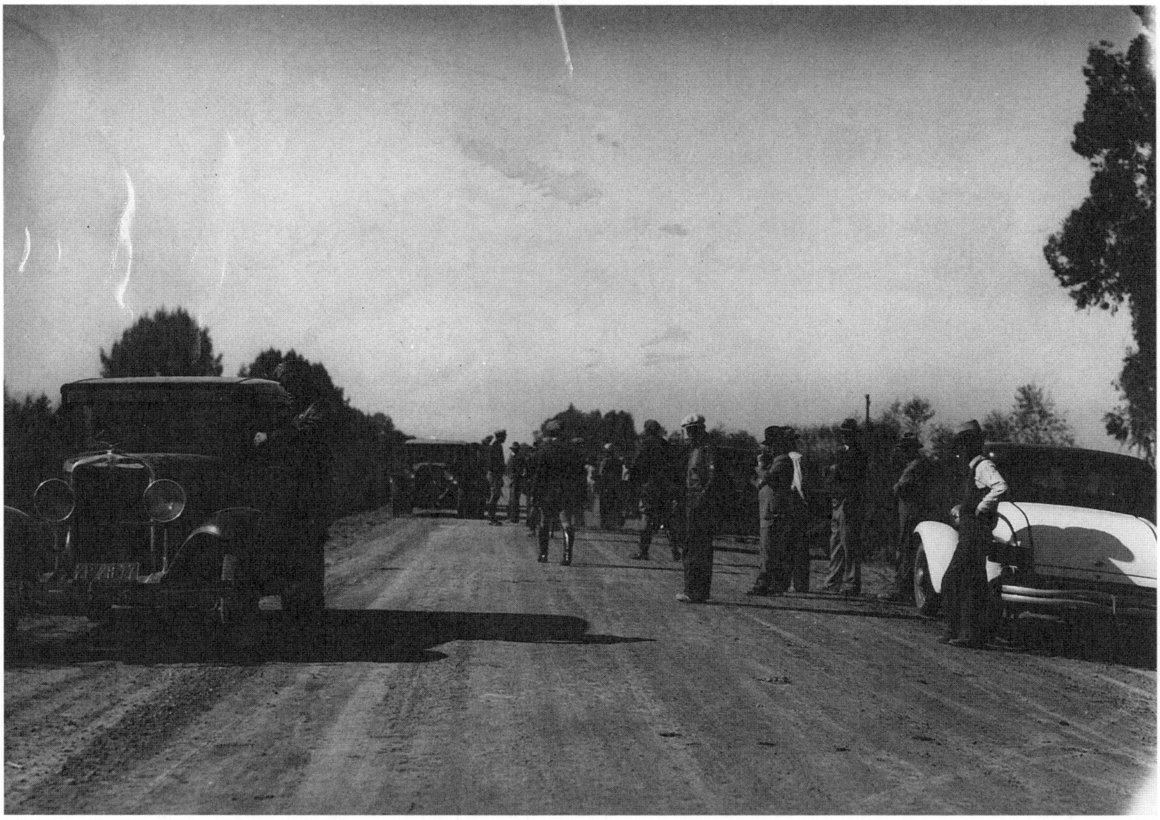

Police roadblock, strike by Imperial Valley lettuce harvesters, January 11, 1934, photographer unknown. Courtesy of *San Francisco Examiner.*

contacted FBI director J. Edgar Hoover. "If you desire," he wrote, "we would be pleased to forward to you, with our compliments, a set of these photographs, together with a descriptive list. While these people are listed in our files as Communists, practically all of them have been involved in other criminal activities, and it is our thought that these records might be of value to you."[34]

Citing lack of jurisdiction, Hoover declined Frazer's photographic dossier. But that did not end efforts to turn photography against farm labor organizing. When Balog attempted to show *Century of Progress* along with other films (*Bonus March,* a film produced by the Film and Photo League, and *Road to Life,* a Soviet feature) to an audience of from seventy-five to one hundred people in a Tulare County Mexican pool hall on May 25, 1934, someone tipped off the police that Pat Chambers was here.

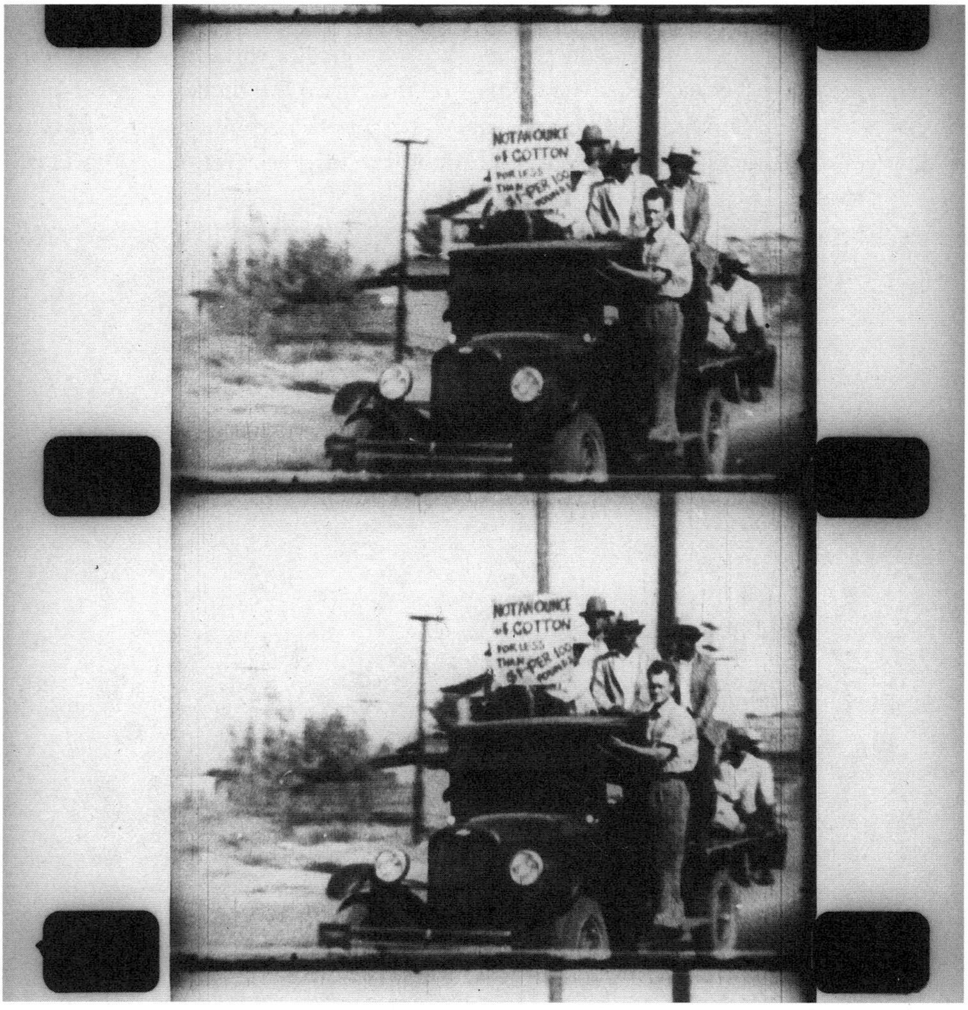

Frames from *Century of Progress* showing the strike by cotton pickers in the San Joaquin Valley, ca. 1933. Filmmakers Otto Hagel and Lester Balog. Courtesy of the Archives of Urban and Labor History, Wayne State University.

Disregarding all First Amendment rights of free speech, Tulare police raided the meeting on the grounds that it was a communist propaganda meeting. "About four troopers came in, big son-of-a-guns, you know?" Balog recalled. "They were about 6 feet, and they stood around me—I didn't know what to do, I finished the film . . . and when it was over they practically picked me up and took me to jail." Although Balog was arrested and charged with operating a business without a license, Otto Hagel, fearing that he would be deported as an illegal immigrant (a tactic employed to remove cotton strike leader Leroy Gardiner the previous year), somehow escaped, along with Pat Chambers. On June 5, Balog and Communist Party organizer Lillian Dinkin were tried for "showing a picture without a license." Convicted by a jury after five minutes of deliberation, both were sentenced to forty-five days in jail and fined one hundred dollars.[35]

As Balog served out his sentence, California slid more deeply into depression. By June 1934, one in five Californians was unemployed and dependent on some kind of public relief. With tensions mounting over providing aid to newly arrived transients, law enforcement authorities launched a statewide crackdown on "subversive literature." Newsboys were harassed for selling the *Western Worker.* Owners of radical bookstores were jailed. Louis Siminow was arrested in San Diego for showing his films. Balog feared that he would be immediately arrested for vagrancy when he was released. Picked up by Joe Wilson of the International Labor Defense, he returned directly to San Francisco, where he resumed showing his films. He spent much of the next year trying to obtain his film *Century of Progress* and equipment from the Tulare Police Department. While some equipment was eventually returned to his lawyers, the film seems to have been sent to Garrison Film Distributors in New York City, which returned it to Balog later that summer.[36]

On October 25, 1934, Avendano Montroni separated from Mieth on the grounds that he had been tricked into marriage and that Mieth had continued to live with Hagel. Following the separation, Mieth and Hagel permanently reunited. Late one night in the fall of 1934, they returned to their Carolina Street apartment to discover that both their film and movie camera were missing. Having lost film and cameras in several earlier burglaries, the two assumed that they had again been victimized by a thief or, more likely, the police. Again, because Otto lacked papers and had immigrated illegally, he was unable to report the theft. But Mieth did, accusing the police of the crime. Although the police denied any involvement, neither Hagel nor Mieth believed them. "It broke us then financially," Mieth recalled. "We returned therefore to still photography."[37]

Forty years later, Mieth learned what had actually happened to the film. Balog had taken it, kept it, and in the early 1970s donated it to Wayne State University Labor Archives after selling publication rights to Tom Brandon. During his negotiations with the archives and with Brandon, Balog never mentioned the role that Hagel and Mieth had played in filming and editing. When Hansel learned of this, she became extremely angry. Concerned about the future of the film, especially the important shots of Pat Chambers and Caroline Decker, and furious that she and Otto were being denied due credit, Hansel telephoned Balog. According to Hansel, Balog said, "My God. Sure. I had the film. I took it with me and all during the war. I had it in my baggage." Because both Balog and Otto Hagel belonged to the Film and Photo League and had edited the film together, Balog believed that it belonged to "labor's cause," not to any one individual. Anyone in the Film and Photo League could, and should, use it, and Balog apparently did, showing it to dozens of audiences throughout the state. Learning all of this, Mieth informed Brandon that he did not have permission to use the film and that he could not use a long and detailed interview he had conducted with her about making the film.[38]

A year after Balog's arrest, an odd turn of events once again linked FBI surveillance and photography. Frightened by the specter of more communist-led strikes, the Associated Farmers, backed by various organizations of employers, goaded law enforcement authorities into suppressing the farmworker movement. Following the bloody San Francisco General Strike, police raided Communist Party headquarters in a half dozen cities. On July 20, 1934, seventy-five police officers and deputies armed with night sticks and tear gas bombs swooped down on CAWIU headquarters in Sacramento and arrested fifteen members, including Caroline Decker and Pat Chambers, on charges of vagrancy and criminal syndicalism. A second raid on a labor camp outside Sacramento netted other labor activists, and smaller raids continued over the next few days. A week later, Caroline Decker was released from jail after providing evidence that she was a paid employee of CAWIU but was again arrested on August 15 and again charged with vagrancy. On August 29, eleven CAWIU members were convicted of vagrancy and given the maximum sentence of six months in jail. Eight others were acquitted but held on criminal syndicalism charges with the eleven previously convicted CAWIU members. Following a long trial that extended from November 26 to April 1, 1935, the eight previously acquitted CAWIU members were convicted of criminal syndicalism. Decker was sent to Tehachapi Women's Prison and Chambers to San Quentin Prison, each for five years. Somewhere along the way, the FBI photographed Chambers and stapled his mug shots into his very thick FBI file. They would remain there, odd surveillance images, unseen by the public, for seventy years.[39]

For contemporaries, the growing concern with images as evidence was a revelation. Even the most stalwart commercial photographers now refused to pass up shots and began contributing their own perspective to the changing picture of life and labor in the fields. A prime example was Imperial Valley photographer Leo Hetzel. Shocked by the Great Depression, Hetzel veered away from standard commercial practices, adopted a documentary perspective, and focused his camera on an important farm tool, the short-handled hoe. Essentially a regular hoe with a twelve-inch handle, the short-handled hoe, or *el cortido* ("the short-one," as it was called), required lettuce and beet thinners to stoop over in the shape of a question mark all day as they weeded and thinned fields. Although at the time it was not considered a symbol of back-breaking labor, the tool attracted Hetzel's attention, and sometime in 1934 he produced a tight shot of a Mexican using the hoe. Recording only the man's hand, his feet, and the hoe itself, Hetzel captured perfectly the nature of stoop labor.

Whether Hetzel was trying to make a point while straying into documentary work or was just using up the last frame of film on something interesting will never be known. Such framing was rare at the time and completely uncharacteristic of Hetzel's work. Whatever the reason, Hetzel seems to have produced the only close-up picture of the short-handled hoe at the time. But he did not stop there. Within months, Hetzel produced a number of other important documentary images. Among the most important are two astounding images showing hundreds of luckless people stranded in the valley while seeking work in the fields and on various canal construction projects. One image shows the men seated at huge communal dining tables while being fed en masse. Another captures them crammed into a work camp in bunks three tiers high and three deep. Among the first such images to graphically depict the appalling conditions faced by farmworkers and migrants, the pictures were so disturbing that Hetzel never published them.[40]

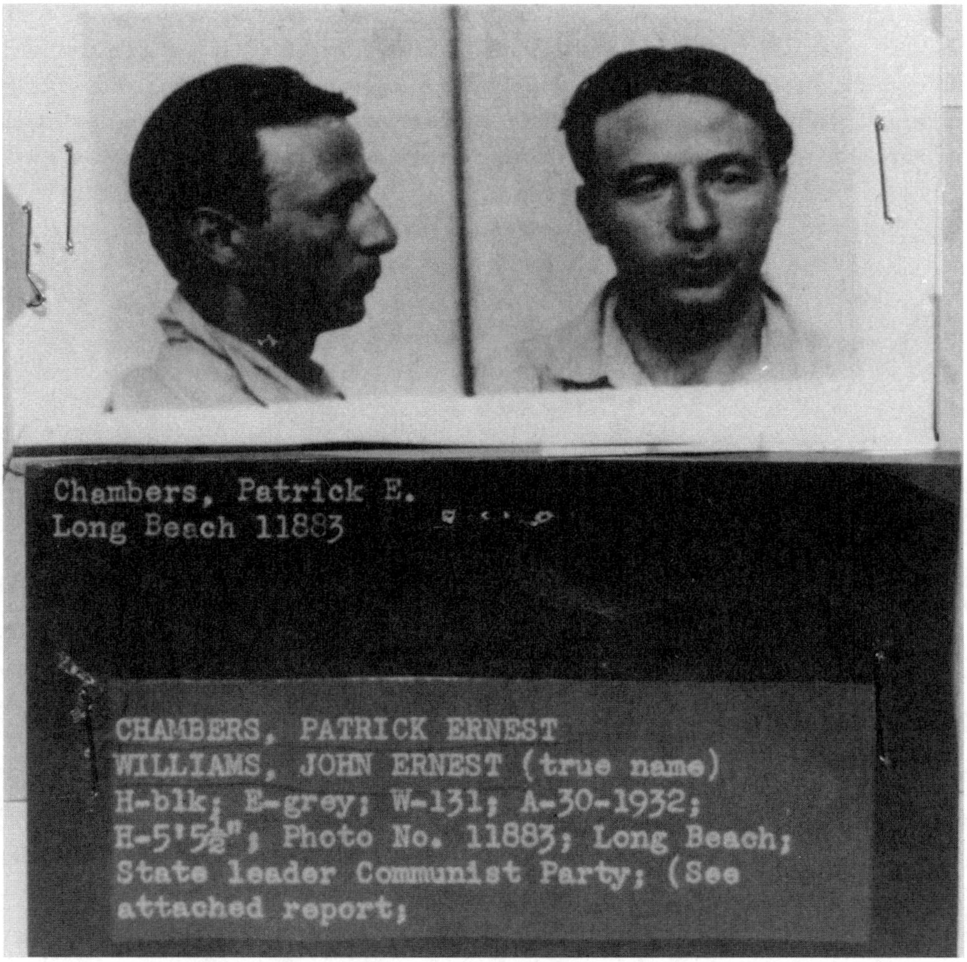

Mug shots of Pat Chambers, a.k.a. Patrick Ernest Williams, a.k.a. John Ernest, 1934, photographer unknown. Courtesy of the Federal Bureau of Investigation.

By the end of 1934, Hetzel and his contemporaries had initiated a new but yet unnamed way of looking at farmworkers. Hardly of one mind, these photographers employed a multitude of approaches, came from a variety of backgrounds, and held as many points of view as they possessed individual goals and aspirations. All shared a humanistic concern and an ability to go far beyond exposé to produce images that are at once beautiful works of art and focused on disturbing, even horrifying and repulsive, circumstances—images that simultaneously evoke strong feelings and make aesthetic statements. Often depicting people sliding into chaos or living a life so hazardous and marginal as to defy belief, these photographers implicitly assigned blame by shifting attention beyond agricultural products to the process by which crops were harvested and the circumstances farmworkers were forced to endure.[41]

And then, having indicted the farm labor system as an instrument of poverty, repression, pain, and exploitation, these photographers moved on. Tina Modotti, who had departed so dramatically from her early photographic training, became involved in extremely dangerous, clandestine, and subversive antifascist work in Europe after she was deported from the United States. Paul Taylor, who had initiated the first sustained work of social science photography, concentrated on teaching and writing about rural California while continuing to search for first-rate photographs. Ansel Adams, who had photographed the first essay on California farmworkers, blossomed

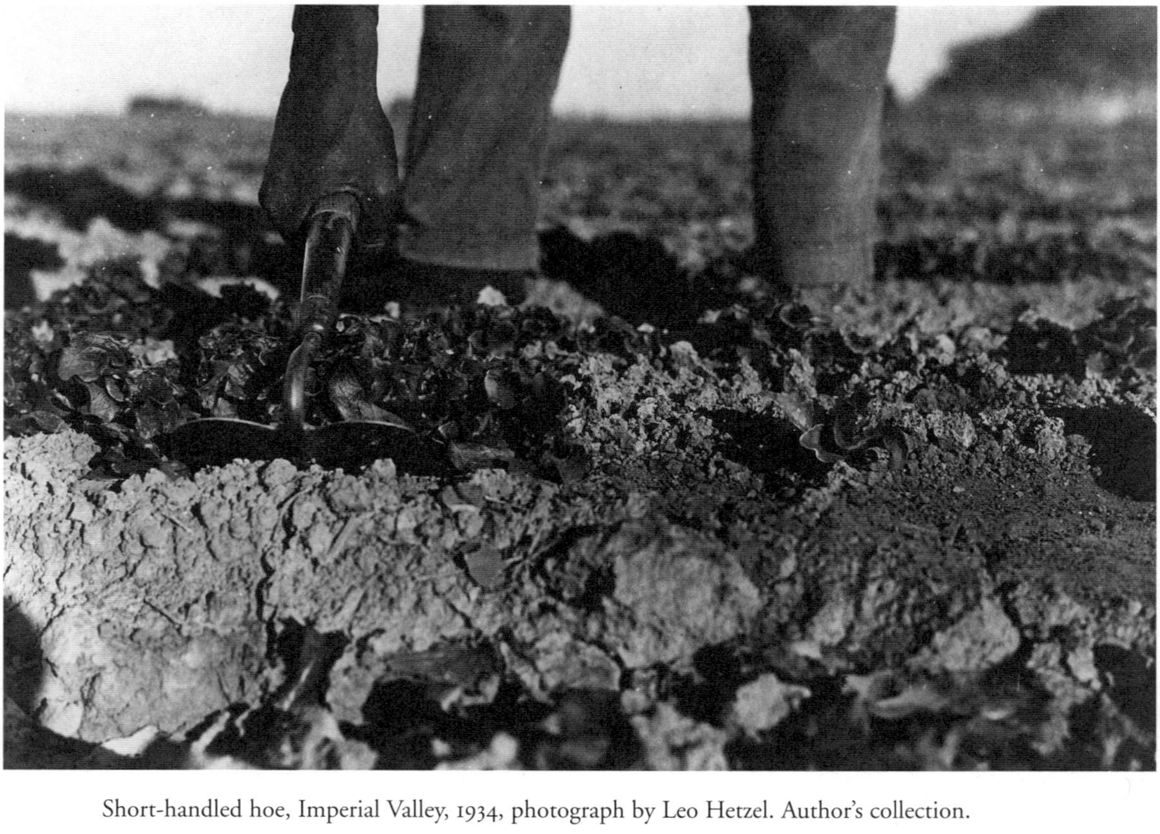

Short-handled hoe, Imperial Valley, 1934, photograph by Leo Hetzel. Author's collection.

as a landscape photographer. Ralph Powell, who had produced the first photo essay of a farm labor strike, went to work as a small-town photographer whose strike photographs were endlessly reproduced without his knowledge. Fred Smith and Harold Ellwood, who had produced some of the first images of violence in the fields, would be kept busy covering the news and were soon in the fields covering another farm labor dispute. Leo Hetzel, who had broken sharply with tradition, returned to the commercial routine.[42]

Only Hagel and Mieth, who had worked in the fields while forging one of the earliest examples of participant–observer photography and lost a child in the process, continued photographing in anonymity. It was a struggle. To make ends meet during the winter of 1934 they became deckhands on Italian and Yugoslavian fishing boats. Mieth recalled staying out all night and bringing back tons of sardines, most of which went to reduction plants to be used as fertilizer. They remained impoverished. For the remainder of the year they continued exploring California farmworkers with fresh eyes, an urgent sense of purpose, and considerable disappointment born of discovering an "invisible America" of poverty, injustice, and incoherence that contradicted their own expectations.[43]

Had these innovators been the only ones covering the state's farmworkers, a more humanistic form of photography might have sputtered to a halt. But they were not. Soon a new photographer, supported by the federal government, would take up the cause. Inheriting the earlier work of commercial photographers, town photographers, social scientists, activists, and photojournalists, Dorothea Lange amplified the nascent humanist perspective. Becoming its greatest exemplar, she transformed this new way of seeing into a powerful and distinct photographic tradition and produced a massive archive that continues to dominate the picture of California farmworkers and inspire countless disciples.[44]

II

THE EMERGENCE OF THE SOCIAL DOCUMENTARY TRADITION

1935–1942

7

Facing People as Human Beings

Dorothea Lange Finds Her Calling

Paul Taylor attended a photo exhibit at photographer Willard Van Dyke's studio, at 683 Brockhurst Street in Oakland, late in the summer of 1934. In 1932, Van Dyke had helped found Group f/64. An alliance of seven photographers in various stages of their careers, Group f/64 was devoted to pure photography at its highest level. Five members—Henry Swift, Sonya Noskowiak, Preston Holder, John Paul Edwards, and Ansel Adams—were just then achieving success. A sixth member, Imogen Cunningham, the senior figure in the group, was shedding her old pictorialist orientation in favor of sharp focus. The seventh member of Group f/64, Edward Weston, was devoted to establishing photography as a pure art form. The group took its name from the principle of precision implied by stopping the lens on a view camera all the way down to f/64, the smallest aperture, which yields maximum sharpness. With the impact of the Great Depression, Van Dyke's aesthetic values had shifted away from pure art and technical details toward social problems. One photographer seemed to embody this orientation more than any other: Dorothea Lange. After seeing some of her street photography, Van Dyke compared her work to Matthew Brady's coverage of the American Civil War. Offering her a solo exhibition in his gallery, Van Dyke later went on to praise her life's work for the way it demonstrated for posterity "the mixture of futility and hope, of heroism and stupidity, greatness and banality that are the concomitants of man's struggle forward." In what would be her first public exhibition, Lange hung her photographs where previously only Group f/64 members such as Ansel Adams and Edward Weston had shown their work.[1]

The exhibition would have a profound effect on the relationship between photographers and farmworkers in California, because it brought Lange to the attention of Paul Taylor. Having deepened his involvement in farmworker photography, Taylor had continued to collect prints and use them in historical publications as well as essays on contemporary events. Now, when news photographers, academic researchers, political activists, and commercial photographers were scrutinizing farmworkers far more diligently than ever before, Taylor saw Lange's work for the first time. He had not the foggiest inkling that the meeting marked a turning point in his life. At Van Dyke's studio, Taylor met the person who, more than any other, would set the standard by which social documentary photography would be measured. He also encountered the woman who would become his wife in an unusually productive union of creative intimacy that amalgamated social science with photography. Together, Taylor and Lange would emerge as leaders of a group of artists and intellectuals that historian Douglas Sackman has labeled "agrarian partisans": people who mobilized facts, images, and literature on the side of farmworkers and small-scale farmers and against what they regarded as a system of exploitative, industrialized agriculture. "The facts they mobilized were political," writes Sackman, "opening up a new way of seeing things so that an alternative reality could be created. Their reports, histories, novels, and photographs were not neutral documents of reality, for they were the sparks of blade touching grindstone."[2]

Lange's path to Van Dyke's studio capped a startling period of artistic change and personal transformation in her life, which began, quite improbably, on the other side of the United States in Hoboken, New Jersey, a city that novelist and poet William Carlos Williams described as full of "immigrants from everywhere under the European sun." The daughter of second-generation German immigrants, Lange was born on May 25, 1895, as Dorothy Nutzhorn, named after her paternal grandmother, Dorothea Fischer. As soon as she could express herself, she voiced her unhappiness with her last name, which seemed harsh, even funny; not until after her death did her husband and any of her children learn of her birth name. She grew up a scarred person, unable to mention her early life even to those close to her. Two traumatic incidents marked her. At age seven, an attack of polio left her with a withered right leg, from the knee down, and a nickname: Limpy. Five years later, her lawyer father deserted the family, leaving her mother to raise two young children. She became a truant who roamed the streets of New York City and prowled its galleries and museums. But she also developed inner resources that would help her later in life, among them her "cloak of invisibility," acquired as she returned home each evening along Christopher Street after riding the ferry from Manhattan to Hoboken.[3]

At first, Lange studied to become a teacher but in 1915 switched to photography, studying with Clarence White at Columbia University. After working for two years in a darkroom fashioned from a rented chicken shed in the Palisades, she left with a girlfriend and fellow truant, Florence Ahlstrom, on a trip around the world by way of El Paso and San Francisco. Lange would later recall the trip as a "very good time," during which complete strangers befriended them. But the first morning in San Francisco in January 1918, Lange and Ahlstrom headed out for breakfast at Compton's Cafeteria, where someone stole all of the money from Ahlstrom's purse. With only five dollars, the two found lodging at the Mary Elizabeth Inn, a home for wayward working girls, but were soon ejected for smoking and leaving an electric iron on in the laundry room. The next day Lange found a job as a photo finisher at Marsh and Company on Market Street, and her friend went to work at Western

Union. While working at Marsh, Lange met many of the people who would figure in her life, among them Roi Partridge, Imogen Cunningham, and Consuelo Kanaga. Joining a camera club to obtain darkroom privileges, Lange soon received financial backing from San Francisco attorney Joe O'Connor and opened a studio at 540 Sutter Street in San Francisco in 1919. She adopted her mother's maiden name and became part of the bohemian art scene. She regarded herself as a tradesman, not an artist. Her clients were mostly drawn from families of the wealthy Jewish merchant, cultural, and artistic class.[4]

A year later she heard some sharp-heeled footsteps in the corridor leading to her studio and asked someone who had those heels? It was Maynard Dixon, who favored western cowboy boots. A tall, lean man with deep blue eyes and a rakish mustache, Dixon was a former newspaper and magazine illustrator, often described as a popular and respected San Francisco figure. His influences were Charles Russell, a legendary and completely inarticulate American painter, and Ed Borein, a verbose society cowboy with an encyclopedic knowledge of the American West. Dixon had no formal training as an artist other than a year spent at the San Francisco School of Design. Born on a ranch north of Fresno, he had traveled widely by horse, wagon, and automobile, financing his journeys with funds earned by the sale of sketches to *Harper's Magazine.* Most of his archive of unpublished and original artwork had been lost in the 1906 San Francisco earthquake and fire, and he was in the process of reestablishing himself by designing billboards with Roi Partridge at the advertising agency of Foster and Kleiser. Lange found him to be bright, witty, interesting, original, and the epitome of what an artist should look and act like. She admired his "extraordinary visual memory" and ability to "capture anything" on a piece of paper. Although Lange would recall being "a little afraid of him" and being "very hesitant," she married Dixon six months after they met. He was forty-five years old and had a daughter by a previous marriage. She was twenty-four. The age difference did not bother her, but it bothered many friends. Dixon discontinued working at his billboard trade and devoted himself to serious painting. Lange kept her maiden name and pursued her career as a studio photographer, producing safe, conventional portraits for wealthy patrons while reserving a small portion of her life, as she would later put it.[5]

In 1925, Dixon and Lange had their first child, a son, Daniel; a second son, John, was born in 1928. Busy with her family, Lange adhered to a routine that allowed Dixon to remain free of the tedium that interfered with his work. During the morning, Lange cleaned house and took care of various chores, then headed off to photograph in her studio in the afternoon, where she worked intensely before returning home in the evening to care for the children. She baked and cooked and tried to keep everything smooth, happy, and enjoyable. She was a fierce housekeeper, allowing no deviation from her schedules and standards. It was too much for Dixon's daughter, who soon began living away in the homes of others. When not away sketching and painting on one of his trips to the Southwest, which were projected to be a month long but often turned into four-month excursions, Dixon helped with the children and various chores in the evening. But as Lange's portrait business began to decline in the first few years of the Great Depression, she grew restless. On a visit to Taos in 1932, she observed the photographer Paul Strand and, energized by his rigorous technical standards and work regime, resolved to "concentrate on people, only people, all kinds of people, people who paid [her] and people who didn't." Dixon had a series of affairs with other women, and Lange also took lovers. She was finding Dixon to be an unnerving mix of snobbishness and populism. With business lagging and more time on her hands, she moved outside her studio and began doing street photography, looking at the dispossessed and photographing them in unusual and beautiful ways. She had plenty to see.[6]

With a population of a six hundred thousand residents in 1933, San Francisco was a vibrant, beautiful, multiethnic, blue-collar city of grand architecture, marvelous civic design, and extensive public works, featuring the vast Hetch Hetchy project, which assured the city a supply of the finest water on earth. Orchestrating commerce from California's huge inland empire and coordinating ocean trade across the Pacific Ocean, San Francisco served as headquarters to numerous companies, including Southern Pacific, Levi Strauss, Crown Zellerbach, Wells Fargo, Bank of America, Stauffer Chemical, S&W Fine Foods, Hills Brothers, and Matson Lines. It had a well-educated, if paranoid, ruling oligarchy and a fiercely independent working class employed in shipping, shipbuilding, insurance, gas and electricity, and the production of blue jeans, paint, and beer. The streets were packed with saloons and boardinghouses, 135 bordellos, and about 150 gambling houses, plus various underground abortion mills, all of which catered to 150,000 blue-collar workers. San Francisco was also a city in crisis. One of four workers was unemployed, but in some professions, such as the building trades, half were out of jobs. Even formerly secure salaried white-collar workers employed by the city's largest corporations now resorted to selling apples and pencils on street corners or seeking tips by cleaning the windows of automobiles stopped at intersections.

Many unemployed survived as "indigent poor," receiving pittance relief payments of no more than pennies a day from the county, or they scraped by working a few days each week at odd jobs. Private charities and church groups also played a key role in providing aid, but none could keep up with the streams of wandering poor families, unattached men, even women and boys who salvaged leftovers from restaurant garbage cans and scoured the produce markets for anything they could find. Along the waterfront, conditions verged on civil war. Seamen had always been among the most exploited workers, and longshoremen endured a system that many compared to slavery. Hired through a shape-up system, thousands of longshoremen arrived on the docks before sunrise in the hope that some foreman would point their way and offer employment as pit donkeys working killing shifts of twenty-four and thirty-six hours. Already, members of the International Longshoremen's Association (ILA), led by the Australian-born Harry Bridges, were engaged in a massive rank-and-file organizing campaign that would dramatically challenge the industry.[7]

These were ominous times, and one of Lange's first pictures, *White Angel Breadline,* San Francisco, 1933, captures the sense of dislocation and uncertainty. Lange would

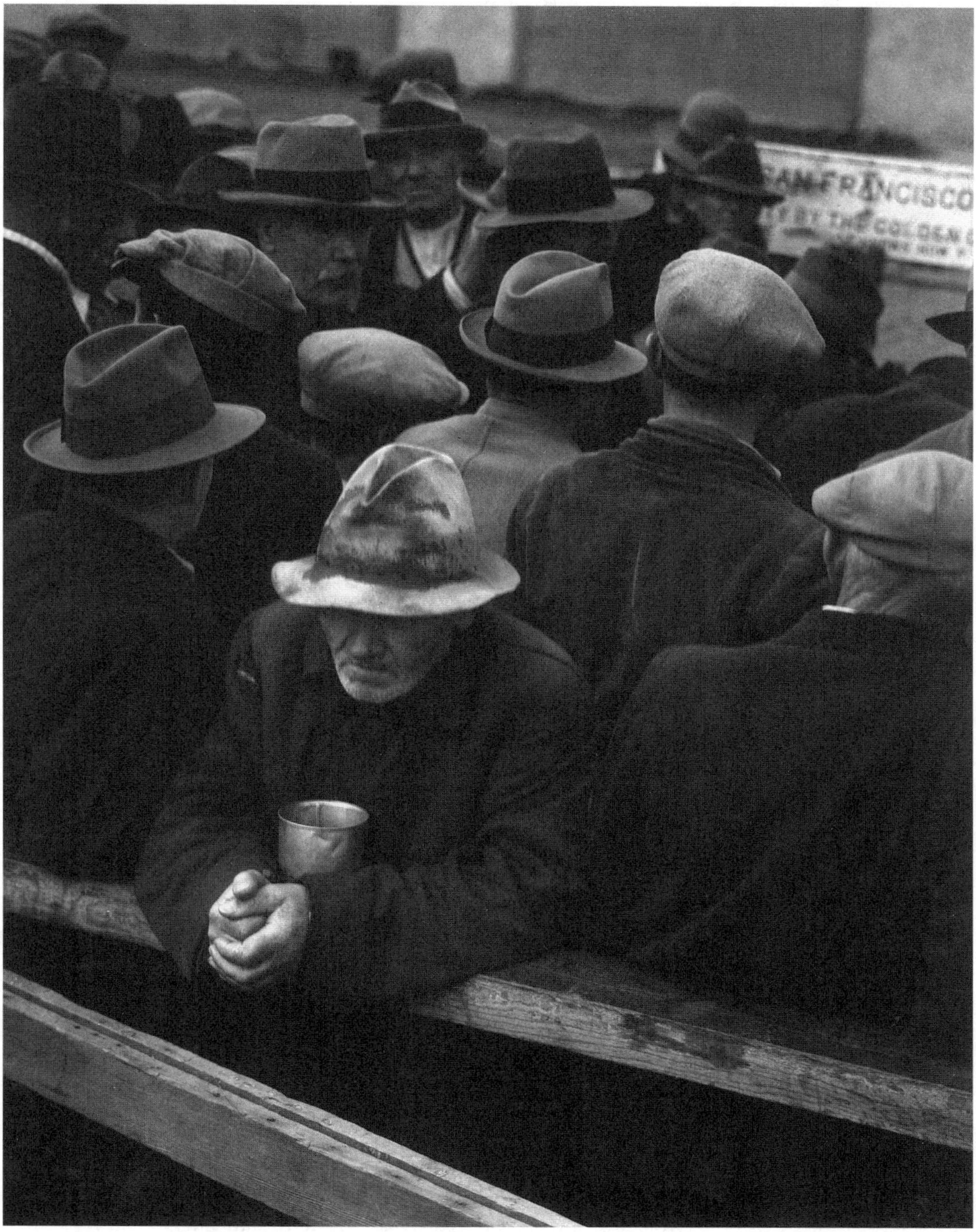

White Angel Breadline, San Francisco, 1933, photograph by Dorothea Lange. Courtesy of the Oakland Museum of California, Dorothea Lange Collection, Gift of Paul S. Taylor.

later describe the picture as a serendipitous combination of intuition and happenstance. She had devoted most of the day to surveying the street from the window of her second-floor studio on Montgomery Street. It was on a corner where the sun entered, and Lange was standing there one day watching people flowing up from the waterfront. The financial district was on her left, Chinatown, the Barbary Coast, and Little Italy straight ahead. "The unemployed would drift up there, would stop, and I could just see they did not know where next," Lange recalled in her oral memoir. "I looked down as long as I could and then one day I said to myself, 'I'd better make this happen,' and that started me." She spotted an unshaven, hunched-up little man in heavy coat, leaning on a railing with a tin cup propped between his forearms, his hands clenched together, his back turned to a crowd of people waiting for a handout at a soup kitchen run by a wealthy matron known as the White Angel. From the landing of her studio steps, Lange made a series of pictures of this scene but initially failed to recognize the iconic nature of at least one of them. Later she removed her film holder and turned it over to Roger Sturtevant, a photographer who shared darkroom facilities with her. Not until he developed her film the next day did the power of the image become apparent. Even after Sturtevant had praised the photograph, Lange's clients, on seeing the slightly cropped image displayed among their portraits on her studio walls, could find neither art nor social value in the image. The reaction was, "What are you going to do with it?" Lange did not yet have the slightest idea. As with Hagel, Mieth, and Modotti, she had no label for the type of photography then germinating in her mind, although she would later identify it as "the very beginning of documentary photography." But within that photograph, Sturtevant perceived the seeds of a new direction. At his prompting, Lange shifted her portrait skills outdoors, where she immediately found her special gift as a photographer. Although she was aware of the work of Jacob Riis and Lewis Hine, she was not copying them or applying to California an approach seen elsewhere. Lange would later recall this shift as her having "grabbed a hunk of lightning."[8]

While Lange expanded her street photography over the next year, her brother Martin accompanied her when she began photographing hobo jungles and defeated men in heavy coats huddled around fires and resting on benches. "I went out just absolutely in the blind staggers," she told interviewer Suzanne Riess. "I had something to do. And I've really kept at it pretty much without an interruption." One of her first photographs was *Slave Market: Howard Street between 3rd and 4th.* But Lange did more than record scenes of down-and-out longshoremen. She thought about the historical significance of her photographs and attempted to place them in time and space. Class conflict seemed inevitable. Passage of the National Industrial Recovery Act (NIRA) as part of President Franklin D. Roosevelt's New Deal was inspiring organized labor to launch an organizing drive without parallel in American history. With thousands of members in locals scattered from Seattle to San Diego, the ILA was preparing to challenge the shape-up hiring system and demand a union hiring hall and industry-wide contract. Inevitably Lange gravitated toward the waterfront, where she would soon be in the middle of a violent confrontation.[9]

When the Industrial Association representing San Francisco employers labeled the ILA's effort "un-American" and refused to bargain, Harry Bridges called a strike, and Lange began photographing picketing along the docks. "I knew there was a great deal of trouble ahead, and that there were going to be demonstrations at the Civic Center by the unemployed, and I said to myself, 'I can't afford (money) to do this and I shouldn't, but I want to.'" About thirty-five hundred longshoremen, sailors, masters and mates, marine engineers and firemen, and stewards went out on strike and shut down all Pacific coast shipping on May 9. The mood was both hopeful and ugly. With ship owners bringing in strikebreakers and mass demonstrations everywhere, Lange could not stay clear of events.[10]

Earlier, on May Day, Lange had photographed massive protest rallies. At San Francisco's Civic Center she found herself in the middle of a sea of pickets shouting their radical messages and carrying placards: AMERICAN WORKERS—JOIN HANDS WITH THE GERMAN WORKERS. DOWN WITH GERMAN FASCISM . . . DOWN WITH AMERICAN PRESS . . . REPEAL CRIMINAL SYNDICALISM LAW . . . DOWN WITH ROOSEVELT'S HUNGER PROGRAM. This was where she made her photograph *Street Demonstration, San Francisco, 1934*. The photograph captures a large policeman, head cocked to one side, his badge prominently displayed, overseeing a line of pickets holding their signs. Another of her photographs captured a Communist orator.[11]

Lange continued to follow events, including the bloody confrontations between strikers and waterfront employees on July 3 through 5, the last day known as Bloody Thursday, when dozens of longshoremen were injured and two shot dead. Although Lange was not a news photographer and shied away from the more dangerous confrontations, where tear-gas grenades and bricks filled the air, she was on hand for many rallies, including the arrival of National Guard troops and the July 16 General Strike, during which tens of thousands of workers closed down the city and paraded in such solidarity with the longshoremen that shippers agreed to an arbitrated settlement. Unaccustomed to being jostled and knocked about by angry and depressed men, Lange found much of the work frightening and had a great fear of losing her camera. "I thought someone might grab it from my back and take it away or hit me, from the back."[12]

Communists were recruiting heavily at this time, and soon Lange's work brought her to the attention of activists of various stripes. Complete strangers began making appointments and while visiting would ask her to attend various Communist Party meetings. "You wouldn't be told at the first visit that they were party meetings," she told Regional Oral History Project interviewer Suzanne Riess. "You would be somewhat flattered and cajoled and it was dangled before you as something that a person like you would be interested in. . . . I had many encounters with this thing." She never went forward with any of these encounters, largely because Dixon was so anticommunist and far less socially moved than Lange. Toward the end of her life, she would confess that she was not sure she had taken the right course. There was much to be said in favor of participating in such groups. But if Lange had done so, she probably would have been a very poor follower, incapable of submitting to party discipline.

Her instinct for freedom was too great, and she was not really interested in politics. Lange was empathetic. Like Taylor, she was an old-line Jeffersonian Democrat.[13]

After Lange photographed the demonstrations and the strike, Van Dyke invited her to exhibit at his gallery and wrote a glowing description of her photography in *Camera Craft,* comparing her attitude to that of "the sensitized plate of the camera itself." Seeing Lange's work, Taylor was awestruck by her street shots. She had an "eye for the essence of a situation," he later recalled. Not only were her photographs interesting and beautiful; they were also valuable as empathetic documents of the times, as contemporary visual history. With Norman Gold, Taylor had just coauthored an article on the San Francisco General Strike. "The manuscript was on Paul Kellogg's desk at the *Survey Graphic* in New York," Taylor recalled years later. "It had some photographic illustrations that I'd made on my own, or picked up one way or another. But at 683 Brockhurst [Van Dyke's studio] I saw this striking array of relevant photographs by Dorothea Lange, whom I had never heard of. One very powerful photograph was of a radical speaker before a microphone."[14]

Asking Van Dyke to put him in touch with the photographer, Taylor spoke to Lange for the first time. "I asked her, could the photograph be used as an illustration to accompany the article on the San Francisco General Strike? She was agreeable and asked the terms. I said I had no authorization, but I would put her in touch with the New York editor, Paul Kellogg, and I thought that they could arrive at a mutually agreeable arrangement, which they did. Her photograph, captioned 'Workers Unite!' became the frontpiece of our article." It showed the dark figure of a man speaking vehemently into a microphone, his mouth stretched open. The orator photographed by Lange turned out to be a brother of one of Taylor's colleagues at the university. *Survey Graphic* eventually paid Lange fifteen dollars for the right to use the photograph. "That was money in those days," Taylor recalled.[15]

Within a few weeks, Lange ventured into the interior valleys to photograph an extraordinary aspect of the Depression. Taylor had been studying the self-help cooperatives that had sprung up as a means of meeting the problems of the unemployed. Organized around the slogan "Self-Help Beats Charity," thousands of families had started bartering their labor for the fruit and vegetables that small farmers could not sell. Soon bakers, barbers, cobblers, carpenters, mechanics, and various professionals were exchanging their services for goods. One project sponsored by the Oakland-based Unemployed Exchange Association (UXA) had developed around a sawmill along the Feather River in the foothills near Oroville. When the owner could not run it profitably, the UXA received a federal grant of seventy-five hundred dollars to buy it and turn it into a cooperative. Collaborating with Clark Kerr, Taylor began studying the cooperative. A few weeks after Willard Van Dyke's Brockhurst exhibition, Taylor invited a group of photographers including Van Dyke, Mary Jeanette Edwards, Imogen Cunningham, and Lange, as well as anthropologist Preston Holder, to accompany him on a two-day expedition to Oroville. "I remember well seeing how the photographers started to work in the very first minutes, each in his own way, and each choosing his own subjects," Taylor recalled in his oral memoir. "The UXA members had been told the photographers were coming and they didn't bat an eye; they didn't put on any show. They just went about their own way. . . . You could see even then the differences in the way they photographed." In particular, Taylor noticed Lange. "Quiet, intent. . . . That's all that I remember. She just quietly went to work." On their return, Taylor submitted his report, which persuaded the federal government to increase grants to self-help cooperatives throughout the state, and then arranged a photo exhibition for Lange and the others on the top floor of Haviland Hall at the University of California, Berkeley.[16]

While at the Unemployment Exchange Association, Lange likewise noticed Taylor, a tall, solid man, extremely cerebral. She was especially drawn to his calm, reserved wit, constant encouragement, and the way he worked with quiet determination and intense concentration. "I remember Paul sitting there in their community house—an abandoned sawmill, so it had that atmosphere—interviewing and speaking to these people. I had never heard a social scientist conduct an interview. I knew about people going and asking questions and filling in questionnaires, but an interview I never heard. And I was very interested in the way he got broad answers to questions without people really realizing how much they were telling him. Everybody else went to bed while he was still sitting there in that cold, miserable place talking with those people. They didn't know they were being interviewed, although he wrote and wrote."[17]

About mid-January 1935, Taylor was asked to head the research program of the Division of Rural Rehabilitation of the California State Emergency Relief Administration (SERA), the state arm of Harry Hopkins's Federal Emergency Relief Administration (FERA). Created in May 1933 to alleviate distress among the unemployed, FERA received five hundred million dollars, to be augmented by three times that amount in matching funds from local governments. To assist with the transient homeless population, FERA created the Federal Transient Service, one of the busiest federal agencies, which handled seventy-seven thousand cases a month by April 1935. The entire state operation was directed by Harry E. Drobish, a public-spirited University of California graduate and associate farm adviser from the Sacramento Valley who would later serve as a state senator. With plenty of individuals who were familiar with family farmers and their needs, SERA needed someone who was familiar with the problems of farm laborers. "It was understood that I would focus on the latter," recalled Taylor.[18]

Developing a rehabilitation program fitted to the needs of rural California, Taylor was to explore and convey a sense of conditions peculiar to the state and largely unknown in Washington, D.C. Who was in distress? What was the nature of their distress? What would be a sensible way to alleviate that distress? In carrying out this new research, Taylor wanted to go beyond what he had done previously when studying Mexican immigration under traditional academic auspices. He had seen the conditions and was sympathetic to the people. He wanted to provide reports that would move people and bring action as well as convey information. "My idea was not just to study the conditions," he later explained. A pragmatic individual who was especially attracted to the way in which Franklin D. Roosevelt appeared to bring the force of mind into closer relation with power, Taylor wanted to use research "to get something *done*." His first task was to assess the situation. After that, the challenge was to persuade government to act. "We had to answer the questions the bureaucracy raised," he stressed. Once appointed as field director, Taylor moved into a dingy office on Fourth Street in San Francisco and set up shop during the bitterly cold winter.[19]

When Taylor began work, Drobish asked what staff he would need? Taylor replied that he would like a few people with academic training and, of course, a secretary to type his letters and reports. Beyond that, he said he wanted a photographer. "Why?" Drobish challenged. Social scientists generally did not use photographs. Conceding the point, Taylor explained that he wanted to compile a visual record of the problems he discovered in the field. This was important because the people who were responsible for making decisions about what to do on the basis of his reports had to see the actual conditions. From his experience in studying the cotton strike, Taylor had learned that words "would not be enough . . . to show the conditions vividly and accurately." Describing the conditions was one thing, but reporting them in a way

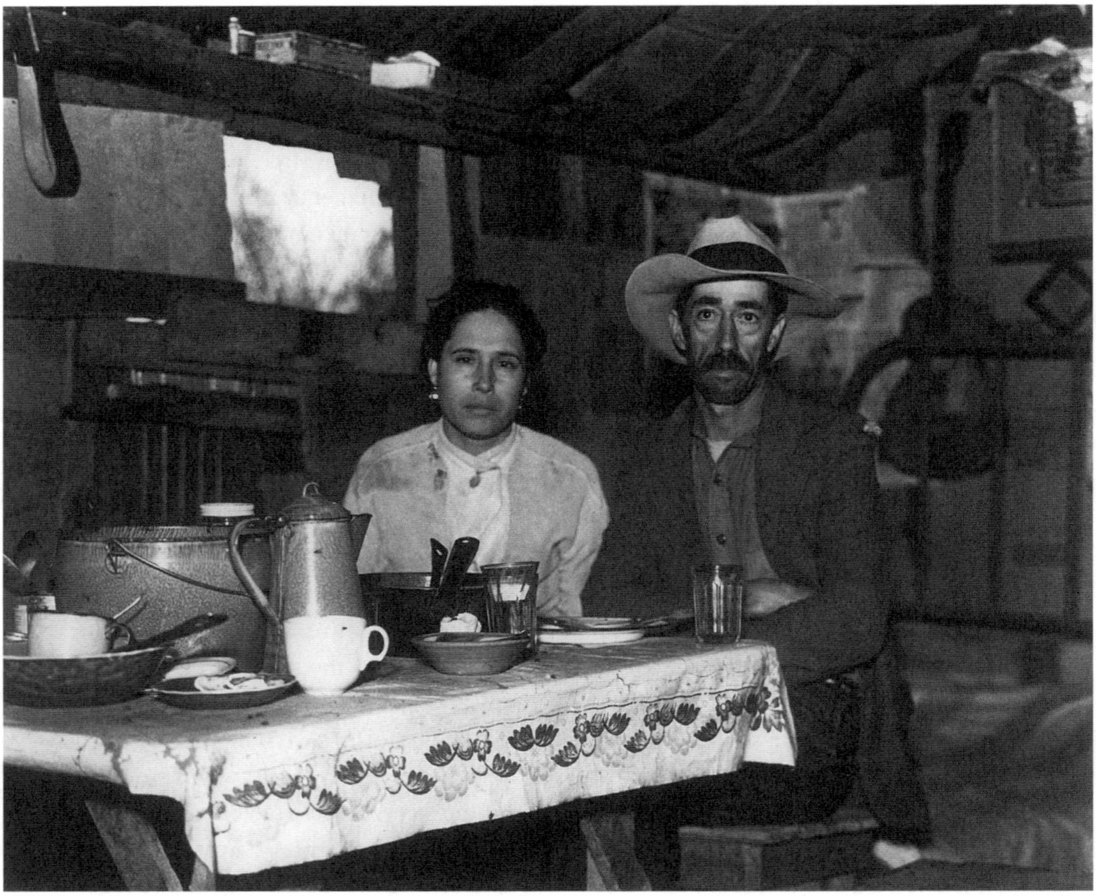

"We are on relief. We are getting 14 and 15 dollars a week now because we have a very good President." Mexican field laborers, Coachella Valley, 1935, photograph by Dorothea Lange. Courtesy of the Oakland Museum of California, Dorothea Lange Collection, Gift of Paul S. Taylor.

to produce action was quite a different task. Back and forth went the debate with Drobish. There was no authority to hire a photographer, no slot, no funds. The situation seemed at an impasse until office manager Lawrence Hewes, a Dartmouth graduate whose career in stocks and bonds had been terminated by the Wall Street debacle, stretched the rules and hired Lange as a clerk–typist at fifteen hundred dollars a year. Taylor later asked her if she had ever typed. She told him that she had once taken some lessons for three days. That was the extent of her typing experience. To get around the problem of expenses in the field, Hewes increased Taylor's per diem allowance for travel and entered Lange's field costs under "clerical supplies." When Drobish learned of the arrangement, he lectured Hewes sternly and warned him, "We'll try it for a month, then we'll see."[20]

About 250,000 farmworkers were in California at this time, and of this number 150,000 to 175,000 were migrants. Many were living in squalid camps that failed to meet even minimal standards of sanitation. The problem had deep historical roots stretching back to even before the turn of the century. But in the Depression years, it had worsened for several reasons: many growers could not afford to maintain or build the most basic accommodations; a large number of homeless male transients were flooding into the state; and Governor James "Sunny Jim" Rolph had drastically and systematically dismantled Progressive regulations and programs, among them the State Division of Immigration and Housing. With its budget severely cut, the division had an entire staff of eleven with just four field inspectors in 1933. As a result, migrants made do as best they could.

They had four options: grower-owned camps; private auto or trailer camps; shack towns, also known as rural Hoovervilles; and ditch-bank or squatter camps. Grower-owned camps were largely unregulated and usually ranged from long lines of one-room cabins in widely varying stages of repair to plank floors on which migrants erected tents; many such camps consisted of little more than vacant outbuildings, old barns, even the spare chicken shed. Auto and trailer camps, conveniently located alongside the main roads, had originally been designed for the tourist trade but, with nobody using them, had been shifted into temporary quarters for migrants and had fallen into disrepair. Shack towns were improvised communities in unincorporated areas, often proximate to city dumps, where migrants erected various kinds of shelters out of anything and everything: old strips of tar paper, double gunny sacks, cement sacks, corrugated iron, fruit-packing crates disassembled and hammered into a new configuration with old burned and rusty nails rescued from cinder piles. Ditch-bank camps were by far the worst. Scattered along creeks and irrigation canals where water was readily available, a clump of trees offered shade, and mere holes in the ground served as toilets, they were an entirely separate reality, completely disconnected from the rural communities nearby.[21]

Life in the camps was hardest on the children. Poverty, constant travel, lack of adequate food, and unsanitary living conditions took their toll. One in three migrant children suffered from malnutrition. Nine had died in California during the 1933 cotton pickers' strike. Makeshift graves marked the path that their parents had followed west along Route 66. Although local health officials constantly rescued migrant children from camps, many of the children nevertheless died from accidents and such simple infections as tonsillitis. As a larger number of people sought work along the migrant stream, more and more children suffered respiratory infections contracted while living in damp sheds and cold shacks. Rickets, diarrhea, and tooth decay were reaching epidemic proportions. Teachers pooled their already meager resources to feed migrant children, but the chronically tired, underfed, often barefoot, and otherwise poorly clothed students could not keep up and were constantly taunted by classmates. Few ever finished the year or semester in the same school.[22]

Reports of poverty, unsanitary living conditions, and malnutrition led reformers such as Simon J. Lubin to scramble into action and call for a return to progressive ideals and policies. But while the Simon J. Lubin Society and other activists championed the cause of the migrants through various publications and fund-raising efforts, they could hardly cope with the scale of the problem. Government action was clearly required. Federal and state officials concerned with these problems met in late January 1935 to weigh their options. At the conference, Chester Moore, a growers' representative whom Taylor had met while studying Mexicans in the Imperial Valley in 1927, suggested that Taylor visit Nipomo, where conditions seemed acute. So in February, Taylor headed into the rural areas to initiate his study of living conditions among migratory farmworkers. He was accompanied by Lange; Maynard Dixon; Harvey M. Coverley, an official with the state agricultural service; Irving Wood, an official with the Division of Rural Rehabilitation who had been one of Taylor's classmates at the University of Wisconsin; Edward Rowell, nephew of *San Francisco Chronicle* editor and University of California regent Chester Rowell; and Tom Vasey, one of Taylor's graduate students. After a day on the road, they reached Nipomo on a Sunday morning.[23]

An unincorporated farm town with a population of five hundred in the heart of the Cayuma Valley, midway between Santa Barbara and San Luis Obispo, Nipomo was described in the 1932 *California Blue Book* as "the center of a rich farming district of high-priced lands." Originally a Chumash Indian *ranchería,* Nipomo (whose name is said to mean "foot of the mountain") remained largely uninhabited until 1837, when the Mexican government granted thirty-eight thousand acres to William G. Dana, a cousin of the writer Richard H. Dana, who promptly named it Rancho Nipomo. With a pleasant, thirteen-room home (known as Casa de Dana) and a commanding hilltop view, Rancho Nipomo boasted lavish hospitality and for many years served as the headquarters for the region and principal stopping place for travelers headed south from Mission San Luis Obispo along El Camino Real. In 1886, the Pacific Coast Railroad extended a line south to the Santa Ynez Valley, unlocking the area's rich agricultural potential. Soon farmers planted thirty thousand acres of wheat, settlers arrived in droves, and in 1889 the heirs of William Dana laid out the modern town. Over the next half century, wheat gave way to more diversified agriculture, and the Nipomo Valley emerged as a center for spring pea production. Migrants arrived every February and remained through late spring, completely overwhelming the limited supply of cheap housing. With few options, workers pitched their tents along the road while bringing in the vegetable crops. These camps had grown to such proportions and spread so far and wide along the coast that nearby Santa Barbara abandoned several years of private relief efforts and formed the Emergency Police Force, which swept through camps, rounding up undesirable single transients and sending them on their way.[24]

Concerned about Lange operating outside her safe studio, Taylor instructed Rowell to look after her. "This is the first time that we've had a photographer out in the field, and I don't know how she will be received," he said. "Will you go with her? Your instructions are, see to it that nothing untoward happens. I don't want anything to disturb the relations between ourselves as a team, and those pea-pickers. Carry her cameras, she'll need somebody to do that. Just quietly stay with her and see that nothing goes awry." He then told Lange, "If you don't make a single photograph the first day, that's all right with me."[25]

At Nipomo, Lange photographed farmworkers for the first time. It was an eye-opening experience for a young woman who had never been on a farm and had previously seen farmworkers only from a distance while inside an automobile on a highway, passing through the rural districts on the way to some destination. Lange instantly recognized that the great impact of her work lay in the "simple drama" that it captured. Here were farmworkers scattered about in torn tents and brush shelters. They lacked access to clean drinking water and had few privies. The camp was muddy, and the people were a sorry sight. Many field hands were ill, and they had little food. Those able to find work earned less than one dollar a day. Everyone was beholding to labor contractors. How best to capture the situation?[26]

Taylor's fears that Lange might be confused, intimidated, or ill-treated proved unfounded. She had no trouble photographing the Nipomo pea pickers. A highly intellectual person, Lange was already trying to define what exactly she was doing. Her working idea was to obtain images that carried the full meaning and significance of the situation at Nipomo. Hard news photographs would not be enough. Artsy photographs would be a self-indulgent crime. Showing how things felt was part of the equation, but that did not go far enough. Lange was trying to open herself to the possibilities and to avoid photographing with preconceptions, which she felt both limiting and false. Her goal was to visually answer the question, What is reality? This required moving beyond the local and specific to capture what was universal. "I had to get my camera to register the things about those people that were more important than how poor they were—their pride, their strength, their spirit," she later told her interviewer. These ideas were a fairly complex first, grappling with what would soon become known as socially oriented documentary photography. Of such moments, Lange would later recall being "thoroughly involved" in something that was not "fun," certainly not "exhilarating," and so intense that it presented "no end to the difficulties" but ultimately offered her "the greatest real satisfaction."[27]

As Lange went about her business, she paid special attention to the behavior of her colleagues. From the beginning of her sojourn, Lange was stunned by the attitudes of several members of Taylor's team. She could not understand how any of them could order meals for $1.75 in their hotel rooms when a fine meal could be had for a $1, which was about the daily wage of the pea pickers they were studying. What most bothered her was how her colleagues referred to the field hands that they interviewed as "informants." Lange had never heard anyone described this way. "What language!" she thought. "What kind of people are these? . . . I knew then that I was with people who were in a different world than mine." One exception was a Mexican woman from

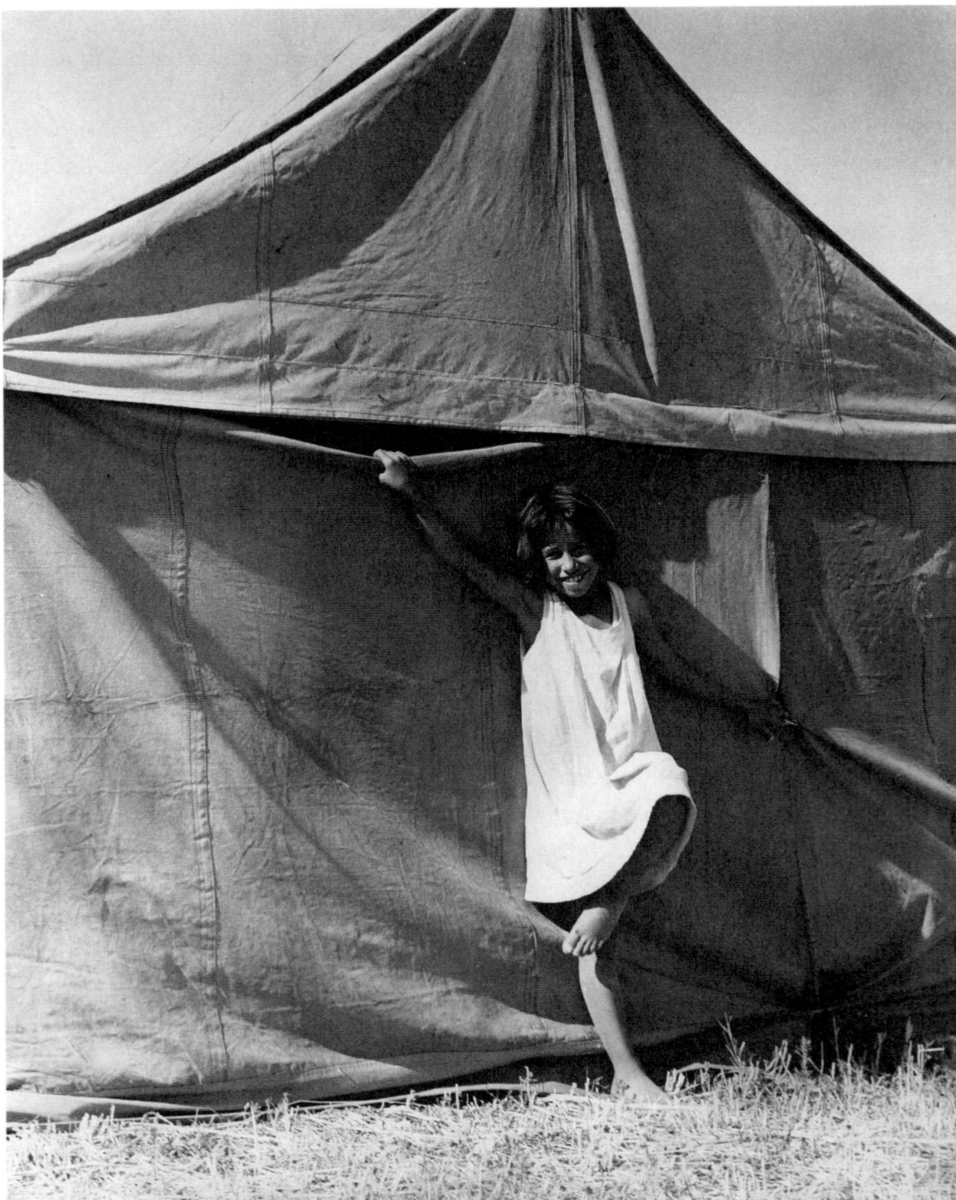

Child in camp of pea pickers near Stockton, 1935, photograph by Dorothea Lange. Courtesy of the FSA/OWI Collection, Library of Congress, Prints and Photographs Division.

San Bernardino. Working by herself among other women in the camp, she did not use the language of the social scientist. "She went off by herself in the morning and came back at night, and she was a wonderful creature," Lange later told her interviewer. "She worked in a very close and intimate relationship. She didn't speak of 'informants.' I think what she came out with was life-histories. She got a lot of them from the women, because the men were working."[28]

From Nipomo, Lange traveled to the Coachella Valley. For everyone, the journey south marked a crucial professional and personal turning point. "I didn't know a mule from a tractor when I started," Lange recalled. But as they traveled, Taylor briefed Lange on the history of farm labor in California, especially the many races and ethnic groups working in the fields. Along the way, Lange saw bindle stiffs tramping the roads and began photographing them, as well as Mexican field hands, Filipino gang laborers, and a large-bellied pea contractor.[29]

Lange's discipline and single-mindedness served her well, allowing her to work as unobtrusively as possible. Her technique was more that of a curious visitor than a photographer. She did not seem to be pushing anything or asking anyone to do much more than visit and share conversation. She was obviously no firebrand from a communist union. Her quiet and unthreatening curiosity would allow her to discover plenty. "One is a photographer second," she was fond of saying, but first and foremost a human being. Being a woman also helped. "I think it made approaches to people easier," theorized Taylor years later. "She stirred up less resistance from people. . . . If she detected any resistance, she folded the camera down, in effect saying, 'Oh, I'm not going to photograph you.'" Lange had no problem keeping up with the work pace set by Taylor. Even her limp helped her, often disarming subjects who otherwise might have been wary but perhaps felt some sympathy for a photographer moving among them.[30]

Another aspect of Lange's working technique, for which she would become famous, also blossomed on this field trip. This was her interviewing and note taking. Lange paid attention to everything she heard. She talked to the migrants. This was very different from her experiences on the streets of San Francisco. "For some reason, I don't know why, the people in the city were silent people, and we never spoke," Lange recalled of her street photography. "But in the migrant camps, there were always talkers. This was very helpful to me, and I think it was helpful to them. It gave us a chance to meet on common ground—something a photographer like myself must find if he's [*sic*] going to do good work."[31]

At Nipomo a migrant said something that deeply affected Lange. She was photographing him leaning against his automobile when he observed of his predicament: "This life is simplicity, boiled down. It seems like God has forsaken us back there in Arkansas." It was the first of many epiphanies. Very quickly Lange recognized that she had to record what she heard. And record it accurately. She wanted to preserve the exact words. Already she understood that the right words could be of enormous value. The problem was that she could not hold the conversations in her head in sufficient detail. Her solution was to record everything in a small, spiral notebook. She called these "jottings" and quickly inserted them between observations on camera shots, technical details, itinerary, and notes on expenses. They allowed her to record people spilling their stories to a friendly ear. But when she could not take notes, Lange spent an hour or two sitting in the car or hotel room recalling conversations and writing them down. If the day was especially hectic, she would reconstruct and transcribe her recollections in the evening. If she forgot her notebook or ran out of paper, or if something cropped up unexpectedly, she stopped photographing and returned to her car to make notes. "She not only saw, but she heard, and she recorded both what she saw and what she heard," Taylor later recalled. "She had no trouble. No problems in her relations with the pea-pickers. It went on that way, always."[32]

After nearly filling up one notebook, Lange began scribbling in a kind of shorthand. A typical entry from her work in the Coachella Valley the following week reads:

> Carrots 14 cents a crate, 48 bunches in a crate, sorted, graded, tied including tag couple [earn] 70 cents in a day. . . .
> They sleep in the rows—for 60 cents a day.
> Fellers, such as me, farmers, such as me, right down on our knees. Got no more chance than a one-legged man at a foot race. They're aimin' at keepin fellas sich as me right down on our knees, aimin at makin slaves of us.[33]

All along the journey, Lange had noticed large numbers of migrants in overloaded jalopies. They were Dust Bowl refugees, the first wave of a growing mass migration that would bring a third of a million people to California. The fear that an army of penniless Americans was about to invade the state in search of relief payments was just then beginning to dawn among Californians.

While returning north, Lange encountered one Dust Bowl couple sitting in their Model-T Ford somewhere along the highway near Bakersfield. Once farmers in Missouri, they had been following the migratory circuit along the Pacific coast but were now unable to move because their old car had broken down. Although the woman seemed distant and not that uncomfortable with her hands tucked in the pockets of her fur-lined coat, the driver was clearly anguished. With his long face, sturdy nose, and wide eyes, he stared past his wife at Lange as she opened the door and looked inside. By world standards, they were well-off, well-dressed, well-clothed, with transportation. After photographing them, Lange later made several prints and then did something that she occasionally did with other images too. Cropping out the woman, she enlarged the portion of the photograph that centered on the driver so that the viewer encountered his gaze. Now the edges of the composition frame the man from just above his cap to just below the steering wheel. The manipulation deletes most of the ragged roof, part of the windshield, and the portion of the seat where his wife sits. This places the viewer much closer and creates a far more intimate connection with his eyes. As a result, the image, titled *Ditched, Stalled, and Stranded,* became a different picture. Rather than showing a married couple, one of whom seems fairly contented, the image was transformed into a slightly deceptive, melancholy metaphor for men thrown into the migrant stream.[34]

Cropping was, at that time, somewhat controversial. Although certain photographers such as Paul Strand were legendary for printing their negatives straight, the truth was that Strand enlarged, cropped, and otherwise manipulated his prints while in the enlarger and felt no guilt about it. Lange did not generally crop her photographs. But she was not adverse to exploring a negative to discover whatever it held. She would often say that while photographing in the field, one did not always see everything. Important elements did not reveal themselves until seen much later in a darkroom enlarger. Additionally, from her experience she knew that field photography was often spontaneous, done quickly under less than ideal conditions, thus capturing a fleeting moment. As a result, an odd lamppost or an extraneous detail often protruded into a picture and would have to be cropped out later. "Why not do that, when the medium

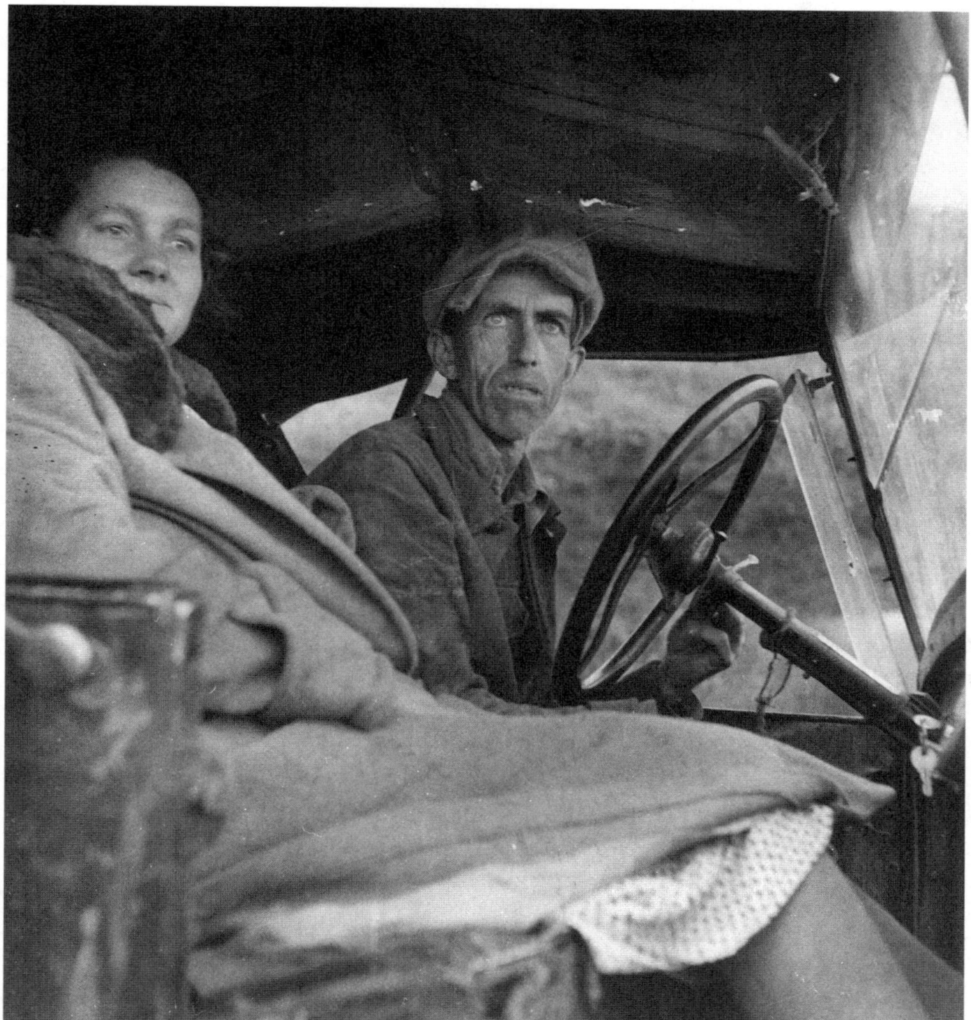

Uncropped version of *Ditched, Stalled, and Stranded,* 1935, photograph by Dorothea Lange. Courtesy of the FSA/OWI Collection, Library of Congress, Prints and Photographs Division.

permits it?" she explained in her oral memoir. "I think it should be explored to the limit. Though, I don't know what the limit of that method is." Lange would crop in order to simplify and amplify her images and eliminate what was irrelevant. In later years she would considerably enhance and improve her work through cropping. She was just beginning to apply the technique to her fieldwork in 1935, and in doing so Lange created one of her most famous early photographs.[35]

If Lange found challenge, inspiration, and a new purpose on the trip, so too did Maynard Dixon. By now approaching sixty years of age and suffering from emphysema, he was no longer calling the shots in his partnership with Lange. An important reversal of roles was occurring. Whereas Dixon had previously guided Lange through the western landscape, now it was Lange who began guiding Dixon away from the awe-inspired environmental paintings and idealized portraits of Native American peoples that had been his stock-in-trade. Within a few months, Dixon had created a number of visually attuned, socially oriented realist paintings. One of the first was *No Place to Go,* an oil on canvas in which a bindle stiff pauses in his trek, leans against a fence somewhere along the Monterey County coastline, and stares off at the Pacific Ocean. Surfacing in his angry poems, such as "Contract" and "Industrial," Dixon's bitterness was not born of a deep commitment to labor or the left. He knew the price to be paid for activist art and was hesitant to paint darker and gloomier scenes, in part because his paintings of men being beaten up, no matter how skillful or moving, failed to command the high prices and attract the wealthy patrons he relied on to earn his living. But as the Depression wore on, Dixon's sense of social responsibility and his involvement with his wife's evolving work overwhelmed his reticence and concern for return on investment, and he continued to explore the harsh realties of life with a series of paintings depicting the reality of the Depression and its effect on people. Among his most important works was *Keep Moving,* in which unemployed workers line up along a street in San Francisco; *Law and Order,* in which striking dock workers attack a policeman; *Free Speech,* in which a policeman in the background seems to monitor a group of workers listening to a labor organizer; and *Forgotten Man,* in which a seasonal worker sits despondently on the curb, waiting in the shadows for work.

After painting *Springtime in California,* a landscape of barren hills in which the dead, dry carpet of grass symbolizes drought, Dixon embarked on his own field trip. Accompanied by his friend Ray Strong of the Art Students League, Dixon visited migrant farm labor camps in the Shafter area, where he painted *Lonesome Ranch, Deserted Sheep Range, Abandoned Ranch,* and *Okie Camp,* the last painting a kind of color version of a Lange photograph. These in effect extended Lange's work, linking Dixon's art to her creative interests. Dixon would continue in this vein and later produce *Destination Nowhere* and *Roadside* (1938), two milestones in Depression-era art that reiterated the dark overtones expressed in *No Place to Go.* He would later refer to these paintings as the Forgotten Man series.[36]

If Dixon's burst of activity was a last desperate effort to supply the kind of direction Lange found in her association with Taylor, it was too late. Having turned forty,

Lange had made the transition from studio portraiture to street photography and, in doing so, found her special gift as a photographer. She was on her way and could not go back. Her relationships had been further complicated by the difficulties and economic uncertainties of making a living in the 1930s. Although she and Dixon had made many attempts to shore-up the family on trips to beloved locations, both understood that their marriage no longer functioned. Having met Taylor in the turbulent, early Depression years following a series of brief affairs, Lange discovered an unusually strong physical and emotional attraction. The two had complementary skills and contrasting personalities. Lange was forever in motion, constantly talking, could react in a flash, completely in the moment. Taylor was quiet, mulled everything over in his mind, spoke softly. Lange found Taylor a solid, emotionally mature man, a one-woman man, a man who never strayed, a happy contrast to Dixon. Although accommodating and unwilling to argue, Taylor was a bulldog on matters close to him. "He embodied intellectual and moral authority," observed the historian John Szarkowski, and "was as fourscore and unbending as one would wish the commander of a company of Marines to be."[37]

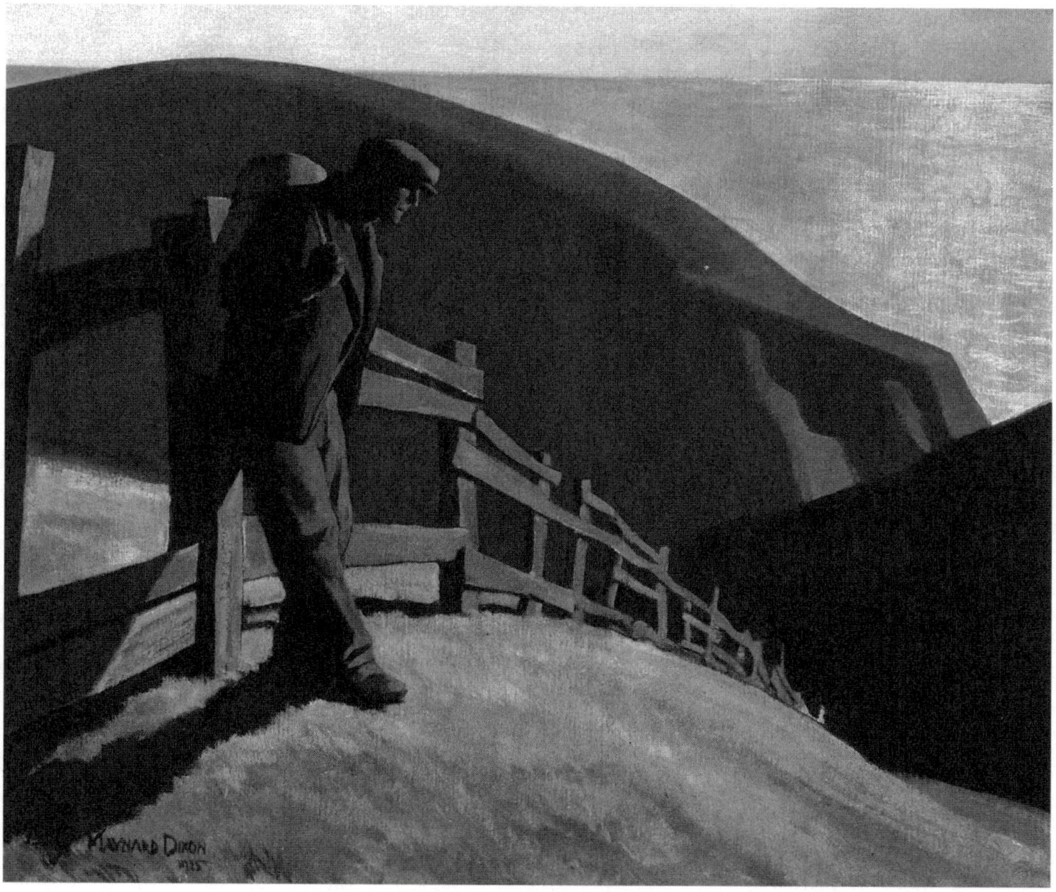

No Place to Go, 1935, painting by Maynard Dixon. Courtesy of the Brigham Young University Art Museum.

The two also exhibited certain similarities: a somewhat refined temperament, a didactic streak, a sympathy for the dispossessed, and a passionate commitment to their work. Neither could separate their values from their life. Each saw knowledge as a form of power that could be used to change the status quo or to maintain it. They believed their work could stimulate action in much the same way a medical diagnosis leads to treatment. Lange also realized that she was the photographer that Taylor needed and that, furthermore, he was a solid anchor in turbulent times, whose life of purpose excited her and presented her with an opportunity to grow as a photographer. Lange had never really felt involved in "the vitals" of Dixon, as she later explained in her oral memoir. Now she knew what it was like to "live with someone with whom you really live, who will share, or wants to share." Lange was falling in love. And Taylor felt a similar pull. His marriage to Katherine Page Whiteside had been faltering for some years before he met Lange. Both were ready to move on.[38]

While all of these relationship changes were transpiring, Taylor and Lange were building an illustrated presentation in support of a plan for a federal program of public labor camps "to accord minimal decencies to workers and access to health and other public agencies." Taylor already had the typed text laying out all of the conditions, giving what history and background there were, presenting statistics or estimates, and recommending certain solutions. But lacking money for fancy advertising programs, he was at a loss about how to proceed. Although he had used photographs to illustrate several articles, he had never made a report amalgamating words and images. Lange came up with a way to do so. Using a new system of wire spiral binding, she obtained strong cardboard covers, waxed them to make them look good, brought in Maynard Dixon to do the lettering to accompany the photographs, and tipped in maps that Taylor had drawn tracing the main migration routes traveled by migrant workers.[39]

Completed on March 15 and soon shown to members of the California State Emergency Relief Administration, the fifty-four-page report contained fifteen pages of text and fifty-seven of Lange's photographs, some dated as recently as March 2. Concentrating on squalid housing, the report presented one photograph after another of crude shelters fashioned out of cardboard, canvas, sticks, poles, packing crates, palm fonds, discarded trash, and even billboards. "The attached photographs, taken in early 1935 by the Division of Rural Rehabilitation, document this condition which words are inadequate to describe," Taylor wrote in his introduction. "The very words of persons photographed are quoted as much as possible in order that the expression of the conditions, needs, and hopes of those in distress may be transmitted faithfully."[40]

One especially strong section dealt with the conditions that Lange and Taylor had encountered in various camps along the way. Taylor wrote:

> We inspected the temporary camps of the pea pickers, and know that they are similar to the camps that will serve as places of abode for workers in the field when melons are gathered. . . . we found filth, squalor, an entire absence of sanitation, and a crowding

> of human beings into totally inadequate tents or crude structures built of boards, reeds, and anything that was found at hand to give a pitiful semblance of a home at its worst.[41]

Evaluating the material and debating a course of action, Drobish dramatically tore out four or five sheets with Lange's photographs on them and passed them around the table. He read some of the quotations: "If I could earn four dollars a week we could get along," vowed one Mexican field hand from the shade of his rickety old shack while his wife and three children listened. Lange's captions, though cryptic, left little to the imagination. Migrant shelters were constructed of rags and weeds; the better ones, from materials salvaged in the adjacent dump. Clean water was a luxury. The report was all that Drobish needed. He passed it along to superiors at FERA, who voted immediately to provide two hundred thousand dollars for establishing twenty sanitary camps for migrant workers. "After that," Taylor recalled, "no question was raised about why I wanted a photographer. It worked."[42]

Taylor certainly treasured the moment, but he also understood that there was much more to do. Even in receiving his allocation of money, he had moved into the field with but a small staff that included a photographer disguised as a typist. He still wondered what he could accomplish. Knowing the conditions and reporting them in a way that produced action were entirely different matters, and the two tasks promised to challenge his resources, both financial and personal. Taylor had to answer all kinds of trick questions, among them whether the conditions he was documenting were new or old. He knew that he was coming close to playing politics and that he would have to say the conditions had long existed, but he hoped to impress critics with evidence revealing that now these conditions had grown into a pervasive emergency beyond anything before. His approach was highly unusual and open to criticism, and he understood that it had a public relations component with no precedent in California. Among government officials, none endorsed photography as a mode of social inquiry, and among fellow social scientists only a tiny minority of anthropologists considered photography more than an illustrative adjunct to written commentary. "In those days whoever saw photographs of a social situation either by professional photographers or anybody else?" Taylor asked interviewer Suzanne Riess in explaining the circumstances. "People out here never had heard of Lewis Hine, most of them. You just didn't see photographs of social situations." And Taylor knew all too well that his fellow economists showed "a resistance to facing people as human beings." By reducing people to numbers, economists all too often abandoned their responsibilities. "You don't have to bother with people," he emphasized. "They are just numbers you can manipulate any way you want. But to associate with people as human beings, that is something else."[43]

8

Under the Most Trying Conditions

Lange's Reports on Migrants and Dust Bowl Refugees

After turning in her report to SERA, Dorothea Lange began preparing for a second trip into the Imperial Valley. It was to last three weeks and required considerable preparation. Someone to care for the children. Film. Tripods. Clothes. Money. Bags. Tools. Back-up cameras. Extra lenses. Notepads. First-aid kit. This was not the bohemian who had once made a living with carefully contrived studio portraits. This was not a studio photographer of local fame preparing to make people look good. This was not someone who had held back part of her self from her husband. This was a totally engaged individual checking equipment and supplies and laying plans the same way a soldier prepares to go into battle. Lange was looking at the world differently. Within a year she had been transformed as a photographer. She had found a purpose for her talents. That sense of purpose had emerged during her street photography and blossomed while she had photographed migrants and Dust Bowl refugees. It had led her to a moment of epiphany and validated her role as a social observer. She was discovering an entirely new world and a new way of looking at it with new people whose interests excited her and were focused on history in the making. She was in on the beginning of something that would soon grow into one of the epic mass population movements in American history. She was no follower. She accepted little discipline except that which was self-imposed. What was now becoming increasingly important to her was the way photography, in conjunction with words and statistics, could convince government officials to build camps for migrants. Everything at this time was directed toward that end. "She wasn't photographing for the Museum of Modern Art," explained Taylor. "She was photographing for . . . the Relief Administration . . . not what you put up in the museum."[1]

Lange and Taylor departed from Berkeley in Taylor's station wagon at 6 A.M. on March 24, 1935. Accompanying them were Vasey, Rowell, Wood, and Lowry Nelson and his wife, Florence. Nelson was a professor of rural sociology at Brigham Young University and was serving as regional representative of the Division of Rural Rehabilitation of FERA for Utah, California, Arizona, and Nevada. Two hours later, while driving through the Santa Clara Valley, they began seeing migrants, most of them camped along the road near row crops interspersed between apricot and prune orchards. Lange remembered thinking to herself, "What is this? What is this?" The deluge of refugees from the Midwest had not yet captured headlines, but Lange knew it was merely a matter of time. She saw refugees everywhere along the four-hundred-mile drive south.[2]

Reaching the Imperial Valley, Lange again focused on housing conditions along with the nature of fieldwork, the multiethnic nature of the farm labor force, and the displaced midwestern farm families who crowded the roads along the route of her journey. Continuing as far as Yuma, Arizona, an entrance point to California for many thousands of families, she was overcome by what she observed. "The cars were hung with kettles, pans, and bedding and loaded with human beings inside," Nelson recalled many years later in his memoir.[3]

Just before leaving Yuma, Lange and Taylor stopped at a gas station. While filling the tank on their automobile, they watched Dust Bowl refugees streaming over a bridge. Toward the end of her life, Lange recalled:

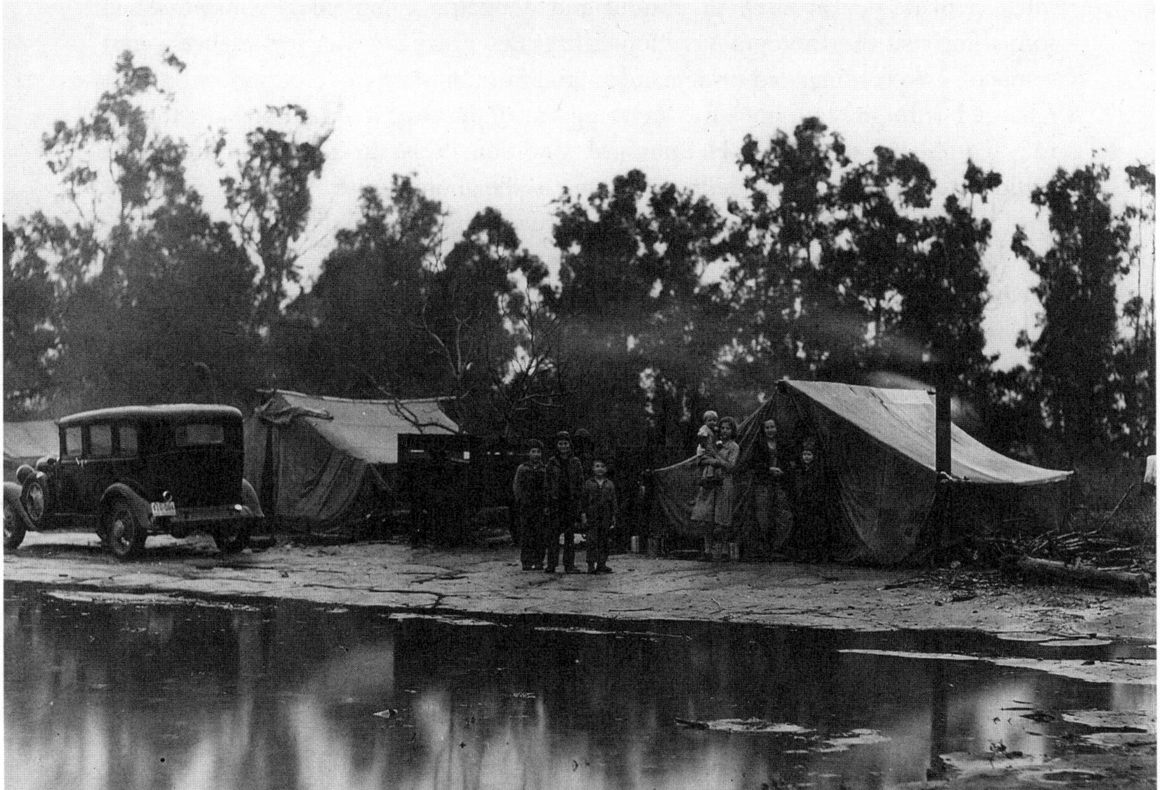

Camp of pea pickers at Nipomo, 1935, photograph by Dorothea Lange. Courtesy of the FSA/OWI Collection, Library of Congress, Prints and Photographs Division.

> There was a car full of people, a family there at that gas station. . . . They had to get out. They looked very woebegone to me. They were American whites. . . . I got out of the car, and I approached them and asked something about which way they were going, were they looking for work, I've forgotten what the question was at the time. And they said, "We've been blown out." I questioned what they meant, and then they told me about the dust storm. They were the first arrivals that I saw.[4]

Lange was tortured by what she saw and found it hard to hold herself together. "Their roots were all torn out," she would later recall of these encounters. "The only background they had was a background of utter poverty. It's very hard to photograph a proud man against a background like that, because it doesn't show what he's proud about." But as Lange gained experience, she began to rely on the "cloak of invisibility" she had developed as a child, photographing confidently among strangers without attracting attention and doing things in ways that did not seem like an intrusion on privacy. Taylor would recall Lange's statement as a mantra that made her feel as if her subjects could not see her. But her method was far more complex than that, requiring her to place two of her most distinguishing characteristics in opposition. Her intellect made her an intensely curious and sympathetic individual who possessed something that the photographer Homer Page described as a "magic presence"—not someone who commanded or demanded attention, but also not a person to be marginalized or forgotten. Lange was anything but timid. And it was impossible for her to go completely unnoticed. Her physical condition always attracted attention. How could anyone ignore a woman limping about as she photographed, however gracefully one limps, carrying cameras and equipment and wearing pants and flat, clumpy shoes?[5]

Lange's disability pervaded everything she did. It inspired her, taught her, humiliated her, helped her, and held her back. She was a woman in pain, which may explain why she went to great lengths to put migrants at ease. Fatigue held her back, so much so that she had felt tired since age ten and could never enjoy enough sleep. What is remarkable about her at this time is how extremely active she was in the fields. Lange not only was up before sunrise and climbing about on top of cars to get her shots; she also shared driving duties. And at that time, maneuvering a car of any kind along two-lane highways required strength and attention.[6]

Arriving at a camp or stopping near a field, Lange would not jump out of the car like a government official, member of law enforcement, or academic investigator. Temperamentally and physically it was beyond her to behave that way. "I'd like to photograph you," she would say. The answer usually would be, "Sure, why not," and then the people would pose a bit. Lange would ignore them and walk around until they forgot about her and became occupied in ways that she wanted to photograph. If she closed up her camera to wait, she would limp down the furrows bantering with harvesters. Her choice of a Rolleiflex camera or a 4 × 5–inch Graflex with a bellows extension facilitated her ability to capture her subjects. Held at her waist, not at eye level, as with a 35-millimeter camera, and sometimes resting on a small tripod, these cameras created a perspective that angled upward toward her subjects, often enhancing the expanse of open sky against which she photographed them. When she photographed with her head lowered to her camera, very quiet, courteous, slightly bent at the waist, she could not have appeared more modest and unthreatening.[7]

As she gained experience on this second trip, Lange considerably expanded her note-taking procedures and adopted the social science interviewing techniques that Taylor employed. From Taylor she discovered that the best way to proceed was "just to go up to them and start talking." A good way to break the ice was to ask a simple question such as, "How far is it to the next town?" After they answered, a few logical questions might follow. "What's the work going on there?" or "Where do the people come from who do this work?" In the fields, Lange asked about clothing, knives, tools. Where was the toilet? What is the hourly pay rate? This was always done in close proximity to the people. Lange never shouted across the fields. She did all of her business within three or four feet of those she photographed.[8]

While informal and proceeding according to no set pattern, many of these encounters yielded substantial interviews. Taylor found them the equal of anything he or any other social scientist produced. One of her first extended interviews carefully noted the tone and slang that a field hand used while explaining his situation:

> Seems funny to me we got so much of everything, including good men with good bodies, and we can't make a living. It's an unfair deal. I can't figger what its' all about. Good God only knows why we come here, xept he's in a movin' mood—Ya mam born and raised in the state of Texas—farmed all my natural life—ain't nothing there to stay for—nothin to eat—sumpin radically wrong. . . . We haven't had to have no help yet. . . . Lots of em have but we haven't. Now all I've got left is my Ford car and I'm figuring to sell that for $10 . . . can't get enough to buy the license."[9]

Taylor remained a constant source of inspiration to Lange. Each day brought a deepening of respect and another lesson. Lange found his energy to be astounding. He worked long hours and was up before dawn, like any good photographer. He was so absorbed in his tasks that he gave no thought about pausing to eat. In her oral memoir, Lange vividly recalled Taylor's fanatical drive and devotion to task. She was sitting in a hotel lobby, watching Taylor standing by the hotel desk, "writing and writing and writing" for several hours. "We first discovered that this man didn't know anything about what people require in the way of food and drink and lodging—very unimportant to him. So we lived without it until finally we called a halt on him."[10]

Back home in early April, Lange prepared a second photo-text with even greater impact than the first. Reporting on the trip, Taylor wrote to Paul Kellogg. Describing the scene at the Yuma crossing, he recalled how

> we watched the drouth refugees stream over the border from Arizona, Texas, Oklahoma, Arkansas, etc. In dire distress, all household goods and the tow-headed children aboard their rattling vehicles. They were fleeing drouth, depression, crop-reduction, oil-control, and everything that has cut employment and livelihood. . . . Would you

> be interested in about 1500 words and photography by Dorothea Lange, who is doing her usual stunning work?[11]

On April 17, Lange completed her essay on the abysmal housing conditions she had photographed. Aiming at narrative coherence, her effort focused on the journey from border inspection stations into the Central Valley. Thirty-nine strong portraits of the refugees and details of their baggage—torn food sacks, wooden water buckets, possessions piled high on top of cars and filling beds of old trucks, photographs from a camp in a Bakersfield dump—carried the story. To underscore the theme of a new westward migration, Lange placed an image of a canvas-topped truck on the back page. Maynard Dixon offered another hand-drawn map. Quotes from the migrants themselves added verity to the photographs. News clippings gathered along the way corroborated the images and statements. The entire package aimed at underscoring the immediacy of the situation and overcoming the inertia of Washington, D.C., bureaucrats.[12]

Taylor's three-page text stressed that a dramatic population shift was under way and argued that rural relief and rehabilitation had now shifted from a state to a national problem. He concluded by stating:

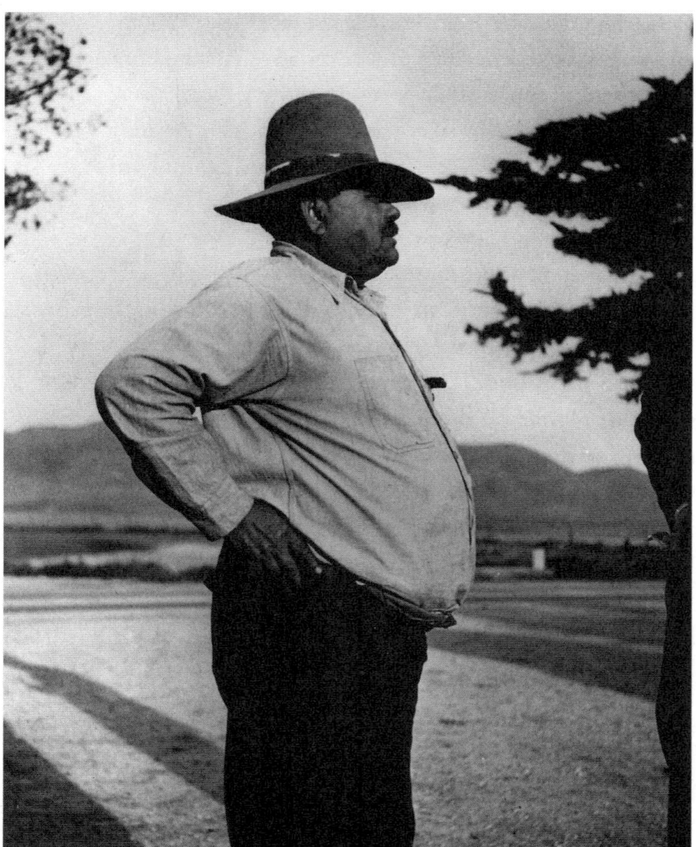

Pea contractor, "One-Eyed Charlie," Nipomo, 1935, photograph by Dorothea Lange. Courtesy of the FSA/OWI Collection, Library of Congress, Prints and Photographs Division.

> THIS PROJECT MEETS A NEED CLEARLY AND PUBLICLY RECOGNIZED BY FEDERAL AND STATE AUTHORITIES, AND BY CIVIC BODIES IN CALIFORNIA. IT IS AN IMPORTANT STEP TOWARD BETTER INDUSTRIAL RELATIONS IN A STRIFE-TORN FIELD, AND TOWARD TRAINING OF TENS OF THOUSANDS OF MEN, WOMEN, AND CHILDREN IN BETTER STANDARDS OF AMERICAN CITIZENSHIP.[13]

A few days later, Lange decided to raise the matter of divorce with Maynard. For their firstborn son, ten-year-old Dan Dixon, the matter was traumatic, and for the rest of his life he remembered it as if it had happened yesterday. He went into his mother and father's bedroom, as was his custom early in the morning, and found them lounging naked on the bed. While they explained that they were going to divorce, Daniel focused his attention on three moles on his father's head, partly hidden in his hairline. After hearing the news, which he did not quite comprehend, he ran from the house. Meeting playmates in the street, he announced the divorce to all present. The children in this Italian, Catholic, working-class section of town reacted with laughter and ridicule, as if young Dan had announced something shameful. He always recalled the moment as humiliating and painful.[14]

With her family matters taken care of, Lange again headed into the countryside with Taylor. Lowry Nelson had asked them to make a supplementary report documenting the rising tide of migrants arriving in California, which he later used to recommend building two migrant labor camps. When Nelson told Taylor that he had asked FERA to allocate twenty thousand dollars for a pilot program at Marysville and Arvin, Taylor was so excited he almost grabbed Nelson by the lapels. Nelson recalled that Taylor "was beside himself with joy" when he learned that funding had been approved. But while Nelson, too, was vastly pleased, growers expressed their deeply felt fear that the camps would become a haven for radical labor organizers. Other problems, mostly in Washington, D.C., also existed. "There were precedents for state and city public housing," recalled Taylor, "but this housing for migrants turned out to be the first federal public housing in the United States." Taylor developed a list of nationwide sites as well as sites for camps in California. After a small landowner in Kern County donated forty acres for the Arvin campsite and Drobish called in favors from his friends on the Marysville Town Council and pried loose from them a piece of land on which twenty-five destitute families had been camping since May 22, FERA gave the California phase of the project a green light. As the first camp to be built, Marysville was to be a showcase for all subsequent efforts. To demonstrate the need for the camp, Lange and Taylor headed into the northern Sacramento Valley. On their way, they stopped to interview fruit tramps camped along Putah Creek in Yolo County. The group was a pitiful sight. "Our government preaches against radicalism," one man told Lange. "But there's nothing more discouraging than to hear your children cry, 'Daddy, I'm hungry.'" The statement inspired Lange to do her best. And it provided Taylor with material he would use in an essay advancing the camp program.[15]

After arriving at Marysville on May 26, Lange proceeded to document squatter camps, Hoovervilles, and "Little Oklahomas," some of them still inundated by spring floods, as well as various nauseating ditch-bank camps in the willow and cottonwood groves along the Yuba and Feather rivers. Continuing to amass interviews, now labeled "notes from the field" or "field notes," she was especially attentive to colorful quotes possessing what the social historian William Stott has described as "an exaggerated folk pungency." While trying hard to delete her own feelings and reactions and to avoid value judgments, she tended to catagorize her subjects, paying close attention to the salient characteristics of age, nationality, family status, previous circumstances, length of time on the road, destination, wages, and experiences. She tended to ask the same questions: How could the government help? What had the migrants experienced while on the road? What had mechanization done to their lives? What had they done back home? Lange's biographers would later cite this as evidence that she was seeking justification for various relief efforts, especially some kind of temporary housing program. But such questions were also the sort of matters any good interviewer would raise under the circumstances.[16]

Unlike many photographers on assignment who developed their film in the bathroom of a hotel room, Lange waited until she was back in her Gough Street studio. During the first few days following their return, Taylor dropped by her studio to see the first prints. When Lange brought the final group to Taylor in his Fourth Street office, the two spent most of the morning discussing the pictures and debating how the government could best improve the appalling housing conditions that they had seen at Marysville. Early in June they finished their report, which was even more elaborate than the previous two. Employing double-page layouts and consolidating quotations and photographs in unified statements, they labeled one section "upward trends" and illustrated it with photographs of migrant "fruit tramps" building houses on wheels in order to follow the crops. Another section, titled "downward trends," contained photographs of workers being evicted from their encampments and local authorities destroying illegal shantytowns. A dramatic image of a father and daughter surrounded by rubble after being evicted ran on the last page. "How can we go when we ain't got no place to go?" read the accompanying caption. Other images captured a rusty water pump and dejected men sitting under lean-tos. A dark green binder tied with a blue cord held the report together. Today the mounting boards are smudged with the marks of countless hands, evidence that the plea for camps and government assistance apparently made the rounds and was widely consulted. "In Washington, they had all kinds of questions, and all kinds of reasons why not to do it, and we had to knock them down one after another," Taylor recalled. "When we showed them a document like this, they couldn't duck it."[17]

Lange did not limit herself merely to providing visual evidence. With Taylor she debated at great length how best to structure the Marysville camp and offered many suggestions about the kind of tent platforms, toilet facilities, wash basins, clothing, and bedding that should be provided. While formulating their camp design, architects Garret Eckbo and Vernon DeMars mulled over these ideas and incorporated them into their design, presenting their final plans in July. The Marysville camp would consist of one-room farm cabins and tent platforms organized around a central cooking shed and a sanitary building. The camp would shelter 230 families, who would have access to indoor toilets, hot showers, and laundry tubs as well as a sewing room, a medical dispensary, a day care center, a central meeting room, even a dance platform.[18]

After finishing her report, Lange tended to family matters and then returned to the fields, this time on her own. On her way through Salinas, she took a photograph that would become her third iconic image. Shot at knee level, with the foreground filled with lettuce and deep furrows, it depicts six Filipino lettuce cutters. Hunched over, they move toward her under lowering skies, a classic image of stoop labor. Reviewing their work, Taylor informed Drobish that the "investigation–photography" by the "superb" Miss Lange was "professional research work . . . not to be confused with mere taking of pictures. A combination rarely found of ability to understand and carry out field investigation in social science, and of ability to do excellent photographic work under the most trying conditions is required."[19]

Lange and Taylor's collaboration was the first extended teaming of a social scientist and photographer. It had few precedents in the academy and today holds special meaning for its relationship to questions of gender and creativity, the latter historically regarded as a solitary male quest for artistic self-expression. With Taylor and Lange, collaboration hinged on their complementary but very different talents and personalities. Lange found Taylor to be a man of quiet and solid convictions, unending devotion to cause, and emotional stability. Taylor found Lange to be creative, exciting, headstrong, living in the moment. These very differences may have been the chemistry that held them together. Lange's biographer Milton Meltzer would speculate that Lange found in Taylor someone she could mother and that Taylor found in Lange a substitute for his domineering mother. But others who knew them say their relationship was much more complicated. From the first, each sensed something extraordinary in their collaborative partnership. It was at the core of their attraction to each other and guided their interactions. They were building an alternate story. For them, creativity flowed not from escaping the confines and constraints of familial and sexual arrangements but from the dynamics of an effective partnership that allowed both to do their best. Plenty of effort went into this union. "Yes," Taylor would later admit, "it was not altogether easy."[20]

Lange was hardly in the shadow of Taylor, although she acknowledged that he was a massive physical and intellectual presence. He was at once lover, companion, and mentor. The combination shaded subtly into each category without any one dominating. Lange found it liberating, even inspiring, and never confining. Not interested in having any more children, Lange had traveled to Seattle for two abortions during her marriage to Dixon. She was entering a new and different phase of her life. For Taylor it was the same. With Lange, he had found the photographer he had aspired to be, someone who made him more than he was on his own and who perfectly represented his visual approach to his research. Each found huge rewards as well as costs in their relationship. Already the two were struggling with the consequences of their partnership. "There were family situations to face," Taylor would later explain. "There were children of two families." But the joys and benefits of a partnership that was both intellectual and sexual opened up the possibility of an extraordinarily fluid, equitable, and mutually enriching union that shattered stereotypes about masculinity and femininity and led to true accomplishment. "We traveled together, we were on the ground together, we saw it together," Taylor explained years later.[21]

In more than the usual ways, 1935 was a turning point in the history of Taylor's and Lange's lives and in the photographic history of California farmworkers. Lange was hitting her stride. Her chance meeting with Taylor allowed her to continue. It is impossible to determine if Lange would have headed in this direction independently of Taylor. What is clear is that Taylor never stopped encouraging and promoting Lange. In late June, Taylor began to send brief reports regularly to Lowry Nelson. Besides advancing the cause of migrant labor, these reports aimed at laying to rest any lingering skepticism about using a photographer. They not only featured Lange's photography but also borrowed Lange's terminology. Taylor called these reports "Notes from the Field," filing them every time he and Lange returned from the field. The first report was filed in just Lange's name. "I wanted to build her up in the mind of the bureaucracy," Taylor recalled. "So I told her to sign this one. Instead of me signing that, we just had her sign it."[22]

With their reports, Taylor and Lange moved into a new area, that of the illustrated book, a venture far more pathbreaking than they realized. Unaware of European publications already following this model and acting entirely on their own instincts, they pioneered a form of communication that soon became well-established in the United States. Now in the thick of the battle for migrant relief, *Survey Graphic* was about to publish another of Taylor's articles, complete with Lange's photographs. Both *Collier's* and *Today* had contacted Paul Kellogg, asking him to forward Lange's images once he was done with them. Because growers were so pathologically hostile to the camps and because leaders in Washington, D.C., were uneasy about launching a massive public housing program, Taylor and Lange spent considerable time defending and protecting the program they had proposed. This became imperative after someone in SERA determined that, because it was a state organization and the money was federal, the administration lacked the authority to spend the two hundred thousand dollars that had originally been allocated to it. Approval would be required from the Federal Emergency Relief Administration director, Colonel Lawrence Westbrook, who oversaw state relief programs.[23]

Neither Lange nor Taylor was confident of success. Describing their odd sense of despair and exhilaration, Taylor wrote to *Survey Graphic* editor Paul Kellogg, explaining:

> We are very eager for publicity on the living conditions of California migrant agricultural laborers, for we have been unable to obtain the support from FERA which we believe warranted to provide camps with sanitary facilities, water, etc. . . . Naturally, we feel the situation keenly. Wish you could travel a week thru California with us. Often I've thought of our days in south Texas, and of how you would "enjoy" the tragedy & human misery which abounds among the migrants & drought refugees. At times one is fairly heart struck over it. Yet the field study of conditions remains thrilling.[24]

In July, Lange used images from the last six months in the field to illustrate Taylor's *Survey Graphic* essay "Again the Covered Wagon." Commenting on the demographic composition of the migrants arriving in California from the Midwest, Taylor observed that they were mostly white Americans, "Oklahomans with small heads, blue eyes, an Abe Lincoln cut to the thighs." Driving home the theme of the earlier covered wagon migration, Lange's photographs suggested the closing of an old frontier of opportunity and the opening of a new one closely aligned with the California Dream. Now following the crops and living out of their jalopies, the newcomers were further evidence of the urgent need for migrant camps. As opposition to the camps built, Taylor fielded inquiries from everyone, from the American Farm Bureau Federation to the American Civil Liberties Union, the former fearing the camps would become havens for labor organization, the latter fearing the camps would impede organizing activity. To counteract these feelings and preserve the program, Taylor and Lange conducted their own public relations campaign. Taylor spoke about the camp program before the Commonwealth Club in San Francisco, distributing fifteen thousand mimeographed copies of his speech, and Lange displayed many of her photographs. "Repeatedly I was asked to speak before this or that group," Taylor recalled. "In that way I was able to handle the public relations, and build enough community support so that the officials could feel that they could go ahead with the program."[25]

Lange and Taylor did more than write, talk, and paste over 150 photographs into five, handmade booklets. They also lobbied. Contacting *San Francisco News* editor George P. West, a friend of Lange's and someone whom Taylor had known as a child back in Sioux City, Iowa, Lange invited West and Taylor to a dinner on August 11 with her and Maynard Dixon, to whom she remained married until later that year. "I remember George paging through this report as Dorothea and I talked to him, wondering if anything would come of it," recalled Taylor. On August 18, West wrote a strong editorial supporting an expanded camp program. Largely as a result of that pressure, Westbrook funded the program, and Taylor immediately began planning the construction of two model camps.[26]

A few days later, Taylor and Dixon accompanied Lange on a trip to photograph the fruit harvest in the Sacramento Valley. Arriving on a large peach ranch, Lange encountered a hostile and suspicious farmer who refused to allow her free access. His workers were hardly enjoying the best of conditions, and he was apparently worried about what might happen if Lange's photographs provoked an investigation. When he demanded to accompany Lange as she interviewed and photographed, Taylor stepped forward and diffused the situation. "I simply explained that I was up there with my team, looking into the field conditions to find out what the problems were, and report . . . what I thought would be a sensible program to help out." Taylor then got into the farmer's truck and drove around with him. "It chanced that he had a niece who was one of my university students," Taylor recalled. "So I was in a natural, normal position, even though he was uneasy about having anybody talk with his fruit pickers." It would not be the last time that Taylor smoothed the way for Lange to work.[27]

When they returned from the Sacramento Valley, Lange sat down to read up on the peach industry. Unlike most social scientists, who prefer to lay a foundation for understanding through study and then apply that knowledge to field observations, Lange, unworried about such methodology, never conducted her research before going out on an assignment. "It is often very interesting," she later recalled, "to find out how right your instincts were if you followed all the influences that were brought to bear on you while working in a region." Those instincts were often extremely acute. She called her approach "blankness" and believed that it allowed her to be as completely receptive as possible. For Lange, images and observation came first, then the research necessary to unlock further meaning. "If I had reading to do, I would do it in the area," Lange explained in her oral memoir. "I couldn't retain it otherwise." Another reason for inverting standard research procedures was her conviction that by studying something ahead of time she arrived on location with preconceptions that prevented her from making insightful observations. "To know ahead of time what you're looking for means you're then only photographing your own preconceptions, which is very limiting, and often false," she explained in her oral memoir. "You force yourself to watch and wait. You accept all the discomfort and the disharmony. Being out of your depth is a very uncomfortable thing." This instinctual form of photography was as close as Lange would ever come to claiming objectivity.[28]

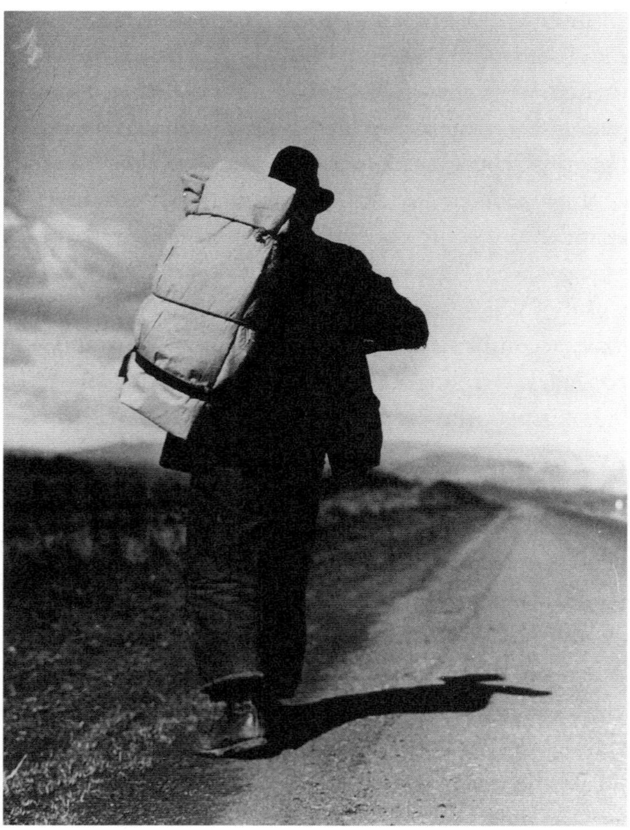

Bindle man on the highway in the Napa Valley, 1935, photograph by Dorothea Lange. Courtesy of the FSA/OWI Collection, Library of Congress, Prints and Photographs Division.

While Lange photographed and prepared her reports, a parallel project was emerging within the Resettlement Administration (RA). One of those vibrant administrative hodgepodges that President Franklin D. Roosevelt cobbled together under executive order and tossed at Depression problems, the RA was a catchall agency headed by the secretary of agriculture and former Columbia University economics professor Rexford Tugwell, also known as Rex the Red. Funded under the Emergency Relief Act of 1935, the RA coordinated relief work among the poorest third of the nation's farm population: the sharecroppers, tenant farmers, and hired hands left out of earlier emergency programs. Assuming control over rural relief and land use programs administered by the Department of the Interior, the Federal Emergency Relief Act, and the Agricultural Adjustment Administration, the RA attempted to integrate the different programs, old and new, into a unified approach. Among its most important tasks were the resettlement of poor farmers, making loans and outright grants to marginal farmers, and helping migrant workers by establishing clean camps, building decent schools, and creating several experimental communities. Needing good publicity for these programs, Tugwell launched a photographic unit in the information department. He called it the Historical Section. Tucked away on page thirty-seven of the First Annual Report of the Resettlement Administration, opposite a photograph of a lonesome cowboy gazing across a valley full of cattle, a thirty-word justification states that the Historical Section would not only keep a record of accomplishments but would also perpetuate photographically "certain aspects of the American scene which may prove incalculably valuable in time to come."[29]

To head the Historical Section, Tugwell chose his former student Roy Emerson Stryker. A pale-skinned, forty-two-year-old man with a big forehead and white hair that stood up in little pig-tailed curls, the former Colorado cowboy and descendant of a Civil War veteran had begun experimenting with photographs as a graduate teaching assistant at Columbia University in the 1920s. While instructing undergraduates, Stryker had grown so dissatisfied with textbooks that he abandoned them and began taking his students on tours of slaughterhouses, slums, and union halls. To amplify understanding, he scrounged up photographs "to show city boys things that every farm boy knows about." In 1925, Professor Harry J. Carman employed him to handle the photographic research for his textbook *American Economic Life,* coauthored by Tugwell, then the economics department chairman. Although not a photographer himself, Stryker was a bright, extremely focused, and highly organized student who believed the camera was a powerful research tool that could make important contributions to understanding contemporary history. Toward that end, he dreamed of producing "a pictorial encyclopedia of American agriculture." The dream never materialized, but his work directing the Historical Section surpassed anything he could possibly have imagined. Between 1935 and 1943, Stryker amassed about 270,000 prints and negatives, all of them noncommercial and humanitarian in nature, which today reside in rows of archival filing cabinets at the Library of Congress. A very large proportion of those images focused on migrants and farmworkers, not only in California, but throughout the United States.[30]

To get the Historical Section up and running, Stryker drew on a wealth of talents. He could, often simultaneously, be moralistic and vivacious, gabby and cryptic, volatile and friendly, generous and parsimonious, articulate but afflicted with writer's block. One biographer, viewing him through the lens of the photographers Stryker supervised, called him "an antibureaucrat's bureaucrat . . . the grand compositor . . . the mind linking far-flung minds . . . the spymaster at his desk keeping his temperamental artists just enough off balance to do their finest work." Stryker himself would say that his job heading the Historical Section (also known as the Photographic Unit) required him to be "one-half editor, one-half papa, one-half hell raiser, one-half purchasing agent, and occasionally [a] psychoanalyst without portfolio." Decades later an entire staff at a major magazine or photo agency would be required to handle a workload equivalent to Stryker's daily regimen.[31]

Stryker commanded comparatively meager resources. His Historical Section consisted of little more than a film lab, a few secretaries and administrators, and lots of filing cabinets. His motley crew of photographers, seldom if ever present at the Historical Section office on Farragut Square in central Washington, D.C., were hardly of one mind. With a few exceptions they did not meet one another at all. But they accomplished a great deal, in no small part because Stryker was such a quick study and quirky personality. Along with his talent for discovering photographers and making them work hard, he seemed to possess a combination of intuitive insight and faith in his own judgment that perfectly suited the task of riding herd on perhaps the single most adept amalgamation of photographers ever assembled in one place at one time on a single project.[32]

From his dingy and claustrophobic Historical Section office, Stryker dispatched his photographers to document everything from radiator caps to Mason jars, cow barns to tractors, but mostly people. He could not have had a more daunting or important task. Ten million people were unemployed. Statistics went only so far in telling the story. The government was trying to get a handle on part of the catastrophe through a project that had no precedent in the annals of modern government. At the beginning Stryker had no clear-cut idea of what he was doing. His assignment was to "direct the activities of investigators, photographers, economists, sociologists and statisticians engaged in the accumulation and compilation of reports." But as the images came back, Stryker was shocked, then inspired, and finally driven to the point that he could not obtain enough photographs to fill his needs. Through a dialogue with his photographers, he developed the goal of amassing a gigantic, ever-widening historical file.[33]

Day and night Stryker poured through big manila envelopes of photographs from Kansas and California, North Dakota and South Carolina. He saw pictures of "destitute migrants, sharecroppers and prosperous farmers, eroded land and fertile land, human misery and human elation." Nostalgia for the lost world of farming and small-town life enveloped him in an ambitious drive to capture what was of timeless and lasting value. To accomplish that goal, his photographers would avoid all fakery and commercial slickness in favor of simple and direct sociological images. In fact, the whole project became infused with tensions and ambiguities, multiple perspectives and layered discoveries, specific and universal meanings, even if these complications and contradictions escaped most viewers of the day along with many subsequent historians. Stryker liked to brag that the files contained only one photograph of President Roosevelt, the most newsworthy individual of the era, no record of the rich or famous or major news events, "no apple salesmen . . . not a single shot of Wall Street, and absolutely no celebrities." But he always wanted more. As has often been said, he wanted to introduce America to Americans.[34]

At the time Stryker presided over the Historical Section and for several generations thereafter, few saw the rich and deep record that he amassed as much more than a catalog of crisis and breakdown during a time of monumental economic collapse and social distress. Fear and sadness, desperation and hunger, and suffering and exploitation are certainly there. But one also finds images of goodness and determination, joy and triumph, smiles and songs, recreation and celebration, neighborliness and kindness, and regional, folk, and ethnic culture. Here were the contradictions of American life. Here was a record that would increase self-awareness, foster responses and actions previously impossible, and move the country further along the path toward a culture of sight and sound, even while supporting conventional American ideals and optimism.

Hardly the uniform edit of the tyrannical Stryker, the archive was the collective take of individual artists, each guided by his or her special vision. Much more than crusaders with cameras, Stryker's photographers more closely resembled a group that the historian James Guimond describes as "a band of good neighbors with cameras." Most of these photographers energetically went about the task of expanding the tradition of humanistic photography. They thought about their predecessors and saw themselves as part of a general movement toward realism. A few were engaged in such an intricate dance that no label or system of classification fits their motives or encompasses the varied original meanings of their images or the subsequent interpretations. In one way or another, they were trying to produce what Library of Congress archivist Paul Vanderbilt called "a kind of timeless life panorama of great dramatic richness." But it is a very complicated panorama. Each photograph holds a unique story. Nothing is self-evident. Political motives sometimes intrude. Aesthetics are always present. Often the motives of individual photographers were so hopelessly mixed as to be indecipherable. Different backgrounds, life experiences, working techniques, camera technology—the components of what is often called style—yielded different takes on reality. "We tried to present the ordinary in an extraordinary manner," recalled Ben Shahn. "We just took pictures that cried out to be taken."[35]

Already Shahn and fellow photographers Arthur Rothstein, Carl Mydans, and Walker Evans were recording astounding images. Stryker had been speaking with Shahn in the spring of 1935 when Lange's illustrated report arrived at Farragut Square. Apparently Taylor himself delivered it. He was in Washington, D.C., when someone said, "You ought to go and see Stryker." So he did. Taylor found Stryker submerged in his work. "Well, in my way, I was already doing it in California, you see. Already

I had a photographer on my staff, and here, in hand, was the report! Already we were doing in California what they had the idea of doing for the United States, and very soon did." Shahn later recalled Lange's work as "a revelation, what this woman was doing." Stryker regarded Lange's work as integral to an epic American story, the westward migration, as well as central goals of the New Deal, such as the exploration of rural poverty.[36]

After contacting Lange late in August, Stryker officially offered her a job on September 19. He explained:

> I hope at last that you have been properly notified by the personnel department of your appointment as photographer with the Resettlement Administration. Mr. [Lawrence] Hewes has probably told you that we would like to have you remain in the west where you can do the photographic work for the various divisions in that area. I am sorry that we are not a little closer together so that we could talk over the plan which we are laying for the photographic activities. I have had the pleasure of looking over the two books which you prepared on the migratory workers. You did a splendid job and it represents the type of thing that we are very anxious to have.[37]

Stryker asked Lange to join a group of photographers who would at various points include John Collier Jr., Jack Delano, Russell Lee, Gordon Parks, John Vachon, Margery Collins, Esther Bubley, and Marion Post Wolcott, as well as Mydans, Evans, Rothstein, and Shahn. Stryker later recalled: "I said, 'I want her,' and I had room for her and I got her. I got Dorothea—I got Walker."[38]

Officially hired at a salary of thirty dollars a week, Lange worked for the RA through the agency's various changes until 1939 and occasionally after that until 1942. Her official title was "field investigator, photographer." Her assignment was not to photograph the unique, odd, or unusual but rather the crucial, everyday occurrences. "Look for the significant detail," was Stryker's admonition. "The kinds of things that a scholar a hundred years from now is going to wonder about." To fulfill that assignment, Lange attempted to penetrate the realities the Great Depression, opening to scrutiny the hard truths of what it meant to be living through those times. "No one was ever given exact directions," Lange recalled. "You were turned loose in a region, and the assignment was more like this: 'See what is really there. What does it look like, what does it feel like? What actually is the human condition?'" But it was really not complicated, because, to a very large extent, Lange simply continued her photographic reconnaissance among California farmworkers.[39]

Lange's first task was to photograph the new camps at Marysville and Nipomo. Just as laborers were beginning to clear the site at Nipomo, a clouded legal title to the land prevented Taylor from going forward with the camp construction. But late in the summer, Taylor succeeded in erecting a camp at Marysville. WPA laborers did most of the work, installing washtubs, toilets, stoves, showers or baths, hot water, laundry sheds, garbage pits, water distribution facilities, and "de-lousing units." They also erected fencing, surfaced roads, and built an administrative quarters, a rudimentary hospital, and tent platforms. Lange's departure for Marysville was delayed when a mob kidnapped and tarred and feathered a Jewish farm labor organizer near Petaluma. Believing this was an important part of their periodic "Notes from the Field," Lange and Taylor appended it to their report with newspaper clippings and pictures of the vigilante action as "part of the temper of the times" that camp program administrators needed to see. After finishing their addendum, Lange and Taylor spent a week at the Marysville camp. Lange provided the RA with a valuable before-and-after record of migrant life. "Anyone studying Dorothea's photography," Taylor later explained, "would see how she fitted it to the program that we were trying to support."[40]

Of all the photographs that Lange took at the Marysville camp, Taylor was especially fond of one showing a Texas tenant farmer working with his wife and two children in the nearby peach fields. Lange's notes appeared on the reverse side of her print of this image. Succinctly encapsulating the plight of thousands of other Dust Bowl refugees, her notes explain:

> 1927—made $7,000 cotton
> 1928—broke even
> 1929—went in the hole
> 1930—still deeper
> 1931—lost everything
> 1932—hit the road
> 1935—fruit tramp in Calif.[41]

After completing her assignment at Marysville, Lange settled into a unique position with the RA. As the only one of Stryker's photographers who continued working out of her home rather than in Washington, D.C., Lange was assigned coverage of California and other western states, with occasional forays into other parts of the country. Stryker reassured her that above all he wanted her to continue taking good photographs but stressed that money was tight. Any cost overrun, he explained, "causes severe headaches here," so Lange would have to maintain a strict expense account and pinch pennies.[42]

Lange's reply initiated a voluminous and at times dizzying exchange of letters, telegrams, memoranda, notes, requests, and packages that would continue over the next five years. Some of it would be stormy and quarrelsome; some of it, mutually complimentary. Most of it would be routine. It began quite cordially. Stryker told Lange that he had enjoyed looking at "Notes from the Field." "You did a splendid job and it represents the type of thing that we are very anxious to have," he wrote. After that they settled into business. Lange needed a darkroom, new supplies, and a new lens. Stryker replied that he had only enough money to allow her to rent darkroom privileges at the University of California for the next two months, a prospect that Lange found depressing. Again he urged her to hold down costs. Stryker explained that he was contending with superiors who did not fully comprehend the expenses

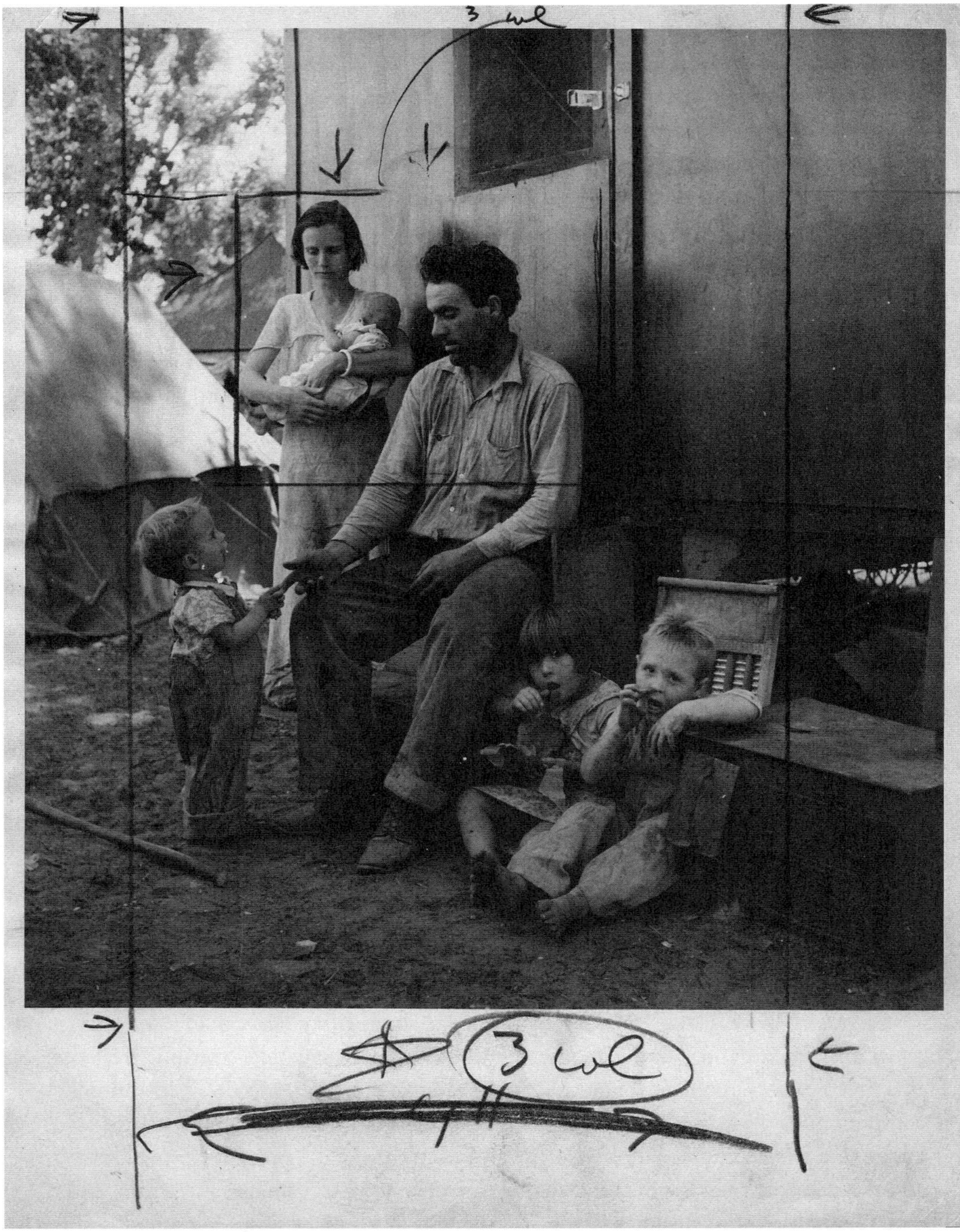

Texas tenant farmer in Marysville camp during the peach season, August 1935, photograph by Dorothea Lange. Note the various cropping marks by an unknown editor. Courtesy of Paul S. Taylor.

involved in photography. After hinting that RA might allow Ansel Adams to print Lange's negatives if Adams kept his charges to a minimum, he asked Lange for a batch of prints. The author of a book entitled *Roots of America* wanted some of Lange's SERA photographs ASAP. Lange made fifty prints and sent them to Stryker three weeks later. The exchange was repeated with minor variations hundreds of times over the next five years.[43]

As she settled into her long-distance relationship with her new boss, Lange could not have been happier. The year had gone by like a dream. Lange's physical appearance had changed radically. She looked healthy. A short, slight, pale woman with freckles who had once sported a cape and beret, she was now suntanned and fit from her travels in the field. She had cut her hair short and lost weight. She was wearing more comfortable clothing and pants, which assisted her work. Much to the consternation of her friends, she divorced Maynard Dixon in October 1935. Dixon accommodated her by obtaining the divorce in Nevada. He wrote in his autobiographical notes: "Tragic interlude: divorce." At sixty, with worsening emphysema, and barely solvent, he was losing both his wife and his children. Living in his studio, he now began a bachelor life of decline. Lange later recalled Dixon as "a very fine man" and admitted that in some way she had failed him, never really pushing him hard enough "so that he would work with his life's blood" or "dip his brush in his own heart's blood" to become an even greater artist. But she never felt that Dixon had shared the "depths of his life" with her.[44]

On October 25, Taylor opened the RA camp at Marysville along with Lange, who was described in a *Sacramento Bee* article as "official photographer." Rexford Tugwell attended the ceremonies. He said very little while there. But at the Marysville railroad station while waiting for his train, he exclaimed to Taylor, "It works." Energized by the endorsement, Lange and Taylor drew further strength from the reaction of the Marysville Farm Bureau's executive secretary, who had initially been apprehensive. But after touring the camp, he told Drobish that he understood the value of having showers for men who had spent a hard day sweating in the fields. It was a good start, even if money was available for just two camps.

When Taylor was next in Washington, D.C., and politicians questioned the utility of the camp program, he fended off pessimists by simply referring to Lange's photography. He made especially good use of Lange's pictures of a shack town that squatters had built around a power plant near Sacramento. The district attorney had come by and threatened to burn it down, and the people had packed up and moved a few miles and rebuilt another shack town. This was happening everywhere. Taylor calculated that on the basis of what he had learned, the RA could alleviate such problems extremely cheaply. "Even if costs at some camps should be quadrupled," explained Taylor, "the expenditure—$8 per family per year, and $1.60 per capita per year—would be entirely justified." Already, he had identified additional camp sites, scattered around the country at locations from Florida and Texas to Arizona and Washington. He began lobbying for an expanded program and more assignments for Lange.[45]

While these elements coalesced, other forms of photography went forward more or less as usual. Still reigning supreme, commercial work continued, although at a reduced pace. Several large Southern California wineries apparently never discontinued their tradition of taking commemorative group photographs during the grape harvest. At Guasti Vineyards, near Ontario, every September from 1934 to 1939, Colton photographer C. N. Jackson arrived to photograph the beginning of the harvest. Using a Cirkut camera, Jackson arranged three hundred or more Mexican, Italian, and Anglo harvest workers in the middle of the winery's five-thousand-acre vineyard and executed a spectacular panoramic portrait. Shot early in the morning, just when the first wagons were overflowing with grapes, and featuring every piece of equipment, foremen mounted on horses, the winery owner standing alone atop a gondola in the center of the photograph, and huge stacks of grapes and grape lug boxes, Jackson's panoramas are full of documentary information. As beautifully executed commemorations of a harvest well done, the panoramas exude memories and inspire long examination and contemplation. But as commercial images paid for by the winery owner, they are not the product of an independent and probing photographic consciousness.[46]

Halfway around the world in the Soviet Union, energetic, idealistic, government-sponsored photographers, despite oppressive censorship, were also merging realism with romance to produce a record of farmworkers engaged in hard work and facing difficulties on the collectivized farms. Taking advantage of the same opportunities—the advent of portable cameras, the changed economic circumstances of the Great Depression, new forms for publication and exhibition (albeit largely government-controlled)—these photographers documented harvest work, living conditions, and moments of leisure and rest. Selecting, framing, cropping, sequencing, and captioning their photographs much as Lange did, Soviet photographer Arkady Shishkin, a former Red Army member who covered peasant life for Moscow magazines, and others like him also shared Lange's belief in the dignity of common labor as well as her hope that government could help alleviate life's harsher aspects. With these motivations uppermost, Shishkin produced many tight, cool, heroically composed images of farm life and labor, which in many ways resemble those of Lange and other FSA photographers. Unlike the relationship of Lange's images to the government, however, Shishkin's earthy images and those of his comrades were designed largely to advance the Soviet utopian dream. Whereas Lange and the FSA photographers emphasized the plight of individuals who were temporarily down but would, through grit and a little help, surely triumph over their circumstances, Shishkin and other Soviet photographers stressed the role of the state, as seen in heroic parades, political rallies, clumps of farmers at work on collectives, huge construction projects, celebrations of the harvest, and echelons of machines moving through the fields. Although each Soviet group certainly exemplified the humble side of life, especially families gathered around tables at home or engaged in neighborly social activities, any aspect of religion was largely omitted from Soviet photos. In contrast, FSA photographers usually included some aspect of religion and seldom took the kinds of heroic documentary shots that Soviet photographers so loved. "Each side had its icons—an American migrant mother, a

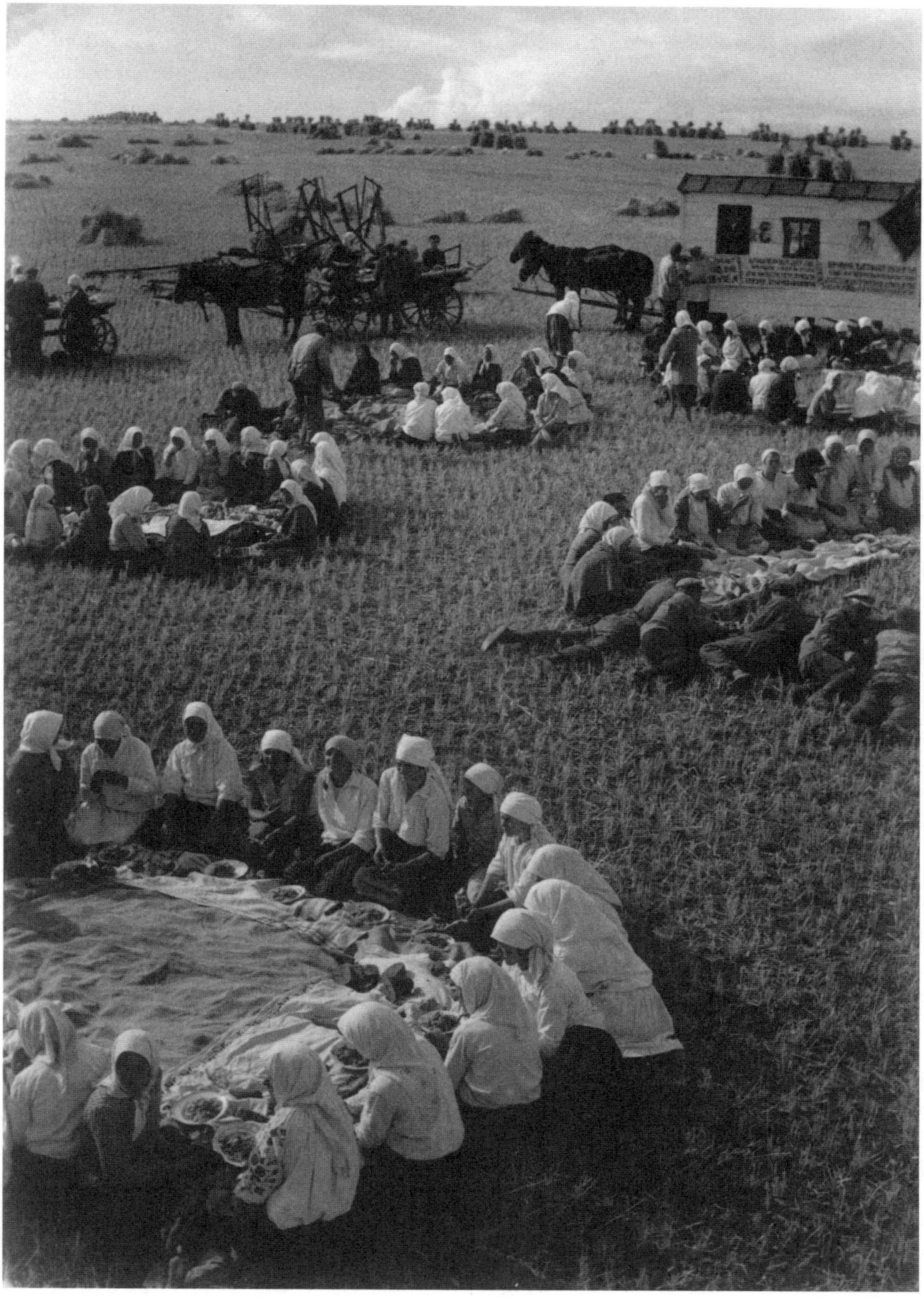

Dinner in the Kolkhoz Field, Ukraine, 1934, photograph by Georgy Petrusov. Courtesy of Gallerie Alex Lachmann, Cologne, Germany.

weather-beaten farmer, a heroically productive Soviet laborer, a Pioneer girl—to extol the government programs of the day," observed Leah Bendavid-Val in *Propaganda and Dreams: Photographing the 1930s in the USSR and US.* "Pictures of individual heroes and victims served to humanize the ideologies and agendas of both countries."[47]

With so many practitioners, the idea of socially oriented documentary photography that was emerging at this time meant many things to different people. Later, in response to being hailed as one of its founders, Lange always replied, "That's nonsense," citing the earlier work of Hine and Riis. Oddly, she did not know of Paul Taylor's photography. Had she understood his contribution and studied his work, she might also have cited it, along with the work of Tina Modotti, Otto Hagel and Hansel Mieth, and the brief but probing work by Leo Hetzel, Ralph H. Powell, even Ansel Adams. Defining documentary photography was not very straightforward. While making the transition from studio to field, Lange certainly realized that she was abandoning her past, charting a new course, and helping to forge a new approach. She really was not imitating anyone or attempting to carry on a tradition. But when she began to contemplate the nature of what she was doing, she faced a dilemma. How could she refer to her work and that of others as documentary when, to some extent, every photograph documents something? She did not even like the word *documentary.* It was more than a problem of semantics. In her new approach to photography, she was not rejecting art. Nor was she even rejecting propaganda. "Everything is propaganda for what you believe in, actually, isn't it?" she would say. "The harder and the more deeply you believe in anything, the more in a sense you're a propagandist." Whatever documentary photography was, Lange never felt she did it as well as she could.[48]

Toward the end of her life, Lange attempted a definition that stressed above all the value of being a spontaneous witness. She wrote:

> For me documentary photography is less a matter of subject and more a matter of *approach.* The important thing is not *what's* photographed but *how.* . . . My own approach is based on three considerations. First—hands off! Whatever I photograph, I do not molest or tamper with or arrange. Second—a sense of place. Whatever I photograph, I try to picture as part of its surroundings, as having roots. Third—a sense of time. Whatever I photograph, I try to show as having its position in the past or in the present.[49]

Rejecting any conflict between art and humanitarian work, Lange argued that she was trying to explore from a humanistic perspective larger societal issues, particularly those involving questions of class, race, and justice. In order to raise issues truthfully, implement reform, and make viewers feel a sense of sadness, pity, or despair, she would show what was wrong, and right, in the hope that by revealing the truth, things would improve. Although going far beyond merely providing visual facts, she was most definitely not engaged in the kind of propaganda being produced by Soviet photographers. Especially wary of the way the totalitarian regimes were employing imagery and slanting captions to cast a favorable light on false and corrupt ideologies, mask repression, and create utopian hopes, Lange rejected any tendency to lie or distort purposefully and believed that good documentary photography was always "buttressed by written material and by all manner of things which kept it unified and solid." At the same time, she recognized the value of public awareness and understanding and of reaching a wider audience with her work.[50]

Never completely comfortable with any definition and rejecting such alternative terms as *historical* and *factual* as too cold and unconcerned with photography's magical power to create images that keep people looking at something again and again (an idea Lange later referred to as "second lookers"), Lange watched with much consternation as the debate over what was and was not documentary photography ebbed and flowed over the next three-quarters of a century: Documentary was a radically democratic genre. No, it was something only a few knew how to practice. Documentary photography dignified the unusual. No, it leveled the ordinary. Documentary photography exalted the common man. No, it saw life from the standpoint of the common man. Documentary made the unremarkable remarkable. No, it made remarkable the unremarkable. Documentary photography explored what was unique and newsworthy. No, it focused on the ordinary and meaningful. Documentary was proletarian. No, it had no particular political bias. Documentary was special. No, it pervaded the culture. Documentary was compelling, persuading truth. No, it was something that moved people to action. About all that anyone could agree on was that a good documentary photographer was concerned mainly with conveying messages and telling stories, usually centered on the less fortunate, that such photography should originate in reality and not one's own inner creativity, and that it should tell an audience what it feels like to be an actual witness. A documentary photographer did not set out to create art, although art might result.[51]

Much haggling would be done over these and other attempts at definition. After thinking about the concept for three years, Lange needed 250 words to explain the concept for Ansel Adams in his 1940 publication *A Pageant of Photography.* The effort left her very dissatisfied. But this was all in the future. What mattered to Lange now was that, at age forty, she was happy, working, and completely energized. She was witnessing an extraordinary moment in time when the good-spirited people of America needed help, and she had found someone who shared her passion. Whatever the labels, documentary photography was far more complicated than she could explain or than anyone has ever been able to put into words.[52]

On December 1, Taylor and his wife divorced. He said nothing on the matter except that it was amiable and that "there was cooperation in both respects." Just before leaving on a "working holiday" to New Mexico, Taylor and Lange rented a two-story, redwood house at 2706 Virginia Street in Berkeley. Perched on a hillside, it overlooked a canyon with a fine view of the university campus below and the San Francisco Bay to the west. On December 6, while in Albuquerque, Taylor and Lange married. That afternoon, she went out and photographed. They traveled on Taylor's expense account, except for the cost of Lange's film. She developed many negatives on the trip, borrowing darkrooms wherever possible and paying for them out of her own pocket. On this trip Taylor took the picture both liked so much—Lange in profile, with the classic beret worn jauntily. Recalled Taylor, "Our work went on from then, together."[53]

Teamwork prevailed. From the start of their collaboration, whenever Taylor had been present during Lange's photographic work, he had often broken the ice by approaching subjects, allowing Lange to take out her camera, and then stepped out of the composition when Lange began photographing. This dynamic was a metaphor for their interactions in the marriage. Dealing with the five children of two marriages involved particular difficulties, which were compounded by Taylor and Lange's devotion to work. Both were holding down full-time jobs, and their work required them to be away from home, alone or together, over extended periods of time. Lange could not leave her children with Dixon, because he was in poor health, and Taylor could not send his children to stay with their mother, because she had left for New York City to study for a PhD in psychology.[54]

Shortly after Christmas, Lange installed a darkroom in the basement of their Virginia Street home, supervising construction of new developing sinks and purchasing a new enlarger. She wrote to Stryker informing him of her marriage to Taylor. Then, in preparing to leave on assignment, she began the practice of dispersing her children and Taylor's among three separate homes of close friends. For many summers before they were eventually able to settle in together, the children would be placed with friends or sent to camp so that Lange and Taylor could continue working in the field. Although Taylor's annual salary of thirty-five hundred dollars was hardly magisterial, in the midst of the Depression it provided a reasonably liveable income for the now-expanded family. And when combined with Lange's twenty-three-hundred-dollar income, it allowed Lange and Taylor to do quite well, compared with others at the time.[55]

Although the marriage would always require considerable cooperation from all involved, Lange and Taylor formed a remarkable team, handling the challenges with grace and generosity. Lange in particular became adept at juggling her career and divergent family responsibilities as mother, stepmother, wife, homemaker, and photographer, although the stress and tension often surfaced in angry explosions, an ulcer, and half-joking, half-serious accusations from her children that she was excessively domineering, "Dictator Dot," as they sometimes called her. Shipped from one household to another, her boys sang mockingly of their fate as children forced to migrate constantly among all the people who cared for them. But Lange never waivered from her chosen course, and Taylor never relented in his commitment to the union. She would be Taylor's spouse, companion, and coworker through the next thirty eventful years, until her death from cancer of the esophagus in 1965.[56]

9

Don't Let Them Break Your Camera

Migrant Mother *and the Dispossessed*

Lange prepared to hire an assistant and head into the winter vegetable-growing districts of Southern California, Arizona, and New Mexico early in January 1936. As she waited for Stryker's telegrams, she kept busy making prints from negatives for various regional outlets. Because she was the sole photographer in the Resettlement Administration's western region, Lange frequently found herself overwhelmed with requests from various publications, conferences, and legislative hearings. Often the requests came in so fast and furious that she confessed to feeling as if she were running a "duplicate [RA] project" in California. Under these pressures, she found it extremely difficult to obtain the required negatives from the RA's headquarters in Washington, D.C., in time to meet her deadlines and quickly grew tired of the added task of packing, sending, unpacking, and requesting materials. Desperate to streamline her work and retain control over it, Lange frequently wrote to Stryker requesting permission to archive her negatives in California. Citing the added expenses of storage, Stryker informed Lange that she would have to follow the same standardized procedures as everyone else and return her negatives to Washington, D.C., as soon as possible. "I fully appreciate how you feel . . . about your negatives," he wrote, "and I wish that there was some way that we could work out a plan so you could keep them." And given his compulsion to impose the general rules on Lange, he doubted that she could ever meet the demand for prints, considering her fieldwork and the time involved in mailing them across country. Although Lange complied, the matter irked her no end, eventually growing into a running dispute with Stryker.[1]

Early in the tussle, Ansel Adams stepped into the picture. Lange had met him in the fall of 1932, when Adams, Willard Van Dyke, and other members of Group f/64 had contacted her. Although Lange's method of shooting quickly on the run with little previsualization stood at odds with Group f/64, she remained friends with most members, who greatly admired her work. This friendship proved especially useful when Lange appealed to Adams and asked him to meet with Stryker and argue her case during a trip to Washington, D.C. Had anyone else attempted to persuade Stryker, he most likely would have been shown the door. But Adams was riding a crest of publicity that had begun building in New York City, where he had so impressed Alfred Stieglitz with his work that Stieglitz had offered him the first solo show in nearly twenty years at Stieglitz's gallery, An American Place.[2]

While in Washington, D.C., lobbying Congress to establish Kings Canyon National Park, Adams met with Stryker and explained that he was intimately acquainted with Lange's work. Frequently printing her negatives and mailing them back to her either in Berkeley or in the field, Adams understood that it was absolutely essential for Lange to evaluate her work quickly in order to make technical adjustments rather than waste time sending negatives across the country. While it is unlikely that Stryker actually believed this technical argument, he could hardly dismiss the country's foremost landscape photographer. Agreeing to allow Lange to develop her

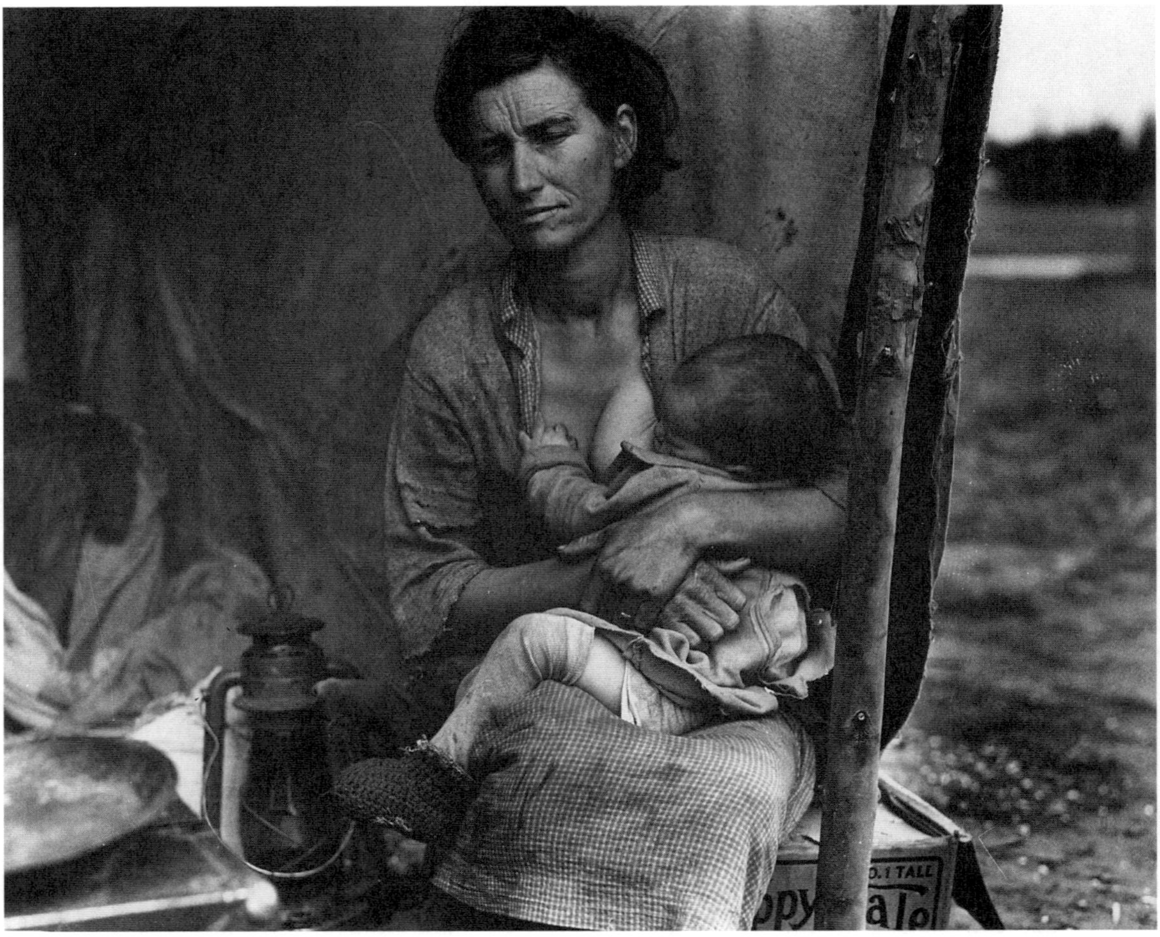

One of a sequence of seven images composing the Migrant Mother series, March 1936, photograph by Dorothea Lange. Courtesy of the FSA/OWI Collection, Library of Congress, Prints and Photographs Division.

negatives at home, he nevertheless placed several restrictions on the arrangement, which Adams conveyed in a letter to Lange. After making three prints from each negative, Lange would have to forward two of them, along with the negative, to Stryker. As a concession, Lange would be allowed to retain one "reference" print to help direct lab assistants printing her work. Lange agreed. But to make up for the loss of her work, she created her own small stash of key prints and negatives that duplicated others sent to Stryker.[3]

After the concession, Lange began preparing for her trip to Southern California. Stryker authorized a budget of six hundred dollars and directed her to leave by February 1 or risk losing her funds. He again urged her to keep careful records of her mileage and expenses and closed with some instructions:

> Would you, in the next few days, take for us some good slum pictures in the San Francisco area? (Of course, no California city has slums, but I'll bet you can find them.) We need to vary the diet in some of our exhibits here by showing some western poverty instead of all south and east. . . . When you get to Los Angeles, I think it might be worthwhile to see if you can pick up some good slum pictures there also. Do not forget that we need some of the rural slum type of thing, as well as the urban.

Before ending his instructions, Stryker shifted from the sociological to the practical. "As you are driving along through the agricultural areas," he concluded, "would you take a few shots of various types of farm activities such as your picture showing the lettuce workers? I think Dr. Tugwell would be very appreciative of photographs of this sort to be used as illustrative material for some things which the Department of Agriculture is working on." With that, Stryker offered some odd encouragement. "Best wishes for a successful trip," he wrote, "and I hope that the cops don't pick you up. Don't let them break your camera."[4]

At the last minute, Stryker inexplicably canceled the trip, finally approving it in mid-February, shortly after Taylor published a report on drought refugees and labor migration to California. Unable to provide a cash advance, he told Lange to pay all costs and submit an expense account on returning. Delayed by stormy weather, Lange printed up more negatives and sent them in with a note reminding Stryker that she had not been paid for the months of September and October. When the weather cleared on February 14, Lange headed south. Lacking funds to hire an assistant, she traveled alone. It was her second solo trip and no small task, given the strength required to drive Taylor's large station wagon.

Following a strict photographic schedule, Lange worked her way down the coast to San Luis Obispo County. Again photographing in a muddy camp of migratory pea pickers at Nipomo, she encountered a labor contractor named One-Eyed Charlie. "I'm making my living off these people," he told her as she photographed him, "so I know the conditions." Barely escaping the coast before the road washed away, Lange then headed east, into the southern San Joaquin Valley. Each night, she loaded and unloaded her film, packed and mailed exposed negatives to Stryker, and checked to make sure she was capturing subjects that Stryker wanted. Exhausted on the evening of February 24, she wrote to Stryker from Bakersfield, describing her struggle to photograph in the rain. She had set her camera on a tripod and shot from the shelter of the back of her station wagon but was certain that she produced mostly blanks and blurs. "I make the most mistakes on subject matter that I get excited about and enthusiastic," she explained to Stryker. "In other words, the worse the work, the richer the material."[5]

From Bakersfield, Lange traveled through the Tehachapi Mountains by way of the grapevine highway. Descending into the San Fernando Valley, she spent several very hot and uncomfortable days photographing homesteads while working her way south to Santa Monica. Stopping frequently for orange juice and ice cream cones, Lange continued toward the Imperial Valley, happy to leave muggy, "vile" Los Angeles. Learning that her back pay had arrived, she no longer had to skimp on film and expenses and spent two weeks photographing Mexican vegetable workers as originally intended. Deeply moved by the people she encountered, she began to form opinions on the value of the various government programs, especially those designed to improve housing. "To my mind," she wrote to Stryker on March 2, "El Monte and San Fernando Homesteads are real achievements. Especially after seeing the misery of the homeless people that I've been meeting and photographing." Over the next few years Lange's already strong commitment to promoting better migrant housing would grow into an all-consuming goal.[6]

After nearly a month on the road, Lange found herself returning home by way of California Highway 101. By March 9 she was "worked out." Driving Taylor's big station wagon over one thousand miles on two-lane highways while working a dawn-to-dusk regimen had taxed her energy. As far as she was concerned, her assignment was over. On the seat beside her in a box were her cameras and dozens of rolls and packs of exposed film ready to mail back to Stryker. "It was a time of relief," she later recalled. "Sixty-five miles an hour for seven hours would get me home to my family that night, and my eyes were glued to the wet and gleaming highway that stretched out ahead. I felt freed, for I could lift my mind off my job and think of home."[7]

Around 9 A.M., Lange reached Nipomo. When she passed through town, she barely noticed a crude wooden sign with an arrow pointing west. "PEA-PICKERS CAMP," it read. But Lange did not stop. It was a cold, miserable, winter morning. Lange had already photographed in the camp a month earlier. She had plenty of photographs of pea pickers. She had seen worse camps. But she could not forget the sign. As the windshield wiper thumped back and forth, an inner dialogue began. Thirty-five years later in a *Popular Photography* article, Lange recalled the thoughts that had flashed through her mind:

> Dorothea, how about that camp back there? What is the situation back there? Are you going back? Nobody could ask this of you, now could they? To turn back certainly is not necessary. Haven't you plenty of negatives already on this subject? Isn't this just one more of the same? Besides, if you take your camera out in this rain, you're just asking for trouble.[8]

Twenty miles later, Lange made a U-turn and drove back. Turning off the highway at Nipomo, she pulled into that miserable, soggy camp and parked her car "like a homing pigeon." With that decision, Lange took her first step toward producing the single most memorable, widely published, and, ultimately, the most debated, studied, and controversial photograph of the Depression years.[9]

Lange immediately sensed something newsworthy. Two weeks of steady rain had caused rust blight to settle into the pea crop, cutting off all harvest work. Nearly twenty-five hundred people, most of them members of families, were stranded in the camp. Spread across the landscape, they huddled around cars and warmed themselves inside makeshift canvas shelters. Apparently destitute and with no prospects of help, one gaunt, sunburned mother and her four children immediately attracted Lange's attention. "I do not remember how I explained my presence or my camera to her, but I do remember she asked me no questions," Lange later recalled. "I did not ask her name or her history. She told me her age, that she was thirty-two. She said that they had been living on frozen vegetables from the surrounding fields, and birds that the children killed. She had just sold the tires from her car to buy food. There she sat in that lean-to tent with her children huddled around her, and seemed to know that my pictures might help her, and so she helped me. There was a sort of equality about it."[10]

After taking her last photograph, Lange left the camp. Spending no more than ten minutes with the family, she never approached the tents and shelters of the other campers and never inquired after their status. Nor did she note the names of the woman's children, ask the whereabouts of her husband and other three children, or inquire where the woman had been or was headed. Such basic questions, Lange believed, were unnecessary. She thought that she had captured the essence of the situation. She had achieved her goal, discovered exactly the image she was prospecting. "I was following instinct, not reason," she later recalled.[11]

Lange had photographed the young mother and her children not as individuals but as anguished types, components of a larger problem. She was not trying to create art. Lange never considered herself an artist. She left any artistic assessment of her work to others. If someone said her work was art, that was fine. "She surely . . . wasn't saying, as she made that photograph, 'Now I am doing a Madonna,'" Taylor later recalled. "That wasn't what she was saying when she went and did it. She was down there, going back to that Nipomo pea-pickers camp where the year before she had had her first day in the field on a new assignment. She had the impulse to return and see again what sort of conditions she might find there."[12]

Lange was emotionally drained by the experience. She wanted people to see the photographs. Time was of the essence. She believed that people's lives were in jeopardy. Her photographs might make a difference. She knew exactly what to do.[13]

With little rest after the long drive home, Lange developed her negatives, made prints, and took the ferry boat from Berkeley across San Francisco Bay, arriving at the *San Francisco News* office with, as she later recalled, "the prints hardly dry." On seeing them, managing editor George West informed the United Press (UP) wire service of the situation at Nipomo. Illustrated with what many regard as the second and fifth photographs from Lange's Nipomo series, the page-three story described how migrant pea pickers, emaciated by hunger, were rescued after weeks of suffering "by the chance visit of a Government photographer." An accompanying story, headlined "FOOD RUSHED TO STARVING FARM COLONY," described how a relief agency representative had arrived at the camp and notified campers that twenty thousand pounds of food and emergency supplies were on their way to them from Los Angeles. Neither Lange's name nor byline appeared anywhere in the story. However, the newspaper went to some pains to thank Lange for her work. "It was not only a good story but a splendid argument for Federal Resettlement Administration camps for such laborers, which I am sure you agree are sorely needed," wrote city editor Morton Sontheimer. "We would appreciate it if you could see your way clear to send us any such similar results of your work in the future. The pictures had tremendous strength and were exceptional photography."[14]

The next day, the last of Lange's images, a vertical composition of the young mother, which would become known as *Migrant Mother,* ran with West's editorial. Asking in its subtitle "What Does the New Deal Mean to This Mother and Her Children?" the editorial stated:

> This remarkable photograph epitomizes the human side of one of California's oldest and gravest problems—the plight of nearly 200,000 men, women, and children who move from valley to valley with the crops and live in wretched impoverished shelters. . . . Here in the fine, strong face of this mother, photographed at the camp of starving pea-pickers in San Luis Obispo County, is the tragedy of lives lived in squalor and fear, on terms that mock the American dream of security and independence and opportunity in which every child has been taught to believe. The shame is that California is not only not tackling this problem but that through its wealthiest and most responsible citizens it is deliberately seeking to block the one constructive step that has been proved to make life a little more secure and a little more decent for these people. We refer to the desire of the Federal Resettlement Administration to build 20 sanitary camps for migratory workers and to the organized opposition of the agricultural section of the State Chamber of Commerce to carrying out this program. The conscience of California should find its voice in a demand that the Federal Government be encouraged to go ahead with its plan for these sorely needed camps.[15]

Whether or not Lange realized what she had accomplished is unclear. Over the next few days, her photographs of the stranded and starving farmworker family ran under a UP byline in newspapers across the United States. Sometime in April she made a number of prints of the as-yet-untitled last image in her Nipomo series. She would identify this picture as *The Oklahoman* for at least the next year and a half. Some time passed before others applied the labels *Migrant Mother* and *Migrant Madonna.*[16]

Considered as *Migrant Mother* and *Migrant Madonna* rather than *The Oklahoman,* Lange's image is transformed from a specific and immediate document into a universal, symbolic, and iconic image. A redemptive power attaches to the abstraction. The

"Madonna of the migrants" seems real, here and now. It allays fears and creates art at the expense of specificity and particularity. People love the image because it has everything. Cradling her baby in the crook of her left arm, the woman comforts the two older children with her presence. Staring off-camera with her right hand pressed to her face, she seems to wonder what she is going to do. Despair and anguish seem to mark her expression, but she also projects inner strength and dignity. Few photographs in American history resonate with such highly charged emotional urgency and power. "When Dorothea took that picture, that was the ultimate," recalled Stryker many years later. "To me, it was *the* picture. . . . The others were marvelous but that was special."[17]

One reason why *Migrant Mother* strikes such a responsive chord is that it has such a beautifully ambiguous quality. Viewers cannot avoid looking into that face and wondering about the social drama surrounding the young mother's plight. They can find whatever they want. Is this a portrait of despair? Does it capture inner strength? Where is this woman's husband, the father of these children? Is she the sole supporter of this family? Is she a symbol of victimization or of dignity? She does not appear

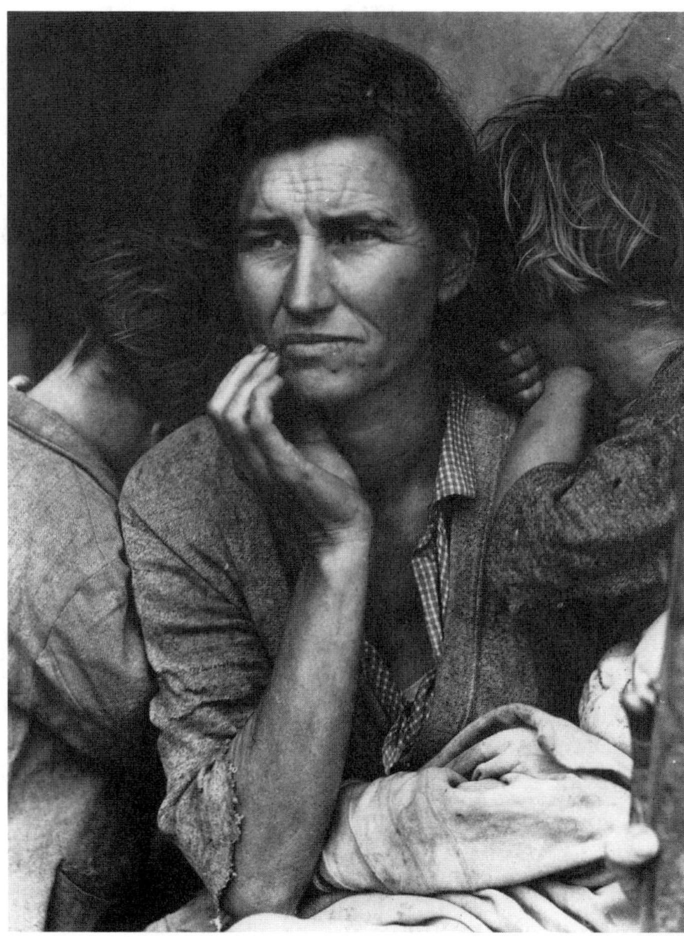

Migrant Mother, unretouched version showing finger, lower right corner, subsequently removed, March 1936, photograph by Dorothea Lange. Courtesy of the FSA/OWI Collection, Library of Congress, Prints and Photographs Division.

delicate, timid, or haggard. She is, in fact, rather handsome. She is not disheveled. She seems puzzled, a woman devoted to her children, doing her best under difficult circumstances. She also appears strong and resolute. Is it pride or fear that we see in the woman's eyes? Is she a symbol of motherhood? family unity? beauty? tragedy? vulnerability? "If one tried to define precisely what that photograph documents," explained John Szarkowski in *Photography within the Humanities,* "one could not locate it in any given decade, one could not with any confidence describe the condition of this woman and her family as being desperately poor." Most of all *Migrant Mother* conjures up a subtle variation on a favorite symbol of Western religion: the Madonna.[18]

Suggesting renewal and regeneration in the face of economic collapse, *Migrant Mother* is such a powerful and appealing image that almost immediately after it appeared artists began appropriating it, copying it, using it for lithographs and paintings, stealing from it, modifying it, coloring it, and adapting it to countless political and artistic purposes. As early as August 1936, a *New York Times* photo researcher who required an illustration for a story on California fruit pickers obtained an RA copy of *Migrant Mother,* which had run in the paper in July. The researcher had a retoucher airbrush away the two children clinging to their mother. He then severely cropped the image and printed it with the caption "A worker in the peach bowl." Lange was not listed as the photographer. The byline read: "Courtesy Resettlement Administration." Two years later a lithograph called *Spanish Mother, the Terror of 1938* appropriated Lange's image to comment on the horrors of the Spanish Civil War. The following year, New York artist Paul Weller created *Noon,* a lithographic print that places the woman of the Migrant Mother series in a field under the burning, midday sun. In 1964 the cover of *Bohemia Venezolana,* a Latin American magazine, transformed *Migrant Mother* into a symbol of oppressed Hispanics. A few years later the photograph became the basis for a psychedelic poster. In 1973 the back page of the *Black Panthers' Newspaper* transformed *Migrant Mother* into a pencil drawing of an African American mother and daughter. A caption read: "POVERTY IS A CRIME, AND OUR PEOPLE ARE THE VICTIMS." As late as 1989, *Time* magazine incorporated a disembodied arm and head from *Migrant Mother* into a collage of famous photographs used to introduce its issue *150 Years of Photo Journalism.*[19]

Lange never received any credit for these uses and appropriations. As time passed, her photograph developed a "life of its own," with "its own message rather than its maker's." *Migrant Mother* appeared so often and in so many different places and was so frequently requested from the RA and later from the Library of Congress that Lange once complained that the picture made her into a "one-photograph photographer." With time, Lange's other images of Nipomo have been forgotten and *Migrant Mother* has grown into one of the most popular images in American history and the central icon of the California farmworker experience. No other photograph has played such an important role in defining the look and feel of a class of people. Few others have been described as something that "has entered Western consciousness."[20]

Endlessly fascinated by the way *Migrant Mother* has been framed, presented, and "appropriated within a symbolic framework," feminist scholars have found that the picture exemplifies "the power of maternal values to overcome the most dire circumstances" and conveys "a searing portrait of poverty and maternal anxiety" while also revealing how much a "damaged femininity came to symbolize the crisis of community for the American public." Some have devoted considerable attention to the "gestural system at work within the image" and how Lange built a narrative around "certain notions of the female body," "renaissance depictions of the Virgin and Child," popular versions that accompanied "the rise of the Victorian cult of domesticity," and how these qualities work within "a protected, interior, feminised space." To photographic historian Weston J. Naef, the image, along with Edward Weston's *Pepper No. 39,* is absolute evidence that photography can produce "great art with extraordinary expressive potential." To others, it personifies the needs of tens of thousands of Depression-era farmworkers and captures perfectly their courage in the face of hardship. The figures in the photograph, wrote Harvard University professor of ethics Robert Coles, "seem so close, so 'tight,' it would be said in the South, yet each seems lost to the others: the children lost in the private world they secure by hiding their

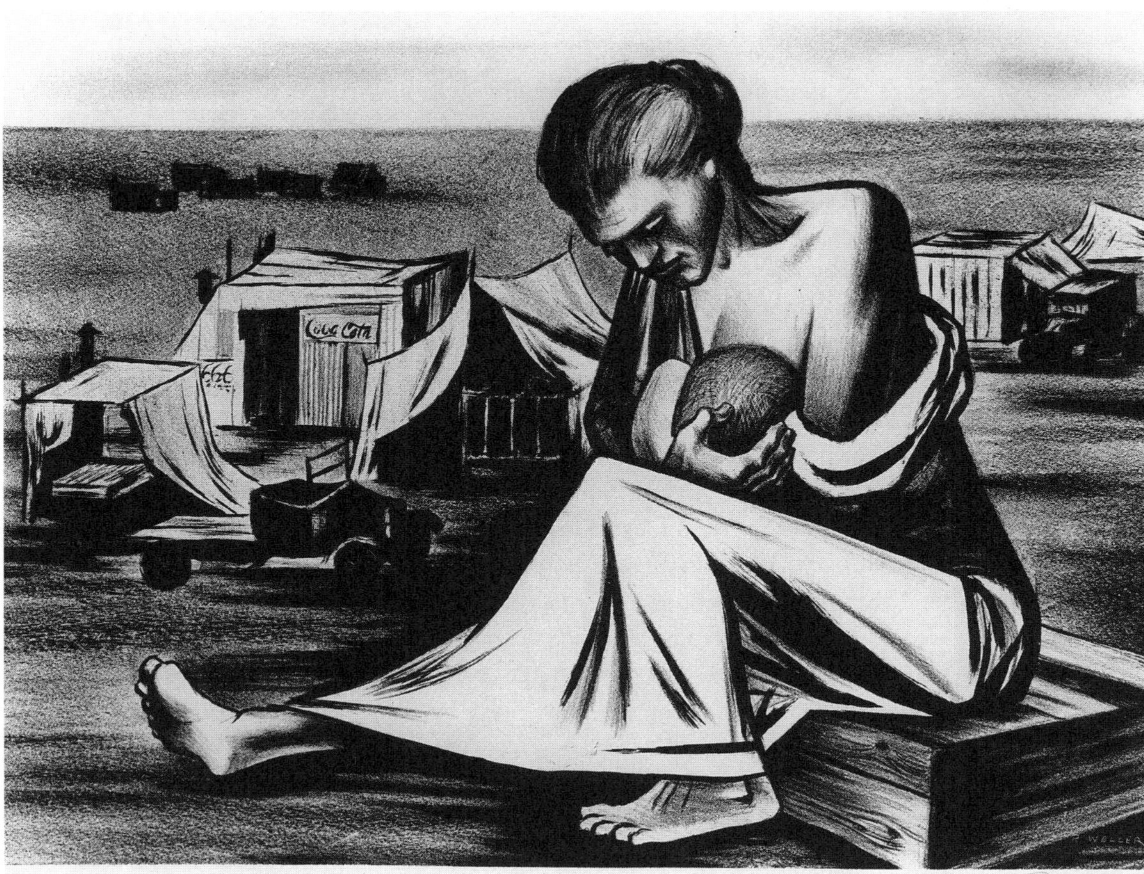

Noon, June 20, 1939, lithograph by Paul Weller. Courtesy of the University of Michigan Museum of Art, Gift of the U.S. Government, W.P.A. Federal Art Project.

eyes, the mother lost in a look that is seemingly directed at no one and everyone, a look that is inward and yet that engages with us who look at her, and maybe with her, or through her, at the kind of life she has been living." The woman in the picture, Lange once said, "has become a symbol to many people, until now it is her picture, not mine."[21]

For more than a half century after Lange made the photograph *Migrant Mother,* no one ever questioned its authenticity. Accepted as an accurate representation of California farmworkers in dire circumstances during the Great Depression, the photograph would grow to such iconic proportions that in 1996 the U.S. Postal Service honored it as one of fifteen postal stamps depicting the 1930s. But *Migrant Mother* derived most of its documentary value from the facts that Lange herself supplied in her captions and field notes. These facts came under scrutiny, first in the talks "Documentary Deception" given by Therese Heyman, curator of the Dorothea Lange Collection at the Oakland Museum, then in a book, *Mind's Eye, Mind's Truth,* by photographic scholar James Curtis, subsequently in questions and discoveries by Lange's biographer Henry Mayer and photographic scholars Sally Stein, Lawrence W. Levine, and Alan Trachtenberg, in several articles in the *Modesto Bee,* and in an article titled "Photographic License" by journalist and scholar Geoffrey Dunn.

Pointing out how, at many important points, Lange's information was either vague or demonstrably inaccurate, these chroniclers dismiss the abstract labels and call for a more specific appreciation of *Migrant Mother.* Seen from this vantage point, *Migrant Mother* emerges as a complicated image that is both more and less than it seems. At the center of this new appreciation is a detailed reconstruction of the photographic sequence of Lange's Nipomo assignment, beginning with the first ten minutes, when she failed to learn that the name of the woman in *Migrant Mother* was Florence Thompson. Perhaps because Lange was tired after her long photographic sojourn and intent on reaching home, she did not follow her usual technique of banter, photography, and diligent note taking. Had she done so, Lange might have discovered that Thompson was not one of the migrant workers at the camp, most of whom were Mexicans, or that she was not a typical Dust Bowl refugee, of European ancestry, who had fled to California from the drought-stricken plains of the Midwest. She might have learned that Thompson, while born in Oklahoma, was in fact a full-blooded Cherokee, displaced from her tribal lands. She had come to California in 1926 with her first husband, Cleo Owens, who had died of tuberculosis in 1931. Although Thompson was six months pregnant when Lange happened by, Lange never learned of her condition.[22]

Had she asked, Lange might have also discovered that Thompson had indeed suffered. Pregnant by a well-to-do Oroville businessman, she had returned to Oklahoma in 1933, where she left her infant son, Charlie, to be cared for by his grandparents. A year later, she left Oklahoma with her parents, seven children, and other relatives. While living in Shafter, a cotton town north of Bakersfield, she met and became pregnant by Jim Hill, a man who was unable to hold a job. To feed and clothe her family, Thompson and Hill began following the crops. "I'd pick four or five hundred pounds of cotton every day. I didn't even weigh a hundred pounds," she told an interviewer later in life. While living under a bridge in Bakersfield, she had walked into downtown to work as a waitress for fifty cents a day, returning each evening with leftovers. To support their family, Thompson and Hill moved constantly, following the crops as far as Arizona.[23]

Many years later, Thompson explained to reporters, and her children confirmed, that they were not verging on starvation when Lange found them, although they were hardly comfortable. The family had become stranded in Nipomo because of a damaged radiator, caused when Jim Hill and Florence's two sons, Leroy and Troy, had removed a broken timing chain. At the time Lange happened by, Hill, Troy, and Leroy were off in Nipomo having the chain and radiator repaired. "I remember that day very clearly," Troy Owens explained to Geoffrey Dunn. "We got the radiator fixed and hurried back to camp to fix the car. When we got there, mama told us there had been this lady who had been taking pictures, but that's all she told us. It wasn't a big deal to her at the time." Even Lange's claim that Thompson had sold her tires and was "living on frozen vegetables . . . and birds that the children killed" appears to be an error. "There's no way we sold our tires," Owens added, "because we didn't have any tires to sell. The only ones we had were on the Hudson, and we drove off in them." Nor did Owens remember that it had been raining that day. "We went off in our regular clothes," he stressed, "and we wouldn't have left Mama and the girls in just the lean-to if it was really raining. We would have pitched our big tent."[24]

By the time the Thompsons learned of the photograph, they were in Watsonville, where Troy and Leroy were making extra money selling out-of-town newspapers. While walking through town, Troy looked at an open copy of an old newspaper as it lay on a lawn and screamed out, "Mama's been shot, Mama's been shot." A printing problem had produced an ink spot on the newspaper picture, right in the middle of their mother's forehead, and it appeared that someone had put a bullet through her. "We ran back to camp, and, of course, she was okay," Troy explained to Geoffrey Dunn. "We showed her the picture and she just looked at it. She didn't say nothn."[25]

For most of the rest of her life Thompson resented her portrait and the way her image had been appropriated to serve larger symbolic, emotional, and political purposes. "That's my picture hanging all over the world," she told a *Modesto Bee* reporter in 1978, "and I can't get a penny out of it. What good is it doing me?" At one point, she threatened to sue Lange, whom she believed had lied to her, distorted history, and made a fortune from sales of the images Lange shot that day. Thompson's children have pointed out that while the photograph may have helped those at Nipomo, it did not help them. They were long gone by the time it appeared. But they would never escape the photograph. Stamping them with an indelible stereotype, the photograph became a source of shame and betrayal and another cross to bear. Wherever they went, it would pop up. "I wish she hadn't taken my picture," Thompson confessed later in life. "She said she would send me a copy. She never did."[26]

Eventually Florence Thompson did benefit from her image. When she was dying of cancer and a stroke in 1983, Thompson's children used her fame and their sales of the photograph to raise money for their seventy-nine-year-old mother's hospital expenses. More than thirty-five thousand dollars and nearly two thousand letters poured into a special Migrant Mother fund established under the auspices of the Hospice Caring Project of Santa Cruz County. Seeing the response from all over the world, Thompson's children finally realized the importance of their mother's image. "None of us ever really understood how deeply Mama's photo affected people," her oldest son told Geoffrey Dunn. "I guess we had only looked at it from our perspective. For Mama and us, the photo had always been a bit of a curse. After all those letters came in, I think it gave us a sense of pride."[27]

Thompson died on September 16, 1983, at the home of her oldest son, in Scotts Valley. When her obituary appeared in newspapers around the country, it was ironically accompanied by Lange's historic image. Soon thereafter scholars began to piece together the entire episode. What they discovered suggests that Lange's photographic methods were anything but objective and far more complicated than she admitted.[28]

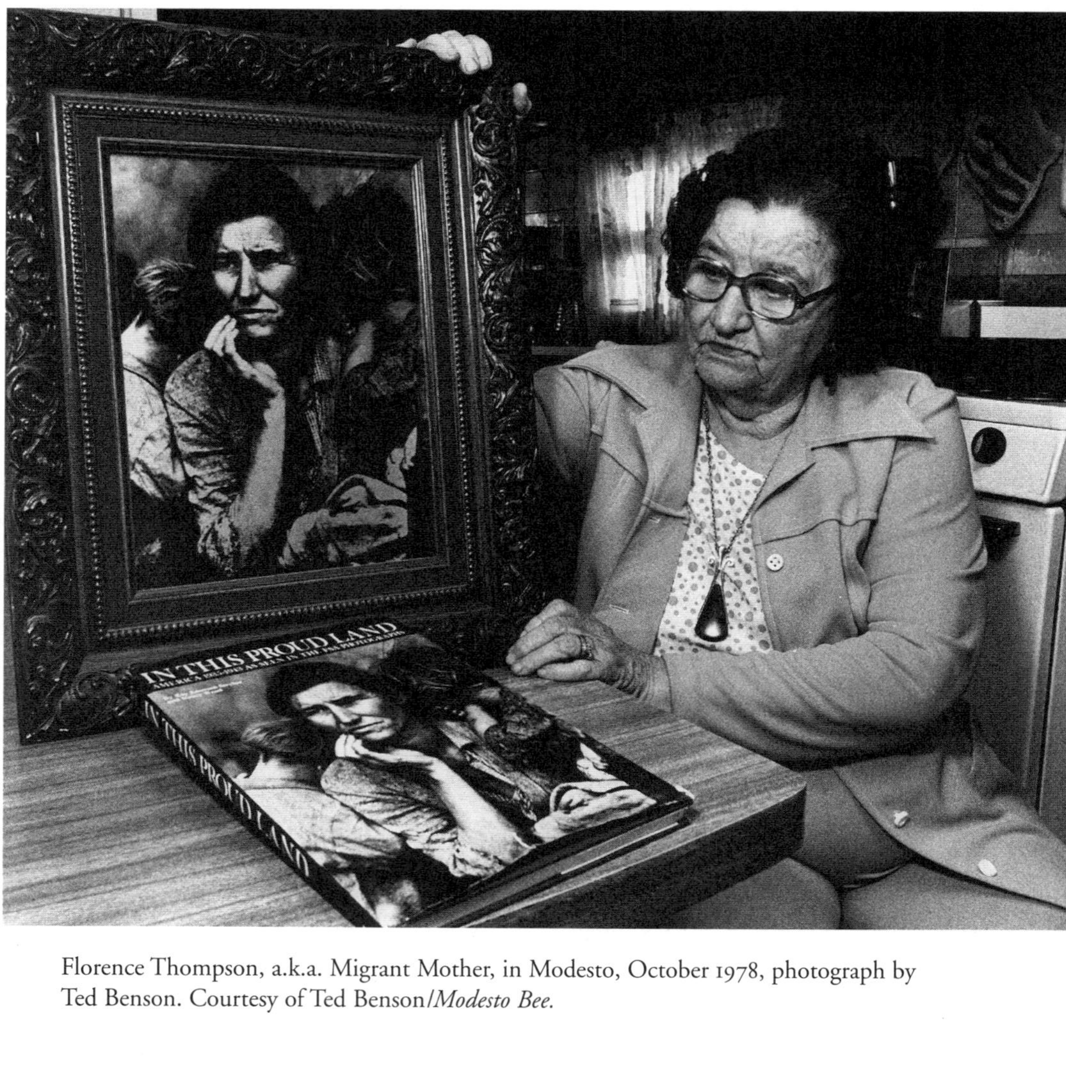

Florence Thompson, a.k.a. Migrant Mother, in Modesto, October 1978, photograph by Ted Benson. Courtesy of Ted Benson/*Modesto Bee.*

What is surprising is the extent to which Lange, having assumed that Thompson and her children were starving farmworkers, orchestrated and designed scenes and possibly coached her subjects in what amounted to a portrait session in the field. On that cold morning, Lange employed all of her photographic talents and otherwise went to great lengths in order to create an image that elicited sympathy, influenced public opinion, advanced political goals, and transformed a mother, who at that time was not a field hand, into a pea picker caught in dire circumstances. While not fabrications, the photographs that Lange shot at Nipomo reveal a great deal about her as a photographer and about people on the move through the California countryside. Although Lange and other documentary photographers of the 1930s have sometimes been described as mere sociologists with cameras, they were in fact driven to communicate effectively with the public by producing images of great technical quality and aesthetic distinction. This is what Lange aimed to accomplish at Nipomo; she created a portrait that is among the most instantly recognized and widely published in photographic history.[29]

Lange accomplished this transformation by making seven images that day, not five as she later claimed, or six, as most scholars note. She used an American Graflex. About the size and shape of a woman's pillbox purse (or a carton of TNT), it weighed about nine and a quarter pounds, had leather straps on each side, and was, according to Lange, "about as awkward a camera as can be." Lange would have kept it folded up inside a camera bag on the seat beside her. To open the camera, she had to depress a hidden bump on top, thus freeing the lens and allowing the collapsible viewing hood to extend upward about ten inches. Then, if the camera was not yet loaded, she had to snap on a film holder, which created a muffled "thunk" when it was securely in place. Finally, she had to withdraw the slide card in the holder, move a sheet of film into position, and cock the shutter. Now she was ready to photograph.[30]

Lange framed her first image from a distance of about seventy-five feet. It was not a very interesting composition. Thompson's eldest daughter reclines in a rocking chair, looking away from Lange toward her mother and baby brother as her younger brother turns toward Lange and smiles and Thompson turns away to confront her daughter behind her. Realizing it was a throwaway, Lange withdrew the slide card on her film holder, moved a second sheet of film into position, cocked the shutter, and framed another picture. In this slightly wider and more successful shot, the eldest girl has taken her rocking chair out of the lean-to and is leaning on it, looking toward Lange coyly, while her brother and sister gather near their mother in the far right corner of the lean-to.[31]

Of all the images Lange made that morning, only the first one seems largely free of manipulation, while the second gives a good sense of the setting, including the fields where the pea pickers are encamped, along with the obvious symbols of migration: a ragged lean-to, a large trunk serving as a table, a half-open trunk full of clothes, an empty pie plate, and a kerosine lantern. Neither image possesses much aesthetic or documentary value, and both were entirely forgettable. No one appears to be suffering or at least suffering enough or suffering in a useful way. Lange later withheld or misfiled the images, along with a third equally forgettable image taken somewhere midway through the sequence. She thought so little of these pictures that she never printed them. But of all the images she made that fateful morning, the first two probably capture the more important truths. They show that in the labor camps under stark and challenging circumstances at the height of the Great Depression during the flood tide of the Okie migration to California, life often resolved into stark black-and-white pictures. Not only does Florence Thompson appear weary, but also her children seem scruffy, dressed in frayed clothes, and anything but neat and clean.[32]

Lange was looking for more. Did she want "symbolic victims," as some assert? Was she prospecting for images of abject poverty, disease, and despair? Her first efforts at Nipomo may have failed to tell the hard story that Lange wanted to tell. They were not useful in marshaling public opinion behind the necessity for massive government assistance. But Lange did not quit. Following her two or three establishing shots, she withdrew the slide card on her film holder, moved another sheet of film into position, cocked the shutter, and began exploring the people in that lean-to according to a process that has been variously described as a sequence of "trial takes" in a standard portrait session leading up to a final image, a multiperspective account of a scene containing one particularly outstanding image, and a "pyramidal process culminating in a masterpiece of direction and manipulation." As part of that process, she now began selecting and excluding details, framing and readjusting her compositions, shifting perspective, and moving progressively closer, always retaining the mother as the central focus of attention. During this time she introduced Thompson and her children to the photographic process, probably talking to the family while she worked. It was an approach she had employed on countless occasions as a studio portrait photographer over the past sixteen years.[33]

How all of this unfolded is not exactly clear and can only be deduced from small clues. Certainly the next three images were made with Lange squinting through her Graflex viewfinder, back bent, legs flexed. With the big camera growing heavy, she slid her palm farther into the side strap, focused tightly on Thompson, and underscored the bond between mother and child by editing out the older children. Their presence would have weakened the intimate portrait of a forlorn farmworker mother tending to a baby that Lange was devising. But Lange may have edited out the older children for sociological reasons. According to this line of thinking, a large family such as this projected an image at odds with the ideal family size that Lange was trying to capture. By shaping the Thompson family to manageable size and eliminating a teenage daughter ready and able to make her own contribution to the family, Lange deleted all of the extraneous visual information that might have detracted from a sympathetic reaction to a needy mother and her small and vulnerable children. She was thinking photographically, much as she had done in studio sessions, when she had learned to make the best possible photograph by "working a situation." Only now much more was at stake. Lange was trying her best to get inside a story, to understand a situation. With each passing moment, she was changing, and her ideas about the situation before her were changing as well.[34]

At some point in this sequence, Thompson bared her breast and began nursing her baby. Most commentators identify this as the fourth image in the series, which may be correct, but it could very well be the third or, most likely, the last picture. Before making the image usually identified as the fifth shot, Lange again readied her camera and shifted slightly left. From this perspective, she then rotated her Graflex from the horizontal to the vertical position and either directed or waited for the boy to place his right hand on his mother's shoulder and his left hand on the tent pole. Thompson now looked directly at Lange in a far more effective rendering of the mother and family bonding theme.[35]

To make the famous sixth image, which is really the seventh, Lange moved still closer. Attracted by Thompson's chiseled beauty and her wrinkled brow, Lange zeroed in on the woman's determined yet haunting gaze at an uncertain fate. Again she removed her film holder slide card, moved a new sheet of film into position, and cocked the shutter. At this point both of the smaller children lean on their mother's shoulders, hide their faces behind their mother, and turn away. Now all of the competing expressions are gone, and Lange can focus on Thompson, who looks slightly to the right of camera while holding her baby bundled in her lap. Spontaneously or under Lange's prodding, Thompson brings her right hand to her face in an expressive gesture suggesting distress. Lange herself had employed the gesture frequently while being photographed by others. Releasing the shutter at that moment, Lange created a powerful and enduring image whose subject cultural historian Lawrence Levine describes as a "perfect victim."[36]

It is hard to believe that this occurred spontaneously, without some gentle coaching, or that Lange did not have something like this in mind almost from the beginning of the session. The nursing Madonna would crop up again and again in her work, in many different contexts, among Dust Bowl migrants and Mexican field hands. But none would have a power equaling that beautiful portrait of Florence Thompson, a.k.a. Migrant Mother.

One scholar credits the image *Migrant Mother* with helping "to awaken Americans to the plight of these particular families and thousands of others facing similar difficulties in depression-torn California." Another labels it as "an instance of photography improving the conditions of real people's lives." Still others declare that it instantly emerged as the key photograph of the California farmworker experience and a symbol for an era. But contemporary newspaper accounts and other commentary reveal that hardly anyone immediately recognized the Nipomo photograph as one of the greatest American photographs. During the six months following its initial publication, the image was published only a few times, always as *The Oklahoman.* Lange herself hardly gave the photograph much thought. She was far too busy traveling widely and completing a string of assignments.[37]

Lange spent the latter half of March and much of April in Utah, photographing RA projects designed to break the cycle of displacement from the land, assignments that she disliked because they bordered on public relations. On returning from Utah, Lange rejoined Taylor. Having transferred to the research division of the Social Security

Board, he had been assigned the task of studying occupations excluded from coverage, particularly farmworkers. Because Taylor's boss thought so highly of Lange's collaboration with Taylor, he allowed the Social Security Board to split the tab for Lange's photography with the RA, effectively doubling the amount of time she could spend in the field. After visiting Stryker at RA headquarters in May, Lange wrote to the *Nation* editor James Rorty, enthusiastically describing the Historical Section as a hot, cramped, disorganized place "where nobody especially knew what he was going to do or how he was going to do it." But the files were "rich," Stryker was inspiring, and the whole operation amounted to a kind of organized chaos devoted to making a difference.[38]

Accompanying Taylor on the journey back to California, Lange photographed steel workers in the East and poor whites, turpentine workers, peach pickers, black churches, revival meetings, and old slaves in the South. Always with a keen eye open for symbolism, she stopped to photograph at a plantation store near Clarksdale, Mississippi. It was late in June or early in July and very hot. A rotund white overseer stands with one foot resting on the bumper of his new car, talking to Lange while she photographs him. Behind him five adult African American field hands, described by the overseer as "my boys," arrange themselves on the porch and steps of the store. In making a picture that perfectly captured the prevailing social order and power relationships of the Deep South, Lange also inadvertently recorded Paul Taylor, whose face and hands barely protrude into the left side of the image. Taylor is the hidden figure behind the composition. He is diverting attention from Lange and putting the overseer at ease. This was his custom when working with Lange. Just how many times he performed this function cannot be estimated. Certainly this was but one of many such instances of his partnership in her photography.[39]

Working her way through northeastern Mississippi, Lange became so alarmed at the conditions she encountered that she sent a three-page report to Washington, D.C. Moving on to Arkansas, she photographed cooperatives formed by tenant farmers who had been evicted from their land, and she produced a long meditation on abandoned farmhouses and other aspects of mechanization and displacement. Driving west through Oklahoma and Texas, she surveyed aspects of cotton culture, then picked up the trail of Dust Bowl refugees and followed them through New Mexico and Arizona.[40]

While Lange photographed in the South and Southwest, about three thousand members of the Confederación de Uniones Campesinos y Obreros Mexicanos (CUCOM) went on strike in the citrus groves of northern Orange County. Blacklisted, evicted, attacked, jailed, and deported by the hundreds, the strikers were ignored by newspaper photographers from the Santa Ana and Fullerton newspapers. When photographers finally appeared on the scene, it was to cover the 119 Mexican men, including three juveniles, who had been arrested on charges of rioting. In a scene resembling that of a crowded movie set, newsreel cameramen, local photographers, and various reporters who had missed the action of the strike surrounded the rear of the Fullerton courthouse on July 9 to record a caravan of the strikers escorted to jail by highway patrolmen. By this time the strike was nearly a month old. When the six-week strike ended in defeat for the union on July 25, the only visual record of the event, which a *Los Angeles Times* reporter described as "a miniature civil war," consisted of a black-and-white block print of a murdered citrus picker. Illustrating a Carey McWilliams exposé published in Helen Hosmer's feisty *Rural Observer,* that single print served as an antidote to a well-organized campaign of disinformation suggesting that oranges and lemons were still being harvested by smiling, red-haired goddesses, not angry Mexican field hands arrested by the hundreds for demanding a decent wage and union recognition.[41]

Lange arrived at the Arizona–California border on August 17. Exhausted and low on film, she paused at Blythe, a small town astride the Colorado River. The area was overrun with drought refuges looking for work in the surrounding fields. Lange focused on members of one Oklahoma family. She described them with the title *Self-Resettlement.* They had picked their way across Arizona, earning just enough to reach California. Lange encountered them sitting beside their hopelessly broken-down car

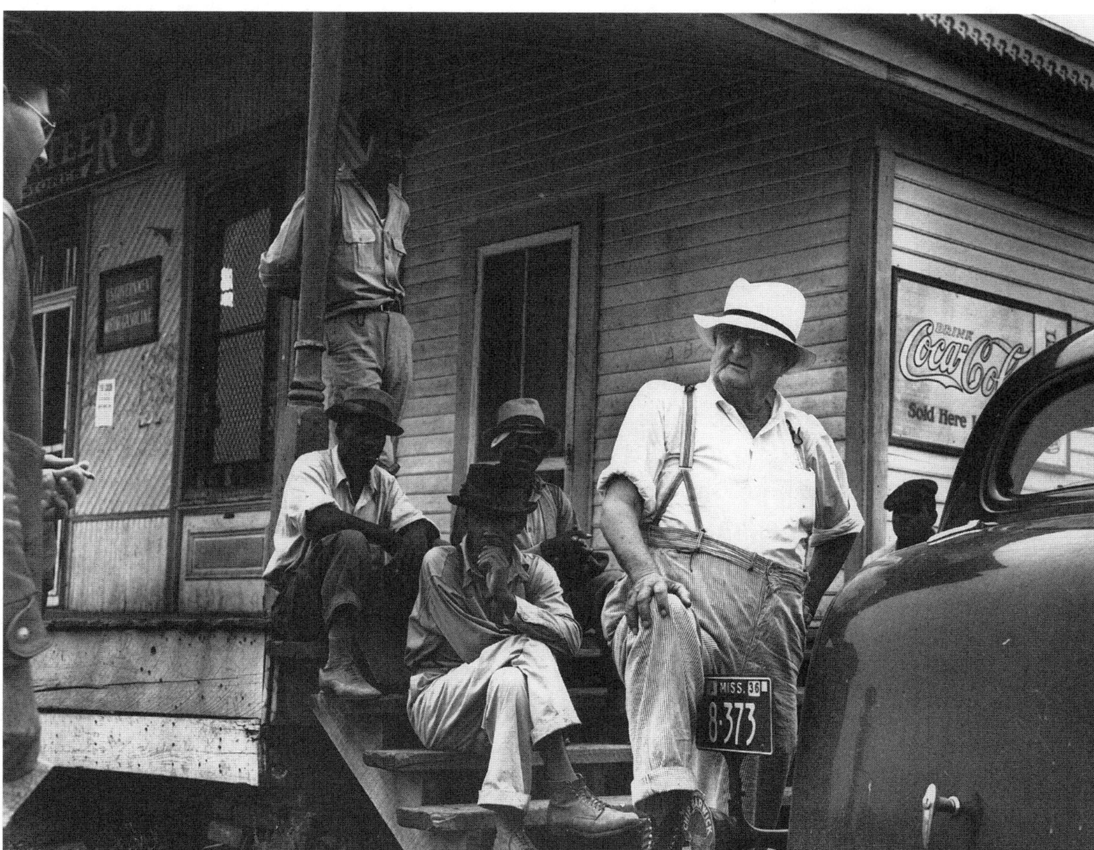

Plantation Overseer and His Field Hands, 1936, photograph by Dorothea Lange. Paul S. Taylor (at left edge of frame) diverts the attention of the overseer and his workers, in Clarksdale, Mississippi. Courtesy of the FSA/OWI Collection, Library of Congress, Prints and Photographs Division.

while they debated walking the rest of the way. About 3 P.M., she happened on the father of one refugee family. Too proud and ashamed, he allowed her to photograph him but not his family. He explained to Lange: "The finest people in this world live in Texas, but I can't seem to accomplish nothn' there. Two years' drought, then a crop, then two years' drought and so on. I got two brothers still tryin' it back there and this year they're sittn."[42]

Working her way home from Blythe, Lange found herself overloaded with lasting impressions of the people she had encountered. She was documenting history. She was in the moment. "And I couldn't wait," she recalled. "I photographed it. I had those first ones. That was the beginning of the first day of the landslide that cut this continent. . . . I went home that day a discoverer, a real social observer. Luckily my eyes were open to it. I could have been like all of the other people on the highway and not seen it. And we don't see what's right before us. We don't see it until someone tells us. But I discovered it myself. This thing they call social erosion. I saw it. It was that day. That was a day."[43]

Two weeks later, Lange reached Berkeley. She was exhausted from driving seven thousand miles and working long days in the heat with few days off. On September 3 she wrote to Stryker of her fear that the trip had been too hard and had taken its toll on her and on her equipment as well. All of her cameras would have to be cleaned. Above all, she worried that her exposed negatives might have been ruined while sitting in her car. She was anxious to have them developed and frustrated by the discovery that her darkroom sinks had dried and leaked. She had to wait several days while a carpenter made repairs; then she purchased some new developing tanks and, "knowing that there was going to be trouble," carefully guided the film through various chemical baths. Disappointed at seeing that many of her negatives were "flat, gray, leaden and overcast," she had her printers use higher contrast paper and directed them in a marathon of contact printing. She did not like the results, which came out "gray and grainy," so she settled on reference prints on defective, medium-grade paper. Late in the month, she sent off a load of photographs to Stryker. Although he complimented her on the work, he expressed puzzlement that her negatives were flawed when those shot by Evans and Rothstein in equally hot and humid conditions "show not the least sign of deterioration." His final comment certainly irked Lange: "Are you sure it isn't the developing rather than the heat?"[44]

The issue of Lange's darkroom techniques, especially her printing and her attention to matters of film exposure, would dog her all of her life. Everyone who knew her expressed an opinion. Fellow photographers who accompanied her into the field agree that her strength was in being there and in interacting with people. Although she used a Weston light meter as soon as it became available, she employed it intermittently and, during the early years in the fields, when no light meters were available, relied on memory, experience, and trial and error. Her type of photography did not allow one to spend much time reading light and worrying about gray scales, which is why she never joined Group f/64. She was first and foremost a shooter interested in the act of photographing people. Her printers all agree that she was no darkroom guru.

Her negatives were uneven and difficult to print, and many required extensive burning and dodging. She knew what she wanted in a negative and interpreted it as well as anyone, but she was never hung up on tonal qualities. She had little interest in chemicals, developing temperatures, and film agitation, and she tended to stick with outdated materials. Still, she knew how to make a great print and often spent days in the darkroom striving for perfection. Sometimes she made final prints, hung them on a wall for weeks, then became dissatisfied with the results or with some flaw that no one else could spot. If she had to make exhibition prints, she drew instructions on a test print to create a printing guide, returned to the darkroom, and reprinted to her satisfaction, then used the master print as a guide for lab technicians. So profound were the memories attached to some of her images that when she printed them she broke down in tears.[45]

While Lange developed and printed, Pare Lorentz released his film *The Plow That Broke the Plains.* Destined to become a classic of the genre, it used a newsreel-like presentation and images of tractors pulling plows across the landscape like tanks moving into battle, to suggest that greed combined with "the machine" had created the great dust storms of the early 1930s. Accompanied by a dramatic and original musical score by Virgil Thompson and seen by audiences in movie theaters across the United States, *The Plow That Broke the Plains* seemed to suggest that the very same instruments of evil that had caused the Dust Bowl could be used constructively under the benevolent leadership of Franklin Roosevelt's New Deal. Toward the end, Lorentz framed a plow, half covered in drifting sand, with a child playing nearby, then cut to final scenes of refugees headed west. "On to the West!" the narrator proclaims. "Once again they headed West out of the Great Plains and hit the highways for the Pacific Coast, the last border. Blown out—baked out—and broke," the final phrase largely borrowed from a caption to one of Lange's images.[46]

If Lange felt slighted by Stryker's comments about her film-developing techniques or pushed aside by a documentary film on the very subject that had occupied her attention for most of the summer, she did not say so to anyone. Her life was moving too quickly, in part because of a sudden interest in her photograph of Florence Thompson. *Survey Graphic* used the untitled image as a full-page illustration in Paul Taylor's essay on the RA. The magazine identified Thompson only as a drought refugee and did not use the term *Migrant Mother.* The magazine also ran three other images by Lange, including a large picture of a sunken-eyed Mexican worker, who explains, "I have worked hard all my life and all I have now is my old body." A few days later *Scholastic: The American High School Weekly* published the Nipomo image in an essay encouraging youngsters to support the New Deal's rural rehabilitation and soil conservation programs. Again the term *Migrant Mother* is absent.[47]

Everyone who saw the image loved the Madonna and child theme and the way it invoked the work of great European masters. But none of the hundreds of requests fielded by Stryker over the next few weeks referred to the photograph as *Migrant Mother.* As the requests multiplied and Lange prepared to exhibit her Nipomo photograph along with three by Arthur Rothstein in a *U.S. Camera* show of the year's best images, she never used the term *Migrant Mother.* Her main concern was not the title of the image but how it would be printed. The exhibition would tour Europe and the United States and was the first time the RA could showcase its work. Lange wanted to submit signed prints and refused to put her name on prints made by the RA photo lab. She induced Stryker to send her the negatives of the Nipomo assignment, then promptly returned them after making prints to her specifications. Even after the image went on tour, no one titled it *Migrant Mother* or *Migrant Madonna.* Those tags came years later, largely at the insistence of editors and museum curators, after the image had been published and exhibited extensively, sometimes dreadfully, to Lange's great consternation and constant embarrassment. As of now, the photograph was still just a beautiful, fairly obscure, and variously titled image.[48]

Throughout all of this, Lange remained anxious to get back on the road. She had a list of ten projects that she wanted to photograph. But as she prepared for her next trip into the field, Stryker wrote with bad news. Budget cuts were threatening the entire RA photographic effort. The money previously allocated to his efforts were now part of the larger information division, and he had no say in the matter. For the umpteenth time, Stryker instructed Lange to count every penny and stay put, which certainly displeased her. At the top of her list of projects were her precious government camps. Lange wanted to produce a comprehensive picture of camps throughout the West. She also wanted to photograph the autumn wine-grape harvest, then under way in the Napa Valley. She had hardly photographed in the Napa Valley previously and realized that the harvest would soon be finished. She was most anxious about the lettuce harvest, then peaking in the Salinas Valley.[49]

Named after the salt deposits near the mouth of the Salinas River, the Salinas Valley encompasses some two hundred thousand acres of deep alluvial soil paralleling the Pacific Ocean for seventy miles between the Gabilan range of mountains on the east and the Santa Lucia Mountains on the west. Cooled by ocean fogs blown in by a prevailing northeastern wind and watered by the intermittent flow of its one meandering river, the valley possesses a mild climate and extended growing season, ill-suited to the bonanza grain farms that dominated agriculture on the old ranchos in the first decades following statehood. Not until 1888, when Claus Spreckels erected a sugar beet factory in Watsonville, did Salinas Valley farmers adopt irrigated agriculture. In 1897, when Spreckels moved his factory south and erected the largest sugar beet refinery in the world ten miles east of the town of Salinas, the valley turned to sugar beet production on a massive scale. Beginning about 1920, sugar beet production shifted to Hawaii and elsewhere in California, and lettuce took its place. Soon farmers were producing half of all the lettuce consumed in the United States and 70 to 80 percent of all lettuce consumed between April and November. By 1929, lettuce had grown into the fourth most valuable crop in California. Producing an annual crop worth twenty million dollars, the Salinas Valley emerged as the self-proclaimed "lettuce capital of the world."[50]

Lange had photographed in the Salinas Valley on several occasions the previous year, when she had made her famous image of stooped lettuce cutters moving through the fields beneath lowering skies. But she had always been dissatisfied with her work. While photographing on her swing through the South, she had devoted more attention than ever before to the nature of field labor, especially work, work tools, and work motion. Now she intended to expand her coverage. The lettuce harvest was a logical starting point, because it was classic stoop labor. Crews of knife-wielding Filipino and Mexican field hands did the work, cutting the crop, quickly placing it in crates, and stacking the crates in trucks. And they had hardly been compliant. In the fall of 1933, Filipinos had organized the Filipino Labor Union, gone on strike, and won a wage increase of ten cents an hour. Angry vigilantes had then organized in Watsonville, burned a labor camp, and herded eight hundred Filipinos out of the valley.

Another dimension to the lettuce industry interested Lange even more than field labor: the work done in the packing sheds. Here Anglo workers, many of them women, trimmed the heads of lettuce, graded them, packed them into wooden crates, and passed them along to men, who iced the lettuce and loaded it into refrigerated railcars for shipment as far as Boston. Because of their control over shed work, Anglo lettuce packers in 1928 had organized the Vegetable Packers Association under a "floating" federal charter from the American Federation of Labor. Restricting their membership to white workers, the Vegetable Packers Association followed the harvest circuit, working in the Imperial Valley during the winter and spring, then spending the summer and fall in the Salinas Valley. Although the union had been involved in two strikes—at Salinas in 1934 (settled by arbitration) and in the Imperial Valley in February 1935 (when two union members had been killed)—it had survived the disastrous anti-union climate in fairly good condition. Reorganized as the Fruit and Vegetable Packers Union (FVPU), Local 18211, it was now the only organized group of agricultural workers in the state.[51]

Early in the harvest season, the FVPU tangled with the Growers and Shippers Association (GSA), an organization of about forty members who coordinated the sales and labor policies of the Salinas Valley lettuce industry. The FVPU struck at several sheds to protest the employment of six men who had acted as strikebreakers during a strike the previous year. When the strike spread to other sheds, the GSA and union met, and after much haggling the GSA agreed to discharge the six strikebreakers and arbitrate the cases of fifteen others. This seemed to galvanize the GSA, which for the next four months worked closely with the rabidly anti-union Associated Farmers. Gearing up for a confrontation with the union, the GSA launched a public relations campaign and, throughout negotiations, refused to concede any of the union requests for higher wages, a closed union shop, and a "preferential employment" clause in the proposed contract. On August 27 and 28, the GSA published full-page advertisements in all of the county newspapers denouncing the union and calling on shed workers to abandon their leaders and settle for what the GSA offered. On September 3, the GSA posted notices around all shipping plants and packing sheds informing everyone that wages and working conditions were set and would not be changed. Anyone arriving the next day would be assumed to have accepted those conditions. The FVPU voted overwhelmingly against the contract and demanded a closed shop arrangement. On

September 4, three thousand members of the FVPU walked out of the sheds, paralyzing packing operations. Small shopkeepers and businesses that catered to their needs lent their support.[52]

On September 5, the anti-union oligarchy implemented its plan for coordinating all law enforcement agencies. To control crowds, Monterey County sheriff Carl Abbott purchased three hundred tear gas rounds from the Lake Erie Chemical Company of Cleveland. Salinas chief of police George Griffin laid in a similar supply of tear gas from Federal Laboratories of Pittsburgh. Local Boy Scout troops mobilized for action, although their exact duties remained vague, and the local high school wood shop was set to work chopping tool handles and manufacturing other clubs. Strikebreakers were recruited in San Francisco and Los Angeles. September 15 was designated as D-Day, when the lettuce harvest would resume. Everything would be sent to three fortified packing sheds: the big Salinas Valley Ice Company sheds in Salinas, and the Marinovitch shed and the Travers and Sakata shed in Watsonville. California Highway Patrol captain Earl Griffin promised to guard the lettuce trucks and protect drivers. All the processing would be done by workers living inside the barricaded sheds.[53]

This was the situation that Lange wanted to cover. But her duties printing *Migrant Mother* and delivering photographs from her long field trip kept her running between the darkroom and the post office, and Stryker had no money to send her out into the fields anyway. Stuck in Berkeley, Lange followed newspaper reports. On Thursday morning, September 10, she wrote to Stryker of her printing problems, her efforts to obtain better paper, and her frustration at being stuck at home. Editors at the *San Francisco News, Call-Bulletin, Chronicle,* and *Examiner,* as well as the *Oakland Tribune* and *San Jose Mercury News* had no such problems. That afternoon they dispatched nearly every available photographer south to Salinas. Several had previously photographed the 1933 cotton strike, and others had covered the San Francisco longshoremen's strike of 1934. The majority were pro-union, having participated in the formation of the Newspaper Guild, often at some danger to their professional careers. Wisecracking *San Francisco News* photographer Eddie Murphy was considered the leader of the pack. They took their first photographs on September 11 outside the Salinas Valley Ice Company sheds, where about one hundred strikers protested the construction of fences and barricades.[54]

On September 12, leaders of the Salinas antistrike coalition contacted Seattle resident Henry Sanborn, a colonel in the United States Army Reserve and a defrocked Episcopal rector. In his considerable experience fighting unions up and down the Pacific Coast, Sanborn had organized and commanded a group of San Francisco vigilantes during the San Francisco waterfront strike and had trained company employees in the use of various weapons during a warehouse strike at the California and Hawaiian Sugar Company in Crocket. In 1935 he started publishing the *American Citizen,* a notorious red-baiting rag whose masthead motto proclaimed that the newspaper existed so that "Fascism would not be necessary to combat Communism"; the paper was largely subsidized through mass purchases by the Industrial Association and the Waterfront Employers Association. During the July antistrike planning, Sanborn had met with William Theile, a leader of the Citizens Association of Salinas. He well understood the task before him when he arrived in town on the evening of September 13, calling himself "Mr. Winter."

Fortified with a $225,000 budget raised by the Citizens Association through an assessment of three dollars per car on lettuce shipped from Salinas, Sanborn first met with Sheriff Abbott, whom he found "scared to death." After reassuring the sheriff, he commandeered the sixth floor of the Hotel Jeffrey, set uniformed sentries at all the doors, and, while consuming massive amounts of food and running up a $113.34 tab for liquor (covered by the association's budget), created an antistrike headquarters, where the telephones rang constantly and town leaders and officials arrived and departed at all hours of the day and night. Either assisting him or directly under his command were Theile; R. L. Hughes, vice president of the Monterey Trust and Savings Bank; Harry Knowland, previous district attorney of Monterey County; Lester Stirling, a local grower–shipper; and Captain Russell Tripp, a long-time personal assistant to Sanborn who specialized in training people to use handguns, clubs, batons, tear gas, and driving tactics. Much to the astonishment of many local residents, chief of police George Griffin, Monterey highway patrol captain Earl Griffin (George's brother), and county sheriff Carl Abbott largely abdicated their responsibilities to this powerful and mysterious unelected outsider, allowing Sanborn and his "general staff" to rapidly transform a quiet little farm town into a bustling military zone prepared for war. More than any other single individual, Sanborn was responsible for subjecting photographers to a dangerous and repressive environment that hometown writer John Steinbeck soon characterized as the type of "Fascist psychology" normally associated with "war-torn Spain" and Nazi Germany but not the "once peaceful Salinas valley."[55]

10

Photo Eye on Salinas

Press Photographers and the Salinas Valley Lettuce Packers' Strikes

Late in the afternoon of September 14, 1936, as the sun dipped behind the fog-topped coastal hills to the west of Salinas, several news photographers staked out positions near the entrance to the Salinas Valley Ice Company packing sheds. Lettuce trucks carrying the first strikebreakers had been spotted passing the Fruit and Vegetable Packers Union headquarters, at the Poodle Dog Café, a mile and a half south of town. Union members inside the café quickly telephoned ahead. By the time the trucks rumbled through the gates of the barricaded packing plant, everyone was ready. Photographers snapped a few pictures of pickets waving their fists and shouting obscenities at the strikebreakers and of trucks slowing to a crawl while they ran the gauntlet along East Gabilan Street. No violence occurred. It was all over in a few minutes. But no one expected the calm to last. Retiring to their hotel rooms that night, photographers readied their equipment, got a good night's sleep, and prepared for the worst.[1]

A half dozen photographers were waiting in the fog at the shed gates the following morning. Most had been there since before dawn. Stomping their feet, they shared the warmth cast by small fires of kindling that pickets maintained in dozens of five-gallon cans. Several had staked out good elevated positions on billboard scaffolding. All of them carried small cotton towels and devoted considerable effort to keeping moisture from accumulating on the lenses of their cameras. They also carried gas masks. They were waiting for the clash that would certainly occur when the Filipinos sent the first truckloads of lettuce off to Salinas. When those trucks rolled into sight, they knew that FVPU pickets were going to jump all over them. They were not going to miss the action. They would need those gas masks. Open warfare was about to erupt on the streets of Salinas.[2]

Photographers took their first pictures at about 9 A.M., when a convoy of lettuce trucks appeared on East Gabilan Street. "Rats! Rats! Rats!" shouted pickets while the trucks approached. A shower of rocks, stones, bricks, and gin bottles followed. These had little effect, because the lettuce companies had encased all of the truck cabs and windshields in heavy chain link and chicken wire. Photographers followed the action through the packing shed gates, taking care to avoid thousands of roofing tacks strewn over the road, and continued to photograph until police chief Griffin stepped forward and warned everyone to back off. Their next series of images came about fifteen minutes later, when police officers fired tear gas bombs toward pickets, and pickets gathered up the bombs and tossed them over the fences into the plant. When Chief Griffin led a contingent of officers through the plant gates and dispersed the crowds with a massive fusillade of tear gas bombs, news photographers backpedaled and dodged projectiles until sundown. "If you didn't zig when they zagged down there," recalled striker Ace Henry, "you were really in trouble, because you might end up with a tear gas canister upside the head."[3]

Photographers worked hard during the opening salvo of what their editors labeled THE BATTLE OF SALINAS. Each one paid a price to get his or her pictures. Ted Smith of the *San Francisco News* waddled around hunched over at the waist while trying to follow the action through his viewfinder and later retired to his hotel room with an aching back and eyes stinging from tear gas. He would later recall how his experience covering sports had been helpful and how the wire sports finder on his camera had made it much easier to follow the action and quickly compose pictures on the run. There had been other impediments, prominent among them the heavy Graflex and Speed Graphic cameras, each weighing five pounds or more, which slowed them down and made them easy targets. Camera film packs holding only six or twelve sheets of film further limited their range, requiring them to carry extra film packs in bulky leather cases that flopped from leather straps dangling about their shoulders. Police and vigilantes were certainly their greatest obstacles. "All news photographers attempting to take pictures were caught by the tear gas," reported the *San Francisco News* on September 15.[4]

Early on Wednesday morning, September 16, photographers were again thrust into the thick of battle when police guarding the entrance to the Salinas Valley Ice Company sheds fired a volley of tear gas to disperse about fifty strikers walking along East Gabilan Street. As the action shifted to the downtown streets, photographers ignored vigilantes wearing blue armbands and brandishing wagon spokes and guns and continued to document a melee that continued the entire day and on into the night. Brave to the point of recklessness, several photographers exhibited unbelievable courage and technical prowess while working under extreme duress. One photographer produced images that had no precedent in the annals of American photography. Another achieved legendary status in his profession by quietly using miniaturized camera technology to photograph with such power and variety that photojournalists have studied his work well into the next century. Local residents noticed the audacity. Writing to her son in New York City, Daisy Mason asked him, "By the way, did the *Times* publish any pictures, and what page?"[5]

One of the most daring of these photographers was the *Chronicle*'s Barney Peterson. A big, gregarious, twenty-four-year-old with a broken nose, baritone voice, and strong opinions, Peterson was later recalled by *Chronicle* reporter Carl Nolte as "the classic vision of the old-time two-fisted newspaper photographer." He had just left the *Examiner* for the *Chronicle* after playing a pivotal role in formation of the San Francisco–Oakland Newspaper Guild and was covering his first labor conflict. Full of daring energy, he followed other photographers from the sheds into the business district, where about five hundred pickets lined Main Street. Shortly after 11:30 A.M., Peterson set up with other cameramen and a motion picture crew on the roof of a building overlooking the intersection of Main and East Gabilan. Within minutes he was photographing three hundred to five hundred pickets unloading a barrage of rocks on a convoy of lettuce trucks that had stopped at a red light. Peterson kept photographing when strikers cut the ropes on the lettuce trucks and dumped entire loads onto the street and squads of police opened fire with tear gas and drove the pickets back. He took some very dramatic shots an hour later, when a second caravan of lettuce trucks

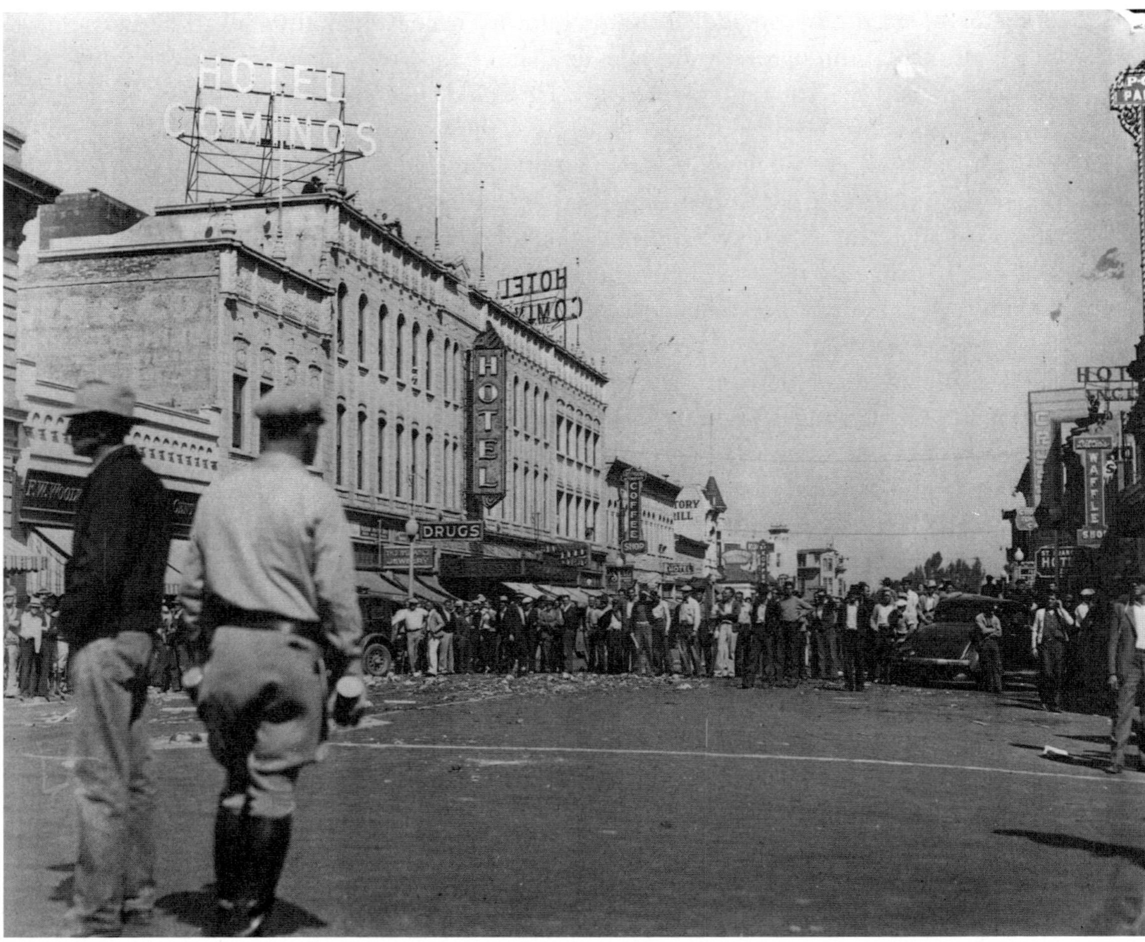

Police and deputies face off against strikers in downtown Salinas shortly after a load of lettuce was torn off a truck and just before pitched battles erupted with tear gassing, September 16, 1936, photograph by Barney Peterson. Note the photographers on the roof of the hotel on the left. Courtesy of *San Francisco Examiner.*

stopped at a red light and strikers began tearing loose crates of lettuce and dumping them onto the road. Several of his exposures capture sheriff's deputies jumping from escort cars and the pitched battles that followed when they waded into the crowd swinging batons and clubs and firing more tear gas. These images are a unique bird's-eye view of violence.[6]

After making his rooftop sequence, Peterson quickly moved down to the street and continued photographing with a half dozen photographers who had taken up positions at the corner of Main and East Gabilan streets. Among them was Harold Ellwood, who, through covering at least three farm labor struggles for the *Examiner,* had developed an uncanny ability to stay cool under pressure. This served him well and allowed him to take one of the two most memorable photographs from the strike. Ellwood kept his camera trained on Henry "Hank" Strobel. A local grower who served as president of the Monterey Associated Farmers, Strobel was a well-known local leader who in 1930 had been elected as the first president of the Grower Shipper Vegetable Association (GSVA). Much hated by the strikers, he drove the first truckload of lettuce

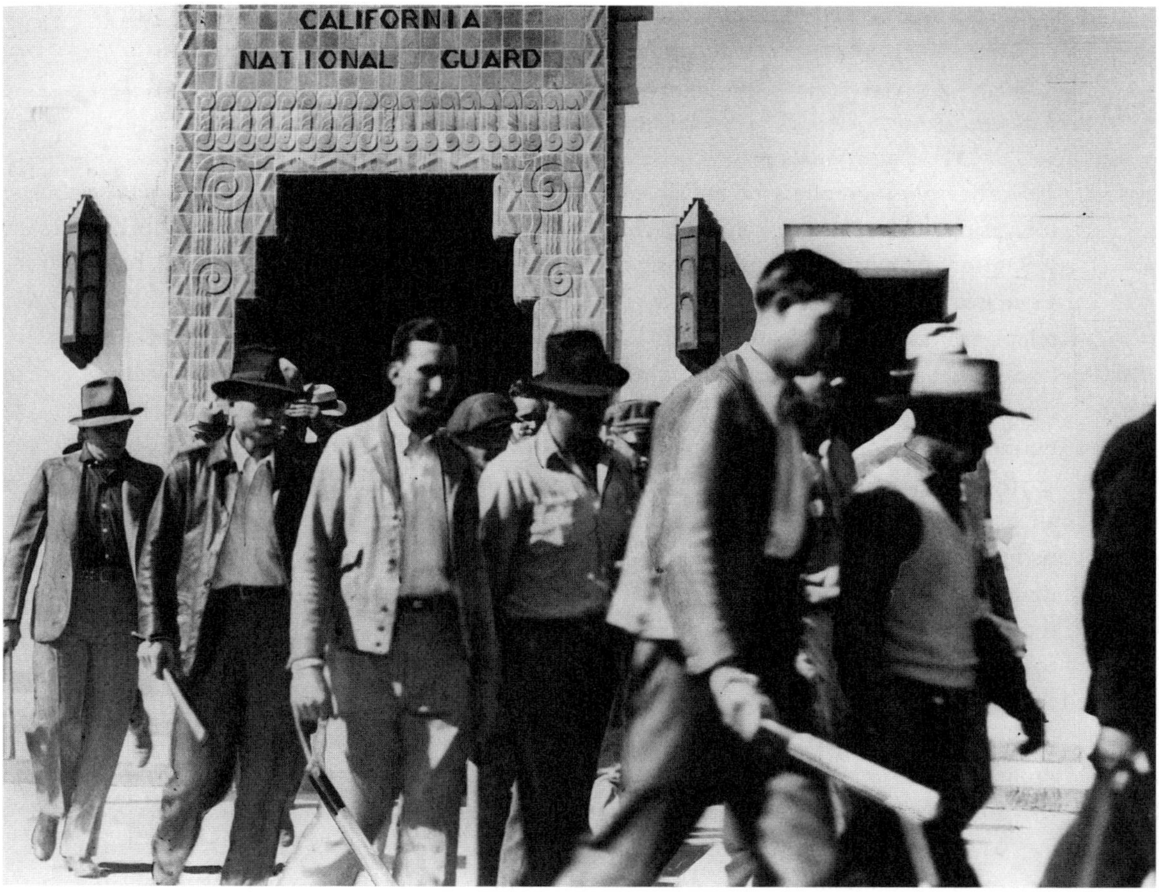

Deputized citizens leaving the California National Guard Armory with clubs, September 16, 1936, photographer unknown. Courtesy of *San Francisco Examiner.*

from the fields to the sheds. The sight of him surrounded by a posse of thirty special deputies carrying shotguns, rifles, and clubs enraged hundreds of pickets who packed the street corners and sidewalks. "Get those damn vigilantes," yelled a lanky lettuce packer. As deputies fought, six men jumped Strobel, knocked him to the ground, and kicked him until twenty-five policemen stepped in and rescued him from serious injury. A free-for-all fight ensued. One vigilante who was knocked down emptied his gun on the nearby crowd, wounding two innocent bystanders. Ellwood captured a picture of Strobel standing defiantly in the middle of the intersection surrounded by debris and angry pickets. Bleeding from the nose, with his shirt torn open, he personified the anti-union stand of the Salinas oligarchy.[7]

As the day wore on, photographers ranged widely throughout the downtown area and into the nearby residential districts. Police cruisers continually checked them out, vigilantes detained them, and road blocks impeded their movement. But they did not back off. Late in the afternoon Ellwood photographed vigilantes and police beating and chasing eight hundred pickets and frightening citizens into the Labor Temple on Pajaro Street. Other photographers recorded squads of recently deputized *posse comitatus* members armed with pick axe handles and pouring out of the National Guard Armory. "BATTLE SCENES," shouted headlines above a massive photo layout in the *San Francisco Examiner.* "CAMERA STORY OF HAND TO HAND FIGHTING," announced the *Call-Bulletin.* "PHOTO EYE ON SALINAS," promised the *Chronicle.*[8]

No other photographers before or since have filled so many pages with so many images of violence in the California countryside. Into the human pathos and issues of migration, immigration, and housing that Lange had captured earlier in the year, San Francisco and Oakland news photographers now injected a strong dose of farm labor relations, hysterical anticommunism, and stark class conflict. Raising questions about power, injustice, and representation, they captivated public attention for weeks, forcing many Californians to reflect on the dark underside of an industry that most had heretofore overlooked or regarded as the personification of wholesome beauty.

By the morning of September 17, photographers were working in what was, for all practical purposes, a combat zone. Every public building, including all schools, had been closed. Most theaters and grocery stores had also shut their doors. There was massive damage to automobiles and trucks, storefronts, fences, lawns, and lamp posts throughout a ten-block area of the city. Broken packing crates littered the roads and tons of lettuce lay rotting in the sun. Police cars prowled about, and officers equipped with loudspeakers demanded to see press credentials and ordered groups of citizens to disperse or risk arrest. Highway patrolmen in radio-equipped cars established check points where convoys of forty or more lettuce trucks assembled and then rolled toward the packing plants. Vigilantes rode shotgun beside each truck driver.[9]

Not an hour passed without some violence. One of the worst incidents occurred late in the afternoon near the packing sheds when deputies fired their shotguns at three automobiles full of strikebreakers mistaken for pickets. Photographers caught the frightened men in midstride when they jumped out and ran for their lives, with highway patrolmen in close pursuit. After a thirty-four-year-old Texan named Albert Blue was badly wounded by shotgun pellets to the head, photographers posed him with his shirt off and men pointing to his wounds. Around sunset, photographers trailed a large group of strikebreakers who had fled into a nearby field. As darkness fell, they were unable to make any pictures of the frightened men refusing to leave their hiding places, even after much urging through police bullhorns. Editors would again collect their images into full-page photo layouts arranged under banner headlines screaming: "BABIES GASSED," "POLICE HURL BOMBS," and "STRIKE BATTLE RAGES."[10]

California Highway Patrol chief Raymond Cato did not appreciate such work. Colonel Sanborn saw photographers and reporters as part of the problem. Other members of the Salinas power elite linked members of the media to communists and agitators. These accusations grew to such proportions that *Chronicle* executive editor Paul Smith flew to Salinas in his private Fairchild airplane to investigate the behavior of his men. A dynamic, eyewitness-type news editor who had assumed leadership of the *Chronicle* at age twenty-five, Smith had ridden the rails with the homeless in 1933, sending out copy from a portable typewriter he packed along. At Salinas he encountered something that suggested to him nothing short of a developing putsch. "Tension permeated every corner of the community," he recalled in his reminiscence. Union leaders were demoralized and defeated, and the city was ringed by roadblocks through which vigilantes refused passage without written passes. "Some streets were blockaded by bands of self-styled vigilantes. The pool halls and bars were overflowing with rugged-looking men carrying everything from baseball bats to 45 Colt automatics."[11]

Rather than identifying media misbehavior, Smith's hard-hitting, four-part series, titled "It Did Happen in Salinas," reported that photographers and reporters had not only behaved admirably but also overcome innumerable threats. Those working out of the Hotel Jeffrey were under constant surveillance by police, who watched them from the roof of a building across the street. Out in the fields, they were harassed by Salinas police and county sheriffs, and press cars were routinely pulled over by California state highway patrolmen, who detained several members of the press and roughed them up.

Stanley Bailey had a particularly rough time on the afternoon and evening of September 17. "Handkerchief to his face, Bailey ducked around the corner of a house, trying to hold his breath," wrote Smith, describing the trouble that photographers had with tear gas assaults. "Stifling, he called out '*Chronicle*' to the advancing officers. The officers halted in their rush toward him, clubs upraised, only when photographer [Barney] Peterson appeared, armed with his news camera, and identified 'Bailey.'"[12]

Safe for the moment, Bailey headed over to the Hotel Jeffrey to speak with a group of strikers. But his work over the previous days, especially his sympathetic portrayal of strikers and his graphic descriptions of tear gassing incidents and riots, made him fair game for a group of vigilantes who planned to "get Bailey and beat the hell out of him," then lynch him. After receiving a severe mauling, Bailey hid out and around midnight appeared at Smith's hotel room, banging on the door and asking for help. Smith stashed him in the trunk of his automobile and drove him to the Salinas airport. At

2:30 A.M., Smith flew Bailey back to San Francisco and drove him to the hospital for emergency medical treatment.[13]

Kidnappings and beatings signaled a new and ominous phase in the relationship between the media and the agricultural industry. For the past eighty-six years, photographers had always been seen as friends. Farmers hardly had reason to feel threatened. But at Salinas, photographers who injected themselves into agricultural labor relations quickly earned the wrath of the town's oligarchy. After Barney Peterson's dramatic pictures of riots along Main Street were published, the mayor of Salinas put out the word that Peterson was a radical who should be detained. On the mayor's orders, police arrested Peterson in the lobby of the Hotel Jeffrey on the afternoon of September 18. Held incommunicado and interrogated for hours, he was not released until the *Chronicle* raised a stink. But the Salinas mayor remained unrepentant, never apologizing. Suspicious characters had to be investigated. After all, numerous agitators were carrying cameras around town.[14]

Several weeks of such treatment left news photographers philosophical and reflective. "A lot of people were kidnapped and detained," recalled Joe Rosenthal, the *San Francisco News* and Scripps–Howard News Syndicate photographer and supporter of the fledgling Newspaper Guild, who arrived several days after Peterson's ordeal. "It was a very negative atmosphere. The sheriffs and the growers were in complete control. They did not like us. They did not want us there. They were entirely against press coverage, especially photography. What happened to Peterson was typical of the atmosphere in Salinas. You had to pick your way through and be calculating. Most of your success came from your personal skills, not your camera techniques. If your camera was smashed or you were smashed, you did no good to your newspaper."[15]

Over the next two weeks, Rosenthal and his colleagues shot hundreds of photographs of armed lettuce trucks, shotgun-toting vigilantes, road blocks, crowds of angry strikers, men being clubbed, rioters and rioting, pickets facing off against sheriff's deputies, and Filipinos harvesting under the watchful eye of gun-toting deputies. "There were probably fifteen or twenty news photographers there in late September," Rosenthal recalled. "We sat together and took pictures of one another. There were newsreel photographers from about five newsreel companies. My activity was on the minor scale compared to others who had been down there a week and gone through the rough stuff. I can still see in my mind's eye during a lull in the action taking a high school graduation-type picture of all the guys with their cameras."[16]

Among the photographers who briefly joined Rosenthal at Salinas was Dorothea Lange. "Am leaving for Salinas tonight, for one working day in the lettuce fields," she informed Stryker on the evening of September 16. "Strike conditions prevailing—if I can make it, i.e., if they'll let me. Since Resettlement has sent out an emissary from Washington on this situation, and politically much hinges on it in California—I thought this expedition would be in line." Lange arrived in the Salinas Valley before dawn on the morning of September 17. Because she was not a news photographer, Lange bypassed the violent confrontations occurring in town and concentrated on the countryside, where she photographed lettuce harvesters and vigilantes watching over the fields. None of her images adds much to an understanding of the strike or to social and economic conditions in the valley.[17]

Unfamiliar with the area, Lange wandered about with little or no guidance. Had she questioned a few strikers, she would have been directed to the now famous Poodle Dog Café. As the unofficial FVPU headquarters, it was precisely the sort of place that Lange loved to photograph and most certainly would have yielded a treasure trove of portraits. And because it was located along a road followed by lettuce trucks headed

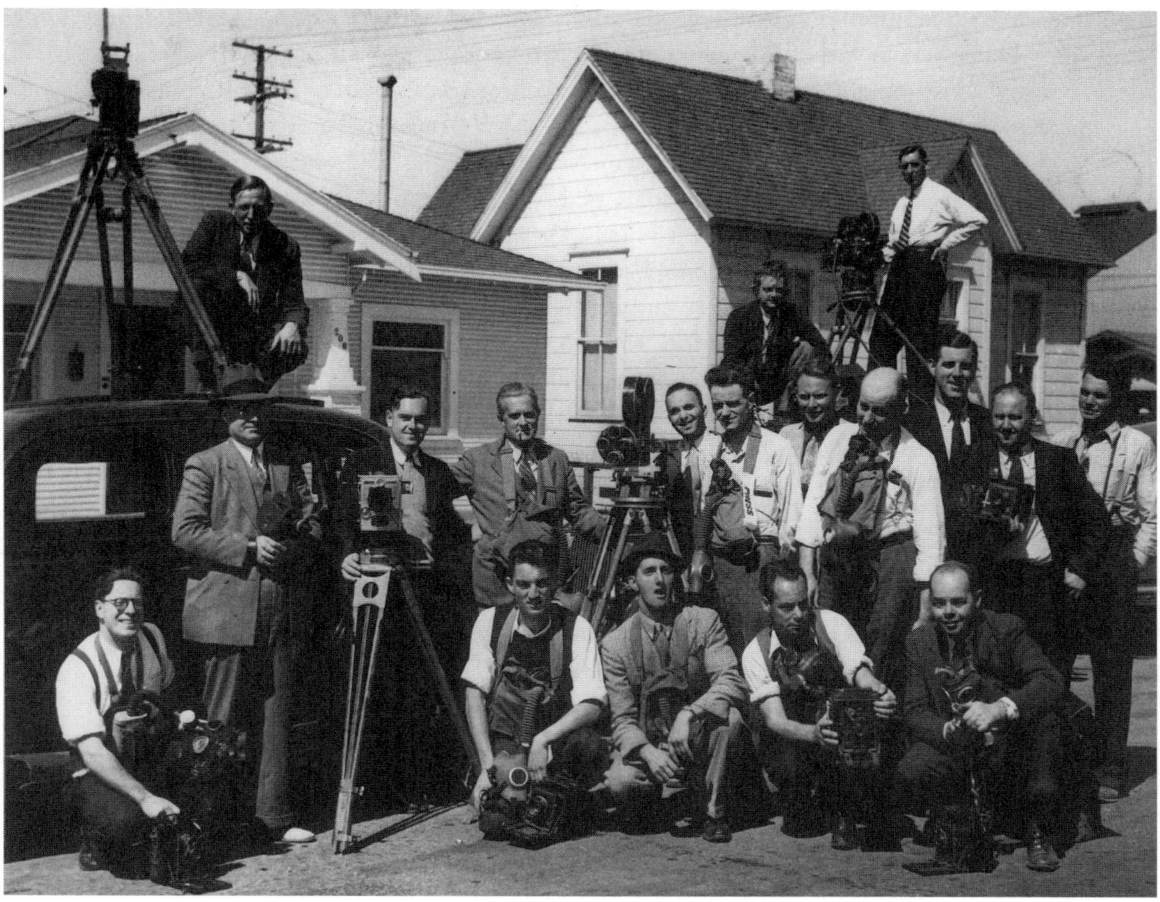

Group portrait of photographers at the strike by lettuce packers in the Salinas Valley, September 20, 1936, photographer unknown (possibly Harold Ellwood). Note gas masks and large cameras. Kneeling, left to right, front row: Joe Rosenthal, NEA/Acme News; Barney Peterson, *San Francisco Chronicle;* Carl Latham, *San Francisco Chronicle;* Eddie Murphy, *San Francisco News;* Ted Smith, *San Francisco News.* Standing, second row: two unidentified movie photographers; Ernest Besig, American Civil Liberties Union; two unidentified movie photographers; Horace Bristol, freelance; Ernie King, Associated Press; Baron Muller, *San Francisco News;* Carl Bigelow, *Oakland Tribune;* Otto Hagel, freelance. Above on cars, third row: two unidentified movie photographers; Keystone News cameraman, top right, in white shirt and striped tie. Courtesy of Joe Rosenthal.

to the sheds, the café was also a place where confrontations between strikers and growers played out on an hourly basis. Whenever a truck loaded with lettuce stopped at the café, angry union members poured through the doors and confronted the driver. This is what happened on the morning of September 17, when lettuce grower L. M. Tracy and his son stalled their truck in the parking lot. Surrounded by strikers poking broomsticks covered in feces toward them while yelling, "Here's your supper," Tracy and his son hauled out their double-barreled shotguns loaded with buckshot and tear gas. Tracy was about to fire on the pickets when his son got the truck running and they sped away. Stopping for a meal, Lange would have found it a relatively simple matter to photograph such scenes throughout the day.[18]

Lange was not the only photographer who missed the action. Photographing and writing about the strike for the *Salinas Index Journal* as well as for San Francisco newspapers and the *San Jose Mercury Herald,* John V. Young had braved thugs, clouds of tear gas, and a close call with vigilantes while helping Paul Smith sneak Stanley Bailey out of town. Early in the strike, he had been on top of a two-story building overlooking a corner in downtown Salinas. He was perfectly set up to take a dramatic picture of a police captain stepping between hundreds of strikers armed with pistols and baseball bats and even better-armed vigilantes. By chance, Young was the only news photographer at that location, with his back to the sun. All of the other reporters and cameramen were on the opposite side, at street level, cut off by a large mob and shooting into the sun. At the climax of the confrontation, when the brave police captain interceded, Young tripped the shutter on his big 4 × 5–inch Graflex and then yanked on the paper tab of the film pack to pull the next exposure into place. In his book, *Hot Type and Pony Wire,* Young recalled what happened:

> I yanked too hard and jerked the entire film pack out of its box. It fell streaming into the street amid the jeers of the crowd, some of whom had been throwing rocks at me earlier. *Index-Journal* reporters were not highly regarded by the workers just then. Quickly I reached for my backup camera, a small folding Kodak of my own, and shot up the rest of the roll of film that was in it. Then I rushed the film to the local commercial photographer for immediate processing, since the newspaper had no darkroom. Later that afternoon I learned to my horror that someone new to the camera shop had developed the film, which was fast panchromatic, under a safe light and it was all fogged beyond recovery. I guess every news photographer has had at least one such experience in his lifetime, to brood about in his declining years.[19]

On September 21, Colonel Sanborn quietly left Salinas in the wake of embarrassing newspaper reports claiming that elected officials had surrendered their authority to a self-appointed dictator. But even while Hollywood personalities, including Gary Cooper, Humphrey Bogart, Boris Karloff, and James Cagney, were raising more than a thousand dollars to assist the strikers, it was clear to most photographers that the strike was failing. Two key Filipino labor activists, C. D. Mensalves and Manuel Luz, had been jailed along with hundreds of other union members on trumped-up vagrancy charges, two men lay in the hospital with shotgun wounds, and Governor Frank F. Merriam was ready to send in the National Guard.

While workers slipped away to find work elsewhere and news photographers prepared to return to their newspapers, the Salinas City Council passed an antipicketing ordinance on the morning of October 5. With the town now transformed into a police state in which large numbers of union members were held in jail for up to a week without any formal charges filed against them, FVPU members poured into the streets. That evening, following several hours of almost nonstop battles, Harold Ellwood waded into a huge riot that spread through the streets in front of the Hotel Jeffrey. Ellwood was one of the few photographers to pack a strobe. Now he made good use of it. At the moment when a man holding a large wrench was about to strike the head of a fallen opponent, Ellwood popped his strobe and captured the single most memorable photograph of the entire strike.

Until then, most photographers had been far away when battles broke out between strikers and nonstrikers. With their normal perspective lenses, their photographs, even when enlarged, failed to capture the faces of those involved. Now, for the first time, a photographer had moved right into a battle and caught the action in mid-punch. "It was the most furious engagement produced by the lettuce strike in more than two weeks," read the caption beneath Ellwood's photograph. "Arrow points to wrench being wielded by second man from right. A score of men were injured and a dozen arrested before deputy sheriffs dispersed the rioters and restored quiet."[20]

Little precedent existed for such images. Even during the bloody waterfront strike two years earlier, press photographers had seldom captured violence as it was happening. Some newspaper readers did not like what they saw. Their gripe was not with the perpetrators. They blamed the photographers. Flooding the *San Francisco News* with their letters, dozens of "spokesmen for the forces of law and order" claimed that such pictures were gross distortions, not news. A typical angry note, from San Francisco resident Helen Dixon, read:

> Sir: I have been a reader of *The Chronicle* for 30 years, but it is fast becoming trash. For years your news, writings and People's Safety valve have been a pleasure to read, but when you give space to some cameraman or reporters who make themselves obnoxious in the time of trouble, thinking the freedom of the press will put them over, it is time to discontinue reading it. . . . Why should newspaper men write up stories . . . and show pictures of some unavoidable disaster? . . . We pay for papers expecting to get something like the truth, not some disgruntled cameraman story.[21]

Newspaper staff photographers were not the only source of these new and highly upsetting images. At Salinas, freelance photographers exerted an impact disproportionate to their relatively small numbers. And among those freelancers, Otto Hagel was certainly the most productive, talented, and explicitly left-wing photographer. On October 25, 1934, he had reunited with Hansel Mieth, whose marriage of less than a year had dissolved. Mieth had steady work documenting the city's various immigrant communities for the Youth Authority, and she was beginning to accept assignments for *Life* magazine. This proved a godsend for Hagel, who for the first time since arriving in California enjoyed a steady income that allowed him to do as he pleased. Although ostensibly employed as a handyman for the R. P. Paoli Company, Hagel would take off for many days and shoot on a freelance basis. He had begun using Agfacolor Neu film and had several projects in the works, among them *Men and Ships,* about San Francisco longshoremen and their victory on the docks, and a series on down-and-out people. In his most well-known photograph, radical socialist leader Tom Mooney, who had been convicted along with Warren K. Billings of planting a bomb that killed ten people and injured forty during the Preparedness Day parade in San Francisco, on July 22, 1916, stares straight ahead at the viewer through his cell bars at San Quentin Prison.[22]

Arriving at Salinas well before the first violence, Hagel is seen in several unpublished news pictures of pickets at the Salinas Valley Ice Company sheds on the morning of September 10. He is wearing a leather coat and has two cameras: a compact 4 × 5 inch–camera with a hand strap and a 35-millimeter Leica dangling around his neck. While he left no written record of his experience at Salinas and never spoke about how he used his equipment, Hagel's contact sheets reveal that he shot almost exclusively with his Leica. His contact sheets also unfold his working methodology and his whereabouts. He was constantly on the move, following the ebb and flow of battles. Climbing on top of cars and drifting in and out of police and picket lines, he used his rapid film-advance mechanism to great advantage, firing off strings of pictures from different perspectives and capturing a sequence of action pictures impossible to obtain with heavy, bulky press cameras. By stopping his lens aperture down to f/8 or smaller, setting his camera at infinity, and preselecting his camera exposure, he was able to ignore many of the technical calculations that slowed down other news photographers. During tear gas incidents, he was able to tuck his camera under his arm and run for safety while other photographers, packing one or more big press cameras and heavy film magazines, could barely totter away.[23]

An unusually alert, innovative, and clever individual, Hagel was well aware of the dangers he faced at Salinas. Somehow, he had to stay clear of trouble and maintain a low profile, but not for the usual reasons: fear of physical injury, even death, at the hands of vigilantes or a tear gas projectile. Unlike everyone else at Salinas, Hagel knew that if arrested and found to be working in the United States without proper immigration papers, he probably would be deported. During the 1933 cotton pickers' strike, several strike leaders had suffered this fate, which was never far from his mind. "He had to be quiet," explained Hansel Mieth years later. "He had an uncanny ability to get himself through unscathed. . . . He had no choice. He was very clever. He had to be. Can you imagine having to go back to Nazi Germany? What would have happened to him? You know where he would have wound up? Where did Erich Salomon [the photographer who used the Ermanox so skillfully] wind up? Where did anyone who was socially progressive and independent-minded wind up?"[24]

Although Hagel appears to have developed his film and made prints in Salinas, then sent his work out by common courier, it is not clear where he worked, if he developed his film in his hotel room, and if he himself made his enlargements and did his printing. He had only a single, normal perspective lens, the telephoto lens being rare at this time. Working quickly, he did not compose his pictures in camera. He realized that he was limited to only a vanishing moment to capture a scene as it was unfolding. He also understood that he would have nothing at all to say about how his images would be used, cropped, or captioned. He carefully scrutinized the individual frames of his contact sheets and extracted usable pictures by considerably enlarging tiny portions of his negatives. His most widely published and powerful image capture tear gassing along Main Street and is taken from about 20 percent of that frame. Although it would become one of two photographs on the front page of the September 16 *San Francisco News,* occupying nearly half the page, the image cannot be seen in the small 35-millimeter frame without using a magnifier or placing it in an enlarger.[25]

Because he knew most of the newspaper editors in the San Francisco Bay Area and was so highly regarded, Hagel was able to place his photographs in a half dozen different newspapers, sometimes under his name, usually not. Often his work appeared

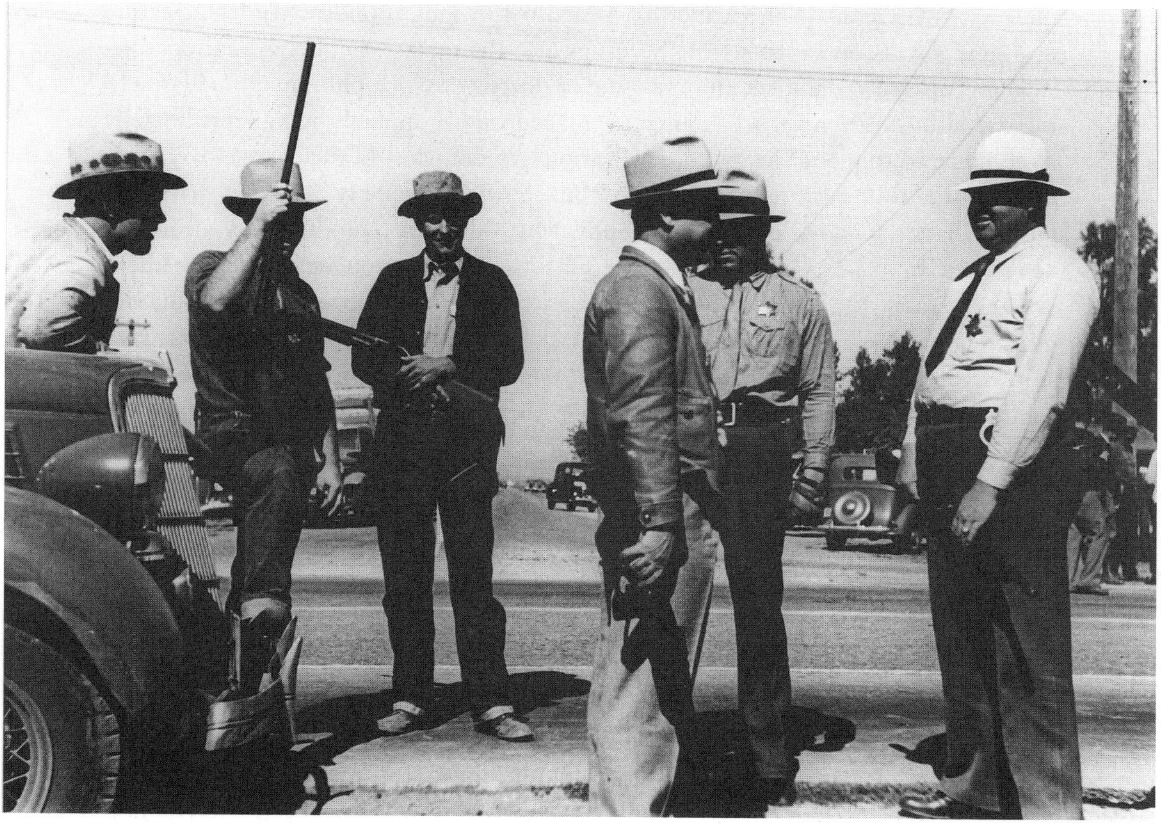

Sheriff and deputies at the strike of lettuce packers in the Salinas Valley, September 16, 1936, photograph by Otto Hagel. Courtesy of Hansel Mieth Hagel.

simultaneously in competing newspapers. The September 17 *Oakland Tribune,* for example, ran Hagel's photographs along with those from the Associated Press, the International News Service (which were often Otto Hagel's work), freelancer Horace Bristol, and its own photographer, Carl Bigelow, as well as shots by *Chronicle* and *Call-Bulletin* cameramen.[26]

Sharing pictures, however, did not mean that the Bay Area newspapers shared the same approach to presenting them. More than size and layout techniques separated the tabloids. Editorial biases determined how news editors assigned meaning to the pictures. Captions, layouts, and texts in the morning *San Francisco Examiner* and the afternoon *Call-Bulletin*—both Hearst-owned newspapers—were extremely progrower in their presentation. The *San Francisco News* adopted a more even-handed approach, and the one independently owned paper, the *San Francisco Chronicle,* was sympathetic to the shed workers and field hands. Virtually identical pictures appearing in any two papers might contain captions suggesting excessive police violence or riotous behavior by howling mobs of agitators, depending on who was writing the copy and setting editorial policy.[27]

Many if not most of the strike pictures were altered in one way or another. This was a fairly common practice in all newspapers of the day. By blocking out parts of images, cutting holes in them and inserting other images, rounding corners, creating ovals and circles, and even setting headings over the images themselves, editors considerably altered the impact and meaning of dozens of strike photographs. Retouching was also common. Artists known as "makeup subs" applied their talents liberally to enhance picture quality and achieve various effects. Most of the changes were cosmetic and of little editorial consequence, but some considerably benefited strikers. A typical change centered on tear gas clouds, which did not reproduce very clearly on newsprint. To make gas show up better against a light sky, retouchers used gray ink to define the shape of the gas clouds. They also used black and white ink to outline riot guns, emphasize facial features, and add back light. Apparently worried about lawsuits, retouchers also eliminated distracting details, such as a Blue Bird Potato Chips sign on the side of a delivery truck caught in the middle of a riot on Main Street.[28]

Twenty miles to the west, in Carmel, fifty-year-old Edward Weston, the renowned environmental abstractionist fond of making peppers look like nudes and nudes look like peppers, sat out the conflict. He not only avoided it; he categorically rejected the idea of using his camera to record hard news. Weston was devoted to the sharply focused negative and the unmanipulated print. He loved and worked with big view cameras. He had begun as a rather conventional portrait photographer in what would become Glendale, California, but had soon become bored with deleting pimples and finding the flattering angle that diminished a portly belly. Becoming a bohemian, he took a series of lovers, among them Tina Modotti, spent years photographing in Mexico among the cacti, trees, and rocks, and returned as an artist devoted to the outdoors. He settled in Carmel in 1929 and lived cheaply while exploring Big Sur and playing with twisted cyprus trees, floating kelp beds, gnarled driftwood, and bleached pelican skulls at Point Lobos. He kept himself physically fit through a vegetarian diet and rugged photographic expeditions into the deserts and mountains and had no social life except for sleeping with a string of amazingly beautiful women, who found him something of a studly monk. "I am not a reformer, a missionary, a propagandist," he wrote in March 1931. "I have one clear way to give, to justify myself as part of the whole—through my work. Here in Carmel I can work, and from here I send out the best of my life, focused onto a few sheets of silvered paper."[29]

Although Lange had discussed her work with Weston during meetings of Group f/64, she was never able to inspire Weston to reassess his photography in light of contemporary events. He refused to directly address political issues, the drama of the Depression, or the plight of California farmworkers, but he was certainly aware of conditions around him. Traveling to and from his home in Carmel and on various photographic excursions around the state, he could not have missed crews in the fields and the thousands of Dust Bowl refugees in the Salinas Valley. Nevertheless, he preferred to maintain a detached and somewhat abstract sensibility. Fascinated by the effects of extreme tonal manipulation and the way light alone can affect even the simplest and most mundane forms, Weston was beginning to experiment with the relationship between nature and eroticism. Stung by French photographer Henri Cartier-Bresson's quip that the world was going to pieces while Weston and Ansel Adams were photographing rocks, Weston wrote to Adams defending creative intuition and the need to follow one's star. "If I saw an interesting battle between strikers and police I might be tempted to photograph it—if aesthetically moved," explained Weston. "But I would record the fight as a commentator, regardless of which side was getting licked."[30]

Never acting on those sentiments, Weston paused to photograph in the fields only when he found some furrows or tomato plants forming into an appealing abstract design. His farm photographs such as *Bean Ranch, Orange County; Ranch, San Simeon Highway; Vineyard, Clear Lake;* and *Tomato Field, Monterey* were studies of tone, shape, and perspective that completely omitted people. Revealing human activity only in the aftermath of trimmed vines, neat rows, and piled hay, these photographs captured symmetry and patterns and were about as close as Weston ever came to farmworkers. As a photographer and citizen, he would have no direct involvement in social documentary or farm labor causes. Objecting violently to political photography and forced to defend his aloofness, he asserted that there was as much significance in a photograph of a rock as in one of a line of unemployed men. "He wasn't going to have some Salinas lettuce thug bust up him and his camera for the sake of photographing strikers," explained Charis Wilson, who was his lover at the time of the strike. "It was only good sense to leave that to the newsmen."[31]

Well into October, at least one photographer was still trying to sell images from the strike. That photographer was F. Hal Higgins, a freelance agricultural reporter whose sympathies were decidedly antilabor and who believed the strike was widely misrepresented, had nothing to do with wages and hours, and was being led by a dozen communists. At Molus, a lettuce shipping point ten miles southwest of Salinas, he documented a group of twenty farmers with rifles and shotguns who had been appointed deputy sheriffs and were under the leadership of a regular police officer. His caption read: "The minute men of Molus. These farmers have kept a steady flow of lettuce to market." A week later he wrote to the editor of the *Chicago Tribune,* offering one or more pictures he had "snapped of armed farmers in California's lettuce strike that has now been on about five weeks." Believing that the *Farm Journal* was not devoted to getting rid of "Ye Olde Newe Deale," he had chosen the *Tribune* because he thought it was interested in the "red" angle. "The reds have been seeping into . . . the Pacific Coast unions at a rapid rate in the past three years until they control the maritime unions in most cases, and from there stick their fingers into all other union arguments they can," he wrote. "Out here, we have reached a point where the farmers have had themselves deputized and armed themselves to protect their crops and insure their marketing to prevent ruin from red-tinged unions that expect to go on and organize all farm labor." Higgins wanted five dollars for each picture. But after reviewing them, the *Tribune* declined to buy any.[32]

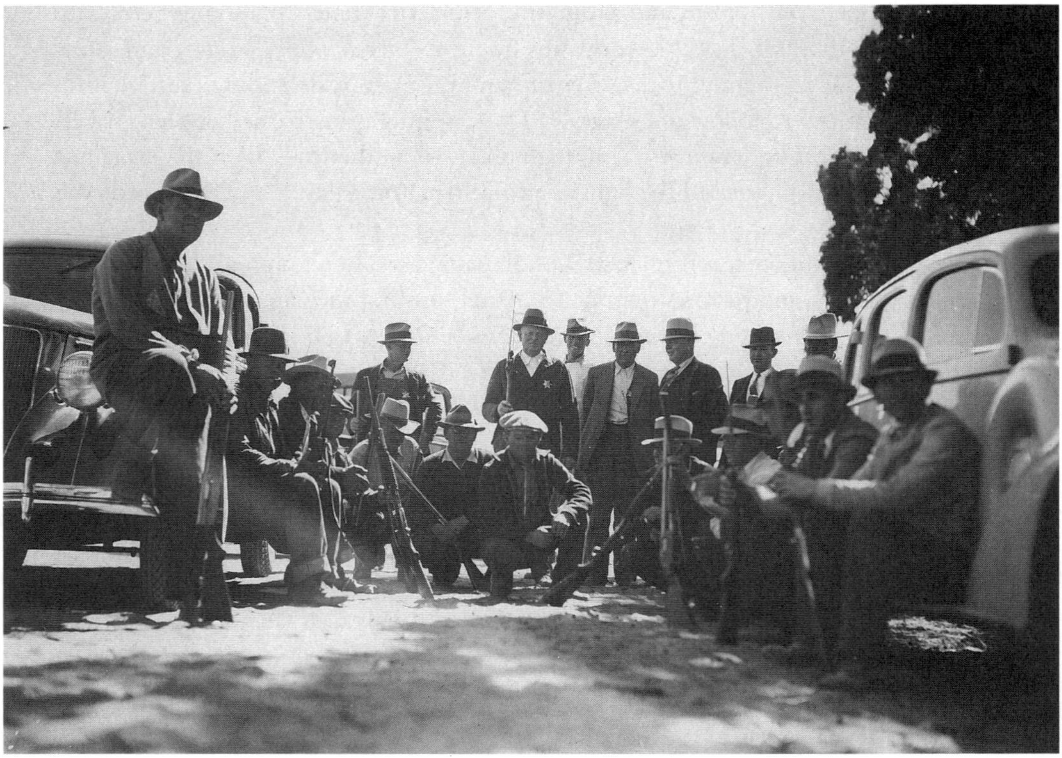

The Minute Men of Molus defending a packing plant, September 14, 1936, photograph by F. Hal Higgins. "Swearing in their farmer neighbors as deputies," wrote Higgins on the reverse side of this photograph, "each farmer reports with repeating rifles, shotguns, and holster guns to see that their crop is packed and shipped in spite of the threats of 3500 unionized workers." Courtesy of Archives and Special Collections, University of California, Davis.

Ellwood, Hagel, Higgins, Lange, Peterson, and Rosenthal were long gone from the Salinas Valley when FVPU members voted to give up the strike on November 3. No press photographer, documentary photographer, amateur photographer, sketch artist, or painter remained to record that sad moment. But the Salinas strike was not so easily forgotten. Pictures distributed outside the Bay Area by the Associated Press, the Hearst newspaper wire services, and the Scripps–Howard chain had circulated as far away as New York. They exerted a profoundly upsetting effect on everyone who saw them. Attorneys for the American Civil Liberties Union, which was defending several strikers, and the LaFollette Civil Liberties Committee, which was investigating abuses of free speech and the rights of labor to organize, found the pictures incontrovertible evidence of "police brutality" and collusion between employers and law enforcement agencies.[33]

At Salinas, photographers broke free from the static, often posed images of victimization that had been carrying the story of farm labor. They captured tension, conflict, organizing, and people taking charge and fighting back. Theirs was an aesthetic based on deadlines, hard news, candid images, and scooping competitors rather than an aesthetic valuing precision of detail, formal composition, and environmental portraiture. With his Leica, Hagel had proven that the Speed Graphic, Graflex, and Rolleiflex cameras, which had long been the standbys of the profession, were simply too slow, awkward, and bulky for the tasks at hand. Only Dorothea Lange refused to follow the trend toward miniaturized equipment. Continuing to document farmworkers in the same ways with the same technology and the same goals, Lange remained a steady and patient force who would not allow the public to forget.

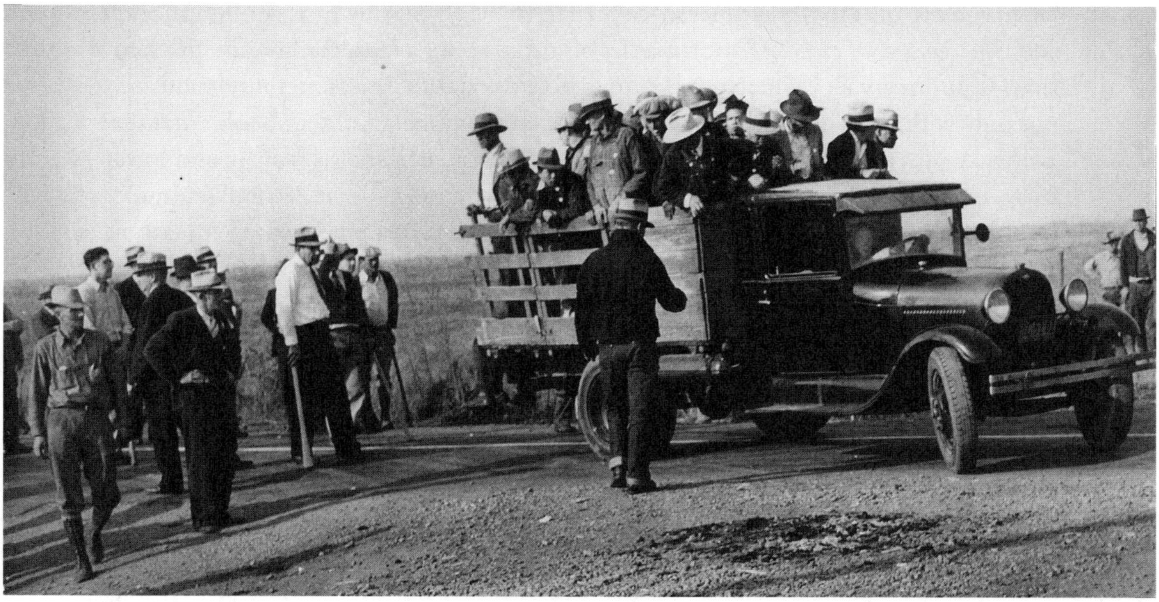

"Strikers in auto turned back by deputies at celery fields, forced to return to Stockton," November 26, 1936, photographer unknown. Courtesy of *San Francisco Examiner.*

11

Always One of Your People

Lange Hits the Road

A month before the Salinas Valley lettuce packers' strike ended, Lange had become involved in a five-part *San Francisco News* report on California migrants and farmworkers. John Steinbeck was the writer. A struggling author who hid his true nature and vast insecurities behind a Hemingwayesque exterior, the thirty-four-year-old Steinbeck had grown up in Salinas, entered Stanford University in 1919, and dropped out six years later, spending much of his spare time working on farms and ranches, where he accumulated a warehouse of experiences and a blur of drinking sessions and hangovers. He began his literary career in 1929 with *Cup of Gold,* a romantic novel based loosely on the life of buccaneer Sir Henry Morgan. His first significant book was *The Pastures of Heaven* (1932), a series of stories about a farm community in a fictitious California valley where people are unable to establish meaningful relationships not only with one another but also with their environment. Another book, *To a God Unknown* (1933), narrates a farmer's adventure in mysticism and paganism, and it was followed by his first big success, *Tortilla Flat* (1935), a humorous, tender, and sentimental account of the adventures and misadventures of down-and-out Mexican Americans around Monterey Bay. Early in 1936 he published *In Dubious Battle,* a highly realistic account of communist involvement in a farm labor strike, which some critics consider his best book. Much of his inspiration had come from interviews with an organizer for the Communist Party's CAWIU, whom Steinbeck had met in Pacific Grove. Grim and violent, the book's unfavorable picture of Communist organizers alienated many radicals and farmworker activists, and its allegedly proworker perspective inspired a flow of invective from agricultural leaders.[1]

At this point in his career, Steinbeck was not very well-known. But his graphic descriptions of life and labor in the fields had caught the attention of *San Francisco News* editor George West, whom Steinbeck had met several years earlier at the Carmel home of Lincoln Steffens. After the Marysville Resettlement Administration camp opened, West had devoted considerable editorial energy to defending it against "powerful influences" aligned against the camp program. After reading *In Dubious Battle,* West thought he might favorably influence public attitudes by sending Steinbeck into the fields to investigate the migrant situation and publicize the RA camp program. Throwing himself into the project, Steinbeck spent most of the summer visiting camps and traveling through the state in an old bakery truck. At the Arvin camp in the southern San Joaquin Valley, he met camp manager Tom Collins. An idealistic, reform-minded individual, Collins had directed a school for juvenile delinquents, distributed relief for the Federal Transient Service, and managed the RA's first migrant camp at Marysville. He was now engaged in building a second RA camp facility at Arvin.[2]

During his research trek, Steinbeck bunked at Arvin for several days. While there he interviewed camp residents, attended camp meetings, tagged along with Collins and read his camp reports, and visited ditch-bank camps in the area. Armed with a wealth of real-life information and personal observations, Steinbeck produced a deeply

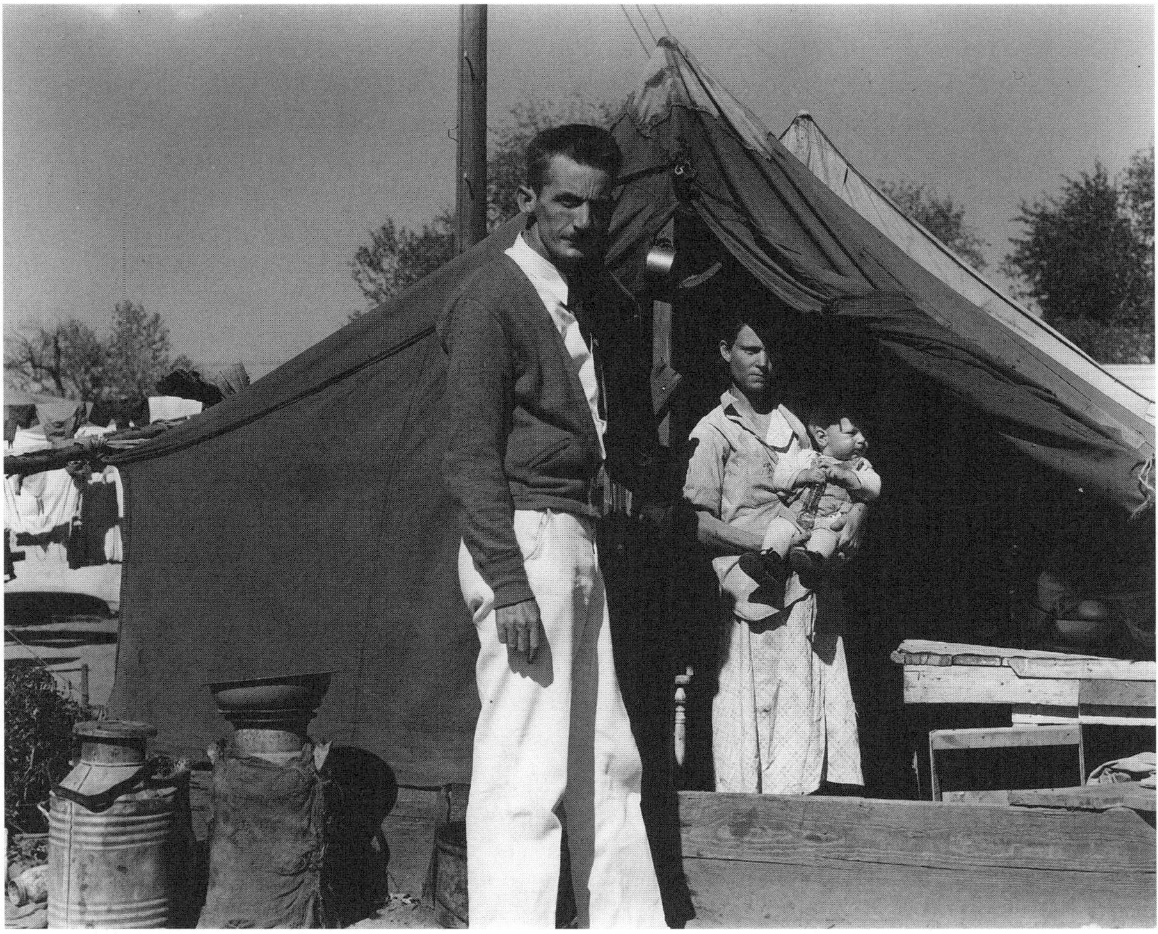

Tom Collins, manager of Kern (Arvin) migrant camp, with mother and child, November 1936, photograph by Dorothea Lange. Courtesy of the FSA/OWI Collection, Library of Congress, Prints and Photographs Division.

descriptive, passionate report tracing the history of farm labor in California. After describing living and working conditions in the fields, Steinbeck dissected large-scale corporate farming, outlined farm labor relations, examined government labor camps, and even offered specific recommendations for alleviating the problems he had encountered. He completed his report late in the summer. The *News* withheld the series during September, when the lettuce strike dominated the front pages of San Francisco Bay Area newspapers, but eventually published Steinbeck's reportage as "The Harvest Gypsies," a seven-part series appearing between October 5 and 12.[3]

Lange's images illustrated each of Steinbeck's articles, playing an especially important role. (They had also influenced how Steinbeck thought and wrote about migrants.) A total of thirteen of Lange's photographs appeared in the series, with *Migrant Mother* running as the lead image in the first article. The fourth article, illustrated by two of her photographs, detailed the safe and welcoming conditions at the RA's camps at Arvin and Marysville, contrasting them with the squalor of ditch-bank camps near Sacramento. It was the first time that Lange had illustrated an entire series on the state's farmworkers, and it may have kindled the idea, now beginning to develop, of merging her photographs into a larger written presentation. Ironically, this pioneering linkage of words and pictures should have enhanced her status and made her indispensable to the RA, but it did not ensure her position. In the aftermath of her most important work, Lange was less secure than ever in her relationship with her boss and her employer, almost entirely because of a crisis brewing back in Washington, D.C., where Stryker was dealing with the aftershocks of a predicament involving one of the RA's photographers.

Early in the year, Arthur Rothstein had been near Fargo, North Dakota, when he discovered and photographed a bleached cow skull on an alkali flat. Looking for good lighting angles, he shifted the skull from the edge of a grassy rise to a flat, cracked patch of earth. At first praised as a dramatic example of the serious drought on the high plains, the image was branded a fake in August, when a Fargo newspaper examined the various exposures and noted that Rothstein had moved the skull in the process of photographing it that spring, long before the drought hit. With charges of faked images receiving wide attention, the integrity of the entire RA came under attack, and the photographic operation suffered considerable damage. Stryker tried to pick up the pieces but was ordered to cut down on the size of his photographic staff. At first he considered resigning. Eventually, he decided to stay and protect his agency, even if he had to sacrifice some photographers and make compromises.[4]

Logic and fairness dictated that Stryker drop Rothstein, who more than any other photographer had jeopardized the RA's photographic work with his actions. But Stryker had praised Rothstein's photographs excessively and could not easily dismiss him without disgracing himself. During this time, Lange kept writing: "How about a letter to your little stepchild?" and "Can I go out in the field now?" and "When will there be money for me to go?" After agonizing over his choices, Stryker sacrificed Lange, a decision that puzzled and infuriated everyone close to the RA. Why Lange? She was one of the best RA photographers. Her bookkeeping, records of vouchers, and accounting for travel and work expenses were precise and comprehensive. She was a conscientious and forthright employee. But she was also far away. Coordinating her work with that of Washington, D.C., had been difficult. Stryker was constantly sending her negatives back and forth, shipping her supplies, and maintaining an extensive correspondence. Her independent spirit probably did not help her cause.[5]

On October 7, Stryker wrote a long letter to Lange. First he told her that his budget had been cut again. It was always being cut and restored. That much Lange knew. Stryker did not mention that Max Waserman, director of finance, was demanding to know who among Stryker's people were worth their pay. Stryker had been placed in an untenable position in which he had to value quantity of output over quality of work. This meant that a photographer, who worked slowly while lugging around a huge view camera and tripod, would have had to be evaluated against a photographer taking many more photographs per day while moving about with a small hand-held Leica. The criteria for Stryker's evaluations would not be easy to explain to any of his staff.[6]

At the end of his letter, Stryker notified Lange that M. E. Gilfond, the new director of information, would be sending her a letter terminating her employment. Two days later Gilfond wrote Lange confirming her termination. With Lange's firing, Walker Evans having been terminated on March 23, and Carl Mydans's departure from the agency that summer, Stryker now had only two photographers, Rothstein and the recently hired Russell Lee. Lange was gracious if not magnanimous. She replied to Gilfond thanking the RA for giving her such an opportunity, promising cooperation, and advising that the RA ought to photograph the construction of the new migratory camps. As these letters were crisscrossing the country, Gilfond received an embarrassing letter from Frederick Soule, information director for the RA's San Francisco region, enclosing a series of John Steinbeck's recent articles on migrant labor, several of which focused on the agency's camps, all illustrated with Lange's photographs, along with an editorial criticizing the slow pace of the camp-construction program. Soule enclosed a duplicate set of articles with the suggestion that Gilfond pass them along to his boss, Secretary of Agriculture Rexford Tugwell.[7]

Further embarrassment came on October 17, when *Mid-week Pictorial* printed *Migrant Mother* to illustrate an essay indicting the inequities of farm tenancy and the need for change. In a caption accompanying the photograph, the magazine urged readers, "Look in her eyes! . . . You can see in her eyes the horror of what is happening . . . for she is not looking at it with the objectivity of the statistician or professor . . . but is feeling its lashings." Citing certain key statistics, the magazine then concluded that only the New Deal could help the "frightened children in this photograph." At the same time, the *Des Moines Register and Tribune* printed Lange's photographs in the supplement it distributed to midwestern newspapers, and the College Art Association organized a large traveling exhibition of 110 RA photographs, many of them Lange's.[8]

Suddenly swamped by requests for Lange's photographs, Stryker found himself in the almost untenable position of having just fired the RA photographer who had produced the most publicity and attracted the most praise and attention to the administration's program. Behind the scenes, Stryker tried to make amends by recommending Lange to other government agencies and even lobbied the Guggenheim Foundation on her behalf. Apparently the letter from Frederick Soule soon prompted Gilfond to speak to Stryker about Lange. On October 22, Stryker placed Lange back in the RA's fold on a per diem basis, making it clear that he was not dissatisfied with her work and that he would rehire her as a staff member as soon as possible. To tide Lange over, Stryker gave her pay for two weeks of furlough and then two weeks of sick leave. When that ran out, Lange could keep going on small individual projects with her per diem. Writing to Lange of his strategy, he explained: "Get all set for your job at the migrant camps. I am asking for two weeks for you to do the work. Then, after the two weeks have been allotted, I will inform them that after all you have to develop and print the stuff, for which I shall have to ask for additional time. You may look for another note along in a couple of days with definite approval on this."[9]

By now the Historical Section was part of the largest bureaucracy in Washington, D.C. The Resettlement Administration, with offices in twenty-seven different buildings and a staff of 12,089, was building and managing migrant camps, issuing emergency loans, constructing flood control plains, making rehabilitation grants, and adding green belts on the edges of cities. While it pursued its work, the RA was constantly attacked in the liberal press for having lost sight of "the human element" and in the conservative press for being a huge and extravagant bureaucracy that made "livid pink" photographs. When Lange was fired, critics increasingly demanded proof that the RA's rapidly expanding archive was worth the cost. Now famous, much admired, and widely respected, Lange could easily have exploited her status and thrown a fit about her treatment. She could have caused plenty of problems for the RA. Look at me? Look at this! But she remained remarkably calm.[10]

If Lange was upset by her firing, she did not reveal it publicly. She had been through this before. All business, she did not waste time protesting. Lange had all kinds of opportunities. She could have quickly gone out on her own. Her style was attracting considerable attention and seemed especially appropriate to the times in general and to the new picture magazines in particular. Americans were demanding to know more about the crisis that faced them, and photographers like Lange were taking their place alongside social scientists and artists devoted to compiling a record of the Great Depression. Already several magazines had made overtures to Lange. Of these, *Life* magazine, which hit the newsstands on November 23, 1936, was especially interested in her work.[11]

Probably the most important general weekly picture magazine of the times, *Life* was the creation of Henry R. Luce, head of the Time, Inc., media conglomerate, whose assets already included the weekly news magazine *Time* (started in 1923), the business monthly *Fortune* (1930), and the radio program and newsreel *The March of Time* (1931). Conceived as a new kind of magazine featuring high-quality pictures arranged in coherent essays, *Life* in fact drew on the experiences of the French magazine *Vu,* the German magazine *Berliner Illustrirte Zeitung,* and the British *Weekly Illustrated,* as well as American publications ranging from *National Geographic* and *Vanity Fair* to *Survey Graphic* and *Charities and Commons.*[12]

Editors at *Life* thought that Lange would well advance the magazine's editorial approach. One West Coast editor wanted her to devote her vacation time to shooting a feature story on migratory labor that would extend and amplify work already under way. Perhaps seeking to show Stryker that she was fully capable of marching out on her own, Lange suggested that Stryker contact *Life.* He could offer her old work to the magazine, and then she could supplement it with recent images. As Stryker evaluated the proposal, Lange considered her future. She wanted to reach a nationwide audience and give the RA greater impact. She dearly wanted to continue her work photographing migrants and briefly considered an offer photographing for the West Coast regional director of Social Security, but she feared that such work might be little more than a "hack job." Confiding in Stryker, she wished that he might be placed in charge of a larger, all-encompassing government department merging all the various agencies that needed photographs. "We could do photographs of historical significance, and chronological significance," she wrote. "It would not be difficult to evoke real enthusiasm."[13]

Early in November, Lange headed to the RA's Arvin Camp, near Bakersfield. Following Tom Collins on his rounds, she made portraits that captured his unpretentious personality and close rapport with everyone. She was especially attentive to his devotion to children. She well captured this relationship in a photograph of Collins drawing on the ground with a stick while a group of surrounding youngsters watch. Returning home, she now began to explore, along with Imogen Cunningham, Otto Hagel and Hansel Mieth, and Ansel Adams, alternative ways of generating income and obtaining assignments beyond her per diem assignments with the RA. But this effort, like her earlier suggestions to Stryker, never amounted to much.

Lange next tried to pry loose her RA negatives from Stryker. She wanted to make additional prints and begin preparing exhibitions. She felt that retaining her work on the West Coast was very important in order to meet local demands quickly without filtering everything first through Washington, D.C. Lange was especially anxious about making a photo presentation to the LaFollette Committee. Scheduled to convene the following year, the committee hearings seemed to offer a "chance of a lifetime for Resettlement to really score." She was momentarily stymied when Stryker refused to forward her negatives. For much of this time, Stryker engaged in a running debate with his boss about whether the RA or its photographers should submit stories to *Life* and other magazines and whether the agency should demand control over the text and images.[14]

Despairing that she might never work again for the government, Lange finally found reprieve that November when Franklin D. Roosevelt won a landslide reelection victory. Transforming the Resettlement Administration, New Deal reformers ended its status as an independent agency created by executive order and shifted it into the Department of Agriculture. In the reshuffle following the change, the director of information, who had previously harassed Stryker and been stingy with funds, was transferred elsewhere in the government. The new director enthusiastically supported Stryker. This was good news for Lange. After taking off December to visit Washington, D.C., with Taylor (her first vacation in seventeen months), she was back on the payroll and anxious to resume her work at the end of January 1937. "What with Stryker's delaying tactics and the leave due her," wrote one of Lange's biographers, "she had hardly been off . . . before she was back on."[15]

Lange devoted the last week of January 1937 to the task of preparing exhibits and newspaper and magazine layouts and editing and captioning photographs. With the WPA sponsoring an exhibition of her images in San Francisco, she was hopeful, energized, and anxious to return to the field. Early in February, she began preparing for a trip into the Imperial Valley and the Southwest. Now that Lange's work had already appeared in a spread in *Mid-week Pictorial, Life* magazine lost interest in publishing it, and Lange was interested in creating a new set of pictures and a fresh perspective that *Life's* editors would want. Originally, she had intended to return to Nipomo but switched to the Imperial Valley after learning that conditions there, "always . . . notoriously bad," had taken a turn for the worse. One-third of the valley's six hundred square miles of cropland was farmed in operations of five hundred acres or more, with a small group of about seventy-four individuals and companies controlling most of that land. Writing to Stryker, who was anxious for her "to get down to the cooperatives and also the pea pickers," she urgently appealed for quick approval of an escort to accompany her on the trip, describing the situation as "beyond belief."[16]

The area was swarming with migrant families, many of them unemployed. Another freeze had wiped out most of the pea crop and delayed the harvest, stranding people and placing them in such dire straits that relief offices had to remain open day and night. To alleviate some of the pressure, the RA proposed to erect one of its camps in the valley. This provoked a storm of opposition from city councils and growers. After the Brawley City Council refused to cooperate with the RA on the grounds that there was no shortage of farm labor housing in the valley, the RA's director of the western region, Jonathan Garst, traveled into the area to see for himself and, according to Lange, promptly "ran into a hurricane" of opposition from growers. All of this made Lange wary. From Taylor and from her study of farm labor history, she knew that just a few years earlier *Nation* writer James Rorty had been kidnapped and that anyone deemed an agitator or union organizer was a target for being tarred and feathered, or worse. "Down there," she informed Stryker, "it is too uncomfortable to be alone. If they don't like you they shoot at you and give you the works. Beat you up and throw you into a ditch at the county line."[17]

Preparing to leave for the Imperial Valley, Lange made arrangements for the care of her children. After having her camera repaired, she took out insurance for it, rounded up film, and obtained letters of introduction to the RA's various field officers. On February 16, she reported to Stryker that "people continue to pour in and there is no way to stop them and no work when they get there." She then headed south, having alerted *Life* magazine that she expected to return with strong images that would make a good story. She would be gone two or three weeks. Without an address where anyone could reach her, she promised to send a postcard each day in order to assure her family that she was safe. To help drive her car and to assist in photographing, developing, and printing, Lange hired Rondal Partridge at one dollar a day. That left her with three dollars a day from her per diem to pay for food and lodging for herself and Partridge as well as film and gasoline. Partridge, a strapping nineteen-year-old, would also provide protection.[18]

Prospecting for images, Lange seldom planned her route in any detail. She simply headed in a certain direction and drove along until she saw something worth looking at. "She never crept up on someone or took a snap shot," recalled Partridge. "She always introduced herself as a government photographer, and told her subjects that the government was interested in them." Bouncing along the narrow back roads, Lange was always on the lookout for pictures. "Go slow, go slow," she would say to

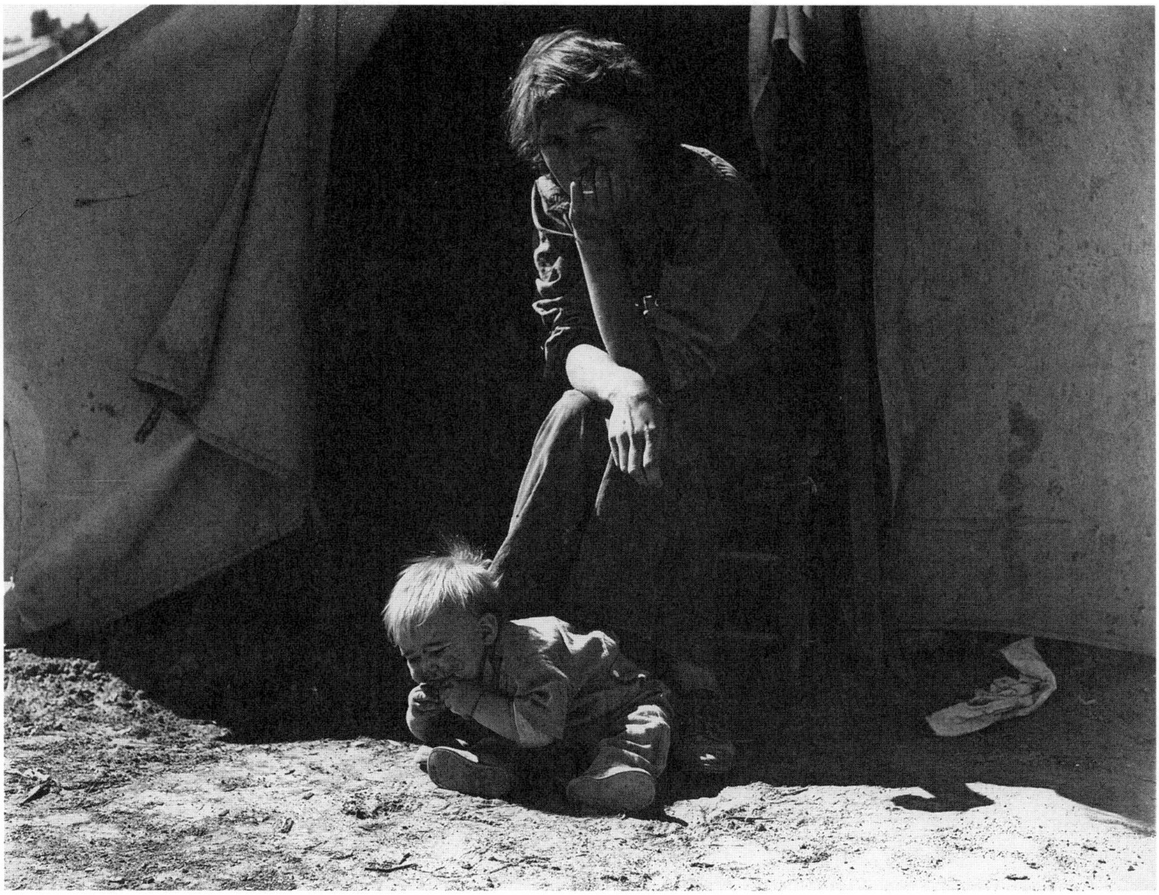

Eighteen-year-old mother from Oklahoma, now a California migrant in the Imperial Valley, March 1937, photograph by Dorothea Lange. Courtesy of the FSA/OWI Collection, Library of Congress, Prints and Photographs Division.

Partridge again and again. Whenever Partridge edged the car above forty miles per hour, Lange would tell him to slow down. "She didn't like to get above twenty-five miles per hour," Partridge recalled. "She was always telling me to slow down."[19]

Spending fifteen minutes, thirty minutes, an hour, a day at one particular site, Lange followed her usual method of listening to her subjects before photographing them in their makeshift camps, standing outside relief offices, or squatting on the edge of fields as they tried to figure out what to do next. Once, while photographing in some fields, Lange gave her camera to a fieldworker and exchanged places, allowing the field hand to photograph her as she dug potatoes. Whether she was working among Okies and Arkies or Mexicans, Japanese, and Filipinos, Lange always photographed with respect and kept up a constant banter. "Do you have trouble getting water? Mind if I photograph your camp? How much do you make a year?" she might say. "What are you picking?" Field hands would toss her whatever fruit or vegetables they were harvesting. Lange would express interest in their clothes, knives, bins, trucks. "How long have you been here?" she might begin. Then she might ask, "When do you eat lunch?" Anything to break the ice. Looking around, she might follow with: "Where do you have to go to find a toilet? How does the heat affect you? Is the boss exploiting you? How much do you get? Sometimes we'd find that out in the course of talk but never by head-on asking. . . . Her presence was the most important thing about her, and by it she would finally work up to photographing them within three or four feet."[20]

Staying in rundown cabins or auto courts with rickety beds and no sinks, Lange and Partridge followed an austere routine. With Partridge bunking outdoors in a sleeping bag and on the cabin floor if the weather was bad, they were an odd couple who attracted attention as they moved about. When desk clerks became curious about the appearance of a forty-two-year-old woman and a younger man, Dorothea would sign the register as "Dorothea Lange and fancy man." But they had little time to worry. At the end of each day in the field they were so tired that all they could do was label film, clean cameras, write a few letters, and eat supper. Occasionally Lange gave Partridge a back massage and vice versa. Up before dawn, they would be on their way with a sip of coffee, an orange, and later a sandwich. "We found our way in, slid in on the edges," recalled Lange. "We used our hunches. And it was hard, hard living. It wasn't easy, but you didn't ever quit in the middle of anything because it was uncomfortable."[21]

On the way south and then on her way back to Berkeley, Lange paid keen attention to signs and billboards along the highways. For the past year the National Association of Manufacturers (NAM) had been hyping American economic life by plastering billboards throughout the countryside with huge images of happy, family-centered, prosperous, white middle-class families. Acutely aware that these conservative, big business clichés bore little resemblance to the realities faced by the migrant farmworkers she was encountering, Lange appears to have launched a kind of counter-billboard project. Already photographer Margaret Bourke-White had skewered the cliché. Photographing a news story on a flood in the Ohio River valley, Bourke-White had recorded a line of poor black people waiting for relief in Louisville, Kentucky. Looming above them in the photograph, a NAM billboard depicting a family in a new automobile proclaims, "WORLD'S HIGHEST STANDARD OF LIVING . . . There's no way like the American Way."[22]

Like most Historical Section photographers, Lange considered the NAM billboards to be absurd. Along with Russell Lee and Arthur Rothstein, she treated them as fair game. While photographing migrants stranded along the road on her trip home, some of them quite desperate if not destitute, Lange found them suggesting a message that ran counter to the signs and billboards of the NAM campaign. She made the first shot somewhere in Riverside County, where she found a NAM billboard displaying a happy housewife waiting at the threshold of her home as her returning husband holds up their daughter. The billboard proclaims, "WORLD'S HIGHEST WAGES . . . There's no way like the American Way." It bears little relationship to the stark and

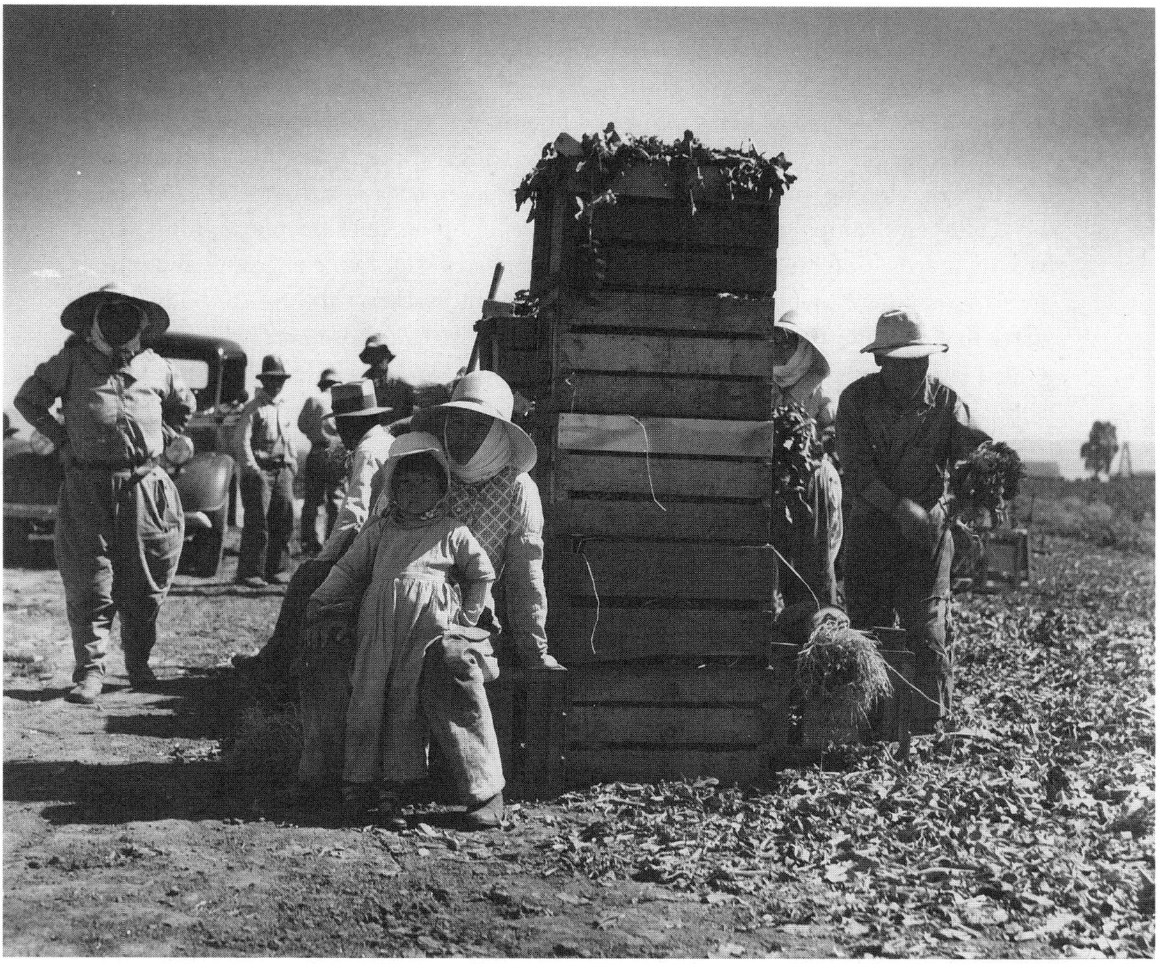

Japanese broccoli workers near Guadalupe, March 1937, photograph by Dorothea Lange. Courtesy of the FSA/OWI Collection, Library of Congress, Prints and Photographs Division.

uninviting surroundings. Her second shot captured an estate sign proclaiming: "A LITTLE FARM WITH POULTRY, FRUIT AND VEGETABLES. YOU ARE SAFE." Located beside the highway, it was seen by hundreds, if not thousands, of drought refugees and seemed to encapsulate exactly what they were seeking. Returning north at the end of her trip, Lange spotted a scene near Los Angeles with the kind of juxtaposition portrayed in the Bourke-White shot. Two bindle men were tramping beside a billboard exclaiming, "NEXT TIME TRY THE TRAIN." Lange parked her car and made two exposures, the first when they approached the billboard, the second a minute or so later, when they passed it. Strong in their ironic juxtaposition, the photographs, and others like them that she made over the next few years, capture the caustic "reality" of unequal travel accommodations in which some people lie back and relax while others trudge the byways with their bindles and suitcases. Lange's billboard images scoff, eviscerate, and jeer at indifferent corporate advertisers. Smile and relax—easy enough if you are traveling oblivious to the miseries of the Great Depression. Lange was ridiculing consumer culture, underscoring the anxieties and longing for security felt by hungry and homeless field hands who were roaming the back roads in search of work.[23]

Back in Berkeley on March 7, Lange had no time to rest. Leaving her bags packed, she headed for the darkroom, where she and Partridge worked nonstop over the next five days, developing, printing, and sorting ninety-seven negatives. Besides documenting ditch-bank camps, men crowded around relief offices, and people washing and bathing in irrigation canals, Lange also photographed a wide range of groups and produced some interesting studies of postures, gazes, and archetypal forms of body language that she later captioned *The Pea Picker* and *The Jobless Man on Relief.* Instinct guided Lange through these encounters. "When you are doing a lot of hard fast field work, it's a physical necessity to forget every day," she later recalled. "You can't try to remember it in any continuity. You get so burdened if you try to do it the other way. You can't dictate to your material, you have to follow this kind of material. You miss it."[24]

At the end of her darkroom marathon, Lange reviewed her prints and wrote to Stryker, advising him that they were "loaded with ammunition." She had discovered abundant evidence of the sense of desperation among the people in the valley and the need for establishing government camps. The whole thing was a "rotten mess." She had not only returned with fresh pictures to replace the older ones that were now being used over and over again but had also collected information from local State Emergency Relief Administration agents, made her usual field notes, and amassed a file of telegrams and letters from Oklahomans and other midwesterners that captured their despair. Lange hoped that her pictures could awaken action and rekindle interest in building camps. Because the situation was so dire, she wanted to send some of her images immediately out to California newspapers and *Life* and to make extra prints for the RA's regional office. "There is considerable heat here on the question of photographs," she wrote Stryker. "They feel that Washington doesn't realize what's happening."[25]

Meanwhile, Lange began preparing a large exhibit of photographs on the drought refugee problem in the Imperial Valley for the California Conference of Social Workers to be held in San Jose. Influential figures such as Paul Kellogg and Isidor Lubin would be present, as would Will Alexander, a top aide to Rexford Tugwell. Lange naturally wanted to make a good showing. It was an excellent opportunity to demonstrate to a very important group of people what sociological photography could do. More important, Lange saw the exhibition as a chance to make those in attendance aware of the problems faced not only by the influx of Dust Bowl refugees but also by the Mexican and Filipino field hands she encountered on her journey. Lange may also have been somewhat concerned by the actions of the RA regional office, which had attempted to hire Mary Jeanette Edwards on a per diem basis. After Washington, D.C., turned down the attempt to hire Edwards, Lange was given free access to her West Coast negatives. She now began printing as much as she wanted for the regional office.[26]

While in the darkroom, Lange looked back over her Imperial Valley sojourn with a mixture of pride and apprehension. The trip had been difficult. She and Partridge had driven several thousand miles and kept constantly on the move. She had scarcely rested and filled every moment with productive work. Now she was being overwhelmed by numerous other projects and problems. Believing that she had risked her safety by venturing into the Imperial Valley, she now grew disillusioned by what she regarded as the RA's betrayal in reneging on a promise to pay her twenty-six hundred dollars that year. There was little that she could do, but she would not let the matter rest. She asked Stryker's permission to write to the individual who had made the promise. "I don't want to make difficult matters more difficult for you—Still I consider this rather shabby business, and I protest all this sort of treatment." Stryker's answer was revealing. He conceded that Lange had in fact been offered twenty-six hundred dollars for her assignment, but his indignation was hollow. "It makes me sore as hell that I am put in a position of having to back down on a promise," he said. Stryker never made any effort to rectify the double-crossing.[27]

Lange worked virtually nonstop through March. During this time she shipped photographs back to Stryker, spotted, mounted, and matted twenty-five 11 × 14–inch exhibition prints, and lobbied for another field trip. As Taylor daily received various revisions of the LaFollette Committee report he was preparing on drought refugees, Lange had to constantly change her photo selections, make new prints, and develop new captions. Early in April, she mailed Stryker fifty captioned and sequenced photographs, together with negatives, so that Stryker's lab assistants could make final prints that were better than the ones she had rushed out using whatever odd printing papers were available. She wrote to Stryker that she was out of darkroom supplies and was working with materials borrowed from other photographers. "I've worked on this job until I'm shaking in the knees," she explained to Stryker.[28]

Demands on Lange's time grew ever more intense with the appearance of her photographs in a wide spectrum of publications. More than anything else, Lange hoped to place her photographs in *Life* magazine. On March 23, still hoping to salvage something, she rushed to *Life* twenty-five new photographs from her Imperial Valley trip illustrating the theme of "human erosion." Without notifying her, Stryker had also sent to *Life* a separate portfolio from Lange's LaFollette Committee report with the provision that *Life* not use them until the report had appeared. Since the report was still months, if not years, in the future, the decision effectively killed Lange's essay for *Life*. After her Imperial Valley images began appearing in newspapers around the country, *Life* apparently lost interest once again. It was typical of how *Life* behaved, encouraging many more picture stories than it could publish, then at the last moment withdrawing support and spiking a story. With *Life*'s gigantic readership and great prestige, photographers like Lange busted their backs trying to be published in the magazine. Lange eventually did have some of her work published in *Life,* but photo essayist Eugene Smith (one of Lange's greatest admirers) always considered it criminal that the country's largest and most influential magazines used Lange's work so sparingly.[29]

Determined to meet all of her deadlines, Lange made a presentation that appeared in the *San Francisco Chronicle*'s rotogravure section in April. She also succeeded in hanging her huge migrant farmworker exhibition on the walls of the San Jose conference room, finishing at midnight before the social workers arrived to begin their proceedings. Anxious to "get out of the darkroom and all this mess of prints," she finished sorting, classifying, and captioning all of the negatives owed to Stryker. After some dental work, she went through her usual drill: make arrangements for the care of her children, service her cameras, and load up on film. At the end of April she prepared to rendezvous with Taylor and travel through the Midwest and South to photograph aspects of farm tenancy, which Stryker regarded as "the biggest issue before RA." She would take Taylor's twelve-year-old son, Ross, along to see the country and spend time with his father and stepmother after having spent the past year in the East with his mother and sisters. Free to photograph, Lange signed her last frantic letters to Stryker before leaving: "Your faithful slave."[30]

Lange now faced a number of challenges, some of them quite threatening. Although her work, as well as that of other RA photographers, was now receiving wide popular praise and dissemination, it was not so highly regarded in agricultural circles. By late spring, the hostility that she had sensed during her trip into the Imperial Valley took several overt forms. Growers and their allies increasingly saw a conspiracy against them. They were infuriated by the photographs that Lange had supplied for Steinbeck's "The Harvest Gypsies" and further angered by the huge controversy and negative attention Lange had caused with her work at Nipomo and her famous Migrant Mother series. Images of the violence at Salinas captured by the San Francisco press corps had made growers so wary of any attention that they threatened Steinbeck with bodily harm. Several farm groups called for a boycott of San Francisco newspapers and loudly condemned Lange's work as fiction, if not communist propaganda. If they could not eliminate the RA entirely, then they would support efforts to cut its funding. And if they could not eliminate uncomfortable RA photographs, then they would have to take the next step. They would create their own counterdocumentary and incorporate cameras into the arsenal of tools employed against farmworker organizations.[31]

For several years, members of the Associated Farmers had been exploring ways to employ photographs to their advantage. Many had already purchased cameras and started using them during labor troubles. Such photographs would prove a deterrent, wrote Associated Farmers executive secretary Fred Goodcell, because "no agitator wants his picture taken." Agreeing with this line of reasoning, the *Pacific Rural Press* suggested that farmers overcome the biases of urban cameramen by arming themselves with cameras and snapping pictures of suspicious people. "Our belief," observed the editor, "is that if the average citizen would carry a small camera in his pocket, one ready to shoot by merely pointing and pressing, that rioting would soon fade, that illegal picketing would stop, and that racketeers with criminal records and those aliens who are illegally in this country would go into seclusion."[32]

Faced with such prospects, Lange had mixed feelings when she left California to photograph through the Southwest and into Texas, Oklahoma, Missouri, Arkansas, Louisiana, Mississippi, Alabama, Tennessee, Georgia, and South Carolina. Because the summer heat and humidity attacked her negatives, Lange departed from her California practice of developing her own negatives and periodically sent the undeveloped film off to the RA for processing. On her way east, Lange photographed Tombstone, New Mexico, once a booming mining town, now largely abandoned. Reaching the Midwest, she concentrated on providing context for what was happening in California. Believing that she could not adequately present the western flow of so-called Okies and Arkies without documenting the land that the newcomers had left behind, Lange expended considerable energy photographing farm tenancy, sharecropping, and displacement. Once in the Deep South, Lange returned to the themes that had most bothered her during her first visit: segregation, backwardness, the legacy of slavery, and the old plantation system.[33]

Lange found one of her most important images while she and Taylor were driving along a back road in Hardeman County, Texas, sometime in June. They had been searching for a house that seemed typical of those inhabited by Dust Bowl refugees arriving in California. Stopping at a dilapidated shack one Sunday morning, they walked onto the porch and looked inside. Through the screen door they saw several men sitting in the dark. None moved until Taylor produced his ID card, poked it through the slightly open door, and explained who they were and why they were there. After asking what Taylor and Lange wanted to learn, the men began talking, and slowly all seven filed out onto the porch. The shack had been abandoned by a family that had left for California after being displaced by large-scale tractor farming. All of them had families to support and were surviving on $22.80 a month from the WPA. One of them lived in the shack in exchange for three days' work for the landlord. The men had been excluded from voting because they could not afford to pay a poll tax. They were talking over their options, engaged in a clandestine political meeting when Lange and Taylor crossed their path. Angered that recent hearings conducted by a special presidential committee on farm tenancy had failed to consider the effects of either mechanization or political disenfranchisement, Taylor became so upset with the political situation that he described it to his superiors in a special "Note from the Field," including with it proof sheets of the negatives Lange had made that day. Looking back on that hot day, months later, Lange and Taylor would identify it as the moment when the idea of doing a book on what they had witnessed finally crystallized. Eventually Lange made seven exposures while the men poured out their hopes and fears to Taylor. "By that time we were just incidentally there," recalled Taylor. "They were so used to us that they went back again to discussing their problem between themselves."[34]

One exposure captures all of the men standing to the left of the shack. In two pictures, six men squat on the ground, discussing their problems. In another, only five appear. A sixth picture, Lange's favorite, has six of the seven men standing in front of the porch. Each man folds his arms or sticks his hands deep inside his pockets. While printing the image, Lange deleted the sixth man on the far right. She never explained why. Possibly because he did not quite fit into the composition. Was it his darker clothing? His pose with his arms behind his back? The space between him and the others? Lange would later explain that she often found it necessary to take multiple images of the same subject because she rarely had enough time to work deliberately; she sometimes photographed knowing full well that she would have to crop "because there'd be confusions . . . awkward portions" that had to be eliminated. Whatever the reason, the tenant farmer on the far right disappears, and the composition is better for it. It says: Here are desperate, unexceptional men who are being bypassed by forces beyond their control, who are trying to figure out their next step, and who do not know what to do or whom to fight. They are the epitome of the people now on their way to California.[35]

On the way back to California, while photographing in Childress County, Texas, Lange happened upon an abandoned farmhouse surrounded by a sea of freshly plowed furrows that ran right up to the farmhouse door. Placing the farmhouse slightly right of center in the treeless, dusty landscape, Lange captured the scene, which instantly summarized what had happened to the people and the land. It would become one of her most widely recognized images. Her title for it, *Tractored Out,* said it all.[36]

A week before Lange returned home, one of her Imperial Valley photographs appeared in the June 21 issue of *Life.* Tacked on to the last page of a highly optimistic six-page layout on various methods to reduce soil erosion in the Dust Bowl, Lange's photograph, published full-page, was a close-up cropped version of a defiant-looking man. The layout suggests that he is not a victim but rather one of the new pioneers making a new life for themselves in California. An accompanying caption, apparently taken from Lange's notes, quoted him as saying, "I heerd about this here irrigation. . . . I figured that in a place where some people can make a good livn' I can make me a livn'." The RA was credited, but Lange received no byline. What bothered her most about the matter, however, was the way her photograph had been detached from the story she had photographed and tacked on to an entirely different story.[37]

As Lange began her usual marathon of darkroom work, an unusual strike erupted in the apricot orchards around the small Sacramento Valley farm town of Winters. This was not a spontaneous strike. It was, in fact, a well-calculated strike that emerged as part of a new organizing strategy. At the center of the strike was Harry Bridges and the longshoremen of San Francisco. Following victories on the docks in San Francisco in 1934, Bridges had left the American Federation of Labor, changed the name of the International Longshoremen's Association (ILA) to the International Longshoremen's and Warehousemen's Union (ILWU), joined the Congress of Industrial Organizations (CIO), and embarked on an aggressive organizing campaign. Following this strategy, the ILWU had chartered dozens of new unions and started organizing warehousemen outside San Francisco in a strategy that some called "the march inland." As part of its

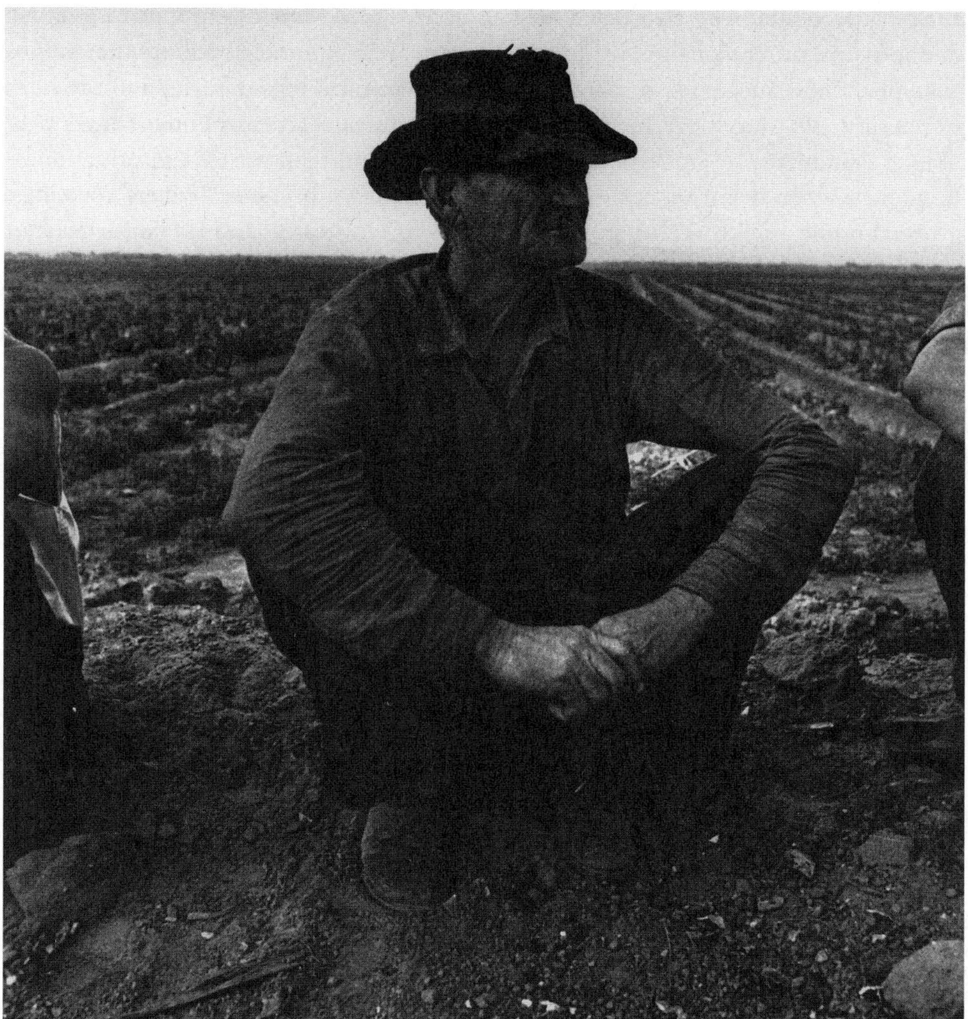

Jobless on the edge of a pea field, Imperial Valley, March 1937, photograph by Dorothea Lange. Courtesy of the FSA/OWI Collection, Library of Congress, Prints and Photographs Division.

strategy, the ILWU chartered the Union of Farm and Field Workers (UFFW). With about five hundred dues-paying fruit pickers in four counties and a half dozen farm towns, the UFFW demanded a raise from thirty-five to forty cents per hour and union recognition. After growers in the Winters area refused to bargain, the UFFW called a strike, and newspapers in Sacramento, Lodi, Stockton, Woodland, and Oakland all dispatched photographers to see what, if anything, was different about the way Bridges and the longshoremen organized in the fields.

They discovered that very little had changed under ILWU leadership. Photographers as usual balanced coverage of the highly effective and coordinated anti-union tactics of the Associated Farmers with sympathetic images of pickers holding large and boisterous outdoor strike meetings. This time, however, they were able to add something to the picture of farmworker strikes that had heretofore been lacking. Unlike their predecessors, who had failed to gain access to the inner workings of Colonel Sanborn and other vigilantes during the lettuce packers' strike at Salinas, news photographers now succeeded in boring into the strike-breaking strategies and activities of Sheriff J. W. Moore and his deputies. Allowed unusual access, photographers were able to document the anti-union planning process and then use that information to be present when deputy sheriffs established road blocks, broke up strikers' meetings, arrested union leaders en masse, dispersed crowds with force, and broke the back of a well-financed, well-led farmworker union.[38]

Whether Lange followed these events or paid any attention to the images appearing in the newspapers is uncertain. She was about to be transferred from the RA to its successor and may have been too preoccupied with the change to pay much attention. This transfer had begun when the RA, an independent agency lacking legislative mandate, was incorporated into the Department of Agriculture. Tugwell resigned, and Secretary of Agriculture Henry Wallace appointed Will Alexander as Tugwell's successor. Wallace changed the name of the RA to the Farm Security Administration, which continued to focus its activities on the underprivileged classes. Like the RA, the FSA maintained a historical section, this one also headed by Stryker. It also continued exploring questions of rural poverty and the solutions offered under the New Deal. But now Stryker's vision became more encyclopedic. He began issuing shooting scripts, directing photographers to document the myriad details of small-town life.[39]

For Lange, the change to the FSA brought more of the same ups and downs, including periodic layoffs. While the economy tanked in the fall of 1937 and two million people lost their jobs, Roosevelt chopped all of the major relief programs by 25 percent. Lange received a pink slip, along with photographer Walker Evans, an RA original who now went on to independent work. The FSA had funds for just two photographers, three laboratory assistants, and five office workers. "I had to cut my staff as far as it will go, believe me," explained Stryker.[40]

Lange remained on the payroll through October. Lacking funds to undertake additional fieldwork, she briefly considered a request by the FSA regional information officer Fred Soule to photograph a cotton strike that had broken out around Shafter and Arvin, in the southern San Joaquin Valley. Recalling her experiences at the Salinas lettuce packers' strike, Lange was not enthusiastic about venturing into photojournalism. She did not waste time arguing with Soule and simply let the matter pass. Perhaps she might continue as a part-time consultant with the office of the western region of the FSA? She was willing, even at "extremely low" pay, she said, if the arrangement allowed her to continue working in the fields, where she was "now so vitally concerned." In the meantime, she devoted all of her attention to developing and printing all of the negatives from her big summer field trip. Depressed at her plight, she faced the fact that after three years of exhausting work, she retained nothing of consequence from her efforts. "I have nothing at all to show for my 3 years of government work in the way of prints," she complained to Stryker. "Wish I could have the time to make a few out of this new series for myself, but I expect you won't be able to permit it, or the time to do it, well, never mind."[41]

Working day and night without a break, she informed Stryker that she would not finish her project by November. When she mailed clusters of negatives and captioned prints to Stryker, she promised somehow to find the funds and time necessary to complete the project. But it was wearing on her. She was reliving the trip, finding holes in her coverage, trying to group the images and place them in proper sequence. "I am not yet through with this god-damn captioning job by any means, although I am working on it just as hard as I can," she informed Stryker. "Sometimes it goes fast but

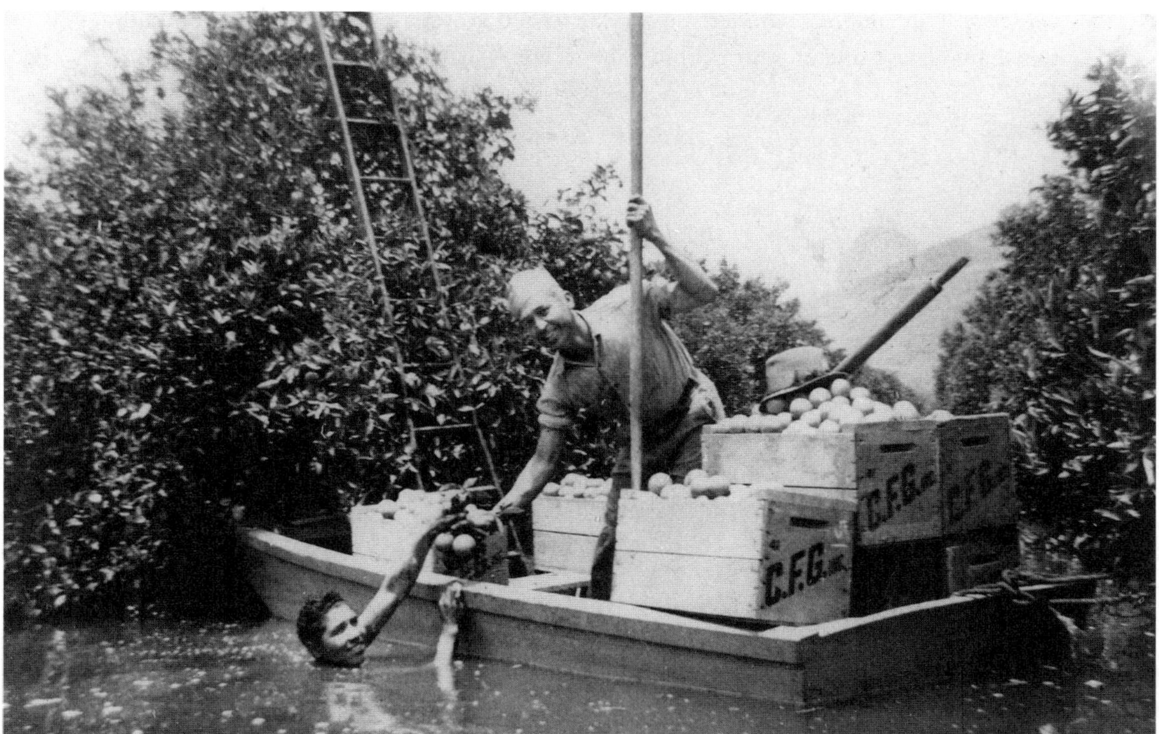

Trinidad Guillen and José Partida picking citrus from a rowboat during the flood of 1937, near Chino, December 1937, photograph by Gavino López. Courtesy of Chino Public Library.

sometimes I get stuck and have to walk around the block or dig in the garden. I write 'tenant farmer' and 'Mississippi' in my sleep."[42]

When floods swept through Chino that winter, drowning the citrus orchards in many feet of water, Lange did not photograph the catastrophe. Given the wide coverage that the flood received, she most likely knew of the situation. Whether she was too busy or too tired or simply not interested, Lange again missed another important part of the farmworker story. By this time, however, citrus harvesters had begun carrying cameras. A few made snapshots of the flood. Some of these snapshots are unlike anything heretofore seen in California. Chino citrus picker Gavino López made the best pictures. When two of his friends rowed a boat into the middle of an orchard submerged under ten feet of flood water, López followed and snapped a picture of the men harvesting citrus. A caption on the mounted and matted photograph reads: "Trinidad Guillen and José Partida picking citrus from a boat after flood waters tore through Chino, 1937."[43]

Just before her last paycheck, Lange assembled a series of photographs illustrating Taylor's report to the Social Security Board on the effects of mechanized farming. For that assignment, she chose her images with the idea that they might be published in a more popular forum, perhaps in *Collier's* magazine. Finishing the project, she looked to the future with considerable trepidation, feelings of betrayal, and a sense of freedom and challenge. As far as she could tell, her career as a government photographer was now at an end. She wondered if Stryker would ever write to her again. "You know that I am always one of your people," she wrote. What next?[44]

12

A Record of Human Erosion

Lange in the American Southwest

After being laid off, Lange fell into a brief depression. Looking back over her work, she lamented that all of her prints and negatives were in Washington, D.C. She had nothing in her possession for two years of hard labor. A strong and determined woman and a true artist, she was inclined to demand possession of what she believed was hers, but she was also a tactful individual who knew the limits of her situation. Lange devoted most of January 1938 to adjusting to her new status as a private citizen. Writing to Stryker on January 12, she explained, "I'm trying to decide what I really want most to do, what is most important to do . . . how I can do it and keep myself and my work financially afloat."[1]

As she assessed matters, Lange recalled her experience in scrutinizing rural poverty. While photographing the federal migrant camps, she had become convinced that they were highly innovative ventures, experiments in rudimentary democracy, the only federal effort to do anything substantial for migrant farmworkers. Besides the shelter they offered, the camps impressed Lange as safe havens where people could talk freely without fear of eviction or reprisal, even hold labor meetings and listen to organizers. During the winter, Lange became convinced that her photography ought to focus on gathering visual information demonstrating the need for a vastly expanded migrant camp program. The question was how to move forward. She had no funds to travel and could not afford to continue at her own expense. She tried to elicit assignments from Stryker with news clippings and outlines of shooting scripts. "Think it over, Roy!" she wrote. When Stryker remained silent, she grabbed some cash off the dresser and headed into the San Joaquin Valley.[2]

Lange spent most of February 1938 photographing around Arvin, on her own or on a per diem basis from the FSA. The forty houses there seemed to her just "one step up from the tent" but certainly a world apart from the ditch-bank camps she had photographed. Enduring endless invitations to take posed pictures of camp managers and residents standing proudly in front of the new kitchen facilities, the dance pavilion, and so on, she adopted a frankly reverent approach that singled out those attributes distinguishing FSA camps from other farmworker settlements. Often in her camp photography, Lange documented buildings and other assets of the camps as well as their layouts. One of her photographs of the welcome sign above the entrance to Arvin Camp as seen in the early morning light was as much a landscape image as a work of documentary photography. Some of her other photographs were second-rate, even banal, moving beyond the normal boundaries of journalism and sociological photography into the realm of propaganda and promotion.[3]

Staying active, Lange assisted relief efforts by cooperating with the Simon Lubin Society. One of the most vocal of the state's reform groups, the Lubin Society took its name from Simon Julius Lubin, a Progressive era reformer, businessman, and civic leader whose Sacramento department store, Weinstock and Lubin, was among the first to implement a medical plan, pension plan, and credit union. Before the Wheatland hop riot of 1913, Lubin had been instrumental in creating the California Commission of Immigration and Housing and in the years after the riot had served as its first chairman. While directing the state Department of Commerce in 1930, he continued to champion the cause of farm labor housing and decent treatment of agricultural laborers. During the Imperial Valley farm labor strikes of 1934, Lubin took to the field as a vehement champion of the migrant cause. At a March 23, 1934, Commonwealth Club of California town hall meeting, broadcast over radio station KPO, Lubin opened the program with a widely reprinted address titled "Can the Radicals Capture the Farms of California?" Squashing fears that the brave but always bickering and highly disorganized communists could accomplish anything, Lubin went on to attack the prevailing climate of "greed and selfishness, the intellectual sterility, the social injustice, the economic blindness, the lack of political sagacity and leadership, and the mock heroics and hooliganism we observe within our State today."[4]

Although he died early in 1938, Lubin was so widely admired and respected for his devotion to the Progressive agenda that a group of social activists led by journalist Carey McWilliams and philanthropist Helen Hosmer created the Simon J. Lubin Society of California. With no paid staff, the society quickly rented office space in the Phelan Building in San Francisco and began publishing the *Rural Observer*, a feisty bimonthly edited by Hosmer and devoted to exposing the stranglehold of "corporate interests" on commercial agriculture. Soon the society was issuing a flood of propaganda, most of it aimed at its arch enemy, the Associated Farmers, while also coordinating private relief activities and serving as an informal research bureau that kept agricultural unions supplied with the latest wage and production information.[5]

In April 1938, the society published two powerful booklets. One was Edith Lowry's *Migrants of the Crops: They Starve That We May Eat,* issued in cooperation with the Council of Women for Home Missions. The other was *Their Blood Is Strong,* a collection of Steinbeck's *San Francisco News* articles, which sold for twenty-five cents and was illustrated with many of Lange's photographs. Her cover shot of an Okie woman illustrates perfectly her attempt to use images that had been made earlier but had remained uncirculated. Lange had made this picture and a very similar one in August

1936, near Blythe, California. The image used on the cover of *Their Blood Is Strong* captures a beautiful young woman seated on a makeshift bed beneath a tent flap as she nurses a baby. Her bare breast is visible and quite shapely. She looks impassively toward the photographer through what William Stott describes as "the innocent trapped eyes of a deer." Her child stares too. It is the same tender and brave look that is found in so many documentary images of the 1930s. To make the second shot, Lange moved several feet to the right and framed the picture slightly differently, with the woman looking off camera as her husband reclines on a makeshift bed, looking directly into the camera.[6]

As Lange had done earlier with *Ditched, Stalled, and Stranded,* she severely cropped the cover picture in such a way as to emphasize certain elements and amplify others. By cropping the picture from its original horizontal composition, Lange eliminated the

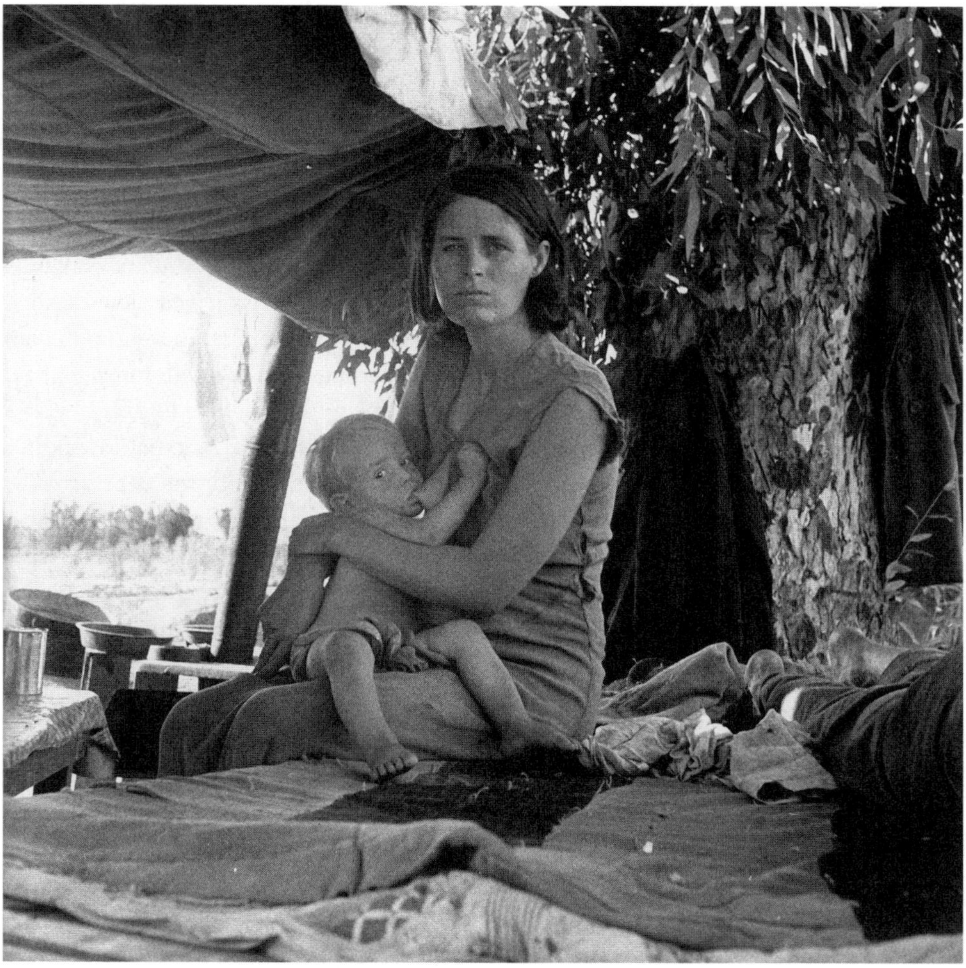

Oklahoma drought refugees camped by the roadside near Blythe, August 1936, photograph by Dorothea Lange. Courtesy of the FSA/OWI Collection, Library of Congress, Prints and Photographs Division.

husband, who dominates the original on the right side. Whereas her uncropped image is essentially a study in family solidarity under stressful circumstances, her cropped image, focusing mostly on the young woman, suggests stoic motherhood.[7]

Reprinted four times, *Their Blood Is Strong* placed Lange's images in even wider circulation than the popular magazines and government publications in which they had been appearing. But while Lange had always derived a great deal of satisfaction in illustrating other people's reports, something was missing for her. She suffered from "mental hunger." She felt most alive on the road, getting up early, recording history as it was unfolding around her. She needed the challenge of that routine. When would she return to the field? What fresh visual discoveries awaited her?

Preparing for a third field trip with Taylor during the summer of 1938, she begged Stryker to hire her back for June, July, and August. She wanted to expand the FSA file on cotton and explore how the poll tax was being used to prevent African Americans from voting in the South. She promised Stryker "dynamite in this one!" But Stryker was under considerable pressures from conservative legislators and more practical-minded superiors. A victim of his own success and the diligence of his photographers, he discovered that when legislators had learned that the FSA had accumulated twenty thousand negatives, some concluded that additional photography would be purposeless. What more was there to photograph? Under these circumstances, the best Stryker could do was agree to purchase one hundred of Lange's negatives at three dollars each. If he could find the funds, he promised to make another three hundred dollars available. This left Lange so poor that she could barley afford a new Zeiss Jewell view camera. Desperate, she again wrote to Stryker. "There was very little cash left in my top bureau drawer, right hand side," she explained. "Just about enough to see me in film. . . . Paul will always feed me, and if you will keep me in film, anything is possible."[8]

At the beginning of May, Lange was at a professional and intellectual low point. Because she would not be able to process her negatives in the field, she contracted to have Ansel Adams do the work. This meant that any remaining funds not spent on film would go to processing and printing. Three months of hot and uncomfortable work in the South would likely leave her in debt and completely dependent on Taylor for financial support. Stryker was touched by Lange's plight but had nothing to offer. It was all he could do to keep the Historical Section alive. "When I look over my list of jobs to be done . . . I become quite bitter," he confessed to Lange. "All I can do is keep pounding away in the hopes that either good luck will come our way, or our bosses will come across, or fire me and close up the damn file."[9]

Facing financial disaster and still tempted by more offers of commercial and editorial assignments outside the FSA, Lange nevertheless stuck with her work. She understood the pressures on Stryker, admired his steady leadership, and told him so. One reason why she kept at it in the midst of all her problems was that she was thinking about producing a book of text and photographs. From the beginning, she did not see this project as a solo effort. Lange had learned much from Paul Taylor. She admired their intimate partnership. She intended to extend their growing collaboration and to further unite social science and photography. These plans had only started to form, and Lange was not yet ready to announce them to Stryker. Although she believed that he would support her effort, she knew that by appropriating her FSA images for private use she was testing the limits of Stryker's goodwill. She also had to consider the issue of what the government would allow her to do with her work. She could not say which of her FSA images she wanted to use; nor did she know who would publish them or how they would be presented. All that was certain was that writers, filmmakers, artists, photographers, even radio broadcasters were coalescing into a new and powerful movement, and Lange wanted to be part of it.

Although permeating the culture, this movement still had no official name and was hard to define or describe. It included proletarian and working-class studies, angry exposés of capitalist exploitation, and worker narratives that conveyed a sense of everyday life. Detached social science essays designed to acquaint the public with significant trends and problems were part of this genre, as were first-person accounts of people triumphing over adversity. Objectivity was not a goal of this discourse, but those pursuing it did not tolerate inaccuracy, falsification, propaganda, fiction, or art for art's sake. Communication had to focus on reality. Substance and content were essential, as were feeling, emotion, and a vivid sense of having lived through an unforgettable experience. But even those things were not enough to define the purpose of this discourse. This was not entertainment. It was not diversion. The goal was to elevate human awareness, promote social engagement, and inspire people to correct wrongs and build a better world.[10]

Already photography had begun to play a role in the new genre of communication. In 1934, Pare Lorentz's *The Roosevelt Year: A Photographic Record* applied photographic coverage in book format to contemporary events, and Charles M. Wilson's *Backwoods America* (1934) and Muriel Sheppard's *Cabins in the Laurel* (1935) used beautifully reproduced photographs by Bayard Wooten to help them explore facets of rural life. Human interest picture books made their debut in 1936 with the publication of Arthur Raper's *Preface to Peasantry,* a sociological tract on tenant farming in Georgia that employs an innovative opening format consisting of two pictures of former slaves who had just posed for their portraits.[11]

Although Lange was aware of these books, none resembled the project she and Taylor had in mind. She probably drew most of her inspiration and ideas from Lewis Hine's six-volume *Pittsburgh Survey* (1909–14), which documents life and labor in the Pittsburgh steel mills, and his *Men at Work* (1932), a tribute to high steelworkers ("all of them persons it is a privilege to know"), depicting them as disciples of the cult of the machine. Carleton Beals's *The Crime of Cuba* (1933), which explores Cuba's misery and suggests that a revolution was just around the corner, also offered her guidance. But Lange was most influenced, inspired, and somewhat appalled by *You Have Seen Their Faces* (1937), a dramatic photo–text study of southern sharecropping that inaugurated a five-year surge of books aimed at providing a first-hand witness to the social realities of the times.[12]

You Have Seen Their Faces features photographs by Margaret Bourke-White. The thirty-four-year-old former zoology student had abandoned academic life in 1929 to become a photographer for *Fortune* magazine, the only one to warrant a byline. Specializing at first in commercial images, she traveled to Russia in 1930 to photograph industrial development. The following year she established her reputation by publishing *Eyes on Russia,* a widely praised book on the Soviet economy. By 1933 she was one of the highest-paid women in America. Known as "the poetess of the camera," she quickly grew uncomfortable with the emphasis on cogs, foundries, and smokestacks and in 1934 accepted an assignment to photograph the drought-stricken Great Plains. Her work attracted the attention of *Tobacco Road* author Erskine Caldwell. Caldwell believed that the public had failed to comprehend that *Tobacco Road* was just a small slice of a larger problem. He wanted to produce an ultrarealistic work of contemporary history that could not be dismissed as fiction. In 1936 he hired Bourke-White to travel with him through nine southern states in search of the grim realities of the Great Depression. She was to provide unbiased photographs, and indeed she would claim that her images were largely mechanical, objective, and uncolored by her biases.

The resulting work in *You Have Seen Their Faces* succeeded in ways that neither Caldwell nor Bourke-White could have anticipated. While Bourke-White's photographs carried much of the emotional impact, they were not presented in the standard classical form used by pure photographers. Rather than publishing each print independent of the others, all in uniform format, *You Have Seen Their Faces* presents photographs in different formats and arranges them in a narrative. When the book appeared in 1937, some reviewers called it a new genre. Caldwell's brutal prose and Bourke-White's mournful portraits of worn, soiled faces make *You Have Seen Their Faces* a kind of *Uncle Tom's Cabin* of southern tenant farmers and sharecroppers, although a few critics thought it cheap, sensationalistic, exploitative, and full of unbelievable captions quoting people saying things they never said. Some also found it highly redundant. Most of the socioeconomic problems it detailed were by then known to almost everyone who read the book.[13]

At the same time that Caldwell and Bourke-White were working on *You Have Seen Their Faces,* Herman C. Nixon, a university professor and small farmer who knew his subject on scholarly and personal levels, published *Forty Acres and Steel Mules.* A sober work of scholarship that deals with the complexities of southern agriculture, *Forty Acres and Steel Mules* was written in a prose style that social historian William Stott describes as "a mixture of social science and Southern orotundity" that shatters the false generalizations found in *You Have Seen Their Faces* and strongly disputes Caldwell's statements that "sharecroppers and share tenants are humanly hopeless." The FSA photographs are the real guts of Nixon's book, accomplishing more than his text. While many of the 150 images show "rural slums" and tenant farmers in gritty circumstances, plenty of pictures also document families enjoying afternoons at the swimming hole, pickup baseball games, homemade diversions, and the natural tempo of field labor. Below one section of happy, healthy tenant farmers, Nixon could not resist ridiculing Caldwell with a caption reading, "Have You Really Seen Their Faces?"—a not-so-subtle jab at the picture of human derelicts created by Bourke-White.[14]

Integrating text and images in this new and creative way, other documentary books extended the tradition in various directions. Alfred Kazin and Pare Lorentz developed the form in *The River,* a 1936 film in which words and images become "not only mutually indispensable, a kind of commentary upon each other, but curiously interchangeable." *Fortune* magazine editor Archibald MacLeish's epic poem, *Land of the Free,* is by far the most coherent. Selecting highly emotional photographs with deep social relevance, MacLeish wove them into a proletarian prose poem, which he called a "sound track"; it begins, "We don't know / We aren't certain," and concludes, "We wonder / We don't know." By the end, community has triumphed over social injustice. A tribute to American diversity and class solidarity overcoming social injustice, *Land of the Free* includes thirty-three images by Lange, along with those of other FSA photographers, exploiting them to great advantage in one section about American liberty now threatened by soil exhaustion and the new westward movement. Early photographs show a beaten, passive, confused people. The book ends with triumphant and energetic images of mass rallies, strikes, and workers organizing. Although *Land of the Free* is not a book of reform, a militant tone not found in other books of this genre runs throughout it, along with an explicit criticism of the capitalist system. Reviewers split on whether or not MacLeish had made much of a contribution to literature. But there was consensus on the images, especially Lange's work. "I give her credit," wrote Lorentz in the *Saturday Review of Literature,* "for putting on celluloid what Mr. MacLeish failed to put in words: the sorrow, and the dignity, and the blood of the people."[15]

Once again, Lange was being hailed for her work in illustrating other people's books. It was a bittersweet acknowledgment. Simultaneously rewarding and frustrating, it strengthened her wish to publish her own images and face down adversity. With three years of work among migrants, Lange now had an awesome archive. This distinguished her from most other photographers of the Great Depression, because, unlike them, her desire to produce a book emerged naturally from what she and Taylor had already seen in the field. She did not go out looking for images to advance a thesis or round out an idea. But in another way, Lange was like her contemporaries. She maintained that she and Taylor were going to create an objective document, even though they were producing a highly slanted description of a regional component of a national problem.

On her upcoming field trip with Taylor, Lange planned to broaden and deepen her picture of rural America. Now their book was becoming clear. It would focus words and images on a social issue. In his oral memoir, Taylor recalled that the underlying message was clear from the first time they discussed it. "These people are worth helping! They are down and out, but they are not the dregs of society. They've hit bottom, that's all."[16]

Just as these ideas crystalized, *Fortune* magazine sent photographer Walker Evans and writer James Agee into the Deep South to collaborate on a series of documentary essays about the life and times of tenant farmers. For about six weeks they lived with three families, identified in the book as the Ricketts, Gudger, and Woods families. At once ill-suited and perfect for the task, Agee and Evans were incapable of typecasting the people they encountered. They refused to approach them as examples of a social problem and tried to connect with them in a scrupulously honest way that respected their humanity and aimed at conveying the specific reality of their lives. Believing the resulting book was "a swindle, an insult, and a corrective," Agee employed an acid prose style that seemed as though it had been composed by flashlight in the dead of night, and Evans, ever attentive to avoiding stereotypes, amplified the text with direct and unadorned portraits. Confused editors at *Fortune* tried to rewrite the impossible and slow-going text but were defeated by writing that delivered facts and self-confessions by the square yard. They gave up and sent the manuscript back to Agee. Over the next two years the difficult and uncompromising book would be rejected and subjected to several rewrites until it was finally published by Houghton Mifflin in September 1941. Titled *Let Us Now Praise Famous Men,* it sold fewer than six hundred copies. Over the next twenty years, average annual sales never exceeded fifty copies. In 1960 the publisher brought out a new edition, which the *New York Herald Tribune* called "the most famous unknown book in contemporary letters," and the book finally garnered the sales worthy of a work that is recognized as an American classic.[17]

Although *Let Us Now Praise Famous Men* appeared too late to shape Lange and Taylor's approach to their own book project, the motivations and struggles of Agee and Evans were immediately known to them and certainly influenced their thinking. Lange was very disturbed by the Caldwell–Bourke-White collaboration but did not agree with the critics who found it an outrageous piece of propaganda that exploited poor tenant farmers. As for the other books, a few had been more or less commercially successful, and those that did not make money had at least attracted considerable attention, even acclaim. Lange and Taylor would guard against the exploitative approach of Caldwell and Bourke-White and take into consideration the criticism that Agee and Evans had leveled at *You Have Seen Their Faces.* They would also attempt to move past fragmentary and thematically limited approaches toward a more global, all-encompassing perspective. As Lange had done in the past, she would take a close look at the most downcast and needy but would also offer an analysis focusing on the industrialization of farming, the decline of family farming, the disruptions of droughts and migration, and chronic rural poverty. The presentation would not threaten the system; rather, it would aim at pushing the system toward reform. Above all, it would make the case for an expanded FSA camp program. By providing a sense of safety, along with shelter, sanitation, and clean drinking water, the FSA camps would help migrants with at least the minimum necessities they lacked.[18]

After evaluating various ways to structure their presentation, Lange and Taylor settled on an extension of what they had already been doing. They would produce a book that was neither text with illustrations nor photographs with captions but an integration of theoretical, visual, and oral information around the theme of "human erosion," a concept they had been thinking about for several years. From Caldwell and Bourke-White they would borrow the technique of quoting from vernacular statements, stressing that their material was based on fact. In contrast to what Agee and Evans would later do in *Let Us Now Praise Famous Men,* they would avoid sentimentality and a realism so exaggerated that it became unreadable propaganda. Unlike MacLeish, whose *Land of the Free* tacked an amorphous and inauthentic perspective onto the problem of the dispossessed, Lange and Taylor would focus on specific geographic areas. Although Lange intended to use many of her existing images in the book, she realized that more work would have to be done.[19]

Before they could launch their book project, Lange and Taylor left for their third summer field trip together. Departing California on June 1, they spent the next six weeks crisscrossing the Southwest, then moved north through Alabama into North and South Carolina. Arriving in Washington, D.C., early in July, they paused for ten days while Taylor, now working for the Social Security Board, testified before the Special Senate Committee on Unemployment and Relief. Hoping to clear the air, Lange again met with Stryker. The two had a heated discussion when he again criticized her negatives. On leaving, Lange was humiliated to discover that one month earlier Stryker had hired Marion Post Wolcott, a beautiful twenty-nine-year-old woman who had worked previously as a freelancer in New York and as a staff photographer for the *Philadelphia Evening Bulletin.* After having just told Lange a month earlier that there was no money to keep her on the payroll and that he could afford to buy only individual negatives, Stryker explained that he had hired Wolcott "to get more photographs of the positive side of the FSA program and something different . . . to contrast with photographs . . . other than the 'lower third' of the country." As Lange departed, she bumped into Wolcott but was cool and abrupt. Wolcott would always regret not getting to know Lange. But Lange felt betrayed. She was looking to the future, intent on making the most of her journey, and she did. On the return trip through Missouri, Arkansas, and Oklahoma, Lange shot many of the photographs that would subsequently appear in her book.[20]

While Lange made her way back to California, Otto Hagel continued to document cotton pickers. During the fall of 1938 he also photographed the grape harvest in Sonoma County. He chose that area and that crop to expand his picture of farmworkers beyond row crops in the San Joaquin Valley. At the same time, a new group of photographers and artists began taking up the cause of farmworkers. One was Marysville photographer Stephen V. Hust, who moved out of his studio during the peach harvest to document organizing activities among migrant peach pickers in Yuba County. Another was Ojai native Horace Bristol, a twenty-eight-year-old from Southern California who had learned photography in night school while putting in a day at several Southern California newspapers. Broke and with two children to support, he set his sights on becoming an advertising photographer. In 1935 he moved to San Francisco. He would later claim to have accompanied Dorothea Lange on several field trips, although Lange does not mention him in her memoirs or any of her correspondence. At the Salinas lettuce packers' strike, Joe Rosenthal photographed him with other press photographers displaying their gas masks, and Otto Hagel grabbed a shot of him sitting atop a telephone pole trying to photograph a convoy of lettuce trucks. About 1937, Bristol's fortunes improved. Between assignments for *Time, Sunset,* and *Fortune* magazines, he read *You Have Seen Their Faces* and resolved to produce a similar picture of Dust Bowl migrants in California. But his proposal to *Life* magazine provoked only mild interest.[21]

Determined to record the suffering and hardship of people in the hinterland, Bristol, during the winter of 1937–38, took the unorthodox step of pitching his project to *Fortune* magazine, a sister publication of *Life,* then asked John Steinbeck, whom he had not met until now, to write a text for the photo essay. Steinbeck was then engaged in revising *Of Mice and Men* and was less than enthusiastic. Suggesting that they work on the project during weekends when Bristol was not on call to *Life* and Steinbeck could take a break from his revisions, Bristol began driving his Buick station wagon to Los Gatos, where he picked up Steinbeck and headed for the Central Valley. Spending three or four days every week working there and in roadside labor camps along the way, the two distributed coffee, beans, flour, and cheap cuts of meat to the migrants. Bristol photographed with a Rolleiflex camera, and Steinbeck casually interviewed but did not take any notes. Paranoid about the Associated Farmers, Steinbeck had Bristol sign motel registers for him under a false name. At the end of the trip, Steinbeck confessed that he did not have the stomach for what he had encountered. Describing his sojourn to his agent, Elizabeth Otis, he explained:

> *Life* sent me down with a photographer from its staff and we took a lot of pictures of the people. . . . I hope this doesn't sound either quixotish or martyrish to you. A short trip into the fields where the water is a foot deep in the tents and the children are up on their beds and there is no food and no fire, and the country has taken off all the nurses because "the problem is so great that we can't do anything about it." So they do nothing. And we found a boy in jail for a felony because he stole two old radiators because his mother was starving to death and in stealing them broke a little padlock on a shed. . . . It is the most heartbreaking thing in the world. If *Life* does use the stuff there will be lots of pictures and swell ones. It will give you an idea of the kind of people they are and the kind of faces. . . . I want to put a tag of shame on the greedy bastards who are responsible for this.[22]

By May, Bristol had shot two thousand or three thousand pictures near Visalia and elsewhere in the San Joaquin Valley. But when he called Steinbeck and told him he was ready to do the book, he got the surprise of his life. "Horace, I'm afraid I have bad news for you," Steinbeck said. "I feel that the material I have been getting is too good to be used just for a photographic book with limited text. I want to write it as it should be written—as a novel." This was unfortunate. Bristol's images were very good and helped fill in the record at a time when Lange was hindered by budget cuts and unable to photograph. But unlike Lange, Bristol had no interest in social issues. He was attracted to the migrant situation mainly only as a dramatic story. "When Steinbeck told me that he was going on to do a novel," recalled Bristol, "I just went

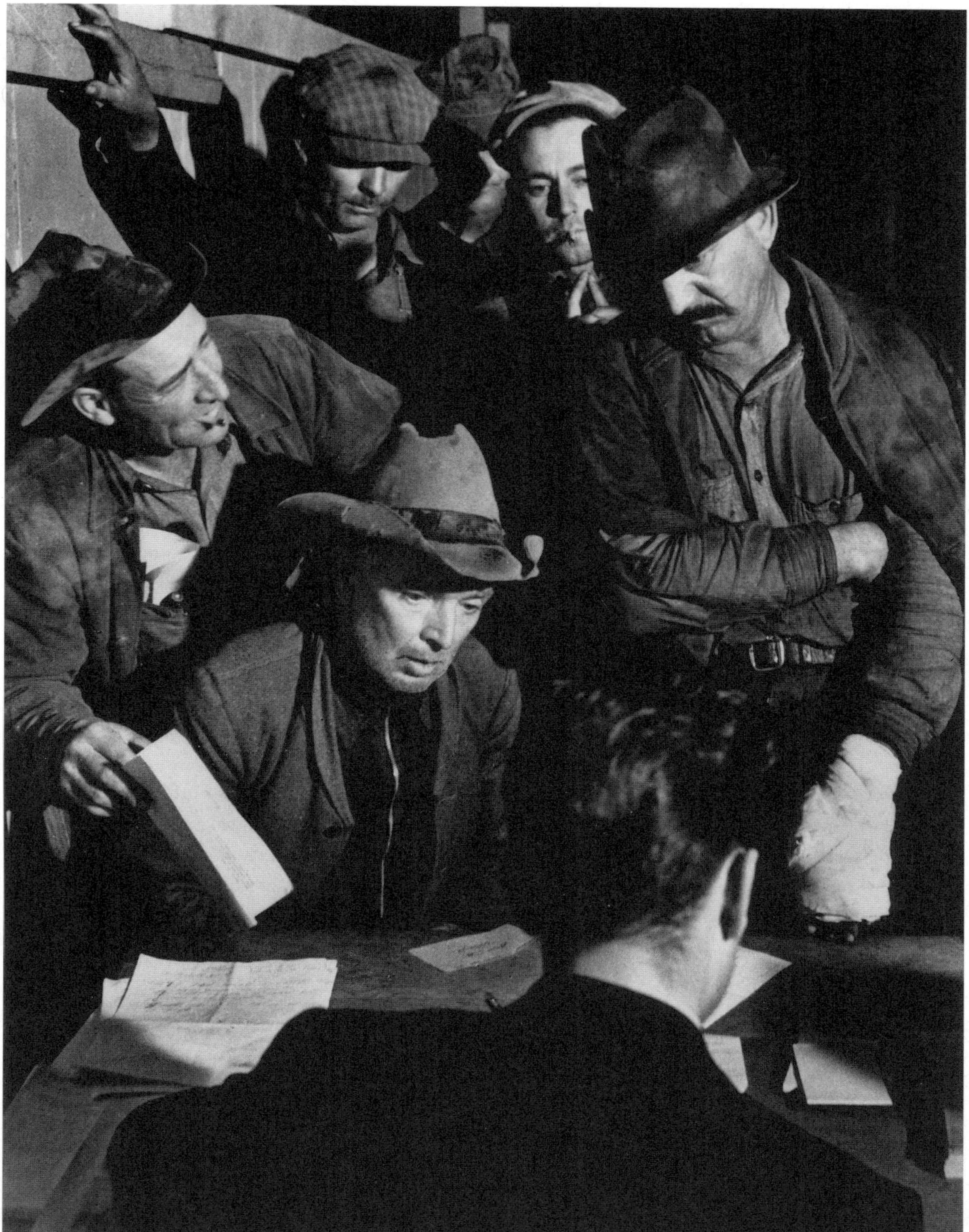

The Grapes of Wrath, March 1938, photograph by Horace Bristol. Courtesy of Horace Bristol.

on to my next *Life* assignment, without looking back." Although Twentieth Century–Fox used his images to cast people for the movie version of *The Grapes of Wrath* and *Life* magazine ran two pages of his images, Bristol never had the impact of Lange or other FSA photographers. Fifty years would pass before anyone even saw his photographs of migrant workers.[23]

Besides Bristol and Hust, other photographers who now followed Lange's footsteps into the fields included freelancers Willard Van Dyke, Paul Strand, Mary Jeanette Edwards, and San Francisco newspaper photographer Edward Mancusco. For *Labor Defender* and other radical publications, Consuelo Kanaga, a well-traveled and widely respected newspaper photographer, produced numerous photographs of jailed farmworkers and union leaders, including portraits of Sam Darcy, leader of United Cannery, Agricultural, Packing, and Allied Workers of America. Alone among the photographers of the day, only Edward Weston remained unmoved by the circumstances of the 1930s. As devoted as ever to the sharply focused negative and perfect print, he never reassessed his photography in light of contemporary events. Awarded a Guggenheim Fellowship in spring 1937, the first ever given to a photographer, Weston traveled thirty-five thousand miles through the desert and mountains of the West with companion Charis Wilson. Camping, backpacking, and lugging fifty pounds of camera equipment up mountainsides and into valleys to get perfect landscape images, Weston still refused to directly address political issues, the drama of the Depression, or the plight of California farmworkers, even while passing through the Salinas, San Joaquin, and Imperial valleys at the beginning of various trips, where he certainly saw migrants working in the fields and camping alongside the highways.[24]

Weston's aloofness was unusual. California farmworkers stirred controversy that attracted many talented artists. Nowhere was this truer than among those painters who earned an income and preserved their skills and self-confidence while employed by one of five overlapping New Deal agencies, which the public mistakenly lumped together as part of the Works Progress Administration. In fact, the public art program was more ambitious and dispersed than most people realized. It began with the Public Works Art Project (PWAP), established in December 1933 with a grant from the Civil Works Administration to the Treasury Department, and was followed by the art program of the Public Works Administration (PWA). A year later the Treasury Department authorized the Section of Painting and Sculpture as part of its Treasury Relief Arts Project. Beginning in 1935, the Federal Arts Project (FAP) of the WPA continued until 1943. (The WPA was renamed the Work Projects Administration in 1939.) Finally, in 1938, the Treasury Department created its Treasury Section of Fine Arts, which was quickly renamed the Public Buildings Administration (PBA). Each agency hired a who's who of California painters to paint murals on the walls of post offices, libraries, courthouses, and public high schools in the state's rural areas, from Eureka south to Calexico. Rather than simply rejecting the unhappy socioeconomic circumstances of rural California, all but a few avoided picturing the politically charged situation, because they knew it would bring extreme censure to their work.[25]

It was not just that these artists saw things differently from the FSA photographers. When the first muralists started their projects, they knew what had happened to Mexican artist David Álfaro Siqueiros in 1932 when he dared to inject farm labor conflict into one of his murals. While teaching at the Chouinard School of Art, Siqueiros was commissioned to paint a mural for the Olvera Street restoration project in Los Angeles. A Marxist who told his students to get out of the studio and encounter life to find inspiration, Siqueiros had his own ideas about art and life and refused to follow traditional mural-painting procedures, even using industrial materials and spray guns in place of wet plaster and paint brushes. Still angry about the treatment of striking Mexican farmworkers in the Imperial Valley, Siqueiros caused a huge furor when he painted an American eagle above the figure of a crucified Mexican peasant in *American Tropicale.* This was deemed so subversive that the eagle was immediately removed, and when that did not appease his critics, the entire mural was whitewashed out of existence.[26]

Realizing the price to be paid for painting anything controversial, muralists, happy to be working, seldom challenged the status quo and rarely engaged historical themes and contemporary topics in any rigorous, critical, or angry way. Adhering to dominant myths and avoiding ideology, they turned to California history, especially the Native American, Spanish, Mexican, and American frontiers that had been so beautifully rendered by Maynard Dixon. A typical mural, like the one painted by Bruce Ariss for Monterey High School, was packed with condescending images: a white priest teaching Indians to plant corn, from which they made tortillas; a Californio couple harvesting corn and grapes before a tile-roofed barn; a contemporary couple loading vegetables into their truck in front of another barn; and in a rare injection of reality, a dark-skinned artichoke picker bent over as he moved through the field. Artists painting murals in Fullerton, Reedley, Selma, San Diego, Vacaville, and Ventura contented themselves with presenting similar scenes of healthy, well-fed workers reaping the bounty of the land. In these murals, farmworkers always seemed to be sharing in the bountiful economy. None was homeless. None went out on strike. None was exploited. They were always equipped with the right tools and depicted performing the correct work motions. In some murals, women did work that was always performed by men. In others, crews were impossibly multicultural. "The peculiarly benign images of farmworkers, the state's poorest workers," wrote historian Steven Gebler in his book on New Deal art in California, "reflected the . . . basic commitment to private employment."[27]

A few painters refused to put a happy face on farm labor and agriculture. One prominent example of visual protest developed while PWAP artists were finishing murals inside San Francisco's Coit Tower, a prominent landmark built during 1932 and 1933 in memory of Lillie Hitchcock Coit, a leading Bay Area philanthropist. Conceived by Herbert Fleishhacker, one of San Francisco's old-guard patrons, the Coit Tower murals were originally seen as a way to occupy leftist artists Bernard Zakheim and Victor Arnautoff, both disciples of Mexican muralist Diego Rivera, as well as less politically doctrinaire artists who went to work in the tower much like a guild of anonymous craftsmen employed under the largesse of federal patronage. Under the leadership of the more left-wing artists, but also reflecting their own private visions and different political loyalties, painters in 1934 created several highly incendiary murals dealing with organized labor, the unemployed, and agricultural strife. Denounced in the press as "Red Propaganda," one mural by Bernard Zakheim containing a hammer and sickle was retouched to eliminate the offending symbols, although the equally offending *Daily Worker* and the *Masses,* pictured on sale at a Powell Street newsstand, were allowed to remain. Another mural, John Langley Howard's *California Industrial Scenes,* injects recent farm labor history into a picture of the northern Sacramento Valley spreading beneath Mount Shasta. Paying close attention to recent events, Howard included a scroll that referred to the 1932 CAWIU pea pickers' strike in Half Moon Bay. It was too much for Fleishhacker, who wanted the entire painting whitewashed.[28]

Perhaps resorting to ridicule that went over the heads of WPA administrators, Maxine Albro painted a flower picker who harvested calla lilies while dressed in a pearl necklace and lace-trimmed dress. At least two post office painters also produced critical murals. Lew Keller's grape pickers, executed for the St. Helena Post Office, well captured the nature of work, especially bending and stooping, while grape pickers race through the vineyards. Henrietta Shore's artichoke pickers, a beautiful mural of oil on masonite originally done for the Santa Cruz Post Office, also stresses the nature of field labor, underscoring the repetitive task of harvesting into large backpacks. Equally critical was Lucienne Bloch, a Swiss-born artist and master printmaker whose cause in life was to create relevant imagery for the masses. In 1936, Bloch created *Land of Plenty,* a sarcastic black-and-white woodcut in which a family of migrant

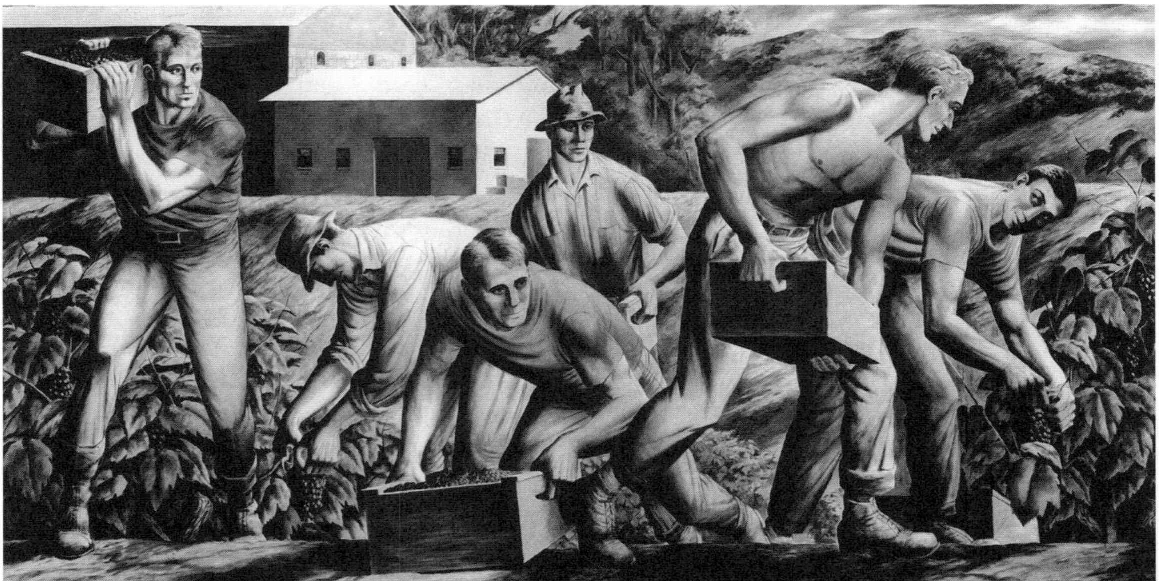

Strong and healthy grape pickers, St. Helena Post Office, 1936, mural by Lew Keller (original in color). Courtesy of Records of Public Building Service, "Photographs of Murals in United States Post Offices, California," Record Group 121, National Archives.

field hands trying to enter a cornfield is dominated by giant looming power lines and impeded by barbed wire.[29]

Such critical imagery was the exception rather than the rule. Continuing the nostalgic theme of nature tamed, painters romanticized the landscape and produced aestheticized views of agricultural enterprise, in some cases comparing the way one farmed to the way one painted, each being a composition of sorts. Whether they adopted a French Fauve palate or a down-home regionalist perspective, painters depicted a farm environment that art historian Sheri Bernstein describes as efficient, productive, and not much different from booster publications issued by the California State Fruit Growers Exchange: a "fantasy land that works itself with remarkably little effort." Even a great muralist like Diego Rivera, who advocated a more socially oriented art, muted his left-leaning politics and dodged issues in some of the murals he painted during his visit to California as part of a U.S. program to reestablish cordial relations with Mexico in 1930–31. One example is the fresco he painted on the walls of the Luncheon Club of the San Francisco Stock Exchange in the spring of 1931. Titled *Allegory of California,* it opted for heroic booster imagery. Featuring a huge woman holding the bounty of the state in her arms, the composition places agriculture on one side, industry on the other, and would have easily pleased members of the Sunkist growers cooperative. On receiving a private commission a few months later to paint *Still Life with Blossoming Almond Trees,* this "Mexican Picasso," as he was often called, continued with his fantasized picture of communal harmony. Neither impassioned nor politically charged, Rivera's mural included a racially integrated harvest crew doing some unknown and concocted labor. A tractor driver tills the soil in the background. And three children of unclear ethnicity help themselves to a basket of fruit. How all of this could be occurring in an almond orchard in full bloom is a question many ask on seeing this pastiche![30]

The painter who more than any other attacked the system of migratory farm labor and agriculture was Ronald D. Ginther. A West Coast casual laborer and member of the Industrial Workers of the World, Ginther had drifted far and wide before settling in Seattle, where he earned his living as a cook and served for many years as an organizer for the Seattle Cooks and Waiters Union. Beginning about 1932 and continuing for most of the Great Depression, Ginther recalled his own personal experiences in the jungle camps, skid rows, and bloody hop picking strikes throughout California and elsewhere in the West by painting graphic watercolor scenes that escaped the camera's lens. He painted on cardboard panels in his basement, late at night, often until he passed out in a drunken stupor, sometimes believing that "he had something going" but never fully understanding the nature of his contribution or talent. At once nightmarish and cartoonlike, Ginther's watercolors, which also draw heavily on his knowledge of labor history, are unlike those of any other artist of his era. Full of destitution, hunger, jails, and bleak surroundings, they are quintessentially Great Depression pictures, but they are also much more.

The people of Ginther's paintings do not head West in their jalopies toward a new life. He painted only one family, few women, and fewer children. None travel by car.

Permanently on the bum in a kind of living hell, they get around by hopping trains and hitchhiking rides. The world he depicted is the world of the single, homeless man who has few possessions other than his bindle and even less hope. Ginther's people do not inhabit Okie camps. Living the life of the casual, migratory worker—a life that had existed for decades before the 1930s—they sleep in hobo jungles and along Skid Road, vomit in dives, search through garbage, and lie dead or dying at the feet of rioting hop pickers. Depressing and realistic propaganda, his images never made it into any gallery or museum. Hanging in his basement, the paintings were not seen until 1969, when Ginther died and the Washington State Historical Society acquired them.[31]

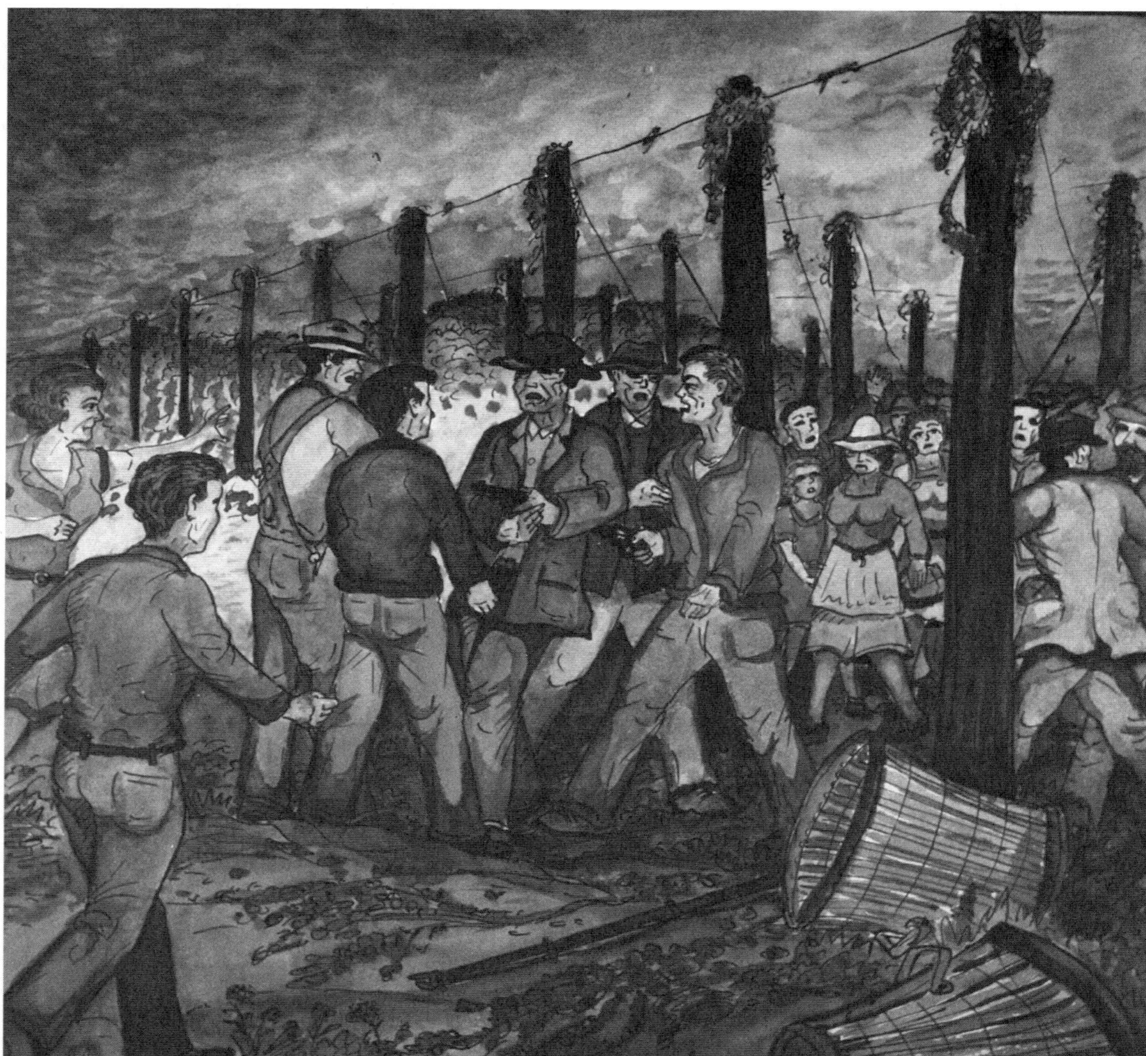

Alcohol-induced watercolor of a strike by hop pickers, composite of memory and experience, 1936, by R[onald] D[ibbs] Ginther. Courtesy of Washington State Historical Society.

Uneasy with New Deal mural painters putting a happy face on rural poverty and frustrated with Edward Weston and other photographers who toured the state prospecting for art, Lange swung back into action in September 1938. Pressing to be rehired and given a raise, she wrote Stryker in mid-September, pleading her case. "Surely neither you nor the Administration are suggesting that my work is below the standards of the other photographers of your staff," she asserted. On September 29, she was back on staff at her original wage of twenty-three hundred dollars, with a promise that she would soon receive a raise to twenty-six hundred. She got the good news and an assignment while flat on her back in the hospital following emergency surgery for an attack of appendicitis. Although she was supposed to spend three weeks in the southern San Joaquin Valley documenting FSA camps and projects, Lange intended to expand her coverage of California agriculture by scrutinizing the small towns she visited along the path of her journey.[32]

Lange hit the road on October 20, accompanied by Rondal Partridge. Very soon the trip turned into a nightmare. Lange discovered families living in the bushes. She saw them in ditches along the highway, beneath billboard windbreaks, and in cheap auto camps. Outside relief offices, she found them waiting early in the morning, long before the offices opened for business. Such scenes led her to conclude that despite all of the relief efforts and the improved economy, little had changed since her last visit. Migrants were as desperate as ever. Around Lindsay, she photographed women living in ragged tent camps, cooking, washing, boiling and carrying water, trying to keep things together in the most alarming circumstances, oddly set amid a sea of the verdant citrus orchards.

Back on U.S. Highway 99 heading south a week later, Lange spotted a large, Southern Pacific billboard reading, "Next Time Take the Train: Travel While You Sleep." Three migrant families were camped around its base. Parking her automobile, Lange made five photographs. The first two are distant, establishing photographs, placing the billboard in its environment. Her third image moves in to tightly frame the migrants, with the sign's message looming above. Walking behind the billboard, Lange made a distant shot and then in her final image focused on one particular family. With only a few tarps, the family had cleverly rigged a tent by hanging everything from the billboard cross beams. A coffee pot sits on an open stove, and a young woman stands beside the shelter and a small table.[33]

Lange spent Halloween in the FSA camp at Shafter photographing a big celebration. While there, she discovered that four thousand workers had gone on strike under the leadership of the United Cannery, Agricultural, Packing, and Allied Workers of America (UCAPAWA). A new CIO-affiliated union, UCAPAWA had been formed when eighteen tiny, independent field worker unions met in Bakersfield during July. By the fall, the union had spread through the southern San Joaquin Valley. When cotton growers cut pay from one dollar to seventy-five cents per hundred pounds of picked cotton, field hands who had previously averaged $1.50 to $2 a day flocked to the union. As the strike spread, flourishing UCAPAWA locals grew in the FSA camps at Shafter and Arvin, and both the FSA and the John Steinbeck Committee to Aid

Agricultural Workers began distributing emergency food rations. Tensions ran high. Growers, fearing that the camps were serving as bases for labor organizing, attempted to boycott the Shafter camp. "The FSA is feeding the strikers and therefore there is hostility—disrupted camp program, and half-empty camps," Lange wrote to Stryker on November 1. "Never worked longer hours, harder—but what the results will be, can only pray to Jesus."[34]

Having done so poorly at the Salinas lettuce strike two years earlier and having missed the San Joaquin Valley cotton strike the previous year, Lange was determined to fully photograph conditions in the cotton district. Now, for the first time, she began documenting organizing activity, often injecting explicitly political symbolism into her compositions. Ever fascinated by signs and posters, Lange made several images incorporating campaign posters and windshield stickers endorsing Democratic candidates. Just after leaving a citrus pickers' camp, she photographed a windshield sticker endorsing Culbert Olson, a state senator running for governor. While

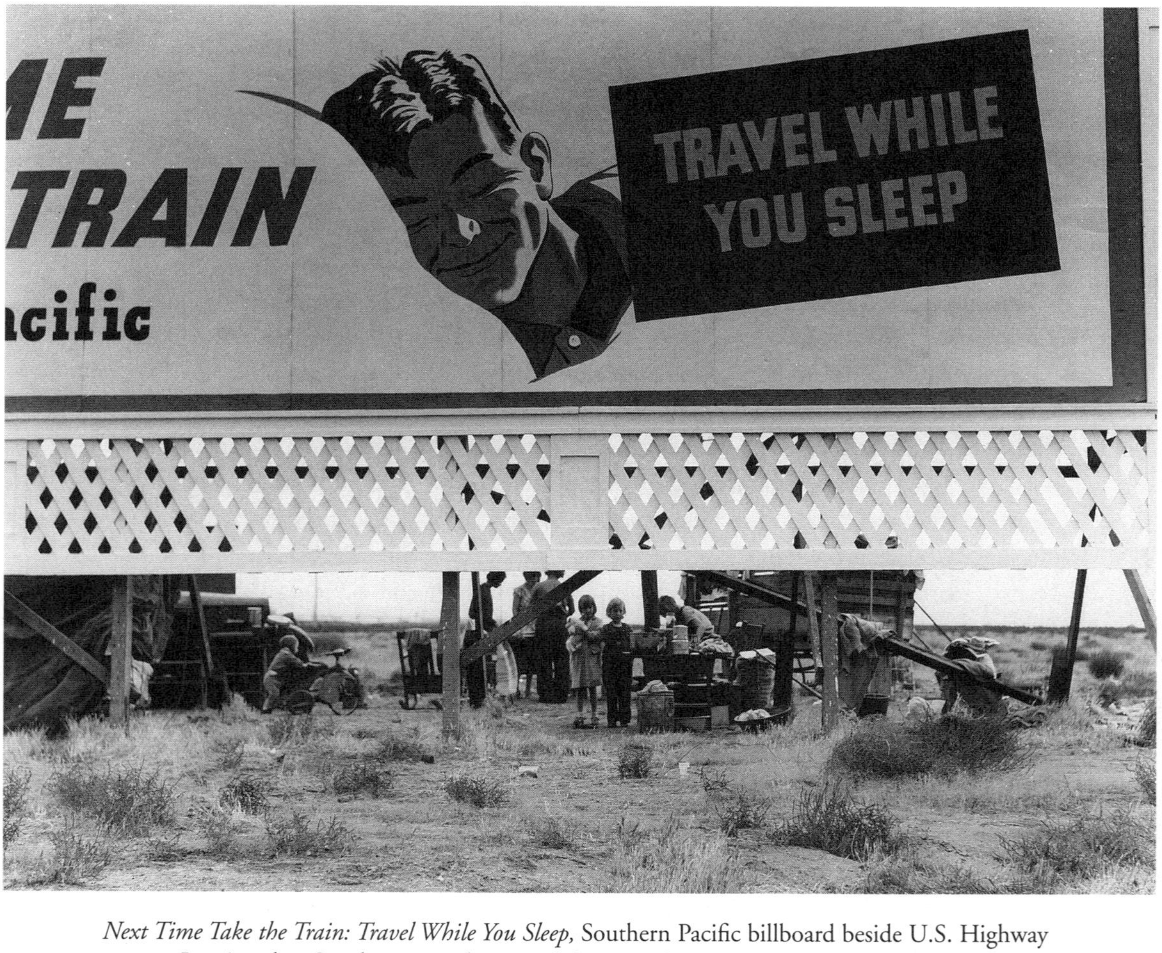

Next Time Take the Train: Travel While You Sleep, Southern Pacific billboard beside U.S. Highway 99 near Los Angeles, October 1937, photograph by Dorothea Lange. Courtesy of the FSA/OWI Collection, Library of Congress, Prints and Photographs Division.

attending a secret nighttime strike meeting in Bakersfield, she and Partridge photographed one Oklahoma refugee addressing a group of strikers. Having only recently joined the union, the Oklahoman had become a leader of a flying squadron of automobiles attempting to picket the cotton fields. Unlike their Mexican counterparts, the Okies had little experience with unions and, on hearing for the first time the call to organize, were uncertain how to proceed.

Accustomed to photographing almost entirely in daylight, Lange had only rarely employed supplementary lighting before this cotton strike. But before leaving on her trip through the South the previous summer she had obtained a Mendelson flash gun, a large and heavy piece of equipment that she used with her Graflex camera. She had also obtained a Kalart speed gun, which was smaller and worked with her Rolleiflex. At another nighttime strike meeting, Lange used one of these strobes, mounted or perhaps held by Partridge off-camera, to take a series of photographs in a "Mexican town" outside Shafter. The following day in Madera, she spotted a sign on a gas

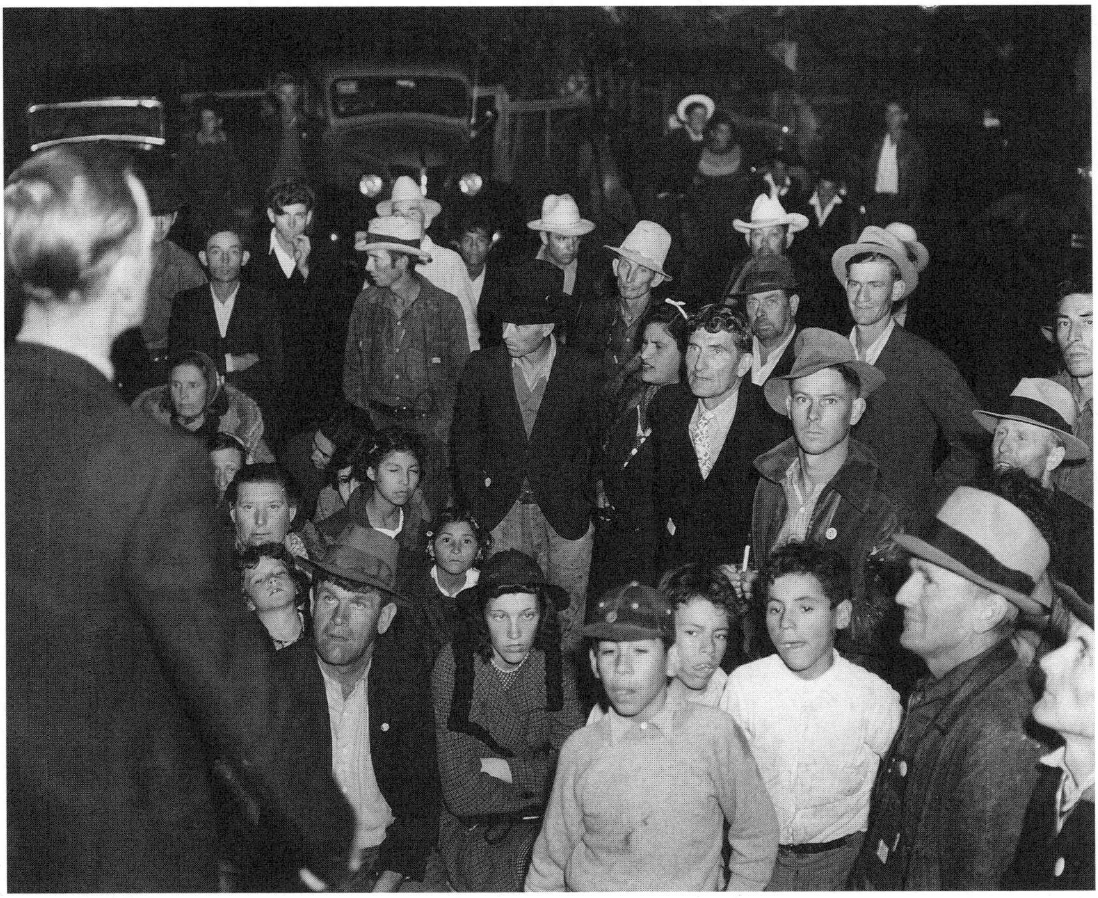

Cotton strikers meeting at night, Kern County, November 6, 1938, photograph by Dorothea Lange. Courtesy of the FSA/OWI Collection, Library of Congress, Prints and Photographs Division.

pump, shouting in bold capital letters: "THIS IS YOUR COUNTRY. DON'T LET THE BIG MEN TAKE IT AWAY FROM YOU." Her photograph would become another of her famous sign shots, much reproduced in photo histories and social histories of the state. Lange also followed the activities of the John Steinbeck Committee to Aid Agricultural Workers, as well as the International Labor Defense.[35]

Eventually growers pressured the State Emergency Relief Administration to deny relief to strikers, and the State Employment Commission, after ruling that no strike existed, referred workers to boycotted ranches. When sheriffs began arresting pickets, Lange was present. She overheard one striker say, "I don't care: let them throw me in jail. There's somebody will take my place." At the Bakersfield Conference to Aid Agricultural Organization, Lange took several dramatic shots of an impassioned cotton strike leader saying, "Brother, it's pick 75-cent cotton or starve." Having ventured out to expand her coverage of FSA camps, she had documented her first farm labor strike meetings and captured some of the few FSA images of farm labor strife. But she did not take the best images at the cotton strike. From the other side of the room at the Bakersfield Conference, Rondal Partridge took a sequence of three images, each within a fraction of a second of one another, capturing the very same impassioned strike leader, raising his hands and gesturing to the audience with his fingers. Apparently produced with an off-camera flash light, the sequence was suggestive of a preacher addressing his congregation at a religious revival meeting. But powerful as they were, Partridge's images were not part of the FSA archive. They would remain unpublished and unseen in his private archive for the next sixty-five years.[36]

Lange's coverage of the cotton strike broke dramatically from her colleagues' approach to their FSA photography, which steered clear of organized responses to wage cuts and unacceptable working conditions. But it did not signal that Lange was shifting her focus away from individual victims and heroes to collective response and organized protest aimed at vast social change. Lange was certainly affected by what she saw and recorded. Several of her images from that strike became personal favorites, full of memories. The whole experience energized and challenged her. She returned to Berkeley determined to effect change. What started out as a routine public relations tour on behalf of the FSA had become a challenging adventure reaffirming her faith in the importance of photography as a medium of communication. Back home, Lange spent four days developing negatives and making contact prints. She then sent them off to Stryker with a note imploring him to return them quickly. She did not want to lose the sense of immediacy and the vividness of the memories recorded in her field notes.[37]

Finishing her darkroom work just in time to vote in the state elections on November 7, Lange was delighted when Californians defeated incumbent Republican governor Frank Merriam and replaced him with Democrat Culbert Olson, whom Lange and Taylor had actively supported. Forty-four years of unbroken Republican rule had finally ended. Olson had swept the state with the help of Okie voters, but his victory with a margin of two hundred thousand votes indicated wide support beyond his huge majorities in the Okie strongholds of Kern, Madera, and Fresno counties. Almost immediately, the new Democratic administration implemented a friendlier position on relief payments to strikers and lent support to UCAPAWA efforts to organize farmworkers. Olson's appointment of Carey McWilliams to run the State Division of Immigration and Housing promised a revitalized attention to substandard housing but infuriated the state's growers. Recalling his muckraking essays from 1935, they denounced him as "Agricultural Pest No. 1, Worse Even Than the Boll Weevil." The new administration even considered bringing its program of progressive reform to the people by establishing a state version of the FSA. Although Stryker lent his enthusiastic support, the idea never amounted to much.[38]

Across the United States, the outcome of the 1938 elections was far less hopeful. Progressives and liberal Democrats were defeated en masse. With Republicans picking up many seats in Congress and capturing many governorships and liberal governments crumbling in Michigan, Wisconsin, and Minnesota, full recovery from the Depression seemed as remote as ever. All of the compassion that the country had expressed for the unemployed in the early years of the Depression now seemed to diminish as Roosevelt, in a calculated move, turned to the conservative wing of the Democratic Party. With progressives unable to push through any new programs and conservatives unable to kill off reforms, the New Deal dissolved into a stalemate. Lange wondered, What, if anything, could her photography do? How much longer would she work for the FSA?[39]

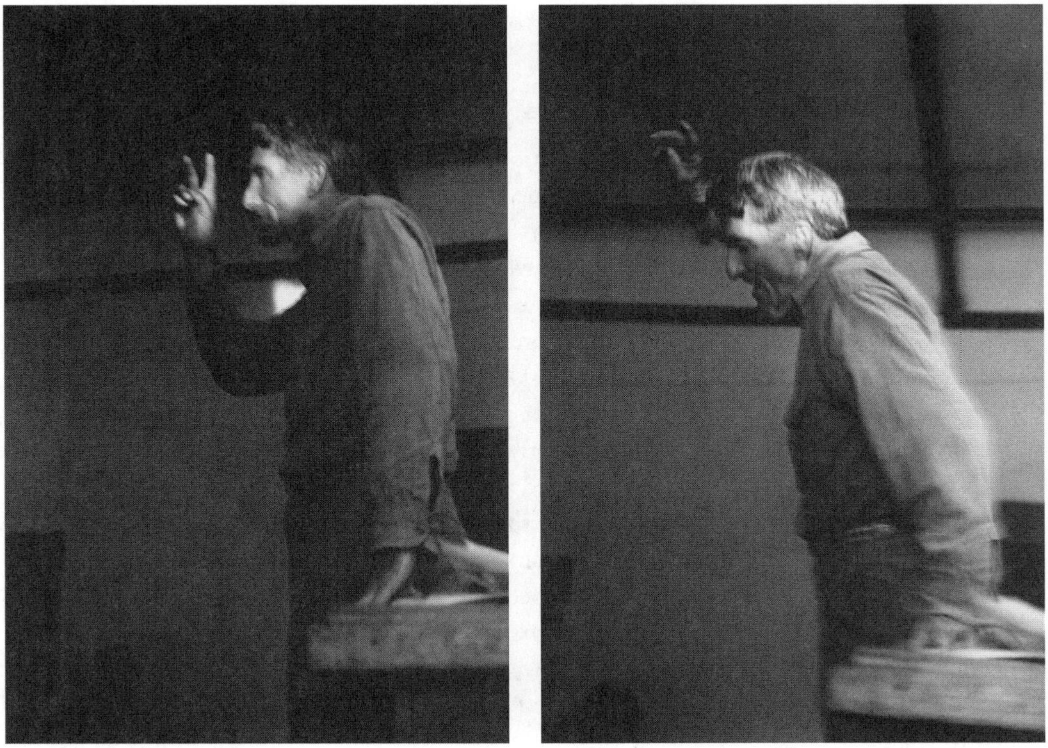

Speaker haranguing a meeting of striking cotton pickers at Firebaugh, October 1938, photographs by Rondal Partridge. Courtesy of Rondal Partridge.

Amid these mixed developments, Stryker saw encouraging results in *U.S. Camera*'s annual publication of the year's best photographs. Edward Steichen, who edited the publication, ran thirty-two pages of FSA photographs, including many by Lange. The year was ending well. Willard Morgan had arranged enlarged FSA images at the International Photographic Exhibit at the Grand Central Palace in New York City, and they had been favorably reviewed by Elizabeth McCausland, one of the country's leading art critics. Stryker sent copies of the reviews and publications to numerous government officials. "Lively times," Lange wrote to Stryker. "Our work . . . has certainly been fruitful." Stryker replied, "I am astounded at the number of people who have been impressed."[40]

Printing her images for exhibitions and government investigations further solidified Lange's devotion to her and Taylor's book project. She wanted to make a coherent presentation that educated the public on issues that the Roosevelt administration had addressed only superficially. Already she had assembled and edited the book and put it aside after becoming bored. In a great fit of energy on December 6, she pulled all of her prints out of storage, spread them across the floor, and reedited the book, this time finding it better than she had initially thought. She wrote to Stryker asking permission to take off a day here and there, sometimes a week, to finish the project. She did not want to pursue it on the sly, without Stryker's knowing what she was doing. "It's all the same job," she wrote, "and when it comes out it will further your purposes, I hope." Stryker agreed. Calling the project an important and mutually beneficial effort, he outlined Lange's FSA work over the next few months. He told her to focus on California and the neighboring states. Rothstein, Lee, and Wolcott would cover the rest of the country. He ended by cautioning Lange to use discretion. He knew of people in the FSA who questioned why a photographer like her was not continuously in the field and had any time for such matters. Other than that, Lange had his blessing. "Really, Dorothea, things are certainly coming along for us."[41]

Lange had already pitched her and Taylor's as-yet-untitled book to Modern Age Books and had been encouraged by the response. To move things along and escape her cramped workspace, Lange rented a one-room apartment near the Pacific School of Religion, about a mile from their Berkeley home. Covering the floor in photographs, she and Taylor spent several weeks moving their images around. Sorting and resorting them, each one enlarged to exactly the size it would be in the book, they experimented with different texts, rearranged various sequences, and laid out the images section by section on facing pages. Slowly the structure and regional movement of the book took shape. That layout owed more to the structure of *Life* magazine and to the forms that Taylor and Lange had developed in their earlier reports than to anything else. The overall goal was to pick images that would stand as independent records but collectively produce a picture leading viewers to take action.

Lange's opening images in the finalized book display gigantic machine-produced cotton and work-scarred hands holding tools. Each following section examines a different agricultural region of the country, moving from the Southeast to the Far West. Six chapter headings detail the subjects: "Old South," "Plantation under the Machine,"

"Midcontinent," "Plains," "Dust Bowl," "Last West." The photographs in "Dust Bowl" move across a desolate landscape and culminate in a vivid double-page layout. On the left is an old windmill. On the right is a gaunt woman, standing tall, arms bent in a gesture of desperation. Other images focus on the exodus from the land, the mass migration of three hundred thousand refugees into California, the ravages of nature, effects of technology, growth of tenant farming, and decline of family farming—all factors contributing to the "social erosion" propelling a great stream of people into the fields of California.[42]

Midway through January 1939, Lange took her first break from the project. Eight million Americans were still without jobs, and politicians in California, organized into the Economy Bloc, were systematically dismantling the Olson administration. When the Workers Alliance, a union of unemployed people, held a mass march in San Francisco, Lange traveled across the bay to photograph the march and a rally protesting relief cuts, as well as down-and-out and homeless people she encountered around the city. In February she took her second break and traveled throughout the state for ten days, documenting FSA camps and migrants harvesting cotton in the San Joaquin Valley and lettuce, carrots, and peas in the Imperial Valley. Near Calipatria on February 18, she encountered a farmer who had left Nebraska the Monday after Easter in 1938. She posed him in hat and overalls, right arm on his hip, then got his story. "I put mine in what I thought was the best investment—the good old earth—but we lost on that, too," he told her. "The Finance Co. caught up with us, the Mortgage Co. caught up with us. Managed to lose $12,000 in three years. My boys have no more future than I have, so far as I can see ahead."[43]

Four days later, near Niland, Lange was in the pea fields photographing men stooped over picking peas; near Calipatria she photographed pea pickers carrying hampers full of peas to a weigh master. On February 23, beside U.S. Highway 80 near the Alamo River outside Holtville, she discovered one truly forlorn Oklahoma family with five children; they had picked their way across Texas and Arizona and had just crossed into California the previous night. A few hours later near Brawley, she photographed a family of eleven in front of their tent. The mother told her, "I want to go back to where we can live happy, live decent, and grow what we eat." The father explained, "I've made my mistake and now we can't go back. I've got nothing to farm with." The next day, in the carrot fields, she found men pulling, sorting, cleaning, and tying carrot bunches for fourteen cents per crate of forty-eight bunches. "They'll sleep in the row (to hold a place in the field) to earn 60 cents a day," one man told her. Another explained, "They're fixin' to free all us fellows—free us for what? Free us like they freed mules. They're aimin' at keeping fellows such as me right down on our knees—aimin' at making slaves of us. We've got no more chance than a one-legged man in a foot-race."[44]

A week later in the Salinas Valley, Lange made some uncharacteristic images of cultivated rows stretching to the horizon. No farmworkers were present. And so it went. Lange was apparently rounding out her picture of industrialized agriculture and needed images illustrating that California had one-third of all large-scale farms in the nation. A few days later, after a marathon of developing and contact printing, Lange made prints of each image and integrated them into the book layout.[45]

When she returned to the book project, Lange was delighted to see that the *Rural Observer,* official publication of the Simon Lubin Society, had made extensive use of her work. A mortal enemy of the Associated Farmers, the *Rural Observer* was already using clever graphics to drive home its critique of corporate farming, but the current editor, Helen Hosmer, went one step further. Selecting images from Lange's series mocking the National Association of Manufacturers in its "American Way" billboard campaign, Hosmer created a countercampaign. First she used a Lange photograph showing migrant families encamped below billboards displaying huge images of attractive family farms that they could never hope to own. The irony was heavy handed. Next Hosmer employed a series of Lange's photographs in a photo essay. The first image showed a plowman. "This is a real farmer," proclaimed Hosmer's caption. Next came a photograph of migrant workers. "This is what happens to the working farmer—foreclosure," wrote Hosmer. Then, using a photograph of a child ready to begin picking cotton at dawn, Hosmer observed, "This is what happens to the working farmer's child." Well into 1941, Hosmer would continue to use Lange's images to great advantage in mocking her "triangle of greed and corruption": the Bank of America, Associated Farmers, and Sunkist.[46]

While her images were being published in the *Rural Observer,* Lange pushed forward with the book project, continuing until she was satisfied that the book's message was conveyed vividly and could be easily and clearly understood. "Dorothea took the initiative here," Taylor stressed. "There was no friction in our collaboration." Lange was concerned less with the artistic and compositional qualities of her images than with their cumulative impact on viewers. Although portraits appeared throughout her still untitled book, Lange did not use a "museum wall" approach in laying them out. Seeking to make the book very much a "human document" (a term that she borrowed from Lewis Hine, who used it to refer to socially oriented photography), Lange excluded some of her most famous images, such as *Migrant Mother,* which might upstage the epic nature of the story she was telling. Concerned more about communities and less about individuals, Lange selected symbolic and panoramic images that amplify themes of community and movement. And because she had not documented certain events, she selected nine photographs by other photographers, among them pictures of the Salinas lettuce packers' strike taken by Otto Hagel and Horace Bristol and a picture of striking cotton pickers taken by Rondal Partridge. Trying to disseminate information and convince people of the need for national action, Lange concluded that the book would not be a work of photographs or an illustrated textbook in the traditional sense. "We use the camera as a tool of research," she and Taylor wrote. "Upon a tripod of photographs, captions, and text we rest themes evolved out of long observations in the field."[47]

On March 30, 1939, Lange informed Modern Age Books that she had finished laying out the manuscript. Using captions and texts and employing the biblical metaphor of the Israelites searching for the promised land, she worked with Taylor to create what was essentially a new medium of communication in which words and pictures did much more than explain and identify. The two understood the synergy between text and photographs and, working hard to link them in a way that reinforced their power, succeeded in creating a third effect, one that allowed readers to meet the people in her book "face to face." During Lange and Taylor's fieldwork, Lange's subjects had frequently asked her to send pictures to President Roosevelt, whom they were convinced would certainly act on their behalf if only he knew what was happening. Captions were constructed to fulfill these requests. Quotations came from the people in the pictures, and end papers are packed with the choral phrases from their subjects, a touch that Lange and Taylor were so proud of that they framed extra sheets and kept them on their workroom walls all their lives. "We adhere to the standards of documentary photography as we have conceived them," they wrote in their foreword, meaning that they would try to respect their subjects and reject the kind of devices employed by Erskine Caldwell and Margaret Bourke-White in their collaboration.[48]

Whenever photographs depict landscapes or landmarks, Lange and Taylor employed captions from persons they encountered along the way. About half of the photographs are accompanied by direct quotations; the other half are accompanied by captions written by Taylor or material taken from newspapers, letters, government documents, scholarly studies, folk songs, and newspaper advertisements. Following their foreword, Lange and Taylor included about twenty pages of text and brief descriptions of conditions found in each of the book's sections involved in the Dust Bowl migration. A typical entry, gathered from a migrant traveling through southeast Missouri, is introduced as "The Question Arises":

> I SAY: A rollin' stone gathers no moss.
> HE SAYS: A settin' hen never gets fat.
> I SAY TO HIM: Better stay here where people know us.
> We'd have to sell our team and maybe we'd be left flatfooted.
> I know about 15 families from Senath that's gone to California.
> Some of 'em made out and some of 'em didn't.

And, beside a photo of the highway stretching to the western horizon:

> They keep the road hot a goin' and a comin'.
> They've got roamin' in their head.[49]

Quite logically, Lange devoted considerable attention to the road that conveyed the most migrants to California. One of her photographs, a section of a New Mexico highway that she encountered in 1938, appears as a kind of long, straight funnel pouring people west. Titled *The Road West,* the image was a strong symbol of both the hopes of a generation and the fears of California residents demanding that their government keep the newcomers out by blocking the highway where it crosses over the Colorado River. Placing *The Road West* alongside a photograph of a road in the

Deep South where an uprooted family walks off toward the horizon, Lange and Taylor drove home a central point of their book: that the small country roads were feeding streams of people onto the highways, all joining in the greatest mass migration in American history.

Lange and Taylor's book is much more than a record of hardship and tribulation. Besides images of desolation and an imploding agricultural order, pictures illustrate the perplexed state of mind of people wondering where they will find their next meal, resenting the cards they have been dealt, even while they demonstrate a stoic vitality and determined resolve. Beauty is not absent from the book. Among the injured and displaced are strong, chiseled faces, graceful women, loving families, thoughtful fathers. Of these people, their times, and their future, Lange and Taylor wrote:

> The old West is gone. The opportunity which the new emigrants find is more in the tradition of industry than of the pioneers on the prairies. . . . The pattern of labor conflict familiar in industry for decades has now spread to the land, but without the tempering effect which the growth of trade unions and long experience in collective bargaining have exerted in industry.[50]

Attempting to summarize and assess the implications of their work, as well as offer some solutions to the problems they described, Lange and Taylor took a fairly radical position in a section titled "Directions." Since its inception, the New Deal government had done little more than enact measures to relieve distress. When Lange and Taylor finished their book, migrants were still arriving by the thousands. Having always made their living from farming, the newcomers did not require public assistance so much as an opportunity for becoming independent. Government policy, Lange and Taylor asserted, should be directed toward that goal, toward programs promoting cooperatives, housing, and family farming.[51]

Not all of the captioning was completely accurate. One example of fudging occurred in the caption for Lange's portrait of Nettie Featherston, which reads: "If you die, you're dead—that's all." Used bluntly, as it is in the book, it considerably enhances the stark image above it, expressing a fairly succinct philosophy of life, meaning enjoy life to its fullest while you can. But Lange's field notes reveal that the expression was part of a larger statement and referred to something quite different from the slant it is given in the book. When interviewed in Texas, Featherston talked at length about the hard life in Childress County and of her desire to leave. She told Lange that Childress was "a hard county," where "you can't get no relief . . . until you've lived here a year," and "they won't help bury you." The phrase "if you die, you're dead" referred not to Featherston's bleak philosophy but to burial practices in Childress County, and it expressed her anger with callous public officials who, in denying a pauper's grave to the poor, seemed also to take an atheistic point of view, rejecting the concept of an afterlife and salvation.[52]

13

Facts and Fiction

An American Exodus *and* The Grapes of Wrath

While Lange was editing images and writing captions for her book, she got into a dispute with Stryker over retouching her famous photograph *Migrant Mother.* When Lange had made her final picture of the Migrant Mother series, Florence Thompson—so the story goes—had reached out with her left hand to grasp a tent post or to hold back a flap. As a result, the blurred image of Thompson's thumb had intruded into the lower right corner of the picture. This was one reason why Lange had withheld the image from circulation, preferring to publish other images from the sequence. There were other reasons as well: Lange found prints varying widely in quality and interpretation and was especially dissatisfied with the published version that appeared in *Land of the Free.* But she could see the potential of the image if the defect could be eliminated. To accomplish that, she borrowed the negative from the FSA files under the pretense that she needed it to make accurate prints for exhibition and to supply various publications and museums, among them the Museum of Modern Art, which intended to add the image to its permanent collection. Lange then hired Roger Sturtevant, "the best retoucher on the Pacific Coast." Sturtevant used emory rouge and a red dye called New Cosine to eliminate most but not all of the thumb. Anyone familiar with the retouching story can find remnants of the thumb in subsequent prints of an image that Lange was still identifying as *The Oklahoman.*[1]

Lange had retouched dozens of images during her career as a portrait photographer. The practice was quite common and hardly new, but there was no consensus on it. Most newspapers and many magazines employed various forms of retouching, often to a degree that the printed image was an amalgamation of the photograph and something created by a layout artist. Certain photographic luminaries clustered around Alfred Stieglitz were vehemently opposed to overt forms of mechanical manipulation, which they saw as dishonest as well as an admission of their technical shortcomings. Reacting against such practices, *Life* magazine adopted a principle that photographs should never be retouched, except to remove distracting elements and when retouching did not affect the integrity of the image. Subscribing to even stricter views, Stryker considered Lange's retouching a major breach of the photographer's code of objectivity and of the FSA's general commitment to truthful documentation. He found the work "a little careless" and called it "dirtying the negative."[2]

More than any other single incident, the retouching episode illustrated the tensions and differences separating Lange from Stryker. Back in Washington, D.C., Stryker was overwhelmed with not only technical matters but also logistics, budgetary pressures, and the bureaucratic problems originating in his status as but a small subdepartment within the vast FSA, which in turn was just part of an even larger arm of the federal government. "He'd sit at his desk and he'd point down the corridor and 'they' were all his enemies," recalled Lange in her oral memoir. "He was guardian at the gates. He was the defender of the files, inviolable, and they were locked up at night. It was a holy crusade. The telephone would ring in his office—he had three or four telephones—he'd pick it up and say, 'Stryker speaking.' And he was just *ready* for whoever it was, any congressman or someone wanting to come in and see what they had on his state of Arkansas or someplace."[3]

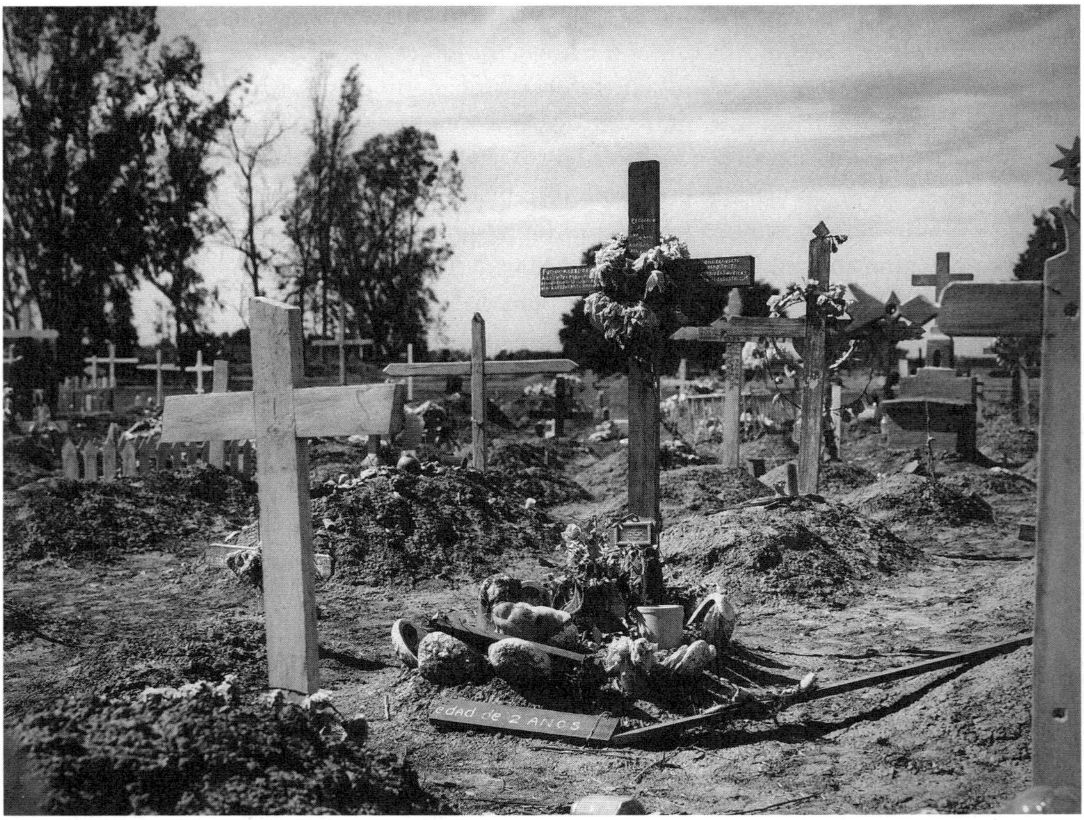

"Victoria Lopez, age 1 year, 9 months . . . She was an angel . . . Imperial valley," February 1939, photograph by Dorothea Lange. Courtesy of the Oakland Museum of California, Dorothea Lange Collection, Gift of Paul S. Taylor.

Stryker was constantly fending off all kinds of irrelevant demands to photograph this or that project, this or that congressman's pet. He often had to jump through the most incredible series of hoops merely to vary, however minutely, from established procedures. To expedite shipments of film and other materials or to use airmail, Stryker avoided the endless labyrinth of supervisors by purchasing the stamps himself and personally mailing the packages and letters. Far away in California, Lange presented special problems often requiring him to write long letters, some going into great detail about assignments, requests for prints, film development, purchasing arrangements, chemical formulas, and a hundred other details. "When you get one thing straightened out," he once explained to Lange, "two more seem to pop up."[4]

Faced with so many problems, Stryker could be crabby with Lange, whom he had always labeled a problem child, a wonderful person, and someone who at times would drive him crazy. He was far less tolerant of her than of other photographers, all of whom were strong personalities. Rondal Partridge always felt that Stryker was an arrogant administrator who could not deal with strong women like Lange. But there were other problems as well. When Stryker raised the issue of retouching, he had still not forgotten the controversy that Arthur Rothstein had caused by moving a cattle skull to make a better image. That incident had nearly ended his project. Ever since then, Stryker had been alert to any error of judgment that critics, of whom there were many in Congress, might use as a pretext for killing the project. Retouching itself was not ephemeral. Photographers debated how and to what extent one could alter an image. While burning, dodging, and cropping were accepted, the physical alteration of a negative was another matter. Raising questions about truth and veracity, it could easily undermine whatever authority Stryker claimed for his photographers as objective, eyewitness observers.[5]

Above all, the retouching incident went to the heart of Stryker's relationship with Lange and their ongoing struggle over final control of her work. As the head the FSA Historical Section, Stryker believed that he supervised the use, production, and printing of images, even going so far as to "kill" certain unacceptable 35-millimeter negatives by punching holes in them. Apparently Stryker never punched any holes in the larger negatives, preferring instead either to discard them, or to return them to their makers, or to leave them in their negative files. As an artist Lange was appalled by such action, especially when she would later find in portions of rejected negatives something that she had originally missed. She was viscerally offended by the idea that anyone would destroy a negative. File it away, yes. But never mutilate it. She could barely bring herself to discard ruined negatives. Most important, as the creator of her images, the person who poured her energy into them, Lange quite understandably did not want to hand them over to someone else. She pointed to what had happened to her 1936 Mississippi photograph *Plantation Overseer and His Field Hands.* When it was published in *Land of the Free,* the black workers were completely cropped out of the picture. This left only the white man, who seemed to be not an overseer in a picture of master and subjects but just an ordinary farmer, standing there with his foot on the bumper of his car, talking to folks. Completely inverting the meaning of the picture, MacLeish's poem on the opposite page further transformed a southern planter lording over his workers into the industrious personification of American values.[6]

Soon many in the Information Division were taking sides. Lange could not see Stryker's point and was deeply upset by his criticism. The dispute so affected her that Paul Taylor asked FSA administrator Will Alexander to intercede. Wisely declining, Alexander remained philosophical. Such differences came with life, he said. We must learn to work through them. Stryker sought support from the director of the western region, Jonathan Garst. Fond of Lange and Taylor, Garst worried that Taylor might withdraw from government service. He tried to smooth over their hurt feelings but was shocked by Taylor's adamant defense of his wife. He had never seen Taylor so agitated. He was especially concerned because Taylor had always seemed to be a stoic and unemotional individual. Garst placated Stryker by informing him that some people in the Information Division "are sort of on your side." It was not exactly a ringing endorsement. Clearly Garst as well as Alexander did not want to jeopardize the photographic project over such a relatively trivial matter. He advised Stryker to back off. "Dealing with fighting cocks, race horses, and lady artists," he wrote, "you will have to make arrangements that they win once in a while."[7]

On Palm Sunday weekend, Lange took her third break from her book project. Traveling to San Francisco, she documented the morning services and open-air meetings at Salvation Army headquarters. Lange apparently selected the assignment herself, which returned her to a location and subject that she had explored six years earlier. She was already traveling across the bay to photograph the new Bay Bridge, from San Francisco to Oakland, as well as various architectural details around the city, and probably spotted advertisements for an open-air meeting that sought new converts. Lange made thirty-nine photographs at an indoor service climaxing in a photograph of a man kneeling in prayer. To light all of the interior shots, Lange used a flash. By this time she may have acquired a General Electric Mazda photo lamp, a long shiny tube with a saucer-sized reflector bowl that held flash bulbs about the size of light bulbs, which Lange carried in an oblong leather case. In most photographs she has bounced her flash off the ceiling, but several images are lit by a harsh, sculpting side light, an effect Lange disliked. Outside, Lange photographed Salvation Army missionaries parading in front of pawnshops and cheap residency hotels along Minna Street toward a section of the city that had been barricaded to allow the missionaries to conduct their meeting. According to Lange's captions, bystanders briefly paused, paid but little attention, then moved along.[8]

A few days after Lange photographed the Salvation Army, *Fortune* magazine published two articles on California migrant labor. Distinguishing "native white" migrants from "foreigners: Chinese, Japs, Hindus, Mexicans," who had long dominated field labor, the articles, illustrated by a selection of Lange's images, along with some by fellow documentary photographer Horace Bristol and watercolors by Millard Sheets, stressed, "These people . . . have become California's sorest social problem." Exemplifying how little control Lange had over how her images were used or where they appeared, the articles, while sympathetic to the plight of the state's farmworkers, bolstered Lange's determination to produce a book integrating her images and experiences with the scholarly insights of her husband.[9]

Further prodding Lange to action was John Steinbeck's *The Grapes of Wrath,* also published in April. After his sojourns with Horace Bristol a year earlier, Steinbeck had gone into seclusion, completed and destroyed a sixty-thousand-word novel, *L'Affaire Lettuceburg,* a "mean, nasty book" about the Salinas Valley lettuce strike, and then gone back to work and finished *The Grapes of Wrath,* the best-known social novel of the 1930s. While neither eloquent nor well-crafted, it possessed an epic story, themes of love, family, and universal friendship, and a political message that struck sympathetic chords among the general public. Becoming an instant success and best seller, the novel was taken as a factual account of the trials and tribulations of the Joad family on their trip from Oklahoma to the fields of California. According to *Publisher's Weekly,* the book figured in so many discussions, editorials, and news stories that the names "Joad" and "Okie" soon became interchangeable. Within two months, 20th Century–Fox's Darryl Zanuck had bought the film rights to the novel for seventy-five thousand dollars. John Ford was going to direct it. Nunnally Johnson handled the task of crafting a script quickly enough for the movie to be completed and released while the novel was still on the best-seller list.[10]

Filming *The Grapes of Wrath* generated a huge body of folklore. One story maintains that Zanuck entirely improvised the ending by transposing a speech from the middle of the novel to the end of the movie. Reassembling the entire cast after finishing the film, he took over for John Ford and created a scene in which Ma Joad rallies her family. "Rich fellas come up an' they die, an' their kids ain't no good, an' they die out," she says. "But we keep a-comin'. We're the people that live. Can't nobody wipe us out. Can't lick us. We'll go on forever. We're the people." While some scholars dispute that this last bit of filming ever happened, without doubt the new ending gave audiences a picture of hope that some found missing from the book. But it did little to mollify hostile farmers and other members of California's agricultural elite, who hated the book with such a passion that, according to a writer for *Collier's,* they would have gladly paid three hundred thousand dollars to "place the book and the book rights in a heavy safe and row out on the Pacific Ocean and dump the whole thing overboard." Agricultural leaders in Kern County called *The Grapes of Wrath* "obscene sensationalism," accused Steinbeck of creating "propaganda in the vilest form," attacked the "Communistic base of the story," and held a book-burning party in August 1939. Many vowed that the movie would never be shown in their part of the San Joaquin Valley and succeeded in banning *The Grapes of Wrath* from public libraries until 1941. So fearful of these actions was Zanuck that he initially stated he would not show the movie in California. When his plans brought a storm of protest, he directed his attorneys to prepare to fight any local censorship.[11]

Caught in a strange nexus of journalism, literature, and cinema, Lange's work became a casualty of the teeter-totter between farmworker fact and fiction. Rather than a pioneer whose work over the preceding five years had served as the raw material out of which Steinbeck had constructed his plot and fleshed out his characters, Lange's images were seen as illustrations affirming *The Grapes of Wrath.* Later scholars would go further with the reverse, attributing Steinbeck's scenes and characters to Lange's imagery. They would point out that when Steinbeck began working on his novel, he had studied the FSA's photo file extensively and come to know Lange's work quite intimately. MacLeish believed that Steinbeck "obviously" became even more familiar with Lange's work by reading *Land of the Free,* which used many of Lange's pictures. Literary scholar D. G. Kehl ingeniously traced the origins of many of Steinbeck's passages to Lange's photographs, especially those in MacLeish's book. According to Kehl's analysis, the description of Tom Joad is rooted in Lange's *Ditched, Stalled, and Stranded,* and Steinbeck's portrait of Preacher Casey is derived at least in part from a picture of an evicted Arkansas sharecropper that Lange had made at Hill House, Mississippi, in 1936. The resemblance between Lange's photography and *The Grapes*

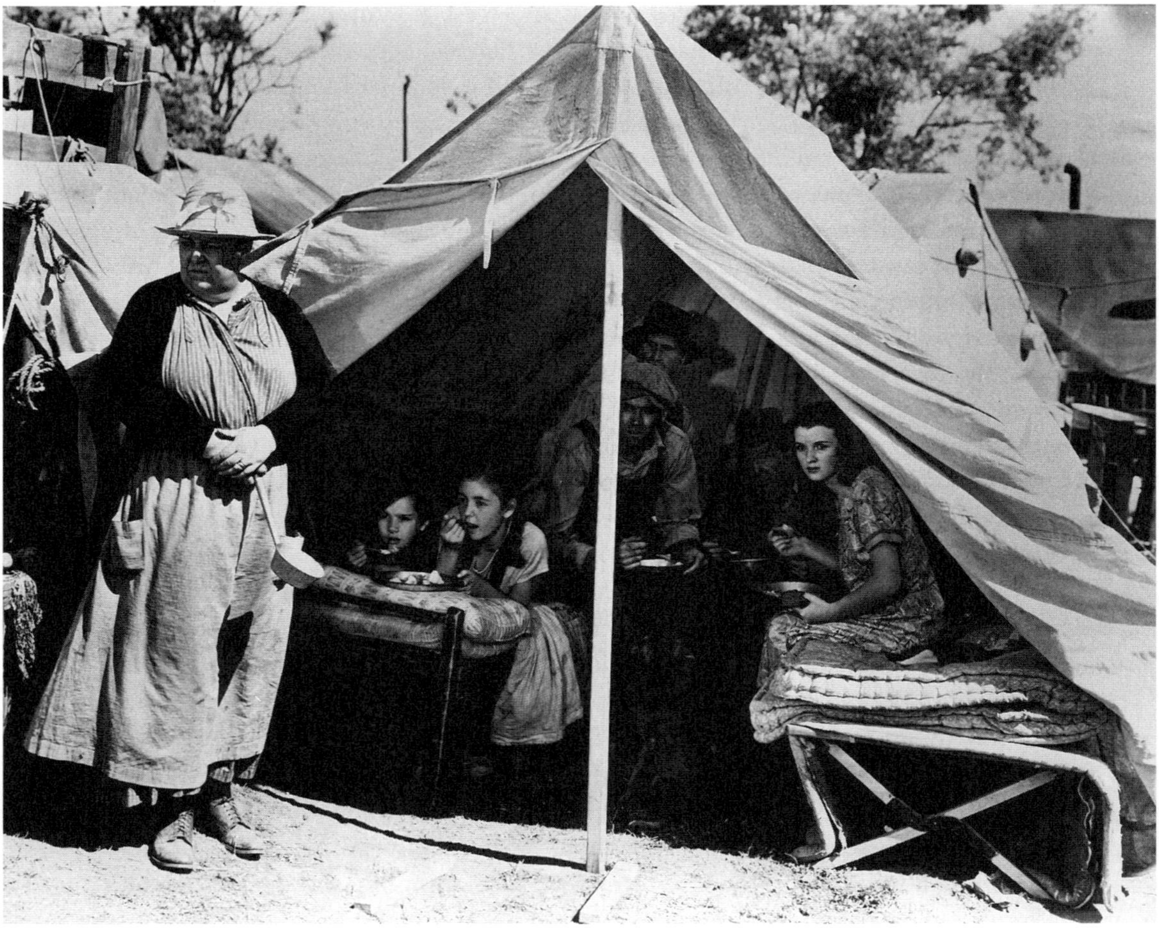

20th Century–Fox, still from *The Grapes of Wrath,* 1940, photographer unknown. Left: Jane Darwell; center, behind pole: Henry Fonda. Courtesy of the Academy of Motion Picture Arts and Sciences.

of Wrath was further strengthened when director John Ford obtained Lange's photographs and used them to construct movie sets. So closely do movie stills approximate reality that the historian Charles Shindo concludes that they "could be presented along with, or mistaken for, photographs by Lange and others of actual migrants. The look of the characters recalls the look captured by most of the FSA photographers: melancholy, questioning, and uncertain." Only the presence of actors Jane Darwell and Henry Fonda in movie stills betrays them as facsimiles rather than authentic FSA images.[12]

Further complicating matters, in early summer *Westways* magazine, heretofore unsympathetic toward such matters, published two of Paul Dorsey's photo essays on migrant workers. Although written by the magazine's ultra-right-wing editor Phil Townshend Hanna, the text accompanying Dorsey's essays cautioned that migrants were "destitute through no fault of their own." At the same time Carey McWilliams published *Factories in the Field: The Story of Migratory Farm Labor in California.* A journalistic account of the industrializing tendency in agriculture and its consequences, *Factories in the Field* also quickly became a best seller. Like Steinbeck, McWilliams had employed Lange and Taylor's fieldwork extensively in writing his book, quoted Taylor frequently, and published some of Lange's photographs. He had also followed Taylor and Lange's field research methodology while writing a series of articles for *Pacific Spectator* with Herbert Klein under the title "Factories in the Fields." And like Steinbeck, McWilliams had caused quite a flap with his references to "farm fascism" and "Gunkist oranges." But by beating Lange's book into print, McWilliams boosted the sense that Lange and Taylor were following others, when in fact their work was entirely original and independent, the culmination of efforts undertaken before either Steinbeck or McWilliams began working on their books.[13]

All of this had a devastating impact on Lange and Taylor's book. Visiting New York publishers at the end of July, they showed their mock-up to *Survey Graphic* editor Paul Kellogg, who immediately supplied the title, *An American Exodus.* But despite, or perhaps because of, the success of *The Grapes of Wrath,* publishers expressed little interest in the odd book of images and text. Tom Maloney, publisher of *U.S. Camera,* would not publish *An American Exodus,* nor would Covici–Friede or Random House. Although every editor expressed interest and praised the book, all claimed that their budgets were bare. Privately they wondered who would buy such a publication. "The book," as Kevin Starr has noted, "had already passed its peak in the market of 1940–1941."[14]

When Hitler launched his war on Europe, Taylor and Lange thought the project finished. "We don't know what to expect in regard to our book, with the war upon us," she wrote to Stryker. Already a publication of a colleague's book had been canceled. Two weeks passed without any word. Eighteen months of hard work seemed lost. Desperate to find a publisher, Lange at one point appealed to Steinbeck. But he was of little help. In September they wrote to a small publisher, Reynal and Hitchcock, describing their book as an independent work, not a follow-up, that would "enable an enlarged audience of readers to answer for themselves, by examining the photographic evidence, whether or not what they read or hear of the migrants is true." Evaluating the manuscript, Reynal and Hitchcock had trouble with the visual narrative but promised to accept it if Steinbeck agreed to write an introduction. After Steinbeck refused, Reynal and Hitchcock accepted the book anyway. Considerable debate then occurred between Lange and the publisher. To conserve space, the managing editor rearranged the "Dust Bowl" section and placed the photographs on the left pages rather than the right, writing blandly to Lange, "We do not think . . . that this is of any vital importance." Lange shot back, yes, it was, put everything back in place, then closely supervised the publishing process, eventually getting the publisher to change the foil on the stamped cloth binding from silver to gold. She told the publisher that she always preferred warm tones.[15]

Although privately expressing reservations about Lange publishing a book using pictures that were in fact the property of the FSA, Stryker was otherwise supportive. So that *An American Exodus* would contain only fresh images, he withheld from circulation all of the pictures that Lange had chosen. He also accommodated Lange's request to purchase special paper on which to print her images. And he wrote to her publisher, arranging a show of FSA photographs at Rockefeller Center to correspond to the date of publication.

Everything seemed to be going well until early October. While on assignment in Oregon, Lange received an unexpected telephone call from Stryker. Without any warning, he informed her that she would probably be laid off. Stryker was expecting his budget to be slashed for the military buildup. When it became clear that he could not keep all four of his photographers, Stryker informed Lange that she would remain on the FSA payroll for only the next three months. He promised her that the Western Regional Office in San Francisco would furnish her with office space and secretarial help to complete the captioning of all the images from her recent fieldwork.[16]

Lange left no written record of her reaction, but Stryker informed Russell Lee that she was devastated. She went into the San Francisco offices and got her work in order but apparently made no friends there. She asked only that Stryker have her cameras cleaned and repaired, fair enough given the circumstances under which she had worked for the past year. Stryker, however, refused on the grounds that such an arrangement went beyond the terms of her employment. At that point Lange started looking to the future. Hoping to obtain a Guggenheim Fellowship, she wired the foundation's headquarters in New York City, only to discover that the application deadline had passed. Her career with the FSA was over, and she had no idea what she would do next.[17]

Alarmed by Stryker's action, FSA officials Jonathan Garst and Walter Packard wrote Stryker and tried to talk him out of his decision. They warned:

> Paul Taylor is in reality the father of our migratory camp program in California. . . . Dorothea Lange has been whole-souled in this enterprise. She has that sort of a nature wherein she can only go pell-mell into something and I certainly think, and you without question will agree, that she has made great contributions through her photography. I can readily believe that Dorothea with her pell-mell enthusiasm may be at times

difficult to work with. . . . The sad part about this is that Dorothea and Paul Taylor feel very much hurt. My first inclination was to tell Dorothea Lange to skip it if she called but after talking it over with Packard we both want to plead with you to see if arrangements cannot be made so that at least there won't be any more bitterness and hurt involved than is absolutely necessary. Packard's suggestion, and I think it is a very good suggestion, is that you might retain her on a W.A.E. [when and as employed] basis. This will give her an official relationship and occasionally you can use her to great advantage.[18]

Pleading lack of funds, Stryker replied that he had no choice in the matter and would have to cut one photographer from the staff. Ironically, at this very moment he was striving mightily to exploit public excitement generated by *The Grapes of Wrath.* Of this opportunity, he wrote to FSA photographer Russell Lee, explaining:

I am fearful that all this fervor over the book and later over the movie may not lead to very serious consideration of the problem. It will be another of America's big excitements, soon forgotten. We should make all possible capital of it and solidify our position.[19]

Rather than enlisting Lange in the cause or promoting *An American Exodus,* Stryker fired her on the grounds that she was the most troublesome and least technically proficient member of his staff. Certainly he had plenty of reasons to single out Lange for termination rather than other staff members. Lange's independent streak and her alleged "artistic" temperament had been constant irritants, and the retouching incident had also irritated Stryker. Lange's insistence on printing her own photographs and retaining her negatives on the West Coast had also been a frequent source of irritation. Now she was working on a book project. But were these reasons to release her rather than someone else?

Marion Post Wolcott had been the last FSA photographer hired. Logically she should have been the first to go. But Wolcott was compliant. Stryker had no problems with her. When he had fired Walker Evans in the spring of 1937, after Evans had been on staff for almost three years, Stryker also cited a shortage of funds. Evans, in fact, had been a rebel, almost impossible to supervise. He hated authority and did not think much of Stryker. His output was low. He hated bureaucratic procedures. He refused to follow shooting scripts. He disappeared for weeks at a time. Stryker had never been able to handle Evans as he had other photographers, but he put up with Evans and paid him considerably more than Lange, his lowest-paid photographer. When Evans used the FSA to further his own interests, Stryker acquiesced for the larger good. He seemed less tolerant of Lange, even though she sacrificed everything for the agency. When Evans fell far short on his assignments, Stryker was silent. But conversely, Stryker showed no appreciation of Lange's sacrifices when she went above and beyond the call of duty in pursuit of her assignments. When Lange begged for work, Stryker stalled. When she asked to print her negatives (something every photographer demanded), he never understood that the only satisfactory prints of a photographer's negatives had to be made by that photographer. Stryker never appreciated Lange's concern for craftsmanship. He belittled her concern for print quality and constantly harped on her alleged technical failures. In addition, he never acknowledged that Lange, unlike Evans or Lee, had already found her vision before he hired her. She had been well on her way toward her accomplishments a year before Stryker hired her, and she did not owe him as much as Evans and others did.[20]

The truth was that Stryker was an enigma. At times agitated, he could also be patient, even tender, and frequently paternal. He vacillated between being supportive and being a tyrant. He was extremely possessive of the FSA archive and was forever telling his photographers to look for this or that. He was accustomed to getting his way eventually. His hiring and firing practices always advanced that end. When he had to eliminate a photographer, Stryker always eliminated the one who was the most intractable. Of those remaining on staff, Lange caused the most problems. "I selected for termination the person who would give me the least cooperation in the job that is laid before me," Stryker explained to Garst. "I can assure you this was not an easy job. I think I appreciate as fully as anyone, perhaps more so, the contribution Dorothea Lange has made to the photographic file of the FSA, and certainly to the presentation of the migrant problem to the people of this country." It was small compensation to Lange. The whole matter sickened her, and Stryker knew it. Writing to Russell Lee, Stryker observed, "I have had no letter in her old style."[21]

What did Stryker expect? A stubborn and independent spirit, hard to direct and very smart, Lange was less an apprentice that Stryker could control than an energetic equal who would not be treated as one of the boys. Lange needed little help from Stryker other than funds and, as the wife of a noted agricultural economist, understood her subject better than Stryker did. Far away in California, she had plenty of disagreements with Stryker that made it easy for him to release her out of smoldering grievances. She remained skeptical of the FSA's use of so-called cookie cutters, a handful of the same images that appeared over and over again. "Stryker was a schoolteacher looking for attentive students," observed photographic historian John Szarkowski, "but Lange had her own live-in schoolteacher. Stryker wanted to gather around him a group of photographers who would describe the texture of quotidian American life, and Lange wanted to give him, again and again, the desperate lives of those on the lowest rung of America's agricultural ladder, those whose plight might serve as a cautionary tale, foretelling the consequences of an industrialized agriculture."[22]

When she left the FSA, Lange certainly drew some compensation from her accomplishments. Largely on her own, she had initiated one of the most significant photographic projects of the 1930s and, in doing so, established a new photographic sensibility. She had developed a coherent, hopeful, substantive photographic style that stressed the production of raw and dense pictures of the realities of rural life. Her images had the ring of truth and a certain edginess that set them apart. "A bitter edge," Lange said of this element of her work. "I liked the bitter edge." Her disdain for obvious propaganda and straight photography, while never ignoring humanistic concerns, exemplified the FSA's photographic mission. The respect that she had shown for her subjects was unique and put her at odds with photojournalistic techniques. She had worked amid the most extreme conditions of poverty, but she had never transferred those circumstances into images of degradation. She had refused to barge in or leap through windows ready to pop a flash in the style of Margaret Bourke-White. She simply could not do it. Going about her business with a kind of self-directed practicality, Lange had avoided rural slumming. She knew who she was, and she had felt no compulsion to shed her comparative sophistication, even while she was putting people at ease and passing up more than her share of sensational photographs. Her collaboration with Taylor had yielded one of the last great "problem books" and a genre of the Great Depression. Her powerful images had established her approach as something worthy of being exhibited or published as art. She had done all of this without compromising her photographic ideals, and now she relinquished all claims to the bulk of her output, which became the property of the U.S. government. Perhaps because of resentment over this, Lange had squirreled away for herself a number of duplicate negatives. As she took stock of her work, she wondered if this was how her career with the FSA was to end.[23]

Proud of the way that she and Taylor had demonstrated the value of photography as a tool for exploring social conditions, Lange invited friends, including Wisconsin senator Robert LaFollette, over to dinner to celebrate their book. LaFollette's presence was yet another reason for celebration. A progressive politician known as the "plumed knight of liberalism," he was chairman of the Subcommittee of the Senate Committee on Education and Labor, also known as the LaFollette Civil Liberties Committee, and had been investigating violations of the rights of labor and free speech. Almost from the start, the committee had wanted to investigate violations of civil rights in California agriculture but was held back until newly elected governor Culbert Olson and newly elected state senator Sheridan Downey had secured fifty thousand dollars for an investigation of agricultural labor relations in California. Now LaFollette was opening offices in San Francisco and Los Angeles and assembling a staff of thirty-five liberal attorneys, highly competent investigators, dogged researchers, and talented writers. Characterized by historian Kevin Starr as "the most dedicated and effective" governmental team of the New Deal, the LaFollette Committee would produce a "documentary masterpiece of the Depression," whose final report rivals *The Grapes of Wrath, Migrant Mother,* and *Factories in the Fields.*[24]

Lange and Taylor were to play important roles in the proceedings. As LaFollette began laying the groundwork for his inquiry into the antilabor activities of the Associated Farmers and, to some extent, the Farm Bureau Federation, Lange helped by supplying twelve large prints of migrant laborers, Dust Bowl refugees, ditch-bank camps, and agricultural strikes. These would eventually become part of 1,747 exhibits, 2,451 pages of testimony, and 5,875 supplementary exhibits compiled by the committee; Lange became, in effect, one of 395 witnesses in the proceedings. Taylor offered his "Documentary History of the Strike of Cotton Pickers, 1933," and then prepared to appear as the lead witness in the San Francisco hearings. Speaking of Lange's images and the circumstances they portrayed, Taylor summarized their significance in eloquent testimony. First, such images were ample evidence that California farmworkers "bear increasingly the mark of a class whose chances of ascending the agricultural ladder, or of finding outlets into industry, grow more difficult." Second, they illustrated the prime question raised by such evidence: "Can a large farm labor class be reconciled with democracy?" Third, they documented the pattern of farm labor disputes, in which "ardent organizers agitate and lead, incensed 'vigilantes' organize and act, growers, officials, and laborers each overstep the law, and citizens finally cry to the State authorities for peace, if necessary at the hands of troops."[25]

As the hearings went forward, Reynal and Hitchcock published *An American Exodus.* The timing could not have been better, or worse. On the one hand, a book, a major film, and a congressional investigating committee were all exploring aspects of California farm labor. On the other hand, the problems of the Great Depression were now rapidly being supplanted by the growing specter of Adolf Hitler and the looming confrontation with Japan. With the public preoccupied by an impending world war, *An American Exodus* never had a chance to reach a wide audience. A masterpiece of art and documentation, it hardly sold. Prowling the Berkeley bookstores, Taylor found a dozen copies remaindered at a dollar each. He bought them all, packing them back home in a sack.[26]

Even as the market for *An American Exodus* shriveled up, reviewers praised the book as a unique and pioneering effort. The *Nation* described it as "one of the best devoted to the dispossessed farmworkers," and, writing in the *New Republic,* Carey McWilliams went on at length about how *An American Exodus* dealt so well with "the tragic exodus so graphically documented," concluding that "the combination of talents that has produced *American Exodus* could scarcely have been improved upon." Beaumont Newhall, author of a pioneering history of photography, called *An American Exodus* a "bold experiment pointing the way to a new medium, where words and pictures do not merely explain and illustrate: they reinforce one another to produce . . . the third 'effect.'" Ansel Adams and Edward Weston, who had earlier derided documentary work as déclassé, wrote to Lange praising the book. Echoing their praise were the *New Yorker* and the scholarly journal *Social Forces.* But Paul Strand, the one photographer Lange truly admired, while warmly welcoming the effort as a "valuable document . . . of integrity and honest feeling," found *An American Exodus* lacking "the impact upon the eye and mind which the subject surely contains." The photographs were very uneven, said Strand, simply paralleling and illustrating the text. This made the book weak, because not every photograph possessed "that unity and intensity of expression which give all works of art their impact." Strand then went on to say the book lacked the kind of "definite approach to the realities of the world" required of good documentary work and was perhaps "mere record making." Pare Lorentz also chimed in with a critique, faulting *An American Exodus* for being disorganized and "not well presented," concluding that economic analysis and photographs did not mix very well and should have been kept separate. Tossing in his two bits, William Hopkins, reviewing *An American Exodus* in *American Economic Review,* labeled Taylor's critique of modern agriculture completely wrong. Devastated by the criticism, Lange drew solace from one West Texas refugee who had provided Taylor with the phrase "tractored out." Sent a copy of the book, his son replied that while his father had recently died, the family found Lange's photographs a "tribute to his . . . memory."[27]

A half century later, the critic A. D. Coleman compared the images in *An American Exodus* with those in *Let Us Now Praise Famous Men.* Discovering in *Let Us Now Praise Famous Men* a quiet and subtler form of terror and grief, Coleman stressed that, while also dealing with brutal conditions, *An American Exodus* suggests that these adverse circumstances were temporary and rectifiable, "that one's sorrow could be tempered with anger—at those standing in the way of change—and hope." Another modern critic, Harvard psychologist and photographic historian Robert Coles, called attention to the prophetic qualities of the book, among them the way it was executed—free of jargon, with compelling photographs. Describing *An American Exodus* as a milestone in photographic history, he praised it as a guide to direct observation by people engaged in firsthand reporting without the intervention of statistics, theory, and methodology. He emphasized:

> Here were a man and woman, a husband and a wife, who drove across our nation with paper, pen, and camera; who had no computers or questionnaires or "coding devices," no tape recorders, or movie cameras, no army of research assistants "trained" to obtain "data." Here were two individuals who would scorn that all-too-commonly upheld tenet of today's social-science research, the claim to be "value-free." They were, rather, a man and a woman of unashamed moral passion, of vigorous and proudly upheld subjectivity, anxious not to quantify or submit what they saw to conceptual assertion but to notice, to see and hear, and in so doing, to feel, then render so that others too, would know in their hearts as well as their heads what it was that happened at a moment in American history, at a place on the American subcontinent. . . . This is documentary study at its revelatory best—pictures and words joined together in a kind of nurturing interdependence that illustrates the old aphorism that the whole is greater than the sum of its parts. . . . We can do no better these days than to look at their book, over half a century after it appeared, not only as an aspect of the past . . . but as a summons to what might be done in the years ahead, what very much needs to be done: a humane and literate kind of social inquiry.[28]

More critically, the historian Kevin Starr found in *An American Exodus* an "exquisitely realized evocation" of documentary art celebrating the white Dust Bowl refugees, the black sharecroppers of the South, and the Mexican farm laborer of the Southwest. Perhaps the best assessment of *An American Exodus* came from Lange's biographer, Henry Mayer, who wrote just before he died:

In its unpretentious approach, in its respect for the wisdom of ordinary people, in its appreciation of the need for stewardship of the land, and in its eloquent visual language, *An American Exodus* remains a profoundly moral inquiry, illuminated by moments of poetry and rooted in Lange and Taylor's unshakeable democratic faith.[29]

Lange certainly derived some consolation from *An American Exodus,* the influence she had exerted on the photographic profession, and the work she had done on behalf of migrant farmworkers. Partly as a result of her example, a group of talented Film and Photo League photographers seceded from the league and established the Photo League as an independent organization. Soon engaged in numerous multiphotographer projects, the Photo League produced series with titles such as Portrait of a Tenement (1936); Rural America (1939), to which Lange herself contributed; The Catholic Worker Movement (1939–40); 16th Street Lost Generation (1939–40); Men at Work (1940); and Harlem Document (1937–40), Aaron Siskind's three-year project.

Struggling to define exactly what constituted this healthy photographic form of activism, Elizabeth McCausland, in a series of articles written for *Photo Notes,* identified what Lange and other FSA photographers had accomplished in just four years. McCausland noted that Lange had not only injected concepts like "truth" and "honesty" into the debate over the photographic medium, in place of useless pictorialism, "rayographs" and "photograms" (filmless pictures popularized by Man Ray), self-centered art projects that led nowhere, and images that made little difference; she had also provided an example of how photographers could excite sympathies, elevate consciousness, "widen the world in which we live," and make a difference without crossing the line into propaganda. From a photographic sensibility that was largely aloof and unconcerned with farmworkers as human beings, Lange had established the model for the informed photographer who, using visual evidence of poverty, unemployment, and various kinds of discrimination, elevated content over form and evoked feelings that conveyed problems as undeniably real.[30]

So widely known and respected was Lange at this time that after leaving the FSA photographic unit, she again could have easily moved on to other subjects. Had she done so, she still would have gone down in the annals of photography as a feisty, morally alert citizen who had done more than anyone else to shape public perceptions of California farmworkers. Able to inspire confidence among her subjects and inject an element of calculated composition into her portraits, she had amalgamated her experience as a studio photographer with a working methodology that was quiet and unthreatening. Capturing a surprising range of images, she allowed viewers to achieve intimate contact with her subjects—the CIO organizer with the look and stance of an assassin and the good-humored Oklahoman who told jokes after losing his farm. Lange's work, Ansel Adams said many years later, "bridged the space between photo-documentation and photo-poetry to an extraordinary degree." Art critic and photographer Van Deren Coke found it as disturbing as that of Lewis Hine, who preceded her by a generation, and as insightful as that of Robert Frank, who followed her by a decade. He wrote, "The somber moods Dorothea Lange caught so graphically on film confirm that photography is a medium of great power not only for the making of vivid documents, but at the same time, is a medium for creating great works of enduring aesthetic value."[31]

Lange's five years of work in the fields had left their mark on her as a person and as an artist, amounting to what she would later characterize as "the greatest education I could ever have been given by anything or anybody." Toward the end of her life, Lange would look back over this time and explain to an interviewer for the Archives of American Art that, during the years the Historical Section was being formed, it was not a public relations success. Stryker had knocked himself out trying to place material, but no one would take it, or magazine editors would sort through stacks of photographs and want to run the same ones over and over again or simply pass on them because they lacked the hard news impact necessary for immediate publication. "Did Roy ever tell you of the many, many trips he made to New York, with pictures under his arm, trying to peddle them to periodicals and to publications, and didn't make it?" she asked the same interviewer. "That's a little bit humiliating, and embarrassing to him."[32]

Those difficulties also gave a sense of failure, but she never considered abandoning her photographic career. Five years with the FSA had a huge impact on her life. Besides placing her in the center of a significant moment of cultural awareness and political ferment, those years had also led her into a completely original collaboration of intimate creativity. While the dissemination of her work and that of other FSA photographers disappointed her, Lange remained upbeat. "Time . . . is a great editor, and a great publicist," she told her Archives of American Art interviewer. "Time has given those things the value."[33]

Lange certainly had plenty of family responsibilities that could have absorbed her energies at this time. As a mother and a photographer, she constantly made very difficult, unpopular choices between her work and family, trying to compromise neither. Nonetheless, she failed often: as a mother, as she admitted, when recalling her many summers away from her own two sons and her stepchildren; and in her work, missing some important moments in history and at times resorting to the same tried and true compositional formulas. But she never wavered from her commitment to her photography or her family.

Farmworker activists already cherished her work and wanted it to continue. So strong and pervasive was Lange's influence at this time that when word of impending budgetary cuts in the FSA reached the West Coast, writers for the Communist Party's *People's World* predicted catastrophe. Left to do as they wanted, farmers would be free to smash farmworker unions at will. The only way to counter this, wrote one correspondent, was to take up the slack and "keep a reporter and photographer in the cotton community and publish material every day just to keep the problem before the public mind." With Lange gone from the FSA, that now seemed highly unlikely.[34]

Unemployed as of January 1, 1940, Lange could have returned to portrait work, studio and commercial photography, or, most likely, gone to work for one of the big news magazines. By now, Carl Mydans had been working for *Life* magazine for three and a half years. She hardly considered these options. To do so would have signaled a retreat from the social science approach she had pursued with Taylor. While Marion Post Wolcott, three months pregnant and worn out from being constantly on the road, was composing a succinct letter of resignation to leave the FSA for magazine photography, Lange remained neither alienated from New Deal field photography nor interested in the larger salary and fast pace of vapid magazine work. Unwilling to forfeit the personal control over her photography that she had long enjoyed, and lacking the ego and ambition required to do fast-paced freelance photography, Lange wondered if she would be able to continue photographing farmworkers and other segments of the dispossessed. But she did not quit. "Once an FSA guy, always an FSA guy," she wrote to Stryker several months later. "You don't easily get over it."[35]

Through a variety of assignments and jobs, Lange was able to continue her photography among farmworkers on a diminished basis over the next three years. Her first photographic assignment began on February 1, 1940, a week after the world premier of *The Grapes of Wrath* at the Rivoli Theatre in New York City, when she was appointed head photographer of the Bureau of Agricultural Economics (BAE), another agency within the Department of Agriculture then engaged in an ongoing study of rural life. Ironically, just as Lange was changing jobs, *Life* magazine published Horace Bristol's photographs in a large essay keyed to the release of the movie version of *The Grapes of Wrath*. Showing that the movie was not an exaggeration, the essay made a point of comparing Bristol's images with certain characters in *The Grapes of Wrath*, particularly the people Steinbeck called Ma and Pa Joad. The most striking similarity was between Bristol's photograph of a middle-aged woman and actress Jane Darwell, who played Ma Joad. Many of Bristol's portraits, in fact, confirmed suspicions that movie director John Ford had carefully examined them, as well as Lange's photographs, before his cameras rolled. "Never before," *Life* magazine observed, "had the facts behind a great work of fiction been so carefully researched by the news camera."[36]

If Lange wondered about the relationship between her photography and the movie, she never said so. Drawing a per diem of $7.22 a day, she threw herself into her work, which she found very similar to what she had done in her FSA days. Over the next five months, from February through June, she made 241 photographs in Kern, Yuba, and Stanislaus counties and another 160 in Pinal and Maricopa counties, Arizona, most of them documenting farmworkers in the fields and camps. Lange paid close attention to developing general captions so that her photography could help justify construction of better housing for migratory laborers while countering bitter criticism and attacks by growers, who labeled the camps dens of communist and subversive activity. One particularly memorable sequence of images documented a family stranded in a broken-down trailer parked in a barren field. Moved by their plight, Lange called the series Children Living in a Democracy.[37]

Midway through her work for the BAE, Lange was driving along Highway 99 when she spotted a large billboard advertising a March 21 opening night for the movie version of *The Grapes of Wrath* at the Princess Theater in Modesto. Like other photographers during the Great Depression, Lange had already used Hollywood billboards as a way to amplify the contrast between myth and reality, although she did not employ the technique to the same extent that others did, for example, the way Walker Evans fitted a billboard advertising *Love before Breakfast* into his 1936 photograph of a rundown residential section of Atlanta, Georgia. But seeing this particular billboard, Lange could not resist. Although she left no recollection of this particular episode, she must certainly have reflected on the extent to which her work had inspired Steinbeck, directing him to important sources of information, as well as helping the director pick certain actors over others for their resemblance to the people she had documented and assisting crews with the construction of movie sets. She might also have taken some pride in seeing her images verified by Twentieth Century–Fox. Possibly with these thoughts in mind, Lange parked her car, walked into a field, and photographed directly opposite the billboard, including a large rundown shed on the left, the billboard on the right, and section of the highway in the foreground. "Surely there was irony in Lange's making this document," wrote the historian Sally Stein. "The photograph's somewhat awkward juggling act leaves us to wonder whether her work had less impact on rural people than on Hollywood sagas."[38]

To some extent Lange's work photographing farmworkers for the BAE was redundant with her FSA work—and humiliating, particularly in March and April, when Stryker dispatched Arthur Rothstein to California to photograph farmworkers in the

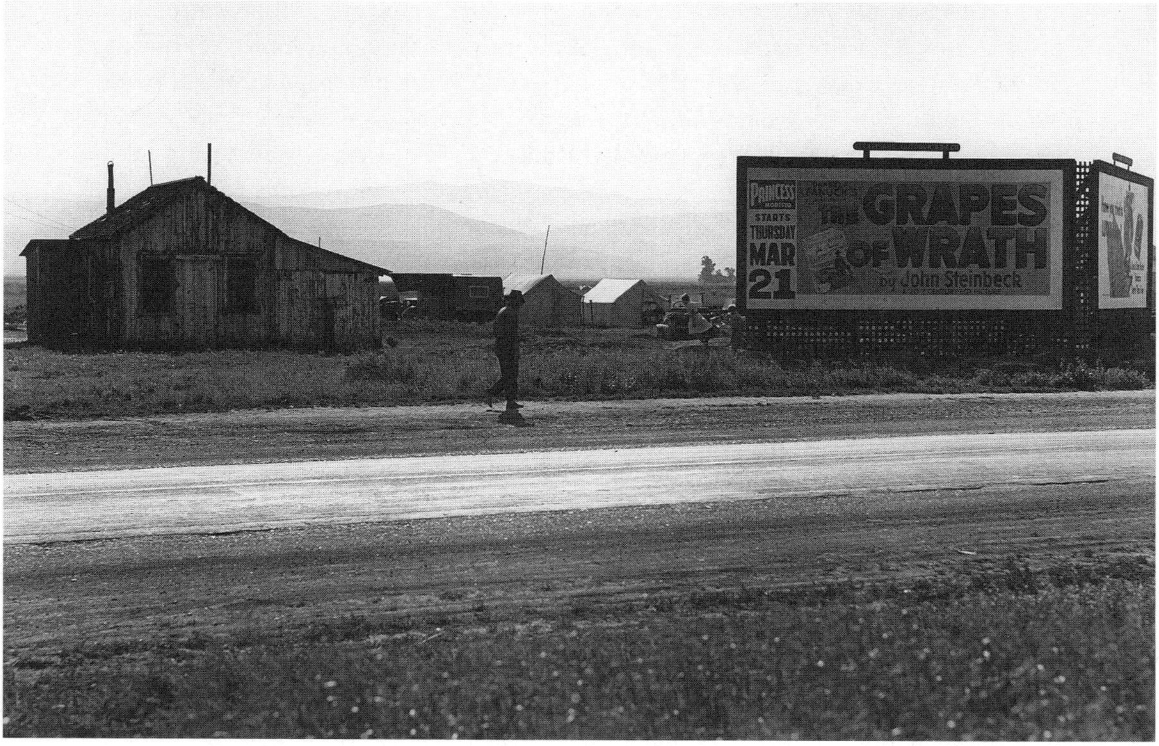

Grapes of Wrath billboard, April 9, 1940, photograph by Dorothea Lange. Courtesy of the Oakland Museum of California, Dorothea Lange Collection, Gift of Paul S. Taylor.

FSA camp at Visalia, ostensibly to fill gaps in Lange's coverage. Ever gracious, Lange met with Rothstein at her home. She knew the Visalia camp well, having visited it several times, and gave Rothstein help setting up for his assignment.

At the time Rothstein arrived at Visalia, the camp was undergoing a transition from temporary housing to a more permanent arrangement that would eventually become the Tulare Migratory Labor Camp. Run by an elected council, the camp stressed democratic participation by committees that ran everything from a cooperative store to a health clinic. Such activities continued to anger and threaten growers, who labeled the camps dens of communism. To counter complaints from agricultural lobbyists and to end the harassment of his agency, Stryker wanted Rothstein to picture migrants in a different and very positive light, "so we will quit being harassed so much by people around Washington [D.C.] for this particular type of photo." Forwarding detailed instructions bordering on a shooting script, Stryker told Rothstein to feature the most wholesome aspects of camp life: "Remember your emphasis is to be on how people conduct themselves in and around the camp. . . . mothers and children are your best bet. Get nurses treating children, mothers coming in for post natal instruction—anything that will demonstrate child welfare work." He then told Rothstein that western regional director Soule would be looking over the work and was especially anxious to see images emphasizing "the positive side."[39]

Following orders, Rothstein flew into a fury of photography, making nearly two hundred images. Corroborating the camp's wholesome and welcoming nature, his scenes show residents respectfully going about their business embroidering, hoeing in the camp garden, repairing trucks, getting out the camp newspaper, ironing in the utility building, putting on a skit, enjoying a Saturday night dance, and both playing and watching baseball. While much of Rothstein's photography was banal, he did complete a remarkable portfolio of close-up portraits showing camp residents, all posed against the same wall of the camp administration building. These are very different from Lange's images. Camp residents appear as well-scrubbed citizens, indistinguishable from other Americans. All are nicely dressed in clean clothes. Most smile. There are no Mexicans, Filipinos, or African Americans. No one looks discouraged or malnourished.[40]

Although Rothstein relayed that he had found the camp the best managed of all he had visited, he hated the assignment. He had made so many pictures of babies and children in nurseries that he quickly exhausted his supply of flash bulbs and wrote to Stryker asking for more. Receiving the bulbs just in time, he finished his work and on April 1 informed Stryker:

> The weather has been terrible. It has rained every day. I like it the least of the western states. My impression is that everything is commercialized, the police & city officials are corrupt grafters, there is little of that gracious western hospitality & most of the people are of that reactionary, super-patriotic, fascist minded type. Practically every newspaper features a daily red-baiting article with 2 inch headlines that condemn Gov. Olson, the NLRB, or Pres. Roosevelt.[41]

Following the assignment, Rothstein left the FSA to work for *Look* magazine. The episode surely hurt Lange, who could have done the work just as well, if not better. And it failed to quiet down congressional criticism.

Oddly, Stryker, Rothstein, and Lange missed an opportunity to photograph Eleanor Roosevelt, who was touring migrant camps in California at this time. Mrs. Roosevelt was concerned with the issues raised by both the book and the movie version of *The Grapes of Wrath.* She had been speaking out on the issue of farm labor and, in early April, had flown to Los Angeles to meet actress Helen Gahagan Douglas, a strong supporter of farm labor issues, who intended to raise the issues during her campaign for a seat in Congress. Roosevelt and Douglas flew to Bakersfield and then toured the southern San Joaquin Valley, accompanied by Mrs. Roosevelt's personal secretary. On their way to the Farm Security Administration camp at Visalia, they visited a ditch-bank settlement, "a cluster of makeshift shacks, constructed of old boards, tar paper and tin cans pounded flat." All along the way a small crowd of reporters and photographers documented their activities, including an incident at one camp where Mrs. Roosevelt lingered at a tent in which children were ill with a contagious disease, then departed in a huff after scolding the camp manager for locating a water faucet beside a privy. A few hours later, at the Visalia camp, Mrs. Roosevelt was greeted by a "blue-jean and calico-clad committee" and escorted about the place. Again photographed everywhere she went, Mrs. Roosevelt replied to a reporter's question about what she thought of conditions. "I never believed that *The Grapes of Wrath* was an exaggeration," she replied.[42]

If Lange was angry at not having the opportunity to photograph Roosevelt's visit and at being pushed aside for Rothstein, she never said so publicly. Ever supportive of Rondal Partridge, who had been assisting her in the fields for the past two and a half years, Lange talked National Youth Authority administrators into providing Partridge with a small stipend in support of a large, if somewhat unstructured, portrait of California youth. Partridge threw himself into the project. He spent most of the spring traveling around the state documenting various adolescent subcultures. Familiar with farmwork, the precocious Partridge used his charm and knowledge to depart somewhat from the FSA tradition. Whereas Lange's photographs typically projected a strong sense of self-possession, Partridge's field photography had a different feel. This was particularly true of photographs he made in a Kern County potato field on April 9. Encountering a girl from Oklahoma, he posed her with her hands on her hips and a large cloth draped over her head in a kind of improvised hat. Slouched over with a large potato picking sack hooked to her belt, she projected a weariness not seen in Lange's work. Partridge's caption noted:

> This girl came from OK state three years ago and lives with her father in a rural slum in Wasco, Kern County, where they have settled down; their jobs in peas, potatoes and cotton are obtained less by the hit-and-miss methods and more by knowing local contractors and independent farmers. They are considered "locals" in the community in which they live. The girl never had a chance to finish high school and will be nineteen

"come August 11." While the girl and her father are away from Wasco on jobs, they live in the trailer in which they came from Oklahoma.[43]

No government agency published *Potato Field Madonna,* as the image was called, or any other of Partridge's images of Kern County, or any of the more than two hundred other photographs he made throughout the state that spring. After returning from the field, his project was terminated, and Partridge moved on.[44]

That summer, when Stryker needed photographers, he did not rehire Lange. Instead, he chose to bring in Jack Delano, a young photographer with exactly one year's experience. Lange certainly had plenty of photographic matters occupying her attention. While moving into a home designed in 1910 by a partner of architect Bernard Maybeck, she supervised construction of a darkroom and studio and shifted away from her involvement with California farmworkers. During this time, Lange no doubt took great pride in, and paid attention to, an investigation by the Select Committee to Investigate the Migration of Destitute Citizens. Popularly known as the Tolan Committee, it took this name from its chairman, Representative John Tolan, a former social worker and Democrat from Alameda County. Under Tolan's direction, his committee held hearings that produced the last great documentary report of the Great Depression. As thorough and revealing as the LaFollette Committee report and even longer, the Tolan Committee report was, according to Kevin Starr, a kind of 5,032-page Pare Lorentz documentary—"realized through transcribed testimony and clean and direct prose refreshingly free of jargon"—that fully corroborated the work of Dorothea Lange, Hansel Mieth, Otto Hagel, and other pioneer documentary photographers.[45]

Applying for a Guggenheim Fellowship to photograph three rural societies (the Amana Colonies, the Shakers, and the Hutterites), Lange won the appointment in March 1941, becoming the first woman and only the third photographer to be so honored. She remained persona non grata with many farmers, particularly the Associated Farmers, who attacked the Guggenheim Foundation for selecting the wife of "Liberal Dr. Paul Taylor," whom they condemned for having previously produced a "grapes of wrathy" book.[46]

Leaving California that summer, Lange photographed her Guggenheim Fellowship project into the fall, traveling extensively in the Midwest and in Utah. During her absence, her work was picked up and carried forward, however briefly and in fragmentary form, by two photographers, Robert Hemmig and Seema Weatherwax. Of Hemmig almost nothing is known. A Ventura photographer, he accompanied City College of New York instructors Charles Todd and Robert Sonkin while they tape-recorded folk music, conversations, and other facets of Okie culture for the Library of Congress Archive of Folk Song. Snapping pictures at Shafter FSA camp in the summer of 1941, Hemmig documented Todd and Sonkin wearing headphones and attentively listening to fiddlers playing regional versions of English ballads and singers sharing down-home folk tunes. But he did not stop there. Following Todd and Sonkin to other camps, he became especially entranced by the El Río FSA camp, in

Ventura County. Perhaps because it was the only FSA camp populated entirely by Mexicans and had not yet been photographed, Hemmig devoted a great deal of time to everyday events, ranging from children in supervised boxing matches to wives watering and tending little gardens outside their tents. Written notes on the back of one Hemmig photograph documenting Charles Todd at a recording machine surrounded by a group of Mexican boys and men read: "El Rio F.S.A. Camp—Cal. 1941—the Mexicans were replacing the 'Okies.'"[47]

Of Seema Weatherwax, more is known. A photographer who had worked for Ansel Adams in Yosemite and San Francisco since 1937, she married radical writer Jack Weatherwax and moved to Los Angeles in early 1941. When she learned of worsening conditions in the San Joaquin Valley, she joined a group that, in September, tried to raise funds to help the residents of the Shafter FSA camp. Folksinger Woody Guthrie agreed to be the big-name draw for a benefit party, which would be held in Los Angeles. Several weeks before the big event, Seema, her husband, and

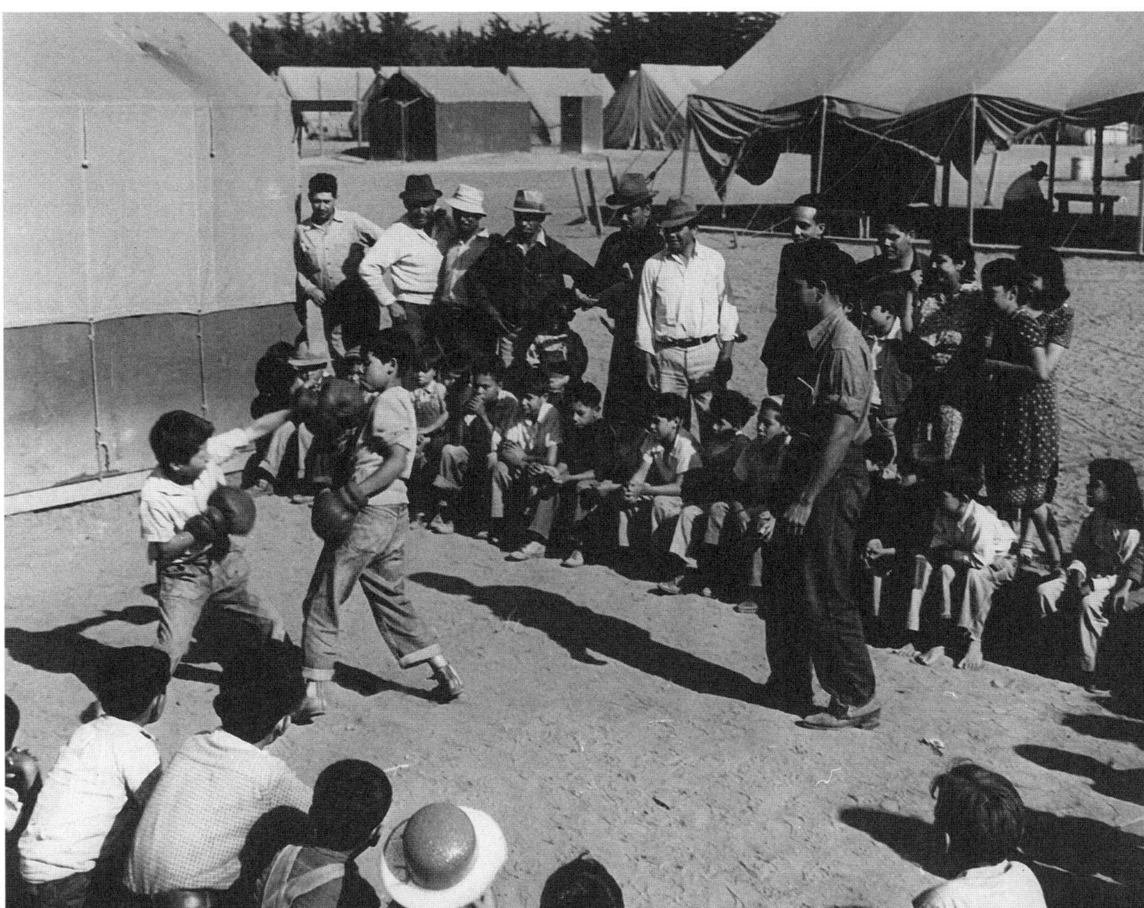

Boxing matches, El Río FSA camp, Ventura County, 1941, photograph by Robert Hemmig. Courtesy of the Ventura County Museum.

Guthrie headed to the camp to meet with its residents. Woody drove and sang at full throttle, remembering and inventing songs all along the way. They arrived in the area after an early spring rain, and the air was clean, with the tingling smells of wet orchards. Just before they arrived at the camp, they passed the outlying squatters' village, where people lived in shacks or vehicles while waiting for spaces to open up inside the camp. But driving inside the wide camp gates, they entered a changed world. Seema recalled:

> I set out, camera in hand, to see the camp. When I took a picture of three little children, other kids saw me and came running from every corner to line up for a photo, with no directions from me. I cooperated and took their picture. . . . Even with my own modest means, I felt like a visiting rich lady. A woman showed me around the showers, wash rooms, and the child care room. Kids napped on rows of cots, and had snacks and planned activities while their mothers did chores. . . . One girl had so many freckles that she inspired us to hold a freckles contest at the party. A beautiful, gaunt woman tentatively told me she made a picture of the rustler's hanging tree in her home town. She slipped off to her house to retrieve it. She had never painted before, but in the camp she had the chance. What emerged from her memory and artistry was a Grandma Moses like rendition of Ada, Oklahoma, a reminder of talents so many people have, without a chance to explore them.[48]

Seema photographed it all, including Woody Guthrie playing a few songs and contemplating the camp entrance with camp manager Fred Ross. Several weeks later, a "Down-Home Gala" party drew a crowd of two hundred to the CIO Hall in Los Angeles. Among those present were four carloads of Shafter camp residents, who listened to Guthrie singing his usual repertoire. With funds raised at the benefit, Shafter camp residents were able to purchase extra supplies, gas, and other necessities.

Lange was unable to cover the Shafter camp celebration or any other important farm labor development that fall. After her brother, Martin, had been arrested and charged with fraud, Lange abandoned her Guggenheim Fellowship project and devoted most of her energies to helping him. Already contemporaries were crediting her with dramatically changing the way photographers worked. By teaching that photographs could be at once beautiful and possess a social conscience and by showing how images could forge deep empathy for human suffering while also generating aesthetic associations, Lange and her peers had established an approach that raised important issues, brought viewers closer to matters otherwise difficult to imagine, and fundamentally improved the lives of California farmworkers. Looking back over her accomplishments at this time, filmmaker Pare Lorentz saw her as a seminal figure. "If there are transient camps, and better working conditions, and a permanent agency seeking to help migratory workers," he argued, "Lange, with her still pictures that have been reproduced in thousands of newspapers, and in magazines and Sunday supplements, and Steinbeck, with two novels, a play, and a motion picture, have done more for these tragic nomads than all the politicians of the country."[49]

When Japan attacked Pearl Harbor on December 7, 1941, and the United States entered World War II, Lange's contributions were quickly forgotten. Shifting its focus away from the problems of Okie, Filipino, and Mexican migrants, the FSA Historical Section refocused its energies on wartime propaganda. To create the kinds of images required for the war effort, Stryker brought Russell Lee to the West Coast. A chemical engineer who had taken up photography after studying art, Lee was known as a "taxonomist with a camera," although his images were anything but neutral and detached. Working for the FSA since 1936, Lee shared Stryker's idealized vision of rural America, a view that emerged in major essays on San Augustine, Texas, in 1939, and Pie Town, New Mexico, in 1940. During this time he had also begun to experiment with color film, something Lange refused to do. Essentially a photo essayist, Lee seldom snapped a single image of anything, preferring to take a series of shots that explored a story or mood, always with an opening and closing shot. During the winter, Lee shot essays on farmworkers in the Imperial Valley and San Benito County and Japanese farmers around the Little Tokyo section of Los Angeles.[50]

Lee was shooting a public relations essay on guayule farming as a new source for the short supply of rubber when President Roosevelt signed Executive Order 9066 on February 19, 1942. Authorizing the establishment of military zones, Executive Order 9066 called for the commander of Western Defense, General John L. DeWitt, to remove anyone deemed a threat to national security. Following orders but also responding to both irrational hysteria following Japan's attack on Pearl Harbor and long-standing anti-Japanese sentiment that had limited Japanese immigration and landownership in California, General DeWitt announced on March 1 that, under the guise of military necessity, all Japanese residents of the Pacific Coast would be relocated to internment camps outside the military zones. The order that DeWitt carried out produced the largest single forced migration in American history, totaling some 110,000 individuals, two-thirds of them Nisei (American-born citizens of Japanese ancestry) and 93,000 from California.[51]

When the government began constructing relocation camps and the U.S. Army started rounding up the Japanese, Lange joined her husband in unsuccessfully petitioning the government to stop the removal and incarceration program. Convinced that the program was a huge mistake, they were further angered by the almost complete denial of due process. Later that March, they joined with the philosopher John Dewey and other prominent Americans in asking that the Japanese at least be given a hearing before a civilian board that could evaluate their loyalty. Then, suddenly, Lange found herself playing a part in the program as one of its photographers.

A new civilian agency, the War Relocation Authority (WRA), led by Milton Eisenhower, took control of the internment program. On WRA's staff was an information officer who had once worked with Paul Taylor at the Social Security Board. When the WRA decided it wanted to document its work, the information officer, who was familiar with Lange's photography, hired her along with several newspaper photographers. Even though she and Taylor were vocal critics of relocation, Lange was assigned to cover the evacuation and relocation. Exactly what motivated the WRA to hire photographers remains a mystery. By now it had become common practice to employ someone to document every government project, even one amounting to a blatant and scandalous violation of justice. But bureaucratic reasons alone did not explain Lange's work for the WRA. While some officials probably wanted to show how humanely the project was being conducted, others no doubt wanted a record of people guilty of no crime who were being imprisoned without trail.[52]

On the staff of the WRA for a year and a half, Lange was one of seven photographers; all the others, former newspaper photographers of varying abilities, each one assigned to a different region and relocation camp. Lange did almost all of her work in three areas of California between March and September 1942. Although Lange had by now seen plenty, she was hardly prepared to bear witness to this mass relocation. Often in complete despair, she slaved away at her task. She began photographing late in April. Much of her work at first centered on the Japanese quarter of San Francisco and other cities in the Bay Area. Lange documented long lines of Japanese assembling to be vaccinated at churches, YMCAs, YWCAs, and various Nisei headquarters. She recalled it as "very difficult" work photographing "baffled, bewildered people" who were "dressed as though they were going to an important event" and who "took huge sacrifices, made practically no demands," and languished in long lines before "oceans of desks and oceans of people with papers." Lange photographed them boarding buses and trains, arriving at assembly centers, and settling down into routines before being moved again to one of the relocation centers.[53]

Early in May, Lange began documenting the relocation of farmers and farm laborers in the Central Valley. Concentrating on the Japanese around Sacramento, she headed ten miles south to Florin, an old center of Japanese farming, where she photographed a Japanese American soldier, in full uniform, standing in the strawberry fields beside his mother. Lange's sad and ironic caption read:

> The soldier, age 23, volunteered at Camp Leonard Wood, Missouri. He was furloughed to help his mother and family prepare for evacuation. He is the youngest of six children, two of them volunteers in the U.S. Army. The mother, now 53, came from Japan 37 years ago.[54]

From Florin, Lange traveled to west to Byron, in the Sacramento Delta, again concentrating on field hands. After taking another photograph that tormented her, she composed a painful caption that read:

> Field laborers of Japanese ancestry from a large delta ranch have assembled at Wartime Civilian Control Authority Station to receive instructions for evacuation which is to be effected in three days under California Exclusion Order No. 24. They are arguing together over whether or not to return to the ranch to work for the remaining days before evacuation, or whether they shall spend that time on their personal affairs.[55]

Over the next four months, Lange concentrated on the temporary assembly centers at Stockton, San Bruno, Turlock, and Woodland, where evacuees were registered and loaded onto trains. Although her photographs would not be used as she wanted, she justified her work on the grounds that it captured a temporary wartime travesty that should not go unrecorded. Although a "minder" at the assembly centers often followed her and an army general continually accused her of various improprieties, such as absconding with negatives and unauthorized publication of images, Lange worked as she had in the past and succeeded in developing a natural relationship with the people she photographed.

While she submerged deeper into her assignment, Lange grew increasingly uneasy about her initial rationalizations. Seeing the evacuation less as a wartime measure and more as part of a racist chapter in the history of California agriculture, to name one locus, she vowed to follow the story into the postwar years. Besides documenting how the experience affected Japanese farmers and farm laborers, she hoped also to stress the various ways in which evacuees were able to overcome the trauma. Toward that end she captured images that disclosed both sadness and pride in the face of degradation. Lange recorded one particularly memorable image in Woodland on May 20. Moving out onto a ranch, she encountered a single Japanese man seated on a block of wood beneath the shade of a tree. His head was downcast. He was obviously in deep reflection. It is unclear whether he is a farmer or a farm laborer. Lange's caption simply states, "Everything is packed, ready for evacuation the following morning."[56]

Three days later, Lange reached a point of complete despair. On the evening of May 23, 1942, in Yolo County, Christina Gardner, who assisted Lange on the assignment, returned from the lobby of the Woodland Hotel to Lange's room to find her in "some sort of paroxysm of fear." The whole assignment had so eaten away at Lange that she could barely continue. Gardner had never seen Lange or anyone else so upset. But by the next morning, Lange had composed herself enough to photograph Japanese farm hands gathering at the Woodland train depot. Most seemed to accept her while she went about her business. She was quiet, fit into the scene, and went to her usual pains to explain who she was and what she was doing. But at least one Japanese American later objected to her photography. In his diary he described her as "a thing in slacks" and hoped that she would just "leave these people alone."[57]

Lange followed the story until September, but she did more than photograph the tragedy. Determined to act as a force for better treatment and early release, she cooperated with Paul Taylor in an essay he published that September in *Survey Graphic* magazine. Entitled "Our Stakes in the Japanese Exodus," the essay labeled the relocation program a colossal mistake that criminalized loyal farm laborers and productive farmers, both of whom would have made substantial contributions to the war effort. As a member of the Fair Play Committee, Taylor worked unfailingly throughout the war on behalf of the internees. Lange shared his position. "It was shameful," she would state many years later in her oral memoir. A fine selection of Lange's photographs illustrated the essay. Because she had signed a statement to seek the permission of the

United States Army before publishing any of her relocation photographs, Lange illustrated the essay with negatives from her FSA work that she had squirreled away.[58]

As Lange struggled at Woodland, Russell Lee stepped back into the picture. How this happened is somewhat of a mystery. Lee was not employed by the WRA. When relocation began, the FSA had recruited thousands of farmers to take over the six thousand farms vacated by the Japanese. As part of that task, the agency also had to supervise the sale of property and various other unpleasant activities associated with the massive transfer of agricultural property to new owners and tenants. All of this had to be documented. Whether or not Stryker authorized it or Lee simply decided to cover it as part of his general duties in California remains a source of much speculation. No surviving letters from Stryker or Lee shed any light on the assignment. Whatever the reason or authorization, Lee brought some unique talents to the task of documenting the relocation of Japanese farmers and farm laborers.[59]

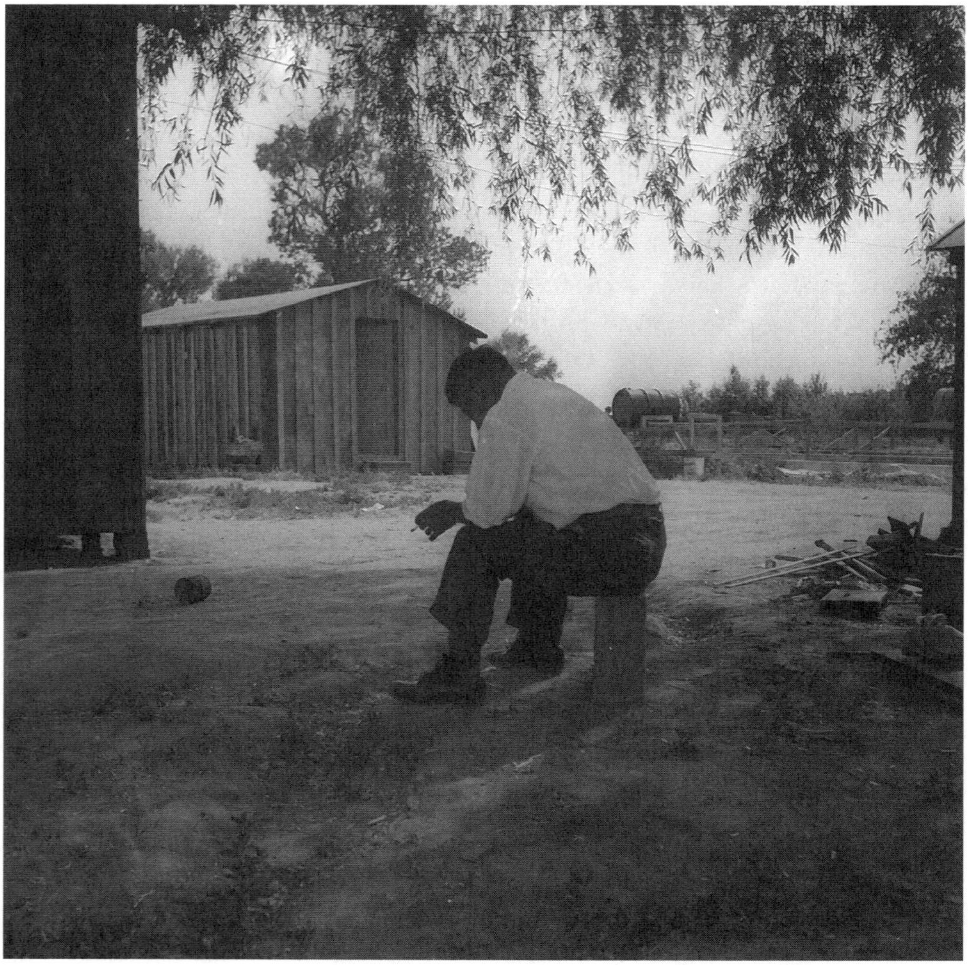

Japanese man awaiting evacuation from a farm near Woodland, May 20, 1942, photograph by Dorothea Lange. Courtesy of the War Relocation Authority Collection, National Archives.

While many of Lee's relocation photographs mirror Lange's, at least two of his photo essays are distinctive. One focuses on a Japanese farm family in Los Angeles County. A group portrait of three generations of the same family sitting on the porch of their farmhouse establishes the price they are about to pay for their nationality. This is followed by a series of photographs of men packing tools and then dickering with Anglo buyers over the price of a harrow. Lee probably found his most ironic images in San Benito County, where he created a photo essay on several Japanese farm families enjoying their last meal before evacuation. To underscore their loyalty, he went to some lengths recording the nature of their last meal in freedom: hot dogs and apple pie![60]

Lee ended his coverage once the Japanese left the relocation centers. But Lange continued to follow them into the Owens Valley, at the eastern base of the Sierra Nevada, where they faced the challenge of growing crops at Manzanar Internment Camp. Photographing at Manzanar on three separate occasions beginning in July, Lange placed familiar scenes in a new context while demonstrating the innovative labor

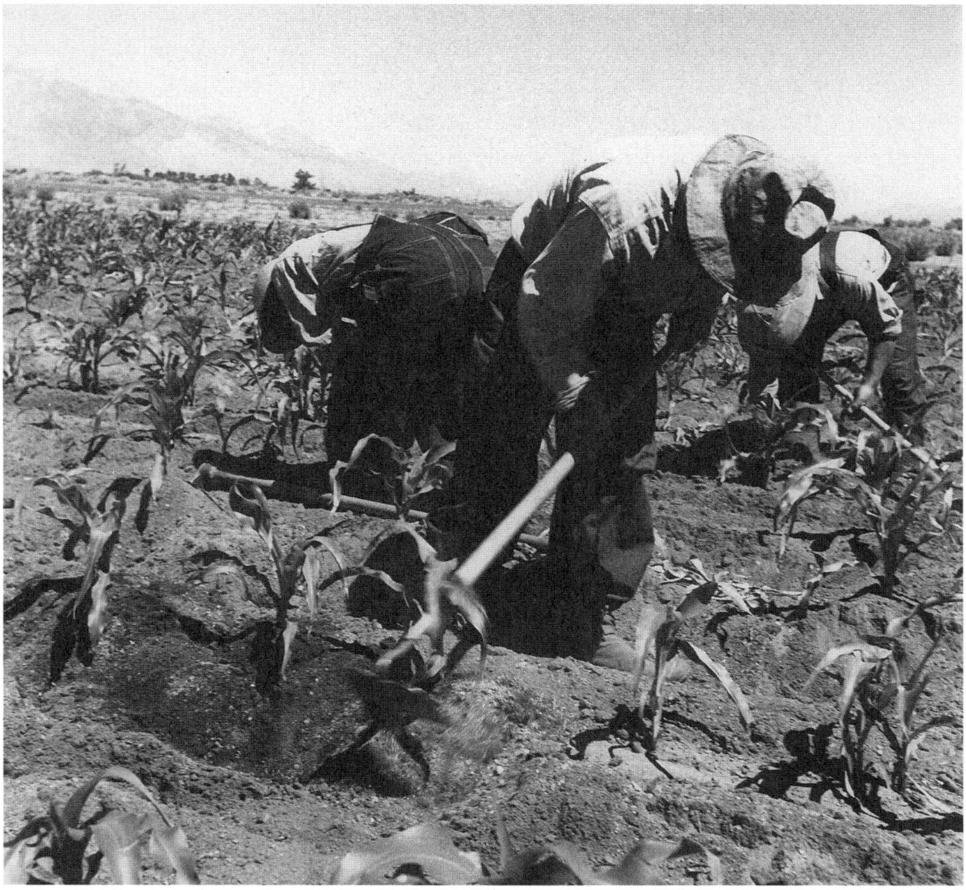

Japanese internees hoeing corn at Manzanar relocation center, July 1942, photograph by Dorothea Lange. Courtesy of War Relocation Authority Collection, National Archives.

exerted in order to survive. Focusing on work developing several large, commercial-scale, irrigated vegetable farms, her images capture scenes of men and women in the fields harvesting lettuce, chard, and various other greens in what was obviously a harsh environment. Hardly celebratory, some of Lange's images of hot, dusty barracks and of crews bent over swinging hoes clearly suggest the unpleasant nature of farmwork in a prison environment. One particularly arresting shot, taken from a low angle, records the backbreaking toil of a crew moving through cornfields, chopping weeds at midday under the blazing July sun. Another shows Japanese in a greenhouse where the shadows cast by the wooden roof slats fall across the men like bars in a jail, so that they appear to be wearing prison stripes. Although Lange failed to photograph the communal toilets, which caused many women inmates considerable embarrassment and distress, that was probably because she realized she could not get them past the censors. One photograph that she made of a wretched outhouse was impounded and not released to the general public until after the war.[61]

By the fall of 1942, Lange was again fully engaged in photographing farmworkers. No longer marginalized by Stryker, she maintained contact with conditions in the fields, even as she probably believed that she was approaching the end of the most vitally important phase of her career. Over the past seven years, Lange had been at the center of a chain reaction of fortuitous events. She had witnessed and recorded one of the great mass population movements in American history. She had played a key role awakening the public to conditions in the fields. And she had made people's lives better. With her images, Lange furnished visual evidence leading to the creation of the FSA labor camp program. While participating in one of the great collaborative efforts in photography, she had helped forge a new photographic sensibility. Few other photographers, with the possible exception of Lewis Hine, had made a greater contribution to documentary photography. Although she had not invented the term, Lange, through her personal example and the example of her work, sharply defined it. Although humble about her achievements, Lange knew that she stood at the center of these developments, that, whether she liked it or not, she was the acknowledged twentieth-century master of the documentary genre.[62]

Just as Lange thought it had all come to an end, she found herself documenting the Japanese farmworkers being relocated to internment camps. Surveying these dramatic events, she might have thought it all a dream: her divorce from Dixon, her marriage to Taylor, her evolution as a photographer, the travels, the family duties, the struggles with Stryker. A less-experienced human being might have concluded that nothing was left to see and record. Encountering the world as if it were an allegory, Lange was one of those individuals who both live history and record it. She was one of those photographers whom the historian Michael Lesy describes as passing through life "as if they were pilgrims on a journey, looking for signs." If she had learned one great lesson from her years in the fields, it was that something new was always just around the corner. The rural environment had a way of surprising even the most experienced observer. Just when someone thought that circumstances had played out, something new would pop up and set in motion a chain of events. This was certainly what had happened almost miraculously to the farm labor force. Whenever it seemed to peter out, whenever it seemed as if all of the possibilities had been exhausted, a new group entered the fields to save the industry from a labor shortage. Now, under wartime pressures, this was about to happen again. The long sequence of catastrophes, dislocations, and tragedies afflicting the state's farmworkers was about to take yet another odd twist. And a new group of photographers would step forward to document it.[63]

III

THE PERSISTENCE OF DOCUMENTARY PHOTOGRAPHY

1942–1965

14

Photographs of Truth and Propaganda

Documentary Continuity and Perversion

While Lange toiled away at Manzanar, Okies and Mexican American farmworkers left the fields for better-paying defense industry jobs or service in the armed forces. Growers noticed the exodus and immediately set in motion a plan that would open up yet another chapter in the history of photographers and farmworkers. Exploiting the wartime crisis, leaders of the American Farm Bureau Federation, the Vegetable Growers Association, the Amalgamated Sugar Company, the National Cotton Council, and other farm groups claimed that a severe labor shortage was placing the harvest in peril. Without a new source of labor, the groups' ability to expand food and fiber production and meet wartime demands would be severely curtailed. After it became apparent that the Mexican government would not allow American growers to recruit their own workers in Mexico, as they had done during World War I, the growers agreed to accept Mexican workers whom the Mexican government would provide to the United States on a temporary basis. Lobbying efforts went forward with great speed. On July 20, 1942, after reassuring the Mexican government regarding the rights of its citizens, the United States signed EAS 278, an executive agreement, not a treaty, thus avoiding confirmation by the United States Senate. Officially referred to as the Emergency Farm Labor Program but generally known as the bracero program, EAS 278 became effective on August 4. It would shape life and labor in the fields for the next generation.[1]

Insulating growers from competing for labor in the domestic labor market, the bracero program was championed not only as an essential component of the wartime effort but also as a positive benefit to poverty-stricken Mexico. The agreement contained several provisions to protect braceros: their round trip, subsistence en route, adequate housing and minimum wages once in the United States, and a minimum number of working days at "the prevailing wage," to be set through public hearings. Because Mexican officials distrusted big growers and insisted that the United States act as the formal employer, the Farm Security Administration was pressed into service.

Besides signing contracts as the employer and then contracting out the workers to various farmers and farm organizations, the FSA also took charge of transporting the men northward from Mexico and then returning them at the end of their contracts. Elated growers and government officials in California laid elaborate plans to welcome the first contingent of men. But it was a different story in Mexico.

Announcement of the bracero program attracted thousands of campesinos to Mexico City and overwhelmed government offices. Few people in the United States were in a position to document the chaos. That task fell to a group of highly politicized, completely independent photographers who had never heard of Dorothea Lange, had no idea of the FSA's work, and had never heard of documentary photography. Familiar with European photographic practices (including the use of the Leica) and unconstrained by wartime priorities, they veered away from their counterparts north of the border. Photographing the farmworker story for the first time through Mexican eyes, they recorded some of the opening scenes of the next great mass population movement into California agriculture. Every bit as dramatic as the Dust Bowl migration, the bracero program brought thousands of men north to work the fields, kept wages low, impeded unionization, and dominated the farm labor relations for the next two decades.[2]

Mexican photographers stepped into the picture for the first time on a cool, rainy morning in mid-August 1942, when the Secretariat of Labor in Mexico City opened offices to select *aspirantes* (candidates) for the bracero labor program. Charged with registering men, assigning quotas from each Mexican state, and creating the Campesino Savings Fund (a kind of Social Security wage deduction system), the secretariat was almost immediately overrun by what newspapers described as "a variegated multitude of potential immigrants," most of them unemployed for the past six months. On the first day, 104 *aspirantes* signed up. But in the following week, their numbers grew almost exponentially, until thousands of *aspirantes,* many of them arriving at 4 A.M. and sleeping on the street, had arranged themselves in long lines stretching around the Secretariat of Labor to López Street and Juárez Avenue. Waiting there in the rain, they were a sight to behold, and their plight made front-page headlines in the Mexico City newspapers.[3]

As their numbers grew, an unusual group of photographers arrived at the Secretariat of Labor building. These photographers were Spanish immigrants who belonged to a photographic collective known as the Hermanos Mayo. The collective was originally composed of brothers from two different families: the Fernández brothers, Francisco (Paco), Julio, and Cándido, and the Cubillo brothers, Faustino and Pablo. These men had fought and photographed in the Spanish Civil War, during which they adopted their nom-de-guerre, the Hermanos Mayo, after Faustino Cubillo had published photographs of the Guardia Civil (Civil Guards) attacking and killing workers during a May Day march in Madrid. Remembered as the "May Day photos," the images provided a good cover for the five brothers, who protected themselves, their families, and comrades from reprisals by calling themselves the Hermanos Mayo—the brothers of May Day.

After the defeat of the Spanish Republicans, the Hermanos Mayo had been forced into concentration camps in France. In March 1939, Julio Fernández was captured at the port of Alicante and imprisoned for several years. Pablo Cubillo remained on the run in Spain and France. Following numerous indignities, three of the Hermanos Mayo—Faustino Cubillo and Cándido and Francisco Fernández—left for Mexico with a group of sixteen hundred other refugees. They arrived in Veracruz onboard the ship *Sinaia* on June 13, 1939. Penniless, with little more than their precious Leicas and the clothes on their backs, the brothers were welcomed by the liberal political environment of Mexican president Lázaro Cárdenas and almost immediately found work as a kind of nascent photo agency. Within a few weeks they had reconstituted their collective as the Foto Hermanos Mayo and began covering Mexico for a wide spectrum of establishment and left-wing publications. Because most of the major Mexican illustrated magazines, such as *Hoy* and *Rotofoto,* paid scant attention to the working class and preferred to glorify industrial development, the Hermanos Mayo had a free run of the factories and countryside. Documenting social struggles that others would not or could not cover, they became the first to use 35-millimeter cameras for Mexican news publications that had heretofore accepted only images recorded on large-format negatives.[4]

When *aspirantes* mobbed the Secretariat of Labor, one of the Hermanos Mayo stationed himself on the street. Although the identity of that brother remains a mystery (because the Hermanos Mayo archive does not link negatives with individual photographers), he went about his business in a highly professional manner. Like any good photographer, the first thing he did was to shoot an "establishing picture"—one that gave a sense of the larger scene. With the streets full of *aspirantes,* this was easy. Stepping to the far side of the street opposite the Secretariat of Labor, he photographed the men clogging the sidewalks, taking care to include large portions of the rain-soaked pavement and the labor building. Moving closer, he then put a human face on the crowd by making several portraits of small groups. Because many of the men lacked hats, he caught them protecting their heads from the rain with newspapers. Finally, he entered the Secretariat of Labor building, made his way to the second floor, poked his Leica out an open window, and made several shots of the *aspirantes* below. Obviously aware of his presence from his ground-level work, the *aspirantes* looked up. Most wore city clothes, including *zapatos de ciudad* (city shoes) rather than *sandalias* (rural sandals). Many smiled. At least five flashed the "V" sign or waved.[5]

Over the next few weeks, as the number of *aspirantes* grew into many thousands, the Hermanos Mayo followed the men everywhere they went. When authorities shifted processing from the Secretariat of Labor building to the National Stadium in the Colonia Roma section of Mexico City, the Hermanos Mayo photographers moved inside the processing center; a few days later when processing shifted to La Ciudadela, an old fortress in the center of the city, the Hermanos Mayo followed. Photographing long lines of *aspirantes* sitting before typists while they filled out forms and read or tried to read their contracts and then signed them, one of the Hermanos Mayo followed events with a sharp eye for the difficulties and tribulations of the bureaucratic process. Continuing to record the ordeal, he documented the *aspirantes* hunching over long tables in crowded, stifling rooms, then stripping naked and being probed, prodded, and tested during a series of medical examinations, and finally being subjected to X-rays and vaccinated against smallpox. Some of the most gripping images record groups of "eligible" *aspirantes* posing for photographs with coded identification tags pinned on their right shoulders.[6]

Because they were good press photographers with an eye for the larger picture, the Hermanos Mayo paid attention to all facets of the bracero story. Finding plenty to document outside the processing centers, they employed their Leicas to great advantage, often firing off strings of images, using telephoto lenses and green and yellow filters to better represent what they were witnessing. To obtain more spontaneous pictures of the *aspirantes* as they congregated in the parks or purchased food and drink from women vendors on the street around La Ciudadela, they avoided trying to gain the *aspirantes'* confidence. Given the huge turnover in *aspirantes,* the photographers saw no way of developing a sense of familiarity with them and struggled to overcome the perennial problems of excessive shyness, reserve, and even fear that the American photographer Paul Strand had faced earlier when photographing Mexican peasants.

Opting for trickery, one of the Hermanos Mayo concealed a camera in a box or bag and tripped the shutter with a cable release. But while he hoped to make candid

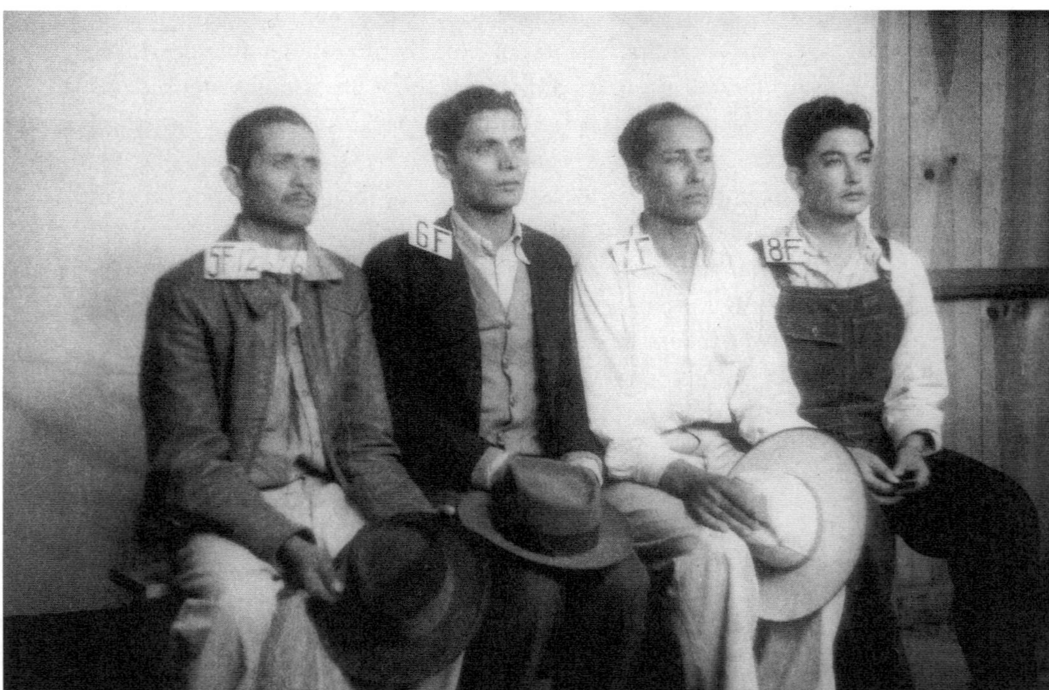

Men waiting to be processed as braceros, Mexico City, August 1942, photograph by the Hermanos Mayo. Courtesy of the Hermanos Mayo Collection, Archivo General de La Nación, Mexico City, and John Mraz.

pictures of men unaware that they were being photographed, he succeeded only in taking a series of not very interesting photographs. The Hermanos Mayo probably made their most dramatic pictures at the Buenaventura train station. Photographing the first groups of seven hundred men getting ready to leave, one of the Hermanos Mayo made gut-wrenching pictures of husbands and wives embracing and crying, men writing letters or dictating letters to public letter writers, and mothers handing babies to men leaning out the windows of train cars for one last parting kiss. But the Hermanos Mayo did not stop there. Providing images illustrating how the surge of *aspirantes* ruptured the contracting system, they paid special attention to the large number of men who became frustrated with bureaucratic delays, engaged in a number of street protests, and were driven away by police water cannons.[7]

Americans saw none of what the *aspirantes* were experiencing in Mexico. North of the border, a different and far more benevolent picture emerged entirely as the result of President Roosevelt's decision to create the Office for Emergency Management (OEM). The OEM took control of various preexisting government agencies and also generated new ones, including the Office of War Information (OWI). Quickly absorbing the remnants of Stryker's FSA photographic unit but leaving Stryker in charge of photographic operations, the OWI stripped the FSA of its probing documentary style and transformed it bodily into a kind of domestic propaganda agency. To disseminate its work, the OWI published *Victory, Photo Review,* and several other magazines that aimed to reach audiences in Europe and North America. To obtain images for the propaganda effort, Stryker hired several photographers, including Dorothea Lange. But he was no longer engaged in mapping out a territory of fundamental social change. Now he was a propagandist for the war effort. Already his guidelines to Lange and other OWI photographers were very different from those he had issued earlier. John Vachon would later comment that Stryker wanted only pictures of "the happy American worker." In a detailed February 19, 1942, memorandum to Russell Lee and Arthur Rothstein, "in particular," Stryker described what he needed:

> People—*we must have at once.*
> Pictures of men, women and children who appear as if they really believed in the U.S. Get people with a little spirit. Too many in our file now paint the U.S. as an old person's home and that just about everyone is too old to work and too malnourished to care much what happens. (Don't misunderstand the above. FSA is still interested in the lower income groups and we want to continue to photograph this group.) We particularly need young men and women who work in our factories, the young men who build our bridges, roads, dams, and large factories . . . more contented-looking old couples—women sewing, men reading . . . coming from church; at picnics, at meetings.[8]

As the program got under way, the OWI sent Fritz Henle to Mexico City to obtain photographs illustrating the positive side of the bracero program. Henle was an outstanding German photographer. On assignment for a German shipping company, he had traveled to Asia late in 1934, where he remained for two years while photographing two books on China and Japan. On returning home, he quickly saw that it was no place for an aspiring photographer interested in doing photo essays on people and social problems. With the blessings of the Gestapo, he managed to leave Germany for the United States, where it was assumed that he would photograph industrial settings and return home with pictures useful to the Third Reich. With no such intentions, Henle discovered Mexico in 1936. Welcomed by the Mexican government, he instantly initiated plans for a photo essay stressing the country's centuries-old cultures. Henle became a staff photographer for *Life* magazine in 1937. He joined the staff of the OWI in 1942, shortly after becoming a naturalized citizen of the United States. All of this made him a logical choice for any assignment in Mexico.[9]

Every bit as good as the work done by the Hermanos Mayo, Henle's photographs are gritty, disturbing, and exactly what the OWI did not want. Henle spent much of

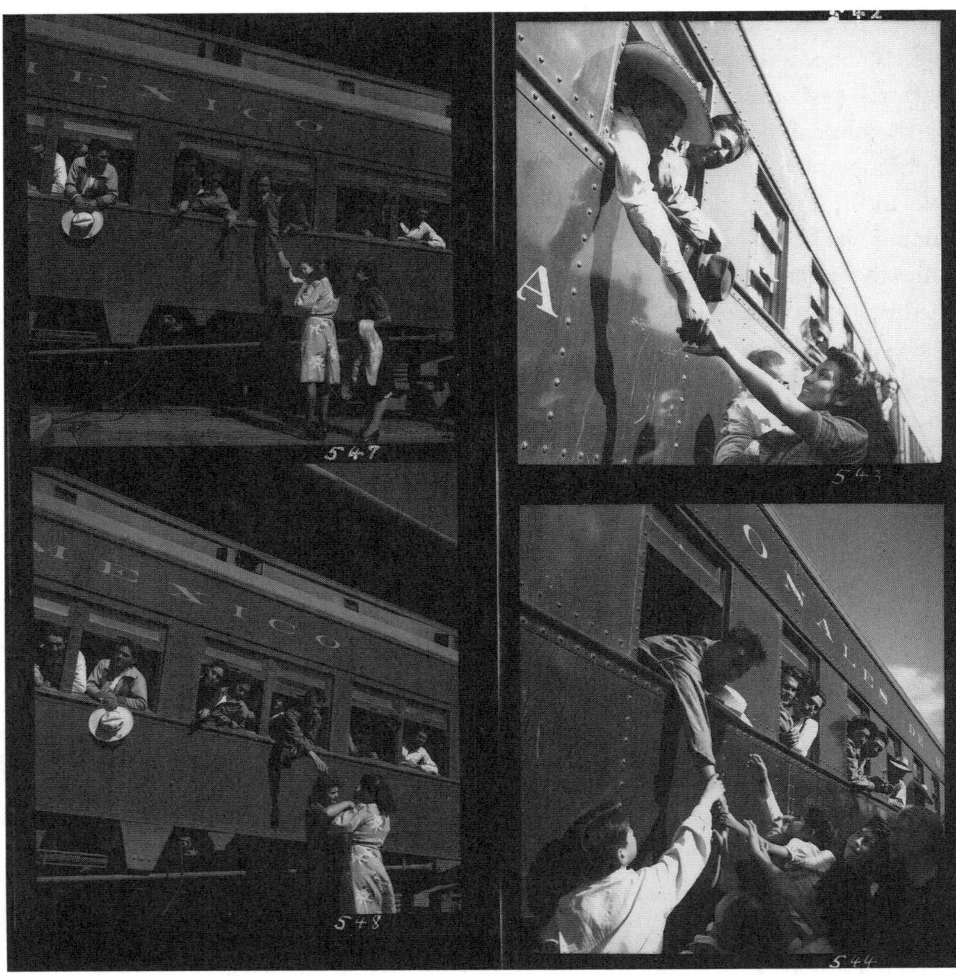

Braceros departing Buenavista train station, in Mexico City, for the United States, 1943, photograph by Fritz Henle. Courtesy of Maria Henle/the Estate of Fritz Henle.

his time inside the processing stations documenting the men filling out forms and waiting in long lines to have their applications typed up. These picturers ooze empathy and suggest a recruitment program resembling a cattle call. Apparently the OWI did not want anyone to see Henle's pictures of men sleeping in the streets outside assembly centers or *aspirantes* being probed, interrogated, and vaccinated en masse before finally embarking for California. Only those images documenting the departure of the first contingent of five hundred braceros from Buenavista train station in Mexico City on September 1 interested OWI officials. But even these went beyond the bounds of what the OWI wanted to show.

To obtain what it wanted, the OWI created a happy and hopeful image from the larger and more tragic picture. A little cropping eliminated hundreds of men hanging from the train car windows and isolated a single family, in which men shake hands with friends and relatives, throw kisses to mothers, daughters, and wives, and wave to everyone as they set out to save the U.S. harvests. No bracero weeps. Mothers and *abuelas* (grandmothers) smile proudly. Children reach to their fathers for a last touch. Everyone is well dressed. Some braceros even wear ties. Poverty, desperation, and the pain of departure are out of the frame. Untainted with sadness, the image bypasses the ordeal of the processing centers. "These workers can afford to leave their families," wrote one enthusiastic supporter of the program. "They are not going to be stranded, and they can make good wages by themselves."[10]

One week later and one thousand miles north, Dorothea Lange waited for the braceros to arrive at a Sacramento train station. The whole affair was going to be stage-managed. Not fully understanding what she was documenting, Lange did not approach the assignment as critically as she had those in the past. Lange's images hardly hint at the tearful partings, bureaucratic humiliations along the way, and trepidations of arrival. There is no sense that the railroad cars smelled of sweat and continuous habitation or that people are arriving at the end of a long trip that began in isolated peasant villages. Lange's braceros smile and wave. They listen to officials greeting them with welcoming speeches, and they lean out the windows of railroad cars displaying coins or holding their fingers in the "V" sign for victory.[11]

Twenty years earlier, Lange had tacked a quotation from Francis Bacon onto her darkroom door:

> The contemplation of things as they are
> Without error or confusion
> Without substitution or imposture
> Is itself a nobler thing
> Than a whole harvest of invention.[12]

But at Sacramento on September 6, 1942, Lange set aside or abandoned her naturally inquisitive perspective and engaged in outright propaganda. One of the greatest ironies of her distinguished career is that when her images appeared in *Survey Graphic, Victory,* and other magazines with captions describing how braceros were arriving "to produce more food for victory," they helped lubricate public acceptance of a scandalous farm labor importation program that even then was being condemned as cheaper and more profitable than slavery.[13]

Missing from these OWI images are all of the great themes of farmworker history. Gone is the emphasis on the problems and dislocations of the Great Depression. In their place, OWI photographers emphasized harmony and national purpose. Accompanying the change in emphasis was a change in attitude. Photographers who just a few years earlier had gone about their business as an act of passion, if not compassion, now did so as an act of patriotism integral to advancing the war effort. Committed to exposing truth and pathos, a photographer like Lange must have found such goals hard to stomach. But if the assignment caused her inner turmoil, she never said so. Failure to publicly comment did not mean that she was pleased with the way independent photography was being subsumed by the war effort. Many years would pass before colleagues such as John Vachon admitted that many of the images he made for the OWI looked depressingly "like those of the Soviet Union."[14]

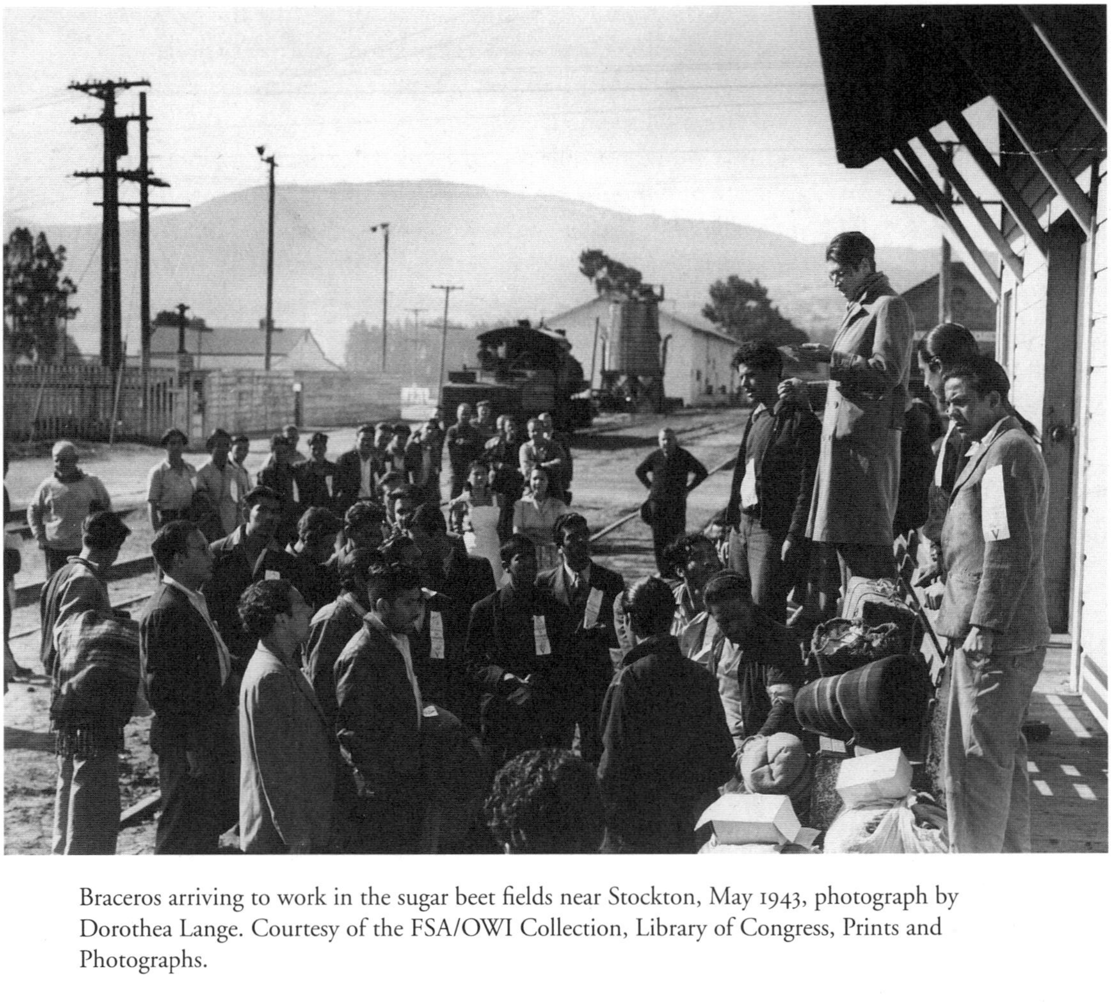

Braceros arriving to work in the sugar beet fields near Stockton, May 1943, photograph by Dorothea Lange. Courtesy of the FSA/OWI Collection, Library of Congress, Prints and Photographs.

Contrasting starkly with what the Hermanos Mayo were producing south of the border, U.S. government photographic coverage of braceros signaled an important change in the relationship between farmworkers and photographers. With socially oriented documentary photography all but gone, it was a relatively simple matter for industry flacks and promoters alike to build on this trend. Taking the lead in this effort, F. Hal Higgins created his own take on the braceros arriving at Sacramento on September 6. Covering the event for *California Farmer,* he photographed virtually side by side with Lange. But unlike Lange, he was not there to cover what he hoped would be a temporary wartime expedient. Higgins had his own agenda. An admirer of the Associated Farmers, who hated what he regarded as communist-dominated agricultural unions, Higgins had been a great champion of labor importation programs since the mid-1930s, and he intended to portray the bracero program as a positive good that should be expanded and made permanent. To advance that goal, he spent several weeks following the braceros not only in Sacramento but also in Stockton, Woodland, and Salinas.[15]

In each location, Higgins did more than photograph braceros pouring off trains. He spent considerable time in and around labor camps and shot roll after roll of film documenting well-staged events: men being welcomed at the gates, men marching off to church for Mass, men enjoying hearty meals in clean, sanitary, spacious quarters. He also made hundreds of pictures in the fields, including some of the most effective shots of sugar beet workers stooped over in the shape of a question mark while bringing in the harvest. Unlike Henle's work, which largely remained unseen, Higgins's photographs were published widely in newspapers and farm magazines across the country, where they represented the bracero program as a positive good. Such images made it a relatively easy matter for caption writers to amplify the message with descriptions of well-equipped camps where men enjoyed recreational activities and access to health clinics and spent their evenings "studying English, their Sundays getting acquainted with America."[16]

As wartime demands grew, photographers who had once been champions of California farmworkers looked the other way. Their willingness to gloss over exploitation in the name of doing their duty reached its apogee the following March, when OWI photographer Jack Delano photographed the citrus industry of Southern California. Having just ridden two thousand miles in the caboose of a train, photographing "a big transportation story" for the war effort, Delano reached San Bernardino with several rolls of Kodachrome, which he used to document the grading and packing operations at the Southern California Fruit Growers Exchange. Oddly, he never left the premises to venture into the nearby groves, where hundreds of newly arrived braceros were harvesting oranges.[17]

Of other government photographers, only those employed by the Department of Agriculture continued to shoot in the fields. Since the mid-1930s, the Department of Agriculture had employed hundreds of people to generate favorable publicity. Photographers played a key part in this effort. Producing countless images of an industrious and proud rural America employing the latest information and up-to-date technology to make a good living, they regarded the harsh conditions of impoverished rural communities as largely outside the scope of their responsibilities. Already disinclined to expose grievous faults and failures or to shed light on problems, they did nothing to advance society's understanding of farmworkers. When they photographed field labor in 1943, it was largely to glorify rural life with more images of smiling braceros washing up after work or sitting down to dinner in surroundings indistinguishable from a summer camp. Department of Agriculture publications like *Fair Is Our Land,* a large-format picture book, further amplify the theme of "a peaceful America—staunch, serene, and comforting" with over three hundred pastoral scenes of bountiful harvests, prosperous farm families, and contented field hands. All was well in such publications. Not one image even hints at poverty, struggle, or exploitation.[18]

Continuing over the next year and a half, this happy imagery culminated in the lavishly illustrated *Report of the Emergency Farm Labor Project of the Agricultural Extension Service, 1943–1945.* Published in 1945 by the University of California in conjunction with the United States Department of Agriculture, *A Report of the Emergency Farm Labor Project* features photographs of "girl volunteers" being trained to pack fruit; smiling and happy milkers in Los Angeles County; industrious prisoners of war being taught to prune fruit trees in Sonoma County; Jamaicans picking citrus around Riverside; Mexican American families picking prunes in the Santa Clara Valley; and soldiers harvesting onions on three-day passes. Out of fifty-one photographs, three depict braceros, all of them sporting new sombreros and looking like they had just come from central casting. The largest and most important photographs fill a half page. One has a group of county extension agents gathered around a table in front of a large graph illustrating harvest labor requirements in Tulare County. Completely staged and apparently lit with an off-camera strobe, this concocted photograph follows equally unbelievable images of people perusing bulletin boards looking for farmwork. In the most fantastic of these images, the man in a well-dressed married couple standing at the counter of a farm labor office is captioned as saying, "I would like to have a job with housing for my family."[19]

About the only place in California where photographers continued to critically explore life and labor in the fields between 1943 and 1944 was at Manzanar Internment Camp. Lange and a half dozen other photographers, including visiting Associated Press photographers and government photographers employed by the WRA, worked at Manzanar. One of these photographers was an internee who photographed surreptitiously: Toyo Miyatake. He had been a successful portrait and wedding photographer in the Little Tokyo section of Los Angeles. At Manzanar, he drew on his years of experience and extensive knowledge of photographic technology to construct a handmade camera. Taking it out when guards were not looking, he used it to record life and labor in the camp and surrounding fields. Miyatake photographed clandestinely for nine months in violation of military regulations. After being discovered, he was allowed to continue after the camp's newly appointed director, Ralph Merritt, assigned a white camp worker to release the shutter once Miyatake had set up his camera. When

Merritt further eased restrictions, Miyatake sent for his equipment, built a darkroom in the ironing building of Block 30, and continued photographing daily work routines (as well as weddings, funerals, and the departure of men for the armed services) as part of an internee-run Manzanar cooperative until he was released from the camp in 1945.[20]

Miyatake's agricultural images stress order and beauty: a Buddhist shrine in a well-tended garden, Manzanar-grown produce in the window of a shop in a nearby town. When focusing on field labor he often included barbed wire fencing and watchtowers. None of his photographs is stage-managed. When a group of young Nisei paused and leaned on a truck while delivering vegetables to the camp mess hall, Miyatake snapped a picture portraying the men as fatigued haulers and packers of row crops, resigned to their work. Hardly taking pride in what they were doing, Miyatake's farm hands readily reveal the sense of deprivation they felt at having to grow their own vegetables in an effort to overcome a non-Japanese jail diet larded heavily with bologna, sauerkraut, shredded wheat, and potatoes. Miyatake reiterated the themes of irony and paradox in a portrait of a chrysanthemum grower, taking a close view that underscores beauty amid ugliness. But at least one of Miyatake's agricultural photographs made a not-so-subtle political statement. Framing the camp barracks through a tractor wheel, Miyatake composed the scene in such a way that the wheel spokes suggest

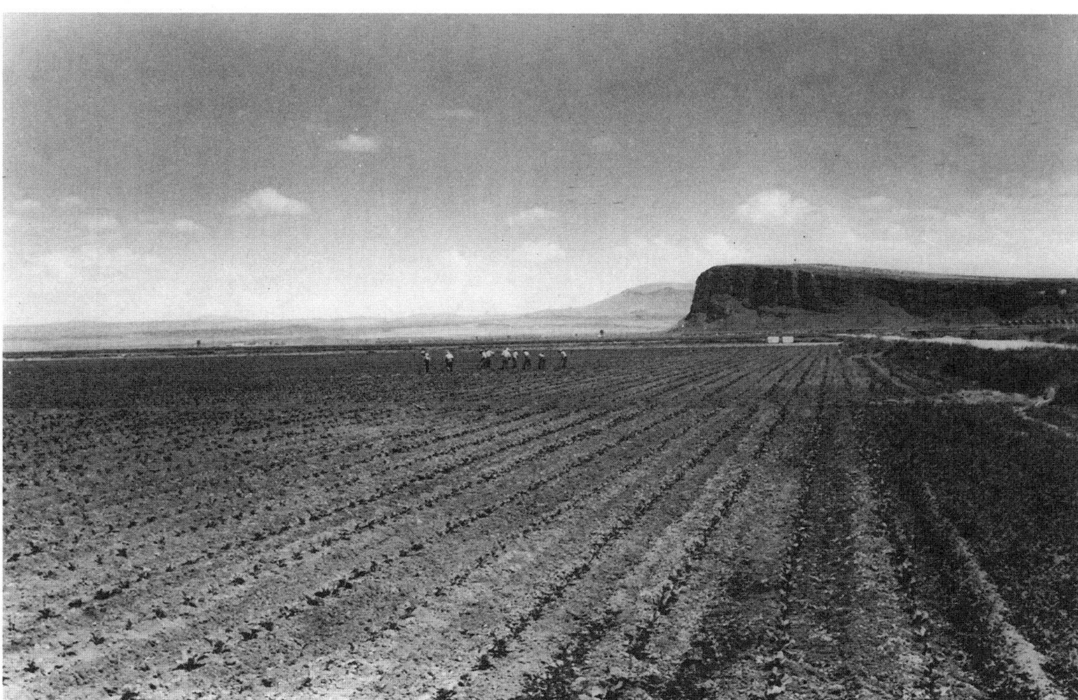

Japanese internees transplanting cabbage from hotbeds at Tule Lake Internment Center, June 24, 1944, photograph by J. D. Bigelow. Courtesy of the War Relocation Authority Collection, National Archives.

the bars of a prison cell. Captioned simply, "from Our World," the image was published in *Valediction,* the Manzanar High School yearbook for 1945.[21]

Ansel Adams also photographed farmworkers at Manzanar. Too old to serve in the armed forces, Adams had been searching for some other way to help with the war effort when Ralph Merritt, an old friend and Sierra Club alley, suggested that he focus on Japanese internees. Adams would later recall his work at Manzanar as "a photographic project where [he] would interpret the camp and its people, their daily life, and their relationship to their community and their environment." Adams financed the project himself, accepting only food and lodging during long visits in the fall of 1943 and spring and summer of 1944.[22]

Willing to excuse the government's relocation program, Adams insisted that Manzanar was "only a rocky wartime *detour* on the road of American citizenship." From this premise he developed a sympathetic and upbeat perspective stressing that the Japanese were engaged in productive agricultural work. To accomplish that, Adams avoided the barbed wire and guard towers out on the farms and discovered perspectives

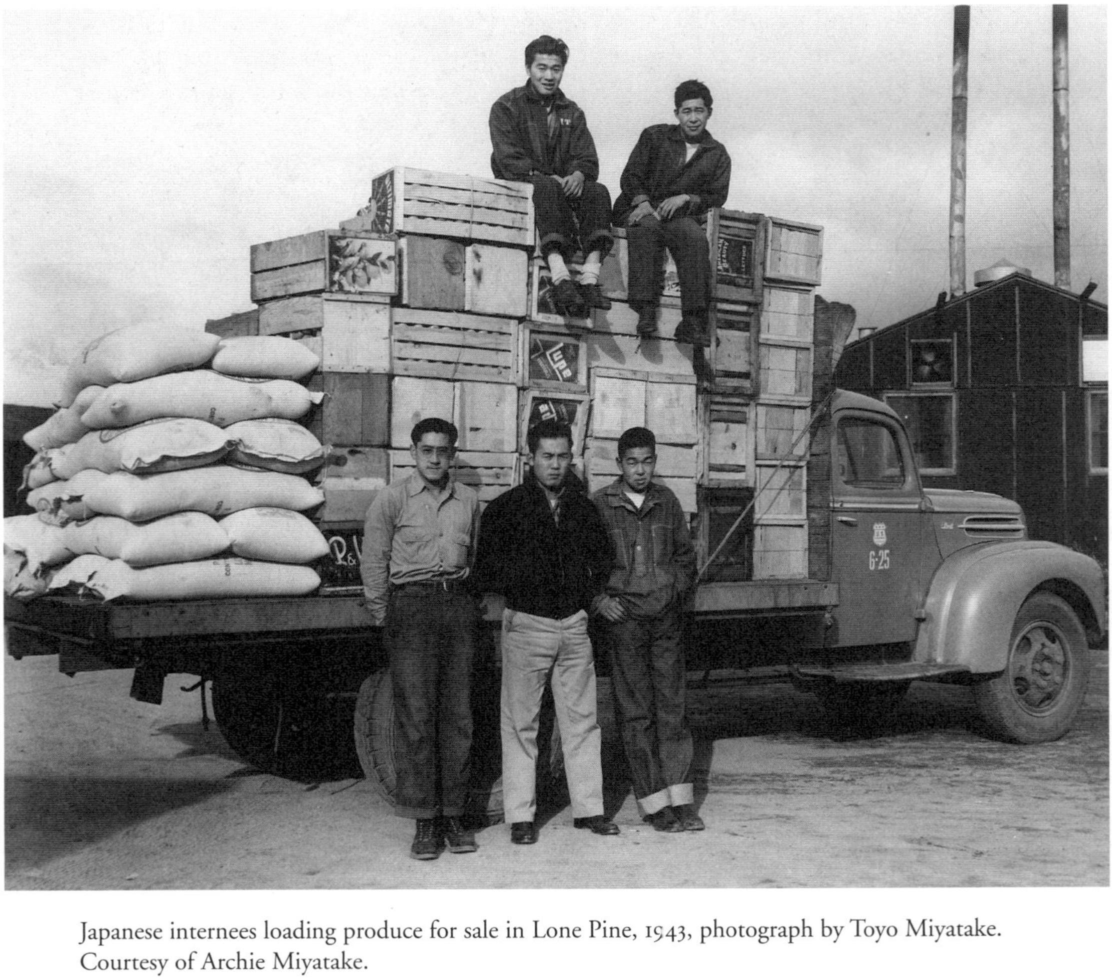

Japanese internees loading produce for sale in Lone Pine, 1943, photograph by Toyo Miyatake. Courtesy of Archie Miyatake.

that transformed fields full of captive Japanese workers into inspirational landscapes where people appeared (much as they had in photographs before the 1930s) as incidental elements amid scenes of enduring, even breathtaking, beauty. No single image more clearly demonstrates this approach than a photograph of the North Farm. Taken from an elevated location, possibly on top of his car in the early morning light, the image creates what is in essence a grand panorama in which industrious Japanese harvest and pack lettuce. Without a caption identifying the workers as internees, a viewer might easily mistake the image as a sublime modernist vision of commercial agriculture. There is no hint that the workers are engaged in unfree labor.[23]

Publishing his work as *Born Free and Equal: The Story of Loyal Japanese Americans,* Adams presented his essay of sixty-six images as a kind of yearbook portrait, encouraging a sense of personal familiarity. Introducing it with a sentimental shot of a young internee gazing across the expansive landscape of cultivated fields spreading to the base of the eastern Sierra Nevada, Adams seemed to suggest that the natural setting of the Owens Valley worked to mitigate the difficulties experienced by relocation and internment. The claim would have seemed ridiculous to men and women swathed in bandannas as they struggled against the choking dust and desert heat. But Adams had more to say. He dismissed his own motivations and faith in the official version of internment and ignored the excessively sentimental nature of his majestic views. Despite the stereotypical stoicism of his camp portraits (including one of Miyatake and his family), Adams nevertheless maintained an independent objective:

> Throughout this book I want the reader to feel he has been with me in Manzanar, has met some of the people, and has known the mood of the center and its environment—thereby drawing his own conclusions—rather than impose upon him any doctrine or advocate any sociological action. I have intentionally avoided the sponsorship of governmental or civil organizations . . . because I wish to make this work a strictly personal concept and expression.[24]

Not everyone found Adams's photographic essay to be uplifting. When Adams hung an exhibition of his Manzanar work at the Museum of Modern Art in New York, museum board members objected to a large panel quoting the Fourteenth Amendment, guaranteeing due process. Canceling the exhibition twice, they forced Adams to remove the offending panel and retitle his exhibit from "Born Free and Equal" to "Manzanar: Photographs by Ansel Adams of Loyal Japanese at the American Relocation Center." Large audiences attended the exhibition, which had to be extended beyond the closing date. Internees also seemed pleased and purchased several hundred copies of the book at the Manzanar camp store. Only Lange seemed dissatisfied. But while finding the exhibition a shameful underpinning of the government point of view, she did nothing to improve the picture.[25]

Over the next three years, documentary coverage of farmworkers in California all but ceased. Adams returned to his environmental work, and Lange stayed close to her home in Berkeley, devoting the last year of the war to documenting the booming wartime shipyards in Richmond. After the end of the war, she shifted her attention to the birth of the United Nations in San Francisco. Also moving on to new subjects, Fritz Henle left the OWI in 1945 and joined the staff of *Harper's Bazaar* magazine, where he shot high fashion for the next five years. On the home front, magazines had little use for documentary work. Dramatic combat images and war propaganda, and eventually the awesome images of the atomic bomb explosions and Nazi concentration camps, war crimes trials, and the start of the confrontation with the Soviet Union, pushed aside images of ordinary people. At the end of the war, newspapers and journals featured pictures of a devastated Europe and Japan. Of those photographers active among farmworkers at the beginning of World War II, only the Hermanos Mayo continued to photograph in the fields when the war ended. By then they had developed a large and complicated essay illustrating how Mexican contract laborers moved quietly, cheaply, and efficiently into the fields of California and the Southwest. They also began to focus on the plight of *aspirantes* who had headed north for the border by foot and boxcar as undocumented workers. Completely unknown north of the border, their work would remain largely unseen for the next half century.[26]

A humanistic concern for farmworkers and the impulse to incite change did not resume north of the border until 1946, when American combat photographers returned from duty in World War II. Some of the bravest and most experienced photographers in the country, they were also among the most creative. Whether serving with the Combat Camera Unit of the Army Air Force, the Combat Photography Section of the Navy, or any of several other military photographic operations, they loved their photographic duties, despite or perhaps because of the dangers, and at war's end, they returned home energized and driven to do their best in peace. Resuming their careers while working for the great mass-circulation magazines, some moved into abstract and personal work. Others followed a variety of conservative activism, asserting that no Americans were forgotten or "no-account" people and that the country was on the path to becoming a truly progressive, cultured, and democratic society. For a few, however, this line of inquiry—largely centered on white, middle-class families—never quite squared with what they saw, and they set about probing the underclass and its struggles.[27]

Many of these photographers cited Dorothea Lange as a source of inspiration. But here the parallels ended. Working in the postwar years, they encountered a far different environment. Gone was the reform impulse that had sustained documentary photography during the Great Depression. Preoccupied with a return to normalcy, Cold War America did not welcome humanistic photographic inquiry. This was a time when a chill fell over critical photography. Campaigns to uncover communists, laws aimed at communist political activity, and the growth of loyalty programs, blacklisting, and FBI surveillance all stifled the once vibrant documentary impulse, generating new ideological considerations and challenges that rapidly altered old ideals and made art itself a suspect. Any continued documentation of California farmworkers required strength of conviction and passion on the part of the photographers. And yet photographers did continue. A tenacious and talented group persevered in this environment and photographed with all of their ideology, without any governmental support. At a time when everything seemed to conspire against them, they produced an unusually strong and enduring body of work that contradicted the idealized American dream of equality, justice, and prosperity, somehow recapturing some of the momentum lost during the war and, in a few cases, going far beyond anything done by Dorothea Lange and other documentary pioneers.[28]

One of the most talented of these photographers was Max Yavno. A prematurely bald, brown-eyed, light-complexioned son of Russian immigrant parents who served as president of the Photo League of New York in 1938 and 1939, Yavno had spent the war in the Army Signal Corps. Because FBI memos stated that Yavno was "reported to be a Communist" and a member of a "the Film and Photo League, a Communistically-dominated organization," and had uncovered evidence that he had falsified his case record while employed as a welfare worker in New York City, Yavno had been denied advancement to officers' candidate school. After being discharged in 1945, he settled in Los Angeles and soon began photographing throughout Southern California. Regarding himself as a "social photographer," he applied for a Guggenheim Fellowship to document the Mexican American community around Los Angeles. Although he failed to obtain support, Yavno managed to launch the project when the UCLA Department of Sociology and Anthropology, with funds from the Haynes Foundation, hired him to photograph Hicks Camp, near El Monte, as well as other Chicano communities. The assignment brought him into direct contact with Anglo and Mexican American farmworkers, as well as braceros, at a key moment in the farmworker story.[29]

Just as Yavno began photographing, Congress allowed the statutory justification for the bracero program to expire. But very quickly, administrative action filled the void, and the government contract system was replaced by direct employer recruitment, supervised and assisted by the Immigration Service, without all of the red tape and safeguards of the wartime program. As the number of men coming north swelled to the tens of thousands and abuses multiplied, braceros soon became a class of uncomplaining, anonymous laborers. Easily dismissed after the harvests and hired on the cheap, braceros were at the complete mercy of growers. With contracting handled by private employers and the government abandoning its responsibility for upholding program guarantees, the bracero program reeked of exploitation. But with magazines like *Look, Life,* and *Fortune* disinclined to undertake a rehash of Depression-era photographic coverage that cut against the optimistic grain, Yavno had virtually no outlet for his work.[30]

With no one to please but himself, Yavno accepted farmworkers as he found them, and he found them everywhere. Many years later, Yavno explained to his biographer, Ben Maddow, how he went about his work. He had met the writer Bea Griffith, and she had asked him to illustrate her book, *American Me,* which called for plenty of images of Mexican Americans. Unlike Lange, who always tried to present a sense of dignity, Yavno followed no central goal. Working with a guide and translator, he photographed men at home, foremen relaxing in bunkhouse doorways, or buddies getting drunk under a shade tree on a Sunday afternoon near Chávez Ravine. Rather than emphasizing the productive labor of these men or their ordeal at the various recruiting and processing centers, his photographs capture the mood and quiet moments of farmworkers away from the fields.

Several of Yavno's best photographs are landscapes. One, a distant view of the Moorpark migrant camp, northwest of Los Angeles, is devoid of all people except for the men who are barely visible as they walk through the camp. Taken in 1946, the photograph is as much a study in beautiful surroundings and graphic layout as it

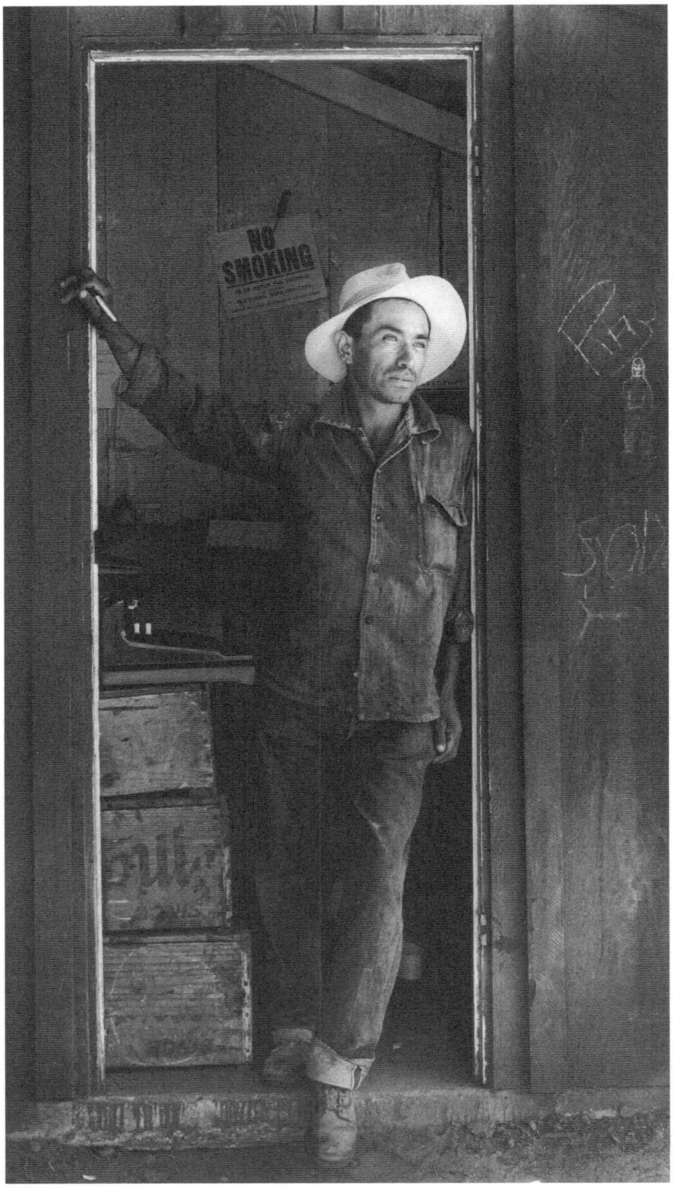

Mexican foreman, Imperial Valley, 1946, photograph by Max Yavno. Courtesy of the Max Yavno Collection. Copyright Center for Creative Photography, University of Arizona, Tucson.

is an exploration of the conditions under which farmworkers lived. Another camp photograph, taken the following year, centers on a young girl. Posed at a water faucet in the dappled shade of towering trees, with her dog lapping up water from a fountain and various campers relaxing in the background, she renders the scene easily mistakable for a children's summer camp.[31]

Aesthetically pleasing and beautifully printed on warm-tone paper, Yavno's farmworker photographs lacked hard news value. Although he exhibited them in galleries around Los Angeles, he could not snag the attention of any newspaper or magazine editors. And because he lacked the kind of government sponsorship that Lange had exploited or the relationship with the press that the Hermanos Mayo had enjoyed, he was unable to sustain his work for more than a few years. When the money ran out, Yavno shifted into commercial work. While maintaining a strong interest in farmworkers and photographing them intermittently for the next thirty years, Yavno would go on to build a reputation as an outstanding commercial photographer of spoons, catsup bottles, and the mundane wares of modern advertising.[32]

Working sporadically and largely at self-assignments, only a few other photographers were able to document the brutally efficient labor system that was developing in the agricultural districts. Two photographers who remained undaunted by their economic condition were Otto Hagel and Hansel Mieth. Since 1937, Mieth had been working as a staff photographer for *Life* magazine. After first working in California, she was stationed in Denver and Chicago before moving to New York City, which became a base of operations for her many assignments. Otto joined her there in 1939 and began shooting on a freelance basis.

One day in 1940, Robert Capa, the legendary Hungarian-born war photographer, who had established his reputation during the Spanish Civil War, stepped into Mieth's cubbyhole office at Forty-eighth Street. Capa explained that his visa had been canceled and that his only chance to remain in the country was to marry a U.S. citizen. Mieth asked if he had any prospects. He had plenty, including the beautiful Toni Sorel, a tall, dark-haired, high fashion model for *Vogue* and *Harper's Bazaar,* whom he had just met. Capa said Sorel would marry him in exchange for a year of dancing lessons. "Are you in love?" Mieth asked. "Well, that's another question," Capa said. "I don't want to discuss it."[33]

At this point in recalling the story, Hagel added his two bits. "If you can help anybody stay out of Hitler's grasp," he asserted, "you do it." Since neither Sorel nor Capa owned an automobile or even knew how to drive, Hagel and Mieth offered to act as chauffeurs in their marriage arrangements and agreed to marry at the same time. On March 28 they all headed off to Elkton, Maryland, where supposedly there was no waiting period to marry. It was a miserable, drizzling day, and they got a late start. On arriving, they discovered that, in fact, Maryland also had a three-day waiting period. Just then several sharpies appeared with a scheme to get around the restriction. For a fee, they would take the two women to a doctor who would declare them pregnant. That would allow them to get married the same day. Mieth and Sorel refused, but Capa insisted, saying, "I need to get married today." So they met the doctor, who, without even looking at them, slipped on his white coat, wrote a note on a piece of paper, and took a wad of cash from Hagel. When Hagel refused to stand before any minister, Capa begged him to relent. They wound up, instead, in front of an old justice of the peace and his sister, who became a witness. "He said a few words, which was supposed to be a marriage ceremony. I saw Otto reach in his back pocket again and pay him whatever he had to," recalled Mieth. Hagel again tried to pay off a bureaucrat to keep the marriage bureau open, but now he was out of money, and Capa was also broke. So Mieth and Sorel financed the marriage by emptying their purses down to the last penny.

On the drive back, no one was happy. Hagel was not driving very well. When he crossed over the center line, Mieth made him stop the automobile and took over the driving. When he got out to enter the passenger side, Mieth took off and left him standing in the rain. After Capa started screaming, Mieth turned the car around and went back. Hagel quietly got in and after a few minutes fell asleep. Moments later Capa tried to kiss his new wife, and they got into a little spat. Mieth stopped the car and broke up the fight. Then everyone sat on opposite sides of the car, and the three passengers fell asleep. At Greenwich Village, Mieth let Sorel out, then drove Capa to his hotel. The next day she left for Montana, and Hagel headed to Cuba on a six-month assignment that had been promised as a marriage gift by the editors at *Life,* thus allowing him to reenter the United States as a citizen. "That was my wedding night," Mieth told *Life* magazine photographer John Loengard a half century later.[34]

Midway through World War II, Hansel transferred to the San Francisco office of *Life* while Otto continued to freelance for *Fortune.* During this time they lived with Dorothea Lange and Paul Taylor. Toward the end of the war, Hansel's relations with Time, Inc., soured and the couple moved to a farm north of Santa Rosa. The challenges and rewards of their attempt to pursue a self-sufficient existence formed the basis of an ongoing essay, later published in *Life* as "The Simple Life." But it hardly satisfied their curiosity.[35]

As assignments dwindled to few and far between, the Hagels suggested stories to their editors. Deeply thought-out and well-researched, these stories increasingly focused on farming and food production. One of the most innovative centered on Huron, a small farmworker community on the west side of the San Joaquin Valley. In the late 1940s, Russell Giffen, "the California cotton king," had purchased fifty-four thousand acres around town, planted cotton to the horizon, and inspired a pack of other big farmers, including Southern Pacific and Standard Oil, to do the same. Fascinated by Huron's transformation every October and November, when ten thousand migrants arrived to work in the center of what amounted to the largest cotton plantation in the world, Otto began spending many weeks in town and its surrounding labor camps. Taking his time, Otto invested most of his energies in building up trust among the people he met. "For days the cameras would stay unpacked in their cases," recalled Hansel. "He mixed with people, talked, asked questions, sat around."[36]

When Hagel finally took out his cameras, he focused on the cluttered sidewalks, where he made a number of highly innovative photographs of men waiting outside hiring offices, searching through surplus clothes in the Salvation Army stores, and moving in and out of bathhouses. Resembling the street photography done by Bruce Davidson in New York City, these shots—many of them lit with off-camera strobes—captured farmworkers in unposed moments while they went about their business, largely unaware of the camera. Photographing on the surrounding labor camps, Otto devoted a great deal of time to recording racist signs proclaiming, "White People ONLY, BRADLEYS CAMP." Approaching the Livingston camp on the Schram ranch early one morning, Otto again recorded signs that read "For Whites Only." He then moved into the camp, climbed to the top of a vehicle, and photographed clumps of cotton pickers departing to the fields. Spending a great deal of time there, he was befriended by a family of cotton pickers in the camp. Again using an off-camera strobe, he recorded several generations of them gathered around the dinner table.

Hagel's most poignant photograph captures a one-legged field hand, Francisco Martínez. His caption, reminiscent of a Dorothea Lange field note, reads:

> Coming off the field upon the highway, a car sideswiped him and left him where he fell. In the morning the Highway Patrol found him and a hospital discharged him early without a prosthesis or medicine. Crutches he begged. Wooden leg he made from scrap he found by the side of the road and was now making his way picking cotton.[37]

Although stunning and remarkably complete, even timely in its depiction of an overnight farmworker boomtown, Hagel's essay on Huron was of little interest to magazine editors. It was the same situation, repeated countless times, for other photographers covering farmworkers at the end of World War II. Occasionally, photojournalists would document a group of farmworkers killed in a horrible bus crash, but their pictures were few and far between and never exerted much of an impact on the public or on government policy. Existing in a kind of netherworld, braceros in particular fell under the thumb of growers offering wages so low that thousands of domestic workers would not go into the fields. As a result, a kind of self-fulfilling prophecy developed. By employing braceros, growers could pay low wages. Because wages were so low, domestic workers avoided farm labor. And because so many domestic workers avoided farm labor, growers appealed for more braceros.[38]

With everything going their way, about the only thing that growers feared was an extended photographic exposé. They had little to worry about until the summer of 1947, when a former leader of the Southern Tenant Farmers Union (STFU), H. L. Mitchell, sent organizers for the National Farm Labor Union (NFLU) into the southern San Joaquin Valley. With a charter from the American Federation of Labor to form a national union of farmworkers, the NFLU set its sights on the state's 5,939 farms that were over one thousand acres in size. Mitchell himself would not handle the field operations. To serve as director of education and research, he chose Ernesto Galarza. Born the son of a campesino in Tepic, Mexico, Galarza had worked as a day laborer, harvest hand, and cannery worker before going on to earn a PhD at Columbia University. Now he would put those talents to work in maintaining a program of information, discussion, and group action. To head organizing activity, Mitchell chose Henry "Hank" Hansiwar, a World War II veteran and member of the United Automobile Workers (UAW) whom Mitchell had met earlier that year at the AFL convention in Memphis.[39]

When Galarza and Hansiwar headed west, they thought carefully about the challenge ahead of them. Almost from the beginning, what they saw and experienced convinced both men that photography and visual evidence would play a key role in the organizing campaign. Hansiwar came to this realization in a moment of great clarification while on his way to a union meeting in the Smokehouse Bar, in Lamont. Passing through the ramshackle collections of shacks, tents, and boxcars that housed farmworkers, he realized that pictures of substandard housing would certainly affect anyone with a conscience. "I did not own a camera then," he later recalled, "but I

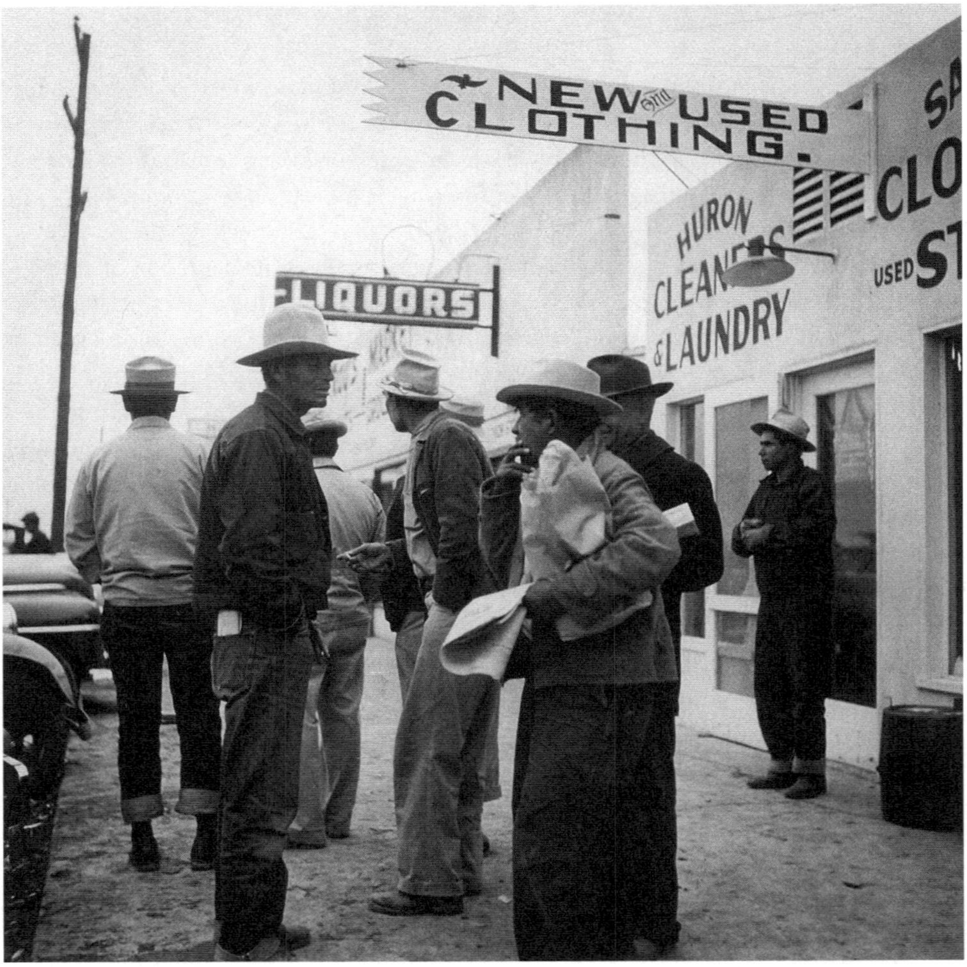

Street scene in Huron during the cotton harvest, 1946, photograph by Otto Hagel. Courtesy of the Otto and Hansel Mieth Hagel Collection. Copyright Center for Creative Photography, University of Arizona, Tucson, Arizona.

vowed to get one and to learn how to use it." For Galarza, photography seemed a logical tool, especially useful in winning public support for any boycott, should that tactic become necessary. He and other NFLU organizers began to pack cameras with them and made sure that every major event was documented.[40]

From the beginning, Galarza and Hansiwar thought photographically. Rather than diluting their efforts, they focused on DiGiorgio Farms. The largest and most modern farming operation in the state, DiGiorgio Farms were the creation of Joseph (Giuseppe) DiGiorgio. A short man with a big forehead, slightly beaked nose, clipped mustache, and thick lips set in a perpetual pucker, DiGiorgio was a living legend. Variously described as "the Kublai Khan of Kern County" and a kind of Italian mafioso "accustomed to controlling everything that was said, thought, and seen," DiGiorgio, known to close friends as Jojo, had come to New York from Corsica in 1888 to sell a consignment of lemons. Remaining in the United States, he worked first as an apprentice fruit jobber in New York and Baltimore, then moved into the banana business, where he acquired a detailed knowledge of marketing. In 1905, he established the Atlantic Fruit and Steamship Company, a firm that soon controlled several fruit shipping operations. His next target was the Earl Fruit Company, a large and very successful produce brokerage that owned or held liens on apple orchards in Oregon and Washington, citrus orchards in Florida, prune orchards in Idaho, and various deciduous fruit-growing operations throughout California. In 1919 DiGiorgio consolidated operations as the DiGiorgio Fruit Corporation, then purchased S&W Fine Foods and began selling his products under that famous label. During the 1930s, DiGiorgio unloaded all of his foreign fruit operations, including a banana business, then diversified into canning and dried fruit. Plowing his profits back into his business, he paid ninety cents an acre for eleven thousand acres of what had once been worthless wasteland and alkaline flats at the base of Bear Mountain, in the southern San Joaquin Valley. By punching down dozens of deep wells, he soon transformed the land into orchards and vineyards worth three thousand dollars an acre. At the end of World War II, DiGiorgio's operations had grown into a quintessential, vertically integrated, family-run, agricultural conglomerate. Annually producing ten million boxes of fruit and five hundred thousand boxes of vegetables worth over twenty-four million dollars, it was the largest farming operation and second largest winemaker in California.[41]

With five hundred permanent employees and several thousand temporary harvest hands, the Bear Mountain ranch, along with dozens of ranches from Borrego Springs to Marysville, appeared to offer a base from which Hansiwar and Galarza could achieve a domino effect. The idea was to organize the largest farming operation in the state and branch out from there. Hansiwar and Galarza believed that other growers, seeing the union's power, would quickly sign union contracts. As a theory of organizing, the domino strategy seemed to make sense and offered certain advantages, among them the possibility of succeeding without laying the careful groundwork necessary for patiently establishing a wide base among the state's agricultural labor force. Within the first month, five hundred employees at DiGiorgio Fruit Corporation's big Bear Mountain ranch headquarters joined Local Number 218. With organizing activities ranging as far north as Marysville and hundreds of Mexican and African American potato harvesters and cotton pickers in Arvin, Weedpatch, and Shafter also joining the union, Local 218 very quickly became the center for farmworker political activity. Overjoyed at the response, NFLU organizers felt a sense of power exceeding their wildest expectations. "Arvin and Lamont," recalled Galarza, "saw faces and heard questions that came out of the long-dormant precincts of the countryside, now filling with new voters."[42]

On August 27, 1947, Hansiwar met with DiGiorgio Fruit Corporation officials and requested a raise of ten cents per hour, seniority rights, and a grievance procedure. After company officials refused to bargain, union members assembled at Grange Hall in Weedpatch and voted overwhelmingly to strike. Five days later, they established picket lines that crippled field and shed operations. By then, however, much of the harvest season was finished, so company officials, realizing that the union could not threaten any crops, refused to permit union elections. Labeling organizers as outside agitators, foremen barricaded ranch gates, evicted union activists, and dumped their belongings onto the county road. That fall the company finished the season with several hundred Filipinos, undocumented workers, Mexican laborers recruited in Texas, and 130 braceros who had remained on the job despite regulations prohibiting them from working during labor disputes.[43]

Up to this point, the strike had proceeded along fairly predictable lines. But as the harvest season ended and the union faced a long hard winter with little leverage over DiGiorgio, it shifted tactics away from the picket lines and launched a public relations blitz. Utilizing photography to carry its message and increase pressure, NFLU leaders appealed to their friends in the media. Lending a hand, former secretary of the interior Harold Ickes denounced DiGiorgio on Thanksgiving Day in a nationally syndicated newspaper column. Telling millions of readers that DiGiorgio's workers were treated "more shamefully than were their prototypes in the dark ages," Ickes relayed to readers his visit with DiGiorgio employee John Gorman, who had gone on strike under the banner of the NFLU. Describing how Gorman, his wife, and four children gave thanks over a few crusts of bread, Ickes went on to elaborate on the one-room shack they rented from their miserly landlord. "The human chattels quit work to force their employer at least to agree to discuss such (to them) life or death matters as better hours, an increase in the pittance they call wages, and more acceptable working conditions," he wrote. And it was all because the Gormans worked for a kind of American version of Ebenezer Scrooge.[44]

For many in the southern San Joaquin Valley, these were fighting words. Once again displeased with unfavorable information, a committee of eleven Kern County agribusinessmen and shopkeepers, led by Walter Kane, publisher of the *Bakersfield Californian,* and including many who had helped ban *The Grapes of Wrath* seven years earlier, visited DiGiorgio Farms with Bakersfield photographer Cal Williams. Hired to refute Ickes's statements, Williams was given unlimited access to the Arvin ranch and several others. During the committee's tour of various farm facilities, he photographed every aspect of life and labor. Hardly curious or probing, however, Williams was a commercial photographer, not a journalist or documentary photographer. Doing the bidding of DiGiorgio, he approached his task much like those who, earlier in the century, had produced bucolic images glorifying agriculture.[45]

At the Poso ranch, one of DiGiorgio's many farming operations, Williams arranged all of the permanently employed men around tables while they played cards and relaxed in a clean recreation room, complete with spittoons. Elsewhere on the ranch he photographed proud families, different grades of employee housing, tree-lined but unpaved roads, other modern recreation facilities such as tennis courts and a swimming pool, and an attractive church. His most effective and widely circulated images display immaculate kitchens, clean beds, employees reading in the living rooms of their apartments, happy children playing in front of well-kept ranch houses, and spotless bathroom facilities with long lines of sinks and wash basins. "This is a more deluxe recreation area than is found in most migratory labor camps," explains a caption affixed to one image. "The recreation room at the Poso Ranch is well-lighted, ventilated and spacious. If more efforts were made such as this, vice and crime amongst migratory labor might diminish."[46]

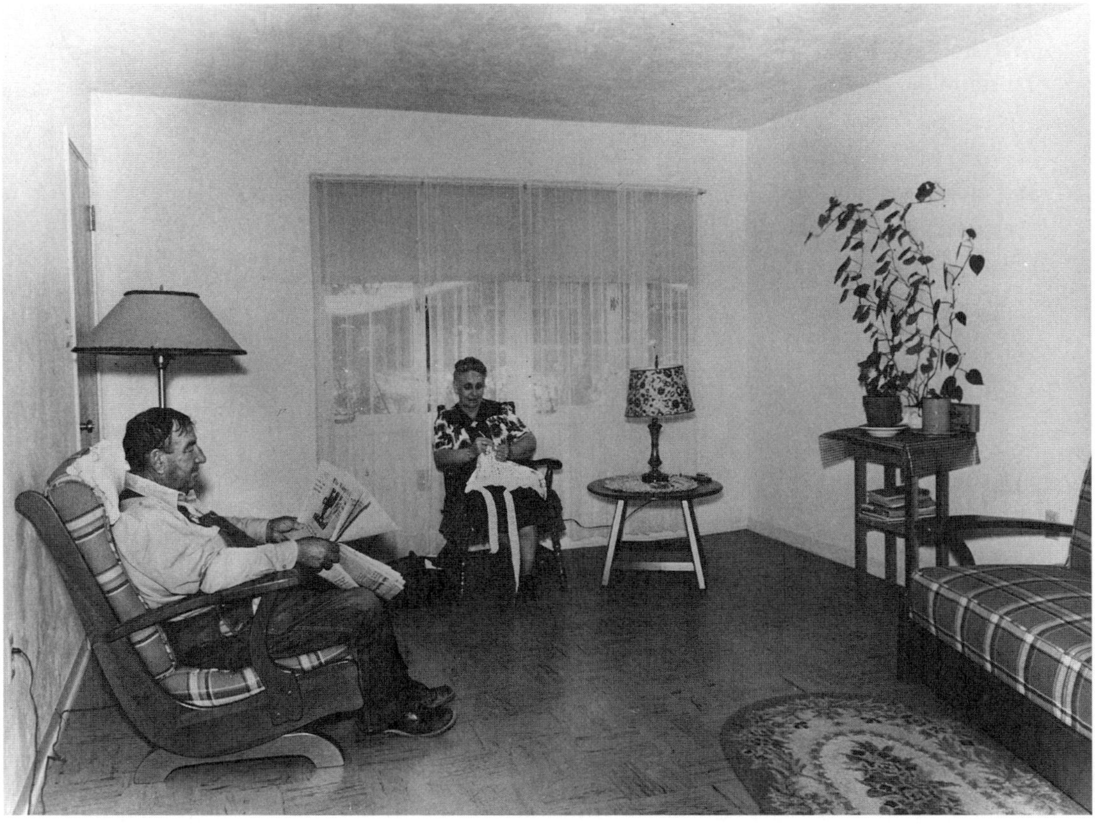

Living room of cook's apartment, Poso ranch, July 1950, photograph by Cal Williams. Courtesy of the President's Commission on Migratory Labor, Dwight D. Eisenhower Library.

One month later, the committee gathered nineteen photographs from this propaganda effort into a handsome, forty-two page pamphlet titled *A Community Aroused.* With an introduction by cotton entrepreneur W[offord] B. Camp, *A Community Aroused* praised DiGiorgio for its program of model housing so expensive that it caused the DiGiorgio Fruit Corporation to incur huge operating losses in the building of bungalows and sanitary barracks. To bolster the thesis that DiGiorgio was a model farm, *A Community Aroused* also featured several photographs that Williams had taken of John Gorman's paychecks from July 15 to September 15, 1947. Attacking NFLU assertions that Gorman was "typical of hundreds of thousands of actual farm slaves in the West," *A Community Aroused* used these photographs as evidence that Gorman was, in fact, a well-paid employee with nothing to squawk about. "To a modern observer who never saw DiGiorgio Farms," wrote the biographers of W. B. Camp, "the truthfulness of these unglamourous photographs, all taken on the same day at a time when the ranch was being picketed, is unmistakable."[47]

Pleased with the excellent public relations material, DiGiorgio distributed the pamphlet along with sets of the photographs to various newspapers and farm journals, where, without byline, the photographs appeared as irrefutable evidence of DiGiorgio's paternal concern. By registered mail Camp also sent copies to Harold Ickes. These photographs, explained the accompanying text, demonstrated that DiGiorgio's farmworkers were among the best treated in California. Pride and anger certainly motivated DiGiorgio's elaborate, illustrated rebuttal. But there were two other reasons why the wily DiGiorgio went to such great lengths to get his point across. One was his character, background, paternalistic resolve, iron will, and, above all, concern for public opinion. He simply was not going to tolerate something he regarded as a libelous fabrication. The other was the NFLU's boycott of DiGiorgio Fruit Corporation products. That fall, after many Kern County stores removed DiGiorgio products from their shelves and the Retail Clerks' Union declared DiGiorgio goods "hot cargo," members of the Winery Workers Union and the Carpenters Union refused to unload DiGiorgio wine sold to Italian Swiss Colony.[48]

As business in California slumped and it seemed that the union might expand its boycott nationwide, DiGiorgio Fruit Corporation mobilized to protect its products and brand name. In the battle for public opinion, photographs were clearly going to play a pivotal role. Eight years after documentary photography had lost its momentum, it was back in the headlines. Only now a gigantic farming corporation with vast resources was going to use photography to its own advantage. Even for those who understood the shortcomings, contradictions, and highly subjective nature of social documentary photography as practiced by the FSA, DiGiorgio's attempt to pass off blatant propaganda as objective truth was too much to stomach. The NFLU would have to strike back. When it did, an epic battle of photographic imagery developed. Competing for public opinion, both sides would mount massive visual campaigns and then settle into a bloody court battle over questions of truth, misrepresentation, and monetary damages. The outcome would shape the course of farm labor relations and influence how photographers worked in the fields for the next two decades.

15

Poverty in the Valley of Plenty

Suppression of the Documentary Ideal

Under the cover of darkness, four men presumed to be strikers moved into the DiGiorgio orchards on January 12, 1948, and cut down 320 plum trees worth eleven thousand dollars. A few days later, pickets smashed the windows in a DiGiorgio truck. Angered by these developments, DiGiorgio employees swinging iron bars and chains charged a group of five strikers on February 8, sending three to the hospital. Five days later, with the DiGiorgio farmworkers' strike entering its fifth month, a team of documentary filmmakers from Hollywood arrived at DiGiorgio's Bear Mountain ranch. Through their documentary film they hoped to help the NFLU and Local 218 counter DiGiorgio's publicity campaign and smear tactics, assist the union by building public support, and force Governor Earl Warren to mediate the strike.[1]

To produce its own documentary film, the NFLU needed about twenty thousand dollars—money it did not have and could not raise. To offset those expenses, all of the Hollywood film unions waived their wage and pay contracts. The Cameraman's Union, Film Editor's Union, and Screen Actors Guild each selected a representative to assist in production. Gaffers, drivers, musicians, and writers also donated time and labor, and suppliers provided much of the material at cost. Also contributing funds to the documentary were the Workers Defense League, the Jewish Labor Committee, the California Federation of Labor, the Los Angeles Labor Council, the American Federation of Labor, and a curious organization called the Hollywood Film Council. Production began on February 23 and proceeded in and around Arvin over the next three days. Within two weeks the film had been edited and a musical score added. Among those considered for the narration of the twenty-five-minute documentary was Ronald Reagan, then president of the Screen Actors Guild. Veteran newsman Harry W. Flannery eventually landed the job.[2]

Consisting of fifty-seven scenes, the documentary was called *Poverty in the Valley of Plenty.* It opened with panoramic shots of rural poverty in the San Joaquin Valley and in sections of Arvin and Weedpatch. Next it shifted to living and working conditions among California farmworkers in general. Contrasting the gorgeous sight of fruit trees and neat rows of crops with close-ups of rundown farm labor camps, Flannery observed of the camps, "Landscaping is done with junk." Touring Arvin, the camera next dwelled on the farmworker shacks that had so affected Hansiwar. Among those singled out was a cold-water shower used by twenty-five to thirty families. "These workers, toiling in a great industry," Flannery explained, "are deprived of the rights and opportunities which are granted to all other industrial workers." The script then turned to the grievances of the DiGiorgio employees, the role of the newly formed Local 218, and DiGiorgio's refusal to bargain. Flannery then contrasted living conditions for farmworkers with the way DiGiorgio handled equipment. "If they were tools," Flannery said, "they would be housed in a nice, clean, water proof shed."[3]

After thirty-seven scenes, the documentary turns to the DiGiorgio strike. Presenting pictures of picket lines, union meetings, a speech to strikers by an organizer and the DiGiorgio head cook, James Price, and ordained minister Phinneas Parks leading everyone in prayer, the film then shows relief caravans from Los Angeles distributing groceries to union members. Rounding out the picture are strikebreaking by braceros and an apparently staged scene in which undocumented workers are being smuggled across picket lines. Here and there Flannery refers to DiGiorgio as "clever and shrewd," the largest grape, plum, and pear grower in the world, and the "richest and most powerful of all corporate farmers." Lines from a popular DiGiorgio strike ballad underscore the spirit of the strikers:

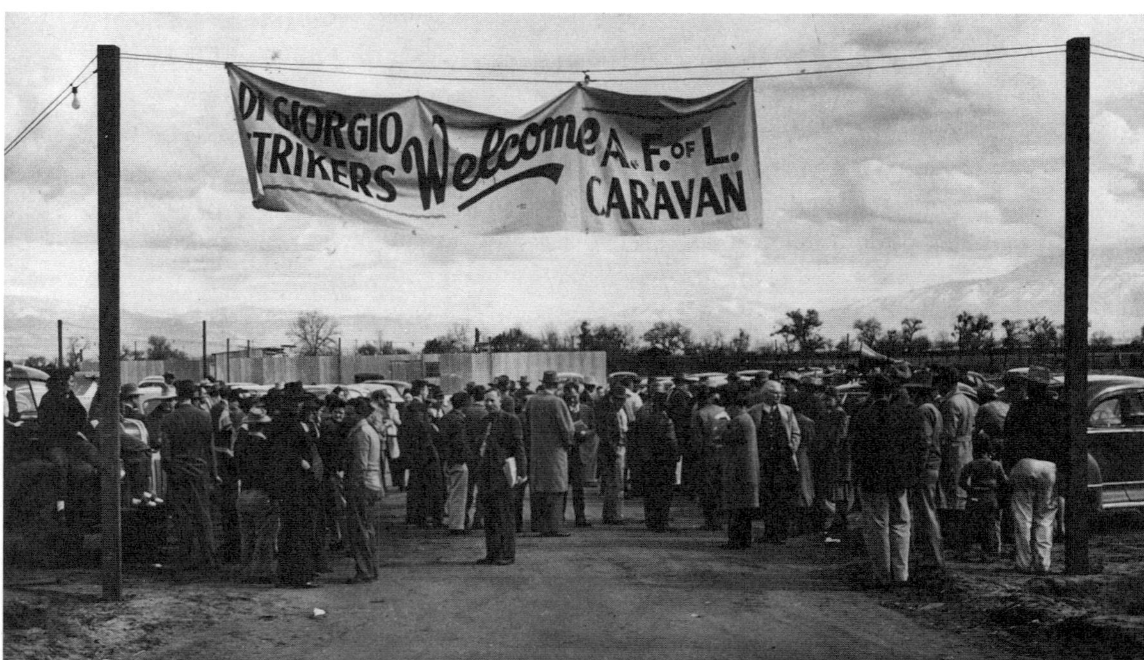

Strike caravan arriving at Arvin, December 1948, photographer unknown. Courtesy of the Southern Tenant Farmers Union Collection, University of North Carolina, Chapel Hill.

God Almighty made the valley
For a land of milk and honey,
But a corporation's got the honey
For to turn it into money.[4]

While the film was being shown, state representative A. J. Elliot visited Arvin. At a meeting of local farmers, Elliot held up a copy of *A Community Aroused,* pointed to the photographs by Cal Williams, pronounced them the true picture of conditions at DiGiorgio's farm, and announced that no legitimate strike existed. Two weeks later, Congresswoman Helen Gahagan Douglas also visited the strikers. Accompanied by CBS reporter Chet Huntley and a camera crew, Douglas began questioning workers while the CBS news crew filmed. But no matter what the CBS crew did, it could not penetrate the DiGiorgio smoke screen. With the local sheriff acting as an interpreter, braceros simply clammed up when questioned on camera. Unable to film inside the farm, camera crews moved outside, where strikers and Los Angeles attorney Robert W. Gilbert discussed the union and strike.

On the basis of these and other interviews, Douglas and Huntley all concluded that DiGiorgio symbolized the repressive, union-busting attitudes of industrialized agriculture. So strong was their condemnation of DiGiorgio and so moving were the CBS images that DiGiorgio now raised the stakes. Unless CBS and other news outlets retracted their lies, corporation lawyers would sue them for libel. Although CBS ignored the threats, newspapers did not. Over the next few months, Ickes's column rapidly dwindled and then completely ceased. But the picketing continued at DiGiorgio Farms, and the NFLU continued to pump out a steady stream of photographs purporting to show deplorable conditions at the ranch. One widely circulated photograph of a rundown shack leaning to one side was published in dozens of newspapers and magazines. Identified as DiGiorgio housing, it was in fact not even on the DiGiorgio property. Union organizers also took pictures of discarded refrigerator cars and rundown buildings in which Mexicans, Okies, Filipinos, and braceros lived. The union made it clear that this was the only type of quarters that farmworkers at DiGiorgio could afford.[5]

In March 1948, two months after its debut, *Poverty in the Valley of Plenty* was shown on the public television station KTLA in Los Angeles. It then went on tour throughout California and as far away as New York, raising about eighty-seven thousand dollars in strike funds. For the first time since the cotton strike of 1938, both filmmakers and still photographers were again playing a role in a farm labor conflict. With both sides battling in the media and the strike eight months old, tensions mounted. On the streets of Arvin, police stopped cars and searched strikers for weapons. All over town, arguments and fist fights erupted, as the hard core of about one hundred militant members of Local 218 carried on the strike.

The wave of violence culminated on the evening of May 17, 1948. While James Price was holding a meeting of the strike committee in the Arvin home of Jimmy Lee

Brasher, two unknown assailants drove by and fired nine shots at the strike leaders. One shot struck Price in the face, emerging near his right ear. As Price lay on the floor in a pool of blood, a union member snapped his picture. Quickly developing the image and making multiple prints, the NFLU bypassed the *Bakersfield Californian,* which it considered an enemy, and distributed photographs to newspapers throughout the state.[6]

Running front page in a half dozen newspapers, the image drove home to the public what was at stake in the strike and the lengths to which some people would go to end it and wipe out its leaders. Responding to calls from AFL president William Green, Governor Earl Warren dispatched a special investigator to Bakersfield. The local Labor Council and NFLU offered rewards totaling a thousand dollars for information leading to the apprehension of the gunmen. Thirty-five years later, Joseph DiGiorgio's son Robert remained unfazed and dismissive. "He was shot, but he was

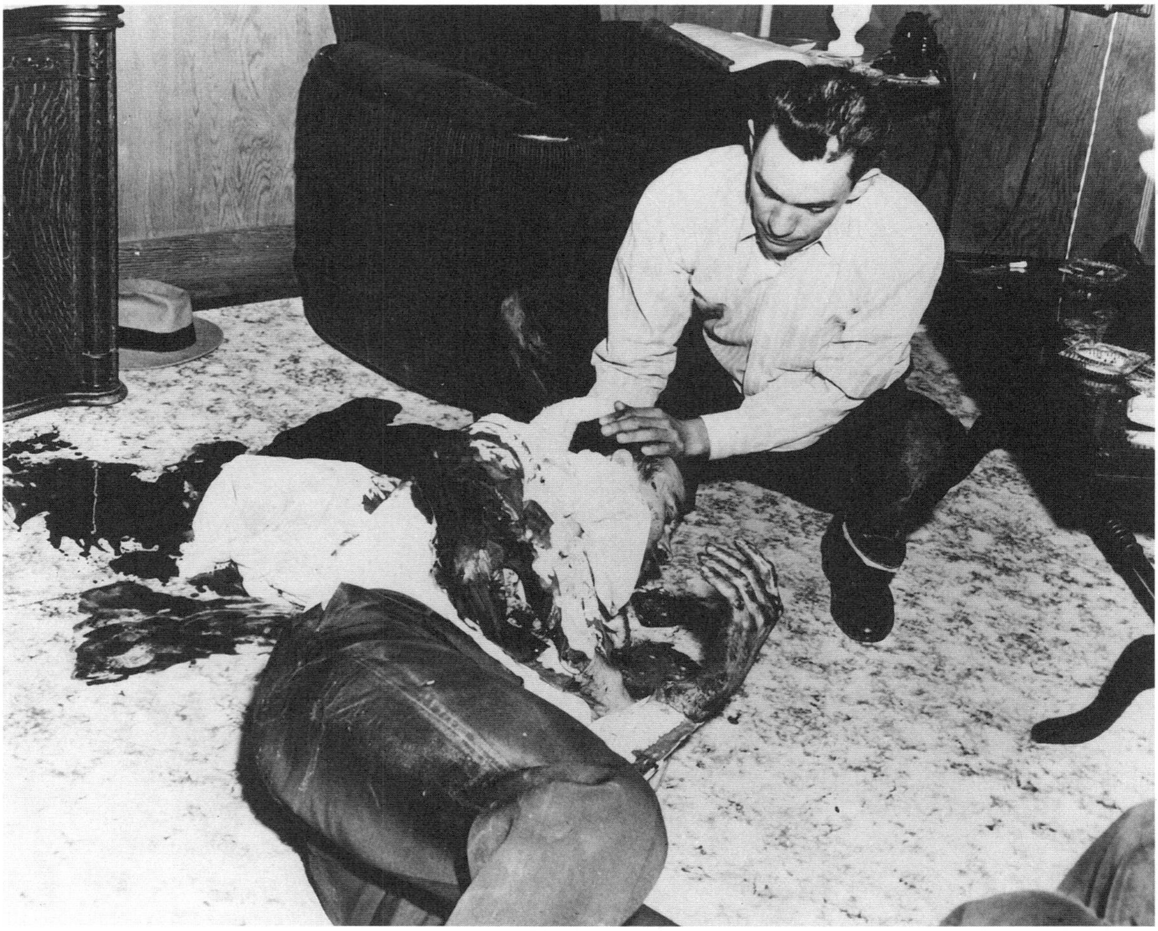

National Farm Labor Union organizer James Price lies wounded from a drive-by shooting, May 17, 1948, photographer unknown. Courtesy of the Southern Tenant Farmers Union Collection, University of North Carolina, Chapel Hill.

not shot by anybody in our organization," he asserted in his Bancroft Library oral memoir. "It was all planned. It was just in the hand, where it would not have been of any great consequence. With a small caliber [bullet]. There were powder burns on him, and so forth. [laughs] So it was shown to be a falsehood, as to who was accused."[7]

Following the shooting, both sides attempted to shift the conflict away from Arvin. For the union, it was a matter of survival. At Bakersfield and Los Angeles late in May and early June, the NFLU was forced to defend itself against state senator Jack Tenney's Committee on Un-American Activities, and the hearings left the union nearly bankrupt. Out on the picket lines, the effectiveness of the strike hinged on barely one hundred men and women who attended meetings, paid dues, and "talked union." Early in the summer, the very premise of *Poverty in the Valley of Plenty* came under attack when a conservative senator dismissed the FSA along with its documentary photographers in a *Life* magazine article. Illustrated by exceedingly trivial FSA images, the article asserted that Stryker and his photographers had wasted $750,000 of government money on "silly" and "ridiculous" pictures, now useful largely to enemies of the country. The implication was that such work was both outdated and worthless. By late summer, everything seemed to be stacked against the union. Staking out a position on DiGiorgio's ranch, Kern County sheriff Johnny Loustalot branded NFLU pickets as "smacking of oldtime I.W.W. methods" and did his best to keep them off corporation property. Ironically, all that sustained the NFLU through the winter and into the following spring were funds and donations raised among labor and liberal groups in Los Angeles who had seen *Poverty in the Valley of Plenty.* To them, the film seemed not only very real but also extremely relevant.[8]

On March 16, 1949, NFLU president H. L. Mitchell showed the documentary to the entire Subcommittee of the Senate Committee on Education and Labor. Chaired by Representative Augustus Kelley, the subcommittee was holding hearings in Washington, D.C., on a resolution to repeal the Labor-Management Relations Act (also known as the Taft–Hartley Act), which had been enacted on June 23, 1947, over President Harry Truman's veto. Thereafter, the film went on the road. While it was being shown in union halls, on college and university campuses, in churches, at state and international labor conventions, and to anyone who wanted to see it, various friends and allies of DiGiorgio, angered by references to *The Grapes of Wrath,* took detailed notes and conveyed them to corporation lawyers. Although denouncing *Poverty in the Valley of Plenty* as a scurrilous propaganda package designed to tarnish his reputation and cripple his business, DiGiorgio nevertheless proceeded carefully. It was one thing to rant about Steinbeck's excesses and distortions but quite another to dispute visual documentation. Most civil codes referred to traditional cases of libelous printed words. Few rules of law guided defamation by a film. How was DiGiorgio to deal with images that were difficult to describe precisely in a written complaint? How was he to handle the matter of a spoken narrative lending meaning to pictures?[9]

For guiding principles, DiGiorgio attorneys from the San Francisco law firm of Brobeck, Phleger, and Harrison searched case law back to 1915. They discovered a case in which a film about prostitution had inadvertently featured a New York factory building identified by a prominent sign. Discovering that factory owner August C. Merle had won a judgment against the Sociological Research Film Corporation on the grounds that he had no connection to prostitution and had been damaged, attorneys found a precedent for bringing a novel lawsuit on the grounds of "libel by visual innuendo." DiGiorgio attorneys also discovered another precedent in a more recent New York case, *Brown v. Paramount Publicity Corporation.* In this 1934 case, the court ruled that the old laws of defamation in print also apply to movies. Studying these cases, attorneys concluded that words and pictures are inextricably connected in effect and meaning. But they were uncertain whether to move forward. After weighing the dangers and advantages of filing a lawsuit, they concluded that *Poverty in the Valley of Plenty* failed to draw a sharp line between generalizations about farm labor conditions in California agriculture and the specific situation at DiGiorgio during the strike. Of all the sequences that carelessly confused the specific and general, attorneys singled out one that implied field hands living in miserable shacks were on DiGiorgio property.[10]

On May 16, 1949, just a few days before the statute of limitations was due to expire, the corporation filed a libel complaint in the Los Angeles Superior Court against Paramount Television Productions. "The statements and representations in the film are grossly misleading, false and defamatory and discredit DiGiorgio Fruit Corporation and all of the farmers of Kern County in the eyes of the public," asserted DiGiorgio attorneys. The film was both libelous and slanderous. DiGiorgio asked one hundred thousand dollars in special damages and another hundred thousand dollars in punitive damages. Potentially the corporation could pursue every person who exhibited the film.[11]

It was a good time to sue. Two years earlier, U.S. attorney general Tom Clark had placed the Film and Photo League on its list of totalitarian, fascist, communist, or subversive organizations, along with ninety other groups. As cultural and ideological conditions worsened and the House Un-American Activities Committee initiated hearings that would ruin the careers of many photographers and filmmakers, DiGiorgio attorneys continued to build their case. Although public television station KTLA immediately broadcast a corrected script with subsequent showings, DiGiorgio attorneys did not relent. Alleging that the film violated section 45 of the Code of Civil Procedure of California, the corporation sued for both libel and slander. An amended complaint asked for a million dollars in general and a million dollars in punitive damages.

The corporation listed fifteen specific "untruths" presented in the film. Among the worst were accusations that DiGiorgio (1) robbed its employees of normal American rights; (2) housed them in unsafe habitations; (3) denied them compensation for injuries on the job; (4) participated in smuggling activities; (5) refused its employees adequate medical care; and (6) deprived children of basic educational opportunities. Threatening to obtain injunctions to prevent further showings of the film in Delano and other valley towns, DiGiorgio also vowed to go after dozens of institutions that had already shown the film. But after evaluating this course, the corporation rejected it as counterproductive. On November 8, it filed its second libel lawsuit, this one against Harry Flannery, the National Farm Labor Union, the Hollywood Film Council, fifty John Does, two John Doe corporations, and five John Doe unions connected with *Poverty in the Valley of Plenty.*[12]

On November 12 and 13, 1949, the Subcommittee of the Senate Committee on Education and Labor met in Bakersfield and, while compiling testimony and other information from both sides, viewed *Poverty in the Valley of Plenty.* Taking a lead in the hearings was a curly-haired first-term U.S. representative from Southern California named Richard Nixon. Demanding that union spokesmen prove all allegations made against the agricultural industry, Nixon dismissed H. L. Mitchell's evidence of children who had starved to death in the Central Valley. Those tragedies, he said, as well as many other incidents named in the film, had not happened on DiGiorgio property and therefore were irrelevant. After returning to Washington, D.C., to review transcripts and draft a report, Nixon obtained the signatures of two of the four other subcommittee members, labeled it a "majority report," and gave it to Bakersfield lawyer Thomas Werdel, who had been elected to Congress the previous year. The report was full of inaccuracies and outright lies: it claimed that the union had presented no testimony from strikers, when in fact several had spoken; it skirted around testimony given by several NFLU members by using the word *employee* when claiming that no DiGiorgio worker had joined the union; and it reported that no union witness described any strike issue, when in fact such testimony had filled many hours. Werdel then received permission from the Speaker of the House to issue the report, including commentary on *Poverty in the Valley of Plenty,* stating, among other things, "that, insofar as it purports to represent conditions existing on DiGiorgio farms, the film *Poverty in the Valley of Plenty* was . . . a shocking collection of falsehoods, almost wholly unrelieved by any regard whatsoever for the truth or facts." Printed in the appendix of the *Congressional Record,* forty-five thousand copies of Werdel's forty-four-thousand-word indictment, bearing the signatures of subcommittee members Richard Nixon, Thurston Morton, and Tom Steed, went out to libraries, colleges, and subscribers throughout the country. "Congressional Committee Bares Facts on Alleged DiGiorgio Ranch Strike," blared headlines in the *Associated Farmer,* copying verbatim the lead caption in the Werdel report.[13]

Werdel's remarks, not part of the official subcommittee findings, were entirely unofficial and unknown to all but a few possessing intimate knowledge of congressional procedure. But this did not stop DiGiorgio Fruit Corporation from seizing an opportunity. DiGiorgio lawyers and other agribusiness interests latched on to Werdel's tract and distributed copies of the statement bearing the signatures of Nixon, Morton, and Steed as official government criticism of *Poverty in the Valley of Plenty.*[14]

DiGiorgio Fruit Corporation did more than initiate a lawsuit and reiterate the so-called Werdel report. Dissatisfied with merely fighting against the film, the corporation hired independent movie producer Frank Walker to film its own version of events. Recalling the episode in his oral memoir, DiGiorgio's son Robert praised Walker for producing the film in under thirty days. Titled *The DiGiorgio Story,* it was twenty-seven minutes long and billed as the "true story" of the so-called strike. After showing it at the Bakersfield hearings, DiGiorgio attorneys provided the film free of charge to any public group. Distributing the film from its San Francisco offices, the corporation attempted to follow up showings of *Poverty in the Valley of Plenty,* so that audiences could "see both sides of the story." In response to these developments, Aubrey Blair of the Hollywood Film Council tacked a new ending on to *Poverty in the Valley of Plenty* and spliced in additional information on violence. But this did not gain them any favor with the DiGiorgio attorneys. Nor did it quiet the mounting wave of criticism raised by the film. This became clear in December, when the Madera County superintendent of schools began showing photographs of decrepit labor camps in order to shock citizens into taking action against them.[15]

As these events unfolded, a Los Angeles photographer identified only as a "Mr. Basset" attempted to get into DiGiorgio headquarters at Arvin. Contacting Bakersfield cotton grower W. B. Camp, he asked to be taken on a tour of the Arvin facility. "Fine. Bring your camera and come to my house alone," replied Camp. "You can take any pictures you want, see anything you want." The photographer arrived early in January 1950, and the pair headed off toward Arvin. Puzzled because the photographer had not first contacted DiGiorgio, Camp stopped his car in front of a shabby cabin at Weedpatch Corner. "Now, you might want to take a picture of that," he said. Although the photographer declined, Camp insisted that he write down the mileage and then, after driving another three miles east, stopped again and pointed out that they had only then reached DiGiorgio property. "The cabin back yonder is the one you people had in all the national magazines, saying it was on the ranch and that's where the labor was living," Camp explained. After a moment of silence, the two continued and, arriving on the ranch, picked up the ranch manager and proceeded to pass the headquarters, various barracks, a swimming pool and tennis court, and a collection of tidy cottages with green lawns and shade trees in the backyards. "Mr. Basset, you want to take some pictures?" asked Camp. Basset again declined. Camp then proceeded to take Mr. Bassett through the single men's barracks and feed him lunch with the workers in the mess hall. During all of this, Mr. Basset never took out his camera. Driving him back to his car, Camp lectured Basset about not taking a single photograph because he could not find anything even remotely distasteful.[16]

Unable to obtain incriminating photographs on the DiGiorgio property, the NFLU began to run out of options during the spring. In a memo, NFLU attorney Alexander Schullman advised union president H. L. Mitchell to withdraw *Poverty in the Valley of Plenty* and accept DiGiorgio's offer of a deal. Reluctant to do so, Mitchell feared that such an agreement would set a bad precedent. If he gave in, every grower faced with an adverse report or unfaltering photograph would sue for libel in order to wipe out a union or kill a strike. To counter the Werdel report, Mitchell asked Senator Dennis Chávez to place items favorable to the union in the *Congressional Record.* He then branded Werdel's report on the film a "falsehood" and challenged Werdel to waive his congressional immunity and defend the report in court. But these tactics had little effect. It was all posturing.[17]

Never very solvent, the NFLU could not afford to continue the court battle. With small financial and legal resources that could hardly match those of DiGiorgio Fruit Corporation, the union realized that it would lose tens of thousands of dollars and end up bankrupt if it fought a long, drawn-out libel case. Putting up a brave front, the union stalled. More than anything else, Mitchell and Galarza and other NFLU leaders wanted the public to absorb the picture presented by *Poverty in the Valley of Plenty.* Unknown to them, three photographers were at that moment probing farmworker communities in Stockton, Los Angeles, and on the west side of the San Joaquin Valley. Working independently of one another and without contacting the NFLU, these photographers confirmed everything that the NFLU had asserted.

One of the photographers to confirm the NFLU's assertions was Wayne Miller. Born in Chicago in 1918, Miller had studied banking at the University of Illinois, Urbana, and there worked part-time as a photographer for the university yearbook and local newspaper. After graduation, he had attended the Art Center School in Los Angeles but was asked to leave because he had not shown proper respect for the school's curriculum. When World War II broke out, Miller joined the United States Navy. Sent to the South Pacific, he served for four years as a lieutenant in Edward Steichen's Naval Aviation Unit. Assigned to photograph a torpedo bombing mission, he gave up his place at the last minute to an enthusiastic photographer who was killed in the attack. That photographer's last image showed a Japanese Zero firing on the plane.[18]

Shaped by his war experiences and deeply troubled by the sight of Hiroshima after it was destroyed by an atomic bomb, Miller had returned to the United States determined to "document the things that make the human race a family." He devoted most of 1946 and 1947 to photographing The Way of Life of the Northern Negro on a Guggenheim Fellowship. Many of his stories appeared in *Ebony,* which was playing a major role in disrupting racist views, although its main focus was on upwardly mobile African Americans.[19]

Miller had met Dorothea Lange during World War II while traveling from Washington, D.C., to the Pacific. He would recall it as "just an afternoon with her with warm pie and coffee in the garden." When Miller decided to leave Chicago, he chose the West Coast over New York largely because of Lange and because he had received a contract from *Life* to work in its San Francisco bureau. Shortly after Miller arrived in California in 1949, *Ebony* editor Ben Burns asked him to photograph black cotton pickers in the San Joaquin Valley. By this time, California had grown into the fourth largest cotton-producing state. Although mechanical cotton pickers were being introduced, full mechanization of the harvest was a long way in the future. Thousands of cotton pickers were still required to bring in the crop. Given the almost complete absence of blacks and other "persons of color" in *Life, Look,* the *Saturday Evening Post,* and other mass-circulation magazines, the editors at *Ebony* saw a major news scoop wrapped around a story almost too incredible to believe. Ben Burns urged Miller to "play up the angle of the South moving to California" and to "get the sharecropper shacks and all the poverty you would find in pictures coming from Dixie" as well as any "Jim Crow signs." Heading into the valley in early November 1949, Miller threw himself into the project.[20]

About thirty thousand black former tenant farmers and sharecroppers had left Arkansas, Oklahoma, Louisiana, and Texas following World War II, and about seven thousand had settled in the Tulare Lake basin. Finding ample work nine months of the year, they thinned ("chopped") cotton in May, harvested onions and potatoes in June, picked grapes from July to September, and moved into the cotton fields each fall. Often joined by busloads of African Americans shipped north from Los Angeles to "blacks only" camps, they picked cotton through the winter, sometimes finishing in February, just as spring plowing began. On foggy winter mornings when the cotton was wet and pickers could not go into the fields, the call would be heard, "Cotton too heavy," and all would spread their sacks on the ground, light a fire, and sleep or gamble until the sun came out. School-aged children worked alongside their parents in the fields while younger children played nearby, with the smallest tots often riding on the tailend of their mother's twelve-foot-long canvas picking sack. Parents tried their best to keep an eye on their children, but accidents happened. Occasionally a toddler wandered away and drowned in a nearby canal. One exhausted youngster sought refuge in a trailer filled with cotton. Falling asleep, he died when the trailer was hauled to a cotton gin and its contents were dumped into a baling mechanism, filled with giant blades.[21]

This was the world Miller encountered when he photographed in the fields and the trailers, tents, camps, abandoned buses, and freight cars that served as quarters for the labor force in and around Firebaugh, Huron, Lamont, Hanford, Tulare, Strathmore, and other southern San Joaquin Valley farm towns. In Corcoran, he worked a section of Whitley Avenue known as the Strip. On the north side were black honkytonks. On the south were the Mexican bars, with names like Mexicolindo, La Palma, and La Frontera. A large Quonset hut named the Chicken Shack was really a house of prostitution where fifteen black prostitutes worked in little plywood booths. Knife fights, fistfights, and mayhem ruled during the cotton harvest, and law enforcement stayed clear. Corcoran was a wide-open town where blacks knew to keep on their side of the tracks.[22]

Recalling the assignment more than a half century later, Miller still remained aghast at what he had seen. "It was as if a part of the Mississippi Delta had been transplanted intact to the Golden State," he explained. "People were living in tents and rickety shacks and abandoned boxcars." They all came from families of plantation slaves and were fed up with sharecropping. But they were not much better off in the San Joaquin Valley. Many of them spoke of returning home. The Klan was still strong in the valley. Migrants joked to Miller that while they still might have to face a cross burning back home at least there were no earthquakes in Texas or Alabama.[23]

Miller photographed stranded cotton pickers at the Corcoran camp, where a four-month-old boy had died of dehydration after being left alone in a hot automobile while his parents were picking cotton. Near Fresno, Miller found a six-year-old cotton picker, Pete Gonzáles, pulling a huge cotton sack through the fields. The boy claimed to be only taking a vacation from school, but Miller suspected he worked in the fields full time. In Huron, he discovered people sleeping in cars. Next to a window in Arvin, he photographed a sign announcing "NO COLORED TRADE SOLICITED!" Along the back roads, he saw unemployed shipyard workers and army veterans buying secondhand shoes out of the car trunks of traveling peddlers. Outside Cottonwood, he used a flash to document union members and their children. Meeting in a partly constructed building with half walls and no roof in the middle of a big field on a cold and windy night, they were discussing whether to protest a cut in pay from $3 to $2.50 per hundred pounds. In a one-room shack, he photographed a discouraged man and his unhappy wife on their bed. By day, while the man worked, she sold her body to make ends meet. Every evening, after picking cotton, the man returned and sat like a prisoner on the edge of their bed without talking. "There's not much I can do," he told Miller. "I need glasses and I can't afford glasses. So I just sit."[24]

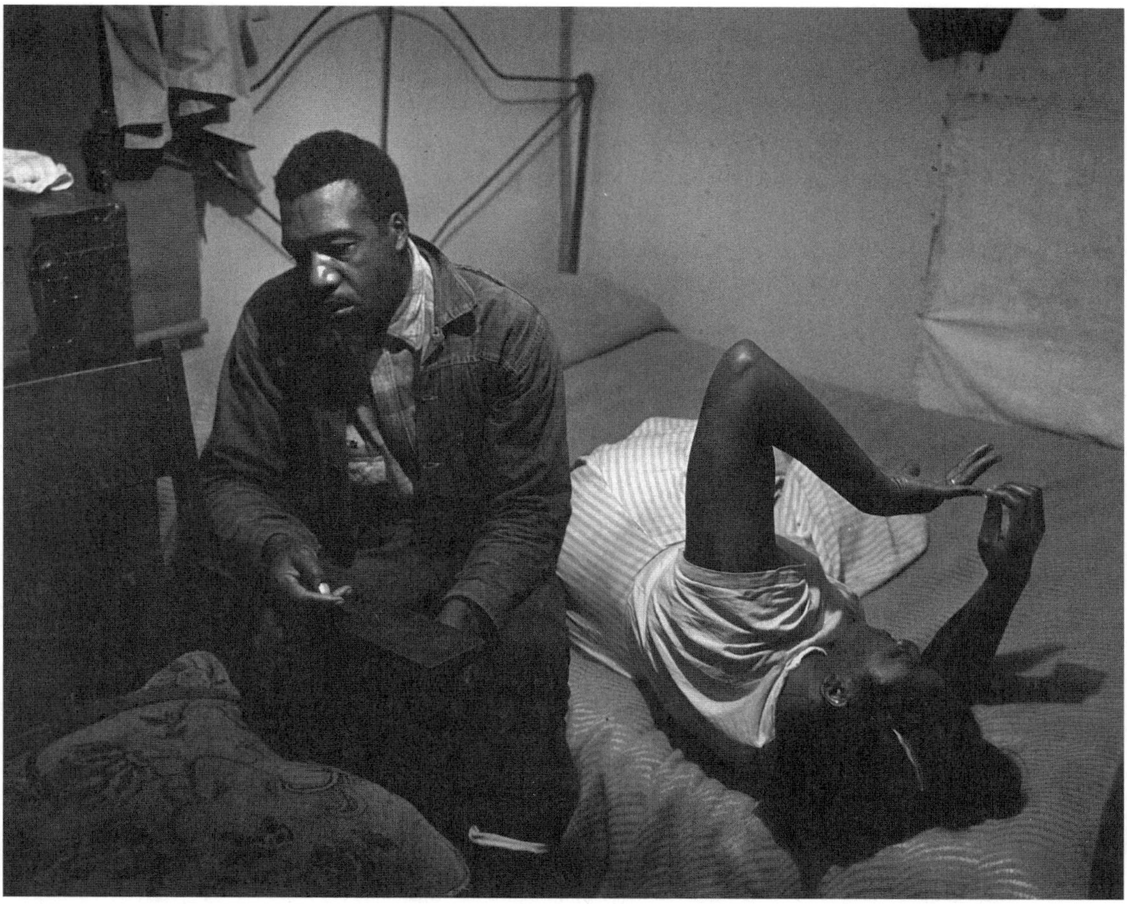

Alonzo Flannigan came to California from Arkansas to pick cotton in 1948. His wife and two children could barely survive on his small income. "This is worse than the early 1930s," he told Wayne Miller. "I can't seem to make a nickel for the winter." Photograph by Wayne Miller. Courtesy of Wayne Miller.

Miller did not have to work hard at finding the subjects of his pictures. He literally walked into their situations wherever he went. Photographing in ways appropriate to these situations, Miller quietly educated *Ebony* viewers with his scrutiny of neglect and misfortune. He took no snapshots. Making people aware of his presence, he gained consent before he photographed, establishing a rapport that was clearly evident in his images. His work had a quiet dignity and emotional power that *Ebony* fully exploited. "There are no sharecroppers, no mules, no plantations in the lush Golden State valleys but the unmistakable spirit of the South is everywhere," reported the magazine. "Too few jobs for too many pickers has resulted in transforming the prosperous valley into a land of want, misery and death."[25]

While Miller was exploring the southern San Joaquin Valley, twenty-year-old photographer Don Normark was developing a photo essay centered on the Hispanic community around Chávez Ravine in Los Angeles. He had been studying at the Los Angeles Art Center when he encountered the images of Eugene Smith and Cartier-Bresson. Bored by the advertising assignments he received at the Art Center, he had started to explore other subjects when he chanced on the little valley with its three Mexican American neighborhoods, scarcely more than a mile from City Hall. Soon he was spending as much time there as he could, a skinny Swede from Seattle, whistling along the paths and dusty roads. Greeting people, Normark paused to record scenes as simple as a kettle being filled at an outdoor tap, an altar to the Virgin de Guadalupe decorated with flowers, and an ancient car being packed for a summer of "las picas"—picking cotton and grapes in Bakersfield, plums and tomatoes in Fresno and Visalia, walnuts and grapes in Chatsworth and Burbank. Favorably impressed, the curator of photographs at the Los Angeles County Museum displayed several of Normark's photographs along with work by Robert Capa and Dorothea Lange in an exhibition called "Photography Mid-century." But no one else was interested. Discouraged by publishers who liked the photographs but refused to publish them, Normark put the project behind him and returned to Seattle.[26]

Also going largely unnoticed was the photographic coverage of Filipino farmworkers that Antonio Peña produced in Stockton. Well established as a commercial photographer, Peña focused mostly on a four-square-block section of downtown Stockton known as Little Manila. Twice every year the area doubled in population: during the spring, when field hands flush with cash packed in to relax and play; and every winter, when cannery workers returned south from Alaska. Peña did plenty of business making studio portraits of field hands and cannery workers wearing their well-cut McIntosh suits while sitting in front of painted backgrounds; he also did a thriving business photographing men in dance halls, shooting pool, playing baseball, and hanging out in the parks. But when the Filipino Agricultural Laborers Association and the Food, Tobacco, and Allied Workers Union (FTAWU) struck against the asparagus industry in the spring of 1948, Peña deviated from his usual pattern. He could hardly miss the action. With FTAWU Local Number 7 headquartered in the hotel one floor above his studio, Peña found it easy to document strikers and supporters preparing to picket the packing plants and farms. Several of his images capture dramatic moments of ethnic militancy and union solidarity. But like the images that Normark shot at Chávez Ravine, Peña's work was not seen by a wide audience. Only the *People's World* and several Filipino newspapers ever published his images. A few survive only because several residents kept the prints, mounted, matted, and framed on the walls of their homes, for over a half century.[27]

With a better outlet for his work, Miller sent shock waves through the state when *Ebony* magazine published his images the following April. Accusations of peonage and modern slavery had accompanied the DiGiorgio fight; it had been a decade since anyone had compared the Golden State to the cotton South or shown that Jim Crow was still alive and well in the heart of California. Now a leading minority publication was again pointing to the bold juxtaposition of lush landscapes and exploited workers to produce a highly negative exposé of the state's cotton industry. But for all of the controversy that Miller's photography provoked, it failed to inspire more coverage or any change. The rapid mechanization of the harvest, which within a few years would eliminate nine out of ten harvest jobs, was making further coverage of cotton pickers of little concern. Also contributing to the lack of attention was the general disinterest in any aspect of agriculture other than production. With photographers working largely independently of one another, there was no way to connect their disparate pictures.

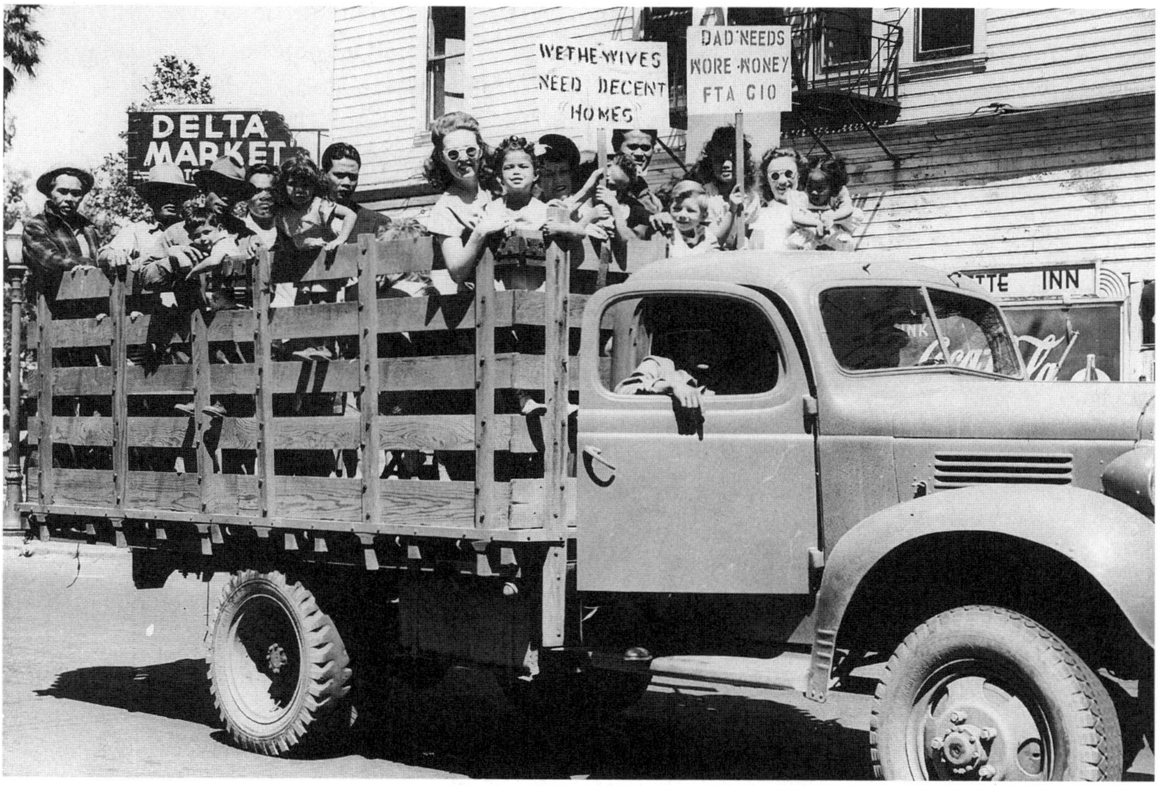

Strike by asparagus workers in Stockton, led by the Food, Tobacco, and Agricultural Workers Union, May 21, 1948, photograph by Antonio Peña. Author's collection.

Had Mitchell or Galarza been aware of this body of work, they might have exploited it to their advantage. But they had no idea that any photographers were out there documenting the same circumstances that they were describing at DiGiorgio. Worn out, facing financial ruin, and running the union from Washington, D.C., with the help of one secretary, Mitchell privately wondered how long the NFLU could continue defending *Poverty in the Valley of Plenty.* Only a few union members remained on the picketline. Every member of Local 218 had been fired. Expenses for fighting the lawsuit were growing larger by the day, and defense funds had long been exhausted. So broke was the union that it had to terminate the services of its attorney, Alexander Schullman, to rely on counsel from the other defendants, principally the California Federation of Labor, the Hollywood Film Council, and the Los Angeles Labor Council. Not only was the union facing a gigantic corporation with apparently unlimited resources, it also had to defend itself against what appeared to be a legitimate congressional report that labeled *Poverty in the Valley of Plenty* an irresponsible, destructive, and libelous misrepresentation.

On May 8, 1950, Mitchell officially ended the strike and boycott. Fifteen days later he signed an agreement with DiGiorgio Fruit Corporation. In exchange for the withdrawal of *Poverty in the Valley of Plenty* from circulation and the destruction of all known prints, including those in libraries, DiGiorgio Fruit Corporation dropped its suit against Paramount Television Products, Flannery, NFLU president Mitchell, NFLU organizers Ernesto Galarza and Hank Hansiwar, and all other parties. In an out-of-court arrangement, the NFLU, Flannery, and the Hollywood Film Council paid DiGiorgio Fruit Corporation a token dollar for the "libel." Under the terms of this agreement, Flannery, the Hollywood Film Council, and the NFLU were immune from liability for unauthorized showings of the film by third parties. As a result of the agreement, the court dismissed DiGiorgio Fruit Corporation's lawsuit against Paramount Televison Productions. In June, the California Federation of Labor notified all of its affiliates to stop showing the film, destroy all prints, and report these actions to the federation's legal department. By the summer of 1950, *Poverty in the Valley of Plenty* was no longer in circulation, and the NFLU had been destroyed.[28]

With the strike over, the DiGiorgio Fruit Corporation refused to rehire any strikers. Out of work, more than one thousand union members scattered to other farm jobs throughout the San Joaquin Valley. "In the short view," wrote Galarza twenty years later, "the loss of the strike was a disaster that could well have banished the National Farm Labor Union from California. In the long view, it was merely a bitter episode in a historic process that had begun long before the NFLU came on the scene, and that would continue after its demise."[29]

Photographers quickly absorbed the message. Because their work had demonstrated great potential for shaping public policy, powerful agribusiness interests extracted a terrible price from anyone who produced an unfavorable picture, especially if it assisted the farm labor movement. Try to cut through the propaganda, photographers learned, and they could expect to be sued and tied up in court for decades. They might never work again and would be ruined financially. Even if those brave or foolish enough to venture into the fields produced something of consequence, they had to contend with the opposing forces of corporate public relations images and films produced with ample resources and pitched to the public as authentic social documentaries. Those able to produce something worthwhile found no one to distribute it. Faced with such obstacles, only the most accomplished, selfless, determined, and politically motivated photographers continued to follow farmworkers. Most simply gave up. During September 1950, when braceros were deployed around Tracy to break a strike by tomato pickers, no photographer was present.[30]

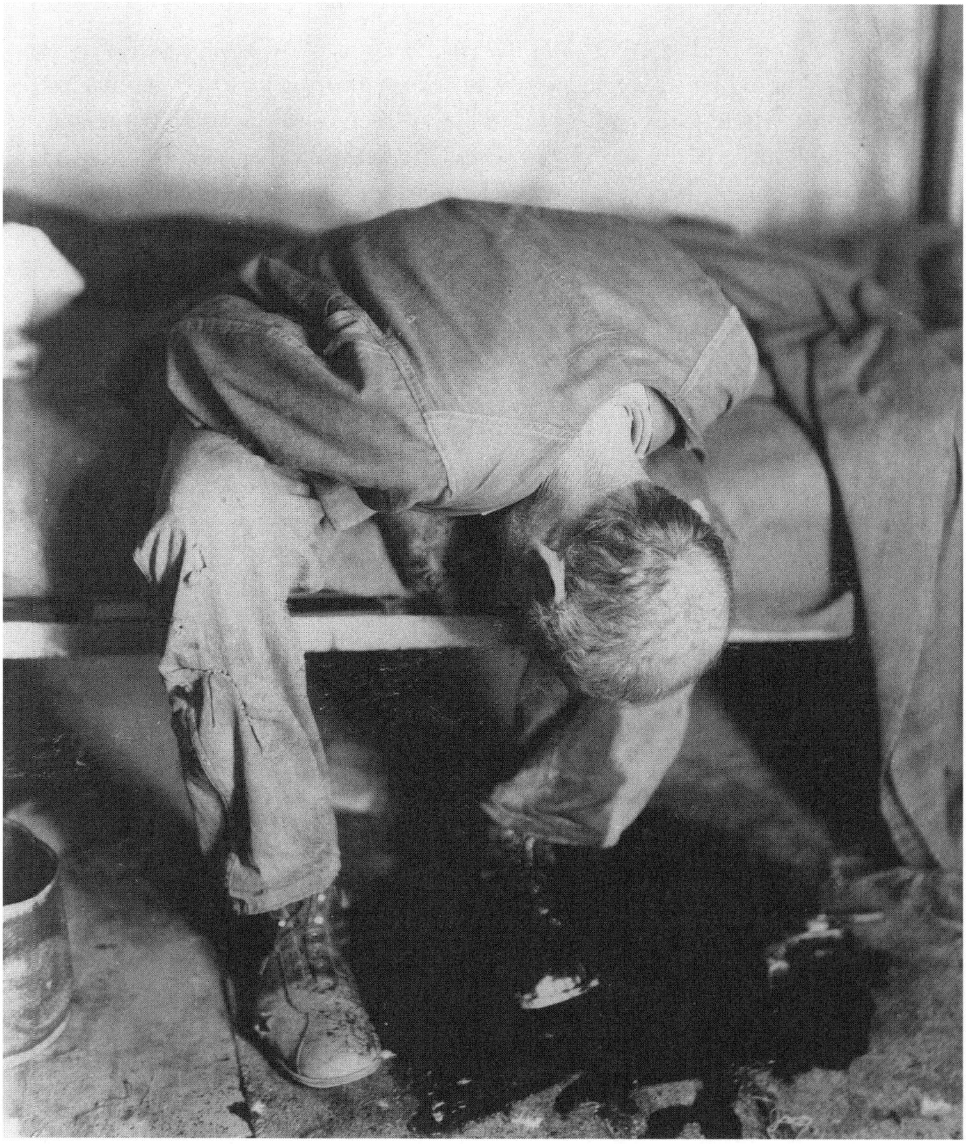

Suicide in a farm labor camp, Ventura County, 1948, photographer unknown. Courtesy of the Coroner's Book of Violent Deaths, Ventura County Museum.

Watching from exile on their small chicken ranch, Otto and Hansel Hagel closely followed these events, even while under constant FBI surveillance. They had compiled a large clipping file on farm labor organizing and desperately wanted to return to the fields if the opportunity presented itself. In the meantime, they kept busy with a series of major projects, including We Return to Fellbach, an exploration of their hometown in Germany in the aftermath of World War II, and *Men and Ships,* Otto's book on the San Francisco waterfront and its workers. When *Fortune* magazine assigned Otto to do a story on cotton farming in October 1950, the Hagels picked up where Otto had left off four years earlier. Only now the focus of their attention shifted to labor organizing.

Making contact with the NFLU, the Hagels began following organizers on their rounds. Wary of vigilantes, organizers were taking great pains to cover their tracks and keep out of sight. Otto and Hansel followed them into the back rooms of cafés and rooming houses, barns and labor camps, and various other clandestine meeting places. Late one night they found themselves at a meeting held at an intersection of two county roads. Only the headlights from a parked car illuminated the scene. Addressing the circle of men and one woman, who listened attentively through a car door window, an NFLU member stood in the bed of a flatbed truck and leaned forward, his hand upraised in a dramatic gesture. At that moment Otto fired an off-camera strobe and snapped a picture. "A second after the picture was taken, they had been discovered and had to disband, at the warning shout, of the lookout," Hansel recalled thirty years later. Few images before or since have so dramatically captured the risks and loneliness involved in organizing field hands.[31]

Far too gritty for *Life* magazine, the photograph and others that the Hagels made during the fall remained unpublished. Had it not been for the President's Commission on Migratory Labor (PCML), most documentary coverage from 1950 might have suffered a similar fate. Appointed by President Harry Truman to explore the plight of migratory agricultural workers, the commission was charged with gathering factual information essential for developing remedial legislation. As part of its investigation, the commission compiled an extensive photographic record. Consisting of hundreds of images depicting everything from farm labor bus accidents and predawn shape-ups to strikes and smuggling, the commission's photographic file was not produced by photographers hired on assignment. Rather, it was more like an archive of existing imagery used to illustrate government publications, including the commission's final report. Although rural spokesmen dismissed commission photographs as FSA retreads, labor and social-reform groups found in them further evidence for ending the bracero program and extending social legislation to farmworkers. Mostly, however, this vast archive, which continued to amass through the commission's activities into the Eisenhower administration, met the same fate as other farmworker photography. It sat, and still sits, largely unused and unappreciated.[32]

A year after Truman created the PCML, a bill to extend the bracero program stalled in the United States Senate, and national attention shifted to the 127,000 "wetbacks" arrested while trying to cross illegally into the United States. Around Calexico, El Centro, and Brawley in the Imperial Valley, the so-called wetback invasion seemed to reach epoch proportions. Constituting about one-third of the sixteen thousand farmworkers in the valley, undocumented farmworkers lived a hideous existence in scrubby hideouts along the banks of the irrigation canals and Alamo River and in gullies around Heber, Holtville, and Westmoreland. Some of these workers excavated caves and camouflaged them with brush; others built straw huts shaped like pup tents, holding them together with Twist-ems purloined from their employers. Everyone cooked over open campfires and washed in irrigation canals. To avoid the Border Patrol, they walked to work through the desert hours before sunrise, all of this to earn a paltry thirty-five to fifty cents an hour for field labor and seventy cents an hour for skilled jobs, such as tractor driving.[33]

Conditions were hardly much better for the local farmworkers who lived in barrios and *colonias* scattered around the valley. Galarza recalled them as men and women accustomed to the most difficult living conditions in the entire state.

> In the dark of the early morning they walked under the stars to climb into trucks and buses so they could be at work an hour or two ahead of the sun. They gathered watermelons in total darkness, testing them for ripeness before wrenching them from the vine by the sound of a middle finger triggered from the thumb against the rind. They topped onions all day, squatting on the rough ground, their shears making a fine drizzle of tinkling music over the baked field. By ten o'clock the cantaloupe pickers had done most of the day's work, carrying sacks that weighed as much as eighty pounds a hundred yards down the row to the trailers in temperatures of 120 degrees. For them the valley was a universe of heat and dust, of short-handled hoes, overloaded crates, sixty-pound lug boxes stacked six and seven feet high, that conditioned their bodies to the strains of hectic work. The veterans of such harvesting measured their days by the thousands of strokes weeding a field, by the endless rows of white conical caps placed gently over young melon plants, or by the bundles of carrots tied with Twist-ems. Their talk was that of people who knew the fields by their first names.[34]

With braceros and undocumented workers holding down two out of three jobs, local farmworkers turned to the NFLU as a last resort. Barely solvent and with less than five hundred dollars in its treasury, the union quickly established three locals and devised a plan to expose the situation. On May 24, 1951, the NFLU announced that it represented farmworkers in the valley and demanded a raise in melon picking wages from twenty to twenty-five cents an hour. The union also called on growers to stop hiring braceros over domestic workers in violation of international agreements. When growers refused, the union set up pickets outside various melon packing sheds. Over the next month, the union extended its picket lines to labor camps, the Holly Sugar refinery, terminals, and several large ranches, using the strike to highlight the way braceros and undocumented workers were being used as strikebreakers. When Teamster Union officials refused to honor picket lines and government officials in Mexico and the United States ignored numerous violations of the bracero agreement, the union realized that it could not succeed in shaming bureaucrats into action. On June 25 it officially ended the strike.[35]

But the NFLU accomplished more than it realized. So great was the ruckus over the effect that braceros and the undocumented were having on American workers that *Life* magazine sent Loomis Dean into the valley to capture the situation. The son of a Monticello, Florida, grocer and schoolteacher, Dean had studied photography at the Rochester Atheneum and Mechanics Institute, the only school in the nation that taught photography in 1937. To pay tuition, he washed dishes and worked at odd jobs. After graduation, Dean put his low-key manner to work as a combination usher–photographer and press agent at Ringling Brothers and Barnum and Bailey Circus. "I was with the circus four years and saw every state in the union before I was twenty years old," he later recalled. "I photographed everything from clowns and acrobats to lion tamers and midgets, processing the pictures in hotel bathtubs." As the result of a contact he made with an army colonel during a stopover in Dayton, Ohio, Dean landed a job with the United States Army Air Force during World War II. After the war, one of Dean's Army Air Force friends, a picture editor who went to work for *Life,* hired Dean to do a story on circus winter quarters. One of Dean's images ran on the magazine's cover, and *Life* hired him in 1947. Assigned to the West Coast, he became a jack-of-all-trades photographer who handled everything from celebrities and breaking news to bat caves and maritime disasters.[36]

While engaged in a series of stories on wealthy ranchers (the "Olive Man," the "Raisin Barron," the "Cotton King"), Dean traveled into the Imperial Valley to cover the Border Patrol's massive campaign to arrest, detain, and deport thousands of undocumented Mexican laborers. Working night and day over a period of several weeks, he thoroughly documented the story, shooting what amounted to the first extended photo essay on undocumented farmworkers in California agriculture. Published under the title "Wetbacks Swarm In: Mexicans Disrupt Border Economy by Sneaking Over for Low Wages," Dean's images competed with the incendiary headlines and advertisements for cars, liquor, perfume, cosmetics, soft drinks, and cigarettes. This was a new development in the visual coverage of California farmworkers. In the pages of *Life,* the pathos and significance of undocumented immigration into the Imperial Valley were presented as part of the larger magazine layout. It was the beginning of a style of graphic equalization that photographic critic David Levi Strauss labels a perverse form of thrill seeking, cultural voyeurism, and "ad-venture." Such layouts, appealing to the consumer–spectator society, would dilute the impact of farmworker photography, no matter how timely and powerful, whenever it appeared in national and regional magazines dependent on advertising revenue.[37]

Despite these problems, Dean's work revealed the desperation and determination of so-called wetbacks. He used a strobe to make nighttime shots of men scrambling under fences to evade Border Patrolmen. By day he photographed serape-clad undocumented workers arrested in raids on labor camps near Holtville and deportees being marched back across the border into Mexico at the Calexico immigration gates. He

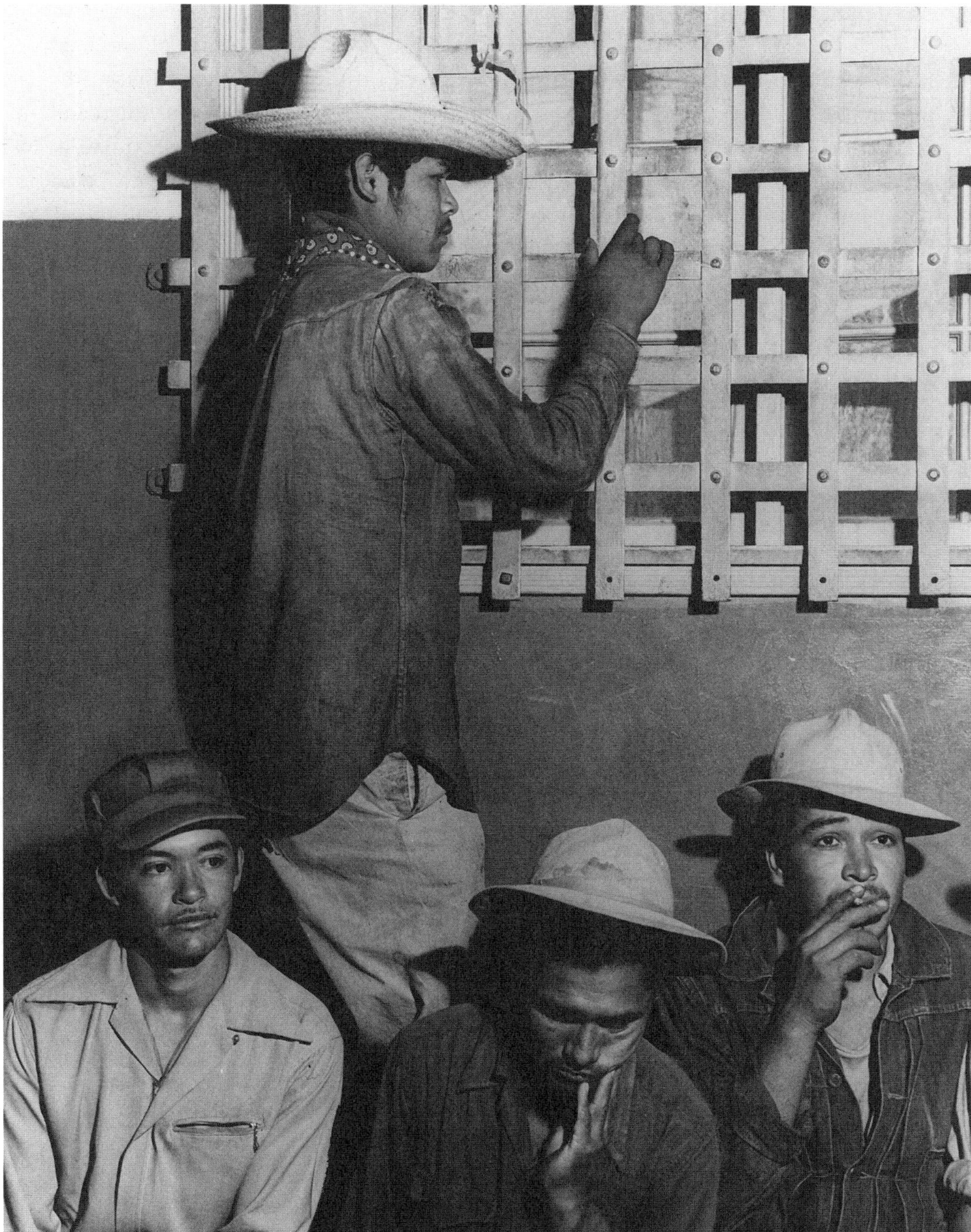

Vicente (standing) and sixty-four other dejected men endure temperatures of 120 degrees in a twenty-square-foot jail cell in Indio while awaiting deportation, June 1952, Willis Photo. Courtesy of the Hearst Newspaper Collection, Special Collections, USC Library.

also discovered a number of stories on his own. One centered on men trekking north on "the Mexican highway," a line of power poles that guided them through the desert. "They would come in by night with a gallon of water, follow those telephone lines north, and end up under the only trees for miles in this exposed spot between the mountains and the Salton Sea, where the Border Patrol would just wait for them and scoop them up as they sat at the only water hole," Dean later recalled. "You had to admire their determination. You felt sad and wondered what circumstances would motivate someone to take such chances. When you take such photographs you always wonder what you would do under those circumstances. You had this feeling of luck and privilege that exposed your own humanity, or lack of it."[38]

After the Border Patrol arrested one group of "wetbacks," Dean followed them south to the Calexico jail. While visiting with them, he noticed the way a single light bulb cast dramatic shadows from the jail cell bars across the room where the men were held. He later recalled:

> I had a Leica and a 28-millimeter lens. I just leaned against the bars and shot at one-half or one-tenth of a second. I knew it was a good picture. The men were so tired they did not even notice that I was there. They just sat there quietly. I knew they would be back. They had too much to gain and nothing to lose. I'm sure they were thinking through their next move. Maybe a different crossing point or a different time of the day or a different day of the week. They were not be deterred. Arrest and detention never intimidated them. One fellow got caught five times in three days.[39]

After completing his assignment, Dean became curious about the ordeal endured by those coming north. Working with a Mexican writer, he traveled deep into Mexico to complete what may have been the first comprehensive American photo essay on undocumented farmworkers. Dean later recalled:

> We followed one man from his village in Oaxaca. We had to be very sensitive. I remember how much he gave up—he had to sell his burro and his saddle and leave his family. I photographed him praying in church, kissing his family, his dog. Those poor guys would get robbed all along the way. My last shot was of all these guys hanging all over the boxcars of this train as it headed south. They had nothing to eat but stolen watermelons. I got up on this boxcar to photograph them and they started throwing pieces of those melons at me. The writer working with me got up with this board and started batting those melons.[40]

Life never published Dean's long essay. When he returned to his old routine, few other photographers followed up on his work. By far the most important reason for the lack of interest was the political pressure that curbed the activity of California artists and intellectuals in the early 1950s. With the FBI investigating anyone deemed a communist or communist sympathizer and the House Un-American Activities Committee hauling people before hearings in Washington, D.C., a staggering number of famous and lesser-known artists found themselves blacklisted for refusing to testify. To be labeled a communist or communist sympathizer, all one had to do was stray from the anointed path. Voicing critical views of economic and social conditions in the California countryside or organizing and photographing farmworkers were certainly actions sufficient to generate reprisals and investigations. And with the dismissal of faculty members from state colleges and the University of California for failing to sign a loyalty oath and some intellectuals feeling so alienated that they left the United States or moved into seclusion, photographers who failed to toe the line had little leeway.[41]

A second reason for this diminishing interest was the timidity of the understaffed and unmotivated state regulatory bureaucracy. Although investigators for the California Department of Industrial Relations packed cameras with them and shot photographs while inspecting farm labor camps, they seldom published their rather amateurish pictures and only rarely employed them as evidence in official publications. The third reason why photographers backed away from their coverage of farmworkers was the lack of sustained interest among the state's newspapers. Just as most U.S. publications paid little attention to segregation and the civil rights movement, so too did they largely ignore both farmworkers and the bracero program.[42]

Max Yavno's struggle to visually depict farmworkers at this time illustrates the frustrations faced by documentary photographers during the early 1950s. Even as a successful commercial photographer with corporate clients, Yavno had never abandoned his political loyalties and constantly searched for ways to return to the fields. When he began photographing for the wine industry, Yavno found a way to combine commercial work stressing technology and landscape with editorial photography focused on workers tending vineyards and bringing in the crops. The arrangement, which several other photographers would soon employ to great advantage, allowed him to maintain contact with farm labor, but it did not provide the kind of long-term contact necessary for producing anything beyond the occasional single image. To overcome this problem, Yavno applied for several Guggenheim Fellowships. He finally won an appointment in 1953 to study "the education, delinquency, mores, achievements, religion, migration, employment, skilled and unskilled labor" of Mexican Americans in the Southwest.[43]

Almost immediately, Yavno inaugurated a project that he had been thinking about since the end of the war. When he began photographing for this project and looking for publishers, Yavno wrote to the editors of *Time, Life, Look, Fortune, Vogue, Holiday,* and the *Saturday Evening Post,* as well as to Houghton–Mifflin Publishing Company. "Coming from one of the most rural and religious backgrounds," he stressed, "these Mexicans were confronted with an alien civilization at the height of its industrialization and secularization. The resulting conflicts," he added, "had their effects socially and economically not only on these people but on the communities in which they lived." But like Paul Taylor twenty-five years earlier—indeed, like anyone who tried to apply documentary photography to social problems at the time—Yavno ran into a wall of opposition. His project was simply too far ahead of its time. Editors unanimously rejected the idea of any survey of Mexican American labor. Only *Harper's Bazaar* art director Alexei Brodovitch, who admired Yavno's photographs and asked to see examples from his published books, seemed even remotely interested. After some discussion, he too passed on the project, consigning Yavno to the same fate as that of so many other photographers working among California farmworkers.[44]

As the years went by, the absence of substantial photographic coverage had disastrous consequences for braceros and undocumented workers. Rarely did photographers question the generally negative picture of these people. Many continued to use loaded terms when captioning their images. Few focused on the contributions, sacrifices, and motivations of the new immigrants. None created photo essays. Producing single, isolated images, photographers illustrated largely negative articles holding undocumented workers responsible for everything from rising crime rates and epidemics to swelling welfare rolls and narcotics trafficking and driving home the themes of an "unchecked tide" that was part of an "alien invasion." Rarely did these photographers show undocumented immigrants as people making a valuable contribution to the agricultural industry, to their families, and to Mexico. During the summer of 1954 this perspective became even further entrenched. Photographers following Immigration and Naturalization Service agents shot hundreds of pictures of them arresting, handcuffing, and shipping home thousands of undocumented Mexican field hands in Operation Wetback, the Eisenhower administration's politically confused, often brutal, mass roundup and deportation program along the U.S.–Mexico border. Superficial and largely reactive, this work reveals little about Mexican farmworkers, why they came north, and the conditions under which they lived.[45]

Faced with this pattern of sensationalism and visual distortion coupled with a lack of outlets for their work, photographers hoping to produce a more complex picture of life and labor in the fields were forced to devise new approaches. One of the most unusual and contradictory approaches was developed by Pirkle Jones. A freelance photographer employed by clients ranging from Tidewater Associated Oil Refinery and IBM to Stanford University and various advertising agencies, Jones accepted a commercial assignment for Kern County Land Company in 1955. It was an odd base from which to engage in documentary work. Hardly the sort of employer to take more than a public relations approach to field hands, Kern County Land Company controlled an empire twice the size of Rhode Island (some twenty-eight hundred square miles of land in fourteen states) and farmed a variety of crops ranging from asparagus to tomatoes.[46]

Much like Carleton E. Watkins three-quarters of a century earlier, Jones surveyed farming operations with an eye for capturing the corporate sublime. And much like Watkins, he photographed planting, plowing, and irrigating in a workmanlike manner, but he never passed up a good picture. Given extensive access to Kern County Land Company property, Jones frequently encountered scenes that were less predictable and more revealing than the commercial images he had been hired to produce. Discovering one Mexican American family waiting in their car beside a large field, Jones paused from his corporate work and made a series of personal photographs recording a young mother and father tending to their infant. Reflecting on that photograph, Jones later described it as neither photojournalism nor documentary work. Rather, it was an example of the peculiar way in which he went about his work. Using commercial photography as a base for more extended work in the California hinterland, Jones obtained access to locations off limits to other photographers and was able to finance other forays and remain in the fields for extended periods.[47]

Of his Kern County Land Company assignment, Jones recalled many years later how he had often encountered scenes that forced him to think about the work of his predecessors, from Lewis Hine to Dorothea Lange, at the very moment he was photographing. Once, after he discovered a cotton picker pulling her long cotton picking sack down a row with a small child sleeping on the sack, the entire heritage of cotton picking photography flashed through his mind. "I could not remember another cotton picking photograph like it," Jones recalled a half century later. "I was compelled, even inspired, to take that picture."[48]

After Jones began using commercial work to advance documentary coverage, the approach caught on, and a number of variations developed. At this point Dorothea Lange stepped into the picture. Although often ill now, she was deeply involved in a *Life* magazine assignment documenting a dam that was about to flood Napa County's Berryessa Valley. When she became fatigued, she asked Ansel Adams to work on the project and, after Adams declined, turned to Jones, whom she had met while teaching at the School of Fine Arts. Offered half of Lange's one-thousand-dollar retainer, Jones jumped at the opportunity. Working side by side, the two at first recorded the same scenes: the destruction of homes and barns, the auction of farm machinery, the demolition of buildings, the clearing of stumps, trees, and orchards by gigantic Caterpillar tractors, and the disinterment of bodies from graveyards and their transfer to new plots above the waterline. But as Lange's health further declined, Jones took over more of the photographic chores. Remaining in the beautiful little valley as the power lines came down and the town of Monticello was burned, the two photographers took their last pictures when the waters began rising and cut off any further access.[49]

Filled with memorable shots, the collaborative essay placed farmworkers at the center of a powerful environmental statement. Lange's angst-ridden pictures of men bringing in the last hay crop captured the sense of sadness that pervaded the valley, and her picture of a terrorized horse being led away by a field hand caught the gut-wrenching trauma that pervaded the valley toward the end. Jones expanded these themes in a series of portraits centering on the grape harvest. Of these portraits, one is especially memorable. Staring straight into the camera, a single grape picker who seems to have a Mona Lisa–like expression displays a box of wine grapes. Other farmworkers stare back with looks of doom and pride and mostly sadness at leaving behind a community they had lived in most of their lives. Many years would pass before the Berryessa Valley images were seen by the public. After Lange and Jones edited their work on the valley and sent it off to *Life,* the magazine, in characteristic fashion, spiked the essay at the last minute, substituting a story on a devastating a flood in Texas.[50]

While Lange and Jones were busy in the Berryessa Valley, Ansel Adams was photographing farmworkers on El Solyo Ranch in Kern County. Most of the assignment was standard commercial work of the type that allowed Adams to make a living in the years before his images commanded huge sums. Always the consummate photographer, Adams did his usual thorough job surveying the property for ranch manager Roy Pike. But Adams did not neglect the people who worked the land. Apparently he stayed overnight at the ranch, because many of his images seem to be taken indoors, after work, on successive days. In one series he used off-camera strobes to photograph men shooting pool, enjoying meals, and bellying up to the bars inside the mess halls. In another he spent considerable time shooting portraits, including one sequence, otherwise completely uncharacteristic of Adams, of a trusted bracero goofing about while smoking a cigar.[51]

Following his assignment at El Solyo Ranch, Ansel Adams made prints for the ranch managers and ranch owners, then filed away his work. Jones did the same with the documentary images of the scenes he had stumbled into while shooting for Kern County Land Company. This pattern was characteristic of humanistic photography among California farmworkers during the decade. While innovative photographers continued to make useful and revealing images and kept the documentary ideal alive, they had no way to place their work before the public or otherwise use it to educate and inform. Frustrated at having to consign useful work to their personal archives and the occasional print displayed on exhibition, Jones and Lange would lash out in frustration against editors, publishers, and the lack of appreciation for documentary work, while Adams, writing it off as part of the price to be paid for doing commercial work, was more philosophical and far less frustrated, since this was not the sort of work that he would be inclined to publish or exhibit.

These problems would also constrain the work of Ernesto Galarza, who, as research director of the NFLU, packed a camera with him on organizing rounds into bars, movie houses, community events, barrios, and *colonias.* Documenting appalling housing conditions and degrading treatment, especially in border recruitment and processing centers, Galarza's images hardly compared to those of Lange, Jones, and Adams. But at this time, quality did not translate into an audience. What mattered was having a way to get the work out to the public. Galarza accomplished this by donating his work to whoever would use it and by publishing it in union pamphlets. In 1956 he published a handful of his images in *Strangers in Our Fields,* a devastating indictment of the bracero program that growers labeled "a pack of lies."[52]

Galarza's photographs exerted their greatest impact not on fellow unionists or the public but rather on another photographer: Los Angeles freelancer Leonard Nadel. Like so many other top photographers of the era, the handsome, worldly, silver-haired Nadel had served in World War II as a combat photographer, slogging his way through New Guinea and the Philippine Islands with the United States Army. After obtaining a teaching credential, he had settled in Los Angeles and worked briefly in the public schools before taking up commercial photography. Never quite satisfied with corporate work, Nadel continued to branch out and soon landed work with *Business Week, Forbes, Fortune,* and other magazines. But even though he was a well-established, widely sought-after corporate photographer, his social values continued to steer him toward the less fortunate members of society.[53]

Shortly after photographing the urban poor for the Los Angeles Housing Authority, Nadel obtained a copy of *Strangers in Our Fields.* An adventurous, creative individual and an avid reader who thoroughly researched subjects before photographing them, Nadel was so taken by Galarza's book that he launched a project that would become the most ambitious, systematic, and explicitly political farmworker photographic exposé of the decade. To fund his project, Nadel contacted the Fund for the Republic, a left-leaning, nonprofit organization created by the Ford Foundation. While concerned with upholding basic principles of the Declaration of Independence, the Constitution, and the Bill of Rights, the Fund for the Republic was then branching out into controversial issues similar to those handled by the American Civil Liberties Union. As part of its support for investigations of immigration policy, the fund granted Nadel a fellowship to study the bracero program and create something that was, in effect, the visual counterpart to *Strangers in Our Fields.*[54]

Nadel devoted six months to his project in the summer and fall of 1956. Concentrating first on conditions in California, he retraced Galarza's steps and photographed all of the labor camps that Galarza had mentioned. Often living with the men there, Nadel documented filthy quarters, overcrowded conditions, inadequate sanitary facilities, how the men were fed and transported, and substandard medical provisions. Attentive to the broader rhythms of life outside work, Nadel also documented braceros at play, gambling and drinking on Saturday evenings. One of his most evocative images captures dozens of braceros on their knees praying and preparing to receive Holy Communion at outdoor masses, conducted by an itinerant Catholic priest in one of the camps.[55]

To help understand why and how braceros traveled north, Nadel did something that only one other American photographer had done: he headed deep into Mexico. After photographing braceros in their home villages, with special attention paid to family life and conditions, Nadel followed the men to the Mexico City recruitment and assembly centers, then on to Monterrey, Mexico, where five thousand men were processed each day. After that he headed north, traveling with braceros in railroad cars carrying seventy men, sometimes more. At the border processing centers, Nadel documented Mexican federal police with rubber truncheons herding men behind barbed wire fences. In one Mexican town, he witnessed police beating a bracero in jail. While photographing at a nearby camp, he was arrested by a Mexican army lieutenant and a squad of armed soldiers. His crime: having failed to obtain permission to climb to the top of a military barracks to take pictures. "It was a ludicrous situation I had gotten into, but not a laughing matter at that moment," Nadel later recalled. "The impasse of the language barrier between the lieutenant and myself was, fortunately for me, soon broken by the arrival of a camp official who rescued me from my predicament."[56]

After traveling five thousand miles and submerging himself in the world of braceros, Nadel abandoned all pretense of neutrality. Braceros, he believed, were essentially modern slaves. Caught between two worlds, kept in line by the fear of being sent home if they complained of ill treatment, they were driven by the goals of escaping

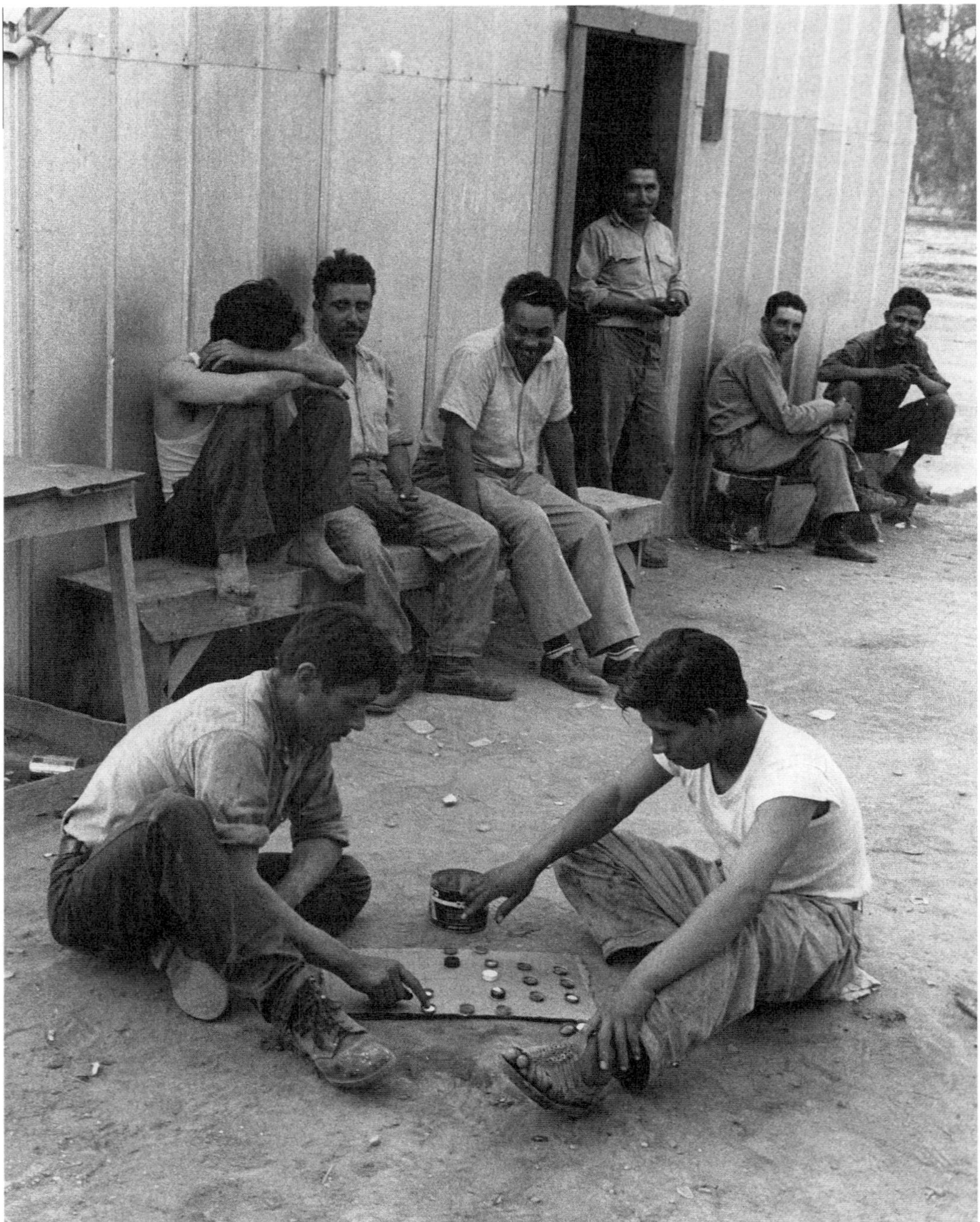

"Work is not always available," wrote Leonard Nadel after taking this photograph in June 1958. "During such lulls the men are not paid and must remain in camp and shift for themselves in trying to fill their time. With bottle caps and the side of a cardboard carton, men improvise their own limited recreation." Photograph by Leonard Nadel. Courtesy of Evelyn DeWolfe Nadel.

the dull and dismal poverty in the Mexican cities or countryside and saving enough money to support their families. Departing for the land of plenty to live a life no better than the one they were leaving behind, they hoped to earn as much as five hundred dollars in two months time, the equivalent of four years of income at home. After purchasing their contracts from local agents, many waited days before their names were ever called, traveled as much as one thousand miles to reach the recruiting centers, and then, after embarking on another arduous trek to the border, were herded into lines for mass examination.

Following braceros on their journey, Nadel shot more than two thousand pictures. By any standard, it was a brave and moving effort. After finishing it, Nadel simply could have walked away, satisfied that he had fulfilled his contract. But he was so deeply affected by what he witnessed that he could not turn his back. Believing that he was duty-bound to make his work available to as many people as possible, Nadel carefully organized his images, aggressively lobbied editors, and eventually created two classic photo essays, which he published in *Jubilee* and *Pageant* magazines. Using small photographs to depict key incidents and capture everyday activities, he structured scenes in a way that tells the story of how and why braceros came north and the price they paid. Certain photographs set the stage as larger images leading to the next scene and finally to a closing statement.[57]

In wrapping up his work, Nadel tried to summarize what he had learned. Writing in *Pageant* magazine, he assessed the bracero program with this powerfully moving message:

> Arriving here, the bracero soon finds that a contract is a piece of paper which may be torn, or burned, or spat upon. His papers assure him a minimum of work hours, paid sick leave, sanitary lodgings, meals at cost, free heat and bedding. But a periphery of profiteers bleeds his paycheck dry. Too often, he is given just enough work to cover his board. He lives in unheated barns and warehouses. He pays dearly for food too rancid to eat, blankets he is too cold to forego and, sometimes, even for the tools of his trade.[58]

Taken together, Nadel's photographs present a comprehensive portrait of a class of people. Everything is there, from quiet moments in small rural communities to the violence and brutality of the processing and recruitment centers. At its core, his work indicts the bracero program as slavery reincarnated. Growers howled at and protested such a perspective, claiming that Nadel, like Galarza and most activists before him, painted a distorted and biased picture. But it was not just Nadel's photo essays that upset agribusinessmen. To exert maximum influence, Nadel provided his photographs to a congressional committee investigating the bracero program. In tandem with Galarza's report, the evidence delivered to Congress was undeniable. Unfortunately, many of Nadel's images were so strong and so disturbing that they could not achieve wider circulation.

One of Nadel's most distressing images captures a group of one hundred naked braceros lined up to be "deloused" with DDT at a border processing center. Without an identifying caption, the photograph, if slightly blurred, could easily have been mistaken for a group of prisoners awaiting execution in a Nazi death camp. Another shocking photograph showed the men as they were being sprayed with DDT. Another documented men lined up in a cinder block room as they were showing the calluses on their hands to prove that they really were experienced farmworkers. No calluses meant no permission to enter California as a bracero, which also meant that men who wished to work would have to cross the border illegally.[59]

Not since Dorothea Lange had a photographer produced such a powerfully moving portrait of farmworkers and provoked such a strong response. Together with Galarza's writing, Nadel's photography kept the issue of bracero labor before the public and fueled demands for reforms, despite official denials of abuses. Unable to dismiss Nadel's photographs of housing conditions, the Department of Labor added more compliance officers, tightened regulations on housing, and either closed or forced owners to clean up or repair more than four hundred substandard camps. But Nadel could not sustain his effort and, like many before him, eventually returned to the commercial photography that paid his bills. He would never again photograph braceros or any other group of farmworkers. Nor would he find much of an audience for the huge photo essay that he had created. With Galarza's union (now renamed the National Agricultural Workers Union, NAWU) barely solvent, holding no contracts, virtually without members, and about to merge itself into the Meat Cutters Union and out of existence, by the 1950s it appeared that whatever photographic momentum had been gained was about to dissipate. Then, as had always happened in the past and would happen again in the future, another photographer stepped forward. That photographer was Harvey Richards.[60]

Of all those photographing in the fields at this time, Harvey Richards was by far the most proletarian and left leaning. Hardened by decades of physical labor, he had served as a merchant seaman during the 1930s and spent World War II installing gun turrets, diesel engines, and propellers on Liberty ships. A man of strong views, he took up photography to serve political and social ends, as he once said, "to open people's eyes to the evils and lies of capitalist society." Father Thomas McCullough, a Roman Catholic priest who ministered to labor camps around Stockton, talked Richards into becoming a photographer. Accepting the challenge, Richards constructed a rooftop platform on his 1957 Chevrolet station wagon and began patrolling the countryside.[61]

Besides the awful living conditions, widespread use of the short-handled hoe, pervasive employment of children, and exploitation of bracero labor, Richards encountered two important new developments in the farmworker story. One was pesticides. Although not unknown to farmworkers, pesticide use was exploding at this time. Richards was probably the first photographer to systematically document the introduction of pesticides on a wide scale and, by implication, their effect on farmworkers. He found farmworkers harvesting fruit in orchards full of signs warning people not to enter, discovered flaggers being covered by poisonous clouds dumped from crop dusters, and stumbled into men picking tomatoes into five gallon cans that apparently had once held some toxic substance.[62]

The other new development among farmworkers, which Richards recorded in great detail and also possibly for the first time on any sustained basis, was the predicament of "bums," alcoholics, transients, and other homeless men who worked as "day-haul" laborers under the so-called wino system around Fresno, Sacramento, and Stockton. Six days a week during February and March 1958, Richards followed the same routine. Taking lodging in one of the cheap hotels in the area, he prowled the rundown rooming houses and soup kitchens in the various skid rows where single men flopped for a night or two. Each morning he rose between 3 and 4 A.M. and accompanied the men out onto the street corners.[63]

Photographing under the dim illumination of street lamps and the harsh glare of automobile headlights, Richards encountered numerous technical problems that threatened to defeat his day-haul project. He could not use strobe or flash lights, because they would have driven the men away. And long exposures from a camera mounted on a tripod would have slowed him down and made a blur of everything. To work unobtrusively and make candid, hand-held exposures documenting the men as they haggled with foremen and paid one dollar for the "day-haul" round trip to and

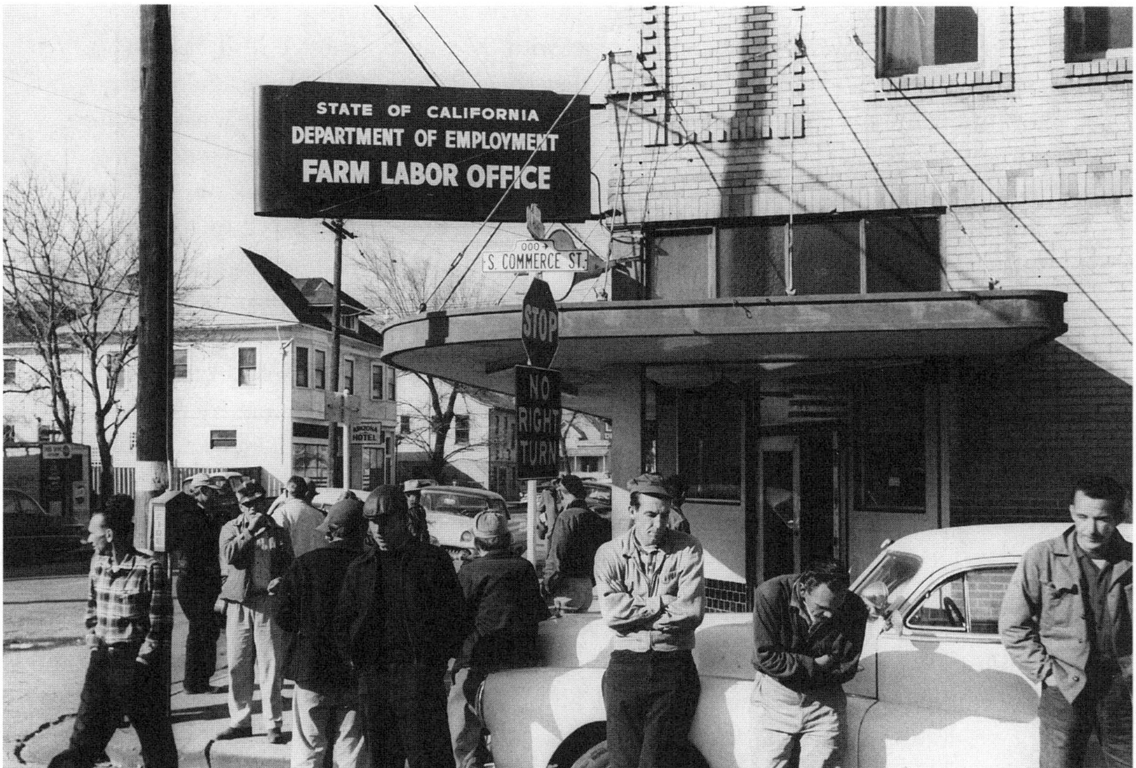

"A hated corner . . . run by the State Employment Office . . . insensitive," wrote Harvey Richards on the back of this March 1959 photograph of the shape-up in downtown Stockton. Photograph by Harvey Richards. Courtesy of Harvey Richards.

from the fields, Richards relied on high-speed black-and-white film, mainly Tri-X. To get the maximum out of his Tri-X, Richards "pushed" it to its limit, overexposing the film and then underdeveloping it in FG-7 developer, thereby achieving a higher film speed, somewhat at the expense of image quality.[64]

When the trucks returned and disgorged the tired men late in the afternoon, Richards was there again. Committed to producing a complete picture, he continued to photograph the men during their daily struggles, even when there was no work. Of his many photographs, probably the most moving ones recorded day-haul laborers warming themselves over garbage cans full of burning debris or waiting in long lines for a free meal under the illuminated cross of the Salvation Army or St. Mary's Rescue Mission.[65]

By the late spring of 1958, Richards had created an activist portfolio, a very effective one, but he did not stop there. Hardly a passive spectator, he set out not merely to criticize farm labor relations but to force dramatic changes. Shattering and pushing aside the view of farmworkers as adjuncts of the landscape, Richards substituted a surreal picture full of bold juxtapositions. Challenging viewers with new and absolutely irreverent images, he turned the pastoral ideal on its head and attempted to nullify much of the agricultural industry's advertising and public relations images. So impressed were several farm labor activists with the way he invested his images with moral authority and political power that they concluded no union campaign could go forward without paying attention to the photographic dimension. This was the conclusion of National Farm Labor Union president H. L. Mitchell. Grateful to Richards and other photographers, he wrote to one of his California organizers on April 11, 1958, advising him to pack a camera. "A picture of a breadline in Stockton and [the] unloading [of] Mexicans," he stressed, "tells the story better than anything else."[66]

After finishing his day-haul project, Richards became a photographer for the Agricultural Workers Association (AWA), a farmworker union organized by Father Thomas McCullough. In the spring of 1959, when the AFL–CIO created the Agricultural Workers Organizing Committee (AWOC) and McCullough's fledgling AWA folded up, AWOC hired several NFLU and AWA organizers, including Richards. Launching a massive, well-financed organizing drive, AWOC provided Richards with a new outlet for his energies. Well endowed by the AFL and boasting a gritty and experienced leadership aware of the complicated and difficult nature of organizing farmworkers, AWOC was probably more cognizant of the complexity of its task than most organizations that had entered the field previously. Writing to AWOC director Norman Smith, field organizer Louis Krainock identified at least one main enemy or obstacle: "the commonly accepted picture of agriculture as being made of the sturdy yeoman, the solid, earthy American family farmer."[67]

Over the next decade, AWOC and other agricultural unions would devote all of their energies to overturning that myth and presenting a fuller and more complete picture of what it meant to be a farmworker in California.

16

Rented Slaves

The Resurgence of Documentary Photography

At a labor convention late in 1959, AWOC director of publicity Louis Krainock made a discovery. Krainock's union had replaced NAWU as the main challenge to corporate farming, and he was searching for ways to build support when he learned of a film about earlier efforts to organize farmworkers. Borrowing the film from the United Automobile Workers union, where it was held in a secure corner of the library at the UAW's Detroit headquarters, Krainock watched what turned out to be a surviving copy of *Poverty in the Valley of Plenty.* An outsider and newcomer to agricultural organizing who was on loan to AWOC from the United Packinghouse Workers of America (UPWA), the craggy-faced Krainock had survived countless union organizing drives and picket-line battles but was unfamiliar with the 1950 ban on the film, its controversial history, and the price to be paid for showing it. He also did not know that Mitchell himself had purchased two prints of the film and destroyed them and that both the Hollywood Film Council and the California Federation of Labor had notified all who had purchased copies to destroy the films. With little contact with Galarza, he had not been told that all concerned with the film assumed *Poverty in the Valley of Plenty* was resting in peace. All Krainock understood was that, after seeing the film, he regarded it as a useful organizing tool, and he wasted little time before showing it to farmworkers and staff members. The film, he said, was a dated but instructive case study of the worst way to go about organizing a large corporate farm.[1]

Beginning on April 6, 1960, AWOC director of organizing Norman Smith took the film to Stockton, Strathmore, Marysville, Olivehurst, Empire, Riverbank, and Westley. Audiences were not large, but there was enough interest for Smith to show the film almost every night to farmworkers and staff members. Word that the film "was out and being shown almost every night" soon reached DiGiorgio's attorneys, who had been alerted after seeing an advertisement for the film in the *Valley Labor Citizen,* a newspaper published by the Fresno County Central Labor Council. To investigate, DiGiorgio dispatched William R. Callan, a private investigator and secretary of the

Orange County Associated Farmers. Moving into the Strathmore area, he provided DiGiorgio with a list of those who were showing the film, who was present, the involvement of AWOC and NAWU in the showings, and evidence that the film had recently been shown in Stockton. On May 12 he recruited several growers who accompanied him to a showing of the film in Woodlake. Everyone took notes, and Callon made a list of all present. The following day, Callan reported his reconnaissance to DiGiorgio's attorneys. On May 14 they viewed the company's print of the film to confirm that it was the same one they had seen. Over the next four days, Callan crisscrossed the valley, gathering up more information and trying to discern Galarza's involvement in the matter.[2]

On May 18, company attorneys filed a two-million-dollar suit against AWOC as well as NAWU for defamation of character. DiGiorgio public relations director Albert O'Dea made the most of the suit with indignant press releases, condemning the showing in scandalous tones: "a shocking collection of falsehoods . . . fraud perpetuated by a handful of men . . . a deliberately fabricated falsehood . . . almost totally unrelieved by any regard whatever for truth and facts . . . a disservice to labor . . ." and a "malicious flaunting of a judgment arising from a similar suit in 1950."[3]

DiGiorgio's rhetoric masked a deeper fear of a resurgence of the farm labor movement. Suddenly farmworker organizing was on the move under the leadership of sixty-two-year-old Norman Smith. A bull-necked, 250-pound, former United Auto Workers leader and close personal friend of AFL–CIO leader Walter Reuther and Director of Organization Jack Livingston, Smith had taken over as AWOC's executive in 1959. To consolidate his power, Smith pushed aside Ernesto Galarza, who had created many enemies within organized labor for his attacks on "labor fakirs" and his insistence on attacking the bracero labor program in order to establish the preconditions for organizing farmworkers. With Galarza relegated to a largely powerless position as director of training, in which he had no duties, Smith moved out from his base in Stockton and began building a base among farmworkers in the Central Valley. With a revolving fund of several hundred thousand dollars a month from the AFL–CIO, he assembled a large staff and planted union locals in farm towns between Yuba City and Dos Palos. Appearing at hearings, Smith scowled and intimidated well-dressed agribusiness lobbyists and verbally fought with State Farm Placement Service personnel.[4]

By the early summer of 1959, Smith was calling California agribusinessmen "robber barons," directing protests that prevented DiGiorgio Fruit Corporation and other growers from hiring braceros in Marysville and Yuba City and stopped the State Farm Placement Service from referring any workers at all to struck farms. Having threatened the cherry crop, AWOC had organizers working on all of the DiGiorgio Fruit Corporation's farms and was preparing actions for the tomato, grape, and peach harvests. When the *People's World* and *San Francisco News* simultaneously characterized the AWOC campaign as "the most concerted drive to organize America's farm workers since the 30s" and predicted that "the Central valley was about to become a battlefield," the DiGiorgio Fruit Corporation noted these developments and decided to act. But rather than confronting AWOC directly, the corporation saw a way to wipe out AWOC the same way it had wiped out the NFLU: by resurrecting the old lawsuit.[5]

As a labor-busting tactic, the lawsuit worked perfectly. With organizers directing over one hundred hit-and-run strikes, which had forced DiGiorgio and other large-scale growers to release hundreds of bracero workers, AWOC leaders suddenly found their energy sapped and their resources exhausted as they shifted their attention away from the fields and reformulated plans. For NAWU, the lawsuit was the last nail in the struggling union's coffin. Facing the possibility of paying a huge monetary judgment, NAWU had to postpone a pending merger with the Amalgamated Meat Cutters and Butcher Workmen that would have injected new money into the campaign. Already contemptuous of AWOC and its leaders, NAWU organizers, including Galarza and Mitchell, were forced to pay for their own legal defense, raising money through personal loans from friends. Galarza claimed malicious prosecution, retained separate council, and filed a countersuit. With little regard for AWOC leaders, whom they regarded as "dumb clucks," neither Galarza nor Mitchell offered support for AWOC and quickly disassociated themselves from its actions.[6]

Although the lawsuit had its desired effect on agricultural unions, it failed to intimidate photographers, filmmakers, and, most important, producers of television news documentaries. A few days after the lawsuit was final, CBS televison began working on a documentary about migrant farmworkers. This was an odd turn of events at CBS, which, like the other television networks, had heretofore run what was essentially an incompatible, antagonistic, and mutually exclusive amalgamation of show business, advertising, and news devoted to creating valuable commercial breaks seen by fifty-four million people and eight out of ten families. But following a series of scandals in which the CBS entertainment division had been caught rigging quiz shows, Executive Producer Fred W. Friendly broke dramatically with an approach to news programming that hardly noticed members of the underclass. To restore the reputation of CBS, Friendly launched a series of bold documentary programs that would take an unusually hard look at complex problems and contemporary issues ranging from airline safety to the funeral industry. Migrant farmworkers came into the picture after Friendly heard a series that radio reporter Edward P. Morgan had been doing. CBS News would expand Morgan's work and adapt it to television.[7]

Problems plagued the effort from the beginning. When production moved forward, CBS News could not find any growers willing to appear on camera. At this point David Lowe entered the picture. An unemployed teddy bear of a producer who appeared weekly at CBS looking for work, Lowe begged for a project, and though Lowe had little or no documentary experience, Friendly, desperate for help, placed him in charge of the story, paying him a one-thousand-dollar retainer. One month later, Lowe had lined up growers and started running film crews up and down the eastern seaboard, following the migrant stream from New Jersey to Florida, with distant detours into California and Arizona to cover AWOC strikes and organizing drives. As filming proceeded, Friendly thought about who to hire as the narrator. Success hinged on this decision. Only one broadcaster seemed appropriate to the task.

That broadcaster was a war-toughened, veteran journalist, the most compelling and dynamic personality to appear in the first two decades of television: Edward R. Murrow. Americans universally trusted Murrow, who had achieved legendary status when his radio reports from London rooftops brought World War II to hundreds of thousands of people back home. Moving into the new medium of television, Murrow admired the documentary work of filmmakers such as Pare Lorentz and John Gierson and transferred those techniques intact to television in 1946, when he established the first CBS documentary unit. He followed this triumph in 1951 by launching the CBS series *See It Now.* For the first time, news producers relied on unrehearsed interviews, shot their own film rather than using film cannibalized from other sources, and unfolded their work according to a prepared script, with story lines arranged into a traditional beginning, middle, and end. Three years later, Murrow almost single-handedly ended Senator Joseph McCarthy's red-baiting activities with a half-hour editorial in which he allowed the senator to hang himself with his own words. After following his McCarthy piece with a half dozen other hard-hitting telecasts, Murrow had taken a six-month sabbatical but, on returning to work refreshed and energized early in 1960, enthusiastically accepted the as-yet-unnamed assignment from Friendly.[8]

More than professional interest underpinned Murrow's involvement in *Harvest of Shame,* the title eventually given the project by Friendly. Reading voraciously about farmworkers, Murrow was transformed from a reporter and television news purveyor into a televison activist. Many years later, Murrow (whose real first name was Egbert) would admit that personal reasons had generated in him a special affinity to the project. Born in a cabin in Greensboro, North Carolina, and growing up watching his father walking behind his mule teams from sunup to sundown, Murrow had a lifelong dislike of farmwork, especially digging potatoes and hoeing weeds, and in general any physical labor under the blazing sun. So deeply did Murrow feel about the project that he insisted on going out into the fields with the CBS crews, often directing the filming himself. After a particularly gritty day interviewing sugar cane harvesters near a shantytown south of Palm Beach, Florida, Murrow seemed to go on a crusade. Virtually living in the editing room, he hammered the script into shape, drafting, redrafting, and tailoring his writing to fit the film tightly.

After completing the filming at the end of the summer, Murrow wove his interviews together so well that when the CBS news team screened a rough cut they cried their eyes out. Despite fever and chills from bronchial trouble that would turn into pneumonia, Murrow continued to work on the final cut. Completing *Harvest of Shame* on schedule, he eliminated a concluding scene with a migrant girl singing a plaintive song as the camera panned across the faces of farmworkers of all races. "You don't need it," Murrow advised. At the end he wanted to provoke anger in the tradition of Ida Tarbell and Lincoln Steffens, not move an audience to tears.[9]

While *Harvest of Shame* was being filmed and edited, Pirkle Jones and Dorothea Lange got out their essay on the Berryessa Valley, reedited it, and showed it to the editors of *Aperture,* the country's preeminent photographic publisher, which immediately published it as *Death of a Valley.* Also coming to fruition after years of work were two book projects integrating farmworkers into portraits of the wine industry. One was *The Story of Wine in California.* Written by M. F. K. Fisher and illustrated with photographs by Max Yavno, *The Story of Wine in California* focuses on life and labor in the vineyards of the Napa Valley. While ninety halftones and sixteen color images unfold stories about winemakers, vineyards, technology, and wineries, several of Yavno's images focus on vineyard workers shoveling pomace, pruning vines, and harvesting grapes. Among these images, a tightly cropped, beautifully composed close-up of a grape picker's hand wielding a grape hook in cutting a bunch of grapes broke new ground with its Aaron Siskind–style amalgamation of aesthetics and documentary intent.[10]

The other big book project was *This Uncommon Heritage: The Paul Masson Story.* Written by Robert L. Balzar and featuring not only the work of Ansel Adams but also that of Pirkle Jones, who had taken leave from his position as instructor of photography at the California School of Fine Art to collaborate with Adams, *This Uncommon*

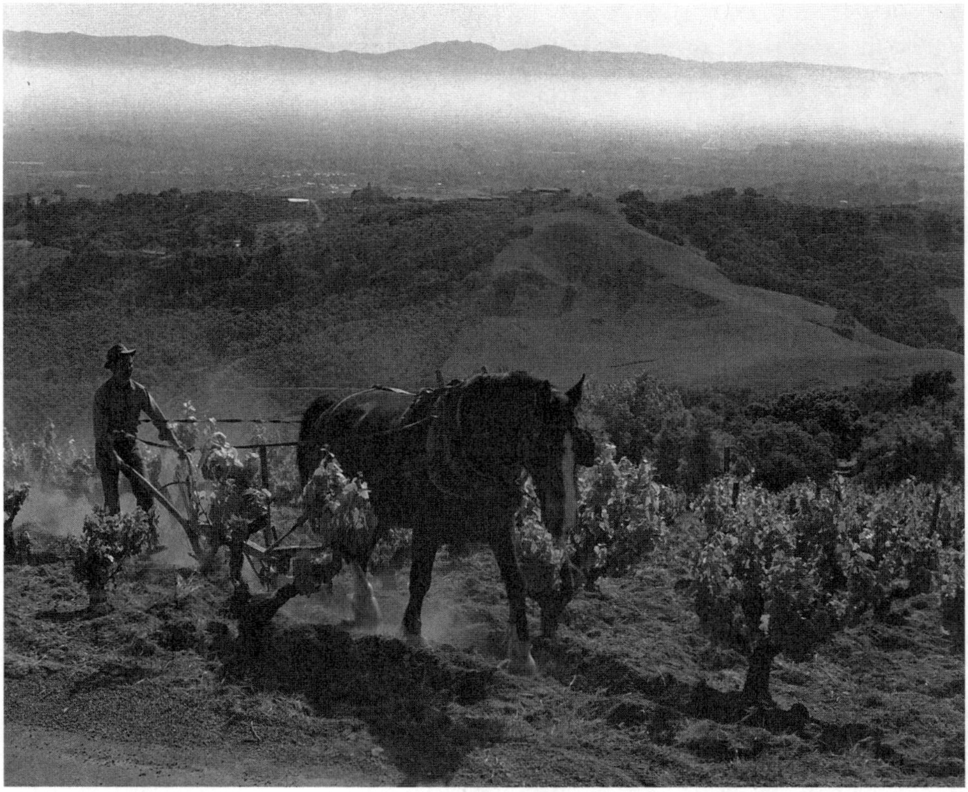

Contour plowing at Paul Masson's Vineyard in the Sky, in the hills above the Santa Clara Valley, 1960, photograph by Ansel Adams. From "The Story of a Winery" (1961). Courtesy of the Ansel Adams Collection, Center for Creative Photography, University of Arizona, Tucson, Arizona. Used by permission of the Trustees of the Ansel Adams Publishing Rights Trust. All rights reserved.

Heritage details the full spectrum of activities associated with wine making. Among the most memorable images are one of a field hand guiding a horse-drawn plow through old vineyards in the hills above Saratoga and another of a young grape picker, beautiful enough to look as if she has just stepped from the pages of *Vogue*. Hardly documentary in nature, such images were hybrids, not easily categorized, often projecting an idealized dimension, as if patterned on a Currier and Ives print. Adams was so uncomfortable with such images that toward the end of the project he wrote to Paul Masson Winery president Otto E. Meyer, emphasizing, "Neither Pirkle nor I would assume it to be an example of free and experimental personal expression."[11]

These projects considerably expanded photographic coverage of California farmworkers. But the resulting publications did not raise issues of power and exploitation, challenge the bracero program, or generate much public concern. When Ernesto Galarza forced the DiGiorgio Fruit Corporation to drop its lawsuit against Mitchell and himself on September 13, newspapers failed to cover the victory. Unfazed, DiGiorgio shifted its attack toward AWOC and the AFL–CIO. For several months it seemed that the photographic campaign was over. This changed dramatically on the evening after the 1960 Thanksgiving holiday, when television viewers turned on the CBS news.[12]

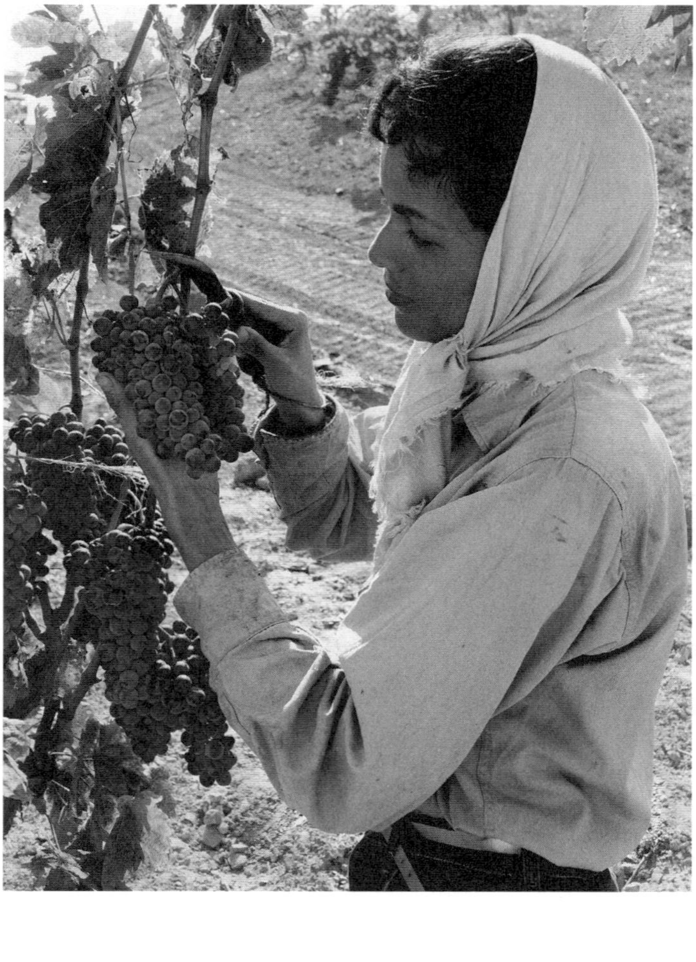

Harvesting grapes at Paul Masson Vineyards, 1961, photograph by Ansel Adams. From "The Story of a Winery" (1961). Courtesy of the Ansel Adams Collection, Center for Creative Photography, University of Arizona, Tucson, Arizona. Used by permission of the Trustees of the Ansel Adams Publishing Rights Trust. All rights reserved.

Confronted by Edward R. Murrow in shirt sleeves, wearing a small microphone around his neck, and standing on the edge of an irrigated field, with furrows stretching to the horizon behind him, the TV audience saw someone resembling a cross between Henry Fonda and Woody Guthrie. Murrow faced the camera straight on and spoke in a dark, slow, and expressive voice that viewers mistook for emotion. Actually, his gruff voice, giving added power and richness to his words, was caused by a lung full of congestion, probably the early stages of the cancer that would kill him.

Murrow's opening words were especially dramatic. "This is the way the humans who harvest the food for the best fed people in the world get hired," he began as the camera followed workers into the fields. He then quoted a grower: "We used to own our slaves. Now we just rent them." Next came the hook. "This . . . has nothing to do with Johannesburg or Capetown," he stressed. "These are citizens of the United States."[13]

Over pictures of an early-morning shape-up, Murrow introduced *Harvest of Shame,* then proceeded to probe the paradox of impoverished farmworkers harvesting bountiful crops to feed the richest nation on earth. With his narration ranging from understated irony to barely restrained anger, Murrow aggressively tackled the subject of American farmworkers in a way that shook the conscience of an entire nation. Using a spare and no-nonsense delivery, he fleshed out pictures of harvest workers stacked in trucks as they rode into the fields; bright children with no hope of a decent education; hovels where farmworkers lived; aged faces; rich farmers; fat lobbyists; earnest missionaries; slippery politicians; and complacent citizens. Although much of his commentary focused on the East Coast, Murrow devoted considerable attention to California. As viewers watched striking AWOC cherry pickers meeting to discuss strategy, Murrow noted that the scene seemed straight out of the Great Depression, when farmworkers had first been excluded from the National Labor Relations Act and had tried unsuccessfully to organize unions. Playing off this theme of exclusion, Murrow's impassioned closing remarks went beyond education and aimed at eliciting change. Addressing viewers, who benefited from the labors of the excluded Americans, he asked them to raise their voice in Congress. Was it not time for the country to extend to farmworkers the rights enjoyed by most other Americans?[14]

Unlike anything ever seen on television, *Harvest of Shame* shocked and sickened all those who saw it. To a stuffed nation still enjoying leftovers from Thanksgiving dinner, Murrow's picture of the filth, despair, and grinding poverty seemed almost un-American. Juxtaposition was everywhere. There were rules for hauling cattle to slaughter and regulations governing the packing of produce, Murrow said, but farmworkers shipped to the fields traveled in haphazard fashion without regulation in dangerous vehicles. Pointing to an anomaly that critics of farm labor had spotlighted for a half century, Murrow observed that while the federal government spent $6.5 million annually to protect migratory wildlife, it failed to appropriate $3 million for migrant education.[15]

The effect of these and other such revelations was stunning, if not inflammatory. Devoting an entire article to the documentary, *New York Times* writer Jack Gould praised Murrow as a democratic voice of reason and the producer of a documentary that was an unsurpassed piece of muckraking journalism, among the finest moments in television history. "With his cameras," Gould said of Murrow, "he showed real-life scenes that could add up only to a terrifying blot on Democracy's escutcheon."[16]

Inspiring calls for legislative action and labor organizing, *Harvest of Shame* opened up an entirely new era in the visual story of California farmworkers. For the first time millions of people who otherwise would never have given farmworkers a second thought were forced to consider them. Many recoiled in horror. Typical of the response was that of Mrs. C. C. Pelt of Long Beach, California, who on the morning after viewing the documentary wrote to President Dwight D. Eisenhower:

> My heart is very heavy this morning. I think it is a picture that should be shown again and again, to awaken *all* people. If only all T.V. channels could show it at one time so that everyone would have to see it in their homes as they are comfortably cozy and perhaps well-fed. In fact it should be shown in schools, churches, labor halls, etc. etc. I guess the reason this has disturbed me so much is because we as children were taught to never waste food since there were many starving people in the world. . . . Now, laborers who are helping to put food on our tables, are in dire circumstances, as revealed in the report![17]

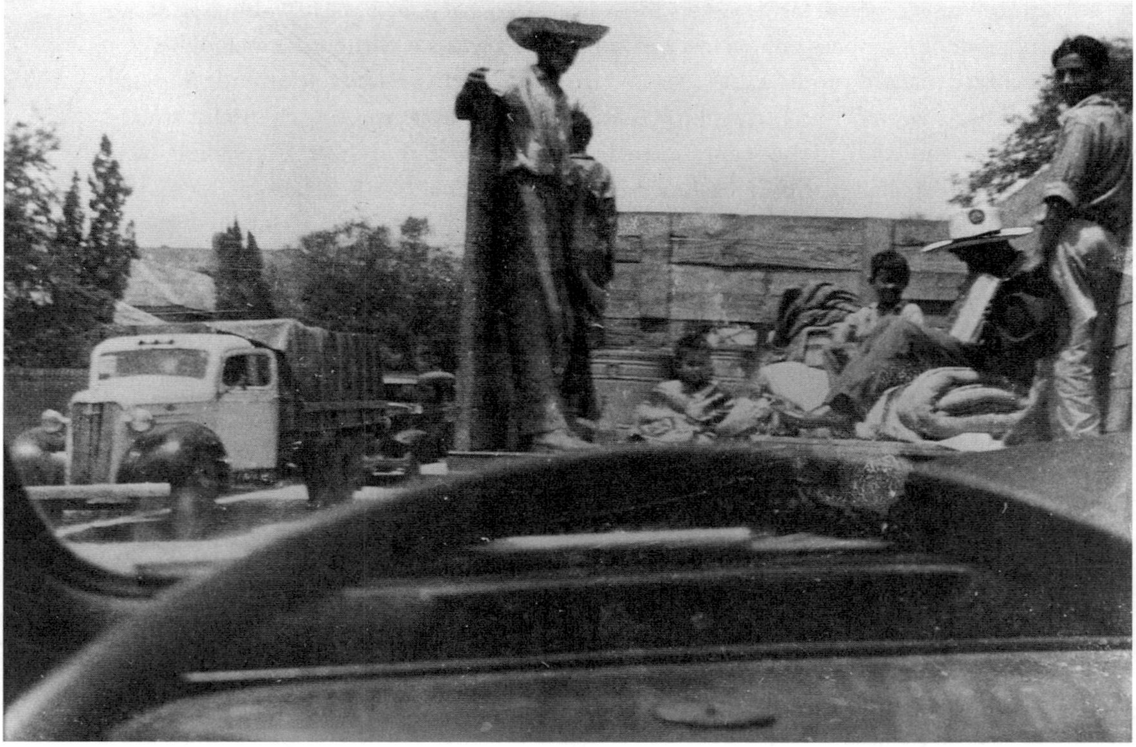

Snapshot of Mexicans being transported in the Coachella Valley, 1958, photographer unknown. Courtesy of the President's Commission on Migratory Labor Papers, Dwight D. Eisenhower Library.

Another viewer wrote to Senator Harrison Williams: "This situation seems to give lie to everything that we believe and stand for. How it can continue to exist is beyond human comprehension." So shocked were members of the Amalgamated Meat Cutters and Butcher Workmen that its leaders announced plans to devote an entire issue of *Butcher Workmen* to the problem in the hope that they could pressure the United States Congress into taking some kind of action. Angered and sickened by what they saw, liberal groups laid plans to hold hearings and petition the government to pass legislation to help the migrants. On December 7, *Variety* magazine reported that of 899 letters received at CBS, only 46 were negative.[18]

When CBS sponsors squirmed and agricultural interest groups cried foul and threatened to pull advertising, two CBS executives headed to Florida and apologized to growers for *Harvest of Shame.* Most vehement of all in its criticism was the American Farm Bureau Federation (AFBF). Accusing CBS of failing to exercise its responsibility for factual reporting, the AFBF pointed out numerous "errors of fact and omission, erroneous inferences," unfair references to slavery, and libelous linkage to *The Grapes of Wrath.* Full of such defects, *Harvest of Shame,* according to the AFBF, was little more than a "rigged documentary" and "highly colored propaganda." Equally incensed, the California Canning Peach Association charged CBS news with a lack of objectivity. Most angry of all, the city Belle Glade, Florida, a barracks community of bars, cafés, and labor camps where eastern migrants spent the winter, protested the way the film depicted life in its area. If CBS did not issue a retraction, the city vowed to boycott the network and the program's sponsor, Philip Morris. At the same time, the U.S. Sugar Corporation, whose headquarters and big refinery were in nearby Clewiston, launched a huge lobbying effort to discredit Murrow, CBS News, and *Harvest of Shame.*[19]

Under great pressure, CBS news publicly refused to knuckle under, apologize to any interest group, change or correct a single word, or cut a single frame. Behind the scenes, however, the news division was in turmoil. Although some members of the documentary team considered following up *Harvest of Shame* with exposés on the bracero program and farm labor organizing, CBS news never produced another comparable program, even though both ABC and PBS would revisit the issue thirty years later.[20]

When CBS was knocked off its perch as the number-one network in the Nielsen ratings that December, its news division chief, William S. Paley, ordered a complete reorganization, including renegotiation of Murrow's contract. At the end of the year, Murrow pulled out of a project documenting racial violence in Birmingham, Alabama, and left CBS to become head of the U.S. Information Agency (USIA), a propaganda arm of the American government. Five months later, CBS news sold rights to *Harvest of Shame* to the British Broadcasting Company (BBC). Ironically, Murrow tried to prevent the BBC from televising the documentary. Official word through press secretary Pierre Salinger was that President John F. Kennedy feared that Murrow's position with USIA would cause audiences to accept the documentary as an official government film. But some people saw a simpler explanation for Murrow's action. According to their view, Kennedy asked Murrow to oppose showing the film in order to curry favor with and maintain support among key southern politicians representing states mentioned in *Harvest of Shame.* Although they could not block Murrow's confirmation as director of USIA, these powerful southern Democrats exerted considerable sway on the Senate Foreign Relations Committee. Among the most important was Florida's Spessard Holland. As payment for his silence, Holland, a Democrat with strong ties to Florida's citrus industry, supposedly demanded that Murrow use his new position to kill foreign broadcasts of *Harvest of Shame.* Without some accommodation to Holland's needs, southern Democrats might make things uncomfortable for Murrow. By holding up his confirmation, they could cause considerable humiliation and embarrassment to the newly elected president. When Murrow's nomination sailed through without a single dissent, some saw this as payoff for his attempt to kill the BBC broadcast.[21]

After the hubbub over Murrow's broadcast died down, the photographer Harvey Richards moved into the Imperial Valley. Hoping to continue the momentum generated by *Harvest of Shame,* he focused his camera on a joint AWOC–UPWA campaign against Public Law 78 (PL 78), the 1951 act allowing the bracero program to continue.

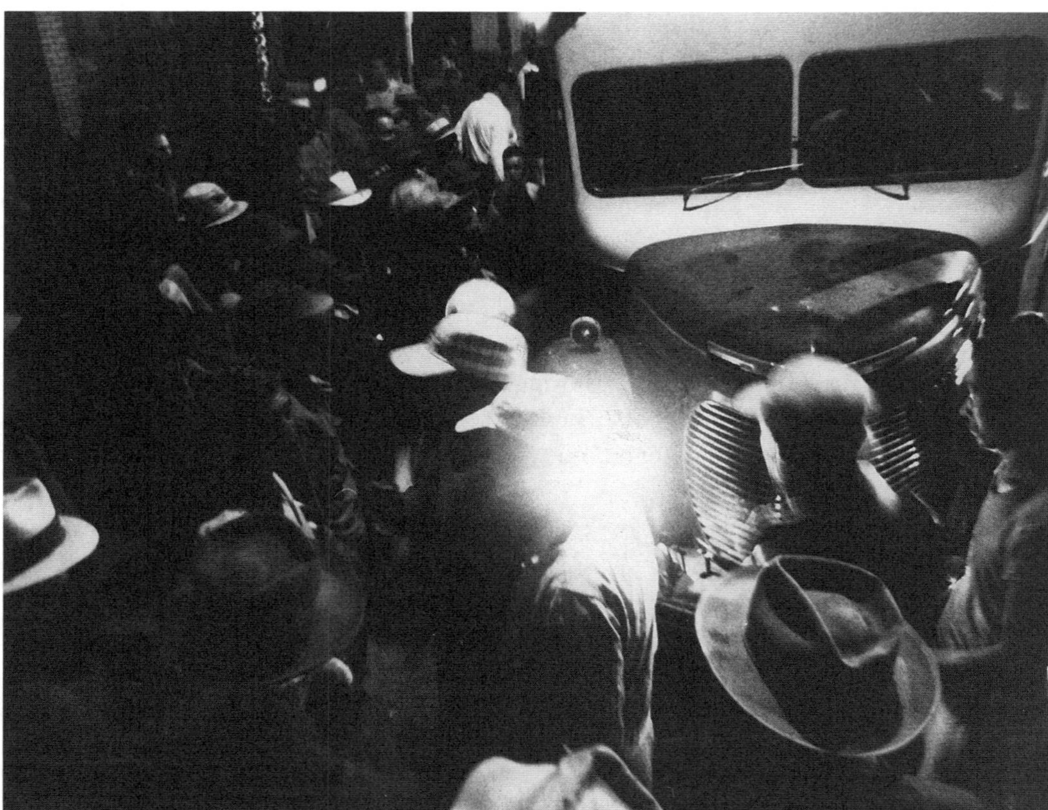

Early-morning shape-up, Stockton, 1959, photograph by Arthur Dubinsky. Author's collection.

Richards knew that with braceros making up 9,000 of the valley's 11,500 farmworkers, a showdown would occur, spotlighting another key issue in the farm labor struggle. Richards took his first photographs on January 5, 1961, at a joint AWOC–UPWA mass meeting at the Calexico Armory, then covered a one-day antibracero strike among lettuce workers and packers. He knew that the two unions had not the slightest chance of winning an increase in wages to $1.25 an hour or of forcing growers to clean up their camps or to provide rest periods, transportation to and from the fields, seniority rights, and a closed shop. He was there because he believed he could use his camera to help expose the extent to which bracero labor dominated picking and packing lettuce and to document the government's response to evidence that braceros were being employed as strikebreakers in violation of the provisions of PL 78.

Paying for his photography out of his own pocket, Richards spent several weeks in the valley from late January until mid-February. On January 7, AWOC–UPWA held a large rally in Calexico, provoking the wrath of the San Diego Catholic bishop, who accused two priests, Father Thomas McCullough and Father Donald McDonnell of San Jose, the so-called bracero priests, of "trespassing" into his diocese to participate in the strike. On January 18, one hundred striking AWOC–UPWA members shut down the harvest on the Bruce Church ranch and forced the U.S. and Mexican governments to withdraw 564 braceros for the duration of the strike. Over the next few days, the strike spread to several smaller farms. On January 21, a fire damaged a cardboard box factory in El Centro, followed by two other fires on January 29, which destroyed a distribution company warehouse and a fertilizer and insecticide storage facility, the latter releasing poisonous fumes that sickened five hundred people. Early in February, El Centro police began rounding up union members as "suspicious vagrants." Arraigned in an open-air court before Police Judge Hugh L. Keating, the men pled guilty to vagrancy and were given suspended sentences ("floaters") on condition that they leave town at once.[22]

Closely following the strikes and arrests, Richards next documented a series of AWOC–UPWA sit-ins. Modeled on tactics used in the 1930s by striking auto workers who took over several Detroit assembly plants, the first of these sit-down strikes closed down the local department of employment office in El Centro. Charging that the office referred workers only to growers associations, thus allowing the associations to weed out activists and hold the number of domestic workers below the 5 percent threshold, at which braceros then had to be removed, two shifts of AWOC–UPWA members swarmed into the department of employment office, occupied every chair, and refused to budge until the department reversed its policy and vowed to refer workers directly to ranches. On February 3, Richards was on hand to document a second AWOC–UPWA sit-in at the Danny Dannenberg Green Barn labor camp near the railyard in El Centro, where between 250 and 300 union members blocked the main gates in order to dramatize the "imprisonment" of braceros inside the camp and prevent them from being taken to struck fields.

As the confrontation escalated, a half dozen other photographers arrived. Among them were freelancer Arthur Dubinsky and Eugene Mackley of the *Los Angeles Times*

Mirror News. For several hours the photographers documented the scene, alternately photographing UPWA leader Clive Knowles while he urged braceros to join the union and then photographing the braceros while they watched from behind the cyclone fence enclosing the camp. After sixteen braceros climbed over the barbed-wire-topped fence, the strikers cheered and remained seated, until about one hundred armed deputies and deputized civilians under the command of Sheriff Herb Hughes arrested them. Richards caught most of the action, which kept several police photographers busy taking mug shots of each arrested striker, front and side, with a docket number hanging around his neck.[23]

Each mug book page holds twelve images and captures a remarkably diverse group (Mexican Americans, African Americans, and Anglos), all sharing the same fate and branded as criminals in a common cause. At least one law enforcement officer later found these photographs to be a "representative cross section of the people engaged in that strike," but they elicited no sympathy among law enforcement authorities and were never even seen by Secretary of Labor Arthur Goldberg and others in a position to act. Relying on the usual channels of advice, Goldberg danced around the issue of bracero strikebreaking. He and other government officials asserted that braceros were never in any danger on most of the ranches where they worked, and they continued to ignore the pleas of organized labor, as well as the Mexican government's requests for the removal of braceros from the areas experiencing labor disputes.[24]

Had government officials looked at the pictures that Richards was making they might have acted differently. But apparently they did not read *Packinghouse Worker* or the other labor journals that ran many of Richards's images, along with those of Arthur Dubinsky and Clive Knowles. Illustrating how the state and federal government abdicated responsibility for monitoring braceros and withdrawing them from labor disputes, these images raised public awareness, at least among UPWA members and their supporters, and helped build momentum against the bracero program. But they and the awareness they raised could not dampen the anger of about fifty union members who were arrested in a police raid a week after they stormed their way into the Joe Corona labor camp, waving brooms and shouting, "Join our union."[25]

After AWOC–UPWA ended picketing on February 13, Richards refused to quit. He did not see the AWOC–UPWA defeat in the Imperial Valley as the beginning of the end for the agricultural unions, even though thirty-six union members were now in the Imperial County jail awaiting trial for riot, assault, and arson. When Goldberg honored requests from the Mexican government and ordered braceros removed from eighteen lettuce fields on March 8, the peak harvest season was long past, and Richards, along with most workers, had moved north to the asparagus fields of the San Joaquin Valley. Looking back over his photographic work in the Imperial Valley, Richards would recall AWOC organizer DeWitt Tannehill's characterization of the place as the "Imperialistic Valley," in effect, another country where "laws did not apply the way they did elsewhere."[26]

After the catastrophe in the Imperial Valley, Richards photographed two hundred AWOC members who walked from Stockton to Sacramento in March to protest the preferential employment of braceros. When AWOC members pitched their tents on the lawn of the state Capitol, Richards recorded what may have been the first mass protest of this kind by farmworkers. Over the next six months, he documented a series of strikes extending the length of the state. But his most important photography focused on working conditions. With AWOC and the UPWA contending that field sanitation was a major problem and growers claiming it was not an issue, Richards decided to bring the situation to the attention of the general public. Using two Nikon cameras, he equipped one with a telephoto lens and mounted it on a tripod. Shooting from the platform he had constructed on the roof of his station wagon, he began looking into fields that he could not physically enter. Everywhere he looked, Richards saw the same woeful lack of sanitary facilities.[27]

Documenting the state of sanitary facilities presented certain problems. How does one document the absence of something? A field without a potty was simply a field. Men without adequate water to wash their hands displayed no obvious or easily identifiable characteristics. Realizing these problems, Richards decided to photograph people in the act of going to the bathroom in the fields. But not everyone. He excluded women and children from these pictures and focused entirely on men. Looking far into fields through his telephoto lenses from his rooftop platform, Richards

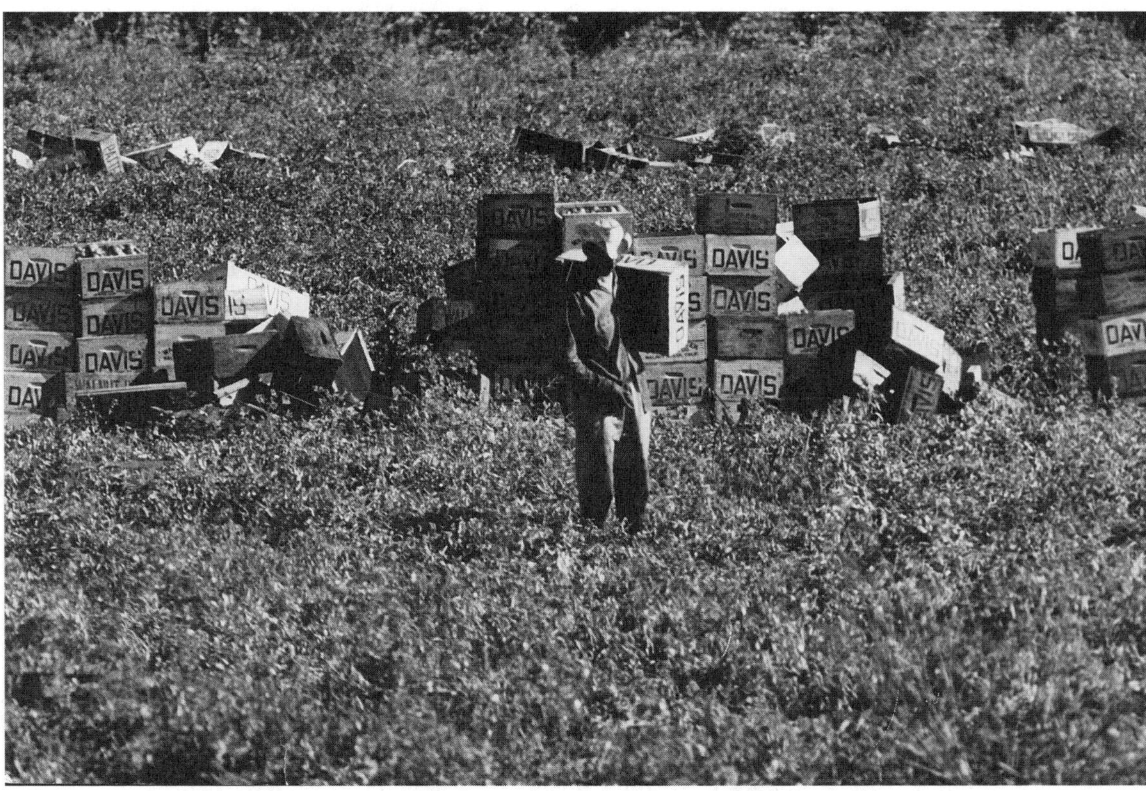

Farmworker urinating in the tomato fields near Stockton, 1959, photograph by Harvey Richards. Courtesy of Harvey Richards/Estuary Press.

shot hundreds of pictures of harvest hands urinating in the fields from late May until September. He found them using the bushes for their bathrooms, trying to hide behind tomato boxes, and squatting over five-gallon buckets. Returning from the fields with what was certainly the first, and probably the last and only, photo essay on the subject, he offered his photographs to editors and reporters throughout California and to some as distant as Moscow in the USSR. But none would publish or even consider them. Like the images that Leonard Nadel had shot of naked braceros being deloused with DDT, the images that Richards made of farmworkers urinating in the fields were too graphic for public consumption.[28]

Eventually Richards managed to publish one of these images in a UPWA pamphlet attacking the bracero program. With the man's face blocked out, the pamphlet announced, "Public Law 78 Means Filth in Your Food. Public Law 78 Must Go." Providing irrefutable evidence of the absence of toilets in the fields, the photograph became the center of a storm of controversy over food safety and contamination. Using his telephoto lens, Richards had demonstrated that field sanitation was a legitimate issue not only for farmworkers but also for consumers—a connection not lost on later organizers seeking to overcome structural impediments to organizing. While artless and hard to look at, his photographs were in many ways as iconic as, if not more than, Dorothea Lange's far more famous *Migrant Mother.*[29]

Besides providing still photographs to AWOC, UPWA, newspapers, and various farmworker allies, including the President's Commission on Migratory Labor, Richards also made a film, *The Harvesters,* an account of farm labor conditions and an exposé of the bracero program. With Arthur Dubinsky and several other well-known photographers joining in the effort, it seemed by the fall of 1961 that photographers were well on their way toward reawakening public concern for farmworkers and marshaling support for agricultural labor unions. At this point, the DiGiorgio Fruit Corporation again stepped into the picture.

Apparently panicked by the appearance of yet another critical documentary, the corporation had kept busy in court. On November 25, 1961, a Stockton Superior Court judge, who was himself from a prominent farm family, found *Poverty in the Valley of Plenty* libelous and ordered the AFL–CIO and other defendants to pay $150,000 in damages. Following a series of appeals, the unions eventually succeeded in reducing the judgment to $60,000, but they could not overturn the decision to suppress the film. Few would dare to show *Poverty in the Valley of Plenty* again.[30]

Photographers quickly absorbed the messages of 1960–61. Visual information had great potential for educating the public and effecting change. But those who crossed powerful agribusiness interests could expect to pay a price. Try to cut through the propaganda obscuring the lives of California farmworkers, photographers learned, and they would to be sued and tied up in court for decades. They might never work again and would be ruined financially. If their images hit the mark, if they were powerful and exposed some awful injustice, they might be ignored or have their discoveries dismissed as propaganda. Only those brave, fanatically driven individuals devoted to exposing the human condition would ever think of tackling such a controversial and provocative subject as the nature of California's farm labor system. Although Richards and AWOC organizers such as Louis Krainock continued to photograph and, indeed, produced some revealing pictures of children out picking fruit when they should have been in school, few others produced similar exposés. Briefly it appeared that Richards, the Hagels, Krainock, Dubinsky, and other documentary photographers had been stymied. At this point, Pirkle Jones stepped forward. With his wife, Ruth Marion Baruch, a German immigrant who had trained with Edward Weston and written her master's thesis on his photography, Jones collaborated on a portrait of Walnut Grove, a small farm town in the Sacramento–San Joaquin Delta.[31]

Trying to capture a sense of place, Jones and Baruch paid close attention to the picturesque architecture and moody river that have given the town its character. But what really interested them was the diverse population of Mexican Americans, braceros, and old Filipino farmworkers. While concentrating on the harvest, they produced a

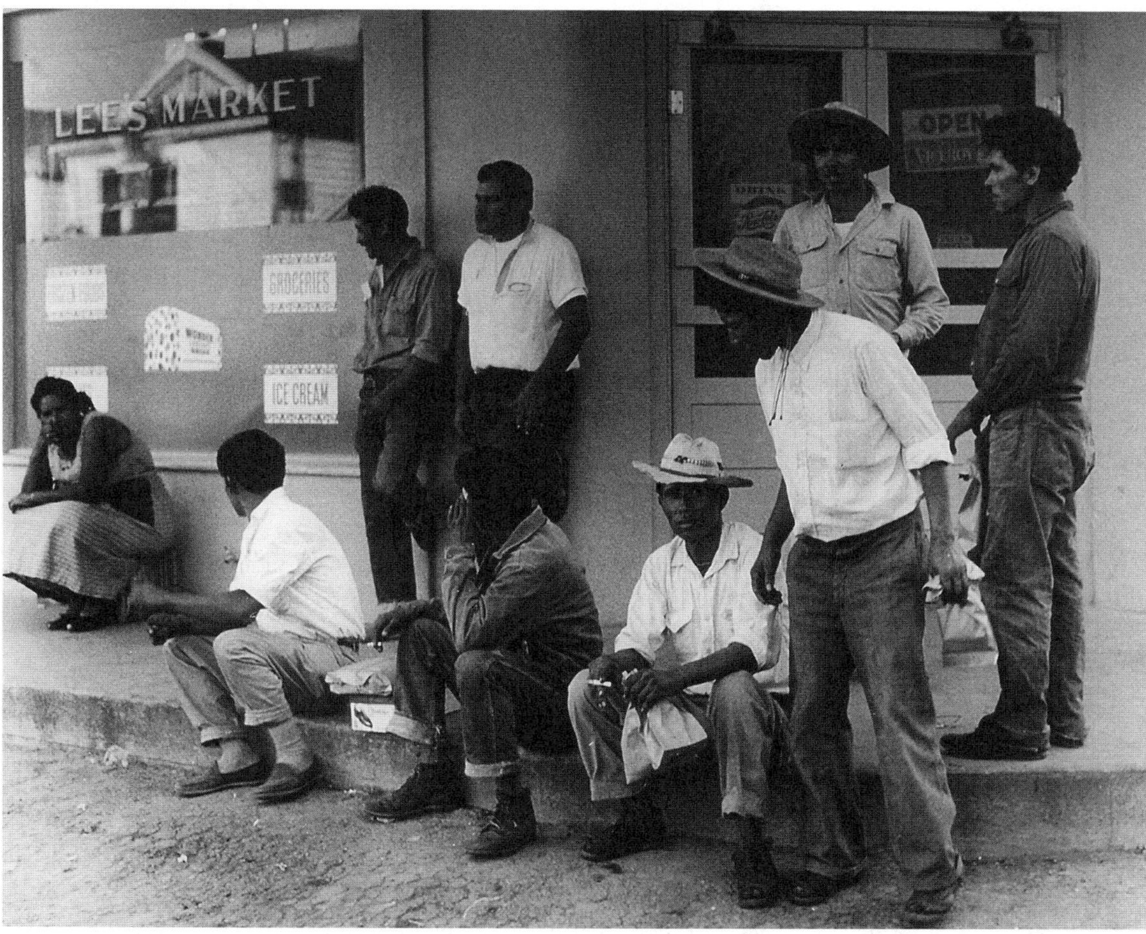

Mexican field hands congregating around Lee's Market in Walnut Grove, 1960, photograph by Ruth Marion Baruch. Courtesy of Pirkle Jones.

series of images that zeroed in on sweat-stained shirts and straining muscles. But they also probed life away from the fields. Documenting farmworkers going about their day-to-day activities, they photographed old Filipinos warming themselves in front of east-facing buildings in the morning of a cold winter day, found young braceros hanging out in pool halls, and followed married couples on their rounds of tending children and doing the wash. Whereas in the past, photographers had emphasized the dramatic and extraordinary aspects of life and labor in the fields, Jones and Baruch turned this around, striving to get at what were, in fact, the normal, regular, and ongoing aspects of existence in a typical small farm town.

During the final stages of editing, Dorothea Lange assisted Jones and Baruch. Looking at their work, Lange said, "Take a stand; at a certain point you must take a stand." Infusing their portrait of Walnut Grove, that advice would lead them to meld two equally strong sets of pictures into a single point of view. They created something that Tim Wride, the photo curator of the Los Angeles County Museum of Art, has described as being "seamlessly woven togther into a visual record that is as much about mood as it is about subject."[32]

At about the same time that Jones and Baruch were zeroing in on farmworkers in a single small farm town, *Life* magazine photographer Truman Moore was moving forward with his project. Regarding the farm labor system as the greatest scandal in America, Moore obtained a contract from Random House to write and photograph a book that would amplify *Harvest of Shame.* To accomplish that he took a leave of absence from *Life* and followed the various migrant circuits for a year. Arriving in California in the spring of 1963, he made contact with AWOC organizers and members of the national Migrant Ministry, then moved into various labor camps and began interviewing and photographing. A statement by a California grower that may have provided the hook for Murrow's opening comments—"We used to own our slaves. Now we just rent them"—supplied the title for his book: *The Slaves We Rent.* Moore later recalled:

> I read *Let Us Now Praise Famous Men* and felt very keenly the concern that Agee expressed about the exploitative nature of writing and photography. I thought being a writer–photographer was the greatest calling on earth and that somehow I could overcome the problems that my predecessors had encountered. But soon I realized how difficult it was. Often, it was impossible. Either the writing would suffer or the photographs. I think the photographs suffered the most. You only have so much time, and I spent most of it interviewing and researching. When the interview session was over, I would grab the camera and make a few shots.[33]

After taking hundreds of photographs, Moore selected twenty-five to illustrate his book. Half were from California. Among them was a portrait of a very young community activist named César Chávez. One notable image captured two proud AWOC organizers in front of a union hall. While posing them, Moore tried to imitate the painting *American Gothic,* by Grant Wood. At other times while photographing, he imitated the work of the Farm Security Administration photographers, whose images Moore recalled as "playing in [his] head like a slide show." Although *The Slaves We Rent* quickly became a best-selling exposé and led an *Atlantic Monthly* editor to offer Moore a contract to produce a second volume concentrating on the California story, Moore was unable to continue his photographic exploration of the state's farmworkers. "My wife and I were starting a family, and the steady work coming in from *Life* took me away from my writing," he later recalled. "I stayed with *Life* until it went out of business. After that I opened a studio in New York City and did mostly corporate photography. I was never able to return to the fields."[34]

A unique and very different perspective emerged through the work of freelance commercial photographer Joe Munroe. For the previous fifteen years, since leaving service with the Army Air Force photographic unit during World War II, Munroe had photographed everything from cattle roundups in California and Arizona to vegetable harvesting in the Salinas Valley for clients ranging from Chevron–Ortho Chemical to *Farm Quarterly.* While he shared many of the same social values as his predecessors, Munroe's commercial orientation kept him focused largely on production agriculture, the beauty of the land, certain technological developments, and the love that farmers had for their soil and work. During this work he captured hundreds of images of farmworkers operating machinery, displaying big bunches of carrots, and posing in what were essentially landscapes resembling an updated version of late nineteenth-century photographs. But Munroe was also a typically curious photographer who often abandoned standard commercial approaches and submerged in issues such as mechanization, pesticides, and unionization. This led him into a unique assignment and the most important of his career: a major photo essay on AWOC executive director Norman Smith.[35]

Munroe could not have chosen a better subject or a more opportune moment. Norman Smith was consolidating his power at this time. He was exploring a merger between NAWU and UPWA, as well as a joint organizing effort between AWOC and UPWA, and he had succeeded in marginalizing Galarza and Mitchell, who now severed all contacts with AWOC and merged NAWU out of existence into the butchers' union. With Mitchell returning to political activities and Galarza departing to write books, Smith ignored a promising community base for organizing that had been developed by Father McCullough and the Agricultural Workers Association and instead launched a novel and some said a foolhardy organizing campaign among day-haul laborers who shaped up for work in Stockton.[36]

To cover Smith's activity, Munroe rose before dawn, made his way to South El Dorado Street, and followed Smith on his rounds while he greeted men emerging from the rooming houses and flophouses at 4 A.M. Milling around the old labor buses, Munroe captured many of the same scenes that had earlier fascinated Richards: contractors selecting men and the men themselves, who, in organized confusion, piled into the buses and trucks and were hauled off to the fields. The arrangement struck Munroe as something "like a mechanized slave market." Once the streets cleared, Munroe trained his cameras on those left behind as they drifted off to the State Farm

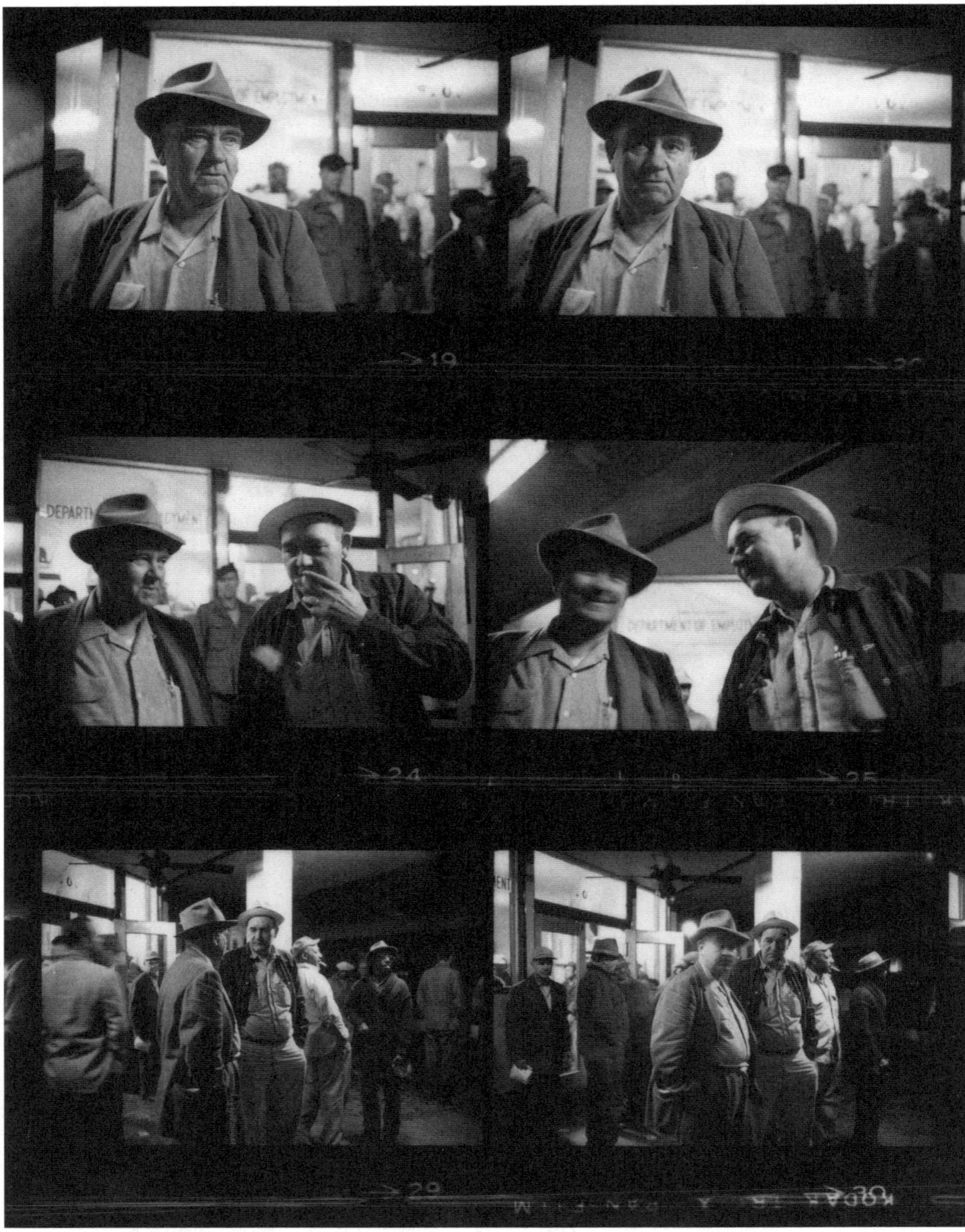

Enlarged frames from the contact sheet of Joe Munroe's essay on Norman Smith's organizing activity in Stockton, 1961, photographs by Joe Munroe. Courtesy of Joe Munroe.

Labor Office, coffee shops, or vacant lots to plop down and drink cheap liquor. Like everyone who saw the day-haul system, Munroe thought the men impossible to organize. He also wondered why anyone would make the attempt. Not only were they among the most casually employed workers in California agriculture; they were also rapidly declining in number and, while given to frequent walkouts, completely lacked any indigenous leadership.[37]

Munroe dogged Smith. He found him in his storefront office, sipping coffee, talking, and planning activities, and outside recruiting new members from the ranks of the transient workers. But Munroe did not stop there. To further illustrate Smith's gritty regime, Munroe followed him into the melon fields. Despite his loyalties and the very considerable commercial work he did for agribusiness interests, Munroe did not sugar-coat his images. Like Pirkle Jones and Ansel Adams, he was above all a consummate photographer who would not pass up a good picture, whatever it revealed. Among his most dramatic shots were those recording men bent over double while hefting melons. Silhouetted against the morning sky, the men leaned forward, straining and sweating, their heads just a few feet off the ground as they pulled their sacks down the long rows.

Tagging along with Smith, Munroe continued well into the night. He took hundreds of images, fully illustrating Smith's exhausting routine. Somewhere along the way, Munroe also made a close-up portrait of Smith. This image ran full-page in *Farm Quarterly,* juxtaposed with a photograph of AWOC pickets strung out along a large tomato field near Tracy. Workers employed by the Cochran Company had worked for one hour, then walked out of the company's fields, demanding higher wages. Wearing signs stating "Calluses, Tears, Tribulations, and $1.00 an Hour, Aren't We Worth $1.25," they were a pathetic sight. Although a dozen of them flanked a field, in Munroe's photograph they appear almost insignificant. Realizing the utter futility of their effort, Munroe stood back and used a telephoto lens to record the men as small figures in the rural environment. His point was both subtle and insightful. No matter how hard AWOC tried, no matter how much support it had among field hands, no matter how just its cause was, no matter how clever and devoted Norman Smith and others like him were, AWOC could never shut down a field the same way the United Auto Workers blocked the entrance to an auto assembly plant or the United Mine Workers tied up the entrance to a coal mine.[38]

Sprawling over some ten thousand square miles, California agriculture had no equivalent of the River Rouge gate or the entrance to a mine. Even the largest and most industrialized farm did not have a single funnel through which field hands passed. Workers came and went helter-skelter by dozens of entrances, and some never even left the property. Distances were huge. An entire steel mill plus several auto assembly plants could be tucked into the average-sized farm, with room to spare. All of this suggested to Munroe, and to many others as well, that agriculture was too big and diverse for traditional trade union tactics and too complicated for traditional trade union organizers like Norman Smith, who drove the back roads of rural California exhausting AWOC's coffers, searching for a nonexistent factory gate and finding nothing better to target than the day-haul system in Fresno, Modesto, Sacramento, Stockton, and a handful of other farm towns.[39]

Without precedent in the annals of farmworker photography, Munroe's work resulted in the first detailed photographic essay on a farmworker organizer. For a brief period, Munroe's humanistic interests had coincided with his technical prowess and allowed him to stray outside the confines of commercial photography. But like Ansel Adams, Loomis Dean, Pirkle Jones, Wayne Miller, Max Yavno, and so many others who ventured into the fields, Munroe could not continue photographing farmworkers. Once his assignment was done, *Farm Journal* sent him in search of bigger peaches, better plows, and the latest chemicals. Resuming his commercial routine, Munroe never completed another editorial assignment on farmworkers. But in his travels, he would continue to shoot individual images as he found them.

That winter, Munroe made some classic shots of men engaged in the odious work of lighting smudge pots used to control frost in the Napa Valley wine-grape vineyards. Six months later he was driving home from an assignment in the rice-growing districts around Colusa, in the northern Sacramento Valley, when he recorded a memorable image, one that instantly conveyed the danger and omnipresence of pesticides. It was late in the afternoon, and the sun was low on the horizon. Off in the distance a crop duster was at work spraying herbicides, directed by a flagger (an assistant who marked the location of each pass by waving a flag). In the quest for greater productivity, farm chemical use was increasing rapidly, from fourteen pounds per acre in 1950 to forty pounds in 1960. Seeing an image that perfectly captured this situation, Munroe stopped his car, climbed onto the roof, and began shooting with a 300-millimeter telephoto lens. Compressing the perspective, Munroe recorded a scene in which it appeared as if the flagger was about to be drenched in poison, when in fact he was a safe distance away.

Over the next two decades, Munroe shifted his attention to mechanization. Beginning first with mechanical potato harvesters, which cut the cost of digging from seventeen to eight cents per one hundred pounds and reduced a normal crew of thirty men to eight, Munroe went on to create a number of other memorable images, including classic shots of the first mechanical tomato harvesters, mobile carrot-picking platforms, and lettuce-packing rigs that allowed twenty-six workers to do the work of forty-five, as well as prune tree shakers, self-propelled irrigation systems, and other devices that improved efficiency and revolutionized the nature of labor in the fields. More than any other single photographer, Munroe provided irrefutable evidence of the benefits of riding through the fields shielded from the burning sun.[40]

17

Photography and César Chávez's Farmworker Struggle

Activists with Cameras

Some observers of rural California believe that by the late 1950s photographers had reestablished documentary coverage of the state's farmworkers. "These photographers were really doing their best to bridge the gap between old traditions and new realities under changed circumstances," explained John Collier Jr., a former FSA documentarian. But while such glowing evaluations are certainly valid, they omit a vital defect. Only within a narrow definition of success did photographers achieve very much; judged in a larger context, they were failures, prime examples of the tragedy of enthusiastic liberals blinded by their own hope. They were out of touch with visual culture, people who loved still pictures at a time when *Look, Collier's,* and *Saturday Evening Post* were being undercut by television. Their most serious flaw, say some commentators, was that (except for Richards) they could not instill a sense of widespread outrage and revulsion sufficient to bring about change or overcome rationalizations of poverty. Being courageous and idealistic and working without benefit of government support or foundation funding, they certainly made memorable images, but their work never pushed aside agricultural advertising. The industry whose beauty and productivity was celebrated on fruit box labels and in festivals could not be so easily shaken from its secure position as a Mediterranean dream personifying all that was good and wholesome in the Golden State.[1]

It was not enough to take great photographs. Without some way to reach the public, photographers working among farmworkers were little more than naive do-gooders. To be effective, to make a difference, they needed a strategy to get their work out. Their problem was that they were contemptuous of marketing and they wanted to maintain control over their work. "We photographed first and thought about what to do with our pictures later," observed Pirkle Jones. They had no ongoing relationship with any news organizations, did not consider themselves news photographers, and, with the exception of Munroe, struggled when not employed by any publication. Trying to find a venue, many went to great pains searching for ways to reach a wide audience. They bombarded book magazine editors, museum curators, and librarians with queries. They donated pictures to unions, investigating commissions, and activist groups. They gave illustrated lectures to audiences ranging from grammar school students to university classes. But they lacked the contacts, range of approaches, and professional associations necessary for influencing public opinion. If they were lucky, they might place a few of their images in beautifully executed documentaries that appeared years too late.[2]

All of these elements were present in the careers of two of the most independent and creative photographers active at this time. One was Ernest Lowe. The son of a Tulare County cattle rancher, at twenty-six Lowe had left the valley to study photography under John Collier Jr. at the San Francisco Art Institute. Like others before and after, he was casting about for a topic when, shortly before graduating in 1958, he heard a public radio interview with Bard McCallister, an American Friends Service Committee representative in Tulare County. McCallister charged that conditions for farmworkers had not improved since the 1930s and in some ways had worsened. Soon thereafter, Lowe became a staff member at public radio station KPFA, in Berkeley. While there, he decided to see for himself if McCallister's accusations were true.[3]

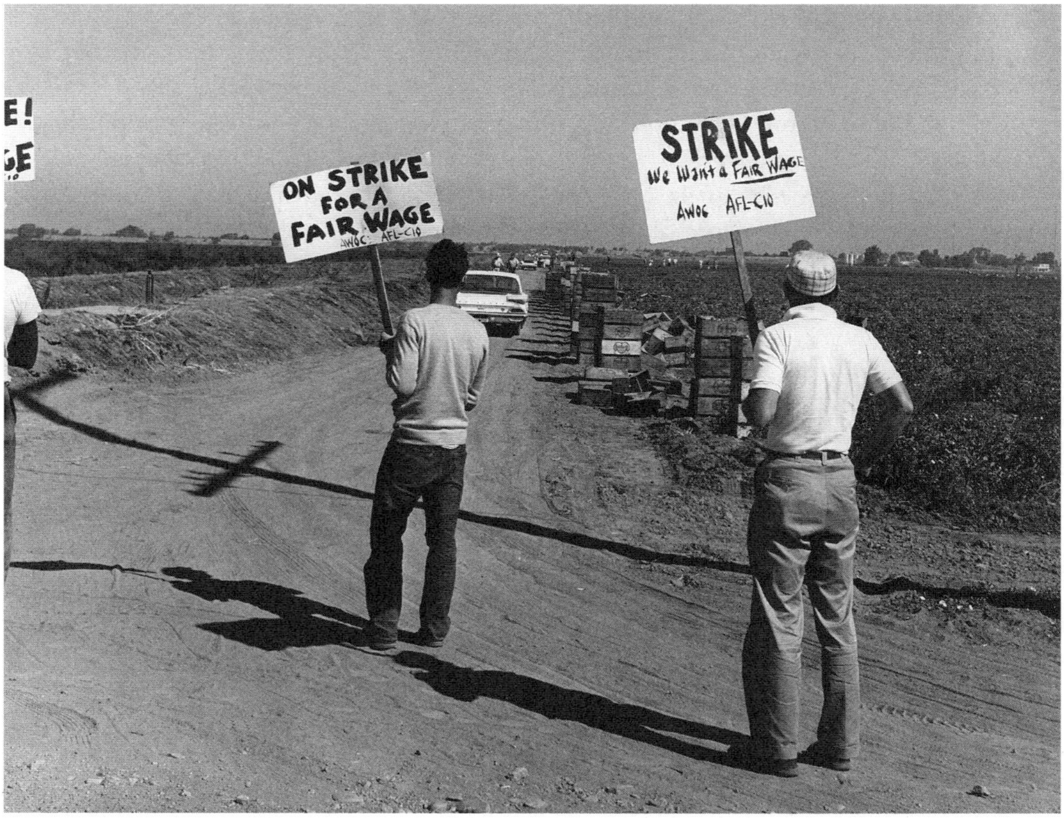

AWOC members picketing against the employment of braceros in the Imperial Valley, 1961, photograph by Arthur Dubinsky. Author's collection.

At first Lowe worked exclusively with a Mamiya twin lens 2¼-inch-format camera. His approach, reminiscent of Lange's, was simple and straightforward. Many years later, he explained:

> I'd just walk up to people in a camp or an orchard and say, "I hear you folks are getting a raw deal. I'd like to take your pictures and talk with you so people back in the city can do something about it." They seldom turned me down. I always shot in available light, no flash. I had some super developer for getting Tri-X way up there [pushing it]. I could handle 1/10th to 1/24th of a second in nighttime meetings inside shacks and get sharp images most of the time. I learned to hold the camera really still. At the shape-up in Stockton, I'd walk around the streets early in the morning until I found some groups of workers waiting for jobs, with lights from stores or the Department of Employment offices shining on them.[4]

During 1960, Lowe made a half dozen trips into the San Joaquin and Salinas valleys, shooting largely while on vacation or on leave from KPFA. After photographing for a year, he visited Dorothea Lange. Seeing his work, she loaned him a 35-millimeter Contax camera and donated film and printing paper. Using Lange's Contax, Lowe photographed and interviewed extensively over the next two years and followed AWOC events closely. He shot some of his most powerful images in December 1961, when AWOC held an organizing conference in the little town of Strathmore, on the east side of Tulare County. Norman Thomas, the perennial socialist candidate for president of the United States, gave a keynote address, recounting his experiences from thirty years in the labor movement. But the real story centered on the two hundred farmworkers attending the conference, particularly María Moreno, who had spent most of her life working in the peach and orange groves around Tipton, and Father McCullough, the farmworker priest who had inspired Harvey Richards to launch his photographic project. Photographing both individuals, Lowe became the first farmworker photographer to document grassroots organizers building a movement from the ground up.[5]

While on a sojourn to Modesto, Lowe met AWOC union research director and organizer Henry Anderson, who provided many contacts within the farmworker movement. Soon Lowe became a familiar figure at union meetings. "I'd go to meetings in Delano, Springville, Porterville, all of the small towns, usually at night," he recalled. By 1962 he had compiled enough information to produce a documentary for KPFA. Splicing his questions among the farmworkers' words, Lowe allowed them to tell their own story. He took his title for his essay, "Sometimes You Work a Day," from an interview with one Tulare farmworker.

> Sometimes you work a day.
> Sometimes you don't work nothn'.
> If you chop beets sometimes you don't find any.
> If you don't find any, you just come home and you don't get nothn.[6]

Although he had trouble selling his farmworker photographs, Lowe kept at his project. Donating images to *Farm Labor,* a journal issued by Citizens for Farm Labor, a group opposed to the bracero program and in support of unionization, he persevered in the belief that a rising tide of interest in rural poverty was occurring. Early in 1963, Lowe acquired a 35-millimeter Nikon camera. Exploiting its portability, he used his Nikon to explore Teviston, an unincorporated African American community of trailers and shacks sprawling along the alkali flats beside Highway 99 between Pixley and Tipton. Entirely self-built, Teviston had only two or three houses that even came close to decent habitation. It was populated mostly by so-called black Okies who had come west after World War II to pick cotton and work in the fields. "Some of those people had it really rough," Lowe observed of his experiences in Teviston. "In the winter they would freeze in their tar paper shacks. I tried to capture a sense of their situation but I also tried to explore their industriousness and sense of community. Poverty created so many obstacles for them, along with race, but they kept at it."[7]

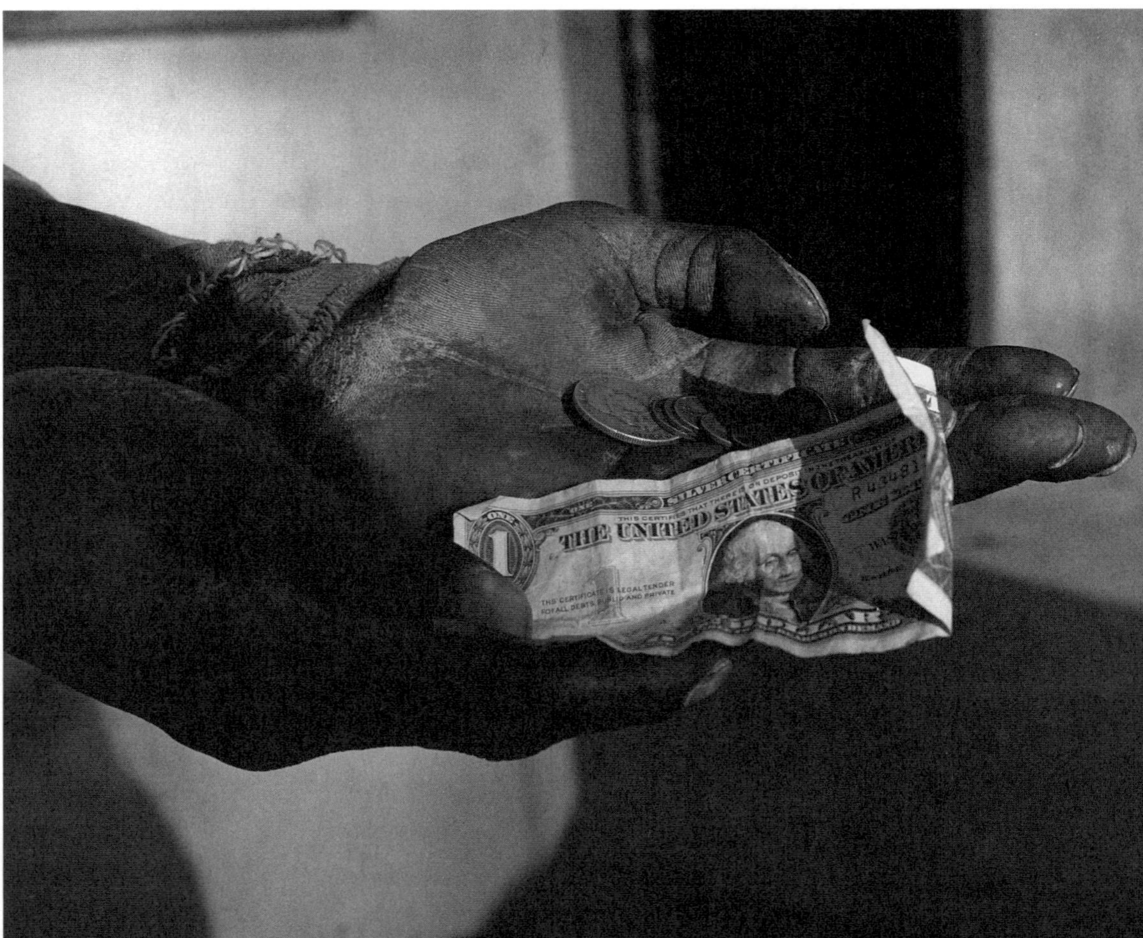

A Day's Wage, 1962, photograph by Ernest Lowe. Courtesy of Ernest Lowe.

At an AWOC meeting sometime in 1960, Lowe met George Ballis, a small man with a perpetual grin and strongly chiseled features that seemed to suggest the innocent wonder of a reporter disposed to have fun while going about his job. Ballis was an intense former Marine with a pixey smile who had first picked up photography while working as a police reporter on a Chicago weekly newspaper from 1950 to 1952. Arriving in Fresno in 1953 to take over as editor of the *Valley Labor Citizen,* an AFL–CIO weekly, he continued his photographic education by studying for six months with Dorothea Lange. Soon thereafter he had an epiphany. "I quickly realized the two most important California issues: 1. Water—its crucial political, environmental, social and economic implications; 2. Farmworkers—the cold exploitation of workers producing food in the world's richest agricultural empire." Moving into the fields, he then started taking pictures. "I set out with my cameras to expose to the world the horrible farmworker conditions in California," he later recalled. "In my cheeriness, I assumed that once the exposure was done, improvements would naturally follow."[8]

Determined to be always ready to photograph under any circumstances day or night, Ballis quickly learned the tricks of the trade. Buying Tri-X black-and-white film in bulk, he pushed it much as Richards, Munroe, and Lewis did, so that he could easily switch between the bright light of the fields and the dim illumination of streetlights, with just one or two cameras, a few lenses, and the same film. But Ballis was never a stickler for technical details. Many of his ideas about photography were very similar to those that had guided Lange. Access was a key to his technique, far more important than equipment. Ballis later recalled:

> I began to consciously develop "invisibility" for photographing people naturally and unposed. This involves turning down my electricity, going physically limp so that people do not feel threatened and, hopefully, my presence is virtually ignored—not always possible, but often enough to get telling photos.[9]

Although a fly-on-the wall observer, Ballis was not impartial. His photographic agenda was quickly transformed by his engagement with his subjects. Honored to be accepted into the lives of the people he was documenting, he intended to make a difference. He wanted to have an impact on society and use photography as a catalyst for organizing. "I was part of the farmworker movement . . . as an organizer, a publicist, always as an advocate," he later recalled. Believing poor farmworkers were not to be pitied or patronized for their poverty, he tried to celebrate their survival culture, in effect to "sell" human dignity and "reflect back to them their dignity, humor, worth, and power." He was fond of saying that farmworkers themselves were his main market and that he "flipped from being an exposé photographer to becoming a friend, an advocate, a *compañero* [comrade]."[10]

During the summer of 1961, San Francisco freelance photographer John Kouns joined Ballis and Lowe in the fields. An Alameda County native who had grown up in the Santa Clara Valley, Kouns had learned photography during a stint in the navy, further honed his skills while studying in New York City, and returned to the Bay

Area in 1958 to take a job with United Press International. Shortly after quitting UPI he embarked on a career as a freelance photographer specializing in social issues, especially the civil rights struggle, the antiwar movement, and the problems of aging. At the beginning of his freelance career, Kouns drove to Tulare County and camped out in a Quonset hut at the Linnell Farm labor camp. The California Migrant Ministry (CMM) was active in the camp and among farmworkers in the area. After meeting CMM leader Sandy Robbins, Kouns joined the group and began documenting the CMM with a used Leica that he had purchased while working as a longshoreman in New York City. He was probably the first photographer to focus on a group that would soon become an important force in the farmworker movement. Kouns remained at the Linnell camp until the early fall. Before returning home, he shot an essay on cotton picking. But like many before and after, Kouns was not done with farmworkers. His experiences and friendships deeply affected him. He had become a supporter of the farmworker cause. Pursuing his assignments back in the Bay Area, he would remain just one telephone call away from returning.[11]

After Kouns left, Ballis continued photographing in the fields for nearly three years. He employed few gimmicks and seldom used a telephoto lens. He shot many of his images with a 21-millimeter lens (just short of being a fisheye), a technique that often placed him so close to his subjects that he inadvertently blocked other photographers. During this time DiGiorgio Fruit Corporation lawyers continued to pursue anyone connected with *Poverty in the Valley of Plenty*, resulting in the 1961 judgment against all those who had shown the documentary to pay $150,000 in damages to DiGiorgio. Undeterred, Ballis continued photographing for AWOC until 1962, when the AFL–CIO, discouraged by the lack of tangible gains, withdrew much of its support. Ballis, like most who had been involved with the farmworker movement, watched in disbelief when Norman Smith was removed from leadership of AWOC and his replacement, Al Green, a gruff, cigar-smoking organizer, subsequently transformed AWOC from a fighting organization that aimed at eliminating the bracero program into a shadow of its former self that quickly signed agreements with 136 labor contractors, most of them in the northern San Joaquin Valley.[12]

Disappointed by these developments and alienated by what they saw as an irrelevant farmworker union movement, Ballis and Lowe, along with Harvey Richards, John Kouns, and many other photographers active among California farmworkers, either left the state to cover the civil rights struggle in Mississippi, Alabama, and Georgia or focused part of their attention on other subjects such as rural poverty and the antiwar movement. During 1963 and 1964, Ballis, Richards, and Lowe rotated among demonstrations, mass marches, church bombings, the Freedom Riders, the Student Nonviolent Coordinating Committee (SNCC), and their ongoing coverage of farmworkers.[13]

Ballis in particular shifted smoothly between the civil rights movement and the farmworker movement. While serving as an SNCC field representative in California, he spent a month in the South photographing with Matt Herron for the Southern Documentary Project (SDP). A kind of FSA project on the cheap, the SDP was funded by the United Auto Workers and had a publishing arrangement with Black Star, the New York photo agency formed in 1936 to market the work of several outstanding German-immigrant photographers. For Ballis, the work was extremely difficult, with constant police surveillance and many encounters with them. Ballis and Herron, being the only photographers who were married, would talk on a daily basis. Many years later, Herron recalled how adept Ballis was in the circumstances of their work. "He would call and say, 'I'm finished here; what do you want me to do next?' And he'd go off on some other mission. He went to Atlantic City to cover the National Democratic Convention and came back with a wonderful collection of images," Herron explained to photojournalist Ken Light. "George and I probably produced the most consistent work."[14]

Photographers who remained in California and continued photographing farmworkers found their work curtailed by problems not faced by photographers in the South. For one, other than a few labor papers and weeklies, they continued to suffer from a lack of outlets for their photographs. Whereas civil rights photographers and African American photographers might place their work in *Ebony* and several other black-owned magazines, farmworker photographers had no similar outlets available to them. For another, farmworker photographers faced continual legal troubles, although they seldom encountered the threats faced by civil rights photographers in the South. Ballis faced legal problems in the spring of 1964 shortly after he returned to California from the South and resumed his duties as editor of *Valley Labor Citizen.*

On April 24, Ballis reprinted an exposé of the DiGiorgio Fruit Corporation by veteran labor reporter Jeff Boehm. Suing Ballis for libel, DiGiorgio lawyers kept him in court for years. Although the lawsuits did not thwart him, they absorbed much time and energy and imposed a severe financial and psychological burden. Ballis later recalled, "Too much is made of the DiGiorgio case. It didn't cause me to miss a photo item. It was a principle." Yet there is little doubt that the case diverted Ballis from farmworkers, forcing him to attend court and sit through depositions at a time when he could have been photographing.[15]

For Ballis, the ordeal imposed by the lawsuits came at a particularly inopportune moment. On December 31, 1964, the bracero program expired, and the traditional oversupply of workers ended, at least for a while. No longer could growers legally drain off the south-of-the-border labor pool that kept wages low. Although Ballis, Lowe, and Richards understood the implications of this development, few other photographers perceived what was happening. Compared with the exciting civil rights developments in the South, the end of the bracero program lacked drama. There were no bloody confrontations to cover, no mass arrests, no police dogs snapping at protestors, no way to reduce the story to an individual image suitable for newspaper reproduction or a series appropriate for a magazine layout—in short, no easy angle. While a few newspaper photographers took pictures of growers plowing under fields to protest the loss of their braceros and others photographed braceros packing up, climbing into buses, and waving to the camera, the departure of 195,000 braceros attracted relatively little photographic scrutiny and produced no memorable published images, although

Ballis in his capacity as editor of the *Valley Labor Citizen* ran stories on the subject almost weekly, much to the disgust of agribusinessmen, who regularly accused him of "distortion"and "deliberate falsification."[16]

Most photographic attention seemed to focus not on the braceros themselves but on Secretary of Labor Willard Wirtz. Appointed to his position in September 1962, Wirtz was a leading figure in the War on Poverty and took seriously his responsibilities under the Civil Rights Act of 1964. When the controversy over the end of bracero labor reached its peak during the spring of 1965, Wirtz flew out to California from Washington, D.C., to inspect personally what was happening. Refusing to be deceived, he was photographed again and again, listening to growers predicting ruin, visiting employment halls, and looking out over fields being harvested by crews of soon-to-be-gone braceros. Some of the last photographs taken of braceros showed 600 of the 1,563 remaining Mexican Nationals lining up outside the State Agrarian League offices in Mexicali, the final quota allowed into California to pick strawberries and asparagus. Following these men north, photographers rounded out their coverage with shots of the last braceros riding labor buses out to the fields, picking strawberries, and standing in long lines with plastic plates to receive lunch dipped out of an insulated bucket.[17]

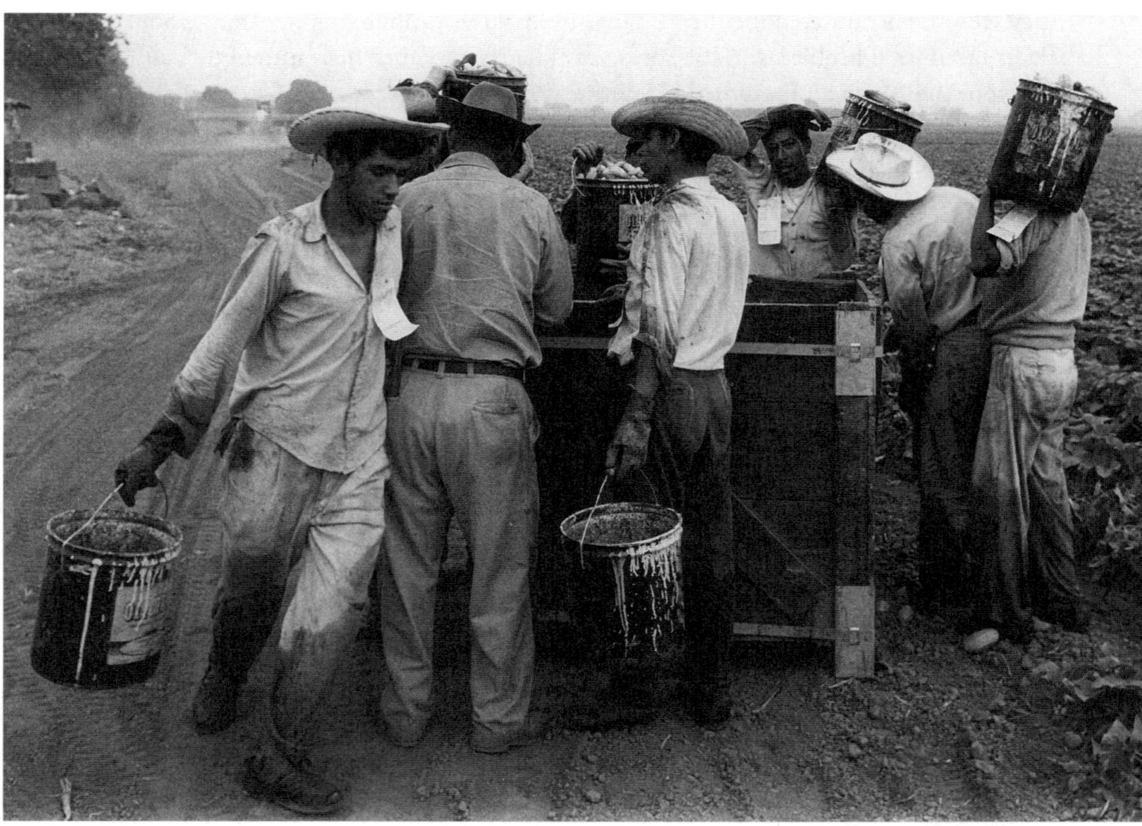

Braceros harvesting cucumbers with used paint buckets, July 1958, photograph by Harvey Richards. Courtesy of Paul Richards/Estuary Press.

Well into spring, photographers covered the end of bracero labor largely with staged shots of Governor Edmund Brown talking with and being confronted by unemployed farmworkers in Stockton and a panel of university professors convening to hear testimony from Stockton asparagus growers, who claimed they faced ruin. In a final desperate attempt to educate the public about the plight of California farmers, ex-actor and now senator George Murphy flew to California and stood on the edge of an Orange County strawberry farm while the grower, Jack Tabata, plowed under a single row of strawberries.[18]

With the bracero program ending, photographers shifted their attention to various labor augmentation schemes. A huge boondoggle organized by the California Department of Employment and funded through the federal Manpower Development and Training Act attracted massive coverage. While documenting the department's efforts to stave off possible labor shortages by recruiting the urban unemployed poor and training them as harvesters, Davis photographer Margery Mann spent several weeks photographing 250 people who attended a two-week course that certified them as tomato pickers. "I did my best photographing the Yolo County farm adviser describing tomato pests and diseases and tomato grading to high school students and unemployed derelicts," she recalled fifteen years later. "The whole thing was an absurd boondoggle."[19]

Ballis also recognized the absurdity of such efforts. If there was one place where plenty of workers could be found it was at a predawn shape-up. When attention shifted to the slave-labor markets of valley towns, Ballis spent several months photographing day-haul laborers. The scenes he captured were memorable ones: cotton choppers push-starting a rickety old labor bus; dejected men leaning against walls after failing to snag jobs harvesting asparagus; and men waiting for work outside a California Department of Employment office. These scenes were also the same ones that his predecessors Munroe, Richards, and Lowe had photographed.

Ballis made some of his most dramatic images at 4:30 A.M. on March 20, 1965, along West Market Street in Stockton. Hundreds of transients, winos, derelicts, and other fruit tramps milled about labor contractors offering work. "How much you paying?" the men asked. "Free transportation?" With the crowds growing larger, Ballis found desperate men either climbing into labor buses or refusing to take jobs, spitting at contractors, cursing them, walking away, purchasing a pint of Tokay wine, and proceeding to get drunk.[20]

After sunrise, Ballis developed his pictures, and later, with the smells of urine, vomit, and automobile exhaust still fresh in his mind, he put in a day at the *Valley Labor Citizen.* When Fresno Labor Council secretary William O'Rear saw the photographs that Ballis had taken, he became so enraged at the spectacle they documented that he wrote an angry letter inviting Albert Tieberg, the unsympathetic director of the California Department of Employment, to witness the spectacle. "Bring your camera," O'Rear advised sarcastically. "It will secure evidence to stiffen your backbone."[21]

Focusing on day-haul laborers at this time, Ballis did not fully recognize the importance of a man whose personality and leadership would dominate the course of farmworker history for the next two generations. That man was a shy, quiet, almost inarticulate community organizer named César Chávez. Along with community organizer Dolores Huerta, he had formed the fledgling National Farm Workers Association (NFWA). As Chávez and Huerta moved forward with grassroots work in helping Hispanic field hands, Ballis slowly expanded his photographic coverage of these two leaders, becoming one of the few photographers to do so in their early stages of organizing activity, although years later he would regret being tardy in covering them. About the only other people who really photographed Chávez during these years were insiders and family members. Their poorly composed, fuzzy, underexposed images, many of which are cracked where they were folded in half, make up the principal visual record of this formative phase in the modern farmworker movement.[22]

Photographic coverage of the movement remained sporadic until May 1965, when Filipino members of AWOC, under the leadership of Andy Imutan, Philip Vera Cruz, Larry Itliong, and Ben Gines, won a wage raise from $1.25 to $1.40 an hour for picking table grapes in the Coachella Valley. With braceros being phased out, Coachella

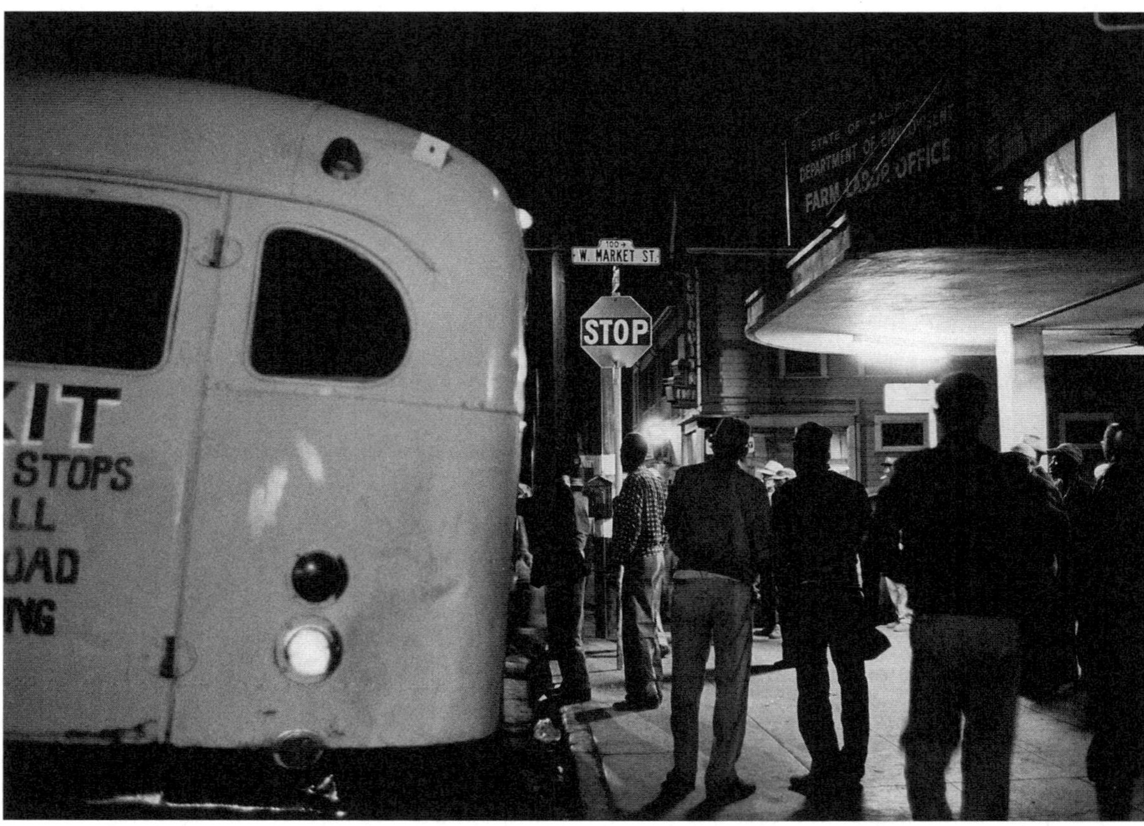

Farm laborers board buses for the fields during the early-morning shape-up in Stockton, 1964, photograph by George Ballis. Courtesy of Take Stock Images.

Valley table-grape growers, accustomed to earning premium profits for the first grapes of the season, had made their calculations and decided not to fight. Two months later, after the Tulare County housing authority raised rents on the old FSA-era tin shacks that sheltered 250 farmworkers in Woodlake and Linnell, two public housing projects near Visalia, members of the newly formed Woodville–Linnell Tenants Committee, along with organizers from the NFWA, the Congress of Racial Equality (CORE), the SNCC, the Citizens for Farm Labor, and various welfare rights organizations, announced a rent strike and marched six miles into Visalia to confront the housing authority. Although Ballis had rarely published his photographs in the *Valley Labor Citizen,* he covered the rent strike extensively, along with Richards, and published front-page photographs of both the march and the deplorable conditions inside the housing projects.[23]

As the harvest moved north, Lowe joined Richards and Ballis and followed developments into the San Joaquin Valley. Over the next three months, there was plenty to document. Arriving in Arvin in mid-June, AWOC had demanded the same wages, only to have growers use labor contractors with Mexican crews to break the strike. Deciding to wait until the September grape harvest in Delano, AWOC organizers called a strike there on September 8, expecting strong support from Filipino farmworkers in their home base of operations. A few days after the strike began, growers began evicting Filipinos from their bunkhouses and labor camps. The Filipinos, infuriated by the action, began picketing at packinghouses reopened with Mexican labor. Hesitating at first, Chávez did not want to jeopardize the three years of work he had put in building up the NFWA. But as more and more NFWA members joined the strike, Chávez met with Itliong and, after thrashing things out, announced that the NFWA was joining the strike.

On Saturday, September 16, about one thousand grape pickers packed into the parish hall at Our Lady of Guadalupe Church in Delano. With the walls decorated with posters of Emiliano Zapata and a huge *huelga* (strike) banner behind the speaker's rostrum, the meeting made for dramatic images. When Chávez called for a strike vote, the hall erupted in pandemonium and broke out in a unanimous "Huelga! Huelga! Huelga!" Chávez then notified Delano-area growers of the strike. But on Monday morning, September 20, only about one hundred of the farmworkers who had attended the strike meeting showed up to begin picketing. Taking the moral high ground, Chávez urged nonviolence, preaching that public sympathy and support would increase if peaceful, powerless farmworkers were seen being subjected to violent repression by wealthy, domineering growers. Although he never said so explicitly, Chávez was already thinking photographically.[24]

To a generation committed to ending the war in Vietnam and the injustices of the poor, Chávez and the farmworker movement became a lightning rod for the spirit of protest. Soon an ever-expanding number of labor, church, student, political, and civil rights groups endorsed the NFWA–AWOC strike. Hundreds of volunteers swarmed into union headquarters at Delano. Attracted to what seemed like a David versus Goliath confrontation pitting an upstart farmworker movement against the huge and powerful table-grape industry, these early volunteers took many of the first photographs documenting strike meetings and organizing efforts during the initial flurry of activity. Picketing and confrontations with police made for dramatic images. So, too, did the forlorn faces of strikers locked out of their labor camps and their winter homes. This work—born of postwar prosperity, Cold War antifascism, optimistic faith in progress, and commitment to the civil rights principles of Martin Luther King Jr.—amounted to a survey of a grassroots labor movement that was unprecedented in the annals of photography in California.[25]

Little photography from the first days of the grape strike ever made it into print, and even less has survived the ravages of time. This was in part the result of the inexperience and bad equipment of volunteers wielding cheap Brownie cameras and plastic knock-offs of professional cameras, their inadequate training, and their lack of connections to news outlets. But if volunteers at first failed to use their cameras effectively, local press photographers did little better. Even when events in Delano captured public attention, photographers from rural newspapers hardly gave the strike much concern. Most news photographs during September were taken by photojournalists from the *Fresno Bee,* the *Bakersfield Californian,* and the *Delano Record,* with occasional forays into Delano by photographers from the *Los Angeles Times,* the *San Francisco Chronicle,* and the *San Francisco Examiner.* Regarding the strike as part of their daily grind and nothing very extraordinary, they covered Delano sporadically, as one of many newsworthy events on their beat.[26]

One photographer who did not miss events at Delano was *Fresno Bee* writer–photographer Ronald B. Taylor. Although he worked for a farm-oriented rural newspaper that devoted the entire Wednesday section of the paper to agriculture, Taylor was able to submerge in the strike story from the beginning. He later recalled:

> The newspaper bent over backwards to report everything fairly. It could have mouthed the grower's side. A second-rate newspaper might have thought "that rabble-rouser Chávez is getting too much attention. We should ignore the guy. He'll go the way of every other farmworker organizer." But the *Bee* did not do that. The newspaper put me on the story, and I stayed on it.[27]

As the action picked up, photographers who had been following the civil rights movement flocked into California. "Delano was lousy with freelancer photographers," recalled one grower. Certain that they were witnessing the first phase of a revolution, these photographers saw the Mexican American and Filipino farmworker movement as a kind of California equivalent of the African American struggle in Selma and Montgomery, Alabama. No strangers to photographing poverty, violence, and injustice, they were part of a generation of photographers who participated in the protest movement and who used their images as an alternate voice to express their outrage and to actively support the causes they championed. Recognizing their dual role, they aimed first at inciting action through their coverage of various incidents and confrontations and second at creating the documents to be used by historians trying to visualize and reconstruct events. Although they were veterans of violent confrontations, mass arrests, and various forms of intimidation and harassment, they were nevertheless astounded by the racism, segregation, and threats that they encountered during the first months of the strike. Most believed that they were in the midst of a unique historical moment, perhaps even a fundamental shift in power. They hoped to provide photographs that would create and re-create the strike indefinitely and allow it to renew itself continually.[28]

As the strike grew, George Ballis spent most of his mornings on the picket lines. When AWOC crews dumped boxes of table grapes at one ranch on September 25, the Kern County Sheriff's Department found Ballis there, along with Terence Cannon, editor of the *Movement,* official publication of the SNCC, and Howard Horowitz, an SNCC photographer and writer. Investigators for the California Senate Subcommittee on Un-American Activities would later cite their presence as evidence of "outside" interference. Well into October, when he documented a Tulare County sheriff's deputy presiding over two very young children harvesting grapes, Ballis remained the principal strike photographer.[29]

Very quickly, law enforcement agencies became preoccupied not only with what was being photographed but also with who was doing the photography. Harvey Richards caused a huge uproar. When photographing strikers beside a field where strikebreakers were at work, he spotted NFWA organizer Dolores Huerta and three other strike leaders standing on top of an old automobile while holding large picket signs exclaiming, "Huelga." Attempting to communicate, Richards was drowned out by the noise of the pickets while he waited for Huerta and another of her companions to raise their signs above their heads. He then began snapping their pictures.[30]

Published on the cover of the October 2 issue of *People's World* and subsequently republished in many other newspapers and magazines, including the *San Francisco Examiner,* one of his dramatic shots of Huerta alone with her picket sign soon caught the attention of an FBI informant. Complaining to FBI director J. Edgar Hoover, the anonymous informant used the photograph as an example of communist infiltration into the farmworker movement. On the basis of the informant's request, Hoover initiated an investigation of Richards and other allegedly subversive photographers and members of the NFWA and AWOC.[31]

After a few weeks, Richards, Ballis, and other photographers settled into a routine. Up at 4 A.M. Meet with pickets at strike headquarters a half hour later. Head out with a picket caravan. Arrive at a farm entrance. Wait for first light. As pickets begin chanting, "Huelga, huelga, huelga, huelga!" scramble after them. Climb on top of cars and move in and out of the vineyards. Shoot every possible angle.

Within ten or fifteen minutes, a deputy would declare the picket line an unlawful assembly, order the pickets to disperse, read the order again, and, when the pickets did not give up, place someone under arrest. All of this would be duly recorded. Then the pickets would disperse and move to another vineyard. When scabs were caught passing through the picket lines, photographers would document confrontations with

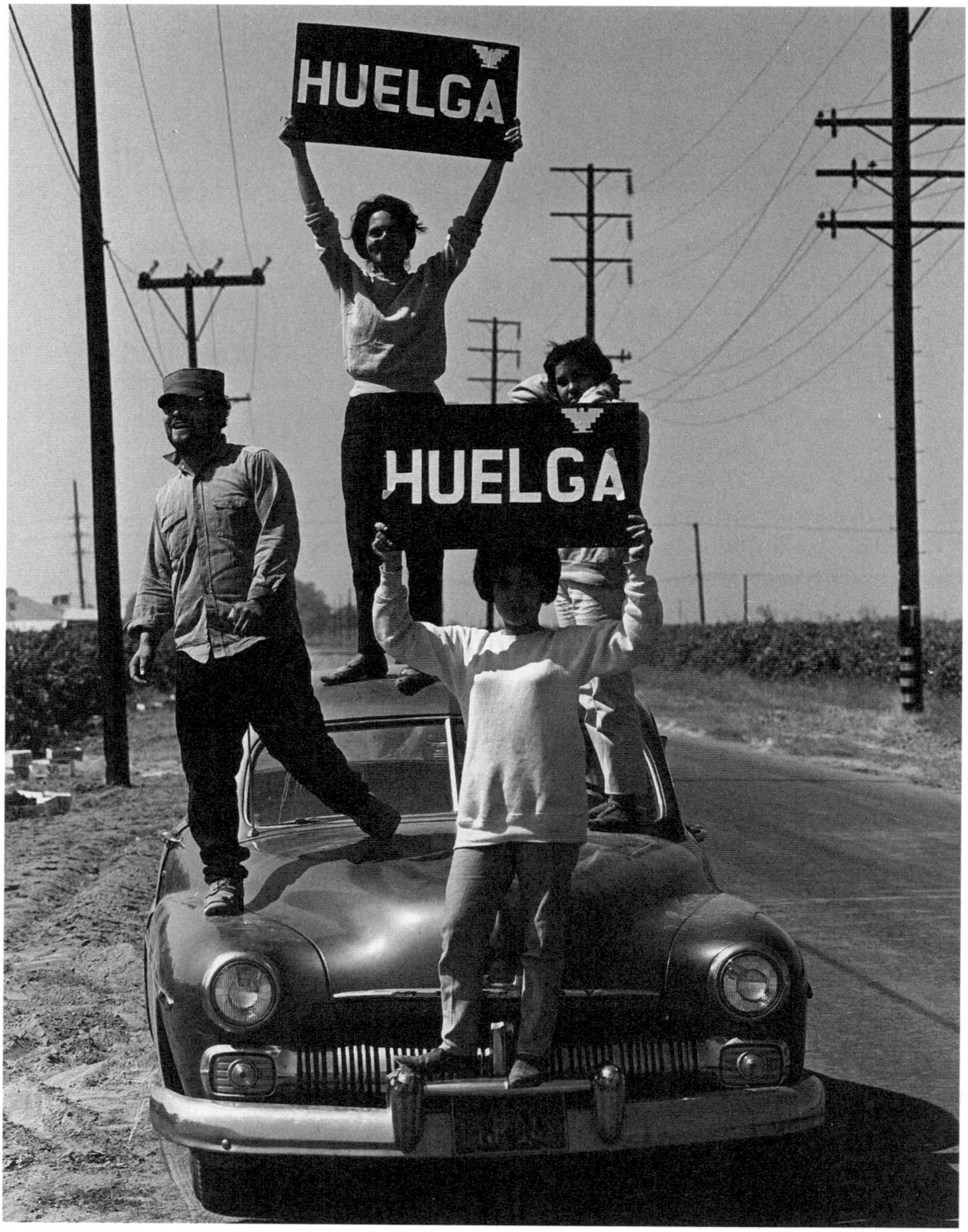

Dolores Huerta (center, on roof of car) holding a "Huelga" sign, September 24, 1965, photograph by Harvey Richards. Publication of this image prompted FBI director J. Edgar Hoover to launch a fifteen-year-long investigation of alleged communist influence on the farmworker movement. Courtesy of Harvey Richards/Estuary Press.

them. They were always alert for angry growers, as well as any guns and weapons. At midmorning they might follow a group of pickets from the farm entrances and begin scouting the back roads. Finding a crew, they paid special attention to picket captains armed with bullhorns trying to induce workers to join the strike. Hand-painted signs with especially clever and dramatic wording would also evoke much attention, as would unique angles on the quickly redundant pictures of picketing.[32]

Continuing throughout the first two weeks of October, these photo confrontations culminated in a series of progressively more violent incidents. Fed up, an angry Ballis could no longer contain himself. On Friday, October 15, he published a short article in the *Valley Labor Citizen.* Titled "Justice, San Joaquin style," it read:

> The *Labor Citizen* photographer has been present on three occasions when grape growers Bruno and Charles Dispoto—in full view of police—have pushed, elbowed, kneed, tripped, and vilified grape strike pickets in the foulest language imaginable. The *Labor Citizen* has pictures of some of this pushing and shoving. Not once in the presence of the *Labor Citizen* photographer have the police said a word to either of the Dispotos until, as noted in the paper last week, one of the pickets warned the police that another of the pickets might kill Bruno Dispoto if he continued the elbow routine. Contrast such casual acceptance by the police of the Dispoto violence with the scene last Monday night. The police arrested picket Jack Delarmente when they saw him strike Charles Dispoto. That's justice, San Joaquin Valley style.[33]

On Saturday, October 16, picket captain Eugene Nelson headed out to the John Dulcich ranch, east of Earlimart. A thirty-six-year-old son of a Modesto grape grower, Nelson had moved to Delano with his wife and daughter after spending several years in Mexico writing his novel *The Bracero.* A kind of jack-of-all-trades (besides picket captain, also a freelance journalist and photographer), he packed a camera wherever he went. He was talking to a group of grape pickers and photographing them at work when a station wagon screeched to a stop a few feet away. Jumping out of the vehicle, George Dulcich, a burly, blond grower with a Slavic accent, cursed Nelson and, after challenging him to a fight, grabbed him by the neck, tried to strangle him, broke his camera strap, and dropped his camera to the ground. Nelson later recalled of the incident:

> I got a good picture of a security guard with a dog going after me. And I got another good picture of a grower striking a middle-aged Mexican woman on the picket line. But when I got the film back from the Delano drugstore the film processor said the pictures didn't come out. I wasn't the only one who had this happen to him. It was all rather suspicious. After that we developed our own film or sent it out.[34]

Returning from Pixley Justice Court that evening, Nelson was detained by Kern County sheriff's deputy Gerald Dodd, who told him that no more shouting of the word *huelga* would be allowed on the picket lines in Kern County, and, furthermore, anyone who read a reprint of Jack London's "Definition of a Strikebreaker" would be arrested. Nelson, frustrated by his failure to produce photographs of the day's incident, now realized a way to strike back. Out on the picket lines on Sunday morning, he prevailed on the Reverend David Havens of the Migrant Ministry to read London's essay "Definition of a Strikebreaker" and submit to arrest. With freedom of speech now an issue, Chávez, Dolores Huerta, Rev. Chris Hartmire, Rev. Jim Drake of the Migrant Ministry, and Nelson met that evening to cook up a photo opportunity. With Chávez scheduled to speak on the steps of Sproul Hall, at the University of California at Berkeley, union leaders decided to exploit the university's recent battles over freedom of speech by having volunteers travel out to the W. B. Camp ranch the next morning and start hollering, "Huelga! Huelga! Huelga!"

Early on the morning of Tuesday, October 19, the NFWA notified the Kern County Sheriff's Department that strikers intended to defy the injunction against the word *huelga.* When sheriff's patrol cars and a paddy wagon predictably appeared at strike headquarters, a large caravan of pickets headed out to the Camp ranch, three miles southeast of Delano. With the police and press watching, forty-four volunteers, including nine ministers and twelve women, parked along the shoulder of the road, walked toward the ranch, held up their "Huelga!" signs, and began chanting in unison, "Huelga! Huelga! Huelga!" When they were arrested, cameramen scrambled over one another, photographing the incident from every possible angle. "Uniformed sheriff's deputies, using small snapshot cameras, photographed each picket," recalled *Fresno Bee* reporter–photographer Ronald B. Taylor. "A CBS-TV camera crew moved boldly into the vineyards, and, ignoring the foreman's protest, they began filming a father and daughter who were harvesting grapes and trying to ignore all of the fuss swirling around them. The two workers tried unsuccessfully to hide their faces from the camera crew."[35]

After Chávez announced the arrests to students at Berkeley, Mills College, and Stanford University, volunteers and money poured into Delano. But that was not the end of the concocted photo opportunities. After thirty-three of the forty-four arrested chose to remain in jail, NFWA leaders further amplified the picture of biased police, intent on denying the rights of free speech, by staging a huge protest outside the Kern County Jail the following day. Singing "We Shall Overcome" and again chanting "Huelga" until they lost their voices, more than 350 NFWA supporters conveyed to the cameras that the strike had overtones of the civil rights movement and was not just a labor dispute. Further adding to the growing drama of the Delano grape strike, such theatrics signaled the beginning of what was to become a long campaign to shape the nature of the images going out to the public. Nelson wrote at the time, "If there was once a press blackout, it is now definitely over. We get calls from the *New York Times, Chicago Tribune, St. Louis Post Dispatch, Kansas City Star,* and from newspapers from coast to coast."[36]

By early December, the desire to control images had become so pronounced that the mere sight of a camera on the picket lines provoked attacks. When the comedian Steve Allen arrived in Delano to compile material for his book *The Ground Is Our*

Table, Chávez watched veteran photographer Arthur Dubinsky going about his business of compiling images for the book and realized that images had become central to the struggle. But with picket teams coming in from the vineyards, grumbling that the harvest was over and there was nothing to do, Dubinsky had to work hard to find his photographs. All of the action was now occurring far from Delano, largely as the result of something Chávez had done a month earlier. Almost in desperation, he had dispatched two workers and a student volunteer to follow a shipment of Schenley table grapes to the Oakland docks and set up a picket line there. To everyone's surprise, the pickets had attracted massive press coverage. When members of the International Longshoremen's and Warehousemen's Union refused to load all one thousand of the pallets holding ten tons of grapes, leaving them to rot on the wharves when the ship left port, Chávez realized something he had long suspected: that when labor struggles in the fields inevitably failed, they could ultimately succeed if the conflict was expanded outside the strike area. Photographs and photographers would be central to that effort.[37]

To launch that effort, Chávez again thought photographically. He asked Walter Reuther, president of the United Auto Workers, to visit Delano on December 16. AFL leader George Meany denounced the visit as "press agentry," which was predictable after the AFL–CIO's withdrawal of support in 1962 but also exactly the response that Chávez wanted. Reuther's presence and the AFL's reaction created another media event. Defying a police ban on marches and carrying a plywood NFWA sign, Reuther joined Chávez, Larry Itliong, and a column of supporters who paraded through the streets of Delano shouting, "Viva Reuther! Viva Chávez! Viva la huelga!" Pausing at the Filipino hall, Reuther addressed a huge crowd of cheering farmworkers and pledged five thousand dollars a month in support of the farmworker movement. So many photographers were present, recalled Ballis, that they fell and tripped over one another and occasionally pushed, shoved, and fought in order to get the best shot.[38]

Drawn to Delano, dozens of photographers who had never seen Chávez got their first extended look at him and found him perplexing, enigmatic, and highly photogenic. A small man whose thick black hair fell carelessly across his forehead and whose chiseled and weathered face could instantly transform from its usual expression of mischief to one of mesmerizing rage, Chávez emerged as a Gandhi-like figure, the Chicano counterpart of Martin Luther King. Whether he was talking through a bullhorn to scabs in the vineyards, praying in church, marching beside Reuther, or addressing strikers, Chávez always made for interesting pictures. He was certainly at the center of everything, and he seemed to be turning the tables on growers with a brilliant, unconventional campaign. With his quiet manner and kind eyes, he was different from any other labor leader, and photographers, who had not seen a Mexican American leader with his commanding presence, followed him everywhere, yet could not get enough of him.[39]

Photographers found that Chávez was widely in demand. His cause was a new one to attract national attention, and it closely paralleled that of the black civil rights movement. His importance would always be overexaggerated, and others of equal importance, including Dolores Huerta, Larry Itliong, and Jim Drake, would be pushed into the background. The media soon used "the Chávez movement" as shorthand and "Chavistas" to refer to members of the NFWA.

Quickly recognizing the key role that photographers played in the struggle, the NFWA–AWOC learned to cultivate press photographers and organize media events. This relationship would prove invaluable in helping the movement that winter, when it shifted the scene of contact into the larger public arena by launching a primary boycott of Schenley Industries and DiGiorgio. Because a wider "secondary" boycott attacking the entire table-grape industry was banned under the Taft–Hartley Act, which amended the National Labor Relations Act, Chávez at first concentrated on two specific products, Schenley's Cutty Sark whiskey and DiGiorgio's Treesweet brand of canned fruit, which were extremely vulnerable and seemed to offer good targets. Dispatched to cities throughout the country, teams of volunteers and union members sustained by local labor unions and sympathetic churches, leafleted, picketed, and harassed grocery and liquor stores, often with help from CORE, the SNCC, and Students for a Democratic Society (SDS), always with a press photographer present.[40]

During the winter of 1965, the NFWA–AWOC began chronicling its own story and disseminating highly favorable, movement-oriented photographs. Just as union leaders welcomed volunteers, religious activists, and members of the SNCC and other civil rights organizations, so too did they cultivate photographers in the hope of building a sense of solidarity and spreading the union's message. As a result, photographers gained unprecedented access and generated an iconography that did more than get the story across to a wide audience.

Growers and their dilemmas would not be part of this picture. Even though the Delano-area grape growers were largely second-generation Croatian immigrants, with their own dramatic story of climbing the agricultural ladder, they would never attract the attention of photographers, even though they were perfectly suitable for a fine *National Geographic*–type color photo essay. This situation was due in part to the prejudices and biases that photographers brought to their task, as well as their urban backgrounds and lack of patience. Also contributing to the skewed picture was the mundane and unnewsworthy nature of such images coupled with the nature of the news business and the market for pictures of the "bleed and lead" type. "Unless a grower was screaming at someone," recalled Delano grape grower Jack Pandol, "he would never get his picture in a magazine or newspaper." Another reason why photographers ignored grape growers was the hostility of growers to all outsiders and photographers. Lagging behind the union, Delano grape growers were slow to realize that their fate hinged on a battleground far from the vineyards, where photographers delivered images that were overwhelmingly sympathetic to the farmworker movement. By the time they recognized this, they had fallen so far behind the union that they would never catch up.[41]

Absent any attempt at balance, photographers conveyed a dramatically skewed picture. By capturing the daily routine of volunteers and union members as well as the work of organizers and union leaders addressing rallies and leading mass marches, photographers crafted images of great passion that collectively forced the public to reflect on what it was like to be a farmworker in California. They also indirectly supported the movement in ways they did not understand. Defiant strikers confronting foremen and growers on picket lines, for example, always knew a photographer was watching. Volunteers preparing meals for pickets or collecting and distributing donations found themselves accompanied by photographers. NFWA members protesting along the highways, parading through Delano, and standing up to police, sheriff's deputies, and private guards no longer felt alone. "Any time something happened," recalled Eugene Nelson, "someone had a camera at the ready."[42]

IV

EVERYONE HAD CAMERAS

1965–2005

18

The Delano Grape Strike and Boycott

Freelancers Step Forward

Grape pickers at Delano had been on strike for two weeks in September 1965 when Eugene Nelson rolled out of his sleeping bag at 4:30 A.M., well into his routine as a picket captain. He grabbed a quick cup of coffee at the NFWA–AWOC strike mess hall, gathered up a bundle of picket signs, and jumped into an old Packard that served as the command vehicle. Seldom able to enjoy more than three or four hours of restless sleep each night, he was tired and wary. Following the same routine for months, Nelson had survived numerous threats, including an incident in which he and several others had been sprayed with sulfur dust and his Packard had been pulled over on the "mistaken" assumption that it was a stolen vehicle. He knew what to expect as he rounded up his pickets and moved along County Line Road toward the Dispoto ranch. Trailing behind were some ever-present members of the Kern County Sheriff's Department, who promptly pulled him over. Asked to provide a list of destinations, Nelson obliged them, joking that law enforcement had already reported spending 2,085 man hours on strike duty, and the union did not want to add unnecessarily to the mounting gasoline bill. "The police continue taking our pictures, thousands of them, with both still and movie cameras," he wrote in his strike diary. "Every Kern County deputy has his own camera now, bought especially for the strike, and they seem to take positive delight in making us feel self-conscious. What are they trying to prove? They seem particularly anxious to snap us when we are walking across the road, and the theory evolves that they plan some massive move designed to shut down our activities altogether on the grounds we are a hazard to traffic."[1]

Nelson's paranoia was well founded. Deputies were, in fact, engaged in massive photographic surveillance. They were stopping entire caravans of strikers on their way to the vineyards, forcing pickets out of their cars, photographing and questioning them, and detaining them for as much as an hour and a half while they filled out field reports. So frequent and widespread was the surveillance that one striker was detained and photographed on at least twelve separate occasions. But law enforcement authorities did not end their surveillance in the fields. The Delano police department photographed license plates of vehicles outside NFWA headquarters and forwarded the information to federal and state authorities, and the Kern County Sheriff's Department compiled a card file of five thousand suspected strike supporters. Each card showed a supporter's name, criminal record (if there was one), and association with groups (if known) and included a mug shot from the dossier of picket-line pictures (if the name and photo could be matched). At the same time, an FBI informant began conducting an extensive photographic surveillance of outsiders in an attempt "to identify some of these people when the strike is over."[2]

So intense and pervasive was photographic surveillance over the next few months that César Chávez raised the matter on March 14, 1966, when New Jersey senator Harrison Williams brought his Senate Subcommittee on Migratory Labor to California. An early supporter of the farmworker cause, Williams had sponsored legislation extending minimum-wage laws and coverage to farmworkers under the National Labor Relations Act. His hearings in Sacramento and Visalia were uneventful, but not so in Delano, where Congressman Harlan Hagan set the tone by questioning Chávez about communist influences within the NFWA. Chávez turned the tables on Hagan by describing how law enforcement authorities were using photography to intimidate and control strikers. Shocked by the accusations, California senator George Murphy, a conservative sympathetic to agriculture, demanded that the subcommittee summon Kern County sheriff Leroy Gaylen. A veteran lawman who had been elected sheriff in 1954, Gaylen had been involved in policing farm labor strikes as a captain of the California Highway Patrol as far back as 1933. A pugnacious and assertive officer of the law, Gaylen did not take kindly to questioning by Senator Robert F. Kennedy, who had arrived at the hearings a day late and immediately seized on the issue of photographic surveillance in an exchange that unfolded as follows:

KENNEDY: Have you taken pictures of the people that were picketing—Sheriff, have you been taking pictures?

GAYLEN: Well, you have people who come in from other places that we don't know, and we keep in touch, find out who they are, why they're here.

KENNEDY: What are you taking their pictures for?

GAYLEN: Just in our files so we will know who they are in case anything happens.

KENNEDY: I can understand you want to take pictures if there's a riot going on, but I don't understand why if someone is walking along with a sign you want to take pictures of them. I don't see how that helps.

GAYLEN: Well, they might take pictures of us, too.

KENNEDY: It's not a question of them wanting to take pictures of you. You're a law-enforcement official. It is in some way an act of intimidation to go around and be taking their pictures.

GAYLEN: I've got to identify those people.

KENNEDY: We're talking about your taking pictures of somebody walking along with a picket sign.

GAYLEN: Well, he's a potential [*sic*], isn't he?
KENNEDY: Well, I mean, so am I. . . . Do you take pictures of everybody in the city?
GAYLEN: Well, if he's on strike or something like that.[3]

Besides being photographed by the police and the FBI, Chávez and other NFWA members were surveilled by professional photographers employed by individual growers and growers associations to document strike-related activities. One of the most vehement anti-Chávez photographers was Gary Allen. A Los Angeles–based film writer and Stanford University graduate, Allen spent several months at Delano while writing and photographing for *The Grapes: Communist Wrath in Delano,* a John Birch Society pamphlet. Designed to tarnish the reputations of Chávez and his followers, Allen's photographs drove home the theme of communist involvement with captions that read, "Communist Larry Itliong," "Cuban-trained Luis Valdez," "Revolutionaries Dolores Huerta and Wendy Gopel," "Marxist attorney Alex Hoffman," and "Kennedy encourages Delano revolutionaries." Other publications also played up Communist Party involvement, evidence of outside agitators, and lack of support for the strike among the workers themselves by featuring photographs of unkempt, long-haired volunteers and bearded students, as well as members of the Student Nonviolent Coordinating Committee and the occasional Communist Party member, such as *People's World* reporter–photographer Sam Kushner.[4]

Strikers never surrendered to photographic harassment. Under surveillance on the picket lines, they fought back in a variety of ways. One course of action was to cooperate excessively with deputies. When stopped while driving out to the vineyards, pickets examined the cards they were forced to fill out, turned them over, read them upside down, corrected spelling, added and deleted information, and took as much time as possible. When asked to pose for mug shots, they would sneeze, frown, pick their noses, close their eyes, or open their mouths wide just at the moment when the shutter snapped, forcing deputies to reshoot pictures again and again. "In my case," explained Chávez to journalist Jacques Levy several years later, "the officer took almost an hour because I went very slowly. I examined the card and the spelling, and I engaged in conversation just to tie him up." After a few weeks of that, the NFWA switched tactics. "We refused to give them any information or let them take our pictures," added Chávez. "We told the inquiring officer from the Kern County sheriff's office that if he wanted more information from us or wanted to take our picture, he would first have to arrest us. And at that point we were able to gain some ground."[5]

From the beginning of the strike, Chávez carried a Nikon camera that someone had donated to the union. Photographing on the picket lines and at various confrontations and union events, he used his camera to level the playing field and expose the myths and lies that he believed agribusiness was concocting to protect itself. But Chávez did more than take pictures and resist photographic harassment. Blessed with an acute sense of history, an understanding of the value of media exposure, and an appreciation of visual culture, Chávez and his cadre of volunteers also designed and created the kind of images that the public saw. From the beginning, religious symbols became part of the strike pageantry. Masses and blessings by priests inaugurated and authenticated every action. Union symbols added punch and assertiveness. Elaborately painted signs and banners, many of them red with a stylized black Aztec eagle in the center to symbolize the union's flag, injected "some color into the movement," as Chávez said. NFWA volunteer Jim Holland made hundreds of circular red and black "Huelga" picket signs, which appeared in virtually every picture and were much appreciated as props and framing devices that turned ordinary photographs into much stronger images. Arrests and harassment were also welcomed and often provoked, with some confrontations playing out like miniature battles. Violent behavior from those within the movement was condemned, but violence against the movement, especially if it was photographed, was regarded as valuable in shaping the public image that Chávez wanted. "We took every photograph of violence and used it to publicize what they were doing to us," recalled Chávez. "We wanted those and other images to be seen by the public."[6]

While exploitation of photographic evidence and development of a visually rich union culture generated plenty of useful pictures, they did not ensure that those images would be published. To achieve that goal, the NFWA formed the Farmworker Press. Bill Esher, who had edited *Farm Labor* before becoming the NFWA's "publicity genius," became the press's managing editor. With little more than a typesetting machine and a homemade layout table, Esher and four volunteers aimed at "challenging the

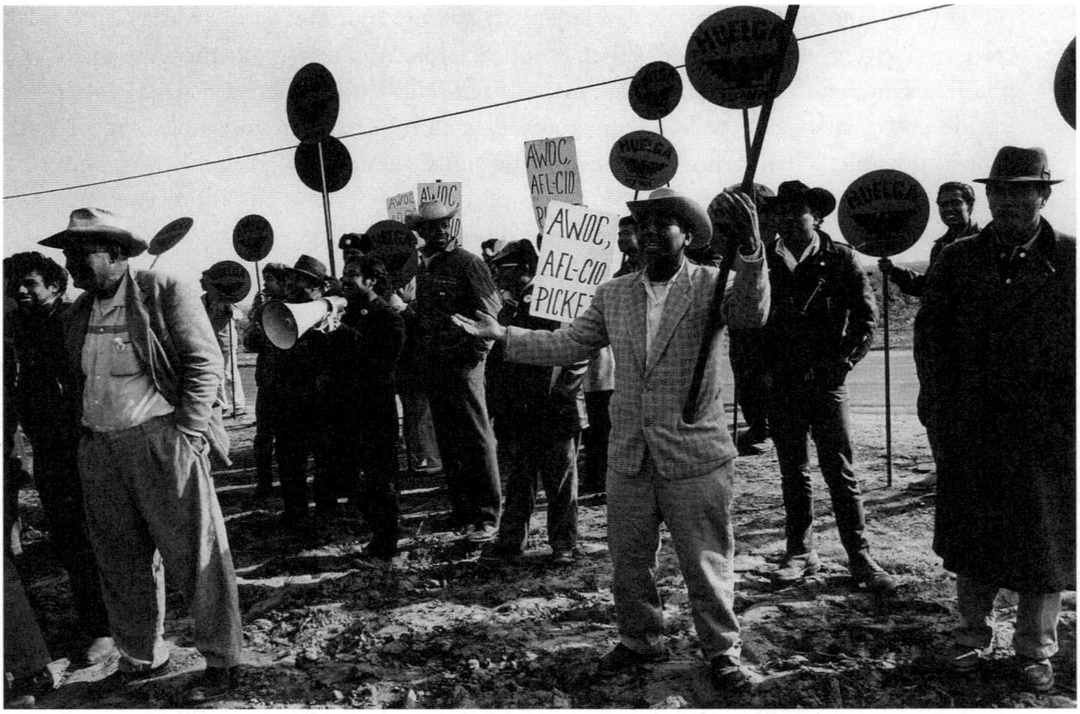

Picket line during the Delano grape strike, November 1966, photograph by John Kouns. Courtesy of John Kouns.

elaborate power structure of California's Central Valley" with a newspaper for farmworkers that could "tell the truth." Published in both English and Spanish, the saucy, free-swinging newspaper first appeared in February and was unlike any other labor paper ever published in the United States, with perhaps the exception of IWW papers such as *Solidarity,* the *Industrial Worker,* and the *Industrial Union Bulletin.* The NFWA called its new paper *El Malcriado.* Full of ironic meaning, the title defied translation into English. Depending on who was explaining, *El Malcriado* meant "the ill-bred" or "the lowly-born" or "we shall inherit the earth, and along the way we'll have a lot more fun than they will." Most simply said it meant "The Bad Boy."[7]

During its first eight months, *El Malcriado* published cartoons, drawings, and irreverent stories, some written with an utter disregard for the facts, most combining editorials with reporting. Farmworkers loved it. Jokes, invective, and slander made the paper a hilarious read but also led to a series of libel suits that forced Esher to suspend publication temporarily. The paper did not actually take the photographs it used beginning in November 1965, when it started running all kinds of them. "*El Malcriado* did not have a camera when I came on board in 1965," recalled staff member Doug Adair. When the paper needed pictures, Esher turned to Ernest Lowe, who was still actively photographing in the fields. Often driving to Berkeley, Esher prevailed on Lowe to make prints for the newspaper. When Lowe became overburdened by the work, Esher developed a "hot list" of sympathetic photographers, who became a de facto staff. "We took the attitude that we could just mooch off all the great photographers who came through, and often used their work without credit," recalled Adair. "We were really shameless. We didn't use bylines, either—revolutionary anonymity or something."[8]

From the beginning, in addition to *El Malcriado,* the Farmworker Press produced "a series of picture books giving the feeling of what it is like to live and work in twentieth century America under feudal labor conditions." The first of such books appeared in February 1966. Titled *Huelga: The First Hundred Days of the Great Delano Grape Strike,* it was written by Eugene Nelson. At the center of operations, Nelson knew all of the union's photographers, photographed key aspects of the strike himself, and kept a detailed daily journal. When he finished the written portion of the book, he collected dozens of photographs by George Ballis, Harvey Richards, Bill Esher, and Bill Berg and integrated them into an admittedly pro-Chávez account. Part personal memoir, part polemic, part journalism, *Huelga* features disturbing images of guard dogs threatening pickets, dark pictures of early-morning shape-ups, and dramatic news shots of priests courting arrest.[9]

Quickly selling out within a month, the book went into a second printing and inspired other photographic accounts. The most important of these appeared in March 1966. Published by the National Advisory Committee on Farm Labor (NACFL), a New York City–based nonprofit organization that had been supporting the farmworker cause for a decade, *The Grape Strike* is packed with pictures of sheriff's deputies and private guards protecting strikebreakers, lines of pickets holding up large "Huelga" signs, farmworkers at union meetings, and the labels and vineyards of grape growers being struck. Featuring a George Ballis photograph of a Kern County deputy sheriff carrying a camera at the Giumarra ranch, the book underscores the way law enforcement authorities employed photography against the farmworker movement. "All deputies carried Instamatic cameras," Nelson explained. "Some had cameras and tape recorders. They took repeated photographs of all pickets, particularly close-up shots."[10]

For some NFWA members, photographs were not enough. To them, no images could possibly convey the anger and sense of powerlessness that they had experienced, and they looked for ways to convey that message. Some found an outlet in El Teatro Campesino (the Farmworker Theater). Founded by Luis Váldez, a twenty-five-year-old member of the irreverent San Francisco Mime Troupe, El Teatro Campesino was a guerrilla theater group that allowed farmworkers to satirize their plight and ridicule their foes. In this amalgamation of commedia dell'arte and Bertolt Brecht, farmworkers themselves became the actors. Assuming the roles of growers, labor contractors, and undocumented workers, El Teatro Campesino members vented their anger from improvised stages thrown together on flatbed trucks. Their role was to instruct as well as entertain fellow workers through broadly caricatured stock parts. Whether playing before pickets at Delano, entertaining students at a California college campus, or performing off Broadway in New York City, the cast of characters was so hilarious, bizarre, and original that they were unforgettable to anyone who saw them.[11]

At the same time that El Teatro Campesino was becoming organized, a steady stream of photographers arrived at Delano and quickly departed. Most were press photographers working for California and national newspapers, especially the *San Francisco Chronicle* and the *Los Angeles Times,* along with contract photographers for magazines such as *Time, Newsweek, U.S. News and World Report,* the *Saturday Evening Post, Look,* the *New Yorker, Business Week,* and *Life.* Recording the farmworker movement according to professional principles of objectivity, these photographers seldom remained more than a few days. Most but not all were typical "parachute journalists." That is, they were the sort who remain aloof, never making contact with farmworkers or strikers, and stay on location just long enough to get a usable picture. They capture part of the news, but photographers of a different cut have to get the rest of the picture.

A reaction against hit-and-run daily news photography shaped and drove a small cadre of talented and dedicated freelance photographers at Delano. An entirely rebellious and stubborn breed, freelancers threw themselves into the grape strike with almost complete abandon. Trading job security for the opportunity to study a subject in depth, many sacrificed personal relationships, left their families, borrowed money, endured financial insecurity, jeopardized their health, took great risks in pursuit of their craft, and, in several cases, expended so much energy that their careers suffered—all just to stay in Delano and document the story as it unfolded. The main reason for this enthusiasm was that, by camping out at Delano, freelancers overcame the main obstacles preventing extended study of an ongoing news event: deadline pressures, lack of access, insufficient funds, and absence when the action occurred. Proud supporters of Chávez and distinctly hostile to agribusiness, with few exceptions freelancers covering Delano crossed the line demarcating participant and observer.

Freelancers made explicit their role as actors in the very drama that they were recording by donating their work to *El Malcriado.* Many also sold their images at union fund-raising functions and allowed the NFWA to transform their best photographs into union posters. Those remaining in Delano for any extended period of time converted to the farmworker cause, became instruments of organizing, and admitted to being extensions of the union. "We were definitely on the union side," admitted Mike Bry, a San Francisco freelancer who took time off from working on his book, *The California Feeling,* to photograph at Delano for several weeks. "All of the photographers I knew helped the union," explained another freelance photographer who arrived at Delano after photographing the civil rights movement in the South. "This business of hiding behind the camera was a crock. . . . You couldn't go out on the picket lines every morning and put up with everything you had to put up with and remain neutral very long."[12]

Seldom acknowledged, this strong political orientation and lack of objectivity was complicated and had important repercussions. Although freelancers never claimed to be neutral, none ever directed or staged pictures. While they took a stand that was most definitely on the side of the farmworker movement, they were "straight" photographers. Their only manipulations consisted of their choice of lens, film, and printing paper, and perhaps the occasional use of a flash to open up shadows during midday or to photograph in union halls during the evening; manipulations never extended beyond an occasional and obvious high-contrast print or artistic "solarization." Freelancers struggled to break into the pages of the large daily newspapers and national magazines. Their photos overwhelmingly dominated certain editorial markets, particularly the labor, radical, and religious press. They sent their work to *Ramparts, Rolling Stone,* the *Catholic Worker,* the *Christian Science Monitor,* and occasionally to *People's World,* and they kept art directors stocked with images of armed authorities, labor camps, harsh working conditions, and, most important, César Chávez. Strong and interesting, their photographs stirred up public opinion and generated additional media attention. Many took pictures that are among the most powerful ever taken of the farmworker movement. For several, their work at Delano was the high point of their career, if not their lives. Nothing they did after that ever compared with the challenges, accomplishments, and friendships from their time covering the farmworker movement.[13]

Although some observers would correctly assert that much picket line activity was largely designed and motivated by the desire to create effective images, photographers were not entirely provocative. Their presence cut in many directions, placing limits on behavior and helping to curb violence. Bill Esher would later argue that by courting photographers and keeping them busy, the NFWA contributed to the safety of pickets, perhaps even saved some lives, since the presence of a photographer on a picket line indicated to foremen and police that they were being scrutinized, which was often all that prevented confrontations from escalating into pitched battles. NFWA strategist Fred Ross made the same point. "The kind of things that the growers used to get away with when they would pick off union activists one by one just couldn't happen when photographers were present," he asserted. "Growers couldn't take the scrutiny.

They ran from photographers to cower behind lawyers and public relations agencies—like cockroaches caught in the light of day—unable to stand exposure and scurrying for places to hide."[14]

Of all the photographers at Delano during the first year of the strike, Jon Lewis was by far the most intrepid, tenacious, dedicated, and important. A Marine Corps veteran with a degree in journalism and social science from San Jose State University, Lewis was about to begin graduate school at San Francisco State University when he visited Delano with activist Marshall Ganz, actor–director Luis Váldez, and a delegation of SNCC members. "It was January 1966," he recalled years later. "I was set to go up to Oregon to photograph the Shakespearean Theater in spring. I intended to spend a week in Delano, do the Shakespearean job, and then return to school. Once I saw what was happening, I said, 'The hell with it. I'm sorry. I'm staying.' I stayed for eight months and shot 256 rolls of film."[15]

Photographing at the DiGiorgio Fruit Corporation's Sierra Vista vineyards ten miles north of Delano during his first week on the job, Lewis got a taste of how growers and Delano residents regarded photographers. As the second largest ranch in the area and one of the most modern and efficient agricultural operations in the state, Sierra Vista

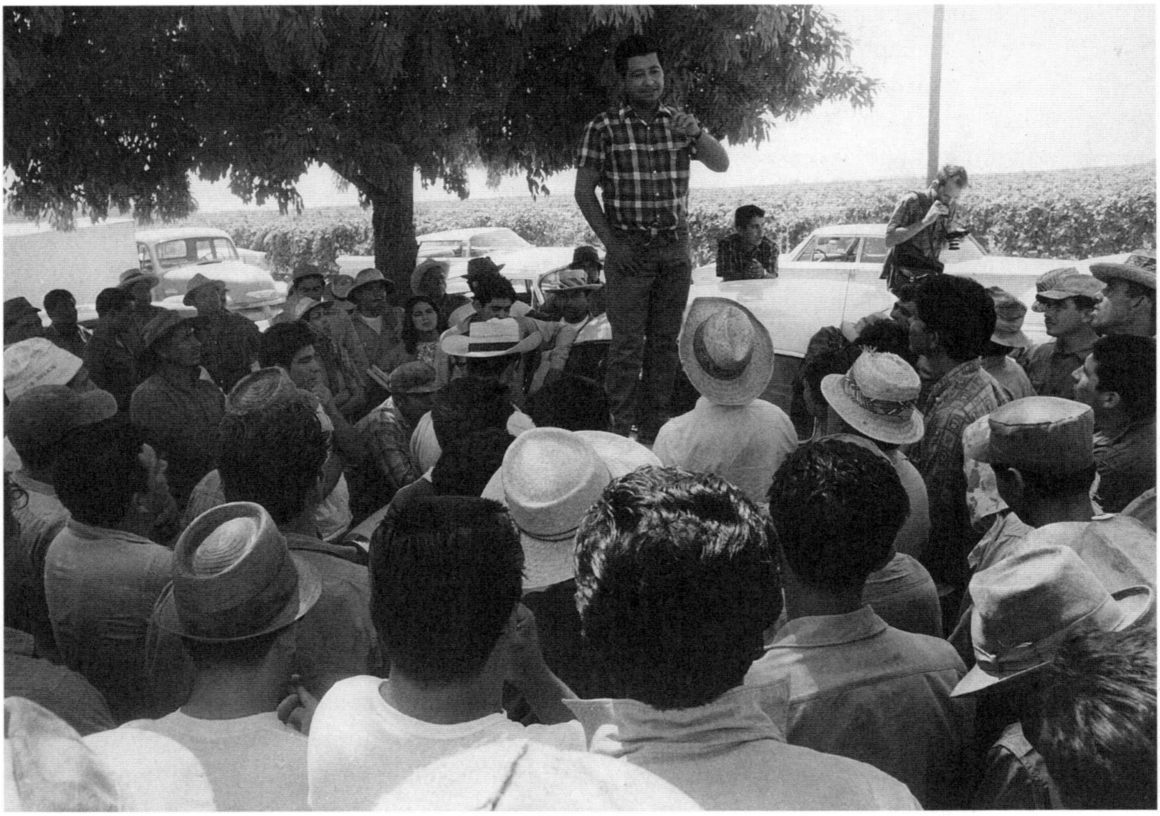

César Chávez addressing strikers at DiGiorgio's Sierra Vista Ranch, as Jon Lewis (toward the right) maneuvers to get a picture, March 1966, photograph by Gerhard Gscheidle.

encompassed forty-four hundred acres and, along with the Schenley Industries ranches, was a prime target for NFWA picketing. As the confrontation intensified, DiGiorgio brought in strikebreakers, some from as far away as Texas. Arriving on the scene shortly after fistfights and shoving matches had erupted on the picket lines, Lewis attempted to photograph nonstrikers pruning vines in the company's vineyards. Already nervous about the role that photographers were playing in the strike, DiGiorgio security guard Herschel Nuñez attempted to prevent Lewis from photographing. Unintimidated, Lewis proceeded, so Nuñez shoved his hand into the camera lens and manhandled Lewis. Lewis explained nearly forty years later:

> I never really got my ass kicked like some other photographers. I was scared some of the time. There were some mean SOB's out there. There were some rednecks. Working with the union and packing a camera, you're a visible target. Plus you're a college student or an outside agitator, someone who's suspicious. You stayed on the other side of town, on the other side of the tracks. You had to be careful. You didn't want to be caught in a dark alley with some of those guys around Delano.[16]

As was also the case during the civil rights struggle in the American South at that time, such fears and efforts at suppression testified to the power of photography and inspired Lewis and those like him to join the NFWA and become advocates. Joining had its advantages. Having no assignment and no connections to news organizations and being so poor he could not even afford to rent an apartment, Lewis's union membership allowed him to flop on the floor at one of two NFWA houses where volunteers congregated. One house was known as the Pink House. Located directly behind the union's storefront headquarters on Albany Street, the Pink House had the most space and operated a medical clinic on the weekends. The other was the Gray House. Located on a neighboring street, the Gray House was where the NFWA had its offset press, and Chávez kept a small office at the end of a dark, narrow hallway. Lewis soon moved into the Gray House. He later recalled:

> It was crowded. We were always cramped for room. People were coming and going all of the time. They would be tossing bedrolls everywhere, in the yard, on the floor, on the lawn, and on couches in all of the rooms. There were at least twenty student workers in every room. It was never quiet. The phones were always ringing. There was always a crisis. A car would break down and need parts. People would be there trying to find money to feed and house strikers. There was nonstop laughter, constant banter in English and Spanish. People would be up all night stuffing envelopes in the living room. *El Malcriado* was coming out weekly. There was activity twenty-four hours a day. The place was just a zoo.[17]

To finance his photography, Lewis borrowed one hundred dollars from one friend and fifty dollars from another. He bought a new lens for his camera and a Durst 606 enlarger, then built a darkroom in a laundry room off the garage at the Gray House.

To help Lewis with supplies, NFWA volunteers rounded up lumber and materials from the community and established a credit account of sorts with a photography shop in Bakersfield. Equipped with a cot, the darkroom/laundry room also doubled as Lewis's bedroom.

From this crude base of operations, Lewis became a veritable one-man photo agency. Besides producing prints for *El Malcriado*, he sent out photo essays, often with extensive typed captions, to news organizations scattered in cities around the country. He also looked after new photographers who could not afford lodging. When the union established its "Forty Acres" headquarters at an old gas station west of town, Lewis moved the darkroom there. For his work, he received the standard five dollars a week and paid for his own film. The only support the union provided was photographic paper.[18]

Working conditions in those darkrooms/bedrooms were, by all accounts, hot, cramped, and difficult. With only a small window leading to the kitchen, the Gray House darkroom became a chemical sauna even on cool days. Unable to install a fan or otherwise improve ventilation, Lewis was forced to do all of his printing and developing during the coolest part of the night, between 1 A.M. and 5 A.M. Often Lewis went straight from an all-night printing marathon out into the sunbaked fields. He later recalled:

> We would meet in the strike kitchen, a mile west of town, where the pickets assembled for a breakfast varying from toast and coffee to eggs and bacon, depending on the donations coming in. There would usually be two caravans: the "Zapatistas" and the "Villaistas." We would often return to the kitchen for lunch, then we would go back out to the fields again. Most days it was just a lot of sweat. You didn't shoot a hell of a lot of film. Some days you didn't take a single picture. When it got warm, you'd get sleepy. Then there would be moments when things broke open and the adrenalin would flow. Occasionally the photography was like combat.[19]

Sometimes Lewis spent long hours just riding in cars with NFWA members along the back roads. Scouting for strikebreakers somewhere within the thirty-eight thousand acres of vineyards around Delano, photographers quickly learned the lesson that previous generations of farmworker activists had learned: picketing farms was not like picketing an industrial plant. One journalist compared his attempt at coverage to trying to cover a factory with one thousand entrance gates spread over forty square miles. The routine reminded Lewis of his stint in the Marines. "You got up early, hurried, then stood around," he recalled. "It was the old 'hurry up and wait' routine. Meals, such as they were, became the big reward of the day. It wasn't all that unfamiliar to me."[20]

After working tirelessly throughout the winter, Lewis became discouraged during the approach of spring. He was exhausted. On his own and without any official backing, he began to wonder how long he could continue and if his photography was having any effect. He was not the only one with doubts. Morale among strikers and union volunteers reached a low point in early March 1966. With the NFWA–AWOC making little headway against the two main targets of the strike, Schenley Industries and the DiGiorgio Fruit Corporation, the cause seemed doomed. "It is very sad and quiet here," Dolores Huerta confessed in mid-March in a letter to AFL–CIO assistant regional director Irwin DeShetler.[21]

One bright spot in the dismal picture came a few days later, when documentary filmmaker Mark Harris flew into Bakersfield from Portland, Oregon, where he was employed at KGW-TV, a local NBC affiliate. Two years out of Harvard University, Harris had been working on a film about "Big Bill" Haywood, founder of Industrial Workers of the World. He was busy tracking down old Wobblies and interviewing them in their rooming houses and shabby, single-room apartments in various skid rows scattered about the Pacific Northwest when he read an essay by sociologist Edgar Z. Friedenberg in the *New York Review of Books.* Titled "Another America," the essay predicted that the impact of the grape strike on labor relations and American democracy "is likely to be out of all proportion to the number of people, strategic import of the industry, or bread-and-butter issues involved." It was a moment of epiphany for Harris. Seeing a chance to film history as it was unfolding, Harris convinced the head of the small documentary division of KGW-TV to let him fly to California and explore the prospect of filming the strike. Forty years later, he recalled:

> I flew into Bakersfield, rented a car, and drove straight to the Albany Street offices of the NFWA. It was only a few minutes before I was shaking hands with César Chávez. "I want to make a documentary about the strike," I told him. As I remember, he agreed at once, although we did discuss the matter more over dinner that night at a Chinese restaurant in Delano. At that point I had little experience as a film maker—only a few documentaries about local issues in Portland—but César didn't hesitate to open the doors of his new union to me. At the time, I wanted to believe it was my youthful idealism that persuaded him to trust me; but looking back, I'm sure it was more his own faith in the justice of his cause. He was confident that if any reasonable person hung around the NFWA with a camera long enough, he couldn't fail to record the truth about farmworkers' struggle and the union battle for recognition.[22]

It would be six weeks before Harris returned to Delano with a crew of camera and sound engineers. In the meantime, Chávez was desperately searching for some way to lift spirits and expand awareness of the strike beyond the borders of Delano. To accomplish that he broke dramatically with traditional labor union approaches. Chávez took his inspiration from field hands who had been sprayed with sulfur dust while picketing the Schenley ranch. Many had vowed to protest by undertaking a cross-country pilgrimage to Schenley's corporate headquarters in New York. Chávez rejected the plan as too dangerous and expensive. But he liked the concept, especially after recalling the publicity generated two years earlier by the Freedom March on Selma, Alabama. Hoping to rekindle interest, generate new imagery, and create what amounted to a massive photo opportunity, Chávez announced a mass march of farmworkers from Delano to Sacramento.[23]

On March 17, seventy-five marchers began a trek that would ultimately cover a total of 280 miles, about the same distance as Gandhi's Salt March to the sea in 1933. The marchers planned to arrive on the steps of the state Capitol on Easter Sunday, where thousands of farmworkers and their supporters would demand that Governor Edmund G. "Pat" Brown intervene in the grape strike. Chávez called the march La Peregrinación (the Pilgrimage), modeled on the Lenten *peregrinaciones* of Mexico. His theme was "Penitence, Pilgrimage, and Revolution." Each night marchers stopped in one of the small towns along the march north. Chávez addressed the public in an attempt to build support for the strike and the boycott of Schenley and DiGiorgio. Nothing of this scale had ever been attempted by a labor organization in California.[24]

As the NFWA prepared for the march, several new photographers arrived in Delano. One was Gerhard Gscheidle, a twenty-three-year-old German with a strong interest in photography and a degree in steel fabrication. Gscheidle had been deeply affected by news of the murder of three civil rights workers in the South. On his own, he traveled by bus to Mississippi, where he photographed for the *Movement,* a Student Nonviolent Coordinating Committee publication. He was exhibiting his work in the Student Union Building at the University of California at Berkeley during the spring of 1966 when the *Movement* editor, Terry Cannon, invited him to join the march and send out photographs along with SNCC press releases. Like most freelancers, Gscheidle was not on the payroll of any publication. Other than the cost of film, paper, and what he would earn from his photographs, he received no compensation. Another photographer operating in this way was Blair Stapp, a San Francisco–based photographer and instructor at the Art Institute. Besides photographing and making sound recordings of the pilgrimage, Stapp also opened his Bay Area darkroom to Gscheidle and other photographers of the farmworker movement. Also present from the beginning of the march was Sam Kushner, who covered the farmworker strike for the communist *People's World.*[25]

Joining Kushner, Bry, Gscheidle, Lewis, and Stapp at Delano for La Peregrinación was John Kouns. No stranger to the movement, Kouns had driven his Volkswagen Bug to Delano in January and camped out in the Gray House with Lewis and other volunteers. Sleeping on the floor and taking his meals at the Filipino Hall, he spent two months, on and off, "doing some picket duty and some photography, sometimes topping off the day with a few beers at People's Bar [Café]." With La Peregrinación shaping up, a telephone call brought him back to cover events through the winter and sporadically over the next two years. At this time he was developing something he would later describe as "Guerrilla Camera." Despite his work for UPI, he did not consider himself to be a news photographer. He rejected any pretense of objectivity. He was trying to help the union with his images, and he credited Chávez with fully understanding his approach and having a similar idea. He later recalled:

> Chávez really knew the value of photography and what it could do for the union. He was very visually aware. I don't think he did anything during the first year of the strike

without considering how it would look on film. To an extent that few realized, much of what the NFWA did was conceived with the idea of shaping the visual record to their advantage. Everyone had cameras. The volunteers knew that if their story was to be understood, they would have to convey it to the public and even illustrate it themselves. NFWA, AWOC, and allies of the farmworker movement took many steps designed to exploit photography and use it to present their point of view. Photography strongly influenced their tactics and thinking. Compared to the agricultural industry, the farmworker movement was much more receptive to photography.[26]

On March 17, photographers were presented with scenes that would soon capture the popular imagination. Chávez was not playing it safe. He was going to kick off the march with appealing and dramatic images. He hoped to provoke an incident and perhaps mass arrests by announcing several days earlier that the NFWA intended to walk down Albany Street in Delano. A farmworker carrying the banner of the Virgin of Guadalupe, patron saint of the Mexican poor and of Emiliano Zapata's armies, would lead the procession. The marchers would then head north. Sixty-seven strikers vowed to march all the way. The youngest, Augustine Hernández, was seventeen. The oldest, William King, was sixty-seven. The average age was thirty-one. Eighteen of the marchers were women. Although AWOC was invited to join the march, its leaders refused, stating that they were engaged in "a trade union dispute, not a civil rights movement or religious crusade." But several AWOC members did participate and selected Manuel Vásquez as their march captain.

Up early for Mass in the backyard of the Pink House, Gscheidle saw only two other photographers present at that historic event. One, John Kouns, wore an old surplus army jacket. Seeing him with two beaten up Leica M2s slung over his shoulder, Gscheidle thought that he must surely be from *Life* magazine. The other photographer, a chain-smoking character whose movements reminded Gscheidle of an ex-Marine, was Jon Lewis. As the marchers prepared to move out, all three photographers got ready for action and then had to scramble when Chávez changed plans. Without obtaining a permit, he led everyone through downtown Delano. With photographers and television crews present, the Delano city manager, already wary of unfavorable images, decided to avoid an incident and allowed the march to proceed. "They wanted us to arrest them," Police Chief James Ailes explained to writer John Gregory Dunne a few months later. "They were all down on their knees with their priests saying all their words and what not. It would make them look good if we arrested them with all that press and TV there."[27]

Of all the photographers present at La Peregrinación, only Jon Lewis and John Kouns intended to walk all the way to Sacramento. As the marchers moved out, George Ballis, Harvey Richards, and Sam Kushner joined their colleagues and began photographing. Doug Adair later recalled Kushner "draped in his camera and with his pipe and notebook." Decades later, the moment remained vivid in the memory of every photographer present. "Wherever you turned, there was something interesting: an old union member, a family, the flags, the march, the cops watching, or some detail," recalled Jon Lewis. "It was an environment rich in photographic material. You had to be a really poor photographer not to see something worth documenting."[28]

Although press photographers enjoyed clean motel rooms and ample meals while intercepting the march at various points along the route, freelancers endured conditions that were raw. "We never knew where we would stay or who would feed us," Lewis recalled. "Some nights we slept in the park. Usually some union supporters would take a couple of us into their homes, give us some tortillas and coffee, and take us back to the start-up point in the morning." The march routine provided freelancers with opportunities to take some intimate photographs, but it also cut into their ability to see the larger picture. Carrying several cameras and gear for ten to fifteen miles each day wore them out, and without cars they could not explore the larger environment that they were passing through. But even though they were limited to their immediate surroundings, they were thrilled to be there and did not deviate from their task.[29]

Most other photographers were not so devoted. Press photographers under deadline would spend a day, then return home to print and edit their pictures. *Time* and

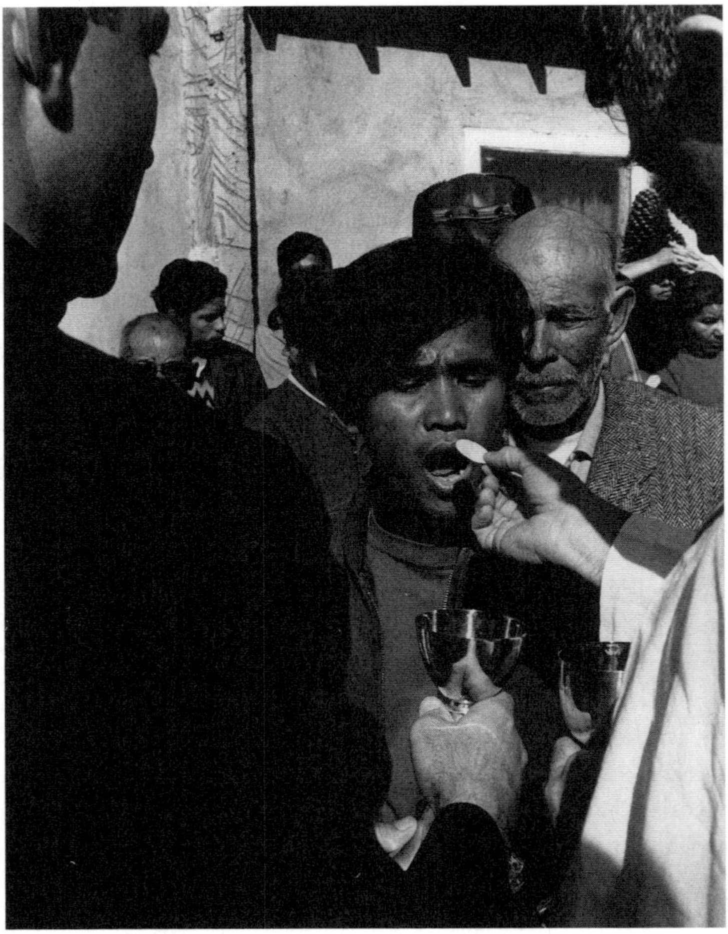

Receiving Holy Communion at the beginning of La Peregrinación, March 17, 1966, photograph by Ernest Lowe. Courtesy of Ernest Lowe.

Newsweek stringers arriving for "snaps" (one or two images produced quickly) rented a pickup truck and driver and sped around for an hour or two up and down the line of marchers. "This got a sorry nod from us three," recalled Gerhard Gscheidle of Lewis, Kouns, and himself. "We considered ourselves part of the farmworker movement and these 'image makers' who joined the march for a couple of hours or even a day on assignment, well, the difference of covering the pilgrimage on assignment and the plain conviction to document the fight of the Mexican American farmworkers for better working conditions made a big difference in my mind."[30]

Only impending deadlines and concern for the large amount of film they were shooting caused Lewis and John Kouns to take a day off late in the march. "We were ahead of schedule," Lewis recalled. "So Kouns and I went back to Delano to shower, get a good night's sleep, and develop film and print photographs. We only missed a couple of hours covering that entire march. I walked with blisters on my feet from the very first day."[31]

Many older photographers could not walk the entire distance. But that did not keep one of them from covering the event. Of Harvey Richards, who drove most of the way, Kouns recalled:

> We would be trudging along and all of a sudden we would see Harvey Richards pull up, climb on top of his station wagon, whip out his tripod, attach a telephoto lens, shoot some pictures, jump back in, and drive five miles to the head of the march. He was twice our age, so I don't think that he could have made the walk. He was really well organized. It got to the point that whenever we'd pull into a little town to camp that evening, he'd be there waiting for us. He probably got the best pictures of the march because he was so mobile, and he was always in position to capture something when it happened, whereas we only saw what was immediately around us.[32]

However, whether they came and went or walked the entire way, photographers recorded essentially the same dramatic scenes. One category of images centered on pageantry. Seeing union members in the countryside carrying banners of the Virgin of Guadalupe, a large cross, and the Mexican, American, and NFWA flags waving in the spring breeze, photographers produced images that could easily have been mistaken for photographs of civil rights marchers moving through the American South. Photographers also found a rich reservoir of subjects in the barrios and *colonias* where the marchers stopped each night, camped out, and were fed and cared for by local farmworkers. And to the joy of audiences and photographers alike, El Teatro Campesino staged lively performances in city parks.

Vividly goofy characters like the *esquirole* (scab), *contratista* (contractor), *huelgista* (striker), and a DiGiorgio Fruit Corporation foreman wearing huge boots, military cap, and dark sunglasses and resembling a cross between a Nazi concentration camp manager and a plantation owner in the American slave South paraded onstage. Photographed from every angle, the skits made good filler on slow news days. Another favorite subject for photographers was Peggy McGivern, the NFWA's nurse, who lanced so many blisters that she would have a recurring nightmare about a giant blister bursting and drowning her in an avalanche of puss. But more than anything else, photographers focused on Chávez. Documenting different variations of his tortured journey, they caught every move, every grimace; even as he sat by the roadside to remove his shoes, massage his aching feet, and apply bandages, photographers would be present recording the moment.[33]

As the march neared Stockton, Rev. Jim Drake became acutely aware that television camera crews were closely following the march. This provoked a change in tactics. After consulting with Chávez and the march leaders, Drake induced the marchers to begin carrying boycott signs. Quickly put together, signs exclaiming, "Boycott I. W. Harper," "Boycott S&W," and "Boycott Treesweet," suddenly appeared alongside the Virgin of Guadalupe, the NFWA eagle, and the American flag on the evening television. At the same time, a half dozen San Francisco newspaper photographers picked up the coverage.[34]

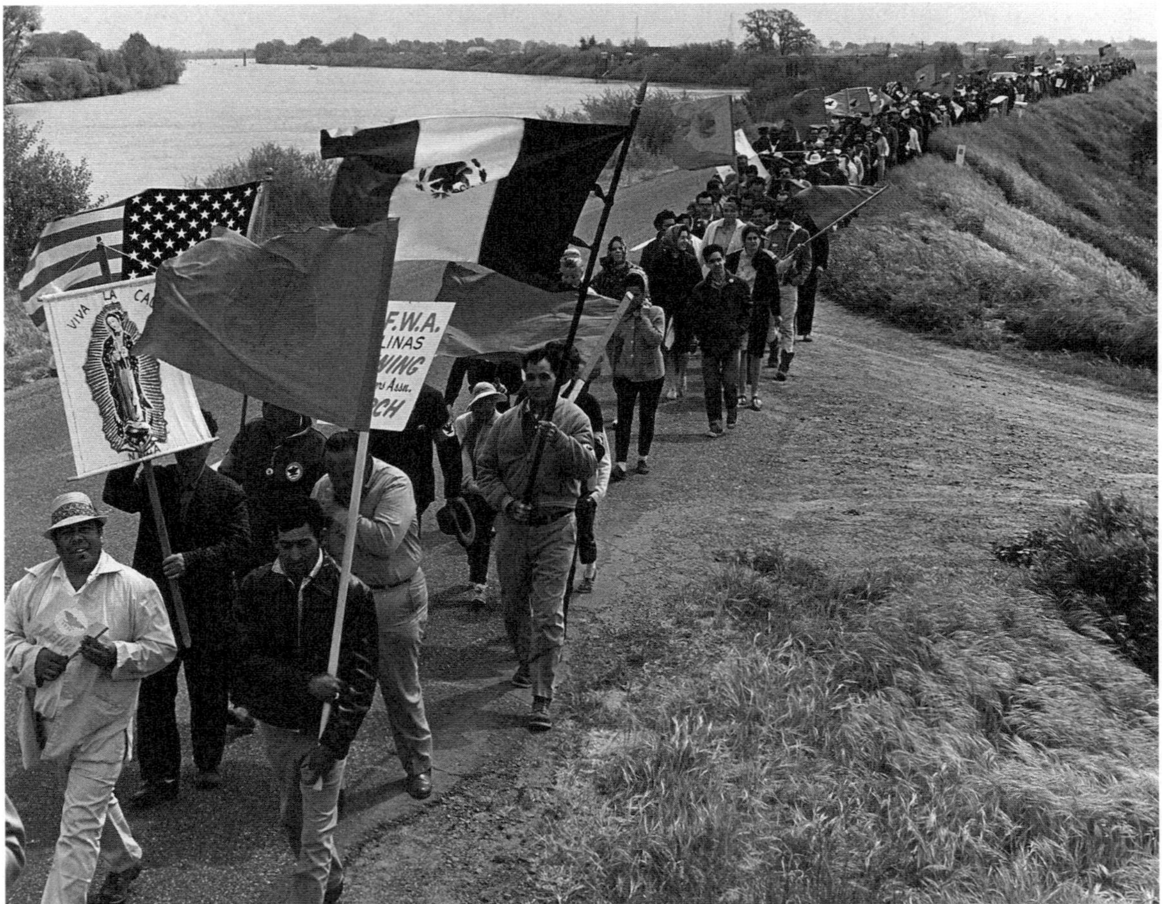

La Peregrinación moving through the Sacramento–San Joaquin Delta, April 4, 1966, photograph by Harvey Richards. Courtesy of Harvey Richards.

Fran Ortiz, a staff photographer for the *San Francisco Examiner,* joined the procession south of Tracy and walked the last fifty miles. Eating, sleeping, and drinking shots of tequila with the marchers and other photographers each night in city parks, Ortiz completely altered his strategy for covering the event. He had arrived with the standard brace of zoom lenses and motor-driven cameras, but on finding that the real story seemed to be in the more intimate moments along the way, Ortiz quickly returned to his old standbys: two quiet Leicas with normal and wide-angle lenses.

While in a small Catholic church where marchers had paused to pray and celebrate Mass on the next to last day of the march, Ortiz employed his Leicas to great advantage. During the Mass, a field hand stood up holding a small crucifix. As the man faced the priest, Ortiz turned around and used his Leica to photograph him deep in prayer. Infused with a sense of honesty and dignity and embodying the theme of penitence, which epitomized the march, the photograph ran in the *Examiner* and later in *Time* magazine. "It became a pretty emotional image," Ortiz later observed. "I could not have made it if the people had not come to trust me."[35]

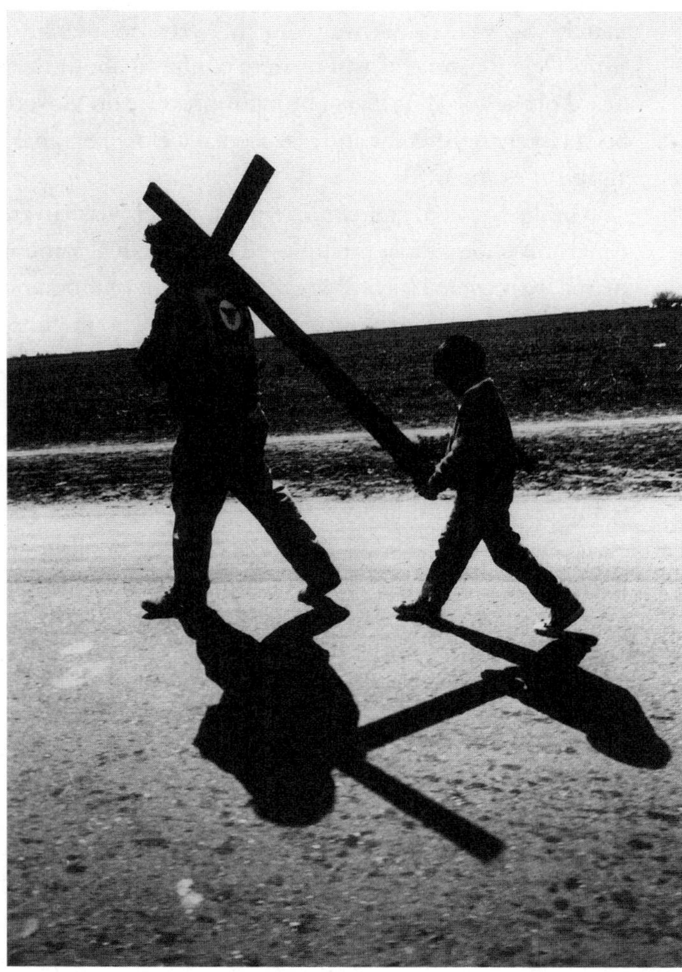

George Ballis's photograph of Roberto Roman carrying a cross on La Peregrinación near Tracy, March 7, 1966. Courtesy of Take Stock Images.

A day after Ortiz photographed in the Stockton church, George Ballis made what many regard as the single most important and memorable photograph of the march. Among a group of farmworkers he was photographing were two who carried a wooden cross, ten feet tall, made of two-by-fours. The two fell behind. Now separated from the march and alone with their burden, one of them, Roberto Roman (who had helped to carry the cross all the way from Delano), so obviously emulated Christ on the way to his Crucifixion that Ballis's image of him was attacked as sacrilegious. But it also drew attention to the sacrifices that farmworkers were making as they fasted and limped along the road. Effective in marshaling support for the farmworker movement, the photograph further confirmed César Chávez and his followers as the Mexican American counterparts to Martin Luther King Jr. and the Freedom Marchers in the South.[36]

As a photo event, the march succeeded on its own merits. There was little advance publicity. "News got around the San Joaquin Valley and certainly in the Mexican American communities, which actually was one of the biggest goals of the pilgrimage—to spread the word about the strike," recalled Gscheidle decades later. "I remember how jubilant Terry Cannon was when the *Los Angeles Times* ran a story after the march was well under way." In this way the march took the strike to workers far from Delano, some of whom were confused about the issues and often had not even heard of the NFWA. It also brought pressure on Governor Edmund Brown, who had been largely indifferent and was seen as a close personal friend of DiGiorgio and other agribusinessmen.[37]

Unlike the civil rights movement, which was covered by a contingent of African American photographers employed by *Ebony* magazine and its competitors, the NFWA march was covered by no Mexican American photographers. With few Hispanic media outlets and no editors from ethnic journals who might sponsor them and publish their pictures, Mexican American photographers were so few and far between at the time that Gscheidle later recalled, "I didn't know or meet a single Mexican American [professional freelance] photographer during my time in Delano." The one exception, after the march, was union volunteer Manuel Chris Sánchez. A huggable, diabetic, teddy bear of a union activist who hung out at the People's Café and was known to everyone as Fats, Sánchez became interested in photography while tending the Porta-John on La Peregrinación. He later purchased an inexpensive camera and learned how to shoot by speaking with Lewis and Kouns and watching them work. "It seemed he was always relaxed, a wry sense of humor carrying him through the stressful times," recalled *El Malcriado* editor Doug Adair many years later. "But he really did not become fluent and productive for several years."[38]

On Easter Sunday, April 10, 1966, photojournalists from dozens of newspapers and magazines joined contract photographers, special correspondents, wire-service reporters, television crews, freelancers, and union photographers on the steps of the state Capitol. Jockeying for position, each tried to capture the drama of ten thousand people welcoming the fifty-two *originales* (the farmworkers who had walked the entire distance, thirteen having dropped out or failed to make it to Sacramento). Countless photographers took exactly the same photograph, from slightly different angles, of Chávez announcing that four days earlier Schenley Industries had agreed to recognize the NFWA and sign a contract raising wages by thirty-five cents an hour. So great was the attraction and so unparalleled in California was the march on Sacramento that it drew every photographer able to attend, among them old veterans who had first photographed in the fields during the Great Depression and young hotshots associated with the counterculture.[39]

Jim Marshall, a budding young photographer accumulating a reputation as a "rock photographer," Marshall hated being pigeon-holed and liked to say that Edward Weston and Ansel Adams were rock photographers, whereas he photographed musicians. Abrupt and patient, generous and hard-assed, and given to drug-induced rants, Marshall would later be recalled by *San Francisco Chronicle* music critic Joel Selvin as "a man who can give being difficult a bad name." He was the last person one would expect to see at a farmworker rally or to associate in any way with photographic coverage of California farmworkers. Human be-ins, rock concerts, love-ins, and various other similar events were his realm. But like all good photographers, Marshall was far more versatile and curious than anyone understood. His interests ranged from current news events to documentary projects. In 1963 he had completed an assignment on Appalachian poverty for the *Saturday Evening Post* and then withdrew the harrowing images and gave them to *Jubilee* magazine editor Ed Rice in order to preserve the integrity of the essay. When La Peregrinación neared Sacramento, Marshall grabbed his Leica and a roll of film and begged a ride to the city. Dropped near a bridge over the Sacramento River, he took a few shots of the march and then tried to zero in on the essence of the event. As he had demonstrated on countless other occasions at innumerable events, he had a unique ability to isolate a single individual in a large gathering. Looking through his battered Leica, Marshall saw Chávez for the first time and never took his eyes off him. Click. A wide shot of Chávez beneath a banner of the Virgin of Guadalupe. Click. A close-up of Chávez listening to speakers. Click. A half roll while following Chávez.[40]

Keeping his focus on Chávez and others near the speaker's microphone, Marshall froze moments, creating silent records full of sounds: the shouts of the crowd; the guitars; the mariachi bands; the crackle of police radios; "Viva La Huelga!"—instants so brief as to suggest a kind of telepathic ability on Marshall's part. Because he hated the darkroom and never developed his film, Marshall left everything to a trusted laboratory technician. Searching the contact sheets, he used a grease pencil to select a single image. Frame 16A is uncropped, showing a young Chávez, who could have easily been mistaken for a Mexican organizer from any of a number of strikes and protests during the preceding fifty years. Only the NFWA eagle on his armband gives any sense of who Chávez represented. No one wanted the picture, and Marshall filed it away with its corresponding contact sheet. Forty years later the public saw the image for the first time when Marshall used it in his retrospective book *Proofs*—yet another example of the extent to which farmworkers attracted the attention of so many of California's best photographers.[41]

Also present at Sacramento, Hansel Mieth Hagel was then in her fourth decade of photographing farmworkers. With Otto, she had just finished a photo essay on the Head Start program in Sonoma County, where she had met many farmworker families living along the banks of the Russian River around Geyserville. No longer close to the dockworkers that Otto had photographed in the mid-1930s and alienated by the "porkchop unionists" that they encountered in the modern longshoremen's union, she had become fascinated by César Chávez. Unlike established unionists, Chávez appealed to her because he seemed to be fighting for basic human rights. Hansel endorsed the NFWA, finding in the farmworker cause "a strata . . . worth further investigation." Now coming out of another period of semiretirement, she was contemplating a book about farmworkers in general and their children in particular. Joining the march at Sacramento, she used a new, motorized 35-millimeter Nikon camera and shot both color and black-and-white film. By far the most experienced photographer on the steps of the state Capitol that day, Hagel brought almost thirty-six years of experience to her work, although few, if any, of the photographers there recognized her. One of her best color shots was a portrait of George Ballis.[42]

A few days after the march ended, Gerhard Gscheidle edited his color photographs of the event and sent them to John Poppy at the San Francisco office of *Look* magazine. Poppy poured over the images, forwarded them to editors in New York City, and proposed an article. But Gscheidle's photographs never appeared in the magazine, because, in Gscheidle's view, management feared losing revenues from the DiGiorgio Fruit Corporation. Not until that fall did Gscheidle place two pages of his color photographs, including a full-page portrait of Chávez and a half-page shot of marchers, in, of all places, *Farm Quarterly.* Also now photographing in color and seeking to crack the national magazine market, Jon Lewis headed to San Jose to obtain a large stock of cheap color 35-millimeter movie film. Spending several days in a friend's bathroom with the lights out, he bulk-loaded his film into hundreds of discarded film canisters. "The first few rolls in effect were lost," Lewis recalled. "We had to experiment and play with different exposures and make a lot of adjustments before we could use the stuff. But it worked just like regular film. It was all to save money. We couldn't just take the color film to a lab and say 'bill me.' We had no funds at all."[43]

Scrounging for film was typical of how impoverished freelance photographers were able to continue covering farmworkers. Few ever had more than pocket change. Their passion and sense of commitment to the farmworker cause kept them going. Kouns later recalled:

> We felt very much a part of the union. All of us were shooting the same thing. We got union cards. We hung out at the Pink House [union headquarters]. We slept on the floor in blankets or sleeping bags, but it was usually so hot that we only slept under a sheet. We got five dollars a week to go out with the pickets in the morning. We would get up before dawn, have some tortillas and coffee, and follow them out to the vineyards,

> another body out there on the line. We really wanted to make this thing go. Some of us even carried picket signs. Everybody would go down to the People's Café and drink and talk in the evening. We were very tight. We took sides.[44]

Over the next few weeks, Kouns recalled that their daily mantra became "obtain more film, stay another day." Focusing not so much on the hard news of confrontation as on the soft news of everyday activities, they were present whenever people gathered together in strike-planning meetings. Often they combined the mundane work of making posters or stapling and addressing mailings with taking an occasional photograph to interrupt the boredom. When union members cooked meals for pickets or held strike-strategy workshops, movement photographers were present. Operating on the edges of everyday union activities, they were able to capture both the day-to-day grind and the charged spirit of the movement. And because they were not working on a deadline and had an insider's view of what was important, they could document quiet moments as well as hot ones. Even though they made no pretense of objectivity, their cumulative effect was to produce a broader and more accurate picture of the grape strike than the one captured by the photojournalists who were constantly arriving and departing.[45]

Their main problem as freelancers was that they remained largely shut out of the major news outlets, which often pushed them aside in favor of photo agency and newspaper staff photographers. While their work was appreciated by fellow union members and used to energize volunteers, most newspaper and magazine editors regarded them as scruffy radicals without portfolios. As outsiders, the best they could do was keep the radical, labor, and church publications supplied with images. They considered themselves lucky every time their work was published.

Toward the end of April, Mark Harris returned to Delano with a documentary film crew consisting of cameraman John Haney, sound man Dick Gilbert, and director Skeets McGrew. By then *la causa* (the farmworker movement) had been profiled on the nightly news shows of all three major televison networks. With Delano awash in reporters and volunteers, Harris could no longer walk right into NFWA offices and see Chávez without an appointment. But the NFWA welcomed his crew, which quickly fell into the rhythm of every other photographer there: cheap quarters, up with the pickets before dawn, meals in the strike kitchen, filming on the picket lines, filming strike meetings at night, hanging around NFWA offices all day "waiting to grab an interview with Chávez." Harris followed the routine for three weeks. Returning to Portland in June, he settled into several months of editing what he believed would be a powerful film.[46]

Of all the freelance photographers who descended on Delano at this time, Ted Streshinsky probably reached the widest audience. Born in Harbin, China, in 1923, Streshinsky was a wiry man with boundless energy, endless curiosity, and a unique ability to capture humanity. Arriving in the United States at the end of World War II, he graduated from the University of California, Berkeley, in 1947, earned a master's degree in political science in 1949, and was working toward his doctorate in the early

1950s when he discovered that he could earn a living taking pictures, something that he had previously regarded as little more than a hobby. Quickly developing a successful commercial business, Streshinsky used his "money work" as a base to pursue stories that interested him. Assigned by the *Saturday Evening Post* to illustrate John Gregory Dunne's essay on the strike (which later became *Delano: The Story of the California Grape Strike*), Streshinsky arrived in Delano on June 17, 1966, a day after marrying his wife, Shirley, in a ceremony in San Francisco City Hall.

Recalling her husband's departure immediately after their marriage and their honeymoon in Delano, Shirley Streshinsky later stressed:

> In those days, if you got an assignment, you were off like that. It wasn't so unusual. Ted wasn't completely unfamiliar with farmworkers. He had photographed them as part of his corporate work for agricultural interests. He regarded Chávez as a civil rights leader. On Easter Sunday [1966], he had driven to Sacramento and photographed the end of La Peregrinacíon. We met Jim Marshall and gave him a lift back to Berkeley. After that, we lobbied the *Post* to do a story on Chávez. Ted really wanted the story. As for spending my honeymoon in Delano, I remember that when Joan Didion [Dunne's wife] picked me up at the train station, the first thing I said to her was, "Is César Chávez for real?" She said, "Yes. This is a man who is destined to lead the farmworker movement." Ted and I stayed in a funky old hotel. Delano was hot and dry. Early in the mornings we would go out on the picket lines. In the evenings we hung out with everyone in a pool hall and bar with other photographers and union members. I remember one evening in an old Grange hall sitting in a circle holding hands with César, Dolores Huerta, and lots of union members singing "We Shall Overcome." All the time while I was there, I had this heightened sense of being in an important place at an important time. It was a wonderful honeymoon.[47]

As Streshinsky and other photographers went about their business, the police continued to watch them. Police surveillance was so common that Tulare County deputy sheriff E. W. Washington explained to John Gregory Dunne that he always packed a camera and photographed everyone he encountered. One afternoon a few days later, Washington approached Dunne and whispered quietly, "You see that guy with the beard and the camera?" He pointed to a freelancer. "How about getting a picture for me. Every time I try, he turns his head."[48]

Although photographers like Streshinsky would soon publish substantial photographic essays on César Chávez and the farmworker movement, the public still remained somewhat visually in the dark. Although not conceived as an explicitly political effort, the photography that Roger Minick completed in collaboration with writer Dave Bohn for their book *Delta West* helped to establish a larger context for understanding farm labor. A word and picture portrait of the Sacramento–San Joaquin Delta, Minick's project merged a historical overview, notes from the field, and transcribed conversations with images to create a book that critic A. D. Coleman described as "virtually a continuation" of *An American Exodus* and *Let Us Now Praise Famous Men.* Among Minick's most memorable images is *Cheng's Hands and Hat.* Focusing on the weathered beauty of an old Chinese man's hands as they cradled a well-worn felt hat, Minick made the image in the open shade after visiting with the man and then asking him to sit and place his hand and hat on a piece of black felt. Exemplifying the point in the photographic story at which the fine arts approach intersected with the documentary tradition as established by earlier photographers, Minick's work defied easy categorization and set in motion an early version of the debate over the aesthetization of poverty.[49]

Also hoping to provide a visual context for what was happening, Ernest Lowe again stepped forward. As Streshinsky photographed at Delano and Minick probed the delta, Lowe organized his work from the previous eight years into a huge exhibition for the M. H. deYoung Memorial Museum, in San Francisco. It began well enough. Thrilled by Lowe's work, museum director Jack R. McGregor promised a budget and, after an initial selection of prints, agreed to an exhibition date. Disappearing into the darkroom, Lowe spent most of the late spring printing and enlarging over one thousand of his five thousand negatives, then enlisted architects Zack Stewart and Dan Osborne to design the show. To provide a context for better appreciating his photographs, Lowe purchased the contents of a shack from a landlord who said the owner had "just up and gone." Inside two scrap lumber walls, he planned to set up an iron bedstead with long johns hanging over the end, worn boots under the bed, a battered icebox, a crooked mirror, a few pots and pans, and government surplus lard and flour on the rickety set of shelves. Posters from the Delano grape strike and letters from migrants on the road were to hang on the outer walls. As visitors walked from one wall of photographs to another, a continuous tape recording of interviews with farmworkers, sounds of their work environment, and snatches of their songs and field chatter would add background material. The idea was to submerge visitors in the farmworker experience. Among the tape recordings was one of a legislator saying, "I'll do everything I can in my power to alleviate your situation."[50]

Pleased by the layout, McGregor laid plans to make Lowe's exhibition into a traveling show that would rotate among a half dozen museums throughout the country. At this point, the museum trustees apparently became alarmed by what they regarded as the controversial nature of Lowe's work. Without warning and without even seeing any part of Lowe's exhibition, the museum canceled it. "I am terribly sorry to tell you that the Executive Committee of the Board of Trustees will not approve showing your exhibition at the museum," wrote Jack McGregor on June 23, 1966. "This is the first time that this has ever happened to me and it came as much of a shock to me as, I am sure, it does to you."[51]

Shattered by the edict and exhausted following hundreds of hours of darkroom printing, an angry Lowe contacted the ACLU and threatened to sue the museum and present his work elsewhere under the title The Exhibition the deYoung Museum Censored. No doubt as the result of the timely intervention of Father Eugene Boyle, a well-known activist Catholic priest, as well as several other influential people, the museum board reconsidered its decision and allowed the show to go forward. On the day of the opening, a DiGiorgio Fruit Corporation annual report that Lowe had attached to one wall mysteriously disappeared. But that was the only problem in what San Francisco art critic Arthur Bloomfield called "a most remarkable documentary photo show."[52]

More than any other single photographic development, Lowe's struggle to show his farmworker photographs and his battle against efforts to censor and suppress his work emerged as the most visible example of how much photographers had to overcome just to reach and educate a very limited audience. Behind the scenes, however, they faced other impediments. Since leaving Delano, Mark Harris had poured his energy into editing the footage he shot two months earlier. But when he screened the first cuts to a test audience, he and his crew were dismayed by the reaction. Most viewers disliked the film. "Why are they so angry? So strident?" they asked Harris. "They can't be that poor. They're riding to the picket lines in cars." Several viewers sided with the growers. "A long strike during harvest could ruin a grower." Harris could not understand why so many people could not identify with the strikers and why so many felt

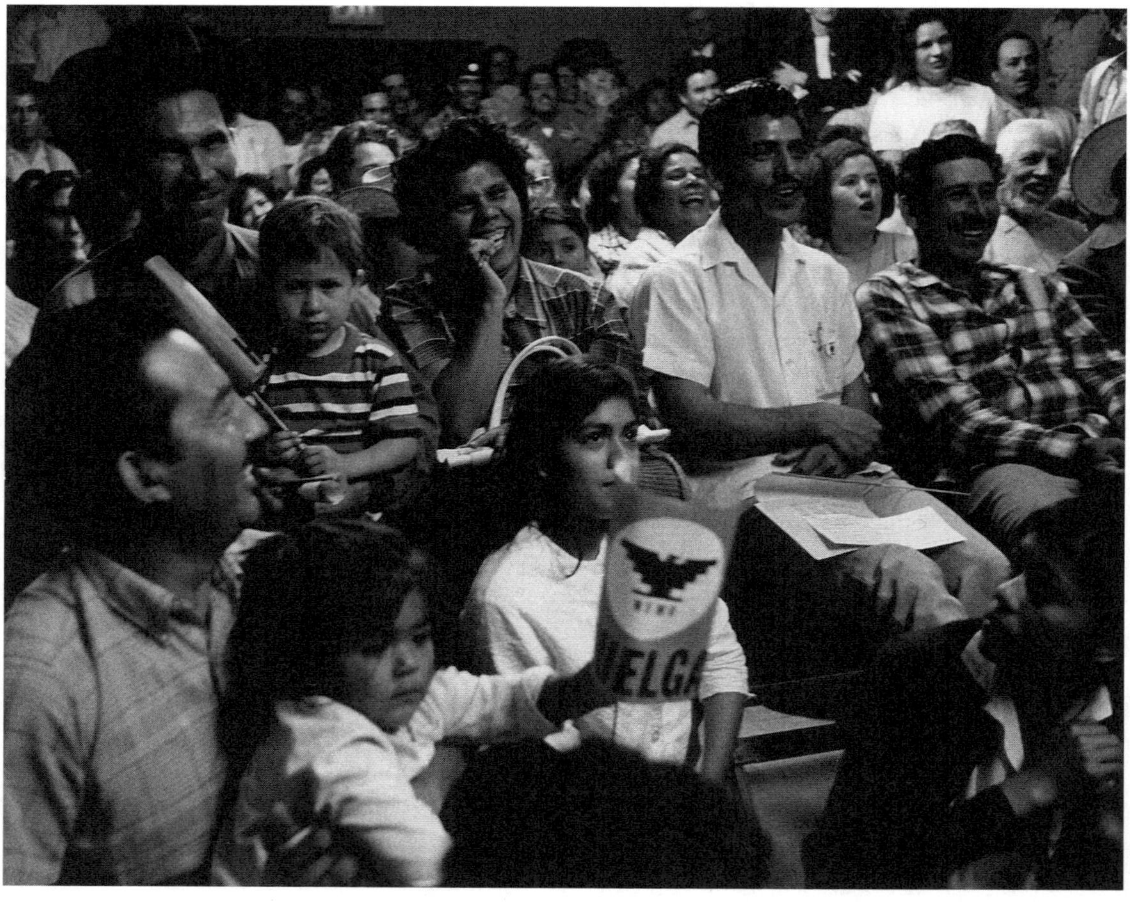

NFWA meeting in Porterville, March 18, 1966, photograph by Ernest Lowe. Courtesy of Ernest Lowe.

that the film was union propaganda and biased against the growers. It was not out of ignorance. Harris had polled his audience and knew that many were familiar with *Harvest of Shame* and had read *The Grapes of Wrath* and *Factories in the Field.* They knew that farmworkers were among the poorest of the working poor. But Harris had failed to hit them in the gut. He had failed to lay the groundwork to justify the strike. For a time he abandoned the effort. When his documentary unit relocated to Seattle to expand its production, he wondered if his film was good enough to broadcast.[53]

What saved Harris and *Huelga* was a chance visit to Seattle by Luis Váldez and El Teatro Campesino. Several weeks earlier, Harris had sent the film to Delano for everyone in the NFWA to view. Váldez had watched the film and seen what was wrong. During their stay in Seattle, Váldez and his troupe met with Harris and suggested ways to improve the film. Within the documentary unit an intense debate broke out over whether or not to make the effort. Some believed it was a hopeless cause and a waste of money. The film was beyond repair, they said; there was nothing to salvage.

Lowe was also depressed. His work at Delano had drained him physically, emotionally, and financially. When his deYoung Museum show ended, he packed it up and stopped photographing farmworkers. As was the case with so many of his predecessors, he simply could not afford to continue. Leaving California, he began a career as an environmental consultant. He would never again photograph in the fields. Jon Lewis was also growing weary. He had been on the verge of quitting when he saw Lowe's exhibition and decided to stay in the Delano area another four months. During that time he concentrated on the competition between the NFWA and the Teamsters Union at DiGiorgio's Sierra Vista Ranch, where the Teamsters had been brought in to undermine the NFWA.[54]

Constantly subjected to harassment, Lewis often mixed it up with Art Chavarria, a big Teamster organizer with a pencil mustache and a mop of black hair, who was always telling Lewis to stand downwind because Lewis stank. "We didn't have the best of bathing and washing facilities, and we probably did start to reek around noon in that heat," Lewis remembered. But Lewis also got his revenge. After taking a close-up photograph of the Teamster organizer, he manipulated the printing process by bending the photographic paper in such a way that Chavarria's smile was distorted to look like a snarling mouth full of fangs. After making dozens of small prints, he scattered them around a befouled toilet on the picket line. Lewis then photographed the scene, made several sets of prints, and made sure everyone out on the picket line saw them.[55]

When the writer John Gregory Dunne met Lewis one afternoon, he extended a hand and tried to introduce himself, only to have Lewis jam his hand into his pocket. "Are you a Teamster?" Lewis snarled. "I don't have enough handshakes to pass any out to Teamsters." Lewis himself was being photographed by two women from Citizens for Facts, the right-wing organization that had been investigating the grape strike. Out on the picket lines, he was under even more intense surveillance. The nature of that surveillance was captured a few days later when John Gregory Dunne observed an exchange between Lewis and Chavarria. As Chavarria shouted insults through a microphone and accused NFWA members of being "Commies," friends of Castro, and allies of the Vietcong, Lewis walked up to his truck and began photographing. Standing nearby, Dunne recorded a dialogue full of implied and overt threats:

> CHAVARRIA: I notice you're the only one here with a Japanese camera. You're not even a good American.
>
> LEWIS: You said it, Art.
>
> CHAVARRIA: Hey, baby, I was a barber once. You need a shave. I'll give it to you. Baby, I don't mind you taking my picture. But you smell. You take my picture, you stand downwind. I'll tell you what. You stand downwind and I'll get you some of that stuff you squeeze under your arm. It's good. It gives one-day protection.
>
> SECOND TEAMSTER: Why don't you bust him in the chops with that mike, Chavarria?
>
> THIRD TEAMSTER: That's right. Jam it right in his mush.[56]

At the end of September, Lewis left Delano. Besides his physical and financial exhaustion, recent developments spurred him to this decision. Most important among these was the merger of the NFWA and AWOC to create the United Farm Workers Organizing Committee (UFWOC), AFL–CIO. With Chávez as president and Larry Itliong, Gilbert Padilla, Dolores Huerta, Tony Orendian, Philip Vera Cruz, and Andy Imutan all serving as vice presidents, the new organization immediately dissolved all of the old AWOC agreements with labor contractors, clearly signaling that UFWOC would pursue a more grassroots policy consistent with NFWA tactics. Within one week, UFWOC had achieved a major victory, defeating the Teamsters Union in representation elections at DiGiorgio's Sierra Vista Ranch by a vote of 530 to 331. Bitter and intense, the election had featured massive amounts of visual and written material, including Teamsters Union leaflets asserting that the farmworker union was a "communist front" led by "beatniks" and "do-gooders" and a Communications Workers Union pamphlet entitled *A Family Portrait* containing portraits of Teamsters Union organizers and their alleged links to gangsters.[57]

All of this convinced Lewis that by the winter of 1966–67, the farmworker movement had reached a major turning point. Now it was time for him to begin raising funds to publish a book of his photographs. Too financially strapped to ship his darkroom equipment to San Francisco, he left it in the Gray House. He was not happy about leaving. "It was a grim time," he would later explain. "I felt like a traitor leaving the union."[58]

A few weeks after Lewis departed, Jonathan Harris returned to reshoot his documentary with a new cameraman, Dick Pierce, recently arrived from New York. By then it was cold and foggy, but the determination and perseverance of the strikers provided fresh material. For a week, Harris filmed winter picketing and the bleak conditions inside labor camps, and, in a stroke of luck, he obtained an interview with the manager of a labor camp. Quickly editing the footage, he entered the recut version into film festivals in Europe, Canada, and the United States, where it was shown on public television. *Time* magazine hated it, comparing it unfavorably with *Harvest of Shame,* but the *Village Voice* hailed *Huelga* as "a movingly candid picture of the material poverty and spiritual pride and persistence of the Mexican American farmworkers who, in the second half of the 20th century, are still living the kind of miserable migratory existence John Steinbeck wrote about 30 years ago."[59]

While Harris moved forward with his film, Lewis was struggling to get by. Arriving in San Francisco with two dollars in his pocket, he pawned one camera for rent money, then started work on his book–thesis. During the fall he designed a small booklet, *La Huelga de la Uva en Delano: The Delano Grape Strike,* and sold it through the farmworker union. With the small profit from that effort and help from the GI Bill, he enrolled in the graduate journalism program at San Francisco State University. Determined to publish his Delano photography, he first learned printing by working at several jobs as a press operator. At night he worked on his book. In the meantime, George Ballis had collected his own images into *Basta: The Tale of Our Struggle.* Issued by the NFWA with a text by Luis Váldez, it was the first published photo essay on the strike.[60]

Inspired by how George Ballis had handled the subject but determined to give the work his own imprint and publish it independently of the union, Lewis decided to emphasize the theme of human relationship to the earth rather than labor organizing. Missing Delano and curious about what had happened there since he had left, Lewis returned that winter to do some additional photography. He spent considerable time trying to make a close-up cover shot of a farmworker sifting soil through his hands. But after many days of photographing the hands of various farmworkers, he could not produce what he saw in his mind's eye. He eventually obtained what he wanted after César Chávez's brother Richard volunteered his hand.

With his cover completed, Lewis then proceeded to print his photographs. His text was a kind of running narrative incorporating photographs with first-person observations from his strike journal in a style reminiscent of *An American Exodus.* Listening to Lewis discuss every page of the book project throughout the winter, Gerhard Gscheidle and his wife, Sandra, began to think of it as a kind of "never-ending pregnancy." Lewis had to ignore important union activities, including a disastrous campaign in Texas during the spring and summer of 1967. But he kept at it. Eventually settling on a layout, he then chose a title. Lewis called his book *From This Earth: Of the Delano Grape Strike.* Also doubling as his master's thesis in photojournalism, *From This Earth* was completely handcrafted—conceived, photographed, composed, written, bound, and marketed by one resolute man. It is perhaps the single most impressive effort in a long line of unique farmworker photo books.[61]

19

A Spirit of Hope among People

Photographers as Organizers

After Jon Lewis published *From This Earth,* he faced the same dilemma that had plagued other photographers. His conscience, his politics, and, most important, his passion for photography and his belief in the farmworker cause told him to keep at it. He had filled his camera frames with people doing honest labor. He was beginning to unravel an aspect of agricultural production that few were willing to admit. But he could do only so much; his financial resources held him back. For all his bravery, persistence, self-sacrifice, and generosity, Lewis could not land a job with a newspaper. No photo agency picked him up, offered him a retainer, or asked for exclusive rights to his work. He had no real marketing plan. He was alone and immobile. Begging rides between Delano and San Francisco, he hung on as long as possible. Even for a hardened Marine, the prospect of another year of long hot days living on beans and tortillas while sleeping in a stuffy darkroom became too much. When he could continue no longer, he moved on. He vowed to return when he had a chance, and he would.[1]

When Lewis departed, photographic coverage almost collapsed. Eugene Nelson was in Texas leading a four-hundred-mile march of farmworkers in the Rio Grande valley and blocking the bridge at El Paso to prevent Mexican strikebreakers from crossing north into Texas. Nelson took his camera with him, leaving Nick Jones to handle most of the photography in the Delano area throughout the winter and into the spring. On the lam after having been drafted by the United States Army, Jones had worked with the SDS in Chicago and was not shy about recording picket line confrontations. Along with Bill Esher and several other volunteers, he managed to keep *El Malcriado* supplied with images until Lewis returned during the summer, when the union began winning contracts through the card check system: obtaining pledge cards from a majority of a company's workers, then asking for collective bargaining without having to go through an election that would inevitably produce a union victory. While hardly the dramatic stuff of the previous year, the card checks won the NFWA contracts with some of the state's major wineries, including Gallo, Almaden, Christian Brothers, Paul Masson, and Franzia.[2]

During the summer of 1967, when Lewis returned to Delano, many familiar faces were away on boycott duty. A new legal staff under the direction of Jerome Cohen was fighting various antipicketing and antiboycott injunctions as well as the Texas Rangers. People's Café still remained the main hangout, always good for a game of pool and a bottle of Mountain Red or Mexican beer. But there was no longer any room for Lewis at the Gray House. Gilbert Padilla needed it. "Gil was on my ass to get my stuff out," Lewis recalled. "I just left the print dryer in the house. I had no way to take it with me on the bus to San Francisco. I hitched a ride with Luis Váldez, an old friend from San Jose State. He and César had parted ways, and I spent a few weeks with him at Del Rey while he relocated El Teatro Campesino. I took my last shots there."[3]

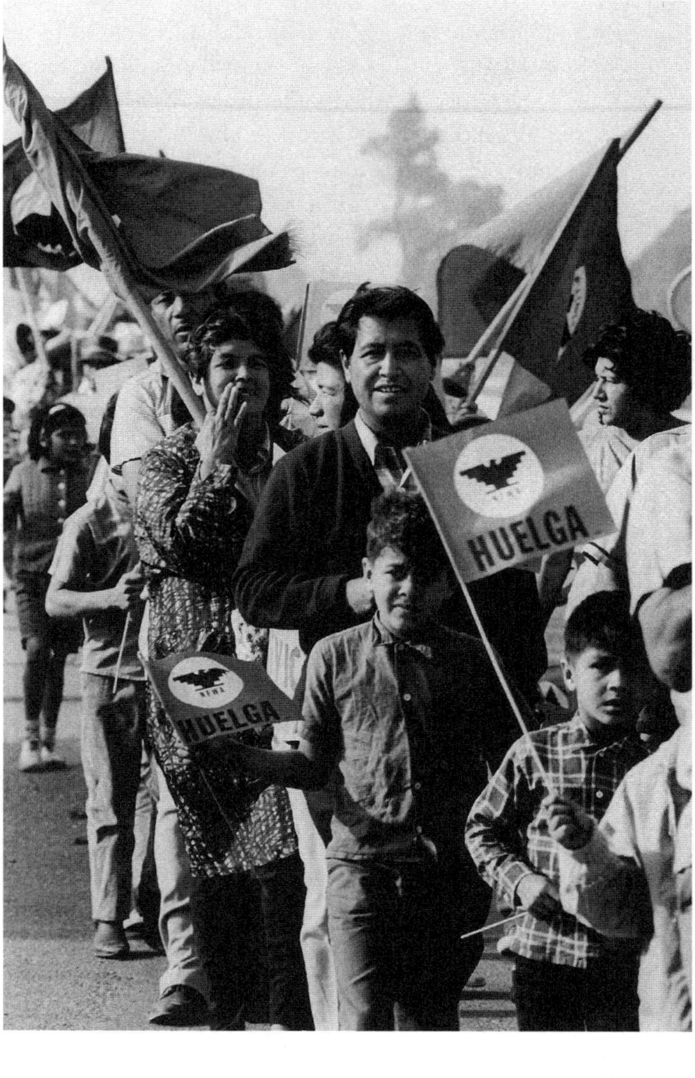

César Chávez leads farmworkers on La Peregrinación, March 17, 1966, photograph by George Ballis. Courtesy of Take Stock Images.

When Lewis returned to his studies at San Francisco State University, Emmon Clarke picked up where Lewis had left off. Clarke had just married a woman from the small town of Dinuba, southeast of Fresno. Living in Mill Valley, just north of San Francisco, he became increasingly curious about agriculture and farm labor while traveling through the Central Valley on visits to his wife's family. He later recalled:

> I wanted to be part of the movement and use my photography to help. So I went to Delano in September 1967 and talked to people in the Filipino Hall. They set me up in a house being used as a barracks for volunteers. The place smelled musty, like dirty socks. It was rough. I said, "I'll give it a try for two months," and if I can't take it, I'll leave. On the second day, I was on the picket line at the Mosesian [Hourigan–Mosesian–Goldberg Company] packing shed. It was located at the far end of the railroad tracks on the south side of Delano, an old shed, operated by a downscale shipper. During the picketing, Manuel Rivera, a pleasant middle-aged man with a large family who lived near the Delano union office [and had been one of the first rose workers in McFarland to support *la causa*], was run down by a truck. Hearing the screech of breaks and cries of pickets, I wheeled around and caught the seriously injured Rivera as he lay under the wheels of the truck. It was right in front of me, and I shot it all with a 28-millimeter lens. I was running backwards, shooting as it all happened. César heard of the incident, and he stepped in to save the driver, who was actually a salesman. The pickets were ready to kill him. César probably saved his life. He let the grower have it. He called him a greedy bastard who had no business having a salesman driving one of those big trucks. I developed that roll of film in the trunk of my car . . . then headed to Dinuba and printed the pictures in a darkroom at my father-in-law's house. As a result of those photographs, I became a part of *El Malcriado* and moved from the barracks into a tract house on the outskirts of Delano, where the newspaper was published. For my work, I received the usual five dollars a week, food, and board, but also an unlimited supply of bulk-loaded black-and-white film.[4]

After the excitement at the Mosesian shed, Clarke shot a series on the now permanently disabled Rivera putting up a brave front while he struggled to get around on crutches with his leg in a cast. Clarke then settled into the same routine as his predecessors. Of the next nine months, Clarke recalled:

> I lived in the darkroom. I had my bed up against one wall. On the other wall was an Omega-D enlarger and a place to soup [develop] prints. As soon as I got them out of the hypo, I'd take them to the bathroom and wash them in the bathtub. Every morning was the same. We would get up early. . . . We'd go over to the Filipino Hall for a cup of coffee and whatever meal was being put together from donated food. Then we'd meet with the picket captains, find out what was going on, and join the picket line. About 10 A.M., a truck would come out and feed us buttered toast or tortillas. Around noon we'd close down. I'd take whatever pictures I could, and immediately go into my darkroom–bedroom to print and develop. I tried to have all of the chemical work done so that I didn't have to breathe the stuff at night.[5]

Over the next seven months, Clarke photographed the ebb and flow of events, including Thanksgiving fund-raisers in Los Angeles, El Teatro Campesino's performances, and picketing in the Perelli-Minetti vineyards, another large Delano-area grape grower. Perelli-Minetti was putting up a stiff fight and, as a last resort, had invited in the Teamsters Union and signed a sweetheart contract. Photographic coverage would prove especially important for the union and a challenge for Clarke. Because the union was boycotting Perelli-Minetti's table grapes, as well as its other products, including premium wines and a special Tribuno label vermouth, Clarke spent much of his time following boycott teams in Los Angeles, New York, and San Francisco, where they wreaked havoc with Perelli-Minetti sales. Most of this photography was uneventful: Chávez speaking, union members picketing and leafleting, fund-raising dinners, meetings with labor officials, and other mundane aspects of the boycott. But at least one assignment challenged Clarke's wits and demanded some quick thinking, even deception.

Clarke was back in Delano photographing boycotted Perelli-Minetti wine labels in a Delano liquor store when the enraged store owner spotted him, locked the doors, and called the police. An officer arrived and demanded his film. Having picked up a few tips from other photographers shaken down by police, Clarke carried a dummy film cannister and deftly substituted it for the real one. Once out of the store, he headed straight for the darkroom. Later that day he made prints of all the boycotted wine labels, cut them out, and pasted them into a mock-up for an *El Malcriado* issue focused on the Perelli-Minetti boycott and for various fliers used in the Perelli-Minetti campaign.[6]

As with his predecessors, Clarke soon wilted under the demands of his job. Burned out and missing his wife (who once visited Delano and was nearly run over while out on the picket lines), Clarke left *El Malcriado* and was replaced by Chris Sánchez, the farmworker who had learned photography from Lewis and Kouns while tending Porta-Johns on La Peregrinación. After Perelli-Minetti abandoned its sweetheart deal with the Teamsters in July 1967, Sánchez covered a representation election that UFWOC won in August, then turned his attention to the struggle with Giumarra Vineyards, the largest table-grape grower in the world. Present at a huge rally on August 3, when two-thirds of Giumarra's five thousand harvest workers went on strike, Sánchez spent most of the next two months patrolling the company's eleven thousand acres of vineyards and following UFWOC organizers into dozens of labor camps while they met with workers. When UFWOC began boycotting Giumarra grapes, Sánchez shifted his attention away from the fields and spent most of the fall documenting union members tracking down and identifying the various labels that Giumarra was using to market its grapes.

His life changed dramatically as a result of a decision made by Chávez in January. With the Giumarra boycott faltering and consumers confused about which grapes to avoid and which to buy, Chávez decided to boycott all California-grown table grapes. Over the next six months, Sánchez criss-crossed the country with Dolores Huerta, Fred Ross, and two hundred strikers and their families. His photographs show union members linking up with students, SNCC activists, and various labor and liberal groups and developing boycotts in forty cities and several hundred communities. Many of his photographs document picketers braving snowstorms outside Boston produce terminals and parading along icy sidewalks in front of Chicago-area supermarkets. Along with Nick Jones, now heading up much of the boycott work in New England, Sánchez produced what is probably the only extended photo essay on the largest consumer boycott in American history.[7]

Out in the fields, the strike was stumbling along. Picket captains were not showing up for duty, morale was low, the boycott was limping, and the union had only a handful of winery contracts. Some union activists grew so angry with the lack of progress that they blew up irrigation pumps, scattered tacks and nails across roads to puncture tires on police and grower vehicles, and roughed up individuals suspected of acting as spies for growers. Although no one admitted to the arson, several mysterious fires that burned grape packing sheds were blamed on the union. After police arrested several union members for hurling marbles and ball bearings at scabs in the Coachella Valley, a tremendous debate developed within the union over how to proceed. As for growers, they seemed as intransigent as ever. So great was the threat of violence that an Indio, California, newspaper reported a ten-thousand-dollar bounty on Chávez's head.

Furious with the violence and fearing that his union was about to fall apart, Chávez embarked on another penitential fast on February 15, 1968, this time vowing to continue until union members renewed their pledges of nonviolence. Six days into the fast, he informed aides of his strategy. For the next thirty-one days, photographers would chart Chávez's health, documenting, perhaps for the first time, the physical changes of a man putting his life on the line for his cause. The "circus aspect" of the fast, as critics referred to it, alienated many supporters but provided photographers with an endless string of subjects, from farmworkers pitching tents and maintaining a vigil for Chávez to elderly women crawling on their knees from a highway to the room at Forty Acres where Chávez resided. Even for veteran photographers who had covered the march on Sacramento, the pageantry of the fast was a visually spectacular admixture of metaphor and document.[8]

With press photographers unable to penetrate union security, freelancers aligned with the union provided most of the images of Chávez at this critical point. Following him through the day, they created a picture of life in the little room at Forty Acres, where he slept on a cot, read, prayed, and greeted visitors. Press photographers, in fact, did not play an important role until, after nine days of fasting, a Kern County Superior Court judge ordered Chávez out of bed to answer contempt charges originating from the union's failure to limit the number of pickets at entrances to the Giumarra ranch. Chávez arrived at the Kern County Courthouse in Bakersfield on February 24. More than three thousand farmworkers packed the corridors. In the cold fog outside, hundreds more knelt in prayer. Countless camera flashes exploded when Chávez left the courthouse. Jerome Cohen, the union attorney who was walking nearby, asked, "Are you okay?" Barely able to walk, César looked up and winked. The camera flashes and media attention were exactly what he wanted.[9]

While the national news media poured into Delano to cover part of what growers labeled a "colossal hoax," magazines and newspapers carried photograph after photograph of the emaciated Chávez, who had lost more than thirty pounds and had fasted longer than Gandhi had in 1924. But his call for nonviolence had been heeded by union members. It was time for Chávez to publicly end his fast. At a rally and Mass in Delano Memorial Park on March 11, 1968, Chávez broke bread with Senator Robert F. Kennedy before more than six thousand farmworkers and supporters. Such was the attraction of Kennedy that when he arrived, farmworkers lined both sides of a mile-long processional path. At least twenty still photographers and a dozen television crews covered the event.

Because of their relationship to the union, freelance photographers grabbed the best spots when the two men sat to break bread and receive the blessing from a Catholic priest. Returning to Delano to cover the event, John Kouns knelt just in front of Chávez. He was in perfect position. Kennedy sat in the center, flanked by Chávez, on his left, with a blanket covering his legs, and Chávez's wife, Helen, on his right, wearing a lace mantilla. A second tier of seven union supporters and an NFWA flag provided context and backdrop. No photographers could block Kouns. Photographing

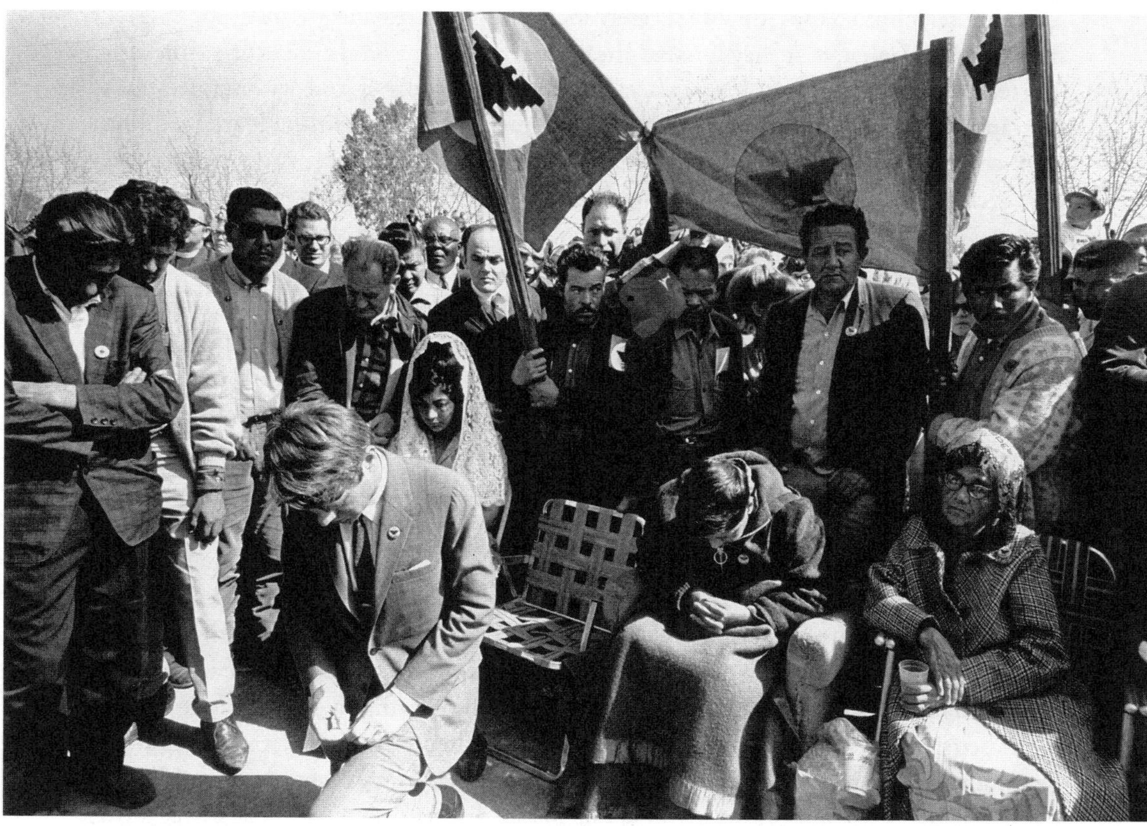

Senator Robert F. Kennedy kneels to pray and accept Holy Communion with César Chávez at the end of his fast, March 11, 1968, photograph by George Ballis. Courtesy of Take Stock Images.

continually, he snapped his strongest image while Chávez moved in and out of consciousness, with two union members ready to grab him when he passed out. So weak that he could barely sit up and hold his mother's hand, Chávez at this point appeared childlike, fragile, and in such obvious distress that even the most cynical person could no longer claim the fast was a fraud. Photographing from a slightly different perspective to the right, George Ballis recorded a series of images, including the moment when Kennedy comforted César's mother and the concluding gesture when Kennedy broke bread with Chávez, symbolically ending the twenty-three-day fast. Back from his boycott duties, Chris Sánchez stood next to Ballis. Photographing from a standing position, he caught another dramatic moment, just as Chávez accepted Holy Communion.[10]

Several months passed before anyone saw these heart-rending photographs of Chávez and Kennedy. By then, the event was cold. For their initial picture, people relied on newspaper and wire service photographers. Less familiar with the union and lacking the connections necessary to stake out those key spots in front of Chávez, newspaper and wire service photographers did one of two things. Shooting from a more elevated and distant perspective, they used wide angle lenses that revealed too much extraneous detail and made Chávez and Kennedy appear small. Or, relying on medium telephoto lenses, they so severely focused on Chávez and Kennedy, or Chávez and his wife, Helen, that they ignored the emotions evident on the faces of union supporters and reporters standing nearby. Either way, newspaper and wire service photographers did not capture the intimacy and drama seen through the lenses of more well-connected photographers. But their work did not go unnoticed. So powerful was the event that it attracted a new rush of union supporters, who now descended on Delano, pledged their support, and reinvigorated the depleted staff of volunteers.[11]

Of all the photographers scrutinizing the Delano grape strike at this time, by far the most famous and influential, if not legendary, was Paul Fusco. After becoming interested in photography in the mid-1940s, Fusco had served in Korea with the United States Signal Corps from 1951 to 1953, then gone on to obtain a master of fine arts degree in photojournalism from Ohio University. In 1957 he became a staff photographer for *Look* magazine. He had been shooting a series of portraits of influential Californians during the summer of 1968 when he learned of the grape strike and used some free time to travel to Delano. "I was very moved by what I saw," he explained many years later. "I asked *Look* if I could do a story on the grape strike. The editor said it was okay. So I spent about three weeks in Delano working with César, the strikers, the people. I wanted people who knew nothing about farmworkers to get a sense of what their life was like, who farmworkers were, and why they were trying to organize a union."[12]

Fusco's presence in Delano, along with *Look* writer Bob Kaiser, created quite a sensation among union members and the staff of *El Malcriado,* who described Fusco as one of the most important members of *Look*'s distinguished staff. Most freelance photographers were equally awestruck. Neither a news photographer nor a photojournalist, Fusco had no central assignment. He was a photo essayist. His working style was basically one of exploration. Famous for following a schedule bordering on obsession and possessed of a competitive spirit that drove him, Fusco had a reputation for thinking like a novelist. He would find people he wanted to photograph—children, Appalachian coal miners, hippies—enter the flow of their lives, and let their story unfold as he saw it. Compared with other photographers grubbing out an existence at Delano, he seemed to be blessed with unlimited resources. Free to do as he liked, he could search out story lines, concentrate on suitable opening and closing shots, and fill in the inner body of his essay. With his presence, Fusco branded Delano a subject important enough to attract coverage by a photographer of one of the country's most important illustrated magazines. Some photographers later claimed that Fusco shot six hundred rolls of film during his first stay in Delano. They were in awe of him.[13]

Wasting little time, Fusco immediately sized things up and went to work. When he first met Chávez and his followers in the vineyards, he saw "a spirit of hope among people who previously had none." To capture that spirit of optimism, he employed an arsenal of different lenses, from wide-angle to telephoto, fitting each one to the task at hand. "Even trudging through the fields, he hauled his bag and his four standard cameras along," wrote one reporter who accompanied Fusco to Delano. "The 28 mm lens caught the look of a mother living in a cardboard house, the 180 mm zeroed in on a rare moment of rest for a grape picker who works in the sun at a frenzied pace for a whole day almost without stopping . . . and the 21 mm caught a moment of the work itself."[14]

As he photographed, Fusco kept a low profile. Living with farmworkers and strikers for three weeks, he got to know them and thus was able to anticipate developments. While photographing, Fusco constantly searched for the "lead" or "opener," a photograph that hooked viewers and introduced a theme or major elements within a story. At the same time, he also looked for "snappers" and "grabbers," memorable images that moved the story along and amplified the central theme, as well as situations with strong symbolic content that conveyed meaning beyond what viewers already knew. Often his main concern was to find subjects that might later prove valuable as links in the overall picture. He wanted to develop a broad perspective, with universal elements, that would not die with the events themselves. He seemed to be everywhere. "Sometimes he was standing on a chair or atop a table, other times, he was lying on the floor or under a desk," recalled UFWOC volunteer LeRoy Chatfield. "It seemed to make no difference, his camera whizzed non-stop, roll after roll. It was my first experience with a professional photographer; I was fascinated."[15]

Fusco definitely operated differently. John Kouns, who encountered Fusco on one of his trips back to Delano, described how all the photographers in Delano wanted to be part of the union. They hung out together, shared stories, drank at the People's Café. But not Fucso. Recalling how he did not mix with anyone, Kouns described him as very independent and very professional:

> He would come in and get out. Nothing disturbed him when he worked. He'd get right straight into a subject. He was very quiet, but his presence demanded attention. He had

> this old canvas camera bag and cameras so worn that the brass shined through the black enamel coating. He was a kind of overpowering and quietly intense photographer.[16]

Although Fusco shot most of his *Look* assignments close up, using wide-angle lenses, he made one of his most memorable images from a distance, with a telephoto lens. During the winter he was out scouting the countryside on a second trip to Delano when he encountered a few farmworker pickets maintaining a round-the-clock vigil on the edge of a vineyard. Nearby was an old automobile that Chávez had once used but was no longer in running condition. The strikers had transformed it into a shrine to the Virgin of Guadalupe. Early the next morning, Fusco rolled out of a dingy motel room long before sunrise and drove through the fog out to the shrine. Realizing that the fog would reduce the contrast in his picture and that he would have to compensate for that flatness later while printing the picture in the darkroom, Fusco decided to take advantage of the diffuse light and emphasize the austere winter conditions. Walking across the two-lane road into a bordering field, he used his 180-millimeter lens to compress the scene, emphasize the gray morning light, and create a timeless symbol of quiet and determined farmworkers manning an isolated and silent outpost in the freezing dawn.[17]

Back at *Look* magazine, Fusco edited hundreds of his pictures in an informal, collaborative arrangement with a staff writer. Evaluating the photo essay with an eye

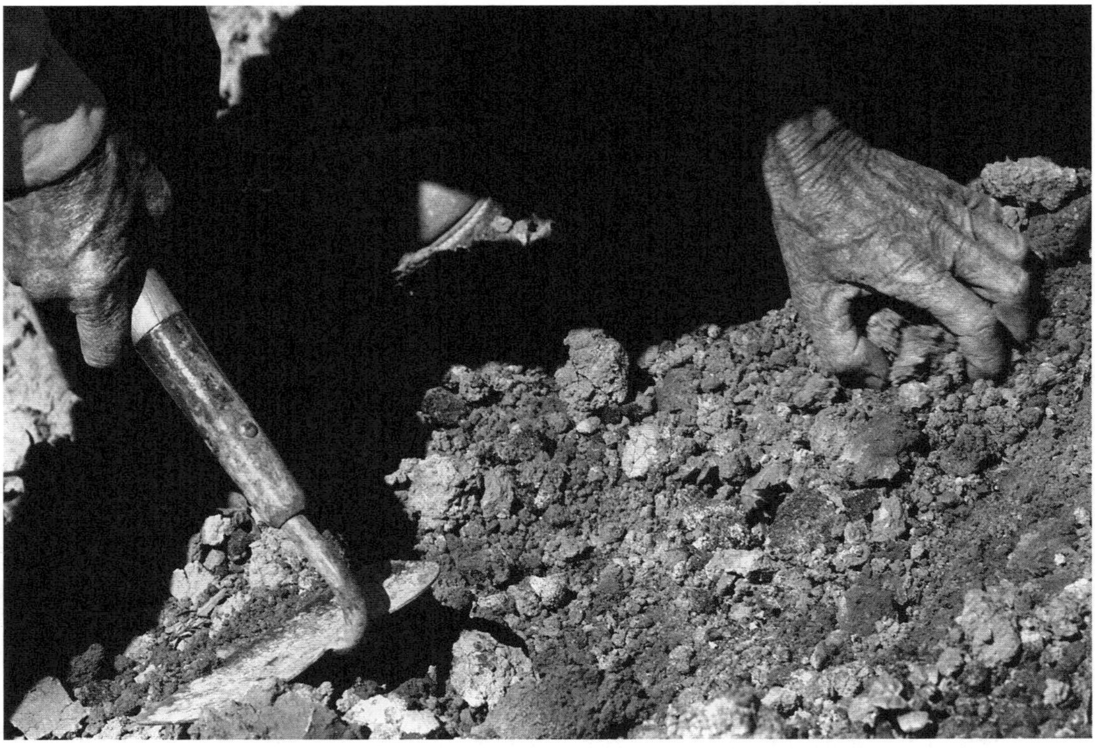

Weeding with *el cortido,* June 1968, photograph by Paul Fusco. Courtesy of Magnum Photos.

toward the way it interacted with the text, the writer often disagreed with Fusco. But Fusco made selections according to a complex series of evaluations, the most important being the content of the photograph. Eventually he and the writer whittled down the images to 150 "selects." At this point, the art director became involved, and the three again debated the various images.

Table-grape growers were well aware that Fusco, the "famous *Look* photographer," had been to Delano. A few had seen him. By now they had become well aware that Fusco and countless other photographers like him were reaching tens of thousands of people who might otherwise have overlooked Chávez and UFWOC. They were not happy. They hated the way they were being portrayed. At their meetings they discussed what was happening. They felt cornered, betrayed, singled out, and unfairly represented. Suspicious of anyone with a camera, they seemed incapable of mounting any kind of visual refutation through their traditional marketing and advertising associations. "We knew we were getting the short end of the picture," recalled Delano grape grower Jack Pandol. "We felt like every photographer was out to get us. We couldn't get a fair shake in the press."[18]

Leading a coalition of growers and businessmen, Pandol helped mount a rebuttal. This took the form of an illustrated booklet titled *The Truth about the Grape Strike.* Featuring photographs of happy and contented field hands and blaming everything on outside agitators, *The Truth about the Grape Strike* argues that, in fact, no strike existed. Chávez was a fraud. The union was run and supported not by farmworkers themselves but by outsiders of dubious character. Most workers, the booklet asserts, did not belong to the union and never participated in the strike. They were well paid and well treated.[19]

If the booklet had any effect on photographers, or if any even saw it, none said so. They continued to arrive at Delano. Another of the most important ones was Hub Segur. A Ventura County activist, Segur had been so touched by the Fast for Nonviolence that he had visited Delano and, after meeting with Chávez and UFWOC volunteer Jim Drake, vowed to return. In February 1969, Segur packed his duffel bag, stored all of his personal belongings, and joined the union as a full-time volunteer. After a few weeks in Delano photographing around town and at Friday evening meetings at the Filipino Hall, Segur was dispatched to the Los Angeles boycott office, where he roomed with two Filipino brothers. "My two 'luxuries' were a small clock/radio and my second-hand Exackta VX 35 millimeter SLR [single-lens reflex camera] with a 135 mm Steinheil lens," he later recalled. "Some five years before a friend had introduced me to basic photography darkroom techniques so that I could at least develop and print."[20]

In April, as Segur photographed boycott activities in Los Angeles, *Look* magazine published ten of Fusco's photographs in an essay titled "Nonviolence Still Works." Laid out in story form, the images were accompanied by an interview with César Chávez. Most found it quite shocking in the way it justified the strike and explained UFWOC's goals. Growers who saw it were furious. They dismissed it as more liberal propaganda from a biased and ill-informed press. But they could not stem the stream of unfavorable images. A month later, UFWOC generated more useful images by laying the groundwork for an organizing campaign in the early table-grape industry with a mass march south from Indio through the Imperial Valley to the border town of Calexico. Diverted from his assignment in Los Angeles, Segur followed the march for eight days. Halfway to Calexico, he ran into Ballis and tagged along with the old master. "Wherever George went," he later recalled, "I followed and took the same shot." Their last shots documented a massive rally in Calexico.[21]

By covering such events, photographers like Segur and Ballis were contributing to a larger awakening of visual awareness, not only in the United States, but around the world. By the summer of 1969, photographers seemed to be everywhere and were assuming a central position in mobilizing popular sentiment. Generating an alternative discourse and serving as an essential social catalyst, they were recording one tragic or stunning event after another: the Tet offensive in Vietnam; the moments following the assassination of presidential candidate Bobby Kennedy by Sirhan Sirhan; police rioting while trying to control student protestors at the Democratic National Convention in Chicago; Russian tanks invading Czechoslovakia to suppress a revolution; and the moments after the assassination of the Reverend Martin Luther King Jr. For those who may have doubted and for those who had not realized it, visual culture was coming of age. Now photographers were embracing the farmworker movement. Entering directly into the organizing drive and helping to shift the locus of conflict from the grower-dominated valleys to the realm of public opinion and public policy, they were helping to create an entirely new farm labor relations dynamic.[22]

On July 4, 1969, the very same day that California table-grape growers filed a lawsuit against UFWOC for twenty-five million dollars in damages, *Time* magazine acknowledged the role that photographers were playing in the farmworker movement. "To enter the public consciousness, a labor conflict must ordinarily threaten the supply of essential goods and services, like steel or coal," reported the magazine. "Politicians and the public take notice only when there is a great impact on the economy, or when spectacular bloodshed occurs. . . . The grape strike seems to meet none of these criteria." With the exception of the civil rights movement, observed the magazine, few other struggles had been so strongly impacted by photographers and photography.[23]

Of all the photographers working at this time, none played a more important role in linking UFWOC with the civil rights movement and protests against the Vietnam War than Bob Fitch. A tall man with bushy, blond hair, a tattered camera bag, and two Nikons hanging from straps around his neck, Fitch was an ordained Presbyterian minister who had learned photography while working for the Southern Christian Leadership Conference. From 1965 until just before Martin Luther King's assassination, Fitch had covered the civil rights movement for the Black Star photo agency. After moving to Oakland in 1968, he had covered antiwar protests and Joan Baez, then shifted his attention to UFWOC.

During the fall of 1969, Fitch traveled with Chávez and five other farmworkers on an eight-week boycott promotion tour of the East Coast and Canada. For much of the trip, Chávez was bedridden with a painful back. Fitch recorded Chávez's daily ordeal as he held conferences in his bedroom. Looking at one of his photographs of Chávez, sitting in his bed dressed only in a white nightshirt with the covers pulled up around him as he spoke to someone off camera, many union members thought the image brought to mind pictures of Gandhi speaking to his followers during one of his fasts. These images helped to solidify the view of Chávez as a kind of Chicano prophet, and they played a significant role in publicizing boycott activity to those in Detroit, Chicago, New York, Boston, Philadelphia, Montreal, and Toronto.[24]

After the long trip east, Fitch returned to California, convinced that the farmworker cause was not just the Mexican American counterpart to the black civil rights movement but a historical event in its own right. Between his coverage of radical politics, war protests, and Berkeley councilman Ron Dellums's campaign for Congress, Fitch continued to document Chávez and UFWOC's organizing campaign. He was welcomed by the union, which often made first use of his work for organizing activities. Occasionally he designed and built portable exhibits of his prints, which the union displayed in its hiring halls and at conventions and rallies.

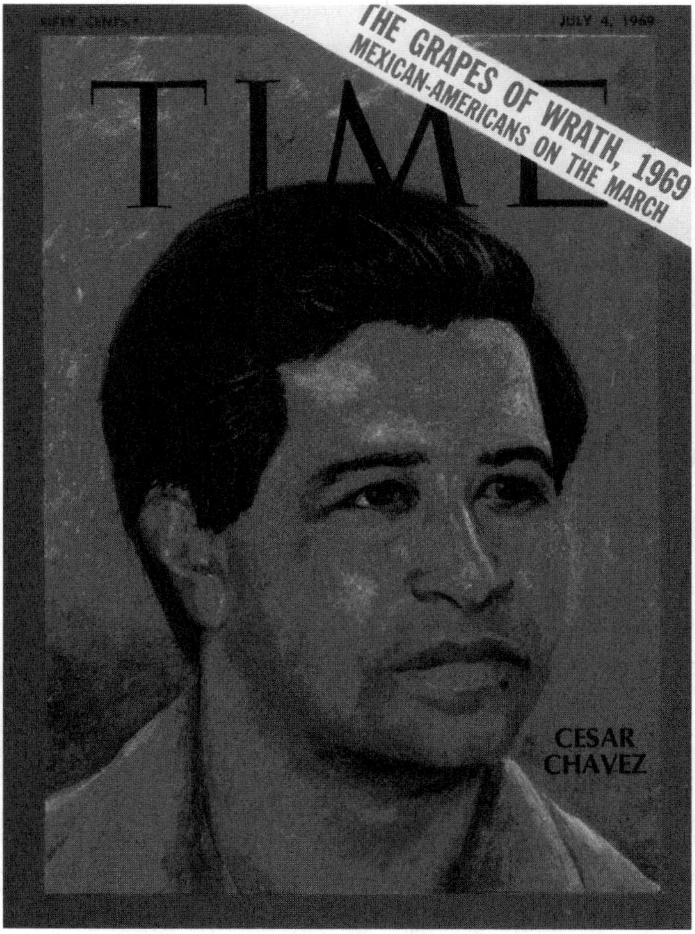

César Chávez on the cover of *Time* magazine, July 4, 1969, artist unknown. Courtesy of *Time* magazine.

By the spring of 1970, Fitch and other farmworker movement photographers were playing a key role in helping UFWOC recruit volunteers, raise funds, and project the kind of image that kept the union struggle before the public. Large agricultural and food production companies were clearly feeling the heat. Coca-Cola was the first to crack. As a consequence of having acquired the Florida orange juice company Minute Maid ten years earlier, Coca-Cola was hard-hit when NBC News aired *Migrant,* a white-paper documentary filled with upsetting scenes from Minute Maid's groves. Appearing just as Senator Walter Mondale was exploring migrant labor problems in a series of hearings before his Subcommittee on Migratory Labor, the documentary placed huge pressure on Coca-Cola chairman Paul Austin, who immediately dispatched foods division head Luke Smith to Florida. After probing conditions in the orchards, a distraught Smith returned to corporate headquarters and told Austin that the situation "could not in conscience be tolerated by Coca-Cola Company." As a result, Coca-Cola sent a second team to Florida. Headed by Joseph Califano, a Washington insider who had served as a White House aide in the administration of Lyndon B. Johnson, and Donald Keough, director of Coca-Cola's public affairs, the team outlined a program of minimum housing, bus transportation to and from the fields, portable toilets, literacy programs, social services, and health care.[25]

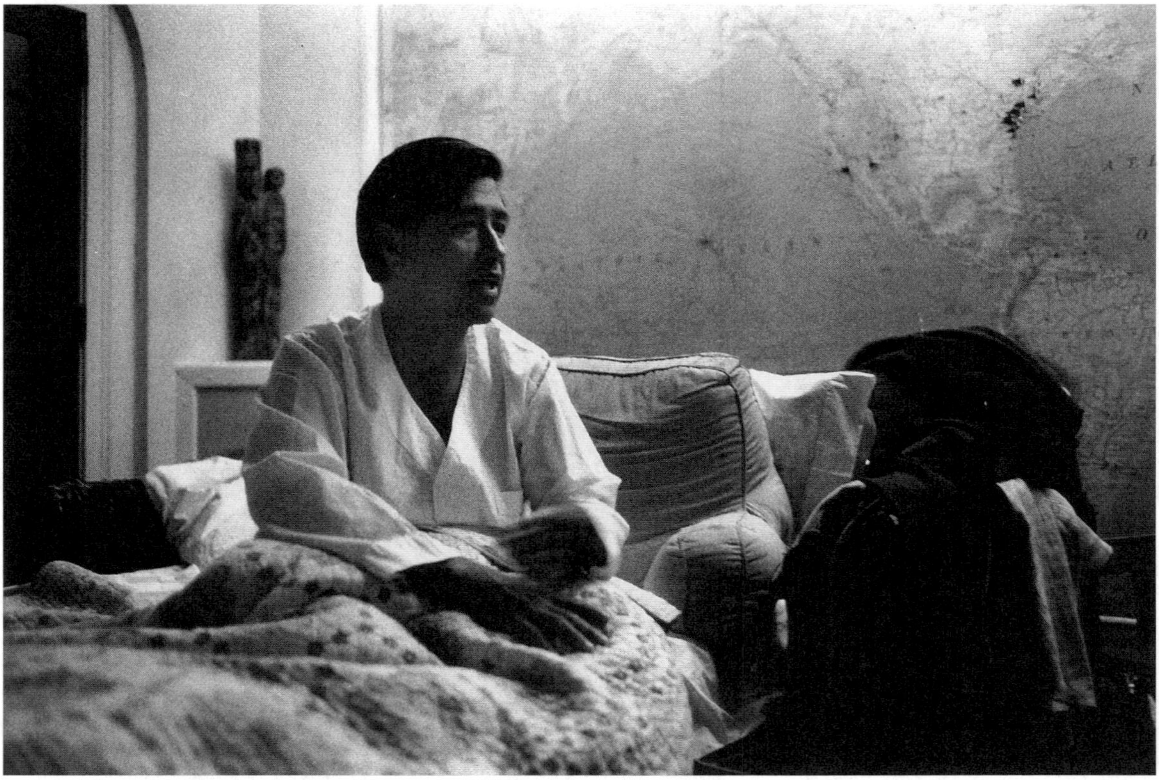

César Chávez looking Gandhi-like while recovering from a herniated disk during boycott activities in New England, October 1969, photograph by Bob Fitch. Courtesy of Bob Fitch.

Over the next few months, photographers recorded countless images of corporate officials being interrogated in congressional hearings, abominable labor practices in Florida citrus groves and California vineyards, and pickets marching outside supermarkets and produce terminals in New York and Philadelphia. By spring, when *Palm Beach Post* photographer Dallas Kinney won the Pulitzer Prize for his graphic black-and-white photo essay on African American migrant laborers following the harvest circuit up and down the East Coast between Florida and New England, the pressure on table-grape growers had built to the breaking point. On April 1, Lionel Steinberg, who owned three large table-grape vineyards in the Coachella Valley, signed a contract with UFWOC. A day later Bob Fitch photographed UFWOC member Richard Chávez carrying boxes of Drake Larson table grapes with the union symbol prominently displayed on the label. Widely circulated in the newspapers, the image would win Larson and Steinberg windfall profits when supermarket chains deluged them with requests for grapes harvested with union labor. It was a nightmare for Delano table-grape growers.[26]

Faced with such images, the agricultural industry began to crack. On the one side were those aligned with the Associated Farmers and DiGiorgio farms. Their approach was to use photography as a tool of surveillance and propaganda. Taking the lead in this effort, the Central California Farmer's Committee hired San Francisco attorney Walter Hoffman on May 25 to begin photographing UFWOC boycott activity in New York City. With this visual evidence, the committee intended to prosecute any labor organization or activist group aiding the boycott. On the other side were large-scale farmers who realized the futility of such action and rejected repressive tactics as counterproductive. This was the course chosen by Coca-Cola CEO Austin. "It was not simply altruism that led to this decision," recalled Califano. "It was also the advantage of having the workers bound by a set of rules, especially when they were being led by such a charismatic leader as Cesar Chavez." But in truth Califano had no other choice. The NBC documentary images could not be denied or brushed aside. On the morning of July 24, 1970, Austin rose from his seat in the Senate Caucus Room of the Russell Building, looked into a blinding flash of strobes, raised his hand to take his oath, and observed that the plight of migrant workers was indeed grave, perhaps so bad that no union could make a difference, then went on to endorse Senator Mondale's request to support the idea of extending the National Labor Relations Act coverage to farmworkers.[27]

A few days later, grape growers were confronted with their worst public relations nightmare when they learned that Paul Fusco was returning to Delano with writer George D. Horowitz to expand Fusco's *Look* magazine photo essay into a book. Rampant speculation held that Fusco would produce a kind of West Coast counterpart to Dallas Kinney's effort. What would happen once Fusco's book appeared? As they asked such questions, many growers began to think about bargaining with UFWOC. They felt beaten. Everything seemed to be turning against them. Chávez seemed to have the grape industry under his thumb. He had cut the number of boxcars of table grapes unloaded in New York by 30 percent and reduced sales in Baltimore by half.

With more and more supermarkets refusing to carry table grapes, Delano grape grower John Giumarra Jr. met with UFWOC on July 25 at 4 A.M. in the Stardust Motel in Delano. He said he was ready to sign a contract.

Jerome Cohen, UFWOC's legal counsel, understood visual culture. He knew that a picture of a contract signing would have a huge impact on the movement, on the public, and, most important, on farmworkers. He was not going to sign a contract out of sight in a motel room in the dead of night. And he was not going to sign contracts individually, according to the agreement among growers. Cohen had read farmworker history. He understood the gravity of the moment. Nothing like this had ever occurred. No grower had ever sat down with a farmworker union leader to sign a contract. Now Cohen had a chance to create a photo opportunity the likes of which had never been seen previously in California. He was not going to miss the opportunity. He told Giumarra to round up all twenty-six Delano grape growers and meet Chávez on July 29 for a public ceremony in Walter Reuther Hall at Forty Acres.

To create the kind of picture Cohen wanted, the union spent the next four days carefully preparing for the big event. Union members began telephoning boycott leaders, asking them to rendezvous in Delano. A crew got busy hanging banners, setting up chairs, laying out microphones, and placing lights around Walter Reuther Hall. At exactly 11 A.M. on the scorching hot morning of July 29, César Chávez stepped before a wildly enthusiastic crowd of two hundred Mexican American and Filipino American field hands. Everything, down to the smallest detail, was stage-managed for the cameras. Next to Chávez at a long table cluttered with microphones and tape recorders sat other UFWOC leaders, and beside them representatives of the AFL–CIO and both the Catholic and Protestant churches. Also present were the grape growers, plain, blunt-spoken men in open-neck shirts. Between the table and the crowd, dozens of photographers maneuvered for position. Every photographer who had ever covered the farmworker movement and could make it to Delano was there to record the historic event. George Ballis was there, along with Ronald B. Taylor and a dozen newspaper photographers, including those from the *San Francisco Chronicle,* the *Los Angeles Times,* and UPI.[28]

Hardly passive observers, photographers exerted a strong influence on the ceremony, a typical gang-bang photo op. As Chávez began to speak, an explosion of strobe flashes greeted him. Over the next few minutes, every gesture inspired a wave of shutter clicks and flashes. Ignoring the commotion, Chávez recalled that when the strike had started, farmworkers asked \$1.40 an hour and twenty cents for each field-packed box of grapes. Now they would receive \$1.80 an hour and twenty-five cents per box. Chávez also stressed that growers had agreed to pay ten cents an hour into the Robert Kennedy Health and Welfare Fund, two cents an hour into a special service fund, and accept a union hiring hall arrangement. With that short speech, he prepared to sign the contract. Sensing the historic picture, photographers crowded even closer. A few fired off "cover your ass" shots of John Giumarra Jr., smiling uncomfortably, as he rose from his seat, addressed the crowd, dismissed the past, and hoped for a new relationship. Chávez then moved to a position alongside him and said a few words. When Bishop Joseph Donnelly, of Hartford, Connecticut, leaned over between Chávez and Giumarra and thumbed through the agreement, after having assisted in its negotiation, Taylor snapped a picture. With that, the scene was set. Most of the photographers had high hopes. They believed that with victory UFWOC would organize farmworkers in all of the major California crops and, from that base, branch out across the country to create the largest labor union in the United States. "Today's really, truly, the beginning of a new day," Chávez announced. "We thank God for all these things, and we thank you, too."[29]

His next words are forever lost, because one photographer, unable to wait for events to unfold naturally, shouted for Chávez to shake hands with Giumarra. At that moment, John Giumarra Sr. threw his hands over his head in a victory sign. His son smiled. Bishop Joseph Donnelly and Monsignor George Higgins started clapping. Larry Itliong beamed. As the audience broke into uproarious applause, photographers let fly with their strobes. Recording the historic moment from every possible angle, they momentarily drowned out every sound in a whir of motor drives advancing film through their cameras.

Within a few days, Paul Fusco was back in Delano and remained there through the fall. Considerably expanding his original project, he shot another four hundred rolls of film. That winter, the Macmillan Company issued his book. Titled *La Causa* (The Cause), it was very much what growers had feared: the West Coast counterpart to Dallas Kinney's essay on African American migrants. "I was not interested in doing an organizing book or a political book," Fusco later said of his approach. "All I wanted to do was show, as best I could, the spirit and character of people involved in a unique battle for human rights." To accomplish that he brought the viewer closer than ever to the reality of farm labor and the long boycott: chilly and damp picketing duties in the fog; long hot days of frantically picking grapes; a lunch break seated on the ground against the rear tires of a bobtail truck for a bit of shade from the sun; and the stoop labor of grubbing out weeds. He also documented families struggling to make ends meet in the labor camps, unemployed husbands, children crawling on the filthy, carpetless floor of what passed for housing, and men waiting in the predawn darkness to ride labor buses to the fields. Organized in a sequence that is almost cinematic, *La Causa* creates a powerful, timely, and compelling portrait. Captions by George D. Horowitz drive home the details, although they take a few liberties. One description of men wielding short-handled hoes reads: "The Bracero Program began in World War II: cheap labor was scarce and Mexicans were imported. After the war, they were still cheap, so the growers cut short the hoe handles. Only a Mexican could stoop so low for a dollar, the growers said. Only a grower would stoop so low to save one, the Mexicans answered. And so the dialogue began."[30]

Other problems emerged during the editing process. Like photographers before him, Fusco emphasized dramatic images over those that more accurately illustrated the truth of the situation. This was particularly true of the way he depicted grape picking. Although he took many photographs of the table-grape harvest, Fusco found them inherently uninteresting, because picking table grapes was a slow process. Workers carefully cut grapes with shears, trimmed off shriveled or undersized berries, and neatly packed them in boxes stored in the shade under the grape vines or in portable packing stands. Picking wine grapes or raisin grapes was dirty, frenzied work. Pickers moved through the vines at maximum speed, cutting the grape bunches with hooked grape knives, not shears. Next, they hefted boxes full of grapes into bins or laid them on waxed brown paper to dry in the sun. While table-grape pickers remained comparatively clean and often included women, who sorted and packed the bunches, wine- and raisin-grape pickers were mostly men, who, within a few hours, became covered in dirt, grime, sweat, and sticky grape juice. Apparently seeing images of table-grape harvesters as too tame, Fusco chose few of them for his book. He preferred instead to mix silhouettes of bare table vineyards and grape vines in wintertime alongside images of exhausted wine- and raisin-grape pickers crawling through the vineyards. Few readers noticed the discrepancy. Believing the implied truth of these images, most who saw the book accepted the slightly skewed picture of labor conditions as an accurate depiction of the table-grape pickers, whom Chávez was seeking to organize.[31]

20

Icons of Struggle

Photographing Thugs and Violence

Shortly after the July 29, 1970, contract signing, photographers headed west from Delano, across the Coastal Range, into the Salinas Valley, where the Salinas Valley Growers and Shippers Association had signed "sweetheart" contracts with the Teamsters Union, which had for many years represented packing shed and packinghouse workers. Not only did the back door deal keep UFWOC out of the lettuce fields; it also violated an agreement that the Teamsters and UFWOC had concluded three years earlier not to infringe on each other's territory. Regarding the deal as a betrayal tantamount to throwing a match into a pile of kindling, Chávez had labeled the sweetheart agreements a "Pearl Harbor attack." On discovering the terms of the agreement, entire crews had refused to sign Teamster authorization cards and were threatening to walk out en masse. All the photographers who had followed the union knew they were about to witness the opening scenes to yet another dramatic chapter in the farmworker saga. Whatever their experience and motivations, which ranged from a junkielike addiction to the action to a deep commitment to the farmworker cause, they were not going to miss the battle.

On Sunday, August 2, photographers walked through the streets of Salinas with three thousand farmworkers, then followed them onto the Hartnell College football field for a mass rally. Over the next few days, they recorded Teamsters Union organizers fanning out across the valley, trying to sign up members, only to be chased out of the fields by angry *lechugeros* (lettuce cutters). Soon much of the action centered on Fresh Pict, a Purex Company subsidiary. After evicting lettuce cutters from labor camps for refusing to sign Teamster cards, Fresh Pict obtained an injunction prohibiting further picketing by evicted workers. When a series of strikes erupted in the strawberry fields, Chávez labeled the injunction an abridgement of constitutional rights and alerted the press that he would defy the court order outside the Fresh Pict office. With photographers watching, Chávez dramatically tore a page out of Jerome Cohen's notepad and scribbled a message: "I am here to be served by the [injunction] order." He then pressed the message against the Fresh Pict office window for all inside to see. Sitting on the office steps, he waited to be arrested. The following day, images of the defiant farm labor leader appeared in newspapers throughout the state.

On August 22, the GSA scuttled efforts by the U.S. Catholic Bishops Committee on Farm Labor to mediate an agreement among United Fruit, Purex, and UFWOC by announcing that, whatever the outcome, all remaining members would honor their contracts with the Teamsters. Two days later, angry UFWOC members met at a mass rally at Hartnell College and voted overwhelmingly in favor of a strike. On Monday, August 24, thousands of farmworkers walked out of the fields, and press photographers began capturing images of pickets confronting harvest crews working under the eye of guards armed with shotguns. With Teamster thugs menacing pickets with baseball bats and generally harassing everyone, photographers did not have to work hard to obtain images suggesting that civil war was about to erupt the length of the valley. Soon they themselves would become targets.[1]

Photojournalist Jacques Levy was well aware of the charged atmosphere when he arrived at UFWOC headquarters in Salinas early on the morning of August 25. On leave from the *Santa Rosa Press Democrat* to write a biography of Chávez, Levy had been interviewing union members and observing events close up and had driven Chávez to Salinas for a mass meeting. When he learned that broccoli harvesters at the Mann Packing Company were threatening to hold a sit-down strike, the first such action in the Salinas Valley, Levy grabbed his camera, joined Jerome Cohen and organizer Venustiano Olguín, and headed out to meet with them. Dodging some sheriff's deputies and private guards, the three found an unguarded road and were walking toward the Mann Packing Company fields when a dozen Teamster thugs and grower Al Hansen confronted them and ordered them to leave. As they turned and headed back to their car, a six-foot two-inch, three-hundred-pound Teamster named Jimmy Plemmens caught Cohen by the neck, held him in a stranglehold, and began bouncing him down the road like a pogo stick. Looking back, Levy saw Cohen's neck twisted grotesquely to one side, seemingly separated from his body by a thick forearm and fist. "Hey, Jacques, take a picture of this!" Cohen cried out. But as Levy focused his camera, one of the thugs threatened, "You take that picture, and I'll smash your camera."[2]

Levy snapped the picture anyway, then started walking down the road, too proud to run, too scared to linger any longer. But right after he began his retreat, someone hit him from behind. Ripping Levy's camera from his hand, the thug sent the photographer sprawling in the dirt and dust. Expecting a beating, Levy curled up in fetal position. When he looked to his left, he saw that Cohen was still being held in a choke grip while being mauled and pounded unmercifully. Levy tried to grab his camera and snap another picture. But one of the thugs smashed it with his boot and kicked it into the brush. Although Levy was unable to take any pictures of the violence that day, *Salinas Californian* photographer Clay Peterson more than made up for it by snapping a chilling image of Cohen in the emergency room at Monterey County General Hospital. The photograph ran front page in the *Salinas Californian* beneath headlines shouting, "Court Bans Pickets as Tension Grows: Attorney Hospitalized."[3]

While Cohen was recuperating and Levy was out searching for a new camera, two other photographers picked up the story. One was Morrie Camhi. A very successful Los Angeles advertising photographer, Camhi had become fed up with the business, models, and art directors that he was dealing with. Following the assassination of Robert Kennedy, he had started to ask himself some hard questions about his chosen profession: "Our society was in turmoil, but my camera, instead of interpreting movements and people that were dynamic forces in our life, was photographing bottles of Scotch, dream trailers, and the newest gadgets," Camhi later explained. To pursue a more meaningful form of photography, Camhi sold his studio, moved north to Petaluma, and began searching for another method to support his family. Landing a job teaching photography at City College of San Francisco, Camhi vowed to make only photographs that were important to him. Soon he headed south to the Salinas Valley. His only goal there was to take meaningful images. They might be unsalable, but they would be substantive.[4]

When Camhi first arrived at union headquarters in Salinas, he encountered a clot of photographers. "You would see so many cameras at all of the gatherings that the farmworkers seemed less the event than the photographers," Camhi recalled. "Many times the farmworkers would strike poses for the photographers. They were all very

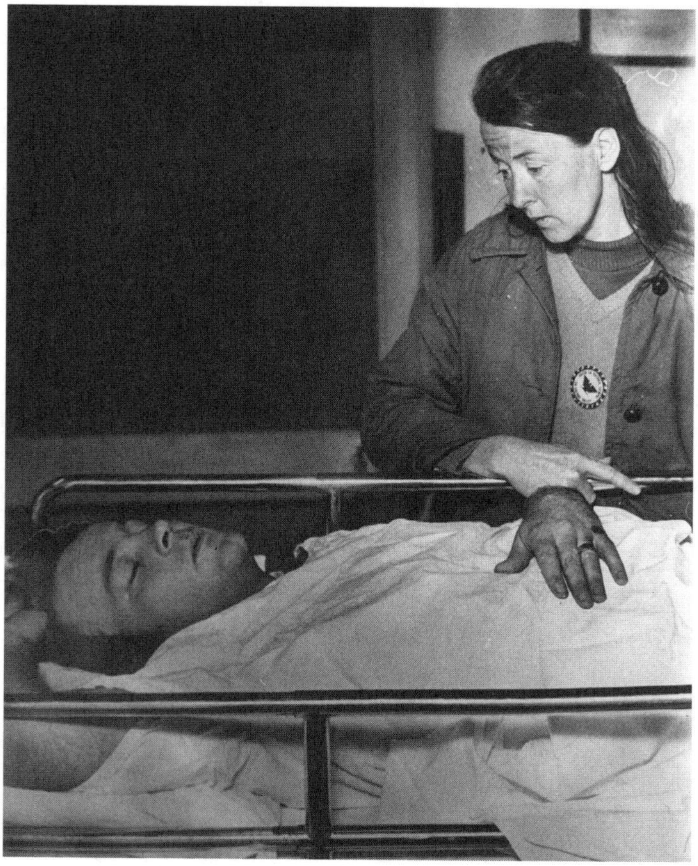

UFWOC nurse Peggy McGivern watches over attorney Jerome Cohen at the Monterey County General Hospital after being kicked in the head earlier in the day on the Al Hansen ranch on Alisal Road, August 25, 1970, photograph by Clay Peterson/*Salinas Californian*. Courtesy of Clay Peterson.

accustomed to seeing cameras." Most of the photographers, in Camhi's opinion, came in search of the violence and other action and the big news events. For many freelance photographers, these opportunities constituted a kind of self-fulfilling prophecy. Of this tendency, Camhi later observed:

> They knew, or felt they knew, what they wanted to see or what their editors wanted, and proceeded to make those photographs. I think most photographers, including myself, were typecasting the struggle in the expected media way of confrontation and physical struggle. Press photographers of the left would show lots of angry pickets—the kind suggesting an irresistible movement—when in fact during the strike most people were still out there harvesting as usual.[5]

While he familiarized himself with the Salinas Valley, Camhi watched many photographers seeking out images of "hard times" to photograph, even when the evidence was to the contrary. Camhi added:

> You would be with photographers in some labor camp or farmworker housing, and you would watch them look at three sides in a room that was well-ordered and well-kept, and they would pick the fourth side and photograph the peeling paint and chipped wall paper. Poverty had to be emphasized. . . . But that was an oversimplification. I was not interested in making political cartoons out of farmworkers.[6]

Determined to overcome these prejudices, Camhi tried to open himself up to the full spectrum of possibilities. A strong supporter of the union, he took very few photos at first. He spent twelve hours each day making picket signs, running errands, driving pickets to and from the fields, and supporting the movement in other ways, much as other photographers had done. Then at night he would flop on a cot, exhausted by the long days, unable to sleep, struggling to decipher what he had seen. Camhi was trying to picture farmworkers on their own merits. He hoped to dispense with preconceived notions and predictable political and artistic agendas. He intended to introduce a new style into the photographic record of California farmworkers. This would require patience, trust, and an eye for small details.[7]

After a few weeks, Camhi began to comprehend several themes. One was the tremendous amount of discussion and thinking that went on among farmworkers and union supporters. Their ability to think through decisions and their ability to measure the risks and rewards of actions were what Camhi called "the intellectual struggle that accompanied the movement." Camhi also turned his lens to the ramifications of going on strike. He wanted to discover the emotional and economic prices that union members paid, the logistics of their struggle, and the sacrifices they made. A third theme was life's daily ritual. Most photographers saw only deprivation. Without glossing over harsh circumstances, Camhi captured examples of a larger humanity: the family ironing board, immaculate clothes hanging on the clothesline ready for Sunday church services, the father outside washing the car, the children inside studying their lessons, a husband and wife relaxing after a hard day in the fields. He sought out the quieter aspects of "the movement": backyard arguments and evidence of union literature left on a table. He did the same out on the picket lines, where he discovered a lonely picket reading a book at a quiet moment when there was no shouting or confrontation.

Narrowing his cast of characters, Camhi sacrificed quantity for quality, breadth for depth. Because of this, his photographs did not so easily serve the cause. Years later, Camhi observed that his approach probably cost him photographs, but it also may have saved him from the beating suffered by Cohen and Levy. He recalled:

> I was about to go onto that farm. . . . As it turned out, something else captured my attention, and I decided not to go . . . but pursue another subject instead. Three hours later, I was visiting the two men [Levy and Cohen] in the emergency ward of a hospital.[8]

Complex and thoughtful, Camhi's photography had little impact on the public. It was too soft, too ambiguous, too intricate. Editors did not want it. They wanted easily captioned hard news photographs, the more confrontational the better. For all the changes of the past few years, conditions in the fields still made people angry, and not

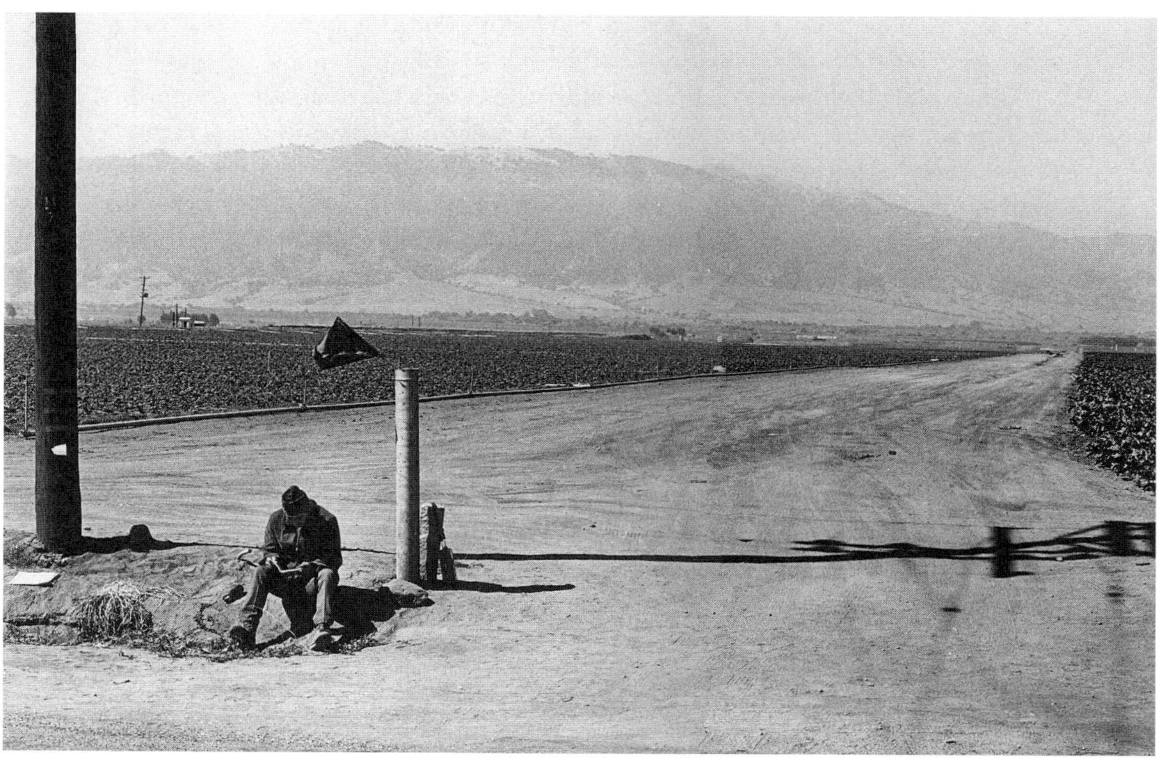

Picket reads at the entrance to a ranch near Salinas, September 6, 1970, photograph by Morrie Camhi. Courtesy of Morrie Camhi.

just in the San Joaquin Valley. When one Santa Rosa photographer got wind of a crew of children cleaning the ground of apples in an orchard near Sebastopol, he scurried over to snap a picture of the "all child crew." Working for seven cents a bucket, the children had organized a strike for eight cents a bucket. By the time the photographer arrived, the grower had refused their demand and ordered them back to work. The youngsters, all under the age of twelve, were dragging buckets and tossing apples at top speed.[9]

But even more than exposés, editors wanted violence, action, and drama. They wanted photographs that shouted. For those characteristics, newspapers and magazines turned to another breed of photographer. They turned to Bob Fitch, whose loud and clear view of California farmworkers and UFWOC during its most difficult phase would dominate public discourse throughout the early 1970s and for generations thereafter.[10]

Shortly after growers obtained their first injunction, Fitch made the first of what would be many dramatic photographs in the Salinas Valley. With armed guards patrolling the fields, farmworkers refusing to obey the injunctions, and violent confrontations erupting the length of the valley, Fitch found images at every turn. "The union often requested that I follow the campaign," he explained. "Contrary to popular myth, violence least occurred when cameras were present. I knew that many times the long hours I spent on the picket lines helped provide a form of protection. It may have seemed dull to other photographers, but it was wonderful for me. I met so many courageous people, learned their stories. Their trust was a very special gift to me."[11]

Wading into the thick of confrontations, Fitch spent much of his time documenting face-offs between Teamsters and UFWOC members. Danger was ever present. A foreman plowed his bulldozer into strikers' cars; a picket accused of throwing rocks was shot in the foot; UFWOC members had their skulls cracked by strikebreakers wielding chains; the union office in Hollister was blown up by dynamite; and three strikers were arrested for shooting a Teamster organizer in Santa Maria. Shifting between these and other confrontations, Fitch somehow managed to avoid trouble. Never personally attacked or hurt, he was frequently threatened. "It was mostly . . . long hot days, waiting and participating," he explained.[12]

Of all the events that unfolded at this time, none reminded Fitch of what he had witnessed in the South more than what happened after Chávez was arrested on December 3 for defying an injunction against boycotting Bud Antle lettuce. Confined to a small cell near the drunk tank in the Monterey County jail, Chávez was reminded of some of the labor camps he had been in, including leaking plumbing, bad lights, and cold. Making the most of his situation, he read books and mail and soon became a martyr to the cause. Across the street, UFWOC members constructed a shrine and sang *correados* (choral songs). On the evening of December 6, Ethel Kennedy arrived to visit Chávez, and photographers poured into town for a well-staged event that began with more than two thousand UFWOC members and supporters greeting Kennedy and then celebrating an outdoor Mass with her. The event almost spun out of control when a vicious crowd converged on Kennedy, her bodyguard Rafer Johnson, and several security guards when she walked to the jail. With Teamsters, members of the John Birch Society, and angry growers and their families waving American flags and shaking their fists while screaming, "Reds go home!" and "Ethel go home!" photographers kept up a steady stream of flash shots, recording a dangerous confrontation that nearly erupted in a riot.

Fitch captured the scene and an even more dramatic one that developed outside the jail on December 24, when the California Supreme Court, in San Francisco, ordered the sheriff to release Chávez. Waiting on the jail steps with Bob Fitch and about four hundred men and women were dozens of photographers, including Jacques Levy, Gene Daniels (also with Black Star), Hub Segur, several San Francisco newspaper photographers, local newspaper photographers Clay Peterson of the *Salinas Californian* and Sam Vestal of the *Watsonville Register-Pajaronian,* and Russ Cain of the *Monterey Peninsula Herald.* When Chávez emerged from the jail at 10:25 P.M., the massed photographers along with hundreds of farmworkers and other spectators simultaneously clicked their shutters. "For about fifteen or twenty seconds, night became day," Fitch recalled. "So many strobes went off that it was almost like a lightning bolt. It was one big blinding flash of light."[13]

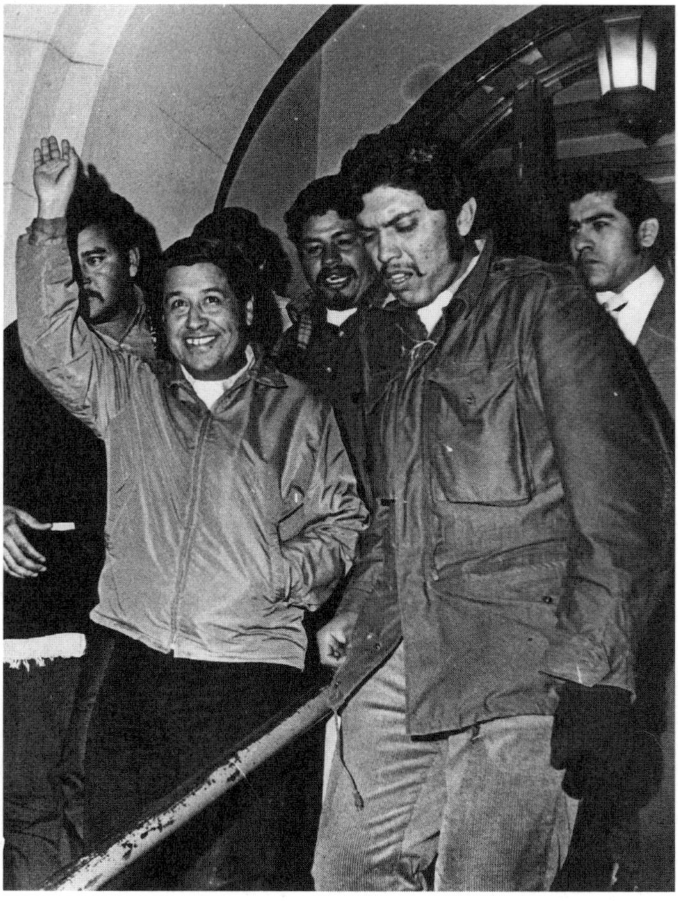

César Chávez leaves the Monterey County jail, December 24, 1970, photographer unknown. Courtesy of the *San Francisco Examiner.*

When the strike petered out and harvest crews headed south to the Imperial Valley, Fitch followed the boycott on nonunion lettuce. Satisfied with his work and believing that his images helped the cause, he continued to chronicle the union but with decreasing effectiveness. Early in 1971 he was shocked and somewhat dismayed when Chávez moved UFWOC headquarters from Delano, in the heart of the San Joaquin Valley, to an abandoned tuberculosis sanatorium in the Tehachapi Mountains southeast of Bakersfield. Fitch thought the location too remote and more of a retreat than a centralized union headquarters. Whereas he had once enjoyed almost unlimited access, Fitch now found bodyguards surrounding Chávez and interceding every time anyone got close. He was not alone in his feelings.

When UFWOC changed from an organizing committee into the United Farm Workers, a chartered affiliate of the AFL–CIO with 147 contracts covering fifty thousand to sixty thousand jobs on farms in California, Arizona, and Florida, photographers long accustomed to having unimpeded access to everything at all hours of the day or night found themselves excluded and cast aside. Whereas volunteers of the farmworker movement had once welcomed them, many field representatives now barred photographers from hiring halls and sent them packing when they tried to document long lines of field hands waiting to be dispatched to jobs. The union itself contributed to the lapse in coverage by inexplicably terminating *El Malcriado.* Suddenly a union that had once been top-heavy with camera-carrying volunteers saw its most talented photographers leaving to work for newspapers and as independent film producers. Suddenly a union that had attracted overwhelming photographic coverage was out of the picture. Suddenly a leadership that had once been warm and welcoming was now aloof from, hostile to, and increasingly paranoid about anyone who was not a loyal insider. Documentary filmmaker Jesús Salvador Treviño discovered this side to the UFW when he tried to contact Chávez to film an interview for his epic *Yo soy Chicano.* He was told by a distrustful member of the legal staff that only people working for the union would be allowed to film or photograph interviews with Chávez. When Treviño volunteered his services to the union in the Los Angeles area, he was rejected, even though union picketing activities were starved for media coverage. "This cooled me on the idea of working for Chávez or the union," Treviño wrote in his memoir of Chicano filmmaking.[14]

Rigorous photographic coverage of the farmworker movement did not resume until César Chávez revived *El Malcriado* and asked UFW aide Richard Cook to recruit a staff. Cook called Susan and Glen Pearcy, two old friends who had attended graduate school with him at Union Theological Seminary in New York City. Working in Albany, Georgia, with the Southwest Project, an African American community-development organization that grew out of the SNCC, the Pearcys were well-versed in the civil rights movement and jumped at the chance to rebuild the newspaper and union printing operations. With two other volunteers, Jack and Nancy Quigley, they rented a large U-Haul moving van, threw all of their possessions inside, set up a baby crib inside a Volkswagen microbus, and headed cross-country with their twenty-month-old son,

Noah. Driving the van, Glen Pearcy bucked heavy headwinds in New Mexico, where he ran out of gasoline twice. Eventually arriving at the UFW's new headquarters, called La Paz, after a seven-day journey, they were introduced to *El Malcriado* editors Venustiano Olguín and Vlaise Bonpane. Moving into two patient rooms in the old hospital building at La Paz, they went to work on a bilingual edition. "We were hired at the standard $5 a week plus room and board," recalled Glen Pearcy. "We shared a refrigerator with another family and cooked on a Coleman camp stove."[15]

As Glen Pearcy supervised construction of a new darkroom, Susan expanded the union's graphics and printing operations in a new building about one hundred yards north of the administration building. "I had a little experience as a filmmaker," recalled Glen Pearcy, "but only a little. I had made two student-experimental films in 16 millimeter." Also responding to the recruiting call was another couple, Gayanne Fietinghoff and Rick Tejada-Flores. Already established photographers, the Berkeley residents moved to La Paz with their eight-year-old daughter. But neither remained at union headquarters very long. Once the darkroom and printing facilities were up and running, both couples headed to Arizona, along with the rest of the union staff. Their assignment was to employ their skills in support of the union's campaign against a hostile new state farm labor law.[16]

Ostensibly modeled after the National Labor Relations Act, the Arizona law in fact aimed to cripple the UFW by eliminating the boycott, its most important weapon. When Chávez announced that he was fasting as part of a campaign to recall Governor Jack Williams for supporting the new law, Glen Pearcy and Fietinghoff shadowed him closely over the next twenty-four days, recording perhaps for the first time the day-to-day physical changes of a labor leader going without food. Breaking from their vigil only to cover rallies and marches, they also documented the union's unsuccessful efforts to forge a coalition of Navajos, African Americans, Chicanos, and angry miners and steelworkers who were attempting to challenge conservative Arizona politicians. Of his coverage of Jerry Pollock's walk across Arizona in an attempt to meet voters during the election campaign for governor, Glen Pearcy recalled him as inept at making human contact with people, a man who just kept walking. The Arizona campaign was little more than a grueling waste of time that produced neither political gains nor labor contracts. But it did yield some useful and revealing images. "We worked eighteen- to twenty-hour days," explained Fietinghoff in an interview thirty years later. "It was a totally exhausting and amazing time. After the union's recall campaign failed [under pressure from state officials, who questioned the validity of large blocks of signatures], we returned to California and began editing the film. We finished it a few months later. You can really see the physical effects of the fast on César. But what comes through is his spiritual character and drive. Considering that we had no money and worked with borrowed and secondhand equipment, I think we did quite a good film."[17]

While Glen Pearcy and Fietinghoff covered the Arizona campaign, old resentments against farmworker movement photographers resurfaced. John Kouns discovered the depth of that anger and the measures that some would take to exact some small revenge when he exhibited his work during the fall. Framing seventy of his prints in redwood prune-drying trays, Kouns created an exhibition entitled "Viva! Farmworkers Union." He then rented a trailer and delivered his exhibition to venues all over the state. Displaying his images at the Longshoremen's Hall in San Francisco and various colleges, union halls, churches, and farmworker benefits, Kouns attracted considerable positive attention and large audiences. But apparently his exhibition was too much for one viewer, who used an X-Acto knife to surgically excise Chávez from seven of the images on display at the College of Marin gallery. "It was very professionally done, nice and neat," recalled Kouns, adding, "The money I got from the insurance settlement was the most that I ever made for my farmworker photographs."[18]

On January 17, 1973, photographers descended on Delano en masse to record the aftermath of a bomb blast that destroyed a wall at the UFW's facility at Forty Acres. It was the strangest of times. On the next day, Yuba City–Marysville labor contractor Juan Corona was convicted of committing the greatest mass murder in California history. Exposing the vulnerability of farmworkers as few other events in their modern history did, the four-month-long Corona trial attracted massive press coverage. Two months later, press coverage shifted to the Coachella Valley, where the Teamsters Union, in a replication of its tactics in the Salinas Valley, signed agreements with most Coachella Valley table-grape growers just nine hours after UFW contracts expired. To enforce the deal, Teamster thugs poured into the valley and began threatening UFW pickets. Chanting, "You stink, you smell, you're a lousy bunch of commies," they quickly earned the label of "los guerrillos." Dangerous and repulsive, they attacked anyone who dared to stand in their way. Every day brought a new escalation. Chávez was shot at, the Reverend John Banks was assaulted in a restaurant by Teamsters Union member Mike Falco, two Teamsters were arrested after stabbing a man they mistook for a UFWOC member, and six others were arrested for throwing rocks at a car in which Chávez was riding.[19]

Throughout the late spring, Glen Pearcy, Fitch, Tejada-Flores, Sánchez, and Fietinghoff (who served as Pearcy's sound recorder) photographed the action. Contact sheets from their work unfold endless scenes of Teamsters stomping effigies of César Chávez, waving clubs, threatening and intimidating UFW members, parading about without shirts, and making obscene gestures to everyone. After an especially violent day, one Riverside County sheriff's spokesman described the situation as a "mad melee of fights and beatings all over the fields." So many clashes occurred between Teamster guards and UFW pickets that Fitch, Pearcy, Fietinghoff, and Tejada-Flores simply could not keep up with developments, despite using two-way radios to track the action.[20]

Working in the hot desert environment and sleeping on the floor of a crowded trailer, the photographers were up every morning at 3 A.M. and out on the picket lines before sunrise. After a month, the long days and constant threats ground them down. Fietinghoff could not sleep and stayed up all night, frightened by what might happen next. Tethered to Glen Pearcy by a sound cable and draped with the heavy recorder and two Nikons, she wilted in the heat while following the action. At times when it became extremely dangerous, *People's World* reporter Sam Kushner would provide her and others with a motel room. "The Teamsters were threatening to kill us every day," recalled Fietinghoff, a small woman weighing barely one hundred pounds. "They were awful people. They were goons. It was very scary. They did not want to be photographed. They didn't like cameras. And the growers. There was one who rode around on a little motor scooter displaying big dollar signs. He was one of the big contributors to the Teamsters."[21]

In the middle of the confrontations, a rift developed between Tejada-Flores and Chávez. Tejada-Flores had also been filming, but when Chávez threw his support to Pearcy's work, Tejada-Flores and his wife split from the filming effort and began shooting their own movie footage in addition to stills. With Fietinghoff gone, Pearcy suddenly needed a sound man. To fill the void in coverage, union volunteer Tom Dalzell called Cres Fraley. A Philadelphia native who had worked on the boycotts during the late 1960s while still in high school, Fraley had known Dalzell since the seventh grade and had worked with him on the boycott in Washington, D.C., Philadelphia, and Baltimore. When the strike had exploded, Dalzell, along with other boycott leaders, had headed to La Paz to help with the fight. "Dalzell contacted me in early June and said César was making this movie on the grape strike and things were getting out of hand and they needed help filming. It was going to be very important, because they were going to use the film for both legal purposes and to raise money," Fraley explained many years later. "I was in San Francisco, and as soon as I hung up the telephone I headed to the public library and took out all the books on filmmaking. I knew nothing about filmmaking. I tried to learn as much as possible so that I could go to work as a sound man. I convinced César that I knew what I was doing. By mid-June, I was in the Coachella Valley."[22]

Other than George Ballis, Sam Kushner, Fietinghoff, Fitch, Sánchez, Tejada-Flores, and Fraley, who packed his own camera while following Pearcy around, the only people photographing developments in the Coachella Valley were law enforcement authorities. Armed with video cameras, several Riverside County deputies recorded picket line confrontations from atop vehicles, and others used police vans as backdrops for mug shots of arrested farmworkers. "When the Teamsters showed up," recalled Fraley, "it got really wild. They would see us filming for the union, and we would have to hotfoot it out. We shot many scenes while we were being chased by those goons. When the Teamsters' goons arrived, Bob Fitch would just walk into the middle of them. So what if he got punched or a black eye. He was after the shot. I would see him at the end of a long day, and we would have these conversations. He would say matter-of-factly, 'Hey, that guy almost got me. How did you do?' I'd say something about our experiences. Then Fitch would say, 'Well, see you tomorrow on the picket lines.' He was completely unfazed by it all."[23]

When the strike followed the grape harvest north into the San Joaquin Valley, much of the violence around the small farm town of Lamont went unrecorded. Neither press photographers nor union photographers caught the first incidents on the Kovacovich ranch, where a foreman pointed a pistol at strikers and threatened to kill them and a private guard nearly ran over a UFW picket captain, or confrontations at the Nalbandian ranch, where Teamsters Union members severely beat several UFW pickets. Two days later, when a picket was hit by shotgun pellets near Delano, no photographer was there to document the violence or its aftermath. With the strike dispersed over such vast distances, photographers found it impossible to monitor police radios and respond quickly enough to capture the action. Several union members tried to fill the gap in coverage by purchasing their own cameras. UFW striker Don Galindo tried to photograph on the Giumarra ranch, but deputy sheriffs impounded his car and removed his equipment.[24]

As the confrontations intensified, union members and supporters were arrested by the thousands. On June 28, Fraley and Tejada-Flores were present on the Kovacovich ranch, near Arvin, when Teamsters attacked UFW pickets. Tejada-Flores captured a series of images at the beginning of the attack showing deputies sitting by in their vehicles when the violence began. In the most dramatic image from that bloody afternoon, Fraley photographed Juan Hernández being placed in an ambulance after a Teamster had fractured his skull. That day, three other union members were hospitalized with serious head injuries. After the attacks were over and twenty-eight Teamsters had been arrested, UFW member Arnulfo Mancha spoke to a Mexican deputy who had been present. "Why don't you give us protection? Where is your gun?" he asked. "You think I want to get killed for one of you guys?" the deputy replied.[25]

Of his experiences on that day, Tejada-Flores later recalled:

> Early in the morning a flatbed truck drove up, and a lot of big Teamsters jumped out. I was with the pickets, and we all started running. Some Teamsters had clubs with nails. I shot a sequence of them beginning their attack and then tried to escape. They beat an old guy. César's wife was injured that day. I got it all. But I never knew whether or not I'd get out with my film or my cameras. I just kept thinking, "They're smashing everything. It's just a matter of time before they go after my cameras."[26]

Five days later, deputy sheriffs at a nearby labor camp arrested and dragged UFW pickets into a paddy wagon. On July 13, an entire picket line on the Sabovich ranch, near Arvin, was sprayed with the pesticide Aldrin. When such incidents had occurred in Riverside County, deputy sheriffs had been relatively balanced in their treatment of the UFW. But now, deputies in Kern, Tulare, and Fresno counties seemed to go on a rampage against union associates. When Rick Tejada-Flores departed to assume a teaching position in Los Angeles, another newcomer, Greg Mengell, stepped in to cover the bloody confrontations. Fraley also attempted to fill the gap by packing a camera and shooting stills during his duties trailing Pearcy with sound equipment.

Early in July, union photographers settled into a routine. Most were living at La Paz, within an hour's drive of Arvin–Lamont. Fraley camped out with all of the single men in one wing of the old tuberculosis sanatorium. On a typical day he would rise at about 4:30 A.M. and be on the road by 5 A.M. Along the way, he and other photographers would debate where to go. "We would check in with Juan Espinoza, who was running the Lamont UFW office," Fraley recalled. "We would figure out where the action was going to happen and try and be there. It was quite frantic. On the really hectic days full of violence and arrests, we would keep at it until we were physically exhausted or we ran out of film or the batteries ran down. We would get back to La Paz dirty and exhausted. We would shower and eat and go to bed and get up and do it all over again."[27]

On July 17, after courts issued injunctions limiting the UFW to one picket every one hundred feet and curbing the use of bullhorns to one hour per day, the UFW launched a massive campaign of civil disobedience, and photographers fanned out across the San Joaquin Valley. Fitch would later recall these days as the worst suppression of the rights of free speech and assembly "since the days of Bull Connor in Birmingham, Alabama." Fietinghoff remembered the picket lines as "shear terror." Over the next two weeks, every photographer took essentially the same picture of UFW members moving onto various farms, defying the injunctions, and provoking mass arrests. With more than twenty-two hundred arrested union members clogging the Kern County jail in Bakersfield as well as smaller facilities in Huron, McFarland, Shafter, and Wasco, photographers also kept busy covering the court hearings.

After most of the farmworkers were released, Fitch followed them to Delano, where he photographed them marching through the streets and gathering for a huge rally in Memorial Park. Two days later, he recorded a crowd of two hundred union members dispersed by deputies when they gathered in the evening to serenade farmworkers held in the Tulare County jail. On July 25, Fitch and Fietinghoff documented the arrest of four hundred UFW members on a farm near Fresno, many for the second time. The next day Fraley, Mengell, and several press photographers and freelancers joined Fitch in following a large UFW caravan while it traveled from farm to farm. Urging field hands to defy the injunctions, caravan leaders provoked more than sixty arrests. One UPI photographer captured farmworker civil disobedience better than any other. Standing near a sheriff's bus, that photographer placed the bus entrance on the far left of his composition and filled the remainder of the frame with a long line of farmworkers, many with their arms upraised in defiant Chicano power salutes, waiting to be hauled off to jail. Stretching to the horizon, the line of farmworkers captured in the image suggests an almost fanatical level of commitment to the cause.[28]

Others besides Fraley saw that Fitch was not timid about wading into the thick of these battles. Fietinghoff herself was the victim of Fitch's bulldozer techniques when he plowed through crowds and inadvertently knocked her aside to get his shots, leaving her bruised by his aggressiveness. Determined not to miss anything and capitalizing on his size and strength, Fitch used his bulk and bulldozing tactics to get pictures that escaped smaller, less determined photographers. To protect the images that he fought so hard to get and to prevent police from confiscating his film, Fitch was always prepared to use the dummy film canister trick. But when it was necessary to avoid arrest on picket lines and escape other tight situations, he could be chameleon-like and do what George Ballis did: make himself small and inconspicuous. He later recalled:

> Photography is a whole body act. I needed all my senses, all my reflexes, all my muscles, all my gray matter functioning very well and in concert. If I had to run and charge forward, I was prepared to do so, and if I had to melt into the crowd, that's what I did. It all depended on reading the situation. And the situation could change in an instant. One moment you'd be standing there talking. Then in a flash all hell would break loose.[29]

While Fitch and Fietinghoff struggled to avoid beatings by Teamster thugs and arrest by Kern County deputies, Fresno County sheriff's deputies moved into the fields with cameras to continue the surveillance of picket lines established by their brethren in the Coachella Valley. Taken for granted by most strikers, police surveillance suddenly emerged as an issue on Friday evening, July 27. When Representative Jerome Waldie, a Democrat from Contra Costa County, spoke to four hundred UFW members in Fresno County's Courthouse Park, a Fresno County deputy attempted to photograph him and make sound recordings. Angry and indignant, Waldie told *Fresno Bee* reporter Jim Boren, "It was incredible that the group could not peacefully assemble without having our picture taken by law enforcement authorities." But when confronted by the charges, Fresno County sheriff Melvin A. Willmirth refused to apologize. Determined to obtain evidence that might be used in court proceedings and to assist in identifying criminals, Willmirth admitted that his department shot hundreds of still pictures and thousands of feet of movie film but claimed that his deputies had monitored the rally where Waldie had appeared merely to identify leaders and strike captains. Echoing what Kern County sheriff LeRoy Gaylen had told Senator Robert Kennedy seven years earlier, he argued that the camera was a powerful investigative tool of law enforcement. According to Willmirth, many people at the rally had previously been arrested, and, given what had happened on the picket lines, there was a good possibility that more violence and arrests would occur. If everything went peacefully, the photographs would later be discarded. Cautioning that there was no secret file, Willmirth further stressed:

> You have to realize under this situation many serious allegations were being made. Some of those who were supposed to have been severely beaten in the jail were out at the rally and weren't being hindered by injuries, our pictures show. It only takes one incident. Somebody faints and before you know it the entire crowd thinks that person has been shot. Anything could happen and we need photography for identification. If the rally had been a one-shot deal, we probably would not have photographed them. If the growers were antagonistic or operating in a militant manner, you better believe we would photograph them at a rally. I don't think any law enforcement official will photograph a certain activity unless there is a possibility that the law will be violated.[30]

On Tuesday morning, July 31, Fitch took some of the most disturbing photographs of the grape strike. Speaking to a crowd of supporters in Parlier the previous evening,

Chávez had announced a new wave of civil disobedience. He said, "The UFW is not going to quit until we arouse public opinion and possibly jail ten thousand or more, and public opinion makes them [county officials] look inward and realize they've made a grave error." That night in Fresno, seventy nonunion melon pickers were eating dinner in a motel when thirty men armed with knives and tire irons attacked them, severely injuring six. The following morning, violence spread throughout the vineyard districts. One of the first confrontations occurred near Richgrove, in Tulare County, where pickets forced a bus carrying strikebreakers off the road and broke all of the windows. On the roads around Delano and in the Arvin–Lamont area, pickets indiscriminately clobbered passing autos and trucks with rocks and bottles. Out at the Giumarra Vineyards, just off Highway 58 near Edison, a group of UFW members was picketing when police helicopters swept in, whipping up a dust storm in an attempt to scatter everyone or herd them toward deputies. Blinded, strikers became enraged and began shouting at police to stop. At that point deputies rushed in. Swinging billy clubs and spraying Mace, they began grabbing strikers. Fitch recalled:

> It smelled like a setup. The police were thumping everyone, jabbing them, beating the shit out of them. I was hunkered down next to a car fender. The dirt was flying, and I had a 28-millimeter lens and shot everything very close, sometimes within three feet of me. . . . That scene was as bad a case of police brutality as any I had personally witnessed.[31]

During the confrontation, Fitch snapped a picture of seventeen-year-old Marta Rodríguez being handcuffed and dragged off, screaming for help. Marta later recalled:

> I was still screaming when the first sheriff nabbed me. The first one pulled my hands behind my back and handcuffed them together very tight. He pulled my arms back until I thought they would break. I was screaming and then the same sheriff hit me in the knees, causing me to fall. Then there were two more sheriffs hitting me. One of them hit me in the side with his stick. I could barely breathe. They were pulling at me so hard.[32]

Fitch got it all. From his position near the car fender, he shot two rolls of film, recording what he regarded as a police riot. Quickly rotating his camera from horizontal to vertical and back again while framing and reframing his scenes, he fired off strings of pictures. Fitch, with no motor drive on his camera, used his rapid-film-advance lever, quickly working the lever with his thumb and the shutter with his index finger. He then quickly reloaded to record one image after another of deputies whacking away at strikers with batons, spraying Mace into their eyes, wrestling them to the ground, dragging them through the mud, and restraining them in choke holds.[33]

At least one other still photographer was present; he can be seen to the left in a Fitch picture of deputies beating, macing, and throwing Frank Valenzuela to the ground, after Valenzuela, international representative from the American Federation of State,

County, and Municipal Employees, had tried to calm an agitated picket. Frozen and out of position, the photographer missed the shot, but the scene vividly remained in the mind of striker Frank Quintanilla. He later recalled:

> I saw the police had a young girl face down on the ground. One cop had his foot on the girl's back and was pulling her arms up. She was crying and begging to be let up. Frank Valenzuela and I asked to talk to the girl and told the cops not to treat her that way. The only response we got was that we were sprayed with Mace. I saw them swinging at Frank. They were holding him face down on the hood of a car and kept hitting him again and again with a nightstick on his legs and head.[34]

Like other photographers covering the farmworker movement, Fitch had no ready outlet for his pictures. But realizing the important news value of his images of Marta Rodríguez screaming for help, Fitch contacted a *Los Angeles Times* photo editor and made a desperate pitch. Not knowing Fitch and only reluctantly accepting his Black Star reference, the editor agreed to use the images if Fitch could deliver them quickly.

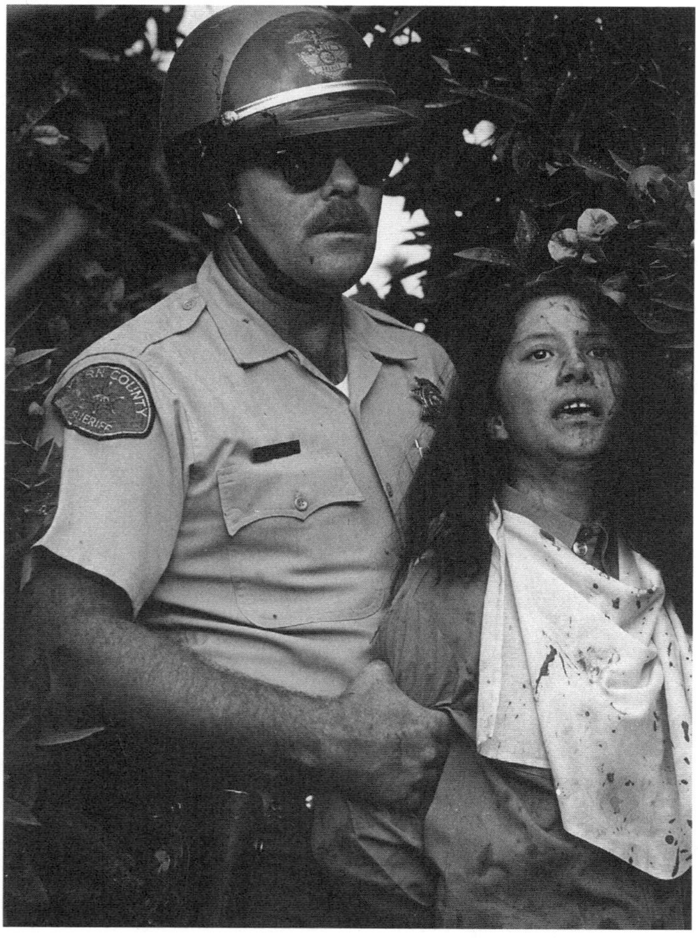

Marta Rodríguez being arrested at Giumarra Vineyards, July 31, 1973, photograph by Bob Fitch. Courtesy of Bob Fitch.

"I got in my little yellow VW Bug and tore down Highway 99 to Los Angeles," he later recalled. "The *Times* ran the photograph of the screaming Marta Rodríguez the next day with the story." Oddly, the newspaper did not run the equally dramatic photograph of deputies beating Frank Valenzuela. Nor did the *Times* run other photographs of farmworkers being thrown to the ground and handcuffed. For some reason, the newspaper chose instead to run a large print of farmworker pickets taunting Sal Giumarra, whose grandson headed Giumarra Vineyards.[35]

Haunted by what he had witnessed, Fitch could not forget the image of Marta's arrest. He later filed a report with the FBI describing the treatment of Rodríguez:

> She appeared to be doing nothing physical, only shouting, when deputies grabbed her. They treated her very roughly. She was crying loudly, like a wounded animal, "Mama, Mama." The deputies dragged her to a grove of trees near the side of the road. Her crying out infuriated the crowd. Frank Valenzuela came to the deputies and said, "You don't have to treat her like that, she's afraid." I remember that Frank always had his hands at his sides or right in front of him. He never raised them. A deputy, whose name I don't know, came up to him and started hitting him with his stick. There were two men on him, but I only remember one hitting him. He was hit on the knees, sides, and back. The deputies then handcuffed him and shoved him down on his knees in the mud. I could see Marta was again face down in the mud behind Frank. It appeared to me that both Marta and Frank were non-aggressive. The physical abuse did not appear to be justified.[36]

Although worried by the level of violence, Chávez refused to back down. Vowing to make the Central Valley into another Selma, Alabama, he called on friends throughout the country to converge on Fresno and participate in mass arrests. Responding to the call, about 143 UFW supporters, including twenty nuns, were arrested early that morning at Anchor and Floral avenues near Reedley for defying the July 17 court order limiting picketing. Among the most famous was Dorothy Day, the venerable seventy-six-year-old pacifist leader of the Catholic Worker Movement, who had led a group of seventy-five priests and nuns from New York to California.

Drawn to Chávez, whom she compared to Mahatma Gandhi, Martin Luther King Jr., and other great mass leaders, Day had picketed in the Arvin–Lamont area on Wednesday, then driven north to Fresno. "I'm happy to be here . . . to be part of the greatest thing to happen in the labor movement yet," she said as deputies surrounded her. "This crowd is not to be denied." As the sun came up, Gayanne Fietinghoff photographed Day holding a union flag while she waited to be arrested. An hour later, Fitch arrived. Crouching and worming his way through the picket lines, he got close enough to photograph her sitting between police. With firearms and batons framing the scene and Day calmly seated, the image quickly became an icon of both the farmworker and the peace movements.[37]

Exhausted by the pace of events and out of money, Fitch was not around a few days later when another battle erupted at Giumarra Vineyards and several pickets were hurt. But in the meantime, his pictures of the July 31 melee had been syndicated by the Black Star photo agency, and Fietinghoff's pictures (including one in which she photographed a Kern County deputy sheriff about to spray her with Mace) were creating quite a stir in *People's World.* When images of the melees appeared in other newspapers across the country, one photograph in particular hit a nerve. Photographing within a few feet of the action, Greg Mengell (or perhaps Cres Fraley or Gayanne Feitinghoff) made a series of revolting pictures on August 7, again in the Giumarra Vineyards. One image shows three Kern County deputies hitting a handcuffed Marcelina Méndez while she was on the ground, then dragging the handcuffed fifty-seven-year-old across the ground to some nearby vines. Another shows her bleeding from a head wound. The photographs shout police brutality, and the union, apparently prepared for the violence, made the most of them by releasing them to the press and then showing Glen Pearcy's film footage of the battles. "We've got movies of them [deputies] rushing a picket line," explained UFW attorney Jerome Cohen to *Fresno*

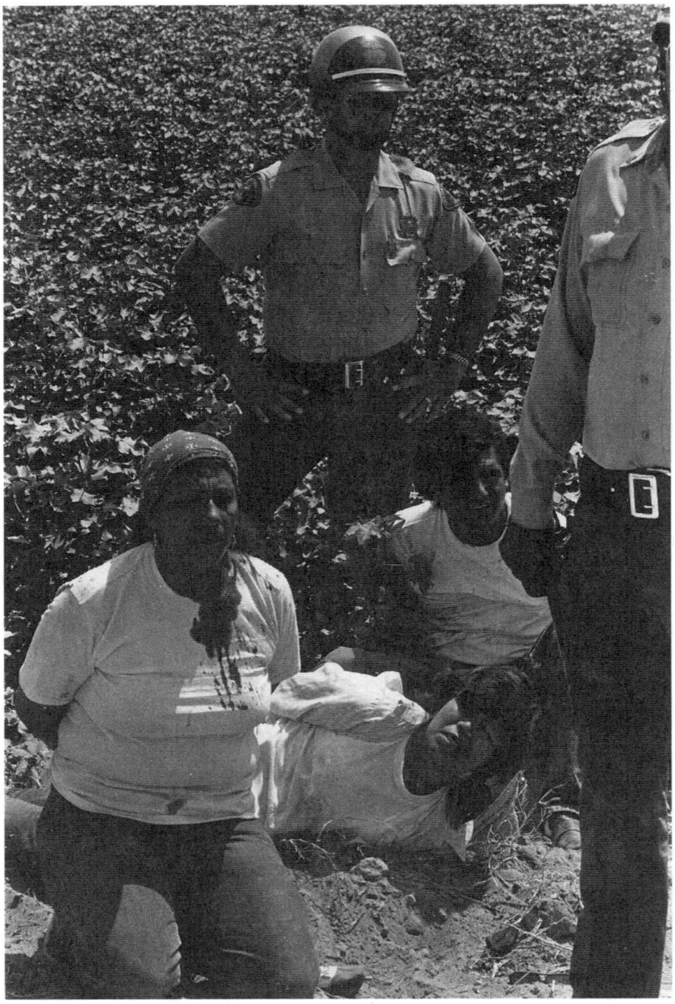

Marcelina Méndez (on the left), bleeding from a head wound after being beaten by Kern County deputies at Giumarra Vineyards, August 7, 1973, photographer unknown (possibly Cres Fraley, Gayanne Feitinghoff, or Greg Mengell). Courtesy of the Archives of Urban and Labor History, Wayne State University.

Bee reporter George Baker. "They ran by Marcelina swinging their night sticks and when they ran into her they just kept swinging. Six stitches were required to close the wound to her head."[38]

According to Cohen, the policy of the authorities was: the worse their brutality against pickets, the more severe the charges they made against them. When Sheriff Dodge dismissed charges of excessive force and indiscriminate beating of women, Cohen simply invited members of the press to look at Pearcy's film and draw their own conclusions about what happened when UFW pickets trespassed into several fields. "You don't have to beat people over the head for that," he snapped. "But that's the way they do it. They go for the head."[39]

Raising the temperature of confrontation to a boiling point, photographs of the July 30–August 7 confrontations—with their freeze frames of helmeted white deputies hauling dark-skinned Mexican farmworkers, women, teenagers, priests, and nuns off to jail—placed the issues of race, class, justice, and nonviolent protest before the public far more effectively than all of Chávez's speeches. They also brought the farmworker struggle to the attention of people who might not normally have been concerned. The frightened face of a Marta Rodríguez, the blood-stained shirt of another middle-aged woman, an old man forced to his knees by three deputies, children being handcuffed, old women battling armed deputies, and farmworkers being arrested by the busload seemed barbarous, even vicious. As with photographs of aggression during the civil rights struggle in the South, what most angered viewers was the sense of overwhelming violence against people unable to fight back. Fully understanding this, UFW members distributed small pamphlets with bloodied farmworkers on the cover and paraded at rallies with enlargements of handcuffed children. Riding the wave of sympathy, Chávez collected thousands of dollars at speaking engagements and used the images to bolster his newest campaign against Safeway stores. So successful was the boycott that by the end of 1973 Safeway claimed it was losing thirty thousand customers per week and filed a suit against the UFW for $150 million in damages.[40]

Employed full-time as a social worker in Oakland, Fitch could not remain in the fields for long periods. As the situation in the San Joaquin Valley worsened over the next two weeks, Fitch missed much of the drama. When Kern County deputies began enforcing injunctions against picketing and skirmishes between pickets and strikebreakers broke out in dozens of vineyards, only Fietinghoff and Pearcy remained to capture the action. While local photojournalists snapped a few pictures of shotgun-toting private guards lording over harvest crews, neither they nor Fietinghoff and Pearcy were present when seventy-five UFW members staged a sit-in to protest the eviction of a fired worker at Gallo's Livingston camp or when strikers armed themselves and launched a campaign of sabotage targeting Teamsters Union members and replacement workers on the Giumarra ranch. So widespread was the violence that only Chris Sánchez photographed eighteen-year-old José Mocón, who was hit in the right shoulder by a shotgun blast while picketing the Tudor ranch, in Tulare County near Richgrove, on August 5. No photographer was present on August 10, when twenty-four-year-old UFW picket Marcelino Barrajas was grazed by a .22-caliber bullet and sixteen-year-old picket Paul Salgado was shot in the hip, both while picketing the Missakian ranch, five miles south of Earlimart. Nor was any in the vicinity when Steve Ruggenburg was shot in the shoulder when he drove a flatbed truck into the Giumarra Vineyards on August 11.[41]

In this poisonous atmosphere, it was only a matter of time before Fitch and other photographers found themselves returning to the fields to document the ugliest of human sins.

21

News Photographers Take Over

Elections and Riots in California

Bob Fitch received a telephone call from the UFW on the morning of August 14, 1973. Something awful had happened, and the union needed him to drop everything and get to Delano as soon as possible. On the previous evening, a twenty-four-year-old Yemeni picket captain, Nagi Daifullah, had been standing outside a bar with a group of friends in Lamont. Celebrating the release of union members jailed over the previous weeks, the group had attracted the attention of Deputy Sheriff Gilbert Cooper, who ordered Daifullah and his friends to disperse. What next happened was and still is passionately disputed. According to police accounts, Daifullah exchanged words with the officer and threw a beer bottle, hitting Cooper in the eye. A scuffle then broke out, Daifullah fled, and the deputy sheriff caught up with him on foot. In the scuffle, the deputy clubbed Daifullah with a flashlight. Law enforcement authorities later claimed that the blows struck Daifullah only on the shoulders, not his head, and that the incident was unrelated to the strike. But UFW witnesses stated that Cooper knocked Daifullah out and dragged him back to the police car, bouncing the young man's head on the concrete pavement. Whatever the exact sequence, Daifullah died of a fractured skull.[1]

Daifullah's death (murder, said many UFW members, but an accident according to the coroner's inquiry) shocked and devastated César Chávez. It also focused attention on Yemeni farmworkers for the first time. Daifullah was one of twelve hundred Yemeni field hands working in the Central Valley. Most were recent immigrants who had taken advantage of their country's liberalized emigration laws in the late 1960s. Largely unknown to the general public, they were highly regarded by growers, who praised them as exceptionally hard-working men who never made trouble. Yemeni field hands lived in isolated labor camps, usually two or three to a room, with at least one small room set aside as a mosque. They were so insulated from the larger society in their barracks existence that, after ten years in the fields, many still did not speak English. Although most labor camps catered exclusively to either Yemeni or Mexican field hands, the two groups did sometimes share quarters, but, even when this was the case, they seldom interacted with one another. Yemeni men were taken aback by Mexican men going naked in communal showers, and Mexicans often resented work days lost to Yemeni religious holidays.[2]

Although many Yemeni field hands had not joined the UFW, their attitude toward the union was not hostile. Men from southern Yemen, who had experienced a Marxist government in their home country, were extremely anticommunist and tended to see unions as threats to their own freedom. To reach them, the UFW brought out two Yemeni organizers from Detroit. But when the Teamsters moved into the fields early that year, many Yemeni field hands left the UFW for the Teamsters. A week after Daifullah's death, Kern County district attorney Albert Leddy announced that Daifullah had worked on a ranch with a Teamster contract. According to the district attorney, Daifullah's foreman had reported to law enforcement authorities that Daifullah was a "spy for the Teamsters." Adding to the controversy surrounding Daifullah's true allegiance, Teamster organizer Cono Macias berated the UFW for claiming Daifullah as a member. While denying that Daifullah had ever been a spy, Macias asserted that Daifullah had been a member of the Teamsters in good standing since May 24.

Enraged by these claims, the UFW pointed out that Daifullah had been a paid-up union member, actively engaged in organizing at the time of his death, and had been living in UFW quarters near Keene. Fraley had made friends with Daifullah when he showed up on the picket line a week before. Whatever Daifullah's history and allegiances, César Chávez considered them irrelevant. More to the point, he explained, Daifullah was yet another farmworker killed in the course of a farm labor dispute. Once again it appeared that the death of a farmworker union member would go unpunished. Daifullah deserved respect, said Chávez, announcing that he personally would fast to honor Daifullah as well as to protest the violence. Chávez also asked pickets to wear black and remain silent. There would be no shouting, no bullhorns. Everyone was to come to Delano for Daifullah's funeral.[3]

On Thursday, August 16, Fitch spent most of the day photographing silent pickets, dressed in black and displaying black flags as they took the message of mourning into the fields. While Fitch was photographing in Delano, another union member was killed. A member of the UFW since its inception, sixty-three-year-old Juan de la Cruz was picketing the Giumarra ranch, twenty-seven miles southeast of Bakersfield. About 3:30 in the afternoon, he was reaching for a drink of water when sixty-four-year-old Fresno resident Ernest Baclig drove by in his pickup truck. From the front seat, twenty-year-old Bayani Advincula leaned out the passenger window and fired four or five shots from a .22-caliber rifle. One shot hit de la Cruz in his chest, just below his heart. He collapsed into the arms of his wife, Maximina. Baclig and Advincula were arrested forty-five minutes later. At about 6 P.M., de la Cruz died in the Bakersfield hospital. It was the third shooting that week.[4]

On learning of the death, Chávez announced that he was switching tactics. Terminating all picketing, he would instead dispatch hundreds of union members to boycotts in dozens of cities nationwide. Hearing the news, Fitch realized that there would be little protest activity worth photographing. But before he departed, he would have to photograph the funerals of Daifullah and de la Cruz. This was not completely unfamiliar territory for Fitch, who, five years earlier, had photographed Dr. Martin Luther King's funeral at the request of the King family. Those services had been long and difficult, with huge and sometimes angry crowds. Despite his reputation for being hard-charging, if not aggressive, Fitch had worked quietly. With more than five thousand union members and supporters now converging on Delano for Daifullah's funeral and a High Requiem Mass, the services promised to be every bit as big and dramatic as the King ceremony. Fitch prepared to deal with the same issues of security, respect, and grief. With multiple controversies complicating an awful tragedy and with countless television crews and photographers sure to be present, including *Fresno Bee* news photographers circling overhead and snapping pictures from an airplane, the question of how to handle these farmworker funerals respectfully weighed heavily on his mind.[5]

To cover Daifullah's funeral as news, Fitch would have to get close to the mourners and family members. Since every other photographer present would also have the same idea in mind, the funerals might easily degenerate into crass publicity events that would cause pain to families, friends, and even strangers attending the services. If that happened, Fitch asked, how could he photograph? Did the news value of the event, which cried out over injustice, outweigh the rights to privacy of those who simply wanted to honor the dead? As a result of having previously proven his ability and cemented his relationship with several key union leaders, Fitch would be accepted into the circle of mourning, whereas other photographers would have to be more cautious. "Trust is the currency of intimate photojournalism," Fitch recalled of this episode many years later, "and that is probably what allowed me to take those photographs. People knew and trusted me, and I knew them."[6]

As he photographed Daifullah's services on August 17, Fitch slowly embedded himself in the funeral procession, which consisted of about three hundred Arab workers followed by thousands of UFW members and supporters, many carrying small black union flags along with the flag of Yemen. Walking with mourners on the dusty two-mile procession from Delano Park to Forty Acres, Fitch photographed Dolores Huerta, Congressman Don Edwards, and various farmworkers paying their last respects. Fitch would later recall Huerta as being "compressed by her grief."[7]

After shadowing pallbearers carrying the flag-draped coffin through the vineyards, Fitch then photographed over the tops of the vines to follow the procession through the streets of Delano. The temperature was around 105 degrees that day, and Fitch later remembered how the UFW, Yemeni, and American flags lay limp in the heat as the pallbearers sweated under their heavy burden and a single Yemeni field hand strained to carry a large portrait of Egyptian leader Gamal Abdel Nasser. While Fitch photographed, he was overcome listening to Chávez's eulogy describing Daifullah as "an immigrant who came here seeking opportunities and fell into the trap of poverty, which has enslaved so many farmworkers in the U.S." The last image that Fitch shot was of a Catholic service, with Muslim prayers, in which Daifullah's Yemeni brothers chanted an Arabic dirge: "There is no god but Allah, and Muhammad is his prophet."[8]

Three days later and sixty miles south, Fitch covered the second funeral. He walked with the funeral cortege for five miles along Bear Mountain Boulevard from DiGiorgio Park to Arvin Cemetery. Along the way he photographed union pallbearers carrying Juan de la Cruz's flag-draped coffin. He made his most lasting images at graveside. One photograph captures Juan's grieving widow, Maximina, her head covered in black widow's lace, sprinkling earth on her husband's coffin. In the background are César Chávez, folksinger Joan Baez, various family members, and numerous priests.[9]

As had been the case with Fitch's past photographs, the public did not see the ones he took of the funerals until many weeks later. But his work continued to resonate for months afterward, with many of his best photographs contributed to a booklet documenting the year's atrocities. Titled *Why We Boycott,* the booklet is packed with images of farmworkers facing down armed growers, bare-chested Teamsters making obscene gestures, and an overwhelming number of law enforcement officers, including photographs by Sánchez, Glen Pearcy, Fietinghoff, Tejada-Flores, Mengell, and Fraley. Hardly a work of detached visual scholarship, *Why We Boycott* notes that 3,538 farmworkers were arrested between April 17 and August 29, 1973, then deploys a barrage of words and pictures that chronicle the tensions, arrests, and mayhem of the year in sickening detail. Introducing the booklet, Chávez wrote an impassioned treatise that serves as a running caption throughout the booklet. It reads, in part:

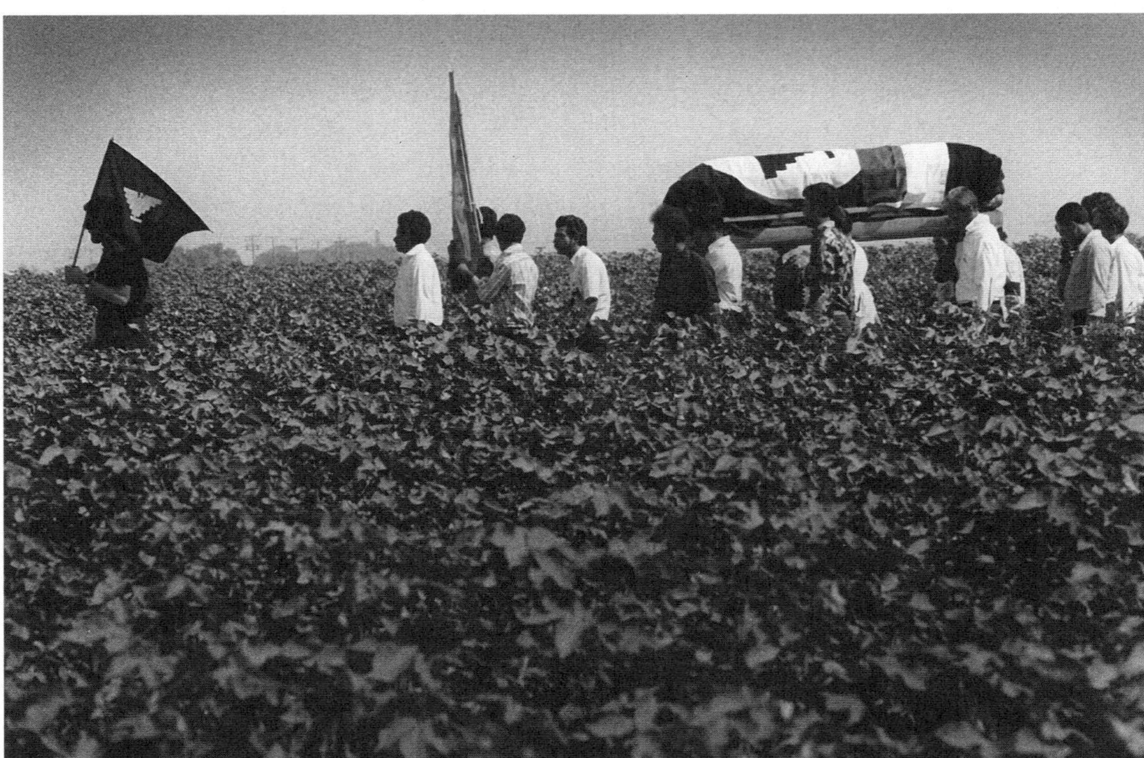

Funeral of Nagi Daifullah, August 17, 1973, photograph by Bob Fitch. Courtesy of Bob Fitch.

> Why another boycott? The Teamsters beat us, while the police watched. The police attacked us many times. A policeman's flashlight and a sniper's bullet changed the course of our struggle. To strike any longer was to invite death. Instead, we left our homes and friends. To 64 cities we have come, to boycott.[10]

Following publication of *Why We Boycott,* Fitch paused to consider his next move. Evaluating the UFW's prospects, he concluded that, although public opinion still remained on the union's side, Chávez now seemed to have poor chances of dislodging the Teamsters Union from its sweetheart deal with vegetable and table-grape growers. With picketing canceled and the confrontation shifting from the fields to the courts and state legislature, Fitch and other photographers determined that little was left to document and so moved on to other projects. But before departing, Fitch and several other photographers remained in the field long enough to cover the UFW's first constitutional convention, which took place in Fresno on September 21 and 22. Sleeping in the homes of union supporters and eating with delegates in the city's convention hall, they recorded the historic and unprecedented process whereby farmworkers created the document that would govern their union. But after making dramatic images of Ethel Kennedy, Senator Edward Kennedy, and United Auto Workers union leader Leonard Woodcock speaking to delegates in front of a huge mural depicting the union's struggle against the agricultural industry, Fitch and most other photographers who had followed the action that summer collapsed in exhaustion. Although Fitch would continue to venture into the fields over the next four years, he had already set a high standard for dramatic action images and left behind a huge legacy of important photographs documenting union operations, life in labor camps, family relations, and violence. He also took some of the few color photographs of Chávez teaching organizers and interacting with his family.[11]

By September, the grape harvest was over. Chávez had now decided to revive the grape boycott. He called UFW members to La Paz, gave them their assignments, and dispersed them around the country. Glen Pearcy filmed the boycott planning meetings and the union members leaving to begin boycotting outside Safeway stores in Chicago and Detroit. When he sat down to assemble his film, photographic coverage of UFW action had reached its nadir, although just five months earlier it had been massive. With Fraley assisting in the film editing process, only Chris Sánchez and Cathy Murphy were available to cover union activities. For three months that fall, Pearcy and Fraley edited thousands of feet of raw film and sound recordings. Using the crudest of equipment, they spent endless days and nights in a small room at La Paz. Of their attempt to make sense out of what they had recorded, Pearcy later recalled:

> It soon became obvious to me that my editing experience was inadequate. . . . A chance encounter on a picket line . . . led me to Bob Dalva, a USC-trained filmmaker who was then head of Francis Ford Coppola's Zoetrope Studios. . . . Dalva gave me unlimited

> access to the proper editing equipment . . . and more important, helped me by giving me and my family living space in their San Francisco home for free. César was well known for holding critical work close at La Paz—so his approval of my move to San Francisco was no small concession. If he had required me to stay in La Paz, with my inadequate equipment and experience I could not have finished. Those weeks and months passed quickly . . . the union was in a fight for its life, and this film was badly needed. I returned to La Paz every couple of months for screenings of the full film. At every deadline, I made progress, but each time I showed the film I could see some great flaw and something more to work on. I was just too inexperienced as a film editor, and I did not realize the true scope of the task. My failure to make deadline was having real consequences, because the union was in the fight of its life, and the film was badly needed to help in the struggle. I'm sure some people must have said kill the project and put someone in charge who was more competent. Finally I finished a short simple version. But every screening of the larger film revealed shortcomings and deficiencies. César kept sending me back for more editing.[12]

After helping Pearcy with the editing in San Francisco, Fraley was called back to La Paz and detailed to duties photographing for *El Malcriado.* As Pearcy slaved away on the film over the next eleven months, his wife, Susan, kept busy in the union print shop. With her infant son in the crib beside her, she cranked out wood block and linocut prints and drawings for use on buttons, bumper strips, and in *El Malcriado.* Her favorites, "Nixon Drinks Ripple" and a head of lettuce styled as a skull, appeared without byline. That winter, Will Kirkland began photographing for the union paper. Much of his work centered on César Chávez. With Fraley and Sánchez covering picketing and boycott activities and volunteers focusing most of their photographic attention on boycott activities in Montreal, Boston, New York, and Chicago, Kirkland handled the darkroom work. "He developed all of César's film," recalled Fraley. "César would come back from these long boycott trips and hand Kirkland thirty rolls of film, and Will would make all of the contact sheets. César was pretty organized. He was pretty careful with those sheets. He could remember images, and he would ask Will to make prints. He'd say, 'Will, remember such and such picture. I need a couple of prints.' And Will would find it and make the prints. César was very involved in photography. He took a lot of pictures."[13]

Pearcy finished *Fighting for Our Lives* in December 1974, a year after the promised delivery date. The final approval screening would remain vividly imprinted in his mind. "When the lights went on," he recalled, "César came over to me, obviously moved, and said, 'You did it, brother.'" Running one hour, *Fighting for Our Lives* was nominated for an Academy Award in the Documentary Feature category; it also won a top prize at the Grenoble Film Festival, in France, and quickly became a staple of the UFW's boycott and organizing efforts. Sadly, farmworkers were again thrust into the spotlight before long. It was not a protest or an arrest that attracted attention. Nor was it the boycott. As had so often been the case, tragedy was what again drew photographers to the farmworker cause.[14]

At 2:30 A.M. on January 15, 1974, an old school bus picked up a crew of lettuce harvesters in downtown Calexico and headed north to the fields near Blythe. Two hours later, the bus missed a sharp right-hand curve, went up onto a canal embankment, and flew fifty-six feet through the air, crashing back to earth on the opposite side of the canal. The bus seats broke loose, catapulting workers forward toward the bus driver and crushing him with the debris. Coming to rest, the bus then flopped over onto its left side and slid into the water. Although twenty-eight passengers managed to scramble free, nineteen were trapped in debris on the submerged side of the bus and drowned in barely two feet of water.[15]

Though this was not the first accident to take the lives of farmworkers, this tragedy was different, because within an hour, photographer Jeanette Hyduke arrived on the scene to record it all. Running a self-described "one-woman, black news bureau" for the *Riverside Press,* Hyduke had cultivated a close relationship with the highway patrol and sheriff's office and used her access to remain on the scene for several hours. Later recalling how she "went into automatic and blocked out the tragedy," Hyduke photographed the crash site throughout the time she was there, recording the recovery

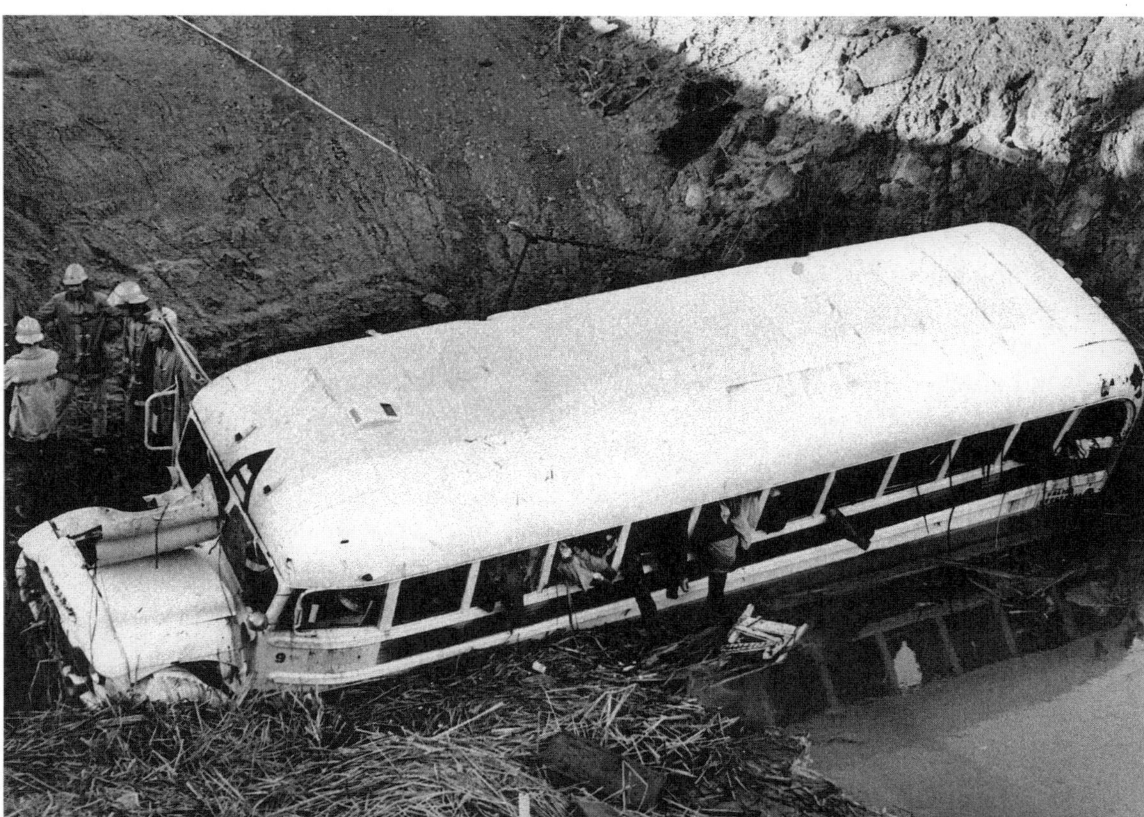

Nineteen migrant farmworkers from Mexicali died in this bus accident near Blythe, January 15, 1974, photograph by Jeanette Hyduke. Courtesy of Jeanette Hyduke.

of the bus, the investigation of the accident scene, and finally the extraction of the bodies. Her grizzly images of arms and legs hanging out of the bus windows when the vehicle was lifted from the canal, as well as shots of the mangled interior of the vehicle and the bus driver jammed up against the windshield behind a wall of debris, provoked a storm of controversy.[16]

The sense of outrage continued to grow after January 19, when dozens of freelance photographers and photographers from the *Los Angeles Times,* the *Imperial Valley Press,* and *La Voz de la Frontera* (Mexico) photographed the mass funeral for the bus accident victims. Mingling with a huge crowd of mourners, the photographers walked from Calexico back into Mexico. Drawn to the sight of farmworkers carrying caskets on their shoulders surrounded by thousands of friends and relatives, they produced images of great power and empathy. Referring to these images again and again, Chávez and the UFW raised the issue of bus transportation safety as well as the agricultural industry's lax occupational safety standards. Always illustrated by graphic images from the bus crash, the debate brought to light the large number of similar accidents that had occurred over the years.[17]

Although images from the Blythe bus accident and funeral shocked everyone who saw them, their impact was short-lived and they were quickly forgotten. With union membership declining, student volunteers departing, and the 1.6-million-dollar strike fund from the AFL–CIO depleted, veteran UFW photographer Chris Sánchez and newcomer Ben Garza had little else to document besides union meetings and car caravans delivering donated turkeys to Delano for Thanksgiving and Christmas. Although there was some evidence that the boycotts on table grapes and lettuce were having an effect, the secondary boycott of Safeway and A&P stores rankled organized labor as a threat to jobs. To placate AFL–CIO president George Meany, the UFW dropped its secondary boycott in March 1974, and the AFL–CIO in return threw its weight behind the table-grape and lettuce boycott. To keep itself in the public eye, the UFW led strikes and marches calling attention to strikebreaking activities by undocumented workers in the Imperial Valley and along the U.S.–Mexico border. Although these tactics produced nothing of consequence, they did buy time for the union to rebuild itself, largely with the help of Catholic priests and nuns, who took over key union staff positions. None of this generated the kind of strategic images that would help the union.

At this point, union strategist Fred Ross decided to reinvigorate the grape boycott by challenging vintners Ernesto and Julio Gallo, the largest winemakers in the world. In 1967, Gallo had been one of the first to sign a contract with the UFW, but in 1973 the winery had turned to the rival Teamsters. Seeking to dramatize the union's campaign, Ross called for a march against Gallo's headquarters in Modesto. Nearly nine years had passed since La Peregrinación had moved up the center of the San Joaquin Valley to Sacramento. Now the union hoped for a similar mobilization. By bringing huge numbers of union members and supporters to the Gallo gates, Ross believed he could attract massive photographic and news coverage that might kick-start a union representation election and force newly elected California governor Jerry Brown to support the UFW's call for an agricultural labor relations law.[18]

While the march cued up on February 22, dozens of photographers milled about the crowd of three thousand forming in San Francisco's Union Square. Suddenly from the top of the St. Francis Hotel, three Gallo employees unfurled a huge banner. In letters three feet tall, it shouted, "Gallo's 500 Union Farmworkers Best Paid in U.S. . . . Marching Wrong Way, Cesar?" Searching for pictures, many photographers seized on the unexpected sight, and their images ran that evening in many of the Bay Area newspapers. Over the next few days, dozens of photographers arrived and departed, just as they had done on La Peregrinación. Recording scenes of the procession passing through the Sacramento River Delta and Stockton, they followed marchers south to Modesto, where the photographers then focused on El Teatro Campesino. The atmosphere was festive on the road, except for one minor controversy in Merced, where the marchers stopped overnight and were photographed by local police while they walked and rested, a routine practice according to the Merced police official who spoke to the press.[19]

Although several of the 130 volunteers who marched all the way from San Francisco to Modesto packed cameras, no professional photographer made the entire trek. Probably the volunteer who photographed the most extensively was Jane Yett. Yett was an experienced amateur photographer and writer who had been active in the union since 1970, and her widely published study of the Safeway boycott, commissioned as part of a student internship, had supported the legitimacy of the boycott, caused the company to rethink its position, gave the union considerable publicity, and caused quite a ruckus. Walking the entire 110 miles with her camera, film, and sleeping bag, Yett ate and slept in church halls and the homes of various volunteers and supporters. She recalled the march as "festive and communal, a joyful time" and felt that she was "part of a wonderful assertion of dignity," which she wanted to capture for subsequent generations. Inspired by the sight of red UFW flags whipping in the breeze as the marchers moved through the green coastal hills, Yett often ran ahead of them and skipped backward and forward along the line of the march to capture key moments, such as an elderly woman's avowal to keep walking in spite of the considerable pain her badly fitting shoes caused. Volunteers and UFW members were friendly and welcoming. Trying to "work in a subtle zone to be sure the subject was agreeable, mostly communicating through body language," Yett often became so engrossed in her work that she lost contact with her traveling companions. "Once I heard a small voice stand out from the singing of hundreds of others, a sound like a clear bell, spiraling upward over the line of the march," she later recalled. "I dropped back in the line to find out where this voice was coming from, and found Joan Baez."[20]

At the end of the march, Yett found herself in a large hall, waiting in the dinner line, plate in hand. Looking up, she discovered César Chávez ladling out beans. "I took a photo of him serving," she recalled. "I understood that was a favorite move of his." Over the years, Yett would find numerous uses for her color slides. Exhibiting, publishing, and donating them to various causes, including the UFW, Yett presented numerous lectures to assorted groups around Monterey Bay and in 1976 used her slides to illustrate a course she taught on farm labor history at the University of California, Santa Cruz.[21]

Most news photographers did not walk all the way to Modesto. Picking the story up around Merced, they came and went as the number of marchers ebbed and swelled. Like other newspaper photographers in communities along the way, twenty-six-year-old *Modesto Bee* photographer Ted Benson covered the march in the midst of his other assignments. Meeting the march near Manteca, he followed it into Modesto, spent the entire evening with the marchers on the night before the Gallo rally, and then photographed on Saturday morning, February 29, at the rally outside the Gallo gates. Along with others who attended the rally that morning, Benson was greeted by another Gallo banner, this one reading: "73 more miles to go. Gallo asks UFW to support NLRA-type laws in Sacramento to guarantee farmworker rights." The attempt to divert media attention succeeded only briefly. Soon the focus shifted to people massed by the Gallo gates. Singing and chanting, "Chávez, sí! Teamsters, no!" they attracted widespread coverage and helped convince newly elected governor Brown and a majority of state

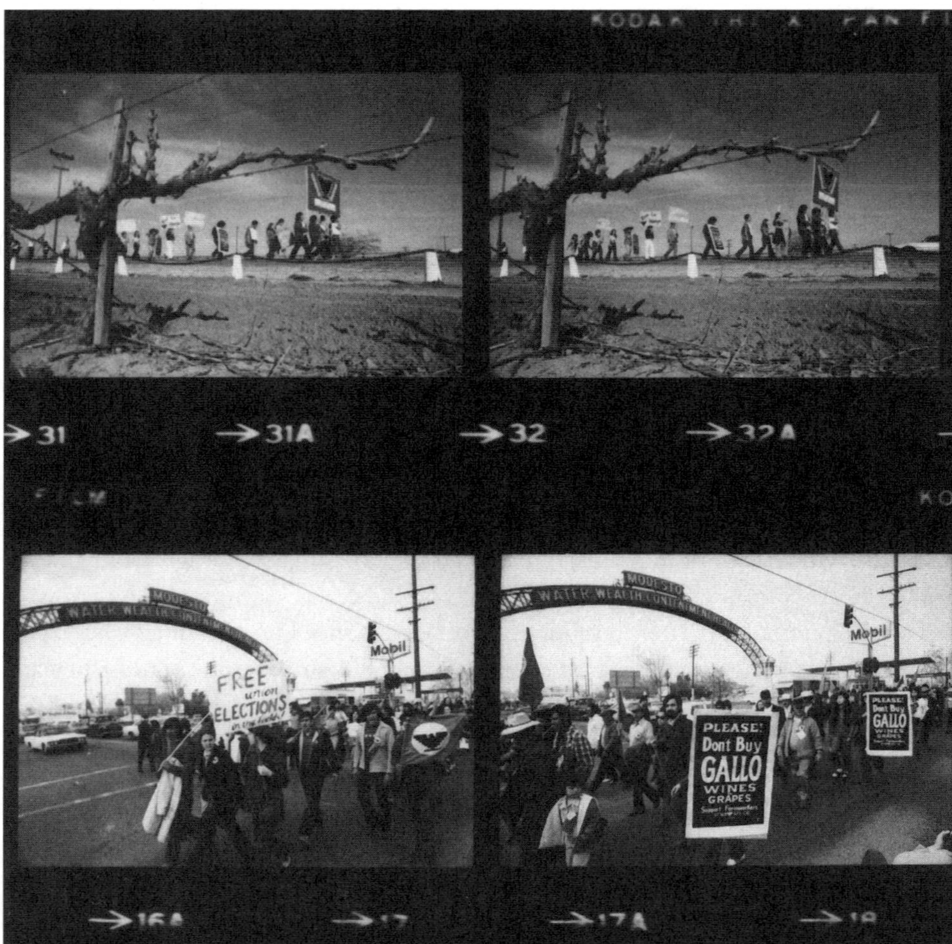

Enlarged frames from Ted Benson's contact sheet of the march against Gallo Winery, February 28, 1974. Courtesy of Ted Benson/*Modesto Bee.*

legislators to draft a law granting farmworkers union representation elections similar to those guaranteed to industrial workers under the National Labor Relations Act. But there was one major difference. Unlike federal labor legislation, the state law allowed farmworkers the right to retain economic weapons such as the boycott, which had been banned under the National Labor Relations Act.[22]

During the summer, when the California Agricultural Labor Relations Act (ALRA) went into effect, photographers once again found themselves embarking on a long march, this time a one-thousand-mile, fifty-nine-day walk, led by Chávez and sixty UFW members, from the U.S.–Mexico border to Sacramento and then back to union headquarters at La Paz. Seeking to inform the state's farmworkers that they now had new rights to bargain collectively, Chávez would meet with union members and supporters in small towns along the way and hold rallies encouraging workers to sign election petitions. The idea was that, by the time all of the bureaucratic problems and legal delays ended at the end of the summer, farmworkers would be well prepared for the ALRA election process. In the meantime, photographers busied themselves with snaps of Teamsters and UFW members waiting with election petitions outside ALRB offices, growers telling organizers to get off their property, and union organizers entering the fields and labor camps to speak with farmworkers about joining the unions.[23]

One of the first photographers to focus on the election campaign was Mimi Plumb-Chambers. A twenty-one-year-old studying under John Collier Jr. at the San Francisco Art Institute, Plumb-Chambers was bogged down in a depressing and horrific photographic study of two adult women still living with their domineering mothers. Unable to conclude the project but still interested in tackling the problems of oppression and victimization, Plumb-Chambers sought out a more positive story. At the start of the farmworker elections, Chávez appointed Venustiano Olguín as the editor of *El Malcriado.* Given free rein to write and illustrate stories as he liked, Olguín initiated a housecleaning at the paper. He replaced Fraley, now delegated to researching the boycott and writing the union's newsletter, and brought in new blood, including Plumb-Chambers, who moved to the UFW in La Paz. Soon after beginning, she was out on assignment with Bob Fitch when the focusing mechanism on her camera broke. Fitch helped her out of the jam by teaching her how to "zone focus," that is, to prefocus her lens to a set distance that could handle most situations and allow her to concentrate on framing scenes.

Plumb-Chambers soon grew disenchanted with life at La Paz. The union headquarters was somewhat removed from the action, and personnel experienced a huge turnover, as loyal and talented union members left or were driven out in droves. "I saw the constant purges of friends and felt the paranoia that resulted," she recalled. Searching for a better window on the day-to-day reality of the farmworker movement, she moved to the Salinas Valley to cover the union election campaign. There she met organizer Ricardo Villapondo. Over a five-month period, Plumb-Chambers followed Villapondo on his rounds of labor camps, pool halls, bars, and other places where farmworkers gathered.[24]

Amplifying the heightened sense of expectation and belief that farmworkers could effectively improve their circumstances, her photo essay all but ignored Chávez and the more famous union personalities. Using her newly learned system of zone focusing, Plumb-Chambers concentrated on the common, everyday occurrences that developed during the union election campaign. At the end of her period in Salinas, Plumb-Chambers exhibited her work in San Francisco. Because it lacked the action and overt drama that the media demanded, her work (like that of Morrie Camhi) sparked little interest among editors. Her main reward came from the farmworkers themselves. "John Collier always stressed that the true test of your photography was how your subjects react to it," Plumb-Chambers recalled. "The heightened sense of pride that farmworkers revealed upon seeing my photographs on the walls of the Salinas union hall was all that I needed to keep going." But when the money ran out that winter, Plumb-Chambers did what Jon Lewis and so many others had done: she stored her farmworker photographs in an attic, where they sat unseen for the next twenty-eight years while she pursued a teaching and art photography career far removed from the farmworker cause.[25]

Soon after Plumb-Chambers left the fields, the elections began. Foremen at Gallo Winery and at other election sites photographed union members and used the images

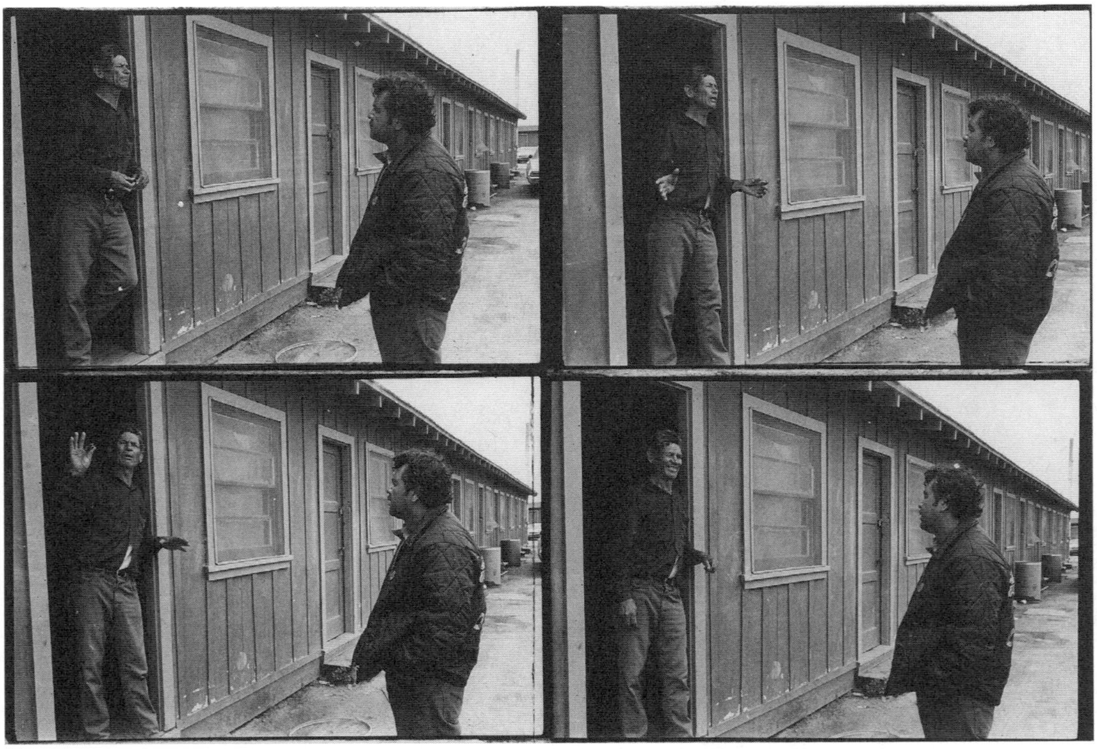

Sequence of images showing a UFW organizer on his rounds through labor camps in the Salinas Valley during union election campaigns, October 1975, photographs by Mimi Plumb-Chambers. Courtesy of Mimi Plumb-Chambers.

to harass and intimidate them. UFW members pointed their own cameras back. News photographers recorded one image after another of thugs wielding baseball bats or blocking access to organizers. The ugliest incidents of the election campaign occurred just as the tomato harvest began in the San Joaquin Valley, near Tracy, where a group of armed men entered the conflict. These men belonged to the Posse Comitatus and were led by Francis Gillings, an angry, "wild-looking," forty-four-year-old, Tracy gas station proprietor who claimed the authority to make and enforce laws, stamp out crime and corruption, oppose the income tax (and indeed all taxes), protect "God-given and constitutional rights," and defend property owners from intimidation by union organizers.[26]

On the morning of September 1, 1975, Gillings and his posse attempted to prevent James Drake and several other UFW organizers from speaking with 145 tomato pickers on a farm east of Highway 99. Having just presented petitions for union representation elections at thirty-seven ranches throughout California, the UFW resolved to speak with the tomato pickers. *Stockton Record* photographer Rich Turner had just gone on duty and was monitoring communications on a police scanner when he learned of the confrontation. Arriving about 9:00 A.M., he found a half dozen deputies facing a group of men wearing polished chrome badges and brandishing clubs, handcuffs, and short-barreled shotguns. Turner feared someone was about to be shot.[27]

About forty-five minutes into the confrontation, Turner began making a series of dramatic photographs. Keeping his finger on the motor drive to his Nikon, he photographed San Joaquin County deputy sheriff Daniel Delfatti attempting to place Gillings under arrest, then documented Gillings calling for his men to back him. A moment after Gilling fired his shotgun, missing deputy Delfatti's ear by about an inch, Turner recorded deputies raising their own shotguns. One image caught a bloodied Gillings being thrown to the ground, handcuffed, arrested, and led out of the field. Another captured Deputy Delfatti aiming his shotgun at Gillings. Also present, *Stockton Record* photographer Dave Evans photographed deputies handcuffing Gilling's son, who had jumped into the fray when his father was being arrested, along with two other Posse Comitatus members. Later that day, these photographs ran on the front page of the *Stockton Record* and were transmitted by the Associated Press to newspapers throughout the state.[28]

No other California news photographers were able to equal Turner's and Evans's photography of the violent confrontation in the Stockton tomato fields. But getting such photographs during union representation elections over the next few weeks proved to be extremely difficult. Following the confrontation, on September 4 the U.S. district court judge M. D. Crocker issued a restraining order denying the UFW further access to farmworkers. "Crocker's ruling subverts our rights," argued UFW attorney Jerome Cohen. "We're not going to stay out of the fields. We've been doing it every day and we're going to continue." After the restraining order, the UFW pressed for immediate elections. One of the first took place on a cold morning late in September at Tri-Valley Produce, about five miles east of Tracy. Surrounded by tomato fields, the polling station consisted of a half dozen voting booths arranged behind a windbreak of trucks and portable toilets. To one side, a clump of lawyers and growers sipped coffee and eyed everyone. On the other side, I spoke with several UFW organizers and field hands.

Still a doctoral candidate at the University of Wisconsin, for which I was writing a dissertation on California farmworkers, I was back in my native California observing things firsthand and writing and photographing for several small weekly newspapers. While I took notes, labor board representatives busily anchored the voting booths so that they would not blow away. Meanwhile, Mexican workers sat on the furrows, slept in cars, milled about the catering truck, and gathered in a circle to shoot craps. Just after sunrise, the labor board representatives kicked out the growers, lawyers, organizers, and myself, the one photographer present. Following several hours of voting, they transported the ballots to Stockton, where they tallied votes at St. Mary's Catholic Church and announced the results at a 3 P.M. press conference. It was a victory for the UFW. Among union members, this inspired much shouting, singing, and guitar playing, all of which spilled outside the church onto the sidewalk. Growers and lawyers, however, promised appeals and challenges. On December 31, the ALRB certified the election at the tomato farm that had been disrupted by the Posse Comitatus and gave the UFW the right to begin collective bargaining. The ALRB also accused Western Tomato Growers and Shippers of threatening union organizers. Ernest Perry replied with a one-million-dollar lawsuit against the ALRB, calling the elections "a fraud and a sham" and alleging a conspiracy against his constitutional right of privacy.[29]

And so it went. Despite a spate of violent confrontations during September, few photographers other than Turner, Evans, and Plumb-Chambers were ever able to capture either the certification process or the union elections. About all that they could manage were a few bland photographs of workers entering and exiting voting booths. When the election process stalled and then broke down entirely under an avalanche of legal challenges, photographers tired of covering the struggle. News editors also found UFW marches to be old news and no longer accorded them as much space. Whereas a few years earlier, photographers had served as strong allies of Chávez and the farmworker movement, by the end of September 1975, this was no longer the case. Although many still admired Chávez and traveled to union headquarters at La Paz to help with *El Malcriado* and to photograph for the union, most press photographers and even long-time followers of the union began to take a more critical view or lost interest. Increasingly drawn to Indian rights, water policy, urban politics, and community self-help projects, George Ballis stopped photographing farmworkers after having amassed an archive of about thirty thousand images, probably the most extensive collection of farmworker photographs by a single photographer other than Dorothea Lange. Twenty-two years would pass before he again took up a camera to document the UFW.[30]

A similar change in attitude affected the work of *Modesto Bee* photographer Ted Benson. Long sympathetic to farmworkers, Benson had grown increasingly disenchanted with Chávez while photographing the UFW for several years. He later recalled:

> Those were very exhausting and interesting years to be photographing. The UFW hadn't quite turned into the new UAW, and as a sympathetic journalist, access was not as limited as it soon became. Then all of a sudden Chávez was surrounded by these bodyguards. Most of this freedom vanished after the march on Gallo. . . . I lost a lot of my own naive idealism in regard to crusading that fall when told by Chávez's bodyguards that it didn't matter how sympathetic I was—they were tired of having me in their face.[31]

Stockton Record photographer Dave Evans felt a similar transformation in his attitude. It began during the Gallo march and intensified while moving among farm labor camps during representation elections. "The numbers grew by maybe a factor of ten as we moved along the hot blacktop, two-lane road connecting the three camps on Matthews Road," Evans recalled. As Chávez spoke from the back of a small pickup truck and Evans shot over his shoulder with a 20-millimeter lens to show the number of people present, he noticed "some of the crowd started to melt away as though tired of the same old rhetoric." The reaction seemed indicative of "deep problems within all of the movement."[32]

As photojournalistic coverage of farmworkers waned, several art photographers moved into the fields. One was Bill Ravanesi. A Boston freelancer, Ravanesi had taken portraits of Angela Davis, Daniel and Philip Berrigan, and other social activists when they spoke at Harvard University and elsewhere in Cambridge, Massachusetts. After Ravanesi's work began appearing in alternative publications, *Boston Phoenix* political writer Flora Haas asked if he would be interested in shooting portraits of César Chávez to illustrate several articles she was planning to write about his visit to Boston in the fall of 1976. When Chávez arrived a week later to tour New England in support of the grape boycott, Ravanesi accompanied him for several days, photographing Chávez walking picket lines, participating in marches, and holding press conferences. "Looking back," Ravanesi recalled in a *Picture Magazine* essay several years later, "I can see that Chávez planted a seed within me. I decided to expand my commitment with the United Farmworkers, from documenting anti–Gallo Winery marches and picket lines in New England to planning a large-format documentary project about farm labor in California. I decided to set aside a hundred days per year to spend on location photographing this UFW project and I estimated that my commitment to farm labor would be five to six years."[33]

Knowing little about farm labor history, Ravanesi drove through the agricultural areas in 1976, photographing from an old truck outfitted with a platform like the one Harvey Richards had used to make many of his photographs. Spending time in Delano during the table-grape harvest, Ravanesi soon became fascinated by aged Filipino agricultural workers. They were single men without wives or children, and their time working in the fields was over. Most spent their days relaxing in the Agbayani Retirement Village, the UFW's Delano facility, which was a tribute to their role in the union and their contributions to California agriculture. Using a Deardorff view camera, Ravanesi made a series of black-and-white portraits of sixty- and seventy-year-old men relaxing in their small rooms, enjoying—perhaps for their first time in their lives—a stable community, support, and companionship.

One morning shortly after shifting his focus from Delano to the Salinas Valley, Ravanesi left a celery field and drove into Soledad looking for lunch. Cruising the back streets, he noticed a small home painted a radiant blue. The scene was so vivid that in order to do it justice, Ravanesi was compelled to reject the standard reliance on black-and-white film and shift to color. It was a hot day, in the midnineties, and all of the doors and windows of the home were closed. Ravanesi wondered if anyone was there? Parking his truck parallel to the sidewalk, he carried his view camera onto the rooftop platform and made one exposure on his old Deardorff. While he rechecked the composition, Ravanesi noticed one of the window curtains being pushed aside. Putting down his dark cloth, he knocked at the front door, hoping to put the occupants at ease. Five minutes later, the door opened. Ravanesi recalled:

> With minimal Spanish and a set of Polaroid prints of campesinos harvesting lettuce, I seemed to make Rafael López feel a little more at ease. Interestingly enough, he was drawn to the wooden view camera. He mentioned that when he was much younger and living in Mexico, his parents had sat him in front of a wooden camera for a family portrait. Rafael's wonder was satisfied as he looked through the viewfinder: "Just like color TV, only upside down!" The next moment the López family filed through the front door, and the setting felt so complete! Rafael López and his brothers are irrigators in King City. Ten people, all close relatives, resided within a one-room house. For the past 25 years the Lópezes have migrated throughout the valleys cutting "salads." Now they are staff irrigators (less stooping) for an independent grower, and they generally work about seven months a year in the Salinas Valley.[34]

Like his predecessors, however, Ravanesi could not sustain his effort. Returning to Boston, he became a curator and photographer with the Boston University School of Public Health. While he continued to pursue documentary projects, including a large essay on asbestos exposure, his work kept him rooted in the Northeast, so he was unable to expand his ambitious farm labor project in California.

At about this time, one of the most celebrated portraits of Chávez was taken. Fifty-three-year-old Richard Avedon had built his reputation in the fashion world before expanding his portfolio to include many icons of American culture, including President Dwight Eisenhower, musician Frank Zappa, civil rights leaders, and African Americans born in slavery. His portraits, usually posed against a seamless white background without dramatic lighting, were often described as cruel, confrontational, lacking sympathy, and revealing every blemish, scar, and pimple. A kind of ringmaster of spectacle and a traveler between the upper crust and the dispossessed, Avedon himself was at a loss for words when trying to explain exactly what his portraits were about, except to say that he was not taking sides, did not want to slant his work one way or another, did not know where his talent and fascination came from, and strove above all to "keep it alive, keep it crucial." Always scared about making portraits on the run, pulling out of himself and his subjects something of interest, his work, he told interviewers, involved little more than paying "intense attention" in the hope of encouraging something to emerge. Observers such as Sandra Phillips, curator of photography for the San Francisco Museum of Modern Art, have been less vague in praising the way Avedon approached people "with some kind of psychological insight," which, for example, transformed Dwight D. Eisenhower, hero of World War II, into a kind of infantile old man. Looking at Avedon's portraits, Black Star photo agency founder and president Howard Chapnick thought, "It seems as if the camera lens becomes a scalpel that goes inside the individual and peels away every layer of artificiality."[35]

All of these elements came together while photographing Chávez on assignment for *Rolling Stone* magazine in 1976. Compiling a series called The Family, Avedon had been making essentially the same straightforward portrait of various celebrities, musicians, politicians, and comedians. Now he would do the same with Chávez. Arriving at UFW headquarters on June 27, Avedon's assistants unloaded such a huge amount of equipment that one UFW member recalled the whole session as causing "quite a commotion," with union members peeking out windows and strolling by to glimpse the famous photographer. When Chávez emerged from his quarters, dressed in an army fatigue shirt, Avedon positioned him in the open shade beside a union building, with white seamless paper behind him, and made a portrait that has been variously described as a "serenely noble," a revolutionary juxtaposition, a unique merger of fashion and the political struggle, a bold challenge to our heroic self-images, and nothing more than the same photograph Avedon had been taking while tracking down his subjects for decades. Praising the way Avedon's straightforward depiction confounds romantic notions that distort reality, some critics have claimed that the portrait forces viewers to wrestle with questions of power and complicity. There is no evidence that Avedon, after publishing his portrait of Chávez in *Rolling Stone* magazine, ever donated a print to the UFW or used the image for anything other than rounding out his portfolio of the rich and famous—or poor and struggling—a portfolio that critic Susan Sontag labeled little more than "class tourism."[36]

In October 1976, the union itself began using photographs to advance a statewide initiative. Known as Proposition 14, the initiative proposed to guarantee permanent funding for the Agricultural Labor Relations Act by merging it into the state constitution, thereby removing the law from the realm of partisan politics. As a key part of its "Yes on 14" campaign, the UFW used a photograph reportedly of a child harvesting onions in 108-degree July heat on the Garin ranch, near Mettler, in Kern County. Although Proposition 14 did not contain any language concerning child labor, the UFW contended that, by preserving the farm labor law, the proposition would ensure wages high enough so that families would not have to supplement their income with money earned by children.

Printed on large posters reading, "Stop Child Labor—Yes on Proposition 14," and also published in *El Malcriado,* the photograph immediately caused a sensation. Posted on telephone and power poles and walls all over the state, the image was further amplified by newspaper photographs of UFW supporters using "human billboard" tactics to display it to passing motorists at busy intersections. Incensed by the photograph, the Garin Company immediately sued the union for libel. Asserting that it did not use child labor, did not farm land at Mettler, did not harvest onions in July 1976, and had no relationship with the contractor named on the poster, Garin claimed general damages of five hundred thousand dollars and punitive damages of one million. Furthermore, the company produced weather service data showing that the temperature never went above eighty-five degrees on the day in question and that the alleged pesticide container shown in the photograph was in fact a discarded adhesive container. On the basis of this information, Kern County Superior Court judge John Benson issued an injunction banning the UFW from using the posters and also ordering that Garin's name be blocked from all posters already on public display.[37]

As election time neared, the union refused to give up. Denouncing Judge Benson's decision as censorship that placed more credence in the oral arguments made by Garin's attorneys than on the sworn statements of twenty adults and children who claimed to have worked in the Garin onion field that day, UFW attorneys also claimed that Garin trucks and tractors were in the onion field and that the company's "no trespassing" signs were evident throughout the area. "Garin is lying, like they always do," Chávez claimed at a San Francisco press conference where he presented three dozen children. "This is an attempt to harass us and confuse the voters," he added, introducing Leticia Galvan of Lamont, the eleven-year-old girl depicted in the poster. To the assembled reporters, Leticia said her entire family, including her younger sister, worked in the fields during summers and sometimes on weekends during the school year. She said her father was credited with the onions she picked. According to her testimony, the Proposition 14 photograph was entirely accurate.[38]

On the basis of this information, the California Supreme Court suspended Judge Benson's ruling and gave the UFW a temporary green light to continue using the allegedly libelous photograph in its Proposition 14 campaign. But the reprieve made little difference. Despite calling in all of its political favors and securing the support of President Jimmy Carter and various Hollywood celebrities, the union's campaign failed dismally in the face of a two-million-dollar opposition mounted by growers and their allies.

Following defeat of Proposition 14, tensions again mounted in the fields, and photographers attempting to cover the UFW routinely found themselves in the middle of pitched battles. Even experienced photographers, such as *Stockton Record* chief photographer Rich Turner, were surprised by the violence. After photographing a tomato strike near Tracy in September 1976, Turner recalled:

> As I arrived on the scene it was evident to me that a confrontation was imminent. The deputies held their ground while the strikers yelled obscenities. The tension was increasing. Then it happened—someone in the crowd yelled something in Spanish and the charge was on. As forty or fifty strikers tried to trespass, the others were busy throwing tomatoes at the deputies. I was standing in the middle of all this, ducking

> tomatoes and dodging strikers who were running in all directions. . . . I did not feel that I was in any particular danger, although I wasn't very happy to be there. In fact, I would not have been there if it were not for my "badge of courage," the camera.[39]

Soon growers stopped complying with the farm labor law. Employing delaying tactics, they pushed aside election results for years, in some cases for decades. Other than dull pictures of ballot boxes, photographers found little to record. Although the UFW continued to win elections and had a clear path, with little or no opposition after the Teamsters withdrew from the fields in the spring of 1977, the declining fortunes of the UFW continued to alienate photographers, who might have otherwise covered union activity. With the UFW in shambles, staff members disagreed over everything from organizing tactics to Chávez's drift toward autocratic control. Many long-time organizers quit or were laid off, including nearly all of the UFW's highly experienced attorneys and most of the volunteer photographers who had followed the union religiously for years. Sympathetic news photographers left as well, bringing coverage of the union to a standstill. For nearly two years, only one photographer remained engaged with farmworkers, more or less full time. That photographer was a University of California, Santa Cruz, photography instructor.[40]

Pam Harris was accustomed to working in a difficult if not adverse environment while documenting community life, having already photographed a book on the Canadian Arctic Indians around Spence Bay, Newfoundland (*Another Way of Being*). But what she encountered in the Pajaro Valley when she began her project on March 1, 1977, severely tested both her artistry and her stamina. Located between the Santa Cruz Mountains and Monterey Bay, the broad valley attracted her attention because it was home to thousands of Mexican field hands who packed into dozens of labor camps and the Watsonville barrio. Photographing first in the Watsonville UFW office, Harris documented union activities and quickly gained the trust of local organizers by placing her images in the union hall for all to see. As she got to know people, Harris began taking portraits of migrants arriving from Mexico to "work the season" while living in homes that she later recalled variously as "shacklike . . . cold in the winter, hot in the summer" and "tiny—the size of a small motel room." At the West Foods Mushroom Company, Harris documented contract-signing ceremonies in a "dirty, dreary, windowless room" and, following the ceremonies, stole a few photographs of the workers and their surroundings, even though company officials refused to allow her to photograph. Slowly expanding her coverage, Harris turned her camera on broccoli harvesting, which seemed "truly like a factory in the fields." In the strawberry fields, Harris found entire families working together, the women seeming very young and shy. Continuing to follow union organizers, she also documented UFW ranch committees, various union meetings, and secret ballot elections to select delegates to the annual union convention, all the time interviewing workers in the style of Dorothea Lange.[41]

During her two years in the fields, Harris never saw another photographer. It seemed to her that farmworkers had been entirely forgotten. And then, as had happened so often in the past, photographic coverage resumed in earnest. After union contracts with lettuce growers expired in January 1979, negotiations broke down and farmworkers walked out of the fields in the Imperial Valley. On February 10, near Holtville, about twenty miles north of Mexicali, twenty-eight-year-old Rufino Contreras and a group of UFW members stormed toward three crews of strikebreakers in a muddy Mario Saikhon Corporation lettuce field. During the confrontation, a frightened strikebreaker pulled a gun and shot Contreras just below the right eye. Contreras fell face down, his body sprawled across three rows, his blood draining into the lettuce. He was the fourth UFW member murdered since the inception of the union. His death brought the total number of farmworkers killed in California agricultural labor disputes to more than a dozen.[42]

No photographer was present when Contreras was shot. Other than the forensic photographs made by Imperial Valley sheriff's deputies, no images document what happened that awful day. One week later, when farm operations completely shut down for the February 14 service, photographers swarmed into the valley. Documenting the early-morning Mass held on the UFW's ever-present flatbed truck, they fanned out over El Hoyo (literally, "the Hole"), a dusty, windswept parking lot for labor buses on the outskirts of Calexico, a hundred yards north of the California–Mexico border, where farmers picked up their workers in the predawn darkness. Focusing on Chávez as he eulogized Contreras, photographers could not miss the giant red and yellow painting of Rufino's face that was stretched over a canvas backdrop above the speaker's podium. Every photographer incorporated that gigantic, sad, unforgettable, and haunting image in his or her composition.[43]

With more than eight thousand farmworkers, strikers, and union supporters weeping and waving black UFW flags and walking four abreast behind the casket, photographers remained busy selecting images and finding shots as the procession moved north along the highway, through the streets of Calexico, and out to Mountain View Cemetery. While they worked, photographers clustered around Chávez, Governor Jerry Brown, Rufino's widow, and countless other dignitaries. After doing a portrait of Rosa Contreras with a large poster of her murdered husband, *Washington Post* contract photographer John T. Barr remained a respectful distance from the funeral and used a telephoto lens to capture the ceremony. Overhead several photographers from the *Los Angeles Times* shot aerial pictures. Published in every newspaper in California, images of the service captured another media event designed both to honor a man and to rally the UFW. One grower labeled it an "emotional circus."[44]

Arriving in Calexico a few days later, *National Geographic* photographer Stephanie Maze noticed crowds gathering in El Hoyo. On assignment shooting for the story "The Mexican Americans," Maze headed over to survey the scene. Shocked and saddened by the murder of Rufino Contreras and resolved to carry on the struggle, several hundred farmworkers had gathered to express their grief. Many held lit candles. While they stood for several minutes in quiet respect, César Chávez joined them. Saddened by the gathering, Maze moved to the front of the crowd and made a simple picture just as Chávez began delivering his eulogy. Soon published in the magazine, the image depicted hundreds of farmworkers illuminated only by the flickering flames of the small candles they held. "Solidarity spoke with silence," explained staff writer Griffin Smith Jr. "Along narrow roads that slice between farms . . . crowds lofted the red flags of the union—while others worked easily in the fields."[45]

Spontaneous and unscripted, such vigils were not photo ops designed for the camera but rather genuine outpourings of passionate resolve and deep despair. And they did not go unnoticed by the UFW leadership. But as picketing increased over the next week, a grassroots anger took hold of the strikers. Many vowed revenge. Returning home, photojournalists missed most of the violent incidents and confrontations over the next few days. But not Maggio personnel. Anticipating the worst and realizing the importance of photographic evidence, Maggio assigned ranch manager David Wells the task of photographing any incidents. On January 15 Wells purchased about sixteen hundred dollars worth of photographic equipment and prepared to document picketing and other activities.[46]

When massive rioting broke out on Wednesday, February 21, only one press photographer was on hand to record what happened. Paul J. Noden, a veteran photographer who had worked for the *Imperial Valley Press* in El Centro since the early 1970s, was listening to the police scanner when he heard a deputy call for help. UFW pickets were massing outside a carrot field operated by Maggio, several miles southeast of Holtville, and several police agencies were responding. One of the oldest and largest Imperial Valley growers, Maggio had been a prime target for farmworker unions since the 1930s. Noden sensed that a dramatic confrontation was shaping up. He grabbed his camera bag and a 50–300-millimeter Nikon zoom lens and sped to the scene. In a separate car was staff writer Don Quinn, also carrying a camera.[47]

As Noden drove east, the confrontation escalated. Converging from three sides of the field, pickets requested access to Maggio's replacement crew of housewives and college students. When Imperial County sheriff's lieutenant Ted Whitmere refused entry, the pickets grew agitated. At about 9:30 A.M., they started throwing rocks. Suddenly, a group of one hundred strikers charged a line of deputies and attempted to enter the field through a recently plowed adjoining field. A second group of eighty to one hundred pickets also tried to enter by crossing a drainage canal parallel to Miller Road. As deputies cut them off, pitched battles erupted. By the time Noden arrived, a full-scale riot was in progress.

Standing on the roof of a sheriff's vehicle to gain a better vantage point and using his telephoto lens to reach into the field, Noden recorded scenes of utter chaos and violence. On Thursday, his photographs of the Chell and Miller Road riot filled two full pages of the *Imperial Valley Press* and *Brawley News* and were carried by the Associated Press to newspapers throughout the state. For the union, the images were a disaster. Despite Chávez's commitment to nonviolence, Noden's lens caught undeniable evidence that UFW members and supporters had broken ranks and attacked strikebreakers, engaged in massive violence, and destroyed property. One of his photographs caught a person throwing a tear gas canister back at law enforcement personnel; the picket got prison time.[48]

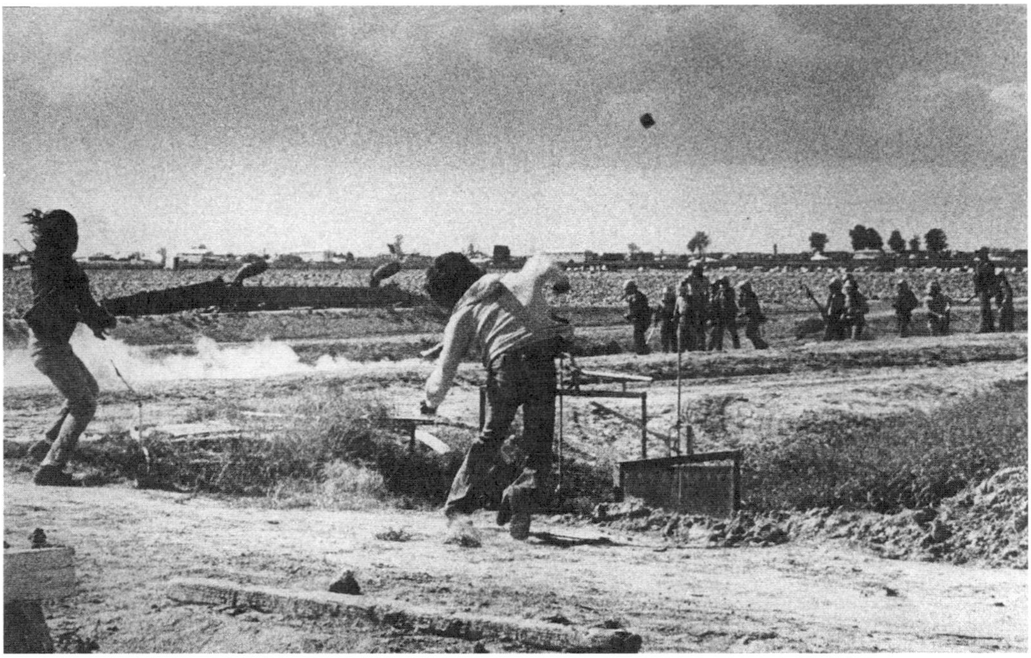

Farmworker hurls a tear gas cannister back at Imperial County deputies during a riot that erupted near El Centro when twelve hundred pickets stormed a field to drive out replacement workers, February 20, 1979, photograph by Paul J. Noden/*Imperial Valley Press.* Courtesy of Paul J. Noden.

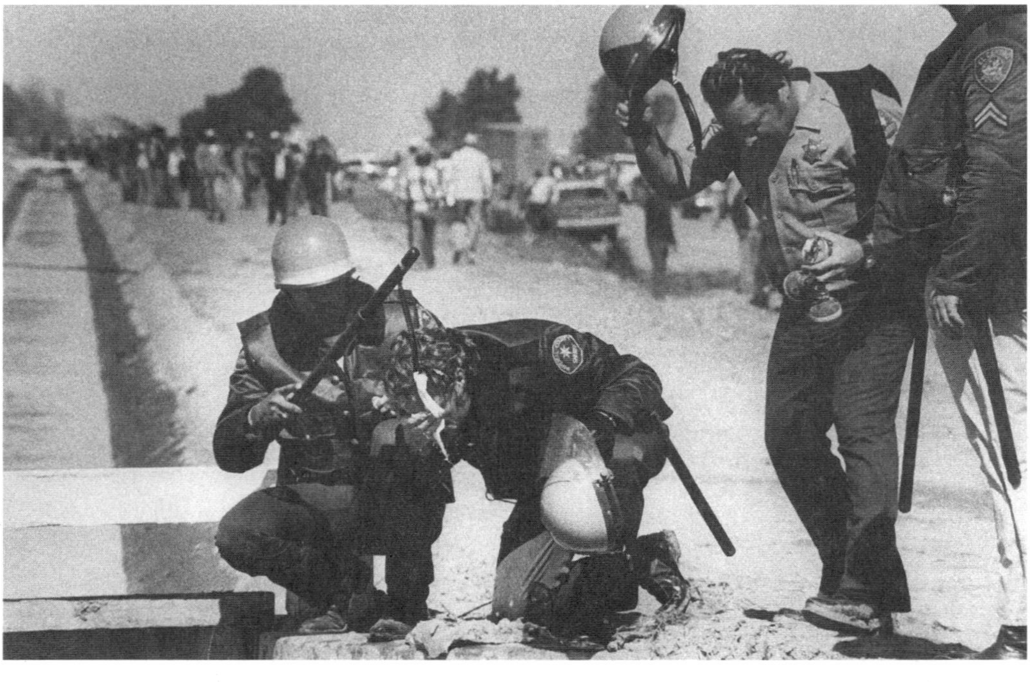

Imperial County deputy sheriffs wash their eyes after being overcome by tear gas blowing back into their faces, February 20, 1979, photograph by Paul J. Noden/*Imperial Valley Press.* Courtesy of Paul J. Noden.

Although Chávez would later call the matter a "police riot," Noden's pictures presented an entirely different and an uncomplimentary picture. With injured sheriff's deputies bathing their eyes in canal water after being blinded by clouds of tear gas and UFW members caught throwing tear gas canisters and holding clubs, it was hard to be sympathetic to the union. Chávez would always be upset by the violence and by images of some of the union's strike leaders behaving as they did. To close friends, he expressed his fear that more than a half century of sympathetic photographic documentation seemed about to unravel.[49]

What happened over the next few months was essentially a rerun of the Imperial Valley episode, except no farmworkers died. As the strike moved east to Blythe and Yuma, then north to Oxnard, Huron, and into the Salinas Valley, press photographers in local newspapers continued to record scenes of confrontation, property damage, personal attacks on farm labor contractors, and vandalism against labor camps housing nonunion workers. After photographers captured images of several fights involving pickets, strikebreakers, and police along a hundred-mile stretch of Highway 101, the *San Francisco Chronicle,* shocked by the images it was publishing, wrote an editorial that the strike had become a "spreading stain that disfigures the important California business that is agriculture."[50]

Commercial agriculture quickly cashed in on this and many similar statements. In dozens of major newspapers including the *New York Times* and the *Washington Post,* growers' public relations agents published full-page advertisements calling for an end to the violence, the strike, and the militancy. Several advertisements advocated intervention by the National Guard, and their public relations firms called for several amendments castrating the Agricultural Labor Relations Board. By late July, many so-called labor experts were writing the UFW off as a lost cause and asking whether the union could survive. So were photographers. They should have known better.[51]

22

Photographing the Human Condition

Undocumented Workers, Pesticides, and Farmworker Communities

Fifteen years of struggle had taught César Chávez plenty of lessons, none more important than the power of photography and the role that imagery had played in advancing the UFW's cause. These lessons had guided his thinking since the beginning of the lettuce strike, when he had started threatening a boycott against Sun Harvest, one of the largest lettuce growers in California. Sun Harvest was extremely vulnerable through its parent company, United Brands, which marketed Chiquita bananas, John Morrell meats, and A&W Root Beer. In early August, Chávez settled on his plan: keep talking strike, engage in sporadic work slowdowns and picketing, develop a general boycott of nonunion lettuce, and hit Sun Harvest hard by pushing a boycott of Chiquita bananas. His problem was that the boycott was a slow, difficult tactic. It required massive publicity, a shift of manpower away from the strike, and deployment of hundreds of UFW members throughout the United States. Chávez needed some dramatic imagery to set the boycott in motion. As he had done so often in the past, he quickly devised a strategy to generate useful images, capture the public's attention, help the UFW regain the initiative, and, most important, launch the boycott.

To convey the right picture, Chávez announced the March on Salinas, actually made up of two segments, one beginning in San Francisco and heading 150 miles south to Salinas, the second starting seventy miles south of Salinas at San Lucas and moving north. The plan was to begin each segment of the march on July 31 and converge three weeks later in Salinas for a huge parade, mass rally, and the UFW's fourth biennial convention, which the union had moved from the Fresno Convention Center to the Hartnell College gymnasium in Salinas because of what it called "an emergency situation." All along the way marchers would visit barrios, *colonias,* labor camps, and Mexican communities, and they would be joined by thousands of urban supporters, church groups, and local trade unionists. In this way, the UFW reasoned, more pressure could be exerted on the growers, the violence defused, and the strike snatched from the jaws of defeat. Not incidental to these goals, countless images of fifteen thousand farmworkers marching for justice would also be generated and circulated in the press.[1]

The plan worked. Photographers swarmed into the valley. Local and national press photographers periodically appeared, made their shots, and disappeared on deadline. Freelancers hung around. They seemed to be everywhere and of all levels of competence, including several barely able to load film into their cameras correctly, apparently on their first self-assignment. Hooking up with Karen Barrell, a Los Angeles graphic artist out of work when her union struck Disney Studios, I saved money by driving with her out to a deserted road near the Salinas River, where we parked our cars rear end to rear end, popped the hatchbacks, threw a tarp over the opening, and camped out to save money on motel rooms. Each morning we were up long before sunrise and headed to Sambos restaurant to freshen up in the restroom and share an omelet and coffee, our only meal of the day. With this regimen we were able to purchase and shoot all of the Kodachrome we wanted. Apparently we were not alone in our poverty and grungy, photographic fanaticism.[2]

To cover the event, we met the marchers each morning as they shaped up along the route. Playing auto leap frog, one of us would drive ahead and pick up the other when the marchers paused for lunch at mile five or six. Often the marchers wound

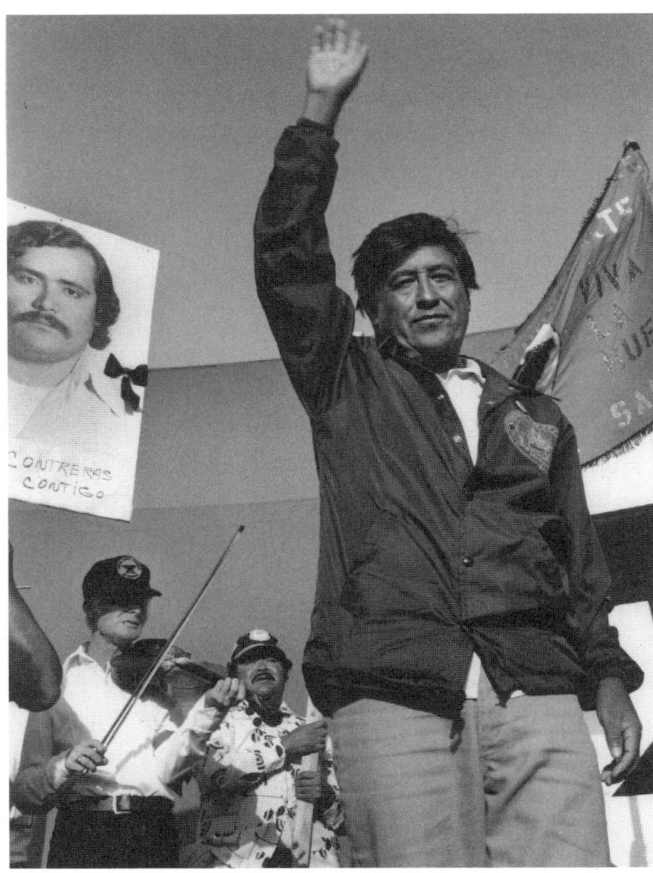

César Chávez at the March on Salinas, August 7, 1979, photograph by Pam Harris. Poster in back left is a photograph of Rufino Contreras. Courtesy of Pam Harris.

through small towns, and we made dramatic shots of families and townspeople standing on sidewalks with American and Mexican flags, cheering the marchers on with shouts and applause or listening to Chávez speak to crowds in parks. But not all the spectators were happy to see the marchers. Passing by some greenhouses, we saw angry-looking foremen guarding entrances and armed with wooden grape stakes. At Greenfields on August 16, I took my first photograph of Chávez. He was on a bandstand, surrounded by farmworkers, gaunt and haggard from his fast, but still looking young and energetic.

Of our days on the march, the one Barrell and I most vividly recall is the morning of August 18. Attracted by hundreds of multicolored banners backlit in the early morning light, we went to work alongside Pam Harris, who had been following the march with us. In a large vacant lot near the lettuce coolers in Salinas, we joined thousands of farmworkers milling about before marching through town. Seventy-three-year-old Amparita Vásquez, a striking Sun Harvest employee who had led the march into Salinas, immediately captured our attention, along with Chávez's mother, Juana. Surrounded by hundreds of red, yellow, and green banners aglow in the soft light, they were such a vivid sight that it was impossible not to produce pictures that were saturated with color and pathos. Later that morning, when the marchers moved out and headed into town, I watched Reesa Tansey and *Salinas Californian* staff photographer Richard Green bounce in and out of the line of marchers, snapping pictures of children. Somewhere back in the march, Barrell was at work, hidden from sight in the sea of signs, flags, placards, and people.

The reason I lost track of my partner was that I was watching twenty-year-old UFW member Elena Solis. Leading the parade, she carried the American flag. Besides her cover girl beauty, what so captivated my attention was her alluring and symbolic attire: she wore a red Growers Exchange cap, a red bandana tied about her face in the way that women do to protect themselves from the sun, and a red turtleneck jersey. Remembering what Ansel Adams had said about color photography ("If you can't make it good, make it red"), I thought Elena Solis was both good and red, and I determined to photograph her. But I did not want to steal a photograph or poke my camera in her face as she walked. During a lull in the march, I approached her, explained what I wanted to do, and made a date to meet her. That night, after I was interrogated by her *abuela* over a dinner of liver tacos with her family in their small Main Street home, her *abuela* permitted me to photograph Elena. The next morning we met before sunrise. After photographing Elena in the open shade, we moved into the fields to complete the session. I have always found the photographs I made during our session to be complex in the way Elena's beauty and the genius of her color scheme transformed common field garb into a fashion statement with highly charged political overtones. I have forever been grateful for the opportunity to have met Elena and her family. It was the last time I ever had liver tacos but the first of many memorable meals shared with farmworkers in austere circumstances.[3]

My efforts and those of Karen Barrell, Lois Nelson, Pam Harris, Richard Green, and others were dwarfed by the exertions of *Salinas Californian* photographer Clay Peterson.

A veteran press photographer who had been covering the Salinas Valley for a decade, Peterson was no stranger to the UFW or agricultural issues. Well versed in his profession, he knew all of the tricks and angles. Determined to get the best picture of all, Peterson knew that the main obstacle to presenting the march was the flat landscape. Like so many photographers before him, he created an elevated perspective. While the rest of us scrambled to the top of highway overpasses to capture the long line of marchers passing underneath, Peterson photographed from a fifteen-foot-high ladder he carried on the roof of his car. Driving to the head of the march and to various points along the way, he unloaded it, set it up, climbed to the top, and exploited the elevated perspective to produce images capturing the widespread support and exciting nature of the mile-long procession as it snaked forward through the cooling plants and fields on the edge of town. Sending his photographs out with the Associated Press, Peterson dominated coverage, even though the march swarmed with photographers.[4]

Along with the work of dozens of other press photographers and freelancers, Peterson's images conveyed yet another media event in which the aspirations of the state's farmworkers built to a dramatic, highly visual crescendo. Exerting the desired effect, these pictures of determined marchers helped Chávez tighten his boycott of Sun Harvest. In response, the growers' united front began to collapse. During a rally at the end of the march, farmworkers employed at Meyer Tomato obtained a contract; a few days later, a contingent of UFW members struck at West Coast farms in Watsonville, and the company signed a contract. By December, the UFW had won contracts with all but a dozen of the most resolute lettuce growers. After fifteen years of struggle, the union suddenly seemed to have made the transition from a movement to a functioning labor union. Membership surpassed one hundred thousand, and unionized lettuce workers were receiving the highest wages of any farmworkers in the country. With new contracts and piece-rate payment, some hard-working lettuce harvesters were earning up to twenty dollars an hour during peak harvest. With benefits including paid vacations and medical coverage, farmworkers for the first time worked under conditions approaching those of employees in nonfarm industries.

Seeing what photographs of the March on Salinas had done to Sun Harvest and other lettuce operations, growers suddenly understood how photography had worked against them and grew even more suspicious of photographers. With the explosive growth of the UFW and farmworker elections becoming a fact of life in the fields, many growers refused to allow anyone with a camera anywhere near their fields. Unwary writers researching topics such as water and land policy soon experienced the consequences of these growers' fears. Taking photographs for his book *A River No More: The Colorado River and the West,* writer Philip L. Fradkin, who was a former *Los Angeles Times* staff writer and editor of *Audubon Magazine* and had shared a Pulitzer Prize for his coverage of the Watts riots eleven years earlier, was kicked out of an Imperial Valley lettuce field by two foremen who believed Fradkin was a UFW organizer.[5]

A year after the march, Pam Harris ran into similar problems while documenting a garlic harvesters' strike in Gilroy. During one picket line incident, she was surrounded by strikers who prevented her from photographing. At the same time a Japanese farmer's son openly violated a provision of the Agricultural Labor Relations Act by using a large movie camera to identify strike leaders and harass them. Harris ran into more problems when she began organizing her work for publication. Struggling with her presentation, she resisted the tendency to turn her project into a sociological tract. Ideally, she wanted to publish just the images and interviews, with perhaps a long "prose poem" that would "flow with the photos." Contacting a dozen writers, she was encouraged by *Salinas Californian* reporter Doug Foster to form the images into a book about creating a home out of what once had been a stop on the migrant loop and how this creation had changed the area and the people. California writer James Houston suggested the theme of survival rather than victimization. Beacon Press editor Marie Cantlon suggested a new approach centered on the issue of "how food is grown" or "the human dimension of food growing" or some other "fresh focus." Harris herself saw the photographs as the avant-garde of an agrarian revolution coming just in time, "as farming gives over to industry and conglomerates swallow control of food." She also thought about Ernesto Galarza, whose book *Barrio Boy* came closest to the kind of writing she wanted to accompany her images. In one book proposal, she wrote:

> From the friends and strangers pictured here, I received this gift and a great deal more—help, encouragement, good conversation, delicious food, a sense of connection. What most impressed me in the time I have spent getting to know and photographing this community is the strength, the vitality, and the kindness of the people I worked with. For me, it has been a great pleasure to photograph the farmworking community of Watsonville. These union families have been endlessly generous of themselves and what is shown here is part of a joint effort. I see these pictures as something we have done together, and it is my hope that the full documentation will eventually be published.[6]

After many publishers expressed initial interest on her project, they all declined to go forward. Most said that there was no longer any interest in farmworkers or that her proposal lacked a hook and needed a greater sense of drama and conflict. To reach at least a limited audience, Harris attempted to exhibit her work. After the Sesnon Art Gallery, at the University of California, Santa Cruz, politely rejected her proposal, the Monterey Peninsula Museum of Art offered her a venue. But when Harris sent a sample set of prints, she ran into trouble. Besides images of farm labor in Chualar, Watsonville, and Salinas, Harris included a unique portfolio of spontaneous portraits centered on César Chávez, Dolores Huerta, and Governor Jerry Brown during the March on Salinas, as well as picket line photographs from the lettuce strike and the Gilroy garlic strike. Reviewing her portfolio, museum curator Rick Deragon and museum director Thomas J. Logan expressed their concern that conservative museum board members would not accept her politically charged images, which Logan characterized as "too hot to handle." Fearing a backlash, he cut out thirty-four of the fifty-three original prints to achieve a "non-political display" of "quiet . . . imagery" with "no UFW flags . . . necessary."[7]

With her original layout eviscerated and a deadline for submitting final prints and for laying out her exhibition, Harris faced a dilemma: cancel her exhibition or cave in and edit out all controversial images. She chose the latter but did slip in one oblique reference to the strike: a photograph of an impromptu altar to the Virgin of Guadalupe on the strike line at a mushroom factory. "Knowing that the farmworkers in Watsonville would have no confidence in going to Monterey, where probably none had been before, though it was just an hour away, we organized a car caravan, meeting at the office in Watsonville and driving over," Harris recalled a quarter century later. "The Museum had laid out food and drink, as it was also the Cinco de Mayo weekend, and this was a celebration. It was a wonderful event, which people enjoyed immensely." Although grateful that the museum showed her work, Harris would always have her regrets. "I have never had a chance to put together the whole show, to give it an accurate shape," she lamented in a memo on her project many years later. "There was a lot of idealism involved."[8]

Along with grower hostility, museum censorship, and corporate timidity, documentary photographers were having other completely unanticipated problems. Suddenly UFW organizers inexplicably became more cautious about allowing photographic access, particularly when pictures did not serve their purposes. This became clear during an ALRB representation election involving seven hundred workers at the Z. B. Zaninovich grape ranch, near Delano, on August 29, 1980. A year earlier, elections at the neighboring M. Caratan ranch were disrupted when some workers attacked ALRB supervisors and stole the ballot box. Attracted as usual to any hint of violence or action, still photographers and television crews from Bakersfield appeared at the Zaninovich ranch just as balloting began. Infuriated by the filming, UFW organizers claimed that the presence of cameras amounted to illegal surveillance and could affect the voting. On these grounds, they demanded that ALRB representatives postpone the election. But ulterior motives were involved. Apparently, the union did not want photographers covering an election that the UFW might lose to the International Union of Agricultural Workers, an independent, grower-backed union with contracts in the Santa Maria area. Although Zaninovich attorneys pressed for the election to go forward, asserting that nothing in the law prohibited the media from entering a polling place, union organizers prevailed on ALRB representatives to confiscate more than 450 ballots and take the matter under consideration.[9]

After the Zaninovich episode, the ALRB allowed photographers to cover farmworker elections from a reasonable distance outside the polling places. But few took advantage of the access. With farmworkers voting overwhelmingly for the UFW, photographers quickly lost interest in what seemed to be a predictable, dull, and undramatic routine. Unable to find in elections the blood and confrontations, arrests and handcuffs, flags, police presence, mass marches, and prominent personalities that so easily suggested people uniting in a common cause, journalistic photographers continued to drop away from the union. Filling the void, a new group of photographers stepped forward. Heirs to the tradition established by Dorothea Lange and other FSA photographers, they conducted their own independent projects. Largely self-financed and extending over several years, these highly emotionally charged projects shifted attention away from organizing and broadened and deepened the picture of California farmworkers at a time when they might well have been forgotten.

Of the photographers working in the early 1980s, none was more daring and original or exerted a greater impact than Roger Minick. Building on his experience of photographing for his collaborative book *Delta West* in the 1960s, Minick returned to the fields as a photographer for the Mexican American Legal Defense and Education Fund (MALDEF) Photo Survey. An increasingly large number of undocumented Mexican immigrants had opted to avoid the dangerous and difficult trek past the immigration stations at San Clemente and Temecula and simply settled in San Diego County, where they found work on the area's strawberry and tomato farms. To shoot his essay, Minick talked a tomato grower into allowing him to enter the grower's property and concentrate on a single group of men living in the ravines and gullies of north San Diego County. Gaining the trust of such people was more important than camera technique. Minick was able to overcome their fears and reticence with a

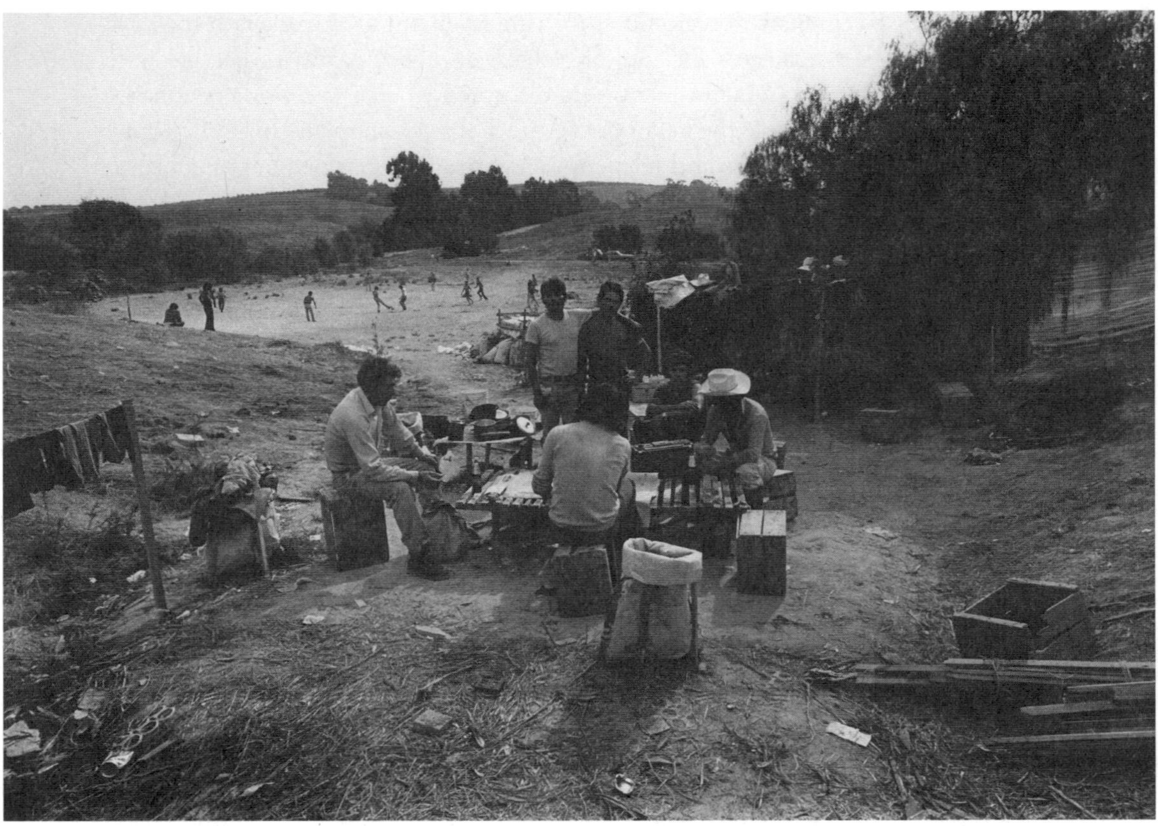

Undocumented farmworkers enjoying Sunday afternoon in a camp near the tomato fields of north San Diego County, June 1978, photograph by Roger Minick. Courtesy of Roger Minick.

strategy commonly used by photographers: shooting pictures with a Polaroid camera. "They had many uses for the Polaroids," Minick later recalled. "They'd use them for identification documents, but mostly they would fold them in half, slip them into a back pocket, and send them home with the next letter as proof that they were well."[10]

After a few days of shooting Polaroids, Minick turned his attention to their daily routine. Following the men into the fields, he documented lunch breaks, the nature of their work, evening recreational activities on improvised soccer fields, and Saturday evening baths in tubs fashioned from fruit bins and plastic sheeting. Paying close attention to their living conditions, Minick shot portraits of the men living in shacks constructed of packing pallets and sometimes in holes in the ground. Underscoring their poverty and determination, as well as their industriousness and sense of community and common purpose, the essay was one of the first to detail the secret lives of undocumented farmworkers. But it would not be the last. Minick had started something. People who had heretofore been overlooked now stepped forward. Shortly after Minick concluded his essay, another photographer began a project that vastly expanded the visual understanding of undocumented workers.[11]

That photographer was a unique figure in the annals of photographers working in the fields, the most compelling person to document farmworkers in the last two decades of the century. Editors did not always understand Len Lahman, but they could not dismiss his work. They admitted a respect for what he did, even when he did it by turning his back on them and one of the most respected news organizations in California. Lahman started out normally enough. A University of Missouri School of Journalism graduate who had worked at various newspapers before landing a job at the *Los Angeles Times,* he had become interested in farmworkers while covering the Imperial Valley lettuce strike. After the strike ended, he began following up rumors of a huge community of undocumented farmworkers somewhere near Del Mar, in north San Diego County. Searching for one of the largest groups of these workers during the fall of 1979, Lahman discovered them nestled in McGoingle Canyon, about three miles east of Interstate 5. Scattered along an intermittent creek that provided both drinking and wash water, their camp housed more than one hundred men, who shaped-up every morning to work in the surrounding tomato fields and nurseries.

Fascinated by their story and believing his photographs would help dispel preconceived notions about immigrant farmworkers, Lahman returned to the canyon many times to photograph. But when his images were published in a story on the camp, they caused disaster for the men. Seeing his images, television news crews aired a report, which was in turn picked up by the networks. After a raid by the Border Patrol, the San Diego County Health Department condemned the camp, and the county's largest truck farmers, Ukegawa Brothers, who leased the canyon along with five hundred acres of surrounding tomato fields, bulldozed it. All that remained on July 23, 1980, when Lahman photographed California lieutenant governor Mike Curb strolling over the area, were a few broken bottles and some crushed pieces of lean-to.[12]

Lahman accepted responsibility for the fiasco. He resolved to "set things right" by throwing himself into the task of understanding the people who had lived in the canyons. He had been pursuing his project for several months when a deadline-conscious editor complained that Lahman had been at the project too long and suggested he get back to work. "He had latched on to something, and he wasn't going to give up before he had done it justice," said one writer with whom he had collaborated. Lahman quit the *Times,* made the transition from photojournalism to documentary photography, and embarked on a project chronicling the sacrifices and fortitude of undocumented farmworkers on both sides of the border. To execute his project properly, Lahman traveled deep into Mexico and became an active participant in the phenomenon he was documenting. He began by photographing men in their home villages, then accompanied one man, Gavino, on his journey north. Along the way, Lahman was arrested and beaten on a bus layover in Nuevo Porvinir, Mexico, an experience that gave him a taste of what the migrants endured from police, "coyotes," and bandits along the way. At the border, Lahman crossed into California by night, photographing Gavino with infrared film and flash so as not to betray his presence.[13]

When Lahman completed his massive project late in 1982 and began looking for a publisher, he encountered the same reactions that had frustrated Pam Harris and others. Every magazine from *GEO* to *National Geographic* rejected his essay. Perhaps it was his refusal to adopt the usual perspective of the superior objective witness that so put off publishers, or perhaps it was his impassioned call for changes in attitudes and policies. Lahman had photographed with ideology. He had not taken the consumerist view that poverty is a sin. He had made every effort to free himself from the idea of recording desperation merely to elicit feelings of guilt and pity. His work was, in fact, quite subversive and considerably ahead of its time. Trying to generate support for it, Lahman showed it at the California Press Photographers Association meeting in San Diego in 1983, where a man claiming to be from the North San Diego County Farmers Association offered to buy all of his images and negatives. Lahman refused. That October he found a publisher, the *Escondido-Times Advocate.*

An innovative newspaper in the heart of the tomato-growing district, the *Times Advocate* ran Lahman's photo essay as a special sixteen-page supplement. Titled *Faces beyond the Border,* the supplement, informed by an extensive text written by journalist Sharon Myers, is notable for several reasons. For one, Lahman completed the project without backing from any journal, institution, agency, editor, or grant. His main source of income during his sojourn consisted of assignments from *Audubon* magazine. Also noteworthy is the way Lahman's photographs stress basic human questions and dilemmas, bypassing stereotypes to create a story that drew readers in and carried them along the journey. His most powerful image shows a group of migrants still carrying their suitcases while being herded away from the border by a low-flying Border Patrol helicopter. But the most controversial aspect of *Faces beyond the Border* flows from the way Lahman's images suggest that undocumented workers demonstrate qualities valued by American society: self-sacrifice, hard work, and perseverance. At a time when the UFW regarded undocumented workers as a threat, mainly because they were so often used as strikebreakers, and the federal government had passed various immigration reform and border control measures, Lahman and Myers rejected the conventional views of undocumented farmworkers as "the silent invasion." After thoroughly probing why Mexicans left home, how they lived in California, how they traveled, and what they lost and gained in the process, Lahman and Myers were compelled to challenge even the word *illegal,* with all its negative connotations. "How can a human being be illegal?" Myers asked.[14]

Lahman's photography never received the wide exposure it deserved. Although he won the Robert F. Kennedy Journalism Award, he could not secure a book contract. When the financial burdens of his years as a freelancer mounted, Lahman took a job at the *San Jose Mercury News* and minimized his coverage of undocumented farmworkers. But as Lahman was moving on to other projects, the controversy over undocumented workers continued to fester. With undocumented immigrants becoming scapegoats for every conceivable social problem and some anti-immigrant groups demanding closure of the border with Mexico, other photographers picked up the story. For many, the subject was highly personal.

One such individual was Harry Polkinhorn. No stranger to the border, farm labor, or undocumented immigration, Polkinhorn had been born and raised in Calexico and had worked in the fields as a teenager. Photographing among people he knew well, Polkinhorn was not interested in evoking feelings that terminate in pity or even compassion but interested rather at leading the viewer into core activities: weddings, birthdays, Sundays at church, casual social occasions, sending money home at the Western Union office. He sandwiched such images between scenes of stoop labor, daring border crossings, the constant search for work, and the ever-present Border Patrol.

Another photographer who stressed the normal and familiar was Elizabeth Sisco. Although not a child of the fields, Sisco was no tourist of despair. Living in the Analos Apartment complex in Solana Beach, near San Diego, she photographed her neighbors, most of whom were undocumented workers. Created in the course of going about her business, her pictures, like those of Polkinhorn, stressed day-to-day routines: heating peppers over the open flame at mealtime, returning from work in the flower gardens, taking in new arrivals, shopping in the supermarket, and losing loved ones to periodic raids by La Migra. No longer abstracted or folded into knee-jerk reactions about securing the border and ending welfare fraud, the undocumented farmworkers portrayed by Sisco, Polkinhorn, and Lahman emerge as hardworking people, neighbors and friends, living a marginal and isolated existence, often beginning their assimilation process by being consumers.[15]

While these projects went forward, photographers continued to highlight abuse and exploitation. None more relentlessly documented the sense of Kafkaesque normality that characterized life and labor in the fields than *Salinas Californian* photographer Clay Peterson. A series of events in 1981 kept him jumping between crises. Following an incident on April 23 in King City, in which unsuspecting field hands had become ill after entering a lettuce field that had been sprayed two hours earlier with Phosdrin, Peterson and other photographers documented farmworkers submitting to blood tests and giving testimony at the UFW's Salinas headquarters. So many photographers showed up that investigators from the Monterey County Agricultural Commissioner's

Office and the California Occupational Safety and Health Administration abandoned any hope of private interviews and postponed talking to victims for several days. On May 21, Peterson received an anonymous tip that led to an even more incredible image. He drove to the nearby Carmel Valley and discovered at least twenty farmworkers using short-handled hoes to weed a lettuce field near the Mid-Valley Shopping Center. Most of the men were undocumented workers. Completely unaware that they were using a tool that had been outlawed years earlier by the State Division of Industrial Safety as the result of a bitter court case, they continued thinning operations while Peterson photographed them moving through the fields. Incredulous readers who saw the photographs in the *Salinas Californian* later that day could not believe that six years after a well-publicized battle banning a tool generally regarded as barbaric, men were still bending over like question marks all day as they chopped away at weeds.[16]

Although most photographers at this time were focusing on working conditions and immigration, at least one developed an entirely different picture. That photographer was a newcomer to California. Her work emerged as the result of something she saw within hours of arriving in the state. Having just finished a stint of photographing the Chamula Indians of Mexico on a Rose McGill Fellowship, thirty-two-year-old Linda Troeller had accepted a teaching position at the University of California at Santa Cruz and was driving up the Pacific Coast Highway early in November when she saw a blue and pink farm labor bus parked beside the deserted highway near Moss Landing. As the early morning light began to burn away the fog, she could just make out farmworkers clad in bright yellow slickers, moving among the lush green artichoke plants. Overcome by the beauty of the sight, she instantly launched an eight-month project and, using a single beaten-up Leica M3, explored everything from the boardinghouses and pool halls along Soledad Street in Salinas to the food processing plants and labor camps of Watsonville. Although she photographed prostitutes, alcoholics, and the seedy side of life as well as hard farm labor, what struck her most was the color of the fields. "I would see workers in a cauliflower field at dawn, and the light would be completely different from the way it struck a tractor driver finishing up late in the afternoon," she recalled many years later. "And throughout the day, because of the marine influence and fog, you'd watch these small changes within a field as the sun broke through in spots."[17]

To capture those dimensions, Troeller broke with traditional black-and-white-oriented documentary photography. Shooting everything in color, she ignored questions of the legal status of the people she was photographing and tried to capture the lighter side of life. Without glossing over the toil involved in harvesting crops, Troeller discovered joy, vivacity, beauty, happiness, group elán, and pride among farmworkers. Morning breakfast breaks were especially memorable. She later recalled:

> I spent time with the people not so much chasing stories as discovering them. I wasn't positioning myself as a news photographer. I was really trying to find the right mood and to not be invasive. I never used a telephoto lens. I shot everything with a moderate wide-angle lens. I wanted to show the people integrated with the crops and what

> they were doing. For me, the project was more like painting than news reporting. I was obsessed with mushrooms, beans, celery. The people I met seemed to be making the best of it, with great cheer.[18]

Like most such personal projects, Troeller's came to an end when her funds ran out at the end of her teaching assignment. When she tried to find a publisher, Troeller encountered the same problems that had thwarted so many before her. Forced to abandon her project, she moved on, eventually becoming a successful commercial photographer in New York City. With its emphasis on happiness and color, her work added a layer of complexity to a black-and-white picture skewed toward pity and compassion. Slowly, haltingly, progressively, from many different photographers, the paradigm of objective photographic coverage was dismantled. By the end of 1981, traditional documentary photography had been infused with a quality that David Levi Strauss calls "collective subjectives."[19]

Over the next few years, several photographers considerably expanded this new subjectivity. One of them, Reesa Tansey, was already well acquainted with farmworkers. She had covered the March on Salinas and gone on to photograph extensively in the fields. Paul S. Taylor, who by now had been a retired and emeritus professor for decades, had supervised Tansey's MA thesis on agricultural cooperatives in the Salinas and Santa Maria valleys, because Tansey was interested in showing migrants struggling to break the cycle of migration. To overcome the outsider's perspective, Tansey lived with these former farmworkers, which allowed her to observe the benefits of their working the land as owners and managers. Tansey found that these proud cooperative members, now in control of their lives and no longer at the mercy of contractors and employers, projected a sense of self-worth when they elected officers and looked after their neighbor's children in the evenings after work.[20]

Another photographer, Ken Light, was, by all accounts, the leader in photographic coverage of the state's farmworkers, a kind of FSA photographer reincarnated a half century later. Photojournalists, art photographers, and documentary photographers all respected the way Light plunged at length into the endless rotation of crop cycles, even if they could not quite agree on a label for his work. His modus operandi, for which he was famous, consisted of grabbing a wad of cash from the kitchen table and heading out whenever possible. This was how Light survived the first few years of a project that seemed in many ways to be a modern counterpart to Dorothea Lange's work. Light's most important contribution was capturing a sense of the great pride that farmworkers expressed in their families and the general competence and industriousness they demonstrated in simply getting through a day. This soon made him curious about the process that brought Mexicans north. To probe this question, Light did the same thing that Dean, Nadel, and Lahman had done: he began traveling widely in Mexico.

While photographing migrants in their home villages, Light switched from a 35-millimeter camera to a Hasselblad, usually on a tripod. Although the switch to a larger format ran against the trend to smaller-format cameras since the mid-1930s, Light chose this approach because the larger negatives provided him with detail that was lacking in smaller cameras. Light also found that the square shape, as opposed to the rectangular 35-millimeter format, proved easier to work with. As for the tripod and big camera, Light developed a way of minimizing the problems that they created by working quickly and, whenever possible, exploiting their commanding presence. In many ways, he adopted an approach that was the opposite of the fly on the wall technique of Lange, Ballis, and other predecessors.[21]

Light's photography broke new ground by showing that, without migration, hundreds of small Mexican villages could not survive. For men in such villages, the decision to leave was not an easy one. Light went to great pains to reveal their tortured thinking, the sacrifices they made, and the distress they felt. Riding with them by bus

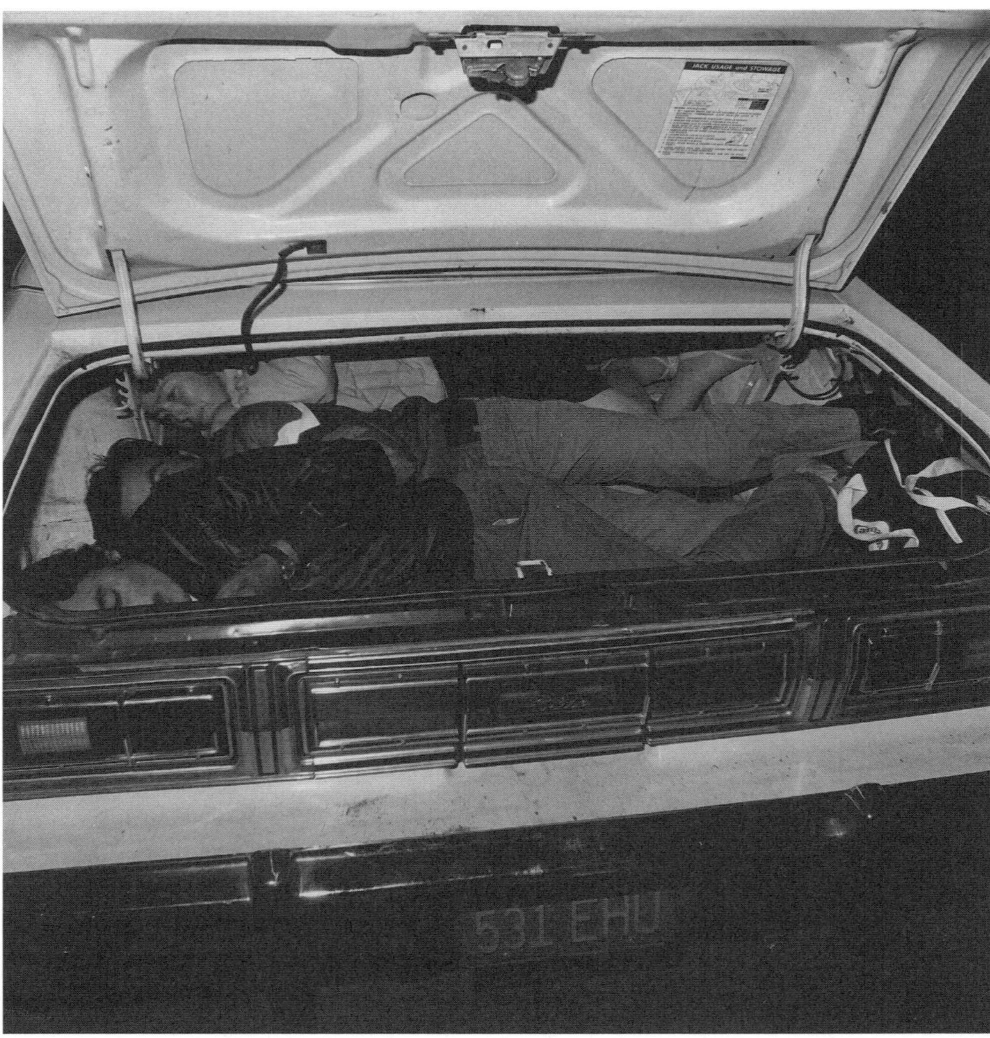

Undocumented workers arrested by the Border Patrol while trying to cross at Tijuana, May 1986, photograph by Ken Light. From the series To the Promised Land (1987). Courtesy of Ken Light.

to the border, he traced their arduous nighttime crossing, much as Lahman had but in even greater detail. At the border he found them crawling through sewage drains, hiding in trucks and railroad cars, cutting holes in the border fence, and wading across the Tijuana River with plastic grocery bags wrapped around their feet. From the border, Light followed men to farms, rural barrios, and labor camps in the San Joaquin, Imperial, and Salinas valleys and to their houses of cardboard in the canyons of north San Diego County. Some of his most disturbing images meditate on the plight of men sitting in the backs of vans, heads bowed, after being apprehended; men and women crammed into car trunks like sardines at the moment a Border Patrol agent discovered them; and men lying prone in the dust on Otay Mesa while being rounded up and "field processed."[22]

Published in *To the Promised Land,* Light's work unfolded a south-of-the-border version of *An American Exodus.* Seeking to defuse anti-immigrant hysteria and humanize a phenomenon that all too often has focused on numbers, the book was so influential at the time of its release that it inspired numerous other photographic probes. Some of these efforts, like the one by *Sacramento Bee* photographer Michael Williamson, suggested that little, if anything, had changed for most farmworkers since the rise of the UFW. In some cases what photographers discovered indicated that conditions were actually worse than those of the Great Depression. This was the implication of a series of pictures that Clay Peterson published in the *Salinas Californian* on September 26, 1987.[23]

Ever on the spy for news pictures, Peterson was at a press conference on a strawberry farm outside Salinas when he recorded a farmworker crawling on all fours out of a small cave dug into a hillside. The cave was his home, and it was not the only one at Rancho de las Cuevas, or Cave Ranch, as it was called. The press conference had been called by the California Rural Legal Assistance (CRLA) to announce a lawsuit against the farm's owners, who had allegedly forced a dozen field hands to "live in holes in the ground and abandoned outhouses and cardboard shacks." The *Salinas Californian* ran the disturbing image to show that, despite the ongoing efforts of the UFW and other advocacy groups, many farmworkers were still struggling to survive under the most adverse circumstances. But to some viewers, this all seemed concocted and unbelievable. Disputing the entire story, readers of the newspaper pointed out that the man crawling out of the cave with blown-dry hair, a fresh shave, and clean clothes, seemed too well-groomed. In reaction to the criticism, *Sacramento Bee* ombudsman Art Nauman contacted Peterson for more details. What Peterson told him raised ethical issues about truthful and responsible photographic coverage of farmworkers.[24]

To bring the issues of government support of low-income housing and stricter sanitary standards to the public and also to announce a lawsuit against the landowner, CRLA attorney Lydia Villareal had invited Peterson and other news photographers, including myself, to a press conference at the farm. The worker pictured was one of those in the lawsuit, a man who claimed to have worked there until the previous week, when he had been fired. He now lived in a shack nearby and had come to the press conference clean and neatly attired. A television cameraman who was also covering the event had asked the man to crawl in and out of the cave, which he did several times. It was during this demonstration that Peterson took his photograph. Therefore, although the image was staged, it was not deceptive, but the accompanying caption should have better explained the circumstances. In this instance the photographer was guilty not of managing the news but of allowing himself to be manipulated.[25]

Photographers continued to focus on migration, border issues, and living and working conditions well into the late 1980s. And then, as had always happened in the past, a new issue emerged. Actually, this one had been there for decades, but now it reached its peak. Exposure to dangerous agricultural chemicals had grown steadily after World War II, when the demand for fresh produce increased exponentially and American farmers nationwide had begun seeking every advantage they could find to meet demand and drastically increase production. New technologies and scientific advances made cultivating and harvesting easier and boosted crop yields far beyond those of any other country. Farmers augmented their bottom line by incorporating drastic chemical components necessary for producing big, cosmetically perfect fruit and vegetables. By the 1980s, they were using 1.2 billion pounds of chemical pesticides per year, with California accounting for about one-sixth of that total. So high was the level of the banned pesticide DBCP in drinking water in the Central Valley that 1,473 wells were condemned as unsafe. As the volume increased, it became almost inevitable that farmworkers would be exposed to the poisons. And indeed, there were hundreds of documented cases, and thousands more described in anecdotal accounts, of farmworkers walking into fields that had recently been fumigated, being doused by an errant crop duster, or being engulfed by drifting clouds of chemicals. As reports of such exposures surfaced, press photographers scrambled to document their effects. Their quest for news would at times assist and at other times hinder those they were trying to help.[26]

Faced with daily deadline pressures, press photographers did not take the lead in this effort. Encountering farmworkers and associated issues in the course of the news cycle somewhere between automobile accidents and sports stories, they basically reacted to events. Shooting one or two images, then moving on to the evening football game and yet another feature portrait, they could not linger long enough to cover pesticide issues in much depth. As a result, freelance photographers seized on the issue of chemical exposure and, as the number of poisonings rose, took the lead in covering the issue with multipicture photo essays.[27]

To develop a more complete picture of the chemical dangers experienced by farmworkers on a daily basis, freelancers began exploring the environmental and human consequences of chemical agriculture, especially the devastating effects that poisons were having on farmworkers' children and the sacrifices that were necessary to care for them. Objectivity was not part of this picture. Freelancers waded into the issue with a crusading conviction in the righteousness of their cause. They made no attempt to mask their biases. By insisting on individual expression and "authorial" control, they hoped to connect directly with an audience on a level that was both intellectual and visceral. Very much attuned to the new human rights politics and aiming at establishing what the critic John Bird calls "a dialectic of gaze," these photographers intended to bear witness and force people to think.[28]

One of the most vehement of these photographers was Lonny Shavelson, a photojournalist and emergency room physician who had previously shot important essays on drug use and abuse. After more than one hundred citrus pickers were burned by chemicals in a San Joaquin Valley orchard in 1986, Shavelson began documenting cases of pesticide exposure as they were brought into the emergency rooms where he was on duty. It was not long before he stopped waiting for victims to cross his path at the hospital and sought them out in the fields and labor camps. Soon his attention settled on farmworker children in one of several "cancer cluster" communities dotting Highway 99 in the Central Valley. Of these communities, McFarland, with a population of just sixty-eight hundred (mostly farmworkers) and thirteen childhood leukemia cases in 1985, seemed to be at the epicenter of everything. But families in a half dozen other communities, including Delano and Tulare, had also been devastated. Shavelson set out to record their plight.[29]

Of all the children he met, none affected Shavelson more than Felipe Franco. Destined to become a poster child for the cancer cluster communities, Franco had been born without arms and legs. But with a wide smile, cheerful nature, and overwhelming support from his family, he seemed able to make the best of his situation and enjoy the unending attention. Visiting the Franco family in Delano, Shavelson simply photographed the youngster seated next to his grandmother on a couch in their home. In an interview, Felipe's mother, Ramona, described picking grapes while pregnant. She later discovered that the vineyard where she was working had been treated with pesticides structurally similar to thalidomide, the drug that had caused severe birth defects in thousands of infants in the 1950s and 1960s.[30]

To amplify Felipe's ordeal and drive it home to viewers, Shavelson engaged in collaborative photojournalism. Encouraging his mothers and fathers to speak directly and emotionally, he published their statements, often in the original handwritten form, alongside photographs of stricken children. By bypassing traditional captioning techniques, Shavelson aimed at narrowing the distance separating photographer and subject. The combination worked particularly well for his portraits of McFarland resident Esmeralda Sánchez, her husband, and their daughter, Mayra. When she was seven years old, Mayra began complaining of severe headaches. Although the McFarland water company warned customers not to give water to children under six months of age, the bills and warnings had been in English, which Esmeralda could not read. By the time Mayra was ten, she had developed a brain tumor requiring an operation. "After the operation she couldn't move at all," Esmeralda told Shavelson. "Now she opens her mouth more," Esmeralda added. "We think she can recognize us."[31]

After Shavelson published his images and stories in his book *Toxic Nation: The Fight to Save Our Communities from Chemical Contamination,* photographer David H. Wells decided to explore the ubiquitous danger of toxic chemicals. With the support of the National Press Photographers Association / Nikon Fellowship, Wells traveled from his home on the East Coast to California, where, in seven separate two-week stints during the spring and summer of 1988, he embarked on a personal crusade to chronicle pesticide use in the most productive agricultural industry in the nation. Explaining his project, he told an interviewer:

> I wanted to see an entire agricultural cycle and photograph the use of the chemicals during the prime planting, growing, and spraying seasons. I also wanted to see how agricultural chemicals affect the farmworkers, their families, and all the residents of the San Joaquin valley. I spent dozens of hours on the telephone, interviewing more than one hundred people who have a professional or personal interest in the issue. While some growers and sprayers chased me off their property, others were amazingly honest about their dependence on chemicals. I was told repeatedly that the consumer was to blame for demanding the kind of cosmetically perfect produce that is only possible with pesticides.[32]

Although Wells also made many extremely disturbing pictures of children who were dying or deformed, his major emphasis was on how, where, and why this happened. Traveling the back roads, Wells documented both careful and irresponsible pesticide use in the agricultural areas of the San Joaquin valley. Compressing perspectives and creating linkages much the same way that Joe Munroe had done in his classic photograph twenty-five years earlier, Wells used a telephoto lens to record flaggers directing crop dusters and spray rigs laying down beautiful diamond spray patterns enveloping grapevines. His strongest and most controversial image, also taken with a telephoto lens, captures an airplane diving across a two-lane highway. The photograph's power derives from the way it suggests the irresponsible chemical drenching of a community, when, in fact, the plane was a safe distance away. But many times while photographing, Wells himself was close enough to be sprayed, and on those occasions he resorted to wearing a gas mask to avoid inhaling the poisons.[33]

To bring his work to the public, Wells relied on Sunday magazines published by major newspapers. "The Pesticide Poisoning of America" is the title of his first essay, which appeared with various other titles in different edited forms, including as a nine-page cover story in the *Philadelphia Inquirer Magazine* and then subsequently in *West* magazine, of the *San Jose Mercury News,* and in various journals and art galleries. Raising important questions about the high human price being paid for aesthetically pleasing fruit, these essays shocked the public but never came close to causing the controversy that developed in November 1986, when Victor Alemán photographed young Felipe Franco, another victim from one of the cancer cluster communities, for the cover of the UFW's journal *Food and Justice.*

Coming from a family of prominent journalists in El Salvador and growing up in a house where photographs were always on display, Alemán was no stranger to conflict. He had been photographing farmworkers since the late 1970s in his capacity as managing editor of *El Malcriado.* With an eye for capturing the human condition and for using his camera in other meaningful ways, Alemán gravitated quite naturally toward the pesticide issue when farmworkers from Earlimart contacted the UFW. As part of the union's campaign against pesticides, Alemán began photographing all of the pesticide victims in California for the union's publication *Food and Justice* as well as for *Vida Nuevo,* a Los Angeles weekly published by the Archdiocese of Los Angeles. During this work, Alemán photographed young Franco three or four times, and Franco's mother gave the union permission to use the images in its video *The Wrath of Grapes.* On the last of these sessions, under the supervision of Felipe's grandmother, Alemán photographed young Franco in the grass on the west side of Delano at Forty Acres. Having relied on Franco's grandmother to carry the youngster to the photo session, Alemán went to considerable pains to explain that the images were going to be used to help all of the victims of pesticide poisoning, not only farmworker children, but all victims. Everything seemed in order.[34]

After Alemán sent Felipe's mother a copy of the *Food and Justice* article in which Felipe's picture appeared, she thanked Alemán and asked for additional copies of the

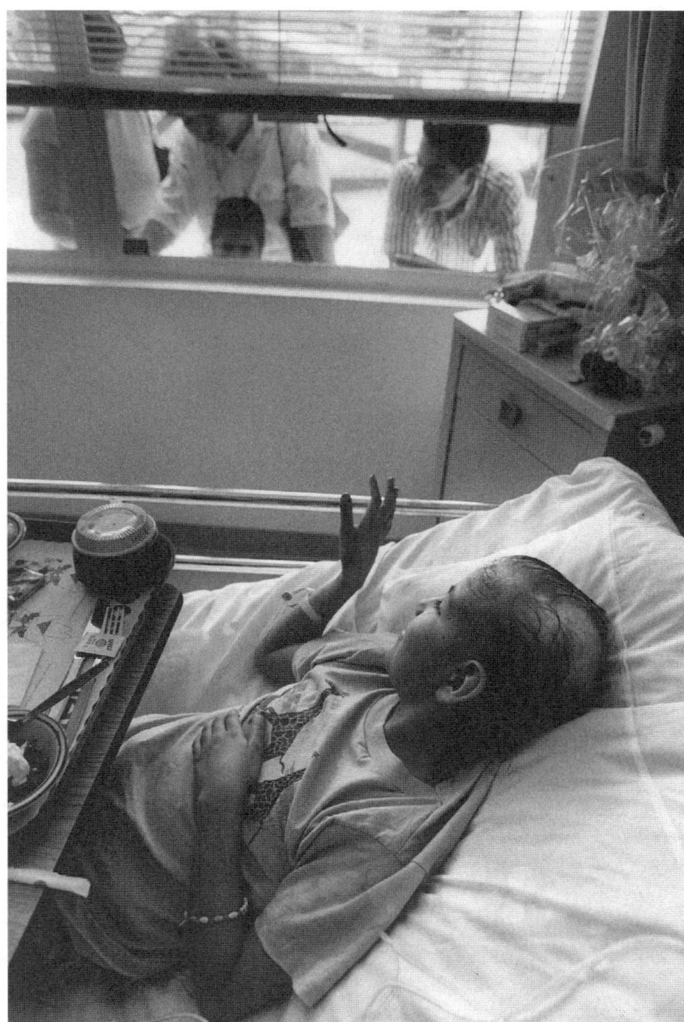

Leukemia victim talking to friends through the window of hospital room, June 1988, photograph by David H. Wells. From the photo essay "The Pesticide Poisoning of America." Courtesy of David H. Wells.

magazine as well as some additional photographs. A year and a half later, some of the union's supporters in Canada and on the East Coast apparently enlarged one of Felipe's photographs to poster size and began using it in boycott activities. Although Alemán had no connection with the incident and had moved on to other projects, he suddenly found himself embroiled in a lawsuit. Claiming that the UFW had misrepresented itself, Felipe's mother denounced the union for invading her privacy and the privacy of her son and for using her son's image without permission. According to her version of events, Alemán had not properly explained in detail how the photograph would be used. When she saw the enlarged version of Alemán's photograph, she sued the union and obtained a temporary restraining order against further use of the photograph.

Over the next three years, Franco and the UFW battled each other in court. In his testimony, Alemán asserted that Mrs. Franco had given her consent many times, that he had even photographed Felipe at least once after the lawsuit, all with permission. How else could he even get access to the young man? The trouble was that Alemán had not obtained written permission, because he had been working essentially as a journalist. "We had a trust," he later explained. "Mrs. Franco understood that these

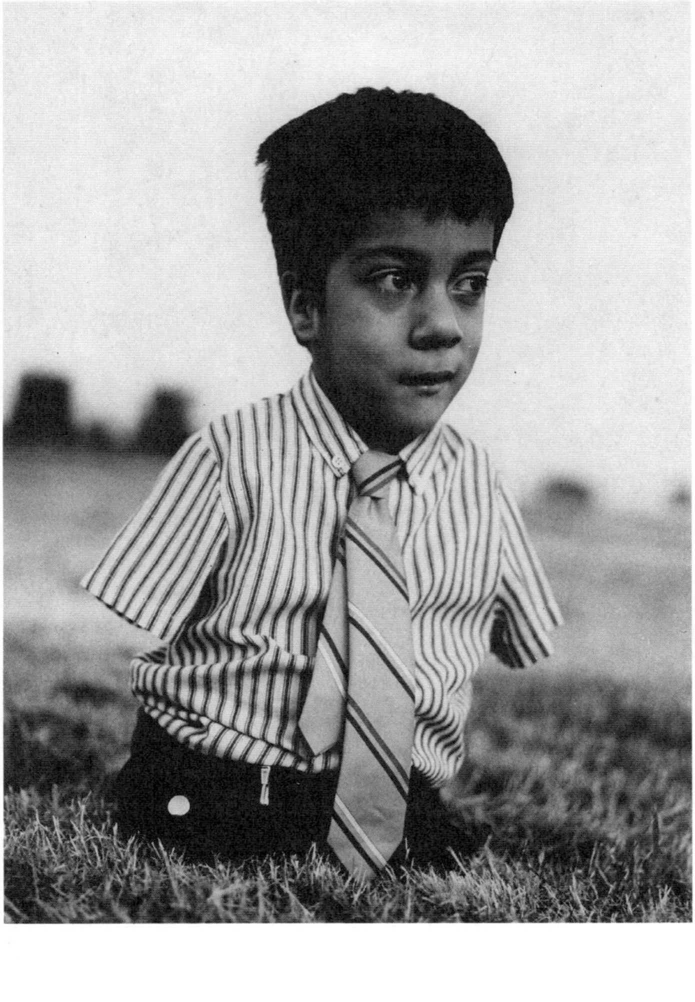

Suppressed photograph of Felipe Franco, June 1986, photograph by Victor Alemán. Original in color. Courtesy of Victor Alemán.

images were important because they [portrayed] victims of these pesticide problems. She knew that I was not taking pictures to exploit them or to commercialize her son. She understood perfectly that, for me, taking pictures is a sacred thing, that I have dedicated myself to recording the human condition, to documenting very delicate situations."[35]

In evaluating Alemán's work, a Kern County Superior Court judge hardly considered the photographer's humanistic concerns. He ruled that Franco's son and the children of other farmworkers who had joined her in a parallel lawsuit had not consented to the use of their likeness. On these grounds, he issued a permanent injunction preventing further publication not only of Alemán's photograph but also of the union's *Wrath of Grapes* video. The decision effectively prevented the UFW from using its main tool for advancing the boycott, which was now being promoted as a campaign against pesticide poisoning. Battling with the Francos for the next two years, Alemán eventually won his case when the Fresno District Court of Appeals overturned the original ruling and allowed the union and its supporters to use its video again as well as the enlargement of Alemán's photograph. But while vindicating both the union and Alemán, the outcome hardly constituted a victory. The union had spent huge sums of money and battled in court for years just to continue using Felipe's image. Few other episodes so clearly illustrate the central importance that photographers and photography played in the farmworker movement—and the lengths to which some people would go to prevent farmworkers from employing effective visual evidence.[36]

By 1987, photographers had vastly expanded on the documentary tradition and created an exceedingly complex picture of California farmworkers. Simultaneously beautiful and disturbing, their work explores a wide range of subjects, many heretofore glossed over and omitted from the record, including entire communities, such as the floating, rootless, proud new Mixtecos arriving in California from Oaxaca, one of the poorest areas in Mexico; the San Joaquin Valley delta remnant town of Locke, which had long been home to one of the last surviving populations of Chinese farmworkers; and Yemeni immigrants, who continued to live and work in isolated farm labor camps. *Santa Rosa Press Democrat* photographer Kent Porter believed that the pictures he made of undocumented workers and other farmworkers living under the Alexander Valley Bridge near Healdsburg while picking wine grapes in the fall of 1988 might somehow help them. But after seeing Porter's images, the Sonoma County Health Department ran the workers off, and the landowner erected a chain-link fence to prevent anyone from using the site. Health officials did not turn their backs on the men, however. Recognizing the important role that undocumented farmworkers played in the wine-grape crop, the health department constructed a temporary camp to house the men during the fall harvest. When photographer Chad Surmick followed up on the evicted bridge campers three years later, he found the same men, only now they camped in dome tents provided by growers. Out under some oak trees a few miles from the bridge, with their red, yellow, green, and blue tents illuminated by battery-powered lamps at sunset, they seemed an almost bucolic sight.[37]

A few photographers produced work that could be described only as bizarre and exploitative. One art photographer got the idea to put a red couch in unlikely situations—a freeway, a back alley, an excavation site, an alligator pond—where celebrities such as Hugh Hefner and Zsa Zsa Gabor were then photographed. Somehow he persuaded César Chávez to recline on the couch outside union headquarters at La Paz. His portrait, which some have described as pure exploitation and others see as part of a general shift in photographic practice away from spontaneous witness toward contrived documentation, did nothing for farmworkers and contributed to the growing speculation that Chávez had lost touch with reality.[38]

Chávez submitted to the indignity because farmworkers needed the publicity. They needed someone to carry on the fight. They needed to overcome their anonymity. Who were these small Mixtecos now arriving from San Agustín Tlacotepec and flowing into the canyons of north San Diego County? What were they doing? Why were they coming north? Farmworkers needed someone to ask these questions, because the UFW was now barely functioning as a labor union. Years of infighting, purges, wasted efforts, direct mailing campaigns, alliances with the drug rehabilitation organization Synanon and its cult figure Charles Dederich, and hostility toward old friends had left the union weak and isolated. Gone were such daunting leaders as Jerome Cohen, who had built the union legal department into something to be feared. Executive board members Philip Vera Cruz, Gilbert Padilla, Jessica Govea, and Marshall Ganz were forced out, leaving the union without most of its founding leaders. Also purged were organizers such as Rev. James Drake, Eliseo Medina, and Mario Bustamonte, dawn-to-dust organizers of the stoutest sort, and Nick Jones, expelled for little more than speaking his piece and alleged communist leanings. Governor George Deukmejian's hostile Republican administration in Sacramento was systematically gutting the Agricultural Labor Relations Board, and growers were defying labor board decisions and refusing to bargain with the union after it won representation elections. Union membership plummeted. By late 1988, the UFW counted only ten thousand dues-paying members, down from a high of one hundred thousand in 1973.[39]

Chávez by this time may well have become a true autocrat, isolated and intolerant. But he understood what worked, and he realized that he could command a hundred photographers and make them all take the same picture, exactly the picture that he wanted. Struggling to rekindle interest in his sagging union, Chávez now did what he had done so often in the past. He tried to reverse fortunes by concocting a snapshot and sending it out to the public. He began as usual with a fast. On July 17, 1988, Chávez vowed that he would fast until growers began talking about contracts and agreed to discuss limiting the use of pesticides. He was guessing that the decision would again attract hordes of photographers and fill newspaper and magazine pages with the kind of images required for rescuing his movement. On the brink, he would pull back from disaster. He knew exactly what he was doing.

Out of sight at first, Chávez deteriorated so quickly that after fifteen days, union leaders called a doctor to monitor his health. With newspapers carrying updates on his condition almost daily and former union leaders streaming in to visit, photographers were desperate to get a picture of the emaciated labor leader, especially after Jesse Jackson, then running for president of the United States, promised that he would visit Chávez in Delano. When the union announced that Chávez had grown ill and would prematurely break his fast at a Mass on August 21, 1988, photographers, including myself, descended on Forty Acres en masse. As we gathered at a news conference on Saturday morning, August 20, Paul Fusco and an Associated Press photographer overheard two union organizers discussing how to allow access to the emaciated labor leader. Wasting no time, Fusco and the AP photographer hitched a ride with the organizers and rode to the house where Chávez was staying. Snapping shots that ran in newspapers and magazines around the country, the two photographers provided the first glimpse of a gaunt and weakened Chávez trying to sit up in his bed.[40]

Early the following morning, I arrived along with dozens of other photographers to photograph the end of yet another Chávez fast. Entering a small room in a building at Forty Acres to hear Jackson discuss his meeting with Chávez, we first had to open our cameras, remove lenses, and show everything to Secret Service personnel. We then packed in tightly and jockeyed for places in front of a bare table. As usual at such convocations, a "gang bang" mentality prevailed. Out-of-town photographers who left to use the bathroom found their spots taken. Only through forceful words and some shoving matches were they able to reclaim their spots, all for rather standard press conference pictures whose sole news value seemed to be the presence of Jackson and UFW vice president Dolores Huerta at the same table. After the press conference, we worked the crowd of three thousand UFW supporters seated inside the UFW's huge circus tent. There was plenty to cover. Besides the banners and pageantry, Ethel Kennedy was present along with state assemblyman Tom Hayden. Onstage were actors Martin Sheen, Eddie Albert, Robert Blake, Mike Ferrell, Emilio Estévez, Edward James Olmos, Luis Váldez, and Rubén Blades, along with welterweight boxer Carlos Palomino. We all snapped away, but besides one photograph of an individual who paraded around the tent carrying a large banner celebrating the union, few if any of our images went beyond the managed "photo op" to record something actually newsworthy.[41]

As Chávez was about to arrive, about fifty other still photographers and I took up positions to the right of a stage behind a rope barrier patrolled by Secret Service agents. For a while we contented ourselves with being led up onstage to take a few pictures behind Jesse Jackson while he addressed the crowd. With television crews and film photographers occupying an elevated platform behind us, we waited in the front row. Late arrivals tried and failed to work their way into position, saying, "Be cool, be cool." One photographer with 1930s Leicas and wearing what appeared to be a Fedora was especially adept. Wiggling his way among, around, over, and under other photographers, he impressed me as a wormlike individual, apparently adept in such gang-bang situations. Others were not so successful. All around me, photographers who had waited all day were now tired and on deadline and would have nothing of this, replying, "Fuck off" and "Don't block me." Refusing to give an inch, we all held our positions. Several photographers threw elbows and shoved the newcomers aside. A few pushing matches occurred. There was no sympathy for photographers flying in from the East Coast and pleading that they had just stepped off an airplane and were disoriented, with only a vague idea of where they were. "It was the first time I had seen so many photographers in one place," recalled Matt Black, a freelancer covering the event for the *Tulare Advance-Register,* "and I remember thinking how everyone's pictures were going to be exactly the same."[42]

By the time Chávez was brought in through a back entrance, everyone was hot, soaked in sweat, thirsty, and impatient. When a Secret Service agent walked directly in front of the bullpen, inadvertently blocking us from a perfect shot of Chávez while he was being assisted to his seat at the front of the tent, a near riot broke out. Yelling "Get out of the way," "Move your ass," and countless other directives and obscenities, we intimidated the Secret Service agent. Immediately stepping aside, he cleared a line of sight allowing us to take pictures of Chávez. When Chávez passed within a few feet, most shot with a 20- or a 28-millimeter lens and a fill flash. Later one agent was overheard exclaiming, "These photographers are animals. I've never experienced anything like this anywhere."[43]

A media circus or moral grandstanding, the whole episode had been staged for maximum effect. During the course of the one-hour service, we made thousands of strobe shots recording every move that Chávez made. Shooting with telephoto lenses and pushed film with shutter speeds of 1/250 second or higher, every photographer exposed several rolls of film documenting Chávez receiving Holy Communion, meeting and greeting friends, being assisted by his son Richard, and seeming to faint and awaken. When Ethel Kennedy reached over to touch Chávez and placed her hand behind his head to prevent him from fainting, we fired off strings of shots. All around, the whir of motor drives and photographers reloading cameras continued for perhaps thirty minutes. None of us even dared to take our eyes from our viewfinders except briefly to wipe away the sweat.

An amalgamation of religion and political action, the event climaxed when Jesse Jackson leaned over and handed Chávez a small cross made of small grapevine canes. Switching to my 180-millimeter telephoto lens, I isolated all but Chávez and Jackson and fired off an entire roll of film, "juicing" every third shot with a flash from an off-camera light. At that moment, a blinding wave of flashes went off. Within the space of a minute, we made thousands of images, with the main differences resulting from the choice of lenses and the various positions we had staked out in the bullpen. Of his experiences at the ceremony, *Bakersfield Californian* photographer Felix Adamo recalled:

> It seems like we waited forever for the shot, which was Jesse passing the cross to César. You just had to have the camera up and ready to shoot when it happened. And when it did, all I could hear was motor drives going off, strobes popping, and batteries recycling. I bet at least forty other photographers have the same shot. What separated one shot from another was what position you happened to be in at the event. The *Bakersfield Californian* ran the photo on the front page the next day and the picture also won an NPPA [National Press Photographers Association] clip contest for that month.[44]

Later, I compared my photographs of the event with Adamo's and also with those taken by Paul Fusco of Magnum and Carl Crawford of the *Fresno Bee.* In the magazines and newspapers that week, my photographs and those of dozens of others displayed César Chávez, Jesse Jackson, and Ethel Kennedy under dramatic headlines: "CHAVEZ ENDS FAST AMID CELEBRITIES." Editors found my work "beautiful and moving." This was history, they said.[45]

Recorded from every angle, in color and black-and-white and in exquisite detail, that instant when Jackson passed the little cross to César may be the single most photographed moment in the history of the farmworker movement. It illustrated just how clever and successful Chávez was at enticing out of the media exactly the photograph that he needed. A scholar looking at one of those photographs without knowing the circumstances under which it was created might regard it as unique, but, in

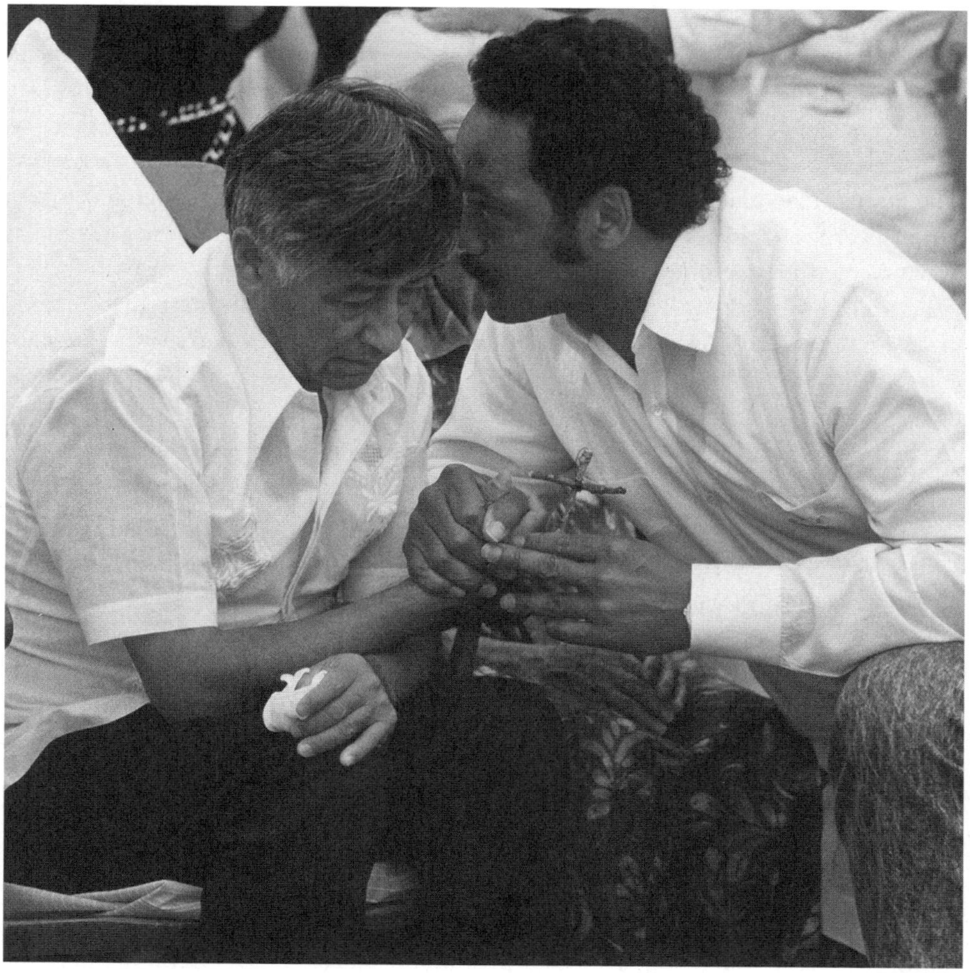

The most photographed moment in farmworker history, when Jesse Jackson passed a small cross of grapevine canes to César Chávez, August 22, 1988, photograph by Richard Steven Street. Original in color. Courtesy of Streetshots.

fact, everything had been carefully choreographed. Had we been hired to do so, we could not have been a better public relations agent for the United Farm Workers union or made the union's case better before the court of public opinion.

Riding the wave of symbolic imagery, the UFW did its best to recapture its lost stature. However, when farmworkers next inspired widespread attention, it was not images of Chávez and the UFW that received public attention but rather a picture of three men operating a "human plow" in a field near Carlsbad, in north San Diego County. *Oceanside Blade-Citizen* photographer Tom Riggs made the photograph in May 1989, after receiving an anonymous tip. "My grandfather had 32 slaves in Mississippi and my father taught me about the abuse of human beings," the informant told Riggs. Heading into the bean fields east of El Camino Real, Riggs did, in fact, find men using an *arado* (plow), with two pulling in front and one guiding the plow from behind. Riggs snapped an astonishing picture of them moving through rolling hills with furrows stretching to the horizon. Running above an article on the plow, Riggs's image provoked a furor and comparisons with farmworkers being treated like animals. But on interviewing the plowmen a few days later, Riggs and a reporter learned that the men were not breaking open, hardened terrain; that job had been done by a tractor. The human plowmen were merely pulling the lightweight device through loose, wet dirt. To confirm this, the reporter had a go at it and found the task nearly effortless. What seemed a relic from the days of slavery was in fact a hand cultivator used for ten years to turn over soft and wet ground. And what had seemed an image reminiscent of slavery turned out, on closer examination, to be more complicated than was apparent at first glance. "We're not slaves," explained one of the plowmen. "Besides animals or tractors would smash the plants."[46]

Two years later, I completed a project photographing in Huron, the poorest town in California and a prime example of the state's persistent pockets of entrenched rural poverty among unskilled immigrant farmworkers, mainly from rural Mexico. Essentially a giant farm labor exploitation camp, Huron is the only town in Westlands Water District, the huge kidney-shaped irrigation territory sprawling over four hundred thousand acres on the west side of the San Joaquin Valley. With fourteen bars, six farm labor camps, and a permanent population of about thirty-five hundred at that time, the town swelled to over ten thousand twice a year, in March and October, when the lettuce harvesters arrived, and virtually all of the lettuce in the United States came out of this one small town. Bitterly divided between a conservative faction of Hispanics who accepted the status quo and did not want to clean up the bars, curb drug dealing, or change anything and an insurgent group hostile to the liquor interests and hoping to build a high school to end the practice of busing the town's teenagers to Coalinga, the town's politics were fascinating in their own right, as were the law enforcement duties of the town police department, with whom I rode nightly. Returning to Huron twice a year for two weeks during the spring and fall lettuce harvest, I stayed with the story for eight years. I eventually published my photographic essay only after the police department had been abolished, a town councilwoman's home had been bombed, and the town's leading businessman had been convicted of drug sales. Eventually the mayor resigned after his automobile had been shot up late one night by two assailants wielding AK-47s. At that point it became too dangerous for me to continue.[47]

Unlike most photographers, I also wrote the long essay that provided context for my photography. As far as I know, I am the first farmworker photographer to link color photography and first-person investigative journalism. Although the reasons for this seemed self-evident to me, a few colleagues subsequently asserted that I was following a strategy of expanding Lange's captioning to its logical conclusion. Others drew parallels between my approach and that of Carl Mydans, the only *Life* photographer who regularly wrote texts for his essays, and Eugene Smith, who demanded complete control over all aspects of his work. In fact, I was imitating no one. I wrote the essay because, like many of my assignments, this one was so demanding of time and commitment that it could only be done solo. There was no room for a partner.[48]

After Huron, I wanted to focus on a more positive side to the farmworker story and continue linking words and images. Having already spent nearly twenty years following the UFW, documenting life and labor in the fields, covering the U.S.–Mexico border, and probing small farmworker communities, not to mention taking thousands of images as part of my advertising and commercial work for California agriculture, I wanted to highlight the day-to-day self-organizing activities and survival culture of the state's farmworkers. Focusing on six different communities in total, I devoted one chapter in my book *Organizing for Our Lives: New Voices from Rural Communities* to the estimated fifteen thousand undocumented Mexican, Salvadoran, and Guatemalan farmworkers who had constructed hundreds of shantytown encampments in the canyons and wooded gullies of north San Diego County.

Since Minick and Lahman had photographed them in the early 1980s, the population of undocumented farmworkers in north San Diego County had grown into the largest single concentration of immigrant squatters anywhere in California, perhaps the entire country. Conditions were raw. Camps lacked electricity and running water. There were few toilets or garbage-collection systems. Meals were prepared over campfires. Mail was delivered by catering truck drivers known as *fayuqueros,* who also supplied low-quality food and bottled water at inflated prices. It was a roughhewn existence, but despite their many hardships and sacrifices, the campers exuded a tenacity and community spirit that seemed worth documenting.

From my experiences in the field and from my knowledge of how my predecessors had worked, I understood that every venture of this type must be negotiated, that it is a complicated act of collaboration. The question was, How could I, as an insider (what critic Andy Grundberg calls a "glorified tourist") deliver anything insightful on what was, for all practical purposes, an alien community? My approach was simply to shed my preconceptions and stylistic tendencies as much as possible. When I began photographing the immigrant campers, I moved into the largest camp, Rancho de los Diablos (Devils' Camp). Helping the men build shelters, driving them to and from medical clinics, shooting Polaroids, translating documents, and making myself as helpful as possible, I soon discovered that what canyon campers needed more than anything else were sheets of plastic to waterproof the roofs of their shelters. Persuading several hardware stores to donate damaged plastic tarpaulins, I distributed them throughout the camp, much to everyone's delight, and became known as El Plastico, a Spanglish reference to the man with the plastic.[49]

During my first few weeks in Rancho de los Diablos, I never took out my cameras. Several photojournalists came and went, including one from Boston, accompanied by gang members from Los Angeles, who were the subject of an essay he was shooting. The man ran through the camp, poking his lenses at people, firing off strings of pictures with his motor drive, and scribbling notes. He did not stay long and returned only to look for the pager that he had lost in the tall grass. The canyon campers despised such photographers. They would turn their backs, spit, and label them vultures. Ashamed to see photographers behave that way, I was determined not to photograph until asked to do so. My opportunity came one Sunday afternoon, several weeks after I arrived. Canyon campers washed their clothes in a creek that ran through their camp and sometimes flooded it. When the most senior member of the camp packed up his clothes and headed off to wash them, he asked me to come along. "Jue take peektures," he said in fractured English, hefting my camera bag and inviting me to follow.

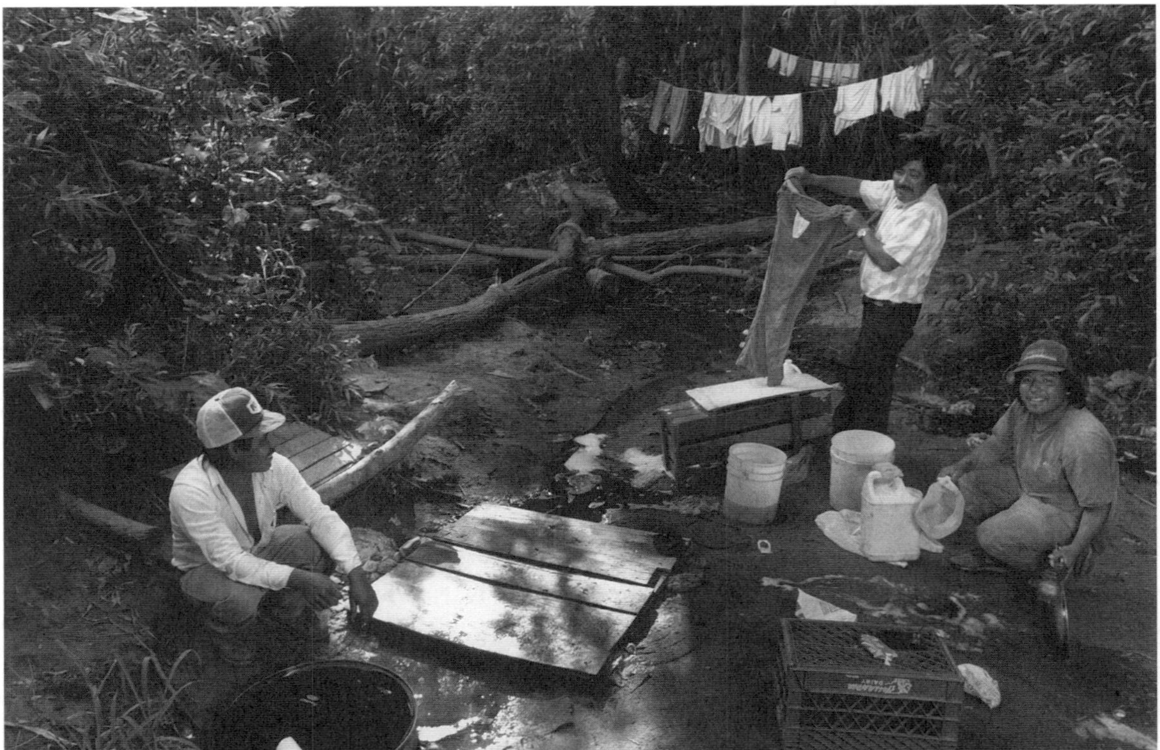

Isidro Rosas (on the right) and friends engaged in their Sunday afternoon washing routine at Rancho Yasecoche, Camp Pendleton Marine Base, Oceanside, July 15, 1991, photograph by Richard Steven Street. From the series Organizing for Our Lives, 1991. Courtesy of Streetshots.

Sunday afternoon washing was a central element in camp routine. Happy to tag along, I quickly set up my soft box, a kind of dome tent that defuses and softens a battery-powered strobe light, and spent several hours chatting in Spanish and shooting pictures. When I finished and began packing my equipment, I became aware that another immigrant camper had been watching us quietly from the nearby woods. Young and bearded, he had a Spanish–English dictionary in his back pocket. In English, frequently consulting the dictionary, he offered to help me pack up my strobes, and as we did so, he asked me for a ride to his home in the camp on the ridge above Rancho de los Diablos. We carried the equipment to my car and headed off to his camp. While we bounced along the dusty, rutted road, I turned on the tape recorder, and he told me his story.

Luis Miguel Rodríguez was twenty-three years old, the youngest of six children, whose parents were schoolteachers. He had just crossed the border. He said that he had been a boxer in Mexico City and was undefeated. We spent the evening together at his camp, stomping aluminum cans and packing them into plastic garbage bags to be recycled for money. When I prepared to leave, Luis insisted that I stay. He dragged out my equipment, directed me to a spot, and told me to set up the strobes and soft boxes. He then took out a long pole and tied a piece of rope to each end. After hanging buckets from the ropes, he placed the contraption on his shoulders and trotted off toward a nursery a quarter mile away to fetch water. It was a routine he followed twice a day. On returning, he stood opposite my lights and directed me to photograph. Bearded, shirtless, and with his arms extended along the pole, Luis looked like Jesus Christ crucified. Personifying suffering and distilling the essence of perseverance, his image shouted the theme of torture ennobled.[50]

What we all want, as Wright Morris once said, is a piece of the cross. We want images that expand our consciousness, not those that are plastered on T-shirts. Reflecting on the episode, I have always felt that it belonged to the former in a way too deep for words. Words, in fact, seem superfluous when desire to have a picture taken and the decision to make it are one and the same, when the poser is the taker. Such moments have very little to do with lighting or camera equipment and everything to do with the standard tools that the professional historian acquires: empathy, attention to detail, a sense of humor, interviewing skills, fluency in a foreign language, and the willingness to follow a story wherever it might lead. Had I not trained as a historian or had I engaged in the hit-and-run photojournalism practiced by the vultures who passed through Rancho de los Diablos without actually seeing it or meeting its inhabitants, I would never have received the gift of that picture.[51]

As for the image itself, which some call "the Crucifixion shot," a few colleagues find it overly symbolic in the way it evokes one man's earthly plight, but at the same time it is never more than an ordinary shot of a man briefly at rest while going about his daily routine. At once a likeness and a document, symbol and self-portrait, it allows Luis Rodríguez to be simultaneously himself and more than himself, to express himself and to allow himself to be represented by someone else. This admixture has always given me the strangest sensation. I believe that, watching me work, Luis felt safe, confident in my abilities. Neither a victim nor voiceless, he had observed me working, assimilated my methodology, and previsualized this image in his mind. He understood its symbolic importance. Luis was no passive victim. Alert and clear-thinking, he was raising a cry of alarm. He had this all figured out in advance. It is his photograph, not mine, further confirmation of the extent to which photographic consciousness—the language of photography—had worked its way deeply into the farmworker experience in California.[52]

23

Photographers and Farmworkers Today

Toward a Global Language

Two years after photographing Luis Rodríguez, I resumed my coverage of the UFW, but under tragic circumstances. On April 23, 1993, César Chávez died near his childhood home in San Luis, Arizona, apparently worn-out by his many death-defying fasts and nonstop schedule. He had been resting from two full days on the witness stand as part of a long, drawn-out legal battle with the Salinas Valley lettuce grower the Bruce Church Company. When he died, his hopes and dreams and aspirations did not die with him. These continued in the UFW and among campesinos and campesinas and a large number of supporters inside and outside agriculture, in California, in Mexico, and across the United States.

So great was the shock and outpouring of genuine grief that his funeral in Delano six days later became the greatest media event in UFW and farmworker history. Every photographer who had ever covered the union, and many more who had not, packed into town the day before the funeral. The sun was topping the Sierra Nevada to the east when I arrived at Forty Acres shortly after 6 A.M. For several hours I kept busy watching people assemble along the two-lane east–west highway that would convey the funeral procession across town. Grammar school children were outside their classrooms, waiting with their teachers behind paper banners bearing messages written in crayon. Families were spreading blankets in the grass and opening umbrellas. Police cars patrolled about, and traffic cops worked side streets. Vans arrived, disgorging people, and left to pick up more. Satellite trucks with their generators making a disrespectful racket packed the dusty parking lot. With all of their antennae extended and pointed skyward, they formed a kind of surreal alcove of media ready to beam the event worldwide. Overhead several airplanes circled. News helicopters hovered on the east side of town.

I tuned my Sony Walkman to Radio Bilingüe. Samuel Orozco was covering the event. Listening to him alternating between English and Spanish, I sensed a kind of Chicano version of Edward R. Murrow pouring his soul into a broadcast. His deep and distinctive voice transported me back to our first encounter on August 12, 1987, when peach pickers had gone on strike against the H. P. Metzler Brothers, and I bumped into Orozco on the picket lines. I was still thinking of that encounter when, around midmorning, glowing spots of color appeared where the road met the horizon several miles east of Delano. Looking through my telephoto lens, I could see that those spots were union banners and flags as they waved and filled in the light breeze. Over the next fifteen minutes, the sea of banners and flags grew into a procession of thirty thousand mourners. The people around me hardly seemed to be attending a funeral. They smiled and held hands. Some wore dark suits, others jeans and white T-shirts. Old friends waved and greeted one another with shouts of "Hola, hola!" A tourist stumbling into the scene might easily have mistaken it for early arrivals at a harvest festival.

Waiting for the procession to cross town, I asked the same questions that I had previously on countless such occasions: What would my predecessors be doing now? Where would Dorothea Lange be? If there ever was a picture that demanded a Carleton E. Watkins–style elevated perspective and a telephoto lens, this was it. I started looking around and found plenty of platforms. Pickup trucks offered limited elevation, so I thought about climbing on top of several buses. I even considered using several trees and one very inviting telephone pole. I had used them all before, at one time or another. I was thinking about Otto Hagel's photograph of Horace Bristol sitting atop a telephone pole during the 1936 Salinas Valley lettuce packers' strike and how Otto had once climbed into the pesticide-dispensing hopper on a crop duster to get a good aerial picture when I spotted an alfalfa loader parked alongside the road near the entrance to Forty Acres. The roof of the cab was fifteen feet above the road and offered a good vantage point. By climbing into the loading bucket, I could add another ten feet and achieve a kind of hovering perspective. Finding the Mexican American owner–operator, I did not have to explain what I wanted to do. He had taken the day off and parked his machine there, hoping to help photographers get their shots, once again evidence of just how deeply photographic consciousness had worked itself into the farmworker community.

When I scrambled from the cab roof into the bucket, several other photographers noticed me and tagged along. Mexican photographer Liliana Nieto del Río was right behind. As she struggled up, I gave her a lift, momentarily alarmed to feel my entire hand fitting around her thin arm. From that vantage point, I began photographing the procession with my 180-millimeter lens. When César's casket rounded the corner several miles away, I could see dozens of politicians, actors, and union members taking their turn as pallbearers. A flatbed truck loaded with photographers and camera crews preceded the casket, and even more photographers walked alongside. For a time I watched those photographers maneuvering for shots of Jesse Jackson, Edward James Olmos, Willie Brown, Jerry Brown, Martin Sheen, the Kennedy clan, and others. Every time photographers got close, UFW guards shooed them away. But one especially persistent paparazzo wearing his baseball cap backward kept circling the casket, working in close. He kept at it for over ten blocks, moving on only after he got the shot he wanted.

Thirty years earlier no one would have imagined a gathering of this sort in Delano. The police would not have allowed it. Now they were scrambling to make it happen. The whole event had an air of unreality about it. I could scarcely believe that César was dead. When the procession came closer, I began photographing. The casket was easy to find in the sea of marchers because of the encircling swath of white and red UFW flags. To the left and slightly behind the coffin was Cardinal Roger Mahony. He was dressed in his magenta religious garments and skull cap, with a small cross hanging across his chest, surrounded by dozens of priests and rabbis in purple, black, and white. Tucked behind his right shoulder was Dolores Huerta, wearing black. Directly behind her, Richard Chávez (César's brother) walked with Arturo Rodríguez, Marshall Ganz, Marc Grossman, Luis Váldez, and Leroy Chatfield. Everyone wore black armbands and red ribbons. Everyone had some kind of UFW symbol: a gold pin, a button.

As the coffin passed below me, I climbed down and followed the procession to a small building on Forty Acres where Chávez lay in the simple pine casket constructed by his brother, Richard. Throughout the day, I greeted one friend after another, including a Los Angeles photographer with whom I had just worked in Haiti. While thousands of union members, friends, and admirers filed past the coffin to pay their last respects, UFW officials periodically invited in several photographers. Escorted by

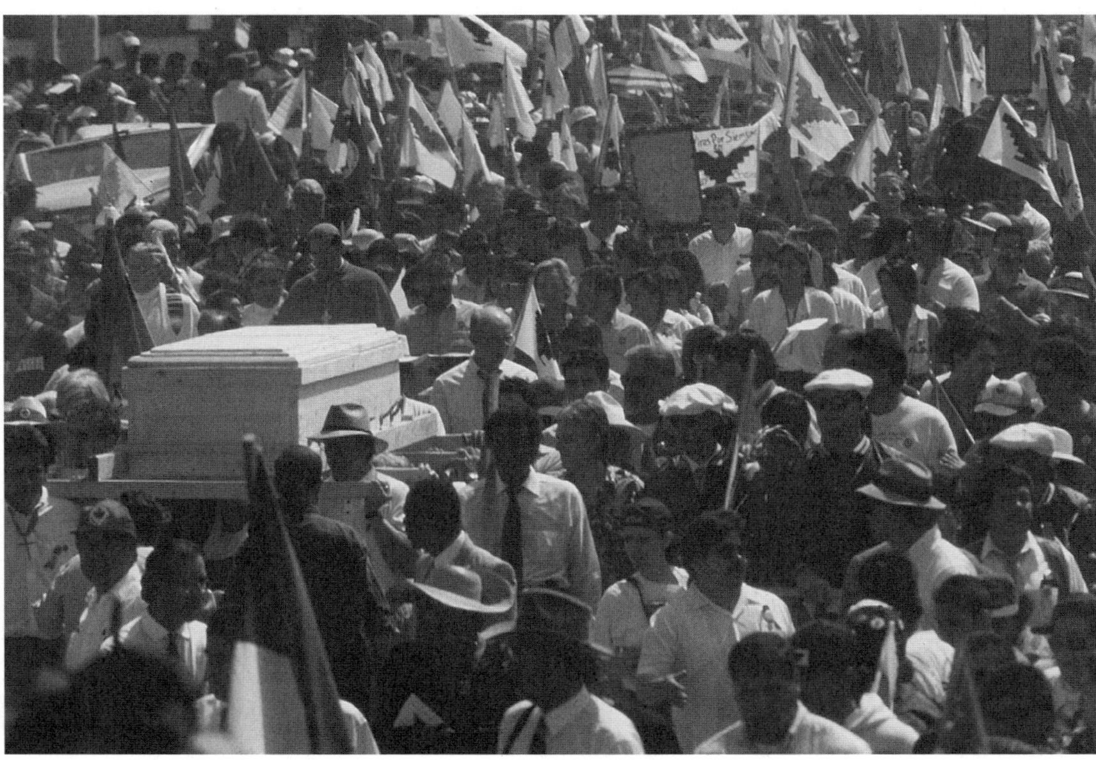

César Chávez being carried in his coffin through the streets of Delano to services at Forty Acres, April 29, 1993, photograph by Richard Steven Street. Original in color. Courtesy of Streetshots.

UFW guards from Delancy Street, the photographers were each given two or three minutes to work. Once again, every photographer took essentially the same shot, but several images did stand out. As an old man lifted his grandchild to his shoulder so that the child could see Chávez, one photographer caught the moment. Another captured elderly farmworkers reciting their rosaries. And so it went. Even in death, Chávez remained photogenic.

Over the next four hours, dozens of photographers and thousands of mourners paid their last respects. Determined not to be rushed, I wanted to take the final and very best picture of Chávez. To do so, I had arrived with battery-powered strobes and soft boxes. Having used the equipment on countless occasions to make beautiful color portraits in extremely difficult circumstances, I decided that the best way to approach the challenge of photographing Chávez in his coffin was to wait until the end, when all the photographers had finished their work. After the last mourners had paid their respects, I would spend more than the allotted five minutes with César. I wanted to do so with minimal interference. I was determined to use the same lighting equipment I would have used to photograph the CEO of a Fortune 500 company or the president of the United States.

As the afternoon wore on, it grew uncomfortably warm, and I began to wither in the heat. Forty Acres was packed with people from all over the country, so I decided to stroll around and look for some drinking water. While listening to a *cantollanista* singing beautiful songs of the farmworker movement, I again encountered *Bakersfield Californian* photographer Felix Adamo. Striking up a conversation, we both agreed that the afternoon had an odd feeling. There was a great sense of sadness and loss. Veteran union members were crying, and some were extremely distraught. *Originales* (farmworkers from the Delano grape strike and the march on Sacramento) had driven across the country to be present. Hispanics from all parts of California had pulled their children out of school, arriving in the middle of the night. The question of what would happen to the UFW, to *la causa,* lingered. But a feeling of reunion and solidarity was also present. The oddest facet to the day was the commercial activity. "It surprised me to see vendors hawking t-shirts, caps, pins, books, flags, and everything else," Adamo later wrote to me. "I realized the UFW was raising funds for their cause, but it struck me as rather strange. But it was nice to see many of the older people, some of whom had actually marched with César, had come to the funeral to pay their last respects to a man who had made their lives and working conditions better."[1]

Late in the afternoon, as the line of mourners trickled to an end, I tucked in behind a group of women dressed in black shawls and a young campesino in a T-shirt. The women carried rosary beads, and the young man carried his three-year-old boy on his shoulder. Working very slowly, I set up my strobe and soft box, made a test flash, and took a meter reading. Next I stood somewhat precariously on a folding steel chair. I was trying to look slightly down on César so that I could clearly see him in his coffin. Then I waited.

As a historian, I was determined not to miss a chance to record history. As a photographer, I wanted to take the very best photograph possible. As a human being, I wanted to respect the man and the moment. All of these goals were in conflict. Physically I was at my limits. Standing on that chair seat was no easy feat. I worried constantly that I might lose my balance or that someone might bump me and I would end up falling onto the coffin and taking down old women and babies. I kept thinking about the photographers present at the funerals of Malcolm X and Martin Luther King Jr. and how important it was for later generations to have pictures of those events. The only way to accomplish that goal was to work as slowly and quietly as possible.

I am not sure the Delancy Street guards understood what I was doing. Had Dolores Huerta been there, she would have instantly recognized my gringo face from our hundreds of encounters over the years and simply smiled and gone about her business. But I had never seen these guards before, and they had no idea that I had been photographing the union for eighteen years, was familiar to most union members, and had many adventures to recount, ranging from the time in the Imperial Valley in 1986 when a large, pear-shaped office manager of Mario Saikhon Inc. became enraged when I entered his office to photograph fired broccoli workers and tried to throw me through a plate glass window to the moment a year later when Dolores Huerta almost choked to death on a fish bone in Perko's restaurant in Reedley while I was interviewing her at 2 A.M.[2]

César's guards had no way of knowing any of this. To them I was probably just some interloper disrespecting the dead to get a good picture. And all that equipment did not endear me to them. When I resisted their efforts to hurry me out, I thought we might get into a tussle. Apparently the balancing act I did on that folding chair put them at ease. For more than twenty minutes I stood there, watching scenes unfold, waiting for each picture to happen. This seemed to prove that I was not out for a cheap shot, that I was not a hit-and-run photographer. I took many pictures of young couples carrying babies. They would pause there and talk to their children, somehow trying to impress on their young minds the gravity of the moment. I watched at least a dozen couples follow the same ritual. I made my best photograph when a young father took his child from his wife's arms and raised the baby up, and two *abuelitas* dressed entirely in black recited the Lord's Prayer. As they made the Sign of the Cross, I snapped a picture. A minute later the coffin lid was closed. I had taken the final image of César Chávez.

That night I retired to People's Café for a beer and a round of pool with old chums from the trail. The next day I went over to the huge tent at Forty Acres, where the funeral service was to be held. Arriving early, I watched Victor Alemán setting up a remote-controlled, motor-driven camera on a cross bar above the stage where the casket would lie. With a wide-angle lens attached, the camera would act like a kind of eye of God, capturing a view of the ceremonies that no photographer elbowing for position at ground level could match. I had no such access and had not brought along my remote equipment. The funeral service was going to be another hot, sweaty affair, with photographers squirming for position, so I walked the grounds and made some mental notes about the best sites. But experience taught me that all of the best vantage points would be taken and that I would have to improvise.

When the funeral service began, hundreds of photographers crowded around the altar. Next to me was KGO-TV's Rigo Chacón, whom I had last seen and photographed fourteen years earlier during the March on Salinas. Magnum photographer Paul Fusco, whom I had seen on and off at farmworker events for more than a decade, was also present, along with George Ballis, the most senior photographer of the farmworker movement. Perhaps the most experienced of all the farmworker movement photographers, Ballis understood the demands of working a mass event and sweating it out under the sun, but he was no longer actively photographing the UFW and lacked the media outlets necessary to get his images out to the public. And he was too grief stricken to stand opposite the open coffin of his old friend with sophisticated strobe lighting equipment to get good color pictures. He was there purely out of respect. Although Bob Fitch had photographed farmworker funerals and certainly knew how to maneuver for position, he was nowhere to be seen.

Many of the photographers present at the funeral were working on deadline. Competing against world events for space, they were under great pressure. But also some were there to witness history and show respect by working more or less as historians with cameras. They did so because of the man—the authentic Mexican American leader inside that plain coffin—and because, like everyone else, they were genuinely moved. They wondered if they were witnessing the end of an era, perhaps the death not only of an old man but also of a declining movement, a major turning point in the farmworker story. In temperament and outlook, they were inclined toward a slower and more personal and artistic view. Covering the funeral with bittersweet images of grief and solidarity and the union in eclipse, they injected questions about the future into coverage long stuck in the past. Through their work, a pivotal moment in the organizing struggle was fixed and preserved. When they thought back over the experience, they never mentioned the money they made from their photographs, if they made any at all. No one who photographed over those two days did so with profit in mind.[3]

While priests moved up and down the isles and dignitaries and old friends filed in for the Mass, photographers kept up a steady stream of flashes. They illuminated every move, documented every expression, caught every tear, recorded every gesture. When César's grandchildren placed a UFW eagle and a short-handled hoe on the altar, hundreds of strobes followed them. When Dolores Huerta eulogized the man she had worked with for over four decades and Luis Váldez announced, "You shall never die," photographers kept clicking away. At the height of the service, when Cardinal Roger Mahony gave his blessing and offered sympathies from the pope, Alemán used his remote device to trigger the camera he had rigged above the casket. Over the next half hour, photographers continued to record every detail. When mourners lit candles, photographers crowded around, firing off flashes to compensate for the rapidly diminishing light. And then with nightfall, the photographers went their separate ways.[4]

Looking back on their two days at Delano, photographers would romanticize what had been a grind, throw in a few anecdotes to embellish the story, and recall evenings in bars, trading shots and replaying tapes of the various songs they had heard. They also recalled a sense of harmony and common purpose, when in fact many had been competing for the same shot. But those who had never before covered a farmworker event did walk through Delano, east to west, every mile from the affluent Anglo section to the barrio near Highway 99. No one who ever made that walk left without some impression of the place where the farmworker movement was born. They ate in the Mexican cafés and sent postcards to friends, relatives, and colleagues, describing their experiences. They purchased union trinkets and stuck them in their camera bags and packed them home. Whatever their previous knowledge and experience, they left Delano with strong memories and images of one of the greatest events in the visual history of the farmworker movement, the Chicano counterpart to Martin Luther King Jr.'s funeral, an event the likes of which had never been seen before and will never be seen again in California. But after converging on Delano to take a last single picture of the most famous farmworker in California, photographers did not stop. They continued, not so much for the union, but for posterity and for themselves. There was a lot more going on and a lot more to see and document.

Constantly adapting not only to changing circumstances but also to changing views of their craft, photographers followed a long series of unpredictable developments. Zeroing in on local communities and adopting a transnational perspective, they probed forgotten eddies in farmworker history while seeking out new ones. They became explorers as well as chroniclers. Opposed to hit-and-run press photography, these photographers worked at their own direction. Seldom content to make a single news photograph, they pursued their work with multiple images acquired by carefully cultivating sources, winning people's trust, and letting things take their natural course over extended periods of time. Only in this way could they amass the experiences and immerse themselves in a situation sufficiently to document how things are, how they came to be, where they were headed, and what they signified. Photographers practice these concepts in varying degrees, but after Chávez's funeral a handful of dedicated photographers undertook projects that went far beyond those of their predecessors.

The best known of these documentarians is Don Bartletti, a bilingual photographer possessing strong political views, tenacious work habits, and an ability to glide between the moving shadows. He had learned his craft while dodging the draft as a student at Palomar Junior College, then served a tour of duty as an army second lieutenant running convoys of explosives and artillery shells near the demilitarized zone in South Vietnam. Back home, he framed a rocket-propelled grenade round that had killed a member of his unit ("small hole in the personnel carrier, nothing but ashes inside"), then tried to dispel his nightmares by using his newly purchased Nikon to photograph clouds, plants, water droplets, and friends. He landed his first photography job in 1973, when an editor at the *Vista Press* hired him to cover local news. In 1977, he moved on to the *Oceanside Blade-Tribune;* the following year he began photographing for the *San Diego Union-Tribune;* in 1983 he landed a job at the *Los Angeles Times,* covering everything from sports and fashion to celebrities and wildfires.[5]

During a summer of picking tomatoes just before graduating from Vista High School, Bartletti first noticed undocumented farmworkers. "Early each morning when the Mexicans marched out of the eucalyptus grove where they were living, I could still see the wisps of smoke wafting above from their breakfast fires," he recalled many years later. "I had never seen a farmworker camp before." Bartletti also got a taste of working with the short-handled hoe, which he used to weed tomato plants. "It was so horrible I couldn't stand it," he recalled. "After two weeks, I quit. I had earned one hundred dollars and that's what I needed. But those workers endured. They had to keep going."[6]

Twenty years later, still living in the old neighborhood where he grew up, Bartletti watched more and more undocumented field hands settling in north San Diego County. He explained to me:

> That's when I realized history was in the making. For decades legal and undocumented farmworkers had passed through the county on their way north. By staying here, they did not have to worry about crossing the highway checkpoints at Temecula and San Clemente. They were finding plenty of minimum-wage work in the nurseries and on the tomato and strawberry farms. To save money, they camped out in the canyons and gullies. Entire shantytown communities grew up overnight. There was a public outcry. Encampments would be a hundred yards from multimillion-dollar hilltop homes. Bus stops became curbside hiring halls. Laborers were riding bicycles home from the fields. Signs changed from English to Spanish. Faces you saw on the streets shifted from Anglo to Latino.[7]

To capture these changes, Bartletti began with the most dramatic and visible component of the larger story, the same place where everyone else began: along the U.S.–Mexico border in San Diego County, where he documented the pattern of migration. Each night it was the same. Having made their way to Tijuana from Oaxaca, Sinaloa, Guerrero, and a hundred other places as far south as Guatemala, immigrants hooked up with coyotes at the Tijuana bus station and headed to the Soccer Field, the nickname for a dusty clearing below Otey Mesa. All day long, enterprising people would sell immigrants tacos, cigarettes, water, soft drinks, marijuana, beer, and tequila. Toward evening, Border Patrol officers began to closely monitor the Soccer Field through hidden censors, helicopters, and night-vision devices. And then, with a whistle or a shout, thousands of migrants—often wearing two pairs of underwear, two shirts, two pairs of pants and carrying everything else stuffed inside a duffle bag—would surge across the fields and gullies into the hills and canyons. One in three would be detained by La Migra. Some would die or succumb to bandits and rapists waiting for them in the darkness. But most would survive the crossing. Within a day, they would be picking strawberries, planting tomatoes, or harvesting gladiolas.[8]

Financing his project out of pocket with additional support from the National Endowment for the Humanities and the San Diego Museum of Photographic Arts, Bartletti plunged into his work and never looked back. Almost immediately he saw things that were almost too incredible to believe. Out searching for farmworker encampments in Rancho Bernardo, an upscale development of homes valued at three-quarters of a million dollars in the late 1980s, he was on a doorstep talking to a homeowner when he spotted a man walking in his direction on the residential street. The immigrant was carrying two large plastic bags full of water obtained from a nearby spigot. When the man turned onto a well-worn dirt path paralleling a neat driveway, Bartletti excused himself for a moment. Stepping a few yards off the doorstep, he composed the scene with a 105-millimeter portrait lens. "Opulence on the left, poverty and struggle on the right," is his accompanying caption. It is the ideal metaphor for what was unfolding all around him, an image symbolizing the growing division between poor immigrant farmworkers and established citizens, right down to the crack in the concrete and telephone pole that neatly bisect the picture. "Sometimes an image is a gift," he recalled of the May 5, 1988, photograph. "This one was a treasure."[9]

Thirteen months later, while climbing an embankment above Interstate 5 near Encinitas Boulevard, Bartletti spotted the crudest example of a camp that he had ever seen. No one was there, so he waited. At around 9 P.M. a group of five men came up a path. Using his usual technique before photographing, Bartletti spent time getting to know these people he hoped to document. Because the Border Patrol often questioned men such as these, Bartletti tried to ease their fears by explaining in Spanish that they were living in one of the most unbelievable places he'd ever seen and that,

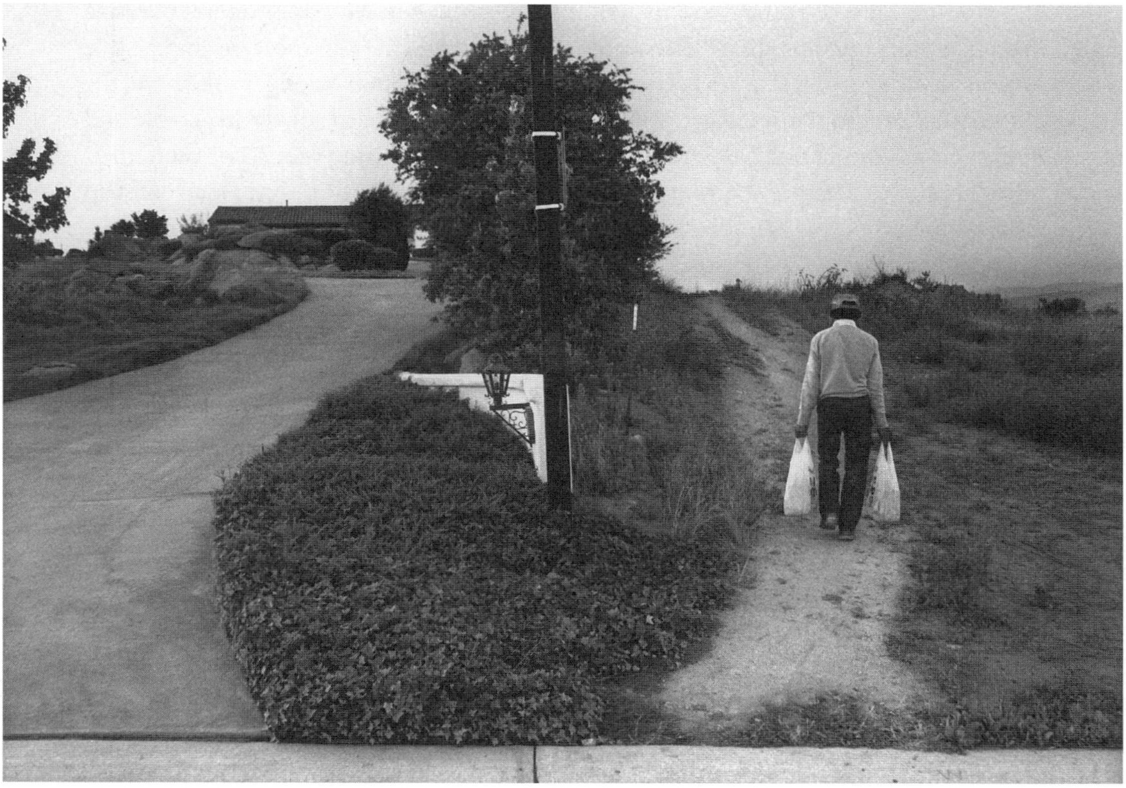

Following a well-worn path, an immigrant field hand carrying drinking water from a sympathetic homeowner's garden spigot heads back to camp near Rancho Bernardo, May 3, 1988, photograph by Don Bartletti. From the series Between Two Worlds. Courtesy of Don Bartletti.

from his perspective, they were part of the changing history of San Diego. If they would allow him to tell their story, Bartletti would do it to the best of his ability. Although the men were Guatemalan Indians who spoke little Spanish, they agreed to let Bartletti sit there with them and take a few pictures.[10]

Bartletti made his first photographs of the men above Interstate 5 in color, without artificial light. Dissatisfied with the results, particularly the lack of detail in the men's faces, he returned the next evening with a strobe, an umbrella reflector, and a light stand and rephotographed the men in black and white. Since they were in total darkness and Bartletti wanted to include lights from the freeway and from the nearby community, he made a timed exposure. Setting his camera on a tripod, he used a small flashlight to help him focus on the men, popped the flash, quickly refocused the lens on infinity, and continued the exposure for about two minutes. By including foreground and background elements, Bartletti captured the dichotomy of desperate men who, though absolutely essential to the local economy, slept on the ground on a hillside above a busy highway next to an affluent suburb populated by Americans who wanted nothing to do with such people. "Every time I drive past that spot," he explained to me many times, "I look up there and remember those men in their dirt bed of hope and despair."[11]

Working closely with *Times* staff writer Patrick McDonnell, Bartletti built outward from these experiences. In Tijuana he documented the circumstances driving people north: families struggling in border factories and vendors hawking trinkets on the streets. Because so many failed in those endeavors and headed for the vegetable and flower farms around San Diego, and because the border crossing was so critical to their immigration experience, Bartletti devoted considerable attention to the narrow strip of territory extending for about one hundred yards on either side of the border line, particularly activities there late at night, when smugglers, bandits, and Border Patrolmen were most active.

At around midnight on June 18, 1992, Bartletti was talking with a group of men through a gap in the ten-foot-high steel fence on the border between San Ysidro and Tijuana. The area was illuminated by huge, stadium-type lights, recently installed by the Border Patrol. Bartletti had just photographed a confrontation between a group called Light Up the Border, who had been pushing for a massive expansion of the border fence, and immigrant rights groups, who labeled such actions racist and un-American. Now he explained his project to the immigrants gathering to rush the fence. Gaining their confidence, he set up to photograph. Suddenly he heard one of the men whistle. It signaled an opportunity to scale the wall. First, a few men slipped over the top, then more. Having caught the Border Patrol during a shift change, the men dropped down the north face of the fence. Bartletti's third tripod-mounted shot in a sequence of six captured that moment when the men topped the wall, cascaded down, and were about to dash past him to begin their quest in El Norte. He called it *La brinca* (The Hop).[12]

Over the next decade, Bartletti amassed thousands of such experiences. Starting at the border and moving north, he documented migration patterns, Border Patrol arrests, encounters with bandits, confrontations with established communities, working conditions on farms, and life in the provisional shantytown communities that dotted the canyons and ravines of north San Diego County. Reactions to his photographs varied. Some viewers praised them as iconic works of art, opening windows into life itself. Others denounced the immigrants they depicted as the dregs of society. Bartletti just saw his neighbors. "If you try to put aside the pathos of life without conveniences," he often explained at lectures, "you will find in the camps and among undocumented farmworkers of San Diego a community of contributors, a spirit of hopefulness, and a degree of happiness."[13]

Gathering together the first installment of his work, he published it as *Between Two Worlds: The People of the Border.* Since then he has continued to expand his photography in articles appearing episodically in the *Times.* One of his photographs had immediate, practical consequences. Because hundreds of undocumented immigrant farmworkers and other recent arrivals had been killed or injured crossing the freeways, the California Department of Transportation (Caltrans) used several of Bartletti's color photographs to create a highway sign and posters alerting motorists to the presence of pedestrians and also warning immigrants of the lethal dangers they might encounter.

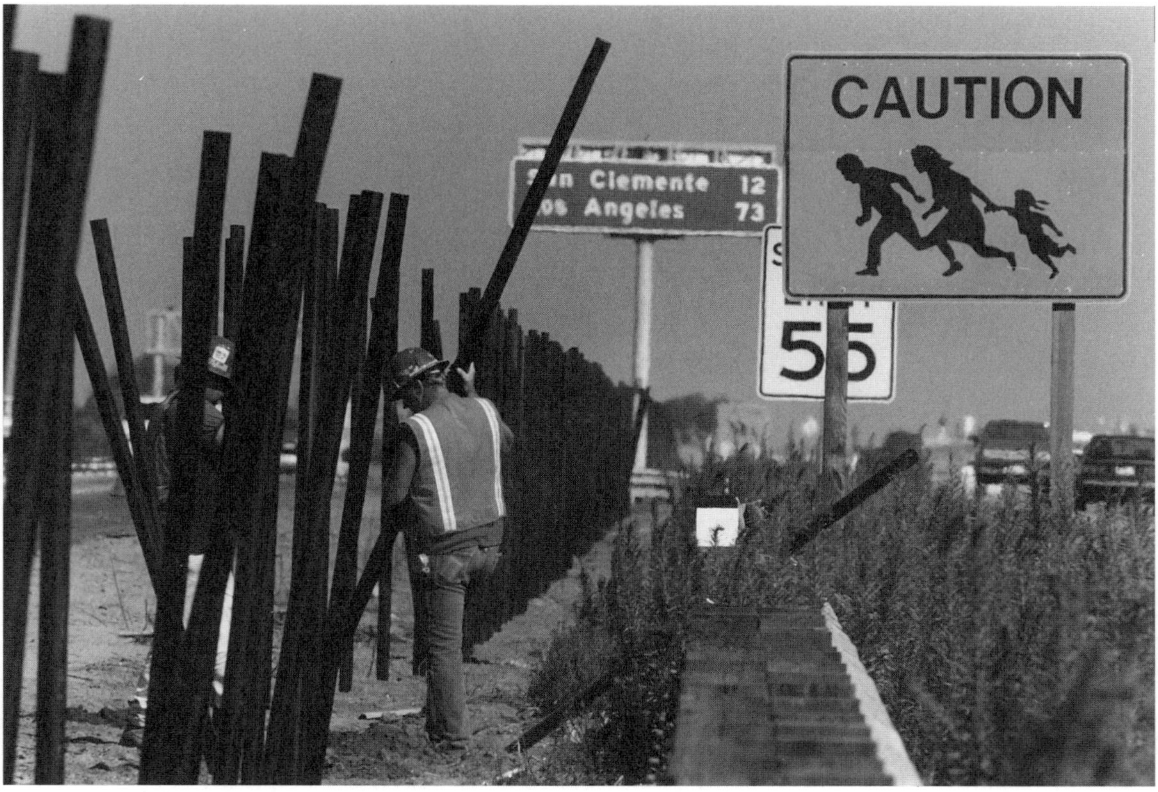

Caltrans warning sign along Interstate 5 near San Diego, based on a Don Bartletti photograph, May 1992, photograph by Don Bartletti. Original in color. From the series Between Two Worlds. Courtesy of Don Bartletti.

Caltrans placed thirty-five of the five-foot wide signs at danger points along several freeways. Those signs, showing pedestrians running, have helped to save countless immigrants from death or injury. A Pulitzer Prize in 2002 acknowledged Bartletti's work as providing an insightful and honest picture of two seemingly separate political territories that are in fact intricately linked through one transnational labor market.[14]

While Bartletti was expanding his documentary project into all corners of north San Diego County's farmworker community, another photographer, Matt Black, was building a smaller but equally intense portrait of farmworkers in his home community in the San Joaquin Valley. Black was twenty years younger than Bartletti but had already contended with him for a Pulitzer Prize. After graduating from San Francisco State University summa cum laude with a degree in history, not photography or photojournalism, Black returned to his home in Lemon Cove, southeast of Fresno. Working briefly for the *Tulare Advance Register* and *Visalia Times-Delta,* he grew increasingly restless as a newspaper photographer. Fed up with the stifling and increasingly cynical attitude toward documentary photography that he encountered, he became a freelancer and began focusing on what he knew and loved: the land and the people of the Central Valley. To his surprise, delight, and occasional dismay, the valley provided an endless reservoir of stories, all of them centered, in one way or another, on farmworkers, farm life, and rural society—ample resources for what he called his "first-person journey through this beguiling place." His chief goal was to address his Tulare County surroundings with the kind of emotional honesty that he found in the work of Dorothea Lange, Walker Evans, and other FSA photographers.[15]

Black's first photo essay focused on Three Rocks, an impoverished farmworker community on the west side of the San Joaquin Valley. Learning that the unincorporated community was holding a festival commemorating the legendary gold rush–era bandit Joaquin Murrieta, Black produced an essay that was less about the legacy of the bandit than about a group of farmworkers struggling to survive hard times in proximity to the spot where Murrieta had been shot and beheaded. Next, focusing on an individual, Black spent long days with Lupe Ortiz, a forty-five-year-old shepherd from Durango, Mexico, who lived in a small trailer surrounded by thousands of sheep and went weeks without seeing or talking to anyone. Shortly after working with *Los Angeles Times* writer Mark Arax on a story about William Saroyan, a freeze struck the orange belt bordering the foothills of the Sierra Nevada, killing off the citrus crop in a one-hundred-mile-long swath between Madera and Wheeler Ridge. Living in the center of the disaster, Black put a human face on the catastrophe by shooting an essay on farmworkers thrown out of work and struggling to survive.[16]

While these and other assignments accumulated, Black began to discover facets of his environment that were strangely overlooked and cried out for photographic documentation. Some he sought out. Others appeared unexpectedly. Perhaps the most important centered on Teviston, a small unincorporated community that sprawls across the alkali flats on the edge of the old Tulare Lake beside Highway 99, on the outskirts of Pixley, and is home to thirteen hundred aging African American Dust Bowl refugees—"black Okies"—and their descendants. His path to Teviston began in another southwestern Tulare County community. He was driving north on Highway 43 one Sunday in 1996 when he spotted an old church with several old cars parked beside it. He stopped and went inside to discover that the church had about eight members, all of them over sixty years of age. He was in Allensworth, remnant of a once-thriving African American settlement founded in 1908 by Colonel Allen Allensworth, a former Kentucky slave and army officer during the Spanish–American War.

Black was affected by the loneliness and isolation of the town, and he returned there over the next year and got to know the church members. Many lived just north of Pixley, in an unincorporated community unlisted on any map. With no sewers, no stoplights, and no businesses other than a single soft drink dispensing machine, Teviston was an odd assortment of tar-paper shacks and outdoor privies that seemed transferred from the Mississippi Delta to the heart of the Golden State. Every third home had burned down, including an old grocery store that Black had passed many times as a child. Touched by what *Los Angeles Times* writer Mark Arax later described as something halfway between a "scattering of country churches and crooked huts" and a "glorified squatter's camp," Black thought to himself, "As a place, it's really not much to look at. It looks like hundreds of other beat-up little towns."[17]

Although too young to have witnessed firsthand Wayne Miller's work on black cotton pickers migrating to California or Ernest Lowe's photographic work in Teviston a decade after Miller's, Black soon recognized that Teviston was, in fact, unlike any other community in the Central Valley. While crime, poverty, misery, and visual pollution were rampant in dozens of rundown, beaten-up farmworker communities, no others even vaguely resembled this faded remnant of broken dreams. Resolving to meet its residents, Black began by first visiting its churches, where, he recalled, "people could see me, and I could see them." Returning so many times that he soon lost count, Black discovered that most of Teviston's residents were in their eighties and nineties and quickly dying off.[18]

Seeking to preserve history before it passed into oblivion, Black began documenting this vestige settlement, with its children, grandchildren, great grandchildren, and memories of a forgotten African American exodus. On one of his visits, Black met a community worker who introduced him to James Dixon, a ninety-five-year-old living in a tiny plywood house with "cobwebs so thick with dust that they seemed to inhale and exhale with each draft." Dixon had come from Louisiana to pick cotton for J. G. Boswell in 1945, one of seven thousand black sharecroppers who had left their homes in the South and Midwest. Black later recalled:

> Dixon was a lonely old man who liked to tell stories and talk about his religion. He had lived the hardest kind of life. I admired him, which I think he knew. He had many ideas about what was wrong with the world. An incredible, Old Testament kind of thinking that you just don't hear anymore. He was Catholic. He would go to a church where the services were in Spanish. He didn't understand a word of it. He was out of his time and place, and his community was gone.[19]

Making Dixon the center of his story, Black returned on many occasions to photograph the old man plugging holes in his shack with flattened Vienna Sausage tins and cardboard boxes or shaving in front of the rearview mirror inside his broken-down 1964 Chevrolet. Before Black could complete his story, someone found Dixon's body on the floor beside his potbellied stove. Having burned the last limbs from an old pecan tree in his yard, Dixon had died of exposure and old age. He would be the first of many others to die while Black photographed. After Dixon was buried in Pixley, his home was ransacked. A few months later, another old resident invited Black to stay with her in her boxcar home while cancer took her life. Of such sensitive situations, Black thought along the same lines that had guided Lange:

> I try to be as quiet as possible, both for their sake and for mine. Lots of people try to play games, but people can see right through that. It takes some courage to keep quiet and put your trust in them as well. People just know if you are for real or not, if you are playing it straight or not. I don't think it much matters what you say.[20]

And so it went, the residents of Teviston revealing their stores, allowing Black to expose his rolls of Tri-X and T-Max film. Conveying these people's sense of decency,

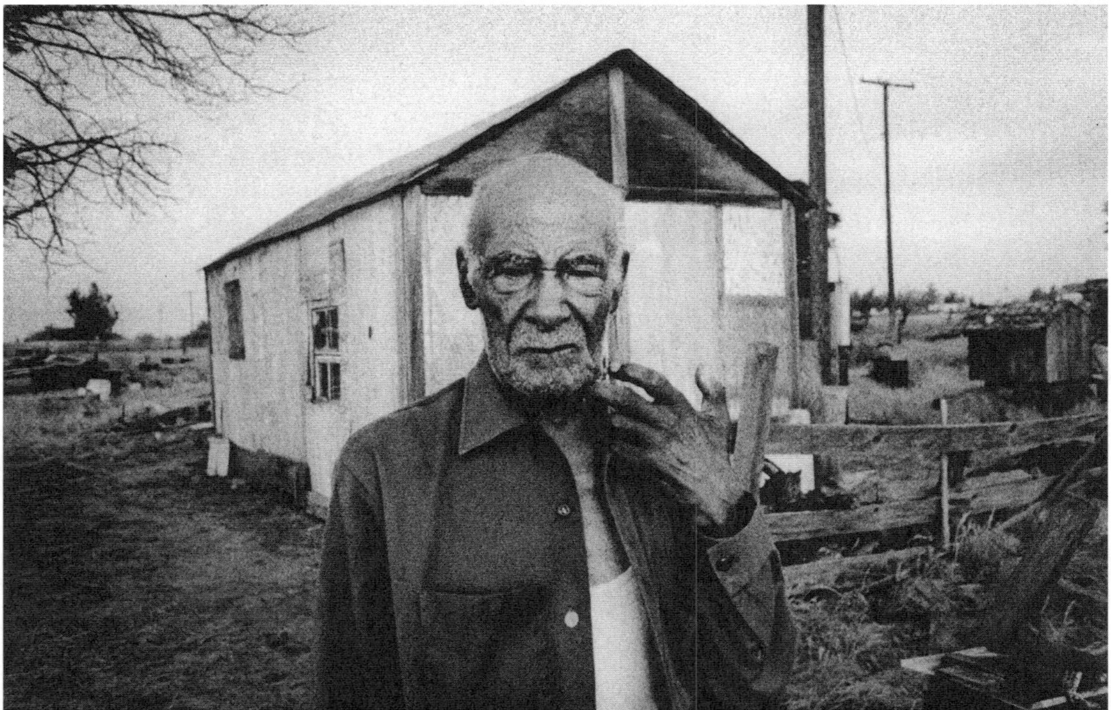

James Dixon, an old African American sharecropper who came west in 1948, in front of his tar-paper and plywood home in Teviston, December 2000, photograph by Matt Black. From the series Black Okies. Courtesy of Matt Black.

even if others had not treated them decently, Black's pictures capture a generation as it was dying off, never one at a time, but always in threes. Published in the *Los Angeles Times Magazine* as "A Broken Bit of the Promised Land," Black's essay contains something that other modern photographers missed: a group bypassed by time, omitted from the War on Poverty, caught in a California variant of the Jim Crow system, and dying out largely unknown to the public. Reflecting on the experience, Black revealed that he enjoyed nothing more than simply being allowed into people's lives. "To me, the actual photos are just an outgrowth of that experience, like a transcription," he explained. "The deeper the immersion, the more attentive the transcription—that's how I think of it. The challenge is not to let your ideas stand in the way of what's in front of you."[21]

Matt Black and Don Bartletti were not alone in discovering new angles to old problems. Following a path similar to theirs, photographer Saundra Sturdevant concentrated on women farmworkers in the Central Valley, particularly those around Lindsay, at the center of the state's citrus, cheese, and dairy industries. With funds from the California Arts Council, she launched the Migrant Photography Project and in the late 1990s began documenting marginal housing conditions, groundwater pollution,

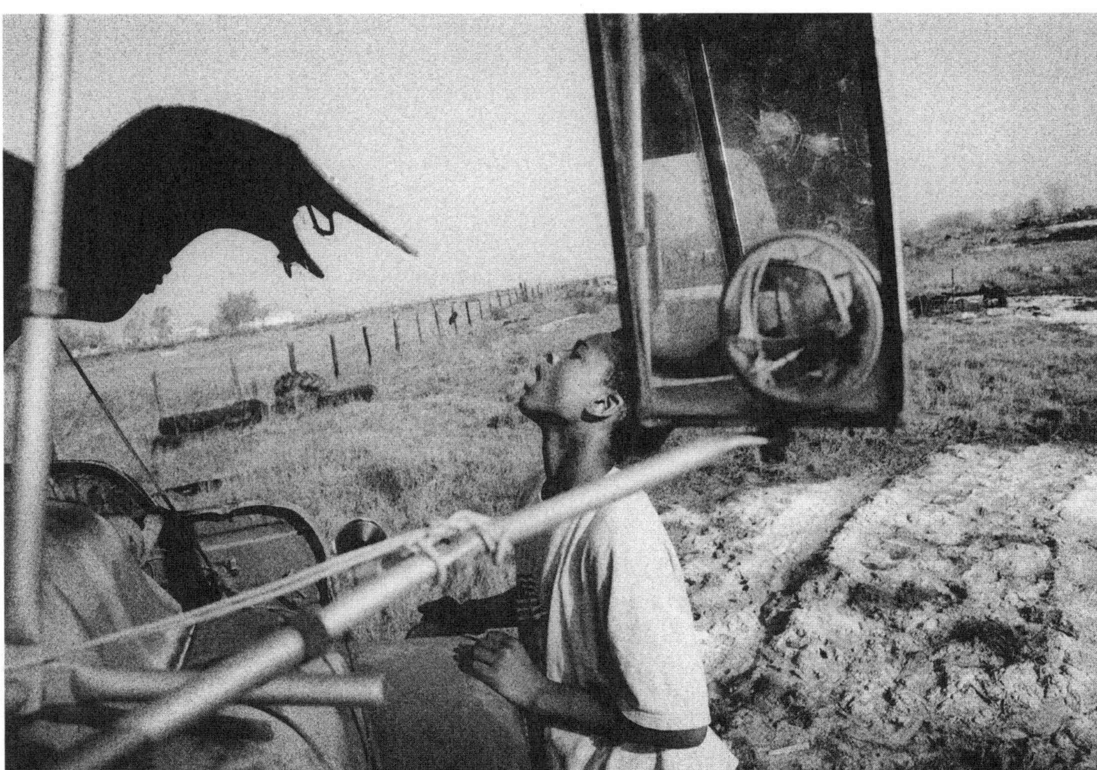

Boy plays on an abandoned farm truck at Teviston, May 2001, photograph by Matt Black. From the series Black Okies. Courtesy of Matt Black.

and bilingual education programs. Paying special attention to Tonyville, a four-square-block section of Lindsay, Sturdevant photographed another of the Central Valley's third world enclaves, one that lacked paved roads and sidewalks and was served by only a single store and a gas station. Uneasy with evoking pious phrases and a few tears, Sturdevant wanted to do more. Photographing from inside the community where she has lived, Sturdevant used her photographs and interviews to obtain a grant to launch a program to teach English- and Spanish-language literacy to residents. She was especially interested in helping women who, lacking immigration papers, struggled to raise children, often as non-English-speaking single mothers. Branching out into public safety issues, she next organized a health fair that in October 2002 provided services to over five hundred farmworkers, then used her photography to help the Pan Valley Institute (an American Friends Service Committee organization based in Fresno) bring Mexican and Southeast Asian women together to advance their mutual interests.[22]

Two years after Sturdevant began photographing in Tulare County, Rick Nahmias launched an ambitious statewide project. A New York University graduate in film and religious studies, Nahmias first became curious about the lives of contemporary farmworkers during the mid-1990s, when, several years after first seeing *Harvest of Shame,* he read a biography of Edward R. Murrow, discovering in Murrow an amazing myth of the flawed American hero. He optioned the book and started working on a screenplay. Finding one Hollywood studio after the next uninterested in a story about the ultimate American truth seeker, Nahmias eventually abandoned the project but could not forget the grittiness and harshness of farmworker life depicted by Murrow. Taking time off from working as a writer and researcher for a political columnist during the winter of 2001, he drove north through the Central Valley to study cooking at the Culinary Institute of America, in the Napa Valley. Sensuous dining experiences were fine so long as he did not think about the deeper implications of food production raised in *Harvest of Shame.* He kept asking himself, Where are those people today?

To answer that question, Nahmias decided to "put a human face on what is sometimes called California's invisible population." After spending eight weeks "buried in every bit of research [he] could find on farmworkers," Nahmias developed contacts among farmworker advocates and academic experts, who led him deeper into the farmworker communities themselves. With funding from the University of California, Berkeley, Center for Latino Policy Research, the Kurz Family Foundation, and California Rural Legal Assistance, Inc., Nahmias made a series of three- to five-day trips to several dozen farming communities over the course of the 2002–3 harvest season. Possessing only a basic competence in Spanish, he relied on community workers to break the ice and used what he calls "a lot of show and tell" to venture on his own into a world totally different from his comfortable surroundings. He recalled:

> I tried to avoid agendas or shot lists, and for the most part succeeded. But halfway through the shoots, my office then literally wallpapered with dozens and dozens of work prints, I realized what I had amassed was a mosaic of sorts: farmworkers at work,

> play, with family, dealing with health issues, housing, recreation, immigration, etc. I only then came to realize that with a bit more focusing on filling the holes I had left, this could be an opportunity to show this community in three dimensions as I had not seen it done before—and in doing so maybe "humanize" them in terms of what our society understands, and ultimately make it harder to keep them invisible or deny their existence and the power of their contributions.[23]

Working in the early-morning hours in Calexico, he encountered workers who had risen before midnight to cross the U.S.–Mexico border and wait for work along the main street in Calexico. Trying to highlight the full range of diversity in the farmworker experience, he sought out those involved in issues of sexuality and the mushrooming AIDS epidemic—people he called "the marginalized within the marginalized." Along the way, he met María, a farmworker and single mother of four, who had unknowingly been infected with HIV by her husband and was struggling to survive and raise her children after her husband had died. In Mecca, a hot and dusty town in the Coachella Valley, he found a man who was living in the dirt, his possessions amassed in three cardboard boxes, and was supporting his family by following the table-grape harvest. On a nearby Indian reservation, he saw farmworkers living in unregulated trailer camps, children playing in the carcasses of rusted automobiles and in stinking trash heaps. Out in the Central Valley, he had to be smuggled into several small, isolated farms, where he found people totally cut off from the outside, completely dependent on their employers or labor contractors. Nahmias called them slaves. Everywhere, he stressed, was "this cloud of oppressive heat surrounding you," impossible to record on film.[24]

A sense of déjà vu pervades Nahmias's photography. Aware that he was carrying on a tradition with deep roots in California photography, he, like Pirkle Jones in the 1950s and myself since 1975, often found himself mentally reviewing photographic history even while he was taking pictures. Of one such occasion, he recalled:

> After a day of shooting Santa Maria strawberry farms under the guidance of Prof. Juan-Vincente Palerm of UC Riverside and UCSB [University of California Santa Barbara], I drove to the center of town looking for farmworkers. I found none. The streets were quiet. I kept walking and soon I found a row of residence motels, their parking lots packed with cars. Outside of each room was a tangle of strawberry harvesting carts and piles of muddy shoes, all drying before another day of working the peak strawberry season, while just inside, their owners, piled in numbers and formations that were not all that different. It didn't take long for me to put the piece together and see the metaphors laid out in front of me—I had read a lot of research stating how overcrowded housing was one of the worst problems faced, as no one is going to build decent housing for a population that is there only 3 months of the year. I was drawn into one pile of shoes after the next, their textures, what they said about their owners, and ended up making the rounds to room after room in at least three adjacent motels. It was only my flash that gave me away, earning me curious stares and glowers from people who darted

> to the window of the rooms they were sharing with a half-dozen others, then shooing me away. Mud-caked shoes never held so much meaning, and undoubtedly never will again. It was the night I returned from this trip that an early edition of *Let Us Now Praise Famous Men* was sitting on my doorstep and I saw Walker Evans's migrant shoe image for the first time.[25]

Such experiences, explains art historian David Lubin, remind us "that images beget images . . . reverberate off one another and draw sustenance from the same deep wellsprings of culture." Extending and amplifying the work that others had done three-quarters of a century earlier, this "weird synchronicity," as Nahmias calls it, continued to haunt him on a daily basis. It would reappear in images that he was not aware duplicated those of his predecessors, for example, in his picture titled *Tomato Tokens.* Showing a man's hands holding small pay tokens, the image is very similar to one shot by Ernest Lowe in 1958. Of the image, Nahmias recalled:

> This is a shot I almost didn't take. I had seen so many images of hands while researching, they were strong but all convey the same thing. There was a deep symbolism and power in dirty calloused hands, but what new could I say that hadn't been said a hundred times before? I loaded the intention into the back of my head and decided to let fate steer me to it if it was meant to be. As it would turn out, I was on the second to the last shoot of the project: covering Stockton, and the northern Central valley, when I was taken by a community worker for the Quaker group American Friends Service Committee into the tomato fields. Once again I was overwhelmed by the sweet smell of hot earth mixed with tomato and the literal army of men who descended on the acres of crop the moment the morning dew had evaporated enough for them to work. Once I had gotten a sense of how the system worked: men crawling through the muck to fill a pair of pails with thirty pounds of green fruit as fast as humanly possible, after which they would dash to the nearby trucks, thrust their pails high above their head, and seeing their fruit replaced with a single tiny token worth ninety five cents, I realized I needed to get a closer look. First came the shots of the field en masse, then the anxious sweating men all lined up at the truck beds and their layers of clothes and those gloved hands. Then I finally found a man hunched over his breakfast—a pair of greasy tacos balanced on his lap while he counted his morning's take—seven tokens. He looked up from under his dirt-caked and sweat-soaked cap and just held out his hand.[26]

Just as *Tomato Tokens* recalls persistent themes and the work of earlier photographers, so too does a photograph titled *Not Forgotten.* Recording a cross marking the grave of one of over twenty-six hundred migrants who have died while trying to cross the southwest desert between Mexico and the United States, the photograph is very reminiscent of a Walker Evans photograph titled *Potter's Grave,* from the mid-1930s, as well as a 1937 Lange photograph, also taken in the Imperial Valley, of the grave of a two-year-old child of migrant farmworkers. Nahmias recalled:

> This shot was taken in the company of one of the community workers. Lupe Quintero, a twenty-plus year veteran of CRLA. She and I had just spent the evening (meeting at 1:30 A.M. on an hour's sleep) in downtown Calexico, traveling the shape-ups and early morning work in the onion and melon fields. After six hours of hopping aboard buses, following workers out some fifty miles from town, shooting them laboring, and when they finished grabbing shots of the glorious little onion sacks as dawn broke, I was seriously dragging. At a gas station I fueled up on coffee, she on O.J., making sure I had enough energy left to visit someplace that was clearly very special to her. We traversed the Imperial valley again, ending up in Holtville. Though it was maybe 10:30 A.M., the sun was high (the temperature had already hit one hundred degrees), and I was truly fighting to keep going. She directed me over to what looked like a small cemetery, full of classic looking headstones. We parked, and then I followed her down a manicured gravel path, through a few trees, and "out back." There before me, under the now baking sun, was maybe a half-acre of parched dirt lined with row after row of little white crosses, all stenciled in black "No Olvidado." Without a word, I realized where I was—a potter's field for unclaimed migrant bodies. Each grave had a roughly hewn brick identifying either a Jane or John Doe, and a small pitcher and saucer where offerings could be left. The power of the place just sucked any reserve of energy and emotion out of me. When I finally got myself togther and slowly began shooting, I watched out of the corner of my eye as Lupe went around to each and every grave, straightening crosses or pitchers which had fallen over. Though I snapped a frame or two of her in the process, when I asked her if I could do a portrait, she very soberly declined, and I clearly understood why, immediately feeling stupid for having asked. More moved by the unnamed dead than I had been by the living, we drove back to her office in El Centro in near silence. And while I retired to my hotel to get a few hours of sleep, she simply and stoically went on with her day.[27]

As he continued his photography, Nahmias often found himself measuring his life against the plight of the people he was documenting. He also found himself growing angry. Appreciating his good fortunes, he realized more than ever before that commercial agriculture rested on the backs of an ever-increasing influx of immigrant workers. He hoped that his images might somehow undermine power relationships and further the cause of farmworkers.[28]

Standing in opposition to cowboy photographers, who climb out of an airplane to fire off strings of images in their frenzied visits to scenes of despair and pity, these photographers are idealists whose values, experiences, and beliefs infuse their work. They are opposed to the quick and superficial glance of those photographers who, as the Uruguayan expatriate writer Eduardo Galeano explains, look without seeing. Black, Bartletti, and Nahmias want to disturb us. They are openly subversive. They intensely dislike cowardly photographers who say a few pious words, congratulate themselves, and move on to the next tragedy. They embrace an entirely different ethic.

Rejecting the myth of objective photography and refusing to be anyone's propagandist, they nevertheless believe that photography can help lift a curtain, undermine complacency, and provoke action. To accomplish these goals, they strive for images that force viewers to wonder if they are allowed to see such things. This requires them not so much to take pictures as to negotiate their way into a photograph. Failure is as important as success. Geopolitics always lurks in the background. History and economics are ever-present. Ideology infuses every picture. Always the goal is to make photographs embodying Sebastião Salgado's idea that good pictures linger in the mind's eye long after the photographer trips the shutter.[29]

Nowhere has this approach been more evident than in the strawberry fields around Watsonville, in the Pajaro Valley. With a large proportion of undocumented workers and countless stories of abuse, the Pajaro Valley has never been out of the picture, but in the late-1990s several developments brought a new wave of scrutiny. Of these, by far the most important was the UFW's organizing campaign. With an annual strawberry crop of seventy-six million boxes (amounting to about one-quarter of the world's production), the industry, with its profits and twenty thousand steadily employed workers with deep roots in their local communities, presented prospects for successful organizing that did not exist anywhere else in the state. When the union attempted to reverse its decline by launching an ambitious organizing drive, a handful of photographers headed south from San Francisco. Of these photographers, two dominated coverage.

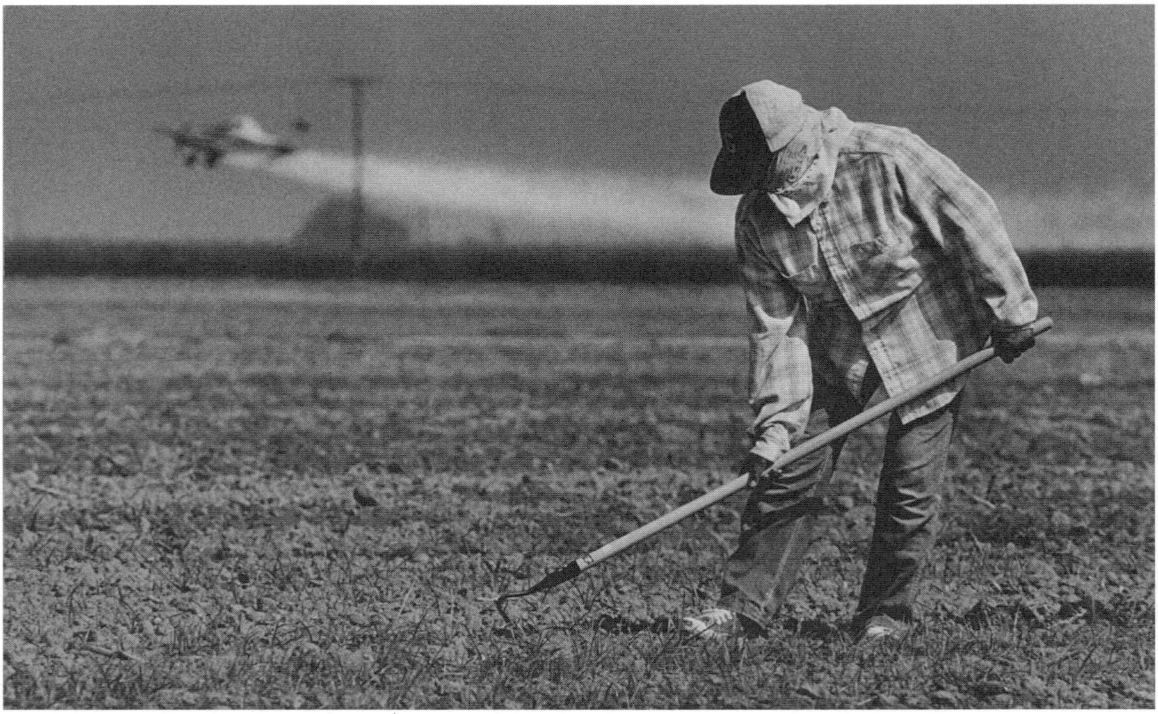

Farmworker hoeing a field near Delano while a crop duster sprays a neighboring field, May 1988, photograph by David H. Wells. From the photo essay "The Pesticide Poisoning of America." Courtesy of David H. Wells.

A former factory worker and union activist, David Bacon was finishing his book *The Children of NAFTA: Labor Wars on the U.S./Mexico Border* when his work brought him into extended contact with farmworkers. Impressed by the extreme youth of a labor force in which the typical worker was a mere twenty years of age and had little if any concept of César Chávez or the UFW, Bacon began a traditional black-and-white documentary essay on the ebb and flow of organizing activities around Watsonville. Big on union marches and symbolism and resembling what John Kouns and Jon Lewis had earlier done during the Delano grape strike, his work dominated coverage until the *Atlantic Monthly* assigned photo essayist Ed Kashi to illustrate an essay that contributing editor Eric Schlosser had written on labor in the strawberry industry.[30]

Since receiving a degree in photojournalism from Syracuse University in 1979, Kashi had become one of the most daring and respected photographers in the United States and gone on to complete nine essays for *National Geographic,* including stories on the Kurds, water problems in the Middle East, and the conflict in the Balkans. Bringing that reservoir of experience to focus on California farmworkers, he broke with the tradition of black-and-white documentary photography and shot his essay entirely in color. To drive home the contradiction of hard labor amid lush fields, he borrowed from a portrait technique that he had popularized: photographing at sunrise or sunset with fill flash to create deceptively beautiful and viscerally gritty images of workers trudging off to or in from the fields.

Back in the small rural slums such as the San Andreas labor camp, Kashi switched to high-speed color film, turned off his strobe, and photographed unobtrusively under natural lighting conditions. He made especially good use of high-speed film while photographing in the Plaza Hotel in Santa Maria, where single men slept three to a bed. Between morning and evening, he remained attentive to small but revealing details, including the blood-colored strawberry stains on the shirts of workers, the pained faces of men whose backs ached from bending over all day, and the spirit of people confronting adversity with determination and a joke. To wrap up his essay, Kashi focused on three women who shared the same room in a dingy labor camp. By following their routine as they dressed for work, pulling on big boots, folding parkas over their heads so that only their eyes were visible, and adding several layers of clothing, bulky gloves, and bandanas to protect themselves against the cold, foggy morning, Kashi elevated the sense of juxtaposition with what developed later in the day, when scenes shifted to hot, sweaty stoop labor so debilitating and draining that workers found it difficult to continue in the fields after reaching thirty-five years of age.[31]

Busy with other assignments, I did not make it to Watsonville until the UFW created another of those spectacles it uses to attract attention, win public support, and shift the scene of conflict beyond the fields. This spectacle occurred in Watsonville on July 8, 1997, when Arturo Rodríguez, the new president of the UFW, met Robert F. Kennedy Jr. ostensibly to commemorate a meeting between Robert F. Kennedy Sr. and César Chávez on March 11, 1966, in Delano. Realizing that Rodríguez's meeting with Kennedy was going to be iconic, I covered it for *California Farmer.* Arriving several hours early to set up a strobe light, I immediately became aware that the UFW had gone to extraordinary lengths to make the meeting especially photogenic. To accomplish this, union members distributed copies of a George Ballis photograph of the earlier meeting between Kennedy and Chávez. Seeing field hands clutching those precious photographs and trying to get Kennedy and Rodríguez to autograph them, both the historian and the photographer in me recognized the unique double picture that was developing. Determined to record the moment, I moved into the middle of the huge crowd encircling Kennedy and Rodríguez and used a 20-millimeter lens to capture a photograph within a photograph. Encapsulating forty years of history, the photograph I made further confirms the depth of understanding of photographic issues that pervades a farmworker community often characterized as fragmented, apathetic, and lacking memory.[32]

When I reflect on that image today, I often wonder if viewers regard it as an objective record of reality. That is not how I would describe something that is, in fact, a political act. It makes me recall something that Pirkle Jones told me long ago in the predigital era, but it still holds true. "You are just wasting film" he said, "unless you move beyond traditional borders and professional boundaries by taking a stand and trying to nudge audiences beyond awareness towards change."[33]

If there is one transcendental lesson that emerges from thirty years of photographing in the fields while also studying and interacting with my peers and predecessors, it is that the failure to become fully integrated with a subject makes for weak photographs. You must become more than a mere observer. You cannot go into the fields for a few days or a couple of weeks, remaining in what David Levi Strauss describes as "linguistic and cultural isolation," and produce anything worthwhile. You must be committed to your subjects. And you must try, insofar as possible, to be what political scientists Margaret Keck and Kathryn Sikkink describe as "activists beyond borders"—people who see with your subjects' eyes or at least in ways that allow others to perceive society from a perspective that is new to them. At a time when photography seems dominant as a universal language, activist work and rejection of the newsperson's deadline inject a depth and complexity that can cut through the sappy bromides and knee-jerk affirmations of the increasingly manipulative and cowardly mass media. This is how Bartletti, Bacon, Black, Kashi, Nahmias, Sturdevant, and those like them use their talents and extract meaning from their photography. Rather than labeling, they bear witness. They open windows on complex, raw, and unpleasant realities. By creating powerful and interesting, even beautiful and durable, images, they provoke thought and establish a human connection that brings us closer to people whose experiences are distant from ours, as well as difficult to comprehend or even imagine.[34]

Challenging ideas of American exceptionalism, such work goes straight to structural problems overlooked by mainstream media, which seldom if ever connect poverty and commercial agriculture. Rather than compartmentalizing each as distinct from the other, modern photographers drive home ideas about an underclass drawn almost entirely from Mexico. They focus on the details of life that are seldom mentioned by news photographers: how an undocumented worker goes about buying a car; why he looks for one with a recent registration; what it is like to hoe fields for ten hours; how one collects aluminum cans and delivers them for cash at recycling centers; where one collects surplus food; how farmworkers save fuel costs by crowding seven to a car to drive to the fields. This perspective shatters the stereotype that the underclass is composed of people who lack the drive and energy required to acquire a piece of the California dream. As the modern counterparts of FSA photographers, these photographers are sympathetic to farmworkers, stressing that they are decent people, victims of collapsing economies, and they try to compensate for their subjects' lack of resources and government support by deeply submerging themselves in their lives, often undergoing the same hardships, from smuggling themselves across the U.S.–Mexico border to spending a Saturday night in a bar in a small town, which serves as the only reward for a week spent harvesting table grapes in the fields. They call commercial agriculture an "illusion." They invite viewers to move past the advertising images and beautiful fields and go where men bunk fifty to a room in labor camps or sometimes live in holes in the ground, to breathe the dusty, pesticide-laden air, to be away from home nine months of the year while following the lettuce harvest, and to make a mad ten-hour drive from Huron south to Calexico to be with family at Easter and then return to the fields after a day's visit followed by a ten-hour drive back north.

As the work of activist photographers becomes imbedded in the public mind, it has the potential to dazzle and divert, to be so overused and common as to become a desensitizing and numbing cliché of rural California. What impresses me about these photographers, and their predecessors, is how, over and over again, they ignore the temptation to sensationalize and ratchet up the horror show. Although not unconcerned with aesthetics, they focus first on content and second on form and style, always fighting the tendency to trivialize through art. With a subtle and steady reiteration of simple and enduring human values, they continually find ways to underscore what is important, ignore what is ephemeral, and embrace apparently contradictory elements such as aesthetics, social conscience, and commercial practice. At times it is difficult to look at their work without flinching in shock and horror, but we must look, and, as has been said of civil rights photography, it is certain that, by looking, answers can emerge. As we search for insight into the problems that surround us, such photography helps strip free the stale exterior of accepted seeing and cuts through to the human condition.[35]

Growers and their allies do not understand this dimension of photographers. Many regard photographers as subversive, menacing, intrusive, and hostile. Labeling them with such sinister names as "camera Cossacks" and "assassins of agriculture," they counterattack with heavy-handed public relations and second-rate photography. Modern critics also attack these photographers, but from a different angle, accusing them of "aestheticizing poverty," engaging in "sentimental voyeurism," capitalizing on the "exploitation of compassion," and generally assisting the liberal corporate state. Picked up and expanded by cultural historian Charles Shindo in his book *Dust Bowl Migrants and the American Imagination,* these critiques have been employed as evidence that photographers who work in the fields are little more than an elite corps

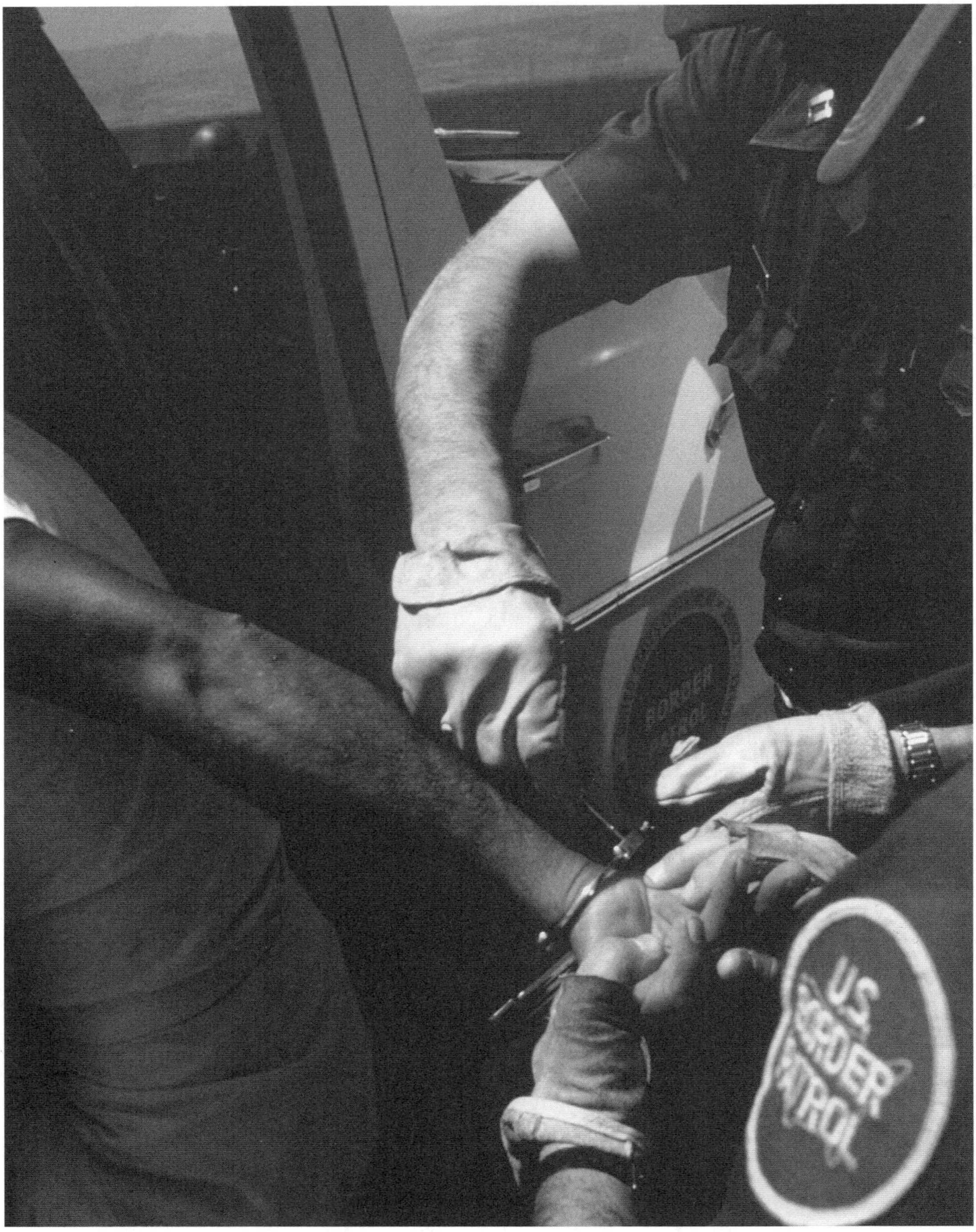

Arrests in the fields near Huron, May 7, 1990, photograph by Richard Steven Street. From the series Knife Fight City. Original in color. Courtesy of Streetshots.

of liberal con artists who appropriate the experience of California farmworkers in order to manufacture enduring symbols of economic dislocation and class exploitation that do little to help farmworkers but considerably advance their own careers and agendas.

No career-oriented photographer chooses farmworkers as a subject. It is too hard to keep going. Nor does it follow that the photographers of California farmworkers appropriate the experiences of others solely for their own purposes, that their work reveals more about them than it does about their subjects, that they lack legitimacy, that they assist rather than subvert the liberal corporate state, or, as John Tagg argues in *The Burden of Representation,* that they objectify and subjugate people in the name of social reform when they are really acting as instruments of social control. Nor does it follow, as Shindo asserts, that their work says more about their intellectual and ethical beliefs than about the actual needs and desires of farmworkers. To claim that they "ultimately failed to perceive . . . humanity" is to shut one's eyes to what they see, ignore the way photography works, minimize how dramatically photography carries on the tradition of visual engagement, assert that photographers create victims where none exist. Such a perspective insults the memory of a field hand photographed while dying in a pool of his own blood; it turns a cold back on an armless, legless child whose life was possibly ruined by his mother's brush with pesticides; and it diminishes the energy, physical challenges, and financial sacrifices required to photograph in the fields.[36]

Watching photographers fighting their way through assignments, we discover much more than the legacy of individual portfolios. Genuinely attentive and open-minded, such people are the opposite of the visual vultures and hit-and-run cowboy journalists that Shindo, Tagg, and others describe. Believing that no detail is too mundane or insignificant, modern photographers of California farmworkers are, with few exceptions, "encounter and witness" documentarians who regard the act of taking pictures as a variety of everyday interaction. Understanding that the most interesting photography is human photography, they do not ignore the great themes or minimize the massive exploitation and oppression of an entire class of people. In their photography, all of the transcendent emotions, from grief and love to terror and compassion, emerge along with the basic everyday realities of birth and death, childhood and old age, health and sickness.

Regarding the challenge of covering farmworkers as a solemn professional duty coupled with a kind of permanent outcast status, these photographers grapple with all of the usual demands, dangers, and obstacles, the most difficult being how to earn a living while doing important work. Passionate in their rejection of national boundaries and narrowly regional identities, they understand the nature of a medium that sparks awareness by pushing the line between art and experience. Concepts like "justice," "solidarity," and "truth," or more commonly "many truths," inform their visual thinking. They do not see art and bearing witness as polar opposites, and they reject the idea that beautiful photographs of suffering shift attention away from the subject. Should they take bad pictures?

By framing images well, they do not become the stars of the story. And by capturing the moment, they hardly wallow in victimization. These photographers are concerned mostly with portraying farmworkers as subjects in their own right. Rejecting a concern for the exotic and the picturesque, they aim at exposing the great differences in class, race, gender, and ethnicity along with appallingly unequal relations of power. For many of these photographers, this amounts to life's central purpose.[37]

Collectively affirming what literary biographer Walter Jackson Bate said of Samuel Johnson, that "hardly a single life had passed from which we could not learn something, if only it were told with complete honesty," these photographers defy the language of academic classification. Whatever the labels—"press photographers," "social documentary photographers," "visual activists," "freelancers," all of the above, or none—every one of them, whether they say so explicitly or not, follows a simple yet profound working philosophy that Dorothea Lange explained this way:

> You put your camera around your neck in the morning along with putting on your shoes, and there it is, an appendage of the body that shares your life with you. . . . You force yourself to watch and wait. You accept all the discomfort and the disharmony. Being out of your depth is a very uncomfortable thing. You force yourself onto strange streets, among strangers. It may be very hot. It may be painfully cold. It may be sandy and windy and you say, "What am I doing here? What drives me to do this hard thing?"[38]

By focusing on a class with a tragic past and a difficult present, these photographers hope to overcome what Gore Vidal labels "the United States of Amnesia." Concerned with the national consensus of American history as one of exceptionalism and unbridled progress, they continue to ask the questions that guide all historically concerned inquiry: Who caused this? How did it come about? How long will it continue? What can be done? By rejecting the immediacy of spectacular news pictures in favor of a slower, long-term, self-financed, self-assigned engagement with their subjects, they steel themselves against the insensitivity, thoughtlessness, and arrogance of their profession.[39]

These are photographers who try to sort out history as it is happening. They want to create a flow of information that communicates something. They love to tell stories. They do not look for one picture. They are not interested in fame. They are not after a name. They never forget. They are Janus-faced, always looking backward and forward. They are disruptive people who believe that disruptive images will educate the public and lead to a better life for farmworkers. This is their way of life. Failing to identify exact solutions or adequately convey what they see, some of these photographers have at times slipped into self-doubt and suggested that perhaps it might be better to do as James Agee suggested in *Let Us Now Praise Famous Men* and Ernest Lowe did in his 1965 photo exhibition: replace their pictures with "fragments of cloth, bits of cotton, lumps of earth, records of speech, pieces of wood and iron, phials of odors, plates of food and of excrement." But in the absence of such an alternative, they keep at it. Angry and nervous in their own complicity and good luck, they try to do their best, not only to record history, but also to shape it and learn from it. Returning home admiring some of the people they have met, many wonder if they could cope with the same overwhelming circumstances. Whether or not they explicitly say so, these photographers are moral pilgrims in the cause of strong, concise, and direct still pictures.[40]

Stubborn and individualistic, they have been slow to shift from film to digital technology. But those who have done so find that being unencumbered by chemicals, paper, film, and processing equipment allows them to travel light. On assignment in some remote location, they can view, delete, or save images, even load them onto a computer and zip them to anywhere on the planet. This frees them from the constraints of "shoot and ship" film-based photography and allows them to remain on assignment longer, often up to the last minute. From this perspective, the digital world is a big gain in efficiency. But it also raises the specter of falsification and manipulation. At stake is the ontological status of the image. With the loss of originality—the sense that an image is created in a particular moment—authorship, ownership, and copyright, along with the authority of the photographer as an observer, come into question. And with the loss of the sense of the real—the belief that a link exists between what is seen and what is in the image—the image as witness dissolves into discussions

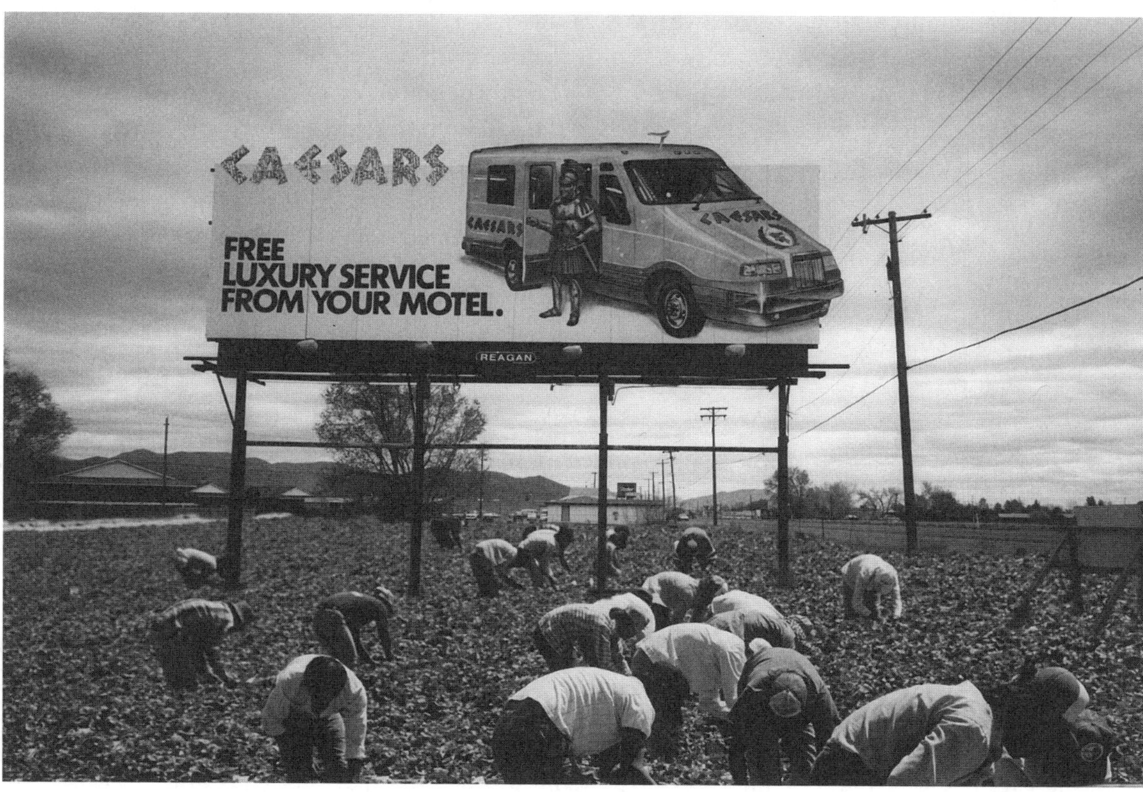

Mexican Migrant Workers, California Highway, 1986/1990 (digital construction), photography by Pedro Meyer. Courtesy of Pedro Meyer.

of how it was created. What is at stake is less how an image comes into being than the ability to claim photographic accuracy.[41]

Rejecting these notions, Mexican photographer Pedro Meyer uses digital imagery to better represent his vision of farmworkers today. In *Mexican Migrant Workers, California Highway* (1986/1990), Meyer used Adobe Photoshop to manipulate the image and challenge traditional documentary photography. Constructing a picture of men stooped over in the fields beneath a billboard ad for Las Vegas, Meyer juxtaposed field hands with a giant Roman gladiator, the latter outlined in glowing neon light and, in this scene, welcoming customers who are obviously too poor and too busy to be interested in the advertised service. This is not classic documentary work. Dorothea Lange discovered her billboard images while out on the road and recorded them in order to exemplify class differences and differences between commercial idealism and reality. Rather than prospecting such images and using them as commentary, Meyer reversed the process. Thinking of two separate images—the billboard sign and the Mexican field workers whom he had photographed about a mile away from it—he associated the two scenes in his mind and then eliminated the spatial separation to create an intellectual connection, or nightmare, much as we experience such connections every day. In speaking of these constructions, Meyer once explained that he created them because he could and because he would not wait days, weeks, months, or even years until he found his decisive moment, if it could even be found. Knowing the point he wanted to make about inequality, he constructed it with his computer.[42]

Meyer's photography involves much more than cutting and pasting. Reflecting on his methodology, he recalled how, as we travel from place to place, we often encounter disparate images evoking strong memories. He stressed:

> If you observe, the association of images from here to there, bring to mind situations that one considers worth thinking about, which is what brought them up in the first place. The art of a novelist, of a poet, and of a journalist, is to find the right association of words to make a good description of that which they want to convey, be this factual or fiction based on facts. We tend to put together a mosaic of experiences, associations which describe in the most efficient way an experience. I could imagine that the combination of these two images could have perfectly well happened at some other place in the agricultural cycle of the area, as the billboard itself was on farmland. The migrant workers would indeed have come to see this billboard. My bringing the two together was not at all just a figment of my imagination.[43]

Because both images had been taken before the digital age, Meyer waited years before linking them and would probably not have thought to link them had he not acquired the means to do so. Although the construction is certainly aimed at making a point about poverty and farm labor, it is primarily a way of opening up memories and creating a new photographic discourse. Contrary to how traditional documentary photographers work, Meyer elevates subjectivity in order to subvert the genre. Alteration of images, he believes, enhances their veracity. All documentary photographs are manipulations, even if the manipulations are made subtly, by moving slightly this way or that to take advantage of better light and perspective.

Impatient, less secretive, and unwilling to trust his work to luck, Meyer takes control. His work is about perception and associations among seemingly unrelated things that we see at different points. To what extent digital manipulation will supplant or add to traditional documentary work, or whether it will even receive much attention or be used outside the art community, cannot be predicted. As an amalgamation of ideas, such work resembles advertising. A point is made, and the image is assembled. As a contrivance, it can be attacked for lacking the foundation in authority essential to veracity. We cannot trust that the image exists anywhere other than in the mind of the photographer or computer technician. As part of the new photojournalism, it certainly breaks with the work of the patron saints of the profession. In the case of *Mexican Migrant Workers, California Highway,* we find ourselves viewing a highly personal, compositionally complex, politically charged work that shouts the following message: hardly able to afford a day in such a place, these immigrant farmworkers both literally and figuratively stoop so that the consumer economy on that big billboard can continue to flourish.[44]

Lacking brevity and objectivity, digital construction, with its tension between reportage and artistic license, shatters the guiding virtues of photojournalism and documentary discourse. With little value to most magazine and newspaper picture editors, it may be destined largely for the exhibition and art book circuit. Easier to use as news, the work of photojournalists, documentary photographers, and concerned photographers still reaches a wide audience. Photographs of Border Patrolmen arresting farmworkers, along with those of pallbearers carrying the coffins of fallen martyrs and dead immigrants mummified in the desert, convey their messages, often in vivid color. So, too, do graphically frank photographs of nonunion workers hired through intermediaries at wages averaging 55 percent of nonfarm rates and photographs of newly arrived immigrants using the short-handled hoe a quarter of a century after it was banned.[45]

Measuring the lasting effects of the photographs of California farmworkers and of the photographers who made them is difficult, if not impossible. Looking back, both friends and foes agree that photographers have amassed an extraordinarily large and significant picture. Some believe that it has helped to permanently unravel the myth of the fruit-crate label showing agriculture as a pastoral Garden of Eden. Others are convinced that by creating a subtly layered portrait of a highly segmented labor force, photographers have pushed society toward a fuller appreciation of the human element in modern fruit and vegetable production. Many see in the work of these photographers vivid evidence of the crucial role that immigration plays in replenishing a labor force in which one segment is constantly moving up while another arrives to take its place. Rather than looking at California agriculture through a prism of triumph and exceptionality, modern photographers reject such flimflam as deeply embedded jingoism born of a long failure to acknowledge an industrial imperialism that anticipated the late twentieth-century search for low-wage workers, only, instead of moving operations overseas, agriculture has benefited from streams of low-wage workers moving into California.[46]

Photographers started working in the fields in an era that placed a premium on growth, promotion, and material development, and they continued into a time when everything was being questioned. Although the first generations of photographers created laudatory images that failed to confront farmworkers in all of their complexities, subsequent generations attacked this simplistic picture by shining a light through the fissures of society. By the end of the twentieth century, photographers had undermined the god of production and destroyed the view of farmworkers as props. Today most noncommercial photographers authenticate the idea of a sustainability in which quality, consequences, and human impact take their place alongside the bottom line. They are an extension of the avant-garde of a movement that started in the 1930s and has expanded ever since. Shedding old forms of representation and employing more critically engaged forms of visual inquiry, they arrived at this ethic the same way that they have explored the countryside: by driving back roads, crisscrossing valleys, sneaking across borders, standing up to bullies, prowling labor clamps. Complicated people, they sharpen their skills learned not from teachers in schools but from experiences in the wider world: from the skin cancer they acquire through years spent under the broiling sun, from the cold they feel in canyon camps, from the fear that they experience on picket lines, from the generosity they receive as guests around campfires, sharing meals prepared under the most austere circumstances.

At a time when many Californians occupy a nebulous space in which deconstruction and cynicism reign, and truth, justice, freedom, and equality are dismissed as merely words, the photographers of California farmworkers put great faith in the fundamental decency of human beings. They are idealists who dream of a better world and believe in a dynamic country capable of solving its problems, and at the same time they are realists who understand that tragedy and inequality persist, that their work reiterates variations on persistent themes and has failed to bring about lasting change. Above all else, these photographers are logical positivists. As we grow increasingly apart in our lives and more specialized in our work, and as we search into the nature of our own being and try to heal a broken world, all of us can benefit by linking arms with such photographers, sitting with them, and extracting whatever lessons we might find. Strong, determined travelers in life's adventure, they believe in the goodness of humanity and continue working toward those goals of truth, justice, and self-fulfillment that are at the core of the California and the American Dream.

Today, their work continues to resonate in odd ways. Those who thought nothing could be new were astounded to see the work of Ricardo O. Alvarado, a Filipino janitor, houseboy, and cook at the Army Hospital in San Francisco. Photographing all aspects of the Filipino farmworker community around Stockton's Little Manila between 1949 and 1959, Alvarado compiled an unparalleled record of daily life that included everything from gambling and cock fighting to Saturday nights in taxi dance halls and Sunday afternoons hanging out in city parks. Unseen except by a small circle of his friends, this important body of images, with its unparalleled focus on everyday activities, was packed inside Alvarado's trunk until his daughter discovered it while cleaning out the basement of the family home and began making it available in 2002. Also packed away for fifty years, Don Normark's photography did not see the light of day until Chronicle Books published it in 1999 as *Chávez Ravine, 1949: A Los Angeles Story.* "I wonder what would have happened if someone had seen those photographs a half century ago," he told me shortly after the book appeared. "Would the city of Los Angeles have been able to so easily knock the neighborhood down and bulldoze it under to build Dodger Stadium on top of it?" Taking the longest time to resurface, Horace Bristol's photography was concealed, for reasons that have never been explained, by none other than John Steinbeck. Sixty years would pass before Chronicle Books resurrected this important record and published it in 1996 as *Horace Bristol: An American View.*[47]

When this work was finally gaining an audience, artists who had grown up in migrant farmworker families in the San Joaquin Valley began producing a series of iconoclastic prints. Using photographs and existing commercial icons, Ester Hernández created *Sun Mad Raisins: Unnaturally Grown with Insecticides, Miticides, Herbicides, Fungicides.* An angry indictment, *Sun Mad Raisins* replaces the well-known Sun-Maid label with a skeleton-like figure suggesting not a healthy snack but one that poses a danger to consumers and field hands alike. Equally disturbing, Vincent L. Méndez focused attention on the open landscape, colors, heat, and nightmares in a series of memorable paintings, including *The Sun's Contempt,* in which a child appears as a tiny figure under a towering sky and a huge, killing sun. Other Chicano and Chicana artists have followed a similar path, each one breaking with dominant romantic landscape motifs. But they have not been content only to create art. They have also defended it. When Corbis Images, which bills itself as having the largest collection of images on the planet, began selling photographs of Dolores Huerta, along with four copyrighted public murals displaying the UFW's trademarked black eagle symbol, mural painters in San Francisco sued the company in November 2000.[48]

The latest installment in this saga came in 2003, when one of Bob Fitch's color portraits of a smiling young Chávez became the basis for a postage stamp issued by the United States Postal Service. Appearing exactly ten years after Chávez died, the stamp was welcomed with speeches and ceremonies that began with an unveiling by his son, Richard Chávez, at the Mission Cultural Center in San Francisco on April 25, 2003, and extended over several days in three Central Valley towns and in San Jose. "It allows us to deliver a message, while delivering the mail," announced Postal Service spokesperson Augustine Ruíz.[49]

The stamp message, however, was considerably different from the original one that Fitch recorded. In constructing the stamp, painter Robert Rodriguez had removed the UFW flag behind Chávez and replaced it with a picture of a lettuce field extracted from a second image shot by freelance photographer Ted Streshinsky and obtained from Corbis Images. Appearing at a time of increased sensitivities following the furor over editorial manipulation of a pyramid to fit a *National Geographic* cover, the darkening of a mug shot of O. J. Simpson for a *Time* magazine cover, and the shifting of silhouetted cowboys to better fit the cover of *A Day in the Life of America* photo book, the beautiful composite raised issues about the power of photographic truth and artistic manipulation. For Bob Fitch, it was almost too much to bear. "The U.S. government," he told reporters on seeing the rendition, "was not ready to put a union label on a stamp."[50]

Apparently, more than the flag had been removed. Observing that the United States Postal Service, in the name of good health, had airbrushed cigarettes out of historical photographs of honored individuals, a *Linn's* writer charged that a gold front tooth seems to have been eliminated from the Chávez photograph. A series of interviews with UFW members close to Chávez established that he indeed had a gold tooth that he did not have replaced until well after the photograph had been taken. However, after viewing a series of Fitch's images taken from different angles, union members concluded that no evidence of the gold tooth appeared in those particular

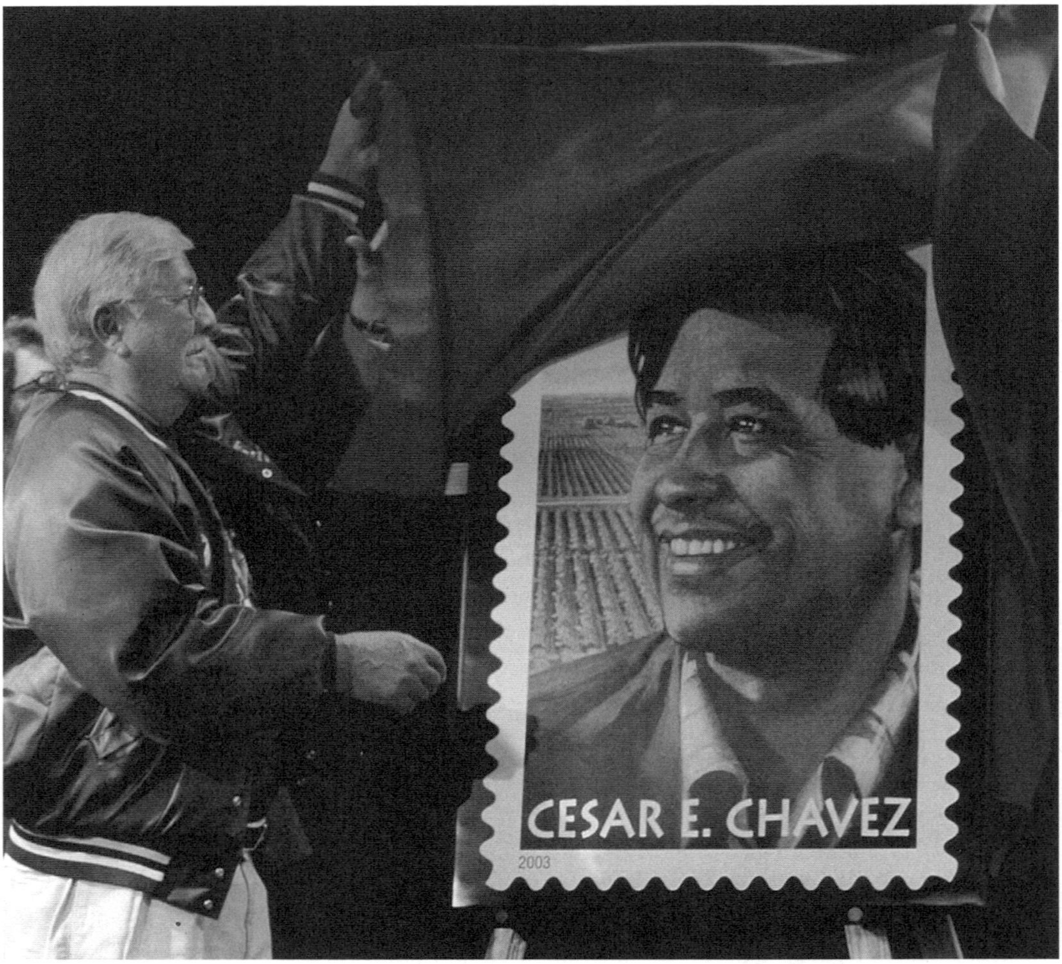

Richard Chávez unveiling a U.S. postage stamp of his father, April 25, 2003, photograph by Fred Larsen, *San Francisco Chronicle*. Original in color. Courtesy of the *San Francisco Chronicle*.

photographs. Regardless of whether or not the gold tooth had been removed from the image used for the stamp, Fitch disliked the Postal Service rendering of his photograph. Speaking to *Linn's* writer Rob Haeseler, he observed that the César Chávez depicted on the stamp looks more like a vineyard owner or *patrón* than the leader of the farmworker movement. "My picture has been neutered," he explained.[51]

Dumbed down, sanitized, decontextualized, and yes, even diminished, that amalgamation—that pastiche—remains a powerful, memorable, and thought-provoking image. Here, affixed to our mail, is a labor leader whose image personifies the ongoing struggle. His dark skin and beaming smile remind us of the succession of immigrants and displaced Americans who have worked in the fields. His name invites us to contemplate the change from a time when power flowed only in one direction to a more hopeful era when farmworkers can hope for a better day. Between our fingers we hold more than an icon. We sense the full weight of an emblematic story that has been at the core of life in the Golden State for more than a century and a half. So small and yet so charged with larger meaning, images like this one point to the great importance of photographers in modern society and of all they must do to make such images. Here is further evidence of what Gordon Parks has long believed: "that no other art form transforms human apathy quicker than photography."[52]

Images such as these help us to see where we have been. They are part of the big picture so essential to becoming more fully human. The best of them hammer their messages in deep. They provide the kind of vision required for thinking politically about the world. Their makers are acutely aware of the commercial deluge that systematically erases reality by pasting the Sun-Maid girl over exploitation. Here, in your face, is the shape and feel of agricultural labor. Here is the hidden side of efficient, large-scale, irrigated fruit and vegetable agriculture. Here is murder and evil and tragedy, the heavy weight of sun burning down on you, the despair and dreams that send you far from home, through deserts, into a form of labor shunned by all except first-generation immigrants. Can you turn away? There is so much here, so much that speaks of life and human spirit, of blood on the lettuce and human sweat dripping into the furrows. We see field hands sleeping, waking up, gathering the children together, going off to work, raising families, praying, wrapping burritos in the kitchen, sitting beneath the vines, chattering, sharing gossip, dozing off, sweating, playing tricks on gringo photographers. We see ourselves, our fathers and mothers and our grandparents, not the other, not "illegals." Respect and admiration emerge naturally when human faces replace the abstraction of agricultural labor. We are grateful. We wonder if we would be up to the challenge. In the specifics of these pictures we begin to shed the tyranny of quantification. We see the qualities of hard work and persistence and self-sacrifice that we all admire. We see hopefulness born of struggle and dignity extending beyond borders and gang code words. If we think about these images in sequence, we can begin to assemble a picture of how the system of farm labor developed, to understand the price it extracts from a class of people, and to see how the blood of the southern hemisphere has been squeezed out to quench our thirsty, profit-driven, ever-expanding consumerist appetite.

Acknowledgments

While photographing agriculture and farm labor, I conducted numerous formal and informal interviews with other photographers, many of whom read the parts of the manuscript that focus on their experiences. A few completely escaped scrutiny or even identification. I never did learn the name of one Filipino photographer I encountered on countless occasions while following the United Farm Workers union, although he appears in dozens of my photographs. I remember most of the hundreds of photographers who worked alongside me, who also spoke to me about their experiences, and in many cases donated photographs. Among these photographers, the following were especially helpful: Felix Adamo, Victor Alemán, George Ballis, Karen Barrell, Don Bartletti, Ted Benson, Matt Black, Mike Bry, Oscar Castillo, Emmon Clarke, Dan Coyro, Carl Crawford, Loomis Dean, Francisco Domínguez, Gayanne Fietinghoff, Bob Fitch, Cres Fraley, Paul Fusco, Richard Green, Gerhard Gscheidle, Joseph Gunterman, Richard Hammond, Jeanette Hyduke, Will Kirkland, John Kouns, Carlos LeGerrete, Len Lehman, Jon Lewis, Ken Light, Ernest Lowe, Margery Mann, Pedro Meyer, Wayne Miller, Roger Minick, Truman Moore, Joe Munroe, Rick Nahmias, Eugene Nelson, Paul J. Noden, Don Normark, Fran Ortiz, Rondall Partridge, Glen Pearcy, Clay Peterson, Mimi Plumb-Chambers, Harry Polkinhorn, Joe Rosenthal, Lonny Shavelson, Elizabeth Sisco, Ted Streshinsky, Saundra Sturdevant, Reesa Tansey, Ronald B. Taylor, Rick Tejada-Flores, Linda Troeller, Sam Vestal, Seema Weatherwax, David Wells, Max Yavno, and Helmut Zingsem. Key nonphotographers who shared stories about photographers from their days in the farmworker movement include Doug Adair, César Chávez, Tom Dalzell, Jim Drake, Susan Drake, Pablo Espinoza, Dolores Huerta, Marcia Lyons, H. L. Mitchell, Chris Schneider, and Jane Yett.

One of my oddest encounters led me to Pam Harris, who photographed alongside me in the Salinas Valley from 1979 to 1981. I did not learn of this until April 2004, when I was finishing a month of research into several hundred boxes of photographic and archival materials at the Henry E. Huntington Library, in San Marino, California.

As part of my fellowship duties, I delivered a slide lecture on farmworker photography. Attending was Randy McCloud, a professor of classics at the University of Toronto. McCloud had been running a large data-mining operation into Shakespearean texts on the table behind me in the Ahumdson research room. Upon completion of my lecture, he informed me that his wife, Pam Harris, had photographed farmworkers extensively and had recently deposited some of her work in the California State Library, in Sacramento. While perusing her work, I discovered yet another first-rate farmworker photographer and learned of her story. I was especially astounded to see on her proof-sheet photographs of myself photographing at the March on Salinas in 1979.

At an early stage of my writing I was assisted by *San Francisco Examiner* editor Jim Willse, who allowed me to copy images from the newspaper's photo archives, which were subsequently transferred to the Bancroft Library, at the University of California, Berkeley, in 2006. At a late stage I was immeasurably helped in working out my ideas on the modern side of the story when Leroy Chatfield asked me to write about my own experiences photographing at César Chávez's fast in 1988 and at his funeral in 1993. Parts of these essays, which originally appeared in his online www.farmworker movement.org anthology and online discussion, are considerably expanded in various parts of this book. I further expanded my ideas when *Visual Communications Quarterly* editor Julianne Newton commissioned me to write about my double life as historian–photographer. Another person who helped me late in the project was John Mraz, a historian of Mexican photography, who shared with me his work on the Hermanos Mayo. Mraz saved me from what was shaping up as a hopeless struggle to pry the Hermanos Mayo images out of the Archivo General de la Nación in Mexico City.

Over the many years of research into the photographers and photography of California farmworkers, I have explored countless archives, exploited a huge body of scholarship, and have been assisted by so many people that I fear I cannot recall them all. Throughout the footnotes the reader will see my dependence on the work of several generations of scholars, including Van Deren Coke, A. D. Coleman, Richard and Maisie Conrat, James Curtis, Geoffrey Dunn, Andy Grundberg, Therese Heyman, Drew Johnson, Lawrence W. Levine, Ken Light, John Loengard, Anne Loftis, Milton Meltzer, John G. Morris, John Mraz, Beaumont and Nancy Newhall, Karen Becker Ohrn, Elizabeth Partridge, David Peeler, Sandra Phillips, Fred Ritchin, Naomi and Walter Rosenblum, Martha Rosler, Martha Sandweiss, Allan Sekula, Charles L. Shindo, Jonathan Spaulding, Maren Stange, William Stott, David Levi Strauss, Leah Bendavid-Val, and Jennifer Watts. Amplifying their contributions and frequently taking issue with their conclusions, I acknowledge that these scholars have excavated the foundation on which all photographic history rests. I also learned more than I expected from my own peers in the photographic profession, including P. F. Bentley, Jay Daniel, Ron Habib, Fred Lyon, Art Rogers, Maggie Steber, and Les Stone, as well as Orrin Moon, Jo Moss, and Douglas Neecke at the Darkroom, and especially Doug Menuez, who taught me more about photography than any other living being. Pirkle Jones argued against the original book title, spoke at length about his experiences working with

Dorothea Lange, and assured me that I had not been the only photographer to finance editorial work and scholarship through commercial assignments. And yes, he too had seen images from the past appearing again in his viewfinder even as he struggled with the decision to press the shutter or not.

Being in the field as an agricultural photographer provided insights into the practical side of my subject that no book or archive could ever approach and also allowed me to participate in the story even as I was studying it. For hiring me, I must thank Charles M. Benbrook, National Research Council; Greg Critser, *California Business, California,* and *Worth* magazines; Lorna Cunkle, Steve McNamara, and Linda Xiques, *Pacific Sun,* who assigned me an ongoing series of essays on photographers that appeared in the newspaper between 1979 and 1982; Tim Driscoll, Driscoll Strawberry Associates, Inc.; Dan Gerawan, Gerawan Farming, Inc.; James Gordon, *Wine Spectator* magazine; Alexandra Gregson, *Forbes* magazine; Des Keller, *Progressive Farmer* magazine; Marcus Moller-Racke, Buena Vista Winery; José Padilla, California Rural Legal Assistance; Steve Pavich, Pavich Family Farms; Harold Rogers, *Western Fruit Grower* magazine; Cheryl Romo, *Sacramento* magazine; Edwin Self, *San Diego* magazine; Elizabeth Kuehner Smith, *Wine News;* and Len Richardson and Richard Smoley, *California Farmer.* They have been completely understanding of and sympathetic to my attempt at merging a life in scholarship and photography, and I thank them for being both generous and flexible in the service of my project.

Two scholars of American visual culture who have helped shape this work are Sally Stein, a friend whose help has extended far beyond the academy, and Sarah Burns, whose scholarship has provided a model of inspiration and who has remained among the strongest and most helpful advocates of my work since our days together at the Stanford University Humanities Center. Dave Evans, Jon Lewis, Harvey Richards, and Rich Turner allowed me to print their negatives. Toward the end of the project, John G. Morris, the legendary photo editor who handled the work of many of the photographers appearing in this book, waded into the manuscript from his post in Paris. I appreciate his critique and cherish his endorsement of my treatment of Otto and Hansel Mieth Hagel. I could not have completed the project without the steadfast assistance and inspiration of Jacqueline Jones, Tom McCormick, Kevin Starr, and Dale Tomich. My editor, Robin Whitaker, improved every page of the manuscript. Of course, I alone am responsible for any errors.

A number of grants and fellowships helped me through the late stages of research and writing. While a fellow in the Stanford University Humanities Center, I was able to formulate many of the ideas about the relationship between photography and the farmworker movement and then test them on a group of excellent students in my courses on farmworkers and agriculture. A Mellon Fellowship at the Huntington Library provided access to that institution's vast resources and the opportunity to share ideas with Jennifer Watts, to present some of them at a bag-lunch slide lecture, and to visit archives in the Los Angeles area. While organizing an exhibition of my farmworker photography for the Thacher Gallery, at the University of San Francisco, in the summer of 2001, I was able to confront how my own work fits into the larger story. Two years later, I concluded my research on Ansel Adams, Otto and Hansel Mieth Hagel, and Max Yavno while serving as the Ansel Adams Fellow at the Center for Creative Photography, University of Arizona, Tucson, Arizona. Two Independent Research and Creative Work Awards from the Charles Redd Center for Western Studies, Brigham Young University, helped me to examine more fully the work of Otto and Hansel Mieth Hagel. A Franklin Research Grant from the American Philosophical Society and the Mark Lynton History Prize from the Anthony Lukas Prize Project, Columbia University Graduate School of Journalism/Nieman Foundation, Harvard University, allowed me to complete the research and writing. A grant from the Puffin Foundation assisted the last stages of writing. I resumed my work in the Leonard Nadel Collection during a stint as a Senior Fellow in the Center for Advanced Study in the Visual Arts at the National Gallery of Art, in Washington, D.C. I finished up as a "We the People" project supported by a National Endowment for the Humanities fellowship. The Wyeth Award from the College of Art Association provided a publication subsidy.

While I worked on this project, farmworkers lost an entire generation of photographers. Before they passed away, it was my great privilege to have met and interviewed Ansel Adams, Horace Bristol, Morrie Camhi, Loomis Dean, Dave Evans, Hansel Mieth Hagel, Peter Leung, Margery Mann, Ralph H. Powell, Harvey Richards, Blair Stapp, Ted Streshinsky, Rich Turner, and Max Yavno. Two important photographic historians and one visual anthropologist also died before I finished writing. Henry Mayer, a new friend who shared with me ideas for his massive new biography of Dorothea Lange (subsequently taken over by Linda Gordon), suffered a heart attack while bicycling in Glacier National Park. Peter Palmquist, an old friend whom I first met while we were both exploring the career of Carleton E. Watkins, was killed by a hit-and-run driver shortly after finishing his encyclopedic second volume on photographers in the American West. John Collier Jr., a neighbor who delighted me with stories about his early years, offered sound advice while I photographed him one afternoon in his hand-built cabin.

I have been helped by countless archivists and librarians stretching from Britain and Germany to Mexico and the Virgin Islands. For providing information, photographs, and leads, I acknowledge Danette Cook Adamson, Special Collections, California Poly Pomona University, Pomona, California; Pat Akre, San Francisco History Center, San Francisco Public Library; Bill Appleton and Pat Havens, Simi Valley Historical Society, Simi Valley, California; Polly Armstrong and Roxanne Niland, Special Collections and Archives, Stanford University; Joseph A. Baird, University of California, Davis; Tracey Baker and Marilyn Ziebarth, Minnesota Historical Society, Saint Paul, Minnesota; Frank Bartholomew, Sonoma, California; Galen Beery, Historical Society of La Verne, La Verne, California; Tom Beck, University of Maryland Archives, Baltimore, Maryland; Linda Blackwell, Southwest Museum, Los Angeles, California; Barbara J. Blankman, First American Title Company, Santa Ana, California; Lynn Housouer, Pioneer's Museum/Imperial County Historical Society, Imperial, California; Trevor Bond, Washington State University Department of Manuscripts and Archives;

Lynn Bonfield, Labor Archives and Research Center, San Francisco State University; Eric Brazil, *Salinas Californian;* Debby Burns, Santa Paula Historical Society, Santa Paula, California; Alexis Buss, Industrial Workers of the World, Philadelphia, Pennsylvania; John M. Cahoon and William Mason, Seaver Center for Western History Research, Los Angeles Museum of Natural History, Los Angeles, California; Karen Carlson, Tenneco West, Bakersfield, California; Leslie Calmes, Denise Gossé, Dianne Nilsen, and Amy Rule, Center for Creative Photography, University of Arizona, Tucson, Arizona; Terry Carter, Ontario Public Library, Model Colony History Room; Rosa Casanova, Fototeca Nacional, Pachuca, Mexico; Howard Chapnick, Black Star Photos, New York City; Heidi Casebolt and Sabine Gerke-Shroeder, Vacaville Museum, Vacaville, California; Lisa Christensen, California History Center and Foundation, DeAnza College, Cupertino, California; Janet Clemmensen, California State Library, Fresno; Jean Coffey, Special Collections, Henry Madden Library, California State University, Fresno; Eileen M. Colla, Wine Institute, San Francisco, California; Carolyn Cole and Kathy Kobayashi, Los Angeles Public Library Photo Collection; Frank Cowsert, Cowsert Studios, Courtland, California; Harry Crosby, La Jolla, California; Donald Cutter, University of New Mexico; Maureen Dilig, National Geographic Society Image Sales, Washington, D.C.; John Dixon, Palm Desert, California; Iris Engstrand, University of San Diego; Thomas Featherstone and Mary J. Wallace, Walter P. Reuther Library, Wayne State University, Detroit, Michigan; Gary Fong and Diane Levy, *San Francisco Chronicle;* Jonathan Friedlander, UCLA Near Eastern Studies; Roy Flukinger and Linda Myers, Harry Ransom Research Center, University of Texas, Austin; Pat Akre, San Francisco Public Library; William Frank, Alan Jutsi, Claire Kennedy, Mona Schulman, Jennifer Watts, and David S. Zeidberg, the Huntington Library, San Marino, California; Jennifer Fukunaga, Chino Branch Library, Chino, California; Genie Orcutt Geer, Santa Paula Historical Society; Tom Gilbert and Kelli Souder, Time–Life Picture Service, New York City; Jann Glissen, Corbis, Bellingham, Washington; Maria M. Gonzalez, Guasti Plaza, Guasti, California; Campbell Gray and Rachel Hoover, Museum of Art, Brigham Young University, Provo, Utah; Marc Grossman, United Farm Workers of America, Keene, California; Al Guillin, Limoneira Company, Santa Paula, California; Bruce Guter, David Streeter, and Susan Hutchinson, Pomona Public Library Special Collections; Dorothy Haase, Fillmore Historical Society, Fillmore, California; Alfred Harrison, North Point Galleries, San Francisco; Michael J. Hart, Sunny Slope Water Company, Pasadena, California; Pat Havens, Simi Valley Historical Society, Simi Valley, California; Hearst Publishing Company, San Francisco, California; Maria Henle, the Fritz Henle Collection, Saint Croix, U.S. Virgin Islands; Matt Herron, Take Stock, San Rafael, California; Melissa Heyman, Campbell Historical Museum, Campbell, California; Dolores Higueras, Museo Naval, Madrid, Spain; James D. Hofer, University of Redlands Archives, Redlands, California; Raymond Hoffman, Pajaro Valley Historical Association, Watsonville, California; Rachael Hoover, Brigham Young University Art Museum, Provo, Utah; J. Horner, Nipomo Public Library, Nipomo, California; Donald F. Houghton, Saint Helena, California; Pat Jacobsen, Millennium Fruit Crate

Label Collection, Weimar, California; Robyn Inglis, Instituto de Historica del Pacífico Español, Vancouver, British Columbia, Canada; Steve Iverson, Rancho los Cerritos Historic Site, Long Beach, California; K. J. Iwagaki, Japanese American Resource Center/Museum, San Jose, California; Charles Johnson, Ventura County Museum, Ventura, California; Drew Johnson, Charles Lokey, Joyce Minick, Bill McMorris, and Therese Heyman, the Oakland Museum, Dorothea Lange Collection; Stephen Johnson, Stephen Johnson Photography, Pacifica, California; Bill Jones, Special Collections, Meriam Library, California State University, Chico; John K. Kallenberg, William B. Secrest, Fresno County Library, California and Local History Room; Shirley J. Kendell, Bidwell Mansion State Historical Park, Chico, California; James E. Kern, Vallejo Naval and Historical Museum, Vallejo, California; Cindy Krimmel, San Diego Historical Society; Martha Krueger, Academy of Motion Picture Art, Hollywood, California; Armand J. Labbé, Bowers Museum of Cultural Art, Santa Ana, California; Glory Laffey, Sourisseau Academy, San Jose State University, San Jose, California; Jerome D. Laval, the Claude "Pop" Laval Collection, Fresno, California; Lila Lee, Held Poage Library, Mendocino County Historical Society, Ukiah, California; Carla Leshne, San Francisco; Peter Leung, University of California, Davis; Emma Lewis, Heritage Centre, Norwich Millennium Library, Great Britain; Dave Lorgang, Yosemite Museum, Yosemite Valley, California; Sandy Lydon, Cabrillo College, Aptos, California; Myra Manfrina, Lompoc Historical Society, Lompoc, California; Thomas Maxwell-Long, University of California, Riverside; Brian McGinty, Scottsdale, Arizona; Donald McGue, A. K. Smiley Library, Redlands, California; Leonard McKay, Memorabilia of San Jose, San Jose, California; Andrea Morris Metz and Sarah Lim, Merced County Historical Society, Merced, California; Archie Miyatake, Pasadena, California; Lynette Miller, Washington State Historical Society, Tacoma, Washington; Vincent Moses and Marvin Powell, Riverside Municipal Museum; John Mraz, Universidad Autónoma de Puebla, Mexico; Evelyn DeWolfe Nadel, Hollywood, California; Jane K. Newell, Anaheim Public Library, Anaheim, California; John Nopel, Chico, California; Kern County Museum, Bakersfield, California; María Ortiz, Fresno Historical Society, Fresno, California; C. C. Keefe-Ostle, Amador-Livermore Valley Historical Society, Pleasanton, California; Breck Parkman, Fort Ross State Park, California; Rondal Partridge, Berkeley, California; Jim Pimentel, *San Francisco Examiner;* David Piff, National Archives, Pacific Region, San Bruno, California; Michael Redman, Santa Barbara Historical Society; Paul Richards, Harvey Richards Collection and Estuary Press, Oakland, California; Charles L. Sawyer, Ralph Milliken Museum, Los Banos, California; Michael Shulman, Magnum Photos, New York City; Steve Simmons, Steve Simmons Photography, Sacramento, California; John Skarstad, Special Collections and Archives, University of California, Davis; Susan Snyder, the Bancroft Library, University of California, Berkeley; Edward Spalding, Fillmore Historical Society, Fillmore, California; Julie Stark, Community Memorial Museum of Sutter County, Yuba City, California; Elizabeth Steward, San Jose Historical Museum, San Jose, California; Kathleen A. Strauss and Don W. Wilson, Dwight D. Eisenhower Library, Abilene, Kansas; Carmen Bambach-Street, Metropolitan

Museum of Art, New York City; David Streeter, Pomona Public Library, Pomona, California; Arne Svenson, Arne Svenson Photography, New York City; Marcicarmen Ruiz-Torres, Ontario Museum of History and Art, Ontario, California; Marilyn Thompson, Yolo County Archives/Records Center, Woodland, California; Robert Thurber, Miami, Florida; Dauce Taube, Ticor Collection, University of Southern California; Genevieve Troka, California State Archives, Sacramento; Rona Tucillo, Getty Images, New York City; Juanita DeValentine, Wheatland Historical Society, Wheatland, California; Crissa Van Vleck, Brendon Williams, California Historical Society, San Francisco.

Notes

Preface

1. Howard Chapnick to author, May 12, 1983, author's possession. See also Howard Chapnick, *Truth Needs No Ally: Inside Photojournalism* (Columbia, Mo., 1994). This comment seems to have made the rounds and appears in many other publications.

2. Quote from Allan Sekula, *Photography against the Grain: Essays and Photo Works, 1973–1983* (Halifax, Nova Scotia, 1984), 7.

3. Andy Grundberg, *Crisis of the Real: Writings on Photography since 1974* (New York, 1999), 263. See also John Berger and Jean Mohr, *Another Way of Telling* (New York, 1982), 100.

4. John Mraz and Jaime Velez Story, *Uprooted: Braceros in the Hermanos Mayo Lens* (Houston, 1996), 17.

5. Quote from Robin D. G. Kelley to author, e-mail, April 12, 2006, author's possession; and elsewhere.

6. Carey McWilliams, Miscellaneous Notes, MS, n.d., Carey McWilliams Collection, Bancroft Library, University of California, Berkeley. See also Carey McWilliams, *Factories in the Field: The Story of Migratory Farm Labor in California,* foreword by Douglas C. Sackman (New York, 1939; Berkeley, 1999), 7; and Carey McWilliams, *California: The Great Exception* (New York, 1949), 150.

1. Before Photography

1. Comments from Sarah Burns to author, e-mail, May 10, 2002, author's possession; anonymous peer review of 2004 National Endowment for the Humanities (NEH) project application, contained in NEH to author, December 15, 2004, author's possession. See also Michael Lesy, *Wisconsin Death Trip* (New York, 1973); and Sarah Burns to author, e-mail, May 2, 2000, author's possession.

2. Quote from Anthony Lloyd, *My War Gone By, I Miss It So* (New York, 2000), 3.

3. Georg Wilhelm Friedrich Hegel, *Philosophy of History* (1821; New York, 1974), 5. See also Michael Lesy, *Bearing Witness* (New York, 1984), xix.

4. David Levi Strauss, *Between the Eyes: Essays on Photography and Politics* (New York, 2003), 17. Cletus Daniel, *Bitter Harvest: A History of California Farmworkers, 1870–1940* (New York, 1982), the standard work on California farmworkers, ignores photographers and does not attribute images. For an early, influential muckraking exposé, see McWilliams, *Factories in the Field,* foreword by

Sackman, who credits some images. Douglas Sackman, *Orange Empire: California and the Fruits of Eden* (Berkeley, 2005), assesses the massive nexus of photography, art, and imagery in the Southern California citrus culture. While valuable as references for farmworkers, none of the other studies pays much attention to photographers. See, for example, Gerald B. Brown, "The United Farmworkers Grape Strike and Boycott, 1965–1970: An Evaluation of the Culture of Poverty Theory," PhD diss., Cornell University, 1972; Linda C. Majka and Theo J. Majka, *Farmworkers, Agribusiness, and the State* (Philadelphia, 1982); Philip L. Martin, *Promises to Keep: Collective Bargaining in California Agriculture* (Ames, Iowa, 1996); Philip Martin and J. Edward Taylor, *Poverty amid Prosperity* (Washington, D.C., 1998); Devra Weber, *Dark Sweat, White Gold: California Farmworkers, Cotton, and the New Deal* (Berkeley, 1994); Miriam J. Wells, *Strawberry Fields: Politics, Class, and Work in California Agriculture* (Ithaca, N.Y., 1996); David Vaught, *Cultivating California: Growers, Specialty Crops, and Labor, 1875–1920* (Baltimore, 1999); Stuart E. Jamieson, *Labor Unionism in American Agriculture* (U.S. Dept. of Labor, Bureau of Labor Statistics, Bulletin no. 836, Washington, D.C., 1946); Gilbert G. González, *Labor and Community: Mexican Citrus Worker Villages in a Southern California County, 1900–1950* (Chicago, 1994); Gilbert G. González, *Mexican Counsels and Labor Organizing: Imperial Politics in the American Southwest* (Austin, Tex., 1999); and Richard Walker, *The Conquest of Bread: 150 years of Agribusiness in California* (New York, 2004). In *Beasts of the Field: A Narrative History of California Farmworkers, 1769–1913* (Stanford, 2004), I make a stab at integrating visual history into the general history of California farmworkers.

5. Drew Heath Johnson, ed., *Capturing Light: Masterpieces of California Photography, 1850 to the Present* (New York, 2001), ix–x; Louise Katzman, *Photography in California, 1945–1980* (New York, 1984), 24; Richard Steven Street, "Valley of the Shadow of Death," *San Diego Magazine* 37 (December 1984): 220–29; "With Our Own Eyes," California Council for the Humanities *Network* (August 2005): 1, 4–5.

6. Troy Jollimore, "Anatomy of a Meal," review of Michael Pollan, *The Omnivore's Dilemma: A Natural History of Four Meals* (New York, 2006), in *San Francisco Chronicle,* April 16, 2006; Steve Allen, *The Ground Is Our Table* (New York, 1966), 30, 43–44. Although the 350,000 figure is commonly cited, it is misleading. Using social security and payroll reporting data, California state statistician Dr. Alfred Kahn estimates that in reality about one million farmworkers are in the state at peak harvest, around August 5. Of those million farmworkers, about one-third are employed at that moment, one-third are unemployed and looking for work, and another one-third are coming off one job and headed to another.

7. Composer, novelist, and photographer Gordon Parks puts it this way: "No art form transforms human apathy quicker. Having absorbed the message of a memorable photograph, the viewer's sense of compassion and newfound wisdom come together like the two lips touching." Gordon Parks, "This Rare Collection," in Life, *100 Photographs That Changed the World* (New York, 2003), 7. See also, Susan D. Moeller, *Compassion Fatigue: How the Media Sell Disease, Famine, War and Death* (New York, 1999), 2, 9–10; and Marianna Torgovnick, "Facing Death in a Culture of War," *Chronicle of Higher Education* (July 23, 2005): B6–B8.

8. Following ideas in Peter Galassi, *Before Photography: Painting and the Invention of Photography* (New York, 1981), 12, 17, 27, 29; and Ann Hyde, *An American Vision: Far Western Landscape and National Culture, 1820–1920* (New York, 1990).

9. Doyce B. Nunis Jr., ed., *The Drawings of Ignacio Tirsch, a Jesuit Missionary in Baja California,* trans. Elisbeth Schultz-Bischof (Los Angeles, 1972), 16, 44–46; Claire Perry, *Pacific Arcadia: Images of California, 1600–1915* (New York, 1999), 9–10.

10. Quote from Brian Lukacher, "Nature Historicized: Constable, Turner, and Romantic Landscape Painting," in Stephen F. Eisenman, ed., *Nineteenth Century Art: A Critical History* (New York, 1994), 143. For the reciprocal relationship among mission building, agriculture, conversion of

Indians, and farm labor, see Robert Archibald, *The Economic Aspects of the California Missions* (Washington, D.C., 1978), 142; Eugene David Burnett, "The Role of Agriculture in the Upper California Mission System as Illustrated at Mission San Diego, 1769–1784," MA thesis, St. Louis University, 1958, 21, 25; and Lionel Rideout, "Fermin Francisco de Lasuén and the Economic Development of the California Missions," MA thesis, University of California, Berkeley, 1940, 16–23. For background, see Clarence H. Harding, *The Spanish Empire in America* (New York, 1947).

11. Ernest J. Burrus, S.J., ed., *Ducrue's Account of the Expulsion of the Jesuits from Lower California, 1767–1769* (Rome, 1967), 16, 42–44, 64, 106; Peter M. Dunne, S.J., *The Black Robes in Lower California* (Berkeley, 1968), 418.

12. Zdenek Kalista, "Commentary," *Edito Cimelia Bohemia* (Prague, 1970); Johann Jakob Baegert, S.J., *Observations in Lower California,* ed. M. M. Branbenberg, trans. Carl L. Bauman (Berkeley, 1952), 204.

13. Miguel Venegas, *Empressas apostolicas de los misiones de la compañía de Jesús de la Provincia de Nueva España obras en la conquista de Californias . . . por el Padre Miguel Venegas de la misma compañía de Jesús, sábado, 7 de noviembre de 1739,* Huntington Library, Los Angeles (incomplete copy), Herbert Bolton Collection (complete copy), paragraph 519, also 516, 523, Bancroft Library, University of California, Berkeley. For a succinct narrative that well describes conditions on the rainy night when the expedition arrived at San Diego, see Miguel Costansó, "Diario histórico de los viajes de mar y tierra hechos al norte de California," MS, 1776, Bancroft Library. For a translation, see Miguel Costansó, *Diario del viaje de tierra,* ed. and trans. Frederick J. Teggert (Berkeley, 1911). By some accounts forty-six campesinos were on the second expedition. See also Francisco Palóu, *Life and Apostolic Labors of the Venerable Fray Junípero Serra,* ed. and trans. C. Scott Williams (New York, 1913), 72. Of about 219 members of the two "sacred expeditions" that started by land and sea, 126 survived the journey, although figures are imprecise. See also Herbert E. Bolton, ed. and trans., *Palóu's Historical Memoirs of New California* (Berkeley, 1926), 1: 30, 295; Antonine Tibesar, ed. and trans., *Writings of Junípero Serra* (Washington, D.C., 1955), 1: 59–61; Luis Navarro García, *Don José de Gálvez y la comandancia general de las provincias internas del norte de Nueva España* (Seville, 1964), 163–69; Herbert I. Priestley, *José de Gálvez, Visitor General of New Spain, 1765–1771* (Berkeley, 1916), 135, 154–57, 279; Harry W. Crosby, *Antigua California: Mission and Colony on the Peninsular Frontier, 1697–1768* (Albuquerque, N.M., 1994), xv; Warren L. Cook, *Flood Tide of Empire: Spain and the Pacific Northwest, 1543–1819* (New Haven, Conn., 1973), 49, also 44–48; Francisco Javier Clavigero, S.J., *Storia della California, opera postuma del Nob. Sig. Abate D. Francesco Clavigero* (Venice, Italy, 1789), 4: 20, later published in Mexico as *Historia de la Antigua ó Baja California obra postuma del Padre Francisco Javier Alegre de la compañía de Jesús,* trans. Nicolas García de San Vicente (Mexico City, 1852); in English as *The History of [Lower] California y Don Francisco Javier Clavigero, S.J.,* ed. and trans. Sara E. Lake and A. A. Gray (Stanford, 1937); and Sigismundo Taraval, *The Indian Uprising in Lower California, 1734–1737,* trans. Marguerite Eyre Wilbur (Los Angeles, 1931), 38. Crespí's diary in Bolton, ed. and trans., *Palóu's Historical Memoirs of New California,* 2: 104, says, "Only fourteen of the forty-four who started with the first expedition and some twelve who went with the second reached San Diego." Hubert Howe Bancroft, *History of California* (San Francisco, 1886), 1: 132–41, 165–68, also cites these numbers. Don DeNevi and Noel F. Moholy, in *Junípero Serra: The Illustrated History of the Franciscan Founder of California's Missions* (San Francisco, 1985), 99–105, claim that twenty-seven of the Baja California Indians survived and that ninety-three started north (thirteen of fifty-one Indians surviving the Portolá march) but cite no sources. DeNevi and Moholy may also be counting the Indian servants assigned to Serra. Various other accounts state that a total of ninety-one campesinos left from Baja California and that forty-nine departed on the Rivera y Moncada expedition. However, the usually reliable Zephyrin Engelhardt, in *Missions and Missionaries of California* (San Francisco, 1912), 1: 14, 16, asserts that

only fourteen campesinos came north with Rivera, and twelve with Portolá, apparently counting only the survivors. My estimate that twenty-seven Baja California field hands were in Alta California in 1770 is based on figures in Bolton, ed. and trans., *Palóu's Historical Memoirs of New California;* Bancroft, *History of California,* 1: 165, 167–68, 175–77; and Charles E. Chapman, *A History of California: The Spanish Period* (New York, 1921), 222–23. The accounting is as follows: twenty-six survivors from the original eighty-six, minus one killed in the attack on Mission San Diego, six who died of sickness that winter, two who went south with Rivera's resupply expedition to Mexico on February 11, 1770, and ten who were dropped off by the ship *San Antonio* on March 19, giving a total of twenty-seven. However, Bancroft's account can be interpreted as indicating that the ten field hands referred to were those left behind when the second Monterey expedition departed on April 17. This would lower the total Baja California campesino force to seventeen. Another accounting discrepancy may involve the presence of three Baja California Indian "boy servants," who seem to have been included in some lists but not others and one of whom was killed in the August 15 attack. I regard these calculations as rough estimates. See Richard Steven Street, "First Farmworkers, First *Braceros:* Baja California Field Hands and the Origins of Farm Labor Importation in California Agriculture, 1769–1790," *California History* 125 (Winter 1996–97): 306–21, 381–83.

14. James A. Sandos, *Converting California: Indians and Franciscans in the Missions* (New Haven, Conn., 2004), xiii, 174–84; Steven Hackel, *Children of Coyote, Missionaries of St. Francis: Indian–Spanish Relations in Colonial California, 1769–1850* (Durham, N.C., 2005).

15. Virginia M. Bouvier, *Women and the Conquest of California, 1542–1840* (Tucson, Ariz., 2001), 1–33; Kenneth E. Pauley and Carol M. Pauley, *San Fernando, Rey de España: An Illustrated History* (Spokane, Wash., 2005); Richard Steven Street, "'We Are Not Slaves': A History of California Farmworkers, 1769–1869: The Formative Years," PhD diss., University of Wisconsin, 1995, 109–12.

16. Arda M. Haenszel, "Visual Knowledge of California to 1700," *California Historical Quarterly* 36 (September 1957): 229–30; James L. Nolan, "Anglo-American Myopia and the California Mission Art," *Southern California Quarterly* 58 (Spring–Summer–Fall 1976): 1–44, 143–204, 261–331. See also Liana Vardi, "Imagining the Harvest in Early Modern Europe," *American Historical Review* 101 (December 1996): 1357–97; Bradley Fratello, "France Embraces Millet: The Intertwined Fates of *The Gleaners* and the *Angelus,*" *Art Bulletin* 4 (December 2003): 685–700; and Margaret A. Sullivan, *Bruegel's Peasants: Art and Audience in the Northern Renaissance* (Cambridge, U.K., 1994).

17. William A. Goetzmann, *Exploration and Empire: The Explorer and the Scientist in the Winning of the American West* (New York, 1966), ix–xi.

18. Quote from Charles N. Rudkin, ed. and trans., *The First French Expedition to California: Lapérouse in 1786* (Los Angeles, 1959), 62. Copies of Vancy's paintings differ substantially from one another in details, clarity, and finish. Compare, for example, the three versions reproduced in Carmen Sotos, *Los pintores de la expedición de Alejandro Malaspino* (Madrid, 1982), figures 624, 625, and 626, which transform soldiers into Indians and edit out and inject various figures. For pointing this out, I thank Robin Inglis of the Instituto de Historica del Pacífico Español, North Vancouver, Canada.

19. Quote from Carey McWilliams, *Southern California Country: An Island on the Land* (New York, 1946), 32. For the debate on Indian labor, see Rupert Costo and Jeannette Henry Costo, eds., *The Missions of California: A Legacy of Genocide* (San Francisco, 1987), ix, 3, 92–93; and Francis F. Guest, "Junípero Serra and His Approach to the Indians," *Southern California Quarterly* 67 (Fall 1985): 223–61.

20. Malaspina visited California twice, the first time in September 1791 and the second time from September 22 to October 26, 1792. Some accounts date Cardero's drawings from his second, more extended stay. However, internal evidence from the view of the Monterey presidio suggests a

1791 date. Specifically, two vessels with three masts are in the anchorage. Since three ships were on the 1791 expedition (two three-masted vessels, the *Descubierta* and *Atrevida,* and one small, two-masted sloop, the *Santa Saturnina*) and their order was reversed in 1792 (two small sloops, the *Suntil* and the *Mexicana,* and one three-masted vessel, the *Santa Gertrudis*), it is likely that Cardero made his drawing in 1791. On the other hand, Cardero had much more time to work during his 1792 visit and had been drawing profusely on the Pacific Northwest coast prior to arriving at Monterey for his second visit. Also, Cardero made two views of the presidio, a rough sketch and a more finished version. He also spent considerable time during 1794–95 completing drawings from his 1791 and 1792 work. For these reasons, the exact date of the first image clearly depicting Alta California field hands remains open to speculation, but it is certainly circa 1791–95. See Donald C. Cutter to author, December 28, 1995, author's possession; Donald C. Cutter, "Early Spanish Artists on the Northwest Coast," *Pacific Northwest Quarterly* 54 (October 1963): 11, 150–55; Sotos, *Los pintores de la expedición de Alejandro Malaspino,* 2; Dionisio Alcalá Galiano and Cayetano Valdés, *Relación del viaje hecho por las goletas "Sutil" y "Mexicana" en el año 1792 para reconocer al estrecho de Fuca* (1802; reprint, Madrid, 1958); John Kendrick, trans., *The Voyage of Suntil and Mexicana, 1792: The Last Spanish Exploration of the Northwest Coast of America* (Spokane, Wash., 1996); Iris W. Engstrand, "Seekers of the 'Northern Mystery': European Exploration of California and the Pacific," in Ramón Gutiérrez and Richard Orsi, eds., *Contested Eden: California before the Gold Rush* (Berkeley, 1998), 100–102; and Henry R. Wagner, "Four Early Sketches of Monterey Scenes," *California Historical Society Quarterly* 15 (September 1936): 213–15; and Henry R. Wagner, "Journal of Tomás de Suría of His Voyage with Malaspina to the Northwest Coast of America in 1791," *Pacific Historical Review* 5 (September 1936): 234–76. *Reception of La Pérouse* disappeared in the 1840s.

21. Iris W. Engstrand, *Spanish Scientists in the New World: The Eighteenth Century Expeditions* (Seattle, 1981), 45, 103; Donald C. Cutter, *California in 1792: A Spanish Naval Visit* (Norman, Okla., 1990), 5, 8–9, 50–51, 65, 68, 75–77; Donald C. Cutter, *Malaspina in California* (San Francisco, 1960), 28, 31, 36; Donald C. Cutter, "Early Spanish Artists on the Northwest Coast," *Pacific Northwest Quarterly* 54 (October 1963): 11, 150–55; "The Art of the Malaspina Expedition of 1791–1792," *Oakland Art Museum Monthly Bulletin* (June 1960): 12–15; Justino Fernández, *Tomás de Suría y su viaje con Malaspina, 1791* (Mexico City, 1939), 16.

22. Jeanne Van Nostrand, *The First Hundred Years of Painting in California, 1775–1875, with Biographical Information and References relating to the Artists,* foreword by Alfred Frankenstein (San Francisco, 1980), 6–7; Anthony Kirk, "Picturing California," in Gutiérrez and Orsi, eds., *Contested Eden,* 359; Ann Jensen Adams, "Competing Communities in the 'Great Bog of Europe': Identity and Seventeenth-Century Dutch Landscape Painting," in W. J. T. Mitchell, ed., *Landscape and Power* (Chicago, 1994), 35–76.

23. Georg Heinrich von Langsdorff, *Langsdorff's Narrative of the Rezanov Voyage to Nueva California in 1806,* ed. and trans. Thomas C. Russell (San Francisco, 1927), 62–63, also 57–59; Georg Heinrich F. von Langsdorff, *Voyages and Travels in Various Parts of the World, during the Years 1803, 1804, 1806, and 1807* (London, 1813–14).

24. Quote from Porter Garnett, *San Francisco One-Hundred Years Ago* (San Francisco, 1913), 93, also 48–49, 55–69, 93–103, reprinted in Julia G. Costillo, ed., *Documentary Evidence for the Spanish Missions of Alta California* (New York, 1991), 145–58.

25. August C. Mahr, *The Visit of the Rurik to San Francisco in 1816* (Stanford, 1932), 61–69; Perry, *Pacific Arcadia,* 16–19; Bancroft, *History of California,* 2: 278–79.

26. Bancroft, *History of California,* 2: 523–25; 653–54; Frank Adams, "The Historical Background of California Agriculture," in Claude B. Hutchison, ed., *California Agriculture* (Berkeley, 1946), 7–15; Edith B. Webb, *Indian Life at the Old Missions* (Los Angeles, 1952); Robert Archibald, *The Economic Aspects of the California Missions* (Washington, D.C., 1978), 184–85; J. N. Bowman,

"The Resident Neophytes (Existentes) of the California Missions, 1769–1834," *Historical Society of Southern California Quarterly* 40 (1958): 138–48; Robert H. Jackson, *Indian Population Decline: The Missions of Northwestern New Spain, 1687–1840* (Albuquerque, N.M., 1994), 60.

27. Kevin Starr, *Inventing the Dream: California through the Progressive Era* (New York, 1985), 58; Thomas Blackburn, "The Chumash Revolt of 1924: A Narrative Account," *Journal of California Anthropology* 2 (1975): 223–27; Sherburne F. Cook, *The Population of the California Indians, 1769–1970* (Berkeley, 1976); Sherburne F. Cook, "Expeditions to the Interior of California: Central Valley, 1821–1835," *Anthropological Records* 20 (1962): 168–80, 205–6; Edward D. Castillo, "The Assassination of Padre Andrés Quintana by the Indians of Mission Santa Cruz in 1812: The Narrative of Lorenzo Aisiara," *California History* 68 (Fall 1989): 117–25; Alan K. Brown, "Pomponio's World," *Argonaut* 6 (May 1975): 1–20; James Sandos, "Neophyte Resistance in the Alta California Missions," in Timothy J. O'Keffe, ed., *Columbus, Confrontation, Christianity: The European-American Encounter Revisited* (Palo Alto, Calif., 1994), 170–78; James Sandos, "Christianization among the Chumash: An Ethnohistoric Perspective," *American Indian Quarterly* 15 (1991): 65–89; James Sandos, "Levantiemento! The 1824 Chumash Uprising Reconsidered," *Southern California Quarterly* 67 (Summer 1985): 109–33; Richard J. Orsi, "Estanislao's Rebellion, 1829," in William A. Burrough, Richard J. Orsi, and Richard B. Rice, *The Elusive Eden* (New York, 1996), 53–68.

28. William O. Goetzmann, ed., *Personal Narrative of James O. Pattie* (Philadelphia, 1962), 194–95; Edward Everett Dale, ed., *The Ashley-Smith Explorations and the Discovery of a Central Route to the Pacific, 1822–1829* (Glendale, Ill., 1941), 195–206, 222, 228. Pattie's narrative may have been concocted by New England minister Timothy Flint.

29. Bancroft, *History of California,* 3, 120–21; Perry, *Pacific Arcadia,* 19–20; Anatole G. Maxour, ed. and trans., "Memoirs of California by K. T. Khlebnikov," *Pacific Historical Review* 9 (1940): 307–36; Maurice H. Grant, *A Dictionary of British Landscape Painters, from the Sixteenth Century to the Early Twentieth Century* (London, 1952).

30. Quotes from Informe, 1826, in *Boletín del Archivo General de la Nación* 30 (1959): 252; Brydges Beechey, *Narrative of a Voyage to the Pacific and Beering's Strait, to Cooperate with the Polar Expeditions, performed in His Majesty's Ship Blossom under the command of Captain F. W. Beechey, R.N., F.R.S., etc., in the years 1825, 26, 27, 28. Published by authority of the Lords Commissioners of the Admiralty,* new ed. (London, 1831), 2: 582–83. In 1841, a supplement to *Narrative of a Voyage* carried twenty-three splendidly colored plates. But these only documented birds and other small animals, plants, and other specimens. Reading the elegant and comprehensive work, one has no idea that Smyth drew and painted field hands extensively at Monterey. For a French artist whose work closely parallels that of Smyth, see Charles Franklin Carter, trans., "Duhaut-Cilly's Account of California in the Years 1827–28," *California Historical Society Quarterly* 8 (1929): 130–66, 214–50, 306–36. For similar developments at Mission San Juan Capistrano, where the Indians would not obey, refused to work, and declared themselves free, see Capt. Juan M. Estudillo to Echeandia, April 25, 1827, San Diego Mission, Department of State, Missions, 2: 20–25, Bancroft Library (copy in Santa Barbara Mission Archive). My thanks to Padre Virgilio Biasiol for the original document and translation. For background, see David Hornbeck, "Economic Growth and Change at the Missions of Alta California, 1776–1846," in David Hurts Thomas, ed., *Columbian Consequences: Archeological and Historical Perspectives on the Spanish Borderlands West* (Washington, D.C., 1989), 1: 423–33; Elizabeth Haas, *Conquests and Historical Identities in California, 1769–1936* (Berkeley, 1995), 38; and Douglas Monroy, *Thrown among Strangers: The Making of Mexican Culture in Frontier California* (Berkeley, 1990), 69.

31. Starr, *Inventing the Dream,* 128, 134. Only one of Smyth's paintings, *Californians Throwing the Lasso,* appears in *Narrative of a Voyage,* along with scattered references to California. Not until 1839 did eight mission scenes based on his paintings appear in Alexander Forbes, *California: A*

History of Upper and Lower California (London, 1839). Sixty-five sketches by Smyth are held in the Bancroft Library. A sketchbook in the Mitchell Library, Melbourne, Australia, contains six of his California scenes, including one of Mission San José.

32. Andrew Rolle, ed., intro., *Life in California: During a Residence of Several Years in that Territory, Including a Narrative of Events Which Have Transpired Since that Period when California was an Independent Government . . . by Alfred Robinson . . . and Chinigchinich, An Historical Account of the Origin, Customs, and Traditions of the Indians of Alta California . . . by the Reverend Geronimo Boscana* (1846; Santa Barbara, 1970), 72–77, 81, 88; Adele Ogden, "Alfred Robinson, New England Merchant in Mexican California," *California Historical Society Quarterly* 23 (September 1944): 202; Henry D. Burrows, "Alfred Robinson," *Historical Society of Southern California Quarterly* 4 (1899): 234–35; Alfred Robinson, "Statement of Recollections on Early Years in California," MS, 1878, Bancroft Library.

33. Ulf Bankmann, "A Prussian in Mexican California: Ferdinand Deppe, Horticulturalist, Collector for European Museums and Artist," *Southern California Quarterly* 84 (Spring 2002): 1–33; Hinrich Lichtenstein, *Ferdinand Deppe's Travels in California in 1837,* trans. Gustave O. Arlt (Los Angeles, 1953). Robinson's original drawings are not in his papers at the Bancroft Library. Their whereabouts is unknown.

34. Bancroft, *History of California,* 2: 779; 3: 644; Nancy Dustin Moure, *California Art: 450 Years of Painting and Other Media* (Los Angeles, 1998), 18. Deppe's painting of Mission San Gabriel is held in both the Santa Barbara Mission Archives and the Orange County Museum of Art. It is not clear which one is the original and which one the replica.

35. Street, *Beasts of the Field,* 93–97.

36. Quotes from *Los Angeles Star,* December 24, 1859, in Van Nostrand, *The First Hundred Years of Painting in California,* 17–18; and Starr, *Inventing the Dream,* 17. See also Kevin Starr, *Americans and the California Dream, 1850–1915* (New York, 1973), 396, 400, 404, 406–7; Monroy, *Thrown among Strangers,* 258–71; Don Mitchell, *The Lie of the Land: Migrant Workers and the California Landscape* (Minneapolis, 1996), 1, 4, also 17–18; John O. Pohlmann, "California's Mission Myth," PhD diss., University of California, Los Angeles, 1974, 1: 1–16; 2: 269–334, 492–527; John H. Kemble, ed., *William Henry Meyers, Journal of a Cruise to California and the Sandwich Islands in the United States Sloop-of-War Cyane by William H. Meyers, Gunner, U.S.N. 1841–1844* (San Francisco, 1955); and Charles Roberts Anderson, ed., *Journal of a Cruise to the Pacific Ocean, 1842–1844, in the Frigate United States, with Notes on Herman Melville* (Durham, N.C., 1937), 84–86. Throughout this volume, artwork measurements are given as width followed by height.

37. Théodore Laplace, *Campaigne de circumnavigation de la frégate l'Artémise pendant les années 1837, 1838, 1839 et 1840* (Paris, 1841–45); Van Nostrand, *The First Hundred Years of Painting in California,* 12–15. Although the last ten years of Mexican rule attracted more foreign attention than the preceding sixty-four years of Spanish colonization, the influx of artists did not alter the skewed picture. Most artists on these expeditions continued to make the same predictable pictures emphasizing mission architecture, Indian dress, and landmarks around Yerba Buena, Santa Barbara, and Los Angeles. See *History of the Coast Counties of Central California* (Chicago, 1893), 196; Erwin Gudde, ed., "Edward Visher's First Visit to California," *California Historical Society Quarterly* 19 (September 1940): 193–216; and William Henry Meyers, *Mission of San Carmel, California,* ca. 1840, watercolor on paper, 13 × 8 inches, Robert Honeyman Collection, Bancroft Library.

38. Richard Henry Dana, *Two Years before the Mast* (New York, 1840), 61–62. See also Robert Lucid, "*Two Years before the Mast* as Propaganda," *American Quarterly* 12 (Fall 1960): 392; Joshua Paddison, ed., *A World Transformed: Firsthand Accounts of California before the Gold Rush* (Berkeley, 1999); James Steele, *Old California Days* (New York, 1939), 116–17; Leonard Pitt, *The Decline of the Californios: A Social History of the Spanish Speaking Californians, 1846–1890* (Berkeley, 1966), 16,

52–53; Alfred Robinson, *Life in California before the Conquest* (1846; San Francisco, 1925), 48; and Charles Nordhoff, *California: A Book for Travelers and Settlers* (New York, 1877), 243–44.

39. Susanna B. Dakin, *The Lives of William Hartnell* (Stanford, 1949), 72, 76, 121, 151 157–58, 181; Adele Ogden, "Hides and Tallow: McCullough, Hartnell and Company, 1822–1828," *California Historical Society Quarterly* 6 (September 1927): 254–64; Webb, *Indian Life at the Old Missions,* 199–201.

40. "Journal of John Henry Hollingsworth," *California Historical Society Quarterly* 1 (September 1922): 255, 268; William Rich Hutton, *Glances at California, 1847–1853* (San Marino, Calif., 1942), 41, 53.

41. Edwin Bryant, *What I Saw in California* (New York, 1848), 308.

42. George W. Patten, "Alfred Sully," in *Annual Reunion of the Association of Graduates, United States Military Academy* (New York, 1879), 90–93; Margaret Koch, *Santa Cruz County: Parade of the Past* (Fresno, Calif., 1973), 11, 15, 17; E. S. Harrison, *History of Santa Cruz County* (San Francisco, 1892).

43. Augustias de la Guerra Ord, "Occurrences in California," MS, 1878, Bancroft Library; Perry, *Pacific Arcadia,* 23–25; *Alta California,* June 3, 1850.

44. J. S. Holliday, *Rush for Riches: Gold Fever and the Making of California* (Berkeley, 1999), 57–111.

45. Georgia Willis Read and Ruth Gaines, eds., *Gold Rush: The Journals, Drawings, and Other Papers of J. Goldsborough Bruff, 1849–1851* (New York, 1949), 546–47, 693, a one-volume, abridged version of the original two-volume edition, published in 1944 by Columbia University Press; Thurston Clarke, *California Fault: Searching for the Spirit of a State along the San Andreas* (New York, 1996), 6–11, 404–14, uncovering some heretofore unknown materials on Bruff. See also George R. Stewart, *The California Trail: An Epic with Many Heroes* (New York, 1962), 277–82.

2. Competing Visions

1. Walter Van Tilburg Clark, ed., *The Journals of Alfred Doten, 1849–1903* (Reno, Nev., 1973), 1: 221, 415, 433. The images were probably pannotypes, underexposed, wet collodion negatives, dried and mounted on the front of a piece of dark leather and contained in polished leather cases. For Hamilton, see Peter Palmquist and Thomas R. Kailbourn, *Pioneer Photographers of the Far West: A Biographical Dictionary, 1840–1865,* foreword by Martha A. Sandweiss (Stanford, 2000), 273–74.

2. Quote from *Alta California,* November 30, [1849?], Bancroft Scrapbooks, Bancroft Library. See also Malcolm J. Rohrbough, *Days of Gold: The California Gold Rush and the American Nation* (Berkeley, 1997), 260–81; Rodman W. Paul, "The Beginnings of Agriculture in California: Innovation vs. Continuity," *California Historical Quarterly* 52 (Spring 1973): 16–27; Samuel E. Gittings, "The Foundations of Placer County Horticulture, 1850–1900," MA thesis, California State University, Sacramento, 1959, 45–46, 64–65; David Vaught, "After the Gold Rush: Replicating the Rural Midwest in the Sacramento Valley," *Western Historical Quarterly* 34 (Winter 2003): 447–68; Edward G. Buffin, *Six Months in the Gold Mines* (Philadelphia, 1850), 98–99; "The Farm of Thomas Knight," *California State Agricultural Society Transactions 1858* (Sacramento, 1859), 11–12.

3. Quotes from *Shasta Courier,* October 29, 1853; and A. G. Tucker to father and sister, November 6, 1861, Rhode Island Historical Society, Providence. See also Richard Rudisill, *Mirror Image: The Influence of the Daguerreotype on American Society* (Albuquerque, N.M., 1971), 131–32.

4. Rudisill, *Mirror Image,* 48, 133–48; Marion Rinehart, *The American Daguerreotype* (Athens, Ga., 1981), 385–397; Beaumont Newhall, *The Daguerreotype in America* (New York, 1976), 34, 70, 76, 85–86, 144, 152–54; Peter Palmquist, "The Daguerreotype in San Francisco," *History of Photography* 4 (July 1980): 209; Malcolm Daniel, "Divine Perfection: The Daguerreotype in Europe and

America," *Metropolitan Museum of Art Bulletin* 107 (Spring 1999): 41–45; George D. Dornin, *Thirty Years Ago, 1849–1879: Gold Rush Memories of a Daguerrotype Artist,* ed. Peter Palmquist (1879; New York, 1995); T. A. Barry and B. A. Patten, *Men and Memoirs of San Francisco in the Spring of '50* (San Francisco, 1873), 143–44; Robert Shlaer, *Sights Once Seen: Daguerreotyping Fremont's Last Expedition through the Rockies* (Santa Fe, N.M., 2000), 35–38, 51–61.

5. *Alta California,* February 1, 1851, and September 23, 1855, Bancroft Library; John Ross Dix [pseud.], *Amusing and Thrilling Adventures of California Artist, While Daguerreotyping a Continent, Amid Burning Deserts, Savages and Perpetual Snows, And a Poetical Companion to the Pantoscope of California, Nevada & Kansas, Salt & the Mormons* (Boston, 1854), 20–22, 35–36.

6. Horace Bell, *Reminiscences of a Ranger, or Early Times in Southern California* (Los Angeles, 1853; Santa Barbara, 1929), 33–36; Harris Newmark, *Sixty Years in Southern California, 1853–1913* (Los Angeles, 1913), 30–31; Michael J. Gillis and Michael Magliari, *John Bidwell and California: The Life and Writings of a Pioneer, 1841–1900* (Spokane, Wash., 2002); Monroy, *Thrown among Strangers,* 180–94, 237–43; Street, *Beasts of the Field,* 696; Dorothy Hill, "Indians of Chico Rancheria: An Ethnohistoric Study," MA thesis, California State University, Chico, 1974, x, 27–33; Jerard D. Wagers, "History of Agricultural Labor in California Prior to 1880," MA thesis, University of California, Berkeley, 1957, 63, 77; George S. Shaw, diary, MS, 1855, entry for May 15, 1855, California Historical Society, San Francisco.

7. Peter E. Palmquist, "The Sad but True Story of a Daguerrean Holy Grail," in Drew Heath Johnson and Marcia Eymann, eds., *Silver and Gold: Cased Images of the California Gold Rush* (Iowa City, Iowa, 1998), 43.

8. Peter E. Palmquist, "Robert Vance: Pioneer in Western Landscape Photography," *American West* 18 (September–October 1981): 22–27; Peter E. Palmquist, "Robert H. Vance: The Maine and Boston Years (1825–1850)," *Daguerrean Journal* (1991): 198–201; Palmquist and Kailbourn, *Pioneer Photographers of the Far West,* 220; R. Bruce Duncan, "Gold Rush Photographer," *Graphic Antiquarian* 2 (October 1971): 14–17.

9. R[obert] H. Vance, *Catalogue of Daguerreotype Panoramic Views in California, by R. H. Vance, on Exhibition at No. 349 Broadway* (New York, 1851), 1–8, New York Public Library. Daguerreotype titles explicitly identified with Hock Farm are: *Indian Hut Near Yuba City; View of Indian Village on Capt. Sutter's Plantation; View of Hock Farm, the residence of Capt. Sutter, on the Feather River; Hock Farm, from the East side of the River; View of Hock Farm from the top of a house and [Showing] the celebrated Bute [Butte] Mountains, sixteen miles distant.* However, views 56, 64, 65, 66, 67, 68, 69, 97, 98, 99, and 101 all seem to pertain to Hock Farm and its environs. Gaps in the sequence suggest that Vance made more than eleven views.

10. Quotes from Vance, *Catalogue of Daguerreotype Panoramic Views in California,* preface; *Photographic Art-Journal* 2 (October 1851): 252–53; and Martha Sandweiss, *Print the Legend: Photography and the American West* (New Haven, Conn., 2002), 85. Overextending himself through excessive speculation in mining stock, Vance eventually gave up his gallery. After 1860 he lived in obscurity, dying in 1876. See Peter Palmquist, "An Account of California's First Photographer," in Palmquist, ed., *Photography in the West* (Manhattan, Kans., 1987), 102–5.

11. Palmquist and Kailbourn, *Pioneer Photographers of the Far West,* 333–34; Rudisill, *Mirror Image,* 145; Catherine Hoover, "Pantoscope of California," *California Historical Courier* (July 1978): 3ff.; Robert Wernick, "Getting a Glimpse of History from a Grandstand Seat," *Smithsonian Magazine* 16 (August 1985): 68–84; John Francis McDermont, "Gold Rush Movies," *California Historical Society Quarterly* 33 (March 1954): 29–38.

12. Quote from untitled lecture notes for the *Pantoscope,* John Wesley Jones Papers, California Historical Society, San Francisco. See also Rudisill, *Mirror Image,* 142–43. The full manuscript is reprinted in Catherine Hoover, "Jones' Pantoscope of California: A 'Lecture' by J. Wesley Jones,"

California Historical Society Quarterly 6 (June 1927): 109–29, 238–53. Departure date taken from *Marysville Herald,* June 3, 1851. For Sutter and his Indian farmworkers at Nuevo Helvetia and Hock Farm, see Albert L. Hurtado, *Indian Survival on the California Frontier* (New Haven, Conn., 1988), 55–71. Paul Emmert was also there while making daguerreotypes for his *Original Panorama of the Gold Mines in 1849.*

13. Perry, *Pacific Arcadia,* 83–84. Bartholomew's 4 × 6–inch pencil drawings on clay-coated paper are in the John Wesley Jones Papers, California Historical Society. For Nahl's translation of Shew's daguerreotype, see *Hutchings' California Magazine* 3 (April 1859): cover; Frank Soulé, John H. Gihon, and James Nisbet, *The Annals of San Francisco* (San Francisco, 1855), 52; and Hurtado, *Indian Survival on the California Frontier,* 160. For Nahl, see Joseph A. Baird, "Charles Christian Nahl: Artist of the Gold Rush," *American Art Review* 3 (September–October 1976): 56–70; Eugen Neuhaus, "Charles Christian Nahl, the Painter of California Life," *California Historical Society Quarterly* 15 (December 1936): 295–305; and Moreland L. Stevens, *Charles Christian Nahl: Artist of the Gold Rush, 1818–1878* (Sacramento, 1976).

14. The Bidwell daguerreotype is in the Special Collections and Archives, Meriam Library, California State University, Chico. See also Palmquist and Kailbourn, *Pioneer Photographers of the Far West,* 276–77.

15. Between 1852 and 1860, studio operators continued to make portraits of farmworkers and visual prospectors continued to frequent Hock Farm. One of the most notable visits occurred in September 1855, when James M. Hutchings, who would soon found *Hutchings' California Magazine,* and Edward Jump, a French immigrant lithographer and sketch artist who would later gain fame for whiskey bottle labels, stopped over at the end of a three-month expedition to produce yet another California panorama. With Sutter's son assisting, they too made a series of five daguerreotypes, several of which included native field hands, all of which subsequently disappeared. See James M. Hutchings, entries for September 1855, in *Journal of 1855,* transcribed by Gertrude Hutchings Mills, James M. Hutchings Papers, Library of Congress; "Guide to the Honeyman Collection," MS, n.d., 55, Bancroft Library; and Palmquist, "Western Photographers, I: Some Stories about Audacious Image Makers," *American West* 28 (May–June 1981): 38–46. On documentary, see Allan Sekula, "On the Invention of Photographic Meaning," in Victor Burgin, ed., *Thinking Photographically* (London, 1982), 84–109.

16. Quoted term from Oliver Wendell Holmes, "Doings of the Sunbeam," *Atlantic Monthly* 12 (1863): 4. See also Peter Palmquist, "Tintype California," *Californians* 2 (November–December 1984): 23–30; Michael L. Carlebach, *Working Stiffs: Occupational Portraits in the Age of Tintypes* (Washington, D.C., 2002), 5; and Robert W. Wagner, *The American Tintype* (Columbus, Ohio, 1999). Melanotypes (early tintypes) were available about 1856. Peter Palmquist to author, September 10, 1998, author's possession.

17. Karen Current and William R. Current, *Photography and the Old West* (Dobbs Ferry, N.Y., 1978), 20–26; John Towler, *The Silver Sunbeam* (1865; New York, 1963); L. P. Clerc, *Photography: Theory and Practice,* 3rd ed. (London, 1954); Clarence S. Jackson, *Picture Maker of the Old West, William H. Jackson* (New York, 1947), vi; William Henry Jackson and Howard R. Driggs, *The Pioneer Photographer* (Yonkers, N.Y., 1929), 112.

18. Quote from Jean Sagne, "All Kinds of Portraits: The Photographer's Studio," in Michel Frizot, ed., *A New History of Photography* (Paris, 1994), 104.

19. Helmut Gernsheim and Alison Gernsheim, *The History of Photography from the Camera Obscura to the Beginning of the Modern Era* (New York, 1969), 153; Towler, *The Silver Sunbeam,* iv, 66, 222.

20. Quote from Françoise Heilbrun, *L'invention d'un regard, 1839–1918* (The Invention of a Gaze, 1839–1918) (Paris, 1989), 16. In some studios farmworkers could sit before cameras having

four, six, eight, or twelve lenses. With each lens exposing different portions of the same negative, farmworkers could obtain an infinite number of carte de visite prints from a single negative. If the lenses were opened at the same time, a farmworker obtained numerous small photos of the same pose. If the lenses were opened sequentially, a farmworker could adjust and change his pose from one exposure to another. After the negative was developed, the resulting images could be printed, mounted, and cut apart. William C. Darrah, *Cartes de Visite in Nineteenth Century Photography* (Gettysburg, Pa., 1981), 1–2, 10–12, 19, 24. Equipment usually included: one 5 × 8–inch camera plus lenses; one 11 × 14–inch or larger camera plus lenses; a dark tent; two tripods; ten pounds of collodion; thirty-six ounces of silver nitrate; two quarts of alcohol; ten pounds of iron sulfate (developer); one package of filters; one and one-half pounds of potassium cyanide (fixer); three yards of flannel; one box of rottenstone (cleaner for glass plates); three negative boxes; six ounces of nitric acid; one quart of varnish; developing and fixing trays; sixteen bottles of various sizes; scales and weights; and four hundred pieces of glass for negatives. See Robert Taft, *Photography and the American Scene: A Social History, 1839–1889* (1938; New York, 1964), 17–26; Gail Buckland, *Reality Recorded: Early Documentary Photography* (Boston, 1974), 40; and *Pacific Rural Press,* January 7, March 4, 1877.

21. Quote from William C. Darrah, *The World of Stereographs* (Gettysburg, Pa., 1977), 2, also 5–6, 145–46, 197. See also Edward W. Earle, ed., *Points of View: The Stereograph in America—a Cultural History* (New York, 1979), 12; Robert A. Weinstein and Larry Booth, *Collection, Use, and Care of Historical Photographs* (Nashville, Tenn., 1977), 187–88.

22. L. J. Rose Jr., *L. J. Rose of Sunny Slope, 1827–1899: California Pioneer, Fruit Grower, Wine Maker, Horse Breeder* (San Marino, Calif., 1959), 52–59. The original Sunny Slope photographs were in the possession of Mrs. Hinda Rose, of San Diego, as well as the Sunny Slope Water Company. Copies were given to the Huntington Library. Jennifer Watts of the Huntington Library provided key details on Godfrey. Sunny Slope allowed me to copy photographs.

23. Arpad Haraszthy, "The Haraszthy Family," MS, 1886, 2, 5–6, 16, Bancroft Library; Arpad Haraszthy, "Early Viticulture in Sonoma," in *Sonoma County and Russian River Valley* (San Francisco, 1888), 77–78; Brian C. McGinty, "A Vintage Life," *Historical Society of Southern California Quarterly* (December 1959): 375–83; *San Francisco Examiner,* September 2, 1867; Theodore Schoenman, ed., *The Father of California Wine, Agoston Haraszthy; including Grape Culture, Wines, and Winemaking* (Santa Barbara, Calif., 1979), 48; Harvey Hansen et al., *Wild Oats in Eden: Sonoma County in the Nineteenth Century* (Santa Rosa, Calif., 1962), 86; Paul Frederickson, "Haraszthy in San Francisco and San Mateo," *Wines and Vines* 28 (July 1947): 15; Paul Frederickson, "Haraszthy's Early Years in Sonoma," *Wines and Vines* 28 (August 1947): 17–18.

24. Vardi, "Imagining the Harvest in Early Modern Europe," 1356–97; Arnold Skolnick, ed., *Paintings of California,* intro. by Ilene Susan Fort (Berkeley, 1993), 13; Arthur Miller, "California Painters—19th Century," *Los Angeles County Fair Exhibition* (catalogue), September 15–October 21, 1939, Pomona Public Library, Pomona, California.

25. Frederick Whymper, drawing, October 21, 1864, Frank H. Bartholomew Foundation, Sonoma, courtesy of Brian C. McGinty. Whymper's rendering is the earliest image (photographic or otherwise) of Chinese working in the fields. See also Arpad Haraszthy, "Wine-Making in California," *Harper's New Monthly Magazine* 29 (1864): 22–30; and Agoston Haraszthy, *Grape Culture, Wines, and Wine-Making* (New York, 1862), frontispiece.

26. Most of what is known about Whymper comes from sketches and maps appearing in the Royal Geographic Society's *Journal* in 1868, Whymper's *Travel and Adventure in the Territory of Alaska* (New York, 1869), which states that he visited San Francisco on numerous occasions between 1862 and 1867, and the *Illustrated San Francisco News,* September 25, 1869, which described his work. See also Mechanics' Institute and Library, *Industrial Exhibition Reports,* 1869, 1870, San Francisco;

and *Alta California,* June 5, 1870, Bancroft Library. When *Harper's Monthly* illustrated a June 1864 article on winemaking in California, it resorted to woodcuts apparently drawn from wet-plate photographs. See also lithograph, *Buena Vista Vinicultural Society's Vineyards and Vaults, Sonoma, California,* Wine Institute, San Francisco.

27. Steven Stoll, *The Fruits of Natural Advantage: Making the Industrial Countryside in California* (Berkeley, 1998), 39; Marjorie D. Arkelian, *Thomas Hill: The Grande View* (Oakland, Calif., 1980); Marjorie D. Arkelian, *The Kahn Collection of Nineteenth Century Paintings by Artists in California* (Oakland, Calif., 1975); Dwight Miller, *California Landscape Painters around Keith and Hill, 1850–1900* (Palo Alto, Calif., 1979). See also Nancy Boas, "The Society of Six and the Birth of California Modernism," *Californians* 5 (May–June 1988): 25–33. For Chinese in the strawberry industry, see Sucheng Chan, *Bittersweet Soil: The Chinese in California Agriculture, 1860–1910* (Berkeley, 1986), 124–31; and Street, *Beasts of the Field,* 606–7.

28. Nostrand, *The First Hundred Years of Painting in California,* 61–62; Kevin Starr and Paul Miller, eds., *O California! Nineteenth and Early Twentieth Century California Landscapes and Observations* (San Francisco, 1991); Benjamin P. Avery, "Art Beginnings on the Pacific," *Overland Monthly* 1 (July 1868): 228–29; Ann Bermingham, *Landscape and Ideology: The English Rustic Tradition, 1740–1860* (Berkeley, 1986).

29. Frank Q. Newton Jr., "William M. Godfrey: Early California Photographer, 1825–1900," *Westerners: Los Angeles Corral, the Branding Iron* 188 (Summer 1992): 2–3; Ralph Andrews, *Picture Gallery Pioneers: First Photographers of the West, 1850–1875* (New York, 1964), 78–79.

30. Roberta Nichols, "William M. Godfrey: Photographer for the Rancheros," *Los Cerritos Docents Publication* (Long Beach, Calif., 1970); Palmquist and Kailbourn, *Pioneer Photographers of the Far West,* 263; Sarah Bixby Smith, *Adobe Days* (Los Angeles, 1925); Loretta Berner, *Rancho los Cerritos* (Ramona, Calif., 1975); Iris H. W. Engstrand, "Rancho los Cerritos: A Southern California Legacy Preserved," *Southern California Quarterly* 77 (September 2003): 1–41, especially 20–26. Steve Iverson of Rancho los Cerritos and Jennifer Watts of the Huntington Library provided key details on Godfrey.

31. Peter Palmquist, *Lawrence and Houseworth/Thomas Houseworth and Co.: A Unique View of the West, 1860–1886* (Columbus, Ohio, 1980), 29–43.

32. Rebecca Solnit, *River of Shadows: Eadweard Muybridge and the Technological Wild West* (New York, 2003), 6–7, 27–28, 38–41, 51; Anita Ventura Mozley, *Eadweard Muybridge: The Stanford Years, 1872–1882,* with Robert Haas and Francoise Forster-Hahn (Stanford, 1972).

33. Quote from Robert B. Haas, *Muybridge: Man in Motion* (Berkeley, 1976), 19, citing brochure in Muybridge Scrapbook, California Historical Society, San Francisco, and advertisement following p. 59 of John S. Hittell, *Yosemite: Its Wonders and Its Beauties, with information Adapted to the Wants of Tourists about to Visit the Valley* (San Francisco, 1868). See also David Harris *Eadweard Muybridge and the Photographic Panorama, 1850–1880,* with Eric Sandweiss (London, 1995), 46; Gordon Hendricks, *Eadweard Muybridge: The Father of the Motion Picture* (New York, 1975); and Buckland, *Reality Recorded,* 39.

34. Chu Limm, "The Images of China and the Chinese in the Overland Monthly, 1868–1875, 1883–1935," PhD diss., Duke University, 1966, 119–60; 305–68; Wei Min She Labor Committee, *Chinese Working People in America* (San Francisco, 1974), 15; Ruthanne Lum McCunn, *An Illustrated History of the Chinese in America* (San Francisco, 1979), 1–29; Clarence Sandmeyer, *The Anti-Chinese Movement in California* (Urbana, Ill., 1973), 45–47. One exception to the omission of Chinese at Promontory Point was among the series Union Pacific R.R. Stereoscopic Views, across the Continent West of Omaha: picture no. 539, *Chinese at Laying Last Rail,* in [S. J. Sedgwick], *Announcement of Prof. S. J. Sedgwick's Illustrated Course of Lectures and Catalogue of Stereoscopic Views of Scenery in All Parts of the Rocky Mountains, Between Omaha and Sacramento* (New York, 1873).

35. William Herman Bradley and Henry William Rulofson, *Catalogue of Photographic Views, Illustrating the Yosemite, Mammoth Trees, Geyser Springs, and other remarkable and Interesting Scenery of the Far West, by Muybridge* (San Francisco, 1873), 28–30, 45, Bancroft Library. See also Ruth Teiser and Catherine Harroun, *Winemaking in California* (New York, 1983), 42–47; Dave Henderson (the Haraszthy Cellars) to author, December 31, 1980, author's possession; Muybridge, stereograph no. 1115, Buena Vista Vineyard, Sonoma, *The "Heathen Chinee" Bottle Washer,* 5 × 8 inches; Muybridge photograph no. 4167, *Buena Vista Vineyard, Sonoma, a Winter Morning, Plowing;* photograph no. 4169, *Buena Vista Vineyard, Cutting Grapes;* and photograph no. 4170, *Buena Vista Vineyard, Loading Grapes for the Press House,* all in Bancroft Library. Muybridge probably did not do the technical work on his Buena Vista survey. Charles Leander Weed, an expert developer and printer, often handled darkroom and printing duties. See Palmquist to author, September 10, 1998, author's possession.

36. Quotes from contract, "Indenture of La-Ache, also known as Jack," to Ira McRay, October 11, 1862, Fresno County Historical Society. See also 1860 MS census, Sonoma County, Healdsburg Township, Healdsburg County Library; *Sacramento Daily Union,* February 4, 1861, list of indentures "to be used in ranching, farming and housework" in Tehama County; *Red Bluff Independent,* n.d., in *Marysville Appeal,* January 4, 1861; *Columbia Times,* January 10, 1861.

37. Quote from J. P. Munroe-Fraser, *History of Santa Clara County, California* (San Francisco, 1891), 23. For general developments, see R. H. Allen, "The Spanish Land-Grant System as an Influence in the Agricultural Development of California," *Agricultural History* 9 (July 1935): 133–34; and Rodman W. Paul, "The Wheat Trade between California and the United Kingdom," *Mississippi Valley Historical Review* 54 (1958): 412. Production figures from Robert Glass Cleland and Osgood Hardy, *March of Industry* (Los Angeles, 1929), 74–75. For local developments, see Will Green, *History of Colusa County* (San Francisco, 1880), 23, 60; E[dward] J. Wickson, *Rural California* (New York, 1923), 75; and Horace Davis, "Wheat in California," *Overland Monthly* 1 (November 1868): 447. For the beginnings of the wheat industry, see Kenneth A. Smith, "California: The Wheat Decades," PhD diss., University of Southern California, 1969, 42–50; Edwin S. Holmes, "Wheat Growing and General Agricultural Conditions in the Pacific Coast Region of the U.S.," U.S. Department of Agriculture, Bureau of Statistics, *Miscellaneous Series,* bulletin no. 20 (Washington, D.C., 1901), 17–19; and Paul, "The Beginnings of Agriculture in California," 16–27. Export value figures from Morton Rothstein, "A British Firm on the American West Coast, 1869–1914," *Business History Review* 38 (1963): 395. See also Effie Martin, "The Development of Wheat Culture in the San Joaquin, 1846–1900," MA thesis, University of California, Berkeley, 1924; and Portia Kellogg, "An Analysis of the Economic Causes of the Rise and Decline of Wheat Growing in the Great Valley of California," MA thesis, University of California, Berkeley, 1946.

38. Joseph H. Hutchinson, "California Cereals," *Overland Monthly* 2 (August 1883): 145; Leo Rogin, *The Introduction of Farm Machinery in Its Relation to the Productivity of Labor in the Agriculture of the United States during the Nineteenth Century,* University of California Publications in Economics no. 9 (Berkeley, 1931), 44–45, 77, 113, 134–37; U.S. Department of the Interior, Census Office, *Tenth Census of the United States, 1880,* "Cereal Production," III, Report on the Production of Agriculture, General Statistics (Washington, D.C., 1880), 457.

39. Unidentified newspaper clipping, F. F. Latta Collection, Sky Farming, Huntington Library. For the migratory workers, see C. F. Menefee, *Historical and Descriptive Sketch Book of Napa* (Napa, Calif., 1873), 217–18; Clark, ed., *The Journals of Alfred Doten,* 1: 339, 364, 402, 412, 420–21, 423, 555. For living conditions, see Nicholas W. Hansen, *As I Remember* (Willows, Calif., 1936), 161–62; Carleton E. Watkins, *The Creasey Farm* (photograph), Prints and Photographs Collection, Library of Congress; and Mary Cone, *Two Years in California* (Chicago, 1876), 132. For parallel developments, see Jack Hurley, *Industry and the Photographic Image* (New York, 1980), 1–2, 79.

40. Thomas D. Isern, *Bull Threshers and Bindlestiffs: Harvesting and Threshing on the North American Plains* (Lawrence, Kans., 1990), 1, 68; *Russian River Recorder* (January 1981): cover, Healdsburg Historical Society, Healdsburg, California; W. R. Nutting Album, Vacaville Museum.

41. George G. Coffom, *Harvester on the Pete Garnett Ranch near Willows in 1899,* photo no. 20,693, Photograph Collection, California Section, California State Library, Sacramento. See also Charles A. Nordhoff, *California for Health, Pleasure, and Residence* (New York, 1873), 187; Ann Morrison Reed, "Opening Address," *California State Agricultural Society Transactions, 1887* (Sacramento, 1888), 15; Edward H. Hall, *The Great West* (New York, 1864), 78; Samuel E. Bowles, *Our New West* (Hartford, Conn., 1869), 439; *Paso Robles Record,* July 13, 1895; and Carl Meyer, "Recollections," n.d., Tehama County Library, Red Bluff, California.

42. Quote from E. Anthony Rotundo, *American Manhood: Transformations in Masculinity from the Revolution to the Modern Era* (New York, 1993), 10–25. See also John Ibson, *Picturing Men: A Century of Male Relationships in Everyday American Photography* (Washington, D.C., 2002), xi, 67.

43. Unattributed photograph of threshing near Chico, circa 1875, provided by John Nopel.

44. Hector Lee and Thelma White, interview with William S. Cornelius, "The Wheat Harvest of 1884 on the Glenn Ranch," 1973, Special Collections, Meriam Library, California State University, Chico; advertisement for G. W. Valleau, *Colusa County Annual Supplement to Weekly Colusa Sun,* July 1878.

45. Williams had been painting California scenes since 1862 and, in 1865, had accompanied photographer Carleton E. Watkins and painter Thomas Hill to the Yosemite Valley. In 1866 he returned to Boston and in 1870 moved back to California following the breakup of his marriage. For Virgil Williams, see Ruth N. Post, "The California Years of Virgil Macey Williams," *California History* 116 (June 1987): 115–29; "Oak Knoll: Items of a Visit There, Agricultural Practices," *California Culturalist* (July 1869): 247–49; and Benjamin P. Avery, "Art Beginnings on the Pacific," *Overland Monthly* 1 (August 1868): 114.

46. Marjorie Arkelian, "William Hahn: German-American Painter of the California Scene," *American Art Review* 4 (August 1977): 109; H. Armour Smith, *William Hahn, Painter of the American Scene* (Yonkers, N.Y., 1942); Marilyn Sommerdorf, *William Hahn, 1829–1887, American Genre Painter* (Sacramento, 1976); Perry, *Pacific Arcadia,* 68–69; Van Nostrand, *The First Hundred Years of Painting in California,* xix, plate 30, 72, 102. For the background to Hahn's threshing painting, see William Hahn Scrapbook, Rostow Collection, Oakland Museum, Oakland, California.

47. *Willows Daily Journal,* October 15, 1917. See also *Pacific Rural Press,* July 26, 1875, and May 6, 1876. Another treatment, although slightly confused, is Higgins, "Dr. Glenn's Million-Dollar Wheat Crop," *Pacific Rural Press,* October 26, 1946. Hoag's record was a remarkable achievement at a time when, in the Ohio River valley, nine hundred bushels were considered the upper limits of threshing in a twelve-hour period. A typical California steam outfit could easily thresh about eight hundred bushels a day. Hoag and others like him are described as tenants in the *Marysville Appeal,* April 4, 1875, and August 9, 1877. But the issues of July 27, 1879, October 12, 1880, and April 25, 1882, refer to Hoag and others like him as renters. Typically Hoag paid all costs and turned over half of his crop to Glenn before expenses. The three small threshers that, bolted together, made up the Monitor included a forty-four-inch-stroke Nichol and Shepherd Vibrator, a forty-inch Buffalo Pitts, and a forty-inch Geyser. The Monitor also had a Jackson feeder that eliminated the need for handfeeding.

48. *Pacific Rural Press,* May 6, 1876. Dr. Joseph Baird has provided more information on the Hill painting; see Street, interview with Baird, March 23, 1985, Tiburon, California, author's possession. On the basis of the painting, Hill's reputation soared. He won more commissions and an armful of medals, including one from the California State Agricultural Society. Among other painters who focused on agriculture and farm labor, Virgil Williams also used the technique of photographing

an event and then later painting from the photograph. Besides his works already mentioned in the text, Williams made the farmworker painting *Farm Yard Scene,* oil on canvas, 10 × 20 inches (1885), last seen at the Kerwin Galleries, Burlingame, California. For Williams's photography, see *Picking Fruit, Foothills of St. Helena,* silver gelatin print, unknown size (ca. 1885), last seen at the Kerwin Galleries, Burlingame. See Gene Dekovic to author, August 15, 1997, author's possession; and Ruth Nicholson Post, *Virgil Williams: He Shaped the Dawn of Western Art* (Calistoga, Calif., 1998), 102–3.

49. Sima Baker and Florence Ewing, *The Glenn County Story, Days Past and Present* (Willows, Calif., 1968), 59–61; "California Harvest Scene—Dr. Glenn's Farm in Colusa County," *Wagon Wheels* 1 (August 1951): 1–4; clipping, F. Hal Higgins, "Honest Heritage," *Implement Record* (April 1947): 23–24, F. Hall Higgins Collection, Archives and Special Collections, University of California, Davis; *Sacramento Bee,* March 7, 1957.

50. Quote from "Andrew P. Hill, Artist and Photographer," *California Country Journal* (June 30, 1899): 37. See also Victoria T. Olsen, "Pioneer Conservationist A. P. Hill: 'He Saved the Redwoods,'" *American West* 14 (September–October 1977): 32–40; and Carolyn de Vries, *Grand and Ancient Forest: The Story of Andrew P. Hill and Big Basin Redwoods State Park* (Fresno, Calif., 1978), 5.

51. Quote from *Pacific Rural Press,* July 26, 1875. Although the lighting would have made sense if the scene had been painted at sunset, the particular combination of light and a perspective that placed the Sutter Buttes in the background could never have occurred as depicted. Considerable controversy surrounds this episode. For a detailed treatment, including the subsequent bizarre history of the painting and two retouchings that eliminated and then restored the rider on the right side, see Richard Steven Street, "Mystery Achievement," *California Farmer* (September 1, 1987): 8–9, 12. An account placing the painting in a wider context is Elizabeth Johns, "Settlement and Development," in William Truettner, ed., *The West as America: Reinterpreting Images of the Frontier* (Washington, D.C., 1991), 230–31, based entirely on my earlier article.

52. Arthur B. Domonoske, "Recollections," 3, F. Hal Higgins Collection, Archives and Special Collections, University of California, Davis; *A California Harvest Scene, Pacific Rural Press,* April 1, 1876; Street, interview with Donald Houghton, January 8, 1985 (during which I shot Kodachrome slides of the painting), San Francisco, author's possession. For Hoag, see unidentified clipping "Old Timer," January 19, 1936, John Waterlund Historical Articles on Butte County, Special Collections, Meriam Library, California State University, Chico, book 1; Amanda Hoag, "Autobiography," MS, n.d., Colusa Historical Society, Colusa, California. The Marcus Hawley and Company lithograph measures 26 × 34 inches. An original is in Archives and Special Collections, University of California, Davis.

53. There are two versions of John R. Key's painting of the Naglee vineyards. The larger one, measuring 16 × 30 inches, was sold by John Howell Books in the 1970s. San Francisco art dealer Alfred Harrison, of North Point Galleries, was given a black-and-white photo of it by Warren Howell. He has not been able to locate the owner. The other, smaller version, dated 1877 and measuring 8¼ × 14 inches, emerged on the art market in 2002 and is now in a private collection in San Francisco. Naglee was the widower of Key's first cousin and became Key's patron during the latter's stay in San Francisco and San Jose during 1869 and 1870. Presumably, the larger 1872 painting was done in Key's Boston studio on the basis of studies (photographs?) taken on the spot in 1869 or 1870. The second painting is apparently a slightly modified copy. In the first and larger version, a harvester sits in the shade of a tree; in the second and smaller version, he hefts wicker baskets full of grapes. Both versions have the same three men carrying and loading grapes onto a wagon, although the perspective and certain details are slightly changed. Otherwise, the two paintings are nearly identical. For the larger painting, I relied on a black-and-white print provided by Leonard McKay. See also Leonard McKay, ed., *Clyde Arbuckle's History of San José* (San Jose, Calif., 1986),

179. For the smaller version, I relied on a copy slide and information provided by Alfred Harrison, of North Point Gallery, San Francisco. See Alfred Harrison to author, January 24, 2003, author's possession.

54. Myron T. Angel, ed., *History of San Luis Obispo County, California, with Illustrations and Biographical Sketches of its Prominent Men and Pioneers,* index and intro. by Louisiana Clayton Dart (Oakland, Calif., 1883; San Miguel, Calif., 1983); Harry L. Wells, *History of Butte County* (San Francisco, 1882); Jesse D. Mason, ed., *History of Santa Barbara County,* intro. by Walter Tompkins (San Francisco, 1883; Berkeley, 1964); Harry L. Wells and William M. Chamberlin, *History of Yuba County* (Oakland, Calif., 1879); Harry L. Wells and William M. Chamberlin, *History of Sutter County* (Oakland, Calif., 1879); Harry L. Wells and William M. Chamberlin, *History of Nevada County* (Oakland, Calif., 1880); *Illustrated Atlas of California* (San Francisco, 1876); Wallace W. Elliot, *History of Kern County California with Illustrations Descriptive of its Scenery, Farms, Residences, Public Buildings . . . with Biographical Sketches* (San Francisco, 1883).

55. For mug book artists and drawings, see *Sacramento Union,* May 7, 1880; *History of Sacramento County, California, with Illustrations Descriptive of Its Scenery,* intro. by Allan R. Ottley (Oakland, Calif., 1880; Berkeley, 1960); *Historical Atlas Map of Sonoma County* (Oakland, Calif., 1877); *Historical Atlas of Santa Clara County* (Oakland, Calif., 1876); *Historical Atlas of Solano County* (San Francisco, 1877); Col. T. F. Gilbert, ed., *History of San Joaquin County* (San Francisco, 1879); *Historical Atlas Map of Fresno County* (Oakland, Calif., 1891); *Official Historical Atlas Map of Tulare County* (Oakland, Calif., 1892); Arthur B. Domonoske, "The Illustrations Remind Me," supplement, *History of Colusa County, California* (1880; San Francisco, 1983), xiv, 151. For Frenzeny, see "The Vintage in California—At Work in the Wine Presses," *Harper's Weekly* 22 (October 5, 1878): 77–78. The drawing was apparently popular enough for Frenzeny to issue a watercolor version measuring 13 × 20⅜ inches. Sketching his adventures as a member of the French cavalry in Mexico, Frenzeny attracted the attention of *Harper's Weekly,* which published his work in 1868, shortly after Frenzeny arrived in the United States. In 1873, *Harper's Weekly* commissioned Frenzeny and another French-born artist, Jules Tavernier, to travel throughout the American West sketching scenes of ordinary activities. During 1877, Frenzeny may have traveled with Buffalo Bill's Wild West Show, completing a series of illustrations for Harrison O'Reilly's *Fifty Years on the Trail: A True Story of Western Life.* For Frenzeny, see Joseph A. Baird Jr., *Catalogue of Original Paintings, Drawings, and Watercolors in the Robert B. Honeyman, Jr., Collection* (Berkeley, 1968), 26; Robert Taft, *Artists and Illustrators of the Old West, 1850–1900* (Princeton, N.J., 1982), 113–16; Patricia Trenton and Peter Hassrick, *The Rocky Mountains: A Vision for Artists in the Nineteenth Century* (Norman, Okla., 1983), 243–47; California Palace of the Legion of Honor, *The French in California, One Hundred Years of Achievement, 1850–1950* (San Francisco, 1950); Betty Hoag, "Jules Tavernier," MA thesis, University of Southern California, 1940; and Robert Nichols, "Jules Tavernier (1844–1889): Painter and Illustrator," PhD diss., University of California, Berkeley, 1978.

56. Quote from Thomas Hardy, "California Vineyards," *San Francisco Merchant,* August 14, 1885, which reports "two old Chinamen" working in the cellar at Gundlach and Company winery but, when questioned, replied, "No savee." See also H. Sherwin, "Observations," *Overland Monthly* 7 (January 1886): 97; Marcia Wilcox, "Blue Gowns and Gold Hills," MS, February 1951, Napa County Historical Society, Napa, California; and Frona Eunice Wait, *Wines and Vines of California, or a Treatise on the Ethics of Wine Drinking* (1889; San Francisco, 1973), 19.

57. Many winemakers built their wineries on hillsides to facilitate the crush and fermentation process. Hauling grapes to the third floor, they removed debris, stems, and leaves and, after sending the grapes through a crusher, used gravity to pipe it from third-floor crushing rooms to second-floor fermenting rooms and later to the first-floor aging cellars. Winemakers also used gravity to dispose of the pomace, which was sent along chutes from the conveyor dump site to pomace piles

farther down the hillside. For production information, see *Annual Report of the State Board of Viticultural Commissioners, 1887* (Sacramento, 1888), 18–20. For further details of harvesting, see sections in the valuable but overlooked Thomas Hardy, *Notes on the Vineyards of America and Europe* (Adelaide, Australia, 1885), American chapters reprinted in *Wines and Vines,* September 1966 to September 1968. For hillside construction, see Wait, *Wines and Vines of California,* 21.

58. Quotes from newspaper clipping, "John Chinaman in the Wine Press," *San Francisco Call,* October 14, 1878, Bancroft Scrapbooks, Bancroft Library; and *Sonoma County Tribune,* September 20, 1891. When the editor of the *Cloverdale Reveille* learned that *Harper's Weekly* was planning another story on the valley, he reviewed the entire episode. See *Cloverdale Reveille,* May 20, 1882. For background, see Richard Holmer, "Currier and Ives Do California," *Californians* 12 (December 1995): 8–11, 51.

59. Paul Mills, *An Introduction to the Art of William Keith* (Oakland, Calif., 1957); Brother Cornelius, *Keith, Old Master of California* (New York, 1942); Emily P. B. Hay, *William Keith as Prophet Painter* (San Francisco, 1916); "William Kieth, 1839–1911," *Bulletin of the California Palace of the Legion of Honor* 3 (July 1945): 34–39; Perry, *Pacific Arcadia,* 77–80.

60. Alfred Runte, "Promoting the Golden West: Advertising and the Railroad," *California History* 70 (Spring 1991): 62–75; Richard J. Orsi, "Selling the Golden State: A Study of Boosterism in Nineteenth Century California," PhD diss., University of Wisconsin, 1973; Perry, *Pacific Arcadia,* 83–86; K. D. Kurutz and Gary F. Kurutz, *California Calls You: The Art of Promoting the Golden State, 1870 to 1940* (Sausalito, Calif., 2000), 22–24.

3. An Old Master in a New Place

1. Husmann's camera produced a negative measuring 6 × 8 inches. See Henry D. Hooker, "George Husmann," *Missouri Historical Review* 23 (April 1929): 353–60; William A. Jones, "Leland Stanford's Tehama County Vineyard," MS, n.d., 1, Special Collections, Meriam Library, California State University, Chico; and Street, interviews with Brothers Peter and Timothy, September 12, 1981, Our Lady of New Clarveaux Monastery, Vina, California, author's possession. See also Vincent P. Carosso, *The California Wine Industry: A Study of the Formative Years, 1831–1895* (Berkeley, 1951), 131. The George Husmann Album (Stanford University Archives and Special Collections) contains thirty-five images, all but one in a horizontal format. Thirty-three of those images range in size from 7 to 8⅞ inches by 4 to 5 inches. One image with a curved top edge measures 8¼ inches by 5⅞ inches at the midpoint of the curve. The image with a vertical format is 6 inches by 8 inches. No dates or information appears in the album itself. The images are pasted on both sides of the album's pages. The album itself is 10⅝ inches by 6⅞ inches and is 1¼ to 1½ inches thick. The phrase "Album of Photographs" is stamped in gold on the cover. Copies of several images are also in the California Historical Society.

2. For the introduction of dry-plate photographic technology, see Naomi Rosenblum, *A World History of Photography* (New York, 1984), 96, 141, 190, 245, 250, 272, 359.

3. Paul S. Taylor and Tom Vasey, "Contemporary Background of California Farm Labor," *Rural Sociology* 1 (September 1936): 284; Robert G. Cleland and Osgood Hardy, *March of Industry* (New York, 1929), 81–93; Alvin Thompson, "Aspects of the Social History of California Agriculture, 1880–1902," MA thesis, University of California, Berkeley, 1953, 237–38.

4. In addition to once owning Williams's silver gelatin print, Kerwin Galleries also owned the painting circa 1990. I was unable to trace its subsequent history, ownership, or whereabouts. See Gene Dekovic to author, August 8, 1997, author's possession; Virginia Post, *Virgil Williams* (Calistoga, Calif., 1998), 43–44, 102; and Benjamin P. Avery, "Art Beginnings on the Pacific," *Overland Monthly* 1 (August 1868): 114.

5. Quote from "California Specimens," *Pacific Rural Press,* January 7, 1871. For other visual materials, see K. D. Kurutz and Gary F. Kurutz, *California Calls You: The Art of Promoting the Golden State, 1870 to 1940* (Sausalito, Calif., 2000), 9; *Scientific American,* supplement no. 399 (August 25, 1883): 6370; *Frank Leslie's Illustrated Newspaper,* supplement, December 24, 1887; and Roger Olmstead, ed., *Scenes of Wonder and Curiosity* (Berkeley, 1962).

6. Quote from the descriptive flier announcing publication of the second edition, Vacaville Museum, Vacaville, California. One view shows grape pickers in the vineyard of L. W. and F. H. Buck on November 3, 1886, harvesting "third growth," late-ripening clusters of Flame Tokay table grapes for the Chicago market. Another captures a crew at the A. McKevitt packinghouse in the upper Vaca Valley on November 8, loading a very late variety of white cling peaches known as Miller's cling. The latest grape shipment depicted in the book was December 22, 1886, an extremely late date to be picking, packing, and shipping fresh fruit. A century later, only a few grape growers specializing in hybrid varieties dared pick grapes into the rainy season. No growers shipped peaches so late in the season. See also E[dward] J. Wickson, *California Illustrated No. 1: Vacaville Early Fruit District* (San Francisco, 1888), i–v; W. R. Nutting, "Vacaville Illustrated in Color," *Vacaville Reporter,* February 9, 1888; W. R. Nutting, photograph, *Packinghouse of A. McKevitt, Shipping Grapes to Chicago, November 8, 1886,* W. R. Nutting Collection, Vacaville Museum.

7. Quotes from Prospectus for the second edition of Wickson, *Vacaville Early Fruit District,* Vacaville Museum; "A Favorable Southern California Opinion," *Vacaville Reporter,* October 11, 1888; and "Vaca Valley Heralded in England," *Vacaville Reporter,* July 10, 1890. See also *Vacaville Reporter,* November 25, 1887, February 3, 1888, and October 11, 1888. Although the lithographs in *Vacaville Early Fruit District* are generally accurate representations of Nutting's photographic compositions, at least one of them omits a Chinese field hand. In the original photograph of peach picking at the Henry Bassford orchard, Bassford himself looks on with another grower as a Chinese picker works on a ladder at the extreme far left side of the frame. But in the lithograph for the book, the left edge is cropped to eliminate the picker. The cropping appears to have resulted from an editor who cut and shaped images into ovals and circles and layered them on top of one another in the kind of layout that editors of the time favored. Many other lithographs depict Chinese field hands exactly as they appear in the original photographs. See Wickson, *Vacaville Early Fruit District,* figure 2323, plate II.

8. Nutting, photograph, *Peach Gathering, Henry Bassford's Orchard,* figures 2333, 2356 (plate A), and 2388 (plate VI), in Wickson, *Vacaville Early Fruit District,* 16, 23, 46; Nutting, photograph, *Mr. Gibbs in the Cutting Shed on the E. R. Thurber Ranch;* Nutting, photograph, *Packing Fruit at L. L. Hatch's Ranch, Upper Vaca Valley;* Nutting, photograph, *H. Bassford Fruit Packing Shed;* Nutting, photograph, *Chinese Houseboys in Front of the Fred Buck Ranch;* all in Nutting Collection, Vacaville, California. For a discussion of Chinese labor, see the *Vacaville Reporter,* quoted in Wickson, *Vacaville Early Fruit District,* 154. See also *Solano Republican,* April 16, 1886; Sucheng Chan, *This Bittersweet Soil: The Chinese in California Agriculture, 1860–1910* (Berkeley, 1986), 272–340; Street, interview with Sabine Goerke-Shrode, August 10, 1998, Vacaville, California; and Street, interview with Peter Palmquist, August 19, 1998, Arcata, California; both in author's possession.

9. Nutting, photograph, *Drying Fruit on Pleasants Farm,* figure 2353, Nutting Collection, Vacaville, California. Ledger books from various farming operations confirm the ages of these children, who earned an average fifteen cents a box. See hundreds of entries in the Luther Harbison Ledgers, Luther Harbison Collection, Vacaville Museum. For typical entries, see Helen Harbison, June 14–15, 17, 20, 27, 28, 1899. Paid the average per box, a six-year-old girl earned fifty cents on July 14, eighty-five cents on July 15, fifty cents on July 17, twenty-five cents on July 20, fifty cents on July 27, and $1.50 on July 28. Children prospered in this work environment, wrote Wickson. They had ample opportunity for amusement and mischief, despite always being under the immediate view

of some adult. No social stigma was attached to their work. As to the effect of the heat on children, Wickson stressed, "The climate is such that very slight shelter is required during the summer, and dwelling in tents are very comfortable. Cot beds and hammocks for sleeping out-of-doors among the trees and vines are common sight" (Wickson, *Vacaville Early Fruit District,* 128; see also 60, 119, 127). "One of the best things to do with children in California is to give them the run of a fruit ranch when the fruit is ripe," wrote Wickson. "It damages the fruit but improves the children. We know of a large family of children who went into Vaca valley last summer when apricots and peaches were in their glory. The children were unused to much fruit and their mother anticipated the direst disaster, but there never was call for a single drop of peppermint. The children would eat fruit until it was a physical impossibility to get another specimen inside them, and yet there was never a squally night all summer" (Wickson, *Early Vacaville Fruit District,* 129). See also Joanne Larkey, "Helen Harbison Power: The Nut Tree and Its Family: An Illustrated Memoir of Helen Harbison Power," oral memoirs, November 27, 29, 1973, March 5, 1974, Vacaville Museum; and various photographs in the Harbison Collection.

10. Quotes from Weston A. Naef and James N. Wood, *Era of Exploration: The Rise of Landscape Photography in the American West, 1860–1885* (Boston, 1975), 79, also 80–124. See also Current and Current, *Photography and the Old West,* 28–48; Peter Palmquist, *Carleton E. Watkins: Photographer of the American West* (Albuquerque, N.M., 1983); and Friends of Photography, *Carleton E. Watkins: Photographs of the Columbia River and Oregon* (Carmel, Calif., 1979).

11. Peter E. Palmquist, "Taber Reprints of Watkins Mammoth Plates," *Photographic Collector* 3 (Summer 1982): 12–20; Charles B. Turrill, "An Early California Photographer: C. E. Watkins," *New Notes of California Libraries* 13 (January 1918): 29–37; Nanette Sexton, "Carleton E. Watkins: Pioneer California Photographer (1829–1916): A Study in the Evolution of Photographic Style during the First Decade of Wet Plate Photography," PhD diss., Harvard University, 1982.

12. David Igler, *Industrial Cowboys: Miller and Lux and the Transformation of the Far West, 1850–1920* (Berkeley, 2001), 92–113; Margaret A Cooper, "Land, Water, and Settlement in Kern County, California, 1850–1890," MA thesis, University of California, Berkeley, 1949, ii–iii, 1, 9, 34, 38–39, 66, 72, 98, 139, 143, 149–51, 156, 158, 173; U.S. Congress, Senate, Committee on Labor and Public Welfare, *Profile of Power Structure in San Joaquin Valley: Hearing before the Subcommittee on Migratory Labor,* 92nd Cong., 1st sess., January 11, 1972, part 3A, 694; James B. Haggin Testimony, December 3, 1877, transcription, Ben Walker Collection, Fresno County Historical Society.

13. *Charles Lux et al. v. James B. Haggin et al., In the Supreme Court of the State of California, Charles Lux et al., Appellants v. James B. Haggin et al., Respondents . . . ,* nos. 8587 and 8588 in the Supreme Court of California, 10 vols. in 6 (San Francisco, 1882–85), 577–81.

14. *Kern County Californian,* February 9, 1889. For a description of Watkins's traveling habits, equipment, and companions, see the extensive correspondence between Watkins and his fiancée/wife beginning in March 1880 and continuing for several years thereafter. This material is in the Yosemite Valley Research Library, Yosemite Valley, California. Copies also in Bancroft Library.

15. The *Kern County Californian* carried one significant piece of information, a reference to Watkins's earlier activity in Bakersfield during the fall of 1887, when he apparently photographed many local homes and estates. During his 1888 sojourn, Watkins probably toured with the same engineers and ranch managers who had escorted him on his 1881 photographic reconnaissance for the Lux and Haggin case.

16. Weather information is from *Kern County Californian,* July, August, and September 1888. For Watkins's physical condition, see his correspondence with his wife, Yosemite Valley Research Library.

17. My tabulation of Watkins's Kern County output is based on the advertisements placed by A. C. Maude in the *Kern County Californian* in October, November, and December 1888. Since

Maude sold the photographs in his stationery store, his account is probably reliable. Other sources simply state that Watkins made about seven hundred pictures. A definitive tabulation is impossible, because none of the various collections of Kern County pictures, including the most complete group at Tenneco West, Bakersfield, contain all of Watkins's images from the southern San Joaquin Valley. See Street, interview with Peter Palmquist, April 24, 1981, Arcata, California, author's possession. Palmquist, *Carleton E. Watkins,* ix, 3, 75–78, is based entirely on information and otherwise unavailable images I provided while researching *A Kern County Diary: The Forgotten Photographs of Carleton E. Watkins, 1881–1888* (Bakersfield, Calif., 1983), 1. Palmquist and Kailbourn, *Pioneer Photographers of the Far West,* 582, inexplicably place the number of images at 415. See also Mary Warren Marien, "Imaging the Corporate Sublime," in Amy Rule, ed., *Carleton Watkins: Selected Text and Bibliography* (Boston, 1993), 1–34.

18. Kevin Starr, *The Dream Endures: California Enters the 1940s* (New York, 1997), 208–9.

19. Watkins always made at least two photographs at any one place. At important sites, he executed as many as fifteen photographs, for example, at the Calloway Canal.

20. The five photographs were part of a larger sequence executed on the 12,800-acre Greenfields Ranch, located eleven miles south of Bakersfield. Beginning with a distant view, taken from the top of his traveling wagon, Watkins moved progressively closer to the threshing crew. In the last three images, shot from ground level and tightly cropped, he focused only on the machinery and the workers. Some commentators see parallels between how Watkins executed these images, gradually isolating his subject, and Dorothea Lange went about making her famous *Migrant Mother* image in 1936.

21. Igler, *Industrial Cowboys,* 1–4, 117, 127, 157.

22. One notable picture of the beginning of the work day in the Great Barnyard at Poso Ranch is both an inventory and a presentation of work relationships. The foreman and his assistants, each handling a team of four horses, pose in the barnyard.

23. Although Watkins had used the elevated perspective since the early 1870s, it would not become common among other western photographers until the 1890s, when several Los Angeles–based photographic studios began employing the technique to photograph homes and buildings. Most landscape photographers, of course, preferred early-morning and late-afternoon light, because it produces dramatic sidelight and reduces the contrast. Watkins did not always use this dramatic lighting, however; his field photographs of threshing and ditch digging are all taken with the sun overhead.

24. The best evidence of Watkins's presence is a beautiful picture of his traveling wagon parked on the bridge spanning Pioneer Canal. Throughout his career, Watkins often recorded evidence of his presence—his photographic tent, camera, and traveling wagon—as an autobiographical habit and as a way of lending scale and depth to his images.

25. There is some evidence that Watkins left the glass plates in Bakersfield, where they resided unknown and unappreciated for over a century in a basement of a Miller and Lux ranch on Stine Road, near the present site of California State University, Bakersfield. I have uncovered contradictory evidence on this matter and have not personally seen the negatives, but several Kern County residences reported examining the collection as late as 1984. See Street, interview with Chris Brewer, March 23, 1984, Bakersfield, author's collection. For printed captions and texts, see Martha Sandweiss, "Views and Reviews: Western Art and Western History," in William Cronon, George Miles, and Jay Gitlin, eds., *Under an Open Sky: Rethinking America's Western Past* (New York, 1992), 196. Photographs taken by Watkins at El Tejon Ranch are published, along with their accompanying captions, somewhat modified, in Frank F. Latta, *Saga of Rancho el Tejon* (Santa Cruz, Calif., 1976), 28, 36, 56, 92, 98, 100, 124, 138, 140, 145, 163, 173, 180, 182, 194, 226. Captions can also be read on the albums at Tenneco West, the Library of Congress, and Kern County Museum,

Bakersfield, California. The Watkins images in the Huntington Library and the Beale Memorial Library, Bakersfield, California, do not contain captions. I discovered a half dozen of Watkins's images scattered through the F. F. Latta Collection, Sky Farming, Huntington Library.

26. Quote from Carleton E. Watkins, photograph, *Irrigating on Panama Ranch,* photo no. 402, Prints and Photographs Division, Library of Congress.

27. Quote from Carleton E. Watkins, photograph, *Stacking Alfalfa Hay: Bellevue Ranch,* photo no. 18, Prints and Photographs Division, Library of Congress. The same caption, slightly modified, was used for Watkins, *Alfalfa Hay-Stacking, Stockdale Ranch,* photo no. 48.

28. *Kern County Californian,* September 1, 1888, citing the *Breeder and Sportsman; Kern County Californian,* October 6, November 10, December 29, 1888, February 9, 1889, and April 2, 1892; *San Miguel Messenger,* September 24, 1888. See also Latta, *Saga of Rancho el Tejon,* 28, 30, 36, 56, 92, 98, 100, 124, 138, 140, 145, 172, 180, 182, 194, 226. Haggin and Tevis also purchased several albums of individual ranches and presented them as gifts to loyal and valued ranch managers. See Mt. View Dairy Album, Kern County Museum. Written inside: "These photos were made for Mrs. Mary Real Pyle, in June 1889. Mr. Pyle was manager of the Mt. View Dairy Ranch with Billy Carr and Haggin. Their cattle brand was J-B." For one publication using Watkins's images without attribution, see Ralph Kreiser and Thomas Hunt, eds., *Kern Panorama* (Bakersfield, Calif., 1961). Some photographs measured 14 × 21 inches rather than approximately 8 × 10 inches. This suggests that Watkins photographed with both an 8 × 10–inch dry-plate camera and a 14 × 21–inch camera. However, he did not use the larger camera for any of his farmworker shots, reserving it for only the more scenic views. Another possibility is that Watkins later copied his mammoth plates with his 8 × 10–inch dry-plate camera. This would explain why some views can be found on both mammoth 20 × 24–inch prints and 8 × 10–inch prints. Trimmed in size from 8 × 10 inches to 6¾ × 8⅝ inches, Watkins's prints have a rich, maroon color. Most, but not all, have titles, a number, a caption, a "Watkins New Series" label, and the address of his San Francisco studio.

29. Quote from *Mt. View Dairy: The Mess House,* Mt. View Dairy Album, Kern County Museum.

30. Time–Life Books, *Documentary Photography* (New York, 1979), 7, 12–13; Naef and Wood, *Era of Exploration,* 12–13.

31. *Frank Leslie's Illustrated Newspaper,* supplement, December 24, 1887; Frona Eunice Wait Lantern Slide Collection, Napa Valley Wine Library, St. Helena, California (35-millimeter color duplicates of lantern slides donated by Maynard Amerine, copied by Gene Dekovic); William Heintz, *California's Napa Valley: One Hundred Sixty Years of Wine Making* (San Francisco, 1999), 108 (for biographical information on Harvey J. Lewelling), 153 (for information on Wait), 216 (for an example of a black-and-white image converted to a colored lantern slide). The H. H. Alexander photograph used by Wait appears in its original black-and-white form on the cover of Vaught, *Cultivating California,* and elsewhere, without Alexander's byline. See also Schyler Rehart and William K. Patterson, *M. Theo Kearney, Prince of Fresno* (Fresno, Calif., 1988), 27. Another photographer who documented farmworkers extensively on glass plates at this time was Frank Hasek. An immigrant from the Czech Republic, Hasek became general manager of Korbel Enterprises, a prominent Sonoma County wine and sparkling wine maker. See Thomas Maxwell-Long, *Napa Valley Wineries* (Chicago, 2002), 29–35. For other hand-colored lantern slides, see *Agua Caliente Indian Hoeing Beans,* no date, collected by George Wharton James, Braun Research Library, Institute for the Study of the American West, Los Angeles.

32. For early halftones appearing in the farm press, see H. S. Crocker and Co., photographs, *Picking Grapes and Curing Raisins in a Riverside Vineyard* and *Dr. Jarvis' Drying Grounds for Apricots and Raisins at Riverside, Cal., Pacific Rural Press,* September 14, 1889. For the influence of halftones, see Sarah Greenough, Joel Snyder, David Travis, and Colin Westerbeck, *On the Art of Fixing a*

Shadow: One Hundred and Fifty Years of Photography (Chicago, 1989), 129, 131, 135; and Vicki Goldberg, *The Power of Photography: How Photographs Changed Our Lives* (New York, 1991), 15.

33. Quote from "The Grape Harvest," *Pacific Rural Press,* July 21, 1888. The photograph was taken in the J. B. J. Portal vineyard near San Jose. See also H. S. Crocker and Co., photograph, *Gathering Apricots for Drying in Dr. Jarvis' Orchard, Riverside;* "Bonnie," photograph, *Sacking Dried Apricots in a Pasadena Orchard,* July 20, 1889; and uncredited photograph, *First Orange Train,* February 18, 1888; all in *Orange County through the Camera* (Santa Ana, Calif., ca. 1900), in Bancroft Library; Michael L. Carlebach, *The Origins of Photojournalism in America* (Washington, D.C., 1992), 3; newspaper clipping, *Orange Grower,* July 1891, in Lewis Ware Scrapbooks, American Crystal Sugar Company Records, Minnesota Historical Society, St. Paul; photograph number 11477, *Apricot Camp, Crawford Ranch, Santiago Blvd., Villa Park, Anaheim* (1904), and photograph number 11478, *Apricot Drying, Lyon's Ranch, Lincoln and Prospect, Villa Park* (1894), both in Mother Colony Collection, Anaheim Public Library; photograph number 1974.1.327, *Ainsley Cannery Foremen* (ca. 1920); photograph number 1974.1.565, *Campbell Fruit Growers Union Drying Yard, Late 1890s;* photograph number 1974.1.567, *Hyde Cannery Drying Yards* (ca. 1893); photograph number 1974.1.323, *Hyde Cannery Drying Yard* (n.d.); photograph number 1974.1.569, Andrew P. Hill, *Prune Drying Campbell Dryer* (also in Coe Collection, California State Library); all in Campbell Historical Museum, Campbell, California.

34. Quote from Peter Turner and Richard Wood, *P. H. Emerson: Photographer of Norfolk* (Boston, 1974), 11.

35. Quote from P. H. Emerson, *Pictures of East Anglican Life* (London, 1888), caption to plate VII, in Nancy Newhall, *P. H. Emerson: The Fight for Photography as a Fine Art* (New York, 1975), 198.

36. See the Emerson letters to Alfred Stieglitz in the Stieglitz Collection, Beinecke Library, Yale University; Robert S. Kahan and J. B. Colson, "Peter Henry Emerson," *Library Chronicle of the University of Texas,* n.s. 5 (September 1972): 69–75; and "Death of Dr. P. H. Emerson, M.D., B.A., a Photographic Pioneer," *British Journal of Photography* (July 3, 1936): 426.

37. Vicki Goldberg and Arthur Ollman, *A Nation of Strangers* (San Diego, Calif., 1995), 23–25.

38. The National Archives, Pacific Region, San Bruno, California, has about 250,000 case files of Chinese who were interrogated and detained between 1884 and 1944. Many of these files include photographs, a large number of which are tintypes. Very cheap and extremely durable, tintypes were largely obsolete by 1870, making the use of this technolgy in the 1880s somewhat of a mystery. See Charles J. McClain, *In Search of Equality: The Chinese Struggle against Discrimination in Nineteenth-Century America* (Los Angeles, 1994), 202–3; Limin Chu, "The Images of China and the Chinese in the *Overland Monthly,* 1868–1875, 1883–1935," PhD diss., Duke University, 1965, 219; Note from Minister Kuo-yin Tsui to Secretary of State James G. Blaine, April 12, 1892, in *Notes from the Chinese Legation in the United States to the Department of State, 1868–1906* (microfilm), Department of State Records, RG 59, National Archives. I have analyzed several hundred photographs pasted inside the judgment of remand documents and shot slide copies of a half dozen. See Records of the District Courts of the United States, Northern District of California, San Francisco, Admiral Case Files (especially box 574), RG 21, National Archives, Pacific Region, San Bruno, California; *Alta California,* August 26, 1885; David Piff to author, e-mail, July 30, 2003, author's possession.

39. Errol Wayne Stevens, "Frederic Hamer Maude: A Photographer and His Collection," *Southern California Quarterly* 82 (Spring 2000): 43–60; Ruth I. Mahood, *Photographer of the Southwest, Adam Clark Vroman, 1865–1916* (Los Angeles, 1961); Nancy Hathaway, *Native American Portraits, 1862–1918: Photographs from the Collection of Kurt Koegler* (San Francisco, 1990), 1–13; William Webb and Robert Weinstein, *Dwellers at the Source: Southwestern Indian Photographs by A. C. Vroman, 1895–1904* (Albuquerque, N.M., 1973). Some photographs of Indian field hands have been

misidentified. See Frederic Hamer Maude, photograph, *Waiting for Work—Migrant Workers' Camp,* identified in W. W. Hutchinson, *California: The Golden Shore by the Sundown Sea* (Palo Alto, Calif., 1980), 146, as a California image from 1918, and in a communication from the Los Angeles County Museum of Natural History stating that the image was taken in Arizona in 1903. Other information from the Los Angeles County Museum identifies the location as Southern California, about 1897. See the Frederick Hamer Maude Collection, Los Angeles County Museum of Natural History.

40. Quote from Jackson to Thomas Bailey Aldrich, May 4, 1883, Houghton Library, Harvard University, cited in Kate Phillips, *Helen Hunt Jackson: A Literary Life* (Berkeley, 2003), 252, the definitive account of Jackson's career. See also 253–64; Don H. Kennedy, "Ramona's People," *Californians* 5 (September–October 1986): 46–49; Albert Carr, "The Genesis and Development of 'Carmelita,' 1886–1892," MS, n.d., Jean Carr Papers, Huntington Library, providing background on the imagery and resources Jackson employed while writing *Ramona.*

41. Brewster was active from 1874 until 1909. See Phil Brigandi, "Rancho Camulos: The Home of Ramona," *Ventura County Historical Society Quarterly* 42 (1998): 5–36; Dydia DeLyser, "A Work of Fiction and the Landscape of Southern California," *Ventura County Historical Society Quartery* 42 (1998): 49–63; and William A. Bullough, "The Photographs of John Calvin Brewster, 1874–1909," *Ventura County Historical Society Quarterly* 41 (1995): 5–34. For photographic appropriation, see James C. Faris, *Navajo and Photography: A Critical History of the Representation of an American People* (Albuquerque, 1996), 17, 42, 74; Joanna Cohan Scherer, "You Can't Believe Your Eyes: Inaccuracies in Photographs of North American Indians," *Studies in the Anthropology of Visual Communications* 2 (Fall 1975): 67; Joanna Cohan Scherer, *Indians: The Great Photographs That Reveal Native American Indian Life* (New York, 1974), 13; and A. C. Vroman and T. F. Barnes, *The Genesis of the Story of Ramona: Why the Book Was Written: Explanatory Text of Points of Interest Mentioned in the Story* (Los Angeles, 1899).

4. Progressive Photography Takes Hold

1. Quote from Dave Larsen, "Raisin Girl Memories Sweeten with Age," *Los Angeles Times,* May 16, 1982. See also "The Face That Helped an Industry," *Fresno Bee,* December 4, 1940; Dick Richardson, "Fresnan Recalls How She Became 'Sun-Maid Girl,'" *Fresno Bee,* January 15, 1978; Nancy Kerr, "Fresno's Sun Maid," *AshTree Echo* 8 (April 1973): 1–2; all in the Fresno County Historical Society; Robin Zehring, "Tales from the Pantry," *California Living/San Francisco Sunday Examiner and Chronicle* (January 2, 1983): 12–13; *San Francisco Bulletin,* August 11, 1915; and George Raine, "A New Raisin in the Sun," *San Francisco Chronicle,* April 23, 2006.

2. Gary F. Kurutz, "'Courtesy of the Title Insurance and Trust Company': The Historical Collection at the CHS' Los Angeles History Center," *California History* 107 (Summer 1978): 188–91; Marlene Smith-Barzanini, "The CHS Southern California Historical Collection: New Location and New Opportunities for Historic Research," *California History* 120 (Winter 1991–92): 397. Because Pierce acquired and copied the works of other photographers, for example, George Wharton James, it is impossible to identify who, in fact, took most of the images in his collection. For Alice Hare, see Alice Hare Collection, Bancroft Library, especially 04947–05133; Peter Palmquist, *A Directory of Women in California Photography before 1902* (Arcata, Calif., 1991), 159–61; and Clyde Arbuckle Collection, box 85, folder 18, San Jose Museum of History. For the photography of H. C. Tibbets, see Charles S. Aiken, "The Surprise of the Desert," *Sunset* 21 (September 1908): 375–98.

3. Jacob Riis, *How the Other Half Lives: Studies among the Tenements of New York* (1890; New York, 1971); Alexander Alland Sr., *Jacob A. Riis: Photographer and Citizen* (Millerton, N.Y., 1974),

4, 45; Robert J. Doherty, ed., *The Complete Photographic Work of Jacob A. Riis* (New York, 1981), 6; Sally Stein, "Making Connections with the Camera: Photography and the Social Mobility in the Career of Jacob Riis," *Afterimage* (May 1983): 9–16; Rosenblum, *A World History of Photography,* 359–61; James B. Lane, *Jacob Riis and the American City* (Port Washington, Wash., 1974).

4. Judith Gutmann, *Lewis Hine and the American Social Conscience* (New York, 1967); Maren Stange, *Symbols of Ideal Life: Social Documentary Photography in America, 1890–1950* (Cambridge, U.K., 1989), xiii, xv, 1, 24; Lewis Hine, "Roving Children," *Survey* 23 (January 1, 1910): n.p.; Lewis Hine, *Child Labor in the Sugar-Beet Fields,* National Child Labor Committee Pamphlet no. 259, n.d., 6, Firestone Library, Princeton University; Verna Curtis, *Photography and Reform: Lewis Hine and the National Child Labor Committee* (Milwaukee, Wisc., 1984), 82; Ralph F. Bogardus and Ferenc M. Szaz, "Reality Captured, Reality Tames: John James McCook and the Uses of Documentary Photography in Fin-de-Siècle America," *History of Photography* 10 (April–June 1996): 131–67; Trudy K. Jones, "Give a Tramp a Chance!" *Landmark* (Fall 1992): 4–11; Todd Allan DePastino, "From Hobohemia to Skid Row: Homelessness and American Culture, 1870–1950," PhD diss., Yale University, 1997, 126–27, 173; "An Old Timer," *International Socialist Review* 9 (August 1914). Henry McGuckin, *Memories of a Wobbly* (Chicago, 1987), 58, runs a photograph by Saffo and describes traveling with him. I have not been able to find Saffo's full name or locate his negatives or original photographs.

5. Although Naomi Rosenblum, Walter Rosenblum, Alan Trachtenberg, and Marvin Isreal's book *America and Lewis Hine: Photographs, 1904–1940* (Millerton, N.Y., 1977), 20, reports that Hine photographed children working in the fields of California sometime between 1915 and 1917, curators at each of the various repositories of Lewis Hine material questioned the claim. I found no evidence that Hine ever worked in California and uncovered no photographs of child laborers in the fields outside Colorado, Texas, Connecticut, Massachusetts, and New Jersey. See Naomi Rosenblum to author, March 6, 1998; Janice Madhu to author, March 6, 1998; Tom Beck to author, February 20, 1998; all in author's possession. Arnold Genthe's work in San Francisco's Chinatown might qualify as an exception to my assertion that California photographers at this time demonstrated no interest in social reform.

6. Esther H. Klotz, Harry W. Lawton, and Joan Hall, eds., *A History of Citrus in the Riverside Area* (1969; Riverside, Calif., 1989), 6–23; Joan H. Hall, *A Citrus Legacy* (Riverside, Calif., 1992), 19, 30–34, 103–7; W. A. Spaulding, *The Orange: Its Culture in California* (Riverside, Calif., 1922); Herbert J. Weber, "History and Development of the Citrus Industry," in Leon Batchelor and Herbert J. Weber, *The Citrus Industry* (Berkeley, 1948), 3: 1–39; J. J. Warner, "The Orange Tree in Los Angeles," *Los Angeles Star,* August 30 and 31, 1871; Ronald Tobey and Charles Wetherell, "The Citrus Industry and the Revolution of Corporate Capitalism in Southern California, 1887–1944," *California History* 124 (Spring 1995): 6; Vincent Moses, "A Citrus Monopoly in Riverside, 1900–1936," *California History* 111 (Spring 1982): 27–35; Gordon T. McClelland and Jay T. Last, *California Orange Box Labels: An Illustrated History* (Santa Ana, Calif., 1985); Thomas P. "Pat" Jacobsen, *Millennium Guide to Fruit Crate Labels: A Price Guide and Collector's Reference* (Weimar, Calif., 2000), 8–9, which is definitive and goes far beyond its title. For a citrus community, see Mark Echeverri, "Pomona, California: The Early Years, 1875–1920," PhD diss., Claremont Graduate School, 1980, 164–95. For the largest lemon grower in the state, see Margo McBane, "The House That Lemons Built: Race, Gender, Citizenship and the Creation of a Citrus Empire, 1893–1919," PhD diss., University of California, Los Angeles, 2002. For another company, see Lorne Allmon, *The Story of Samuel B. Hampton and the California Citrus Industry, 1887–1918* (Riverside, Calif., 1994). See also Jesse E. Boyd, "Historical Import of the Orange Industry in Southern California," MA thesis, University of California, Berkeley, 1922. For Sunkist, see Josephine K. Jacobs, "Sunkist Advertising," PhD diss., University of California, Los Angeles, 1966; Rahno M. MacCurdy, *The*

History of the California Fruit Growers Exchange (Los Angeles, 1925), 60–63, 82; H. E. Erdman, *The California Fruit Growers Exchange: An Example in Cooperation in the Segregation of Conflicting Interests* (New York, 1933); Albert J. Meyer, "History of the California Fruit Growers Exchange, 1893–1920," PhD diss., Johns Hopkins University, 1950, 151–83; and Starr, *Inventing the Dream,* 140–47. For the citrus belt, see Clifford Zierer, "The Citrus Fruit Industry of the Los Angeles Basin," *Economic Geography* 32 (January 1934): 22–39.

7. Karen Demichelis, "Early Stockton Photographers," senior thesis, San Joaquin Delta College, 1981, 7–11; R. Coke Wood and Leonard Covello, *Stockton Memories: A Pictorial History of Stockton, California* (Fresno, Calif., 1977), v–vi, 87–98; Margarett Loke, ed., *The World as It Was, 1865–1981: A Photographic Portrait from the Keystone-Mast Collection,* foreword by Paul Theroux (New York, 1980); Edgar Cohen, "Playing Tricks on Nature," *Country Life in America* 23 (December 1913): 74–75; "A Change in Photographic Circles," *Oxnard Courier,* June 13, 1903; Peter Palmquist, *Fine California Views* (New York 1979); V. Covert Martin, *Stockton Album through the Years* (Stockton, Calif., 1959), 11; clipping, Tweedy's Studio, "Lemons Are Handled Almost as Carefully as If They Were Eggs," *California Citrograph,* n.d., F. Hall Higgins Collection, Archives and Special Collections, University of California, Davis; Richard Street, "Pop Laval and His $5 Crackerbox: A Photographer of California's San Joaquin Valley," *History of Photography* 6 (July 1982): 195–210. Candid photography, photojournalism, and social documentary photography at this time were practiced in California by only one man, Arnold Genthe. While photographing San Francisco's Chinatown, Genthe initiated a new approach, that of the unrehearsed opportunistic snapshot. Prowling the streets and alleyways of Chinatown with his Zeiss camera and using a lens that allowed him to photograph in low light, Genthe unobtrusively documented his subjects unaware of his presence. But Genthe was an urban photographer. Had he left the environs of Chinatown and ventured into the countryside, he would have initiated a new tradition in coverage of farmworkers. But after two decades in Chinatown, he abandoned San Francisco and candid photography and spent the remainder of his career as a fashion photographer in New York, thus ending any possibility that pre-1900 California farmworkers might be portrayed sympathetically, compassionately, and realistically. See Richard Dillon, *Images of Chinatown: Louis J. Stellman's Chinatown Photographs* (San Francisco, 1976), 9, 11, 13, 15, 17–18, 21; Arnold Genthe, *Pictures of Old Chinatown* (New York, 1908); Arnold Genthe, *Old Chinatown: A Book of Pictures* (New York, 1913), with essays by Will Irwin; Arnold Genthe, *As I Remember* (New York, 1936); all in the Arnold Genthe Collection, California Historical Society.

8. Raffi Zinzalian, "Fraser's Fotos," *LaVerne Magazine* 3 (February–March 1979): 14–18; Russ Leadabrand, "Photographer of the Desert," *The Westerners: Brand Book Number 11* (Los Angeles, 1964); Anthea M. Hartig, "'In a World He Has Created': Class Collectivity and the Growers' Landscape of the Southern California Citrus Industry, 1890–1940," *California History* 114 (Spring 1995): 100–103.

9. See countless photographs in the C. C. Pierce Collection, Huntington Library. These may or may not be by Pierce, who acquired the work of several other photographers and marketed it under his imprint. Street, interview with Peter Palmquist, March 23, 1993, San Rafael, California, author's possession. For one example of commercial portraiture applied elsewhere, see the photographs in the John Calvin Brewster Collection (Ventura County Museum) of Japanese workers beside a new steam engine that the American Crystal Beet Sugar Company used to haul beet wagons out of the fields in 1901.

10. Street, interview with Pierre Biane, May 17, 1974, Brookside Winery, Cucamanga, California; Street, interview with Harry Bachigalupi, May 12, 1977, San Bruno, California; both in author's possession; Lanier Bartlett, "An Immigrant in the Land of Opportunity," *World's Work* 17 (April 1909): 11379. Copies of photographs of harvesting into gondola cars are in the Department

of Special Collections, Ontario Public Library, Ontario, California, in the Seaver Center for Western History, Los Angeles Museum of Natural History, and in Guasti Plaza, Guasti, California. Following a suggestion of Jennifer Watts, the Huntington Library curator of photographs , I examined the Burton Fraser Collection, Pomona Public Library, Department of Special Collections, Pomona, California, and concluded that Fraser was not the photographer hired to document the Italian Vineyard Company's railroad. Other photo curators in Southern California were unable to identify the photographer. For photographs of railroad cars used to haul grapes out of the vineyards at El Pinal Winery, near Stockton, see Teiser and Harroun, *Winemaking in California,* 150.

11. Quote from Peter B. Hales, *William Henry Jackson and the Transformation of the American Landscape* (Philadelphia, 1988), 264, also 275, 329; William Henry Jackson, photograph, *Raisin Drying, Fresno, California,* ca. 1901, William Henry Jackson Collection, Library of Congress. See also Jackson, diary entries for September 29 and October 3, 4, 5, 1901, William Henry Jackson Diaries, New York Public Library Manuscripts Collection. A useful but not entirely reliable version of the diaries is Leroy R. Hafen and Ann W. Hafen, eds., *The Diaries of William Henry Jackson, Frontier Photographer* (Glendale, Calif., 1959). William Henry Jackson, *Time Exposure: The Autobiography of William Henry Jackson,* intro. by Ferenc M. Szasz (New York, 1940; Albuquerque, N.M., 1986), 325, omits Jackson's work photographing in California orange groves, packing sheds, and raisin vineyards. See also Jeff Burdick, *The Handbook of Detroit Photographic Company Postcards: A Guide for Collectors* (Essington, Pa., 1955), 5–8, 54–55.

12. Fraser's work is surveyed in Raymond Holt, "Fraser's Fotos—Postcard King of the West," *Pomona Valley Historian* 4 (April 1968): 71–78. For examples, see Edwin F. Mitchell, *Indians Picking Hops,* Harvest Scenes Folder, Ukiah Historical Society, Ukiah, California; postcards published in *Wheatland Historical Society, Wheatland: 1874–1974* (Wheatland, Calif., 1974), 53–55; and *Marysville: An Historical Sampler* (Marysville, Calif., 1978). For messages, see the many postcards in the Covina Public Library, Western History Collection, Covina, California.

13. For postcards in general, see Hal Morgan and Andreas Brown, *Prairie Fires and Paper Moons: The American Photographic Postcard: 1900–1920* (Boston, 1981); George Miller and Dorothy Miller, *Picture Postcards in the United States, 1893–1918* (New York, 1976), 146; Monica Highland, *Greetings from Southern California: A Look at the Past through Postcards* (New York, 1988); and Mary Price, *The Photograph: A Strange, Confined Space* (Stanford, 1994), 143.

14. "Agrilithologist" Pat Jacobsen's *Millennium Guide to Fruit Crate Labels* is the definitive work. He kindly allowed me to research his vast collection at his Weimar, California, archive. See also John Salkin and Laurie Gordon, *Orange Crate Art* (New York, 1976), 7–13; Joe Davidson, *Fruit Crate Art* (Secaucus, N.J., 1990), 10–12; and Gordon McClelland and Jay Last, *California Orange Box Labels* (New York, 1985).

15. See the fruit box labels in the collections at the Huntington Library, San Marino, California; California Historical Society, San Francisco; Smithsonian Institution, Washington, D.C.; Library of Congress, Washington, D.C.; Riverside Museum, Riverside, California; Riverside Public Library, Riverside, California; Archives and Special Collections, University of California, Davis; Special Collections, California State University, Fullerton; Pomona Public Library, Pomona, California; Ontario Public Library, Ontario, California.

16. Photographer unknown, *Apricot Drying Yard,* ca. 1895, photograph number 15024, First American Financial Corporation Photo Collection, Santa Ana, California; A[ndrew] P. Hill, photograph, *Prune Drying Campbell Dryer,* ca. 1903, Coe Collection, California State Library.

17. Quotes from W. R. Nutting, photograph, *Dipping and Peeling Peaches, H. A. Bassford Packing House,* ca. 1886; W. R. Nutting, photograph, *Packing House of A. McKevitt. Shipping Grapes to Chicago,* November 8, 1886, Vacaville Museum; photographer unknown, E. M. E., *Fruit Drying Crew, Drago Fruit Company,* August 29, 1892, Fresno County Historical Society. See also photograph,

Berryessa Fruit Growers Union, n.d., San Jose Historical Museum; photograph, *Snyders Pitting Shed, Near Aromas, Cal.,* ca. 1900, California State Library, Sacramento; Lock, photograph, *Frank Duncan's Dryer,* ca. 1900, Campbell Historical Museum, Campbell, California, emphasizing "*Duplicates Of This Can be Had At Any Time.*" Also useful are Jerome D. Laval, *As Pop Saw It: Photographs of the San Joaquin Valley from the Files of Claude C. "Pop" Laval* (Fresno, Calif., 1975), 2: 134; photograph no. 3914, *Canet Ranch, Ventura Avenue, West Ventura, Apricot Drying, 1906,* Ventura County Museum; and W. R. Nutting, photograph, *A. Bassford's Packing House,* ca. 1887, Vacaville Museum.

18. Allan Sekula, "The Body and the Archive," in Richard Bolton, ed., *The Contest of Meaning: Critical Histories of Photography* (Cambridge, Mass., 1989), 347, 363–65.

19. Denied parole in 1907 and 1908, Hankins was finally released on November 14, 1914. Becoming a merchant seaman, he moved to Seattle and never got into trouble again. Hankins died in 1964 in Seattle, having worked most of his life as a seaman. See Arne Svenson, *Prisoners* (New York, 1997), 44, 138–40; clippings, *Marysville Appeal,* July 20, 22, 23, 24, 1904, October 14, 15, 19, 22, 1904, November 6, 1904, and July 20, 1906, copies courtesy of Arne Svenson.

20. Quote from *Marysville Democrat,* July 14, 1906, copies courtesy of Arne Svenson, New York City. (Eventually the *Marysville Democrat* merged with the *Marysville Appeal* to become the *Marysville Appeal-Democrat.*) For Smith, see Peter Palmquist, *Shadowcatchers: A Directory of Women in California Photography before 1901* (Eureka, Calif., 1990), 202–4; and Nikki Pahl, Mary Swisher, and Genevieve Troka, *Camera Craft: Commercial Photography of the Sacramento Valley, 1900–1945* (Sacramento, 1982), 5.

21. Photographs, Agricultural Laborers in California, BANC PIC 1905.02634–.02731, Bancroft Library; Corrine Gibb, "Ira B. Cross: Portrait of an Economics Professor," oral interview, Regional Oral History Project, 1967, Bancroft Library; U.S. Congress, Senate, Immigration Commission, "Immigrants in Industries," part 25, vol. 2, *Japanese and Other Immigrant Races in the Pacific Coast and Rocky Mountain States: Agriculture,* 61st Cong., 2nd sess., 1911, S 633.

22. In several conversations, Paul Taylor has referred to the photographs that Cross had taken early in his career, citing them as one of the influences on his own photographic work. For Hine's photographs, see H. Parker Willis, "The Findings of the Immigration Commission," *Survey* 15 (January 7, 1911): 571–78.

23. Some evidence indicates that Marysville photographers C. C. Green and Clara Sheldon Smith had photographed earlier at the Durst hop camp. For Green and McCurry, see Pahl, Swisher, and Troka, *Camera Craft,* 4–6. I have based my conclusion that McCurry or one of his assistants photographed at the Durst hop camp on two elevated views of the camp with negative numbers 7947 and 7948. They were first published in Robert Coe Jr., "Once the Largest Producer of Hops," *Wheatland News,* July 13, 1973. The numbers on these photographs match the McCurry Foto Company negative list in the California Room, California State Library, Sacramento. But there is no identifying information next to the numbers. Research in Wheatland failed to discover the originals or copies of them. The maker of these views therefore remains open to speculation and could also have been one of McCurry's many assistants. See Street, interview with Marianne Leach, May 26, 1982, California State Library; Street, interview with Robert Coe Jr., May 23, 1982, Wheatland, California; both in author's possession. I have scrutinized the McCurry Collection in the Sacramento History Center, Sacramento, California, but turned up no additional information.

24. Street, "'We Are Not Slaves,'" 214–15.

25. Gail Buckland, *First Photographs: People, Places, and Phenomena as Captured for the First Time by Camera* (New York, 1980), 114–15.

26. This photograph was published in Chicano Communications Center, *450 Years of Chicano History in Pictures* (Albuquerque, N.M., 1976), 96.

27. This is my "reading" of the photograph. No identifying information appears on the back. The location seems to be on the west side of the Durst camp, near town.

28. A vast literature describes conditions in the camp at Wheatland. My analysis is based on manuscript reports in the Commission on Industrial Relations Papers, State Historical Society of Wisconsin, Madison; Wheatland Hop Field Riot Scrapbooks, Bancroft Library; various publications issued by the California Commission of Immigration and Housing; Carleton Parker, *The Casual Laborer and Other Essays* (New York, 1920), 169–99; David John Vaught, "California's Specialty Guardians: Growers, Specialty Crops, and Labor, 1875–1920," PhD diss., University of California, Davis, 1997, 194–96; and the unedited manuscript version of an essay published as Richard Steven Street, "Wheatland: Birth of the Farm Labor Movement," *Sacramento Magazine* 10 (December 1984): 38–42, 63–66.

29. Preserved in the Juanita [Neyens] DeValentine Album, Wheatland, the photograph is cracked and suffering from severe fading. Mrs. Juanita DeValentine, who owns the print, recalls that Yuba County sheriff John Dower rescued the picture from the archives of the Marysville Courthouse, just before the building was demolished. According to DeValentine, the picture is one of the original exhibits used in the court case that grew out of the riot. See Street, interviews with Mrs. Juanita Neyens [DeValentine], October 27, 1980, January 5, 1981, and July 24, 1982, Wheatland, California; Neyens to Street, December 21, 1980; Juanita DeValentine to author, July 12, 1998; all in author's possession.

30. Quote from Dick Meister and Ann Loftis, *A Long Time Coming: The Struggle to Unionize America's Farm Workers* (New York, 1977), 12. This quote is widely cited in numerous sources. For Elizabeth Carney, see Street, interview with Juanita Neyens [DeValentine], October 27, 1980.

31. DeValentine Album, Wheatland. See also Orrin Rounds Album, in possession of Orrin Rounds, Chico, California; and Meriam Griffin Album, Special Collections and Archives, Meriam Library, California State University, Chico (originally consulted in Wheatland). Before I discovered these images, historians had mistakenly assumed two other images were the first photographs of striking farmworkers in America. Both fail to withstand scrutiny. One of them, appearing in Buckland, *First Photographs,* 115, was in fact nothing more than a placid group portrait taken at Wheatland, probably a few days before the strike. Another appeared first in the *Marysville Appeal-Democrat* accompanying an article by Howard T. Johnson Jr., titled "Wheatland Hop Riots 55 Years Ago Today," and later in Paul S. Taylor and Ann Loftis, "Migratory Farm Labor in the Wheat Belt: Early Twentieth Century," in Edward and Frederick Schapsmeir, eds., *Agriculture in the West* (Manhattan, Kans., 1980), 105. Showing a crowd of men, their right hands raised, gathered around a speaker who stands addressing them on an elevated podium, it clearly illustrates field hands in a defiant mood, united in action. Supposedly the man standing on the elevated platform was Richard "Blackie" Ford, the IWW organizer who presented strike demands. Three fold marks crease the center of the photograph, breaking the emulsion and making the image look old, as if it was packed about by some agitator, now long-dead. One can easily imagine such a person, by campfire, late at night, in a hobo jungle, slowly taking the picture from his pocket, passing it around, then launching into a story about the Wheatland hop riot. The photograph has been frequently published and represented as a scene at Wheatland, but a close examination raised doubts. First, the absence of any of the prominent landmarks of the Wheatland area, particularly the many water towers that were scattered about or the hop trellises that surrounded the camp on three sides, indicate the picture was not taken at Wheatland. Second, accession records for the original place it not in California but two thousand miles to the east, somewhere in the Midwest "sometime after 1915." See Richard Steven Street to Thomas Featherstone, September 28, 1981; Featherstone to Street, October 26, 1981; Featherstone to Street, July 2, 1982; Margery Long to Street, July 2, 1982; all in author's possession; accession notes, and Howard Johnston to Fred Thompson, March 26 and April

20, 1968, Fred Thompson Papers, Archives of Urban and Labor Affairs, Wayne State University, Detroit, Michigan.

32. Adopting a less literal translation, I read the sign as saying, "We are not slaves." The somewhat polite grammar used on the sign raises questions about who wrote it and to what extent it expressed the feelings of common people.

33. As with most snapshots, years passed before Carney's images fell into the hands of historians capable of making them accessible, people asking the kinds of questions and supplying the proper historical context that elevated them beyond family mementos into the realm of historical icons and mileposts in the evolution of a class of people.

34. Photographs appeared in the *Sacramento Bee, Sacramento Star, Marysville Appeal-Democrat, San Francisco News, Harper's Weekly, International Socialist Review, Outlook,* and *World's Work.* I have not used any of these photographs, mainly because of the problem of "lifting" prints from published work and because the technical quality of such prints is poor. Original photographs or high-quality copies are in the Wheatland Historical Society; Mildred Phillips Collection, Wheatland; Dam Family Collection, Wheatland; Juanita DeValentine Album, Wheatland; Miriam Griffith Collection, Wheatland; Emma Hutchinson Collection, Marysville; Mary Aaron Museum, Marysville; and Robert V. Howard, "Bloody Sunday: The Wheatland Hop Fields Riot," unpublished research paper, California State University, Sacramento, 1973.

35. Quote from Mitchell, *The Lie of the Land,* 14–15. See also California Commission of Immigration and Housing, *Advisory Pamphlet on Camp Sanitation* (Sacramento, 1914), 7–12; and California Commission of Immigration and Housing, *Second Annual Report of the California Commission of Immigration and Housing* (Sacramento, 1915), 13, 15.

36. Samuel Wood, "The California Commission of Immigration and Housing: A Study of Administrative Organization and the Growth of Function," PhD diss., University of California, Berkeley, 1942; Christina Krysto, "California's Labor Camps," *Survey* 43 (November 8, 1919): 70–73, 76–78; Laval, *As Pop Saw It,* 1: 124–34.

37. Quote from Bertha H. Smith to C. C. Leffingwell, December 8, 1914, Leffingwell Ranch Collection, Album 104, Huntington Library.

38. Brian Coe and Paul Gates, *The Snapshot: The Rise of Popular Photography, 1888–1939* (London, 1977), 13, 107–13.

39. Alice Prescott Smith, "The Battalion of Life: Our Women's Land Army and Its Work in the West," *Sunset* 41 (November 1918): 30–33; Margo McBane, "The Role of Women in Determining the California Farm Labor Structure: A Case Study of the Women's Land Army of America during World War I," MA thesis, University of California, Davis, 1978.

40. Catherine G. Kipp, "Women on the Land: The Woman's Land Army: California, Northern Division, 1918–1920," MA thesis, California State University, Sacramento, 1960; Kevin Starr, *Endangered Dreams: The Great Depression in California* (New York, 1996), 46–47; M. F. Tarpey, "Some Possibilities of the Development of New Labor during the War," *California State Fruit Growers Convention Proceedings, 1917* (Sacramento, 1917), 78, 102.

41. For the changes in farm labor during World War I, see "Labor Conditions," *Monthly Labor Review* 2 (November 1920): 221–23; Kathryn Cramp, Louise F. Shields, and Charles Thompson, "A Study of the Mexican Population in Imperial, California," MS, March 31–April 9, 1926, Bancroft Library; and Camille Guerin-Gonzales, *Mexican Workers and American Dreams: Immigration, Repatriation, and California Farm Labor, 1900–1939* (New Brunswick, N.J., 1994), 41–47.

42. Richard Steven Street, *Photographing Farmworkers in California* (Stanford, 2004), 86; George J. Sánchez, *Becoming Mexican American: Ethnicity, Culture, and the Identity in Chicano Los Angeles, 1900–1945* (New York, 1993), opposite 206. See also cards in the Arizona Historical Society, Tucson, Arizona.

43. A. D. Shamel, "Housing the Employees of California Citrus Ranches," *California Citrograph* (February 1918): 70–71, and (March 1918): 96; A. D. Shamel, "Those Who Have Achieved in the Citrus Industry," *California Citrograph* (May 1918): 96–97, and (June 1919): 204; A. D. Shamel, "Co-operative Handling of Labor," *California Citrograph* (August 1920): 389, and (August 1924): 390–91; Hartig, "In a World He Has Created," 100–111; Richard Steven Street, "Into the Good Land: The Emergence of California Agriculture, 1850–1920," MS, 1979, 521, in author's possession. For biographical information on Shamel, see John Brown and James Boyd, *History of San Bernardino and Riverside Counties* (Los Angeles, 1922), 1: 487; and Klotz, Lawton, and Hall, eds., *A History of Citrus in the Riverside Area,* 16.

44. Some of Shamel's original negatives are in the A. D. Shamel Collection, Archives and Special Collections, Tomás Rivera Library, University of California, Riverside. The citrus village negatives, along with 230 others, are in the Riverside Museum, possibly donated by Harry Lawton, and consist of 8 × 10–inch glass plates. The work of other photographers, principally Avery Edwin Field, a Riverside photographer, and a man named Metcalf, are interspersed among the collection. For Shamel's photography in the 1920s, see A. D. Shamel, "The Aesthetic Side of Orange Growing in the Southwest," *California Citrograph* (January 1928): 79, (February 1928): 110, (March 1928): 154, (June 1928): 281, and (November 1929): 4. See also J. D. Culbertson, "Housing of Ranch Labor," *First Annual Report of the California Citrus Institute* (June 1, 1920): 97–99; and González, *Labor and Community,* 8–9, 41.

45. H. Vincent Moses, "'The Orange-Grower Is Not a Farmer': G. Harold Powell, Riverside Orchardists, and the Coming of Industrial Agriculture, 1893–1930," *California History* 124 (Spring 1995): 34–35.

46. Carey McWilliams, *North for Mexico: The Spanish-Speaking People of the United States* (New York, 1940); Carey McWilliams, *Brothers under the Sun,* rev. ed. (New York, 1951); Albert Camarillo, *Chicanos in California* (New York, 1984); Matt Garcia, *A World of Its Own: Race, Labor, and Citrus in the Making of Greater Los Angeles, 1900–1970* (Chapel Hill, N.C., 2001); José Amarillo, "Bitter-Sweet Communities: Mexican Workers and Citrus Growers on the California Landscape, 1880–1941," PhD diss., University of California, Irvine, 2000.

47. Laval learned photography while working as a foreman at the Coshocton Iron Works in Monongahela, Pennsylvania. An acquaintance who had an apparently broken 8 × 10–inch "crackerbox" camera sold it to Laval for five dollars. Examining it, Laval discovered that the ground-glass focusing screen had been reversed, corrected it, and had a fine piece of equipment that he used regularly for more than sixty years. Leaving the ironworks, Laval spent nine years learning his craft at the R. W. Johnson studios in Pittsburgh. He moved to Fresno in search of a climate with warmer winters. See *Fresno Morning Republican,* August 18, 1918; Richard Steven Street, "Pop Laval," *American Heritage* 31 (October–November 1980): 60–61; Street, "Pop Laval and His $5 Crackerbox"; Laval, *As Pop Saw It,* 1: 234.

48. A few glass plates and prints are in the Frank D. Robinson Collection, Merced County Historical Museum, Merced, California. A larger collection of glass plates is in the possession of Stephen Johnson, Pacifica, California. For Robinson, see "Frank D. Robinson," in John Outcalt, *A History of Merced County California . . . Illustrated* (Chicago, 1925), 693.

49. Quotes from Otis B. Tout, *The First Thirty Years in Imperial Valley, California, 1901–1931* (1931; Imperial, Calif., 1990), 375–76. The title of the photograph depicting the Japanese women and children reads simply: *Picking Winter Strawberries in Imperial Valley.* The gender of the workers and the nature of their exertions are not mentioned. Hetzel's prints are from 6 × 10–inch glass plates. After purchasing Hetzel's studio in 1950, Warren Rhodes declared Hetzel's acetate negatives a fire hazard and destroyed thousands of them. Hetzel's collection is in the Imperial Valley Historical Society, Pioneers Museum, Imperial, California (originally consulted in Imperial Valley

College). See also Paul S. Taylor, *Mexican Labor in the United States: Imperial Valley* (Berkeley, 1928); and Joe Livernois, *Hetzel, the Photographer: Impressions of Imperial Valley* (Fresno, Calif., 1982), 6, 73–74, 80, 113, 118, 120. A large man who bore a striking resemblance to William Jennings Bryan, Hetzel faced huge technical obstacles from 1913, when he began his career in El Centro, until 1949, when he died. Working in a hot environment, Hetzel often had to buy three hundred pounds of ice every other day during the summer simply to process his film and maintain darkroom chemicals at the proper temperature.

50. Kenneth L. Roberts, "Wet and Other Mexicans," *Saturday Evening Post* 200 (February 4, 1928): 10–11; Kenneth L. Roberts, "The Docile Mexican," *Saturday Evening Post* 200 (March 19, 1928): 39–41; John J. Hader, "Honk Honk Hobo," *Survey* 60 (August 1, 1928): 453–55; Adaline A. Buffington, "Automobile Migrants," *Family* 6 (July 1925): 152, 149.

51. Thomas McGeough (of Ewing Galloway) to author, March 26, 1980, author's possession; clipping, October 20, 1920, Pajaro Valley Historical Society, Watsonville, California; captions from Keystone–Mast Collection, California Museum of Photography, University of California, Riverside, California.

52. For Keller, see Kenneth Keller to Mr. Clifton Heard, March 3, 1924, Kenneth Keller Correspondence, Huntington Library. Much is known about Appleton. Born in Newburyport, Massachusetts, in 1867, Appleton arrived in the Simi Valley in 1887, a year before the first influx of settlers. After working for several years driving cattle and tending bees, Appleton purchased 160 acres of land, cleared it of sagebrush and cactus, began dry farming grain, then moved into apricots, walnuts, alfalfa, and honey. After he married his childhood sweetheart, Laura Jacques, in 1894, Appleton went into the honey business on a large scale, annually producing sixty-nine tons of white sage honey. When the old Appleton land was sold in the 1960s, a developer began demolishing various outbuildings, barns, and migrant workers' quarters to make way for construction grading. Behind the old ranch house, in one of the smaller buildings, workers discovered boxes containing 450 of Appleton's glass-plate negatives. Failing to understand their value, the workers tossed the boxes into the nearby creek, along with tons of other trash, before the creek was to be backfilled, graded, and paved. At about this time, Appleton's son happened by while hunting quail. On discovering the glass plates, he rescued them, although hundreds had been ruined. Now in the possession of Bill Appleton, an industrial photographer and great-grandson of John Appleton, the glass plates have been cleaned and cataloged. In 1997 the Simi Valley Historical Society exhibited enlarged prints from the original negatives. See Patricia Havens, *Simi Valley: A Journey through Time* (Simi Valley, Calif., 1997), 74–75, 83–85, 108–9, 112, 117, 118, 119, 124, 142, 173, 193, 247, 249, 250; Bill Appleton to author, May 11, June 19, 26, and July 12, 2002, author's possession; notes from Appleton Diaries, March 10, 1990, Simi Valley Historical Society.

53. Emilio Zamora, *The World of the Mexican Worker in Texas* (College Station, Tex., 1993), 40–41; Sánchez, *Becoming Mexican American,* 36–58; Alexandra Minna Stern, *Eugenic Nation: Faults and Frontiers of Better Breeding in Modern America* (Berkeley, 2005), 57–79.

54. Hugo Summerville Collection, Harry Ransom Humanities Research Center, University of Texas, Austin.

55. Jennifer Watts and Claudia Bohn-Spector, *The Great Wide Open: Panoramic Photographs of the American West* (New York, 2001), 66. For Summerville, see Marguerite Davenport, *The Unpretentious Pose: The Work of E. O. Goldbeck, a People's Photographer* (San Antonio, Tex., 1981), 12–13, 133–37, 144–45; Goldberg and Ollman, *A Nation of Strangers,* 71–73; and the Hugo Summerille Collection, Harry Ransom Research Center, University of Texas, Austin. Texas played such a significant role as a demarcation point for California, because the railroad system directed immigrants to Texas and did not connect to California in any easily accessible way.

56. For Goldbeck, see Roy Flukinger, "Only a Crazy Man Would Do What I Do," in Kitti

Bolognesi and Jordi Bernardo, eds., *Goldbeck* (Lugano, Switzerland, 1999); and Clyde W. Burleson and E. Jessica Hickman, *The Panoramic Photography of Eugene W. Goldbeck* (Austin, Tex., 1986), 116. For the Border Patrol, see Kelly Anne Lytle Hernández, "Entangling Bodies and Borders: Racial Profiling and the U.S. Border Patrol, 1924–1955," PhD diss., University of California, Los Angeles, 2002; and Stern, *Eugenic Nation*, 57–81.

5. An Attitude of Engagement

1. Born in Italy, Modotti immigrated to the United States in 1913. After working as a seamstress in San Francisco, she landed a part as an actress in the 1921 Hollywood movie *Tiger Lady*. Shortly after meeting the photographer Edward Weston, she followed him to Mexico, where she studied with him and became his lover, then struck out on her own as an independent photographer. See Patricia Albers, *Shadow, Fire, Snow: The Life of Tina Modotti* (New York, 1999), 87–118. The sombreros photograph is incorrectly dated as 1928 in Carole Naggar and Fred Ritchin, *Mexico: Through Foreign Eyes, 1850–1990* (New York, 1993), 205; and as 1929 in Peter Stephan, ed., *Icons of Photography: The 20th Century* (Munich, 1999), 44–45; Michael C. Meyer and William H. Beezley, eds., *The Oxford History of Mexico* (New York, 2000), 560–61; and James Oles, with Karen Cordero Reiman, *South of the Border: Mexico in the American Imagination, 1914–1947* (Washington, D.C., 1993), 89. *Mexican Folkways* published the art, drawings, poetry, and photographs of such stellar individuals as Diego Rivera, José Clement Orozco, and Carleton Beals.

2. Andrea Noble, *Tina Modotti: Image, Texture, Photography* (Albuquerque, N.M., 2000), 87–89; Margaret Hooks, *Tina Modotti: Photographer and Revolutionary* (San Francisco, 1993), 122; Joan Smith, "Tina Modotti's Revolutionary Journey," *Image/San Francisco Examiner*, November 14, 1993, 20–25; John Mraz, "Tina Modotti: En el camino hacia la realidad," *La Jornada Semanal* 7 (July 30, 1989): 18; Laura Mulvey and Peter Wollen, *Frida Kahlo and Tina Modotti* (London, 1982), 12–16; Mildred Constantine, *Tina Modotti: A Fragile Life* (New York, 1975), 99–171. See also Bonnie Hayman and Andrea Alessandra, *Tina Modotti's Mexico: A Tale of Love and Revolution* (New York, 2003); and Sarah M. Lowe, *Tina Modotti and Edward Weston: The Mexico Years* (New York, 2004).

3. Henry (Yoshitaka) Kiyama, *The Four Immigrants Manga: A Japanese Experience in San Francisco, 1904–1924*, trans., intro., and notes by Frederik L. Schodt (Berkeley, 1991). I first encountered these cartoons in the Japanese American Research Project Collection in 1976, at which time I shot 35-millimeter copies of them. Professor Tasura Namura, a Japanese scholar at Achi Prefecture University, Japan, whom I met in 1975 while working in the Wayne State University Archives of Labor and Urban History, translated the cartoon captions. The original listing is Henry Yoshita[ka] Kiyama, *Manga Yonin Shosei* (Four Immigrants Comic) (Oakland, Calif., 1931), Japanese American Research Project Collection, Archives and Special Collections, University of California, Los Angeles.

4. Ventura County Coroner's Book of Violent Deaths, 1926–31, Ventura County Museum, Oxnard, California.

5. Quotes from Roy W. Hammack, MD, Coroner's Report no. 2228; Oliver Reardon, Coroner's Report no. 2191; courtesy of John Nichols Gallery, Santa Paula, California.

6. William Stott, *Documentary Expression and Thirties America* (New York, 1973), 9. The International News Pictures was the visual component of the International News Service, a Hearst newspaper picture service. Wide World Photos was a *New York Times* picture service. Acme Newspictures became United Press. See Wilson Hicks, *Words and Pictures: An Introduction to Photojournalism* (New York, 1952), 25; and Suzanne Riess, "Dorothea Lange: Making of a Documentary Photographer," Regional Oral History Project, 1968, 155, Bancroft Library. See also Maren Stange, "Documentary Photography in American Social Reform Movements: The FSA Project and Its Predecessors," in

Daniel P. Younger, ed., *Multiple Views: Logan Grant Essays on Photography, 1983–89* (Albuquerque, N.M., 1991), 195; Miles Orvell, *The Real Thing: Image and Authenticity in American Culture, 1880–1940* (Chapel Hill, N.C., 1989), 230; Beaumont Newhall, "A Backward Glance at Documentary," in David Featherstone, ed., *Observations: Essays on Documentary Photography* (Carmel, Calif., 1984), 2–3; Roy Stryker, "Documentary Photography," in Willard Morgan, ed., *The Complete Photographer* (New York, 1952), 4: 1369; and Roy Stryker, "The FSA Collection of Photographs," in Vicki Goldberg, ed., *Photography in Print: Writings from 1816 to the Present* (New York, 1981), 350.

7. Quote from Antonio Rodríguez, "La glorificación de lo insignificante," *El art fotográfico: Exposición de Nacho López,* Fototeca del Instituto de Antropología e Historia, Mexico (Mexico City, n.d.).

8. Quote from Suzanne Riess, "Paul S. Taylor: California Social Scientist: Education, Field Research, and Family," oral interview, Regional Oral History Project, 1973, 1: 41, Bancroft Library. See also Paul S. Taylor to author, February 2 and 28, 1978, author's possession; testimony of Paul S. Taylor, *Hearings before the United States Senate Subcommittee on Migratory Labor,* Committee on Labor and Public Welfare, Senate, 92nd Cong., 1st sess., January 11, 1972, part 3A, 782. For background on Commons and the University of Wisconsin, see Benjamin Rader, *The Academic Mind and Reform: The Influence of Richard T. Ely in American Life* (Madison, Wisc., 1966), v, 10, 2–23, 217.

9. Richard Steven Street, "Paul S. Taylor and the Origins of Documentary Photography in California," *History of Photography* 7 (October–December 1983): 293–308; Richard Steven Street, "The Economist as Humanist: The Career of Paul S. Taylor," *California History* 68 (Winter 1979–80): 350–70; Paul S. Taylor, "Nonstatistical Notes from the Field," *Land Policy Review* 5 (January 1942): 13–19; Taylor, *Mexican Labor in the United States.*

10. Clark A. Chambers, *Paul U. Kellogg and the Survey: Voices for Social Welfare and Social Justice* (Minneapolis, 1971), 7, 23–27, 32, 49, 84–85; Edward T. Devine, *When Social Work Was Young* (New York, 1939), 108–12; Stange, *Symbols of Ideal Life,* 47–55, 63, 67, 90. For information on turn-of-the-century illustrated magazines, see Edward Earle, "Halftone Effects: A Cultural Study of Photographs in Reproduction, 1895–1905," *California Museum of Photography Bulletin* 8 (1989): 1–24.

11. Quote from Riess, "Paul S. Taylor: California Social Scientist," 1: 115.

12. Quotes from ibid., 1: 113–14; Clark Kerr, preface, in Paul Taylor, *On the Ground in the Thirties* (Salt Lake City, Utah, 1983), vii, ix. See also Richard Steven Street, interview with Paul S. Taylor, May 27, 1979, Berkeley, California, author's possession.

13. Quote from Taylor, *On the Ground in the Thirties,* ix. See also Street, interview with Clark Kerr, April 11, 1976, Berkeley, California, author's possession. For the Imperial Valley at this time, see Governor C. C. Young, Mexican Fact-Finding Committee, *Mexicans in California* (Sacramento, 1930), 17–18; Street, interview with Luis Block, March 12, 1974, San Francisco, California, author's possession; and Max S. Handman, "Economic Reasons for the Coming of the Mexican Immigrant," *American Journal of Sociology* 35 (January 1930): 605.

14. Listening to people talk and continuing to ask questions, Taylor broke through the barriers of language and culture and, in doing so, developed a style of reporting that preserved the content and flavor of his subjects' words, a style that in many ways anticipated the "field notes" that his second wife, the photographer Dorothea Lange, compiled while documenting Dust Bowl refugees. In this way, when field hands relaxed and Taylor was no longer an intruder, he would make a picture, usually after first asking permission. Street, interviews with Paul S. Taylor, May 23 and June 15, 1975, August 7, 1977, and September 26, 1979, Berkeley, California, author's possession. For examples of Taylor's photographs, see Paul S. Taylor, "Making Cantaros at San José Tateposco," *American Anthropologist* 35 (1933): 33–35. Although most of Taylor's negatives were destroyed in the Oakland Hills fire of 1989, small collections are held by Rondal Partridge, the Oakland Museum,

Bancroft Library, John Dixon, and myself. Taylor's interviews can be found in Paul Taylor Field Notes and Interviews, Paul Taylor Papers, Bancroft Library. See also Abraham Hoffman, "An Unusual Monument: Paul S. Taylor's Mexican Labor in the United States Monograph Series," *Pacific Historical Review* 45 (May 1976): 255–70. Taylor's fieldnotes and papers in the Bancroft Library have been considerably altered since I first worked with them in 1974–75. Two other scholars were also using small handheld cameras while working among the Mexicans at this time. One was geographer Stanley W. Cosby, who illustrated "The Imperial Valley of California: An Example of Geographic Instability," PhD diss., University of Chicago, 1930, with pictures he shot himself and with others he acquired from Imperial Valley photographer Leo Hetzel during 1927–29. The other was agricultural scientist Wofford B. Camp. In 1927, while working as a U.S. Department of Agriculture scientist, Camp documented Alcala cotton culture at the Shafter Experimental Farm in Kern County, including numerous images he photographed of Mexican harvest workers there. See William J. Briggs and Henry Cauthen *The Cotton Man: Notes on the Life and Times of Wofford B. ("Bill") Camp,* intro. by Paul Smith (Columbia, S.C., 1983), figures 19–20. At the time of this writing, Camp's photographs were held in a private collection. Manuel Gamio, a Mexican anthroplogist also studying Mexican labor at this time, did not employ a camera as part of his research methodology. See Manuel Gamio, *The Life Story of a Mexican Immigrant,* intro. by Paul S. Taylor (1929; New York, 1971), v–ix.

15. Quotes from Riess, "Paul S. Taylor: California Social Scientist," 1: 117. See also Eugenia P. Janis and Wendy MacNeil, eds., *Photography within the Humanities* (Danbury, N.H., 1977), 27; Street, interview with Paul S. Taylor, February 17, 1976, Berkeley, California, author's possession; and Mary Ellen Leary, "The Power of a Tenacious Man," *Nation* 219 (October 1974): 337. Taylor's negatives measured 3 × 5 inches. His lens was of a normal perspective, used at a medium aperture. Although Taylor recalls it as a Kodak "postcard camera," it was likely a 3B Quick Focus, which went into production in 1906. The hairlike flaw later became useful in attributing many uncredited photographs to Taylor. My understanding of Taylor's photography has also been influenced by my interviews with Rondal Partridge, March 12, 1975, and July 6, 1998, Berkeley, California, author's possession.

16. Stephanie Barron, Sheri Bernstein, Ilene Susan Fort, et al., *Made in California: Art, Image, and Identity, 1900–2000* (Berkeley, 2002), 81.

17. Quotes from Riess, "Paul S. Taylor: California Social Scientist," 1: 238–238A; and Irving Stone, ed., *There Was Light: Autobiography of a University, Berkeley, 1868–1968* (Garden City, N.Y., 1970), 35. See also Willard Van Dyke, "The Photographs of Dorothea Lange—a Critical Analysis," *Camera Craft* 41 (October 1934): 461–67; and Street, interview with Paul S. Taylor, March 23, 1981, Berkeley, California, author's possession. Van Dyke's key role in California photography has never been adequately explored. For slivers of information, see Leslie Calmes, *The Letters between Edward Weston and Willard Van Dyke* (Tucson, Ariz., 1992), 22–23, 57; and Michel Oren, "On the 'Impurity' of Group f/64 Photography," *History of Photography* 15 (Summer 1991): 119–27.

18. Quotes from Riess, "Paul S. Taylor: California Social Scientist," 1: 116.

19. Ibid., 1: 117, also 116.

20. Quotes from *Exeter Sun,* October 31, 1929; and unidentified clipping, James E. Woods Papers, Bancroft Library. See also *Watsonville Pajaronian,* January 24, 1930; various other clippings and interviews, James E. Woods Papers, Bancroft Library; Charles N. Wollenberg, "Huelga, 1928 Style: The Imperial Valley Cantaloupe Workers' Strike," *Pacific Historical Review* 38 (February 1969): 45–58; *Stockton Record,* October 26, 1929; George W. Missemer, "Why the Californians Mob the Filipinos," *China Weekly Review* 51 (1930): 353; *Los Angeles Times,* January 31, 1930; *San Francisco Chronicle,* January 30, 1930; Hicks, *Words and Pictures,* 23–27; and Tim M. Gidal, *Modern Photojournalism: Origin and Evolution, 1910–1933* (New York, 1973).

21. Riess, "Paul S. Taylor: California Social Scientist," 1: 238–238A; Paul S. Taylor, "Mexicans North of the Rio Grande," *Survey Graphic* 19 (May 1931): 135–40, 197, 200–202, 205; Janis and MacNeil, eds., *Photography within the Humanities,* 27. For Taylor's photographs among the San Francisco longshoremen, see Paul S. Taylor and Norman Leon Gold, "San Francisco General Strike," *Survey Graphic* 23 (September 1934): 405–11. For modernism, see Naomi Rosenblum, "F.64 and Modernism," in Therese Thau Heyman, *Seeing Straight: The f.64 Revolution in Photography* (Oakland, Calif., 1992), 34–41. For the photo essay, see Maitland Edey, *Great Photographic Essays from Life* (Boston, 1978), 37–38. For repatriation, see Abraham Hoffman, *Unwanted Mexican Americans in the Great Depression: Repatriation Pressures, 1929–1939* (Tucson, Ariz., 1974).

22. Jonathan Spaulding, *Ansel Adams and the American Landscape: A Biography* (Berkeley, 1995), 70–91, 117–21; Jonathan Spaulding, "The Natural Scene and the Social Good: The Artistic Education of Ansel Adams," *Pacific Historical Review* 110 (February 1991): 15–42; Mary Street Alinder and Andrea Gray Stillman, eds., *Ansel Adams: Letters and Images* (Boston, 1988); Ansel Adams, *Ansel Adams, an Autobiography,* edited by Mary Street Alinder (Boston, 1996), 64–77. For information on the San Francisco art scene in the late 1920s, see Lawrence Ferlingetti and Nancy J. Peters, *Literary San Francisco* (San Francisco, 1980); and Kenneth Rexroth, *An Autobiographcal Novel* (New York, 1978).

23. Adams exposed ten negatives, each measuring 3¼ × 4¼ inches. These negatives are very thin, suggesting they were in a film pack. Although in a letter to me Adams stated his belief that the negatives had been destroyed in a darkroom fire, they are preserved in the Ansel Adams Collection (AG 31), Center for Creative Photography, University of Arizona, Tucson. Mary Street Alinder (to Richard Steven Street, January 28, 1981, author's possession) describes the commission by Mrs. Charles Felton. According to Alinder, Adams did not meet Taylor until 1935 and did not see the text for the article until after it had appeared with his images. See also Therese Heyman, "Ansel Adams Remembers Dorothea Lange," in Elizabeth Partridge, ed., *Dorothea Lange: A Visual Life* (Washington, D.C., 1994), 155. This phase of Adams's work is not mentioned in any of his biographies. Nor do his biographers devote much space to his subsequent photographic work among farmworkers, largely for California wineries and corporate farms, extending over the next thirty years.

24. To follow the work Adams did among farmworkers, consult the Ansel Adams Collection, Center for Creative Photography, especially his commercial work at El Solyo Ranch in 1950, and Ansel Adams to Otto E. Meyer at Paul Masson Vineyards, February 28, 1963, delineating his work photographing the Paul Masson Winery in 1960. See also Street, interview with Pirkle Jones, April 15, 2003, Mill Valley, California, author's possession; Kent Kay, "Photographers Tell Story of a Winery," *San Francisco Chronicle,* June 9, 1960; Elsa Gridlow, "The Story of a Winery," in *U.S. Camera Annual, 1963* (New York, 1963), 40–51; and Robert Lawrence Balzar, *This Uncommon Heritage: The Paul Masson Story* (Los Angeles, 1963), especially 38, 41, 81.

25. Quotes from Janis and MacNeil, eds., *Photography within the Humanities,* 27; and Street, interview with Paul S. Taylor, March 23, 1981, Berkeley, California, author's possession. It should be noted here that Adams would make another contribution to the photographic study of California farmworkers by developing hundreds of negatives for Dorothea Lange between 1935 and 1940. For Taylor's photographs among the San Francisco longshoremen, see Paul S. Taylor and Norman Leon Gold, "San Francisco General Strike," *Survey Graphic* 23 (September 1934): 405–11. For Adams, see Adams to Edward Weston, November 29, 1934, Ansel Adams Collection, Center for Creative Photography.

26. Quote from Riess, "Paul S. Taylor: California Social Scientist," 1: 238–238A. For a discussion of the term *documentary photography,* see Robert Coles, *Doing Documentary Work* (New York, 1997), 5; Mary Ellen Mark, "Streetwise Photographer," in Ken Light, ed., *Witness in Our Time: Working Lives of Documentary Photographers* (Washington, D.C., 2000), 81, 107; Riess, "Dorothea

Lange: The Making of a Documentary Photographer," 155, 159; and Stott, *Documentary Expression and Thirties America,* 5–17, 20–21.

27. Paul S. Taylor and Clark Kerr, "Uprisings on the Farms," *Survey Graphic* 24 (January 1935): 19–22, 44.

28. Quote from Hansel Mieth Hagel, "The Woman," MS, n.d., 22, Otto and Hansel Mieth Hagel Collection, Center for Creative Photography, University of Arizona, Tucson. See also Grace Schaub, "Hansel Mieth and Otto Hagel: A Story of Love, Commitment and Search for Truth," *Photographer's Forum* 17 (November 1994): 26; and Dolores Flamiano, "Too Human for Life: Hansel Mieth's Photographs of Heart Mountain Internment Camp," *Visual Communication Quarterly* 11 (Summer–Autumn 2004): 4–17.

29. Quotes from "Otto Hagel and Hansel Mieth," in Center for Creative Photography, *Reframing America* (Tucson, Ariz., 1995), 30; and Street, interview with Hansel Mieth Hagel, January 9, 1980, Santa Rosa, California, author's possession. See also John Loengard, "Hansel Mieth," in Loengard, *Life Photographers: What They Saw* (New York, 1998), 75; and in Otto and Hansel Mieth Hagel, Declassified FBI Files, FOIPA no. 981877: Report, May 13, 1949, San Francisco, file no. 65–2427, Espionage, 9; and San Francisco Agent to Director, FBI, December 13, 1951, enclosures; all in author's possession.

30. David Mellor, ed., *Germany: The New Photography, 1927–1933* (London, 1978).

31. For German 35-millimeter press photography at this time, see Leah Ollman, "The Worker Photography Movement: Camera as Weapon," in Younger, ed., *Multiple Views,* 236–37; Leah Ollman, *Camera as Weapon: Worker Photography between the Wars* (San Diego, Calif., 1991); and John Font, "The Berliner Illustrirte and Photojournalism in Germany, 1929–1935," in Catskill Center for Photography, *Picture Magazines before Life* (New York, 1982), 1–5.

32. Kim Sichel, *Germaine Krull: Photographer of Modernity* (Cambridge, Mass., 1999), xxii, 16–40; Inge Bondi, *Chim: The Photographs of David Seymour,* foreword by Cornell Capa, intro. by Henri Cartier-Bresson (Boston, 1996), 19–20; Terrence Pitts, "Reframing America," in Center for Creative Photography, *Reframing America,* 15–16, 50; Richard Whelan, *Robert Capa* (New York, 1985), 27–58; Jan Herz and Dirk Halfbridt, *Fotografie und Revolution: München 1918/19* (Munich, 1988); Daniel D. Mich, "The Rise of Photojournalism in the United Sates," *Journalism Quarterly* 24 (September 1947): 205; Sandra J. Phillips, "The *Berliner Illustrirte, Vogue,* and *Vu:* Pictorial Magazines in Europe before World War II," in Martin Taureg and Jay Ruby, eds., *Visual Explorations of the World* (London, 1985), 140–66; Keran Becker, "Forming a Profession: Ethical Implications of Photojournalistic Practice on German Picture Magazines, 1926–1933," *Studies in Visual Communication* 11 (1985): 44–60; Sandra J. Phillips, "The French Picture Magazine *Vu,*" *Studies in Visual Communication* 11 (1985): 6–9; John Four, "The *Berliner Illustrirte* and Photojournalism in Germany, 1929–1935," in Catskill Center for Photography, *Picture Magazines before Life* (Woodstock, N.Y., 1982); Street, interview with Vilem Kriz, May 2, 1983, Berkeley, author's possession.

33. Zoe C. Smith, "Émigré Photography in America: Contributions of German Photojournalism from Black Star Picture Agency to *Life Magazine,* 1933–1938," PhD diss., University of Iowa, 1983; Gisele Freund, *The World in My Camera* (New York, 1974); Gisele Freund, *Photography and Society* (Boston, 1980); Whelan, *Robert Capa,* 17–18.

34. Otto's trip across the Atlantic Ocean and adventures as a window washer are described in E. K. T. [Edward K. Thompson] to Hansel Hagel, n.d., Otto and Hansel Mieth Hagel Collection, Center for Creative Photography. Although many publications place Otto's photograph of himself as a window washer in New York City and date it to 1929, various buildings and scenes in the image definitively place it in San Francisco. See *Window Cleaner, Self-Portrait, 1928,* "Old Ermanox Camera," Photographic Materials: Special Negatives, Otto and Hansel Mieth Hagel Collection, Center for Creative Photography. Adding to the confusion, Hansel dated the image as 1929 in

"Deed of Gift," June 27, 1992, *Window Washer, PG&E Building, San Francisco, 1929.* For Otto's employment with Crosetti and his uncle Roth, see San Francisco Office of the FBI, Espionage-R, April 12, 1951, enclosures, 11–12, file no. 65-2427, Declassified FBI Files; E. K. T. [Edward K. Thompson] to Hansel, n.d., Otto and Hansel Mieth Hagel Collection, Center for Creative Photography; and Grace Schaub, "Hansel Mieth and Otto Hagel: Never Just Art," *View Camera* (January–February 1996): 20–27.

35. Quote from Loengard, "Hansel Mieth," 77. See also Mieth Hagel, "The Woman," 22.

36. Loengard, "Hansel Mieth," 77. Hansel's cousin, the daughter of her aunt Victoria Golle, recalled a different version of Hansel's cross-country trip. Interviewed in 1950 by the FBI as part of an investigation into Hansel's alleged communist sympathies, she stated that Hansel had stayed with her mother for two weeks, only to leave suddenly for California by Greyhound bus. See Report Made at Philadelphia, October 27, 1950, Espionage, file no. 65-4239; Report Made at Baltimore, Maryland, June 30, 1949, Espionage, file no. 65-1672; Report Made at San Francisco, n.d. [September 1950], and enclosures, file 65-2427; all in Declassified FBI Files, San Francisco Office of the FBI.

37. Quotes from Hansel Mieth Hagel to Sally Stein, September 28, 1978, Otto and Hansel Mieth Hagel Collection, Center for Creative Photography. The arrest story is from E. K. T. [Edward K. Thompson] to Hansel, n.d., Otto and Hansel Mieth Hagel Collection, Center for Creative Photography. See also Schaub, "Hansel Mieth and Otto Hagel: Never Just Art"; Schaub, "Hansel Mieth and Otto Hagel: A Story of Love, Commitment and Search for Truth"; and Street, interview with Hansel Mieth Hagel, January 9, 1980, Santa Rosa, California, author's possession.

38. Street, interview with Hansel Mieth Hagel, August 12, 1983, Santa Rosa, California, author's possession; Ellen Liebman, *California Farmland: A History of Large Agricultural Landholdings* (Totowa, N.J., 1983), 111–13.

39. "On the Life and Work of Otto Hagel and Hansel Mieth as Narrated by Hansel Mieth," *Left Curve* 13 (1988): 12; Tom Brandon, interview with Mrs. Hansel Hagel, December 7, 1974, 8, Otto and Hansel Mieth Hagel Collection, Center for Creative Photography; Ken Light, "Hansel Mieth: The Depression and the Early Days of Life," in Light, ed., *Witness in Our Time,* 18. See also Bob Sylva, "Harsh Light: The Stark Days of Sacramento and the Depression Are Frozen Forever in Hansel Mieth and Otto Hagel's Photographs," *Sacramento Bee,* May 2, 1994.

40. *Sacramento Bee,* November 3–7, 1932; Irving Bernstein, *The Turbulent Years: A History of the American Worker, 1933–1941* (Boston, 1971), 149–52; Stuart E. Jamieson, *Labor Unionism in American Agriculture,* U.S. Bureau of Labor Statistics Bulletin no. 836 (Washington, D.C., 1945), 81–95.

41. Quotes from "On the Life and Work of Otto Hagel and Hansel Mieth as Narrated by Hansel Mieth," 12; Tom Brandon, interview with Mrs. Hansel Hagel, December 7, 1974, 8; and Mieth Hagel, "The Woman," 6–7; all in the Otto and Hansel Mieth Hagel Collection, Center for Creative Photography. See also Light, "Hansel Mieth," 18; and Street, interview with Hansel Mieth Hagel, August 12, 1983, author's possession.

42. Quote from Hansel Mieth Hagel to Naomi Rosenblum, April 30, 1987, Otto and Hansel Mieth Hagel Collection, Center for Creative Photography. See also Street, interview with Sally Stein, April 2, 1999, Del Mar, California, author's possession.

43. Quote from Hansel Mieth Hagel, "Toward Clarification—a Question of Reality" MS, December 7, 1966, 142–43, Otto and Hansel Mieth Hagel Collection, Center for Creative Photography. See also Mieth Hagel, "The Woman," 6–7.

6. Photography and the Great Depression

1. Michael McCabe, "A Life in Pictures," *San Francisco Chronicle,* This World section, March 27, 1994, 8–11; Mary McChesney, interview with Hansel Mieth Hagel, October 8, 1964, 12, Archives

of American Art, Smithsonian Institution; Alexander Alland, *Reframing America* (Tucson, Ariz., 1995), 30.

2. I have not been able to find the Ermanox negatives, along with much work from 1930–33, despite a complete sifting of their archive. See "Old Ermanox Camera," Otto and Hansel Mieth Hagel Collection, Center for Creative Photography, University of Arizona, Tucson. Any surviving material may have been lost in several burglaries to their apartments in the early 1930s and in a fire at their Santa Rosa ranch in the early 1950s. See Rosenblum, *A World History of Photography,* 603–4.

3. Hicks, *Words and Pictures,* 29–32; Erich Salomon, *Portrait einer Epoche* (New York, 1963); Van Deren Coke, *Avant Garde Photography in Germany, 1991–1939* (New York, 1982), 39–40.

4. Because lenses for 35-millimeter cameras did not have to be very large in diameter in relation to the small negative size, they could sustain very fast shutter speeds and larger apertures useful in working under dim light. See Loengard, "Hansel Mieth," in Loengard, *Life Photographers,* 76; Tom Brandon, interview with Hansel Mieth Hagel, December 7, 1974, unedited transcript, 11, Otto and Hansel Mieth Hagel Collection, Center for Creative Photography.

5. Quotes from Brandon, interview with Mieth Hagel, December 7, 1974, 11, Otto and Hansel Mieth Hagel Collection, Center for Creative Photography; Light, "Hansel Mieth," 19; Street, interview with Hansel Mieth Hagel, August 12, 1983, Santa Rosa, California, author's possession; Nancy Schiesari, *Hansel Mieth: Vagabond Photographer,* video (Independent Lens Television, 2003). I have found no evidence of any foreman ever using a whip at this time or at any other time.

6. Quotes from Light, "Hansel Mieth," 19; Brandon, interview with Hansel Mieth Hagel, December 7, 1974, 11–12, Otto and Hansel Mieth Hagel Collection, Center for Creative Photography. Because they lacked a proper negative carrier, Otto and Hansel found it difficult to print the small negatives shot with their Leica and Ermanox. "We tried to construct one," recalled Hansel, "but it was hard to keep them (the negatives) in place." See "Photographic Materials: Special Negatives," Otto and Hansel Mieth Hagel Collection, Center for Creative Photography.

7. For the El Monte berry pickers' strike, see Ronald López, "The El Monte Berry Strike of 1933," *Aztlan: Chicano Journal of the Social Sciences and the Arts* 1 (Spring 1970): 101–14; Abraham Hoffman, "The El Monte Berry Pickers' Strike, 1933: International Involvement in a Labor Dispute," *Journal of the West* 12 (January 1973): 71–84; and Gilbert G. González, *Mexican Consuls and Labor Organizing: Imperial Politics in the American Southwest* (Austin, Tex., 1999), 82–121. For the number of strikes, see Jamieson, *Labor Unionism in American Agriculture,* 39.

8. Quote from clipping, *Experimental Cinema,* February 1931, Otto and Hansel Mieth Hagel Collection, Center for Creative Photography. For the Film and Photo League, see Leah Ollman, "The Photo League's Forgotten Past," *History of Photography* 18 (April–June 1994): 73–86; Russell Campbell, *Cinema Strikes Back: Radical Filmmaking in the United States, 1930–1942* (Ann Arbor, Mich., 1982); Anne Tucker, "The Photo League," *Modern Photography* 43 (September 1979): 88–92, 173–84; Anne Tucker, "Photographic Crossroads: The Photo League," *Afterimage* 5 (April 1978): 2, 6–8; William Alexander, *Film on the Left: American Documentary Film from 1931 to 1942* (Princeton, N.J., 1981), 17–18; Neil C. Trager, "The Curators," in State University of New York, *The Photo League, 1936–1951* (New York, n.d.), 5; and Lili Corbus Bezner, *Photography and Politics in America: From the New Deal into the Cold War* (Baltimore, 1999), 33.

9. The Los Angeles Film and Photo League is obscure. Its members often used aliases. Apparently the league consisted of two groups. One was centered in Boyle Heights, the "Jewish East Los Angeles." The other, which worked out of Hollywood, was composed mostly of actors and film industry members. Siminow was affiliated with the East Los Angeles group. See Sarah Cooper to Richard Steven Street, April 22, 1993, author's possession; and Carla Leshne, e-mail to author, November 14, 2002, author's possession. For the Film and Photo League film on the El Monte strike, see *El Monte Berry Pickers' Strike* (1933), Southern California Library for Social Studies and

Research, Los Angeles, California. Not a documentary, the twenty-minute film was more accurately described as a dramatization. It lists no credits. Some evidence indicates that the Hollywood group attempted to produce a film on the Imperial Valley melon workers but failed to finish it. Seymour Stern produced and directed this film. See Leshne, e-mail to author, November 6, 2002, author's possession; and Leshne, "The Worker's Film and Photo League in California," MS, 2002, 1–3, in Leshne's possession.

10. Starr, *Endangered Dreams,* 72. Glouck committed suicide, and police cleared strikers of any involvement. See also Lynn Burkett, interview with Carl Smith, June 12, 1977, John Steinbeck Library, Salinas, California; Norman Lowenstein, "Strikes and Strike Tactics in California Agriculture: A History," MA thesis, University of California, Berkeley, 1940, 86–89.

11. "Reds Deported," *Oakland Tribune,* October 6, 1933; "Mopping Up Lodi," *Stockton Record,* October 7, 1933; *Sacramento Bee,* October 5 and 6, 1933. See also Taylor and Kerr, "Uprisings on the Farms," 19–22, 44.

12. Mark Arax and Rick Wartzman, *The King of California: J. G. Boswell and the Making of a Secret American Empire* (New York, 2003), 150–57; Paul S. Taylor and Clark Kerr, "Documentary History of the Strike of the Cotton Pickers in California, 1933," in U.S. Congress, Senate, Subcommittee of the Committee on Education and Labor to Investigate Violations of the Right of Free Speech and Assembly and Interference with the Right of Labor to Organize and Bargain Collectively, *Hearings Pursuant to S. Res. 266,* "Violations of Free Speech and Rights of Labor," 74th Cong., 1st sess., 1940, appendix, exhibit 8764, part 54: 19994 (hereafter cited as LaFollette Committee Hearings).

13. Walter J. Stein, *California and the Dust Bowl Migration* (Westport, Conn., 1973); James M. Gregory, *American Exodus: The Dust Bowl Migration and Okie Culture in California* (New York, 1989); Donald Worster, *Dust Bowl: The Southern Plains in the 1930s* (New York, 1979).

14. Quotes from *San Francisco Chronicle,* October 11, 1933; and *San Francisco News,* October 11, 1933. See also Accession Papers, Corcoran Strike Photographs, October 1933, R. H. Powell Studio, Hanford, California, and Library of Congress; *La Opinion,* October 12, 13, 14, 1933; *Los Angeles Times,* October 11, 1933; and Taylor, *On the Ground in the Thirties.* At least one of the killings on October 10 was at the hand of cotton farmer Clarence "Cockeye" Salyer. A third striker, Pedro Subia, was killed in Arvin. See Arax and Wartzman, *The King of California,* 153–54.

15. "Federal and State Authorities in Move to End Cotton Picking Strike," *Bakersfield Californian,* October 12, 1933, credits NEA photographer Fred Smith with taking the photograph of growers and vigilantes beating up Pat Chambers in Pixley. Three images appear in the sequence. "When Opposing Factions Saw Red," *Sacramento Bee,* October 12, 1933, published the first two images of the dying striker but not the last one. See also *Los Angeles Times,* October 11, 1933; *San Francisco Chronicle,* October 13 and 15, 1933; *Modesto Bee,* October 12, 1933; *San Francisco Examiner,* October 12, 1933; and "Valley Strife Ended as Pickers Accept Compromise Pay Scale," *San Francisco News,* October 27, 1933. For the epistemology of death images, see Susan Sontag, *Regarding the Pain of Others* (New York, 2003), 59, 70.

16. *San Francisco Examiner,* October 12 and 13, 1933.

17. For Lew Hegg's work, see "State Seeks Strike Peace as 3 Die," *Fresno Bee,* October 10, 1933. I believe that all of the images in the layout illustrating "Strikers Set Up Corcoran Tent City" are by Ralph H. Powell. Anne Loftis to Lynn Bonfield, December 29, 1989, Otto and Hansel Mieth Hagel Collection, Center for Creative Photography, notes the similarity between frames from *Century of Progress* and certain still pictures appearing in Paul Taylor and Clark Kerr's documentary history of the cotton strike. While Otto Hagel could have sold many of his photographs for two or three dollars apiece to newspapers, he apparently had neither the connections necessary to market his images nor the darkroom facilities required to develop and print his work in time to meet newspaper deadlines.

18. In Powell's description of the Cirkut print, the length is actually the width and the width is the height; that is, the print was panoramic. And although Powell referred to the camp as the Pixley camp, it was in fact the Corcoran camp. Quotes from Powell to author, June 12, 1980, author's collection. For Powell's family history, see clipping, obituary, *Fresno Bee,* n.d., Ben Walker Collection, Fresno County Historical Society, Fresno. Illustrating dozens of histories and government reports and published again and again over the next half century, Powell's photographs appear without attribution in McWilliams, *Factories in the Field,* after page 219; Weber, *Dark Sweat, White Gold,* cover and after page 136; Ann Loftis, *Witness to the Struggle: Imaging the 1930s California Labor Movement* (Reno, Nev., 1998), cover, 27; and Daniel, *Bitter Harvest,* after page 196. I obtained prints of Powell's original negatives from his brother. The Powell photographs deposited in the Prints and Photographs Division, Library of Congress, attribute the images to the International News Service (INS), which apparently distributed Powell's images to the newspapers.

19. Quote from Street, interview with Ralph H. Powell, January 27, 1981, Hanford, California, author's possession. I photographed Powell in his studio at the conclusion of the interview.

20. Quote from ibid. See also clipping, "Strikers Set Up Corcoran Tent City," *Fresno Bee,* October 10, 1933, Paul Taylor Papers, Bancroft Library. Camp condition description from *San Francisco Call-Bulletin,* October 16, 1933. For Bañales, see Weber, *Dark Sweat, White Gold,* figure 4.

21. *San Francisco Examiner,* October 14, 1933. Although Loftis, *Witness to the Struggle,* 26, suggests this was taken by an *Examiner* photographer, it was actually R. H. Powell's photograph. Exactly how the *Examiner* obtained it is a mystery. Powell could not recall selling it to the *Examiner,* although he acknowledged that was his practice. On the reverse of the Bancroft Library photograph *We Want Food,* the Powell Studio stamp appears along with a handwritten description: "A crowd of young Mexican women out for the picket lines. There [*sic*] sure fighters when they get mad. Some are educated." See BANC PIC 1945.0007:4-PIC.

22. Malca Chall, "Paul Taylor: California Social Scientist; California Water and Agricultural Labor," oral interview, Regional Oral History Project, 1975, 2: 1–4, Bancroft Library. See also Taylor and Kerr, "Uprisings on the Farms," 19–22, publishing a picture of the attack on Pat Chambers. The photographs that Taylor collected have been transferred from the Paul Taylor Material relating to Agricultural and Maritime Strikes in California Collection to the photographic collection under the heading Photographs relating to Agricultural Strikes in California, BANC PIC 1945.007-PIC. Neither Taylor nor Powell remembered the other when I interviewed them.

23. For Hansel Mieth recollections, see "On the Life and Work of Otto and Hansel Mieth as Narrated by Hansel Mieth," 12, Otto and Hansel Mieth Hagel Collection, Center for Creative Photography. In her oral memoirs many years later, Mieth somewhat confused the issue of who was where doing what in her recollection to Ken Light: "So many times in the cotton-picking picture, you see me either picking cotton or Otto doing the work amongst the other people. Or you see me standing out in a picture with a Rolleiflex up in the air to get a better view." Still photographs in the Hagel Collection depict these activities, but they appear to be from 1935 or later. Film shot in 1933 contains no scenes of either Otto or Hansel, although there is ample evidence that Otto shot film footage of the cotton strike. For Hansel's confusing recollections, see Light, "Hansel Mieth," 18.

24. For more on Balog, see Anne Tucker, interview with Lester Balog and Sam Brody, September 23, 1974, transcript in Department of Photography, the Museum of Fine Arts, Houston, Texas; San Francisco Office to FBI, October 30, 1951, Espionage-R, Internal Security Act of 1950, enclosures, 16, file no. 65-2427/65-4387, Declassified FBI Files.

25. Quotes from Brandon, interview with Hansel Mieth Hagel, December 7, 1974, 14, Otto and Hansel Mieth Hagel Collection, Center for Creative Photography.

26. Quote from Leslie Balog, comp., "Lester Balog," *Left Curve* 7 (1978): 16. When Balog spoke of getting the camera ready, it is unclear if he was referring to a movie or a still camera.

27. Quotes from ibid.; and Leshne, "The Worker's Film and Photo League in California," 6. Information on Decker is from Ella Winter, *And Not to Yield: An Autobiography* (New York, 1963), 186. I used a process of deduction to exclude Balog as the source of any photographs before October 11, because he was not on the scene until then and did not have a history of selling to newspapers and news services. I disagree with those scholars who believe that some of the unattributed images of the 1933 cotton strike published under the NEA logo before October 11 were by Otto Hagel or Hansel Mieth. This is possible only if those images were among the photographs that Hagel and Mieth lost in one of several burglaries they suffered in 1934 and 1935 or in a fire at the Hagels' home in the 1960s. They are not in the Otto and Hansel Mieth Hagel Collection, Center for Creative Photography. However, it is more likely that these images are by a *Fresno Bee, Sacramento Bee,* or *Stockton Bee* photographer, most likely Powell, because these newspapers had a relationship with the NEA and published Powell's work under the NEA logo. Most of the images used by Paul Taylor and Clark Kerr were probably shot by R. H. Powell. Paul Taylor often obtained photographs from other photographers, including Hagel and Mieth, and would later obtain Otto's negatives from his coverage of the 1936 Salinas Valley lettuce packers' strike.

28. Information on Hansel Mieth Hagel's loss of her child is from Street, interview with Sally Stein, March 23, 1999, San Diego, California, author's possession; Street, interview with Ken Light, May 12, 1997, Berkeley, California, author's possession; and Sally Stein, interview with Hansel Mieth Hagel, n.d. (ca. 1978), Otto and Hansel Mieth Hagel Collection, Center for Creative Photography. See also Susan Ehrens, "Hansel Mieth," *Photo Metro* 5 (May 1987): 5–9; and Horace Bristol, "Otto Hagel and Hansel Mieth: Two Unrecognized 'Greats,'" MS, June 20, 1986, courtesy of Horace Bristol, Ojai, California, in Bristol to Street, June 16, 1986, author's possession.

29. Quote from Dear Otto [1933], Otto and Hansel Mieth Hagel Collection, Center for Creative Photography. I have my doubts about this letter, which is written in Hansel's poststroke handwriting. Whether it is a postdated piece of history or an attempt to support her version of events by re-creating from memory something she had earlier written is impossible to say. Another problem with Hansel's version of events is her assertion that she refused to take any more photographs for at least a year after the tragedy, when the photographic record indicates that she was again shooting by the spring of 1934. A final problem with this account is that I was unable to find any reference to this tragedy in local newspapers from the period.

30. There is a mass of excellent information in Otto and Hansel Mieth Hagel's declassified FBI file no. 0981877-000/01. Montroni had his marriage to Mieth annulled on July 19, 1935. See, for example, San Francisco Office to FBI, April 12, 1951, Espionage-R, enclosures, 1–2, File 65-2427, Hagel Declassified FBI File.

31. Quote from Jesse Hamlin, "The Graphic Arts Workshop Presses Forward," *San Francisco Chronicle,* September 25, 2002. Slowly returning to photography, Hansel regained her courage, picked up her camera, and began photographing antifascist rallies, where she met photographers Dorothea Lange and Peter Stackpole. Paying particular attention to the slave market, where unemployed longshoremen crowded, hoping to be chosen for the few jobs available, Hansel made dramatic pictures of men jostling one another and extending their hands to receive a pass for a day's work. When the longshoremen's strike broke out, Otto and Hansel again used a 16-millimeter movie camera to record strike agitators and police activities. To process their film, they improvised a darkroom in the bedroom of their apartment, rented out the other room, and used the remaining space for editing and printing. See Light, "Hansel Mieth," 18. "Having been out in nature so long," Hansel later recalled, "we got claustrophobic and we actually put up a tent on the roof and lived on the top floor." Quote from Hansel Mieth Hagel to Tom Brandon, August 27, 1975, Otto and Hansel Mieth Hagel Collection, Center for Creative Photography. See also Hansel Mieth Hagel to Cornell Capa, March 6, 1975, Otto and Hansel Mieth Hagel Collection, Center for

Creative Photography. Powell can be seen photographing in the Hagel–Balog film footage when Hagel, Balog, and Powell photographed a striker blowing a bugle to call workers out of the fields. Toward the end of his life, Balog claimed most of the credit for the film, explaining in a letter to a film historian that "*Century of Progress* . . . was started in Chicago at the '33 World's Fair. Then a Milwaukee antifascist demonstration by yours truly. Next scenes of rusting heavy equipment and WPA [Works Progress Administration] pick and shovel project by Otto Hagel. Also by Hagel, a march in Sacramento. Finally my own stuff: the 1933 San Joaquin valley cotton strike." Transcribed letter courtesy of Carla Leshne. However, Hansel asserted on many occasions that Otto also shot footage at the strike and, in a letter to Cornell Capa, founder of the International Center for Photography, summarized Otto's work as "a fine two-reeler"—a description suggesting extensive filming over a long period of time. "We made the film of our own private resources, with financial help of others," Hansel emphasized in a letter to Brandon. See also Brandon, interview with Hansel Mieth Hagel, December 7, 1974, 14–15; and Hansel to Sir, May 17, 1976; both in Otto and Hansel Mieth Hagel Collection, Center for Creative Photography. The billboard shot in the film very closely resembles one by Dorothea Lange. Titled *The American Way,* it was taken along US Highway 99 in March 1937. This may indicate that Otto Hagel and Balog were still filming at that late date. For the San Francisco Workers School, see *Western Worker,* February 12 and December 11, 1934, and clippings provided by Carla Leshne, who has researched documentary filmmaking in the early 1930s and believes that *Century of Progress* was combined with a documentary farmworker film called *Migratory Worker,* which depicts events in 1932 and 1933. Leshne, e-mail to author, November 11, 2002, author's possession. Campbell, *Cinema Strikes Back,* mistakenly lists a 1938 documentary titled *Cotton Pickers' Strike* as a 1933 product of the Los Angeles Fim and Photo League.

32. "Organizers for Union of Mexican Field Workers," *Calexico Chronicle,* November 27, 1933; "Speakers Urge Mexicans to Unionize by Themselves," *Calexico Chronicle,* March 22, 1934; Jerome Wolfe, "The Imperial Valley as an Index of Agricultural Labor Relations in California," PhD diss., University of Southern California, 1964, 142. For background on Terrazas, see González, *Mexican Consuls and Labor Organizing,* 177–78.

33. Quote from Campbell MacCulloch to the NLRB, February 24, 1934, National Labor Relations Board Correspondence, Records of the Department of Labor, RG 25, National Archives. For photographs, see MacCulloch to B. M. Stern, February 24, 1934. I have not been able to locate the photographs MacCulloch referred to or determine who made them. See also Louis Bloch to Taylor, January 13, 1934, Taylor Papers, Bancroft Library; and Street, interview with Louis Bloch, March 12, 1974, San Francisco, California, author's possession.

34. Quotes from Guernsey Frazer to J. Edgar Hoover, April 11, 1935, Declassified FBI File 61-6742-3, Associated Farmers. Hoover wrote to the special agent in charge of the investigation, "With reference to Mr. Frazer's desire to obtain criminal records of known Communists from the Bureau files, you should diplomatically point out to Mr. Frazer that by statute this Bureau is permitted to furnish criminal records only to duly constituted law enforcement officers." Replying directly to Frazer, the special agent wrote, "At present time, there is no federal statute which makes it illegal to engage in the so-called Communistic or radical activities." Quotes from Hoover to Frazer, May 18, 1935; Hoover to special agent in charge, May 18, 1935; both in Declassified FBI File 61-6742-3.

35. Quote from Leshne, "Workers Film and Photo League," 10. For Balog's arrest, see R. L. Hill to Mrs. Y. Balog, July 19, 1934, in Balog, "Lester Balog," 18; "Communist Film Seized at Tulare: Pat Chambers Escapes after Presenting Show," *Visalia Times-Delta,* May 25, 1934; and *Western Worker,* June 18, 1934, courtesy of Carla Leshne. For deportation as a threat, see Taylor, *On the Ground in the Thirties,* 54. In Brandon's interview with Hansel Mieth Hagel, she described Otto and Balog traveling together and showing the film (Brandon, interview with Hansel Mieth Hagel, December 7, 1974, 13, Otto and Hansel Mieth Hagel Collection, Center for Creative Photography). Arrest

date is from San Francisco Office to FBI, October 30, 1951, Espionage-R, Internal Security Act of 1950, enclosures, 16, Declassified FBI Files 65-2427 and 65-4387.

36. "Arrest of Newsboy in Attempt to Halt Communist Papers," *Western Worker,* February 15, 1932; "Arrest of Tulare Worker's Book Shop Agent," *Western Worker,* January 15, 1934; "San Diego Police Raid Anti-Fascist Movie Showing," *Western Worker,* July 16, 1934.

37. Quotes from Hansel Mieth Hagel to Cornell Capa, March 6, 1975, Otto and Hansel Mieth Hagel Collection, Center for Creative Photography. According to Therese Thau Heyman, Sandra S. Phillips, and John Szarkowski, *Dorothea Lange: American Photographer* (San Francisco, 1994), 18, 38, Balog saved the film from the police raid on the Hagels' home. No sources are cited. Like all other accounts of the Hagels, this episode has subtle variations, including statements by Hansel that the film was taken from their car.

38. Quotes from Hansel Mieth Hagel to Cornell Capa, March 6, 1975, Otto and Hansel Mieth Hagel Collection, Center for Creative Photography. One copy of *Century of Progress* is in the Archives of Urban and Labor History, Wayne State University, Detroit, Michigan. See Margery S. Long to Richard Steven Street, October 29, 1980; and Thomas Featherstone to Richard Steven Street, October 30, 1980; both in author's possession. Video copies are in the Labor Archives Research Center, San Francisco State, and the Oakland Museum. For Balog, Hagel, and the Film and Photo League, see "Proposed Plan of Work," *Film Front* (March 15, 1935): 11; and Leshne, e-mail to author, November 6, 2003, author's possession. See also Hansel Mieth Hagel to Mr. Brandon, March 15, 1975; Hansel Mieth Hagel to Sir, May 17, 1976; Hansel Mieth Hagel to Marjorie Long, September 14, 1978; Leslie Balog to Marjory Long, January 4, 1979; and Marjory Long to Hansel Mieth Hagel, January 31, 1979; all in the Otto and Hansel Mieth Hagel Collection, Center for Creative Photography. In an interview with Grace Schaub, Hansel stated that Otto had filmed the San Francisco General Strike of 1934. See Schaub, "Hansel Mieth and Otto Hagel," 33, Otto and Hansel Mieth Hagel Collection, Center for Creative Photography. Balog had apparently shown *Century of Progress* as late as 1966, when a jam-packed meeting in Filipino Hall at Delano saw the film along with a second film on migrant farmworkers from the 1930s. See John Gregory Dunne, *Delano: The Story of the Grape Strike* (New York, 1968), 163. In a letter to Brandon, Hansel describes seeing two films, *Century of Progress* and *Migratory Workers,* which Brandon had forwarded for her viewing. I have not located the *Migratory Workers* film footage. See Hansel Mieth Hagel to Brandon, August 27, 1975, Otto and Hansel Mieth Hagel Collection, Center for Creative Photography.

39. I am not arguing that the FBI was acting in a documentary manner but rather that it had, inadvertently, created images with documentary value to later generations and that, in doing so, had become part of the ongoing debate over the changed uses of photography in farm labor disputes. For the Sacramento criminal syndicalism trials, see Marion Hardy, "The Politico-economic Implications of the Pat Chambers Criminal Syndicalism Trial," MA thesis, California State University, Sacramento, 1964, 34–37, 40, 116–18; and Ellen Lois Halcomb, "Efforts to Organize the Migrant Workers by the Cannery and Agricultural Workers' Industrial Union," MA thesis, California State University, Chico, 1963. I obtained Chambers's declassified FBI file and prison mug shots through an Freedom of Information Act request. See Allen H. McCreight to Richard Steven Street, June 5, July 28, August 16, September 28, and October 11, 1978, and September 20, 1979, all in author's possession.

40. Tout, *The First Thirty Years in Imperial Valley,* 375–76. As mentioned in chapter 4, Hetzel's collection is in the Imperial Valley Historical Society, Pioneers Museum, Imperial, California.

41. Charles N. Wollenberg, review of Charles Shindo, *Dust Bowl Migrants and the American Imagination* (Lawrence, Kans., 1997), in *Pacific Historical Review* 67 (December 1998): 639–40. See also Shindo, *Dust Bowl Migrants and the American Imagination,* 2, 7–9, 218; John Berger, *About Looking* (New York, 1980); and Sontag, *Regarding the Pain of Others,* 117, 119.

42. Only now, looking back over a story thought to be understood, have historians begun to revise their view of social documentary photography among farmworkers in California as a New Deal offshoot, tied specifically to developing state liberalism and related reform movements, to see it more as a process that had diverse roots and had been under way in the state for perhaps a decade.

43. Loengard, "Hansel Mieth," in Loengard, ed., *Life Photographers,* 77.

44. For Lange's evolution as a photographer prior to her FSA work, see Van Dyke, "The Photographs of Dorothea Lange," 462–67. Taylor considered Van Dyke's essay the best single piece ever written on Lange. See Riess, "Paul S. Taylor: California Social Scientist," 1: 123.

7. Facing People as Human Beings

1. Quote from Van Dyke, "The Photographs of Dorothea Lange," 462. See also Leslie Calmes, *The Letters between Edward Weston and Willard Van Dyke* (Tucson, Ariz., 1992), 22–23, 57; Michel Oren, "On the 'Impurity' of Group f/64 Photography," *History of Photography* 15 (Summer 1991): 119–27; and Heyman, *Seeing Straight.*

2. Sackman, *Orange Empire,* 182–83.

3. Quote from Robert Coles, *Dorothea Lange: Photographs of a Lifetime,* Aperture Monograph (Millerton, N.Y., 1982), 9.

4. Riess, "Dorothea Lange: The Making of a Documentary Photographer," 78–92; Riess, "Paul S. Taylor: California Social Scientist," 1: 225; Van Deren Coke, *Photography in New Mexico: From the Daguerreotype to the Present,* foreword by Beaumont Newhall (Albuquerque, N.M., 1979), 24; Beaumont Newhall and Nancy Newhall, *Masters of Photography* (New York, 1958), 10; George P. Elliot, *Dorothea Lange* (New York, 1966), 9; and Joan Murry, "Looking at Lange Today," *Art Week* 9 (July 1978): 1–3.

5. Wesley M. Burnside, *Maynard Dixon: Artist of the West* (Provo, Utah, 1974), 126–28; Patricia Janis Broder, *The American West: The Modern Vision* (New York, 1984); Donald J. Haggerty, *The Art and Life of Maynard Dixon* (New York, 1993); Riess, "Dorothea Lange: Making of a Documentary Photographer," 94–123.

6. Quote from Coles, *Dorothea Lange,* 14. See also Melton Meltzer, *Dorothea Lange: A Photographer's Life* (New York, 1978), 3–78; and Riess, "Dorothea Lange: Making of a Documentary Photographer," 104–6, 138–39, 140.

7. Starr, *Endangered Dreams,* 84–85; Starr, *The Dream Endures,* 118–19.

8. Quotes from Riess, "Dorothea Lange: Making of a Documentary Photographer," 144–46, also 150–67. See also Sally Stein, "Starting from Pictorialism: Notable Continuities in the Modernization of California," in Johnson, ed., *Capturing Light,* 128; Arthur Miller, *Maynard Dixon: Painter of the West* (San Francisco, 1945), 3; and Street, interview with Paul Taylor, January 21, 1981, Berkeley, California, author's possession.

9. Quote from Riess, "Dorothea Lange: Making of a Documentary Photographer," 147. See also Meltzer, *Dorothea Lange,* 80–82.

10. Quote from Riess, "Dorothea Lange: Making of a Documentary Photographer," 150.

11. Quote from Meltzer, *Dorothea Lange,* 77–78. See also Riess, "Paul S. Taylor: California Social Scientist," 1: 222.

12. Quote from Riess, "Dorothea Lange: Making of a Documentary Photographer," 149. See also Mike Quinn, *The Big Strike* (San Francisco, 1949); Charles P. Larrowe, "The Great Maritime Strike of '34," *Labor History* 11 (Fall 1970): 403–51, and 12 (Winter 1971): 337; and Bruce Nelson, *Workers on the Waterfront: Seamen, Longshoremen, and Unionism in the 1930s* (New York, 1988).

13. Quote from Riess, "Dorothea Lange: Making of a Documentary Photographer," 151. See also Meltzer, *Dorothea Lange,* 78; and Riess, "Paul S. Taylor: California Social Scientist," 1: 222.

14. Quotes from Van Dyke, "The Photographs of Dorothea Lange," 461–62; Newhall and Newhall, *Masters of Photography,* 140; and Riess, "Paul S. Taylor: California Social Scientist," 1: 112, also 122. See also Beaumont Newhall, "Historians, Curators, Dealers," in Judy Dater, ed., *Imogen Cunningham: A Portrait* (New York, 1979), 91; and Street, interviews with Rondal Partridge (Imogen Cunningham's son), March 12, 1975, July 6, 1998, Berkeley, author's possession.

15. Quote from Riess, "Paul S. Taylor: California Social Scientist," 1: 112, also 154, 222. See also Burnside, *Maynard Dixon,* 67, 26–28; Elliot, *Dorothea Lange,* 6–9; F. Jack Hurley, *Portrait of a Decade: Roy Stryker and the Development of Documentary Photography in the Thirties* (Baton Rouge, La., 1972), 52, 72; Edith Hamlin, "Maynard Dixon, Artist of the West," *California Historical Quarterly* 103 (Winter 1974): 365–68; and Lou Maclean, "Portrait of a Liberal," *People's World,* October 19, 1939. *Survey Graphic* ran Lange's image with its own caption, "Workers of the World, Unite!" which gave the image a twist that caused Lange to reflect on the importance of captioning and retaining control over identifying information. See Paul S. Taylor and Norman L. Gold, "San Francisco and the General Strike," *Survey Graphic* 23 (September 1934): 404–11.

16. Quotes from Riess, "Paul S. Taylor: California Social Scientist," 1: 120–25. See also Paul Hill and Thomas Cooper, *Dialogue with Photography* (New York, 1979), 302; Annegret Ogden, "Dorothea Lange on Documentary Photography v. Photojournalism," *Californians* 3 (March–April 1985): 7–10; and Clark Kerr, "Productive Enterprises of the Unemployed," PhD diss., 4 vols. University of California, Berkeley, 1949.

17. Quote from Riess, "Dorothea Lange: Making of a Documentary Photographer," 1: 166.

18. Quotes from ibid., 1: 25, 126, 142. See also J. Hauss, "Unemployed, 1933, Model," *Nation* 173 (November 8, 1933): 541; SERA, "Migratory Labor," 1935; SERA, "Unemployment Relief," 1935; SERA, "Transients in California," 1936; all SERA documents located in Bancroft Library and California State Archives.

19. Quote from Riess, "Paul S. Taylor: California Social Scientist," 1: 142. See also Irving Stone, ed., *Let There Be Light: Autobiography of a University Berkeley: 1868–1968* (New York, 1970), 40.

20. Quotes from Riess, "Paul S. Taylor: California Social Scientist," 1: 127–29. See also Alan Temko, "Walter Packard: Land, Water, and Power Development in California, Greece, and Latin America," Regional Oral History Project, 1970, 306–12, Bancroft Library.

21. Duncan Aikman, "California Sunshine," *Nation* 132 (April 22, 1931): 448–50; Lillian Creisler, "Little Oklahoma: A Study of the Social and Economic Adjustments of Refugee in the Beard Tract, Modesto, Stanislaus County," MA thesis, University of California, Berkeley, 1940; Albert Croutch, "Housing Migratory Agricultural Workers in California, 1913–1948," MA thesis, University of California, Berkeley, 1948.

22. James E. Siedel, *Pick for Your Supper* (New York, 1939); Farm Security Administration, *A Study of 6,655 Migrant Households in California* (San Francisco, 1939); Ruth A. Molander, "A Study of 101 Migrant Families Receiving Assistance under the Regulations of the California Aid-to-Needy Children Law in Kern County in June 1940," MA thesis, University of California, Berkeley, 1943.

23. Quotes from Riess, "Paul S. Taylor: California Social Scientist," 1: 130, also 175.

24. *California Blue Book or State Roster* (Sacramento, 1932), 736. See also Myron Angel, *History of San Luis Obispo County, California, with Illustrations and Biographical Sketches of Its Prominent Men and Pioneers* (Oakland, Calif., 1883), 11, 51, 64, 67, 102, 107, 129, 132, 133, 217–18, 242, 301, 321; Daniel Krieger, *San Luis Obispo County: Looking Backward into the Middle Kingdom* (San Luis Obispo, Calif., 1990), 63, 83; Judy Walker, "The Historical Heritage of Nipomo," MA thesis, California State Polytechnic University, San Luis Obispo, 1965; Laura C. Abele, *Jens and Mette Jensen: Their Family Record from Denmark to California* (Los Alimitos, Calif., 1997); and Ronald Nye, "The Challenge to Philanthropy: Unemployment Relief in Santa Barbara, 1930–1932," *California Historical Society Quarterly* 56 (Winter 1977–78): 310–27.

25. Quotes from Riess, "Paul S. Taylor: California Social Scientist," 1: 130, 2: 23. See also Zoe Brown, "Dorothea Lange: Field Notes and Photographs, 1935–1940," MA thesis, John F. Kennedy University, 1979, 1: 68, copy in the Dorothea Lange Collection, Oakland Museum (volume 1 is an analysis of Lange's field notes; volume 2 is a transcription); Dorothea Lange, "Lucretia Penny: Pea-Picker's Child," *Survey Graphic* 24 (July 1935): 352–53; and Lowry Nelson to Paul V. Maris, Weekly Report for Week Ending February 16, 1935, Harry Hopkins Papers, Franklin D. Roosevelt Library, Hyde Park, New York.

26. Riess, "Paul S. Taylor: California Social Scientist," 1: 134.

27. Quotes from Meltzer, *Dorothea Lange,* 97; and Riess, "Dorothea Lange: Making of a Documentary Photographer," 156, 158, 163.

28. Quotes from Riess, "Dorothea Lange: Making of a Documentary Photography," 161. I have been unable to identify the Mexican woman Lange referred to or to track down the life-histories the woman compiled. These would be extremely valuable, if not a gold mine of information, useful in re-creating the situation at Nipomo.

29. Quote from Partridge, ed., *Dorothea Lange,* 114. Coverley concluded a report on the trip by describing housing conditions as "squalid" and calling for more sanitary labor camps. Harvey Coverley, "Report on Investigation of Housing Conditions for Agricultural Workers in Coachella Valley from Feb. 27 to March 3, 1935," March 7, 1935, Irving R. Wood Papers, Bancroft Library.

30. Quotes from Stott, *Documentary Expression,* 228–29; Riess, "Paul S. Taylor: California Social Scientist," 1: 134, also 149; and Janis and MacNeil, eds., *Photography within the Humanities,* 31. See also Karin Becker Ohrn, *Dorothea Lange and the Documentary Tradition* (Baton Rouge, La., 1980), 56, 72, also 233.

31. Quote from Meltzer, *Dorothea Lange,* 97.

32. Quotes from Riess, "Paul S. Taylor: California Social Scientist," 1: 131, 132, 178, also 177. See also Rondal Partridge's recollection in Meltzer, *Dorothea Lange,* 167.

33. Quote from entry for February 22, 1935, in Brown, "Dorothea Lange: Field Notes and Photographs," 2: 375, 379.

34. This photograph, taken in 1935, has also been dated February 1936. See Heyman, Phillips, and Szarkowski, eds., *Dorothea Lange: American Photographer,* 188. Both Loftis, *Witness to the Struggle,* 135, and Coles, *Doing Documentary Work,* 106–9, discuss this image and Lange's cropping. Both date it as 1935, as does Meltzer, *Dorothea Lange,* 201. See also Stein, *California and the Dust Bowl Migration,* 81–82.

35. Quote from Riess, "Dorothea Lange: Making of a Documentary Photographer," 202–3. See also Meltzer, *Dorothea Lange,* 201–2; and Mark Hawoth-Booth, *Paul Strand* (New York, 1974), 34.

36. Linda Jones Gibbs, *Escape to Reality: The Western World of Maynard Dixon* (Provo, Utah, 2002), 150; Donald J. Haggerty, "Maynard Dixon and the Changing West, 1917–1935," *Montana* 51 (Summer 2001): 36–51; Hamlin, "Maynard Dixon, Artist of the West," 365–68; Edith Hamlin, "Maynard Dixon: Painter of the West," *American West* 19 (November–December 1982): 50–60; Grant Wallace, *Maynard Dixon,* WPA Project no. 2874 (San Francisco, 1937), 82.

37. Quote from John Szarkowski, "Dorothea Lange and Paul Taylor," in Heyman, Phillips, and Szarkowski, eds., *Dorothea Lange: American Photographer,* 53.

38. Quotes from Reiss, "Dorothea Lange: Making of a Documentary Photographer," 122–23. See also Street, interview with John Collier Jr., March 23, 1980, Muir Beach, California; Street, interview with Winona Tomanocz, May 12, 1978, San Francisco, California; both in author's possession. Although I generally agree with the portrait of Lange and Taylor's evolving relationship that is developed in Meltzer, *Dorothea Lange,* 125–27, the theory about Taylor bending to her will, as he had supposedly bent to his mother's, and the suggestion that the relationship between Taylor and

Lange was anything less that a partnership of equals are at variance with the observations of many who knew Taylor and Lange as a married couple.

39. Quote from Taylor, "Notes from the Field," in Drobish to McLaughlin, March 15, 1935, lot 879, Prints and Photographs, Library of Congress. See also Harry Drobish Papers, Bancroft Library; Riess, "Dorothea Lange: Making of a Documentary Photographer," 175; Riess, "Paul S. Taylor: California Social Scientist," 1: 138.

40. Quote from Taylor, "Establishment of Rural Rehabilitation Camps for Migrants in California," 5, in Harry Drobish to Frank McLaughlin, March 15, 1935, lot 879, Prints and Photographs Division, Library of Congress.

41. Ibid.

42. Quotes from ibid.; and Riess, "Paul S. Taylor: California Social Scientist," 1: 212, 138–39, also 207–8. See also Janis MacNeil, eds., *Photography within the Humanities,* 29; Harry Drobish, "A Review of Steps Taken in the Development of the Program for Farm Laborers," n.d., Harry Drobish Papers, Bancroft Library; and Croutch, "Housing Migratory Agricultural Workers in California, 1913–1948."

43. Quotes from Riess, "Paul S. Taylor: California Social Scientist," 1: 128, also 126, 142, 145, 180, 212.

8. Under the Most Trying Conditions

1. Quote from Riess, "Paul S. Taylor: California Social Scientist," 1: 214, also 222. See also Partridge, ed., *Dorothea Lange,* 41.

2. Quote from Riess, "Dorothea Lange: Making of a Documentary Photographer," 175; and Richard K. Doud, interview with Dorothea Lange, May 22, 1964, 58–62, Archives of American Art, Smithsonian Institution (copy in Oakland Museum). See also Taylor to Kellogg, April 7, 1935, Survey Graphic Papers, Social Welfare History Archive, Department of Special Collections, University of Minnesota.

3. Quote from Lowry Nelson, *In the Direction of His Dreams* (New York, 1985), 265. See also Street, interview with Paul S. Taylor, March 12, 1976, Berkeley, California, author's possession.

4. Quote from Doud, interview with Dorothea Lange, May 22, 1964, 11, Archives of American Art, Smithsonian Institution. Lange never gave an exact date for this encounter.

5. Quotes from Riess, "Paul S. Taylor: California Social Scientist," 1: 133, also 225; Meltzer, *Dorothea Lange,* 97; and Riess, "Dorothea Lange: Making of a Documentary Photographer," 156, 158, 163.

6. Sally Stein, "Peculiar Grace: Dorothea Lange and the Testimony of the Body," in Partridge, ed., *Dorothea Lange,* 58–59; Riess, "Paul S. Taylor: California Social Scientist," 1: 225.

7. Quotes from Taylor, prologue to Dorothea Lange, "The Assignment I'll Never Forget," *Popular Photography* 46 (February 1960): 43, 45. See also Street, interview with Rondal Partridge, March 12, 1983, Berkeley, author's possession; Riess, "Paul S. Taylor: California Social Scientist," 1: 224, 226; and Riess, "Dorothea Lange: Making of a Documentary Photographer," 73.

8. Quotes from Riess, "Paul S. Taylor: California Social Scientist," 1: 132–33.

9. Quotes from Brown, "Dorothea Lange: Field Notes and Photographs," 2: 2, 9, 13, 18. Russell Lee also took extensive field notes while photographing. His wife, Jean, who often accompanied him on his photographic assignments, would transcribe these notes at night while Lee developed his film in the bathrooms and closets of the hotels and cabins where they stayed.

10. Quotes from Riess, "Dorothea Lange: Making of a Documentary Photographer," 160–61.

11. Quote from Paul S. Taylor to Paul Kellogg, April 7, 1935, Survey Graphic Papers, Social Welfare History Archives, University of Minnesota.

12. Riess, "Paul S. Taylor: California Social Scientist," 1: 215; and "Notes from the Field, Migration of Drought Refugees to California," April 17, 1935, in Henry E. Drobish to Dr. Lowry Nelson, with report by Paul S. Taylor, April 17, 1935, lot 879, Prints and Photographs Division, Library of Congress.

13. Quote from Paul S. Taylor, "Application for Funds for Rural Rehabilitation Camps for Migratory Laborers in California," April 17, 1935, Irving R. Wood Papers, Bancroft Library. In her captions, Lange used the term *social erosion* for the first time. Lange and Taylor would later modify this to "human erosion" and employ it as the subtitle to their pioneering collaborative work of text and images, *An American Exodus: A Record of Human Erosion* (New York, 1939; New Haven, Conn., 1975). See also Coles, *Doing Documentary Work,* 110–11.

14. Meltzer, *Dorothea Lange,* 126.

15. Quotes from "Native American Fruit Tramps on Putah Creek," May 25, 1935, Lange Field Notes, Dorothea Lange Collection, Oakland Museum; Riess, "Paul S. Taylor: California Social Scientist," 1: 137, 140, 210; and Nelson, *In the Direction of His Dreams,* 266. See also Paul S. Taylor, "Establishment of Rural Rehabilitation Camps for Migrants in California," March 15, 1935, in Taylor to Frank Y. McLaughlin, lot 879, Prints and Photographs Division, Library of Congress; Brown, "Dorothea Lange: Field Notes and Photographs," 1: 26; and Tom Collins, "The Human Side of the Operation of a Migrant's Camp," October 12, 1935, MS, Irving R. Wood Papers, Bancroft Library.

16. Quote from Stott, *Documentary Expression and Thirties America,* 228–29. See also Paul S. Taylor, "Again the Covered Wagon," *Survey Graphic* 24 (July 1935): 248–351, 368.

17. Quotes from Taylor to Drobish, "Status of Research in Agricultural Labor," June 8, 1935, Paul Taylor Papers, Bancroft Library; Riess, "Paul S. Taylor: California Social Scientist," 1: 137, 215.

18. Street, interview with Vernon DeMars, April 17, 1978, Berkeley, author's possession; Riess, "Paul S. Taylor: California Social Scientist," 1: 137.

19. Quote from Taylor to Drobish, "Status of Research in Agricultural Labor," June 8, 1935, Paul Taylor Papers, Bancroft Library. See also Taylor to Kellogg, June 3, 1935, Survey Graphic Papers, Social Welfare History Archive. I am not entirely convinced that this photograph dates from 1935. Before he died, Lange biographer Henry Mayer said it could have been taken anytime in 1935, when Lange passed through the Salinas Valley on numerous trips, or in September 1936. Henry Mayer to author, e-mail, March 16, 2000, author's possession.

20. Quote from Meltzer, *Dorothea Lange,* 149, also 126, 128. See also Clark Kerr, "Paul and Dorothea," in Partridge, ed., *Dorothea Lange,* 39; Street, interview with Rondal Partridge, May 22, 1984, Berkeley; Street, interview with Vernon DeMars, April 11, 1976, Berkeley; Street, interview with Alma Lavenson, March 6, 1980, Larkspur, California; and Street, interview with Hansel Mieth Hagel, March 12, 1981, Santa Rosa, California; all in author's possession.

21. Quotes from Riess, "Paul S. Taylor: California Social Scientist," 1: 149, 212, also 210. See also Street, "Paul S. Taylor and the Origins of Documentary Photography in California." For the husband and wife collaborative process, see Whitney Chadwick and Isabelle de Courtivron, eds., *Significant Others: Creativity and the Intimate Partnership* (London, 1993), 7–11.

22. Quote from Riess, "Paul S. Taylor: California Social Scientist," 1: 212. See also 1: 209, 213, 215; and "Notes from the Field, Migration of Drought Refugees to California," April 17, 1935, in Henry E. Drobish to Dr. Lowry Nelson, with report by Paul S. Taylor, April 17, 1935, lot 879, Prints and Photographs Division, Library of Congress.

23. Wilson Hicks, *Words and Pictures* (New York, 1952), 5, 34; Stott, *Documentary Expression,* 120–75; Taylor, "Again the Covered Wagon," 348–51.

24. Quote from Paul Taylor to Paul Kellogg, June 3, 1935, Survey Graphic Papers, Social Welfare History Archives, University of Minnesota. See also Taylor, "Again the Covered Wagon," 348–51, 368.

25. Quotes from Taylor, "Again the Covered Wagon," 348–51; and Riess, "Paul S. Taylor: California Social Scientist," 1: 146, also 212. See also *Redding Independent,* November 27, 1935; J. Earl Coke, "Reminiscences of People and Change in California Agriculture, 1900–1975," oral memoir, 1976, 245, Archives and Special Collections, University of California, Davis; Florence Loeb Kellogg to Taylor, June 4, 1935; Taylor to Kellogg, June 9, 1935; Taylor to Kellogg, April 7, 1935; and Taylor to Kellogg, May 11, 1935; all in Survey Graphic Papers, Social Welfare History Archives, University of Minnesota.

26. Quote from Riess, "Paul S. Taylor: California Social Scientist," 1: 138, also 145–46, 180, 209, 212. See also *San Francisco News,* August 10, 1935, and February 13, 1936.

27. Quotes from Riess, "Paul S. Taylor: California Social Scientist," 1: 134–35.

28. Quotes from Riess, "Dorothea Lange: Making of a Documentary Photographer," 174, 177–78. See also Coles, *Dorothea Lange,* 31.

29. Quote from Paul Hendrickson, *Looking for the Light: The Hidden Life and Art of Marion Post Wolcott* (New York, 1992), 54. See also James L. McCamy, *Government Publicity: Its Practice in Federal Administration* (Chicago, 1939), 119–20; Hurley, *Portrait of a Decade,* 68–72; Rexford W. Tugwell, *The Brains Trust* (New York, 1968), 14–19; Richard S. Kirkendall, *Social Scientists and Farm Politics in the Age of Roosevelt* (Columbia, Mo., 1966), 42–44; Rexford W. Tugwell, "Unions of Agricultural Workers," *American Federationist* 43 (June 1936): 632; and Rexford W. Tugwell, *To the Lesser Heights of Morningside: A Memoir* (Philadelphia, 1982). Taylor dates the transfer to the RA as July 1. See Riess, "Paul S. Taylor: California Social Scientist," 1: 139.

30. Quotes from Roy Emerson Stryker and Nancy Wood, *In This Proud Land: America 1935–1943 as Seen in the FSA Photographs* (New York, 1973), 7. See also Robert J. Doherty, "Farm Security Administration Photographs of the Depression Era," *Camera* (October 1962): 9051; Werner J. Severin, "Photographic Documentation by the Farm Security Administration, 1935–1941," MA thesis, University of Missouri, 1959; James C. Anderson, *Roy Stryker: The Humane Propagandist* (Louisville, Ky., 1977); and Ulrich Keller, *The Highway as Habitat: A Roy Stryker Documentation* (Santa Barbara, Calif., 1986), 24–52.

31. Quotes from Hendrickson, *Looking for the Light,* 46, 48. See also Arthur Rothstein, *Documentary Photography* (Boston, 1986), appendix A, 163–68; Thomas Garver, *Just before the War* (Balboa, Calif., 1968), n.p.; and Roy Emerson Stryker, "Documentary Photography," *Complete Photographer* 21 (April 10, 1942): 1364–74, subsequently revised, expanded, and reprinted in Willard D. Morgan, ed., *The Encyclopedia of Photography* (New York, 1971), 7: 1179–83.

32. Alan Trachtenberg, "From Image to Story: Reading the File," in Carl Fleischhauer and Beverly W. Brannan, eds., *Documenting America, 1935–1943* (Berkeley, 1988), 43–73; James Guimond, *American Photography and the American Dream* (Chapel Hill, N.C., 1991), 124–25.

33. Quote from Stryker and Wood, *In This Proud Land,* 11.

34. Quotes from Stryker and Wood, *In This Proud Land,* 14, 15, also 7, 8, 9, 187, 188. See also FSA photo editor Edwin Rosskam's comments in Sherwood Anderson, *Home Town* (New York, 1940), 144. Stange, *Symbols of Ideal Life,* 106, is the source of the interpretation of the RA/FSA as both inheritor and creator of the documentary tradition in photography. In many ways Stryker was running an early, noncommercial version of a photo agency like Magnum Photos or Black Star. I have applied this idea to the evolution of social documentary photography among California farmworkers in Richard Steven Street, "Lange's Antecedents: The Emergence of Social Documentary Photography of California's Farmworkers," *Pacific Historical Review* 75, no. 3 (August 2006): 385–428.

35. Quotes from Guimond, *American Photography and the American Dream,* 101; Paul Vanderbilt, "Memorandum on the Photography of America," February 7, 1963, 2, Paul Vanderbilt Papers, Archives of American Art, Smithsonian Institution; and Davis Pratt, ed., *The Photographic Eye of*

Ben Shahn (Cambridge, Mass., 1975), x. See also Time–Life Books, *Documentary Photography* (New York, 1972), 56.

36. Quotes from Riess, "Paul S. Taylor: California Social Scientist," 1: 149; and Richard K. Doud, interview with Ben Shahn, April 14, 1964, 16, Archives of American Art, Smithsonian Institution.

37. Quote from Roy Stryker to Lange, September 19, 1935, Stryker–Lange Correspondence, Roy Stryker Papers, University of Louisville Photographic Archives (hereafter cited as UL Photo Archives).

38. Quote from Hendrickson, *Looking for the Light,* 53.

39. Quotes from Roy Stryker to Lange, October 30, 1935; Lange to Stryker, December 31, 1935; both in Stryker–Lange Correspondence, Roy Stryker Papers, UL Photo Archives; and Partridge, ed., *Dorothea Lange,* 111. See also Naython Lyons, ed., *Photographers on Photography* (Englewood Cliffs, N.J., 1966), 90.

40. Quotes from Riess, "Paul S. Taylor: California Social Scientist," 1: 143, 215. See also *Santa Rosa Press Democrat,* August 22, 1935.

41. Quote from Lange's penciled notes on the extensively cropped version of RA 9066E, courtesy of Paul S. Taylor. Lange made several exposures. See also RA 2534E. These notes are more extensive than those appearing in Heyman, Phillips, and Szarkowski, eds., *Dorothea Lange,* 69.

42. Quote from Stryker to Lange, September 19, 1935, Stryker–Lange Correspondence, Roy Stryker Papers, UL Photo Archives.

43. Stryker to Lange, October 30, 1935, and January 1, 1936; Lange to Stryker, December 31, 1935; all in Stryker–Lange Correspondence, Roy Stryker Papers, UL Photo Archives.

44. Quotes from Meltzer, *Dorothea Lange,* 126; and Riess, "Dorothea Lange: Making of a Documentary Photographer," 99, 101, 126.

45. Quote from Riess, "Paul S. Taylor: California Social Scientist," 1: 143, also 1: 141–45, 211. See also Lange Field Notes, May 20–25, June, September, October 1935; and *Sacramento Bee,* October 25, 1935; and Street, interview with Vernon DeMars, March 3, 1977, Berkeley, author's possession.

46. In 2002, I made copy negatives and scanned digital files of the sequence of four panoramas shot by Jackson at Guasti Vineyards. I was unable to locate any information on Colton in the Colton Public Library. I originally photographed these on 35-millimeter film circa 1977.

47. Quote from Leah Bendavid-Val, ed., *Propaganda and Dreams: Photographing the 1930s in the USSR and US* (Zurich, 1999), 76.

48. Quote from Riess, "Dorothea Lange: Making of a Documentary Photographer," 181, also 146–47, 158, 181, 205.

49. Dorothea Lange, *Dorothea Lange: Photographs of a Lifetime* (New York, 1982), 46. See also Dorothea Lange, *Dorothea Lange Looks at the American Country Woman,* commentary by Beaumont Newhall (Los Angeles, 1967), 5.

50. Quote from Riess, "Dorothea Lange: Making of a Documentary Photographer," 155, also 146–59. See also Beaumont Newhall, *History of Photography: From 1839 to the Present* (New York, 1964), 137; Stott, *Documentary Expression and Thirties America,* 5, 11, 14, 26, 29–30, 56, 61, 119; Allan Sekula, "On the Invention of Photographic Meaning," in Goldberg, ed., *Photography in Print,* 452–73; and Guimond, *American Photography and the American Dream,* 4–5. For propaganda, see Bendavid-Val, ed., *Propaganda and Dreams,* 8–9, 66–69; and Leslie C. High, "The Documentary Idea in Depression America," PhD diss., University of Michigan, 1973, 61.

51. Riess, "Dorothea Lange: Making of a Documentary Photographer," 146–59; Stryker, "Documentary Photography," in Morgan, ed., *Encyclopedia of Photography,* 7: 1179–83; Newhall, "A Backward Glance at Documentary," 2–3; Stott, *Documentary Expression and Thirties America,* 49–53; Arthur Rothstein, *Photojournalism* (Garden City, N.Y., 1974), 27.

52. Stryker to Lange, October 22, 1936, Stryker–Lange Correspondence, Roy Stryker Papers, UL Photo Archives; Newhall, *History of Photography,* 137; Riess, "Paul S. Taylor: California Social Scientist," 1: 238A.

53. Quote from Riess, "Paul S. Taylor: California Social Scientist," 1: 149, also 143. See also Joyce Eli, "Dorothea Lange and Paul Taylor: Chroniclers and Conscience of a Decade," *Californians* 3 (March–April 1985): 16.

54. Riess, "Paul S. Taylor: California Social Scientist," 1: 149–50.

55. Lange to Stryker, December 31, 1935, Stryker–Lange Correspondence, Roy Stryker Papers, UL Photo Archives. Regarding Lange's salary, see Stryker to Lange, December 17, 1941, Dorothea Lange Collection, Oakland Museum.

56. Lange, "Field Notes," September–October 1935; Ansel Adams in Dater, ed., *Imogene Cunningham,* 47.

9. Don't Let Them Break Your Camera

1. Quote from Stryker to Lange, January 3, 1936, Stryker–Lange Correspondence, Roy Stryker Papers, UL Photo Archives. See also Stryker to Lange, September 19 and October 30, 1935; Lange to Stryker, December 31, 1935; and Stryker to Lange, January 1, 14, and 31, 1936.

2. Nancy Newhall, *Ansel Adams: The Eloquent Light* (San Francisco, 1964), 124, also 82. For background on Adams, see Spaulding, *Ansel Adams and the American Landscape,* 129–34, which omits the visit with Stryker.

3. Ohrn, *Dorothea Lange and the Documentary Tradition,* 102. Lange's third biographer, Henry Mayer, theorized that Lange now began a practice of shooting duplicates in the field whenever she felt that she was achieving something especially good. See Street, interview with Henry Mayer, March 22, 2000, Stanford. This practice of witholding prints would bear fruit when most of her Office of War Information negatives and prints were lost in shipment to Washington, D.C. See Riess, "Paul S. Taylor: California Social Scientist," 1: 235–36.

4. Quotes from Stryker to Lange, January 14, 1936, Stryker–Lange Correspondence, Roy Stryker Papers, UL Photo Archives. See also Paul Taylor, "Drought Refugee and Labor Migration to California, June 16 to December 15, 1935," with Tom Vasey, *U.S. Monthly Labor Review* (February 1936): 7–8.

5. Quote from Lange to Stryker, February 24, 1936, Stryker–Lange Correspondence, Roy Stryker Papers, UL Photo Archives. See also Lange to Stryker, March 2, 1936. For the photographs in the camp at Nipomo, see LC-USF34-T01-001787-C; 001817-C; and 001818-C, Prints and Photographs Division, Library of Congress.

6. Quote from Lange to Stryker, March 2, 1936, Stryker–Lange Correspondence, Roy Stryker Papers, UL Photo Archives.

7. Lange, "The Assignment I'll Never Forget," 42–43. See also Janis and MacNeil, eds., *Photography within the Humanities,* 38; Riess, "Dorothea Lange: Making of a Documentary Photographer," 1: 199; and Dorothea Lange, "Dragging around People," *Survey Graphic* 25 (March 1936): 524–25.

8. Lange, "The Assignment I'll Never Forget," 42.

9. Quote from ibid., 42. See also Lange Field Notes, March 9, 1936, Dorothea Lange Collection, Oakland Museum.

10. Lange, "The Assignment I'll Never Forget," 43, 128. See also James Curtis, "Dorothea Lange, Migrant Mother, and the Culture of the Great Depression," *Winterthur Portfolio* 21 (Spring 1988): 1–20.

11. Quote from Richard K. Doud, interview with Dorothea Lange, May 22, 1964, Archives of American Art, Smithsonian Institution (copy in Oakland Museum). See also Street, interview with

Paul S. Taylor, May 12, 1981, Berkeley, author's possession; Paul S. Taylor, "Migrant Mother: 1936," *American West* 7 (May 1970): 41–45; and Meltzer, *Dorothea Lange,* 132–36. The criticism that Lange failed to caption her image adequately and to obtain all of the information that we subsequently demand strikes me as typically academic. Only those who have never been in such situations could, from the distance of a half century, demand more. Given the volume of her work and her state of exhaustion, it is remarkable that Lange recalled as much as she did.

12. Quote from Riess, "Paul S. Taylor: California Social Scientist," 1: 294.

13. Ibid., 1: 294, also 1: 138, 209.

14. Quotes from "Starving Pea-Pickers," *San Francisco News,* March 10, 1936; and Morton Sontheimer (*San Francisco News* city editor) to Lange, March 10, 1936, Dorothea Lange Collection, Oakland Museum, thanking her for her photographs and information on Nipomo. Scholars borrow the sequencing of the Nipomo series from James Curtis, *Mind's Eye, Mind's Truth: FSA Photography Reconsidered* (Philadelphia, 1989), 45–68. See also Meltzer, *Dorothea Lange,* 133; and Janis and MacNeil, eds., *Photography within the Humanities,* 38. Sally Stein has questioned whether the alleged relief was delivered and found no corroborating evidence in local newspapers. See Street, interview with Sally Stein, March 12, 1999, Del Mar, California, author's possession.

15. Quote from George West, editorial, "Ragged, Hungry, Broke, Harvest Workers Live in Squalor: What Does the New Deal Mean to This Mother and Her Children?" *San Francisco News,* March 11, 1936. Henry Mayer questioned whether Lange could have made the long drive back to Berkeley, developed and printed her work, and delivered it across the bay to the *San Francisco News* in time to meet the March 10 publication date—all in less than twenty-four hours. Average speed on the highway then was about thirty-five miles per hour, not the sixty-five miles per hour that would have put her in Berkeley that evening. On the basis of such calculations, Mayer dated the Migrant Mother shots to about March 7. See Street, interview with Henry Mayer, April 4, 2000, Stanford, California. Taylor did not know whether Lange took all of the prints, including *Migrant Mother,* to the *News,* or why George West picked the two that ran first. He theorized that the two that ran might not have been high art on the plane of *Migrant Mother* but that they may have "showed the situation better." Quote from Riess, "Paul S. Taylor: California Social Scientist," 1: 295.

16. Helmut Gernsheim and Allison Gernsheim, *A Concise History of Photography* (London, 1965), titles Lange's *Migrant Mother* image as *Seasonal Farm Labourer's Family,* which is considerably less dramatic and memorable.

17. Quote from Stryker and Wood, *In This Proud Land,* 19. See also Lawrence W. Levine, "The Folklore of Industrial Society: Popular Culture and Its Audiences," *American Historical Review* 97 (December 1992): 1386; Lawrence W. Levine, "The Historian and the Icon: Photography and the History of the American People in the 1930s and 1940s," in Fleischhauer and Brannan, eds., *Documenting America, 1935–1943,* 15; Meltzer, *Dorothea Lange,* 133; Goldberg, *The Power of Photography,* 136; and Lange to Stryker, April 24, 1936, Stryker–Lange Correspondence, Roy Stryker Papers, UL Photo Archives.

18. Quote from John Szarkowski in Janis and MacNeil, eds., *Photography within the Humanities,* 95. For more on the ambiguous quality of *Migrant Mother,* see Stryker and Wood, *In This Proud Land,* 19; Roger Sprague, "The Picture," *Californians* 14 (April 1996): 39; Robert Coles, "Dorothea Lange and the Politics of Photography," *Raritan* 1 (Fall 1981); 39–40; Starr, *Endangered Dreams,* 223–24; and Wendy Kozol, "Madonnas of the Fields: Photography, Gender, and the 1930s Farm Relief," *Genders* 2 (Summer 1988): 1–23.

19. For the earliest mutation, see *New York Times,* August 30, 1936. For the Spanish version, see Diane Thorne, *Spanish Mother, the Terror of 1938* (1939), the lithograph protesting the Spanish Civil War, Study Collection, Department of Photography, Museum of Modern Art, New York City. This lithograph is now missing. See John Benicewicz and Ryan Jensen to author, June 10, 2003, author's

possession. For a 1939 mutation, see Lisa Dorrill, "Picturing the Dirty Thirties: Paintings and Prints of the Dust Bowl," PhD diss., University of Kansas, 1998, 75, 252, original in the University of Michigan Museum of Art (1943.148). The Hispanic adaptation appears on the cover of the Latin American magazine *Bohemia Venezolana* (May 10, 1964), Astor, Lennox, and Tilden Foundations, Central Research Division, New York Public Library. For the Black Panther version, see *Black Panthers' Newspaper,* 1973, Dorothea Lange Collection, Oakland Museum. For the latest mutation, see the *Time* issue *150 Years of Photo Journalism* (Fall 1989), discussed in Amy Rule and Nancy Solomon, eds., *Original Sources: Art and Archives at the Center for Creative Photography* (Tucson, Ariz., 2002), 117. For an excellent summary of the various uses of *Migrant Mother,* see Goldberg, *The Power of Photography,* 138–41. Some humorous mutations are recounted in Margery Mann, "Dorothea Lange: Camera with a Purpose," *Popular Photography* 66 (March 1970): 84, 99–101. See also Lawrence W. Levine, *The Unpredictable Past: Explorations in American Cultural History* (New York, 1993), 283, 308.

20. Quotes from John Roberts, *The Art of Interruption: Realism, Photography and the Everyday* (Manchester, U.K., 1998), 85; Lange, "The Assignment I'll Never Forget," 42; and KQED (television station), *The Closer to Me* (National Educational Television, 1964), video.

21. Quotes from Halla Beloff, *Camera Culture* (New York, 1985), 15; Paula Rabinowitz, *They Must Be Represented: The Politics of Documentary* (London, 1994), 86; Elliot, *Dorothea Lange,* 7, 25, 103; Graham Clarke, *The Photograph* (New York, 1997), 153; Liz Wells, ed., *Photography: A Critical Introduction* (New York, 1996), 44; John Pails, *The Body and the Lens: Photography 1839 to the Present* (New York, 1995), 93; David M. Lubin, *Shooting Kennedy: JFK and the Culture of Images* (Berkeley, 2003), 87; Coles, *Doing Documentary Work,* 101–3; John Bloom, "An Interview with Weston J. Naef," in John Bloom, ed., *Photography at Bay: Interviews, Essays, and Reviews* (Albuquerque, N.M., 1993), 33; and Andrea Fisher, *Let Us Now Praise Famous Women* (London, 1987), 140–41. See also Lange to Stryker, September 3 and 30, 1936, Stryker–Lange Correspondence, Roy Stryker Papers, UL Photo Archives; Edward Steichen, "The F.S.A. Photographers," in T. J. Maloney, ed., *U.S. Camera Annual 1939* (New York, 1938), 44; Levine, "The Folklore of Industrial Society," 1386; and Anne Tucker, "Photographic Facts and Thirties America," in Featherstone, ed., *Observations,* 50–51.

22. Curtis, *Mind's Eye, Mind's Truth,* 45–68; Barbara O. Natanson, "Exploring Contexts: Migrant Mother," in *American Women: A Gateway to Library of Congress Resources for the Study of Women's History and Culture in the United States,* http://memory.loc.gov/ammem/awhhtml/awpnp6/migrant_mother.html, accessed 1998. Lange's field notes variously identify the photographs as having been taken in February and March. See Dorothea Lange Collection, Oakland Museum. I am indebted to Henry Mayer for raising many issues concerning Lange's work at Nipomo. As Mayer saw it, the debate over *Migrant Mother* essentially forces a choice between Lange's field notes made on the spot and oral history offered forty years later. See also Ohrn, *Dorothea Lange and the Documentary Tradition,* 85–87; and Colin Jacobson, "A Different Way of Seeing," *Lancet* 357 (May 5, 2001): 1454–55.

23. Quote from Bill Ganzel, *Dust Bowl Descent* (Lincoln, Neb., 1984), 3. See also Harold Evans, *The American Century* (New York, 1998), 658.

24. Quotes from Geoffrey Dunn, "Photographic License," *Metro* 10 (January 19–25, 1995): 22. Thompson's eldest son disputes Lange's claim that the camp was muddy or that it had been raining the day that Lange photographed. See also caption to photograph 9098C, FSA/OWI Collection, Prints and Photographs Division, Library of Congress; Geoffrey Dunn, "The Heart of a Woman," *Santa Maria Sun,* February 15, 2002; and Roger Sprague, "*Migrant Mother:* The Story as Told by Her Grandson," www.migrantgrandson.com, accessed 2002.

25. Quote from Dunn, "Photographic License," 22. One implication of this story is that it confirms Henry Mayer's suspicion that many days transpired between the photographic session at Nipomo and the time that *Migrant Mother* made it into print. It certainly would have taken several

days for the Thompsons to travel up the coast, get settled in camp, and for the boys to begin their newspaper business. See also "Migraine Mother," *American Photographer* 1 (July 1980): 9; Emmett Corrigan, "Migrant Mother Tells Story behind Famed Photo," *Modesto Bee,* October 23, 1978; Emmett Corrigan, "A Noted 'Working Mother,'" *Modesto Bee,* November 4, 1979; and "Dust Bowl Update," *Life* 2 (August 1979): 9.

26. Quotes from Martha Rossler, "In, Around, and Afterthoughts on Documentary Photography," in Martha Rossler, *Three Works* (Halifax, Nova Scotia, 1981), 75, reprinted as Rossler, "In, Around, and Afterthoughts (on Documentary Photography)," in Bolton, ed., *The Contest of Meaning: Critical Histories of Photography,* 315; and Dunn, "Photographic License," 23. To her death, Thompson failed to understand why she never received a penny from the photograph. See Ted Benson to author, August 23 and October 11, 1985, author's possession; and Street, interview with Florence Thompson, November 12, 1978, Modesto, California, author's possession. In addition to claiming that Lange promised to send her a copy of one of the images, she claimed that Lange vowed not to sell any of the photographs. Thompson's lawsuit and accusations hurt Lange very much. Some basis for claims that Thompson demanded compensation can be found in Janis and MacNeil, eds., *Photography within the Humanities,* 41. Taylor discusses the threatened lawsuit in Street, interview with Paul S. Taylor, May 12, 1981, Berkeley, author's possession. On this matter, see Ruby Sprague (Florence Thompson's daughter), interview (tape), 1989, Dorothea Lange Collection, Oakland Museum.

27. Quote from Dunn, "Photographic License," 24. See also Sprague, "*Migrant Mother.*" During the late 1930s, Thompson moved with the crops and became involved in several cotton strikes, probably the 1938 and 1939 Madera cotton strikes. After World War II, she settled in Modesto. When Hill left, she married George Thompson, a quiet and stable manager at the state hospital, where Florence worked as a laundry maid.

28. "Appeal for the Symbol of the Depression," *San Francisco Chronicle,* August 23, 1983; "'Migrant Mother,' Symbol of Depression, Dies at Age 70," *San Francisco Chronicle,* September 17, 1983; *Los Angeles Times,* September 17, 1983; "An Appeal for a Face from the Depression," *New York Times,* August 24 and September 17, 1983; Jack Foley, "Migrant Mother Now Lies Dying: Subject of Photo Racked by Cancer," *San Jose Mercury News,* August 21, 1983.

29. Curtis, *Mind's Eye, Mind's Truth,* 47; Peter Stepan, ed., *Icons of Photography: The 20th Century* (New York, 1999), 70; Clarke, *The Photograph,* 153.

30. Quote from Riess, "Dorothea Lange: Making of a Documentary Photographer," 197.

31. A modern photographer equipped with a telephoto lens and a 35-millimeter camera could have easily zoomed in to the corner of the tent and tightly framed an effective picture of mother and her child as seen in the second image. Lange, in "The Assignment I'll Never Forget," 42, claims to have made only five images. Theresa Heyman, *Celebrating a Collection: The Work of Dorothea Lange* (Oakland, Calif., 1978), refers to five images, as does Coles, *Dorothea Lange,* 20; Meltzer, *Dorothea Lange,* 133; and Ohrn, *Dorothea Lange and the Documentary Tradition,* 79–88, 251n.18. The first scholar to call attention to the sixth image was Hank O'Neal, in *A Vision Shared: A Classic Portrait of America and Its People, 1933–1943* (New York, 1976), 76. O'Neal located the image in the Dorothea Lange Collection, Oakland Museum. Curtis, in *Mind's Eye, Mind's Truth,* 66, also adds in the sixth image. Lange, "The Assignment I'll Never Forget," 44, publishes the first image in the sequence. Sally Stein discovered the seventh image tucked inside a photo sleeve in the Dorothea Lange Collection. Some Graflex film magazines held eight shots; some twelve. Rondal Partridge has identified Lange's camera as a 4 × 5–inch Graflex with a holder containing twelve negatives in a leather bag. See Street, interview with Rondal Partridge, April 12, 2005, Berkeley, California, author's possession.

32. Quotes from Levine, "The Historian and the Icon," 20; Maurice Berger, *FSA: The Illiterate Eye: Photographs from the Farm Security Administration* (New York, 1985), n.p.

33. Quotes from Trachtenberg, "From Image to Story," 68. For the mechanics of operating a Graflex and a Speed Graphic, see Hendrickson, *Looking for the Light,* 75–77; and Time–Life Books, *The Camera* (New York, 1970), 7, 162.

34. Curtis, *Mind's Eye, Mind's Truth,* 52–53; Curtis, "Dorothea Lange, Migrant Mother, and the Culture of the Great Depression," 1–20; Shindo, *Dust Bowl Migrants in the American Imagination,* 37–55.

35. Unlike modern 35-millimeter images, which have frames imprinted with sequential numbers, Lange's big negatives bore no such numbering code. Before he died, Lange's biographer Henry Mayer disputed the generally accepted version of the sequence leading up to *Migrant Mother,* which he believed was the middle image, not the last image. Taylor also expressed his puzzlement at the exact sequence. "In what order I do not know; she never said." Quote from Riess, "Paul S. Taylor: California Social Scientist," 1: 295. Mayer also believed that the nursing image may have been simulated, as the infant appears to be asleep. Mayer found it unlikely and against common sense for Thompson to have taken out her breast, nursed, and then cuddled with her children during the last two shots. See Street, interview with Henry Mayer, April 4, 2000, Stanford, California, author's possession.

36. Levine, "The Historian and the Icon," 8. See also Robert Coles, "The Human Factor," *Camera Arts* 3 (February 1983): 34–49. McWilliams, *Factories in the Field,* 312–13, erroneously states that Lange made her *Migrant Mother* image at Nipomo in 1937.

37. Quotes from Gregory, *American Exodus,* xiii; and Bezner, *Photography and Politics in America,* 6. See also David P. Peeler, *Hope among Us Yet: Social Criticism and Social Solace in Depression America* (Athens, Ga., 1987), 64–65, 81–82.

38. Quote from Lange to James Rorty, May 29, 1936, Stryker–Lange Correspondence, Roy Stryker Papers, UL Photo Archives. See also Doud, interview with Dorothea Lange, May 22, 1964, Archives of American Art, Smithsonian Institution.

39. Daniel Dixon, "Dorothea Lange," *Modern Photography* 16 (December 1952): 72, 138.

40. Metzler, *Dorothea Lange,* 140–49.

41. Quote from *Los Angeles Times,* July 7, 1936. See also Louis Reccow, "The Orange County Citrus Strikes of 1935–1936: The Forgotten People in Revolt," PhD diss., University of Southern California, 1971, iii, 197; Gonzáles, *Labor and Community,* 135–60; Sackman, *Orange Empire,* 221–24, 254; *Santa Ana Journal,* July 9, 1936; Frank Stokes, "Let the Mexicans Organize," *Nation* 143 (December 19, 1936): 732; Carey McWilliams, "Gunkist Oranges," *Pacific Weekly* (July 20, 1936): 38–39; and "Cooperation at a Profit," *Fortune* 17 (July 1936): 47–55, 90, 92, 95.

42. Quote from Meltzer, *Dorothea Lange,* 150. See also Sidney Baldwin, *Poverty and Politics: The Rise and Decline of the Farm Security Administration* (Chapel Hill, N.C., 1968); and Riess, "Paul S. Taylor: California Social Scientist," 1: 148–49.

43. Quote from O'Neal, *A Vision Shared,* 111–12.

44. Quotes from Lange to Stryker, September 3, 5, 10, 30, 1936, Lange Collection; Stryker to Lange, October 7, 1936, Stryker–Lange Correspondence, Roy Stryker Papers, UL Photo Archives.

45. Street, interviews with Vilem Kriz, May 22, 1982, and March 23, 1983, Berkeley, author's possession; Street, interview with Richard and Maisie Conrat, March 11, 1976, Berkeley, author's possession; Street, interview with Rondal Partridge, June 18, 1982, Berkeley, author's possession; Van Deren Coke, "Dorothea Lange: Compassionate Recorder," *Modern Photography* 37 (May 1973): 90–91; Janis and MacNeil, eds., *Photography within the Humanities,* 79–80; [Deschin Jacob], "Dorothea Lange and Her Printer," *Popular Photography* (July 1966): 28, 30, 68, 70.

46. Quotes from Worster, *Dust Bowl,* 96. See also Paul Rotha, *Documentary Film* (New York, 1952), 38; and clipping, *McCall's* (July 1936), FSA/OWI Scrapbook, FSA/OWI Written Records, FSA/OWI Collection, Library of Congress.

47. Clipping, *Scholastic: The American High School Weekly,* September 26, 1936, FSA/OWI Scrapbook, Library of Congress; Paul Taylor, "From the Ground Up," 25 *Survey Graphic* (September 1936): 524–26, 537–38; Hurley, *Portrait of a Decade,* 130.

48. *Mid-week Pictorial,* October 17, 1936, FSA/OWI Scrapbook, Library of Congress; Meltzer, *Dorothea Lange,* 134; Lange to Edwin Locke, September 10, 1936, Dorothea Lange Collection, Oakland Museum.

49. Lange to Stryker, September 16, 1936, Dorothea Lange Collection, Oakland Museum; Stryker to Lange, October 7, 1936, Stryker–Lange Correspondence, Roy Stryker Papers, UL Photo Archives.

50. Francis James Smith, "The Impact of Technological Change on the Marketing of Salinas Valley Lettuce," PhD diss., University of California, Berkeley, 1961, 33, 48; William O. Jones, "The Salinas Valley, Its Agricultural Development, 1920–1940," PhD diss., Stanford University, 1947; Sidney Hoos and H. Fisk Phelps, *Commercial Head Lettuce Economic Status 1947, and Statistical Supplement,* California Agricultural Experiment Station Circular no. 378 (Berkeley, 1948), 3, 15–18; LaFollette Committee Hearings, part 62: 22667, part 74: 27083–27109, exhibits 13782 and 27100.

51. Judith C. Glass, "Conditions Which Facilitate Unionization of Agricultural Workers: A Case Study of the Salinas Valley Lettuce Industry," PhD diss., University of California, Los Angeles, 1966, 73–79; Howard Dewitt, *Violence in the Fields: California Filipino Farm Labor Unionization during the Great Depression* (Saratoga, Calif., 1980), 74–112.

52. Cletus Daniel, "Organized Anti-unionism in Triumph: The Salinas Lettuce Packers' Strike," MA thesis, San Jose State University, 1969, 77–78; Frank J. Taylor, "Hot Lettuce," *Collier's* 26 (September 1936): 23; Frank J. Taylor, "Green Gold and Tear Gas," *California: Magazine of Pacific Business* 36 (November 1936): 17; Jack Tracy, "Strikebreaker!" *Stanford Daily,* October 5, 1936.

53. Helen B. Lamb, "Industrial Relations in the Western Lettuce Industry," PhD diss., Radcliffe College, 1942; McWilliams, *Factories in the Field,* 254–55; John V. Young, *Hot Type and Pony Wire: My Life as a California Reporter from Prohibition to Pearl Harbor* (Santa Cruz, Calif., 1980), 75–83; "Lettuce Strike Facts," *Salinas Index-Journal,* September 8, 1936; *Los Angeles Times,* September 17, 18, 1936.

54. Lange to Stryker, September 10, 1936, Dorothea Lange Collection, Oakland Museum; Richard Steven Street, "Salinas on Strike: News Photographers and the Salinas Lettuce Packers' Strike of 1936: The First Photo Essay on a California Farm Labour Dispute," *History of Photography* 12 (April–June 1988): 165–74; "Strikers Jeer as Lettuce Fence Is Erected" and "6 Lettuce Strikers Jailed," *San Francisco News,* September 14, 1936; "Police Guns," *Oakland Tribune,* September 14, 1936.

55. Quotes from John Steinbeck, "Poison Gas in America's Salad Bowl: Vigilantes Hunt Reds in the Lettuce Fields of California," *Literary Digest* (October 10, 1936): 5–6. See also Street, "Salinas on Strike," 165–74; and Edward Robbin, "The General Staff Takes Charge," *Nation* (October 31, 1936).

10. Photo Eye on Salinas

1. Richard Steven Street, "The Battle of Salinas: San Francisco Bay Area Press Photographers and the Salinas Valley Lettuce Strike of 1936," *Journal of the West* 26 (April 1987): 45.

2. Street, interview with Ted Smith, October 6, 1977, Santa Rosa, California, author's possession; "Lettuce Harvest Resumed," *Oakland Tribune,* September 15, 1936; Stanley Bailey, "Fighting Begins When Growers Start Moving Produce," *San Francisco Chronicle,* September 15, 1936.

3. Quote from Melissa Christine Lambert, "Fascism, Communism, and Collective Bargaining: The Salinas Lettuce Strike of 1936," senior honors thesis, Stanford University, 2002, 19. See also "Where Officers Dispersed Crowds" and "Lettuce Strikers Gassed," *Oakland Tribune,* September

15, 1936; "State Patrol Guns, Bombs Menace Mob," *San Francisco News,* September 15, 1936; and *Salinas Index-Journal,* September 15, 1936.

4. Street, interview with Ted Smith, October 6, 1977, Santa Rosa, California.

5. Quote from Daisy Mason to Alvin Mason, September 18, 1936, in Lambert, "Fascism, Communism, and Collective Bargaining," 53. See also *New York Times,* September 17, 1936.

6. Quotes from Carl Nolte, "Photographer Barney Peterson," *San Francisco Chronicle,* February 14, 1990. Peterson had a large Graflex worth two hundred dollars. His photographs ran in the *Chronicle* and the *Oakland Tribune.* For photographers on the roof of one building, see Alexander B. Hawes, Proposed Findings of Fact, Proposed Conclusion of Law, and Proposed Order of NLRB, 311-D-220, 26, American Civil Liberties Union Papers, California Historical Society, San Francisco; and NLRB, *Decisions and Orders of the National Labor Relations Board* 15 (Washington, D.C., 1939), 350.

7. Biographical information on Ellwood from Street, interview with Rosenthal, June 22, 1986, San Francisco, author's possession. See also "Memorandum on Lettuce Bowl Strike Pictures," n.d., 3, American Civil Liberties Union Papers, California Historical Society; Lambert, "Fascism, Communism, and Collective Bargaining," 39; and various statements from victims of tear gassing, Grossmen–Gladstein Papers, Labor Archives Center, San Francisco State University.

8. Headlines from the San Francisco *Examiner, Chronicle, News,* and *Call-Bulletin,* September 16, 1936. See also "Strike Riot," and "Gas Bombs," *Oakland Tribune,* September 16, 1936; Richard Steven Street, "Salinas on Strike: News Photographers and the Salinas Lettuce Packers Strike of 1936: The First Photo Essay on a California Farm Labor Dispute," *History of Photography* 12 (April–June 1988): 172–73; and Lynn Burkett, interview with Carl Smith, 1977, Salinas, California, in Lynn Burkett, "The Okies? Why They're Some of Salinas' Best Citizens," senior thesis, University of California, Santa Cruz, 1978. For a fictionalized account, see Haakon Chevalier, *For Us the Living* (New York, 1949), 237–319, in which the Battle of Salinas becomes the Battle of Querco, and the Salinas Valley is renamed Salsipuedes Valley.

9. "Armistice in Salinas," *Oakland Tribune,* September 17, 1936.

10. LaFollette Committee Hearings, 1366–67; and *San Francisco Examiner,* September 19, 1936. A collection of newspaper clippings on the strike, originally held at the Pajarao Valley Historical Society, Watsonville, where I first consulted it in the 1977, was later transferred to the Archives and Special Collections, University of California, Davis, where the material was misplaced. Burton Anderson's *The Salinas Valley: A History of America's Salad Bowl* (Salinas, Calif., 2000), 113–14, does not mention the strike but contains useful information on the industry.

11. Paul Smith, *Personal File: An Autobiography* (New York, 1961), 176. Although Chief Cato claimed that two dozen red agitators had supposedly been identified and that others were being trucked down from San Francisco, and Los Angeles Police captain William Hynes asserted that armed communist agitators were disguised as tourists on their way north from Los Angeles "bent on making trouble," there is no evidence of any significant communist involvement in the strike. Governor Merriam certainly provided the silliest evidence for communist involvement with his claim that red flags along the highways identified assembly points for agitators, when in fact they had been placed there by the Division of Highways to check traffic flow. See Porter M. Chaffee, "A History of the Cannery and Agricultural Workers Industrial Union," Oakland, Federal Writers' Project, 1939, 2 vols., Bancroft Library, an account written by a communist organizer who had worked in the Salinas–Watsonville area in 1932.

12. Paul Smith, "How the Chronicle Handled News and So-Called Forces of Law and Order Handled Chronicle Staff," *San Francisco Chronicle,* September 24, 1936.

13. Quote from Bailey, "Fighting Begins When Growers Start Moving Produce." See also Street, interview with Joe Rosenthal, June 22, 1986, San Francisco, California, author's possession; and

Street, interview with Barney Peterson, November 12, 1974, San Leandro, California, author's possession. Smith's series was a parody of the famous 1935 antifascist Sinclair Lewis book *It Can't Happen Here.*

14. Starr, *Endangered Dreams,* 187–88; Smith, *Personal File,* 171–77; *San Francisco Chronicle,* September 19, 1936; "Raid on Home Laid to Unpaid Rent" and "Merriam Investigation," *Oakland Tribune,* September 19, 1936.

15. Quote from Street, interview with Joe Rosenthal, June 22, 1986, San Francisco, California. Rosenthal later won the Pulitzer Prize for his photograph of United States Marines raising the American flag atop Mount Suribachi on Iwo Jima on February 19, 1945. See also Street, interviews with Rosenthal, May 5 and June 10, 1986, San Francisco, California, author's possession; Street, interview with Ted Smith, October 6, 1977, Santa Rosa, California, author's possession; "Scram!" *Oakland Tribune,* September 22, 1936; "2,842 Spent by Highway Patrol," *Oakland Tribune,* September 22, 1936; "Valley Strife," *Oakland Tribune,* September 27, 1936; "Firing of Tear Gas," *Oakland Tribune,* September 25, 1936; and *California Farmer,* September 26, 1936.

16. Quote from Street, interview with Rosenthal, June 22, 1986, San Francisco. At least three newsreel crews, including one from Keystone Movie Company, were also present. Northern California American Civil Liberties Union lawyer Ernest Besig shot an 8-millimeter motion picture camera. For Besig's film, see Street, interview with Ernest Besig, May 12, 1978, San Francisco, author's possession; "Memorandum of Lettuce Bowl Strike Pictures," n.d.; and ACLU to John T. Dunlap, March 1, 1937; both in American Civil Liberties Union Papers, California Historical Society.

17. Quote from Lange to Stryker, September 16, 1936, Stryker–Lange Correspondence, Roy Stryker Papers, UL Photo Archives. See also Jamieson, *Labor Unionism in American Agriculture,* 139–40; LaFollette Committee Hearings, 27236–38. Lange's work at Salinas is hard to pin down. See *Salinas Lettuce Fields—Where One of the More Interesting Strikes in California History Is Now Going On,* LCUSF34-9700, LCUSF34-9703; and *Deputized Vigilantes Armed with Clubs, Guard Entrance to Lettuce Fields during Lettuce Strike,* LCUSF34-19288E; both in FSA/OWI Collection, Prints and Photographs Division, Library of Congress.

18. Jack Tracy, "Strikebreaker!" in Lambert, "Fascism, Communism, and Collective Bargaining," 37.

19. Young, *Hot Type and Pony Wire,* 82. Young recalled the strike as "one of the largest civil rights violations by constituted authority in California history."

20. Quote from photo *Center of Battle* caption, accompanying "Action Contingent on Vote, Official Approval," *San Francisco Chronicle,* October 6, 1936.

21. Helen Dixon, "Disgruntled Camera Man," *San Francisco Chronicle,* September 25, 1936. Other similar letters debated news and photographic coverage.

22. The FBI was interested in Mieth and believed that she was closely connected to Communist Party District 8 organizer Sam Darcy. The bureau was in close enough contact to note that Mieth had sought public relief following the annulment of her marriage and that she spoke English carefully but with a heavy German accent. This file contains a mass of excellent information, much of it pointing up discrepancies in aspects of Mieth's official biography. It also contains specific assignments, addresses, and occupations, including dates that Mieth received assistance (October 4 to November 6, 1933; September 7 to October 9, 1934; and June 1935 to January 1936). The report also gives the name of Mieth's sponsor in Philadelphia and the makes and years of Hagel's cars, as well as the names of various friends. Of the reasons why Montroni had his marriage to Mieth annulled, the San Francisco FBI agent noted that Mieth "had told him and introduced him prior to the marriage to another man as being a relative of herself, whereas Montroni learned subsequently that this man was not a relative but a man with whom she had been living and to whom she returned upon leaving Montroni." See San Francisco Agent Report, "Otto Fritz Hagel,"

Espionage-R, 2–3, Internal Security Act, 1950, June 30, 1950, and enclosures, Declassified FBI File, author's possession; also San Francisco Agent Report, "Otto Fritz Hagel," Espionage-R, 1–3, April 12, 1951, Declassified FBI File 0981877-000/10. For Mieth's "bum" shots, see the seven images appearing in *Life* (January 11, 1937): 29. A good biographical treatment of Hagel is in Mamoru Inouye, *The Heart Mountain Story,* essay by Grace Schaub, photographs by Hansel Mieth and Otto Hagel (Los Gatos, Calif., 1998), 1–13. See also "On the Life and Work of Otto Hagel and Hansel Mieth as Narrated by Hansel Mieth," 4–17; and Ken Conner, "Hansel Mieth—Admired Photojournalist," *San Francisco Chronicle,* March 15, 1998. The work provided enough financial stability for Hagel and Mieth to start a project they called the Great Hunger. At one point Mieth had concealed herself inside a parked automobile and documented the reactions of pedestrians to a man (Hagel) lying face up on the sidewalk, appearing to be either dead or unconscious. Hagel worked differently from Mieth. "He made up his mind in advance just about what three or four or six things he wanted to show," recalled Paul Taylor, who knew and respected Hagel. "That is the way Otto Hagel worked and he is a very good one at it. His wife Hansel didn't work that way, and Dorothea didn't work that way." Quote from Riess, "Paul S. Taylor: California Social Scientist," 1: 241. Similar information from Street, interview with Hansel Mieth Hagel, January 9, 1981, Santa Rosa, California, author's possession. Information on Hagel's experimentation with color comes from Photographic Materials, Color Transparencies (AG170:64), Otto and Hansel Mieth Hagel Collection, Center for Creative Photography, University of Arizona, Tucson. Contained in this uncataloged box of materials are 35-millimeter slides from 1977 to 1979 and from 1981 to 1982 and seven color transparencies measuring 2¼ × 2¼ inches in aluminum mounts. These transparencies, fading to sepia with green entirely gone but with yellow and blue still visible, depict cotton picking and match exactly a series of black-and-white shots dated 1934. Because color was not available until 1935 or 1936, the black-and-white photographs could not have been made in 1934. This work appears to predate the FSA/OWI experimentation with color photography by several years. See Paul Hendrickson, *Bound for Glory: America in Color, 1939–1943* (New York, 2004). For early color, see Henry Wilhelm, *The Permanence and Care of Color Photographs: Traditional and Digital Color Prints, Color Negatives, Slides, and Motion,* with contributing editor Carol Brower (Grinnell, Iowa, 1993), 19–20. See also San Francisco Bay Area District Council no. 2, Maritime Federation of the Pacific Coast, *Men and Ships: A Pictorial of the Maritime Industry* (San Francisco, 1937), International Longshoremen's Union Library, San Francisco.

23. My analysis of Hagel's photographic technique is from his contact sheets in the Dorothea Lange Collection, Oakland Museum; a contact strip of five negatives in the Otto and Hansel Mieth Hagel Collection (AG 170:38/1), Center for Creative Photography; and Street, interview with Rosenthal, June 22, 1986, San Francisco. Hagel's film was DuPont 35-millimeter type 527 Panchromatic nitrate base, with a film speed of approximately 25 or 32. Hagel employed his 4 × 5–inch camera to photograph the stockade erected around the lettuce packing sheds on September 10. See *Stockade: 1936 Lettuce Strike,* in Photographic Materials: Special Negatives, Otto and Hansel Mieth Hagel Collection, Center for Creative Photography.

24. Quote from Street, interview with Hansel Mieth Hagel, January 9, 1981, Santa Rosa, California, author's possession. Also, Rosenthal recalled of Hagel, "He was one of those who flocked in and out of our group"; see Street, interview with Rosenthal, June 22, 1986, San Francisco. Rosenthal also had a 35-millimeter camera as "backup." Rosenthal would photograph farmworkers sporadically for the next forty years. Some of his last work before he retired focused on the United Farmworkers Union campaign to organize Gallo Winery. See *San Francisco Chronicle,* April 12, 1974. Salomon died in a Nazi concentration camp.

25. Although it is unclear where Hagel developed his film, the assumption is that he shared processing facilities with others in Salinas.

26. Stein, "Starting from Pictoralism," in Johnson, ed., *Capturing Light,* 138.

27. Horace Bristol's photographs may have run in the *Call-Bulletin,* where his mother worked as an editor on the "women's page." I discovered one of his Salinas lettuce strike photographs in the San Francisco Public Library Photo Archives. Since Bristol destroyed much of his life's work in a fit following the suicide of his first wife, this may be the one surviving print from his Salinas sojourn. The image first ran in Lange and Taylor, *An American Exodus,* 138 upper.

28. Based on a personal inspection of the original photographs in the *San Francisco Examiner* library in 1975. My thanks to editor James Willse for facilitating the search.

29. Quotes from Starr, *The Dream Endures,* 211–15. See also Hilton Kramer, "Edward Weston's Privy and the Mexican Revolution," *New York Times,* May 7, 1972; Charis Wilson and Edward Weston, *California and the West* (Millerton, N.Y., 1978), 23, 65, 75, 134, 136, 176; Nancy Newhall, ed., *The Daybooks of Edward Weston* (Millerton, N.Y., 1961), 1; Amy Conger, *Edward Weston in Mexico: 1923–1926* (Albuquerque, N.M., 1983); Amy Conger, "Edward Weston's Early Photography, 1903–1926," PhD diss., University of New Mexico, 1982; Ben Maddow, *Edward Weston, His Life* (Millerton, N.Y., 1989), 236–37; Spaulding, *Ansel Adams and the American Landscape,* 137–38; and Calvin Tomkins, *Paul Strand: Sixty Years of Photographs* (Millerton, N.Y., 1976).

30. Quotes from Edward Weston to Ansel Adams, December 3, 1934, Ansel Adams Collection, Center for Creative Photography. See also Ansel Adams to Edward Weston, November 29, 1934, and August 6, 1935; and Weston to Adams, December 3, 1934; all in Edward Weston Archive, Center for Creative Photography.

31. Quote from Gideon Bosher and Stu Levy, "Charis Wilson Weston," *American Photographer* 3 (August 1979): 59. For a similar view, see "Recollections of Charis Wilson at Program Group f.64: 1932 Origins/1992 Inspirations," October 24, 1992, Art Department, Oakland Museum, which also notes that Weston turned down invitations from his radical friends in Carmel to photograph strikes because he feared his equipment would be harmed.

32. Quotes from F. Hall Higgins to Frank Ridgeway, farm editor, *Chicago Tribune,* October 9, 1936, F. Hal Higgins Collection, Archives and Special Collections, University of California, Davis; and *Pacific Rural Press,* September 26, 1936.

33. "LaFollette Civil Liberties Committee Seeks Source of Tear Gas Used in Salinas and San Francisco Dock Strike," *San Francisco News,* September 25, 1936.

11. Always One of Your People

1. Jackson Benson, *The True Adventures of John Steinbeck: Writer* (New York, 1984), 347. See also, Donald N. Noble, ed., *The Steinbeck Question: New Essays in Criticism* (Troy, N.Y., 1993); Jay Parini, *John Steinbeck: A Biography* (New York, 1995).

2. *San Francisco News,* February 20, 1936; Brian Q. Cannon, "Keep on A-Going: Life and Social Interaction in a New Deal Farm Labor Camp," *Agricultural History* 70 (Winter 1996): 1–32; Walter Rundell, "Steinbeck's Image of the American West," *American West* 1 (Spring 1964): 4–17, 1–79; Jackson Benson, "'To Tom, Who Lived It': John Steinbeck and the Man from Weedpatch," *Journal of Modern Literature* (April 1976): 184–86.

3. John Steinbeck, "The Harvest Gypsies," *San Francisco News,* October 5–12, 1936, reprinted in Charles N. Wollenberg, ed., *The Harvest Gypsies: On the Road to the Grapes of Wrath* (Berkeley, 1988); Loftis, *Witness to the Struggle,* 144–54; Meltzer, *Dorothea Lange,* 155; Benson, "'To Tom, Who Lived It,'" 151–210; John Steinbeck, "Dubious Battle in California," *Nation* 143 (September 12, 1936): 302–4; Elaine Steinbeck and Robert Wallsten, eds., *John Steinbeck: A Life in Letters* (New York, 1975).

4. Arthur Rothstein, "The Assignment I'll Never Forget," in Harvey Fondiller, ed., *The Best of Popular Photography* (New York, 1979), 215–17; Hurley, *Portrait of a Decade,* 86–87.

5. Quotes from Meltzer, *Dorothea Lange,* 155–56.

6. Belinda Rathbone, *Walker Evans: A Biography* (New York, 1995), 147.

7. Lange to M. E. Gilfond, October 19, 1936; Frederick Soule to Gilfond, n.d. (enclosures), stamped as received September 16, 1936; both in Stryker–Lange Correspondence, Roy Stryker Papers, UL Photo Archives.

8. *Mid-week Pictorial,* October 17, 1936, FSA/OWI Scrapbook, Written Records, FSA/OWI Collection, Library of Congress.

9. Quote from Stryker to Lange, October 22, 1936, Stryker–Lange Correspondence, Roy Stryker Papers, UL Photo Archives. See also Hurley, *Portrait of a Decade,* 78–80, which is sympathetic to Stryker.

10. Quote from *New York Times,* June 18, 1936. See also Hendrickson, *Looking for the Light,* 56; and Riess, "Dorothea Lange: Making of a Documentary Photographer," 171.

11. Meltzer, *Dorothea Lange,* 156–57; Street, interview with Paul Taylor, April 11, 1980, Berkeley, author's possession.

12. Loudon Wainwright, *The Great American Magazine: An Inside History of Life* (New York, 1986), 15–16; James L. Baughman, *Henry R. Luce and the Rise of American News Media* (Boston, 1987), 92–93, 170.

13. Wendy Kokol, *Life's America: Family and Nation in Postwar Photojournalism* (Philadelphia, 1994), 23–50; Erika Doss, ed., *Looking at Life Magazine* (Washington, D.C., 2001), 1–24.

14. Lange to Stryker, December 7 and 13, 1936, Stryker–Lange Correspondence, Roy Stryker Papers, UL Photo Archives.

15. Quote from Meltzer, *Dorothea Lange,* 158. See also Loftis, *Witness to the Struggle,* 134–35.

16. Quotes from Stryker to Lange, February 13, 1937; and Lange to Stryker, February 8 and 16, 1937; all in Stryker–Lange Correspondence, Roy Stryker Papers, UL Photo Archives. See also Federal Writers' Project, *California: A Guide to the Golden State* (New York, 1939), 639–40.

17. Quote from Lange to Stryker, February 16, 1937, Stryker–Lange Correspondence, Roy Stryker Papers, UL Photo Archives. For a first-person account of his kidnapping, see James Rorty, *Where Life Is Better* (New York, 1936), 322. See also Starr, *Endangered Dreams,* 68–69; and Meltzer, *Dorothea Lange,* 165.

18. Quote from Lange to Stryker, February 16, 1937, Stryker–Lange Correspondence, Roy Stryker Papers, UL Photo Archives. See also Street, interview with Rondal Partridge, June 3, 1998, Berkeley, author's possession; and Meltzer, *Dorothea Lange,* 166–67.

19. Quotes from Meltzer, *Dorothea Lange,* 167.

20. Quotes from Meltzer, *Dorothea Lange,* 167; supplemented and verified in Street, interviews with Rondal Partridge, July 6 and August 12, 1998, Berkeley, California, author's possession. See also Elizabeth Partridge and Sally Stein, *Quizzical Eye: The Photography of Rondal Partridge* (San Francisco, 2003), 21.

21. Quotes from Lange to Stryker, February 21, 1937, Stryker–Lange Correspondence, Roy Stryker Papers, UL Photo Archives; and Richard K. Doud, interview with Dorothea Lange, May 22, 1964, Archives of American Art, Smithsonian Institution (copy in Oakland Museum). See also Street, interview with Partridge, March 12, 1975, Berkeley, author's possession.

22. Guimond, *American Photography and the American Dream,* 112–15.

23. Images LC-USF34-016237-E; LC-USF34-016316-E; and LC-USF34-016317-E; all in FSA/OWI Collection, Library of Congress; Heyman, Phillips, and Szarkowski, *Dorothea Lange: American Photographer,* 1, 106.

24. Partridge, ed., *Dorothea Lange,* 112.

25. Quotes from Lange to Stryker, February 16 and March 12, 1937, Stryker–Lange Correspondence, Roy Stryker Papers, UL Photo Archives. Also Lange to Stryker, March 9, 19, and 23, 1937.

26. Meltzer, *Dorothea Lange,* 168.

27. Quotes from Lange to Stryker, March 17, 1937, Stryker–Lange Correspondence, Roy Stryker Papers, UL Photo Archives; and Linda A. Morris, "A Woman of Our Generation," in Elizabeth Partridge, ed., *Dorothea Lange: A Visual Life* (Washington, D.C., 1994), 22, 33, but exact letter not cited. For the letter, see Stryker to Lange, March 24, 1937, Stryker–Lange Correspondence, Roy Stryker Papers, UL Photo Archives.

28. Quote from Lange to Stryker, March 12, April 2, 1937, Stryker–Lange Correspondence, Roy Stryker Papers, UL Photo Archives. For Lange's description of her trip see Lange to Stryker, April 6, 1937, Stryker–Lange Correspondence, Roy Stryker Papers, UL Photo Archives; and Lange Field Notes, February 20–March 1937, Dorothea Lange Collection, Oakland Museum.

29. Lange to Stryker, March 9, 19, and 23, 1937, Stryker–Lange Correspondence, Roy Stryker Papers, UL Photo Archives; Eugene Smith, "One Whom I Admire: Dorothea Lange," *Popular Photography* 58 (February 1966): 86; Meltzer, *Dorothea Lange,* 171; Doss, ed., *Looking at Life Magazine,* 1–25.

30. Quotes from Lange to Stryker, March 24, April 6 and 27, 1937; also April 23; all in Stryker–Lange Correspondence, Roy Stryker Papers, UL Photo Archives.

31. Steinbeck to George Abee, [1936] and January 11, [1937], in Steinbeck and Wallsten, eds., *John Steinbeck,* 132–34; Street, interview with Paul Taylor, February 11, 1978, Berkeley, California, author's possession; Street, interview with F. Hal Higgins, May 23, 1970, Woodland, California, author's possession; James Rorty, *Where Life Is Better* (New York, 1936), 322; Lange to Stryker, February 16, 1937, Stryker–Lange Correspondence, Roy Stryker Papers, UL Photo Archives.

32. Quotes from "The Candid Camera," *Apathy,* bulletin no. 40 (April 13, 1937), citing John Pickett, editorial, *Pacific Rural Press,* April 3, 1937; Fred Goodcell to Associated Farmer county units, June 1, 1937, in LaFollette Committee Hearings, part 69: 25283–84.

33. Brian Q. Cannon, "Casa Grande Farms," in Katherine G. Morrissey and Kristen M. Jensen, eds., *Picturing Arizona: The Photographic Record of the 1930s* (Tucson, Ariz., 2005), 61–79; Meltzer, *Dorothea Lange,* 172–77.

34. Quote from Riess, "Paul S. Taylor: California Social Scientist," 1: 136. The ideas about the moment that Lange and Taylor conceived of doing their own picture book are from Henry Mayer. A dummy layout of an early version of Lange and Taylor's *An American Exodus* narrated the encounter at length. See Taylor, "Note from the Field on Seven Texans," in Taylor to Thomas C. Blaisdell Jr., June 8, 1937, FSA/OWI Written Records, FSA/OWI Collection, Library of Congress, reiterated in Taylor to Blaisdell, June 14, 1937, Paul Taylor Papers, Bancroft Library.

35. Quote from Riess, "Dorothea Lange: Making of a Documentary Photographer," 177, also 208. See also Elliot, *Dorothea Lange,* 8; Meltzer, *Dorothea Lange,* 173–75; and Ohrn, *Dorothea Lange,* figures 28–29. Lange made seven photographs at this site, one of which shows the entire group, and various prints that include six, five, and four-and-a-half men. Considerable debate surrounds her cropping, whether it was done for aesthetic reasons or simply to accommodate a book layout.

36. Meltzer, *Dorothea Lange,* 173–74.

37. "The U.S. Dust Bowl," *Life* 21 (June 1937): 60–65, FSA Scrapbook; Lange, "Migrant Workers," in Fleischhauer and Brannan, eds., *Documenting America, 1935–1943,* 116–17. A subsequent example of altered meaning occurred when *U.S. Camera* published a feature on Lange's work and mixed up her captions so that those referring to the Dust Bowl appeared under her portraits of people on the streets in San Francisco. See Pare Lorentz, "Dorothea Lange: Camera with a Purpose," *U.S. Camera Annual, 1941,* vol. 10 (New York, 1941), 93–98. In May 2004, more than fifty vintage Lange press prints from her RA assignments were discovered in a filing cabinet in Thousand Oaks, California, among the papers of Elmer E. Lore, a newspaper linotype operator and California assemblyman from 1934 to 1940. As chairman of the State Assembly Committee on Social

Service and Welfare, Lore had become interested in the plight of migrants and taken the initiative of writing to Paul Taylor requesting information. See *Ventura Star,* May 29, 2004.

38. "Counties Oust Farm Strikers," and "In Fruit Crop Conflict," *Oakland Tribune,* June 23, 1937. Lange's thinking can be followed in Lange to Stryker, May 28 and June 3, 1937, Stryker–Lange Correspondence, Roy Stryker Papers, UL Photo Archives.

39. Stryker and Wood, *In This Proud Land,* 187. See also Hurley, *Portrait of a Decade,* 96–98.

40. Quote from Meltzer, *Dorothea Lange,* 180.

41. Quotes from Lange to Stryker, October 6 and October 20, 1937, Stryker–Lange Correspondence, Roy Stryker Papers, UL Photo Archives.

42. Quotes from Lange to Stryker, October 6, 10, and 20, 1937, Stryker–Lange Correspondence, Roy Stryker Papers, UL Photo Archives.

43. Quote from photo documentation files, Chino Public Library, courtesy of Jennifer Fukunaga. For Lange, see Lange to Stryker, June 3, 1937; and Taylor to Tom Blaisdell Jr., June 3, 1937; both in Stryker–Lange Correspondence, Roy Stryker Papers, UL Photo Archives. For the Farm Security Administration at this time, see Baldwin, *Poverty and Politics,* 193.

44. Quote from Lange to Stryker, November 16, 1937; also October 20, 1937; both in Stryker–Lange Correspondence, Roy Stryker Papers, UL Photo Archives. See also Coke, "Dorothea Lange: Compassionate Recorder," 90–95.

12. A Record of Human Erosion

1. Quote from Lange to Stryker, January 12, 1938, Stryker–Lange Correspondence, Roy Stryker Papers, UL Photo Archives.

2. Quote from Lange to Stryker, January 12, 1938; see also October 20, 1937. For Lange's devotion to California, see Richard K. Doud, "Interview with Dorothea Lange," in Howard M. Levin and Katherine Northrup, eds., *Dorothea Lange: Farm Security Administration Photographs, 1935–1939* (Glencoe, Ill., 1980), 1: 7.

3. Quote from Meltzer, *Dorothea Lange,* 181. See also Reiss, "Paul S. Taylor: California Social Scientist," 1: 143–44. For the camps, see Gregory, *American Exodus,* 9, 39; Ann Loftis, "Steinbeck and the Federal Migrant Camps," *San Jose Studies* 16 (Winter 1990): 76–90; and Benson, "'To Tom, Who Lived It,'" 151–94.

4. Quote from Simon J. Lubin, "Can the Radicals Capture the Farms of California?" speech before the Commonwealth Club of California, March 1934, Simon J. Lubin Papers, Bancroft Library.

5. "Lubin Society-History," n.d., Lubin Papers, Bancroft Library; [Helen Hosmer], "Who Are the Associated Farmers?" *Rural Observer* (September–October 1938), Helen Hosmer Papers, Stanford University Archives and Special Collections; Walter J. Stein, *California and the Dust Bowl Migration* (Westport, Conn., 1973), 76, 97, 202, 244–45.

6. Quote from Stott, *Documentary Expression and Thirties America,* 59. For the second photograph, see Edward Steichen, ed., *The Bitter Years, 1935–1941* (New York, 1962), n.p. Edith Lowry, *Migrants of the Crops: They Starve That We May Eat* (New York, 1938), also includes a photograph of a Mexican mother and her child that some call a precursor image to *Migrant Mother.*

7. Steinbeck added an epilogue titled "Starvation under the Orange Trees." Lange contributed photographs to the front and back covers. Like many of Lange's photographs, the cover shot is somewhat a mystery. Usually dated 1935, the Oakland Museum copy is titled *Drought Refugees Hoping for Cotton Work, Blythe, California, 1936.* The photo is also dated 1936 in David P. Peller, *Hope amongst Us Yet: Social Criticism and Social Solace in Depression America* (Athens, Ga., 1987), 65, 115. Lange could have chosen other images for the cover. She had taken plenty of pictures of

bindle stiffs, drifters, tramps, and unfortunate, aimless down-and-outers. But she apparently did not want to use any photographs of people who seemed poor through laziness or moral dereliction. She wanted an image projecting the simple dignity of people who had "leaned against" the wind, as she put it, honest, straight-talking, accommodating, and decent people who worked in the sun.

8. Quotes from Lange to Stryker, May 2, 1938, Stryker–Lange Correspondence, Roy Stryker Papers, UL Photo Archives. See also Carle Zimmerman and Nathan Whetten, *Rural Families on Relief* (Washington, D.C., 1938), 93; and Ronni Ann Frankel, "Photography and the Farm Security Administration: The Visual Politics of Dorothea Lange and Ben Shahn," senior honors thesis, Cornell University, 1969.

9. Quote from Stryker to Lange, May 17, 1938, Stryker–Lange Correspondence, Roy Stryker Papers, UL Photo Archives. See also Lange to Stryker, May 23, 1938.

10. Stott, *Documentary Expression and Thirties America,* ix–x, 3–4, 6–7, 9–14, 23, 26.

11. Gernsheim and Gernsheim, *The History of Photography,* 447; Robert H. Bremner, *Up from the Depths* (New York, 1956), 196.

12. Quote from Stott, *Documentary Expression and Thirties America,* 213, also 30, 212–14. See also James Korges, *Erskine Caldwell* (Minneapolis, 1969), 14.

13. Erskine Caldwell and Margaret Bourke-White, *You Have Seen Their Faces* (New York, 1937), 77, 108, 111, 165, 167, 187; John Rogers Puckett, *Five Photo–Textual Documentaries of the Great Depression* (Ann Arbor, Mich., 1984), 87, 91; Margaret Bourke-White, *Portrait of Myself* (New York, 1963), 122, 126, 137; Margaret Bourke-White, "Notes on Photographs," in Caldwell and Bourke-White, *You Have Seen Their Faces,* 187; Susan Kaplan, "Study and Comparison of Margaret Bourke-White and Dorothea Lange," MA thesis, Goddard College, 1976, including eleven pages of notes from an interview with Paul S. Taylor, January 22, 1976; Stott, *Documentary Expression and Thirties America,* 211, 216, 220–21; Elliot, "On Dorothea Lange," *Dorothea Lange,* 8–9.

14. Quotes from Stott, *Documentary Expression and Thirties America,* 223–24. See also H[erman] C[larence] Nixon, *Forty Acres and Steel Mules* (Chapel Hill, N.C., 1938), 3, 19, 26, 35, 45, 60; H. C. Nixon, *Possum Trot, Rural Community, South* (Norman, Okla., 1941); and H. C. Nixon, "Whither Southern Economy," *I'll Take My Stand* (New York, 1930).

15. Quotes from Stott, *Documentary Expression and Thirties America,* 222–23, 310, 313; and Meltzer, *Dorothea Lange,* 185. See also Archibald MacLeish, *Land of the Free* (New York, 1938); Stott, *Documentary Expression and Thirties America,* 224–25; and T. K. Whipple, review of *Land of the Free, New Republic* (April 13, 1938): 311–12.

16. Quote from Riess, "Paul S. Taylor: California Social Scientist," 1: 217.

17. First quote from James Agee and Walker Evans, *Let Us Now Praise Famous Men: Three Tenant Families* (New York, 1940), inside front page, xiii–xvi; and Stott, *Documentary Expression and Thirties America,* 290, see also 262–66; second quote from Rathbone, *Walker Evans,* 155, also 134–38.

18. Walker Evans, *American Photographs* (New York, 1938), 197; James R. Mellow, *Walker Evans* (New York, 1999), 307–31; Dale Mahridge and Michael Williamson, *And Their Children after Them: The Legacy of "Let Us Now Praise Famous Men": James Agee, Walker Evans, and the Rise and Fall of Cotton in the South* (New York, 1989).

19. Pare Lorentz, "We Don't Know," *Saturday Review* 2 (April 1938): 6; Riess, "Paul S. Taylor: California Social Scientist," 1: 217, 295; Meltzer, *Dorothea Lange,* 183–86; Stryker to Lange, May 17, 1938, Stryker–Lange Correspondence, Roy Stryker Papers, UL Photo Archives; Puckett, *Five Photo–Textual Documentaries,* 83–109. Besides evaluating *An American Exodus* alongside the work of four other photo documentaries, Puckett's work compares the first and second editions of *An American Exodus.*

20. Quote from Hank O'Neal, *A Vision Shared* (New York, 1976), 175. Hendrickson, *Looking for the Light,* 44–45, 58–64, does not mention the incident with Lange. See also Meltzer, *Dorothea Lange,* 185–87; *San Francisco Examiner,* April 26, 1938; and Stryker and Wood, *In This Proud Land,* 708.

21. Taylor and Lange, *An American Exodus,* 136; Stephen C. Hust, *This Is My Own, My Native Land* (Yuba City, Calif., 1956); Ken Conner and Debra Heimerdinger, *Horace Bristol: An American View* (San Francisco, 1996), 9–13, 37–41, 55–57; Horace Bristol, "Steinbeck and Other Recollections," MS, n.d., 1–14, courtesy Horace Bristol. See also David Sheff, "Fifty Years of John Steinbeck's *The Grapes of Wrath:* 1939–1989, The People Who Lived His Story . . . and Are Living It Now," *California* 14 (October 1989): 93; and Steinbeck and Wallsten, eds., *Steinbeck,* 158–59.

22. Quote from Steinbeck to Elizabeth Otis, March 7, 1938, in Steinbeck and Wallsten, eds., *Steinbeck,* 161. For similar sentiments, see Steinbeck to Otis, February ? and 14, 1938, ibid.; Steinbeck to Pare Lorentz, March 6, [1938], in Pare Lorentz, *FDR's Moviemaker: Memoirs and Scripts* (Reno, Nev., 1992), 122, 157–59; and Thomas Kiernan, *The Intricate Music: A Biography of John Steinbeck* (Boston, 1979), 228.

23. Quotes from Horace Bristol, "Faces of the Grapes of Wrath," *This World: San Francisco Chronicle* (October 25, 1987): 14; and John Loengard, "Horace Bristol," in Loengard, *Life Photographers,* 68. Slightly corrupting and skewing this episode, Jay Parini, *John Steinbeck: A Biography* (New York, 1995), 199, reports that *Life* killed Steinbeck's story as too "liberal." There is no documented explanation why *Life* nixed Steinbeck's words but later ran Bristol's photographs. See also Horace Bristol, "Documenting the Grapes of Wrath," *Californians* 12 (January–February 1988): 40–47; Benson, *The True Adventures of John Steinbeck,* 422; David Roberts, "Travels with Steinbeck," *American Photographer* 19 (March 1989): 45; and "Speaking of Pictures: These by *Life* Prove Facts in *Grapes of Wrath,*" *Life* 22 (February 19, 1940): 10–11.

24. Newhall, ed., *The Daybooks of Edward Weston,* 1; Conger, *Edward Weston in Mexico;* Conger, "Edward Weston's Early Photography, 1903–1926"; Spaulding, *Ansel Adams and the American Landscape,* 137–38; Tomkins, *Paul Strand;* Ansel Adams to Edward Weston, November 29, 1934, and August 6, 1935; Weston to Adams, December 3, 1934; both in Edward Weston Archive, Center for Creative Photography, University of Arizona, Tucson. Contrary to Beaumont Newhall's claim in *History of Photography,* 146, Lange was never a member of Group f/64. For Mancusco, see Jerome Prescott, ed., *America at the Crossroads: Great Photographs from the Thirties* (New York, 1995), 81. Mancusco's photographs are in the San Francisco History Center Archives, San Francisco Public Library. For Kanaga, see Barbara Head Millstein, *Consuelo Kanaga: An American Photographer* (Seattle, 1992), 35–36; Paul Dorsey, "Waifs in the Winds," *Westways* 31 (June 1939): 16–17; and Paul Dorsey, "Bindle Stiffs," *Westways* (October 1939): 8–9.

25. Patricia Junker, "Celebrating Possibilities and Controlling Limits: Painting of the 1930s and 1940s," in Steven A. Nash et al., *Facing Eden: 100 Years of Landscape Art in the Bay Area* (San Francisco, 1995), 66; Marlene Park and Gerald Markowitz, *Democratic Vistas: Post Offices and Public Art in the New Deal* (Philadelphia, 1984).

26. Alma Reed, *The Mexican Muralists* (New York, 1960); Melba Levick and Stanley Young, *The Big Picture: Murals of Los Angeles* (New York, 1988); Orville Clarke Jr., "Social Statements in Art: WPA Murals," *Antiques and Fine Art* 5 (November–December 1987): 54–59.

27. Steven Gebler, "Working to Prosperity: California's New Deal Murals," *California History* 105 (Spring 1977): 117. See also Steven Gebler and Lydia Modi Vitale, *New Deal Art: California* (Santa Clara, Calif., 1976), 23–24, 110–17. The government first began subsidizing unemployed artists with the Public Works Art Project. After that agency folded in 1934, artists found work with the State Emergency Relief Administration, then in 1935 with the Treasury Relief Arts Project and the Federal Arts Project of the WPA.

28. For Coit Tower, see Anthony W. Lee, *Painting on the Left: Diego Rivera, Radical Politics, and San Francisco's Public Murals* (Berkeley, 1999), 92–93, 134–59. See also Renee Ann Koury, "Faulty Tower," *California Living Magazine* (October 2, 1983): 15–17.

29. For Shore, see Sylvia Moore, ed., *Yesterday and Tomorrow: California Women Artists* (New York, 1989); and Patricia Trenton, ed., *Independent Spirits: Women Painters of the American West, 1890–1945* (Berkeley, 1995). For Bloch, see Lucienne Bloch, "Murals for Use," in Francis V. O'Conner, ed., *Art for the Millions: Essays from the 1930s by Artists and Administrators of the WPA Federal Art Project* (New York, 1973). Photographs of murals are in "Photographs of Murals in United States Post Offices, California," looseleaf, 2 vols., Records of the Public Building Service, RG 121, National Archives.

30. Quote from Stephanie Barron, Sheri Bernstein, and Ilene Susan Fort, eds., *Made in California: Art, Image, and Identity, 1900–2000* (Los Angeles, 2001), 118. A fine discussion of Diego Rivera's murals *Allegory of California* and *Still Life with Blossoming Almond Trees* is in Sackman, *Orange Empire,* 1–10. See also pp. 123–26 for a critique of New Deal murals citing the insightful observations of a prominent orange grower. See also Laurance Hulburt, *The Mexican Muralists in the United States* (Albuquerque, N.M., 1989), 100, 107; Bertram Wolfe, *The Fabulous Life of Diego Rivera* (New York, 1963), 285; and Mark Dean Johnson, ed., *At Work: The Art of California Labor* (Berkeley, 2003), 16–18.

31. "R. D. Ginther, Workingman Artist and Historian of Skid Row," *California Historical Quarterly* 104 (Fall 1975): 263–66; Wallace Stegner, "Depression Pop: Bad Times and the Art of R. D. Ginther," *Esquire* 35 (September 1975): 79–83, 154. Biographical details supplied by the Washington State Historical Society, Tacoma, Washington.

32. Quote from Meltzer, *Dorothea Lange,* 188. See also Stryker to Lange, October 7, 1938, Stryker–Lange Correspondence, Roy Stryker Papers, UL Photo Archives.

33. Ever attentive to irony and juxtaposition, Lange was traveling past Shafter in February 1937, when she spotted a billboard advertising Cyanogas, a new spray used to control infestations of leaf hoppers in table-grape vineyards. Migrants were using the billboard as a shelter. Bedding, mattresses, and tools are strewn about. Apparently tidying up their makeshift shelter, two girls had just finished wrapping the bottom of the sign in burlap. As Lange photographed, one of the girls peeked around the billboard corner while the other adjusted a burlap cover stamped with "Shafter Long White Potatoes." See LC-USF34-016463-E.

34. Lange to Stryker, November 1, 1938, Stryker–Lange Correspondence, Roy Stryker Papers, UL Photo Archives. See also Lange to Stryker, October 19, 1938; O'Neal, *A Vision Shared,* 175; and Stryker to Tugwell, June 29, 1938, Rexford Tugwell Papers, Franklin D. Roosevelt Library, Hyde Park, New York. *Kern County Cotton Strike* (silent film, 20 minutes, [1939]), Southern California Library for Social Studies and Research, Los Angeles, has shots of Dorothy Ray Healey, picketing, arrests, and fieldwork. See Sarah Cooper to author, April 22, 1993, author's possession.

35. For Lange's photographs at Madera, see the collection of unpublished pictures given to me by Paul S. Taylor, author's possession, some of which appeared in *People's World* during November 1939.

36. Quotes from Lange to Stryker, November 12, 1938, Stryker–Lange Correspondence, Roy Stryker Papers, UL Photo Archives; and LC-USF34-018383-E, FSA/OWI Collection, Library of Congress. See also Street, interview with Partridge, April 12, 2005, Berkeley, California; Weber, *Dark Sweat, White Gold,* 182; and Robert Burke, *Olson's New Deal for California* (Berkeley, 1953), 22. For flash equipment, see Meltzer, *Dorothea Lange,* 171.

37. Lange to Stryker, November 12, 1938, Stryker–Lange Correspondence, Roy Stryker Papers, UL Photo Archives. For background, see Terence Edwin Smith, "Making the Modern: The Visual Imagery of Modernity, U.S.A., 1908–1939," PhD diss., University of Sydney, Australia, 1985, 342–43;

and Maren Stange, "'The Record Itself': Farm Security Administration Photography and the Transformation of Rural Life," in Pete Daniel, Merry A. Foresta, Maren Stange, and Sally Stein, *Official Images: New Deal Photography* (Washington, D.C., 1987), 3–4.

38. Quote from Carey McWilliams, "California Pastoral," *Antioch Review* 2 (March 1942): 103. See also Burke, *Olson's New Deal for California,* 90–91, 119–21, 138; and Stein, *California and the Dust Bowl Migration,* 92–97, 117, 247.

39. Lange to Stryker, November 12, 1938, Stryker–Lange Correspondence, Roy Stryker Papers, UL Photo Archives; Lange Field Notes, 2: 360–72, Dorothea Lange Collection, Oakland Museum; David M. Kennedy, *Freedom from Fear: The American People in Depression and War, 1929–1945* (New York, 1999), 344–50, 420–23, 782.

40. Quotes from Lange to Stryker, November 12, 1938, and Stryker to Lange, December 12, 1938; both in Stryker–Lange Correspondence, Roy Stryker Papers, UL Photo Archives. See also Steichen, "The F.S.A. Photographers," 43–65; and *Springfield Union and Republican,* September 12, 1938.

41. Lange to Stryker, November 12, 22, and December 7, 22, 1938; Stryker to Lange, December 22, 1938; all in Stryker–Lange Correspondence, Roy Stryker Papers, UL Photo Archives; Street, interview with Taylor, June 22, 1976, Berkeley, author's possession.

42. Heyman, Phillips, and Szarkowski, eds., *Dorothea Lange: American Photographer,* 29.

43. Quote from Lange Field Notes, February 18, 1939, Dorothea Lange Collection, Oakland Museum. See also Lange and Taylor, *An American Exodus,* 129; and Meltzer, *Dorothea Lange,* 196–99.

44. Quotes from Lange and Taylor, *An American Exodus,* 111–15, 129.

45. Ibid., 130.

46. Quote from Street, interview with Helen Hosmer, March 12, 1975, Redwood City, California, author's possession. See also clipping, *Rural Observer,* March and December 1939, Helen Hosmer Collection. I consulted this collection when I met Hosmer at her home in the mid-1970s. It is now at Stanford University.

47. Quotes from Riess, "Paul S. Taylor: California Social Scientist," 1: 217–18, 295; and Lange and Taylor, *An American Exodus,* 5–6.

48. Quotes from Lange and Taylor, *An American Exodus,* 36, 65, see also 4–6, 152–56.

49. Ibid., 135.

50. Ibid., 144–49.

51. Lange, *Dorothea Lange Looks at the American Country Woman,* 7; Alfred Kazin, *On Native Grounds: An Interpretation of Modern American Prose Literature* (New York, 1942), 494; Lorentz, "Dorothea Lange," 93–116, 229.

52. Stange, *Symbols of Ideal Life,* 120–22; Robert L. Reid, *Picturing Texas: The FSA–OWI Photographers in the Lone Star State, 1935–1943* (Austin, Tex., 1994), 23–24.

13. Facts and Fiction

1. For Sturtevant's role in the retouching incident, see Street, interview with Rondal Partridge, March 23, 2001, and April 12, 2005, Berkeley, author's possession. Henry Mayer argued that the object in question was not Florence Thompson's thumb but may have been Lange's finger or thumb. I think it is a right thumb. However, this makes no sense unless Lange was holding her camera in her left hand and arm and balancing by holding on to the tent pole with her right hand. Henry Mayer to author, April 11, 2000, author's possession. See also Riess, "Dorothea Lange: Making of a Documentary Photographer," 1: 199.

2. Quote from Meltzer, *Dorothea Lange,* 200. The rift between Lange and Stryker can be followed in Stryker to Lange, December 22, 1938; and Lange to Stryker, December 7, 1938, and May

16, 1939; all in Stryker–Lange Correspondence, Roy Stryker Papers, UL Photo Archives. See also Hurley, *Portrait of a Decade,* 142–43. For retouching at this time, see Hicks, *Words and Pictures,* 42. For examples of the print before retouching, see James L. McCamy, *Government Publicity: Its Practice in Federal Administration* (Chicago, 1939), opposite 238; and MacLeish, *Land of the Free.* Also, a vintage print in the Sotheby 1999 catalog clearly shows a thumb or finger (slightly out of focus) in the lower right corner, as does the image on the cover of *U.S. Camera Annual, 1936,* and an unretouched print in the FSA/OWI Collection, Library of Congress. See also "Look in Her Eyes," *Mid-week Pictorial,* October 17, 1936, FSA Scrapbook, FSA/OWI Collection, Written Records of the Farm Security Administration, Historical Section—Office of War Information, Overseas Picture Division, Washington Section Collection, Prints and Photographs Division, Library of Congress.

3. Quote from Riess, "Dorothea Lange: Making of a Documentary Photographer," 172. See also Ohrn, *Dorothea Lange and the Documentary Tradition,* 102.

4. Quote from Stryker to Lange, December 22, 1938, in Stryker–Lange Correspondence, Roy Stryker Papers, UL Photo Archives.

5. Newport Harbor Art Museum, *Just before the War: Urban America from 1935 to 1941* (Balboa, Calif., 1968), 8–9; Street, interview with Rondal Partridge, May 12, 1981, Berkeley, author's possession.

6. Reiss, "Paul S. Taylor: California Social Scientist," 1: 124; Riess, "Dorothea Lange: Making of a Documentary Photographer," 171–72; Elliot, *Dorothea Lange,* 9–10; O'Neal, *A Vision Shared,* 46; Anette Melville, *Farm Security Administration, Historical Section: A Guide to Textual Records in the Library of Congress* (Washington, D.C., 1985), 12–13.

7. Quote from Garst to Stryker, May 13, 1939, Stryker–Lange Correspondence, Roy Stryker Papers, UL Photo Archives.

8. Ohrn, *Dorothea Lange and the Documentary Tradition,* 72; FSA/OWI Collection, caption file for negatives 16043–20268, A–E series, box 9, FSA/OWI Written Records, Library of Congress.

9. "I Wonder Where We Can Go Now," *Fortune* 19 (April 1939): 91–95 (illustrated with watercolors by Millard Sheets); "Along the Road: Extracts from a Reporter's Notebook," 96–100 (illustrated with photographs by Lange and Bristol).

10. Horace Bristol, "Travels with Steinbeck," *People* (May 1, 1989): 67–73; Dean Brierly, "Horace Bristol: Eye on an Era," *Photo Metro* 2 (August 1993): 3–15; Robert T. Elson, "Remembrance of LIFE Past," *f.y.i.* (December 11, 1972): n.p.; Mark Edward Harris, "Picture Stories: The Life and Times of Horace Bristol," *Camera and Darkroom: The Magazine for Creative Photography* (August 1993): 23–28; Laurence J. Pett, "Horace Bristol and the Great Old Life," *Photo District News* (April 1989): 96–98; *Publisher's Weekly,* April 13, 1940. Scholars later linked passages in *The Grapes of Wrath* to some of Lange's images and captions. See D. G. Kehl, "Steinbeck's String of Pictures in *The Grapes of Wrath,*" *Image* 17 (March 1974): 2. Zanuck's movie adaptation of *The Grapes of Wrath,* which many found superior to the book, opened at the Rivoli Theater in New York City.

11. Quotes from Frank Condon, "The Grapes of Raps: Hollywood Makes a Picture Strictly under Blankets," *Collier's* 27 (January 1940): 32; Frank J. Taylor, "California's Grapes of Wrath," *Reader's Digest* (November 1939); *Publisher's Weekly,* April 13, 1941; and *New York Times,* April 27, 1939. See also Stein, *California and the Dust Bowl Migration,* 116–17; "Is the Grapes of Wrath Too Hot for Hollywood?" *Look* 2 (October 24, 1939): 12–22; Janis and MacNeil, eds., *Photography within the Humanities,* 31; Tim Kappel, "Kern County's Ban on *The Grapes of Wrath,*" *California History* 61 (Winter 1982): 210; Steinbeck to Elizabeth [Otis], December 15, 1939, in Steinbeck and Wallsten, eds., *Steinbeck,* 195; and interview no. 204 with Catherine Sullivan, February 27, 1981, California Odyssey Project, California State University, Bakersfield.

12. Quote from Shindo, *Dust Bowl Migrants in the American Imagination,* 118–19. See also Kehl, "Steinbeck's 'String of Pictures' in *The Grapes of Wrath,*" 1–10; Lorentz, "Dorothea Lange,"

93; Gary C. Davis, "John Steinbeck in Films: An Analysis of Realism in the Novel and the Film—A Non-textual Approach," PhD diss., University of Southern California, 1975, 66–75; and 20th Century–Fox, publicity photographs from *The Grapes of Wrath,* 1940, Academy of Motion Picture Arts and Sciences, Los Angeles.

13. *Factories in the Field* was published in July. See Greg Critser, "The Political Rebellion of Carey McWilliams," *UCLA Historical Journal* 4 (1983): 34–65; Greg Critser, "The Making of a Cultural Rebel: Carey McWilliams, 1924–1930," *Pacific Historical Review* 55 (May 1986): 226–55; Carey McWilliams, *The Education of Carey McWilliams* (New York, 1978), 74–78; and John E. Pickett, "Termites Steinbeck and McWilliams," *Pacific Rural Press,* July 29, 1939. Pare Lorentz, *FDR's Moviemaker: Memoirs and Scripts* (Reno, Nev., 1992), 122, discusses how he, Lange, and Steinbeck borrowed from one another. Writing to Stryker, Edwin Locke concluded that it was mostly Steinbeck borrowing from Lange. "I am reading Steinbeck's great book, and it is great," he wrote. "When you read it, notice how like the pictures of D. Lange it is." Edwin Locke to Stryker, April 28, 1939, Roy Stryker Papers, UL Photo Archives. For Dorsey's work, see Dorsey, "Waifs of the Winds"; and Dorsey, "Bindle Stiffs."

14. Quote from Starr, *Endangered Dreams,* 265.

15. Quotes from Lange to Stryker, September 7 and 9, 1939, Stryker–Lange Correspondence, Roy Stryker Papers, UL Photo Archives; Lange and Taylor to Reynal and Hitchcock, September 6, 1939; and J. A. McKaughan to Lange and Taylor, September 22, 1939; both in the Dorothea Lange Collection, Oakland Museum. See also Lange to McKaughan, September 25, 1939; exchanges of September 28 and October 4 and 7, 1939; all in the Dorothea Lange Collection; Steinbeck to Pascal Covici, n.d., 1939, John Steinbeck Papers, Harry Ransom Humanities Research Center, University of Texas, Austin; Riess, "Paul S. Taylor: California Social Scientist," 1: 218; and "Migratory Labor: A Social Problem," *Fortune* 19 (April 1939): 97–99.

16. Stryker to Lange, October 6, 1939, Stryker–Lange Correspondence, Roy Stryker Papers, UL Photo Archives; Metzler, *Dorothea Lange,* 205–6.

17. O'Neal, *A Vision Shared,* 61; Ohrn, *Dorothea Lange and the Documentary Tradition,* 109–11; Stryker to Lee, January 11, 1940, Stryker–Lange Correspondence, Roy Stryker Papers, UL Photo Archives. Stryker seems to have sanitized that portion of his correspondence surrounding Lange's termination.

18. Quote from Jonathan Garst and Walter Packard to Stryker, November 21, 1939, Stryker–Lange Correspondence, Roy Stryker Papers, UL Photo Archives.

19. Quote from Stryker to Russell Lee, May 17, 1939, quoted in Sally Stein, "FSA Color: The Forgotten Document," *Modern Photography* 43 (June 1979): 95.

20. Mellow, *Walker Evans,* 265, 267, 272, 281, 285, 381; Rathbone, *Walker Evans,* 147–48, 153–54, 165, 190, 209, 234, 247; Hendrickson, *Looking for the Light,* 58–61.

21. Quotes from Stryker to Garst, November 30, 1939; and Stryker to Russell Lee, January 11, 1940; both in Stryker–Lange Correspondence, Roy Stryker Papers, UL Photo Archives. See also Richard K. Doud, interview with Roy Stryker, October 17, 1963, Archives of American Art (copy in the Oakland Museum).

22. Quotes from O'Neal, *A Vision Shared,* 10; Szarkowski, "Dorothea Lange and Paul Taylor," 51.

23. Quote from Guimond, *American Photography and the American Dream,* 121.

24. Quotes from Starr, *Endangered Dreams,* 266, 269. See also Chall, "Paul Taylor: California Social Scientist; California Water and Agricultural Labor," 2: 53–64, Bancroft Library; and Jerold Auerbach, *Labor and Liberty: The LaFollettte Committee and the New Deal* (Indianapolis, 1966), 75–77, 177–96.

25. Quotes from LaFollette Committee Hearings, part 54: 17283, 19947. See also Paul Taylor and Clark Kerr, "Documentary History of the Strike of the Cotton Pickers in California, 1933,"

ibid., 19945–20036; Auerbach, *Labor and Liberty,* 185–86; Kerr, "Paul and Dorothea," in Partridge, ed., *Dorothea Lange,* 39; and Riess, "Paul S. Taylor: California Social Scientist," 1: 203.

26. O'Neal, *A Vision Shared,* 61; Lange to Stryker, January 19, 1940, Stryker–Lange Correspondence, Roy Stryker Papers, UL Photo Archives; *Photo Notes* (February 1940): 3; Street, interview with Paul Taylor, May 10, 1977, Berkeley, author's possession; Nunnally Johnson, "Will 'The Grapes of Wrath' Be Shelved?" *Photoplay* (November 1939), in Richard Griffith, ed., *The Talkies: Articles and Illustrations from a Great Fan Magazine, 1928–1940* (New York, 1971), 260–61, 320; Warren French, *Filmguide to the Grapes of Wrath* (Bloomington, Ind., 1973), 18.

27. Quotes from *Nation* (January 20, 1940): 77; *New Republic* (February 12, 1940): 54; Newhall, *Dorothea Lange Looks at the American Country Woman,* 7; Paul Strand, "An American Exodus by Dorothea Lange and Paul S. Taylor," *Photo Notes* (March–April 1940): 2–3; Riess, "Paul S. Taylor: California Social Scientist," 1: 219, 233; and Lorentz, "Dorothea Lange," 97. See also William S. Hopkins, "Review of *An American Exodus,*" *American Economic Review* 30 (June 1940): 385; Ansel Adams to Lange and Taylor, January 25, 1940; Edward Weston to Lange and Taylor, April 1 and June 1, 1940; clipping, Paul Strand, *Photo Notes* (March–April 1940); all in Dorothea Lange Collection, Oakland Museum; and *Social Forces* 12 (May 1940): 598–99. For a discussion of problems with the 1970 edition reissued by the Oakland Museum and Yale University Press, see *New York Times Book Review,* March 8, 1970.

28. Quotes from A. D. Coleman, review, *New York Times,* February 14, 1971, 38; and Coles, *Doing Documentary Work,* 112–15.

29. Quotes from Henry Mayer, "The Making of a Documentary Book," MS, n.d., author's possession; and Starr, *Endangered Dreams,* 264–65.

30. Stott, *Documentary Expression and Thirties America,* 21, 49, 56, 61; *New Masses* 31 (May 16, 1939): 10; Elizabeth McCausland, "Documentary Photography," *Photo Notes* (January 1939): 6; Elizabeth McCausland, "Hine's Credo," *Photo Notes* (May 1940): 5.

31. Quotes from San Francisco Center for Visual Studies, in *Perspectives* 7 (1978): 8; and Coke, "Dorothea Lange: Compassionate Recorder," 90–91. See also Stott, *Documentary Expression and Thirties America,* 229; and W. Eugene Smith, "One Whom I Admire: Dorothea Lange," *Popular Photography* 58 (February 1966): 88.

32. Quotes from Alice Caton, "Wants More Publicity on Straits of Migrants," *People's World,* October 16, 1939; and Richard K. Doud, interview with Lange, May 22, 1964, 56, Archives of American Art, Smithsonian Institution (copy in Oakland Museum). Contrary to Lange's claim that the FSA public relations effort had failed, the FSA/OWI Supplementary Reference files and agency scrapbooks contain innumerable examples of FSA images being placed in the mass media. A partial publication record of Lange's March 1937 Imperial Valley photography shows it appearing in the *St. Louis Post-Dispatch Sunday Magazine,* April 17, 1938; *Current History* (April 1939): 33; *Social Work* (April 1939); *St. Louis Post-Dispatch Sunday Magazine,* January 28, 1940; *Country Gentleman* (February 1940): 9; and the *Democratic Digest* (June–July 1940): 46. Tracing the exact dates and locations of Lange's images is difficult, because many clippings do not provide proper identifying information.

33. Quote from Doud, interview with Lange, May 22, 1964, Archives of American Art, Smithsonian Institution.

34. Quote from Starr, *Endangered Dreams,* 270. See also Doud, "Interview with Lange," in Levin and Northrup, eds., *Dorothea Lange,* 1: 77, 85; Therese Heyman, interview with Rondal Partridge and Christina Gardner, August 6, 1975, Dorothea Lange Collection, Oakland Museum; and *CIO News,* November 6, 1939.

35. Quotes from Dixon, "Dorothea Lange," 138; and Lange to Stryker, March 31, 1940, Stryker–Lange Correspondence, Roy Stryker Papers, UL Photo Archives. See also Street, interview with

John Collier Jr., May 6, 1979, Mill Valley, California, author's possession; F. Jack Hurley, *Marion Post Wolcott: A Photographic Journey* (Albuquerque, N.M., 1989), 122–29; and Hendrickson, *Looking for the Light,* 202–3.

36. *Life* 2 (June 5, 1939): 22; *Life* 3 (January 22, 1940) (three-page spread of Bristol's photographs): 23; *Life* 3 (February 19, 1940): 11; Goldberg, *The Power of Photography,* 141; Kehl, "Steinbeck's 'String of Pictures' in *The Grapes of Wrath,*" 2; Robert DeMott, *John Steinbeck's Working Days: The Journals of the Grapes of Wrath* (New York, 1990), 174–75; Joseph Millichap, *Steinbeck and Film* (New York, 1983), 26–50; Warren French, *A Companion to the Grapes of Wrath* (New York, 1963), 163.

37. An index to the photographs Lange made for the BAE is in the Audio–Visual Division, Records of the Bureau of Agricultural Economics, RG 83, National Archives; and Lange Field Notes, 1: 639–63, Dorothea Lange Collection, Oakland Museum. Some photographs from her BAE work are also in the Lange Collection. The problem in dating this image is that the BAE photographic file records the date as April 9, 1940, suggesting that it was probably shot during the time Lange was on the BAE payroll. Most likely, this was part of Lange's personal archive. See Records of the Bureau of Agricultural Economics (83-G-41450), National Archives.

38. Quote from Sally Stein, "On Location: The Placement (and Replacement) of California in 1930s Photography," in Stephanie Barron, Sheri Bernstein, and Ilene Susan Fort, eds., *Reading California: Art, Image, and Identity, 1900–2000* (Los Angeles, 2001), 192–93. For an interesting if forced comparison of how Lange and Steinbeck went about their work, see Carol Schloss, *In Visible Light* (New York, 1987), 200–231. A mystery surrounds Lange's famous billboard photograph advertising a March 21 showing of the movie *The Grapes of Wrath* (O.M. 35003 in the Dorothea Lange Collection).

39. Quotes from Stryker to Rothstein, March 2, 5, and 19, 1940, Roy Stryker Papers, UL Photo Archives.

40. Charles L. Todd, "Trampling Out the Vintage," *Common Cause* 8 (July 1939): 7–8, 30; clipping, *Los Angeles Times,* July 9, 1939, Charles Todd Scrapbook, Charles L. Todd Collection and Robert Sonkin–California Migrant Labor Collection, Archive of Folk Culture, Library of Congress; Charles Todd, "The Okies' Search for a Lost Frontier," *New York Times Magazine* (August 27, 1939): 10–11. Charles Todd recalled Rothstein using a "snapshot" technique while photographing. See Margaret and Gerald Parsons, notes from an interview with Prof. Charles L. Todd, August 16, 1985, Archive of Folk Culture, Library of Congress.

41. Quote from Rothstein to Stryker, April 1, 1940, Roy Stryker Papers, UL Photo Archives.

42. Photographs of the visit are in the Eleanor Roosevelt Papers, Franklin D. Roosevelt Library, Hyde Park, New York; and the Helen Gahagan Douglas Collection, Carl Albert Center for Congressional Archives, University of Oklahoma. See also Helen Gahagan Douglas, *A Full Life* (New York, 1982), 146, 154; and Street, interview with Paul Taylor, February 23, 1979, Berkeley, author's possession.

43. Quote from Sally Stein, "Figures of the Future: Photography of the National Youth Administration," in Pete Daniel, Merry A. Foresta, Maren Stange, and Sally Stein, *Official Images: New Deal Photography* (Washington, D.C., 1987), 111; see also 92–113.

44. "She was bound to get exploited, pregnant, and wrinkled under the sun," Partridge recalled of the young girl sixty-three years later in *Quizzical Eye,* the quasi-biography written by his daughter and photographic historian Sally Stein. Quote from Elizabeth Partridge and Sally Stein, *Quizzical Eye: The Photography of Randol Partridge* (San Francisco, 2003), 133; see also plates 17–18. Partridge's work can been seen on its original mount boards in California subgroup, National Youth Authority Collection, RG 119, National Archives.

45. Quote from Kevin Starr, *Endangered Dreams: The Great Depression in California* (New York, 1996), 270. See also Meltzer, *Dorothea Lange,* 233–37.

46. Lange to Henry Allen Moe, September 5 and October 13, 1941, January 10 and April 14, 1942, Dorothea Lange Collection, Oakland Museum.

47. Quote from handwritten notes on reverse of photographs AFC 1985/001:P12 and AFC 1985/001:P16, El Río FSA Camp, Ventura, the Charles L. Todd and Robert Sonkin—California Migrant Labor Collection, Library of Congress Archive of Folklore. For Robert Hemmig, see Shindo, *Dust Bowl Migrants in the American Imagination,* 143–44. Whether photographs 7454 and 7450, Ventura County Museum, taken at the El Río FSA Camp, are by Hemmig or Russell Lee is in question. I am convinced they were taken by Hemmig. One listing for Hemmig appears in the 1941–42 *Ventura County Directory,* which finds him at 952 Poli Street, an apartment complex, nothing before or after. My thanks to Ventura County Museum librarian Charles Johnson for these leads.

48. Quote from Seema Weatherwax as told to Jane Yett, "In Touch with the Human Spirit: On the Road with Woody Guthrie," *Californians* 10 (January–February 1993): 25–30, 35. See also Ed Cray, *Ramblin' Man: The Life and Times of Woody Guthrie* (New York, 2004), 204–5, 226; Huell Howser, *Weedpatch,* California's Gold #601, video (Los Angeles, 1995); Street, interview with Seema Weatherwax, May 12, 1993, Santa Cruz, author's possession; Street, interview with Fred Ross, September 27, 1978, Kentfield, California, author's possession; Street, interview with Jane Yett, September 15, 1994, author's possession; Yett to author, e-mail, November 16, 2003, author's possession; and Dave Marsh, ed., *Pastures of Plenty* (New York, 1990), 261. Many prints that Weatherwax made at the Shafter (Arvin) FSA camp are in the Seema Weatherwax Collection, Archives and Special Collections, Stanford University, and in the Woody Guthrie Archives and Foundation, New York City. Her negatives are in her own private archive in Santa Cruz, California.

49. Quote from Lorentz, "Dorothea Lange," 93.

50. Quote from F. Jack Hurley, *Russell Lee, Photographer* (Dobbs Ferry, N.Y., 1978), 14; see also 9–22, 58–61; William Wroth, ed., *Russell Lee's FSA Photographs of Chamisal and Peñasco, New Mexico* (Santa Fe, N.M., 1985); Mark Adams and Russell Lee, "Our Town in East Texas," *Travel* (March 1940): 5–12; Russell Lee, "Pie Town," *Creative Camera* 193–194 (July–August 1980): 246–53; and F. Jack Hurley, "Pie Town, N.M., 1940," *American Photographer* 10 (March 1983): 76–85.

51. Roger Daniels, *Concentration Camps, North America: Japanese in the United States and Canada during World War II* (Malabar, Fla., 1981), 104–17, 122–29; Dorothy Swain Thomas and Richard Nishimoto, *The Spoilage: Japanese American Evacuation and Resettlement during World War II* (Berkeley, 1946); Jeanne Watatsuki Houston and James D. Houston, *Farewell to Manzanar* (Boston, 1973), 163. For Russell Lee's California sojourn, see Hurley, *Russell Lee,* 21. A good example of his farmworker photography is *Bundling Carrots, Imperial Co., Calif.,* March 1942.

52. Paul Kellogg to Paul Taylor, June 18, 1942; Taylor to Kellogg, July 26, 29, and September 17, 1942; all in Social Welfare History Archives, University of Minnesota; Reiss, "Dorothea Lange: Making of a Documentary Photographer," 186, 191; Reiss, "Paul S. Taylor: California Social Scientist," 1: 228.

53. Riess, "Dorothea Lange: Making of a Documentary Photographer," 186–89. The other WRA photographers were Hikaru Iwasaki, Tom Parker, Frank Stewart, Charles Mace, Fred Clark, and Clem Albers. Albers had been a photographer for the *San Francisco Chronicle.*

54. Quote from Lange caption, Florin, California, May 11, 1942, War Relocation Authority Photographs, National Archives, cited in Richard Conrat and Maise Conrat, *Executive Order 9066: The Internment of 110,000 Japanese Americans* (San Francisco, 1972), 114.

55. Quote from Conrat and Conrat, *Executive Order 9066,* 115. See also Edward H. Spicer et al., *Impounded People: Japanese-Americans in the Relocation Centers* (Tucson, Ariz., 1969).

56. Quote from Conrat and Conrat, *Executive Order 9066,* 115. See also Sylvia F. Danovitch, "The Past Recaptured: The Photographic Record of the Internment of the Japanese-Americans," *Prologue* 12 (1980): 91–103.

57. Quotes from Partridge, ed., *Dorothea Lange,* 49–50; and John Modell, ed., *The Kikuchi Diary, Chronicle from an American Concentration Camp: The Tanforan Journals of Charles Kikuchi* (Urbana, Ill., 1973), 52.

58. Quote from Riess, "Dorothea Dixon: Making of a Documentary Photographer," 190. See Paul Taylor, "Our Stakes in the Japanese Exodus," *Survey Graphic* 31 (September 1942): 373–78, 396–97.

59. Lee describes his work in some detail in F. Jack Hurley, untranscribed tape recording with Russell Lee, interview no. 1, May 15–17, 1973, Austin, Texas, deposited in Mississippi Valley Archives, Memphis State University. Lee to Stryker, December 19, 1941, Roy Stryker Papers, UL Photo Archives, sheds some light on Lee's work in the Salinas Valley. For the FSA's work in rounding up replacement field hands in the relocation centers, see Supplementary Reference File 292, box 19, FSA/OWI Written Records of the Farm Security Administration, Library of Congress. For background on the FSA's role in disposing of Japanese farm property and finding temporary tenants, see Baldwin, *Poverty and Politics,* 227–28.

60. Quote from "Japanese Relocation: Russell Lee," in Fleischhauer and Brannan, eds., *Documenting America,* 240–47. Lee took 263 photographs showing Japanese farm laborers wearing big identification tags; farmers and their families standing in long lines while soldiers guard them and inspect their luggage; tenants disposing of their property; owners walking the land with buyers; evacuees surveying endless rows of barracklike buildings that would serve as their quarters at the Santa Anita racetrack; and grandmothers and grandfathers being read evacuation orders.

61. Riess, "Dorothea Lange: Making of a Documentary Photographer," 182–83, 188, 190; *New York Times,* September 16 and 24, 1972. For the jail bar reference and impounded pictures, see Reiss, "Paul S. Taylor: California Social Scientist," 1: 230. For the corn-hoeing image, see *Field Laborers Hoeing Corn, Manzanar Relocation Center,* July 1942, Photo no. 210-C-764, War Relocation Authority Photographs, Records of the War Relocation Authority, RG 210, National Archives. See also U.S. Army, Western Defense Command and Fourth Army, *Final Report: Japanese Evacuation from the West Coast, 1942* (Washington, D.C., 1943), with the seventy-seven page "Pictorial Summary," a kind of annual business report on the evacuation and internment.

62. Hendrickson, *Looking for the Light,* 57.

63. Quote from Lesy, *Bearing Witness,* xix. See also Guimond, *American Photography and the American Dream,* 140; and John Szarkowski, *Looking at Photographs: 100 Pictures from the Collection of the Museum of Modern Art* (New York, 1973), cited in Hendrickson, *Looking for Light,* 207, asserting that few photographers have a genuinely creative period exceeding ten or fifteen years.

14. Photographs of Truth and Propaganda

1. Otey Scruggs, *Braceros, "Wetbacks," and the Farm Labor Problem: Mexican Agricultural Labor in the United States, 1942–1954* (1955; New York, 1988); Otey M. Scruggs, "Evolution of the Mexican Farm Labor Agreement of 1942," *Agricultural History* 34 (July 1960): 141–42; Barbara A. Driscoll, *The Tracks North: The Railroad Bracero Program of World War II* (Austin, Tex., 1999); Wayne Rasmussen, *A History of the Emergency Farm Labor Supply Program, 1943–1947* (Washington, D.C., 1951); Robert C. Hayes, "Mexican Migrant Labor in the United States: Historical Notes on the Bracero Problem," MS, December 1950, 20–25, Division of Historical and Policy Research, Office of Public Affairs, Department of State Papers, RG 59, National Archives.

2. Ernesto Galarza, *Merchants of Labor: The Mexican Bracero Story* (San Jose, Calif., 1964); Peter N. Kirstein, *Anglo over Bracero: A History of the Mexican Worker in the United States from Roosevelt to Nixon* (San Francisco, 1977), 12; Richard B. Craig, *The Bracero Program: Interest Groups and Foreign Policy* (Austin, Tex., 1971), 43–45; Maria Herrera-Sobek, *The Bracero Experience: Elitelore*

versus Folklore (Los Angeles, 1979); Kitty Calavita, *Inside the State: The Bracero Program, Immigration, and the I.N.S.* (New York, 1992), 1–4; Pedro de Alba, *Siete articulos sobre el problema de los braceros* (Mexico City, 1954); Ignacio García Tellez, *La migración de braceros a los Estados Unidos de Norteamérica* (Mexico City, 1955).

3. Robert C. Jones, *Los braceros mexicanos en los Estados Unidos durante el periodo bélico: El programa Mexicano-Estadunidense de prestación de mano de obra* (Washington, D.C., 1946); Blanca Torres Ramírez, *Historia de la segunda revolución mexicana: México el la segunda guerra mundial, periodio 1940–1952* (Mexico City, 1979), vol. 19; George C. Kiser, "The Bracero Program: A Case Study of Its Development, Termination, and Political Aftermath," PhD diss., University of Massachusetts, 1974, 88–115; Otey M. Scruggs, "The Bracero Program under the Farm Security Administration, 1942–1943," *Labor History* 3 (Spring 1962): 149–68.

4. *Fotografía de prensa en México: 40 reporteros gráficos* (Mexico City, 1992), 93; John Mraz and Jaime Vélez Storey, *Uprooted: Braceros in the Hermanos Mayo Lens* (Houston, Tex., 1996), 5–53; John Mraz, "From Positivism to Populism: Towards a History of Mexican Photojournalism," *Afterimage* 18 (January 1991): 23–28; Cándido Mayo, *Yo soy la opinión pública* (Mexico City, 1982), 77.

5. John Mraz placed the original transcripts of his extensive interviews with the Hermanos Mayo in Fondo Mayo, Departamento de Imagen y Sonido, Archivo General de la Nación. See also "Presentación," in *Testimonio sobre México* (Mexico City, n.d.), 127–29.

6. John Mraz, "Close-up: An Interview with the Hermanos Mayo, Spanish-Mexican Photojournalists (1930s–Present)," *Studies in Latin American Popular Culture* 11 (1992); John Mraz, "Aceramientos: Entrevista con los Hermanos Mayo," *La Jornada Semanal* 27 (December 17, 1989).

7. Manuel García, *Foto Hnos. Mayo* (Valencia, Spain, 1992), 34–35. Although most scholars believe that it is impossible to compare "Mexican" photography to "foreign" photography (because each has fed off the other), in this case the Mexican perspective was so intimate and so comprehensive in its treatment of events south of the border that it certainly represents an exception to the dictum. See also Carole Nagger and Fred Ritchin, eds., *Mexico through Foreign Eyes, 1850–1990* (New York, 1993), 47, 97, 271; and John Mraz, *Nacho López: Mexican Photographer* (Minneapolis, 2003), 2, 13–17.

8. Quote from John Vachon, "Tribute to a Man, an Era, an Art," *Harper's* 247 (September 1973): 99, in Guimond, *American Photography and the American Dream,* 138; quote from Stryker memorandum to Lee and Rothstein from Wood, *In This Proud Land,* 188. See the previous page for a different shooting script from 1936. See also Stryker to Lange, September 16, 1943, Stryker–Lange Correspondence, Roy Stryker Papers, UL Photo Archives.

9. Fritz Henle, *Mexico: 64 Photographs by Fritz Henle* (New York, 1945), ii–iii; Fritz Henle, *Fritz Henle,* foreword by Allan Porter (New York, 1975); Vivienne Winterry, *Fritz Henle's Rollei* (New York, 1950); Maria Henle to author, January 3 and August 24, 1998; Street, interviews with Maria Henle, May 21 and September 30, 1998, St. Croix, U.S. Virgin Islands; all in author's possession.

10. Quote from Wallace Stegner, *One Nation* (New York, 1945), 111. Unpublished photographs and contact sheets, Fritz Henle Collection (uncataloged), Harry Ransom Research Center, University of Texas, Austin. Henle's daughter believes that the published versions were cropped by the OWI and others, not by her father. See Street, interview with Maria Henle, September 30, 1998, St. Croix. The Henle Collection, Center for Creative Photography, University of Arizona, Tucson, holds nothing relevant to this matter.

11. Anne R. Issler, "Good Neighbors Lend a Hand: Our Mexican Workers," *Survey Graphic* 32 (December 1943): 389–94; [Dorothea Lange], "Americans of Spanish Descent," *Victory* 1 (1943): 26–30; Records of the Office of War Information, RG 208 (section 10), National Archives.

12. Quoted in Elliot, *Dorothea Lange,* 6.

13. Quote from Stegner, *One Nation,* with the editors of *Look* (New York, 1945), 111, also 25–26, 114–15, 61–62. For background on Stegner's involvement with *One Nation,* see Jackson J. Benson,

Wallace Stegner: His Life and Work (New York, 1996), 148–50, 152. Because the government apparently lost most of Lange's negatives, very little of her work from this period survives in its original form and must be followed in the published record. Lange donated "rejects and duplicates" of the OWI negatives to the Oakland Museum, where the September 6 date on her photographs of braceros arriving in Sacramento became October 6, 1942. See Meltzer, *Dorothea Lange,* 246; and David G. Gutiérrez, *Walls and Mirrors: Mexican Americans, Mexican Immigrants, and the Politics of Ethnicity* (Berkeley, 1995), 134–51.

14. Quote from Vachon, "Tribute to a Man, an Era, an Art," 99, also cited in, Stange, "'The Record Itself,'" 4; and Guimond, *American Photography and the American Dream,* 139.

15. While the standard source is the F. Hal Higgins Collection, Archives and Special Collections, University of California, Davis, published and unpublished photographs are also in the American Crystal Sugar Company Records, Minnesota Historical Society, St. Paul; the Yolo County Archives, Woodland, California; and *National Beet Grower.* Higgins used 4 × 5–inch negatives.

16. Quote from Stegner, *One Nation,* 113, also 100–115.

17. Jack Delano's work with Kodachrome in Redlands, California, can be followed in FSA/OWI Color Photographs, OWI Shooting Assignments, Prints and Photographs, Library of Congress, LC-USW36-884; and Jack Delano, *Photographic Memories* (Washington, D.C., 1997), 93–94. For color, see Hendrickson, *Bound for Glory.*

18. Pete Daniel, "Command Performances: Photography from the United States Department of Agriculture," in Daniel, Foresta, Stange, and Stein, *Official Images,* 36–41; Deborah Bright, "Victory Gardens: The Public Landscape of Postwar America," in Daniel P. Younger, ed., *Multiple Views: Logan Grant Essays on Photography, 1983–89,* intro. by Alan Trachtenberg (Albuquerque, N.M., 1991), 335–37.

19. Quote from *A Report of the Emergency Farm Labor Project of the Agricultural Extension Service, 1943–1945* (Berkeley, 1945), 9. See also Richard Lacayo and George Russell, *Eyewitness: 150 Years of Photojournalism* (New York, 1990), 127–28; and Bezner, *Photography and Politics in America,* 1–5, 26.

20. Born in Japan in 1895, Miyatake had come to California with his family in 1909. First studying photography at age twenty-one, he apprenticed to photographer Harry Shigeta until 1923, when he won considerable local notice for his work and opened his own studio. In 1932, he photographed the Olympics on assignment for *Asahi Shimbum.* Miyatake and a carpenter friend fashioned his camera from wood scraps, spare drainpipe, and a lens and 3¼ × 4¼–inch film holder smuggled into Manzanar. For Miyatake's background and career, see Dennis Reed, *Japanese Photographers in America, 1920–1945* (Los Angeles, 1985); Dennis Reed, "Southern California Pictorialism: Its Modern Aspects," in Michael G. Wilson and Dennis Reed, eds., *Pictorialism in California: Photographs, 1900–1945* (Los Angeles, 1994); and Helen Caldwell, *Michio Ito* (Berkeley, 1972). Details of his work are from Archie Miyatake to author, June 23, 1998, author's collection. For various drawings and sketches made by internees at different camps, see Deborah Gesensway and Mindy Roseman, *Beyond Words: Images from America's Concentration Camps* (Ithaca, N.Y., 1987); Karin Higa, *The View from Within: Japanese American Art from the Internment Camps, 1942–1945* (Los Angeles, 1992); and Mine Okubo, *Citizen 13660* (New York, 1946). Clem Albers, about whom little is known, also photographed Japanese farm laborers at Manzanar. The equally obscure J. D. Bigelow did the same at Tule Lake Internment Center. See Albers, *Evacuees on Their Way to Clear Land of Brush,* April 2, 1942, and Bigelow, *Transplanting Cabbage from Hot Beds at Tule Lake Center,* June 24, 1944, both in Records of the War Relocation Authority, RG 210, National Archives; and Conrat and Conrat, *Executive Order 9066,* 79, 83, 118.

21. Toyo Miyatake Collection, Miyatake Studios, San Gabriel, California; John C. Welchman, "News from No-Place . . . Ideological Formations in the Photographic Representation of the

Other," in Warren Neidich, *American History Reinvented* (New York, 1989), 48–49; Toshio Yatsuhio, *Politics and Cultural Values: The World War II Japanese Relocation Centers and the United States Government* (New York, 1978), 11, 344, 339, 486; Graham Howe, Patrick Nagatani, and Scott Rankin, eds., *Two Views of Manzanar: An Exhibition of Photographs by Ansel Adams/Toyo Miyatake* (Los Angeles, 1987), 9–10. So successful were Japanese farmworkers that they produced a surplus. Although they sold part of it in nearby Lone Pine, their crop of acorn squash was so large that the weight of the stacked vegetables pushed out the sides of a large storage shed, causing it to collapse. See Street, interview with Archie Miyatake, June 16, 1998, San Gabriel, California; and Archie Miyatake to author, June 23, 1998; both in author's possession.

22. Quote from Ansel Adams, *Ansel Adams, an Autobiography* (Boston, 1985), 258. See also Ansel Adams, Manzanar Relocation Center Collection of Manuscripts, Correspondence, and Ephemera, Special Collections and Archives, UCLA; Adams to David McAlpin, January 10, 1943, and Nancy Newhall to Adams, November 11, 1944, both in Ansel Adams Collection, Center for Creative Photography, University of Arizona, Tucson; and Alinder and Stillman, eds., *Ansel Adams: Letters and Images,* 141–43.

23. Quote from Ansel Adams, *Born Free and Equal: The Story of Loyal Japanese Americans* (New York, 1944), 25.

24. Quote from ibid., 9. See also Ansel Adams, *On the North Farm at Manzanar,* Prints and Photographs Division, Library of Congress; John Hershey, "Commentary," in John Armour and Peter Wright, *Manzanar* (New York, 1988), xvii–xx; and Sylvia E. Danovitch, "The Past Recaptured: The Photographic Record of the Internment of the Japanese Americans," *Prologue* 12 (1980): 91–103. Because Adams was not on the government payroll, his images remained his own property. Later he donated them to the Library of Congress.

25. Ohrn, *Dorothea Lange and the Documentary Tradition,* 148. See also Adams, *Born Free and Equal,* 9; Nancy Newhall, review, *Photo Notes* (June 1946): 3–5; and "Pictures Available," *Manzanar Free Press,* April 29, 1944. Adams's concern with landscape at Manzanar can also be deduced from two of his best-known images: *Mount Williamson, the Sierra Nevada, from Manzanar, California, 1944* and *Winter Sunrise, the Sierra Nevada, from Lone Pine, California, 1944.* See also Spaulding, *Ansel Adams and the American Landscape,* 201–7; Stott, *Documentary Expression and Thirties America,* 214; Riess, "Dorothea Lange: Making of a Documentary Photographer," 190–91, 200–201; and Ansel Adams to Nancy Newhall, July 23, 1944, Ansel Adams Collection, Center for Creative Photography, University of Arizona.

26. For Lange's postwar career, see Charles Wollenberg, *Photographing the Second Gold Rush: Dorothea Lange and the Bay Area at War, 1941–1945* (Berkeley, 1995); and Jon Carroll, "Dorothea Lange Comes Home Again," *San Francisco Chronicle,* June 3, 1994. Henle's bracero photographs appeared in Wallace Stegner's *One Nation,* 111–12, and in Anita Brenner's *The Wind That Swept Mexico* (Austin, Tex., 1943), 163. See also Carole Nagger and Fred Ritchin, *México: Through Foreign Eyes, 1850–1990* (New York, 1993), 297; and Guimond, *American Photography and the American Dream,* 141. When Julio Fernández made his way to Mexico in 1947, he also made his contribution to the Hermanos Mayo's portrait of braceros, as well as undocumented workers, as did Pablo Cubillo, who was unable to join the Hermanos Mayo until 1952. When they finally gave up photography in 1985 and deposited their archive of over five million negatives in the Archivo General de la Nación in Mexico City, the Hermanos Mayo had more than four hundred images of braceros. Although not produced for political reasons, these images, as historian John Mraz has pointed out in his and Vélez Storey's pioneering work on Mexican photojournalism, *Uprooted: Braceros in the Hermanos Mayo Lens,* nevertheless marked a tradition of independent humanistic photography that would provide middle-class reformers with a powerful indictment of the farm labor system and would contribute to its eventual demise. For the Hermanos Mayo after World War II, see Mraz,

"Fotos Hermanos Mayo," *History of Photography* 17 (Spring 1993): 81–89; Geoffrey Dunn, "Working Images," *Metro* (February 20–26, 1997): 6–8; and Carlos Monsivais, "Los fotógrafos Mayo: Invención y rescate del pasado," *Siempre!* 1652 (February 20, 1985): 8–9.

27. Peter Maslowski, *Armed with Cameras: The American Military Photographers of World War II* (New York, 1993), 9; Francis Fralin, *The Indelible Image: Photographs of War: 1846 to Present,* essay by Jane Livingston (New York, 1985), 7–13; Guimond, *American Photography and the American Dream,* 165–244. For an example of a former military photographer who slid into personal and quizzical work, see Partridge and Stein, *Quizzical Eye,* 22.

28. Robert Justin Goldstein, *Political Repression in Modern America from 1870 to the Present* (Boston, 1978), 287–99; William Haupton, "The Suppression of Art in the McCarty Decade," *Artforum* (October 1973): 48–52; Bezner, *Photography and Politics in America,* 71.

29. Charlie Haas, "A Vision of California," *New West* 4 (June 6, 1977): 20–23; Constance Wolf, "The Photography of Max Yavno," in Max Yavno, *Photographs at the Museum of Contemporary Art, Los Angeles* (Los Angeles, 1989), 5; index to the Max Yavno Collection, Max Yavno proof sheets, Center for Creative Photography, University of Arizona; Ben Maddow, interview with Max Yavno, September 16, 1980, 21–22, Max Yavno Collection, Center for Creative Photography.

30. Calavita, *Inside the State,* 2; Meister and Loftis, *A Long Time Coming,* 74; Robert D. Tomasek, "The Political and Economic Implications of Mexican Labor in the United States under the Non Quota System, Contract Labor Program, and Wetback Movement," PhD diss., University of Michigan, 1957, 52, 88, 107, 132; Guimond, *American Photography and the American Dream,* 152; Brett Gary, "The Pitiless Spotlight of Publicity," and Wendy Kozol, "Gazing at Rage in the Pages of Life," in Doss, ed., *Looking at Life Magazine,* 79–101, 159–78.

31. Margaret Whitehead, "Max Yavno—Views of People and Their Lives," *Art Week* (March 4, 1978): 13.

32. Ben Maddow, *The Photography of Max Yavno* (Berkeley, 1981), 115–17. Because of his membership in the Hollywood Artists, Sciences and Professions Council, an organization the FBI deemed a "Communist front," Yavno was investigated by the FBI in the 1950s. Placed under physical surveillance, he also had his mail intercepted and monitored. In 1958 he was dropped from the FBI Security Index, although the Los Angeles FBI office retained a photograph of Yavno in its files. Yavno requested his FBI file on May 17, 1978, and received it on December 1, 1978. See file number 65,558, Max Yavno Declassified FBI File 65-558, author's possession.

33. Quotes from Loengard, "Hansel Mieth," 84–85.

34. Quotes from ibid. See also Robert Whelan, *Robert Capa: A Biography* (New York, 1985), 206–8. Sorel's real name was Nona Teilenbogen. A *Life* editor also sent Capa to Mexico for a six-month waiting period so that he could reenter the United States legally, much like Hagel.

35. Riess, "Paul S. Taylor: California Social Scientist," 1: 241; Sally Stein, "Hansel Mieth and Otto Hagel," in Rule and Solomon, eds., *Original Sources,* 127–30; "Otto Hagel and Hansel Mieth," in Andrei Codrescu and Terence Pitts, eds., *Points of Entry: Reframing America* (Tucson, Ariz., 1995), 30–31; Report of San Francisco Office, November 11, 1949, "Administrative Page," 7–8, Espionage-R, Otto and Hansel Hagel, Declassified FBI File 65–2427.

36. Quote from Mieth Hagel, "The Woman," 15. See also Richard Steven Street, *Photographing Farmworkers in California* (Stanford, 2004), 78–81, 125–26, 135–37.

37. Quote from *Francisco Martínez,* Photo File no. 98:107:052, Otto and Hansel Mieth Hagel Collection, Center for Creative Photography, University of Arizona, Tucson. See also *Livingston Camp,* Photo File no. 98:107:071; *Davidson Family,* Photo File nos. 98:107:076 and 98:107:07; *Salvation Army Store,* Photo File no. 98:107:061; *Cotton Pickers Wanted,* Photo File nos. 98:107:059–98:107:065; and Huron street shots, Photo File nos. 98:107:054, 98:107:056, and 98:107:058.

38. Larry Manuel García y Griego, "The Bracero Policy Experiment: U.S.–Mexico Responses

to Mexican Labor Migration, 1942–1955," PhD diss., University of California, Los Angeles, 1988, 226; Street, interview with James Price, May 23, 1974, Bakersfield, California, author's possession.

39. *Farm Labor News* issues: (January 1946): 1; (November 1946): 2; (January 1947): 2; (March 1947): 1; (April 1947): 1; (June 1947): 4; "Report of the Executive Council to the 12th Annual Convention of the American Federation of Labor," December 11–13, 1945, 2; Gardner Jackson, telegram to H. L. Mitchell, December 11, 1945; Frank McCallister, telegram to H. L. Mitchell, December 10, 1945; Mitchell, telegram to President Harry S. Truman, December 11, 1945; J. E. Clayton to Mitchell, May 1, 3, 5, 12, 27, 28, 1945; all in Southern Tenant Farmers Union Papers, Special Collections, University of North Carolina, microfilm (hereafter this holding is cited as STFU); Carlos Muñoz Jr., *Youth, Identity, Power: The Chicano Movement* (New York, 1989), 43, 129; Ernesto Galarza, *Barrio Boy: The Story of a Boy's Acculturation* (Notre Dame, Ind., 1971).

40. Quote from Street, interview with Hank Hansiwar, June 12, 1977, Bakersfield, California, author's possession. Some of Galarza's photographs are in box 65, folders 3–5, Ernesto Galarza Collection, Stanford University Archives and Special Collections. He would later use some of his photographs to illustrate his *Strangers in Our Fields* (Washington, D.C., 1965), 5, 9, 22–24, 26, 34, 52–55. See Street, interview with Ernesto Galarza, May 11, 1976, San Jose, author's collection. Hansiwar also packed a camera but subsequently lost his negatives.

41. Quotes from Ruth Teiser, "The DiGiorgios: From Fruit Merchants to Corporate Innovators," intro. by Rudolph A. Peterson, Regional Oral History Project, 1983, 100, Bancroft Library. See also Ruth Teiser, "Joseph DiGiorgio," Regional Oral History Project, 1975, 97–103, 205, Bancroft Library; Ruth Teiser, "Antonio–Perelli–Minetti: A Life in Winemaking," Regional Oral History Project, 1975, 36, 53–55, 61–69, 72–73, Bancroft Library; Hans Christian Palmer, "Italian Immigration and the Development of California Agriculture," PhD diss., University of California, Berkeley, 1965, 234–41; Sheridan Downey, *They Would Rule the Valley* (San Francisco, 1947), 186–89; "Joseph DiGiorgio," *Fortune* 26 (August 1946): 97; "The Fruit King," *Time* 37 (March 11, 1945): 80; DiGiorgio Fruit Corporation, *The DiGiorgio Story* (San Francisco, 1959), 5; and DiGiorgio Fruit Corporation, Notice of Annual Meeting of Stockholders, March 23, 1948. For the Earl Fruit Company, see Harper Leech and John C. Carroll, *Armour and His Times* (New York, 1938), 154–59.

42. Quote from Ernesto Galarza, *Spiders in the House and Workers in the Fields* (Notre Dame, Ind., 1970), 74. See also NFLU, "Statement on the DiGiorgio Strike," November 12–13, 1949, STFU; *Associated Farmer,* October 25, 1947; and Ernesto Galarza, "Big Farm Strike," *Commonweal* 46 (June 4, 1948): 178. For the relationship between Dust Bowl migrants and labor organizing, see Walter Goldschmidt, *As You Sow* (New York, 1947), 232; and Stein, *California and the Dust Bowl Migration,* 220–74.

43. *Farm Labor News* (August 1947): 2, 4; *Farm Labor News* (November 1947): 1; NFLU, confidential memo, "Plans for Organization of Agricultural Labor," n.d. [1947], STFU; "DiGiorgio Strike Report No. 2," n.d. [November 2, 1947], STFU.

44. Street, interview with Hank Hansiwar, March 22, 1974, Bakersfield, California, author's possession; clipping, Harold Ickes, "The Plight of the Migrant Farm Laborers," *Atlanta Constitution,* November 27, 1947, STFU. See also "New Grapes of Wrath," *Fresno Labor Citizen,* November 14, 1947; "Chronological Summary DiGiorgio Strike," in *NFLU Strike Bulletin;* Kern County Labor Union Local 218, press releases: "DiGiorgio Strike Bulletin Number 8," December 20, 1947, and "DiGiorgio Strike Bulletin Number 3," November 13–15, 1947; Robert Gilbert to H. L. Mitchell, December 1, 1947; and unidentified clipping, November 23, 1947; all in STFU.

45. Stein, *California and the Dust Bowl Migration,* 116–17; "Is the Grapes of Wrath Too Hot for Hollywood?" *Look* 2 (October 24, 1939): 12–22; Tim Kappel, "Kern County's Ban on the Grapes of Wrath," *California History* 61 (Winter 1982): 210; Steinbeck to Elizabeth [Otis], December 15, 1939, in Steinbeck and Wallsten, eds., *Steinbeck: A Life in Letters,* 195; interview no. 204 with Catherine

Sullivan, February 27, 1981, California Odyssey Project, California State University, Bakersfield; John Pickett, editorial, *Bakersfield Californian,* December 16, 1947; and DiGiorgio Photographs, President's Commission on Migratory Labor, Dwight D. Eisenhower Library, Abilene, Kansas; "DiGiorgio Workers Not on Strike at Arvin," *Associated Farmer* 8 (October 25, 1947); and "Out Go Mexicans," *Associated Farmer* 8 (November 15, 1947). For union radio broadcasts, see Kern County Council, Relief and Strike Fund, "To All Central Labor Councils," October 31, 1947; and John Holmes to Citizens Committee on the DiGiorgio Strike, March 1948, and enclosures, STFU.

46. Quote from photograph 2835-D, Migrant Labor Photographs, President's Commission on Migratory Labor, Dwight D. Eisenhower Library, Abilene, Kansas.

47. Quotes from Kern County Citizens, *A Community Aroused,* intro. by W. B. Camp (Bakersfield, Calif., 1947), n.p., Bancroft Library and California State University, Bakersfield; and William J. Briggs and Henry Cauthen, *The Cotton Man: Notes on the Life and Times of Wofford B. ("Bill") Camp,* foreword by Paul Smith (Chapel Hill, N.C., 1983), 207. See also Ross E. Kinney to Earl Warren, December 20, 1949, Earl Warren Papers, California State Archives, Sacramento.

48. *Associated Farmer,* October 23, 1947; NFLU press release, January 1, 1948; DiGiorgio Strike Bulletin no. 2, April 18, 1948; both in STFU.

15. Poverty in the Valley of Plenty

1. DiGiorgio Strike Bulletin no. 11, January 18, 1948; Jim Wrightson to H. L. Mitchell, January 11, 1948; Hank Hansiwar to Mitchell, July 4, 1948; press release, n.d. [July 4, 1948]; all in STFU; *Farm Labor News* (July 1948): 1; *Farm Labor News* (August–September 1948): 2; Bert Seidman to Tom Keehn, March 5, 1948; Zane Meckler to Rowland Watts, February 1, 1948; DiGiorgio General Correspondence, March 5, 1948; all in Workers Defense League Papers, Archives of Urban and Labor History, Wayne State University.

2. Jim Wrightson to Mitchell, February 23, 1948; DiGiorgio Strike Bulletin no. 17, February 29, 1948; rough draft statement by Galarza, March 1948; Aubrey Blair to Ernesto Galarza, April 15, 1948; Galarza to Blair, April 20, 1948; Aubrey Blair to Galarza, April 22, 1948; Blair to Bob Delson, May 18, 1948; all in STFU; *Oakland Tribune,* February 26, 1948.

3. Quote from transcript of *Poverty in the Valley of Plenty,* MS, n.d., n.p., STFU. California Federation of Teachers historian Fred Glass argues that *Poverty in the Valley of Plenty* was not simply a liberal attempt to help the strikers but also the product of a clever right-wing effort to head off radical unionism. He came to this conclusion while tracking down surviving copies of the documentary. After discovering a copy in the Wayne State University Archives of Urban and Labor History, Glass interviewed Roy Brewer, a notorious "red baiter" and leader in the International Alliance of Theatrical Stage Employees (IATSE), who had been brought in to battle left-wing unions in Hollywood. Brewer told Glass that he was the one behind *Poverty in the Valley.* "The Communists were still active in the field," he told Glass, "and I wanted to make sure that they did not take charge and I had this film to head them off at the pass. I rounded up the people, got funds, and sent them to Arvin. I was head of the Hollywood Film Council." Quote from Street, interview with Fred Glass, January 15, 2002, Sacramento, author's possession. Galarza did not mention Brewer's role. For Brewer and the IATSE, see Gerald Horne, *Class Struggle in Hollywood: Moguls, Mobsters, Stars, Reds, and Trade Unionists, 1930–1950* (Austin, Tex., 2001), 48, 134–56, 163, 165, 174, 176, 184, 195, 200, 204–5, 211, 218, 222–24, 239.

4. Quoted from Hollywood Film Council et al., *Poverty in the Valley of Plenty* (1948), California Federation of Teachers Archives, Sacramento, video copy courtesy of Fred Glass. See also Galarza to Helen G. Douglas, May 26, 1948; Mitchell to Blair, November 1, 1948; Blair to Mitchell, May 18, 1948; Blair to Robert Delson, May 18, 1948; and Blair to Mitchell, November 8, 1948; all in STFU.

5. Ulla E. Bauers Jr., "The DiGiorgio Strike," MA thesis, University of California, Berkeley, 1949.

6. The photograph ran in many newspapers, including the May 18, 1948, *Los Angeles Herald-Examiner.* See *Los Angeles Herald-Examiner* Photograph Collection, Los Angeles Public Library; Galarza, *Spiders in the House and Workers in the Fields,* 24; and Ernesto Galarza, *Farmworkers and Agri-business in California, 1947–1960* (Notre Dame, Ind., 1977), 113. Those present at the meeting were L. E. Leonard, Arvin; W. A. Swearingen, Oildale; George Watson, Oildale; Hattie Shadowens, Arvin; W. Vanvickle, Arvin; and Rev. Phinneas Parks, Arvin. Police identified the weapons as .32-caliber and .22-caliber pistols. See "Strike Leader Shot Down in Attack on Union Meeting," *Bakersfield Californian,* May 18, 1948; "State Agents Join Hunt for Strike Meet Gunmen," *Bakersfield Californian,* May 19, 1948; and "Union Offers Reward in Shooting," *Bakersfield Californian,* May 21, 1948. Who took the photograph is unclear.

7. Quote from Teiser, "The DiGiorgios," Regional Oral History Project, 1983, 98, Bancroft Library.

8. Mitchell to Hank Hansiwar, May 6, 1948; Mitchell to Dean Bough, September 10, 1948; Arthur Churchill to Chief Film Division, U.S. Department of Agriculture, October 7, 1948; Mitchell to Blair, June 7, 1948; all in STFU; "Senator on the Warpath," *Life* (June 7, 1948): 40–44.

9. H. D. Gower, L. Stanley Jast, and W. W. Topley, *The Camera as Historian* (New York, 1916), 1–4; Richard M. Barsom, *Nonfiction Film: A Critical History* (New York, 1973), 4–5, 194, 396; Ella Cooper Thomas, *The Law of Libel and Slander* (New York, 1963); John Hall, "Pleadings in Libel Actions in California," *Southern California Law Review* 22 (March 1939): 225; John Hall, "Proof in Libel Actions in California," *Southern California Law Review* 33 (July 1951): 339.

10. Mitchell to Galarza, March 15 and 17, 1949; Galarza to Mitchell, January 13, 1950; press release, March 16, 1949; W. B. Camp, "The Fight to Preserve American Freedom," address before the Northern California Agri-business Relations Conference, April 27, 1951; all in STFU; LaFollette Committee Hearings, 619–37, 643–58.

11. Complaint for Libel, Superior Court of California, County of Los Angeles, *DiGiorgio Corporation v. Paramount Television Producers,* May 16, 1949, no. 559 852, STFU; telegram, DiGiorgio to Thomas Werdel, March 18, 1949; Joseph DiGiorgio to Earl Warren, March 21, 1949; Paul Scharrenberg to M. F. Small, April 13, 1949; Warren to Werdel, May 3, 1949; Warren to DiGiorgio, May 23, 1949; all in Earl Warren Papers, California State Archives, Sacramento.

12. William Hauptman, "The Suppression of Art in the McCarthy Decade," *Artforum* (October 1973): 48–52; Gordon Pates, This World section, *San Francisco Chronicle,* June 26, 1949; *Farm Labor News,* June 1948; DiGiorgio Fruit Corporation, complaint for libel, *DiGiorgio v. Harry Flannery et al.,* November 7, 1949, STFU.

13. Quotes from U.S. Congress, House, Extension of Remarks of Thomas H. Werdel of California in the House of Representatives, 83rd Cong., 1st sess., *Congressional Record* 82 (March 9, 1950): H 3157, in appendix 1, Galarza, *Spiders in the House and Workers in the Fields,* 292–93; and "Congressional Committee Bares Facts on Alleged DiGiorgio Ranch Strike," *Associated Farmer* 12 (March–April 1950): 1–4. See also *Los Angeles Times,* March 11, 1950; and *Bakersfield Californian,* November 12, 1949, and March 11, 1950.

14. Gregory Harrison to Louis A. Nissen, April 3, 1950; Alex Schullman to Mitchell, April 21, 1950; Mitchell to Schullman, May 3, 1950; all in STFU; *California State Federation of Labor Bulletin,* June 14, 1950, International Longshoremen's Union Library, San Francisco.

15. Ross E. Kinney to Warren, December 20, 1949, Earl Warren Papers, California State Archives, Sacramento; "DiGiorgio Film Set for State Showings," *Associated Farmer* 10 (June–July 1949): 2; Willa K. Baum, "Wofford B. Camp: Cotton, Irrigation, and the A.A.A.," intro. by Dr. Paul S. Smith, Regional Oral History Project, 1971, 234, Bancroft Library; Wofford B. Camp, "The

Fight to Preserve American Freedom," address before the Northern California Agri-business Relations Conference, April 27, 1951, San Francisco; Teiser, "The DiGiorgios," Regional Oral History Project, 1983, 95, Bancroft Library. For the Associated Farmers, see Clarke A. Chambers, *California Farm Organizations: A Historical Study of the Grange, Farm Bureau and Associated Farmers, 1929–1941* (Berkeley, 1951), 39–52, 70–81, 196–202.

16. Quotes from Briggs and Cauthen, *The Cotton Man,* 231–33. See also Baum, "Wofford B. Camp," Regional Oral History Project, 1971, Bancroft Library.

17. Quote from press release, Mitchell to Werdel, March 27, 1950, STFU. For the union response, see Robert Gilbert to Mitchell, January 13, 1950; telegram, Mitchell to Galarza, March 10, 1950; Alexander Schullman to Mitchell, April 21, 1950; all in STFU. For union efforts to counter the report using the same tactics, see Mitchell to William Becker, April 12, 1950, STFU. See also statement of Ernesto Galarza, August 12, 1950, Records of the President's Commission on Migratory Labor, 1950–51, Harry S. Truman Library, Independence, Missouri.

18. Sam Whiting, "History through a Lens," *San Francisco Chronicle,* January 23, 1997; Nancy Nadel, "Cultivating New Ground," *F-Ten Forum* (Fall 1991): 8–10; William Manchester, *In Our Time: The World as Seen by Magnum Photographers,* with essays by Jean Lacouture and Fred Ritchin (New York, 1989), 28, 451.

19. Ken Light, "World War II and the Family of Man," in Light, ed., *Witness in Our Time,* 46–53. See also Edward Steichen, *The Family of Man* (New York, 1955), 129; and Walter Goodman, "Ebony: Biggest Negro Magazine," *Dissent* (September–October 1968): 403–9.

20. Quotes from Light, "World War II and the Family of Man," 49. See also Guimond, *American Photography and the American Dream,* 173.

21. Quote from Ben Burns to Wayne Miller, December 10, 1949; see also Wayne Miller to Ben Burns, December 16, 1949, and January 1, 1950; all courtesy of Wayne Miller. For the cotton industry, see John Turner, *White Gold Comes to California* (Bakersfield, Calif., 1981); and Steven John Zimrick, "The Changing Organization of Agriculture in the Southern San Joaquin Valley, California," PhD diss., Louisiana State University, 1976. The stories about children are from Arax and Wartzman, *The King of California,* 264–79, a work of great insight. See also William L. Preston "Land and Life in the Tulare Lake Basin, California," PhD diss., University of Oregon, 1979, 335–37.

22. Street, interview with Wayne Miller, May 19, 1981, Orinda, California, author's possession. Corcoran descriptions from Arax and Wartzman, *The King of California,* 273–74; and Street, interview with Ramón Mares Sr., July 7, 1991, Kettleman City, California, author's possession.

23. Quote from Street, interview with Wayne Miller, May 19, 1981, Orinda, California, author's possession. See also Herb Nipson to Wayne Miller, November 30, 1949, courtesy of Wayne Miller. For blacks and the mass-circulation photo magazines, see Guimond, *American Photography and the American Dream,* 170.

24. Quote from Street, interview with Wayne Miller, May 19, 1981, Orinda, California, author's possession. Ironically, Miller's work closely duplicated what Otto Hagel had done several years earlier. Lacking an assignment, the Hagels could not get their work published.

25. Quotes from "Dixie Comes to California," *Ebony* 26, April 1950, 15–16. See also Miller to author, July 15, 1998, author's possession.

26. Don Normark to author, September 17, 2003, Seattle, Washington, author's possession. See also Don Normark, *Chávez Ravine, 1949: A Los Angeles Story* (San Francisco, 1999), 62, also 11–12, 14, 34, 37–38.

27. Dawn Bohulano Mabalon, "Stockton Is in the Heart," *Filipinas Magazine,* May 2002, www.filipinasmag.com; Mabalon to author, e-mail, July 26, 2004, author's possession; Huell Howser, "Little Manila," *California's Gold,* program no. 5008; *People's World,* May 7 and 21, 1948; mounted photographs, People's World Collection, Labor History Archives Center, San Francisco

State University. For Filipinos in Stockton, see H. Brett Melendy, "Filipinos in the United States," *Pacific Historical Review* 43 (Spring 1974): 520–47; Bruno Laskker, *Filipino Immigration to Continental United States and Hawaii* (Chicago, 1931), 21, 53–64; Carlos Bulosan, *America Is in the Heart* (New York, 1941), 275–77; and Paul Cressey, *The Taxi Dance Hall: A Sociological Study in Commercialized Recreation and City Life* (Chicago, 1932). For the strike, see Jamieson, *Labor Unionism in American Agriculture,* 181–83. The best recent treatment, especially strong for the Japanese versus Filipino angle, and vice versa, is Eiichiro Azuma, "Racial Struggle, Immigrant Nationalism, and Ethnic Identity: Japanese and Filipinos in the California Delta, 1930–1941," *Pacific Historical Review* 67 (May 1998): 163–200, especially 177–83.

28. According to Robert DiGiorgio, the AFL sent DiGiorgio a check for seventy-five thousand dollars. See Teiser, "The DiGiorgios," Regional Oral History Project, 1983, 95, Bancroft Library. I have been unable to verify this. Although several commentators believe this is the first instance in which an employer suppressed a film, I have not found any guidance on this point in the standard reference, Buckland, *First Photographs.* For the final suppression of *Poverty in the Valley of Plenty,* see Galarza, *Spiders in the House and Workers in the Fields,* 64–66; Joan London and Henry Anderson, *So Shall Ye Reap: The Story of Cesar Chavez and the Farm Workers' Movement* (New York, 1970), 45; Mitchell to Schullman, April 12, May 30, 1950; copy of agreement in *DiGiorgio v. NFLU,* May 8, 1950; both in STFU; and *California State Federation of Labor Bulletin* (June 14, 1950): 1–2. Many copies of the film survived.

29. Quote from Galarza, *Spiders in the House and Workers in the Fields,* 73. The number of braceros employed in the United States peaked in September 1959 at 265,000. See also Ernesto Galarza, *Merchants of Labor* (Santa Barbara, Calif., 1964); and Ernesto Galarza, *Strangers in Our Fields* (San Francisco, 1957).

30. Galarza, *Farmworkers and Agri-business in California,* 150, also 190; Ellis Hawley, "The Politics of Mexican Labor Issue, 1950–1965," *Agricultural History* 40 (July 1966): 159–60.

31. Many published versions of *Night Meeting* are dated 1934, 1936, and 1939 and titled *Night Meeting at the Crossroads, Cotton Strike, Great Central Valley, California, 1934* and *Salinas Lettuce Strike, Night Meeting, 1939.* For the former, see *Passing Torches: The Diverse Sources of Documentary, the Mother Jones 1998 Fine Print Portfolio* (San Francisco, 1998), 5; for the latter, see Mark Dean Johnson, ed., *At Work: The Art of California Labor,* foreword by Gray Brechin, afterword by Tillie Olsen (San Francisco, 2003), 36–37. All of these years are erroneous. In a February 12, 1990, letter to me, Hansel Hagen firmly rejected them, stating that she was tired of the misdating and wanted to set the record straight. According to her, she (or Otto) made the photograph in 1961, on the west side of the San Joaquin Valley. However, the Hagel FBI file, along with various lists in the Hagel Collection, provides convincing evidence for 1950 having been the year the photograph was taken. Also internal evidence in the image (for example, the style of an automobile's headlights and fenders and the style of dress) indicates that this could not have been taken in the 1930s. See Otto Hagel, "The Farm Surplus You're Paying For," *Life* 47 (November 30, 1959): 22–23; photographic prints sent to Jim Hughes, editor, *Camera Arts,* February 15, 1983; and Alice Richards to Otto and Hansel, September 8, 1960; both in Otto and Hansel Mieth Hagel Collection, Center for Creative Photography, University of Arizona.

32. Julian Samora, *Los Mojados: The Wetback Story* (South Bend, Ind., 1970), 33; Ellis Hawley, "The Politics of Mexican Labor Issue, 1950–1965," *Agricultural History* 40 (July 1966): 159–60; Commission on Migratory Labor, *Migratory Labor in American Agriculture* (Washington, D.C., 1951), 180; Records of the President's Commission on Migratory Labor, 1950–51, Harry S. Truman Library, Independence, Missouri.

33. Robert D. Tomasek, "The Political and Economic Implications of Mexican Labor in the United States under the Non-quota System, Contract Labor Program, and Wetback Movement,"

PhD diss., University of Michigan, 1957, 22; Lyle Saunders and Olen E. Leonard, "The Wetback in the Lower Rio Grande Valley of Texas," *Inter-American Education, Occasional Papers* 7 (July 1951): 33; *Excelsior,* February 1 and 2, 1951.

34. Quote from Galarza, *Farm Workers and Agri-business in California,* 148–49.

35. Quote from ibid., 149–50, also 151–70. See also NFLU, "The Wetback Strike: A Report on the Strike of Farmworkers in the Imperial Valley of California," May 24 and June 25, 1951, Records of the President's Commission on Migratory Labor, 1950–51, Harry S. Truman Library, Independence, Missouri; and *Imperial Valley Press,* May 17, 24, 31 and June 6, 8, 9, 1951.

36. Street, interview with Loomis Dean, February 3, 2000, Venice, Florida, author's possession; Loengard, "Loomis Dean," Loengard, *Life Photographers,* 277–85; Steve Rubenstein, "Loomis Dean—*Life* Magazine Photographer," *San Francisco Chronicle,* December 15, 2005; Juan Ramón García, *Operation Wetback: The Mass Deportation of Mexican Undocumented Workers in 1954* (Westport, Conn., 1980), 171, 176, 193–94, 214.

37. Quotes from "Wetbacks Swarm In: Mexicans Disrupt Border Economy by Sneaking Over for Low Wages," *Life* 30 (May 21, 1951): 33–38. See also Strauss, *Between the Eyes,* 23–28; and John Berger, *Ways of Seeing* (New York, 1977), 130.

38. Quote from Street, interview with Loomis Dean, May 12, 1999, Venice, Florida, author's possession. Dean's film was Kodak XX rated at ASA 160.

39. Quote from Street, interview with Loomis Dean, May 12, 1999, Venice, Florida. See also Richard Lacayo and George Russell, *Eyewitness: 150 Years of Photojournalism* (New York, 1990), 140.

40. Quote from Street, interview with Loomis Dean, May 12, 1999, Venice, Florida. Dean left the West Coast in 1956 to head *Life*'s bureau in Paris. While sailing across the Atlantic Ocean, he photographed the sinking of the *Andrea Doria* ocean liner.

41. Richard C. Ehret, "A Descriptive Analysis of the Hearings Held by the House Committee on Un-American Activities in 1947 and 1951 on the Communist Infiltration of the Motion Picture Industry and Their Relationship to the Hollywood Labor Movement," MA thesis, University of California, Los Angeles, 1969; John Gerard, "A Program of Cooperation: The FBI, the Senate Internal Security Subcommittee, and the Communist Issue, 1950–1956," PhD diss., Marquette University, 1993; Joseph Greco, "The File on Robert Siodmak in Hollywood: 1941–1951," PhD diss., State University of New York, Stony Brook, 1995, 179–80; Ralph Van Deman Collection, RG 46, National Archives.

42. John F. Baxter photographs, *Triple S Mexican Nationals Camp, Oxnard, California,* March 31, 1955 [June 1, 1955], California Department of Industrial Relations, Records of the President's Commission on Migratory Labor, 1950–51, Harry S. Truman Library, Independence, Missouri. Among those artists who focused on farmworkers, Alfonso Santos, talented though a convicted heroin dealer, was probably the most unusual. Santos spent two years painting a remarkable six-panel mural, ninety-five feet long that depicts aspects of California history, including immigrants crossing the border from Mexico and farmworkers stooped over in the fields. At about the same time, Domingo Ulloa, often called the Father of Chicano Art, painted *Bracero,* an oil on canvas close-up of workers held behind barbed wire and living in substandard shacks. Long active as a graphic artist specializing in labor, Emmy Lou Packard made *Half Moon Bay,* a color linocut placing field hands, antlike, in an immense field of artichokes below lowering clouds. See Kelly St. John, "San Quentin Prison Was His Art School," *San Francisco Chronicle,* July 27, 2003; Mark-Elliott Lugo, "El Centro's Ulloa an Undiscovered Master?" *San Diego Tribune,* May 31, 1985; Elise Miller, "Chicano Artist Portrays the Struggle of His People," *Los Angeles Times,* January 28, 1981; Geri DePaoli, *Emmy Lou Packard: 1914–1998* (Davis, Calif., 1998); and Pat Pfeiffer, "Emmy Lou Packard's Palette of Paint and Politics," *San Francisco Sunday Examiner and Chronicle,* May 2, 1982.

43. Quote from Max Yavno, Guggenheim Fellowship application, 1953, Max Yavno Collection. Yavno had become enchanted by the wine industry while shooting for *The San Francisco Book,* text by Herb Caen (New York, 1948), and *The Los Angeles Book,* text by Lee Shippey (New York, 1950).

44. Street, interview with Max Yavno, September 22, 1985, San Francisco, author's possession; the following from the Yavno Collection, Center for Creative Photography, University of Arizona: Margaret Whitehead, "Love, Honor, and Obey That Impulse," MS, n.d., Margaret Whitehead File; Douglas Borgstedt to Yavno, May 16, 1953; Lou Merciel to Yavno, May 18, 1953; Arthur Rothstein to Yavno, May 18, 1953; Alexander Liberman to Yavno, May 19, 1953; John Allen to Yavno, June 8, 1953; Alexei Brodovitch to Yavno, May 19, 1953; and Wallace Stegner to Yavno, May 22, 1953.

45. García, *Operation Wetback,* 169–79; Tomasek, "The Political and Economic Implications of Mexican Labor in the United States under the Non-quota System, Contract Labor Program, and Wetback Movement," 271; Nelson Copp, *Wetbacks and Braceros* (San Francisco, 1971), 40; Gladwin Hill, "Plan Gains to End Use of Wetbacks," *New York Times,* June 27, 1954; Gladwin Hill, "Rio Grande Wetbacks," *New York Times,* August 12, 1954, 9; Marion Wilhelm, "Wetback Tide Overflowing Rio Grande Again," *Washington Post,* Sunday, June 7, 1953; Gladwyn Hill, "Two Every Minute across the Border," *New York Times Magazine,* January 31, 1954, 13; Richard P. Eckels, "Hungry Workers, Ripe Crops, and the Non-existent Mexican Border," *Reporter* (April 13, 1954): 28; Peter Odens, *The Desert Trackers: Men of the Border Patrol* (Yuma, Ariz., 1975), 2, 30, 61.

46. James Guimond describes these photographers as people seeking "an honorable synthesis" between the older FSA approach and the new imperatives of daily photojournalism. See Guimond, *American Photography and the American Dream,* 148. For Jones, see Ansel Adams, "Pirkle Jones: Photographer," *U.S. Camera Magazine* (October 1952): 40–42; Robert Holmes, "Pirkle Jones," *British Journal of Photography* (October 17, 1980): 1040–41; and Nancy Newhall, "Pirkle Jones Portfolio," *Aperture* 4 (1956): 49–57. Born in Shreveport, Louisiana, in 1914, Jones grew up in Indiana and Ohio and, following graduation from high school in 1931, operated a shoe-trimming press at the Lima Sole and Heel Company in Ohio until 1941. Following service as a cryptographer in the United States Army Signal Corps, Jones took advantage of the GI Bill to further his education and became one of the first to study with Ansel Adams in the newly established photography program at the California School of Fine Arts, in San Francisco.

47. See also Tim B. Wade, *Pirkle Jones: California Photographs* (Millerton, N.Y., 2003).

48. Quote from Street, interview with Pirkle Jones, April 8, 2003, Mill Valley, California, author's possession.

49. Pirkle Jones and Dorothea Lange, "Death of a Valley," *Aperture* 8 (1960): 127–65; Alfred Frankenstein, "Acquisitions at the de Young," *San Francisco Chronicle,* November 6, 1960, 23; James Breckenridge, "Photography Art Exhibit Provides Meaningful Message," *Chicago's American Sunday* (January 27, 1963); Ohrn, *Dorothea Lange and the Documentary Tradition,* 189, 195; Meltzer, *Dorothea Lange,* 299–305.

50. Meltzer, *Dorothea Lange,* 302–3; Pirkle Jones and Ruth Garner Begell, eds., *Berryessa Valley: The Last Year* (Vacaville, Calif., 1994), 54; Bob McKenzie, "Demise of Berryessa Valley," *Napa Register,* July 24, 1994.

51. El Solyo negatives, Ansel Adams Collection, Center for Creative Photography; Elsa Gridlow, "The Story of a Winery," *U. S. Camera Annual, 1963* (New York, 1963), 40–51. Santa Cruz photographer Al Lowry remembers Adams in the fields photographing farmworkers as late as 1967. "There were about twenty of us enrolled in 'The Making of a Photographic Book,' with Ansel Adams, Nancy Newhall, Beaumont Newhall, and Adrian Wilson (a very highly regarded book designer of the day)," recalled Lowry. "The year was 1967. . . . We were to produce a book during

the ten-day workshop and as a group decided to do a book on Santa Cruz County and split into groups to photograph the various aspects of the county. My group (four or five) headed north along Highway 1 and just out of Davenport found a crew planting Brussels sprouts. Eager to show my leadership skills, I volunteered to talk to the crew to ask permission to photograph them. I barged out into the field and the crew stopped to see what I wanted. I determined who the head guy was and asked if we might photograph them for a class project. He said no. I tried to explain (in English) what the project was about and he said no. I tried to further explain what we were doing again and he said no and motioned his crew to continue work. Much chagrined, I went back to the group with my tail between my legs. Another group member, Marion Patterson, asked if she could try. We waited for the crew to return to our end of the field and Marion stepped forward to speak to the head guy. She again tried to make our case (this time in Spanish) and within a minute or two the boss agreed and continued with his planting while we photographed until we had enough." Lowry to author, e-mail, January 23, 2005, author's possession.

52. Stephen J. Pitti, *The Devil in Silicon Valley: Northern California, Race, and Mexican Americans* (Princeton, N.J., 2003), 136–47.

53. Ibid., 145. See also newspaper clipping, Richard Warren Lewis, "The Quality of Compassion," California Living section, *Los Angeles Herald-Examiner,* July 2, 1978, 1–32; Nadel, "Pueblo del Rio," MS; and Nadel, "Alisio Village, USA," MS; all in Leonard Nadel Collection, courtesy Evelyn DeWolfe Nadel, Hollywood, California.

54. Only sporadic references to Nadel can be found in the Fund for the Republic Archives, Seeley Mudd Manuscript Library, Princeton University. For background, see Thomas Reeves, *Freedom and the Foundation, the Fund for the Republic in the Era of McCarthyism* (New York, 1969).

55. Street, interview with Evelyn DeWolfe Nadel, March 9, 1994, Hollywood, California, author's possession.

56. Quote from Leonard Nadel, "Liaison—New Role for the Photographer," MS, n.d., 5, Nadel Collection, Smithsonian Institution, Washinton, D.C. (This collection was held by Evelyn DeWolfe Nadel in Hollywood at the time I consulted it.) See also Leonard Nadel, "Strangers in Our Fields," MS, n.d., 4; and Evelyn DeWolfe Nadel, "Bio Sketch on Leonard Nadel," MS, n.d., 1–6; both in Leonard Nadel Collection, Hollywood, California. After I completed my research, Nadel's photographs were deposited in the Smithsonian Institution. Some of his research notes are also in the Research Library, Getty Research Institute, Los Angeles, California.

57. Evelyn Nadel to author, July 25, 1998, author's possession. For a discussion of the photo essay layouts, see Hicks, *Words and Pictures,* 63–79.

58. Quote from clipping, Leonard Nadel, "Between Two Worlds," *Pageant,* n.v., n.d., 140–46, Leonard Nadel Collection, Hollywood California.

59. Galarza, *Farmworkers and Agri-business in California,* 250–56; Leonard Nadel to Mark Strage, editor, *Pageant* (May 17, 1957); Strage to Nadel, April 27, 1957; both in Leonard Nadel Collection, Hollywood, California.

60. Meister and Loftis, *A Long Time Coming,* 84; Paul Richards, *Critical Focus: The Black and White Photographs of Harvey Wilson Richards* (Oakland, Calif., 1986), 5–6.

61. Paul Richards, *The Harvey Richards Film and Video Collection* (Oakland, Calif., 1991), 1–4; Street, interviews with Harvey Richards, May 17, 19, and 21, 1978, Menlo Park, California, author's possession; Matthew Taylor, "Harvey Richards," obituary, *San Francisco Chronicle,* April 29, 2001.

62. Paul Richards, "Primary Source Documents: The Making of *We'll Never Turn Back* (1963) and *Dream Deferred* (1964), Films by Harvey Richards," MS, 1998, 1–3, courtesy of Paul Richards, Oakland, California; Street, interview with Paul Richards, July 12, 1998, Oakland, California; Street, interview with Harvey Richards, August 12, 1978, Palo Alto, California, author's possession. I printed Richards's images at the Darkroom, San Rafael, California, in September and October 1978.

63. For the day-haul system, see Paul Mapes, Silas Ragster, et al., *Who Are Men: A Study of the Tramps of Downtown Stockton and the Agencies That Serve Them,* Department of Applied Behavioral Sciences Research Monograph no. 10 (Davis, Calif., 1973); Charles Anderson, Tony Coya, Willie Little, Willie Lasby, Manuel Fernández, and Jerry Costa, *Housing Sacramento's Invisible Men: Farmworkers, Hustlers, and Misfits,* Department of Applied Behavioral Sciences Research Monograph no. 9 (Davis, Calif., 1970); Glenn R. Hawkes, Minna Taylor, and Beverly E. Bastian, *Patterns of Living in California's Migrant Labor Families,* Department of Applied Behavioral Sciences Research Monograph no. 12 (Davis, Calif., 1973); and Galarza, *Farmworkers and Agri-business in California,* 30–31, 135, 235.

64. Street, interview with Harvey Richards, July 1, 1978, Atherton, California, author's possession.

65. Street, interview with Harvey Richards, August 12, 1978, Atherton, California, author's possession.

66. Quote from H. L. Mitchell to Ernesto Galarza, April 11, 1958, STFU.

67. Quote from memo, "An Analysis and Report, with Suggestions," Louis Krainock to Norman Smith, October 9, 1959, STFU.

16. Rented Slaves

1. Galarza, *Spiders in the House and Workers in the Fields,* 4–5, 88, 95–96; *Valley Labor Citizen,* May 6, 1960.

2. *Stockton Record,* May 19, 1960; *Valley Labor Citizen,* May 6, 1960; *San Francisco Chronicle,* July 31, 1960; *California Farmer,* June 18, 1960; Brobeck, Phleger, and Harrison to Gilbert, May 18, 1960; Galarza to Mitchell, May 20 and July 11, 1960, November 29, 1961; all in STFU.

3. Quote from press release, DiGiorgio Fruit Corporation, May 18, 1960, STFU. See also Galarza, *Spiders in the House and Workers in the Fields,* 98–102, 147–50, 156.

4. Galarza, *Spiders in the House and Workers in the Fields,* 93–97, 148.

5. *People's World,* June 6, 1959; *San Francisco News,* June 15, 1959.

6. Quote from Mitchell to Galarza, May 25, 1960, STFU. See also Mitchell to Galarza, May 23, 1960; Galarza to Mitchell, May 23 and 24, 1960; Mitchell to Galarza, May 25 and June 16, 1960; Mitchell to Harry Poole, June 3, 1960; all in STFU; London and Anderson, *So Shall Ye Reap,* 139. For one writer–photographer who continued to work, see Truman E. Moore, *The Slaves We Rent* (New York, 1965), photographs after page 78, also 123, 128–30, 135, 151, 156–58. Louis Krainock of AWOC and John F. Baxter, California Department of Industrial Relations, also photographed farmworkers at this time. For their photographs, see Migrant Labor Photographs, box 98, Records of the President's Commission on Migratory Labor, 1950–51, Harry S. Truman Library, Independence, Missouri. See also Joseph Gunterman to author, March 23, 1976, author's possession; AP Wirephoto mcwc41721pool, *First Hand Look,* March 24, 1965; *Valley Labor Citizen,* April 24, 1964; and *Santa Clara County Union Gazette,* April 17, 1964.

7. Marshall McLuhan, *Understanding Media: The Extensions of Man* (New York, 1964), 308–37. See also Erik Barnouw, *Documentary* (New York, 1993); Raymond Lee Carroll, "Factual Television in America: An Analysis of Network Televison Documentary Programs, 1948–1975," PhD diss., University of Wisconsin, 1978; Tom Mascaro, "Lowering the Voices of Reason: The Decline of Network Televison Documentaries in the Reagan Years," PhD diss., Wayne State University, 1994; William A. Bluem, *Documentary in American Television* (New York, 1965); Barsom, *Nonfiction Film,* 247–48; and Roper Organization, *Changing Public Attitudes toward Television and Other Mass Media, 1959–1976* (New York, 1977).

8. Alexander Kendrick, *Edward R. Murrow, Prime Time* (New York, 1969); Joseph E. Persico, *Edward R. Murrow: An American Original* (New York, 1989); Bob Evans, *Edward R. Murrow and*

the Birth of Broadcast Journalism (New York, 2004); Robert Smith, *Edward R. Murrow: The War Years* (Kalamazoo, Mich., 1978); David Halberstam, *The Powers That Be* (New York, 1979); Robert Lichello, *Edward R. Murrow: Broadcaster of Courage* (Charlottesville, Va., 1971). Neither of the two repositories of Murrow materials (Department of Archives and Special Collections, Mount Holyoke College, Massachusetts; and the Department of Manuscripts, Archives, and Special Collections, Washington State University, Pullman) contains any material pertinent to Murrow's involvement with *Harvest of Shame.*

9. Quotes from A. M. Sperber, *Murrow: His Life and Times* (New York, 1986), 603–4, also 13, 594–95, 607–8.

10. M. F. K. Fisher, *The Story of Wine in California* (Berkeley, 1960); Street, interview with Max Yavno, May 12, 1983, San Francisco, author's possession; Max Yavno Collection, Center for Creative Photography, University of Arizona, Tucson.

11. Quote from Ansel Adams to Otto E. Meyer at Paul Masson Vineyards, February 28, 1963, Ansel Adams Collection, Center for Creative Photography, University of Arizona. See also Kent Kay, "Photographers Tell Story of a Winery," *San Francisco Chronicle,* June 9, 1960; Robert Lawrence Balzar, *This Uncommon Heritage: The Paul Masson Story* (Los Angeles, 1963); and Street, interview with Pirkle Jones, April 15, 2003, Mill Valley, California, author's possession.

12. For Galarza, see Gorman to Mitchell, July 26, 1960; Galarza to Poole, September 13, 1960; Galarza to Fay Bennet, August 11 and September 22, 1960; Galarza to Mitchell, August 13, 1960; and Mitchell to Bennett, August 27, 1960; all in STFU.

13. Quotes from Edward R. Murrow et al., *Harvest of Shame,* text of script, CBS News (New York, 1960), 13; and Sperber, *Murrow,* 610.

14. Edward Bliss Jr., ed., *In Search of Light: The Broadcasts of Edward R. Murrow, 1938–1961* (New York, 1967). See also Malvin Wald, "Shootout at the Beverly Hills Corral: Edward R. Murrow versus Hollywood," *Journal of Popular Film and Television* 28 (Fall 1991): 16–22.

15. Les Brown, *Television* (New York, 1972), 196; Edwin Diamond and Alan Mahony, "Once It Was 'Harvest of Shame'—Now We Get 'Scared Sexless,'" *TV Guide* (August 27, 1988).

16. Quote from Jack Gould, "TV: *Harvest of Shame,*" *New York Times,* November 26, 1960.

17. Quote from Mrs. C. C. Pelt to President Eisenhower, November 26, 1960; also numerous other letters to Eisenhower; all in President's Commission on Migratory Labor Papers, Dwight D. Eisenhower Library, Abilene, Kansas.

18. Quote from L. D. Schur to Senator Harrison Williams, December 8, 1960, President's Commission on Migratory Labor Papers, Dwight D. Eisenhower Library, Abilene, Kansas. Department of Labor officials received requests from twenty congressmen for more information on farmworkers. See also U.S. House of Representatives, Committee on Agriculture, *Mexican Farm Labor Program,* 87th Cong., 1st sess., 1961, 70–71, 127, 318–21; Frank P. Gorman to International Executive Board, January 26, 1961; Gorman to local unions, November 17, 1960; Harry R. Poole to Mitchell, November 28, 1960; Gorman to Mitchell, December 8, 1960; Mitchell to Gorman, February 21, 1961; Mitchell to CBS News, November 1, 1960; all in STFU; clipping, *Variety,* December 7, 1960, United Packinghouse Workers Union Papers, State Historical Society of Wisconsin, Madison.

19. Farm engineers who were engaged in research on mechanization used *Harvest of Shame* as a reason to proceed apace with their work. See Roy Bainer, "The Engineering of Abundance," oral interview, 1975, 275, Archives and Special Collections, University of California, Davis. See also "Analysis of *Harvest of Shame,*" in Actions of the Board of Directors, American Farm Bureau Federation, January 4, 1961, United Packinghouse Workers Union Papers, State Historical Society of Wisconsin, Madison; "Lost Fight for Itching Pills," *Valley Labor Citizen,* May 28, 1965; and Leslie O'Rear to Virgil Mitchell, November 29, 1960, United Packinghouse Workers Union Papers, State Historical Society of Wisconsin, Madison.

20. CBS News, *Harvest of Shame,* December 17, 1988, West 57th Transcripts (New York, 1988), 5–8; ABC News, *American Migrant Workers: Continuing the Harvest of Shame,* July 17, 1989, Nightline Transcripts (New York, 1989), 2–9; PBS, Hector Galan, *New Harvest, Old Shame,* narration by Dave Marsh (1990), tape no. TV-8293, Museum of Broadcast Communications, Chicago.

21. Murrow remained at USIA until he died in April 1965. Ironically, the televison network that ultimately had no place for a reporter interested in farmworkers and never again probed their place in society would later remember him as the "patron saint of American broadcasting" and *Harvest of Shame* as an exemplar of televison journalism. See Sperber, *Murrow,* 628–29; clipping, Henry Anderson to *Washington Post,* April 3, 1961, Anne Draper Collection, Stanford University Archives and Special Collections; and Gary Edgerton, "Edward R. Murrow: U.S. Broadcast Journalist," www.museum.tv/archives/etv/M/htmlM/murrowedwar/murrowedwar.htm, accessed 1999. Subjecting the documentary to close scrutiny, the *Palm Beach Post* was able to point out one factual error. Contrary to Murrow's claim that no migrant child had gone beyond high school, the *Post* found several children of Florida migrant parents who had graduated from college. See "The Glades Side of the Story," *Palm Beach Post,* February 8, 1961.

22. Mark Thompson, "The Agricultural Workers Organizing Committee, 1959–1962," MA thesis, Cornell University, 1963, 142–43; Jerome Wolf, "The Imperial Valley as an Index of Agricultural Labor Relations in California," PhD diss., University of Southern California, 1964, 330–56; Chris Paige, "Farmworker Organizing and the AWOC," MS, History Department, University of California, Berkeley, 1968, 20–21; clippings, Floyd McCracken, "California Valleys Echo to Lettuce Fight," *Christian Science Monitor,* February 7, 1961; McCracken "Bracero Issue Keys California Lettuce-Harvest Dispute," *Christian Science Monitor,* February 11, 1961; both in Anne Draper Collection, Stanford University Archives and Special Collections.

23. Sheriff Oren Fox to Lynn Bodgen, enclosed in Bogden to author, March 2, 1995, author's possession.

24. Quote from Street, interview with Oren Fox, June 17, 1995, Brawley, California, author's possession. See also the following clippings: "Farm Unions Used Sit-Ins in Imperial," *Cascade Labor News,* March 21, 1961; "El Centro Demonstration," *Packinghouse Worker,* February 1961, 1; "Arrest of Clive Knowles" and "Striking Lettuce Workers," *Packinghouse Worker,* March 1961, 1–2; "Lettuce Sitdown—13 Jailed," *San Francisco Chronicle,* February 3, 1961; "Mexico Plea Brings 2800—Bracero Shift," *San Francisco Chronicle,* March 5, 1961; "150 March in Lettuce Protest," *San Francisco Examiner,* February 20, 1961; "Goldberg Move in State Farm Rift," *Oakland Tribune,* March 4, 1961; "Farm Pickets Pulled Out," *Oakland Tribune,* February 13, 1961. All of these and the police mug books are in the Herb Hughes Scrapbooks, Imperial Valley Historical Society. Another collection of photographs in the Herb Hughes Scrapbooks documents the Danny Dannenberg labor camp sit-in. Both are now in the Pioneers Museum, Imperial, California.

25. Quote from clipping, California Labor Federation, *Weekly News Letter* 6 (January 6, 1961): 1, 5, Anne Draper Collection, Stanford University Archives and Special Collections. See also *Imperial Valley Press,* January 1, 5, 6, 8, 26, 31 and February 3, 1961; and *Packinghouse Worker* (February 1961). While searching for photographs of his father photographing in the fields, Paul Richards attempted to obtain the photo file compiled by the Imperial Valley Sheriff's Department but was told that the file had been destroyed. See Paul Richards to author, June 7, 1998, author's collection.

26. Quote from Street, interview with Harvey Richards, May 11, 1979, Atherton, California, author's possession. See also "Committee to Shift Organizers to San Joaquin Valley Farms," *Los Angeles Examiner,* February 17, 1961, Anne Draper Collection, Stanford University Archives and Special Collections; and *Imperial Valley Press,* February 2, 1961.

27. John Walsh to Harvey Richards, March 3 and 9, 1960; Richards to Walsh, February 25, 1960; Walsh to Klive Knowles, January 14, 1960; Walsh to Arthur Dubinsky, February 10, March 3,

and June 8, 1960; Dubinsky to Walsh, December 31, 1959, February 3 and May 8, 1960; April 1, 1961; all in President's Commission on Migratory Labor Papers, Dwight D. Eisenhower Library, Abilene, Kansas; newspaper clippings, *Packinghouse Worker* 21 (February 1961) and 21 (March 1961), Anne Draper Collection, Stanford University Archives and Special Collections.

28. Street, interview with Harvey Richards, January 12, 1978, Atherton, California, author's possession; Street, interview with John Kouns, March 24, 1981, Mill Valley, California, author's possession.

29. United Packinghouse Workers of America, *Public Law 78 Means Filth in Your Food* (Huntington Park, Calif., 1960), 1–3.

30. *New York Times,* November 26, 1961. I have located several surviving copies of *Poverty in the Valley of Plenty,* one in the Labor Archives, San Francisco State University, another in the archives of the California Federation of Teachers. Fred Glass generously provided a copy.

31. Street, interview with Margery Mann, March 23, 1978, Dixon, California, author's possession. For Krainock's photographs of child labor, see *School-Age Worker, School in Session, June 1961,* California, Child Labor, and Migrant Labor (poor child care), box 98, President's Commission on Migratory Labor, Dwight D. Eisenhower Library, Abilene, Kansas.

32. Quotes from Street, interview with Pirkle Jones, March 7, 2002, Mill Valley, California, author's possession; and Tim Wride, "Black Panthers: Photographs by Ruth Marion-Baruch and Pirkle Jones," *18th Street Arts Center Bulletin* (May 15, 2004): n.p. See also Jorie Parr, "Husband, Wife Photogs Not Always 'a Team Thing,'" *Mill Valley Record,* January 21, 1981; and Wade, *Pirkle Jones: California Photographs,* 108–9. Katherine Peake of the Los Angeles–based Emergency Committee to Aid Farmworkers also photographed extensively at this time and shot a series of unique photographs at various strikes. I have been unable to track down her work.

33. Quote from Truman Moore to author, July 24, 2003, author's possession.

34. Quote from ibid. Moore lost all of the negatives from his book project when he closed his New York City studio and moved to Charleston, North Carolina. See Moore to author, July 25 and 26, 2003; and Truman Moore, *The Slaves We Rent* (New York, 1965), 70, 128–31.

35. David Oltman, "Farm Frames," *California Farmer* 277 (December 1994): 36–42; Nancy Nadel, "Hard Work, Dedication Pay Off for Munroe," *F/Ten Forum* 12 (Winter 1991): 16–17.

36. Galarza and Mitchell moved their union into the Amalgamated Meat Cutters and Butcher Workmen, because it had been friendly to them in the past and even held a single contract with field hands at the Campbell Soup Company in Seabrook, New Jersey.

37. Grant Cannon, "Farm Labor Organizes," *Farm Quarterly* 16 (Spring 1961): 60–64, 160; Richard Mines, "The AFL–CIO Drive in Agriculture (1958–1961)," MA thesis, Columbia University, 1974, 37–65.

38. Cannon, "Farm Labor Organizes," 60–64, 160. Cold and technically challenging, the work required Munroe to "push" his film as Richards had earlier done.

39. "AFL–CIO Organizers Go After Farm Labor," *Business Week* (September 24, 1960): 50–54; London and Anderson, *So Shall Ye Reap,* 48–49; Joe Munroe, *Changing Faces on Our Land* (Des Moines, Iowa, 1990), 172–73.

40. Street, interview with Joe Munroe, February 13, 1995, Orinda, California, author's possession; Munroe, *Changing Faces on Our Land,* 86–89.

17. Photography and César Chávez's Farmworker Struggle

1. Quote from Street, interview with John Collier Jr., May 8, 1981, Muir Beach, California, author's possession. See also Street, interview with Ernest Lowe, May 12, 1999, Oakland, California, author's possession.

2. Quote from Street, interview with Pirkle Jones, March 12, 1981, Mill Valley, author's possession. See also John Kenneth Galbraith, *The New Industrial State* (Boston, 1967), 218, 302; Leo Bogart, *The Age of Television* (New York, 1972), xi–xiii, 1, 8, 184; Robert MacNeil, *The People Machine: The Influence of Television on American Politics* (New York, 1968), 77; Brown, *Television*, 58–66, 125, 196–97; Daniel Boorstein, *The Image: A Guide to Pseudo Events in America* (Chicago, 1961), 13; Daniel Boorstein, *The Americans: The Democratic Experience* (New York, 1973), 392–94; and Mary Ann Watson, *The Expanding Vista: American Televison in the Kennedy Years* (New York, 1994).

3. Street, interview with Ernest Lowe, March 14, 1995, Oakland, California, author's possession. See also Street to Lowe, October 8, 1976, author's possession; Munroe, *Changing Faces on Our Land*, 100–101; and Street, interview with John Collier Jr., March 12, 1978, Muir Beach, California, author's possession.

4. Quote from Lowe to author, June 5, 1998, author's possession.

5. Ibid. See also Riess, "Dorothea Lange: Making of a Documentary Photographer," 163.

6. Quote from handwritten notes from Ernest Lowe interview, ca. 1961, Ernest Lowe Collection, Oakland, California. Photographs originally consulted in his possession, in Oakland; now at Take Stock, San Rafael, California. Other written materials in Lowe's possession.

7. Quote from ibid. For Lowe's photographs, see London and Anderson, *So Shall Ye Reap*, 61–63. For an account of Teviston, see Richard Hammond and Nick Zachreson, *The San Joaquin Valley* (Visalia, Calif., 1979), 22. For Lowe's work in *Farm Labor*, see the covers of 1 (January 1963) and 1 (November–December 1963).

8. Quotes from Ann McGregor, comp., Cindy Wathen, ed., *Remembering Cesar: The Legacy of Cesar Chavez*, photography by George Ballis (Clovis, Calif., 2000), vi. See also Galarza, *Spiders in the House and Workers in the Fields*, 213; "Prints as Politics," *Fresno Bee*, September 30, 1973; and Street, interview with Ernest Lowe, March 14, 1995, Oakland, California.

9. Quote from George Ballis, "Narrative of Career," MS, n.d., 1, George Ballis Collection, Fresno, California; originally consulted in his possession, now at Take Stock, San Rafael, California.

10. Quotes from ibid.; Ballis to author, July 6, 1998, author's possession; and McGregor et al., *Remembering Cesar*, vi.

11. John A. Kouns, "John A. Kouns," in LeRoy Chatfield, *Farmworker Movement Documentation Project*, www.farmworkermovement.org, accessed 2005.

12. Galarza, *Spiders in the House and Workers in the Fields*, 100, 106, 112, 120, 127; Paul Richards, *Critical Focus: The Black and White Photographs of Harvey Wilson Richards* (Oakland, Calif., 1986), 38; Meister and Loftis, *A Long Time Coming*, 107–9.

13. Quote from Ballis, "Narrative of Career." See also Ballis to author, July 6, 1998; Citizen Editor on Photo Project, *Valley Labor Citizen*, July 31, 1964; *New York Times*, November 26, 1961.

14. Quote from Ken Light, "Matt Herron: The Civil Rights Movement and the Southern Documentary Project," in Light, ed., *Witness in Our Time*, 66–67. See also Ballis, "Narrative of Career," 1.

15. Quote from Ballis to author, July 6, 1998. See also *Valley Labor Citizen*, April 24, 1964; *Santa Clara County Union Gazette*, April 17, 1964; Galarza, *Spiders in the House and Workers in the Fields*, 196–276; Street, interview with George Ballis, May 23, 1981, Fresno, California, author's possession; and George Ballis, *Dream What We Can Become and Rejoice* (San Rafael, Calif., 1995).

16. Quotes from "Large Landowner Mouthpiece Accuses Citizen Editor of 'Distortion' and 'Deliberate Falsification,'" *Valley Labor Citizen*, July 31, 1964. See also Moore, *The Slaves We Rent*, photographs after page 78, also 123, 128–30, 135, 151, 156–58.

17. *Stockton Record*, April 20, 1965; Kiser, "The Bracero Program," 177–277.

18. Frank L. Hull, "The Effects of Braceros on the Agricultural Labor Market in California, 1950–1970: Public Law 78 and Its Aftermath," PhD diss., University of Illinois, 1973, 144–64; UPI

Telephoto HCPO51806, *Mexicali, Mexico,* May 19, 1965; UPI Telephoto SXPO61704, *Salinas, California,* June 19, 1965.

19. Quote from Margery Mann to author, March 23, 1977, author's possession. See also typed captions on Margery Mann's photographs taken in August 1965, consulted when in her possession.

20. Quote from Street, interviews with George Ballis, May 2, 1982, Fresno, and March 12, 1998, Toll House, California, both in author's possession. See also Mary Rudge, "Their Art Comes from the Fields," *San Francisco Examiner,* California Living section, May 17, 1981; clipping, "Stockton Hub for State Farm Labor; Contractors Bid for Migratory Workers," *Stockton Record,* n.d., Raymond P. Roth Collection, Archives and Special Collections, University of California, Davis. For one published photograph of the 4:30 A.M. shape-up in Stockton, see London and Anderson, *So Shall Ye Reap,* 64.

21. Quote from William T. O'Rear to Albert Tieberg, March 22, 1965, California Migrant Ministry Papers, Archives of Urban and Labor History, Wayne State University. See also "O'Rear: Tieberg Should See Farmworkers," *Valley Labor Citizen,* March 26, 1965; and Street, interview with Ballis, August 1, 1997, Tollhouse, California, author's possession.

22. Jacques Levy, *Cesar Chavez: Autobiography of La Causa* (1975; Minneapolis, 2007), after 148. Although not a photographer, Henry Anderson, editor of *Farm Labor* and chairman of the Citizens for Farm Labor, also photographed farmworkers extensively at this time. San Francisco photographer Richard Weymouth Brooks provided a highly abstract shot of the deteriorating wall of a farmworker house for the February 1964 cover of *Farm Labor* (vol. 1), an example of an Aaron Siskind–type composition that also illustrates how some photographers found even abstract art in the fields. See *Farm Labor* 2 (October 1964): 12.

23. "Protest March against Rent Hike on 27-Year-Old Metal Shacks," *Valley Labor Citizen,* July 23, 1965.

24. *Fresno Bee,* September 18, 20, 1965; *Los Angeles Times,* May 13, 1965; *Valley Labor Citizen* issues: June 4, September 17, October 1 and 8, and November 5, 1965; *People's World,* October 2, 8, and 23, 1965; *California Farmer,* September 17, 1965; UFW, "A Summary of Events in the Grape Strike," mimeo, n.d., n.p.; UFW, "A History of the Delano Grape Strike and the DiGiorgio Evictions," mimeo, n.d., 1; both mimeos located in the California Migrant Ministry Collection, Archives of Urban and Labor History, Wayne State University.

25. Craig Scharlin and Lilia V. Villanueva, *Philip Vera Cruz: A Personal History of Filipino Immigrants and the Farmworkers Movement* (Los Angeles, 1992), 34–36; Richard Griswold del Castillo and Richard A. Garcia, *César Chávez: A Triumph of Spirit* (Norman, Okla., 1995), 38–39; Philip L. Martin, *Promises to Keep: Collective Bargaining in California Agriculture* (Ames, Iowa, 1996), 86–87. Some sources put the number of strikers present at Guadalupe Church at twenty-seven hundred.

26. At least one of these photographers was commissioned by union supporters. Requiring good photographs of a food caravan to Delano in December 1965, Anne Draper, regional director of the Amalgamated Clothing Workers of America, hired San Francisco photographer Larry Kenney to document the event. Although one picture appeared in a Clothing Workers union publication, most remained unseen by the public and sat unused in Draper's archive for the next forty years. See Larry Kenney, proof sheets, Anne Draper Collection, Stanford University Archives and Special Collections.

27. Street, interview with Ronald B. Taylor, May 23, 1974, Fresno, California, author's possession. See also Ronald B. Taylor, *Chávez and the Farmworkers* (Boston, 1975); and *Fresno Bee* clipping files and photo morgue files, *Fresno Bee,* Fresno, California.

28. Quote from Street, interview with Jack Pandol, November 11, 1987, Delano, California. See also del Castillo and Garcia, *César Chávez,* 45; and John Bloom, *Photography at Bay: Interviews, Essays, and Reviews* (Albuquerque, N.M., 1998), 172–74. Several photographers got their start at

Delano, including one who arrived with a little plastic Koni camera. Driving 250 miles by motor bike from San Rafael, Happ Stewart learned photography at Delano and later went on to a photographic career in New York City. See Street, interview with Jon Lewis, August 9, 1998, San Francisco; Street, interview with John Kouns, August 23, 1998, Sausalito, California; both in author's possession. A preliminary list of photographers, volunteers, and NFWA members with cameras who were at Delano on and off between September 1965 and September 1966 includes Henry Anderson, George Ballis, Bill Berg, Mike Bry, Gene Daniels, Anne Draper, Arthur Dubinsky, Bill Esher, Gerhard Gscheidle, Joseph Gunterman, Howard Harowitz, Nick Jones, John Kouns, Jim Kunz, Sam Kushner, Jacques Levy, Jon Lewis, Ernest Lowe, Eugene Nelson, Lauri Oman, Steve Pinskey, Harvey Richards, Victor Salandini, Chris Sanchez, Eric Schmidt, Blair Stapp, Ted Streshinsky, Hap Stuart, Ronald Taylor, and Bob Thurber. Stapp's work is in the Oakland Museum.

29. "Six-Year-Old Strikebreakers," *Valley Labor Citizen,* October 1, 1965; California State Legislature, Senate, *Fourteenth Report of the Senate Fact-Finding Subcommittee on Un-American Activities* (Sacramento, 1967), 28–29; *People's World,* October 16, 1965; *El Malcriado,* no. 27 (n.d.); Eugene Nelson, *Huelga: The First Hundred Days of the Great Delano Grape Strike* (Delano, Calif., 1966), 81; Kern County Sheriff's Office Records, September 25, 1965, in Records of the California Senate Fact-Finding Committee on Un-American Activities, California State Archives, Sacramento.

30. *People's World,* October 2, 10, and 30, 1965; *San Francisco Examiner,* October 17, 1965; *El Malcriado,* no. 21 (n.d.). For a wider photograph from the sequence, see newspaper clipping A. V. Krebs, "Strikers Seek Church Help," *National Catholic Reporter* 50 (October 20, 1965): 6, Victor Salandini Collection, Stanford University Special Collections and Archives. See also William O'Brien, "The Grapes of Wrath in Delano," *San Francisco Examiner,* October 17, 1965.

31. Hoover's men would eventually compile a file of about fifteen hundred pages that uncovered not one instance of subversive or illegal activity among photographers or anyone else. See Richard Steven Street, "The FBI's Secret File on César Chávez," *Southern California Quarterly* 128 (Winter 1996–97): 347–84; FBI director to special agent in charge of field office, Los Angeles, October 11, 1965; Catha DeLoach to Milton Jons, "Communist Infiltration of the National Farmworkers Association, Delano, California, Internal Security—C," October 15, 1965; Hoover to special agent in charge of field office, Los Angeles, October 18, 1965; all in Declassified FBI File 100-444762 (César Chávez). Besides discovering Richards's home address at 14 Flood Circle, Atherton, California, the FBI noted that he drove a 1965 Oldsmobile station wagon, California license plate S75763. For later concerns with Richards, see A. Jones to Robert Wick, March 11, 1965, Declassified FBI File 100-444762. One informant supplying information on Richards was apparently close to Chávez, because he "asked" Chávez about the photographer and was "told" he was a freelancer. I have not been able to identify the informant.

32. Street, interview with George Ballis, June 6, 1979, Fresno, author's possession; Street, interview with Eugene Nelson, August 12, 1979, Sebastopol, California, author's possession.

33. Quote from "Justice, San Joaquin Style," *Valley Labor Citizen,* October 15, 1965. See also "Citizen Fouls Up on Dispoto Bullying," *Valley Labor Citizen,* November 19, 1965; and *Movement* (December 1965).

34. Quote from Eugene Nelson to author, October 24, 1976, author's possession. The recollection bears an eerie resemblance to what had happened to *Salinas Index* photographer John V. Young during the 1936 lettuce packers' strike. See Nelson, *Huelga,* 94–95. Doug Adair recalls that after using the Richards photograph of Huerta on the cover of Nelson's *Huelga,* the Farm Worker Press dropped the photograph in favor of a panorama of a picket line for the cover of the second edition. "I can't remember why we changed," he recalled decades later, "since the photo of Dolores is much more dramatic." Adair to author, e-mail, July 20, 2004, author's possession.

35. Quote from Taylor, *Chávez and the Farmworkers,* 143. See also Nelson, *Huelga,* 104.

36. Levy, *Cesar Chavez,* 192–93; *People's World,* October 23, 1965; Nelson, *Huelga,* 100–104. Nelson died in 1999. Kathy Muriaga to author, e-mail, December 27, 2004, author's possession.

37. On December 2, *El Malcriado* editor Bill Esher discovered just how far some would go to eliminate unfavorable images. While photographing badly packed table grapes being dumped into gondolas headed for a local winery, Esher was chased back to his car by an irate company employee, who then followed him down the highway and tried to run him off the road. See Nelson, *Huelga,* 119. For Dubinsky, see Steve Allen, *The Ground Is Our Table* (Garden City, N.Y., 1966), 95–99. See also J. Craig Jenkins, *The Politics of Insurgency: The Farmworker Movement in the 1960s* (New York, 1985), 142–43; Majka and Majka, *Farm Workers, Agribusiness, and the State,* 174–75; Street, interview with Ballis, June 6, 1979, Fresno; and Sam Kushner, *Long Road to Delano* (New York, 1975), 153.

38. Nelson Lichtenstein, *The Most Dangerous Man in Detroit: Walter Reuther and the Fate of American Labor* (New York, 1995), 410; Arthur Schlesinger Jr., *Robert F. Kennedy and His Times* (Boston, 1978), 790–92; United Automobile Workers, *Proceedings of the Twentieth Constitutional Convention, Long Beach, California* (May 16–20, 1966), 230; UPI Telephoto DEP121602-12-16-98, *Delano, Calif.* December 16, 1965.

39. Street, interview with Jon Lewis, March 4, 1981, San Francisco, author's possession.

40. Street, interview with Fred Ross, September 17, 1979, San Anselmo, California, author's possession.

41. Quote from Street, interview with Jack Pandol, November 13, 1986, Delano, California, author's possession. See also, Street, interview with Stephen Pavich Jr., September 27, 1989, Richgrove, California, author's possession.

42. Quote from Eugene Nelson to author, October 29, 1976, author's possession.

18. The Delano Grape Strike and Boycott

1. Quote from Nelson, *Huelga,* 73.

2. Quote from Catha DeLoach to Milton Jons, "Communist Infiltration of the National Farmworkers Association, Delano, California—Internal Security—C," October 20, 1965, Declassified FBI File LA-100-444762. See also National Advisory Committee on Farm Labor, *The Grape Strike* (New York, 1966), 29; Taylor, *Chávez and the Farmworkers,* 165; A. V. Krebs, "Strikers Seek Church Help," *National Catholic Reporter* 50 (October 20, 1965): 6; Kushner, *Long Road to Delano,* 137–39; Dunne, *Delano,* 28; *Valley Labor Citizen,* October 1, 1965 (describing one incident); Levy, Cesar *Chavez,* 190; "Dear Don," memorandum, California Migrant Ministry Papers, Archives of Urban and Labor History, Wayne State University; and A. Phillip Randolph to Dear Friend, March 30, 1966, Raymond P. Roth Collection, Archives and Special Collections, University of California, Davis.

3. Quote from U.S. Senate, Committee on Labor and Public Welfare, *Hearings of the Subcommittee on Migratory Labor,* 89th Cong., 2nd sess., 1966, 369. See also Taylor, *Chávez and the Farmworkers,* 165–66.

4. Quotes from Gary Allen, *The Grapes: Communist Wrath in Delano* (Belmont, Mass., 1968), 3–12, Raymond P. Roth Collection, Archives and Special Collections, University of California, Davis. See also Gary Allen, "The Grapes: Communist Wrath in Delano," *American Opinion* 9 (June 1966): 1–14; DeLoach to Jons, "Communist Infiltration of the National Farmworkers Association, Delano, California—Internal Security—C," 3, October 20, 1965, Declassified FBI File 100-444762; and California State Legislature, Senate, *Fourteenth Report of the Senate Fact-Finding Subcommittee on Un-American Activities* (Sacramento, 1966), 42, 68–69, 72–75.

5. Quote from Levy, *Cesar Chavez,* 190. See also Street, interview with Henry Anderson, May 22, 1978, Berkeley, California; Street, interview with George Ballis, March 17, 1981, Fresno; and Street, interview with Sam Kushner, August 7, 1973, Arvin, California; all in author's possession.

6. Quote from Street, interview with César Chávez, August 7, 1979, Salinas, California, author's possession. See also Meister and Loftis, *A Long Time Coming,* 122; Street, interview with Jon Lewis, August 8, 1998, San Francisco, author's possession; and Jon Lewis, "Jon Lewis Photos, 1966–1968," in Farmworker Movement Documentation Project, www.farmworkermovement.org, accessed 2004. For a photograph of Chávez photographing organizers departing California in the grape boycott of 1969, see the UFW Collection, Archives of Urban and Labor History, Wayne State University. See also Susan Ferriss and Ricardo Sandoval, *The Fight in the Fields: Cesar Chavez and the Farmworkers Movement* (New York, 1997), 151, 175. The whereabouts of much of the UFW photographic material still remain a mystery. For example, NFWA volunteer Father Victor Salandini packed a camera and shot hundreds of photographs, but after searching the Salandini Collection I failed to find his negatives. For an anecdote describing his photography, see Dunne, *Delano,* 126. Leroy Chatfield has copies of some of Chávez's photographs. See Chatfield to author, January 2, 2005, author's collection.

7. Quotes from Nelson, *Huelga,* 129; and London and Anderson, *So Shall Ye Reap,* 173.

8. Quotes from Adair to author, e-mail, August 1, 2004, author's possession; and Street, interview with Bill Esher, May 29, 1981, Sebastopol, California, author's possession. See also Bill Esher, "Coyotes in the Cantaloupes: Notes from the Melon Harvest," *Farm Labor* 2 (August 1964): 9–10.

9. Quote from Nelson, *Huelga,* 129.

10. Quote from National Advisory Committee on Farm Labor, *The Grape Strike* (New York, 1966), 29. See also A. Frank, P. Graham, and Philip Randolph to Friend, March 30, 1966, Raymond P. Roth Collection, Archives and Special Collections, University of California, Davis.

11. Yolanda Broyles-Gonzales, *El Teatro Campesino: Theater in the Chicano Movement* (Austin, Tex., 1994), 13, 27, 76, 13–20, 235–36; Betty Ann Diamond, "Brown-Eyed Children of the Sun: The Cultural Politics of El Teatro Campesino," PhD diss., University of Wisconsin, 1977; Street, interview with Felipe Cantu, August 23, 1987, Sanger, California, author's possession. For an early published photograph from El Teatro's New York City tour, see Edwin Bolwell, "Strike Message Put to Music Wins Cheers," *New York Times,* July 22, 1967, photograph by John Orris. See also John Hoagland, "Farmworkers Dramaticize Discontent," *Los Angeles Times,* July 23, 1967. One of the few women photographers active among the farmworker movement at this time was Stockton-based Elizabeth Sunflower, who did a long interview and photo essay on Luis Váldez and El Teatro Campesino for the *Tulane Drama Review.*

12. Quotes from Street, interview with Mike Bry, April 22, 1982, San Francisco; and Street, interview with Bob Fitch, March 22, 1982, San Francisco; both in author's possession. See also Street, interview with Ernest Lowe, April 12, 1999, Oakland, California, author's possession; and Street, interview with Doug Adair, May 22, 1986, Thermal, California, author's possession.

13. Al Howard, "Delano: The General Strike in the Grapes," *Insurgent* (January–February 1966); Al Howard, "Delano: Bread and Justice," *Insurgent* (May–June 1966): 16–17; Al Howard, "Profile of a Striker," *Insurgent* (May–June 1966): 18–19; National Advisory Committee on Farm Labor, *Farm Labor Organizing, 1905–1967: A Brief History* (New York, 1967), 51, 65; John Gregory Dunne, "Strike!" *Saturday Evening Post* 240 (May 6, 1967): 32–68.

14. Quote from Street, interview with Fred Ross Sr., May 20, 1979, Kentfield, California, author's possession. See also Street, interview with Bill Esher, May 29, 1981, Sebastopol; and Street, interview with Ernest Lowe, March 14, 1995, Oakland, California, author's possession.

15. Quote from Street, interview with Jon Lewis, March 4, 1981, San Francisco, also July 9, 1998, author's possession. See also Jon Lewis, "Jon Lewis Photos, 1966–1968," Farmworker Movement Documentation Project, www.farmworkermovement.org, accessed 2004.

16. Quote from Street, interview with Lewis, March 4, 1981.

17. Quote combined from Street, interviews with Lewis, March 4, 1981, San Francisco, and August 23, 1998, Oakland, California, author's possession. See also LeRoy Chatfield, "John A.

Kouns Photos, 1966–1970, 1973–1974, 1995–1996," in LeRoy Chatfield, Farmworker Movement Documentation Project, www.farmworkermovement.org, accessed 2003.

18. Susan Drake to author, May 23, 2003, author's possession. See also Doug Adair to author, June 3, 2003, author's possession; Jon Lewis, *From This Earth* (San Francisco, 1969); Street, interview with Gerhard Gscheidle, May 8, 2003, Stuttgart, Germany, author's possession; Gscheidle to author, May 15, 2003, author's possession; and Jon Lewis photo essay on DiGiorgio's Sierra Vista Ranch (extensively captioned sequence of eleven photographs), Anne Draper Collection, Stanford University Archives and Special Collections.

19. Quote from Street, interview with Lewis, March 4, 1981. See also Bill Esher to Lowe, n.d., Ernest Lowe Collection, Oakland, California.

20. Quote from Street, interview with Lewis, August 23, 1998, Oakland. "It was day to day," recalled Lewis. "You would wait for the weekends. Everyone would go to People's Café. The strike caravans would come in. There would be food. Groovy chicks. I had a cigarette habit and the five dollars a week wage was tough. You were just like one of the pickets. It was the experience of a lifetime" (Street, interview with Lewis, August 8, 1998, San Francisco). Lacking in resources, Lewis shot Tri-X developed in Acufine. This developing practice irritated Jack Welpott, his photography instructor at San Francisco State University, who accused Lewis of compromising quality. But Lewis had no choice. He had to develop his film with whatever was available. This was also true of his print-drying techniques. Because he lacked an electric drum dryer, Lewis improvised, placing his still-wet prints face down on a plate of stainless steel out on the lawn in the hot sun. "I got pretty fair glossies that way," he later recalled (Street, interview with Lewis, March 4, 1981, San Francisco). See also Jon Lewis, "From This Earth . . . from the Delano Grape Strike," MA thesis, San Francisco State University, 1969; and Street, interview with Sam Kushner, November 12, 1973, Los Angeles, author's possession.

21. Quote from Dolores Huerta to Irwin DeShetler, March 13, 1966, Irwin DeShetler Papers, Archives of Urban and Labor History, Wayne State University.

22. Quotes from Edgar Z. Friedenberg, "Another America," *New York Review of Books* (March 3, 1966): 23–25; and Mark Jonathan Harris, "On Making *Huelga*," MS, July 2005, in Farmworker Movement Documentation Project, www.farmworkermovement.org, accessed 2005.

23. Jerald Brown, "United Farm Workers Grape Strike and Boycott, 1965–70: An Evaluation of the Culture of Poverty Theory," PhD diss., Cornell University, 1972, 161–62; Marshall Ganz, "Five Smooth Stones: Strategic Capacity in the Unionization of California Agriculture," PhD diss., Harvard University, 2000, 337–40.

24. Ferriss and Sandoval, *The Fight in the Fields*, 117–23; Peter Matthiessen, *Sal si puedes: Cesar Chavez and the New American Revolution* (New York, 1969), 127–29. Some question the assertion that the march on Sacramento was the longest mass march in American history up to that point. To some extent it depends on how one defines a protest march. See Lucy G. Barber, *Marching on Washington: The Forging of an American Political Tradition* (Berkeley, 2003).

25. Gerhard Gscheidle to author, May 7, 28, and June 3, 2003, author's possession.

26. Quote from Street, interview with John Kouns, March 24, 1981, Mill Valley, California, author's possession. See also Kouns, "John A. Kouns," in Chatfield, Farmworker Movement Documentation Project, www.farmworkermovement.org; and Street, interview with Chris Schneider, March 22, 1987, El Centro, California, author's collection.

27. Quotes from Brown, "United Farm Workers Grape Strike and Boycott," 168; and Dunne, *Delano*, 133. Information on the marchers is from *El Malcriado* 33 (April 10, 1966).

28. Quotes from Doug Adair to Marshall Ganz, e-mail, June 8, 2004, UFW Documentation Project, nfwaleroy@listerve.com; and Street, interview with Jon Lewis, August 8, 1998, San Francisco. See also Fran Ortiz daily journal, March 20–22, 1966, courtesy of Fran Ortiz, San Francisco;

Gerhard Gscheidle to author, May 1 and 28, 2003; and Street, interview with Gerhard Gscheidle, May 12, 2003, Stuttgart, Germany; all in author's possession.

29. Quote from Street, interview with Jon Lewis, August 8, 1998, San Francisco.

30. Quote from Gerhard Gscheidle to author, June 3, 2003, author's possession. See also Street, interview with Jon Lewis, August 8, 1998, San Francisco; and Street, interview with John Kouns, March 26, 1981, Mill Valley, California, author's possession.

31. Quote from Street, interview with Jon Lewis, August 8, 1998, San Francisco.

32. Quote from Street, interview with Kouns, March 26, 1981, Mill Valley. See also Street, interview with Harvey Richards, May 13, 1978, Atherton, California, author's possession.

33. *Time* (March 1, 1966): 28–29; Street, interview with Kouns, March 26, 1981, Mill Valley; Street, interview with Jon Lewis, August 23, 1998, Oakland. For the work of *Sacramento Bee* photographer Ward Sharrer, see the April 11, 1966, issue of that newspaper. For the DiGiorgio sequence, see the captioned photographs by Jon Lewis, Anne Draper Collection, Stanford University Archives and Special Collections. "There was no question that the symbolism . . . provided dramatic visual scenarios," recalled Gscheidle, "but this was a side product of the event itself. I never had the impression that we as photographers were only welcome because we provided the union with photographs, but that the human element was a strong connection. We came down from the big city and became part of a movement to further the cause of the farmworker without any immediate financial reward." Quote from Gerhard Gscheidle to author, June 3, 2003, author's possession.

34. Jenkins, *The Politics of Insurgency,* 155; *Stockton Record,* March 21 and 22, 1966; *San Francisco Examiner,* March 21 and 22, 1966; *San Francisco Examiner, California Living,* December 21, 1980; Street, interview with Rich Turner, March 12, 1976, Stockton, California, author's possession.

35. Quote from Street, interview with Fran Ortiz, March 22, 1989, San Francisco, author's possession. The *San Francisco Examiner* lost both Ortiz's negatives and prints. See Street, interview with Elizabeth Martin, May 23, 1998, San Francisco, author's possession.

36. For religion and popular culture, see Warren Susman, *Culture and Commitment, 1929–1945* (New York, 1973). For the Virgin Mary motif, see Maria Warner, *Alone of All Her Sex: The Myth and the Cult of the Virgin Mary* (New York, 1976), 203, 223; Pat Hoffman, *Ministry of the Dispossessed: Learning from the Farm Worker Movement* (Los Angeles, 1987), 35. For the crucifixion photograph, see George Ballis, *Basta! La historia de nuestra lucha (Enough! The Tale of Our Struggle),* text from the Plan of Delano (Delano, Calif., 1966), 52. See also Paul Jacobs, "Clear the Dignitaries! Clear the Dignitaries! The Platform Is Reserved for the Originales!" *Ramparts* 5 (July 1966): 32. Several days earlier, the ever-present Jon Lewis framed a scene in Stockton with the very cross that Ballis had so dramatically documented. See Street, interview with Jon Lewis, August 23, 1998, San Francisco, author's possession.

37. Quotes from Gerhard Gscheidle to author, May 28 and June 3, 2003. See also Doug Adair to author, June 3, 2003, author's possession; Street, interview with John Kouns, March 26, 1981, Mill Valley; and Street, interview with Jon Lewis, August 23, 1998, San Francisco.

38. After the march, Sánchez went on to document the union's day-to-day activities for the next five years. "As he got better and better," recalled Doug Adair, "he let it be known he preferred being called 'Chris' [his name was Manuel Cristóbol Sánchez]. . . . He actually did some of his best photography after I left the *El Malcriado* staff in 1970." Quote from Adair to author, June 3, 2003, author's possession. Besides Chris Sánchez, a short list of Mexican American photographers who covered the NFWA and its successors includes Victor Alemán, Oscar Castillo, Ben Garza, Alexis Gonzáles, and George Rodríguez.

39. For Blair Stapp's work, see his disorganized but extremely valuable collection in the Oakland Museum. For press photographers, see the work of Joseph A. Frisina and Walt Porter in the *Fresno Bee,* March 25, 1966. Some photographers recall the atmosphere on the steps of the state

Capitol as resembling that of a class reunion, as old radicals and liberals put aside animosities and jeered Governor Brown for refusing to meet the marchers in favor of spending Easter at Frank Sinatra's home in Palm Springs.

40. Quote from Jim Marshall, *Proof,* intro. by Joel Selvin (San Francisco, 2004), 119–20, back page. See also Street, interview with Jim Marshall, October 15, 2004, San Francisco, author's possession; and Marshall to Street with enclosures, October 18, 2004, author's possession.

41. Marshall, *Proof,* 121–22; Street, interview with Shirley Streshinsky, August 12, 2003, Kensington, California, author's possession.

42. Hansel Mieth Hagel Contact Sheets and Color Slides: *Grape Strike March,* March 10 and 28–30, 1966; *César Chávez, San Francisco,* June 1966; *Farmworkers Grape Strike, San Francisco,* July 1966; Hansel Mieth Hagel, "Toward a Conclusion" MS, December 8, 1966, 48; Hansel Mieth Hagel, "The Headstart Story, a Reappraisal," MS, July 14, 1969, 5–6; Hansel to Otto (handwritten, undated); "A Publishable Story," (handwritten notes), December 1968; all in Otto and Hansel Mieth Hagel Collection, Center for Creative Photography, University of Arizona. Frames 25 and 28, her color transparencies, depict George Ballis photographing the march.

43. Quote from Street, interview with Jon Lewis, March 4, 1981, San Francisco. See also Gerhard Gscheidle to author, June 3, 2003; and Grant Cannon, "Labor—Strike, Boycott and Contract," *Farm Quarterly* 21 (Fall 1966): 20–26. As one of his last projects in Delano, Gerhard Gscheidle photographed the Schenley elections on assignment for *Newsweek,* snagging the job through a connection that the SNCC's Los Angeles office had with the local *Newsweek* office.

44. Quote from Street, interview with John Kouns, March 26, 1981, Mill Valley.

45. Ibid.

46. Quote from Harris, "On Making *Huelga.*"

47. Quote from Street, interview with Shirley Streshinsky, August 29, 2003, Kensington, California, author's possession. See also Street, interview with Shirley Streshinsky, August 25, 2003, Kensington, California, author's possession; and Kelly St. John, "Ted Streshinsky—Noted Photojournalist," *San Francisco Chronicle,* March 2, 2003.

48. Quote from Dunne, *Delano,* 85–86. See also Street, interview with Jon Lewis, September 6, 1998, San Francisco; and Street, interview with Ted Streshinsky, September 15, 1998, Kensington, California, author's possession. Despite their poverty, poor equipment, lack of media contacts, and ongoing harassment by law enforcement, freelancers were dogged in their commitment to the cause and extremely patient in their work. Contrasting their behavior with that of several photojournalists, Dunne and Streshinsky encountered one reporter–photographer team for a national magazine that seemed to epitomize the cowboy approach. "The photographer was surprised to learn that he was in the San Joaquin valley, which he had thought was in the state of Washington," recalled Dunne in *Delano,* "and the reporter, in the words of one observer, 'wouldn't know a grape if he saw one in the Safeway.' I saw them the following morning at 102 Albany trying to hire a picket line for a photograph, advising the NFWA magnanimously to 'send the bill for the gas to New York.'" Quote from Dunne, *Delano,* 58.

49. Quote from A. D. Coleman, *Light Readings: A Photographic Critic's Writings, 1968–1978* (New York, 1979), 39. See also Dave Bohn and Roger Minick, *Delta West* (Berkeley, 1969).

50. When Lowe complained that he could not possibly reduce his show to sixty or seventy images, Stewart and Osborne said, "Let's see hundreds of them. These are too good not to use." Completely redesigning the layout, the architects dramatically expanded the number of images to include two full galleries for a total of between three hundred and four hundred photographs. One wall would hold 16 × 20–inch prints. Another would hold 30 × 40–inch prints. Several long lines of 8 × 10–inch prints would weave between the two walls, providing an environment for the larger pictures. Jack R. McGregor to Lowe, November 5, 1965, and January 5, 1966; Lowe to McGregor,

February 25 and June 29, 1966; press release, M. H. deYoung Memorial Museum, September 3, 1966; all in Ernest Lowe Collection, Oakland.

51. Quote from Jack R. McGregor to Ernest Lowe, June 23, 1966; McGregor to Beaumont Newhall, June 23, 1966; both in Ernest Lowe Collection, Oakland.

52. Quote from Arthur Bloomfield, "Message of Misery," *San Francisco Examiner,* September 19, 1966. See also Lowe to Ernest Besig, June 27, 1966; and Besig to Public, June 29, 1966; both in Ernest Lowe Collection, Oakland; Street, interview with Lowe, April 6, 1998, Oakland, author's possession. Through no fault of his own, Lowe's photography would remain hidden and suppressed. Nearly forty years would pass before it finally surfaced for public view. Shortly after the exhibition debacle, and in part because of it, Lowe turned over his entire archive of some five thousand negatives to the Oakland Museum. As he went about his business, he believed that the museum was making the material available to scholars and students of farm labor. But lacking space and short on funds, the museum filed the entire collection away in a warehouse, where it sat, unused, unseen, uncataloged, and unknown for more than a generation. After searching for the material over three decades, I tracked down Lowe and contacted museum director Robert Powers, who located the collection in a warehouse. Lowe then withdrew his collection and placed it with Matt Herron/Take Stock Collection, San Rafael, California. See Street to Lowe, October 8, 1976; Lowe to Street, November 15, 1976; Street to Heyman, December 8, 1976, March 5, 1977, and July 8, 1982; Street to Powers, March 5, 1995; and Drew Johnson to Street, June 12, 1998; all in author's collection.

53. Quotes from Harris, "On Making *Huelga.*"

54. LeRoy Chatfield, "Mark Jonathan Harris Photos 1966," in Farmworker Movement Documentation Project, www.farmworkermovement.org, accessed 2004; Bill Esher to Lowe, n.d., Ernest Lowe Collection, Oakland. Harris went on to a distinguished career and won three Academy Awards for documentary filmmaking.

55. Street, interview with Jon Lewis, August 8, 1998, San Francisco.

56. Quote from Dunne, *Delano,* 159, 162. Like the good former Marine that he was, Lewis stoically endured the harassment at Sierra Vista Ranch. In July, *Ramparts* illustrated an essay by Luis Váldez and a reminiscence by César Chávez with his color photographs and black-and-white photographs by Kouns.

57. Majka and Majka, *Farmworkers, Agribusiness, and the State,* 182–84.

58. Street, interview with Jon Lewis, April 9, 2006, San Francisco, author's possession.

59. Quote from Chatfield, "Mark Jonathan Harris Photos 1966." See also Bill Esher to Lowe, n.d., Ernest Lowe Collection, Oakland.

60. For a photographic collaboration between Kouns and Lewis, see Luis Váldez, "Huelga! Tales of the Delano Revolution," *Ramparts* 5 (July 1966): 37–50. For Lewis's photographs at Sierra Vista, see *AFL–CIO News,* October 29, 1966. See also, Ballis, *Basta,* 4.

61. Quote from Gerhard Gscheidle to author, June 3, 2003, author's possession. A year later Lewis used his still photographs to produce an eleven-minute film, *Nosotros venceremos!* (We shall overcome), Third World Cinema Group (Berkeley, 1969), copies in San Francisco Public Library and Labor Studies Archive, San Francisco State University. For the atmosphere at Delano during the summer of 1967, see *New York Times,* July 30, 1967. For Texas, see Ray Robert Leal, "The 1966–1967 South Texas Farm Worker Strike: A Case Study of Farm Worker Powerlessness," PhD diss., Indiana University, 1983, 280–305.

19. A Spirit of Hope among People

1. Street, interview with Jon Lewis, April 9, 2006, San Anselmo, California, author's possession. See also Jacques Levy Research Collection on César Chávez, series I, audiotape 47, transcript

file 15, box 5, folder 141, Yale Collection of Western Americana, Beinecke Rare Book and Manuscript Library, Yale University.

2. LeRoy Chatfield, "Nick Jones Photos, 1966–1976"; and Nick Jones, "Nick Jones, 1966–1976"; both in Chatfield, Farmworker Documentation Project, www.farmworkermovement.org, accessed 2004. Before his camera was lost or stolen in 1975, Jones shot over fifteen hundred photographs, many of them documenting the boycott in Boston and Oregon. See also London and Anderson, *So Shall Ye Reap,* 158.

3. Quote from Street, interview with Jon Lewis, April 9, 2006, San Anselmo.

4. Quote from Street, interview with Emmon Clarke, March 4, 2001, Rohnert Park, California, author's possession. For more on Clarke, see Street, interview with John Kouns, March 22, 2000, Sausalito, California, author's possession; Street, interview with Emmon Clarke, April 27, 2001, Rohnert Park, California, author's possession; and Doug Adair to author, e-mail, August 1, 2004, author's possession. For a photograph of Emmon Clarke and the *El Malcriado* staff, see folder 5, Anne Draper Collection, Stanford University Special Collections and Archives.

5. Quote from Street, interview with Emmon Clarke, March 4, 2001, Rohnert Park. See also César Chávez, "The Case against Perelli-Minetti: An Appeal for Justice," January 19, 1966; and various enclosed materials containing Clarke's photographs, Irwin DeShetler Papers, Archives of Urban and Labor History, Wayne State University.

6. Street, interview with Emmon Clarke, March 4, 2001, Rohnert Park. See also Jenkins, *The Politics of Insurgency,* 163–66; Taylor, *Chávez and the Farmworkers,* 218–21; London and Anderson, *So Shall Ye Reap,* 173.

7. UFWOC, *Sons of Zapata: A Brief Photographic History of the Farmworkers Strike in Texas* (Rio Grande City, Tex., 1967).

8. Meister and Loftis, *A Long Time Coming,* 151–55; Majka and Majka, *Farm Workers, Agribusiness, and the State,* 186–87.

9. Quote from Ferriss and Sandoval, *The Fight in the Fields,* 144.

10. Photographing in both color and black-and-white, Ballis made close-up portraits showing the strain on the face of César Chávez, wide views of the large scene, and side-by-side portraits contrasting Kennedy's Irish Catholic face with the Mexican face of Chávez. For more on Ballis, see Kushner, *Long Road to Delano,* 137, 187.

11. For press coverage, see *San Francisco Examiner,* March 11, 1968; *Fresno Bee,* March 10, 1968 (photographs by Ronald B. Taylor), reprinted in Taylor, *Chávez and the Farmworkers,* 221–22; UPI Telephoto HCP1585938, March 10, 1968; and UPI Telephoto HCP031031, March 10, 1968. For volunteers, see Hub Segur (a.k.a. Ojo Negro), "Hub Segur Photos, 1969–1973, 1987–1989," in Chatfield, Farmworker Movement Documentation Project, www.farmworkermovement.org, accessed 2005.

12. Quote from Street, interview with Paul Fusco, February 19, 1980, Mill Valley, California, author's possession.

13. Clipping (with photograph), "Los ojos de *Look* sobre Delano," *El Malcriado,* Anne Draper Collection, Stanford University Archives and Special Collections; Street, interview with Jon Lewis, March 4, 1981, San Francisco, author's possession; Street, interview with Emmon Clarke, April 27, 2001, Rohnert Park, contrasting Fusco's three Leicas and unlimited film supply with his one Nikon, three cheap lenses, and bulk-loaded film. See also LeRoy Chatfield, "Paul Fusco Photos, 1967–1988," in Chatfield, Farmworker Movement Documentation Project, www.farmworkermovement.org, accessed 2005.

14. Quotes from Tom Moran, *The Photo Essay: Paul Fusco and Will McBride* (New York, 1974), 26, 30.

15. Quote from Chatfield, "Paul Fusco Photos."

16. Quote from Street, interview with John Kouns, March 22, 2000, Sausalito, California, author's possession. See also Street, interview with Fusco, February 19, 1980, Mill Valley.

17. Moran, *The Photo Essay,* 30, 74.

18. Quote from Street, interview with Jack Pandol Sr., November 13, 1986, Delano, California, author's possession. See also Street, interview with Steven Pavich, September 22, 1989, Richgrove, California, author's possession.

19. Delano Grape Growers, *The Truth about the Grape Strike* (Delano, 1968); Cletus Healy, "Subversion in the Grape Industry," *The Truth about Communism, Nos. 39–41* (Milwaukee, Wisc., 1969); Allen, *The Grapes;* all in Raymond P. Roth Collection, Archives and Special Collections, University of California, Davis.

20. Quotes from Segur, "Hub Segur Photos"; and Segur to author, e-mail, May 3, 2006, author's possession.

21. Quote from Segur, "Hub Segur Photos." See also César Chávez, "Nonviolence Still Works," *Look* 33 (April 1, 1969): 52–55; and Street, interview with Jack Pandol Sr., November 13, 1986, Delano, California.

22. Hal Buell, *Moments: The Pulitzer Prize–Winning Photographs: A Visual Chronicle of Our Time* (New York, 1999), 78–84; Peter Stepan, ed., *Icons of Photography: The 20th Century* (New York, 1999), 160–61; Life, *100 Photographs That Changed the World,* 71–74, 134–35; William Shawcross, "A Tourist in the Refugee World," in Carole Kismaric, ed., *Forced Out: The Agony of the Refugee in Our Time* (New York, 1986), 30; Fred Ritchin, "The Unbearable Relevance of Photography," *Aperture* 171 (Summer 2003): 62–73.

23. Quote from "The Little Strike That Grew into *la Causa,*" *Time* 94 (July 4, 1969): 16. See also, Doug Adair, "California Vineyards Revisited," *Catholic Worker* 33 (September 1967): 5; Henry Schacht, "Labor Strife Moving North with Harvesters," *San Francisco Chronicle,* April 5, 1961; "Chavez Protests Television Segment," *San Francisco Chronicle,* April 25, 1991; and Street, interview with Jocelyn Sherman, August 3, 1998, Los Angeles, author's possession.

24. Quote from Fitch biography, www.takestockphotos.com/pages/fitch.html, accessed 2003, largely based on the biography I supplied to Take Stock. Bob Fitch to author, May 5, 2003, author's possession.

25. Quote from Joseph A. Califano, *Inside: A Public and Private Life* (New York, 2004), 210. See also Memorandum for Joseph Califano, for both November 21 and December 14, 1966; Memorandum for Honorable W. Willard Wirtz, October 4, 1966; and Summary: Task Force, November 22, 1966, Migratory and Farm Workers; all in Lyndon Baines Johnson Records, Office Files of Joseph Califano, box 63, and other materials, Lyndon Baines Johnson Library and Museum, Austin, Texas.

26. Ferriss and Sandoval, *The Fight in the Fields,* 155; Buell, *Moments,* 89–90.

27. Quote from Califano, *Inside,* 211–12. See also *AFL–CIO News,* April 4 and May 9, 1970; Walter Hoffman to NLRB, May 25, 1970, Victor Salandini Papers; both in Archives of Urban and Labor History, Wayne State University. According to Califano, when photographers recorded Austin and him trying to make their way through the sea of spectators and reporters, they missed one incident: halfway down the aisle, a young, dark-haired woman with thick glasses blocked their way and yelled at Califano, "You sold out, you motherfucker, you sold out." He identified that woman as Hillary Rodham, a Yale Law School student, who would later to marry Bill Clinton, support his rise to the presidency, and go on to become a senator from New York. Quote from Califano, *Inside,* 211–12. See also, Levy, *Cesar Chavez,* 453; *New York Times,* July 23, 1970; *Migrant and Seasonal Farmworker Powerlessness: Hearings before the Subcommittee on Migratory Labor of the Committee on Labor and Public Welfare,* 91 Cong., 1st sess., July 24, 1970, 5884–86.

28. Street, interview with George Ballis, March 17, 1981, Fresno, author's possession; Street, interview with Ronald B. Taylor, May 28, 1974, Fresno, California, author's possession.

29. Quote from Meister and Loftis, *Long Time Coming,* x. See also Street, interview with Sam Kushner, August 7, 1973, Arvin, California, author's possession; "Beyond Peace at Delano," *America* 123 (August 22, 1970): 80; Roy Bongartz, "La Raza in Revolt," *Nation* 210 (July 1, 1970): 664–66; William F. Buckley, "Victory of César Chávez," *National Review* 22 (September 8, 1970): 965; "The Candor That Refreshes," *Time* 96 (August 10, 1970): 59; "César Chávez: La Causa and the Man," *American Labor* 4 (February 1971): 20–30; and "Chávez Strikes Again," *Newsweek* 77 (January 25, 1971): 64–65. I have not been able to identify all of the photographers present at the contract signing. In the center was Chris Sánchez. Far right of the table was a *Delano Record* photographer. Also present was George Ballis.

30. Quotes from Street, interview with Paul Fusco, February 19, 1980, Mill Valley; and Paul Fusco, *La Causa: The California Grape Strike,* text by George D. Horowitz (New York, 1970), 44–45. See also Fusco to author, August 28, 1998, author's possession.

31. Fusco, *La Causa,* 5–6, 8–11, 66–75.

20. Icons of Struggle

1. Bob Fitch contact sheets, Bob Fitch Collection, Take Stock Images, San Rafael, California; Segur, "Hub Segur Photos"; Street, interview with Bob Fitch, May 12, 2006, Santa Cruz, California, author's collection; Street, interview with Clay Peterson, August 10, 1979, Salinas, California, author's possession.

2. Quote from Levy, *Cesar Chavez,* 382–84. See also Ferriss and Sandoval, *The Fight in the Fields,* 161–62. Levy's work can be followed by consulting various materials, newspaper clippings, affidavits, and especially his personal notes in the Jacques Levy Research Collection on César Chávez, Yale Collection of Western Americana, Beinecke Rare Book and Manuscript Library, Yale University.

3. "Court Bans Pickets as Tension Grows: Attorney Hospitalized," *Salinas Californian,* August 25 and 26, 1970. See also Taylor, *Chávez and the Farmworkers,* 259–60.

4. Quote from Street, interview with Morrie Camhi, May 2, 1984, Petaluma, California, author's possession. See also Milton Meltzer, *The Eye of Conscience: Photographers and Social Change* (New York, 1974), 166–71; and *Pacific Sun,* April 3, 1972.

5. Quote from Street, interview with Morrie Camhi, May 2, 1984, Petaluma. See also Camhi to author, July 22, 1998, author's possession.

6. Quote from Street, interview with Camhi, May 2, 1984, Petaluma. For an approach similar to Camhi's, see the photography of Harvey Saul Columbus in David O. Weber, *Health for the Harvesters: A Decade of Hope, 1960–1970* (Sacramento, 1970), Raymond P. Roth Collection, Archives and Special Collections, University of California, Davis.

7. Camhi to author, June 23, 1998, author's possession.

8. Quote from Street, interview with Camhi, May 2, 1984, Petaluma.

9. "Ground Crew," *Fresno Bee,* January 4, 1971.

10. Street, interview with Matt Herron, July 8, 1998, San Rafael, California, author's possession.

11. Quote from ibid.

12. Quote from Street, interview with Bob Fitch, May 26, 1981, San Francisco, author's possession. See also *Salinas Californian,* November 3, 4, and 5, 1970.

13. Quote from Street, interview with Bob Fitch, May 26, 1981, San Francisco. See also Street, interview with Russ Cain, July 9, 1998, Monterey, California; Street, interview with Clay Peterson, August 4, 1979, Salinas, California; Sam Vestal to author, November 30, 1976; all in author's possession; *Salinas Californian,* December 5 and 7, 1970; *Watsonville Register-Pajaronian,* December 7, 1970; and "My Spirit Was Never in Jail," *San Francisco Chronicle,* December 24, 1970.

14. Quote from Jesús Salvador Treviño, *Eyewitness: A Filmmaker's Memoir of the Chicano Movement* (Houston, 2001), 262.

15. Quote from Glen Pearcy, "Glen Pearcy, 1972–1975," in Chatfield, ed., Farmworker Movement Documentation Project, www.farmworkermovement.org, accessed 2004.

16. Quote from Glen Pearcy to author, August 25, 2003, author's possession. See also Street, interview with Gayanne Fietinghoff, August 31, 2003, Los Angeles, author's possession; and Taylor, *Chávez and the Farmworkers,* 280–84.

17. Quote from Street, interview with Gayanne Fietinghoff, August 31, 2003, Los Angeles, author's possession. See also Glen Pearcy to author, August 25, 2003, author's possession. While the Pearcys, Fietinghoff, and Tejada-Flores were editing the film, the union was campaigning against Proposition 22, a California version of the dreaded Arizona law, which California voters overwhelmingly defeated on November 7.

18. Quote from Street, interview with John Kouns, March 4, 1981, Mill Valley, California, author's possession. See also Street, interview with John Kouns, April 18, 2003, Sausalito, California, author's possession.

19. Ed Cray, *Burden of Proof: The Case of Juan Corona* (New York, 1973), argues that Corona was innocent. Tracy Kidder, *The Road to Yuba City: A Journey into the Juan Corona Murders* (New York, 1974), makes the case for Corona as a monster. For developments on the Coachella Valley, see John Bank, "Coachella Valley: Struggle for Self-Determination," *Christianity and Crisis* 33 (July 9, 1973): 132–35; César Chávez, "A Romance Rekindled," *Nation* 216 (March 19, 1973): 366–70; and "Teamsters, Growers Renegotiate," *Monthly Labor Review* 96 (March 1973): 73–74. For the bombing, see *El Malcriado,* January 26, 1973, Jacques Levy, Notebook 52, Jacques Levy Research Collection on César Chávez, Yale Collection of Western Americana, Beinecke Rare Book and Manuscript Library, Yale University.

20. "Teamsters Sign with Growers," 96 *Monthly Labor Review* (June 1973): 73–74; Harry Bernstein, "Duel in the Sun: Union Busting, Teamster Style," *Progressive* 37 (July 1973): 17–20; *San Francisco Chronicle,* April 21, 1973; Street, interview with Rich Tejada-Flores, August 28, 2003, Berkeley, author's possession.

21. Quotes from Street, interview with Gayanne Fietinghoff, August 31, 2003, Los Angeles, author's possession. See also, Street, interviews with Gayanne Fietinghoff, August 28, 2003, and July 26, 2004, Los Angeles, author's possession; and Street, interview with Rick Tejada-Flores, August 30, 2003, Berkeley, author's possession.

22. Quote from Street, interview with Cres Fraley, May 10, 2006, Santa Cruz, California, author's possession. See also Cres Fraley to author, e-mail, May 15, 2006, author's possession; Street, interview with Tom Dalzell, May 16, 2006, Berkeley, author's possession; and UFW, *Why We Boycott* (Keene, Calif., 1973), 14.

23. Quote from Street, interview with Cres Fraley, May 10, 2006, Santa Cruz.

24. *Wall Street Journal,* June 29, 1973. For the press and union photographers, see Bob Fitch, contact sheets, Bob Fitch Collection, Take Stock Images, San Rafael, California; Street, interview with Clarke, March 4, 2001, Rohnert Park, author's possession; *People's World,* August 7, 1973; and *San Francisco Chronicle,* August 4, 1973. See also *El Malcriado,* December 28, 1973. After replacing Gayanne Fietinghoff as Pearcy's sound recorder, Cres Farley continued in that capacity as the strike moved north. Fietinghoff covered events as a still photographer well into September and produced an archive of several thousand images. Farley also shot stills, as did César Chávez, who was often seen with a Nikon hanging around his neck. I have not been able to discover what happened to Chávez's photographs.

25. Quote and photograph in UFW, *Why We Boycott,* 14.

26. Street, interview with Rick Tejada-Flores, September 30, 1998, Emeryville, California, author's

possession. See also the video by Glen Pearcy, *Fighting for Our Lives* (Keene, Calif.: UFW Production, 1974).

27. Quote from Street, interview with Fraley, May 10, 2006, Santa Cruz. See also Street, interview with Juan Espinoza, May 7, 2006, Woodville, California, author's possession.

28. Quotes from Street, interview with Bob Fitch, May 26, 1981, San Francisco; and Street, interview with Gayanne Fietinghoff, July 26, 2004, Los Angeles. See also *New York Times,* July 19, 1973. For UPI photographs, see *San Francisco Chronicle,* July 26, 1973; see also July 5, 18, 19, 20, 21, 23, 24, 25, 27, and 28.

29. Quote from Bob Fitch to author, May 5, 2003, author's possession. See also Fitch biography, www.takestockphotos.com/pages/fitch.html, accessed 2004; and Street, interview with Gayanne Fietinghoff, August 29, 2003, Los Angeles, author's possession.

30. Quotes from Jim Boren, "Sheriff: Camera Is legitimate Tool," *Fresno Bee,* July 27, 1973.

31. Quotes from "Pickets Flock to Table-Grape Ranches," *San Francisco Chronicle,* July 31, 1973; and Street, interview with Bob Fitch, May 26, 1981, San Francisco. Berkeley freelance photographer Gayanne Fietinghoff and photographers from the *Los Angeles Times* and *Fresno Bee* also recorded the violence. Fietinghoff did excellent work covering Chávez addressing strike meetings in various parks in small farm towns throughout the southern San Joaquin Valley. Probably most of the images in *El Malcraido* 6 (June 15, 1973), 6 (July 13, 1973), and 6 (October 19, 1973) are hers. August 7 was a particularly hard day for her, photographing unending violence and mass arrests. She and her husband, Rick Tejada-Flores, made the 1973 film *Si se puede.* The random violence is described in "50 Arrested in 2 Days of Farm Strife," *Bakersfield Californian,* August 1, 1973.

32. Quote from Marta Rodríguez statement, August 2, 1973, courtesy of the UFW. See also Street, interview with Marta Rodríguez, May 17, 2006, Arvin, California, author's possession.

33. Bob Fitch, contact sheet image no. 6510224, along with numerous other images on contact sheets, Bob Fitch Collection, Take Stock Images, San Rafael, California.

34. Quote from UFW, *Why We Boycott,* 17. Fitch's work can be followed in his contact sheets in the Bob Fitch Collection, Take Stock Images, San Rafael.

35. Quote from Fitch, e-mail to author, May 25, 2003, author's possession. For his work in the *Los Angeles Times,* see Frank Del Olmo, "Arrests, Trouble Mark Second Day of Escalated Grape Strike," August 1, 1973. Several photographers who saw Fitch's proof sheets have remarked that bad editing and photo selection possibly cost Fitch a Pulitzer Prize in spot news photography. Years would pass before photographic historians would rediscover Fitch's work and begin to reconstruct the photographic record, seldom accurately. See for example *450 Years of Chicano History* (Albuquerque, N.M., 1976), 154–55. Readers of the *San Francisco Chronicle* and other newspapers saw only a few wire-service photographs of pickets being arrested, loaded into buses, and hauled away. Far less dramatic, these images hardly captured the terror of that hot and bloody day. Neither the *Stockton Record* nor the *Sacramento Bee* carried any photographs from the confrontation. For the August 1 shooting, see "UFW Back on Lines," *Sacramento Bee,* August 2, 1973.

36. Quote from Statement of Bob Fitch to FBI, October 9, 1973, Declassified FBI File SC 44-580, courtesy of Bob Fitch. The file contains two hundred pages of affidavits and interviews with those present, including strikers, observers, private security guards, and sheriff's deputies, the last two groups laying the onus of violence on strikers and the UFW and denying any use of excess force.

37. Quote from *San Francisco Chronicle,* August 3, 1973. See also *San Francisco Chronicle,* July 23 and 31, 1973; *New York Times,* July 19 and 31, 1973; *Los Angeles Times,* July 20, 26, and 31, 1973; Robert Coles, *Dorothy Day: A Radical Devotion* (New York, 1989); and Street, interview with Gayanne Fietinghoff, August 29, 2003, Los Angeles. For *Fresno Bee* photographer Edward Nold's photograph of Day being led away, see Mike Lassiter, "Seeks Arrest: Elderly Crusader for Poor Happily Goes to Jail," *Fresno Bee,* August 2, 1973.

38. Quote from George Baker, "Farm Strike: Bitterness Grows between Valley Pickets, Lawmen," *Fresno Bee,* August 19, 1973. For Fietinghoff's photographs, see *People's World,* August 8, 1973, People's World Collection, Labor Archives and Research Center, San Francisco State University.

39. Quote from Baker, "Farm Strike." UFW member Juan López also photographed at this time and took important pictures at a Kern County vineyard where three union members were struck by a car driven by a private security guard. See "Huelga Violence Escalates," *El Malcriado* 6 (August 24, 1973).

40. On the relationship between photographs of aggression and public reaction, see Alan Lincoln and George Lovinger, "Observers' Evaluations of the Victim and Attacker in an Aggressive Incident," MS, May 1972, in David Garrow, *Protest at Selma: Martin Luther King and the Voting Rights Act of 1965* (New Haven, Conn., 1978), 153.

41. Street, interview with Bob Fitch, May 8, 2003, Santa Cruz, California, author's possession; Street, interview with John Kouns, April 18, 2003, Sausalito; Richard Steven Street, "Jack Be Nimble," *California Business* 4 (April 1988): 32–40, 48–50; Street, interview with Jack Pandol Sr., November 13, 1987, Delano, California, author's possession. For the shootings and violence, see *San Francisco Chronicle,* August 10 and 11, 1973. For Sánchez's work, see "Huelga Violence Escalates." Ben Garza was the other photographer who photographed extensively in the fields at this time.

21. News Photographers Take Over

1. *Delano Record,* August 14, 1973; George Baker, "FBI Probes Death of Kern Farmworker," *Fresno Bee,* August 16, 1973; *San Francisco Chronicle,* August 17, 21, and 30, 1973. In apparent retaliation, seven automobiles owned by replacement workers were torched the following evening at the Sierra Vista labor camp near Richgrove. UFW spokesman Rev. John Banks later claimed that Cooper allowed Daifullah to lie on the sidewalk for twenty minutes before calling an ambulance and that the Kern County General Hospital waited two hours before placing Daifullah in the intensive care unit. Daifullah died following surgery. UFW attorney Jerome Cohen labeled the incident part of the policy of harassment by sheriff's deputies against union members and supporters. See also Declassified FBI File 44-57484, enclosed in David M. Hardy to author, August 4, 2003, author's possession; Street, interview with Juan Espinoza, May 7, 2006, Woodville, California, author's possession.

2. A typical strategy was to immigrate for a three- to five-year period, live a spartan existence, save as much money as possible, and send it to families in Yemen, returning home to visit whenever possible. Carpooling and migrating along well-established routes in tight groups, a typical Yemeni picked grapes in Delano from July to November, remained into January to prune vines, harvested asparagus around Tracy between February and May, picked cherries around Patterson in June, and detoured as necessary into the spring carrot and vegetable harvest around Holtville or summer cannery work in Modesto. See Jonathan Friedlander, ed., *Sojourners and Settlers: The Yemeni Immigrant Experience* (Salt Lake City, 1988), 69–99; Mary Bisharat, "Yemeni Farmworkers in California," *MERIP Reports* (January 1975): 22–26; and Juan Sánchez and Saul Solache, "Yemeni Agricultural Workers in California: Migration Impact," *Journal of Ethnic Studies* 8 (1980): 85–94.

3. Frank Del Olmo,"UFW Starts Fast for Fatally Injured Worker," *Los Angeles Times,* August 21, 1973. See also Jacques Levy, Notebook 57, Jacques Levy Research Collection on César Chávez, Yale Collection of Western Americana, Beinecke Rare Book and Manuscript Library, Yale University; and Street, interview with Cres Fraley, May 10, 2006, Santa Cruz, California, author's possession.

4. George Baker, "UFW Picket Is Slain Near Arvin," *Fresno Bee,* August 17, 1973; *Los Angeles Times,* August 17, 1973; Taylor, *Chávez and the Farmworkers,* 310–13; Ferriss and Sandoval, *The Fight*

in the Fields, 187–89. After his arrest, Baclig was released without charges. Advincula stood trail and was acquitted of the charge of murder. Defense attorneys argued that pickets had thrown rocks at the car in which he was riding, and therefore he had acted somewhat in self-defense. He was then convicted of manslaughter. Three years later, he was cleared after a jury ruled that he had fired in self-defense after being hit by rocks thrown by pickets.

5. For the *Fresno Bee* aerial photographs, see *Fresno Bee,* August 18, 1973.

6. Quote from Fitch to author, May 25, 2003, author's possession. See also Street, interview with Bob Fitch, July 10, 1998, Berkeley, California, author's possession; and Street, interview with Marc Grossman, April 12, 1996, Watsonville, California, author's possession.

7. Quote from Street, interview with Bob Fitch, May 8, 2003, Santa Cruz, California, author's possession. See also *Sacramento Bee,* August 18, 1973; and *Fresno Bee,* August 18, 1973.

8. Quotes from Street, interview with Bob Fitch, May 8, 2003, Santa Cruz. See also "Farm Worker's Huge Funeral," *San Francisco Chronicle,* August 18, 1973; *New York Times,* August 20, 1973; and Pearcy, "Glen Pearcy, 1972–1975."

9. Street, interview with Fitch, July 11, 1998, Berkeley, California, author's possession. See also Ferriss and Sandoval, *The Fight in the Fields,* 186–88; Taylor, *Chávez and the Farmworkers,* 310–12; *Fresno Bee,* August 14 and 17, 1973; *Bakersfield Californian,* August 14 and 17, 1973; and *San Francisco Chronicle,* August 22, 1973.

10. UFW, *Why We Boycott,* 1, 12–13, 16–17, 20–21, 25. Tabulation of the total number of arrests varies according to the source but generally hovers around thirty-five hundred.

11. *New York Times,* September 24, 1973. "There is a tendency for people to glamorize the photographers who documented the farmworker movement," Fitch recalled. "I turn that around. The real heroes were the people in the photographs—they made it happen." Quote from Fitch to author, July 10, 1998, author's possession. Today, Fitch often takes stacks of his photographs into school classrooms and shares stories of the people seen in those images.

12. Quote from Glen Pearcy to author, August 25, 2003, author's possession.

13. Quote from Street, interview with Fraley, May 10, 2006, Santa Cruz. See also Street, interview with Will Kirkland, May 16, 2006, San Rafael, California, author's collection; and Ken Schroeder, "Ken Schroeder, 1974–1989," in Chatfield, ed., Farmworker Movement Documentation Project, www.farmworkermovement.org. See this Web site also for the following reminiscences: of "Helmut Zingsem-Eick, 1974–1975"; "Richard B, Cook, 1972–1983"; and "Mark Pitt, 1972–1977."

14. Quote from Glen Pearcy, "Glen Pearcy," in Chatfield, ed., Farmworker Movement Documentation Project, www.farmworker movement.org, accessed 2006.

15. Thirteen of the bus accident victims (six of the dead, seven of the injured) were current or former members of the UFW. See "19 Lettuce Workers Die in Contractor Bus Massacre: Drowned in 'Prison of Seats,'" *El Malcriado,* February 22, 1974; *Los Angeles Times,* January 15, 1974; and *Imperial Valley Press,* January 15, 1974.

16. Street, interview with Jeanette Hyduke, April 12, 2004, Palo Verde, California, author's possession; Hyduke contact sheets, Palo Verde. Hyduke used a Rolleiflex.

17. Street, interview with J. Paul Noden, March 13, 1997, Imperial Valley, California, author's possession. One year later, a bus accident at Wasco injured five farmworkers. The worst such accident had occurred at Chualar, in the Salinas Valley, on September 17, 1963, causing the death of thirty-two braceros when their bus was struck by a Southern Pacific freight train. See Ernesto Galarza, *Tragedy at Chualar: El crucero de las treinta y dos cruces* (San Jose, Calif., 1977); Galarza, *Spiders in the House and Workers in the Field,* 164–65, 196; and "Farm Workers Should Be Promoted in Law from Category of Things to Persons," *Valley Labor Citizen,* May 22, 1964. Photographic coverage of bus accidents again made headlines on January 16, 1975, when four farmworkers were injured after their van collided with the back of a truck near Lost Hills, on the west side of the San

Joaquin Valley. Occurring almost exactly one year after the Blythe fiasco, the accident briefly became news when *El Malcriado* published photographs of the smashed van and Chávez held a press conference to explain that over thirty-five farmworkers had been killed in bus and car accidents since the beginning of the year. See "Another One in Wasco," *El Malcriado* (January–February 1975). Continuing unabated in the pages of *El Malcriado* and the rural press over the next quarter century, debate over labor bus safety eventually culminated in the enactment of strict farmworker transportation laws and tough enforcement by the California Highway Patrol.

18. *Los Angeles Times,* March 29 and April 9, 1974; *San Francisco Chronicle,* February 22 and March 27, 1974.

19. "Winery Talks in on March by UFW," *Fresno Bee,* February 24, 1975; "UFW March Nears Gallo Showdown," *Fresno Bee,* February 27, 1975; "Photo Is in Error," *Fresno Bee,* February 28, 1975; Mike Musura (photo), *At Gracead Park, San Francisco Chronicle,* March 2, 1975; UPI Photo, *Banner-Bedecked UFW Supporters March into Modesto, 10,000 Strong, San Francisco Examiner,* March 2, 1975; Street, interview with Jane Yett, March 17, 2004, Santa Cruz, California, author's possession.

20. Quote from Jane Yett to author, e-mail, June 19, 2004, author's possession. See also Yett to author, e-mail, November 16, 2003, author's possession; and Jane Marie Yett, "Farm Labor Struggles in California, 1970–1973, in Light of Reinhold Niebuhr's Concepts of Power and Justice," PhD diss., Graduate Theological Union, 1980, 138, 149–52.

21. Quote from Yett to author, June 12, 2004, author's possession.

22. Shooting Tri-X 400 (pushed to 1,600 for the low light of the evening rally) and walking backward with a twenty-pound camera bag and several cameras draped around his neck, Benson, like other photographers, had to do a kind of ballet, photographing while he made sure that he did not trip over anyone. What impressed him most at the Gallo march was his complete access to any one of the more than fifteen thousand people who gathered at the Gallo gates. "I was still naive enough to figure long hair and a sympathetic stance was enough to get me in, and that was pretty much the case," he remembered years later. "People were open about their feelings, and it came across pretty well." Ted Benson to author, April 23, 1995, author's possession. See also *San Francisco Chronicle,* September 25 and November 13, 1975, March 10, 1977, and December 9, 1978; *University of California San Francisco Synapse,* August 14, 1975; Ellen Hawkes, *Blood and Wine: The Unauthorized Story of the Gallo Wine Empire* (New York, 1993), 273–74; *Tracy Press,* February 28, 1975; and Street, interview with Martin Wybert, October 3, 1975, Tracy, California, author's possession.

23. *Modesto Bee,* August 24, 1975; *Sacramento Bee,* August 31, 1975; *Fresno Bee,* September 2, 1975. Jim Kuntz photographed the Modesto rally for *El Malcriado.* I have not been able to track him down. Cathy Murphy, who covered the boycott and union for *El Malcriado* at this time, exhibited her work at La Paz in 2005.

24. Quote from Mimi Plumb-Chambers statement, n.d., author's possession. Along with UFW archivist Barbara Pruett, Fraley helped archive the UFW materials that were soon shipped to the Archives of Urban and Labor History, at Wayne State University. Street, interview with Fraley, May 10, 2006, Santa Cruz.

25. Quote from Street, interview with Plumb-Chambers, August 14, 2003, Petaluma, California, author's possession. See also Street, interview with Plumb-Chambers: May 23, 1977, Point Richmond, California; July 28, 1979, Salinas, California; and May 22, 1982, Point Richmond, California; all in author's possession; and Street, interview with Morrie Camhi, May 2, 1984, Petaluma, California, author's possession.

26. Quotes from "Return of the Posse?" *Newsweek* 85 (May 26, 1975): 54; and "Field Showdown," *Stockton Record,* September 2, 1975. See also Winthrop H. Segur, "Representation Elections for Farmworkers: Voting Power under Alternative Rules Eligibility," PhD diss., University of California, Davis, 1980, iii–iv, 15–25; Meister and Loftis, *Long Time Coming,* 218–19; Philip Martin and

Susan Vaupel, "Agricultural Labor Relations in California," in Walter Fogel, ed., *California Farm Labor Relations* (Los Angeles, 1985), 1–51; and Rex L. Cottle, Hugh H. Macaulay, and Bruce Yandle, *Labor and Property Rights in California Agriculture: An Economic Analysis of the CALRA* (College Station, Tex., 1982). Citing photographic intimidation, the California Agricultural Labor Relations Board set aside a Teamster election victory over the UFW at Gallo and ordered a new election.

27. For Turner's work leading up to the confrontation, see *Stockton Record,* July 24, 26, and 30; August 1 and 8; September 10, 11, and 12, 1974; and August 2 and 26, 1975.

28. Street, interview with Rich Turner, September 28, 1975, Stockton, California, author's possession. See also *Stockton Record,* September 2, 1975. The *Record* also announced that the California secretary of state had officially filed access regulations guaranteeing organizers the right to contact workers. See also *Stockton Record,* September 3, 5, and 12, October 17, 28, and 29, November 11, 16, 20, 21, and 27, December 5, 18, 19, 23, and 31, 1975; *Tracy Press,* September 3, 1975; *Lodi News Sentinel,* September 3, 1975; *Oakland Tribune,* September 3, 1975; *San Francisco Chronicle,* September 3, 1975; Street, interview with Martin Weybert, September 29, 1975, Tracy, California; and Martin Weybert, notes on Francis Gillings and the Posse Comitatus; both in author's possession.

29. Quote from Gene Turner, "Farm Union to Ignore Writ," *Stockton Record,* September 4, 1973. See also *Stockton Record,* December 10, 17, 18, 19, 23, and 31, 1973; and notes by the author taken while photographing and reporting at Tri-Valley Produce in September 1975. Eight years later, all of the appeals and challenges had not yet been fully resolved at either the Perry ranch or Tri-Valley Produce. The workers by this time had scattered, and the union elections had been effectively stymied.

30. *Stockton Record,* September 4, 1965. See also Ballis to author, July 6, 1998, author's possession; the following books by George Ballis: *The Dispossessed* (Piedmont, Calif., 1970); *Oakland* (Oakland, 1970); *If I Had a Hammer* (Washington, D.C., 1971); and *The Seed of Life Cooperation: Lanare Community Organization* (Riverdale, Calif., 1975); George Ballis, *I Am Joaquin* (Tollhouse, Calif.: Ballis Productions, 1969), film; George Ballis, *The Richest Land* (Tollhouse, Calif.: Ballis Productions, 1972), film; Margo McBane, *Talking Farmworker Blues* (Davis, Calif.: McBane Productions, 1978), multimedia program; and James Motlow, "The Orchard Workers," *San Francisco Examiner, California Living Magazine* (December 16, 1973): 12.

31. Quote from Benson to author, October 11, 1985, author's possession.

32. Quote from David Evans to author, September 8, 1983, author's possession. See also Rich Turner to author, September 3, 1981, author's possession.

33. Quote from Bill Ravanesi, "A Farm Labor Project," *Picture Magazine* 7 (1978): 4. At this time, Santa Cruz commercial photographer Alexander Lowry photographed farmworkers in the wineries around the Santa Cruz Mountains and a crew of Filipino asparagus harvesters near Greenfield. He also photographed farmworkers and agricultural subjects from the air for his stock photo agency, Photo Researchers. Alexander Lowry to author, e-mail, January 18, 2004, author's possession; Alexander Lowry, *Little Histories: Photographs of Santa Cruz County, 1966–1997* (Santa Cruz, Calif.: Museum of Art and History at the McPherson Center, February–April 15, 1997).

34. Quote from Ravanesi, "A Farm Labor Project," 4.

35. Quotes from Howard Chapnick, *Truth Needs No Ally: Inside Photojournalism* (Columbia, Mo., 1994), 273–74; and Sylvia Rubin, "Richard Avedon: Photographer of Fashion and Real People," *San Francisco Chronicle,* October 2, 2004. Also borrowing from Andy Grundberg, "Richard Avedon's Portraits: Inverted Fashion, Fashionable Mud," in Grundberg, *Crisis of the Real: Writings on Photography since 1974* (New York, 1999), 92–93. See also Charlie Rose, interviews with Richard Avedon, *The Charlie Rose Show* (KQED Public Television), October 5, 1993, November 1, 1995, January 19, 1996, and November 11, 1999. For Avedon's published portrait of Chávez, see "The Family, 1976," *Rolling Stone* (July 4, 1976).

36. Quotes from Street, interview with anonymous UFW member, March 23, 1987, La Paz, California, author's possession; Susan Sontag, *On Photography* (New York, 1978), 57, also 58; and Mark Williams, "Richard Avedon," in Rule and Solomon, eds., *Original Sources,* 50–52. I attempted to use this photograph but gave up when presented with a two-thousand-dollar publication fee along with demands to control reproduction and review my text.

37. "Farm Union Sued for Libel—Poster on Onion Field," *San Francisco Chronicle,* October 14, 1976; "UFW's Prop. 14 Poster Gets OK," *Fresno Bee,* October 24, 1976.

38. Quote from "Judge Bans Farm Union's Poster on Child Labor," *San Francisco Chronicle,* October 21, 1976. See also "Reprieve for Farm Union Poster," *San Francisco Chronicle,* October 23, 1976.

39. Quote from Rich Turner to author, undated [1982], author's possession.

40. del Castillo and Garcia, *César Chávez,* 164–84; Street, interview with Rev. James Drake, September 22, 1976, Stockton, California, author's possession.

41. Pam Harris diary, entries for March 1 and 4, April 2, June 11, July 22, and September 3, 1977; August 4, 1980; "Crosetti Lettuce," n.d.; September 2, 1981; in the Pam Harris photograph collection (private), Toronto, Canada.

42. "Investigation of the Rufino Contreras Case," Declassified FBI File 44-79199, contained in J. Kevin O'Brien to author, May 30, 1995, author's possession.

43. Richard Steven Street, "The Lettuce Strike Story," *Nation* 230 (January 19, 1980): 45–49. See also the photographs by John T. Barr in Lou Cannon and Carl Cannon, "Doubts Raised by Transcript of Dismissed Case," *Washington Post,* September 16, 1979; Len Lahman, photographs in the *Los Angeles Times,* February 13–16, 1978; and John W. McDonough to author, January 19, 1983, author's possession.

44. Street, "The Lettuce Strike Story," 45–49; Street, interview with Len Lehman, April 10, 1981, Tucson, Arizona, author's possession; photographs by John T. Barr in Cannon and Cannon, "Doubts Raised by Transcript of Dismissed Case."

45. Quotes from Griffin Smith Jr., "The Mexican Americans: A People on the Move," *National Geographic* 157 (June 1980): 788, 796. See also Street, interview with Stephanie Maze, May 12, 1999, Washington, D.C., author's possession.

46. Reporter's transcript of the witness Carl Maggio, in *Maggio, Inc., et al. v. UFW,* January 22 and 23, 1986, case no. 51761, Imperial County Superior Court, 1: 20, 80; January 24 and 29, 1986, 2: 186–89. My thanks to attorney Jay Jeffcoat for providing copies of the voluminous court case.

47. Richard Steven Street, "Maggio Strikes Back," *California Farmer* 256 (December 13, 1986): 6–7, 16–20; reporter's transcript of the witness Oren Fox, in *Maggio, Inc., et al. v. UFW,* April 9 and 10, 1986, 1: 6, 57, 60–63.

48. Street, interviews with Paul J. Noden, May 29 and July 16, 1998, El Centro, California, author's possession; Noden to author, August 13, 1998, author's possession; Street, interview with Richard King, May 13, 1986, El Centro, California, author's possession; Street, "Maggio Strikes Back." Pickets tore out one hundred feet of a nearby sheep corral and used the metal fence posts as clubs and spears and also threw them at the sheriff's helicopter hovering low overhead. To drive the pickets off, deputies fired tear gas grenades, but the wind blew the gas back into their faces. As rocks and tear gas canisters flew back and forth, several deputies attempting to rescue an injured officer drew their handguns and fired shots into the air.

49. *Imperial Valley Press,* February 22, 1979; *Brawley News,* February 22, 1979; Street, interview with Marc Grossman, April 15, 1997, Watsonville, California, author's possession; Street, interview with Chris Schneider, April 26, 1986, El Centro, California, author's possession; Noden to author, August 13, 1998, author's possession.

50. Quote from *San Francisco Chronicle,* March 31, 1979.

51. Numerous clippings, California Agricultural Labor Relations Board Clipping Files, Sacramento, California.

22. Photographing the Human Condition

1. Street, "The Lettuce Strike Story," 45–49; "Smashing the United Farm Workers," *Pacific Sun* (June 29, 1979): 5–11.

2. Karen Barrell to author, February 25, 1980, author's possession.

3. Street, interview with Reesa Tansey, September 22, 1983, Oakland, California; Street, interviews with Richard Greene, October 29 and November 6, 1983, Salinas, California; Street, interview with Eric Brazil, February 16, 1982, Salinas; all in author's possession.

4. Street, interview with Clay Peterson, August 17, 1979, Salinas, California, author's possession; Pam Harris to author, e-mail, May 25, 2004, author's possession. At one point in the march, I commandeered Peterson's ladder to photograph a huge crowd of farmworkers attending a big UFW rally in a Salinas park. While examining Pam Harris's contact sheets twenty-five years later, I was amazed to find several images of me on that ladder and photographing at the UFW convention. See Pam Harris Collection, California State Library, Sacramento. See also Pam Harris diary, entries for August 4, 1980; "Crosetti Lettuce," n.d.; and September 2, 1981; in the Pam Harris photograph collection (private), Toronto, Canada.

5. Philip L. Fradkin, *A River No More: The Colorado River and the West* (New York, 1981), 289.

6. Quotes from Harris, "These Photographs," "United Farm Workers Union," and various undated memos, Pam Harris Collection, California State Library, Sacramento. See also in that collection: Harris to Frederick Hill, May 25, 1983; Harris to Marie Cantlon, April 2, 1981; memo on Steve Stevonovich, April 25, 1983; Book Proposal Notes, n.d.

7. Quotes from Rick Deragon to Pamela Harris, November 10, 1983, Pam Harris Collection, California State Library. See also Harris to Deragon, November 30, 1983, February 7, 1984, and March 9, 1984; Deragon to Harris, November 19, 1983, and April 25, 1984; Harris to Rolando Castellon, October 17, 1983; Castellon to Harris, May 8, 1984; hand-drawn layout scheme; *Monterey Peninsula Museum of Art Calendar* (May 1984), n.p.; and various interviews, proof sheets, photographs, and correspondence; all in Pam Harris Collection, California State Library, Sacramento.

8. Quotes from Harris, "Farm Workers/Watsonville, California, 1977–81," Pam Harris Collection, California State Library; and Pam Harris, e-mail to author, May 25, 2004, author's possession. Harris continued to photograph in and around Watsonville until 1985, while also interviewing a number of farmworker families. Although both the Sierra Club and the California Historical Society expressed interest, the fuller exhibition project fell apart. "It was not a time when black-and-white photos of farmworkers were highly salable," she recalled. "I heard phrases like 'no one is interested in farmworkers anymore'" (Street, interview with Pam Harris, June 6, 2004, Toronto, Canada, author's possession). Eventually Harris abandoned her project, which she considered her most important body of work. After marrying a professor of classics, she moved to Canada but continued her documentary photography. Always haunted by her failure to produce a major exhibition or book, she eventually deposited copies of her images and transcribed interviews in the California State Library, where they are now available to researchers.

9. "Dispute over Filming," *Fresno Bee,* August 30, 1980; Street, interview with Ed Pérez, September 2, 1980, Sacramento, California, author's possession.

10. Quote from Street, interview with Roger Minick, January 30, 1981, Berkeley, author's possession.

11. Fragments of Minick's essay appear in Ken Light, Roger Minick, and Reesa Tansey, *In the Fields,* intro. by Paul Taylor and Anne Loftis (Oakland, Calif., 1982). See also A. D. Coleman, *Light*

Readings: A Photography Critic's Writings, 1968–1978 (New York, 1979), 39; and Street, interview with Roger Minick, December 8, 1982, Vallejo, California, author's possession.

12. *Los Angeles Times,* September 16, 1979; Street, interviews with Sharon Myers, May 4, 1981, Tucson, Arizona; February 14, 1982, San Jose, California; both in author's possession.

13. Quote from Street, interview with Sharon Myers, May 4, 1981, Tucson, Arizona, author's possession.

14. Quote from Street, interview with Phil Garlington, October 11, 1983, Petaluma, California, author's possession. See also "Faces beyond the Border," *Escondido-Times Advocate,* September 1980; Street, interview with Len Lahman, November 22, 1980, Tucson, Arizona, author's possession; Lahman to author, June 10 and November 21, 1980, author's possession; and Richard Steven Street, "Illegal Collaborations," MS, 1982, 1–7, author's possession.

15. For Elizabeth Sisco, see Sisco to author, September 6, 1983, author's possession; and Joseph Nalven and Craig Frederickson, *The Employer's View: Is There a Need for a Guest Worker Program?* (San Diego, 1980). For Harry Polkinhorn, see Harry Polkinhorn to author, June 8, 1980, author's possession; Harry Polkinhorn, *La Frontera* (San Diego, 1983); and *La Prensa,* January 15, 1982.

16. Paul Engstrom, "Media Circus Halts Probe of Poisoning," *Salinas California,* May 1, 1981; Roberto Robledo, "Banned Hoes Sighted in Local Fields," *Salinas Californian,* May 21, 1981.

17. Quote from Street, interview with Linda Troeller, March 30, 2003, New York, author's possession.

18. Quote from ibid. Recording the banter and camaraderie among crew members, Troeller paused one morning to eat breakfast with some field hands she had been photographing since sunrise. Offering to share their breakfast tortillas with Troeller, they also offered a few tiny red peppers. Blazing hot and generally unknown to the Anglo population, the little peppers set her mouth on fire, much to the delight of the field hands, who laughed uncontrollably, then immediately offered her sips of milk to put out the flames. I had this same trick played on me numerous times. See ibid.; Kurt Ellison, "Photographer Captures Love Affair with Valley," *Watsonville Register-Pajaronian,* November 6, 1981; and Diane Valeska, "Finding Beauty in the Fields," *Salinas Californian,* September 25, 1981.

19. Quote from Strauss, *Between the Eyes,* 49.

20. Light, Minick, and Tansey, *In the Fields,* n.p.; *Afterimage* 12 (February 1983): 50. See also Reesa Tansey, "Families on the Land: A Study of Mexican Farm Laborers Who Are Striving to Create New California Farm Cooperatives," MA thesis, University of California, Berkeley, 1982; and Miriam Wells, "Mexican Farmworkers Become Strawberry Farmers," *Human Organization* 49 (1990): 149–56.

21. Ken Light, *With These Hands,* text by Paula DiPerna, preface by César Chávez (New York, 1986); Light, Minick, and Tansey, *In the Fields,* n.p.; *Afterimage* 12 (February 1983): 19; Arthur Bloomfield, "Photos of Fantasy and Fact," *San Francisco Examiner,* July 6, 1978; A. D. Coleman, "In the Field," *Photo Metro* (May 1983): 7; Paul Raedke, "Ken Light," *Photo Metro* (May 1983): 3–15. Some reviewers complained that the body of work in *With These Hands* was inadequately captioned and failed to scrutinize work motions and that the method of presentation—one image per page, with little identifying information—was antiseptic and too much like a museum presentation. Most viewers found it stunning in the way it captured the desperation of men living in huts made of garbage, the aches and pains of bending over all day while planting seedlings, the drive and ambition of men leaving their families behind to cross the border illegally and work in the fields of California, and the aspirations involved in breaking free from wage labor and becoming tenant farmers on small agricultural cooperatives.

22. Ken Light, *To the Promised Land,* intro. by Richard Rodriguez (New York, 1988), 52–57; Street, interview with Ken Light, September 4, 1998, Orinda, California, author's collection.

23. Willy Morris, "Ag Worker Field Sanitation Rules Sought," *Imperial Valley Press,* January 24, 1985; *San Francisco Chronicle,* September 24, 1985; Jerome Cohen, "Once Again, Farmworkers Must Fight for Protection," *Los Angeles Times,* October 14, 1985; Edgar Sanchez, "Farmworkers Reap Broken Dreams," *Fresno Bee,* August 18, 1988; Richard Hammond and Jeff Zachreson, *The San Joaquin Valley . . . a Portrait* (Visalia, Calif., 1979); Michael Franklin's photo essays in the *San Diego Union;* Robert M. Young, *Alambrista!* (The illegal) (Bobwin-Film-haus, 1978), a film that tells the story of a Mexican farmworker who comes illegally to California; Susan Ferris, *The Golden Cage: A Story of California's Farmworkers* (Golden Cage Productions, 1989), a film about the state's Mexican farmworkers.

24. Quote from editorial, "Another View of America," *Salinas Californian,* September 26, 1985.

25. Notified early in the afternoon, I was unable to make the long drive to Salinas in time for the evening press conference. See Art Nauman, "Cave Dweller," *Sacramento Bee,* October 6, 1985; and Fred Ritchin, "What Is Magnum?" in William Manchester, *In Our Time: The Word as Seen by Magnum Photographers,* with essays by Jean Lacouture and Fred Ritchin (New York, 1989), 422.

26. California Department of Pesticide Regulation, *Pesticide Use Reports* (Sacramento, October 31, 2002). See also Lawrie Mott and Karen Snyder, *Pesticide Alert: A Guide to Pesticides in Fruits and Vegetables* (San Francisco, 1987), 5.

27. For discussion of the photo essay, see Glenn G. Willumson, *W. Eugene Smith and the Photographic Essay* (Cambridge, U.K., 1992), 1–7, 268.

28. Quote from John Bird, *Leon Golub: Echoes of the Real* (London, 2000), 45.

29. California Department of Pesticide Regulation, *Pesticide Use Reports.*

30. Lonny Shavelson to author, May 22, 1989, author's collection.

31. Quote from Lonny Shavelson, "Poisoned Lives: Six Stories from Toxic California," *Image/San Francisco Examiner,* July 26, 1987, 22–26. See also Lonny Shavelson and Fred Setterberg, *Toxic Nation: The Fight to Save Our Communities from Chemical Contamination* (New York, 1993).

32. Quote from Street, interview with David Wells, May 23, 1999, San Anselmo, California, author's possession. For similar statements, see David H. Wells, "Feature," *News Photographer* 44 (May 1989): 48–49; and David Wells, "From a Photo Essay on the Pesticide Poisoning of America," Boston University School of Public Health: Department of Environmental Health, www.bumc.bu.edu/SPH/Gallery/Introw.html, accessed 2001. See also "Pesticide Poisoning to Be Subject of New Documentary Award," *News Photographer* 43 (June 1988): 14; and Michael Thrihey, "Chemical Firms Agree to Pay Limbless Delano Boy $800,000," *Bakersfield Californian,* November 7, 1987.

33. David Wells, "Professional Statement," MS, 1988, author's possession. See also David Wells, "The Killing Fields," *Philadelphia Inquirer Magazine* (January 29, 1989): 20–29; David Wells, "Deadly Harvest," *West* magazine, *San Jose Mercury News* (May 21, 1989): 12–17; and David Wells, "The Spraying Fields," *California Magazine* 22 (June 1990): 94–95.

34. Quote from Street, interview with Victor Alemán, September 14, 1998, Los Angeles, author's possession.

35. Quote from Street, interview with Victor Alemán, September 16, 1998, Los Angeles, author's possession. See also Dianna Lyon, Victor Alemán, et al., trial notes and interviews by the author, August 25, 1989, Bakersfield, California, author's possession; *Food and Justice* 6 (December 1986): cover; *Food and Justice* 7 (March 1987): 3–5; and Street, interview with Connie Rosales, November 15, 1986, McFarland, California, author's possession. According to UFW members and lawyers, Mrs. Franco's motives were not so innocent. Although Felipe had just won a settlement of eight hundred thousand dollars from a chemical company, his grandmother, not his mother, was the executor. With mounting expenses for a special wheelchair, a van with a hydraulic lift, and costs that would only increase as Felipe grew older, the Francos were going through large amounts of money, and the settlement was looking slim indeed. Although Felipe's mother denied any ulterior

motives underlying her lawsuit, UFW members maintained that advisers to the growers convinced Mrs. Franco to sue the UFW as a way to rake in a pile of money from the funds that the union was supposedly taking in from supporters everywhere. See *Bakersfield Californian,* July 21, and November 7, 1989; *San Francisco Chronicle,* June 24, 27, and July 28, 1989; Dianna Lyon to author, November 6, 1989, enclosure of *Connie Rosales et al. v. UFW,* August 25, 1989, Superior Court of California for Kern County, case no. 207218, author's possession.

36. According to the appellate court, Mrs. Franco and other mothers had consented to the filming and had, in at least one instance, voluntarily appeared on camera. The appellate court further ruled that Alemán had in no way violated Franco's privacy, stating flatly that there was "simply no substantial evidence to support the minor plaintiffs' claim that their mother's consent was exceeded or fraudulently obtained." See Steven Rosenlind, "Court Rules Film's Use of Minors Not Fraudulent," *Fresno Bee,* August 27, 1991.

37. Jeff Gillenkirk and James Motlow, *Bitter Melon: Stories from the Last Rural Chinese Town in America,* intro. by Sucheng Chan (Seattle, 1987); Friedlander, ed., *Sojourners and Settlers,* ix, 69–99, 113; Eniac Martínez Ulloa, "The Mixtecs," in Kerry Tremain, ed., *World Views: The First Mother Jones International Documentary Photography Awards,* intro. by Carole Nagger (San Francisco, 1991), 22–25; Alvarado Delgado, "Spartan, Dusty Home under Bridge," *Santa Rosa Press Democrat,* September 4, 1988; Delgado, "Tent City Improves Harvest Conditions," October 20, 1991. See also Laura Myers, "Migrant Workers Live in Squalor," *San Jose Mercury News,* September 22, 1999. For trends, see Gretchen Garner, *Disappearing Witness: Change in Twentieth-Century American Photography* (Baltimore, 2003), xv–xvi.

38. William Least Heat Moon, *The Red Couch: A Portrait of America* (New York, 1986). Oddly, *The Red Couch* went into a second edition.

39. *Los Angeles Times,* January 8, 9, and 10, 2006; Jeff Coplon, "Cesar's Fall from Grace," *Village Voice,* August 14 and 21, 1984; Frank Bardacke, "Cesar Chavez: The Serpent and the Dove," in Clark Davis and David Igler, eds., *The Human Tradition in California* (Wilmington, Del., 2002), 209–25. A voluminous exchange between old UFW members in Chatfield, ed., Farmworker Movement Documentation Project, www.farmworkermovement.org, accessed 2005, contains a vast amount of new information on all aspects of the union's disintegration during these years.

40. "Jackson Praises Chavez," *Fresno Bee,* August 15, 1988; "Jesse Jackson Visits Chavez," *San Francisco Chronicle,* August 15, 1988; Richard Rodriguez, "One Man's Cause," *Los Angeles Times,* August 28, 1988.

41. Joe Rosato, "Stars Come Out to Support Chavez," *Fresno Bee,* August 9, 1988; also August 21 and 22, 1988.

42. Quote from Matt Black to author, March 26, 2004, author's possession.

43. Personal observation while photographing on assignment, August 21, 1988, Delano, California; Street, interview with Felix Adamo, July 8, 1998, Bakersfield, California; Street, interview with Carl Crawford, August 18 and 21, 1998, Fresno, California; Street, interview with unidentified Secret Service agent, August 21, 1988, Delano, California; Felix Adamo to author, November 25, 1998; all in author's possession.

44. Quote from Felix Adamo to author, August 24, 1998, author's possession. Also from Adamo's recollections: "When César ended his hunger strike, the thing that I remembered the most was how crowded it was under that tent. Photographers were elbow to elbow. I left Bakersfield early to get a good spot, only to find the place was packed when I arrived. Luckily though, I found a place on the front line and didn't have to shoot over anyone. I used a 300-millimeter lens on a Nikon and was shooting transparency film. What made the shoot hard was the lighting. It was under a tent, and it seemed to cast a strange yellow cast on the film. To add to that, both César and Jesse were wearing white shirts and both have dark complexions. So the slide has always been tough to print."

45. For examples of such photographs, see, for example, those by Carl Crawford in the *Fresno Bee,* August 22, 1988; and by Felix Adamo in the *Bakersfield Californian,* August 22, 1988; both in author's possession. Quote from John G. Morris to author, August 25, 1988, author's possession.

46. Quotes from Dan Trotta, "'Human Plow' Image Ignites Furor," *Oceanside Blade-Citizen,* May 16, 1989.

47. Richard Steven Street, "Knife Fight City," *West* magazine, *San Diego Mercury News* (July 28, 1991): 8–13, 22–24; Richard Steven Street, "Agriculture's Wild West Town," *California Farmer* 272 (March 17, 1990): 14–16, 26. See also J. Edward Taylor, Philip L. Martin, and Michael Fix, *Poverty and Prosperity: Immigration and the Changing Face of Rural California* (Washington, D.C., 1997), xi.

48. For other examples of my approach, see Richard Steven Street, "Maggio Strikes Back," *California Farmer* 265 (December 13, 1986): 6–7, 16–19; Richard Steven Street, "The Border," *California Farmer* 265 (September 6, 1986): 10–11, 36–39; and Richard Steven Street, "SAW's Edge," *California Farmer* 269 (October 15, 1988): 8–9, 37–39.

49. Quote from Grundberg, "The Foreign and the Fabulous," in Grundberg, *Crisis of the Real,* 183. See also Richard Steven Street, *Organizing for Our Lives: New Voices from Rural Communities,* intro by César Chávez, interviews by Richard Steven Street and Samuel Orozco (Portland, Ore. 1992), 66–79; Richard Steven Street, "Life in the Canyons: Photographs of San Diego's Shantytowns Communities," *Labor's Heritage* 11 (Winter 2001): 36–59; Richard Steven Street, "'Something Better Than We Are': Latino Workers in California," *Culturefront* 3 (Fall 1994): 92–101.

50. Richard Steven Street, "Framing Farmworkers through a Historian's Lens," *Chronicle of Higher Education* (June 7, 2002): B13–B15.

51. Wright Morris, "In Our Image," *Massachusetts Review* 19 (1978), in Goldberg, ed., *Photography in Print,* 534–45; Richard Steven Street, "A Photographer's Double Life: The Historian as Photographer, the Photographer as Historian," *Visual Communication Quarterly* 13 (Spring 2006): 32–33.

52. Several months later, when I returned to give Luis some prints, his camp had been destroyed, and he was long gone. I never saw him again.

23. Photographers and Farmworkers Today

1. Quote from Felix Adamo to author, November 24, 1998, author's possession. See also Street, interviews with Liliana Nieto del Río and Scott Fortner, April 27, 1993, Delano, California, author's possession; and Richard Steven Street, "The Last Time I Saw César," in Chatfield, ed., Farmworker Movement Documentation Project, www.farmworkermovement.org, accessed 2005.

2. The pear-shaped office manager who tried to shove me through the plate glass window also tried to have me arrested on the grounds that I had attacked him. After interviewing witnesses and observing me waddling around with three cameras around my neck and a large camera bag, the Mexican American deputy sheriffs concluded the charge was ridiculous and sent me on my way. "It's not like the old times, when the largest employer in town just got his way," said one deputy. "You were insane to go into that building." That evening, on assignment photographing a farmworker rally in Calexico for *California Farmer,* an intoxicated field hand threatened to kill me if I did not stop photographing César Chávez. I refused. Such episodes occurred frequently and came with the territory. See *Imperial Valley Press,* February 12, 1985; Richard Steven Street Diary, notes on the February 12, 1985, Saikhon Incident, author's possession; and Chris Schneider to author, February 27, 1985, author's possession.

3. Out in the Central Valley, two of the state's preeminent landscape photographers, Robert Dawson and Stephen Johnson, were returning to the environment of their childhood with the idea of rediscovering a place that neither knew very well. Using large-format view cameras and the

latest digital technology, they finished a massive, ten-year-long visual survey, much of it focused on the agricultural environment, that explored the nexus of land, water, agriculture, racism, poverty, and abundance. Published in 1993 by the University of California Press as *The Great Central Valley: California's Heartland,* their project was a modern, activist counterpoint to what Carleton E. Watkins had done a little over a century earlier, only now much of it was recorded in color. With a stunning layout that vastly improved and restored old images by removing cracks, scratches, mold, and other defects and with computer manipulations that adjusted many of the duotone curves (and in at least one case altered an original document by shifting text from a following page onto the preceding one), *The Great Central Valley* depicts one of the most technologically altered, massively productive, and agriculturally varied landscapes on earth. See Stephen Johnson, Gerald Haslam, and Robert Dawson, *The Great Central Valley: California's Heartland* (Berkeley, 1993), 233; and Stephen Johnson, *Making a Digital Book: Art, Computers, Design, and the Production of the Great Central Valley: California's Heartland* (Pacifica, Calif., 1993), 9, 18–19, 33–36, 43.

4. Personal observations while photographing on April 29, 1993, Delano, California. See also Street, "The Last Time I Saw César," in LeRoy Chatfield, ed., *National Farmworker Documentation Project* (Sacramento, 2004), DVD. For a full presentation of my photographic work, see "The Photographer's Double: The Photographer as Historian, the Historian as Photographer," *Visual Communication Quarterly* 13 (Spring 2006): 66–89.

5. Quote from Street, interview with Don Bartletti, August 25, 1998, Vista, California, author's possession.

6. Quote from Street, interview with Don Bartletti, August 2, 1998, Vista, California, author's possession.

7. Quote from Street, interview with Don Bartletti, August 9, 1998, Vista, California, author's possession.

8. Richard Steven Street, "The Border," *California Farmer* 265 (September 6, 1986): 10–11, 36–39; Peter Andreas, *Border Games: Policing the U.S.–Mexico Divide* (Ithaca, N.Y., 2000), 3–15; Ken Ellingwood, *Hard Line: Life and Death on the U.S.–Mexico Border* (New York, 2004), 9–40.

9. Quote from Don Bartletti, *Between Two Worlds: The People of the Border* (Oakland, Calif., 1992), 33. For background, see Oscar Martínez, *Border People: Life and Society in the U.S.–Mexico Borderlands* (Tucson, Ariz., 1994); Oscar Martínez, *Troublesome Border* (Tucson, Ariz., 1991); Daniel Arreola and James R. Curtis, *The Mexican Border Cities: Landscape, Anatomy and Place Personality* (Tucson, Ariz., 1993); and County of San Diego, Human Resources Agency, *Illegal Aliens: Impact of Illegal Aliens on the County of San Diego* (San Diego, Calif., 1977).

10. Bartletti, *Between Two Worlds,* 33; Street, interview with Bartletti, August 2, 1998, Vista, California, author's possession.

11. Quote from Street, interview with Bartletti, August 2, 1998, Vista, California.

12. Ibid., 21. Bartletti used a tripod-mounted, motor-driven camera, 24-millimeter wide-angle lens, slow shutter speed of about 1/30th second, and T-Max film exposed at ASA 400.

13. Quote from Street, interview with Bartletti, August 25, 1998, Vista.

14. Kevin Brass, "'Uneasy Neighbor' Tells San Diego Migrants' Plight," *Los Angeles Times,* May 11, 1989.

15. Quote from Matt Black to author, March 26, 2004, author's possession.

16. Matt Black, "Homage to an Outlaw," *West* magazine, *San Jose Mercury News* (January 7, 1996); Matt Black, "Keeping the Sheep," *Los Angeles Times,* December 1, 1996; Matt Black, "After the Freeze," *Los Angeles Times,* June 20, 1999; Mark Arax, "City of Exiles," *Los Angeles Times Magazine* (November 22, 1998).

17. Mark Arax, "A Broken Bit of the Promised Land," *Los Angeles Times Magazine* (August 25, 2002).

18. Quote from Street, interview with Matt Black, March 18, 2004, Lemon Cove, California, author's possession.

19. Quotes from Matt Black to author, March 26, 2004, author's possession.

20. Quote from ibid. See also Street, interview with Matt Black, March 18, 2004, Lemon Cove, California, author's possession; and Mark Arax, "Life and Death of a Guardian Angel," *Los Angeles Times Magazine* (August 27, 2002).

21. Quote from Black to author, March 26, 2004, author's possession.

22. Saundra Sturdevant, "Herstory: Migrant Photography Project," ssturdevant@mindspring.com, accessed 2001. See also LA Writers Collective, "Fields of Hunger: Lives of Fresno Farmworkers," *Revolutionary Worker* 1213 (September 21, 2003), at www.rwor.org. The California Council for the Humanities sponsors photographic projects that encourage farmworker children to illustrate their lives in Mexico and the United States, allow farmworker women to document their political activity in the Coachella Valley, and support photographers compiling a comparative "then and now" record of farmworkers in Santa Barbara County. See the following traveling exhibitions funded by the council: Sandra Sturdevant, "Herstory," 2005, Migrant Photography Project, Lindsay, California; Jacalyn Lopez, "Life Cycles: Reflections of Change and a New Hope for Future Generations," 2005, University of California, Riverside; Melinda Burns, "The New Okies," 2005, Santa Barbara County Arts Commission; and David Bacon, "Living under the Trees," 2005, California Rural Legal Assistance.

23. Quotes from Nahmias to author, e-mail, August 13, 2004, author's possession.

24. Quotes from Kitty Felde, interview with Nahmias, *Talk of the Town,* August 18, 2003, KPCC Radio, www.publicradio.org/columns/kpcc; and Nahmias to author, e-mail, August 13, 2004, author's possession. See also "Shadowed Lives," *Orange County Register,* August 3, 2003, www.rcnphoto.com.

25. Quote from Nahmias to author, e-mail, August 13, 2004. For background on the shoe images, see Stott, *Documentary Expression and Thirties America,* 273; Stryker and Wood, *In this Proud Land,* 11, 14; and Fredric Jameson, *Postmodernism: Or, the Cultural Logic of Late Capitalism* (Durham, N.C., 1991), 6–11. For the original image, see Agee and Evans, *Let Us Now Praise Famous Men,* 12.

26. Quotes from Lubin, *Shooting Kennedy,* 284; and Nahmias to author, e-mail, August 13, 2004, author's possession.

27. Quote from Nahmias to author, e-mail, August 13, 2004.

28. KCET interview with Nahmias in "Life and Times," *Los Angeles Times,* December 10, 2002; and Sandra Mubilio, "Migrants' Lives as Seen through Camera Lens," *Los Angeles Times,* October 20, 2002. See also Nahmias to author, e-mail, July 29, 2004, author's possession; and "The Human Cost of Agriculture," *Santa Maria Sun,* April 17, 2005.

29. Hal Foster, "Postmodernism: A Preface," in *The Anti-aesthetic Essays on Postmodern Culture,* ed. by Hal Foster (Port Townsend, Wash., 1983), xv; Ingrid Sichy, "Good Intentions," *New Yorker* (September 9, 1991): 92; John Berger and Jean Mohr, *Another Way of Telling* (New York, 1982), 100; Sebastião Salgado in Fred Ritchin, "The Lyric Documentation," and in Eduardo Galeano, "Salgado 17 Times," trans. Asa Zatz, both in Galeano and Ritchin, *Sebastião Salgado: An Uncertain Grace* (New York, 1990), 11, 147; Strauss, *Between the Eyes,* 8–9; Sebastião Salgado, *Migrations: Humanity in Transition* (New York, 2000). Also part of this group of photographers is Carol Peterson. From 1995 to 2003 she photographed farmworkers around Oxnard, as well as UFW leader Dolores Huerta during her appearances on the UCLA campus. In 2003 she and a UCLA film student installed a photo quilt in the new commons building of De Neve Plaza. The quilt was arranged in the shape of the UFW eagle and consisted of one hundred of her photographs in sets and composites.

30. David Bacon, "Every Worker an Organizer: Farm Labor and the Resurgence of the United Farmworkers," exhibition, Oakland Museum, March 30–April 26, 2001; David Bacon, *The Children of NAFTA: Labor Wars on the U.S./Mexico Border* (Berkeley, 2004); Bill Gillette, *Las manos de la tierra: Land and Labor in the San Joaquin Valley,* California Institute for Rural Studies (Davis, 1990).

31. Ed Kashi photographs in Eric Schlosser, "In the Strawberry Fields," *Atlantic Monthly* 276 (November 1995): 80–108; Eric Schlosser, *Reefer Madness: Sex, Drugs, and Cheap Labor in the American Black Market* (Boston, 2003), 75–109; Kashi to author, e-mail, June 6, 2003, author's possession. Kashi frequently exploited a technique for which he had become famous: shooting at sunrise or in the early-morning light, underexposing his color transparencies one stop or more to achieve maximum color saturation, and then adding light from an off-camera strobe. I have copied this technique and used it extensively in my commercial work.

32. Richard Steven Street, "Jose Ballin: Strawberry Field of Terror," *California Magazine* 13 (December 1988): 76. See also Wells, *Strawberry Fields,* the definitive account of labor in the strawberry industry. Mitigating against successful organization is the extensive use of tenant farming and share cropping arrangements.

33. Quote from Tim Wride, "Black Panthers: Photographs by Ruth-Marion Baruch and Pirkle Jones," *18th Street Arts Center Bulletin* (May 15, 2004): n.p.

34. Quotes from Strauss, *Between the Eyes,* 14, also 42; and Margaret Keck and Kathryn Sikkink, *Activists beyond Borders: Advocacy Networks in International Politics* (Ithaca, N.Y., 1998). See also Mark Philip Bradley and Patrice Petro, eds., *Truth Claims: Representation and Human Rights* (New Brunswick, N.J., 2002), 1–7.

35. Mark Philip Bradley and Patrice Petro, *Truth Claims: Representation and Human Rights* (New Brunswick, N.J., 2002), 1; David H. Wells, "Professional Statement," MS, 1988, author's possession; Barbie Zelizer, *Remembering to Forget: Holocaust Memory through the Camera's Eye* (Chicago, 1998), 15. See also Julianne H. Newton, *The Burden of Visual Truth: The Role of Photojournalism in Mediating Reality* (Mahwah, N.J., 2002), ix; John L. Ward, *The Criticism of Photography as Art: The Photographs of Jerry Uelsmann* (Gainesville, Fla., 1970), 30; and Strauss, *Between the Eyes,* 48.

36. Quote from Charles N. Wollenberg, review of Charles Shindo, *Dust Bowl Migrants and the American Imagination* (Lawrence, Kans., 1997), in *Pacific Historical Review* 67 (December 1998): 639–40. See also John Tagg, "The Currency of the Photograph," in John Tagg, *The Burden of Representation: Essays on Photographies and Histories* (London, 1988); Shindo, *Dust Bowl Migrants,* 2, 7–9, 218; John Berger, *About Looking* (New York, 1980); Stange, *Symbols of Ideal Life,* xv; and Julian Stallabrass, "Sebastião Salgado and Fine Art Photojournalism," *New Left Review* 1, no. 223 (May–June 1997): 136.

37. Rodríguez, "La glorificación de lo insignificante."

38. Quotes from W. Jackson Bate, *Samuel Johnson* (New York, 1975), xix; and Dorothea Lange Field Notes, in Coles, *Dorothea Lange,* 7. See also John Bloom, "An Interview with Sebastião Salgado," *Photo Metro* (October 5, 1990): 7; W. Eugene Smith, "Photography as We See It," *Photo Notes* (June 1948): 4; John Szarkowski, introduction to the "New Documents Exhibition," February 28–May 7, 1967, Museum of Modern Art, New York City; Garner, *Disappearing Witness,* xviii; Inge Biondi, *Chim: The Photographs of David Seymour,* edited by Catherine Chermayeff, Kathy McCarver Mnuchin, and Nan Richardson, foreword by Cornell Capa, intro. by Henri Cartier-Bresson (Boston, 1996), 9; Light, ed., *Witness in Our Times,* 8; Carole Kismaric, *André Kertész* (Millertown, N.Y., 1997), 12; George Rodger, *Humanity and Inhumanity: The Photographic Journey of George Rodger,* text by Bruce Bernard, foreword by Henri Cartier-Bresson, picture research by Peter Marlow in association with Magnum Photos (New York, 1999); Sebastião Salgado, T. J. Clark, Orville Schell, Nancy Scheper-Hughes, Candace Slater, and Michael Watts, *Migrations: The Work of Sebastião Salgado* (Berkeley, 2002), vii–x, 6, 8, 24.

39. Quote from Amy Goodman, interview with Gore Vidal, May 13, 2003, *Democracy Now!* WBAI Radio, New York City, at www.democracynow.org/history.shtml.

40. Quote from Agee and Evans, *Let Us Now Praise Famous Men,* 13. See also Roland Barthes, *Camera Lucida* (New York, 1992), 12; and "Future Stock," *American Photo* (September–October 1996): 80.

41. Fred Ritchin, *In Our Own Image: The Coming Revolution in Photography* (New York, 1999), xii, 4; Martin Lister, "Extracts from Introduction to the Photographic Image in Digital Culture," in Liz Wells, ed., *The Photography Reader* (New York, 2003), 198, 219–27; W. J. T. Mitchell, *The Reconfigured Eye: Visual Truth in the Post-photographic Era* (Cambridge, Mass., 1992).

42. Pedro Meyer, *The Real and the True: The Digital Photography of Pedro Meyer* (New York, 2004); Pedro Meyer, *Truths and Fictions: A Journey from Documentary to Digital Photography* (New York, 1995).

43. Pedro Meyer to author, e-mail, April 24, 2005, author's possession.

44. In my discussion of Pedro Meyer's digital photography, I draw heavily on Mraz, *Nacho López,* 185–89, a fine and highly original work that goes far beyond its ostensible purpose. See also Pedro Meyer, "Redefining Documentary Photography," editorial, *Zonezero,* April 2000, www.zonezero.com.

45. This trend has parallels in other genres of western photography, for example, the way Robert Adams uses images of the violated landscape as a counterpoint to the primordial views of Ansel Adams. See also Richard Avedon, *In the American West, 1979–1984* (New York, 1985); Max Kozloff, "Through Eastern Eyes," *Art in America* 75 (January 1987): 91–97; Martha Sandweiss, "Views and Reviews: Western Art and Western History," in William Cronon, George Miles, and Jay Gitlin, eds., *Under an Open Sky: Rethinking America's Western Past* (New York, 1992), 185–202; Philip L. Martin, *Promises to Keep: Collective Bargaining in California Agriculture* (Ames, Iowa, 1996), v, 104, 112; and John Annerino, *Dead in Their Tracks: Crossing America's Desert Borderlands* (New York, 1999), xii, 16, 46, 48, 51, 56, 64, 79, 113, 118–19, 121–22, 125–26, 128–29.

46. Tony Platt, "History—It's Not Just about Us," *San Francisco Chronicle,* April 23, 2006, review of Thomas Bender, *A Nation among Nations: America's Place in World History* (New York, 2006).

47. Quotes from Don Normark to author, September 17, 2003, author's possession. See also K. Patrick Conner, "The Two Lives of Horace Bristol," *This World: San Francisco Chronicle* (September 2, 1990), 10–14; Conner and Heimerdinger, *Horace Bristol;* Jeff Bruel, "Through My Father's Eyes" and the Alvarado Project featured in *Filipinas Magazine* (May 10, 2002); Monica Sagullo, "A Journey Back in Time," May 1, 1999, www.thealvaradoproject.com/news//news_id=4; and Normark, *Chávez Ravine, 1949,* 62, also 11–12, 14, 34, 37–38. The film that Normark set out to make, *Chavez Ravine: A Los Angeles Story* (Tiny Projects, 2003), is now complete, with music by Ry Cooder and narration by Cheech Marin.

48. Quote from "Huerta, UFW, Muralists Sue Internet Image-Vendor," *San Francisco Chronicle,* November 10, 2000. See also David Hale, "Family Roots Resurface in Artist's Work," *Fresno Bee,* August 25, 2002; Chicana 2000: Emerging Voices, "Mi alma, mi tierra, mi gente: Contemporary Chicana Art," exhibition, October 6–November 3, 2002, Moreau Art Galeries, Saint Mary's College, Notre Dame, Indiana; Stephanie Barron, Sheri Bernstein, and Ilene Susan Fort, *Made in California: Art, Image, and Identity, 1900–2000* (Berkeley, 2001), 116–17, 197, 224–25; and Richard Griswold del Castillo, Teresa McKenna, and Yvonne Yabro-Bejarano, eds., *Chicano Art: Resistance and Affirmation, 1965–1985* (Los Angeles, 1991), 143.

49. María García, "Chávez Stamp Feted across Bay Area," *San Francisco Chronicle,* April 25, 2003.

50. Quote from Fitch to author, May 25, 2003, author's possession. See also Tom Wheeler, *Phototruth or Photofiction? Ethics and Media Imagery in the Digital Age* (Mahwah, N.J., 2002). See also Street, interview with Shirley Streshinsky, August 26, 2003, Orinda, California, author's possession.

51. Quote from Fitch to author, May 25, 2003, author's possession. See also Rob Haeseler, "Chavez Had Gold Tooth When Photo Was Shot," *Linn's Stamp News,* June 23, 2003; and Street, interview with Matt Herron, July 14, 2003, San Rafael, California, author's possession. I proposed several of my own photographs for this stamp, which were rejected outright, along with those of other photographers and artists, in a selection process that many of us regarded as highly suspicious.

52. Quote from Gordon Parks, "This Rare Collection," in Life, *100 Photographs That Changed the World,* 7.

Index

Richard Steven Street is founder, owner, and manager of Streetshots agricultural photography. He has been an Ailsa Mellon Bruce Senior Fellow at the National Gallery of Art, Center for Advanced Study in the Visual Arts, and is currently a National Endowment for the Humanities Fellow. He has devoted the past thirty years to creating and studying the visual record of rural California. He is the author of *Beasts of the Field: A Narrative History of California Farmworkers, 1769–1913; Photographing Farmworkers in California; Organizing for Our Lives: New Voices from Rural Communities; A Kern County Diary: The Forgotten Photographs of Carleton E. Watkins;* and the forthcoming *Knife Fight City and Other Essays: An Independent Life Adrift in the California Agro-industry at Millennium's End.*